W9-ARJ-841

THE YALE EDITION

OF

HORACE WALPOLE'S

CORRESPONDENCE

EDITED BY W. S. LEWIS

VOLUME TWENTY-SEVEN

HORACE WALPOLE'S
CORRESPONDENCE

WITH

SIR HORACE MANN

AND

SIR HORACE MANN THE YOUNGER

XI

EDITED BY W. S. LEWIS
WARREN HUNTING SMITH
AND
GEORGE L. LAM
WITH THE ASSISTANCE
OF EDWINE M. MARTZ

NEW HAVEN
YALE UNIVERSITY PRESS
LONDON · OXFORD UNIVERSITY PRESS

1971

La Baccano:
Filorandi flees to, ii. 532
La Bossier or Laboussiere, Carlo de, papal surgeon:
Clement XIV dissected by, viii. 42
Labour:
cabinet-makers' and journeymen carpenters' strikes, vi. 49
strike by journeymen tailors, vii. 31
Labour in Vain. See under Williams, Sir Charles Hanbury
Laboussiere. *See* La Bossier
La Bruyère, Marquise de. *See* Gérente-d'Andréa, Marie-Thérèse de
La Bruyère de Court, Claude-Élisée de (ca 1664–1752), French naval officer:
Alicante said to be reached by fleet of, ii. 415
Mathews may attack, at Toulon, ii. 443
ordered to fight, better, ii. 443
Rowley attacks, ii. 414
La Calmette, Mme de:
convent of Saliciennes to be founded by, in Vienna, iv. 333–4
Maria Theresa summons, to educate her daughters, iv. 325–6
La Calprenède. See Costes de la Calprenède
La Cattolica. *See* Cattolica
Lace:
adrienne to have head of, ii. 334
Brussels, on wedding gown, vii. 93
coat trimmed with, iv. 342
custom house officers search for, vii. 296
for waistcoats, copied from frieze, vi. 218
gold: broad, on silk waistcoat, iv. 396; from Palazzo Pitti, made into plate, ix. 231; on Young Pretender's theatre cushion, ix. 536
green, Lorenzi uses, in chariot, v. 501
HW's goldfish may burn like, iv. 188
liveries trimmed with, iii. 507
Mann adds, to gala liveries, viii. 239
Mann to refrain from, to buy silver, ii. 472
Modenese princess gives, to Mme Grifoni, i. 70
silver: i. 183, 453; bought by Pamfili from Jews, iii. 445
waiters wear, on clothes, iv. 209
La Cerda. *See* Cordova Spinola de la Cerda
La Chalotais. *See* Caradeuc de la Chalotais
La Chavanne. *See* Borré de la Chavanne
La Chétardie, M. de. *See* Trotti, Joachim-Jacques
Lacing:
Lucchi, Angiola, resorts to, to appear at opera, ii. 368
tight, Craon, Princesse de, suffers from, iii. 145
La Clocheterie. *See* Chadeau de la Clocheterie
La Clue. *See* Bertet de la Clue Sabran
Lacon, Hester (ca 1707–1805), m. (1726) Sir Francis Edwardes, 3d Bt:
daughter maintains, vi. 210–11

second match of, leaves her destitute, vi. 210–11
La Condamine, Charles-Marie de (1701–74), traveller and mathematician:
Damiens's execution attended by, vi. 147, 153
deafness of, vi. 146, 151
England probably left by, vi. 155
English abused by, in letter to newspaper, vi. 147, 151
executioners' witticism about, vi. 147
HW condemns absurdity of, vi. 151
HW to deliver letter to, through Hertford, vi. 151
inoculation promoted by, vi. 150
Lami gives data to, about inoculation, vi. 150
landlady tries to expel, vi. 146–7, 151, 153
letter of, published in Leyden gazette and French Court gazette, vi. 153
London streets walked by, with ear trumpet, map, spectacles and hat, vi. 146
Lorenzi's letter to, forwarded by Mann, vi. 149
—— to tell, of daughter's smallpox, vi. 153
—— wants HW to meet, vi. 149, 151
Mann knew, slightly, vi. 152–3
La Croix, Charles-Eugène-Gabriel de (1727–1801), Marquis de Castries; Maréchal de France:
Du Barry, Comtesse, has new military post created for, vii. 169
Karl Wilhelm Ferdinand defeated by, v. 444
Lacuadra. *See* Llano y Lacuadra
La Curne de Sainte-Palaye, Jean-Baptiste de (1697–1781), French lexicographer:
uncertainty of, in Provençal, v. 186
Lacy, James (d. 1774), theatre manager:
rioters' demands upon, vi. 120–1
Ladbroke, Sir Robert (?1713–73), Kt, 1744; M.P.:
London council instructs, v. 546
London election candidate, vii. 5–6
Powell formerly clerk to, vi. 176
Ladder:
accidents on, ii. 148
Conway awkward at climbing, into frigate, ix. 115
Louis XV said to be carried home upon, vii. 90
See also Scaling-Ladder
Ladies:
Florentine, ranks of, in court ceremonial, vii. 583–4
Ladies of the Bedchamber:
Albemarle, Ds of, treats her maids as, ix. 564
Lading, Bill of. *See* Bill of lading
Ladles:
Mann's, acquired from Fane, ii. 472

Lady Great Chamberlain of England:
  Bertie, Lady Priscilla Barbara Elizabeth is, viii. 499
Lady Mayoress:
  George II's levee resembles visiting-day of, ii. 95
  Richmond, Ds of, costumed as, iv. 49
Lady of the Bedchamber. See under Bedchamber
Laeffeld:
  battle of, iii. 423-4, 425-6
La Ensenada. See Somodevilla y Bengocchea
La Eraga, Don Emanuelle:
  Neapolitan queen's physician, v. 325
La Fayette, Comtesse de. See Pioche de la Vergne, Marie-Madeleine
La Fayette, M. de. See Du Motier, Marie-Joseph-Paul-Yves-Roch-Gilbert
La Florta. See La Storta
Lafões, Duque de. See Bragança Sousa Ligne Tavares Mascarenhas da Silva, João Carlos de (1719-1806)
La Fontaine:
  Fables: Rominagrobis in, vi. 119
  'Fiancée du Roi de Garbe,' Craven, Bns, resembles, ix. 655
La Frenaye, Léonor or Pierre (d. before 1778), jeweller:
  Mann advises Lincoln to buy scissors from, i. 98-9
La Frenni. See La Frenaye
La Galaisière, M. de. See Chaumont, Antoine-Martin de (1697-1783)
La Galissonnière, M. de. See Barrin, Roland-Michel
La Garde, Baronne de:
  Terray sacrifices, because she sold preferments, vii. 339
Lage de Cueilly, Gil Fernando (d. 1753), Chevalier; naval officer:
  fleet of, to be attacked by Townshend, iii. 253
  St Isidore commanded by, ii. 189
  Townshend avoids ships of, iii. 325
Lagusius. See Hasenöhrl, Johann Georg
La Hougue. See Hogue, La
La Houze, Baron de. See Basquiat de la Houze
Lainsborough. See Lanesborough
La Jamaïque, M. de. See Fitzjames, Charles-Bernard-Pascal-Janvier (1751-87)
La Jamaïque, Marquise de. See Stolberg-Gedern, Karoline Auguste of (1755-1829)
La Jonquière, Marquis de. See Taffanel, Clément de
Lake, Gerard (1744-1808), cr. (1804) Bn and (1807) Vct Lake; army officer; M.P.:
  Pulteney recommends, to father, vi. 146
Lake, Warwick (1745-1821):
  Pulteney recommends, to father, vi. 146
Lake Champlain, Battle of:
  Americans defeated in, viii. 261

La Lippe. See Lippe-Bückeburg
Lally, Thomas-Arthur (1702-66), Comte, Baron de Tollendal:
  execution of, vi. 421
  intercepted letter from, shows insolence, vi. 516, 523
  Lorenzi says, is Irish, vi. 523
Lama. See Grand Lama; Teshoo Lama
La Mani, Lt:
  captured at Velletri, ii. 491
La Mar, Mlle. See Lemaure
La Marche, Comte de. See Bourbon, Louis-François-Joseph de (1734-1814)
La Marche, Comtesse de. See Fortunata Maria
Lamb:
  roasted on London's artillery ground, v. 121
Lambart, Richard (ca 1722-78), 6th E. of Cavan, 1772; army officer:
  toast proposed by, to Louis XV, v. 251, 255
Lambergh, Contessa di. See Khevenhüller, Ludovica
Lambert. See Lambart
'Lamberti'. See Benedict XIV
Lamberti, Maria (fl. 1764-ca 1777), ballerina at Venice:
  Lincoln poxed and cheated by, vii. 368, 378
Lambertini, ——, niece of Benedict XIV:
  Pisa baths benefit, iii. 487
Lambertini, Prospero. See Benedict XIV
Lambro, river:
  Charles Emmanuel III attacks Spaniards near, iii. 279
Lamb's brains:
  Mann eats, at dinner, i. 104
Lamesan, Gaetano Carlo (d. 1755), Conte de Salins; army officer:
  Florentine fiddlers threatened by, iii. 365
  Kilmorey, Vcts, calls, 'monseigneur,' iv. 298
  Mann about to receive call from, iii. 466
Lami, Dr Giovanni (1697-1770), writer and antiquary:
  Almada's secretary's book corrected by, v. 476
  anti-Jesuit champion, v. 475-6
  Francis I's pension to, probably a bribe to procure favourable notices in periodical, vi. 13-14
  ——'s teologo, vi. 13
  HW must have known, as Riccardi's librarian, v. 476, vi. 13
  La Condamine furnished by, with data on inoculation, vi. 150
  Mann will communicate to, HW's notes on Sir Robert Walpole, vi. 35
  Novelle letterarie: Buondelmonte criticized in, iv. 117-18; published weekly, vi. 14
  Palombo's billet from, vi. 13, 15, 24
  panegyric of Sir Robert Walpole wanted by, vi. 15

Riccardi's librarian, v. 476, vi. 13
Richecourt has, as interpreter at *giuoco della sibilla*, iv. 477
La Mina, Marquis de. *See* Guzmán, Don Jaime Miguel de
Lamina:
 gold, by Cellini, vii. 407
Lamo, Jean de, Lt:
 captured at Velletri, ii. 493
Lamoignon de Malesherbes, Chrétien-Guillaume de (1721–94); official in the Cour des Aides and Louis XVI's Household:
 good but lacks ambition, viii. 208
 HW praises, as a true philosopher, viii. 133
 Maurepas and Vergennes incite, to ask Marie-Antoinette to dismiss Guines, viii. 207
 resignation of, viii. 140n, 207
La Mothe-Fénelon, M. de. *See* Salignac, François-Louis de (1722–80); Salignac, Gabriel-Jacques de (1688–1746)
La Motte, Comtesse de. *See* Saint-Rémy de Valois, Jeanne de
La Motte. *See also* Cahideuc
La Motte Fouquet, Henri-Auguste (1698–1774), Baron de; Prussian general:
 defeat of, at Landeshut, v. 419
La Motte Picquet, Comte de. *See* Piquet de la Motte, Toussaint-Guillaume
Lamp; lamps:
 antique brass, HW buys, at Oxford's sale, i. 374
 English glass, ii. 478, 485
 in D. of Newcastle's dessert, iv. 126
 in orange trees, at Ranelagh, iv. 47
 London houses decorated by, for Keppel's acquittal, ix. 438
 Mann's garden lighted by, ii. 478, 485
 of teakettle, v. 451
 silver, in Cordon's chapel, ix. 55
 Vauxhall, ii. 485
Lampoons:
 political situation will arouse, vi. 444
Lampugnani, Giovanni Battista (1706–81), composer:
 Roxana by, ii. 342
Lanbi. *See* Lante
Lancashire:
 cobalt and zinc said to be in, ii. 284
 Dutch troops ordered to, iii. 109
 Ligonier to defend, iii. 160
 rebels may hope for uprising in, iii. 159
 rebels oppress people of, iii. 193
 Roman Catholics in, threaten loyal citizens, iii. 172
 Towneley joins rebels in, iii. 179
Lancaster, D. of. *See* John (1340–99) of Gaunt
'Lancaster, D. of':
 newspaper term for D. of Gloucester, vi. 264

Lancaster, Dukes of:
 bagnios and taverns will be frequented by, iv. 155
Lancaster, English ship:
 at Port Mahon, i. 283
Lancaster, Lancs:
 rebels reported near, iii. 159
Lancaster, Duchy of:
 Edgcumbe chancellor of, i. 399n, ix. 518n
 Strange's death leaves chancellorship of, vacant, vii. 313
Lancaster, House of:
 histories biased in favour of, vi. 253
Lancaster. *See also* Carvajal y Lancáster
Lancelloti, Anton Domenico; Leghorn merchant:
 ship of, v. 269
Lancet:
 used to bleed people, viii. 79
Lanci, Hieronyma (d. 1743), m. Marchese Bichi:
 (?) lottery ticket of, ii. 206
 (?) of Siena, ii. 206
Lancing:
 occurrence of, v. 369
Landaff, Bn, Vct and E. of. *See* Mathew, Francis
Landaff. *See also* Llandaff
Landau:
 burned, ii. 241
 priest takes, to Cameron's execution, iv. 384
Landau-and-six:
 Ferrers rides in, to execution, v. 399
Landi, Francesco (1682–1757), cardinal, 1743:
 Benedict XIV's witticism on death of, v. 69–70
Landsberg:
 Frederick II expels Russian garrison from, v. 247
Landscape:
 English painters sometimes paint, well, viii. 93
 Louterbourgh paints, well, viii. 93
 Müntz's genius for, v. 239
Landscape effects:
 at Hounslow Heath, i. 441–2
 at Pope's house in Twickenham, v. 417, ix. 177–8
 at SH, iv. 380, 386–7, ix. 532
 bad, at Florentine villas, iv. 166, 191
 Chinese want of symmetry in, admired by HW, iv. 127
 England greatly improves, iv. 166
 English, uncommonly luxuriant, ix. 321
 HW satirizes, v. 418
 Kent's, at Euston, ii. 254–5
 Richelieu's garden pavilion, v. 172n, vii. 329
Land's End, Cornwall:
 Brest fleet appears off, ii. 392
Landeshut:
 battle of, v. 419

Land tax. *See under* Tax

Lane-Fox, Mrs James. *See* Pitt, Marcia Lucy

Lanesborough, Cts of. *See* Rochfort, Lady Jane (1737–1828)

Lanesborough, E. of. *See* Butler, Brinsley (1728–79); Butler, Robert Herbert (1759–1806)

Lanfranc. *See* Lanfranco

Lanfranchi, Carlo, *or* Federigo, *or* Ranieri Lanfranchi Poggi (1718–93):
HW's letter from, forwarded by Mann, probably contains some commission, ix. 468

Lanfranchi, Federigo:
house of, *see under* Pisa: Mann's house at

Lanfranco, Giovanni (1582–1647), painter:
Parker may have a painting by, ii. **275**
picture by, of St Anthony: Mann advises HW not to buy, ii. 296–7; Mann hears nothing from Rome about, ii. 290; Mann to write about, to Rome, ii. 275; quarantine would prevent, coming from Rome, ii. 297; Walpole, Sir Robert, does not want, ii. 311

Lángara y Huarte, Juan de (1736–1806), Spanish naval officer:
rewarded for bravery, though his temerity was costly, ix. 25–6
Rodney defeats, ix. 16

L'Ange, Mlle:
Du Barry, Comtesse, formerly known as, vii. 75

Langeac, Marquise de. *See* Cusack, Marie-Madeleine de

Langio, Carlo Niccolò:
Gualtieri's book aided by, ii. 88

L'Angle. *See* De L'Angle

Langley, William (d. 1770), Mayor of King's Lynn 1766–7:
HW's letter to, printed in newspapers, vi. 531–2

Langley. *See also* Langlois

Langlois, Benjamin (1727–1802), M.P.; undersecretary of state 1779–82:
Cadogan, Lady, entertains, ix. 246
HW told by, of Mann's promotion, ix. 246

Langlois, Christopher:
arrested and sent to Florence, iii. 366
Gondrecourt insults, at Leghorn theatre, iii. 366
Mann keeps, as prisoner, iii. 374

Langlois, Jacky:
Acciaioli, Mme, has, as cicisbeo, iv. 284

Language; languages:
English should learn, iii. 12
in England and France, more refined than in Italy, ix. 193
modern, Francis II learns, ix. 282
necessity for learning, when young, v. 409
universal, French may become, vi. 218

Languedoc:
Beauvau removed from government of, vii. 321–2

fatal and contagious malady in, reported, ix. 304
sailors from, join Toulon fleet, ii. 396
scheme for insurrection in, iii. 310

Lannoy, Mrs James. *See* Frederick, Jane

Lansdown, Bn. *See* Granville, George

Lansquenet:
momo resembles, i. 194
played, i. 414

Lante, Federigo Marcello (1695–1773), cardinal, 1743; protector of England:
Benedict XIV consults, about Young Pretender, iv. 22
Cavalchini to be told by, of his defeat, v. 216
—— upheld by, despite French pressure and threats to his French benefices, v. 220

Lante della Rovere, Maria Cristina, m. (1750) Averardo Salviati, Duca di Giuliano-Salviati:
refuses to live in Florence, vi. 467

Lantern:
at Houghton, iv. 163
at SH, iv. 375
dark, Mann carries, on visit to Theodore of Corsica, ii. 190

Lanti. *See* Lante

Lanza, Jean de, Lt:
captured at Velletri, ii. 493

Lanze. *See* Delle Lanze

Lanzi, Luigi Antonio (1732–1810), Abate; writer:
Real galleria di Firenze accresciuta, La, given to HW by Hamilton, ix. 530

Laocoön:
duplicate of, at Rome, finer than Florentine one, vi. 71
fire breaks out near, vi. 67
in Uffizi gallery, ix. 171
Walpole, Sir Robert, has, at Houghton, ii. 326

La Pace, Tuscan ship:
seizure of, v. 274

Lapdogs:
taming of, iv. 454

Lapeggi. *See* Lappeggi

La Perrière, Barone de. *See* Viry, Francesco Maria Giuseppe Giustino di (1736–1813)

Lapier, Bettina, dancer:
(?) dances in new opera, i. **256**
(?) Neapolitan footman of, absconds after her illness, i. 421
(?) Neapolitan prince may have had, poisoned out of jealousy, i. 421

Lapis lazuli:
beads of, given by Benedict XIV to Lobkowitz, ii. 447
Mann buys handles of, for dessert knives and forks, i. 73
pocket flask of, ii. 139

Laplanders:
women of, compared to those of Florence, iv. 427

La Plata, Duque de. *See* Guzmán, Don Jaime Miguel de

La Porte, —— de:
Estevenon accompanied by, to Florence, i. 200

Lappeggi:
Richmond, Mrs, takes things to, iii. 238
Tuscan Court prefers, to Petraia and Castello, vi. 412

Lara, (?) Aaron, Jewish merchant in London:
daughter of, deserted by husband, ix. 601

Lara, Deborah (living 1790), m. John King, divorced ca 1785:
husband pursued by, to Leghorn, ix. 601

La Reginella, Nicolò (d. ?1751); singer:
English opera acted by, iii. 370

Lares, Gothic:
HW's term for SH, v. 433

Larga, Via:
Medici cousin lives in, ii. 170

Larine, Casimiro:
captured at Velletri, ii. 493

Lark:
HW's bones as little as those of, viii. 71

Laroche, James (1734–1804), cr. (1776), Bt; M.P.:
North saved by, from mob, vii. 290

La Roche de Kerandraon François-Yves, Marquis de, naval ensign:
(?) wounded, viii. 395

La Rochefoucauld, François (1630–80), Duc de; author:
reflections by, on self-love, viii. 373

La Rochefoucauld, Frédéric-Jérôme de Roye de (1701–57) Abp of Bourges, 1729; cardinal, 1747; French ambassador to Rome 1745–8:
celebrations for Francis I's election opposed by, iii. 183
Louis XV threatened by, to separate him from Mme de Pompadour, iv. 530
Old Pretender confers with, iii. 85
—— reassured by, iii. 268

La Rochefoucauld-Liancourt, François-Alexandre-Frédéric de (1747–1827), Duc de:
Macaulay, Mrs, and HW to dine with, vii. 92

La Rochelle:
Hawke's victory off, iii. 445

La Rocque, Conte di. *See* Cacherano d'Osasco, Giuseppe Ottaviano

La Rocque de Varengeville, Jeanne-Angélique de (ca 1674–1763), m. (1702) Louis-Hector, Duc de Villars, Maréchal de France:
hot rolls served by, at dinner for Ds of Bedford, vi. 105, 113

La Rode. *See* Sénezergues de la Rode

Larpent, John (1710–97), government official:
HW can send letters to Mann through, vi. 449
HW receives Mann's letter through, vii. 65, 73
Mann hears from, that his packet has arrived, vii. 65

——'s correspondence with, about HW, vi. 461, 466, 468
——'s correspondence with, over successor in secretary of state's office, vii. 443
—— sends batch of private letters through, vii. 60
——'s letters and office affairs entrusted to, vi. 449
——'s packet to, delivered by a woman, vii. 67
—— tells, to advise HW of courier's return to Florence, vii. 52
'old good-natured man,' vi. 468
Shadwell, Richard, recommended by, to Mann, vii. 443
to retire from conduct of Mann's affairs, vii. 443

Larpent, John (1741–1824):
Hertford, Cts of, hears from, of Mann's letter to father, vi. 461

La Santa Fortunata, Tuscan ship:
seizure of, v. 273–4

Lascelles, Gen. Peregrine (ca 1684–1772):
exonerated, at court martial, iii. 320

Laschi, (?) Filippo; comedian:
HW praises, iv. 41

La Siette, Col de:
French attack upon, repulsed, iii. 426–7, 431–2, 441

Las Minas. *See* Guzmán, Don Jaime Miguel de

Las Torres. *See* Torres

La Storta:
Austrians camp near, ii. 534
Filorandi flees to, ii. 532

Last Supper:
Mann to get painting of, for Chute's chapel at the Vyne, iv. 485, 489, 529, 539
See also under Santo di Tito

Late Gallant Exploits, The:
HW quotes, i. 187–9
Mann comments upon, i. 208

Latimers, Buckinghamshire:
Conway rents, iv. 163n

Latin language:
absurdity of Englishmen talking, to their kings, vi. 84
Aulic matrons' jury would speak, barbarously, v. 258
Cambridge tutor does not speak, because of sore mouth, ii. 148
Capello and Sir Robert Walpole talk, ii. 459
Cerretesi does not speak, i. 503
Damer, Mrs, writes, ix. 184
Dashkov, Ps, knows, vii. 249
George I and Sir Robert Walpole converse in, i. 503n
Gray to compose inscription in, for Bianca Cappello's portrait, iv. 407
HW belittles advantages of, v. 409
HW does not know mathematical terms in, v. 353
HW not commentator enough to wrap licentious allusions in, v. 489–90

[Latin language, *continued*]
HW's inscription for Benedict XIV translated into, vi. 88
lawyers dispute in barbarous, vii. 11
Orford lacks taste in, iv. 481
proverb in, quoted by HW, vii. 208
Richelieu's son boasts of father's ignorance of, iv. 339
St John writes letters in, to confessor, ii. 205
Scaliger's and Scioppius's invective in, ix. 438
verses in, Christian VII unable to hear, at Cambridge, vii. 48
La Torre, Don Ferdinand de (d. 1752), Marqués di Campo Santo:
sent to Spain with news of Campo Santo battle, ii. 161
La Touche, Marquis de. *See* Le Vassor, Louis
La Touche. *See also* Gervaise de la Touche
La Tour d'Auvergne, Henri de (1611–75), Vicomte de Turenne; Maréchal de France:
conversion of, for political reasons, viii. 255
Craon brings verses on, i. 153
English publicity worthy of, iv. 199
ghost of, will be shamed by Necker's holding office in France, though Protestant, viii. 255
La Tour d'Auvergne, Henri-Oswald de (1671–1747), cardinal, 1737:
pope to be chosen from faction of, i. 21
La Tour d'Auvergne, Marie-Sophie-Charlotte de (1729–63), called Mlle de Bouillon, m. (1745) Charles-Just de Beauvau, P. de Beauvau:
daughter of, vi. 341n
father-in-law to pay tax on fortunes of, iii. 23
Louis XV congratulates fiancé of, on his approaching marriage, iii. 1
parents-in-law visited by, at Petraia, iii. 500
uncle leaves property to, iii. 426
Young Pretender related to, iii. 262
La Tour du Pin-Gouvernet, Jean-Frédéric de (1727–94), Comte de Paulin; army officer:
Lyon visited by, with munitions, iv. 536
La Tour en Voivre de Savonnières, Comtesse. *See* Nay, Louise-Charlotte de (1729–57)
La Tour en Voivre de Savonnières, François-Hyacinthe (d. 1778), Comte de:
father-in-law followed by, to Lorraine, v. 80
marriage of, iv. 451
wife dresses wounds of, after coach accident, v. 442
wife's devotion from, v. 43
La Tournelle, Marquise de. *See* Mailly-Nesle, Marie-Anne de
Laud, William (1573–1645), Abp of Canterbury:

HW ridicules tyranny of, ix. 605
HW would like repetitions of trial of, vi. 284
perishes before his cause succeeds, vi. 200
Laudanum:
Clive takes, by physician's orders, for pains, viii. 60–1, 68
Crawford takes overdose of, iv. 110
Kingston, Ds of, once resorted to, viii. 152
Mann, Lady Lucy, takes, to make her sleep, viii. 199
Molesworth, Henrietta, given, vi. 145
Thomas prescribes, for Chute, viii. 210–11
Walpole, Bns, may take, i. 89
Laudohn. *See* Loudon
Laugier, Leopold, French ensign:
Lee duels with, iv. 363–4, 372
La Ulla. *See* Aulla
Launceston, Cornwall:
Bedford, D. of, attacks, iv. 113
Morice family borough, iv. 113
Laundresses:
Châteauroux, Duchesse de, recommends, to future Dauphiness, ii. 523
Laurel; laurels:
boar's head covered by, v. 301
HW does not decorate windows with, at Christmas, iv. 16
kept in portmanteaux, ii. 61
Mann should wear, v. 232
Laurence, French (1757–1809):
Rolliad and other verses by, ix. 612n
Laurence, Capt. (?) William:
Florence visited by, on way to England, iii. 192
Mann lodges, and sends him to opera, iii. 192
Laurence. *See also* Laurens
Laurens, Henry (1724–92), statesman:
American ambassador to Holland, ix. 91
imprisoned in Tower, ix. 91, 212
Keppel captures, ix. 91
President of Congress, ix. 91
Laurens, John (1754–82), general; American army officer and envoy to France:
signed capitulation which made Cornwallis a prisoner, ix. 212
Laurenzo:
Bronzino sold by, to Mme Suares, i. 128–9
Mann gets confession from, about Bronzino sale, i. 128
Lausanne:
Herbert, Lady Charlotte, to consult Tissot at, ix. 493
Morice writes from, ix. 432
Lauzun, Duc de. *See* Gontaut, Armand-Louis de
La Vallée. *See* Valle
La Vauguyon, Duc de. *See* Quélen de Stuer de Caussade, Antoine-Paul-Jacques de (1706–72)
Lavendar, spirit of:
HW bathes his eyes with, v. 139, 147
white, resembles Hungary water, v. 147

Lavendar drops:
  Pelham, Lady Catherine, might give, to distracted daughter, iv. 114
Lavendar water;
  spirit of lavendar not to be confused with, v. 139
L'Averdy or Laverdy, or La Verdy. See Del' Averdi
La Victoria, Marqués de. See Navarro, Juan José
La Ville, Abbé Jean-Ignace de (ca 1690–1774); Bp of Trichonium, 1774:
  Parallèle de la conduite on Kloster-Zeven attributed to, v. 235–6, 245
La Vrillière, Duc de. See Phélypeaux, Louis (1705–77)
Law, Joanna (d. 1823), m. (1772) Sir Thomas Rumbold, cr. (1779) Bt:
  tours Italy for son's health, ix. 651
Law:
  called 'shameless profession' by HW, ix. 297
  common: common sense has no relation with, v. 374; equity as good law in England as, ix. 217; Thirlby studies, iv. 215n; will and declaration of Cts of Orford in accordance with, ix. 169
  courts of, more lax in Tuscany than in England, ix. 131
  degree in, HW scoffs at, ix. 316
  English: defective in not giving relief to deserted wives, vi. 22; Italians wonder at severity of, iv. 356; marriage witnesses not required by, vii. 484
  equity and dispatch of, in England, deplorable, ix. 191
  Foote scrupulous about profession of, vii. 100
  HW and Sir Edward Walpole to obey, literally, in E. of Orford's case, viii. 295
  HW does not understand, vii. 122
  HW's satirical remarks on, vii. 11–13, 29–30
  'horrid liar,' viii. 56
  international, England violates, by destroying French ships on Portuguese coast, v. 334
  North Briton violates, vii. 28
  terms of, could not be translated into Italian or into sense, ix. 473
  young man studies, by being read to, v. 139
Lawes. See Laws
Laws, Capt. William:
  Turkey merchant hears from, of English loss of Cartagena, i. 71
Lawson, Elizabeth (d. 1759):
  Maid of Honour, iii. 63
Law suit:
  Mann to decide, i. 102
Lawyer; lawyers:
  army formed by, under Willes to guard royal family at St James's in George II's absence, iii. 180
  Bolton, Ds of, unable to persuade, to draw up her will, v. 365

deaf, while justice is blind, ix. 307
delaying tactics of, ix. 200
despotism supported by, vii. 376
English: dispute in barbarous Latin and half English, vii. 11; Italians allowed no rights by, against an Englishman, ix. 328; Mozzi's ignorance of, indicated by his thinking affairs could be concluded quickly, ix. 265
excellent at evading laws and settlements, viii. 249
fire at Lincoln's Inn will give business to, iv. 321
Florentine: doubt validity of Cts of Orford's will, ix. 123; Migliorucci's, commit rogueries, iv. 266; Mozzi and Mann open Cts of Orford's will in presence of, ix. 114; Mozzi consults, on interest on jointure arrears, ix. 456; Mozzi pays, ix. 512
Fox disliked by, out of respect to Hardwicke and Murray, iv. 412
HW contrasts, with gentleman, ix. 158
HW resists fraudulent schemes of, vii. 528
HW's, see Dagge
HW satirizes, viii. 71
HW's life invaded by, vii. 497
HW's poor opinion of, ix. 441
HW's reflections on evasions of, ix. 131
HW tries not to be involved by, vii. 522
have combined the ideas of gaining time and gaining money, ix. 297
honesty unusual in, v. 365
lying is merely an expletive for, ix. 298
Mann consults, about Cts of Orford's will, ix. 120
Mann, Edward Louisa, brings, to Galfridus Mann, v. 32
Mann, Galfridus, recommends, to HW, v. 365
Orford, Cts of, may consult, viii. 91
Orford, 2d E. of, fees, in preparation for wife's arrival, iii. 61
prediction by, of Appleby election expense, iv. 435–6
trial of, would not consider character, ix. 342
Layard, Mary Anne (1743–1804), m. (1769) Lord Brownlow Bertie, 5th D. of Ancaster, 1779:
  lady's woman or governess, viii. 500
  Waldegrave, Lady Anna Horatia, told by, that nephew would have married her, viii. 494
Layton. See Leighton
Lazaretto; lazarettos:
  at Leghorn, vii. 24
  letters from Rome held up at, ii. 282
  ships permitted to land only at, ii. 252
Lazaro. See San Lazaro
Leach, Dryden, printer:
  damages recovered by, vi. 188–9
Lead:
  coffins of, melted for musket balls, iv. 428
  white, death caused by, vi. 484

Leadenhall St, London:
HW has little sympathy for East India Company in, ix. 578
to be pointed out in schoolboys' lesson, vii. 400
League, ('Ligue'), the:
Bourbon, Cardinal de, styled 'Charles X' by, ix. 482, 520
of Cambrai, iv. 571, 582, 585
See also Holy League
Leake, Stephen Martin (1702–73), Garter King-of-Arms:
advertisement by, for peeresses' names, v. **535**
(?) Selwyn's witticism on, iv. 391
Leake, Staffordshire:
rebels retreat to, iii. 178
Leap frog:
Ramsay plays, with brats, ix. 540
Lease; leases:
delay in, inconsequential, i. 113–14
Donegall's Irish tenants refuse to pay fines for renewal of, vii. 391
fines on renewal of, paid to Cts of Orford instead of to son, ix. 335
HW's at SH, iii. 486
HW will not bore Mann with news of, vii. 515
Orford, Cts of, receives, ii. 39, iii. 272
—— to renew, on Florentine house, iii. 97, 101
—— to receive, for signing, i. 108, 115
Leather:
case of, vii. 286
pouch of, ii. 148
red turkey, bindings of, ii. 126
Leatico. *See* Aleatico
Le Blanc, Jean-Bernard (1707–81), abbé:
England visited by, iv. 228
Lettres d'un français . . . sur les Anglais by, iv. 228
Vandières accompanied by, to Florence, iv. 228
Le Bovier de Fontenelle, Bernard (1657–1757), author:
Cornbury's retort to, iv. 213
Thétis et Pelée, revival of, at Paris, iv. 213
Voltaire's verses mention, vii. 306
witticism of, on death-bed, v. 52
Lechmere, Bns. *See* Howard, Lady Elizabeth
Leclerc, Jean-Louis (1707–88), Comte de Buffon:
European animals said by, to degenerate when taken across Atlantic, ix. 47
Leda and the Swan:
statues of, iv. 547
Le Despenser, Bn. *See* Dashwood, Sir Francis (1708–81)
Le Despenser, Bns. *See* Gould, Sarah
Le Despenser, Hugh (1261–1326), cr. (1322) E. of Winchester:
HW satirizes, ii. 357

Le Despenser, Sir Hugh (d. 1326), Kt, 1306:
HW satirizes, ii. 357
Lee, ——:
Cholmondeley totally attaches, vii. 357
Gloucester, D. of, and Lord Cholmondeley accompanied by, to Florence, vii. 353
HW knows horrible story about, vii. 364
Lee, Dr. *See* Lee, Sir George
Lee, Arthur (1740–92), M.D.; American deputy:
French ambassador introduces, at Vienna, viii. **390**, 395
Maria Theresa may not have seen, viii. 390
—— refuses to receive, viii. 396
Lee, Gen. Charles (1731–82), American general:
American colonies favoured by, in public letter, viii. **128**
Americans accuse, of treachery, viii. 215
Americans may court-martial, viii. 286
character of, viii. 128
Clinton said to have captured, in Carolina, viii. 215
confirmation of news of capture of, viii. 285
Florentine nobles would be less belligerent to, than Lorraine officer was, iv. 372
half-pay commission of, viii. 129
Lorraine officer's duel with, iv. 363–4
Mann knew, intimately, viii. 128–9
ward of Galfridus Mann, iv. 363, viii. 128
wound of, improves in Venice, iv. 364
Lee, Sir Charles. *See* Lee, Sir George
Lee, Lady Elizabeth. *See* Harcourt, Lady Elizabeth (1739–1811)
Lee, Hon. Fitzroy Henry (1699–1751), naval officer:
Richecourt's correspondence with, i. 455–6
surly, ii. 234
Lee, Sir George (?1700–58), D.C.L., 1729; Kt, 1752; M.P.:
Admiralty appointment of, i. 242n, 333, 355–6, 366, 451, ii. 550, iv. 30
(?) Argyll's friend, i. 355–6
attached to Frederick, P. of Wales, iv. 493n
Augusta, Ps of Wales, favours, iv. 412
—— has, as head of her ministry, and teaches George II to praise him, iv. 245–6
—— makes, treasurer, i. 242n
Bute's favour with Ps of Wales makes, jealous, v. 104
Carteret (Granville) friend of, i. 242n, iii. 241
dean of the arches, knight, and privy councillor, i. 242n
death of, v. 261
election of, i. 242–3
Exchequer chancellorship declined by, iv. 493
Exchequer chancellorship to go to, v. 92
Falmouth opposes, i. 451

Frederick, P. of Wales, has, in his ministry, iv. 30
—— prefers, as Truro candidate, i. 451
—— probably chose, as future prime minister, i. 242n, iv. 419
——'s papers burned by, iv. 239
—— would have made, Chancellor of the Exchequer, v. 261n
German treaties opposed by, iv. 501
HW called on by, iv. 246
HW's opinion of, iv. 30
health of, gout, iv. 32
Methuen and Wynne propose, as chairman, i. 243
Newcastle's attentions to, iv. 245
Parliamentary debate by, on privately-raised regiments, x. 16, 17, 18
Parliamentary opposition wants, to be chairman of the Committee of Elections, i. **220**, 242–3
Pelham may be succeeded by, as prime minister, iv. 412, 419
Pitt opposed by, in Parliament, iii. 241
speech by, against Pelham over Buckingham assizes, iii. 470–1
Stuart Mackenzie said to succeed, as treasurer to Ps of Wales, v. 104–5
unfit to be prime minister, iv. 30, 431
Lee, George Henry (1690–1743), 2d E. of Lichfield, 1716:
death of: ii. 210; expected, ii. 168
Gower succeeds as Board president, ii. 186
mob incited by, i. 390
son of, i. **247n**
Lee, George Henry (1718–72), styled Vct Quarendon 1718–43; 3d E. of Lichfield, 1743; M.P.:
Cignani painting bought by, from Arnaldi collection, v. 231
Court will support, in getting Chancellorship of Oxford, vi. 72
Hamilton said to have bought Cignani painting for, v. 208
Jacobites may not now favour, vi. 72
Lichfield earldom inherited by, ii. 210
named in Secret Committee lists, i. 385
Opposition supported by, i. **247**
uncle of, i. 455–6
Walpole, Bns, connected with, ii. 210
witticism by, to Winnington on Bell's release, i. 502–3
Lee, Matthew (d. 1755), physician:
Frederick, P. of Wales, attended by, iv. 232
Lee, Nathaniel (ca 1653–92), dramatist:
Alexander the Great, Statira character in, v. 517
HW prefers, to Glover and Thomson, iii. **27**
Princess of Cleve, indecent play by, iv. 481
Lee, Sir William (1688–1754), Kt, 1737; lord chief justice of King's Bench; M.P.:

brother of, i. 242n
death of, iv. 453n
Ryder succeeds, as lord chief justice, iv. 453n
Lee family:
HW gets story from, about their son, vii. 364
Leeches:
for bleeding, i. 48
Leeds, Ds of. See Godolphin, Lady Mary (ca 1723–64)
Leeds, D. of. See Osborne, Francis Godolphin (1751–99); Osborne, Peregrine (1659–1729); Osborne, Thomas (1713–89)
Leeson, Joseph (1711–83), cr. (1756) Bn of Russborough, (1760) Vct Russborough, and (1763) E. of Milltown:
(?) goods of, captured by French on merchant ship, iii. 13
(?) scagliola tables made for, iii. 423
Leeuwenhorst, Dutch ship:
involved in war, ii. 458
Leeward Islands:
fleet from, arrives safely, ix. 191, 306
Le Febre. See Le Fevre
Le Fevre, Dr —— (b. ca 1731), quack; of Liége:
called to England, vii. 244
Constable hears of, in Brussels, vii. 244
gout remedy of, vii. 243–4, 251, 310
HW considers, a quack, vii. 251
medicine of, noxious, vii. 251n
prices charged by, vii. 251
reputation of, exploded at London and Liége, vii. 310
Leg:
Benedict Arnold's, wounded in American service, to have been cut off and buried with military honours before hanging him, ix. 241–2
Damer, Mrs, injures, ix. 645, 650
Lorraine, Primate of, injures, i. 12, 17
Orford's, swollen, ix. 266
servant to Marchesa Bichi breaks, iii. 408
swollen, see Swollen leg
wooden, sailor mends, with tar and oakum, viii. 283–4, 290
See also Discharge from legs; Disorder in legs; Mortification in the legs; Sore leg; Swollen ankle
Legate:
at Bologna: bars Lee, iv. 364; disputes with Bologna senate, ix. 85; may see Young Pretender, iv. 15
perpetual, York, Cardinal, may become at Bologna, iv. 332
York, Cardinal, may be, at Avignon, iii. 416
See also Vice-legate
Legge, George, Capt. (naval), 1756:
misbehaviour of, v. 296
Legge, Hon. Henry Bilson (1708–64), politician:

[Legge, Hon. Henry Bilson, *continued*]
Admiralty lord, iii. 34, 256, 457n
Bath, Exeter, London, Worcester, and Yarmouth give freedom of city to, v. 87
Bedford and the Pelhams courted by, iii. 458
Berlin to be post of, as envoy extraordinary, iii. 457
career of, iii. 457n
Chancellor of the Exchequer, iii. 457n, iv. 417, 453, 493n, 512, v. 12, 18, 24, 486n, 490, 492–3, vi. 252n
dispute with Pitt and Fox avoided by, iv. 453
Edinburgh may give freedom of city to, v. 87
embassy of, delayed, iii. 464
following of, exclusive of Leicester House, v. 12
George II cannot endure, iv. 39
Hessian subsidy opposed by, at Treasury meeting, iv. 501
Hessian treaty not signed by, iv. 493
London Common Council gives freedom of city to, v. 77
Newcastle and Fox opposed by, iv. 509–10
Newcastle, D. of, former protector of, frowns upon him, iv. 493
—— replaces, in Treasury, v. 103
out of favour with George III's court, v. 486
Parliamentary debates by: on amendment to the Address, x. 23; on privately-raised regiments, x. 18; on Scotch Bill, x. 32
peerage not given to, v. 486
Pitt demands peerage and Admiralty post for, v. 92
—— ignores, vi. 161
Prussian affair mismanaged by, iv. 39
resignation to be avoided by, iv. 503
secretary to the Treasury, i. 492–3, iii. 457n
surveyor of the Roads, iii. 457n
treasurer of the Navy, iv. 39, 417n
Treasury lord, iii. 256, 457n
Walpole, Sir Robert, called on by, ii. 244–5
—— makes, secretary to the Treasury, iii. 457n
—— turned against, because of courtship of his daughter, iii. 458
Whitworth succeeded by, as surveyor of the Forests, i. 493
witticism by, on death-bed, vi. 252
Legge, William (1672–1750), cr. (1711) E. of Dartmouth:
Anne's secretary of state, iv. 208n
Bolingbroke's book arouses sarcasm of, iv. 208
death of, from old age, iv. 208
son of, iii. 457n, iv. 417n
Legge, William (1731–1801), 2d E. of Dartmouth, 1750:

almost became secretary of state for America, vi. 444
Board of Trade resigned by, vi. 444
Germain succeeds, as secretary of state for American province, viii. 142
Grafton succeeded by, as lord privy seal, viii. 142
Legghorne. *See* Leghorn
Leghorn:
Agdollo formerly prisoner at, i. 168n
air of, bad in midsummer, viii. 318
alabaster vases and books for Conway to be sent from, iv. 329
Algerine-Tuscan treaty injures trade at, iv. 472
American colonies send grain to, vi. 486
American news from, i. 35
American patriots sail directly to, viii. 88
Archinto and Richecourt often meet at, i. 490
bark reaches, from Marseille, i. 407
barks fail to reach, iii. 360
barracks at, Jews to build new front to, vi. 418, 423
Beauchamp's body to be shipped from, to England, ii. 510
best port for English ships, v. 59
Birtles arrives at, iii. 76
box for Mann arrives at, i. 183
Braitwitz confident of resistance of, i. 267
—— dismissed from, i. 406
—— resists Traun's order to withdraw troops from, ii. 85
—— returns to, i. 192, 195
——'s troops' barracks destroyed by earthquake at, i. 293
Cambridge to take HW's things home from, ii. 196, 200
Campbell, Lady William, to be sent home by sea from, ix. 263
cannon at, v. 16
cannon firing from Marciana audible at, ii. 28
Capponi's regiment sent to, i. 214, 266
captain of *Great Duchess of Tuscany* is hissed at, ix. 480
captain of *Guarland* brings news to, i. 269
carnival at, ii. 526, vi. 354
casino at, York, D. of, passes evening in, vi. 221
cathedral at, design of, vi. 40
Charles Emmanuel III and Mann might land army at, v. 266
Charles Emmanuel III may be on man of war at, ii. 145
Chelsea china reaches, by unknown ship, vi. 181
church attendance at, i. 260
Chute hears gossip at, about Walpoles, i. 146
—— may go to, ii. 27
—— might land at, to make acquaintances at Pisa, iv. 114

—— soon to send HW's eagle to, iii. 149

Cocchi's books wait at, iv. 437

commerce of, might be ruined by loss of English at, iv. 278

consuls to, *see under* Consul

Conway misses boat to, iv. 280

——'s intention to visit, unknown to Arbuthnot, iv. 284–5

Cooper refits his bomb ships at, iii. 81

corn surplus at, viii. 106

Corsican galley at, made to fly French colours, vii. 56

Corsicans at, ii. 145, ix. 196

couriers from: ii. 506; awaited by Mann, ix. 15; frequent, ii. 37; to Florence, prevented by floods, iii. 131

Craon, Princesse de, blamed by HW for considering a trip to, ii. 61

—— sends furniture, plate, and equipage by sea to, vi. 536

—— wants to see English fleet at, i. 443

Craons may go to, ii. 27, 38, 503

crowds at, for reception of Modenese princess, i. 66

cuirassiers at, i. 214

Cumberland, D. of, may visit, vii. 53

—— to embark at, probably for Marseille, ix. 645

customs at, i. 130, v. 115

Danish ship at, reports action at Cape St Vincent, ix. 9

defences of, i. 179–80, 192–3, 198, 204, 206

Dick and Rutherfurd are Russian commissaries at, vii. 222, viii. 114, 453

Dick consul at, iv. 527, vii. 41n

Dicks break up house at, viii. 239

disputes at, fomented by Goldsworthy, i. 456

drams for E. of Hertford to be sent from, v. 49, 69

drawings of, Mann to send, to HW, vi. 20

Du Châtelet to defend, i. 182

Dutch merchants at, give boat race for Tuscan court, vi. 418, 423

Dutch ship brought to, by privateer, ix. 120

Dutch ships at, to be reported to Mann for use in conveying Domenichino painting, ii. 116

Dutch vessel at, detained by Spanish ships and meets French ones, viii. 541

eagle to be sent from, iii. 197, 200, 216

earthquake at: i. 284, 293, 303–10, 334, vii. 261–2; Del Fantasia's letter about, i. 307–8; not preferred to London one by Francesco, iv. 130

Electress's jewels to be safeguarded at, i. 241

enemy vessels cruise between Minorca and, ix. 205

England hated by Tuscans despite her benefits to, iv. 581

England might exchange Port Mahon for, i. 267

English affairs at, at stake, v. 10

English alleged to ruin trade of, v. 274

English at: dispute over citizenship of, iv. 266–7, 272, 275–6, 277–8; to be respected by Spaniards, i. 214

English attack upon: expected, v. 134; predicted by French to Francis I, v. 176

English burying ground at: Mann sends Orford design of mother's monument in, ix. 345; not to be mentioned by HW, ix. 213; not walled, ix. 206; Orford, Cts of, has noble tomb in, ix. 436; Orford, E. of, to erect monument in, to mother, ix. 195, 219

English captain at: gives Mann false information about Townshend, iii. 359; Mann's orders disregarded by, with excuses to Goldsworthy, ii. 288, 300

English captain brings captured prisoners to, ii. 354

English captains at: ii. 38–9; blunder in their letters, ii. 461; Braitwitz entertains, ii. 98; Cascine dinner attended by, ii. 98, 100; Craon entertains, at supper, ii. 98; disobey Mann, ii. 507; Du Châtelet entertains, ii. 78; Goldsworthy deludes, ii. 77; Goldsworthy told by, that there are too many ships at Leghorn, ii. 106–7; HW attributes Mann's illness to, ii. 117, 119, 123; HW tells Mann not to offend, ii. 97; Mann called on by, ii. 238; Mann conciliates, at Florence for curbing Martin, ii. 100; Mann tells, that they are protecting English merchants, not Francis I, ii. 92, 106; Mann tells, to preserve Tuscan neutrality, ii. 92; Mann to be visited by, at Florence, ii. 92–93; Mann to write to, ii. 77; Mann visited by, at Florence, ii. 98, 99–100, 106–7, 115; not of Anson's party, v. 123; play cards at Mann's, ii. 98; Regency council's hand to be kissed by, ii. 92–3, 99; share prizes with Townshend, iii. 277; succeeded by new ones, ii. 106; Theodore of Corsica's cause injured by, ii. 188; Vernon revered by, ii. 151

English clergyman at, *see* Horton, ——

English fleet captures provision ship from, iii. 82

English fleet's reception at, pleases Francis I, v. 128

English fleet welcomed at, for protecting commerce, v. 114–15

English frigates at, vii. 108

English man of war at: arrives from Gibraltar, vi. 12; brings news, v. 197; convoys ship to Gibraltar, v. 132; does not go to England, ii. 106

Englishman's suicide at, iv. 1, 14

Englishmen at, send home story about Lincoln, vii. 368

English merchants at: angry, ii. 437; apply

[Leghorn, *continued*]

to Goldsworthy, i. 179; asked by Mann to send an address, i. 260, ii. 151; attend church, i. 260; defend Langlois, iii. 366; drink toasts, iii. 151-2; entertained by Goldsworthy on King's birthday to propose address, ii. 151; expect peace, vi. 69; frightened, i. 179, 193, 199, 204, 258; give *calcio* for Tuscan Court, vi. 417, 423; have copy of Byng's process, vi. 81-2; hear of Braddock's defeat, iv. 497; hear of English fleet for Mediterranean, v. 58; indemnified for French blockade, v. 69; Mann asked by Turin court to borrow money from, iii. 215, iv. 386; Mann tells Goldsworthy to reassure, i. 405; Mann tells news to, i. 282; Mann to consult, about shipping HW's things to England, ii. 178; Mathews orders fleet to protect, ii. 92; may be alarmed, iii. 2; may send goods to Genoa and Lucca, i. 199; Newcastle to receive letter of thanks from, i. 260-1; not safe from Spaniards, i. 209; receive answers to letters, iii. 148; receive mail regularly, ii. 443; Richecourt submits to Mann in dispute about, iv. 522; Sturgis and Bns Walpole told lies by, i. 462; suspect King and Cts of Lanesborough, ix. 601; to be asked by Mann for money for Corsican conquest, iii. 183; to be protected by English fleet, ii. 92, 106; York, D. of, welcomed by, vi. 220

English purchase of, rumoured, i. 267

English ship, ships at: brings Gibraltar news, vi. 577; fire salutes, v. 123; leave, to blockade Genoa, ii. 244; ordered by Mathews to await Mann's directions, ii. 59, 67; take French prizes, ii. 438; transferred to Austrian service, iv. 162

English-Spanish naval fray reported at, viii. 307

English supplied, with fish, when in control of the Mediterranean, ix. 21n

English trade with: benefits, both sides, v. 176; will suffer from French control of Corsica, vii. 27

English treated insolently at, v. 31

English war ships at, i. 455

expense of shipping to, from Florence, i. 130

express from: iii. 136, viii. 380, ix. 249; Mann awaits, ix. 9; Mann receives, about Rodney's victory, ix. 24

factory of, *see* English merchants at

fair at, for Leopold II, vi. 417-18, 423

felucca brings Genoese news to, iii. 338

Ferdinand and Maria Carolina to attend dances at, ix. 594

Ferdinand and Maria Carolina to sail from, to Naples, ix. 594, 600

Ferdinand to give entertainment on shipboard at, for Maria Louisa, ix. 600

fire in harbour shipping at, iii. 472-3

fishermen to be enticed to new suburb at, to make sailors, iv. 217

fish ships expected by, now that Newfoundland is recovered, vi. 100-1

flag on belfry of, v. 278

fleet conference at, may be attended by Mann and Villettes, i. 443

Florentine money to be deposited at castle at, i. 428

Florentine news eagerly awaited at, iv. 445

Florentines have 3 days of devotion for relief of, i. 304

fortifying and provisioning of, i. 192-3, 206

Fox's urns shipped from, v. 97, 123, 133

——'s wine at, v. 304

Francavilla statues shipped from, iv. 314

France and Spain have no subjects at, vi. 351

France may blockade, unless Leopold annuls neutrality edict, viii. 508

Francis I appoints governor for, v. 125

—— does not want Tuscan troops kept in, iii. 11

——'s fleet at, iv. 162

——'s maritime power to be established at, iv. 98

—— tells Braitwitz to defend, i. 229

French bark at, i. 179, 407

French conquest of Corsica may injure, vii. 54

French frigates and privateers menace English ships sailing from, iv. 577, v. 16, 49, 69, 264, 334, 524, vi. 88, viii. 352, 375, 397, 437, 443, 476, 508, ix. 199, 205, 429

French may cut Minorca's communications with, viii. 443

French merchants at, give chariot race for Tuscan court, vi. 418, 423

French prisoners at, ix. 207

French ship brings plague to, i. 105, vii. 24

French ships take refuge at, iv. 320

frigate at, awaits Stanley, vi. 326

frigate to be launched at, vi. 548, vii. 72

Gardes Vallones take refuge in, iii. 55

Genoa supplied by, with provisions, iii. 409

Genoese foreign merchants flee to, iii. 338

Genoese refugees at, iii. 401

George II expects, to be defended by garrison, ii. 77

German troops sent away from, i. 214, 229

Ginori 'buried' by governorship at, iv. 77

—— expected from, iv. 463

—— made governor of, iii. 322

——'s funeral planned at, v. 81

—— to build houses at, iv. 217

Glasgow to visit, for repairs, v. 292

Gloucester, D. of, to give dinner and ball at, for Leopold and Maria Louisa, vii. 353

—— to visit, vii. 294

Goldsworthy and friends from, visit Mann, ii. 17, iv. 70

—— fails to meet Conway at, iv. 290

—— hopes for naval conference at, i. 444

——'s house at, prepared, i. 381

—— temporarily leaves, for Florence, i. 342–3

Goldsworthy, Mrs, describes state of, i. 313

—— learns Italian at, v. 353n

goods sent from, to Trieste, i. 380

Gorsegno tells Mann to confer at, with Townshend, iii. 183

gossip at, about HW, i. 146

Gott and Howe ship HW's art objects from, x. 3, 6

governor of, see Capponi, Giuliano Gaspero (1667–1745); Del Monte, Giovanni Battista Filippo (1708–80); Ginori, Carlo (1702–57)

Great Duchess of Tuscany boarded by Slavonian sailors at, ix. 479

Greek church at, iii. 13

guards from, to go to St Martin's, ii. 66

Guarland sent with news from, i. 305–6

gun barrels at, ii. 325, 329

HW does not like rejoicings at, over Prussian defeat, v. 118

HW may step to, on marine belt, vi. 333

HW might have been insulted if he had gone to, i. 146

HW's drams at, iii. 238

HW's gesse figures ready to go to, iii. 59

HW's purchases sent to, for shipment, ii. 177, x. 3, 6

HW's shipment to Mann awaits quarantine at, vi. 109

HW's statue to be shipped from, ii. 79, 106, 133, 177, 178

HW's things ready to go to, ii. 161

HW tells Mann to go to, for sea air, viii. 311, ix. 49

HW threatens to return Riccardi's jewels to, iii. 74

HW to send books for Mann to, ii. 464

HW to send maps to, for Mann, vii. 411

HW to send puppies to, vii. 40, 45, 72

HW visualizes Toulon fleet at, ii. 384

HW wants eagle left at, for man of war, iii. 229–30

HW wants to be kept informed about, i. 186

Haddock sends ship to, i. 380

Haite sent from, with letters by Mann, i. 258, 264

healths drunk at, iii. 151–2

Herculaneum and Caserta books for HW go from, v. 319, vi. 477, 533

hurricane at, vi. 77

India travellers reach, viii. 509

inn at, i. 263

Ipswich at, ii. 42

Irish merchants at, v. 269

iron to be sent to, from Magona, i. 304

Jackson at, i. 145

—— seeks post at, i. 186, 218, 409

Jermy makes fortune at, ix. 206

——'s monument to be at, ix. 206

Jewish merchants at: give horse race for Tuscan court, vi. 418, 423; repair barracks, vi. 418, 423; St John wants to convert, i. 292

Jewish quarter of, damaged by earthquake, i. 293

Jones, Inigo, said to have designed buildings at, vi. 9, 20, 40, 104, 147

Joseph II and Leopold to visit, to see war ships, vi. 108

Joseph II to visit, vi. 556

Karl Wilhelm Ferdinand to visit, vi. 458

keys of, Du Châtelet to turn over, to Rinuccini, i. 199

King denied permission at, to print libel, ix. 601

Kingston, Ds of, sends treasure to, to be embarked for Calais, viii. 404

—— to bring treasure back to Rome from, now that Russian ship has sailed, viii. 409–10

ladies quarrel on road from, i. 37–8

Langlois insulted by officer in theatre at, iii. 366, 374

Leopold and Maximilian to visit, viii. 130

Leopold, Maria Louisa, and Maria Carolina set out for, ix. 600

Leopold may visit D. of Gloucester at, vii. 335, 342

—— represented at, on medal, viii. 469

—— to stay at Pisa and, till February, vii. 71

—— to visit, vi. 453

letters from: about English fleet, iii. 334; reach Florence, i. 84

letters received at, by sea, subject to quarantine, viii. 461

lies from, i. 417

Long and Mann confer at, ii. 477

Lorenzi scolded for embroiling Viennese court in affair about, v. 475

—— urges Regency to expel English fleet from, v. 274

Lorraine guards sent to, i. 182, 198, 204, 214, 239, 266

Lorraine officer kept at, iii. 374

Lyttelton, Sir George, owns gesso statues detained at, iv. 577

Lyttelton, Sir Richard, at villa near, v. 511

Malta's Grand Master entertains Leopold at, vi. 556

Maltese cats go to, i. 394, 462

Mann absorbed by naval transactions at, iii. 56

Mann and Fordwich to visit, when D. of York arrives there, vi. 170–1

Mann and Rowley friendly since their meeting at, iii. 9

Mann and Rowley to confer at, ii. 503

Mann and Townshend to confer at, iii. 183

Mann avoids visitors from, at Pisa, iii. 487, iv. 85, 91

[Leghorn, *continued*]
—— borrows 6 numbers of the *Whisperer* from, vii. 219
—— consults Long at, ii. 469
—— defends people of, against Tuscan government over Port Mahon packet-boat, viii. 416
—— deluged with letters from, iii. 216
—— does not want HW's statue to be kept at, ii. 57
—— fails to get tea from, i. 59
—— gives his own opinion only in regard to trifles regarding ships and merchants at, v. 475
—— hears accounts from, of Russo-Turkish battle, vii. 232
—— lends money to Fermor at, ii. 509
—— may be besieged in, iii. 3
—— may go to: ii. 27, 38; to see D. of Gloucester, vii. 333
—— may seek secretary at, i. 157, 172, 207
—— may send eagle from, in man of war, iii. 122, 246
—— meets Capt. Pet at, ii. 509
—— might have to take his servant to, to get clothes, iv. 205
—— orders English captain at, to watch Civita Vecchia, ii. 287–8, 296, 300
—— persuades Regency to permit amusements at, iii. 1
—— plans Sir Robert Walpole's trip from, ii. 212
—— receives *Constitutional Queries* from, iv. 234
—— recovers from fatigues of, at Pisa baths, vi. 427
—— says that George II expects garrison to be kept at, ii. 77
——'s correspondence with, increases, ii. 92
—— sends cases to, for HW, iii. 329
—— sends Cocchi's book to, to be forwarded to HW, iv. 158
—— sends express to, to send ship to Civita Vecchia, ii. 296, 300
—— sends letters through, ii. 377
—— sends ship from, to recall English fleet, ii. 559
——'s pedigree to arrive at, iv. 205
—— spends fortnight at, v. 122
——'s proximity to, causes Gorsegno to write him, iii. 150
——'s secretary should deal with affairs of, i. 157–8
——'s ship from, to visit Port Mahon, iii. 206
——'s ships sail from, ix. 249
——'s success at, pleases HW, v. 131
—— tells Chute to send Pergolesi's *Serva Padrona* to, i. 262
—— to receive D. of York's commands at, vi. 180
—— to send gesse figures to, for shipment, iii. 34

—— to send HW's statue to, ii. 106
—— to send sailors to, i. 158
—— to visit, to see Osborne, v. 117
—— tries to send fleet from, to help Rivarola, iii. 162
—— visits English fleet at, ii. 506–7
—— wants funeral to be at, ix. 665
—— wears tricolour cockade at, ii. 544
—— writes from, ii. 473, vii. 336–7
Mann, Horace II, would have sailed to, if wife had died, viii. 233, 238
Maria Louisa too pregnant to attend celebration at, vi. 556–7
Martin may be sent to, ii. 26
—— to protect, ii. 100
Mathews alone cannot defend, ii. 77
—— may be on man of war at, ii. 145
—— sends ship to, ii. 26, 37
——'s instructions read aloud to war council at, ii. 484
medal sent from, to Lady Orford, i. 426
Medici, Ottajaro de', dies at, ii. 173
Mediterranean ports to be eclipsed by, iv. 102
Medley sends ship to, from Port Mahon, iii. 192
melon seeds shipped from, for Hartington, ii. 428
militia regiments at, i. 266, 288
Mill expected to attack Indian trade from, iv. 101–2
ministry of, i. 476
Minorca cut off from, by hostile ships, ix. 429
Minorcan females evacuated to, viii. 453, ix. 179, 180
Minorcan prisoners reach, ix. 430
Minorcan supplies gathered at, viii. 375, ix. 249–50
mole at: i. 303, ii. 27, 38; Ferdinand goes to his barge at, ix. 581
Montemar stays in port of, in Genoese galley, i. 214
Nardini violinist of, vi. 537
neutrality of: disputed, ii. 438; Mann tells English captains to guard, ii. 92; should be preserved, v. 112; used to be disputed, vi. 156
Newcastle brings prize to, ii. 448
Newcastle puts in at, ii. 182
Newfoundland ships at, vi. 100–1, viii. 246
news from, of Spanish troops in Majorca, vii. 261
news of Richecourt eagerly awaited at, iv. 445
no prizes at, to squabble about, v. 507
not a safe port, v. 36
old woman prophesies fall of, vii. 261–2
opera at: i. 259–60; restored, iii. 1; Sani sings in, ii. 160; to be given, for Carnival, vi. 354
Order of St Anne of Holstein more impressive at, than in London, viii. 96

Orford, Cts of, buried at, ix. 114, 195
——'s death, probably reported to England from, ix. 129
Orlov leaves, just before courier arrives, vii. 204
——'s letters reach, vii. 226
Osborne's fleet to get provisions at, v. 114
palace at, design of, to be brought to HW by D. of Grafton, vi. 40
Paoli's followers near, vii. 159
pedestal of Vespasian bust sent from, v. 521, vi. 6
Percy, Lord Algernon, sends case from, containing *Illustri fatti Farnesiani*, ix. 420
Pertici, Mme, sings at, iv. 357
Philibert may replace Braitwitz at, i. 406–7
pilots sought at, for Adriatic, i. 455–6
plague discovered on French ship at, i. 105
plague ship repelled from, ii. 262
population of, i. 303
Porto Ferrajo next best port to, v. 59
post for Germany awaits letters from, vii. 232
post from: i. 47, ix. 313; brings news of Sir Robert Walpole, iii. 22
Preston leaves off business at, iv. 499
Prince George plies between London and, v. 414
privileges of, extend to fugitives whose crimes were committed out of Tuscany, ix. 602
provisions scanty at, i. 304
provisions sent from: for expedition to Provence, iii. 352; for Genoa, iii. 409; for Minorca, viii. 375, ix. 249–50; for Russian fleet, vii. 172
Prussian consul at, with arms over his door, v. 112
quarantine (lazaretto) at, vi. 109, vii. 24, viii. 461, ix. 42
Regency Council urged by Mann to defend, i. 259
rich ships from Gibraltar expected by, viii. 397
Romney to disembark troops at, ii. 26
Russian fleet gets provisions from, vii. 172
Russian fleet to visit, vii. 148, ix. 84, 160, 415
Russian frigates reach, from Paros, vii. 326
Russian long-boat sinks at, ix. 493
Russian officer and courier arrive from, vii. 235
Russian remittances to, for use of fleet, vii. 222
Russian ships at: vii. 192, 202, 307, 308, viii. 114, 404; to fetch Orlov and Dolgoruky, vii. 191
Russians spend lavishly at, viii. 95
Rutherfurd in business at, viii. 453
sailors sent on to, i. 158
St Quintin sails to, i. 394, 419
salt meat supplied to, i. 193
San Giovanni de' Padri Agostiniane, church of, falls on people in earthquake, i. 304, 307
Santini's watch to be conveyed to, v. 302
Sardinian galleys at, iii. 82
Savona bark reaches, iii. 434
scagliola tables sent from, iv. 27
sea engagement not reported from, ii. 406
sepulchral altar sent to, from Rome, iv. 365
ship from Marseille arrives at, v. 242
ship from Newfoundland reaches, viii. 246
ship from Port Mahon visits, i. 314, iii. 132
ship loses mast in approaching, iii. 235
shipments for HW wait at, ii. 329–30
ship not yet due at, iii. 258
ship sails from, to pursue pirates, ix. 480
ships arrive at, after Rodney's victory, ix. 24
ships at: to evacuate English merchants in emergency, ii. 27, 38; unnecessarily numerous, ii. 106–7
ships dare not leave, for fear of privateers, viii. 437
ships from, not going to join English fleet, ii. 175
ships from Sicily not permitted to land at, because of plague, ii. 252
ships not to sail from, with valuable cargoes, for fear of French, v. 69
Sisson's plan should not be sent by ship unless going directly to, v. 375
slaves at, iv. 83
Spaniards hire transports at, iii. 304
Spaniards may find weak garrison at, iii. 11
Spaniards might march to, ii. 77
Spaniards store supplies at, iii. 10–11
Spanish expedition may reach, i. 196, 198–9, 212
Spanish men of war near, i. 182, 212
squadron of, to investigate Benedict XIV's relations with Charles of Naples, ii. 67
square at: Madonna di Monte Nero worshipped in, i. 303; residents sleep on, in chairs or coaches, i. 303
Stampa rents villa between Florence and, iv. 116
Stosch's brother's corpse sent to, iii. 358
Stuart subjected to 25-day quarantine on arriving at, in privateer, ix. 42
Sturgis sent to, i. 95, 107
suburb of, to be built by Ginori's plans, not Richecourt's, iv. 217
Swedish captain reports Rodney's victory to, ix. 24
Te Deum sung in, v. 112
Theodore of Corsica may be on man of war at, ii. 145
—— near, iii. 132
—— pretends to expect fleet of ships at, iv. 378
—— sails from, ii. 174
'titular' at, *see* Dick, Sir John
toasts drunk at, iii. 151–2

[Leghorn, *continued*]

Toulon squadron may intercept ship to, vi. 88

Townshend does not leave, iii. 169

—— returns to, iii. 277

—— sends express from, to Mann, iii. 136

trade of, almost annihilated by French privateers at Corsica, viii. 476

troops from, mostly reach San Martino, ii. 76

troops reinforce, iii. 245

troops sent back to, ii. 85

troops to be left at, iii. 11

Tuscan Court visits, vi. 417, 422–4, vii. 80

Tuscan defenders may retire to, ii. 295

Tuscan ships at, load French goods for the Levant, v. 273–4

Tuscan ship to depart from, ix. 138

Tuscan troops to defend, ii. 77, 530, iii. 2

Tuscan war ship at, vii. 108

Udny succeeds Dick as consul at, viii. 233, 251

Uguccioni's poems at, ii. 554

Venetian ship destined for, iii. 81

Venetian vessel from, with English engineers, intercepted by French on way to Minorca, viii. 476–7

vessel may be on way to, with news of Eliott and Howe, ix. 330

vessel sent to Gibraltar from, arrives, ix. 303

visitors to: Braitwitz, i. 106, 117, 179, 260–1; Bridgwater, Ds of, v. 501; Cameron, Jeanie, vi. 453; Charles III, vii. 238; Charlton, vii. 334; Cholmondeley, vii. 335, 336–7, 342–3; Davison, iii. 407; Edgcumbe, iv. 536; Erne, Vcts, ix. 652; Eszterházys, iv. 351; Ferdinand, ix. 581, 600; Ferdinando II, i. 305; Fox, Capt., ii. 182; Francis II, ix. 499, Gloucester, D. of, vii. 332–7, 341–2, 345, 347, 393–4, 405; Hamilton, Lady, vi. 259; Hamilton, Sir William, vi. 259; Hervey, Bns, ix. 652; King, John, and family, ix. 601; Kingston, Ds of, viii. 398, 404; Lanesborough, Vcts, ix. 601; Leopold II, vi. 417–18, 422–4, 548; Lindsay, Sir John, ix. 499; Lyttelton, Sir Richard, v. 501, 507, 509; Mann, i. 258–64, ii. 506–7, 544, v. 122–3, 499–500, vi. 220–1, 422–3, vii. 72, 80, 333–7, 347–8, 394; Mann, Horace II, viii. 94, 292; Mann, Lady Lucy, viii. 292; Maria Carolina, ix. 581; Maria Louisa, vi. 423; Medici, 'Ottaviano' de', ii. 160; Mill, iii. 407; Modenese princess, i. 66, 70; Moroccan ambassador, viii. 469; Murray, Gen. James, ix. 269, 271; Murray family, ix. 179, 180; Nomis, ii. 110; Osborne, v. 123; Paoli, Clemente, vii. 130; Paoli, Pasquale, vii. 130; Pitt, Thomas, v. 500; Richecourt, iv. 162; Sani, ii. 160; Serristori, iv. 442; Spiridov, vii. 233; Suckling, ii. 182; Theodore of Corsica, ii. 145, 188; Uguccioni, ii. 509–10; Vandières, iv. 236; York, D. of, vi. 155, 170–1, 220–1, 223

Wachtendonck commands Maria Theresa's troops at, i. 467n

Walpole, Bns, corresponds with, about her allowance, ii. 39, 272

Walpole, Sir Robert, may be on man of war at, ii. 145

—— wishes to go to Italy by, ii. 202

Walsegg to command at, i. 130

wateridge expense between Florence and, i. 130

water supply of, i. 304

Whithed may go to, ii. 27

William IV may visit, ix. 590

Winchelsea reaches, vii. 233

wind may injure ships at, iv. 25

Young Pretender may be intercepted by vessel from, i. 14

'Leghorn':

Mann's code name for Spain, ix. 43

Leghorn Gate, at Florence:

floods at, iii. 131

Spaniards to pass, i. 342

Tempi's villa near, ii. 228

Legislators:

Europe prefers, to heroes, viii. 391

Legonier. *See* Ligonier

Legout:

Lorraine, Primate of, described by, i. 17

Leheup, Isaac (ca 1686–1747), M.P.; diplomatist:

recalled from Hanover for indecent behaviour, iii. 111n

remark by, on his not calling on Cts of Orford, iii. 112

Walpole, Horatio (1678–1757), brother-in-law of, iii. 111n

Leicester, Cts of. *See* Tufton, Lady Margaret

Leicester, E. of. *See* Coke, Thomas

Leicester Fields:

Capello visits Frederick, P. of Wales, at, iii. 134

George II's invitation to George III at, iv. 562

Gower, Cts, takes niece to, iii. 447

houses in, illuminated for fear of mob, vii. 7

men in, discuss Frederick, P. of Wales's death, iv. 240

Leicester House:

angry, v. 75

Augusta, Ps of Wales, entertains at, after her delivery, ii. 358

coachman at, ii. 232

courtiers kiss hands at, at George III's accession, v. 443

dissension at, iv. 39

Fox not forgiven by, v. 99

Frederick, P. of Wales's children at, ii. 219

HW taken to, in childhood, to play with D. of Cumberland and Ps Mary, ix. 647

Karl Wilhelm Ferdinand calls on Augusta, Ps of Wales, at, vi. 197

Legge's following at, v. 12

new household rudely treated by, v. 13
Niccolini will not revisit England when denied access to, iv. 285
opposition to be raised at, v. 98
pacific measures may be preferred by, v. 13
Pitt and Legge supposed to be countenanced by, v. 12
St James's Palace no longer at odds with, iv. 549
Thomas, Bp, read prayers at, to George II, iv. 348
visitors to: HW, ii. 358; Rich, Sir Robert, ii. 219
Leichtenstein. See Liechtenstein
Leiden. See Leyden
Leiden, Jack of. See John of Leiden
Leige. See Liége
Leigh, ——, father of Mgr Leigh:
Irish merchant at Cadiz, iii. 416
Leigh, Mgr:
York, Cardinal, to have, as maestro di camera, iii. 416
Leigh, Cassandra (1723–70), m. (1739) Sir Edward Turner, 2d Bt:
Spanish privateer captures, between Dover and Calais, i. 153
Leigh, Peter (1710–59); High Bailiff of Westminster:
Cooke's letter to, iv. 224
Crowle, Gibson, and Murray named by, iv. 224
Trentham's friends summon, iv. 225
Westminster election scrutiny to be settled by, iv. 108
Westminster election vote of, iv. 131
Westminster scrutiny delay explained by, iv. 123
Leighlin and Ferns, Bp of. See Carmichael, Hon. William (1702–65); Robinson, Richard (ca 1708–94); Stone, George (ca 1708–64)
Leighton, Mrs. See Thorold, Jane
Leinster, Ds of. See Lennox, Lady Emilia Mary
Leinster, D. of. See Fitzgerald, James (1722–73)
Leipzig:
Frederick II's victory near, v. 158
Seckendorf's plan for seizing, v. 266
Leith:
Dutch troops land at, iii. 131
Leitrim, Bn, Vct, and E. of. See Clements, Robert
Le Jumel de Barneville, Marie-Catherine (1650 or 1651–1705), m. (ca 1665) François de la Motte, Baron d'Aulnoy:
Chatte blanche, La, Mann alludes to, ii. 303
Nain jaune, Le, HW mentions, ii. 238
Leman, James (fl. 1720–ca 1770):
stuffed birds of, auctioned, vii. 210
Le Marchant, Sir Denis (1795–1874):
HW's letters seen by, x. 39, 41, 43
Lemnos:
Russian fleet at, vii. 245

Russians said to have burned Turkish fleet at, vii. 319
Lemon; lemons:
Brown, Sir Robert, saves money by not having, on his sideboard, ix. 609
for punch, at Cambridge banquet, iv. 83
Lemonade:
Conway, Hon. Jane, dies from eating, iv. 58–9
HW takes, for gout, vii. 252
Mann serves, i. 95, 104
served at subscription masquerade, iv. 59
Lempster, Bn. See Fermor, George (1722–83)
Le Neve, (?) Elizabeth (1720–before 1759), m. (between 1743 and 1748) Hugh Pigot:
comet played by, at Houghton, ii. 36
Leneve, Isabella (ca 1686–1759):
aged 73, v. 316
annuity to, from Customs place, x. 53
Churchill, Lady Mary, brought up by, v. 353n, ix. 609n
comet played by, ii. 36
Giberne, Mrs, comforted by, ix. 82
HW and Sir Robert Walpole lived with, v. 316, 353n, ix. 609n
HW told by, not to waste coal, v. 353
HW visits, in last illness, v. 316
health of, bad, v. 316, 324
Houghton visited by, ii. 36
understanding and wit of, v. 353n
unused turkey-pouts counted by, after dinner at Houghton, ix. 609
Walpole, Lady Anne, brings up, v. 353n
Leneve, Peter (1661–1729), Norroy King-at-Arms:
epitaph by, for Craggs, iv. 181
Leneve family:
ancient family in Norfolk, v. 353n
Lennox, Lady Anne (1703–89), m. (1723) William Anne van Keppel, 2d E. of Albemarle:
Altena visited by, with Ps Louisa, ii. 341
Caroline, Q., has, as lady of the Bedchamber, ii. 341n, iv. 111n
children of, honoured, vi. 94, 101
Cumberland, D. of, congratulates, in Drawing-Room, vi. 94
finances of, iv. 459–60
George II gives pension to, iv. 460, 466–7
—— gives watch and chain to, iv. 111–12
——'s favourite, iv. 112, 269
HW and two ladies congratulate, in Spring Garden, on son's acquittal, viii. 442
HW knows, well, ii. 341
health of, blooded, viii. 442
husband obtains offices through influence of, iv. 269
husband's death dreamed by, iv. 460
Lincoln talks with, about Bury, ii. 166–7
Richmond receives letter from, ii. 341
Richmond, Ds of, entertains, ii. 166
robbed in Great Russell St, iv. 111
son announces husband's death to, at breakfast, iv. 460

[Lennox, Lady Anne, *continued*]
son of, v. 285n, ix. 508n
three sons of, at Havana capture, vi. 82
Yarmouth, Cts of, friend of, iv. 112, 269
Lennox, Lady Caroline. *See* Lennox, Lady
Georgiana Caroline
Lennox, Lady Cecilia Margaret (1750–69):
birth of, iv. 125, 131
mother has dropsy at birth of, iv. 131
Lennox, Charles (1672–1723), 1st D. of Richmond:
body of, exhumed from Westminster Abbey,
iv. 182
daughter of, v. 285n, vi. 82n, ix. 508n
Lennox, Charles (1701–50), 2d D. of Richmond, 1723:
Albemarle, Cts of, writes to, ii. 341
Caroline displeased by statement of, that
his children would precede D. of Cumberland's grandchildren, iii. 20
Charles II grandfather of, ii. 450n
costumed as Henry VIII, i. 338
daughter of, iii. 28n, v. 530
daughter of, elopes, ii. 450
daughter's elopement may make, sensitive
about King Charles spaniels, iii. 71
daughters of, i. 184
Dayrolles's relations with, iii. 403
death of, i. 338n, iv. 182
fireworks by, at Whitehall, iv. 56–7
Frederick, P. of Wales, does not speak to,
at Carlton House, i. 337
—— offends, i. 391
French embassy refused by, iv. 28
Goldsworthy, Mrs, to urge, to intercede
for her husband, ii. 13
Hanover to be visited by, with George II,
ii. **209**
horses sent to Flanders under care of, for
George II's visit, ii. 69
influence of, on foreign appointments,
slight, ii. 31
Kildare refused by, as son-in-law, iii. 241
Lincoln to 'bring' Bury to dinner given by,
i. 377–8
Mann gratified by behaviour of, i. 348
Marlborough friendly with, ii. 451
Master of the Horse, i. 319, 338n, ii. 209
Modenese Duke unworthy of elaborate en-
tertainment of, iv. 75
Newcastle may be influenced by, against
Mann, i. 334
Norfolk, Ds of, entertains, i. 338
Pelhams friendly with, ii. 451
Radcliffe entertained by, iii. 241
—— related to, iii. 241n
rebels do not forgive, for Carlisle surrender,
iii. 296
resignation of, falsely reported, i. 319, 330
resigns, iii. 211
Robinson entertains, i. 184
—— gives ball for daughter of, i. **174**, 184
Sandwich aide-de-camp to, iii. 176

sister of, iv. 111n, 459n
viceroy of Ireland, ii. 556
Walpole, Sir Robert, defended by, in **House**
of Lords, i. 330
—— not a personal friend of, i. 319
—— told that mastership of the Horse is
resigned by, i. 319
wife's devotion from, i. 184, iv. 125
wife's intention to visit Ds of Norfolk
during his absence in the army worries, iii.
176
Lennox, Charles (1735–1806), 3d D. of Richmond, 1750; Duc d'Aubigny:
abuse of, by both parties, indicates his
virtue, ix. 295
anxiety over military campaign of, v. 316
audience of, postponed, vi. 364
balls given by, for approaching wedding,
v. **67**
Bauffremont recommends Soyres to, ix. 518
casts of antique statues collected by, in
garden room, for use of artists, v. 173
Conway aided by, vi. 507
courier summons, to Fontainebleau, vi. 364
Damer, Mrs, models sleeping dogs in
marble for, ix. 576
—— sister-in-law of, ix. 576n
declines to secede from government after
Rockingham's death, ix. 294
denounced to Gordon rioters, ix. 54
England visited by, from Paris, vi. 399, 400
fireworks by, on Thames, vi. 148–9
Garter given to, ix. 273
gazettes say, is in Paris, vi. 369
George III adds, to Bedchamber, v. 460
Grafton succeeded by, as secretary of state,
vi. 419–20
HW calls on, at Paris, vi. 364
HW content with any ministry that satis-
fies, vi. 436
HW entertains, at dinner at SH, vi. 322
HW hears from, that Conway is recovering,
vi. 413
HW pleased by promotion of, vi. 420
HW's only political connection is with
Conway and, vi. 359n
HW to tell, of Clement XIII's deference
to George III, vi. 393
HW wishes well to, in new administration,
ix. 310
Louis XV asks impertinent questions of,
about George III, vi. 163, 170
Mann compliments Conway on stepdaughter's marriage to, v. 82
—— kindly treated by, vi. 374
—— knew, at Florence, vi. 427
—— pities, vii. 102
—— pleased by promotion of, vi. 427–8
—— reassured about his packets under
cover of, to Conway, vi. 405
—— sends copy to, of his letter to Albani,
vi. 385

—— sends letters through, to HW and Conway, vi. 397

——'s letters received by, vi. 400

——'s letters to HW sent to, without knowing of his return to England, vi. 399

—— writes to, about Young Pretender's Roman negotiations, vi. 369, 374

masquerade given by, vi. 148-9

Master of the Ordnance, ix. 262, 296, 392

ministry defeated by, over India House, vii. 546

North administration severely handled by, for their flippancies, ix. 284

Paris not yet reached by, vi. 341

Paris post accepted by, vi. 323

Paris visited by, vi. 163

Parliamentary motion of, to put Ps of Wales in Regency Bill, rejected, vi. 297

Pitt has fit when replying to, viii. 371

Pitt, William II, adopts fortification plan to please, ix. 629-30

prime ministership should have gone to, instead of to Rockingham, ix. 296

resignation of, from Ordnance, ix. 392

resignations of ministers under Shelburne opposed by, ix. 294

Rockingham faction deserted by, ix. 294, 295

rumoured as Rockingham's successor, ix. 289

secretaries to, at Paris, vi. 405

servant of, robs and sets fire to Conway's house, vi. 588

sister of, v. 517n

step-father-in-law better-looking than, vi. 67

willingness of, to retain post of Master of Ordnance, shows his disinterestedness, ix. 296

Lennox, Lady Emilia Mary (1731-1814), m. 1 (1747) James Fitzgerald, 20th E. of Kildare; cr. (1761) M. of Kildare, (1766) D. of Leinster; m. 2 (1774) William Ogilvie:

Dayrolles takes, for walk in park, iii. 403

father repulses suitor of, iii. 241

Florence to be visited by, with family, for summer, viii. 181

Holland visited by, iii. 404

Kildare weds, iii. 371

Mann finds villa for, viii. 181

Queensberry, Ds of, invites, to ball, iii. 28

Robinson entertains, i. 174, 184

sister of, v. 154n

sister seen by, iii. 371

subscription masquerade attended by, iv. 49

Lennox, Lady George. See Ker, Lady Louisa (1739-1830)

Lennox, Lord George Henry (1737-1805), army officer; M.P.:

Cumberland, D. of, takes, to Hanover, v. 78

(?) Mann hoped for acknowledgement from, vi. 405

wife of, vi. 148n

Lennox, Lady Georgiana Caroline (1723-74), m. (1744) Henry Fox, cr. (1763) Bn Holland; cr. (1762) Bns Holland, s.j.:

Aiguillon, Duchesse d', procures ticket for, to see Paris fireworks, vi. 163

barony granted to, vi. 31

Beaufort, Ds of, told by, in letter, about older sons' ingratitude, viii. 30

Boufflers, Comtesse de, asked by, about SH, vi. 270

Caligula's bust pleases, vi. 524

casts of Caligula's bust taken by, vi. 528

Dayrolles takes, for walk in park, iii. 403

death of, viii. 25

debts of elder sons cleared by, viii. 25

dying, viii. 19

elopement of, ii. 450-1

father's rage at marriage of, iii. 71

Florence visited by, vi. 466-7, 473, 528

Fox, C.J., and Stephen, wound, by their ingratitude, viii. 22

Fox, Henry Edward, the only good son of, viii. 5

HW, Cts of Orford, and Mozzi call on, vii. 229-30

HW not told by, of Leopold's favour procured by Mann for her husband, vi. 540-1

HW receives Caligula's bust through, vi. 522

HW's great friend, vi. 466

health of, cancer, viii. 5

Holland visited by, iii. 404

husband to be joined by, at Naples, vi. 466-7

husband wants peerage for, v. 75

Mann entertains, at Florence, vi. 467, 528

—— grieved for, vii. 102

—— hopes that fortune of, is not injured by husband's generosity to sons, vii. 536

—— hopes that husband's fortune will not be left by, to her older sons, viii. 29-30

—— pities, for hopeless illness and husband's death, viii. 22

—— sent compliments by, vi. 524

—— takes, for country jaunts in Tuscany, vi. 528

—— will like, vi. 473

Robinson entertains, i. 184

rôle of, in English political drama, v. 53

Rome to be visited by, vi. 467

Shelburne's legacy to, iv. 248

sister of, v. 154n

sister sees, iii. 371

sons will probably dissipate inheritance from, viii. 31

vases liked by, v. 212

Lennox, Lady Louisa Augusta (1743-1821), m. (1758) Rt Hon. Thomas Conolly:

Dayrolles takes, for walks in park, iii. 403

Lennox, Lady Sarah (1745–1826), m. 1 (1762)
Sir Thomas Charles Bunbury, 6th Bt (divorced, 1776); m. 2 (1781) Hon. George
Napier:
  appearance of, v. 530
  beauty of, unlikely to last, vi. 8
  Bunbury to wed, vi. 8
  Charlotte's bridesmaid, v. 529
  (?) Dayrolles takes, for walks in park, iii.
  403
  George III's alleged love affair with, v. 517
  (?) Mann shocked by follies of, vii. 102
  'Statira,' v. 517
  Westmorland mistakes, for Q. Charlotte, v.
  531
Lennox family:
  glow of beauty peculiar to, v. 530
Le Normand d'Etiolles, Charles-Guillaume
(1717–99):
  opera girl not kept by, iv. 340
Le Normant, Mme. See Morphy, Marie-Louise
Lenox, ship:
  expected at Port Mahon, i. 285
Lent:
  'burial of Carnival,' the one day in, when
  amusements are permitted, viii. 281
  Clement XIII allows Spaniards to eat meat
  4 days a week in, vi. 5
  concerts during, iii. 374
  fasting during, iii. 129
  fish shortage might compel Clement XIII
  to allow meat in, vi. 101
  Florentines dread, iii. 465
  Florentines want Leghorn devotions postponed till, i. 304–5
  invalids in Florence likely to be visited
  during, vii. 458
  Italy lacks fish for, ix. 17
  Leopold dispensed from maigre dinners in,
  vi. 409
  Mann gives routs during, vii. 458
  passion play presented during, in all Italian
  churches and convents, vii. 459
  Pius VI permits meat during, ix. 17, 21
  Protestants interfere with fasting during,
  ix. 21
  solemn tranquillity of, iv. 465
  theatres open after, vi. 224
  Thurn's death increases solemnity of, in
  Florence, vi. 400
Lentulus, Robert (Rupertus) Scipio (1714–?86),
Freiherr von, Prussian army officer and envoy; governor of Neuchâtel:
  England receives news from, of Lobositz
  battle, v. 4
  Frederick II's victory exaggerated by, v. 14
Leominster, Bn. See Fermor, Thomas (1698–
1753); Fermor, William (1648–1711)
Leominster, Bns. See Jeffreys, Hon. Henrietta
Louisa
Leominster. See also Lempster
Leon, ship:
  in Spanish fleet, i. 286

Leonidas:
  Russian fleet to arouse ghost of, vii. 212
Leonidas. See under Glover, Richard
Leonora, Ps. See Eleonora Luisa
Leopard, ship:
  eagle shipped on, iii. 268
  HW's cases taken by, to Mahon, iii. 268
  involved in war, iii. 232
  prizes captured by, iii. 245–6
Leopold (d. 1136), saint; Margrave of Austria:
  celebration on day of, at Florence, vi. 367
  festival of, in Florence like that of St
  Joseph in Vienna, vi. 371
Leopold II (1747–92), Grand Duke of Tuscany
1765–90; Holy Roman Emperor 1790–2:
  ability of, high, vii. 372
  Accademia dei nobili gives celebration in
  honour of, vi. 367
  accession not yet announced by, out of
  deference to brother, vi. 345
  accoucheur accompanies, on travels, vii. 220
  affability of, Medicean, vi. 390
  affairs diligently conducted by, vi. 353–4
  Albani and Clement XIII not to be visited
  by, at Rome, vii. 2
  Albany, Cts of, puts herself under protection of, ix. 101, 108n, x. 47
  Alfieri imposes upon, ix. 397
  announcements of accession of, delayed, vi.
  350, 353, 356, 367
  arrival of, in Florence, vi. 330, 334, 336–8
  audiences given by, to servants and tribunal
  heads, vi. 340
  bal masqué and supper to be given by, at
  great theatre, for D. and Ds of Cumberland, ix. 644–5
  Beauchamp to avoid route of, vi. 336
  Beaufort, Ds of, befriended by, vii. 372
  Bonechi agent of, at Naples, vii. 254
  Borghese entertains, at villa, vii. 23
  Botta busy preparing for, vi. 123, 157,
  166–7, 246, 334, 337
  —— disliked by, vi. 337, 398, 454
  ——'s conduct disapproved by, vi. 379
  —— to be grand maître to, vi. 246
  —— to meet, at Pietra Mala, vi. 334
  —— visits Vienna probably to arrange
  coming of, vi. 87
  brothers to be met by, at Venice, and
  escorted to Florence unless Bohemian affairs
  interfere, viii. 95
  busy because he is his own prime minister,
  vii. 372
  carnival diversions eagerly enjoyed by, vi.
  486, 491
  Castello visited by, ix. 421, 644
  ceremony performed by, of taking possession of duchy, vi. 412
  chambellan rebuked by, for wrongly announcing Guasco, vi. 531
  Chartres slights, ix. 417
  china factory of, see China factory

Cholmondeley tells Mann to inform, of D. of Gloucester's plans, vii. 397

Clement XIII quarrels with, over disposal of church plate, vi. 475

—— thanked by, through Schwartzenberg, vii. 23

Clement XIV's dispute with, over Arezzo bishopric, vii. 504

coachman of, is Clement XIV's relative, vii. 118

cockades given to, at Leghorn, vi. 423

Coke, Lady Mary, regards, as her persecutor, vii. 553

collection of, Mrs Damer may wish to copy statues in, ix. 184

comment of, on D. of Cumberland's journey, vii. 513

comptroller of, serves beer and punch to Cowper and Tylney, vi. 379

Conway awaits announcement of, to forward Mann's new credentials, vi. 376

Córdoba's unwillingness to risk battle foretold by, to Mann, ix. 155

Corpus Domini procession at Florence to be attended by, vi. 418

Corsican seizure by France should be resented by, viii. 477

Corsica's French ownership now regretted by, vii. 54, viii. 437

Corsini to entertain, vii. 95

costume regulated by, ix. 174–5, 183

councils of, held at Florence for form's sake, and results sent to him, ix. 548

courier expected by, with news of war in Germany, viii. 389

court of, will enliven Tuscany, vi. 134

court procedure of, vi. 366–7, vii. 535

Cowper communicates Mann's dispatch to, urging that Charles III be persuaded to stop war with England, ix. 43

——'s burletta not attended by, for fear of reprimand from Vienna, vi. 393

—— visits, in country, vii. 335

Cowpers favoured by, over Young Pretender, viii. 245

Craon, Princesse de, pays court to, at Poggio Imperiale, vi. 537

crystal vase esteemed while in *tribuna* of collection of, ix. 169

Cumberland, D. and Ds of, to be received by, ix. 644–5

Cumberland, D. of, might not be permitted by, to stay with Mann, vii. 50

Damer, Hon. Mrs, should be asked by, for piece of statuary, ix. 613

decree of, forbidding high head-dresses, ix. 174–5, 183

dinner invitations of, sent only a few hours in advance, vi. 390–1

dispensed from eating *maigre* dinner, vi. 409

Doria to entertain, vii. 95

duchy ruled by, like a private estate, viii. 343

economy practised by, to amass fortunes for his children, vii. 502

Elector Palatine requires first visit from, at inn, viii. 164

English change in administration astonishes, ix. 396

English honours undervalued by, vii. 502

English visitors offended by haphazard invitations of, vi. 482

envoy to be appointed by, to England, vi. 345–6

expenses of, immoderate, vi. 340

father-in-law convinced by, that English war is a mistake, ix. 43, 58

father-in-law esteems, ix. 43

father's annual requiem attended by, at Florence, ix. 600

father will get part of Tuscan revenue even during reign of, vi. 255

Ferdinand and Maria Carolina of Naples to be entertained by, ix. 594, 598

Ferdinand and Maria Carolina will relieve, by their departure, ix. 600

Ferdinand's popularity at Florence may displease, ix. 600

Ferdinand, Archduke, and wife escorted by, on Bologna road to Naples for carnival, ix. 2

fiancée of, 3 years old, iv. 393–4

Florence disliked by, vii. 72, 79, 94–5, 123, 278, 296, ix. 421, 425

Florence may be visited by, to take Joseph II to Pisa, ix. 367

Florence prepares for, vi. 206, 254–5, 258–9, 273, 290–1, 306, 327, 333–4

Florence thought by, to dislike him, ix. 425

Florence to be revisited by, before Holy Week, viii. 453–4

Florence to be visited by, for St John's day festivities, vi. 424, 427

Florence welcomes, as relief from Lorraine control, vi. 336

Florentine public entry of, vi. 424

Florentine theatres disgust, vi. 477

Florentine theatre visited by, in chaise and pair without attendants, vii. 112

Fortescue and Gore invited by, to dinner at Florence, vi. 482

France and Spain complain to, about supplying St Philip's, ix. 250

France and Spain remonstrated against, for treatment, viii. 509

France tells, to annul neutrality edict, viii. 508

Frascati visited by, vii. 23

freedom permitted by, in writings about princes, ix. 193

French threat conveyed to, by Barbantane's valet-de-chambre, viii. 505

Gaddi busts, pictures and torso bought by, ix. 170

[Leopold II, *continued*]

Galluzzi's history of Medici family, commissioned and encouraged by, ix. 59, 81, 87n, 202, 205–6, 214

—— told by, to tell the truth, ix. 205–6, 214

garde noble of, vii. 253

Gatti rewarded by, for inoculating his sons, vii. 7

Genoa may reject letter of, vi. 379

Genoese loan obtained by, at 4 per cent, vi. 526

George III announces brother's death to, vi. 391, 556

——'s letter to, viii. 530

——'s notification from, vi. 362, 367, 378

—— to call, 'brother,' vii. 47

German qualities shown by, in disliking Florence, vii. 79

Gloucester, D. of, asked by, to get honours for Cowper, vii. 502

—— entertained by, vii. 405

—— exchanges civilities with, vii. 294, 304, 332–3, 335, 342, 348, 352, 355–6, 357, viii. 291, 297–8

—— invites, to dine on shipboard and attend *bal masqué* at Leghorn, vii. 353

—— probably will not be seen by, viii. 129

—— tells, at Vienna, of marriage, vii. 308

Grand Ducal title not permitted until accession of, is announced, vi. 330

Grand Maître of, Thurn to be, vii. 253

Guasco often spoken to, by, vi. 531

HW admires, for mourning Thurn's loss, vi. 404

HW asks Mann about china in collection of, ix. 215

HW belittles pretensions of, vi. 483

HW does not care a straw about royal visitors to, ix. 602

HW esteems, for having commissioned Galluzzi's history of Medicis, ix. 202

HW expects paragraph in *London Gazette* about Mann's investiture by, vii. 57

HW fears that Ferdinand's and Maria Carolina's visits to, may inconvenience Mann, ix. 583

HW regrets Mann's ill-success with plan about, ix. 48–9

HW's message to, through Mann, about Octavius's death, ix. 413

Hamilton and Mann have audience with, ix. 425

Hancarville gets patent from, for fish supply, vii. 448

health of: not quite well, ix. 600; not robust, vi. 337; often out of order, vi. 559

Holland, Bns, forgets to tell HW of kindness of, procured by Mann for her husband, vi. 540–1

household of, furnished with plate made from gold taken from Palazzo Pitti, ix. 231

House of Austria may no longer need heirs from, vi. 526

Ingenhousz inoculates, vii. 120, 122

—— to inoculate, vii. 91, 108

inoculation's benefits to family and subjects of, ix. 420

Inquisition suppressed by, ix. 81

'in villa,' ix. 548

Italians adopt pro-British sentiments of, ix. 383

itinerary of: from Florence to Naples, vii. 17–18; on Tuscan tour, viii. 343

Jesuit confessor still employed by, vi. 519

Jesuits suppressed but kindly treated by, vii. 512–13

Joseph II accompanied by, to Pisa and Leghorn, vii. 108

—— and, probably agreed regarding Galluzzi's history, ix. 238

Joseph II and D. of Gloucester, to meet, at Milan, vii. 331

Joseph II at odds with, vi. 375

—— discusses heir's education with, ix. 474

—— exhausts treasury of, vi. 446

—— forbids, to negotiate with Spain, ix. 46

—— gives little aid to, vi. 526

—— might urge, to make Siena agreeable to D. of Gloucester, viii. 125

—— nurses, vii. 120

—— prejudiced by, against Florence, ix. 474

—— proclaims, as Grand Duke of Tuscany, vi. 329, 330

—— received by, in Boboli Gardens, vii. 108

—— regulates policy of, ix. 383, 389

——'s acknowledgement of, as Grand Duke, doubtful, vi. 330

—— said to be trying to make Francis II King of Romans instead of, ix. 613n

—— said to have reported Polish disturbances to, ix. 44

——'s deputy, in giving *toison d'or* to son, vii. 55, 59

——'s letter to, about Paoli, vii. 137, 154

——'s relations with, to be settled by Rosenberg, vi. 393–4

——'s simplicity copied by, vii. 220

—— to be accompanied by: at Verona, vii. 105; to Leghorn, vi. 548, vii. 108; to Pisa, ix. 367, 468; to Venice for the Ascension, vii. 105, 108, viii. 105

—— to be consulted by, about Mann's dispatch, ix. 43

—— to be shown new frigate by, vi. 548

—— to renounce Tuscany to, vi. 123

—— to stay for inoculation of, vii. 111

—— to visit, viii. 123, ix. 350, 367, 468

—— visited by, at Mantua, ix. 593

—— visits, vii. 108, 111, 120, ix. 468

Karl Wilhelm Ferdinand declines invitation of, but is well received at Court, vi. 457–8

Keppel said by, to have blockaded Brest, viii. 395

ladies never received by, vii. 535

learned Jesuits invited by, to Tuscany, vii. 512
Leghorn and Lucca to be visited by, viii. 130
Leghorn governor asks, for instructions in case of D. of Gloucester's death, vii. 341–2
Leghorn merchants give shows for, vi. 417–18, 423
Leghorn to be visited by, vi. 453, vii. 71, 108, ix. 600
Leghorn visited by, vi. 422–3
Leghorn visited by, to see frigate launched, vi. 548
letters opened by, ix. 412n, 566
Leyden gazette's account of Octavius's death alarms, ix. 405, 412n
Liechtenstein, P. of, may prepare Florence for arrival of, vi. 153
life of, dull, vi. 354
limited amusements of, during mourning period, vi. 340
lives at his villa like a country gentleman, ix. 498–9
Lunigiana visited by, ix. 318
maigre dinner not joined by, vi. 409
maître d'hôtel of, see Julien
Maltese Grand Master sends Rohan to, with galleys, vi. 556
Mann accompanies: to Pisa and Leghorn, vi. 422–3; to Pisa but not to Siena, vi. 515
Mann and Murray meet, in Grand Chamberlain's apartment, vi. 350
Mann and other English received by, vi. 345
Mann and P. of Mecklenberg entertained by, at Poggio Imperiale, vi. 437–8
Mann argues with, about taking medicine, vi. 459
—— asks HW to reassure, about Octavius's inoculation, ix. 405–6, 412, 420
—— dines with, vi. 379
—— discusses Clive's death with, viii. 68
—— dreads return of, from Pisa, ix. 393
—— gives Chinese pheasants to, vi. 368
—— gives code name for, ix. 43
—— has had no instructions about his behaviour to, vi. 319
—— hears Spanish news from, viii. 530, ix. 145
—— invested by, with Bath insignia, vii. 63
—— invited by, to dinner, vi. 390
—— must use more obsequious language to, than to other foreigners, ix. 393
—— persuades, to urge Charles III to cease supporting France against England, ix. 43
—— presents Herbert and George III's letter to, viii. 530
—— presents young Chernyshev to, ix. 84
——'s Bath ribbon pleases, vii. 9
——'s correspondence with HW known to, ix. 412n
——'s credentials as minister plenipotentiary presented to, ix. 249

—— seeks promotion too late when Florence is about to receive, vi. 341
——'s expense allowance for marriage of, vi. 356–7
——'s failure to be promoted might be considered disrespectful to, vi. 352
—— should get Bath ribbon before return of, vii. 36–7
——'s promotion might induce, to appoint new envoy to England, vi. 345–6
——'s servants exempted by, from inheritance tax, ix. 666
—— tells, of Rodney's victory, ix. 24
—— tired by standing long periods when introducing strangers to, ix. 425
—— to be invested by, with Bath insignia, vii. 48, 59–60
—— to have audience with, to deliver George III's notice, vi. 391
—— told by: about Paoli's supposed Vienna visit, vii. 140; about Russo-Prussian interference in Sweden, vii. 439; of D. of Gloucester's marriage, vii. 308; of Joseph II's praise of Paoli, vii. 137, 154; of Russian-Turkish war, ix. 415, 420
—— to thank, for letting son dine on board Sir John Lindsay's squadron, ix. 499
—— well treated by, vi. 367–8
—— will never have to follow, to an army camp, vii. 92
—— would be embarrassed to answer, about peace treaty, ix. 383
(?) Mann, Horace II, discusses Parliamentary freedom with, ix. 58
—— thanked by, for making fund of Mann's servants' legacies, ix. 670
mantle of, may be rumpled by France, viii. 515
Mantua to be visited by, ix. 593
Maria Amalia visits, ix. 299, 301, 307n
Maria Carolina entertained by, at Florence, vii. 17–18
—— to be accompanied by, to Naples, vii. 2, 11
—— to meet, at Bologna, vii. 15
Maria Josefa to visit, vi. 492
Marino visited by, vii. 23
maritime ambitions of, vi. 548
marriage of, vi. 319, 321, 343n
marriage of, planned, iv. 393, vi. 123, 125
masking enjoyed by, vi. 477, 486, 491, viii. 343
Maximilian escorted back to Florence by, part way from Rome, viii. 123
medal struck by order of, to commemorate Moroccan ambassador's reception, viii. 469, 478, 500
Medicean collection assembled and augmented by, ix. 530–1
Medici guardaroba sold by, ix. 531
medicine taken frequently by, vi. 459
memorials presented to, requesting ban on extravagant dress, ix. 175

[Leopold II, *continued*]

Milan duchy to be administered by, for Francis III, iv. 393

Mill and Lowther still get salaries from, vi. 548

minchiate played by, vi. 340

ministers' reports to be heard by, in person, vii. 220

Modenese princess not to wed, vi. 125

Moroccan emperor presents horse to, viii. 469

mother gives trunk-load of medicines to, vi. 459

mother may be visited by, in Vienna during war, viii. 389

mother sends courier to, to tell him that she cannot meet him at Gorizia, viii. 200

mother's will favours, ix. 107

mother tells, to go to Parma to lecture sister, vii. 411–12

mother thanks Ingenhousz for inoculating, vii. 123

mother to be visited by, vii. 214

mother to meet, at Gorizia, with his family, viii. 191

name-day of, to be celebrated, vii. 342

neutrality of: disapproved by French ministers, viii. 508–9; does not prevent son from congratulating Mann on Rodney's victory, ix. 281–2

Niccoli's dispatch informs, of high price of food, viii. 106

—— the Paris agent of, viii. 362

Niobe group in Uffizi dispersed by, ix. 170–1, 530

nuncio gives papal bull to, vii. 507–8

nuncio's relations with, vi. 319

opera regulated by, vi. 559

Order of Marie-Thérèse brought to, by Kinský from Vienna, vi. 362

Order of St Stephen to build church for, vi. 258

Orford, Cts of, allowed by, to use Pratolino apartment, vii. 23

Orlov gives Egyptian horse to, vii. 228

out of humour and perplexed by failure of Florentine mills, ix. 318

Palestrina to entertain, vii. 95

Paoli talks with, vii. 130, 136–7

Parma dislikes accession announcement of, vi. 378–9

Passion Play in Lent forbidden by, vii. 459

Patch would be permitted by, to copy paintings, vii. 268

people meet, in lanes and roads near Poggio Imperiale, giving coins, vii. 122

Pisa abbey suppressed by, vii. 504

Pisa balls end at retirement of, vii. 171

Pisa baths to be visited by, for wife's health, vii. 108

Pisa but not the Pisans liked by, vii. 254

Pisa gives more liberty to, vii. 278

Pisa illuminated for visit of, vi. 422

Pisan Battle of the Bridge displeases, vi. 515

Pisan Battle of the Bridge to be deferred by, until Ferdinand's visit, ix. 569

Pisans may erect statue of, vii. 95

Pisa to be visited by, vi. 453, 459, vii. 71–2, 108, 336, 342, 348, ix. 421, 425

Pisa visited by, vi. 422–3, 515, vii. 91, 171, 185, 422–3, viii. 129, ix. 383, 421

Pitti Palace disliked by, vii. 253–4

Pitti Palace refurnished for, v. 556–7

Pitti Palace scene of New Year's ceremonies of, viii. 346

Pius VI not complimented by, with suppression of carnival, ix. 243

Poggio a Caiano visited by, vii. 296

Poggio Imperiale must be summer residence of, vii. 296

Poggio Imperiale visited by, vi. 424, 427, 526, vii. 111–12, 122, 449, ix. 421, 594, 598

porcelain factory of, ix. 590

Porto Longone not to be visited by, to see P. of Piombino's iron mines, vii. 131

portrait of, should be painted, investing Mann with Bath order, vii. 48

Pratolino visited by, vi. 334, 337, 350

private messenger received by, from Vienna, every fortnight, ix. 44

public works program to be started by, ix. 314

reception to be given by, followed by Drawing-Room, vi. 362

repose preferred by, ix. 600

return of, to Tuscany, unexpected, ix. 515

returns to Florence from Vienna, but still in retirement, viii. 250

riding the only amusement of, vi. 353–4

Rohan, P. Camille de, invites, to supper and illumination at Leghorn, vi. 556–7

Roman court dislikes letter from, vi. 378

Roman nobility prepare festivals for, vii. 95

Rome not to be visited by, vii. 2, 17

Rome's dictates opposed by, ix. 81

Rome visited by, vii. 23, 91, 95, 103, 108–9

Rosenberg accompanies, vii. 253

Rosenberg and German physician fear attack of smallpox for, vi. 559

——'s inefficiency displeases, vii. 220

—— told by, of print satirizing three abbés' mutual admiration, vi. 531

royal rank of, acknowledged, vii. 293

Russian victory announced to, vii. 478–9

sale of collection of: deplored by HW, ix. 215, 531; from Palazzo Vecchio, ix. 230–1

Salviati to entertain, vii. 95

seclusion of, vi. 353–4, 526, viii. 250

Siena and seacoast to be visited by, viii. 343

sister-in-law's death may injure inheritance prospects of, vi. 526

smallest theatre preferred by, vi. 477

son of, ix. 281–2

sovereigns all address, as 'brother,' vii. 55

stables of, visited by Maria Amalia, ix. 301

strangers affably entertained by, ix. 425

supper guests of, not restricted, vii. 191

supper taken by, at 9 P.M., vi. 354

Te Deum not to be sung for arrival of, at Florence, vi. 334

theatre attendance may be denied to, by orders from Vienna, vi. 407

theatre attended by, in great simplicity, with Joseph II, vii. 112

theatre balls attended nightly by, in mask, vi. 486

Thurn, Anton, to be *grand maître* to, vii. 253

Thurn, Franz, former governor of, vi. 398

——'s death distresses, vi. 397–8

Thurn, Comtesse, rewarded by, vii. 253

travels *en bourgeois*, by Joseph II's example, vii. 220

tunny fishing to be watched by, at Porto Ferrajo, vii. 131

Tuscan drainage project of, expensive and fruitless, viii. 343

Tuscans vainly ask relief from, for bread shortage, vi. 448

Tuscany given to, by father, vi. 412

Tuscany to be ruled by, v. 556, vi. 123, 125

Uffizi collection increased by, ix. 230, 530–1

Uffizi collection rearranged by, ix. 169–71, 530–1

Vienna has probably told, how to receive D. of Gloucester, viii. 129

Vienna to be visited by, vii. 220, viii. 389, 409

Vienna visited by, vii. 332, viii. 240, 505, 515

Viennese instructions awaited by, for announcement of accession, vi. 350, 353, 356

Viennese mourning regulations awaited by, before seeing visitors, vi. 337

Viennese permission awaited by, vii. 91, 413

violent in his exercises, vi. 559

war council at Vienna may be led by, in case of war, viii. 370

wife follows, in coach to Florence, vi. 427

wife left by, to attend balls, vi. 486

wife's dinner not shared by, because male servants are not allowed in her chamber, vi. 529

York, D. of, to be offered an apartment by, vi. 417

younger children of, about to be inoculated, ix. 406, 412n

Young Pretender complains to, through his first minister, ix. 102

—— said to have bequeathed kingdoms to son of, ix. 394–5

——'s request for dais or baldacchino over theatre boxes denied by, ix. 536

Zoffany should have put, in painting of Tribune, viii. 539

Leopold I (1679–1729), D. of Lorraine 1690–1729:

Charles VI persuaded by, to make Craon a prince, ii. 298n

Craon ejected by, from wife's bed, ii. 298n

——'s 'children' resemble, ii. 298n

Craon, Princesse de, bears twenty children to, ii. 298n, iv. 326

—— mistress of, i. **17,** 60, 189n, ii. 298n, iv. 213n, 236, 326, vi. 324n

—— occupies apartment near, iv. 116

—— receives homage of, vi. 536

death of, ii. 298n

health of, operated upon for piles, i. 60

Lunati, Mme, flees from advances of, iv. 351

Mann hopes that Francis I will spare Beauvau out of respect for, i. 481

son of, vi. 324n

Walpole, Bns, exhumes stories about, i. 327

wife jealous of amours of, ii. 298n

Leopold Friedrich Franz (1740–1817), P. of Anhalt-Dessau as Leopold III:

Albani's letter to, enclosed by Mann, vi. 478

brother accompanies, to Florence, vi. **418**

England to be visited by, in summer, vi. 418

England visited by, vi. 437, 450

English cultivated by, vi. 418

London lodging of, is in Suffolk St, vi. 437

Mann encloses letter to, vi. 437, 450

—— entertains, vi. 418

Lepage, Mme. *See* Éremans, Mlle

Le Page, Anne-Marie (1710–1802), m. (1727) Pierre-Joseph Fiquet du Boccage:

England visited by, iv. 142

Les Amazones by, a failure, iv. 142

Milton translation by, praised by Chesterfield, iv. 142

Lepell, Mary (1700–68), m. (1720) John Hervey, styled Bn Hervey of Ickworth:

Bourbon, Duc de, receives allegorical dialogue in form of letter from, ii. 517–18

death of, vii. 58, 60, 76

family of: vii. 58n; suffer from gout, viii. 86

favourite son of, v. 233

Frederick, P. of Wales, does not speak to, i. 391

George II told by, of HW's joke on Churchill, i. 359

HW entertained by, i. 275

HW fears that Montesquieu's letters may hurt, because of her friendship with Mme Geoffrin and Duchesse d'Aiguillon, vi. 524

HW's regard for, v. 233, vi. 82, vii. 58–9, viii. 475

health of: gout, vii. 76; gout and rheumatism, vii. 58

physicians say, died of bootikins not diarrhœa, vii. 76

son of, vi. 82

[Lepell, Mary, *continued*]
son's letter from, x. 29–30
son's sincerity probably not reverenced by, viii. 475
Ussons and Comtesse de Boufflers often at house of, vi. 135
Lepell family:
gout the ailment of, viii. 86
Lepidus, Marcus Æmilius (d. 13 B.C.), triumvir:
Octavius and Antony struggle over, v. 79
Lepri, Marchesa. *See* Cherufini, Vittoria
Lepri, Marchese Don Amanzio (d. 1785), priest of order of Malta:
Pius VI gets donation from, for nephew, ix. 384, 568, 589n
——'s donation from, declared invalid, ix. 587–8, 589
repents of giving wealth to Pius VI, ix. 588
Lepri, Anna Maria *or* Maria Anna (b. ca 1773), m. (1789 or after) —— Cusani:
Sforza engaged to, ix. 384
uncle tries to deprive, of inheritance, ix. 384
Lepri, Marchese Giuseppe (d. before 1783):
England visited by, ix. 384
Lercari, Giovanni (d. 1802), Abp of Adrianople; Abp of Genoa, 1767:
Old Pretender wants to remove, from Cardinal York's entourage, iv. 354
Lercari. *See also* Imperiale Lercari
Lerici:
Bute to embark from, for Genoa, vii. 103
Charles of Naples and Don Philip to meet near, v. 280
Coke, Lady Mary, expects murder at, because boatmen will not sail, vii. 552
—— to embark from, to Genoa, vii. 545
inn at, miserable, ix. 204
Mann, Horace II, detained at, ix. 204, 210
passage from Genoa to, i. 393
'Le Roi Pepin':
fashionable French race-horse, viii. 266
Le Sage, Alain-René (1668–1747):
Gil Blas, HW refers to Archbishop in, who resents imputation of senility, vii. 216, ix. 483
Leson. *See* Leeson
Lessines:
English army awaits recruits at, iii. 52
Lesson for the Day, by HW:
Coke given a copy of, ii. 33
HW writes copy of, for Mann, i. 491–3
printed, with additions not by HW, ii. 33
Lessons, Biblical:
parodies of, popular, ii. 33
Lestevenon, Mme. *See* Windsor, Hon. Catharine
Lestevenon de Berkenroode, Matthijs (1719–97), Dutch ambassador to France 1749–92:
burletta attended by, i. 200
Florence visited by, i. 200

La Porte and Schulenburg accompany, i. 200
Lincoln's marriage to Lady Sophia Fermor predicted by, i. 217
Mann's call belatedly returned by, i. 217
opera attended by, i. 217
Pomfret, Cts of, related to, i. 200
Uguccioni repulsed by, i. 217
Lestock, Richard (ca 1679–1746), vice-admiral, 1743; admiral, 1746:
acquittal of: at court martial, expected, iii. 33; party affair, iii. 321
Craon sends news of, to Francis I, i. 315
East India Company's magazines said to be destroyed by, iii. 330
England reached by, ii. 496
English fleet not joined by ships of, ii. 413, 414
English messenger brings orders to, to defend Hungary and Tuscany, i. 405
failure of, to arrive, may endanger English naval battle, ii. 416
French invasion to be led by, iii. 319
Haddock to be joined by, i. **221**, 290
Mann's shipments to HW not delivered by, ii. 496
—— wants to hear English comments on, ii. 444
Mathews criticized by, ii. 432
naval officers recalled from Mediterranean to be examined about affair of, iii. 12
orders too literally obeyed by, for fear of censure, iii. 33–4
Osborne conveys, to England, ii. 477, 514
Parliamentary investigation vindicates, iii. 33–4
Port Mahon to be visited by, i. 290
Scottish officer comments on, iii. 25
Spanish barks captured by, i. 433
Whigs uphold, iii. 33
Le Sueur, Eustache (1616–55):
Cipriani's paintings to replace those by, at Houghton, ix. 316
Le Tellier, François-Louis (1704–67), Marquis de Souvré; Lt-Gen.:
witticisms by, v. 514, 520
Le Tellier, François-Michel (1639–91), Marquis de Louvois:
successor to, will rise in France, viii. 208
Le Tellier de Louvois, Louis-Charles-César (1695–1771), Comte, Duc, and Maréchal d'Estrées:
Broglie and Soubise compared with, vi. **47**
Ferdinand must be dislodged by, or retreat will be necessary, vi. 50
Maillebois quarrels with, over battle of Hastenbeck, vii. 283
Lethargy:
apoplectic, occurrence of, vi. 17
Lethieullier, Sarah (d. 1788), m. (1746) Sir Matthew Fetherstonhaugh, cr. (1747) Bt:
Mann visited by, at Fiesole, iv. 194

Le Tonnelier, Jacques-Laure (1723–85), Bailli de Breteuil; Maltese ambassador to Rome 1757–ca1778, to France 1778–85:
Clement XIII persecuted by, to make him acknowledge Young Pretender, vi. 386
Mann told by, of Old Pretender's income, vi. 385
mother of, a Fitzjames, vi. 385
Young Pretender attended by, in France, vi. 385
Le Tonnelier, Louis-Auguste (1730–1807), Baron de Breteuil, French diplomatist:
Lee introduced by, at Vienna, viii. 390
Maria Theresa rebukes, for American-French alliance, viii. 390
might become prime minister, viii. 10
Le Tourneur, Pierre-Prime-Félicien (1737–88):
Shakespeare traduit de l'anglois, Shakespeare gets French encomiums as a result of, viii. 267
Letter; letters:
address upon, now greatly abbreviated, ix. 608
bombastic, not in English taste, ii. 558
circular: sent to English ministers to announce George III's coming marriage, v. 520; usually sent by retiring secretary of state to correspondents, ix. 299
complimentary endings of, vii. 550
compliments no longer customary in, ix. 608
cover of, should be sealed on the inside, i. 98
HW's, see under HW
should not be published while they may offend living persons, vi. 524
See also Correspondence
Letter-book:
Mann's: letter mislaid in, iv. 275; Palombo has access to, iv. 275
Lettere pittoriche. See Bottari, Giovanni Gaetano: Raccolta di lettere
Letter from Mr Cibber to Mr Pope, A. See under Cibber, Colley
Letter from Xo Ho, by HW:
HW sends, to Mann, v. 91
Leyden Gazette publishes French translation of, v. 108
Mann thanks HW for, v. 101
Letter of attorney. See Attorney, power of
Letters and Negotiations of M. Van Hoey:
Mann asks HW about, ii. 337
Letters concerning the Present State of Poland. See under Lind, John (1737–81)
Letters from Italy. See under Riggs, Anne (1741–81)
Letters of credit:
Orford, Cts of, takes, iii. 49
Letters of marque:
Holland has not yet issued, ix. 116
Letters of Neptune and Gracchus. See under King, John

Letters to his Grace the D—— of N——.
See under Shebbeare, John
Letter to . . . Lord North, A. See under Dobbs, Francis
Letter to Sir William Windham. See under St John, Henry
Letter to the Clergy and People of London. See under Sherlock, Thomas
Lettre de cachet:
(?) Matignon, Mme de, would shudder at, i. 152
Lettres du Marquis de Roselle. See under Morin-Dumesnil, Anne-Louise
Lettres . . . sur les Anglais. See under Le Blanc, Jean-Bernard
Leutron. See Leutrum
Leutrum, Friedrich (d. 1755), Bn de, Sardinian general ('Lutrum'):
Asti captured by, iii. 227
Belle-Isle forces, to retreat towards Ventimiglia, iii. 409
Brown to reinforce, iii. 436
Nice to be invaded by, iii. 432
troops needed by, iii. 422
Valenza to be besieged by, iii. 237
Ventimiglia to be besieged by, iii. 436, 441
Le Vallois, Philippe (ca 1632–1707), seigneur de Vilette:
widow of, iv. 136n
Levant, the:
commerce with, to be opened, iii. 437
Dutch convoy to, ix. 3
England's trade with, will suffer from French control of Corsica, vii. 27, 36, 47
French convoy from, eludes English ships, iii. 367
French ships from, in Pope's ports, should be burned by English, ii. 453
French trade with: carried on under Francis I's flag, v. 273–4, 282; resumed after Tripolitan incident, iv. 320
Mathews seizes rich French ships from, ii. 452
privateers expect harvest in, v. 335
prizes from, disputed about in Tuscany, v. 280
ships from, for Marseille, captured by privateers, viii. 437
Toulon fleet pursued towards, by Saunders, v. 431
Le Vassor, Louis (d. 1781), Marquis de la Touche; French naval officer:
Martinique defended by, vi. 21, 29–30
Levee; levees:
Carteret gives, ii. 349
Christian VII holds, at St James's, vii. 41
death will never find HW at, vii. 41
etiquette for, i. 210
Frederick, P. of Wales, to give, i. 338, 369
George II's, i. 173, 210, 337, 502, ii. 14, 94–5, 102, iii. 165
George III cancels, because of mother's illness, vii. 375

[Levee; levees, *continued*]
—— insolently treated at, by Diede, vii. 402
——'s: v. 530–1, vi. 161; after Du Châtelet-Chernyshev quarrel, vii. 126; attended by HW and Lord Howe, vii. 250; Mann, Horace II, to attend, ix. 659
HW abhors, v. 79
Karl Wilhelm Ferdinand gives, at Somerset House, vi. 197
Newcastle's: iv. 20; deserted by bishops, vi. 36–7
none, in court of Tuscany, ix. 340
Pelham gives, ii. 349, iv. 20
Richecourt's, v. 9
Russell's, in Newgate Prison, vii. 82
Sandys pretends to be having, ii. 232
Walpole, Sir Robert, gives, i. 318, ii. 349
Lever, John (d. 1745), high bailiff of Westminster:
clerk of, makes election return, i. 272
serjeant-at-arms has, in custody, i. 251, 272–3
vote of censure on, i. **251**
Leveson-Gower, Hon. Baptist (? 1703–82), M.P.:
Gower sends, to vote for Hessians, x. 24
Leveson-Gower, Lady Elizabeth (1723–84), m. (1751) Hon. John Waldegrave, 3d E. Waldegrave, 1763:
Anson, Bns, dances louvre with, iv. 121
marriage of: arranged by Sandwich, iv. 258; father probably regrets, more than his own dismissal, iv. 266
Leveson-Gower, Hon. Gertrude (1715–94), m. (1737) John Russell, 4th D. of Bedford, 1732:
Bolingbroke, Vcts, receives watch from, to be shown to Q. Charlotte, vi. 104–5
brother of, iv. 113n, 124
Carteret, Robert, awakens, after cropping horses' ears during visit, ii. 501
cousin lends to, Lady Mary Wortley Montagu's letters, iv. 281
daughter-in-law accompanied by, to opera, at time of son's accident, vi. 498
George II entertained by, iii. 464
—— supports precedence dispute of, iv. 122
Guerchy compliments, on fender at Woburn, vi. 218
HW obtains from, a glimpse of Lady Mary Wortley Montagu's letters, iv. 281
HW visits, at Woburn, iv. 281
Marlborough dislikes, iv. 73n
masked ball given by, iii. 464
Mirepoix, Duchesse de, disputes precedence with, at Sandwich's ball, iv. 122, 144
Newcastle, Ds of, meets, iv. 201
niece of, vii. 121
Paris to be visited by, vi. 78
Sandwich governs husband through, iv. 120
Selwyn accompanies, to Paris, vi. 105
son's death distresses, vi. 506

Villars, Maréchale de, entertains, in Paris, vi. 105
Leveson-Gower, Granville (1721–1803), styled Vct Trentham 1746–54, 2d E. Gower, 1754; cr. (1786) M. of Stafford:
Admiralty appointment of, iv. 100n
Admiralty declined by, vi. 449
Bedford, D. of, brother-in-law to, iv. 113n
Bedfords receive overtures through, vi. 537
bill for doubling militia opposed by, viii. 497
Dashwood to succeed, in Great Wardrobe, vi. 130
election of, iii. 425
father breaks with, iv. 258
French actors championed by, iv. 100n
friends of, summon high bailiff of Westminster, iv. 224
Gower sends, to vote for Hessians, x. 24
lord president of the Council, vi. 569, 571, viii. 497, 534
not yet gone over to the enemy, viii. 534
Pitt sends, to Woburn with overtures to Bedford, vi. 472
prime ministry rejected by, ix. 379
Privy Seal rumoured to go to, vi. 130
resigns: as Admiralty lord, iv. 258; as lord chamberlain, vi. 311; as lord president of the Council, viii. 526, 533
Rockingham refuses Shelburne's request to ask Cabinet post for, ix. 261
rumoured as Rockingham's successor, ix. 289
Vaughan dismissed for voting for, iv. 122
Westminster candidate, iv. 113n
Westminster election of, endangered by his championing of French actors, iv. 100n
Westminster election won by, iv. 107–8, 156
Leveson-Gower, John (1694–1754), 2d Bn Gower; cr. (1746) E. Gower:
Bath visited by, with Hervey, ii. 89
Board elects, president, ii. 186
brothers, sons, and Chetwynds sent by, to vote for Hessians, x. 24
Cobhamite dismissal wished by, iii. 188–9
daughter of, matched to Waldegrave by Sandwich, iv. 258
daughter's wedding probably more regretted by, than his own dismissal, iv. 266
Dorset succeeded by, as Master of the Horse, v. 104
George II assured by, of his loyalty, iii. 128–9
gout prevents: from leading his regiment, iii. 161; from taking Privy Seal, i. 478
HW to accompany Ds of Grafton to seat of, v. 427
inarticulate from palsy, iv. 418
Jacobites renounce, iii. 26
Jacobites renounced by, iii. 189
lord privy seal, i. 457, 492, 494, ii. 70, 89, 186, 551, iii. 211, iv. 517

Mann admires HW's joke about 'kissing hands' by, ii. 10

Manners family demands Rutland's substitution for, iv. 418

New Ode, A, satirizes, ii. 51

opposition party joined by, ii. 159

Pelhams control, iv. 258

privately-raised regiments defended by, iii. 154

Privy Seal resigned by, iv. 417–18

Pulteney and Hervey join, at Bath, ii. 89

Pulteney may succeed, as lord privy seal, ii. 96

—— opposes Privy Seal appointment of, ii. 70

Purnell's trial pressed by, iv. 18

Regency includes, ii. 218

regiment of: may be mustered, x. 15; mutinies, iii. 209

resignation of, as lord privy seal: ii. 356, iii. 211, iv. 417–18; expected, ii. 118, 159

Roman dispensation jokingly suggested as delaying assumption of office by, i. **494**

Ryder's conversation with, about Purnell's trial, iv. 18

Sandwich's quarrel with, iv. 258

son and Bedford break with, iv. 258

Temple to succeed, as Master of the Horse, v. 104

Tories drop affair of Hanoverian troops in deference to, ii. 141

Walpole, Horatio (1678–1757), receives witty answer from, to abusive letter, iv. 563

Westminster scrutiny paid for by, iv. 113

wife of, iv. 281n

Leveson-Gower, Lady Mary (d. 1778), m. (ca 1774) Sir Richard Wrottesley, 7th Bt:
Denbigh, Cts of, confuses, with Lady Mary Wortley Montagu, v. 540

Leveson-Gower, Hon. Richard (1726–53), M.P.:
Bedford House visited by, iv. 135
Nugent insulted by, at masquerade, iv. 124
Waldegrave mistaken for, iv. 156
watchman's earthquake warning imitated by, iv. 135

Leveson-Gower, Hon. William (ca 1696–1756), M.P.:
Gower sends, to vote for Hessians, x. 24

Leveson-Gower family:
Pelham makes invectives against, iv. 201

Levi. *See* Lévis

Leviathan:
parson compares, to Sir Robert Walpole, i. 197

Levinge, Mary (d. 1740), m. (ca 1704) Washington Shirley, 1st E. Ferrers:
daughter lives with, in France, iv. 298

Lévis, Marc-Antoine (b. 1739), Comte de:
(?) HW takes, to Pantheon, vii. 298

Lévis, Philippe de (d. 1203):
picture showing meeting of, with the Virgin Mary, iv. 88

Lévis de Lomagne, Gaston-Charles-Pierre de (ca 1699–1757), Marquis de Mirepoix; Duc de Mirepoix, 1757; Maréchal de France; French ambassador to England:
ambition of, to be Duc, iv. 28–9
appointment of, to London embassy, iv. **13,** 15, 55
ball may be given by, for nephew's birth, iv. 116–17
dancing the chief pleasure of, iv. 106
English manners and costume aped by, iv. 89
English ministers receive complaints by, of attack on French ships, iv. 489
France not notified by, of English belligerency, iv. 491
French lightness to be demonstrated by dancing of, iv. 117
George II congratulates, on dukedom, iv. 281
—— to be attended by, to Hanover, iv. 116
HW describes, iv. 87
HW thought that France depended on secret informants instead of, iv. 491
letters from, at Toulon, v. 141
Lorenzi to accompany, to England, iv. 67, 68
—— visits, iv. 87
malapropism of, iv. 289
Putney the residence of, iv. 87
White's Club's chess players invited by, iv. 289
wife gets no Court tabouret through, iv. 92
wife of, iv. 144
Yarmouth, Cts of, visited by, iv. 96

Lévis family:
family pride of, iv. 88
relationship of, to the Virgin Mary, iv. 88, 92

Lévis-Léran, Louis-Marie-François-Gaston, Marquis de:
Mirepoix accompanied by, to England, iv. 87

Levites:
Florentine ladies dress in, ix. 175

Levorirne. *See* Leghorn

Levshin, Petr Georgievich (1737–1812) ('Father Platon'), Bp (1770) and Abp (1775) of Tver; Metropolitan of Moscow, 1787:
discourse by, at Peter I's tomb, vii. 249

Lewen, Laetitia van (1712–50), m. (1729) Rev. Matthew Pilkington:
Sherlock, Bp, caricatured by, iv. 134

Lewes, Sussex:
races at: Newcastle, D. of, chats about, to Sussex men, iii. 495; Taaffe and D. of Newcastle attend, iv. 289

Lexington:
battle of, viii. 110

Ley, John (ca 1732–1814), assistant clerk of House of Commons 1767–1814:

[Ley, John, *continued*]
Speaker attended by, in empty House, ix. 573

Leyden, [? Cornelies Pieter (1738–90), Rijksbaron van]; Dutch emissary to Austria:
Joseph II to receive, ix. 593

Leyden:
English packets retarded at, iii. 257
John of, *see* John of Leiden
Van Heck to forward HW's letters from, iii. 145–6

Leyden Gazette; Leyden gazettes. *See Gazette de Leyde*

L'Hôpital, Maréchale de. *See* Mignot, Marie or Claudine-Françoise

L'Hôpital, François de (1583–1660), Comte de Rosnay; Maréchal de France:
marriage of, iv. 130

L'Hôpital, Paul-François de [Galuccio de] (1697–1776), Marquis de l'Hôpital; French ambassador to Russia and to Naples:
young men brought by, to Russia, v. 53

Libel; libels:
political situation will arouse, vi. 444
Wilkes's trial for, vi. 137
See Constitutional Queries

Liberty:
English, foreigners cannot understand, vii. 15
HW calls, charter obtained only by bloodshed, ix. 237
HW does not pant after, except that of his limbs, ix. 235
HW pleased by survival of, on one side of Atlantic Ocean, viii. 448
unwarranted riots injure cause of, vii. 22

Liberty cap:
masquerader carries, on pole, in imitation of Wilkes, ix. 193

Libri, (?) Girolamo Francesco (1699– living 1744), banker:
Gabburri to make, her cicisbeo, i. 150

Libri. *See also* Compagni and Libri

Libro, Lorenzo:
arrest of, for grain scandal, iii. 473

Libro d'Oro:
Mann's pedigree worthy of, iv. 197
Tuscan nobility may ignore, iv. 193

Licanians:
Spaniards capture, ii. 459

License:
export, needed to send art objects from Tuscany, v. 208

Lichfield, Bp of. *See* Chandler, Edward (1668?–1750); Cornwallis, Hon. James (1742–1824); Hough, John (1651–1743); Hurd, Richard (1720–1808); North, Hon. Brownlow (1741–1820)

Lichfield, E. of. *See* Lee, George Henry (1690–1743); Lee, George Henry (1718–72)

Lichfield:
near Stone, iii. 173

Lichtenstein. *See* Liechtenstein; Löwenstein

Liddell, Hon. Anne (ca 1738–1804), m. 1 (1756) Augustus Henry Fitzroy, styled E. of Euston, 3d D. of Grafton, 1757 (divorced, 1769); m. 2 (1769) John Fitzpatrick, 2d E. of Upper Ossory:
Acciaioli, Mme, to attend, vi. 27
airings to country places declined by, to save her strength for evening entertainments, vi. 29
altered appearance of, on her return to England, vi. 80
Branchi, Mme, charms, vi. 35, 50
coach easily tires, vi. 29
Corsi, Marchesa, invited to meet, vi. 28
divorce of, v. 506n, vii. 66
father visited by, instead of attending Garter installation, vi. 80
Florence reached by, vi. 27
Florence to be visited by, on way to Rome, vi. 554
gazettes report arrival of, in England, vi. 88
Geneva left by, for Turin, v. 537
Geneva's vicinity visited by, vi. 40
Genoa to be visited by, for health, v. 506
HW anxious about his letter to, vi. 2
HW delivers Mann's letter to, vi. 109
HW mistaken about package from Mann supposedly carried by, vi. 94
HW receives through, the drawing of Leghorn casino, vi. 104
HW's correspondence with, v. 548, 554, vi. 2, 12, 27
HW's letter to, received by her, vi. 27
HW's 'passion,' v. 506
HW's praises of, vi. 38–9
HW to accompany, to D. of Devonshire's, E. Gower's, and E. of Hertford's, v. 427
HW told by, of Mann's attentions, vi. 38–9
HW wishes well to, vii. 66
horse to be ridden by to Petraia, vi. 29
Huber's silhouette of, sent to HW, v. 548, 554
husband hurries, from Florence, vi. 39
husband separates from, vi. 269, 279–80
Italian and music studied by, vi. 29
itinerary of, from Florence, vi. 34
jointure of, vi. 269
loo the passion of, v. 427, vi. 17
Mann encloses letter to, vi. 202
—— entertains, at dinner, vi. 33
—— fails to receive letters of, vi. 202
—— given Chelsea china by, vi. 180–1, 191, 202
—— inquires about HW's letter to, vi. 12
—— orders music for Mme Branchi because of, vi. 50
—— recommends Manzoli to, vi. 173
——'s attentions appreciated by, vi. 80
——'s conversazione to be attended by, vi. 28
——'s correspondence with, vi. 191, 202
Naples to be visited by, v. 550

other road to Rome taken by, v. 565

Pitt, George, awaited by, at Turin house, vi. 2

plays cards instead of attending concert in Rome, vi. 17

public diversions and private study both enjoyed by, vi. 40

Riccardi's letter to, enclosed by Mann, vi. 108

Richmond's masquerade attended by, as Cleopatra, vi. 148

Rome visited by, v. 565, vi. 12, 17, 22

Turin visited by, v. 537, 554, 557, vi. 2

Voltaire called on by, vi. 40

Liddell, Sir Henry (1708–84), 4th Bt, 1723; cr. (1747) Bn Ravensworth; M.P.:

Bedford asks Parliament to investigate papers of, iv. 366

daughter of, v. 506n

daughter visits, in Northumberland, vi. 80

Fawcett's assertions should not have been accepted by, so readily, iv. 365

Hanoverian reinforcements suggested by, in Parliament, iv. 526

Johnson, Murray, and Stone accused by, of toasting Old Pretender and Dunbar, iv. 360–1, 365

named in Secret Committee lists, i. 384, 386, 391

peerage granted to, iii. 419

Liechtenstein, Joseph Wenzel Lorenz (1696–1772), Fürst:

cannon awaited by, iii. 258

Charles Emmanuel III brings, to save Alessandria, iii. 231

Florence visited by, to prepare for Leopold's arrival, vi. 153–4

Gages defeated by, iii. 266

—— opposed by, iii. 245

Naples may be attacked by, iii. 324

Pisa baths visited by, vi. 154

Spaniards to be attacked by, iii. 258

Townshend congratulates, iii. 269

Tuscan regency warned by, iii. 245

York, D. of, will eclipse, in Italy, vi. 154

Liechtenstein, Karl Borromäus Joseph (1730–89), Fürst; Austrian General:

Berlin entered by, v. 445–6

Liége, Bp of. See Johann Theodor (1703–63)

Liége:

battle near, iii. 318

bishopric of, coveted, vi. 119

English and Hanoverian troops may go to, ii. 142

France has great weight in chapter of, vi. 119

HW's works said to be published at, vi. 273

Le Fevre abhorred at, vii. 310

Roman disputes as uninteresting as those of canons of, v. 491

Young Pretender said to have renounced Roman Catholicism at, vii. 402

Liegnitz:

battle of, v. 432, 434–5

Lieutenant de police, French. See Sartine

Lieutenant-general of the Ordnance. See under Ordnance

Life:

HW considers, to be like a chess-board, ix. 510

HW's definition of, as comedy to those who think, tragedy to those who feel, vii. 166

HW's reflections on, iv. 256, 462

See also under World

Life and History of Theodore the First. See History of Theodore I

Life of Edward, Lord Herbert of Cherbury. See under Herbert, Edward (1582–1648)

Lighters:

convicts confined on, acquire added villainy, ix. 316

HW calls, colleges for undergraduates in villainy, ix. 316

on Thames, for D. of Richmond's fireworks, iv. 56

Light Horse:

stationed near London in case of riots, vii. 205

Lighthorseman:

Karl Wilhelm Ferdinand greets, vi. 197

Lightning:

damage done by, in England, ix. 419, 427

Portsmouth fire supposedly caused by, v. 419–20

strikes Lady Mary Fox's dressing-room, vii. 392

Lightning Bomb, English ship:

sinking of, iii. 269

Ligne, Léopold-Philippe-Charles-Joseph de (1690–1754) Duc d'Arenberg:

ancestor of, iv. 195

dines at 11 A.M., ii. 97

England visited by, ii. 79

entertained at suppers only, ii. 97

French forces considered inferior by, ii. 250

HW has not seen, ii. 97, 115

HW sees, at opera, ii. 137

Richmond, Ds of, does not invite, to dinner because he wants it at 11, ii. 97

Stair reconciled with, ii. 278

Wade quarrels with, ii. 440

Walpole, Sir Robert, does not see, ii. 115, 137

wounded at Dettingen, ii. 258, 265

Ligneville. See Ligniville

Ligniville, Comtesse de. See Capoue, Béatrix de

Ligniville, Anne-Marguerite de (1686–1772), m. (1704) Marc de Beauvau, P. de Craon:

age of, vi. 324, 536

anecdote by, about Catherine of Braganza, iii. 500–1

[Ligniville, Anne-Marguerite de, *continued*]
Antinori accompanies, to Artimino, ii. 329, 521
—— at odds with, i. 203
—— cultivated by, ii. 101
—— flirts with, despite her son's death, i. 463
—— more affectionately treated by, ii. 353
—— retires with, ii. 318
—— suggests improper ideas to, i. 313
apartment of: near Leopold of Lorraine's, iv. 116; often shown, ii. 110; remodelled, ii. 78
appearance of, altered, iv. 213
appetites of, 'unchristian,' iii. 369
Artimino visited by, ii. 324, 329, 521, iii. 455, 466
assemblies of, i. 16
ball given by, i. 416
ball may be given by, i. 56
Barbantane hears complaints from, vi. 537
barenecked and crowned with jewels, iv. 213
Beauvau, Chevalier de, not a favourite of, ii. 298
berceau brought by, to rented villa, iv. 116
berceau of, iv. 387
Bocchineri, Mme, protégée of, iv. 447
Bolognetti, Mme, calls on, i. 37
—— entertains, i. 10, 16
—— refuses to visit, first, ii. 65
Braitwitz's affair with Mme Vitelli pleases, ii. 353
candles intolerable to, when unshaded, ii. 228, 242
Capuchin resembled by, ii. 109
cards played by, i. 178, 463, vii. 23
Carteret to receive thanks of, for aiding son, ii. 286
Carteret, Bns, surpasses, in grandeur, ii. 464
Chenevix toys coveted by, iv. 24
children of: Leopold's, ii. 298n, iv. 326; 'unlawful,' iii. 369
china packed by, for flight, i. 193, 199
Chute to be entertained by, ii. 372
colic of, used to support her dignity, iii. 36
collections of, ii. 78
Colonna, Mme, tiresome guest of, ii. 545
Corsi entertains, at ball, i. 137
corso at Rome taken by, as compliment, i. 3, iii. 358
costume of: as Maria Theresa's representative at ceremony of the *doti*, ii. 196; for cocchiata, discussed with Antinori, ii. 485–6; for cure of eyesight, ii. 228; for opera, iii. 357–8; indoors in winter, ii. 109
cradle of: i. 178; new, ii. 78; occupied in illness, i. 481, iii. 369
curtain's rising taken by, as compliment to her entrance into theatre, iii. 358

Cybo, Maria Anna Matilde, entertained by, iii. 475–6
daughter fills former rôle of, vi. 243
daughter-in-law visits, iii. 500
daughter leaves, in pitiful state, iv. 213
daughter may be displaced by, in Stanislas I's affections, iv. 26
daughter of, to start convent in Vienna, iv. 334
daughter to visit, in Lorraine, iv. 116
death of, vii. 425–6
devotion of, ii. 298n, iii. 161, 243, 369
devotion the only amusement of, in retreat, v. 249
diamond drops lost by, iii. 8
does not look her age, iv. 26
Electress shown HW's presents by, i. 424
Empress sends chocolate to, i. 205
English cocchiata honoured by, ii. 485
English visitors at Florence will not be as well received by, when refugees, ii. 459
épuisements described by, iv. 234
equipage of, on display, v. 179
equipage sent by, by sea to Leghorn, vi. 536
Eszterházy, Ps, compared to, iv. 351
ex-Jesuit and Irish officer accompany, vi. 536
eyes of, prevent her from entertaining for Coronation, ii. 240, 242
faro and lansquenet partners of, i. 414
faro played by, i. 16, 29, iv. 106, v. 533
fires not provided by, in winter, ii. 109
fireworks attended by, ii. 242
Florence to be destination of, by way of Loreto, i. 22
Florence to be visited by, to entertain Vorontsov, iii. 184
Forrester boasts to, of wife-beating, iii. 500
Forzoni emissary of, i. 60, iii. 357
—— told by, to maim gnats, iii. 369
Franceschi's jewels displayed by, i. 413
Francis I and Maria Theresa honour, at Frankfurt and Innsbruck, vi. 537
Francis I asked by, to promote nephew, vi. 324
—— gave life use of Petraia to, vii. 296
—— invites, to Vienna, iv. 25
Frankfurt visited by, to see Joseph II elected K. of the Romans, vi. 324, 537
French abbés entertained by, i. 16
French in her sympathies, ii. 427
Gastin de Paris accounts believed by, iii. 197
gentleman usher of, *see* Forzoni
Goldsworthy, Mrs, called on by, i. 316 317–18
—— calls on, i. 316
grief feigned by, for daughter-in-law's uncle, iii. 426
grows scrupulous, vi. 246
guests of: Antinori, i. 413; Buondelmonti, i. 414; Chute, i. 443, 498, (?)ii. 1; Forzoni,

i. 414; Grifoni, Mme, i. 416; Guadagni, i. 413; Mann, i. 443, 498, ii. 1; Pugi, i. 414; Sade, i. 413; St Jean, i. 414; Sarrazin, Mme, i. 414, 498; Whithed, (?)ii. 1
HW accompanies, to St Peter's to see relics, i. 4
HW agrees with criticism by, of the Tesi, ii. 318
HW asked by, to thank Carteret for helping her son, ii. 312
HW asks about, i. 402
HW asks about fasting and appetite of, iii. 161, 243
HW blames, for considering a trip to Leghorn, ii. 61
HW calls, 'Princesse épuisée,' ii. 561
HW contrasts Duchess of Modena with, ii. 246
HW discusses La Chétardie with, i. 20
HW dreams of visit of, to Houghton, ii. 91
HW fears he is forgotten by, ii. 267, 277
HW fears that Mann will be murdered by cold rooms of, ii. 136
HW forgotten by, iii. 243
HW hopes for throne for, iv. 126, 132
HW imagines, as wife of Stanislas I, iv. 132
HW leads secluded life after departure of, from Rome, i. 28
HW mimics, ii. 298
HW often plays faro with, in Casa Craon, v. 468
HW paid court to, at Petraia, vi. 29
HW plays faro with, i. 29, iv. 106, v. 533
HW quotes letter of, ii. 291
HW regrets departure of, from Florence, iv. 34
HW's correspondence with, i. 409, 417–18, 422, 435–6, 463, 505, ii. 15, 291
HW sends compliments to, ii. 91, 194, 371–2, 432, 529
HW sends presents to, i. 189
HW sends thanks to, i. 24
HW's expenditure on Japan ware and fans for, i. 506
HW's presents to, delivered by Mann, i. 413–16
HW's recommendations honoured by, iii. 253
HW subject of inquiries by, iii. 402
HW suspects loyalty of, to Mann, i. 419
HW thanked by, in letter, for Chinese present, viii. 6
HW thinks Maria Theresa has summoned, to educate her daughters, iv. 326
HW to receive compliments of, ii. 371–2, iv. 23
HW wants introduction to her daughter from, iv. 13
health of: ailments described, iv. 401; ailments discussed publicly, ii. 98; ailments numerous, ii. 122; colic, i. 37, 481, ii. 318, iii. 369; confined to her bed, i. 122,

ii. 109–10; épuisements, i. 481, ii. 1, 61, 115, iii. 357, 369, 476; épuisements cured, iii. 500; eyes, i. 78, ii. 28, 240, 242, 277; Sarrazin, Mme, explains, ii. 175; sickness caused by tight lacing, iii. 145; tired, iii. 407; vomiting, i. 37
Hobart welcomed by, iii. 253
house of, altered by Botta, v. 557
husband and Châtelet cannot pacify, iii. 440
husband calls, 'm'amie,' ii. 298n
husband compelled by, to leave her at Poggio Imperiale after cards, and go home to bed, viii. 23
husband influenced by, to refuse Richecourt's request for certificate, ii. 216
husband's death might be followed by remarriage of, iv. 116, 132
husband's dinner viewed by, from gallery, i. 155
husband tells, her hair is too scanty for Tesi's coiffure, ii. 263
husband warned by, against Richecourt, iv. 220
husband watched by, with Stanislas I, iv. 92
illnesses of, conceal her poverty, ii. 242
in bed, on reentering Florence, i. 122
India cabinets of, ii. 78
Indian things coveted by, iii. 330
Kaunitz attracts visitors to house of, i. 37
Leghorn may be visited by, i. 443, ii. 27, 38, 503
Leopold II paid respects by, at Poggio Imperiale, vi. 536
Leopold of Lorraine allots apartment to, iv. 116
—— ejects husband from bed of, ii. 298n
—— fears that his piles may disgust, i. 60
—— pays homage to, vi. 536
——'s mistress, i. 17, 189n, 213n, 236, 298n, 326, vi. 324n
L'Hôpital, Maréchale de, compared with, iv. 131–2
Lorraine family hardly rewards, for 71 years' service, iv. 26
Lorraine may be revisited by, iii. 467
Lorraine residence of, in height of her beauty, i. 28
Lorraine to be home of, iv. 24
loves everything royal, viii. 23
Lunéville seldom visited by, through jealousy of daughter, vi. 243
Madame Royale mourned by, iii. 1
Madonna exposition not to be missed by, i. 100
Madonna of the Annunciata besought by, to preserve husband's resolution, ii. 216–17
maids and parrots of, odorous, ii. 78
Mann accompanies, to opera, iii. 357–8
—— afraid of squeezing, in coach, iii. 358
—— apparently deserted by, iii. 457

[Ligniville, Anne-Marguerite de, *continued*]

— calls on, i. 36–7, 122, 463, 481, ii. 175, iii. 500, vi. 537

— cannot tell improper story to, ii. 307

— dines with, on Francis I's birthday, i. 217, ii. 348

— discusses HW with, i. 33–4, 67

— discusses Richecourt's return with, i. 236

— entertained by, at breakfast, ii. 78

— entertains, at dinner, iii. 502

— gives barrel of beer to, ii. 228

— has not lately seen, ii. 65

— helps arrange pillows of, i. 481

— never mentions, iii. 243, 497

— plays berlan with, i. 179

— pleases, with gooseberry tarts, iii. 402

— quotes, on subject of attending Corpus Christi procession, iii. 407

— receives compliments from, during illness, iii. 466–7

— receives pity and *chaud d'eau* from, iii. 385

— recommends Lucca as refuge for, i. 178

—'s attentions from, surprise HW, iii. 503

— sends news of HW's illness to, i. 51

— shows Houghton plan to, i. 463

—'s innocence of sonetto authorship asserted by, iii. 498

— sits and talks with, on cradle, i. 178

—'s visits embarrass, iii. 197

— takes Mme Antinori to Artimino to dine with, iii. 145

— tells, that heavy clothing causes her ailments, ii. 109–10

— to entertain, ii. 353

— to give plum cake to, i. 263

— told by, to give compliments to HW, iv. 23

— to present English visitors to, iv. 14–15

— to see, i. 433

— to show Houghton plan to, i. 443

— to take, to see English fleet at Leghorn, i. 443

— to tell, about HW's success at faro, iii. 494–5

— twitted by, on sheltering Goldsworthy children, i. 313

— urged by, to visit Petraia, i. 443

— will be as *épuisé* as, v. 326

Maria Theresa represented by, at ceremony of the *doti*, ii. 196

—'s gala not celebrated by, ii. 324

marriage of, to Stanislas I would increase her fondness for Young Pretender, iv. 132

Mass attended by, before going to bed, ii. 115

Maynard dropped by, ii. 440

— introduced to, by Mann, ii. 371

— to be entertained by, ii. 372

— to be introduced to, by Mann, ii. 367

may retire, i. 236, 283

medicine taken by, ii. 98

midnight supper taken by, ii. 122

Mirepoix, Mme de, to be told by, about HW, iv. 23

Modena, Ds of, entertained by, ii. 228

Modenese princess avoided by, i. 60, 65

Modenese princess offends, iii. 476

momo played by, i. 218

mourning costume got by, for Court presentation, vi. 536

mourning directions expected by, from Vienna, ii. 175

oculist repulsed by, ii. 240

Old Pretender called on by, at Rome, i. 9

— friendly with, i. 25

— might have prayers from, iii. 161

— 'old tenant' of, iii. 108

—'s restoration may please, iii. 108

—'s sons may be helped across Tuscany by, i. 15

ombre faithfully played by, ii. 101

opera attended by, i. 40, 83, ii. 302, iii. 357–8, 439–40, 502

opera attended by, to avoid giving fête for Maria Theresa's delivery, ii. 302

opera incidents offend, iii. 439–40

Paris post brings few letters of condolence to, i. 463

Petraia briefly revisited by, vi. 536–7

Petraia supplied by, with furniture, iv. 116

Petraia the summer residence of, vi. 224–5

Petraia visited by, i. 109, 443, 463, 481, ii. 1–2, iii. 407, 500, iv. 14

Pitt, Anne, resembles, viii. 6

Poggio Imperiale apartment obtained by, for herself only, viii. 23

Pomfret, Cts of, disputes with, over precedence, iv. 132n

Prague's siege and son's danger make, anxious, ii. 1–2

Prague visited by, to see Joseph II crowned as K. of Romans, vi. 324

(?) prior's affair with, i. 17

receives ladies, ii. 348

religious turn of, after Leopold's death, ii. 298n

returns to Nancy *via* Bologna after paying court to Leopold at Poggio Imperiale, vi. 536–7

Richecourt does not yet permit, to resume faro, iii. 501

— may yet be triumphed over by, iv. 326

— mortifies, i. 189n

—'s designation by, iv. 197

Rinaldi, Mme, entertained by, i. 217–18

Roman adulation of, i. 28

Roman flight would be disliked by, i. 178

Rome visited by, i. 3, 9–10, 16, 20, 22, 25, 28–9, iii. 358

Rosenberg drives, from Petraia, vii. 296
Rowley sends beer to, iii. 9
Russian news commented upon by, i. 20
Sade and Bp of Apamea employed by, to negotiate etiquette with Modenese princess, i. 60
Sade dissuades, from Leghorn trip, ii. 38–9
—— would be told by, to read Mme de Sévigné's letters to her, iv. 387
St-Aignan and Lorenzi taken through Corso by, in phaeton, i. 83
St John plays faro with, v. 533
Salviati, Duchessa, serves, i. 4
Salviati, Mme, entertained by, i. 218
Salviatis entertained by, iii. 145
Sansedoni favoured by, iv. 228
Santa Croces meet, i. 3
Sarrazin, Mme, companion to, i. 436n
—— dismissed by, ii. 361–2
—— tired of illnesses of, ii. 122
—— tires, with compliments, ii. 362
seclusion of, in last years, vii. 426
seldom writes, iv. 23
servants of, i. 9, ii. 196
Siena lady calls on, i. 481
sister-in-law of, iv. 118
son of, dies, i. 454, 463, 468, 480, 481
son pursued by, to Florence, iii. 502
son's arrival cures, of épuisements, iii. 500
son's future marriage pleases, iii. 1
son visits, at Petraia, iii. 500
Spanish invasion feared by, i. 178
Stanislas I courts, iii. 467
—— gives Queen's apartment to, at Nancy, iv. 116
—— may wed, iv. 116, 132
—— said to be in love with, iv. 126n, 132
stays in bed to keep warm, ii. 110
SH would delight, iv. 387
sups at midnight by bedside, ii. 122
teeth and hair lost by, iv. 213
tenebræ attended by, with Shrewsbury, i. 4
Tesi calls on, ii. 263
——'s acting criticized by, ii. 302
——'s costume envied by, ii. 263
theatre to have been attended by, in mask, iii. 8
Venice to be visited by, at Ascension, i. 25, iv. 29
Vernon liked by, iv. 305
Vienna visited by, to ask Francis I to promote nephew, vi. 324
Villa Patrizi entertainment attended by, i. 25
Viviani's desertion scandalizes, i. 239
Vorontsov, Mme, quarrels with, after calling and being made to wait, v. 248, 259
weeds will be worn by, after husband's death, iv. 418
Whithed to be entertained by, ii. 372
(?) —— visits, at Petraia, i. 443, ii. 1
Young Pretender's arrest displeases, iv. 22
——'s journey might be facilitated by, i. 17

Ligniville, Eugène de, Princesse de Craon's nephew:
(?) aunt wants Francis I to promote, in army, vi. 324
Ligonier, Vcts. See Pitt, Hon. Penelope (b. 1749)
Ligonier, Edward (1740–82), 2d Vct Ligonier, 1770; cr. (1776) E. Ligonier; army officer:
Alfieri fights duel with, over wife, ix. 538n
Ferdinand's victory to be announced by, v. 314
pension conferred upon, vi. 450
wife divorced by, vii. 451n, ix. 538n
Ligonier, Sir John Louis (1680–1770), K.B., 1743; cr. (1757) Vct Ligonier and (1766) E. Ligonier; M.P.; army officer:
armour buckled on by, v. 305
army of; halts at Coventry, iii. 160; to defend Lancashire, iii. 160
Cumberland, D. of, served by, iii. 20
—— to command, iii. 167
Durand sends express to, at Preston, iii. 166
earldom conferred upon, vi. 449–50
farrier of, iv. 204
Granby's promotion mortifies, vi. 449
Harrington plays whist with, at Petersham, iii. 166
Sackville informed by, about court martial, v. 328
two regiments under, x. 17
Ligonier du Buisson, Marguerite de (d. 1793), m. 1 —— de Panne; m. 2 (ca 1740) Sir Luke Schaub, Kt:
Cholmondeley said to pursue, i. 185
HW and 'King' Theodore to be entertained by, at coffee, iv. 40
Robinson entertains, i. 185
Ligue, the. See Holy League; League
'Ligur-Napolispani':
Spanish and Neapolitan and Genoese army called, iii. 82
Lilacs:
at SH, HW cannot miss, vi. 289
Lilburne, John (ca 1614–57), political agitator:
Gordon acts as, to Scottish Presbyterians, ix. 11
Lilford, Bn. See Powys, Thomas (1743–1800)
Lilford, Bns. See Mann, Eleanor (1747–1823)
'Lilliput.' See under Swift, Jonathan, Gulliver's Travels
Lily:
lilia jacobæa, HW mentions, v. 113
Lima:
Hermione sails from, vi. 45
traveller from, may visit England's ruins, viii. 62
'Limbo':
Italian, understood by no one, iii. 504
Limerick, Vct. See Hamilton, James (d. 1758)
Lime-trees:
at SH, iv. 382, 387

Limewater:
remedy beneficial to Horatio Walpole (1678–1757), iii. 510n
Lincoln, Bp of. *See* Gibson, Edmund (1669–1748); Thomas, John (1691–1766)
Lincoln, Cts of. *See* Fitzgerald, Lady Elizabeth (ca 1528–90); Pelham, Catherine (1727–60); Pelham, Lucy (d. 1736); Seymour-Conway, Lady Frances (1751–1820)
Lincoln, E. of. *See* Clinton, Henry (1684–1728); Clinton, Theophilus (ca 1600–67); Fiennes Clinton, Henry (1720–94); Pelham Clinton, Henry Fiennes (1750–78); Pelham Clinton, Lord Thomas (1752–95)
Lincoln, earldom of:
abjudication of barony of Saye and Sele occasions examination into, ix. 165
Lincolnshire:
Day's estate at, i. 49
Lincoln's Inn:
fire at: consumes legal documents, iv. 321–2, 331–2; nearly destroys papers of Sharpe and Duane, ix. 350
Lincoln's Inn Fields:
Somerset, D. of, leaves house in, to daughter, iv. 10–11
Walpole, Hon. Thomas, lives in, ix. 55
Lind, John (1737–81), political writer:
Letters concerning the Present State of Poland, Mann reads, vii. 502–3, 564
Murray's chaplain at Constantinople, vii. 564–5
——'s quarrel with, vii. 565
Polish Partition, The, vii. 556, 564
Stanislas II takes, as preceptor to P. Stanislas Poniatowski, vii. 565
'Lindamira,' character in Swift's *Memoirs of Martin Scriblerus*:
Newcastle called, iv. 214
Linden, ——, Lt Maréchal Comte de:
Velletri attacked by, ii. 488
Linden und Aspermont, Cts. *See* Eszterházy von Galantha, Theresia (d. 1746)
Lindsay, Hon. Mrs. *See* Bingham, Hon. Margaret (d. 1839)
Lindsay, John (1702–49), 20th E. of Crawford:
affairs of, embarrassed, iv. 110
death of, iv. 109–10, 118
laudanum overdose taken by, when wound opens for 17th time, iv. 109–10
life of, by Rolt, iv. 110n
Marchmont to succeed, as representative Scottish peer, iv. 110–11
Scotland's premier earl, iv. 110n
servant rescues, iv. 110, 118
Turks fought by, in Hungary, iv. 110
Lindsay, Sir John (1737–88), Kt, 1763; K.B., 1771; rear-admiral, 1787:
Francis II entertained by, on board squadron at Leghorn, ix. 499
Linen:
gown of, vi. 148

HW's, at Arlington St, just come from the wash, vii. 285
Lorraine officials sell, at Florence, ii. 270
Mann must replenish his stock of, vi. 166
screen of, iii. 357
settees covered with, at SH, iv. 382, 387
sold in Florence, i. 53
York, D. of, does not change, after sweating at dance, vi. 553
Lingdeen, ——, captain of Swedish ship *Esperance:*
bill of lading for Van Dyck portrait may have been signed by, ix. 501
Link; links (torches):
Neapolitans told not to carry, in religious demonstration, viii. 541
North Briton set on fire with, vi. 188
Link-boys:
English warriors become, v. 213
saying of, at Vauxhall, iv. 91
Linlithgow, Cts of. *See* Hay, Lady Margaret
Linton, Kent:
chimney piece at, Cicero bust to adorn, iv. 86
church at: Mann family pew in, iv. 250; sepulchral urn for Galfridus Mann at, designed by HW and Bentley, v. 128, 142, 157, 250, ix. 668, 678; sepulchral urn for Mann at, ix. 665–6, 668, 670
'citadel of Kent,' v. 129
Croft to carry Edward Louisa Mann's will to, viii. 154
entail of: always implied by Galfridus Mann, vii. 76, 120; Chute and HW sure about, vii. 101; HW thinks that Mann's allusion to, is to French designs on Corsica, vii. 60, 65, 71, 73, 76; HW would not advise Mann to break, viii. 266; Hull consults lawyers about breaking, viii. 240; Mann and Horace Mann II cut off, viii. 257, 259, 266n; Mann indifferent about, vii. 112; Mann, Edward Louisa, mentions, in letter, iv. 306–8, vii. 51, 71, 112, 120, 129, viii. 172; Mann, Horace II, has no doubts about, vii. 408
Fiesole fogs remind Mann of, vi. 117
Foote offers to leave, viii. 180
furniture at, to go with the house, vii. 172
HW asks if Mann will bring over things for, viii. 175
HW determines to send Mann's next present to, ix. 74
HW visits, v. 128
income from: according to old rent roll, viii. 160; smaller than was believed, viii. 257
Mann always kept in uncertainty about inheritance of, viii. 183
—— does not wish to relinquish, entirely to Horace Mann II, viii. 240
—— has collected no fine things to furnish, viii. 180–1
—— must cut off entail of, to benefit

Horace Mann II's daughters, viii. 225, 240, 257
—— offered an apartment at, by Edward Louisa Mann, viii. 166
—— promises use of, to Horace Mann II, viii. 169–70, 180
—— relieved to find that Horace Mann II will have succession to, viii. 166
——'s body to be sent to, by Horace Mann II, ix. 665
——'s family affairs at, iv. 306–8
—— should come to take possession of, viii. 160
—— should send his portrait to, vii. 48
——'s portrait will go to, not to SH, viii. 27
—— to get income from Galfridus Mann in case he loses salary before inheriting, viii. 172–3
—— to have life use of, vii. 172
—— urges Foote to stay at, until Horace Mann II arrives, viii. 169, 180
—— wants sepulchral urn at, v. 142, ix. 665–6
Mann, Edward Louisa, always wrote of entail of, as settled, viii. 172
—— charges, with annuity to Mary Mann, viii. 160, 168, 176, 181, 187, 258
—— claims to have disposal of, vi. 564, 568, 576, viii. 146, 154–5, 172, 259
—— dies at, viii. 154, 165
—— does not cut off entail of, viii. 159
—— establishes Mrs Foote at, v. 129
—— refuses to let Horace Mann II live at, viii. 169–70
—— reoccupies, for first time in 4 years, viii. 120
—— says that purchase of, was made in his own name, viii. 146
—— stricken at, with gout, viii. 145, 146
Mann, Galfridus, should have annexed his estate to, v. 61
Mann, Horace II, may be carousing with electors at, when wife's body arrives, viii. 381, 398
—— might marry again to produce an heir to, viii. 358
—— to inherit, after Mann, vii. 172
Mann, Lady Lucy, to be buried at, viii. 363, 381, 398
Mann, Robert, disposes of, by will, iv. 306–8, vi. 576, vii. 51, 71, 112, 120, 129, viii. 147, 172
view of Kent from, in fog, vi. 117
Westmorland, Cts of, visits Mrs Foote at, vi. 72
Linz:
Catalogue of French Books, A, mentions, ii. 54
Francis I ordered back from, to Vienna, i. 316
news of distressed garrison at, arouses Frederick II, i. 315

surrender of, expected, i. 288
surrenders, i. 315
Tuscan troops to take oath at, v. 180
Lion, English ship:
Brett commands, iii. 91, 95
Elizabeth forced back to Brest by, iii. 87, 88, 91, 95
loss of, in West Indies, reported, viii. 516
Lion; lions:
fable about, ix. 152–3
in Tower of London, i. 233, vi. 135
Lion d'Argent, Calais inn:
beef unloaded for, iv. 13
Lionel (1338–68), cr. (1362) D. of Clarence:
counterparts of, v. 57
Lions. See Lyon
Liotard, Jean-Étienne (1702–90), painter:
beard, girdle, and Turkish habit worn by, iv. 362
Constantinople visited by, iv. 362
crayons, enamels and water-colours of, iv. 362
Genévois, iv. 362
HW commissions Churchill to have Crébillon's and Marivaux's portraits painted by, iv. 324–5, 362
Marivaux intimate with, iv. 325
prices of, extravagant, iv. 362
Lipari, island of:
earthquake account mentions, ix. 376
Lippe, river:
Frederick II said to be sending army to, vii. 466
Lippe-Bückeburg, Gräfin von. See Schulenburg-Oynhausen, Margarete Gertrud von
Lippe-Bückeburg, Albert Wolfgang (1699–1748), Graf von:
son of, vi. 43n
Lippe-Bückeburg, Friedrich Wilhelm Ernst (1724–77), Graf von:
birth of, in England, vi. 43n, 48
Portuguese troops to be commanded by, vi. 43
sash torn by, from cowardly Portuguese general, vi. 94
Tyrawley disgusted by appointment of, vi. 48
Westphalia left by, vi. 43
Lip-reading:
(?) Pitt, Mrs, practises, vii. 456
Lipyeatt, Rev. Jonathan (d. 1812):
Ailesbury, E. of, intimate with, iv. 331
Bruce accompanied by, to Florence, iv. 331
Liqueur; liqueurs:
citrons in, i. 317, 322, 398, 439
HW never drinks, v. 222
HW's, Mann encloses bill of lading for, v. 220, 225
HW's countermand of order of, came too late, v. 231
HW wants case of, v. 203
HW will pay Mann for, but will not use it, v. 227
See also Drams

Liquor; liquors:
strong: Cocchi cautions Mann against, vi. 469; Young Pretender takes extra quantity of, on St Andrew's Day, ix. 100
Lirici. *See* Lerici
Lisbon:
Acciaioli expelled from, v. 476
Charles III may send French fleet against, viii. 224
Clement XIII expects courier from, v. 430
earthquake at: iv. 511–12, 519–20; Acciaioli writes about, iv. 519; Charles III has no sympathy for victims of, vi. 49; England has no masquerades since, iv. 539, vi. 17, 49, vii. 58
earthquake spoils advantage of, as health resort, iv. 536
England sends relief ship to, iv. 512
English capture packet boat from, iv. 320
English expedition to, a mystery, vi. 18
Fane said to be new ambassador to, i. 135
Gage's sloop may have gone to, viii. 110
Goldsworthy said to be transferred to, iv. 433n
Grosett is Scottish merchant at, ix. 410
HW refuses to send Riccardi's gems to, iii. 273
Howe is reported to have passed, ix. 320
Kinnoull and Pitt to visit, v. 364
Kinnoull to visit, v. 352
merchant of, marries Miss Giberne, iv. 82
Norris, Sir John, and sailors call, ungrateful, i. 456
Northampton may visit, vi. 151
nuncio at, *see* Acciaioli, Filippo (1700–66); Tempi, Luca Melchior (1688–1768)
patriarch of, *see* Saldanha, Francisco de
ships arrive at, from America, iv. 498
Spain might dethrone royal family at, v. 560
Spain's armada probably bound for, viii. 111
Spanish threat to, minimized by HW, vi. 23–4
Tyrawley to go to, vi. 7
visitors to: Keppel, Hon. William, iv. 460; York, D. of, vi. 179
Walpole, Hon. Robert, has post and marries at, ix. 410
Lisburne, Vcts. *See* Nightingale, Elizabeth (d. 1755)
Lisle, Hon. Mrs. *See* Cholmondeley, Hon. Hester (1755–1828)
Lisle, Guillaume de (1675–1726):
geography of, iv. 501
Lisle, William Clapcott:
wife of, vi. 210n
Lismore, E. and Cts of. *See* O'Brien, Daniel; O'Brien, Margaret Josepha
Lister, James, HW's printer:
(?) runs away, v. 300
Litany:
HW quotes, ix. 387

Litchfield. *See* Lichfield
Litchmore. *See* Lismore
Lit de justice:
Louis XV holds, v. 56, vi. 415n
Louis XVI speechless with rage at, viii. 102
mob intends to draw Louis XVI's coach to, viii. 61–2
Selwyn's witticism about Pitt and, v. 43
Literati:
literary squabbles are meat and drink to, vi. 465
Litter:
Mann might be carried in, i. 66
Pius VI's, Orford, Cts of, carried in, viii. 317
Richecourt enters, in bedchamber, v. 80
—— to go in, to Lorraine, v. 62, 80
Walpole, Bns, gives, to Salimbeni, i. 116
Walpole, Sir Robert, must use, to go to Houghton, ii. 538
'Little friend,' Mann's:
spies on Old Pretender at Albano, iii. 140–1
Little John, English tartan:
Butler sent by, from Gibraltar to Leghorn, ix. 303
Littleton. *See* Lyttelton
Lively, English ship:
England reached by, with books and vases from Mann to HW, ix. 635
Mann sends china to HW on, ix. 619
not expected in England before February, ix. 620
Liverpool, E. of. *See* Jenkinson, Charles (1729–1808)
Liverpool:
Irish resent Britain's commercial favour to, viii. 473
New York gazette arrives at, viii. 334
Liverpool, English ship:
involved in war, iii. 207, 232, 292
Livery; liveries:
Botta's attendant pages and dukes to wear, vi. 330
Bristol's servants in, v. 202
footmen's, iv. 181
for Papal bargemen, vii. 566
Francis I's, i. 68, ii. 196
gala: Mann adds lace to, viii. 239; Mann gets, vi. 357; Mann's, for Maria Carolina's reception, to be worn at his investiture, vii. 60
HW does not wish footman to spoil, by fighting, ix. 337
Kingston's, vii. 99
laced, worn by 'Onslow's' servants, iii. 507
Lucchese servants wear, to attend D. of York, vi. 222
Mann's, Davenport sends materials for, from London, vii. 295, 304, 308
valet-de-chambre for Mann is not to wear, i. 207
Van Hoey offers to renew, for French victories in Flanders, iii. 91

Livery of London:
Opposition escorted by, vii. 200
presents petition to George III, vii. 132
quarrels with George III, viii. 116
Livery servants. See under Servants
'Livia':
model of statue of: ii. 178-9, 190, 197, 200, 210; at Leghorn, awaiting shipment, ii. 329; crumbling and rotten, vi. 111; HW receives, broken, ii. 560-1, vi. 98; Rysbrach mends, iii. 63; Valle to get inquiry about, vi. 107
statue of: Domenichino painting to be accompanied by, ii. 89, 152; embarked, ii. 190; expected from Rome at Leghorn, ii. 161; finished, ii. 56-7; Genoese vessel takes, from Rome to Leghorn, ii. 178; HW hopes to receive, by Dutch ship, ii. 119; HW mentions, iii. 347; HW not pleased by execution of, ii. 292, 303; HW receives, ii. 292; HW wants, sent to Leghorn to be shipped with Domenichino painting, ii. 79; HW wants cast of, in bronze, vi. 98; Mann continues work on, in absence of instructions, i. 317; Mann expects Parker to report shipment of, to Leghorn, i. 133; Mann has not drawn money for, ii. 201; Mann pays for, ii. 175, 177-8, 214; Mann to be reimbursed for, ii. 193; Mann to inquire at Rome about mould of, vi. 98; Mann to send, to Leghorn, ii. 106; Parker advances money for, x. 4; Parker's delay may prevent shipment of, from Leghorn, ii. 177; polishing of, prolonged, ii. 127; price of, ii. 177-8, 197, 214; to be on Dutch ship, ii. 89; to be procured for HW by Parker, i. 82, 212, 268, 291, 317, ii. 56-7; Valle gives mould of, to Mattei, vi. 115; Valle not to send, until paid for it, ii. 152; Valle to varnish, ii. 116
Livingston, Lady Anne (1709-47), m. (1724) William Boyd, 4th E. of Kilmarnock, 1717: husband staggered by, iii. 300
Livingstone, Charlotte Maria (1694-1755), Cts of Newburgh, s.j.; m. 1 (1713) Hon. Thomas Clifford; m. 2 (1724) Hon. Charles Radcliffe, titular 5th E. of Derwentwater: daughter of, i. 28
son of, iii. 241n
Livizzani, Giuseppe (1688-1754), cardinal, 1753: death of, iv. 429
Livy (Titus Livius) (59 B.C.–A.D. 17), historian:
HW mentions, i. 300
modern occurrences parallel those in, vi. 186
schoolboys thrilled by lies of, about Brutus, Camillus, and Fabius, v. 541
strange stories told by, iv. 142
Lixen. See Lixin
Lixin, P. de. See Lorraine, Jacques-Henri de (1698-1734)
Lixin, Princesse de. See Beauvau-Craon, Anne-Marguerite-Gabrielle de

Lizard; lizards:
on Cellini's bell, vii. 383
Lizard Point:
religion at, i. 477
Llandaff, Bp of. See Ewer, John (d. 1774); Gilbert, John (1693-1761); Mawson, Matthias (1683-1770); Shipley, Jonathan (1714-89)
Llano y Lacuadra, Don José Agustin de, Marqués de Llano:
Charles III sends instructions to, by courier, vii. 446
Du Tillot chooses, as successor, vii. 325
Ferdinand of Parma forced by wife to dismiss, vii. 445
Florence visited by, to give Maria Louisa the instructions from Charles III, vii. 446
return of, to Parma, vii. 518
Lloyd, Henry (ca 1720-83), Gen.:
Conway writes to, about maps, vii. 421-2
Lloyd, Katherine (d. 1791), m. (before 1743) Jeffrey French:
Mann asks about, ii. 151
marital troubles of, ii. 135-6
Lloyd, Sir Richard (?1696-1761), Kt, 1745; M.P.; King's counsel:
Frederick, P. of Wales's lord of the Bedchamber, i. 250n
Mansfield answered by, in Parliament, i. 250, 344
solicitor-general, i. 250n, 344n
Lloyd's Evening Post:
(?) HW's illness reported in, vi. 459, 461
(?) Mann has, sent to him, vi. 326
Loan:
England gets, at 8 per cent, viii. 448
See also Silesian loan
Loano:
Spaniards reach, ii. 559
Lobkowitz, Johann Georg Christian (1686-1753), Fürst; army officer:
adjutant of, see Rifler
Albani's and Thun's letters referred to, by Viennese court, ii. 515
Albani visited by, ii. 447
Albano approached by, via Lunghazza Frascati, Zagarola, and Marino, ii. 447
Alessandria may be approached by, over Po bridges, iii. 41
Alessandria may be occupied by, iii. 37
Althan sent by, to Vienna with dispatches, ii. 486, 489, 491
Amor, Don Theodore, captured by, ii. 505
army of: advances, ii. 330; dwindles, ii. 515; Fano and Pesaro reached by, ii. 542; moved to Bologna, ii. 322; near Rome, ii. 473; reinforced, ii. 336; to cross Tronto, ii. 438; wears tricolour cockade, ii. 544
artillery endangered by misconduct of, ii. 541
Artimiso mountain attacked by, ii. 488
Austrian army joined by, ii. 302

[Lobkowitz, Johann Georg Christian, *cont.*]
Austrian army safely brought by, to Monte Rosi, ii. 525
Batthyáni to replace, iii. 23, 41
Bavarians perhaps defeated by, ii. 230
Benedict XIV gives audience to, ii. 446–7
—— gives permission to, ii. 437
——'s gifts to, ii. 447
Braitwitz gets courier from, iii. 11
cavalry of, superior, ii. 312
cavalry to be sent by, to Charles Emmanuel III, ii. 509, 513
Cesena revisited by, ii. 331
Charles III attacked by, at Velletri, ii. 486–7, 488–94, 504
—— may be attacked by abler general than, iii. 237
Charles Emmanuel III ignores weakness of, ii. 515
——'s army to be joined by, at Pavia, iii. 55
—— to be aided and Tuscany to be protected by, ii. 512–13
—— to be assisted by troops from, ii. 502
—— to be imitated by, ii. 324
desertions from army of, ii. 513, iii. 23
detachment sent by, reaches Aquila, ii. 454
dispatches of, to Turin, brought by son, ii. 486, 489, 491
Fermo visited by, ii. 419
Fiorenzuola occupied by, iii. 47
Foligno, not Tuscany, to be line of retreat of, ii. 520
Francis I's men might not accept artillery of, ii. 529–30
French defeated by, i. 451, 457
Gages may be attacked by, ii. 324
—— pays men to desert from, iii. 23
—— permits retreat of, to Pesaro and Fano, ii. 542
—— prevents, from inciting Neapolitans, ii. 471
——'s army equalled by that of, iii. 41
—— told to attack, iii. 15
Gorani sent by, to Pontremoli to defend La Ulla, iii. 36
HW grateful to, for preserving Tuscany, ii. 343
HW impressed by Mann's negotiations with, ii. 467
Imola visited by, ii. 555
inactive, ii. 397
invalid soldiers not to be embarked by, at Fiumicino, ii. 519
Königseck visited by, i. 205
Licanian captives estimated by, ii. 459–60
Lombardy cannot be left unguarded by, ii. 405
Lombardy the destination of, ii. 502, 509, 515
Lombardy to be defended by, besides maintaining garrisons, ii. 512–13

Mann blames, for ill success at Velletri, ii. 514–15
—— flattered by, ii. 461
—— friendly with, iii. 13
—— receives courier from, ii. 453
—— receives five couriers from, about invalids, ii. 519
—— restrains impatience of, ii. 471
—— satisfies demands of, for English naval help, ii. 470
——'s correspondence with, ii. 405, 453, 459, 470–1, 474–6, 484, 519
——'s letters to Long intercepted by, ii. 514
—— to notify, if he finds Francis III's pictures, ii. 323
—— to send courier to, ii. 508
Mantua to be garrisoned by, ii. 513
Maria Theresa orders, to retire to Lombardy, ii. 508
——'s armies should no longer be led by, ii. 519
Mathews asked by, for loan of ships, ii. 438
——'s friendship doubted by, ii. 476
——'s plan of making descents unknown to, ii. 484
——'s remonstrances against Neapolitan expedition of, sent by courier, ii. 444
—— to refuse to lend ships to, ii. 443
Milan and Modena to be garrisoned by, ii. 513
Milan to be visited by, ii. 555
Modena near station of, iii. 35
Naples expedition of, assembles at Monte Rotondo, ii. 443
Naples may be taken by, ii. 419
Naples to be taken by, to compensate for Villa Franca loss, ii. 437
Neapolitan conquest and dispatch of regiment to Piedmont simultaneously expected of, ii. 512–13
Neapolitan invasion required of, ii. 271, 434–5
Neapolitan prince's birth reported by, ii. 478
Neapolitans would revolt if encouraged by, ii. 460
Panaro crossed by, iii. 30
Panaro to be defended by, iii. 22
Parma near station of, iii. 36–7, 40, 47, 50
Perugia visited by, on way to Gubbio, Umbria, and Fano, ii. 529
Pizzighettone to be garrisoned by, ii. 513
Regency dislikes discard of artillery by, ii. 529
reinforcements received by, ii. 336, iii. 30
retires to the Panaro, iii. 22
retreat of, from Faiola and Genzano, ii. 530
Rimini occupied by, ii. 331, 339
Romans acclaim, ii. 447
St Castaldo occupied by, near Modena and the Naviglio, iii. 30
Schulenburg replaces, iii. 41, 50, 55, 58
Silesian affair to be mended by, iii. 58

son of, ii. 487, 489, 491, 564
Spaniards and Neapolitans ready to pursue, if he falls back, ii. 508
Spaniards await advance of, ii. 335
Spaniards cut off, from Foligno, ii. 529
Spaniards if not pursued by, would return, ii. 413
Spaniards not sufficiently crushed by, ii. 359
Spaniards retreat from, ii. 412–13
Spaniards to be driven by, to Naples or Pesaro, ii. 405
Spanish cavalry inferior to that of, ii. 312
Spanish infantry outnumbers that of, ii. 312
successor to, not appointed, iii. 50
Terra del Sole to be crossed by, iii. 11
Tiber to be bridged by, ii. 437
Traun to be replaced by, ii. 279–80, 285, 302
Tuscan troops to be ready to join, iii. 11
Tuscany may be entered by, ii. 339, 508, iii. 11
Tuscany may be exposed by retreat of, into Lombardy, ii. 502, 508
unpreparedness of, blamed on Vienna, iii. 22
Velletri victory of, ii. 486–7, 488–94
'victory' of, may be costly, ii. 486
Vienna does not reinforce army of, iii. 22
Vienna orders, to enter Tuscany, iii. 11
Lobkowitz, Joseph Maria Karl, (1725–1802), Fürst; army officer; Austrian minister to Russia 1763–77:
apothecary and surgeon accompany, ii. 564
English arrival of, interests Mann, iii. 13
Harwich visited by, ii. 564
Joseph II and Maria Theresa send, with ultimatum to St Petersburg, vii. 310
Turin to be visited by, with father's dispatches, ii. 487, 489, 491
Lobositz:
battle of, v. 14, 72
Lobster:
Mathews's letter looks as if written by claw of, ii. 195
Locatelli, Andrea (1695–1741):
views of Rome by, i. 395, ii. 214
Lock. See Padlock
Locke, John (1632–1704), philosopher:
prerogative defended by, x. 24
Lockhart, George (1726–61), of Carnwath; Jacobite:
Corsini recommends, in Florence, iv. 78
deserted from the Guards to the rebels, iv. 78
Florence visited by, from Rome, iv. 78
Young Pretender sends, to Benedict XIV, iv. 27
Lock-jaw:
occurrences of, ix. 281
Lockman, (?) John (ca 1721–1807), D.D.; Canon of Windsor:
Pulteney's bequest to, vi. 146

Lodge. See Loggia; Porter's lodge
Lodi:
Spaniards pillage, iii. 267
Lodiggiano:
French and Spaniards invade, iii. 269
Loggia:
Craon's, i. 79
Mann's: Mann exercises in, i. 30; unpleasant in bad weather, i. 154
of Santo Spirito convent, iv. 446
Loggia dei Lanze:
Mann advises Botta to put Centaur and Alessandro Magno in, vi. 124
Perseus and Rape of the Sabines in, vi. 123–4
staircase to Uffizi to be made from, vi. 123
Lombard, Mary Magdelaine (ca 1695–1783), m. (1720) Horatio Walpole, cr. (1756) Bn Walpole of Wolterton:
age of, at death, ix. 385
apothecary paid by, for the first time, when she had a fever at 86, ix. 385
bathing and fires disliked by, ii. 47
blind, ix. 385
brother-in-law charged by, for his grandson's riding her son's horses, ii. 70
HW spends an hour with, ix. 385
house of, visited and described by HW, ii. 47
husband calls, 'Pug,' ii. 47n
Mann's old acquaintance, ii. 70, ix. 385
Marie Leszczyńska's conversation with, vii. 435
stay-maker's daughter, vii. 435
tailor in Drury Lane farce recalls family of, iv. 342
Lombard, Peter (1643–1725), tailor ('French staymaker'):
daughter of, vii. 435
Lombardy:
Austrian army in, estimated, i. 291
Austrians may retire to, ii. 413
battle expected in, i. 424
clergy of, i. 446
convents' wealth from, will not satisfy Joseph II, ix. 594, 595
couriers from, do not go through Padua, viii. 136
Croats en route to, i. 206
Elizabeth Farnese expects conquest of, ii. 195–6
Elizabeth Farnese may order seizure of, ii. 161
English demand withdrawal of Neapolitan troops from, ii. 15
Ferdinand VI's policy in, iii. 278
Florence cut off from news of, iii. 206
Florentines astonished at affairs in, iii. 230
Foligno gives access to, i. 261
Francis I's troops may march to, v. 9–10
French and Spanish troops may invade, vii. 469, 474
Gages may invade, ii. 556, iii. 31

[Lombardy, *continued*]

Genoese mob tries to bar troops' approach from, iii. 343

German troops sent to, i. 154, 214, iii. 200, 206

Joseph II contemplates restoring kingdom of, ix. 556n

Lobkowitz cannot leave, unguarded, ii. 405

—— may retreat to, ii. 502, 508–9

——'s army in, will be small, ii. 515

—— to send cavalry from, to Charles Emmanuel III, ii. 513

Mann, James II, to tour, before returning to Florence, ix. 598

Maria Theresa orders Lobkowitz to retire to, ii. 508

——'s affairs in, i. 427

—— sends troops to, v. 271

——'s troops to march through, i. 154

military forces in, iii. 258, 262–3

military situation in, not known, ii. 271

Neapolitans may invade, iii. 364, 367

Neapolitans on way to, iii. 237

Neapolitan troops may march towards, iii. 378, 402

news from, discredits peace rumours, iii. 225

Orsi faction lose hope of getting, through Montemar, i. 481

peace said to be declared in, iii. 504

Philip, Don, may be ruler of, i. 427

Sardinian successes in, iii. 237

Spaniards may exchange, for Tuscany, i. 206

Spaniards may invade: ii. 547; from Naples, iii. 367

Spaniards to return through, ii. 45

Spanish expedition may be headed for, i. 180, 192, 198, 204, 206, 208, 213, 219, 229, 261, 266, 311, 323, 341, 350, ii. 76

Spanish invasion diverted to, from Tuscany, iii. 22

Spanish victories in, iii. 119–20

Traun to defend, ii. 295

troops for Tuscany said to assemble in, iv. 320

victories in, reported in England, iii. 291

Lomellini, Agostino (fl. 1739–62), Doge of Genoa 1760–2:

Corsicans reject conciliation by, iv. 509

Lomellini, Bartolommeo; governor of Novi:

(?) follies of, iii. 76

Schulenburg's letter from, iii. 67

Lomellini, Pellina, m. (1738) Rodolfo Emilio Maria Brignole Sale:

(?) expected at Florence, i. 151

(?) Francis III admires, i. 44

(?) HW mentions, i. 43

Lommellino. *See* Lomellini

London, Bp of. *See* Gibson, Edmund (1669–1748); Hayter, Thomas (1702–62); Sherlock, Thomas (1678–1761); Terrick, Richard (1710–77)

London:

air of, 'purified' by fires in winter, ix. 542

alarm in, over rebels' advance, iii. 178

aldermen and Lord Mayor of: refuse to give banquet for Rodney, ix. 343; to present address to Q. Charlotte, v. 531

aldermen and members of Common Council of, to inspect Carte's history, ii. 480

American events unimportant to, viii. 385

American merchants numerous in, viii. 116

American news from, i. 35

Amherst's success celebrated by, v. 437–8

Amsterdam Gazette prints address from, ii. 418

apothecaries' and fishmongers' malpractices in, viii. 71

architecture in, flimsy, viii. 228

artillery ground at, v. 121

balloons absorb attention of, ix. 542–3

barbarity of, vi. 421

Barnard formerly lord mayor of, vi. 252n

Beckford alderman of, vi. 39n

Bedford attacks Lord Mayor, aldermen, and Common Council of, for permitting riot in Wilkes's favour, vi. 188

better than the country in wintertime, vi. 456–7

bishopric of, brings 'fat fines,' iii. 511

Blakiston an alderman of, iv. 261n

bonfires in, *see under* Bonfire

Brentford election will make roads unsafe for HW to go to, viii. 47

brokerage, privateering, contracts, and insurance upheld in, v. 549

Brown, Sir Robert, maps by-lanes of, for consumptive daughter's rides, to avoid turnpike fees, ix. 609n

Carte employed by, to write English history, ii. 480

charity in, for French prisoners, v. 367

citizens of, revolt from Court, viii. 535

city feast at, attended by Marlborough's general and stupid alderman, v. 198, viii. 29

city of: America and Ireland should sympathize with, vii. 292; banquets and sermons of, attended by Wilkes, vii. 208; Bute's downfall hastened by petitions from, vi. 129; change of ministers pleases, moderately, ix. 264; does not choose to be burned for Lord George Gordon's amusement, ix. 187; elation in, over victories, v. 518; factions in, vii. 151, 330; fire strikes family in, ix. 242; Fox, C.J., notifies, of peace proceedings, ix. 428; George II addressed by, on Minorca's capture, iv. 585; George III given remonstrances from, vii. 196–7, 199–200, 203, 215, ix. 218; gives pro-Jacobite instructions, iv. 12; Gordon, Lord George, candidate for, ix. 183, 187; Guadeloupe's retention wanted by, vi. 106; Havana's capture will not satisfy greed of, vi. 83; House of Commons quarrels with, over Wilkes, vii. 283; Howe's health probably drunk by, v. 226; Keppel's address from, too exultant,

viii. 446; Keppel to be banqueted by, viii. 445; Keppel voted freedom of, viii. 444; land tax defeat displeases, vi. 489; Mann disapproves of policy of, v. 90, vii. 305; mob comes from, vii. 290; 'money in their right, constitution in the left,' x. 24; moody on war prospect, viii. 361; mourning for Pitt's resignation proposed in, v. 540; petition from, vii. 133; Pitt abuses, vii. 251; Pitt lures, by hope of Spanish plunder, v. 549; Pitt's grave desired by, viii. 382; Pitt's peerage disliked by, vi. 442–3; popular party of, may defeat Court in sheriffs' election, vii. 419; sedition in, mentioned by newspapers, viii. 117; Townshend has not told, that peace negotiations are over, ix. 355; Townshend notifies, of peace, ix. 355n
coal-heavers in, all Irish whiteboys, vii. 33
coal-heavers terrorize, vii. 21, 33, 39
Common Council of: entertains Rodney at London Tavern, ix. 343; meeting of, i. 329, 331; not much altered by new election, vii. 164; Pitt and Legge receive freedom of city from, v. 77, 87; receives Pitt's letter explaining his acceptance of pension, v. 546
Court candidates elected by, iii. 425
crime prevalent in, ix. 316–17, 343, 619
Cumberland, D. of, may be given honours by, iii. 288
—— saves, from rebel army, iii. 178
curious about news, but indifferent to it afterwards, ix. 373
decline of noble houses in, ii. 316
deserted: after Birthday, vi. 422; after rising of Parliament, ii. 211, vii. 416; around New Year's, iii. 455; at Christmas, vi. 191; due to Easter and Newmarket, ix. 639; during shooting season, viii. 335, ix. 433; in August, v. 427, vi. 550, vii. 230; in autumn, vi. 256; in December, till Parliament meets, iv. 209, ix. 105; in early January, ix. 354, 619; in Easter holidays, i. 398, 399, ii. 429, vii. 401; in summer, ii. 7, iii. 118, 418, 430, 435, iv. 89, 163, v. 118; until Birthday, ix. 354
divided between politicians and 'pleasurists,' viii. 89
driest spot in the nation, viii. 278
dromedary and camel exhibited in, v. 199
dullness of, iv. 291, 360
earthquake drives people from, iv. 130–1, 134, 136–7, 147
English army used to return to, in winter, v. 362
English vitality drained by, in winter, vii. 121
epidemics in, ii. 200, 213, v. 312, ix. 284
epigram on Pitt's gift from, v. 87
favourites of, constantly change, ix. 133–4
ferment in, caused by Parliament's dissolution, viii. 44–5
Florence compared with, vii. 569, viii. 228
Fogliani's mission to, ii. 183

follies of, do not vary, ix. 133
Frederick II's victory celebrated in, v. 452
French actors opposed in, i. 166, ii. 305, iv. 100n
French allowed to go to, despite undeclared war, viii. 399
Frenchman encourages mob in, to break windows, vii. 111
full of balls, shows, breakfasts, and joys, ix. 502
geese and turkeys to race from Norwich to, v. 7
George II's return to, celebrated by illuminations and bonfires, ii. 340
—— tells, that victory is caused by unanimity, v. 347
George III's wedding will make, the centre of diversions, v. 520
Gordon riots in, ix. 52–7, 61–4, 66, 67, 131, 187, 559
gossip of, soon forgotten, iii. 460
growth of, rapid, vii. 569, viii. 228
guards overawe, iii. 118
HW better in, than at SH, vi. 451
HW detests, vi. 451
HW has seen sights of, fifty times over, viii. 55
HW prefers, to the country, ii. 211
HW's affection for, ii. 315–16
HW's house-breaking at Arlington St puzzles, vii. 286
HW speculates about Rousseau's opinion of, viii. 62
HW spends but 3 days in, in a month, iii. 494
HW to return to, from travels, i. 142
hackney chairmen in, are mostly Irish, ix. 489n
half starved by delay of colliers, because of bad weather, ix. 274
Hamerani's medal to depict, x. 3
houses in: ii. 315–16; re-painted, v. 427; ridiculous for size and flimsiness, vi. 143; too flimsy to last long, v. 108n
hurricane loss makes little difference to people of, ix. 109
illuminations in, see under Illumination
inquiry to have been demanded by, about Rochefort attempt, v. 154–5
Keppel's dinner from, marked by riots, viii. 449
livery of, see Livery of London
Lord Mayor of, see Lord Mayor of London
Mann's banker in, see Croft, Richard
—— would be at a loss in, viii. 166
Mathews to send couriers to, ii. 325
meeting of, to propose address, iii. 106–7
melancholy, iii. 177
merchants of: loyal, ii. 408; object to precautions against plague, ii. 282; subscribe to raising troops, iii. 106
military camps at, resented, ix. 75
Mill familiar with, iii. 407

[London, continued]
mob of: given money for bonfires, i. 390; governs it, ii. 305; may upset King's Bench proceedings, vii. 15; should have America's and Ireland's sympathy, vii. 292; see also under Riots
Newcastle, D. of, and the English-French hostilities approved by, iv. 493
Nineveh compared with, iv. 469, vii. 133
nobody leaves, till July, ix. 641
Oliver, alderman of, vii. 291
Orford, Cts of, cannot endure one night in, vii. 492
Paris compared with, vii. 121
Parliamentarians flee, when no longer exempted from arrest for debt, iii. 418
Parliamentary members of, vote for address, ii. 125
Parliament attracts few spectators in, iii. 118
Parliament not to leave, at Christmas, viii. 543
Parliament's dissolution will empty, ix. 461
peace celebration in, iv. 46–50
people of: must carry arms at night against footpads, ix. 316–17; used to be lively after long vacation, ix. 558
Pitt's restoration expected by, viii. 366
plague in, ix. 423
politicians of, warm about C.J. Fox's India bill, ix. 448–9
Prince George plies between Leghorn and, v. 414
public diversions in, more than would suffice for two capitals, ix. 317
rebels may march to, iii. 160
rebels said to have reached, iii. 190, 196
remonstrance of, see under London: city of
riots in, see under Riot
Roman Catholic uprising expected at, iii. 138
Rome compared with, viii. 228
Scotch and Irish come to, vii. 569
spirit of, rises in 1745, iii. 105
stagnates at Christmas and autumn, but is feverish from February through May, viii. 149
street cries of, v. 154
streets in: dirty, iii. 317; re-paved, v. 427
Strozzi, Principessa, seeks stolen jewels in, iii. 350
trooper prophesied ruin of, iv. 137, vii. 261
troops summoned to, ii. 400
Tullie brings new guineas from, vii. 498
visitors to, no longer in danger of mobs, vii. 360
Walpole, Sir Robert, confused by new streets and squares of, viii. 228
weekends unfashionable when spent in, iv. 63–4, v. 118
Whitsuntide exodus from, i. 450
Wilkes becomes sheriff of, vii. 317
—— defeated as candidate for, vii. 5–8
—— elected alderman of, vii. 81–2, 317
—— in political control of, viii. 45–8
——'s dignity as alderman of, vii. 208
—— to be chamberlain of, viii. 535
Young Pretender unlikely to conquer, iii. 398
London Chronicle:
Evening Post reprints, vi. 326
Mann's recall from Florence rumoured in, vi. 315
London Evening Post:
Amelia, Ps, attacked by memorial in, iv. 322
Concord battle revealed by, viii. 109
Fane's Treasury appointment said by, to be reward for uncle's silence, ii. 33
Kingston, Ds of, writes letter to, viii. 126
Mann takes, vi. 326
Roman letter to Goldsworthy would look ridiculous in, iii. 226
London Gazette:
bad news palliated in, ix. 88
Battle of Lake Champlain will be described in, viii. 261
Battle of Long Island described in, viii. 248–9
censored and unintelligible, viii. 282
Charles of Naples's manifesto may be printed in, ii. 420
Conway's regiment mentioned in, iv. 297
Cornwallis's dispatch abridged in, ix. 158
Cowper's principality noticed in, ix. 606
Cumberland's dismissal not in, v. 150
English political changes announced in, ix. 469
extraordinary: announces Estaing's defeat, viii. 544–5; brags of captured fortresses, ix. 145; Clinton's and Howe's accounts in, viii. 408; describes Montreal's capture, v. 438, 445; Dutch-English war announced by, ix. 104–5; Mud Island and Red Bank announced by, to be captured, viii. 351–2; on Montreal's capture, received by Mann, v. 445; on Quebec's capture, received by Mann, v. 342
French must get idea of Quebec's possible recapture from, v. 421
Goldsworthy's transfer announced by, iv. 433
Guadeloupe fully treated in, v. 301
HW knows no more than, about Martinique, vi. 16
HW need not copy news which Mann will see in, ix. 433, 462, 542
HW writes letter to explain events in, viii. 405
Havana accounts in, vi. 86
Hawke's victory fully described in, iii. 445
Hessians said by, to be leaving, iii. 222
Howe's intention to start campaign reported by, viii. 315
Indian war in America noticed in, vi. 177
India success proclaimed in, v. 337
lies about American war, viii. 232

Mann can make nothing of, ix. 94
—— cannot err while he sticks to, viii. 249
—— hopes for, to inform him of new administration, ix. 300
—— must believe rumours only when confirmed by, vi. 315
—— questions article in, about Electress's wealth, ii. 205–6
—— reads in: of Bath ribbons conferred, vi. 390; of Cholmondeley's Berlin embassy, ix. 333; of Fitzroy's death, i. 116; of Rodney's victory, v. 309
——'s 'Bible,' viii. 216
——'s investiture as K.B. described in, vii. 57, 63, 70
—— to receive, iii. 44
—— will find new appointments in, ix. 264
—— will read in: about battle at Camden, ix. 92; about Elliot's defeat of Thurot's fleet, v. 376; about new peers, viii. 205; about Pondicherry, v. 516; about Quebec's capture, v. 338; of administration's dissolution, ix. 461; of Byron's victory, v. 433; of Cape Breton capture, v. 233; of Cornwallis's activities, ix. 158–9
Mitchell's knighthood announced in, vi. 380
Pigot's capture of schooner should not be in, ix. 318
plague warnings sounded by, ix. 422
proclamation in, about expected French invasion, viii. 500
publication date of, ix. 92
Rodney's letter in, v. 309
secret expedition suggested by, v. 437–8
Stosch contributes Florentine reports to, ii. 206
Ticonderoga defeat described in, v. 233
too prudent to print war news, iv. 484
victories in, not found elsewhere, ix. 76
Washington's total defeat not proclaimed by, viii. 339
London Tavern:
Rodney dines at, with Common Council, ix. 343
supporters of Bill of Rights meet at, and use its name, vii. 114
Long, Lady. See Bouverie, Harriet (1736–77)
Long, Charles (d. 1783):
uncle to provide for, vii. 22–3
Long, Mrs Charles. See Phipps, Hannah
Long, Emma (d. 1837) m. (1793) William Scrope:
(?) mother's only child, viii. 182
Long, Harriet Etruria (b. and d. 1776):
(?) mother's only child, viii. 182
Long (later Tylney-Long), Sir James (1736–94), 7th Bt, 1794:
Tylney accompanied by, viii. 312
—— doubtless makes, heir to English possessions, ix. 533
——'s will taken to, by courier, ix. 533
uncle always intended to leave Wansted to, vii. 22–3

Long, Robert (d. 1771), naval officer:
Admiralty lord criticized by, ii. 470
Leghorn visited by, ii. 477
Lobkowitz intercepts Mann's letters to, ii. 514
Mann confers with, at Leghorn, ii. 477
—— consults, at Leghorn by Mathews's request, ii. 469–70, 473, 475
—— praised by, for his lucid instructions, ii. 470
——'s correspondence with, ii. 473–4, 483
Mathews gives command of Nettuno fleet to, ii. 476
——'s instructions to Mann read aloud by, at war council, ii. 484
Naples to be attacked by, ii. 476–7
Long-boat:
Russian, sinks at Leghorn, ix. 493
Long Island, New York:
battle of: Americans defeated at, viii. 248–9; France will not permit England to have too many victories like, viii. 253; Newfoundland ship brings rumour of, to England, viii. 246
Estaing said to have captured, viii. 528
Long Island, South Carolina:
English troops land at, viii. 236
Longitude:
Macclesfield investigates, iv. 359
Longleat:
Weymouth retires to, viii. 534
'Long live George the King':
French horns unable to play, ix. 70
Longone. See Porto Longone
Long Story. See under Gray, Thomas
Lonsdale, Cts of. See Stuart, Lady Mary (1740–1824)
Lonsdale, E. of. See Lowther, Sir James (1736–1802)
Lonsdale, Vct. See Lowther, Henry (1694–1751)
Loo:
HW and Ds of Grafton to play, at D. of Devonshire's, E. Gower's and E. of Hertford's, v. 427
HW plays, till 2 or 3 A.M., v. 368
HW uses term from, iv. 453, vii. 382, ix. 539
Maria Louisa plays, with D. of Gloucester, vii. 352
Looking-glass:
HW's verses on Lady Bingley's search for, iv. 141
See also Mirror; Pocket-glass
Lopdell, Alexander, navy-yard clerk:
Mann sends, to England with letters, ix. 219
return of, delayed by lameness, ix. 227, 228
Lorain. See Lorraine
Lord advocate. See Dundas, Henry (1742–1811)
Lord chamberlain:
designs for Wolfe's tomb submitted to, v. 428
Devonshire, D. of, is, v. 91, 428, vi. 96n
Grafton is, i. 274n, iii. 125, iv. 120

[Lord chamberlain, *continued*]
heading of a party by, implies waning of opposition, iv. 120
Henry VIII's, Sandys was, iv. 485n
Hertford, acting as, receives Christian VII at St James's, vii. 42
——'s duty as, to supervise Augusta, Ps of Wales's funeral, vii. 381
Marlborough becomes, vi. 103
—— may be succeeded by Devonshire as, vi. 130–1
Pomfret, Cts of, not notified by, of Emperor's death, iii. 53
Portland resigns as, vi. 471
to Q. Charlotte: Harcourt may be succeeded by Lord Charles Spencer as, vii. 66; Manchester becomes, v. 517; Northumberland becomes, vi. 103
Lord chancellor; lord chancellors:
appointment of, not yet made, vii. 251
Bathurst formerly was, viii. 534
—— to succeed father as, vii. 268
De Grey not to be, vii. 247
George III demands Thurlow's continuance as, ix. 381
—— insists on keeping Pratt as, vi. 538
Hardwicke resigns as, iii. 211
Henley formerly was, vi. 500
mace of, i. 174
Mansfield declines to become, vii. 174
North cannot make, vii. 268
Norton does not wish to be, vii. 179
Pitt names Pratt for, vi. 161
Pratt (Camden) dismissed from post of, vii. 174
—— formerly was, viii. 103n, ix. 440n
—— remains as, vi. 538, vii. 65
Pulteney refuses to become, ii. 72
Thurlow remains as, ix. 262
—— succeeds Bathurst as, viii. 385
when ill, sometimes carried to woolsacks, ix. 347
Willes refuses to be, iii. 212
Yorke, Charles, accepts as, after declining, vii. 175
—— kisses George III's hand as, vii. 178
See also Yorke, Philip (1690–1764), E. of Hardwicke; Talbot, Charles (1685–1737)
Lord chancellor of Ireland. *See* Jocelyn, Robert
Lord chief justice. *See under* Court of Common Pleas; Court of King's Bench
Lord high steward:
Dorset again to be, iv. 470
Hardwicke becomes, at trial of rebel lords, iii. 280
Henley is, at Ferrers's trial, v. 388
wand of, broken, vii. 99
Lord justice:
Bessborough and Jocelyn nominated as, in Ireland, iv. 426
Walpole, Sir Robert, acts as, in absences of George I and George II, vi. 26

Lord keeper:
appointment of, not yet made, vii. 251
Bathurst becomes, vii. 251, 259, 268
De Grey hesitates to accept post of, vii. 247
Henley becomes, v. 110
Seals to be put in commission if not given to, v. 18
Smythe to be, vii. 248
See also Henley, Sir Robert
Lord lieutenant of Ireland. *See under* Ireland
Lord marshal. *See* Keith, George
Lord mayor of London:
at liberty, when Parliament is prorogued, vii. 303
ball given by, i. 183–5, 208, vii. 200
Barnard formerly was, vi. 252n
dinner given by: for Opposition, vii. 200; Lyttelton and Temple attend, vi. 464; Marlborough's general dines at, v. 198, viii. 29, 414, ix. 340
gold chain of, i. 295
Wilkes almost becomes, vii. 441, 520, viii. 45
—— becomes, viii. 48
See also Blakiston, Matthew (ca 1702–74); Bridgen, William (ca 1709–79); Bull, Frederick (ca 1714–84); Crosby, Brass (1725–93); Fludyer, Sir Samuel (ca 1705–68); Godschall, Sir Robert (d. 1742); Harley, Thomas (1730–1804); Heathcote, George (d. 1768); Kite, Sir Robert (d. 1772); Newnham, Nathaniel (ca 1741–1809); Walworth, Sir William (d. 1385)
Lord mayor's show:
Mann's investiture compared to, vii. 60
Lord of the Bedchamber. *See under* Bedchamber
Lord of the Treasury. *See under* Treasury
Lord of trade; lords of trade:
Burke's bill opposed by, ix. 26–7
Pitt, John, among, iii. 458n
Rice, George, becomes, v. 489, 490
Robinson, Sir Thomas, becomes, iv. 17
Talbot, Jenyns, and Rigby succeed J. Grenville, T. Pitt and Edgcumbe as, iv. 517
Thomas, Sir Edmund, becomes, v. 490
Yorke, John, becomes, v. 490
see also First Lord of Trade
Lord president of the Council. *See* President, lord, of the Council
Lord privy seal:
Carlisle, 4th E. of, is, iii. 211
Carlisle, 5th E. of, is, ix. 365n, 391
Cholmondeley may succeed Gower as, if Pulteney refuses, ii. 159
Dartmouth succeeds Grafton at, viii. 142
Gower is, i. 457, ii. 89, 186
—— resigns as, iii. 211
—— succeeds Hervey as, i. 492, ii. 70, 89
—— succeeds Marlborough as, iv. 517
Grafton is, viii. 139, ix. 262
Hardwicke may become, v. 541

Hervey was, in George II's reign, ix. 503n
Pitt becomes, vi. 442
Pulteney may succeed Gower as, ii. 73, 96
Suffolk becomes, vii. 268
Temple to succeed Gower as, v. 104
See also Cholmondeley, George (1703–70), E. of Cholmondeley; Leveson-Gower, John (1694–1754), E. Gower; *see also under* Privy Seal
Lord's prayer:
Ferrers consents to use of, at his execution, v. 401
Lord's supper:
painting of Catiline's conspiracy mistaken for, ii. 41
Lord steward of the Household:
Carlisle resigns as, ix. 365
Marlborough succeeds Devonshire as, iv. 66–7
Rutland, D. of, resigns as, v. 98
Talbot becomes, v. 489
See also Cavendish, William (?1698–1755), D. of Devonshire; Sackville Lionel Cranfield (1688–1765), D. of Dorset
Lord treasurer:
green velvet bags used by, ii. 225n
Hardwicke or Newcastle may become, iv. 412
Southampton was, iv. 282n
Lorenzi, Chevalier de. *See* Roland, Jacques (d. 1784)
Lorenzi, Conte. *See* Roland, Luigi (d. 1766)
Lorenzi, Contessa. *See* Ughi, Maria Minerva
Loreto:
Acciaioli, Mme, sets out for wedding at, i. 474
—— visits, for daughter's wedding, ii. 65
Acciaioli wedding to take place at, i. 444
Austrians seize magazines near, ii. 419
Chute and Whithed to visit, iii. 48
Craon, Prinecsse de, to pass through, i. 22
Gloucester, D. of, to visit, vii. 370, viii. 130
Lorenzi, Comtesse de, visits, iv. 437
Madonna di: visits to, induce pregnancy in women and mares, iv. 437; York, Cardinal, will give jewels to, ix. 526
Pitt, Thomas, intends to visit, v. 543
Pomfrets to visit, i. 41
Spanish cavalry to pass through, ii. 45
Strange will regard Albano as his, v. 404
Wales, Ps of, taken for Lady of, by Cts of Pomfret, i. 343, 368, 370
Young Pretender to meet bride at, vii. 406
Lorne, M. of. *See* Campbell, John (1723–1806)
Lorrain, Claude (Claude Gelée) (1600–82), landscape painter:
Chesterfield buys painting attributed to, vii. 466
Cipriani's paintings to replace those by, at Houghton, ix. 316
paintings by, not to be found despite Hoare's order to Mann, v. 209

Whithed collects paintings by, iv. 142
Lorraine, Duchesse de. *See* Bourbon d'Orléans, Élisabeth-Charlotte de (1676–1744)
Lorraine, D. of. *See* Leopold I (1679–1729)
Lorraine, Primate of. *See* Beauvau-Craon, François-Vincent-Marc de
Lorraine, Emmanuel-Maurice de (1677–1763), Prince d'Elbeuf; antiquarian:
Caligula's bust discovered by, vi. 528
Lorraine, Jacques-Henri de (1698–1734), P. de Lixin:
death of, excludes wife from French court, iv. 92
widow of, iv. 122n
Lorraine, Louis-Marie-Léopold de (ca 1720–1747), P. de Guise:
death of, iii. 426
Lorraine:
archives of, to be secured, i. 199
calcidonio said to be in mountains of, ii. 207
Charles, P., threatens, ii. 457
—— unlikely to threaten, ii. 297
Craon gets leave to go to, iv. 25
Craon, Princesse de, lived in, at height of her beauty, i. 28
Craons hope to return to, iv. 24
Craons may revisit, iii. 467
Du Châtelet's troops of, to go to Leghorn, i. 182
Eszterházy, Ps, born in, iv. 351
faction of, at Florence: Botta opposed by, v. 424, vi. 13; despair about Francis I's favours to Tuscans, v. 125; English picque noticed by, in Florence, iv. 9; Florentine society consists only of, iv. 115; Florentines shun, iii. 457n; George II's speech pleases, i. 38; Leopold welcomed as relief from, vi. 336; Mann disclaims attachment to, v. 148; Mann 'frequented' by, iii. 79–80; opera supported by, in Florence, ii. 555; Orford, Cts of, tells, that she will return after recovering English estates, iii. 75; sell off all Florentine supplies, ii. 270; Spanish attack not expected by, i. 204; told of Cts of Orford's plans, iii. 75; trust in Maria Theresa, v. 360; Uffizi treasures not collected by, vi. 71
Francis I keeps regiment from, in Florence, iii. 457n
Gondrecourt, an officer, from, insults Langlois, iii. 365–6, 374
HW pleased by end of supremacy of, in Tuscany, v. 138
HW surprised at Mann's fondness for ladies of, iii. 457
Irishman from, sent to Vienna to protest to Francis I, v. 125
Joseph II demands restitution of, from France, vi. 395
ladies from: Mann frequents, iii. 452; Mann

[Lorraine, *continued*]
to entertain, in dark room to hide their ugliness, iv. 370; more sociable than Italians, iii. 466
Lottinger from, vi. 345
man from, tells Mann that Frederick II must be punished, iv. 589
Mann hopes that the French may lose, ii. 290
Mirepoix, Duchesse de, to visit parents in, iv. 116
Morehead, Mrs, treated as a 'lady of condition' in, iii. 489
Nancy in, viii. 131
officer of: fights Capponi, ii. 182, 202; talks to Frenchman about Vandières, iv. 228; *see also* Laugier
officers of: cat calls of, at theatre, i. 162; more courageous than Florentines, iv. 372
officials of, in Florence sell kitchenware, linen, and wood, ii. 270
Old Pretender lived at Craon's in, iii. 108n, iv. 132, 332
Pitt, Anne, leaves, for Pisa, viii. 188
Richecourt and Traun hope for recovery of, ii. 285
Richecourt from, i. 189n, 409n, ix. 122n
—— to go to, v. 62, 80, 85
Sarrazin, Mme, from, i. 436n
—— to be tended by daughter in, ii. 361
Stanislas I's death will be mourned by, because of his generosity and economy, vi. 402
Tuscany hates rulers from, but is anti-British, iv. 581
Lorraine, House of:
Craon's, Princesse de, ill rewarded by, iv. 26
Medici history discouraged by, v. 284
Lorraine Guards:
encampment of, ii. 98
gens d'armes: countryman's ill-treatment by, at Florence, i. 79; Dumesnil major of, i. 225; Givrecourt colonel of, ii. 368; officers of, offended by valet's arrest, i. 225; Tesi insulted by, at opera, ii. 368
sent to Leghorn, i. 182, 198, 203–4, 214, 239, 266
Lorrainer; Lorrainers:
'little,' HW sends letter to Mann through, i. 18
Milan predicted as station of, i. 380
peace between England and Spain would alarm, ii. 107
Los Balbases, Marquesa de. *See* Colonna, Maria Vittoria (1721–77)
Lothian, Marchioness of. *See* Darcy, Lady Caroline
Lothian, M. of. *See* Ker, William (1661–1722); Ker, William Henry (ca 1710–75)
Lottery:
English ministers propose, ii. 141
Florentines sacrifice snuff for tickets for, iv. 389

HW compares remedies to, ix. 428
Suares family supposedly adept at, ii. 351
Vitelli, Mme, makes, ii. 340, 351
Lottery ticket:
Bichi, Mme, has, ii. 206
Lottinger, Giovanni Stefano, Tuscan consul at Genoa 1757–64; chargé d'affaires in England 1764–ca 1770:
Francis I appointed, to succeed Pucci as Tuscan envoy to England, vi. 345
'Lorrainer,' vi. 345
Loudon, Gedeon Ernst (1716–90), Freiherr von; field marshal:
army command declined by, v. 470
Frederick II defeats, v. 331–2, 434–5, vi. 70
Kunersdorf victory attributed to, by Austrians, v. 331–2
Maria Theresa faints at news of defeat of, v. 435
—— should have, instead of Daun, v. 428
Loudon. *See also* Loudoun
Loudoun, E. of. *See* Campbell, John (1705–82)
Loughborough, Bn. *See* Wedderburn, Alexander
Louis, St, order of. *See* St Louis
Louis VI (1081–1137), 'le Gros,' king of France 1108–37:
Courtenay the heir of, iii. 309n
Louis XI (1423–83), K. of France 1461–83:
Pitt's despotism compared with that of, vii. 100
Louis XIII (1601–43), K. of France 1610–43:
Galluzzi bitter against, ix. 225
Louis XIV (1638–1715), K. of France 1643–1715:
Bussy's stories about, ii. 131
Charles II 'sells' British Isles to, ii. 247
Coke, Lady Mary, visits vault of, at St-Denis, vii. 14
France could admire, viii. 140
Genoa's submission to, iii. 313
George II compared with, ii. 71
health of: operated upon for piles, i. 59; piles, ii. 71
James II could not be restored by, to English throne, viii. 127
life of, *see* Voltaire: *Siècle de Louis XIV*
Maintenon, Marquise de, marries, morganatically, vi. 126, 144, 270n
medal struck by, for Siamese ambassadors' reception, viii. 469
mémoires of the minority of, resemble English political gossip, v. 13
saying of, about bestowal of places, viii. 5
Louis XV (1710–74), K. of France 1715–74:
absolution *in articulo mortis* wanted by, vii. 518, viii. 8
accident of, may be considered a chastisement for adultery, vii. 90
age of, should make him favour Princesse Louise rather than Comtesse du Barry, vii. 399

Aiguillon gains little ground with, vii. 321

Aix treaty probably facilitated by aversion of, to army, iii. 482

amatory career of, vii. 87–8

ambassador represents, in England, iv. 144

anxious to stop bloodshed, vi. 60

Argenson remonstrates with, about Young Pretender, ii. 415

Argenson's and Machault's dismissals by, will antagonize all parties, v. 59

Argenson thinks that devotion of, to Roman church is necessary for monarchy, v. 48

arm injured by, in fall from horse, vii. 90

army of, ii. 456

assassination of: attempted by Damiens, v. 43–4, 48–9, 52, 59, 79–80, vi. 65; French fashions might be inspired by, v. 52; proves that he was not *bien aimé*, vii. 4; would be the least bad of murderers, v. 79

Austria quelled by negotiations of, with Turks, ii. 543

Beauvau congratulated by, on future marriage, iii. 1

—— pleases, ii. 216

Belle-Isle's estates said to have been given to illegitimate son of, vi. 4

Benedict XIV's letter to, v. 59–60

Bernis dismissed by, v. 265

book on Kloster-Zeven will not help cause of, v. 236

bread carried by, in pocket, iv. 340

Broglie banished by, vii. 521

Brown said to be rewarded by, for news of Falkirk, iii. 217

Buondelmonte's answer to question about French devotion to, v. 48–9

'cabinet' of, see *Recueil d'estampes d'après les plus beaux tableaux*

Carrickfergus now belongs to, v. 371

catafalque of, avoided by Ducs d'Orléans and de Chartres, vii. 25–6

Cavalchini excluded by, from papacy, v. 216, 224

Charles III's advice asked by, vii. 277

—— said to be about to meet, at Lyon, v. 283, 289, 318

—— said to be influenced by, about Papal election, i. 20–21

—— sees reluctance of, to aid him, vii. 277

——'s relations with, over Jesuits, vii. 414

Charles, P., to have been driven by, across the Rhine, ii. 505

Charolais's dogs given by, to aggrieved Président, iv. 340

Châteauroux, Duchesse de, dismissed by, through Bp of Soissons' intervention, ii. 523, 544, vii. 87

—— mistress of, said to be poisoned, ii. 552

Choiseul reproached by, for fomenting war, vii. 258

——'s Corsican drive feared by, to provoke war, vii. 62

——'s dismissal by, aids England, vii. 314

——'s would-be visitors not forbidden by, vii. 321

civil list of, pruned by financiers, iv. 500

Clement XIII tells Aubeterre that he will acknowledge Young Pretender if example is set by, ix. 526

Clement XIV influences, through Princesse Louise and Comtesse du Barry, vii. 372

—— may be asked by, for absolution, viii. 8

—— to tell Princesse Louise and Comtesse du Barry to influence, against Charles III, vii. 430–1

clergy at odds with, iv. 199, 206, 293–4

clergy told by, to grant him money, vii. 399

college of cardinals asked by, to await his cardinals, v. 207

confessor of, see *under* Confessor

Conflans offers his head to, for Quiberon Bay disaster, v. 358–9

conquests planned by, make him an object of great interest, v. 335

Condé influences, vii. 265

Conti says, could give crown to Charles X instead of Louis XVI, vii. 304

council said to be attended by, v. 44

Damiens's attack on, makes past crimes more credible, vi. 65

daughter-in-law begs, to avenge her father against Frederick II, v. 5

daughter of, vii. 398

daughters do not address their mother across, at dinner, iv. 340

daughter's entrance into convent opposed by, vii. 207

daughter's letter from, about escape from assassin, v. 48

daughters tend, although they have never had smallpox, viii. 1–2

death of: at Metz, wished, ii. 502, 504; chief topic of conversation in Florence, viii. 9; confirmed, viii. 5; rumoured, viii. 1

despised, vii. 270

Devil feared by, iv. 236

devotional turn of, iv. 530

displeasure of, at Benedict XIV's acknowledging Francis I's election, iii. 183

Drummond to be commander for, in England, iii. 187

Du Barry, Comtesse, and Ps Louise persuade, vii. 321, 414

Du Barry, Comtesse, can still be enjoyed by, despite war, vii. 253

—— flings powder in face of, vii. 85

—— influences, vii. 284, 320–1, 414

—— may celebrate installation by, by displacing Choiseul, vii. 90

—— may reunite, with Jesuits, vii. 94

—— reproved by, for making faces at Choiseul at whist game, vii. 157

—— said to keep, diverted or drunk, vii. 270

[Louis XV, *continued*]

——'s presentation to, arranged, vii. 85, 94, 115

Easter confession of, awaited, iv. 542

end of, contemptible, viii. 36

England may be pardoned by, for aggression, iv. 497

England tries to exclude, from America, v. 335

English and Scottish Jacobites said to have influenced, ii. 426

English fleet may soon be captured by, iii. 71

English invasion said to be the aim of, v. 309

English might compel, to take refuge, in Holland, v. 228

English paper on, prevented by French officers' threat to printer, vii. 230–1

English to be chased by, from Mediterranean, iv. 588

epigram on statue of, at Bordeaux, i. 125

expenses of, iv. 500

Fitzjames said to have been sent by, to Young Pretender, vii. 337–8

France may rebel against, vi. 415

Frederick II not making terms with, v. 159

——'s peace overtures to, v. 366

French cardinals protest to, against Cavalchini's appointment, v. 224

French medals would depict, with Neptune, v. 357

French opponents subjugated by, vii. 320–1

French people curse, vii. 320

French prisoners in England abandoned by, v. 367

Gallican church's liberties upheld by, vii. 81

Génie de France extols, at Genoa, iii. 505

German defeats probably regarded by, as inconsequential, vi. 51

German Empire to be conciliated by, in sending them a royal general, v. 176

HW and Mann know more about, than about each other's friends, vii. 260

HW calls, 'Solomon,' vii. 157

HW does not see, i. 152

health of: hiccup, viii. 1; ill at Metz, ii. 502–3, 504–5; smallpox, viii. 1, 2, 8

Holland told by, not to send troops to England, v. 298

humanity of, touched by Mme de Pompadour's love of peace, iv. 530

illegitimate son said to have been avowed by, vi. 4

indifference of, to public affairs, v. 358

Irish mistress provided for, by Mme de Pompadour, iv. 542

Jesuit confessor's lessons retained by, vi. 415

Jesuits subject of complaints by, vii. 507

La Chalotais provokes Aiguillon to be tried before, at Versailles, vii. 206

Lambert proposes toast to, v. 251

La Rochefoucauld said to have frightened, into discarding Mme de Pompadour, iv. 530

La Tournelle, Marquise de, to be mistress of, ii. 102–3

lit de justice held by, v. 56, vi. 415n

Lorenzi, Comtesse, reveres, iv. 276

Maillebois and Monteynard first sustained, then punished by, vii. 283–4

Mailly, Comtesse de, disgraced by, ii. 102, vii. 87

Maria Amalia's dismissal of Du Tillot from Parma offends, vii. 445

Maria Theresa asks, for ladies to educate her daughters, iv. 326

Marie Leszczyńska celebrates recovery of soul and body of, ii. 524

—— and daughters do not speak across, at table, iv. 340

Masserano signs declaration on warrant of, vii. 269

Maupeou advises, to remove Choiseul to make parliaments submit, vii. 259

Maupeou and Comtesse du Barry almost alone with, at Versailles, vii. 298

Maupeou meets, often, in Princesse Louise's cell at St-Denis, vii. 321

——'s conduct would not be imitated by, vii. 359

millions of lives sacrificed by stewards of, vi. 81

ministerial choices of, aid England, vii. 314

ministers referred by, to Belle-Isle, v. 358

mistresses kept openly by, in wife's lifetime, vii. 78–9

mistresses of, enumerated, vii. 87

Monteynard's plea to, vii. 284

Montfort's obesity insulted by, iv. 156

new regime not creditable for, vii. 260

Noailles accompanies, to Valenciennes, ii. 441

nurse's letter from, published, ii. 544

pacific intentions of, iv. 480, vi. 60, vii. 157, 258

Paoli would be undone if Comtesse du Barry were expelled by, vii. 90

Papal election said to be influenced by, i. 20–1

Paris mob tramples old woman for cheering, v. 56

Parliament forbidden by, to dispute his acts, vi. 415n

Parliament of Paris opposes, iv. 293, 440, vi. 153, 412

parliaments' rage survived by, vii. 329

Parsons noticed by, i. 185n

peasants cry to, for bread, v. 520

Philip V of Spain said to be influenced by, about Papal election, i. 20–1

Pitt almost tossed, in blanket, vi. 276

Pompadour, Marquise de, made by, *dame du palais* to his wife, iv. 530

—— manages, to the advantage of the English, vi. 30
—— may be displaced by Mme de Guerchy with, vi. 239
—— mistress of, iv. 227–8, vi. 212n
—— said to be separated from, iv. 530, 542
—— said to have abandoned, iv. 236
—— said to have introduced mistress to, vi. 4
Princes of the Blood do not endanger, by their opposition, vii. 320
Raphael painting owned by, v. 200
Rena may have had designs on, v. 162
returns from Choisy, vii. 115
Richelieu suggests Comtesse du Barry's presentation to, vii. 115
Richmond, D. of, and Fox asked impertinent questions by, vi. 163, 170
Rome kept on good terms by, to insure absolution, vii. 518
sobriquet of, should be changed from *Well-beloved* to *Well-beloving*, vii. 79
Soissons, Bp of, confined by, to diocese, ii. 523n
—— promised by, that mistresses would be dismissed after his recovery, ii. 504–5
—— will repent having separated, from Duchesse de Châteauroux, ii. 544
son less desirable than, v. 44
son tells, that he will obey the Pope in all, v. 44
Souvré angers, by witticism, v. 514
Stanislas II's misadventure must alarm, vii. 359
Stormont said to have been asked to take Sutton to, viii. 2
Tencin probably persuaded, that Young Pretender's attempt would divert English military strength, ii. 379
Trianon given by, to wife, i. 126–7
Turks and Polish confederates vainly encouraged by, vii. 331
(?) Tuscany guaranteed by, against Spanish invasion, i. 197–8
verses threatening, iv. 287, 387–8, v. 48
Victoire, Princesse, betrays Bp of Orléans to, vii. 321
—— loved by, vi. 164
weakness of, increases, vii. 283
Young Pretender hated by, v. 44, 59
——'s pretensions said to be supported by, in letter to Tencin, i. 114
(?) Zurich may seek aid of, ii. 290
Louis XVI (1754–93), K. of France 1774–93:
advocates burning authors instead of their books, viii. 10
Albany, Cts of, pensioned by, ix. 150
Artois informs, of destruction of floating batteries, ix. 325
aunts of, govern his wife, vii. 321
balloon operators commemorated by, in statues, ix. 450

Bernis said to have been recalled by, ix. 222
Catherine II should be dethroned by, viii. 35
Charles III not pleased with, ix. 21
—— would not allow Jesuits to be restored by, viii. 9–10
Choiseul reported to have had conferences with, ix. 291
church may be championed by, viii. 10
Conti's retort to, vii. 304
Court reformation and economies of, viii. 12, 18
Du Barry, Comtesse, released by, viii. 99
—— should be released by, viii. 35
English said to be disliked by, viii. 17
European despots should be dethroned, and Corsica freed by, viii. 35
Europe concerned only with public policies of, viii. 18
faultless, viii. 133
Ferdinand of Naples said to be told by Charles III and, to exclude Russian fleet, ix. 616n
Francis II's French uncle, ix. 282
French defeat at Jersey not the fault of, according to Barbantane, ix. 127
generous principles embraced by, viii. 124
Gloucester, D. and Ds of, invited by, to Paris, viii. 125
Guines thanked and made a Duc by, viii. 208
Gustav III should be dethroned by, viii. 35
impotence of, alleged, viii. 208n
Jesuits might be restored by, viii. 3, 9–10
Joseph II may influence, viii. 3, 17
La Vauguyon the governor of, vii. 87
Mann calls, simple, ix. 128
Marchais first valet-de-chambre to, viii. 266
Marie-Antoinette's influence over, viii. 3, 17, 208
——'s match with, vi. 404, viii. 54
Maupeou and Terray banished by, viii. 34
Maupeou said to be liked by, viii. 1
may be Wilkes's French equivalent, viii. 62
ministers not to be seen by, for 9 days, viii. 5
mob besieges, at Versailles, viii. 112
mob intends to draw coach of, to *lit de justice*, viii. 61
Parliament of Paris infuriates, by examining rioters, viii. 102
policies of, still unknown, viii. 1, 12
Polish war might be embraced by, in order to destroy dissidents, viii. 11
propagation discovered by, viii. 393
Resurrexit on Henri IV's statue a compliment to, viii. 19, 36
said to be 'obstinate,' or 'firm,' about making peace, ix. 285

[Louis XVI, *continued*]
  speechless with rage at *lit de justice*, viii. 102
  Stuart, Charlotte, allowed by, to inherit father's French possessions, ix. 536–7
  unpromising, vii. 322
Louis (1661–1711), Dauphin:
  Choin, Mlle, thought to have married, vi. 270n
Louis (1729–65), Dauphin:
  bigotry of, ameliorated before his death, v. 44n
  change of air and ass's milk improve, vi. 348
  comment of, on Nero, v. 44
  death of: expected, vi. 342, 364, 369; irony of, vi. 404
  extreme unction administered to, vi. 364
  father preferable to, v. 44
  father told by, of subservience to Pope, v. 44
  funeral oration for, in Paris, vi. 403
  Jansenists disliked by, v. 44
  Metz visited by, ii. 502
  wedding of: Lorenzi celebrates, iii. 14; Lorenzi to celebrate, ii. 559
  wife of, v. 5n
  Young Pretender would be aided by, v. 59
Louis (-Joseph) (1781–9), Dauphin:
  death of, falsely reported, ix. 583
Louis (-Joseph-Xavier) (1751–61), D. of Burgundy:
  birth of, celebrated, iv. 276, 280, 286, 287
Louis —— (d. 1767), HW's Swiss servant:
  message taken by, iv. 554
Louis, Don. *See* Luis Antonio
'Louis, Master.' *See* Wallmoden, Johann Ludwig
Louis, of the Palazzo Vecchio. *See* Siries, Louis
Louis, French frigate:
  capture of, vi. 82
Louisa (1724–51), of England, m. (1743) Frederik V, K. of Denmark, 1746:
  becomes queen, iii. 295
  clothes bought by, for wedding, ii. 305
  Delorain, Cts of, governess to, ii. 82n
  husband shorter than, ii. 341
  Mann wants news of, ii. 303–4
  marriage of: contract for, signed, ii. 218–19; expected, ii. 277; rumoured, ii. 203; Riccardi asks Mann about, ii. 289
  summer spent by, at St James's Palace, ii. 218
Louisa (1773–1802) of Naples, m. (1790) Ferdinand III of Tuscany:
  inoculated, viii. 330
Louisa Ann (1749–68) Ps, daughter of Frederick, P. of Wales:
  (?) brother may accompany, to Spa, vi. 524
  Coke, Lady Mary, enters Westminster Abbey vault at death of, viii. 14
  father survived by, iv. 233

health of, consumption, vii. 22
pretty, but small and unhealthy, vi. 275
Louisa Maria Theresa (1751–1819), of Parma, m. (1765) Charles IV, K. of Spain 1788–1808:
  father's death told to, vi. 313
Louisa Ulrica. *See* Louise Ulrica
Louisbourg:
  Boscawen may attack, iv. 511
  —— the conqueror of, v. 292
  capture of: Botta's satisfaction over, v. 244; Cherbourg's capture eclipsed by, v. 234; English impatient for, v. 226; Ticonderoga defeat dampens joy over, v. 241; will enable England to send troops to Germany, v. 236
  England would not exchange Carrickfergus for, v. 371
  English besiege, v. 229–30
  French depreciate, now that it is no longer theirs, v. 343
  French fleet reaches, iv. 484
  French lose spirit at, v. 233
  French proclaimed English repulse at, vi. 21, 89
  French well informed about events at, v. 230
  Loudoun abandons attempt on, v. 130
  Mann reminds Botta of false rumours about, vi. 89
  ship from Marseille brings false news of relief of, v. 242
  standards taken at, carried to St Paul's Cathedral, v. 237, 238
  starvation to speed capitulation of, v. 204, 218
  supplies relieve, v. 218
  Wolfe does well at, v. 267
Louise Augusta (1771–1843), m. (1786) Friedrich Christian, D. of Holstein-Sonderburg-Augustenburg:
  legitimacy of, doubtful, vii. 386
Louise-Marie (1737–87), Ps, dau. of Louis XV:
  Beauvilliers scratched by, from party list, vii. 115–16
  Carmelite convent entered by, vii. 207, 321n, 398
  centre of clerical intrigue, vii. 398
  Clement XIV may influence Louis XV through, vii. 321, 372, 414, 431
  Du Barry, Comtesse, contends with, for Louis XV, vii. 399
  expense of coffee for, iv. 500
  Louis XV and Maupeou often meet at cell of, at St-Denis, vii. 321
  Marie-Antoinette governed by, vii. 321
  Maupeou influences, vii. 398
  mother not addressed by, across father at dinner, iv. 340
  'papal agent,' vii. 321
  Young Pretender's wife may have sprung from cell of, vii. 399

Louise Ulrica (1720–82), of Prussia, m. (1744) Adolf Fredrik, K. of Sweden, 1751:
(?) Cumberland, D. of, may wed, ii. 62
marriage of, ii. 219n
Loutherbourg, Philip James de (1740–1812), painter:
landscape and cattle well painted by, except for overdoing one colour, viii. 93
'Swedish' artist in England, viii. 93
Louvois, M. de. See Le Tellier, François-Michel
Louvre (palace in Paris):
threatening verses posted at, iv. 287
Louvre (dance):
Anson, Bns, proposes, at Sandwich's ball, iv. 121
'Louvre editions':
HW will print, exclusively, at SH, v. 131
Lovaine, Bn. See Percy, Lord Algernon (1750–1830)
Lovat, Bn. See Fraser, Simon (1726–82)
Lovatini, (?) Giovanni, opera singer:
Buona Figluola played by, vii. 42
HW praises, vi. 474
Love:
HW's reflections on, viii. 324–5
HW's reflections on male and female attitudes towards, ix. 424
impossible at threescore, except of oneself, ix. 173
Mann's reflections on, iv. 105
Love Elegies. See under Hammond, James
Lovel, Bn. See Coke, Thomas
Lovel, Bns. See Tufton, Lady Margaret
Lovelace, Hon. Martha (d. 1788), m. (1739) Lord Henry Beauclerk:
Dick attached to, iv. 527, v. 10, vi. 511
—— sends thanks to, for Mann's civilities, iv. 550
——'s letters to, may mention Mann, v. 10
HW's old and great friend, iv. 527
Mann's kindness to Dicks will please, v. 19
Love-Letters between a Nobleman and his Sister. See under Amis, Aphra
Love-matches:
HW's reflections on, ii. 367
Love Song. See under Swift, Jonathan
Lovendal, Freiherre Ulrik Frederik Woldemar (1700–55), Maréchal de France:
print of, iii. 395–6
Lowendal, Comtesse de. See Szembeck, Barbe-Madeleine-Élisabeth de (d. 1762)
Lowendal. See also Lovendal
Löwenstein-Wertheim, Christian Philipp (1719–69), Prinz von; Austrian army officer:
Genoese peace terms brought by, to Vienna, iii. 306, 313
Lower classes:
ingratitude of, Mann's reflections on, iv. 264
Lowestoft, ship:
vessels captured by, iii. 82, 277

Lowther, Henry (1694–1751), 3d Vct Lonsdale:
whist played by, at house on Richmond Green, iv. 63
White's Club member, iv. 63
Lowther, Sir James (? 1673–1755), 4th Bt; M.P.:
heirs of, iv. 550
Lowther, Sir James (1736–1802), 5th Bt, 1751; cr. (1784) E. of Lonsdale; M.P.:
extravagance of, v. 200
HW mentions, v. 528
in English invasion of France, v. 204
inheritance of, iv. 550
marriage of, v. 527, 531
Orford bets, will not have child before George III does, v. 531
peerage to be given to, vii. 58
Portland's quarrel with, compromised, vii. 58
'prince of the coal pits,' v. 527
Thanet contests Appleby election with, iv. 435
'young Crœsus,' iv. 435
Lowther, Katharine (ca 1736–1809), m. (1765) Lord Harry Powlett, 6th D. of Bolton, 1765:
ball by, for D. and Ds of Gloucester, to be attended by HW, ix. 22
Lowther, Lady Mary. See Stuart, Lady Mary (1740–1824)
Lowther, Sir Thomas (ca 1699–1745), 2d Bt, 1705; M.P.:
nephew of, fetches him to vote, i. 244
Lowther, Sir William (ca 1727–1756), 3d Bt; M.P.:
death of, iv. 550
Patch tries to buy Poussin paintings for, v. 209
Lowther, William (d. 1768), maritime official:
East India Company's former employee, vi. 548
Leopold still pays, vi. 548
Loyalists, American:
England's dereliction of, opposed, ix. 365, 369
in Georgia, reported abandoned to Americans, ix. 306
Loyd, Mr ——:
K.B. predicted for, iv. 136
Loyd. See also Lloyd
Lozenge:
to be used in arms on Cts of Orford's monument, ix. 240
'Lozenge coach':
dowagers have, iii. 298
Lübeck, Bp of. See Adolf Fredrik
Luc, M. de. See Vintimille, Charles-Emmanuel-Marie-Madelon de
Lucan, Bn and E. of. See Bingham, Sir Charles (1735–99)
Lucan, Bns and Cts of. See Smith, Margaret (d. 1814)

Lucan, E. of. *See* Bingham, Hon. Richard (1764–1839)

Lucan (Marcus Annæus Lucanus) (A.D. 39–65), author:
HW's edition of, HW gives, to James Mann, for Mann, v. 472
Pharsalia, HW quotes, iii. 119

Lucas, Charles (living, 1797), E. of Orford's lawyer:
apparent zeal of, for noble client, well paid, ix. 200
caveat against Cts of Orford's will probably suggested by, ix. 137, 143
Cony dissuaded by, from writing to Lady Mary Cholmondeley, x. 55
—— may arouse jealousy of, ix. 147
demands stretched too far by, ix. 391
dilatoriness of, ix. 172, 200, 315, 433
division of money held by Hoare unlikely to suit, ix. 426
Duane and Sharpe to meet, at HW's, ix. 391
Duane concedes some claims to, ix. 414
—— disputes with, over Mozzi's claims, ix. 397–8, 404
—— praised by, ix. 216, 315
—— probably would not be approved by, ix. 304
—— rejected by, ix. 235
HW called on by, ix. **123**
HW cheated by, out of interest on father's legacy, ix. 637
HW condemns, for forcing Mozzi to come to England, ix. 315
HW confers with Duane, Sharpe, and, over Mozzi's affairs, ix. 419, 421, 439–41, 444–7, 448, 471–2
HW glad to sow division between Sharpe and, ix. 315
HW hopes, will be afraid of Duane, ix. 331
HW's correspondence with, ix. 131, 186, 195, 510
HW's previous receipt of part of father's legacy unknown to, ix. 637
HW's relations with, over Mozzi's negotiations with Lord Orford, ix. 124, 126, 131, 143, 147–8, 154–5, 156, 157–8, 166, 167, 172, 176, 184, 186, 195, 213, 215–17, 235, 266, 286, 315, 331, 404, 427, 439–41, 444–7, 448, 471–2, 477–8, 495, 505–6, 509–11, 515, 516, 519
HW suspects, of lying, ix. 315
HW suspects trick of, ix. 320
health of, gout, ix. 195
'immovable intrepidity' of, ix. 297
interest on interest will not be relinquished by, ix. 462
Mann thinks, invented tale that Sharpe wanted Mozzi to divide Cts of Orford's English funds with, ix. 160
—— to be consulted by, ix. 126, 160
—— will obey Orford's commands conveyed by, ix. 137

money in Hoare's bank to be contested by, ix. 143
Morice and HW can get papers from, ix. 289
Morice and Sharpe scold, for his delay, ix. 286
Morice's correspondence with, ix. 286
——'s illness exaggerated by, ix. 217
Mozzi cannot speed up, by bribery, ix. 200
—— drained by, for back interest, but HW gets insufficient interest from him, ix. 637
—— glad to escape from, ix. 161
—— said to blame, for delay, ix. 216
——'s compromise proposals to, ix. 478
——'s reasonableness arouses suspicions in, ix. 298
—— suspects Sharpe and, of wishing him to go to law, ix. 322
Orford, Cts of, jointure deficiency of, examined by, ix. 176
Orford, E. of, instigated by, to contest mother's will, ix. 510
—— refers Horace Mann II's claims to, ix. 155
—— reproves, for delay, ix. 168, 181
——'s boroughs tended by, in the west, ix. 462
——'s claims produced by, ix. 143, 341
——'s claims summarized by, and delivered to Duane, ix. 335
——'s creditor told by, that money would come from Mozzi, ix. 286, 439
——'s demands against Mozzi at last given in by, ix. 333
—— sends, to announce arrival in Devon and Dorset, ix. 227
—— suggests tossing, in blanket, ix. 322, 328
—— to be seen by, ix. 286
—— to get letter from, ix. 472
—— too indolent to oppose, ix. 456
—— would probably be favoured by, ix. 421–2
sangfroid of, greater than that of a Stoic, ix. 307
Sharpe acts in concert with, ix. 286, 328
Sharpe and, had settled on £6,000 for Orford, HW thinks, ix. 335
Sharpe and, to defer to Duane, ix. 232
Sharpe cannot agree with, ix. 150–1
—— less zealous than, ix. 200
—— prepares discharge paper with, for Duane's consideration, ix. 500
——'s approval of Duane sought by, before Orford's, ix. 217
——'s negotiations with, displease Mozzi, ix. 492
—— to deliver summary by, to Duane, ix. 335

Lucas, Charles (1713–71), apothecary:
apothecary who made a noise in Ireland, v. 200–1

Dublin mob favours, iv. **156**
Swift's history written by, v. 200–1
Lucca:
ambassadors from and to, *see under* Ambassador
Austrian archduke would not be sent to defend, v. 96
baths of: Clerici, Mme, to visit, ii. 252; Richecourt visits, i. 468; Strathmore visits, vi. 69
concert at, by Genoese musicians, for D. of York, vi. 221–2
Diodati sent by, to Antibes, to compliment Montemar, i. 207
envoys to and from, *see under* Envoy
Florence's war with, iv. 514–16, 521, 525
Francis I permits, to build new road, iv. 514
Frederik IV entertained by, in palace, vi. 222
Genoese refugees at, iii. 401
Gloucester, D. of, invited by, vii. 348
gonfalonier at, i. 449
Karl Wilhelm Ferdinand to visit, vi. 458
lady of: (?) Kilmorey, Lady, struggles to kiss hand of, iv. 352; receives absurd letter from Lady Kilmorey, iv. 352
Leghorn merchants send goods to, i. 199
Leghorn residents flee to, i. 303
Leopold and Maximilian to visit, viii. 130
Mann complimented by 2 senators of, on D. of York's visit, vi. 222
—— may flee to, i. 196, ii. 398
—— recommends, as refuge to Princesse de Craon, i. 178
ministers to and from, *see under* Minister
Modenese princess to visit, i. 56
Patch seeks Fra Bartolommeo's paintings at, vii. 371
Richecourt persecutes, iv. 521
rumours of Austrian-Prussian peace and Charles VI's death come from, i. 134
secretary of, tells Palombo of lack of news, iv. 465
Spaniards advance towards, ii. 35
Tuscan regents divert Serchio river into, in revenge for new road to Modena, iv. 514–16, 521
Tuscany could be conquered by, if Lucca imitates Genoa, iii. 120
Tuscany may make Bientina lake overflow into, iv. 515
Vanneschi cheats Middlesex and Raymond at opera at, i. 216
Venturinis at, ii. 391
visitors to: Bruce, iv. 336; Eszterházys, iv. 351; Mann, vi. 221–2; Richecourt, i. 468; York, D. of, vi. 221–2, 223
Wright expected to storm, i. 449, 460
Lucchi, Angiola, Whithed's mistress:
certificate by, vi. 267
Chute made Whithed provide for, vi. 265
—— the sole protector of, iv. 306

Florentine girl, vi. 268n
Mann advances money to, on annuity, vi. 266, 279
—— afraid to break news to, iv. 244
—— hopes to console, with news of her fortune, iv. 264
—— persuades, to retire to country for health, iv. 264
—— tormented by, about daughter's fortune, vi. 278
—— to tell, of lover's death, iv. 241
—— tries to comfort, iv. 251
—— tries to get money for, from Chute and Thistlethwayte, iv. 330
—— wants copy of Whithed's will for, iv. 254
Mann, Galfridus, looks after interests of, iv. 312
masses arranged by, for deceased lover, iv. 254
opera appearance of, requires tight lacing, ii. **368**
Whithed has child by, ii. 406, vi. 268n
——'s annuity to: of £120 a year, iv. 238; Thistlethwayte brothers obstruct, iv. 312n, vi. 266, 278
——'s generosity to, revealed by Mann, iv. 251
—— to have child by, ii. 368
Lucchi, Sophia (b. 1744), Whithed's natural daughter:
birth of, ii. **406**
Chute and Galfridus Mann trustees for, iv. 246
Chute ignores Mann's pleas to secure fortune of, v. 412–13
—— rescues, from foundling hospital, vi. 265
—— urges Thistlethwaytes to pay fortune of, vi. 268
Dagge and HW confer about fortune of, v. 416, 420–1, 430
legacy of, withheld by Thistlethwayte's legal devices, vi. 288–9
Mann sends picture of, to her father, iv. 244
—— wants copy of Whithed's will for, iv. 254
—— writes to brother about affairs of, vi. 370
—— writes to Thistlethwayte about, iv. 330
marriage impossible for, without dowry, v. 413, vi. 265, 278
Morice to intercede for, with Chute, iv. 266
old maid at nineteen, vi. 265, 278
parentage of, vi. 268n
pretty girl, iv. 244
Whithed's bequest to: announced, iv. 238, 246, 251; Thistlethwayte brothers make difficulties over, iv. 246, 254, 312n, 330, v. 412–13, 416, 420–1, 430, 433, vi. 265–6, 268, 278–9, 370

[Lucchi, Sophia, *continued*]
—'s generosity to, revealed by Mann, iv. 251

Luci, Filippo (1674–1750), Florentine auditor fiscal 1737–46:
Mann asked by, about criminal who wears tricolour cockade, ii. 544
Regency council urged by, to forbid masks, ii. 372

'Lucia':
rôle of, in Addison's *Cato*, v. 327

Lucian (Lucianus) (fl. 2d century A.D.):
Lyttelton's *Dialogues of the Dead* mention, v. 408

Lucifer:
Devil's name as lawyer, viii. 71

Lucius Verus:
Vere pedigree starts with, iv. 181

Lucretius (Titus Lucretius Verus) (ca 96–ca 55 B.C.), Roman poet:
De rerum natura: HW quotes, vii. 151, viii. 48

Ludlow, Edmund (ca 1617–92), regicide:
HW as agitated as, about modern affairs, vi. 303

Ludwig (1753–1830) of Hesse-Darmstadt; Landgrave of Hesse-Darmstadt, 1796; Grand Duke of Hesse, 1806:
(?) Mann entertains, at Florence, viii. 164

Ludwig Joseph Anton (1784–1864), archduke:
birth of, ix. 549

Luis Antonio (1727–85) Cardinal, 1737 ('Don Luis'):
Viviani instructs, ii. 129

Luise (1722–80) of Brunswick-Wolfenbüttel, m. (1742) August Wilhelm of Prussia:
wedding of, i. 315

Luise (1726–56), of Denmark, m. (1749) Ernst Friedrich III, D. of Sachsen-Hildburghausen:
Adolf Fredrik's rumoured marriage proposal for, ii. 304
Cumberland, D. of, rumoured to be marrying, iii. 20

Luján Silva y Góngora, Pedro Francisco (1727–94), 6th Marqués de Almodóvar, cr. (1780) Duque de Almodóvar:
couriers received by, viii. 460
England to be visited by, viii. **366**
English Court told by, of Charles III's intentions, viii. 495
niggardly fees paid by, at brothel, viii. 413
small size of, viii. 413
stays in England despite war, viii. 487
writes much, viii. 460

Luke, saint:
picture supposedly painted by, ii. 207

Lullin, Mme. *See* Fatio, Alexandrine

Lumber:
Kent's architecture deals in, viii. 93

Lumisden, Andrew (1720–1801), Jacobite:
Young Pretender drives away, x. 47

Lumley, Hon. James (d. 1766), M.P.:
HW mentions, v. 503

Lumley, Richard (ca 1688–1740), 2d E. of Scarbrough:
suicide of, vi. 312

Lumley-Saunderson, Richard (1725–82), 4th E. of Scarbrough, 1752:
resigns, as Cofferer of the Household, vi. 471
Thomond succeeded by, as Cofferer, vi. 311

Lumley-Saunderson, Thomas (ca 1691–1752), 3d E. of Scarbrough, 1740:
address of approbation moved by, in House of Lords, ii. 159
Frederick, P. of Wales, accompanied by, to George II's levee, i. **337**
—'s treasurer, i. 337, ii. 159

Lumsden. *See* Lumisden

Lunardi, Vincenzo (1759–1806), æronaut:
Blanchard's rival, ix. 543
cat and dog exhibited by, in Pantheon, ix. 543
cat taken by, in balloon, ix. 528
first balloon ascent in England made by, ix. 528
investments bought by, with balloon proceeds, ix. 543
Neapolitan secretary in London, ix. 528n, 543

Lunario per la Toscana. See under Paperini,—

Lunati-Visconti, Marquise de. *See* Roquefeuille, Jeanne-Thérèse de

Lunati-Visconti, Ferdinand (d. 1732), Marquis de:
wife tells, to remove her from Leopold of Lorraine's advances, iv. 351–2

Lunati-Visconti, Marchesa Maria Anna Luisa (d. after 1780), m. (1734) Paul Anton Prince Eszterházy von Galántha:
Antinoris, Pandolfini, and Corsi entertain, iv. 351
Craon, Princesse de, compared to, iv. 351
Florence visited by, iv. 349–52
Pisa, Leghorn, and Lucca visited by, iv. 351
Viviani entertains, at *festino*, iv. 350–1

Luneggiana. *See* Lunigiana

Lunéville:
Craon, Princesse de, seldom visits, from jealousy of daughter, vi. 243

Lung; lungs:
coughs clear, in elderly people, ix. 652
effusion of blood from, ix. 567

Lung'arno:
serenade at Corsini house on, i. 97, 105

Lunghazza:
Lobkowitz marches to, ii. 447

Lunigiana:
Fivizano in, iii. 35
Francis I may barter Corsica for part of, vi. 157
Leopold visits, but will not find people satisfied, ix. 318
Richecourt gets fief in, iii. 385

Spanish army threatens approach from, to Tuscany, i. 289

Spanish troops store provisions in, iii. 10

Traun's troops must enter Tuscany through, ii. 76

Lupi smascherati, I:
Jesuits attacked by, v. 476

Lusatia:
Frederick II invades, v. 254

Lustre; lustres:
in every Paris hotel, vii. 312
of rock-crystal, Riccardi puts, in gallery, vi. 157

Lutestring:
white, Richelieu's pavilion hung with, vii. 329

Luthens. *See* Luytens

Luther, Martin (1483–1546), reformer:
alleged painting of, banished at Pitti Palace, vi. 179, 246, 291
church property probably inspired Reformation by, ix. 544

Lutheran:
Young Pretender's wife said to be, vii. 398

Lutrum. *See* Leutrum

Lutterberg:
battle of, v. (?) 246, 251, 254

Lutterel. *See* Luttrell

Luttrell, Anne (1743–1808), m. 1 (1765) Christopher Horton; m. 2 (1771) Henry Frederick, D. of Cumberland:
actors insult, at Calais, vii. 519–20
Arras visited by, vii. 349
brother of, viii. 383, ix. 29
brother of, cause of Opposition's dislike of her marriage, vii. 434
Calais visited by, vii. 344, 351, 519–20
candlesnuffer tries to give bouquet to, vii. 519–20
Clement XIV to have shown attentions to, vii. 559
Coke, Lady Mary, quarrelled with Huntingdon for waiting on, vii. 550n
Court attendance denied to, vii. 358
Cumberland, D. of, announces marriage to, vii. 344, ix. 629
embarked for Italy, vii. 505
finances exhausted by waste of, at Milan, vii. 559
Genoa to be visited by, vii. 553
George III deserted by, for P. of Wales and Opposition, ix. 140
HW glad that Mann will have no trouble with, vii. 531, 539
husband to be joined by, at Besançon, for trip to Spa, ix. 645
King libels, ix. 601
landed in England, viii. 3
Leopold and Maria Louisa come to Florence to receive, ix. 644
Leopold and Maria Louisa to give *bal masqué* and supper for, at great theatre, ix. 644–5

Mann offers to pay duty to (if carried up and down stairs) but is called upon instead, ix. 644
—— seeks instructions about his treatment of, vii. 501–2
—— should not try to entertain, vii. 500
Milan to be visited by, vii. 500, 505, 511, 513, 519
Milan visited by, vii. 543, 553, 559
Naples visited by, ix. 618, 628
not pregnant, vii. 344n
not yet sailed, vii. 511
Pitt, Anne, may take liberties with, vii. 558
pretensions of, provoke second circular letter from secretary of state's office, vii. 543
Rome may not receive, well, vii. 502
Rome visited by, vii. 559, 564, 565
St-Omer visited by, vii. 520
seclusion said to be planned by, at Rome, vii. 559, 564
Tuscan and Viennese courts may be embarrassed by, vii. 502

Luttrell, Col. Henry Lawes (1737–1821), 2d E. of Carhampton, 1787:
Court candidate for Middlesex election, vii. 104–5
Court puts into House of Commons, in Wilkes's place, vii. 344
election of, offensive but does not produce disturbances, vii. 114
Holland House gives public breakfast for supporters of, ix. 11
Middlesex sheriffs summon Wilkes instead of, vii. 475
Opposition dislikes D. of Cumberland because of his alliance to, vii. 434
sister of, vii. 344
Townshend refuses to pay tax in protest against election of, vii. 346
Wilkes's friends petition against, vii. 114–15

Luttrell, Simon (1713–87) cr. (1768) Bn Irnham; (1781) Vct Carhampton; (1785) E. of Carhampton:
son of, vii. 104n

Luttrell, Hon. Temple Simon (?1738–1803), M.P.:
Germain's quarrel with, viii. 383
North accused by, of buying a borough supposedly bought by Luttrell, ix. 29

Luttrell family:
Gloucester, D. of, will not become involved in politics of, viii. 77
newspaper contributions of, inflame George III against D. of Gloucester, viii. 77

Luxborough, Bn. *See* Knight, Robert (1702–72)

Luxborough, Bns. *See* St John, Hon. Henrietta (1699–1756)

Luxembourg, Duc de. *See* Montmorency-Luxembourg, Charles-François-Frédéric de (d. 1764)

Luxembourg Palace, Paris:
  Modena, Ds of, to have apartment at, ii.
  222
Luxemburg:
  France may take, iii. 88
Luxury:
  London's evils aggravated by, vii. 151
Luynes, Cardinal de. *See* Albert, Paul d'
Luytens (Luthens), Heinrich Christian, Prussian consul at Leghorn:
  arms over door of, v. 112
Luzac, Étienne (1706–87), editor:
  HW's *Xo Ho* translated by, v. 108
Lymington, Vct. *See* Wallop, John
Lynch, Sir William (ca 1730–85), K.B., 1771;
  M.P.; English envoy to Sardinia 1769–79:
  Carlisle, E. of, may succeed, at Turin, viii.
  36
  English minister at Turin, vii. **272**
  made K.B., vii. 272
  Mann gets letter from, about Lady Mary
  Coke, vii. 553
  plenipotentiaryship obtained by, vii. 293
  Strange's letter to, sent by mistake to
  Mann, viii. 140
Lynn. *See* King's Lynn
Lynn, Mayor of. *See* Langley, William
Lyon, Abp of. *See* Guérin de Tencin, Pierre
  (1680–1758)
Lyon, Charles (1699–1728), 4th E. of Strathmore:
  wife wounded when intervening in Carnegie's quarrel with, v. 364n
Lyon (after 1767, Bowes), John (1737–76),
  7th E. of Strathmore, 1753:
  Bouverie to demand HW's letters from, vi.
  88
  Foley tells, of Paris visitors' heavy remittances from England, vi. 152
  French passport procured by, after long
  wait at Parma, for journey to England,
  vi. 22–3
  HW prefers Thomas Pitt to, vi. 152
  HW receives letters through, vi. 152, x. 36
  HW to receive pastilles and letters through,
  v. 565
  Lucca baths visited by, vi. 69
  Mann gives HW's letters to, but now must
  demand them back, vi. 88
  —— presents, to Botta, v. 564
  ——'s correspondence with, v. 501
  —— to entertain, in garden, vi. 45
  Naples and Rome visited by, v. 564
  Parma left by, for Florence, v. 524
  Pitt, Thomas, awaited by, v. 524
  —— friend of, v. 543
  —— separates from, in Spain, v. 501
  —— to be accompanied by, to Italy, v.
  364
  —— visited by, vi. 152
  returns to England after calling at Florence, vi. 69
  Rome to be visited by, v. 543

Sanvitale, Cts, accompanied by, to Florence,
  vi. 45
—— detains, at Parma, v. 524, vi. 88
—— enthralls, vi. 145
—— will accompany, to call on Mann, vi.
  69
  sets out for England with HW's letters, vi.
  145
  too much a Celadon, vi. 152
Lyon (Lyons)
  Charles III, Charles Emmanuel III, and
  Louis XV said to be planning to meet at,
  v. 283, 289
  Hamilton, Ds of, and husband, may not
  pass, v. 466
  Mann gets 3 suits from, vi. 357
  Mann, Horace II, to meet young Hull at,
  viii. 258
  —— writes from, viii. 265, ix. 421
  stuffs from, at Leghorn fair, vi. 423
  Tencin retires to, iv. 255
  trade of, interrupted, v. 123
  Veers deceives bankers of, iii. 507
  visitors to: Holdernesses, vi. 172; Hull
  (nephew), viii. 265; Mann, Horace II, viii.
  265, ix. 421; Orford, Cts of, vii. 152
  Voyer and Paulin pass, with armament,
  iv. 536
  Young Pretender passes through, iii. 368
Lyon, Gulf of:
  Spanish expedition reported in, i. 179
Lyons:
  'triple of,' *see under* Cockade
  See also Lyon
Lyppiat. *See* Lipyeatt
Lysistrata:
  beard worn by, in drama, v. 53
Lyttelton, Bns. *See* Rich, Elizabeth
Lyttelton, Lady. *See* Fortescue, Lucy (ca
  1718–47); Rich, Elizabeth (ca 1716–95)
Lyttelton, Charles (1714–68), Bp of Carlisle
  1762–8:
  Venice might be converted by, after its
  quarrel with Benedict XIV, iv. 163, 177
Lyttelton, Sir George (1709–73), 5th Bt, 1751;
  cr. (1756) Bn Lyttelton:
  Bedingfield's alleged letters by Bower exposed by, as forgeries, iv. 532–4
  bill of lading for vases and gesse for, iv.
  577, 582
  Bolingbroke's and Pope's friend, iv. 61
  Bolingbroke's letters to, iv. 59–60
  —— told by, not to publish reflections
  against Sir Robert Walpole, iv. 59
  Boughton, Mrs, the 'ancient Delia' of, v.
  532
  Bower a friend of, iv. 532
  —— obtains a government post through,
  iv. 533
  brother of, iii. 189n, iv. 33n, v. 54n, 505n
  Campbell will reimburse Mann for gesse
  expenses, iv. 577, 582
  chancellor of the Exchequer, iv. 512, 517

characters worn by, iv. 52
Chesterfield defended by, i. 232
death of, vii. 511
Dialogues of the Dead: HW's criticism of,
v. 408–9; HW sends, to Mann, v. 407;
Mann receives, v. 446; Nivernais translates,
vi. 79–80; Voltaire called an exile in, v. 486
Doneraile plagues, in Parliamentary committee, iii. 388
Fortescue, Lucy, to marry, i. 338
Frederick II's poetry praised by, v. 408
Frederick, P. of Wales, dismisses, ii. 551
—— has, as secretary, ii. 118
—— may dismiss, ii. 118
——'s follower, ii. 102
—— warns, ii. 102
HW hears from, of plot against Bower, iv.
532
HW reads to, part of Mann's letter, iv. 554
habeas corpus voting shunned by, ii. 409
Hackman's murder would have been attributed by, to diabolical spirit, viii. 477
Hanoverian troop bill supported by, iii.
241
History of Henry II, Mann likes, viii. 477
Leeds, D. of, succeeds, as Cofferer, iv. 517
Legge succeeds, as chancellor of the Exchequer, v. 24
long speeches of, vi. 567
lord of the Treasury, ii. 551
Mann asked by, to get gesses and vases for
his hall, iv. 539, 547, 554, v. 40
named in Secret Committee lists, i. 384
Navy office coveted by, iv. 39
Parliamentary debate by, on privately-
raised regiments, x. 18
Parliamentary opposition includes, ii. 102
Parliamentary proceedings heralded by, at
the Treasury, iii. 168
Parliamentary vote by, on privately-raised
regiments, x. 19
Parliament members cannot divide with,
iii. 4
peerage granted to, v. 18, 24
Persian Letters, Stamp Act protest should
be bound with, vi. 410
Pitt faction abandoned by, iv. 512
——'s friendship with, iii. 27
——'s rift with, iii. 194
Pitt, Thomas, loses borough to, iv. 39
Pope suppresses panegyric on, in Bolingbroke's *Letters,* iv. 61
Regency bill provokes motion by, in House
of Lords, vi. 296
Secret Committee proposed by, ii. 117
son of, vi. 251
Stamp Act repeal opposed by, vi. 410
Temple accompanied by, to Lord Mayor's
feast, vi. 464
Voltaire writes to, from hovel in France,
v. 486
wife dislikes Pitt's domination of, iii. 194
wife of, i. 166n, v. 409

wrong party always supported by, vi. 567
Lyttelton, Mrs George. *See* Fortescue, Lucy
(ca 1718–47)
Lyttelton, Hon. Lucy Fortescue (1743–83),
m. (1767) Arthur Annesley, 8th Vct Val-
entia:
husband of, elopes, viii. 15
Lyttelton, Sir Richard (1718–1770), K.B., 1753;
M.P.:
Argyll's aide-de-camp, i. **356**
Breadalbane succeeded by, as Master of
the Jewel Office, iv. 25
confined at villa near Leghorn, v. 511
Cumberland, D. of, antagonizes, iv. 33
death of, leaves K.B. vacancy, vii. 240
depositions collected by, against D. of
Cumberland, iv. 240
Essex, Cts of, told by, not to meddle in
politics, v. 54
Frederick, P. of Wales, deals with, iv. 33
HW asks about, v. 517, 542
HW praises, v. 505
health of: fatigued, v. 545; gout, v. 501,
507, vi. 247, vii. 240
Jewel Office may be resigned by, v. 548,
557
K.B., iii. 189n, iv. 33n
Leghorn visited by, v. 501, 507
Mann need not tell, of HW's opinion about
Pitt, v. 542
——'s correspondence with, v. 507–8
marriage of, iii. 189, iv. 33n
Methodism attracts, iv. 52
Mutiny Bill attacked by, iv. 33
Naples visited by, v. 545
Neapolitan neutrality not trusted by, vi. 12
patriot officer, iv. 240
Pitt sends messenger to, with Turin offer,
v. 507–8
——'s relationship with, v. 542n
Pitt, Thomas, leaves, at Leghorn, v. 501
Queensberry, Ds of, sends card to, about
step-daughter's omission from ball, iv. 226,
235–6
Rome revisited by, vi. 12
San Casciano baths visited by, with Thomas
Pitt, v. 524
Temple, Cts, entertains, at Stowe, vi. 247
Turin post declined by, v. 507–8, 511
use of limbs lost by, vii. 240
Wood's correspondence with, over Turin
post, v. 507–8, 511
Lyttelton, Sir Thomas (1686–1751), 4th Bt,
1716; M.P.:
son of, iv. 33n
Lyttelton, Thomas (1744–79), 2d Bn Lyttel-
ton, 1773; M.P.:
administration attacked by, though justice
in eyre, viii. 536
Court opposed by, because he is not made
secretary of state, viii. 464–5
Court party attacked by, in House of
Lords, viii. 139

[Lyttelton, Thomas, *continued*]
death of, viii. 536–7, ix. 2
Florence visited by, vi. **251**, viii. 103n
HW sarcastically calls: 'bashful,' viii. 151;
'virtuous,' viii. 139
justice in eyre, viii. 141, 464, 536
Kingston, Ds of, denied compassion by,
viii. **151**
pretends to reform, viii. 20
retires with nymphs to Epsom house, viii.
537
rhubarb taken by, viii. 537
Savoir Vivre club led by, viii. 103
shunned, vii. 511
speaks for and against the Americans, de-
pending on whether he gets a place, viii.
151–2
talents of, nullified by vices, ix. 2
temper of, alienates everybody, vi. 251
whitewashing of, attempted, viii. 139
Lyttelton faction:
does not resign, iii. 27
Regency bill opposed by, iv. 248
Lyttelton family:
army increase voted by, i. 410
Egmont's *Faction Detected* never forgiven
by, iv. 31
Pitt drives, iii. 194
——'s only allies, iii. 169
Secret Committee hearing not shunned by,
i. 366

M——, Lady:
Sundon, Bns, leaves nothing to, i. 276
Mabuse. *See* Gossaert, Jan
Macanis, Eugene, Lt:
captured at Velletri, ii. 492
Macanis, Frans, Ensign:
captured at Velletri, ii. 492
Macanis, Hugh, Lt:
captured at Velletri, ii. 492
Macaroni:
Compoflorido, Ps, cannot get, in Paris, ii.
315
pie of, iv. 219
Macaronies:
Clive 'begot,' resulting in poverty, vii. 400
England tolerates, ix. 23
English ladies may aspire to be, vii. 527
extravagance of, at height, vii. 498
France dreads, vii. 476
India's wealth emptied by, vii. 499
lethargy of, viii. 547–8
new dresses and nosegays the only extravagance of, vii. 467
races run by, in Kensington Gardens, vii.
491
unseasonable products of hothouses preferred by, vii. 392
Macartney, Bns, Vcts, and Cts. *See* Stuart,
Lady Jane (1742–1828)

Macartney, Frances (d. 1789), m. (1748)
Fulke Greville:
Italy to be visited by, iv. 58
(?) Osorio pursues, i. **186**
Phelps accompanied, in Italy, v. 124
'pretty,' iv. 58
(?) Richmond, Ds of, has, as companion, i.
186
Macartney, Sir George (1737–1806), Kt, 1764;
cr. (1776) Bn, (1792) Vct, and (1794) E.
Macartney; M.P.:
Cathcart succeeds, in Russian post, vi. 586
marries Bute's daughter, vi. 586
Parliament to be entered by, vi. 586
Macartney, Lady Jane. *See* Stuart, Lady Jane
Macaulay, Mrs. *See* Sawbridge, Catherine
Macbeth. See under Shakespeare, William
Maccaronis. *See* Macaronies
Maccarty, Robert (1685–1769), titular 5th E.
of Clancarty:
family of, forfeits property for James II,
iii. 160
made vice-admiral at Brest, iii. 160
Macclesfield, Cts of. *See* Nesbitt, Dorothy
(d. 1779)
Macclesfield, E. of. *See* Parker, George (ca
1697–1764)
Macdermoch, King:
title of, to Irish throne, v. 371
Macdonald, Æneas (d. 1746), Col.:
death of, iii. 208
Macdonald, Capt. Archibald (d. 1746) of
Keppoch:
wounded at Prestonpans, iii. 117
Macdonald, Donald (d. 1746) of Kinlochmoi-
dart:
clans not raised by, iii. 167
Macdonald, Hugh (1701–73), Bp of Diana,
1731; vicar of the Highland districts of
Scotland 1731–73:
baggage of, seized, iii. 242
rebels joined by, iii. 242
Macdonald, Sir James (ca 1742–66), 8th Bt:
Beauchamp's friend, vi. 344
death of, at Rome, vi. 447
Florence to be visited by: after Easter, vi.
407; from Paris, vi. **343**; in summer, vi.
418
HW recommends, to Mann, vi. 343–4
HW's correspondence with, vi. 396, 402,
411
health of, bad, vi. 402, 407
learned, vi. 447
Mann to tell, that HW has answered his
letter, vi. 396, 402, 411
Naples visited by, vi. 407
Macdonald clan:
retires from rebel army on chieftain's
death, iii. 208
MacDonel, Don Rainaldus (d. 1745), Lt-Gen.
in Spanish service:
Macdonald confused with, iii. 117
retreat of, causes his disgrace, ii. **336**

Macdonnel, Patrick Randal (d. 1786):
(?) friends of, break into prison to avenge his murder on Fitzgerald, ix. 631
Macé, François:
Histoire des quatre Cicérons, L', v. 57
Mace:
lord chancellor's, i. 174
Pulteney refuses, ii. 72
Speaker's: Cust returns, on resigning, vii. 175; not respected, by Washington, Gates, or Cromwell, viii. 356
Macerata:
Young Pretender conducts bride to, vii. 406
Macgregor (otherwise Drummond), William (1698–1765) of Balhaldies, 2d Bt (Jacobite), 1749:
Rome visited by, ii. 380
Macguire. *See* Maguire
Machault, Jean-Baptiste de (1701–94), financier:
disgrace of: rumoured, v. **56**; undesirable, v. 59
parliamentary faction led by, v. 56
Rena mistress to, v. 162
Macheath. *See* Gay, John: *Beggar's Opera*
Macheronis. *See* Macaronies
Machiavelli, Niccolò (1469–1527), author and politician:
Bute imitates policy of, vi. 401
Clive's policy would be approved by, vii. 484
English events will recall, to Florentines, viii. 48
Hastings' defence rested on code of, ix. 642
Mann quotes, vii. 516
Machine:
for raising water: at Marly, v. 354; 'fire machine,' Perelli wants Sisson's design and model for, to be procured from England by HW and Mann, v. 348, 352–4, 375–6, 379, 384, 390, 407, 414, 418–19, 429–30
steel, used to pick up handkerchiefs, iv. 203
to pick up coals from the hearth, iv. 203
Machines, political:
Cumberland, D. of, uses iv. 417
Macinghi, Elena (1720–89), m. (1740) Ferdinando Carlo Federighi, Conte:
Suares turns to, ii. 345
Macinghi, Ottavia (1717–77), m. (1735) Francesco Gaspero Pepi:
child of, attributed by her husband to Suares, ii. 345
husband of, i. 137
Parigi to be shot by, for giving disease to Pecori, i. 444
—— would have been killed by, because of Pecori, iii. 136
Pecori cicisbeo to, ii. 150
——'s engagement to, broken, i. 111, 136
—— to be killed by, for deserting her, i. 136–7

sbirri arrest, i. 136, 444
MacIntosh, Lady. *See* Farquharson, Anne
MacIntosh, Æneas (ca 1702–70):
government supported by, iii. 233
MacIntosh. *See also* Macdonald, Donald
MacIntosh clan:
head of, *see* Mac Intosh, Æneas
Mackdonnell, Edmond, Lt:
captured at Velletri, ii. 492
Mackenzie, Lady Anne (d. 1768), m. 1 Hon. Edmond Atkin; m. 2 (1764) Dr John Murray:
beauty of, iii. 281
Mackenzie, Lady Betty. *See* Campbell, Lady Elizabeth
Mackenzie, Lady Caroline (1746–91), m. 1 (1760) Capt. Drake; m. 2 (1776) Walter Hunter:
beauty of, iii. 281
Mackenzie, Lady Elizabeth. *See* Campbell, Lady Elizabeth (ca 1722–99)
Mackenzie, George (ca 1703–66), 3d E. of Cromarty, 1731:
capture of, iii. 254n
imprisoned in Tower, iii. 272, 281
Receiver of Rents, iii. 284
reprieve of, iii. 296, 302, 387
Sutherland, Cts of, in bed with, iii. 296
trial of, iii. 281–7
Wales, P. of, secures reprieve for, iii. 296, 302
Mackenzie, Lady Isabella (1725–1801), m. (1760) George, 6th Bn Elibank:
beauty of, iii. 281
Mackenzie, Hon. James Stuart. *See* Stuart Mackenzie, Hon. James
Mackenzie, John (1727–89), styled Bn Macleod; cr. (in Sweden) Count Cromarty; M.P.; army officer:
brought to London, iii. **272**
father pleads for, at rebels' trial, iii. 285
mother sees, at Woolwich, iii. 272
Mackenzie, Kenneth (1717–61), styled Lord Fortrose; M.P.:
Cumberland, D. of, accompanied by, iii. 233
restored to his fortune and admitted to Parliament, iii. 233
troops raised by, to oppose Young Pretender, iii. 102
Mackenzie, Kenneth (1744–81), 1st Vct Fortrose, n.c. (1766); 1st E. of Seaforth n.c., 1771; M.P.:
Highlanders led by, defend Jersey, viii. 472
Mann to be accompanied by, at investiture, vii. 60
Mackenzie, Lady Mary, m. 1 (1750) Capt. Clark; m. 2 (1757) Thomas Drayton; m. 3 (1762) John Ainslie; m. 4 —— Middleton:
beauty of, iii. 281
Mackenzie, William (d. 1740), 5th E. of Seaforth:
attainted, iii. 233

Mackenzie clan:
rebels joined by, iii. 233
Mackerel-boat:
French lose, v. 214
Macklish, Robert, sea-captain:
Happy Jennet commanded by, x. 6
Mackreth, Sir Robert (?1725–1819), M.P.; Kt, 1795:
expected to retire, as candidate for Castle Rising, viii. 60
former waiter at White's, viii. 53n
Orford, E. of, gives Castle Rising borough to, for loan of money, viii. 53n
—— says that his mother borrowed money from, viii. 53
Maclaine Miss (daughter of James Maclaine, highwayman):
family of, iv. 168
Maclaine, Rev. Archibald (1722–1804), divine:
Calvinist minister at The Hague, iv. 168
Maclaine, James (1724–50), highwayman:
career of, iv. 168–9
condemned to be hanged, iv. 188
faints from crowd of visitors, iv. 199
family of, iv. 168–9
Grub St ballad commends HW for not prosecuting, iv. 188
HW robbed by, in Hyde Park, iv. 99, 101, 106
HW's witticism about being hanged for, iv. 184
hanged, iv. 199
Mann wishes, to be saved, iv. 206
print of, with HW's quotation from Gay, iv. 184
suicide would have been committed by, if he had shot HW, iv. 184
visitors to, iv. 169, 199
Maclaine, Mrs James. *See* Maclogen, Miss
Maclaine, Rev. Thomas (d. 1740):
family of, iv. 168
said to be Irish dean, iv. 168
Maclane. *See* Maclaine
Maclane, Donald, grenadier:
Allen's death blamed upon, vii. 20
Maclanghlin, Jean, Lt:
captured at Velletri, ii. 492
Maclaughlin, Peter, corporal:
Allen's death blamed upon, vii. 20
Maclean. *See* Maclaine
Macleod, Bn. *See* Mackenzie, John (1727–89)
Macleod, Norman (1706–72), Laird of Macleod; M.P.:
Lovat writes bitter letter to, iii. 381
Maclogen, Miss (d. 1748), m. (ca 1746) James Maclaine:
family of, iv. 168
MacNamara, John (ca 1690–1756), Vice-Adm. in French navy:
fleet taken back to Brest by, iv. 482–3
Macquart, Philippe-Charles-Félix (1744–81), Bn de Rullecourt; chevalier:
failure of, at Jersey, ix. 127–8
privateer, according to Barbantane, ix. 127

Macreth. *See* Mackreth
MacSwinny. *See* Swinny, Owen Mac
Madame Royale. *See* Bourbon d'Orléans, Élisabeth-Charlotte de
Maddocks. *See* Madocks
Mad dogs. *See under* Hydrophobia
Maddox, Isaac (1697–1759), Bp of St Asaph, 1736; of Worcester, 1743:
HW remembers, chaplain to Bp of Chichester, ii. 246
translation of, to Worcester, ii. 246
Madeira:
Acciaioli born in, i. 477n, ii. 65
—— speaks only the language of, i. 444, 474, 477
Madhouse:
Pitt, Anne, dies in, ix. 127
Madocks, John (ca 1723–94), M.P.; King's counsellor:
legal opinion by, viii. 258
Madonna; Madonnas:
and Child, painting of, *see under names of painters*
HW embarrassed by number of, sent by Mann, ii. 201
painting of, in Giovanni Gastone's oratory, iv. 489
Pergolesi's 'office' of, i. 408
Sassoferrato's paintings of, ii. 94, 214
soldier steals jewels from church, and tells Frederick II that they were a gift from, ix. 499–500
Madonna dell' Annunciata:
Craon, Princesse de, prays to, to preserve husband's resolution, ii. 216
exposition of, i. 100
Madonna della Imprunetà:
brought to Florence after flood during HW's visit, v. 276
Florentines worship, i. 303
Florentine weather attributed to, v. 276
too expensive to invoke, to stop winter rains, v. 359
Madonna della Seggiola. *See under* Raffaello Sanzio
Madonna di Loreto. *See under* Loreto
Madonna di Monte Nero:
Leghorn inhabitants worship, in public square, i. 303–4
Madonna di Valentano:
Inquisition officers to examine, at Monte Fiascone, viii. 30, 39–40, 42
Madras:
English said to lose, v. 214
French expect to capture, v. 279
Rumbold under prosecution for corruption at, ix. 400
See also Fort St David
Madrid:
Bristol, E. of, not likely to stay long at, v. 556
Byng's conversation with Bucareli reported to, iv. 566

Catalogue of French Books, A, mentions, ii. 53

Charles III avoids, vi. 414–15

—— will treat, with great condescension, vi. 441

Clement XIII's answer to Charles III offends, vi. 532

—— sends expostulations to, about Jesuit expulsion, vi. 518

Clement XIV's treatment of threats from, vii. 221

Conclave sends courier to, to complain of Bourbon cardinals, viii. 79

courier brings news to, of Philip Anton's death, viii. 330

Court of, carts Clement XIII, vii. 32

Cumberland's negotiations with, ix. 82

Egmont sent to, by Richelieu, iv. 572

etiquette of, does not allow early announcement of pregnancy, vi. 427

Gages awaits orders from, iii. 10

Grantham ambassador at, like his father, ix. 296n

Gray, Sir James, may go to, as ambassador, v. 150, 159, 165–6, 556, vi. 112

—— to have post in, since peers reject it, vi. 463

Hervey later minister at, iii. 372n

insurrection at: against Squillace, vi. 414; blamed on the Jesuits, vi. 509, 518–19

La Ensenada to replace Campillo at, ii. 253

Montemar's army prepared at, ii. 5

——'s attempted relief of Modena reported by courier to, i. 501

Mount Stuart gets post at, ix. 363, 398

news of Lisbon earthquake comes from Keene at, iv. 512

Ossun at, vii. 264

Pulteney dies at, vi. 121

royal academy of, Sloane's museum offered to, iv. 359

Spanish army sends standards and kettle drums to, as victory tokens, ii. 161

Spanish army to get orders from, i. 265

Squillace's letter from, vi. 99

Tanucci could not compete with grandees of, v. 330

Te Deums sung at, for Spanish landing on Minorca, ix. 189

treaty of: terms of, unknown, iv. 320; to be for pacification of Italy, iv. 294–5

Venetian ambassador at, i. 84

Viviani visits, ii. 129

Young Pretender ill-received at, iii. 392

Madwoman:
imagines herself to be Q. Elizabeth, viii. 361

Maecenas:
niece of, in *Ballet de la Paix,* ii. 496

Maestricht:
Joseph II said to have invested, ix. 566

negotiations over siege of, iii. 480

Maestro di Camera:
York, Cardinal, has Angelelli as, vi. 374

—— to have, iii. 416

Maestro di Camera, Papal. *See* Borghese, Scipione

Maffei ('the Great'), Scipione (1675–1755), Marchese di; author:
quarrels of, i. 150

Walpole, Bns, praised by, i. 150

Magazine; magazines (of ammunition):
American: British try to seize, at Concord, viii. 110; destroyed by British, viii. 306; Tryon burns, viii. 309

at Cherbourg, blows up, v. 226

at Perugia, iii. 10

Austrians seize, at Ancona and Loreto, ii. 419

French lack, in Germany, v. 499

Hanoverians preserve, v. 228

in Minorca, captured, ix. 198

Lestock destroys, iii. 330

Magazine; magazines (periodicals):
HW called 'learned,' in, v. 368

HW fears to see his inscription for Benedict XIV printed in, v. 132

HW leaves, with Galfridus Mann, for Mann, ii. 31

HW to send, to Mann, ii. 9

Mann wants, since opening of Parliament, i. 396

North Briton No. 45 printed in, vi. 196

Magazines (store-houses):
of corn, iv. 507n

of pitch, ix. 577

Magdalen:
Guido's painting of, v. 532–3

head of, HW receives, ii. 292

Torri's, i. 268

Magdalen College, Oxford:
Parker becomes Master of, under James II, iv. 188

Magdalen House:
HW visits, v. 368

Magdalenes:
Mann to bequeath, to HW, ii. 93

Magdeburg:
Seckendorf sent to, v. 266

Magellan, Straits of:
kings may dispute territory near, viii. 154

Maggio, Via, Florence:
notice posted in, satirizing Mann's parties, iii. 499

Magistrates:
rural, refuse to billet foreign troops, v. 13

Magliabechi, Antonio (1633–1714):
Spence's book about, v. 289

Magnan, Marquis de (fl. 1708–61):
Caroline, Q., and Sir Robert Walpole employ, ii. **548**

Carteret to receive letter from, ii. 549

'conseiller du commerce,' ii. 548

Florence visited by, ii. 548–9

[Magnan, Marquis de, *continued*]
Francis I gives position to, to get rid of him, ii. 549
George II tires of pensioning, as spy, ii. 564
Greek Orthodox, ii. 564
Greek Orthodox Church at Leghorn to be headed by, iii. 13
HW receives letter from, ii. 563
linguistic abilities of, ii. 548
Mann hears boast of, of protection from Walpole family, ii. 548–9
—— persecuted with letters from, iii. 13
—— refuses to be godfather to child expected by, iii. 13
——'s coach used by, iii. 13
Regent employs, to teach his son Russian, ii. 563–4
Remarks of a Persian Traveller, ii. 548
salaries of, ii. 548–9
Ulfeld recommends to Francis I, at Vienna, ii. 564
Venice and Vienna visited by, ii. 563–4
Waldegrave sends, to England, ii. 564
Walpole, Horatio (1678–1757), said to be chief protector of, ii. 549
—— to receive letter from, ii. 549, 563
Magnan, Marquise de:
child expected by, iii. 13
Florence visited by, ii. 548–9
'St-Germain lady,' ii. 549
Magona, Francis I's iron works:
Leghorn to be sent iron by, i. 304
Maguignon, Mme. *See* Matignon, Mme
Maguire, Hugh (d. 1766), army officer:
Cathcart, Bns, marries, i. 420n
Charles VI's service entered by, i. 420n
Gibson, Bp, receives, from Roman Catholic Church, i. 420
Mahmud I (ca 1696–1754), Sultan of Turkey 1730–54:
Catalogue of French Books, A, satirizes, ii. 53
Francis I's treaty with, iii. 437
Louis Siries makes razors for, iii. 437
Mahogany:
chair of, iii. 9
Mahon, Duc de. *See* Berton de Balbe, Louis de (1718–96)
Mahon, Vct. *See* Stanhope, Charles (1753–1816)
Mahon, Vcts. *See* Pitt, Lady Hester (1755–80)
Mahon, Mahone. *See* Port Mahon
Mahone, Cts. *See* Clifford, Anne
Mahoni, Comte. *See* Mahony, James Joseph
Mahonnoises:
style of, in France, v. 52
Mahony, Cecilia Carlotta Francisca Anna (d. 1789), m. Principe Benedetto Giustiniani:
England visited by, vii. 287
relatives of, among spurious royal family, vii. 287
Mahony, James Joseph (1699–1757), Comte Mahony:
marriage of, i. 28

Mahony, Mary Anne (d. 1751) m. 1 Richard Cantillon; m. 2 (1736) Francis, Comte de Bulkeley:
family of, ii. 429n
Maid. *See under* Servant
Maida ['Maide']:
earthquake account mentions, ix. 375
Maid of Honour:
Anne of Orange's, Anne Whitwell was, vii. 269n
Augusta, Ps of Wales's: Chudleigh, Elizabeth, v. 487, viii. 196, 203; Drax, Elizabeth, ii. 441; Granville, Hon. Elizabeth, i. 402, iii. 63; Lawson, Elizabeth, iii. 63; Nevill, Hon. Catherina, iii. 63; Pitt, Elizabeth, iv. 507; Young, Lucy, i. 431n, iv. 58n
Caroline's: Fitzwilliam, Hon. Mary, iv. 281n; Howe, Mary, i. 495n; Mordaunt, Anna Maria, iv. 208n, vi. 163n
coachman forbids his son to marry, ii. 232
George II gives faulty topazes and amethysts to be raffled by, iv. 112
HW ridicules chastity of, i. 411
HW ridicules modesty of, i. 496
Kingston, Ds of, may bring, to her trial, viii. 187
—— might again become, viii. 464
Maria Theresa's, *see* Pálffy, Maria Anna
Mary of Modena's, Modena, Ds of, questions Old Pretender's legitimacy in conversation with, i. 44
Maidstone:
electors of: Mann, Horace II, may offend, viii. 225, 240; Mann, Horace II, must carouse with, at Linton, viii. 381, 398
Mann, Horace II, abandons, ix. 488
—— going to, to settle constituents' subscription, viii. 513
—— writes from, ix. 494
mayor of, *see* Stevenson, Samuel
riotous meeting at, attended by Horace Mann II, ix. 290
soldier held at, *see* Schroeder, William
Mail; mails:
five, arrive together in Florence, ix. 344
French throw, overboard from captured packet-boat, v. 451
from England, loiters, ix. 348
See also Post
Mail, Coats of:
at SH, iv. 381
Maillebois, Comte de. *See* Desmarets, Yves-Marie
Maillebois, Marquis de. See Desmarets, Jean-Baptiste-François (1682–1762)
Mailly, Comtesse de. *See* Mailly-Nesle, Louise-Julie de
Mailly, Augustin-Joseph (1707–94), Comte and Maréchal de; Marquis d'Haucourt:
made director of troops, vii. 283
Mailly-Nesle, Louise-Julie de (1710–51), Comtesse de Mailly; m. (1726) Louis-Alexandre de Mailly, Comte de Rubempré:
Louis XV's affair with, vii. 87

sister said to have been poisoned by, i. 125
sister succeeds, as Louis XV's mistress, ii. 102
Mailly-Nesle, Marie-Anne de (1717–44) cr. (1744) Duchesse de Châteauroux; m. (1734) Louis, M. de la Tournelle:
created Duchesse de Châteauroux, ii. **102n**
exile of, rumoured, ii. 503
laundresses recommended by, to future Dauphiness, ii. 523
Louis XV's affair with, ii. 544, vii. 87
'poisoned,' ii. 552
sister supplanted by, as Louis XV's mistress, ii. 102
Soissons, Bp of, dismisses, with Louis XV's acquiescence, ii. 523–4
stipulations of, on becoming mistress, ii. 102–3
Mailly-Nesle, Pauline-Félicité de (1712–41), m. (1739) Jean-Baptiste-Félix-Hubert, Marquis de Vintimille:
death of, i. 125
Louis XV's affair with, vii. 87
sister said to have poisoned, for being more ugly than herself, i. 125
Mailly-Rubempré, Comtesse de. See Mailly-Nesle, Louise-Julie de
Main, river:
French try to cross, ii. 258
Maine, Duchesse du. See Bourbon, Anne-Louise-Bénédicte de
Mainz:
Abp and Elector of, see Eltz, Philipp Karl von (1665–1743); Ostein, Johann Friedrich Karl von (d. 1763)
Cours de l'Europe satirizes, i. 177
English may cross Rhine near, ii. 290
English troops to go to, ii. 102
Stair to visit, ii. 102
Maison Carrée. See under Nîmes
Maître d'hôtel:
Leopold's, see Julien
to Cts of Orford, see Waters, Charles
See also under Servants
Majendie, ——, m. Philemon Pownall:
marriage of, vi. 45
Majoli or Mayoli, Clemente, Jesuit:
imprisoned, viii. 30
Major, English army:
would refuse to serve for a mere 6 months, x. 14
Major, Florentine. See Pellegrini, Ignazio
Majorano, Gaetano. See Caffarelli
Majorca:
Spain sends troops to, vii. 261
Spaniards seize English merchant ship near, ii. 354
Spanish fleet at, eludes Mathews, ii. 244
Spanish reinforcements expected from, ii. 106
Spanish xebecs escape from, ii. 287, 300
Major-domo:
Clement XIII's see Bufalini, Giovanni Ottavio

Corsini is, to Maria Louisa, vii. 294
Rosenberg to replace Botta as, in Florence, vi. 447–8, 453–4
York, Cardinal, to have, iii. 416
Major-general:
militia officers cannot be, viii. 372
Malabar:
French expelled from coasts of, v. 523
Malaga
Foudroyant said to have reached, v. 193
Malagrida, Gabriel (1689–1761), Jesuit:
Portugal does not release, v. 341
Malaria:
armies ruined by, ii. 454
HW afraid of, i. 22
HW hopes that D. and Ds of Gloucester escape, viii. 186
Mann, James II, could not visit Rome and Naples before season of, if he lingered at Pisa, ix. 581
Malaspina, Signora. See Fregosa, Rosa
Malaspina, Azzolini (1697–1774), Neapolitan minister to Saxony 1738:
'Cleosa' marries, i. 150
Malaspina, Margherita (ca 1723–74), m. (1724) Carlo Bardi, Conte:
marriage of, ii. 60
Malaspina, Matilde (1693–1772), m. Francesco Feroni:
Lorenzi entertained by, i. 317
Mann entertained by, i. 32–4, 317
—— receives cedrati from, from Bella Vista, i. 317
opera attended by, in Mann's box. i. 81
opera seldom attended by, i. 81
Malavolti. See Ugurgiere Malavolti
Malborough Fort, English xebec:
captain of, receives patent from Mann, ix. 199
gets in and out of Minorca, ix. 219
Mann has vessel named, for relief of Minorca, ix. 199
—— sends, to Minorca, ix. 204
'small scuttling vessel,' ix. 205
Malcolm, Sarah (ca 1710–33) murderess and washerwoman:
forgotten, iii. 460
Temple washerwoman, iii. 460n
Maleager. See Meleager
Malesherbes. See Lamoignon de Malesherbes
Mall, the:
citizens watch fireworks from, iv. 48
Mallet, David (ca 1705–65), poet:
Bolingbroke bribes, iv. 62
——'s letters sold by, to bookseller, iv. 62
Flobert banished from Tuscany for trying to fight, v. 377
—— meets, at Chesterfield's, v. 377
—— quarrels with, over girl, v. 386
Marlborough, Ds of, leaves money to, to write husband's life, ii. 528, iv. 62
Pope's relations with, iv. 62
Mallet:
pirates kill helmsman with, ix. 479

Mallevadore:
accademici demand, from Filippo de' Medici, ii. 439
Malling Abbey, Kent:
(?) Foote may move to, viii. 180
Mal maritate, le:
Vernaccia, Mme del, may be released from, by husband's wish, ii. 121–2
—— sent to, ii. 112
Malone; Maloney. *See* Molone
Malovitio:
Jesuits involved with, x. 49
Malpas, Vct. *See* Cholmondeley, George (1724–64); Cholmondeley, George James (1749–1827)
Malpas, Vcts. *See* Edwardes, Hester (ca 1727–94); Walpole, Mary (1705–31)
Malsan. *See* Maltzan
Malta:
agents of, buy provisions, v. 494
ambassadors from and to, *see under* Ambassador
cats from, i. 181, 212, 394, 462
Charles V's grant to, iv. 406
consuls from and to, *see under* Consul
cross of, given to Albani, iii. 475
English fleet cruises near, ii. 559
English ships fired upon by, v. 225
English squadron goes to, on errand to English consul, vi. 201
France offers Lérins islands to, iv. 406
French convoy expected from, ii. 559
French ships at, may go to Tripoli, iv. 319–20
Grand Master of, *see* Pinto de Fonseca, Emmanuel (1681–1773)
HW's arms and quarterings will entitle him to be Grand Master of, iv. 372
health office at, visited by Capt. Bodie, vii. 227, 232
isolated because of plague, ii. 252
knights summoned by, to defend island against Turks, v. 493–4
La Rose driven ashore at, v. 225, 335
Mann receives account from, of Russo-Turkish naval battle, vii. 226–7, 232
Maria Theresa forbids knights of, to fight Turks, v. 505
Naples tries to starve, iv. 405
Neapolitan dispute with, over right of Bp of Syracuse to visit cathedral, iv. 405–6
Neapolitans send valuables to, i. 501
orange flower water from, iii. 330
Russian squadron may move to, from Port Mahon, to scare Turks, vii. 189
Saunders pursues Toulon fleet from, v. 431
Sicily provides all supplies for, iv. 405
visitors to, Mann, Horace II, and Lady Lucy, viii. 233
Malta, Knights of. *See* St John of Jerusalem, Knights of
Maltese cats. *See under* Cat

Malton, Bns and Cts. *See* Finch, Lady Mary (d. 1761)
Malton, E. of. *See* Watson-Wentworth, Charles (1730–82); Watson-Wentworth, Thomas (ca 1690–1750)
Maltzan (*or* Maltzam *or* Malzen), Catherine (b. ca 1735, living 1810), Baronne de; canoness:
(?) Albany, Cts of, has as *dame de compagnie*, ix. 522
Maltzan, Joachim Karl (1733–1817), Graf von; Prussian minister to England:
Austrian-Prussian war expected by, viii. 393
Diede laughs at, at George III's levee, vii. 402
(?) sister of, ix. 522
Malvezzi, Vincenzo (1715–75), cardinal, 1753; Abp of Bologna:
Jesuits' college's director refuses to obey orders of, without Pope's authorization, vii. 487
Jesuits' revenues in Bologna to be under the arbitration of, vii. 494
Malyn, Elizabeth (1691–1789), m. 1 James Fleet; m. 2 Capt. William Sabine; m. 3 (1739) Charles Cathcart, 8th Bn Cathcart; m. 4 (1745) Lt-Col. Hugh Maguire:
Maguire marries, i. 420n
Mamamouchi. *See* Molière: *Bourgeois Gentilhomme, Le*
'M'amie':
Craon's name for his wife, ii. 298
Man:
HW calls, an *aurivorous* animal, ix. 400
wicked wit of, HW's reflections on, ix. 451
Man, Isle of. *See* Isle of Man
Manchester, Ds of. *See* Montagu, Lady Isabella (d. 1786)
Manchester, D. of. *See* Montagu, George (1737–88); Montagu, Robert (ca 1710–62)
Manchester:
House of Commons hears counsel from, against taxes, ix. 573
rebels joined by people from, iii. 179–80
Manciforte (*or* Mancinforte *or* Marcinforte) Sperelli, Giovanni Ottavio (1730–81), nuncio to Tuscany, 1771–5; cardinal, 1777; titular Abp of Teodosia:
Clement XIV orders, to welcome D. of Gloucester, vii. 343
Leopold II receives Papal brief from, vii. 508
suppresses satire on Conclave, viii. 69
Mancini, Rosa:
opera performance of, ii. 342
Mancini-Mazarini, Louis-Jules-Barbon (1716–98), Duc de Nivernais:
Bedford, D. of, to meet, at Dover, vi. 55, 69–70
Bute dines with, vi. 82
Choiseul said to be succeeded by, vii. 62
England might be considered reasonable by, vi. 117

Éon affair makes, ridiculous, vi. 273
—— publishes Praslin's correspondence with, and other letters, vi. 217–18
—— secretary to, vi. 190, 216
France advised by, to conclude peace as soon as possible, vi. 89
Frederick II's witticism about small size of, when minister at Berlin, vi. 84–5
—— wants Valory as minister instead of, iv. 541–2
French trip of, disarranged by news, iv. **286**
Garter installation at Windsor not attended by, because of ill health, vi. 79
Guerchy disparaged by letters of, vi. 218
HW called on by, at SH, on way from Hampton Court, vi. 136
HW describes, but has not met him, vi. 79
HW's poor opinion of, vii. 62
Lyttelton's *Dialogues* translated by, vi. 79–80
Mann regrets that Havana's capture was celebrated in presence of, vi. 90
Maurepas brother-in-law of, ix. 212
—— may be succeeded by, as minister of finance, ix. 212
St James's Coffeehouse waiter says he could thrash, vi. 84
secretaryship of state for foreign affairs expected by, in vain, iv. 286
to be ambassador extraordinary to arrange peace with England, vi. 55, 69–70
Man-dancer:
arrested for debt, iii. 294
Manège:
Maria Theresa's ladies practise at, for *carrousel*, ii. 99
Manelli. *See* Mannelli
Manetti, ——, Mann's landlord:
Mann's bed from, v. 447
Manetti, Col. Antoine:
captured at Velletri, ii. 493
Manetti family:
Mann rents house of, iii. 317n
Mange:
puppies may get, vii. 40
Mangle, Capt. ——:
Cameron, Jeanie embarks on ship of, from Leghorn, vi. 453
Mani, La. *See* La Mani
Manifesto (invoice):
for box, i. 183
Manifesto; manifestos:
Burgoyne's, viii. 320
Catherine II's, on Peter III's death, vi. 64, 71, 74, 209, 570n
Charles of Naples's, ii. 420
English, to Holland, ix. 104–5, 112, 142
Frederick II's, fail to justify him, ii. 511
Genoa's, iii. 65
Prussian: Mansfield's answer to, v. 286; stops payment on Silesian loan, iv. 348
Spain's: on rupture with England, v. 563;

Portuguese campaign fails to live up to, vi. 66
Venice prepares, iv. 176
Wilkes prints, against House of Commons, vii. 205
Young Pretender's, iii. 103
Manila:
Draper the conqueror of, vi. 383n
—— to receive share of ransom of, vi. 344
Mann, Alice (1739–63), m. John Apthorp:
father's legacy to, v. 34
Mann estate should not be entailed upon, v. 61
mother benefits, by accepting jointure, v. 41
obstacle to parents' separation, v. **29**
Mann, Catherine (d. 1776), m. (ca 1752) Rev. Francis Hender Foote:
brother's bequest to, vi. 226, 234, 240–1
child when Mann left England, viii. 220
death of, viii. 205, 214, 220
HW and Mann not acquainted with, viii. 205
Linton entailed upon, vii. 51, 112
Mann's intended bequest to, ii. **93**
Mann, James, persuaded by Edward Louisa Mann to make, a residuary legatee, viii. 225–6, 271
—— unduly generous to, in will, viii. 257–8
marriage portion of, ii. 308, iv. 308
virtues of, viii. 214
Mann, Catherine (1742–1811), m. (1771) Rev. Hon. James Cornwallis, 4th E. Cornwallis, 1823:
father's estate settled on, vi. 563
father's legacy to, v. 34
Foote, Mrs, summons, to reading of Edward Louisa Mann's will, viii. 159
HW to be godfather to, ii. **31**
Mann estate should not be entailed upon, v. 61
Mann reads of marriage of, but is sent no notice of it, vii. 354
mother benefits, by accepting jointure, v. 41
obstacle to parents' separation, v. 29
Mann, Edward (d. 1761), of Chelsea; Mann's uncle:
death of, v. **555**
Mann hardly knew, v. 555
Tortola lands granted to, viii. 168, 173, 199–200, 202
Mann, Edward Louisa (1702–75), of Linton; Horace Mann's brother:
Allen's application to be rejected by, vii. 366
at Richmond, vii. 305–6, 340, 379, viii. 36
Boothby preferred by, as Mann's proxy at Bath installation, vii. 356, 371, 385, 389
—— tells, of D. of York's intended visit to Italy, vi. 165
bootikins not used by, viii. 71
breaches of promise by, to Mann and

[Mann, Edward Louisa, *continued*]

Horace Mann II, do not surprise HW, viii. 276

business manager to be procured by, for Mann and himself, vi. 231

Challis obliged to pay bond to, for place in his Customs House department, viii. 276-7, 284, 292

Chute confers with, about letter to Thistle-thwayte, vi. 316

Croft calls on, at Richmond to settle proxy choice, vii. 379

——— writes to Mann of preference by, of Sir William Boothby over Horace Mann II as his proxy, vii. 371

Customs place of, viii. 177-8, 276-7, x. 53, 54

daughter of, viii. 101

daughter's match with nephew contrived by, vii. 100, 112

death of: falsely reported, v. 555; Foote announces, to Mann, viii. 165, 168; HW hears of, viii. 154; Mann awaits letter about, from Horace Mann II, viii. 172; requires Horace Mann II's presence in England, viii. 225

executor of James Mann's will, vi. 240

expense of nephew's knighthood dreaded by, vii. 390

face of, fresh and juvenile, viii. 148

father assigns Sussex estate to, for his maintenance, viii. 168

father compares Mann's income with that of, ii. 307

father's deeds must decide right of, to Sussex estate, viii. 176

father's will declared by, to be invalid regarding Linton, viii. 146

faults of old age intensified in, viii. 131

Foote, Mrs, established by, at Linton, v. 129

Footes' share in James Mann's estate regretted by, viii. 271-2

HW asked by, to recommend 3 Englishmen to Mann, vii. 129, 138

HW called on by, at Arlington St, vii. 32

HW calls on, vi. 226

HW congratulated by, i. 321

HW discusses Mann's Bath ribbon with, vii. 47-8

HW dropped by, vi. 196

HW entertains, at SH, iii. 503, iv. 63

HW hears nothing from: about Horace Mann II, vii. 359; about Horace Mann II's Italian trip, vi. 237-8; about proxy for K.B. installation, vii. 350

HW ignorant about mistresses and illegitimate children of, vi. 242

HW not surprised at behaviour of, v. 384, viii. 276

HW pushes, to oppose Thistlethwayte over Sophia Lucchi's legacy, vi. 288-9

HW reproached by, for giving Bentley income from Customs House, viii. 276

HW's alarm over Galfridus Mann's health surprises, v. 30

HW's correspondence with: about Bath proxy, vii. 45, 340-1, 346, 364, 407-8; about James Mann's death, vi. 226; about dogs, vii. 45; note during gout attack, vii. 76

HW's neglect from, distresses Mann, vii. 353

HW's offers to visit him refused by, at Richmond, vii. 305-6, 408

HW's relations with: bad, vii. 340; beyond surprise, v. 384; civil but distant, vii. 418; cool but civil, vii. 408; very distant till healed, vi. 226

HW tells, that nephew's scruples may be sincere, vii. 101

HW tells Mann to have nephew placate, viii. 37

HW tells Mann to thank, vii. 49

HW told by: about Galfridus Mann's estate, v. 57; about stocks in Mann's name, v. 54-5, viii. 176; that nephew is more prudent, vii. 506

HW to pay: for Beauchamp's wine, vii. 200; for Masaccio engravings, vii. 268

HW to talk with: about nephew, v. 409; about proxy for Bath installation, vii. 327-8

HW visits, at Linton, v. 128-9

HW would never try to get back money from children of, viii. 286

health of: bad, ii. 308, v. 47, vii. 354; bootikins tried by, vii. 231, viii. 71; gout, ii. 197, v. 50, vi. 260, 568, vii. 76, 231, 340, 408, 495; viii. 71, 72, 145, 146; ill, vi. 563, vii. 25; ill, making him unfit for business, vi. 228; pleurisy, vi. 560; recovered, according to Croft, viii. 148; too ill to be brought to Richmond, viii. 165

Houghton visited by, iii. 510

illegitimate children of: vi. 240, 242, 247, viii. 264-5, 277, 286, 320, ix. 583n; arouse brother's fears, vi. 568; can be well provided for, vii. 576; said to be well provided for, viii. 154-5, 159

in country, vi. 260

indolent and retired, v. 158

lawyer brought by, to brother at Richmond, v. 32

life of, miserable to himself and to all about him, viii. 165

Linton bought in name of, to exempt him from sheriff's duties as Sir Robert Walpole's esquire of the Bath, viii. 146

Linton estate of: apartment at, offered to Mann, viii. 166; charged with annuity in return for his outlay on it, viii. 160, 176; claimed by him to be at his own disposal, vi. 563-4, 568, vii. 129, viii. 146, 159, 259; entail of, cannot be cut off, though nephew may be threatened with it, vii. 76; entail of, clearly proved by his letter, vii. 51, 120;

entail of, not cut off, viii. 159; mortgages on, declared illegal, viii. 258

Linton reoccupied by, for first time in 4 years, viii. 120

Linton said by, to have been purchased in his own name, viii. 146

Linton visited by, when stricken with gout, viii. 145, 146

lives out of the world, v. 178

longevity was little consolation to, for gout, viii. 189

looks young and well, vii. 101

Mann advised by: not to marry, vii. 113; to seek promotion, vi. 318

—— commissioned by, to get painting for Royston, v. 532, 539, 540, 545

—— encouraged by, to consider future of Horace Mann II, viii. 271

—— esteems, v. 41

—— ill-used by, viii. 266

—— may be represented by, at installation of Knights of the Bath, vii. 327

—— may mention HW's name to, but not to others, vi. 372, 376

—— offered an apartment at Linton by, viii. 166

—— refers would-be purchaser of Tortola lands to, viii. 169, 200, 220

——'s age close to that of, vii. 79–80, 112

——'s Bath ribbon pleases, vii. 55

——'s cool relations with, vii. 353, viii. 154, 176

——'s correspondence with: v. 168, vi. 338, 353, 376; about Angiola Lucchi, vi. 370; about Bath installation, vii. 327–8; about Bath ribbon, vii. 32; about brothers' deaths, v. 41, 42, 47, 49–50, vi. 240; about brothers' healths, iv. 543, 544, vi. 228; about D. of York's trip to Italy, vi. 165; about father's will, and Linton entail, iv. 301–2, 306–8, vii. 50–1, 65, 71, 79–80, 112–13, 129, 172, viii. 146–7, 154, 165–6, 172–3; about nephew's misbehaviour, vi. 305, 563; about picture for Royston, v. 545; through Croft, vii. 356, 410–11, 417

——'s intention to stay in Italy misinterpreted by, v. 175

——'s portrait sent to, vii. 155, 565

——'s portrait would please, vii. 48

—— succeeds to place of, in Custom House, viii. 177–8

—— thanks HW for news of, vii. 36

—— to leave bijoux to, ii. 93

—— urges, not to give in to sister-in-law, iv. 536

Mann, Galfridus, discusses business with, iv. 556

—— makes, his executor, iv. 34, v. 72

—— more apt than, to find information, v. 178

—— persuaded by, to take tar-water, v. 30

Mann, James, induced by, to leave money to the Footes, vi. 240–1, viii. 225–6, 271–2

mistress might be married by, to legitimate her son, vi. 242

mistress of: and children, to be provided for, vi. 240–1, 242; provided for in his will, viii. 160

mortgages illegally placed by, on Linton, viii. 258

nephew asked by, to be Mann's proxy, vii. 346

nephew cannot depend upon, viii. 131

nephew corresponds with, vii. 366

nephew excluded by, from James Mann's bedchamber, viii. 271–2

nephew might be disinherited by, to help illegitimate children, vi. 242, 563–4, 576, vii. 76, 80, viii. 172

nephew no longer displeases so much, vii. 172, 506

nephew not notified by, of opportunity to be Mann's proxy, vii. 366

nephew prevented by, from living at Linton, viii. 169–70

nephew probably threatened by, with loss of entail, to make him more economical, viii. 154–5

nephew's affairs taken away from guardianship of, vii. 36

nephew's affairs to be managed by, to repay loans, vii. 576

nephew seen by, and sent to HW, vii. 408

nephew's future prospects mentioned by, v. 129, 142, vii. 408

nephew's marriage considered too expensive by, vi. 305

nephew's marriage flatters, vi. 242, 245–6

nephew's promises from, broken, viii. 169–70, 181

nephew's proxyhood for Mann's Bath installation disapproved and then endorsed by, vii. 379, 385, 410–11

nephew's unpaid bills irritate, viii. 36–7

nephew to be considered by, as son, vii. 113

Radnor entertains, at dinner, iv. 456

Rochford's letter from, written by HW and transcribed by daughter, vii. 408

sister-in-law asks money from, v. 60

sister-in-law could not be restrained by, v. 19

sister-in-law's bad temper not mentioned by, iv. 544

sister-in-law's opposition dreaded by, v. 47

Sussex estate's income awarded to, for life, iv. 307, viii. 168, 173, 176

temper of: abominable, viii. 266; caused by his sufferings, viii. 284–5; insupportable, vi. 196; spoilt, vii. 353

testamentary intentions of, vii. 100–1

Tortola lands 'inherited' by, viii. 168–9, 173, 200, 220, 264–5

Walpole, Sir Robert, attended by, as esquire of the Bath, viii. 146

[Mann, Edward Louisa, *continued*]
Walpole family occasioned financial loss to, viii. 287
will of: viii. 154–5, 158–9, 160, 166, 168–70, 172–3; Mann, Horace II, the object for Mann's rectifying, viii. 181; Mann, Mary, applies for grant of Tortola lands according to, viii. 264; nephew excluded from, viii. 160, 225; sister summons nieces and their husbands for reading of, viii. 159
Mann, Eleanor (d. 1789), m. (ca 1724) Sir John Torriano, Kt:
caveat entered by husband of, against James Mann's will, vi. 240, 241–2, 245, 247, 271
father's will omits, vii. 51, 112
Mann's bequest to, ii. **93**
Mann, Eleanor (1747–1823), m. (1772) Thomas Powys, cr. (1797) Bn Lilford:
father's estate settled on, vi. 563
father's legacy to, v. 34
Foote, Mrs, summons, to reading of Edward Louisa Mann's will, viii. 159
husband of, ix. 475n
Mann estate should not be entailed upon, v. 61
mother benefits, by accepting jointure, v. 41
obstacle to parents' separation, v. 29
Mann (otherwise 'Gilmore'), Eleanor, m. (ca 1773) Capt. John Rogers of the East India Company:
Bentley's bond might have gone to, viii. 277
father may disinherit nephew to aid, vii. 76, 80
father's bequest to, viii. 168
father's fondness for, alarms uncle, vi. 568
father to provide for, vi. **240**
Mann, Emily (?1772–1847), m. (1792) Robert Heron, 2d Bt, 1805:
father hurries home to, viii. 530
father joins, in Kent, ix. 539
father leaves, happy, ix. 662
father visits, in country, ix. 229
father will come to London for the sake of, ix. 363
HW would not have advised Mann to break Linton entail for sake of, viii. 266
Mann must leave his money to, viii. **225**
—— wishes to secure Linton to, viii. 240, 257, 266
Mann, Galfridus (1706–56), army clothier; Horace Mann's brother:
Ædes Walpolianæ to be forwarded by, to Mann, iii. 511, iv. 64
affairs of, worry him, iv. 526
American map to be sent by, to Mann, iv. 497
ass's milk taken by, for cold, iv. 520
Baker, Dr, consulted by, iv. 523, 525
baronetcy reversion to go to, iv. 458n
Bath to be visited by, iv. 537, 544, 549

Bentley to design urn for monument of, at Linton, v. 157
Bologna banker to draw upon, i. 228
Boughton Malherbe bought by, iv. 166–7, 308
Bristol visited by, iv. 551, 556, 563, 564, 569, 574, 586, v. 1
brother-in-law manages new purchase by, iv. 308
brothers less well placed than, to collect information, v. 178
brother's love for illegitimate children feared by, vi. 568
brother's marriage to mistress feared by, vi. 242
Bubb Dodington tells, of disappointment over P. of Wales's death, iv. 244, 253
business still transacted by, though at Richmond, iv. 549
Chute and HW told by, that Linton estate is entailed, vii. 101
Chute calls on, iv. 523, 529
——'s kindness gratifies, iv. 540
—— to reduce, to abstinence and health, iv. 63
—— urged by, to secure Sophia Lucchi's fortune, v. 412
Cicero bust to be shown by, to HW, iv. 86
Cocchi a help to Mann in grief for, v. 58
Dacres urge, to come to Italy, iv. 564
Dagge recommended by, v. 365, vi. 268
—— treats with, about Sophia Lucchi, vi. 265
daughter loved by, iv. 499
daughters of, v. 29
Day persuades Robert Mann to add Mann's portion to that of, for marriage settlement, viii. 183
death of: v. 34, 38, 40–1, 42, 54–5; HW reminded of, by James Mann's death, vi. 226; HW's heaviest blow next to deaths of parents, vi. 226
Designs by Mr R. Bentley . . . to be forwarded by, to Mann, iv. 367–8
domestic troubles of, concealed from brother, v. 40–1
Egmont's pamphlet to be forwarded by, to Mann, iv. 43
estate of: keeps brothers busy, v. 50, 72; large, v. 50; settled on daughters, v. 61, vi. 563; should have been annexed to Linton, v. 61
Faction Detected mentioned by, ii. 334
family all taken by, to Bristol, iv. 574
Fane's affair with Mann to be told by, to HW, ii. 17
——'s departure from England expected by, i. 135
father on bad terms with, ii. 273
father's will explained by, to Mann: entails Linton estate, iv. 301–2, vi. 564, 576, vii. 51, 79–80, 112, 129, viii. 147, 172; obliges him to provide for Mann, iv. 302,

306–7, vii. 50–1, 76, 112, 113, 120, viii. 167, 172–3, 183

Forth, Mrs, leaves little to, despite promise, iv. 556, 564

Fox does not favour, v. 166

friends' concern over health of, iv. 523, 526

Giberne restrained by, from calling on HW at SH, iv. 98

—— to get passage money from, i. 216

Giberne, Mrs, will give money to, to increase her son's allowance, iii. 93

goodness of, inexhaustible, vi. 50

gout called 'a cold' by, iv. 79

Gray repays, for HW's advances, i. 445

HW accompanied by, to see Astley's paintings, iv. 341

HW and Mann could discuss, v. 506

HW asks about bill of exchange to, for Riccardi's payment, iii. 435

HW called on by: at SH, iv. 456; during illness, ii. 147; in Arlington St, iv. 474

HW calls on, iv. 63, 523, 529, 538, 549, 554, v. 27, 32

HW cherishes memory of, vi. 196

HW consulted by, about Mann's idea of going to Hanover, iv. 150–1

HW contrasts James Mann with, vi. 133

HW converses with, about family fortunes, iii. 496

HW defends, against Mann's charge of lack of generosity, viii. 176

HW dines with, v. 1

HW discusses Mann's affairs with, daily, i. 212

HW discusses with, the sending of things to Mann, i. 439

HW entertains: at Arlington St, iv. 234; at breakfast, iv. 360; at dinner, v. 1; at SH, iv. 63

HW excuses Edward Louisa Mann because he is brother of, vii. 340

HW forgets to ask, about copies of Ædes Walpolianæ, iv. 64

HW gives translated paper to, ii. 225

HW hears rumour from, that Mann goes to Rome, iv. 470

HW leaves pamphlets and magazines with, for Mann, ii. 31

HW may have given bill of lading to, v. 118

HW may have heard from, that Elizabeth Pitt is in Florence, iv. 406

HW may pay, when he pleases, iii. 441

HW pays Mann through, ii. 366, 386

HW praises, iii. 442

HW receives condolences of, i. 321

HW receives Cours de l'Europe from, i. 177

HW receives letter from Mann through, i. 496, ii. 140, 267

HW receives Mann's letters through, ii. 342, iii. 348, iv. 234

HW's affection for, iii. 503, v. 32

HW's correspondence with, iv. 523

HW sees more of, when at Twickenham, iii. 442

HW sends word of Sir Robert Walpole's death through, iii. 24, 31

HW's excuses to, for not seeing Pelham and Milbanke, iv. 200

HW's eye-trouble known to, ii. 365

HW's health not mentioned by, ii. 546

HW's illnesses would be reported by, to Mann, ii. 140

HW's letters to Mann to be consigned to, in case of any emergency, iv. 442

HW's monument to: design to be made for, by HW, v. 128; HW pleased that Mann approves of, v. 262; HW's inscription for, v. 157; Mann frames design of, for his bedside, v. 253; Mann wants description of, v. 142; placed in Linton church, v. 249–50, ix. 668

HW's reasons for not writing to be conveyed by, to Mann, iii. 16

HW's regard for memory of, v. 79, viii. 54

HW takes, to Richmond, iv. 63

HW tells: of talk with Mann's father, ii. 244; to complain to Prevereau about mail, ii. 448; to write Mann of Johnson's victory, iv. 511

HW the friend of, ix. 461, 668, 670, 671, 677

HW to be absent sponsor at baptism of child of, ii. 31

HW to be shown Mann's letter by, i. 382

HW to be told by: about Mann's hopes from Stone, iii. 221; of Mann's affairs with P. of Wales, iv. 242

HW to bring, to SH, iv. 525–6

HW to entertain, at SH, iii. 503

HW to hear from: about Leghorn fire, iii. 472; about Mann's efforts to get his arrears, iii. 474

HW to hear news through, of Cts of Orford, iii. 54

HW to hear progress of Mann's affair with Fane from, ii. 553

HW told by: about Mann's toothache, iv. 87; of letter sent to Mann, iii. 103; of Mann's defence of Northumberland's gallery, iv. 340–1; of Mann's failure to receive letters, i. 196, ii. 166; that Linton estate was entailed, vii. 76

HW to pay: for cases shipped from Leghorn, ii. 343; for Domenichino painting, ii. 45; for commissions, i. 166; for Domenichino painting and Livia statue, ii. 119; for Livia statue, ii. 79; for scagliola tables, iv. 37; for sepulchral altar, iv. 388

HW to pay Riccardi through, iii. 420

HW to receive letter and office of the Madonna through, i. 408

HW to receive Mann's letters through, ii. 232

HW to repeat Mann's news to, ii. 486

Handel's overtures to be sent to Mann by, ii. 31

[Mann, Galfridus, *continued*]
health of: asthma, iv. 522, 540, 543, 549,
551, 554, 564; better than Mann's, iii. 442;
cold, iv. 79, 520, 569, v. 30; consumption, iv.
523, 525, 527, 529, 536, 537–8, 540, 543,
544, 547, 549, 551, 554, 556, 559, 563, 564,
569, 574, 582, 586, 591, v. 1, 8–9, 16, 19,
22, 27, 29, 30, 32–3, 35–6; cough, iv. 525,
v. 1; emaciated, iv. 551; eruptions, v. 30,
35–6, fever, iv. 525, v. 30; foreign tour
might improve, iv. 526, 527–8, 536, 569,
582, 586, v. 1, 33, 36; gout, iv. 79; gout in
ankle, iv. 63; looseness and salivation, iv.
537, 543; shortness of breath, iv. 523, v. 1;
sore mouth, iv. 543
Houghton visited by, iii. 510
Keene fond of, v. 166
kindness of, to family on death-bed, v. 32–3
lawyer brought to, by brother, v. 32
Lee a former ward of, iv. 363, viii. 128
lent all the world money for nothing, v.
178
letter of, i. 24
London visited by, from Richmond, iv. 30
lottery ticket to be investigated by, ii. 206
Lucchi affairs transacted by, as trustee, iv.
246, 312
Malpas sees, iv. 554
Mann abused to, by father, ii. 190
—— advised by HW and, not to give
presents to Newcastle, ii. 137, 152
—— alarmed at not hearing from, iv. 252,
520, 525
—— discouraged by, from assuming name
of Guise, iv. 408, 415
—— draws bills on, for purchase of
Domenichino painting, ii. 57–8
—— draws money upon, i. 269
—— draws on, for money for Livia statue,
ii. 177
—— encloses bill to, in letter to HW, ii.
224
—— fond of, though he inherited nothing
from him, viii. 167, 170, 183–4
—— has no letters from, ii. 229
—— has not heard from, about his letter
to his father, ii. 152
—— has no time to write to, ii. 375, 386
—— hears from: of Orford's and Whithed's
deaths, iv. 243; of Sir Robert Walpole's
death, iii. 34
—— left annuity by, in case of recall from
Florence, v. 38n
—— left £100 a year by, v. 38, 61, viii.
173
—— may have heard from, of Houghton
lantern, iv. 163
—— misses attentions of, vi. 122
—— not expected by, to be shifted to
Genoa, iv. 272
—— receives news of baronetcy in letter
from, iv. 467

—— receives news of Chute from, iv. 251
—— resembles, iii. 442, 503
——'s affection for memory of, prompts
him to break Linton entail, viii. 271
——'s baronetcy concealed by, until negotiations are complete, iv. 462
——'s collection of salary arrears to be
assisted by, ii. 517
——'s conversation resembles that of, iii.
496
——'s correspondence with, i. 49, 51, 98,
222, 246, 255, 269, 321, 382, ii. 45, 189–
90, 206, 347, iv. 270, 306, 313, 329, 467,
520, 522, 527, 535, 540, 543, 544, 547, 551,
559, 564, v. 158, 168, vii. 51, 129
——'s correspondence with his family
chiefly confined to, vii. 353–4
——'s devotion to, v. 41, viii. 167
—— sends seeds to, ii. 330, 560
——'s funeral monument to be the twin
of that of, v. 142
—— shielded from afflictions of, viii. 97
——'s investments judiciously managed by,
v. 61, viii. 176, 183
——'s letter about Genoa brought by, to
HW, iii. 92
——'s letters to HW promptly forwarded
by, ii. 71
——'s letter to government official shown
by, to HW, i. 396
——'s portrait discussed by, iv. 313
——'s situation worries, v. 31
——'s twin brother, iii. 442n, iv. 522n, v.
142
——'s uneasiness always quickly removed
by letters of, v. 168
—— tells: to call on HW with letter about
snuff-box, ii. 330; to find out about his
alleged commission to Genoa, iv. 270
—— to draw upon, i. 228
—— told by: about Cts of Orford, iii.
200; about Stone, ii. 115; of sister's marriage, ii. 354
—— to leave bijoux to, ii. 93
—— to receive chair pattern from, iii. 20
—— to receive *Life and History of Theodore* (and other things) through, ii. 303
—— to receive prints of HW's eagle
through, iv. 485
—— to send bill of lading to, for Cocchi's
books, iv. 438
—— will recognize, in his son, viii. 27
—— writes to, to find successor to Giberne,
iii. 83
Mann, Edward Louisa, discusses business
with, iv. 556
—— writes to Mann at time of death of,
viii. 172
Mann, James, not as delicate as, in friendly
attentions, vi. 25
—— sees, weekly, iv. 523
Middleton's book to be forwarded by, to
Mann, iv. 185

mistake by, about cobalt and zinc, ii. 216
money for Domenichino painting received
by, ii. 79
Moyzer recommended by, i. 408
Neapolitan snuff-box received by, ii. 496
Newcastle's request to Mann given by, to
HW, iv. 459
Orford, 2d E. of, asks, to ask Mann if
proof of wife's infidelity is obtainable, iii.
200
—'s death would injure, iv. 233, 242
Orford, 3d E. of, might help the finances
of, by rich marriage, iv. 250
—— recommends Knight to Mann through,
iii. 462
Oswald to pay, for Mann, i. 228
paper for Mann's room in hands of, iv. 367
pedigree expense not mentioned by, iv. 194
Pelham to be pressed by, about Mann's
affairs, iv. 211
Pembroke's arrival announced by, to HW,
ii. 267
perfection of, in kind offices, vi. 42
Pitt's relations with, v. 166
Pomfret, Cts of, apologizes for rudeness to,
iii. 148
postal delays to be investigated by, ii. 233
Prevereau the forwarding agent of, i. 98
Pringle, Dr, consulted by, iv. 523, 525–6,
529, 540, 543, 544, 551, 559, v. 36
—— wanted by Cocchi to give medical
description of case of, iv. 544, 554, v. 36
quicksilver taken by, iv. 523, 527, 537,
543, 551
Radnor entertains, at dinner, iv. 456
—— praises appetite of, v. 1
regimental clothier, v. 50n
Richmond scene of illness of, iv. 520, 522,
549, v. 27
rides daily, iv. 554
riding may be tried by, for health, iv.
549, 551
riding used by, to cure cold, iv. 520
seal ordered by, for Mann, iv. 480
secretary for Mann to be found by HW
and, i. 157, 172, 189, 190, 207, 430
seeds procured by, for Duncannon, Whithed
and others, iv. 25
servant of, cuts his bread and butter, iv.
554
sleeps in closet after dinner, iv. 525
son loves Mann as much as, viii. 423
son may dissipate fortune of, vi. 563
son of: equivalent to Mann's own son, ix.
610; HW would never prevent, from collecting just debts, viii. 82; Mann could
easily be patient with, viii. 60; Mann's
esteem for, equal to that for father, viii.
167; pleases HW, vii. 408, viii. 265–6
son probably resembles, more strongly after
being with Mann, viii. 413
son resembles, v. 129, 409, v. 56, viii. 27,
91, 97, 104

stocks in Mann's name not the gift of, v.
61, viii. 183
stocks supposedly put by, in Mann's name,
v. 54–5, viii. 176
tar-water taken by, v. 30, 36
temper of, good, iv. 556, v. 129
Whithed accompanies, to select Cholmondeley's pictures, iii. 405
——'s loss grieves, more than Orford's, iv.
243
—— supposes that Mann is kept informed
by, iii. 444
——'s will seen by, iv. 251
widow of, ix. 343n
wife makes scenes when lawyer is drawing
will of, v. 54–5
wife never mentioned by, to Mann, iv.
535, 544, v. 29, 40
wife persuaded by, to accept a jointure, v.
32–3, 41
wife's temper a trial to, iv. 525, 535, 538,
556, v. 1, 9, 19, 29, 32, 40
will of: drawn up, iv. 32–3, 34–5, 38, 54,
60–1; son's daughters given no provision
in, viii. 257; unfair to Mann, viii. 167,
170, 183–4
World issues sent by, to Mann, iv. 395,
399
Mann, Mrs Galfridus. See Gregory, Sarah (ca
1716–1804)
Mann, Harriette (d. 1810), m. (1801) Col.
John Staunton Rochfort of Clogrenane Co.
Carlow, Ireland:
father hurries home to, viii. 530
father joins, in Kent, ix. 539
father leaves, happy, ix. 662
father visits, in country, ix. 229
father will come to London for the sake
of, ix. 363
HW would not have advised Mann to break
Linton entail for sake of, viii. 266
Mann must leave his money to, viii. **225**
—— wishes to secure Linton to, viii. 240,
257, 266
Mann, Sir Horace (1706–86), cr. (1755) Bt;
K.B.; HW's correspondent:
age of, ix. 656
amiable and agreeable, according to Mrs
Damer, ix. 287
apartment of, over the river, see Ambrogi,
Casa
appearance of: clumsy embonpoint, viii.
430; compared to 'wrinkled parchment,'
viii. 148; fatter, vii. 231; Mann, Horace II,
will describe to HW, as no longer 'slick
and bonny,' ix. 523; plump and portly, viii.
423; portly in Zoffany's painting, viii. 529;
Zoffany probably lessens potbelly of, viii.
540
appointment of: as envoy, vi. 371, 376; as
minister plenipotentiary, ix. 246, 248–9,
257; as resident, i. 2, 6–7

[Mann, Sir Horace (1706–86), *continued*]
assemblies of, well attended by Court officials, vi. 350
aversions of: to retirement, viii. 166; to travelling, iv. 473
baronetcy of: HW congratulates Mann upon, iv. 458–9, 461, 468, 471; Mann, Galfridus, conceals negotiations about, iv. 462
body of: reaches England, ix. 671; to be embalmed and sent to Linton, ix. 665; to go to England on shipboard, ix. 668
box of, at opera and theatre, *see under* Opera, Florentine; Theatre, Florentine
chapel of, Te Deums may be sung in, viii. 216
cicisbea of, *see* Acciaioli, Clarice
constitution of, 'unathletic,' v. 326
costume of: cloak, ii. 98, 187; cloth coat, iv. 69; furs, iii. 391; galoshes worn over shoes, viii. 79; great coat, vii. 72; 'old finery,' ii. 115; suits of clothes from Lyon, vi. 357; weepers, v. 165, 174
credentials of: arrive, v. 463; on their way, i. 6–7, 24; render request for promotion useless, v. 468–9
Customs place of, x. 53
death of, ix. 664
diet of: i. 78, 100, 104, 218, viii. 430; apples, i. 218, ii. 132; ass's milk, ix. 560; bacon and beans, v. 10; bread and butter, i. 104; broths, ix. 547, 560; chicken, i. 61, iv. 308; currants, i. 218; goat's whey, ix. 560; gooseberry tarts, i. 57, 61, iii. 261, v. 10; grapes, i. 218; ice cream, ix. 560; lamb's brains, i. 104; meat avoided, i. 78; pudding, i. 57; ravioli, i. 218; soup, i. 104; stewed peaches, i. 104; tea, i. 104
diplomatic correspondence of, carried on in quadruplicate, to avoid loss, ix. 339
dispatches for England being prepared by, ix. 196
England not soon to be revisited by, vii. 222
England would have afforded no society for, vii. 222, viii. 166, 221–2
Englishman nearly challenges, because of not being invited to dinner, ix. 341
English of, considered good for a foreigner, viii. 438
Eton days of, ii. 477
family of: unjust to him, viii. 131, 166, 170, 183; will treat him as a stranger, vii. 222
finances of: allowance for secret service work, v. 149–50; annuity accepted in lieu of Linton, viii. 257, 259; annuity considered, vii. 129, 134; art purchases for himself not permitted, viii. 180–1; bills for extras paid, iii. 220; bills for extras unpaid, ii. 484, 516; brother's annuity to, in case of recall from Florence, v. 38n, viii. 172–3; draws bills at 6 per cent because brother does not remit money, vi. 125; English visitors at Florence strain, iv. 8, 15; expense allowance for festivities of Leopold's marriage, vi.

356–7; expense of new Court at Florence will ruin, vi. 273, 291, 355; expenses of, in entertaining, ii. 78; father gives portion of, to Galfridus Mann, viii. 183; father's provision for, i. 27, iv. 301–2, 306–8, vii. 112–13, viii. 167, 172–3, 183; father to leave miserable pension to him, ii. 152; HW concerned over, i. 27, ii. 105, vii. 134; income increased by being made minister plenipotentiary, ix. 246; Mann, Galfridus, conceals extent of, for fear of making Mann extravagant, v. 61; Mann, Galfridus, invests savings in old and new annuities, for use after retirement, viii. 183; Mann, Galfridus, manages, v. 61, viii. 176, 183; Mann, James, to have charge of, v. 41, 47; Orford, Cts of, leaves legacy, ix. 124; Pisa sojourns hard on, vii. 92, 129, 134, 150, 254, 278, 293; plenipotentiaryship needed to restore, vii. 293; power of attorney sent by, to England, v. 71, viii. 219; salary arrears as chargé d'affaires, ii. 516–17, iii. 56, 71, 220–1, 338, 474, 483–4, 490, iv. 8, 24–5, 173, 180, 195–6, 211, v. 370, 483; salary as chargé des affaires and as resident, ii. 516–17; stocks put by Galfridus Mann in name of, v. 54–5, vii. 129; stocks represent father's legacy to, v. 61; tries to save a pittance for retirement, viii. 170; Tylney's legacy, ix. 534, 537
first foreign tour of, i. 161–2
Florentines revere, ix. 625
fondness of: for elderly sensible women, vii. 564; for hot weather, v. 310
friendships of, iii. 443
funeral monument of, to be the twin of his twin brother's, v. 142
garden of: assemblies in, i. 94–5, 104, ii. 281, 332, 462, iii. 15, 66, 115, 277; assemblies in, on special occasions only, iv. 191; assemblies in, will be enjoyed by D. of York, vi. 236; assembly in, for Mrs Barrett and Signora Capello, iv. 174, 191; bench in, scene of illicit relations, iii. 497–8, 502–3; bob cherry walk, iii. 277; Chute and Whithed walk in, iii. 252; cocchiata to be given in, i. 499; concert in, iii. 421; conversazioni in, ii. 478–9; conversazioni to be held in, ii. 281, iii. 66; currant and gooseberry bushes in, are in bud in February, iv. 25; double chairs in, ii. 332, 479, 485; Drummond compares, to Vauxhall, iv. 427; English glass lamps for, ii. 478, 485; evening party to be given at opening of, for first time, below stairs, vi. 45–6; evenings too inclement for use of, iv. 69; Florentine ladies to frequent, instead of the bridge, i. 498; Florentines regret exclusion from, iv. 162; gallery built in, iii. 115; greenhouse in, collapses while being built, iv. 94; HW against renewal of assemblies in, iv. 169; HW imagines Signora Grifoni in, ii. 497; illuminated, ii. 1, 478–9, 485, iii. 115; lemonade served in, i. 104; lodge

of Santo Spirito convent overlooks, iv. 446; Mann and Horace Mann II walk in, by moonlight before supper, viii. 517; Mann and Richecourt talk in, iv. 273; Mann and Signora Grifoni walk in, i. 100; Mann has dinner under tents in, in October, v. 10; Mann invites guests to walk in, i. 117; Mann sends seeds from, to friends, iv. 25; Mann wants double windsor chairs for assemblies in, ii. 332; *musa ragionevole* in, i. 100; music performed in, i. 112, 483, 499, ii. 1, iii. 277, 421; nuncio watches Saturday night party in, from convent lodge, iv. 446; orange trees in, i. 104, 499, ii. 230; Salimbeni and Amorevoli sing in, i. 240; table in middle of, i. 498; Thursday assemblies in, to end for season, iii. 115; to be 'packed up,' i. 151; 'Vauxhall in miniature,' ii. 478, 497, iv. 427; vine branches surround lamp posts, ii. 479, 485

HW advises, not to seek greater rank, iv. 16, v. 465, vi. 363

HW chilled by refusal of, to come to England, viii. 176, 182, 194

HW compares, to sheet of wet brown paper, ii. 467, iii. 61, 127, viii. 66, 521, ix. 656

HW expects, to come to England, vii. 218, viii. 155, 160, 173-4

HW has seen, patient though in torture, ix. 620

HW jokingly threatens to publish correspondence of, with celebrities, ii. 504

HW mentioned by, in last lucid intervals, ix. 664

HW's gifts from: HW embarrassed by, ii. 201, viii. 15, ix. 56, 165-6; HW regrets Mann cannot see, displayed, ix. 165; list of, x. 56; may be needed to furnish Linton, viii. 176

HW's procedure with, in recommending friends, iii. 250

HW's relations with: friendship like that of Orestes and Pylades, vi. 274, vii. 309, viii. 283, ix. 5, 9, 312, 615; friendship of long standing, vi. 280, ix. 332; HW wounded by remark, v. 79, 89; Mann's inviolable affection for HW, ix. 192; Mann's inviolable attachment, ix. 203

HW the best friend of, ix. 461

HW the only friend of, in England, viii. 166

HW thinks, should be minister to Spain, v. 166

habits of: abstemious in diet, viii. 430; bathing feet in cold water, vi. 266, 313, 322, 335-6; carried up and down stairs, ix. 585; drinks iced water, viii. 430; eats tarts and puddings, i. 57; gives routs during Lent, vii. 458; goes to Cascine gardens at sunset, ix. 585, 597; has not dined at table with anybody since October, ix. 581, 599, 611 horseback riding, iv. 143, 172, 191, v. 58, *see also under* Horse; keeps free from quarrels with Englishmen, ix. 341; lives on

boiled chicken and tarts, i. 61; meat-eating avoided, i. 78; removes from bed a few hours a day, ix. 574; sees dinner guests but does not sit at table, ix. 599; serves sherbets before theatre opening, ix. 585; snuff-taking, i. 317, iv. 376-7, 389, 392; takes the air and returns visits when sure of not being admitted, ix. 567; washes head and neck, viii. 430; water-drinking, vi. 114, 266, 335; wine-drinking avoided, i. 78, 155, vi. 469; writes in bed, iv. 216, ix. 547, 555

health of: ache, iv. 22; admirable, viii. 423; aged and infirm, ix. 171; attack in breast, ix. 626; bled, i. 48, 316, ix. 321, iii. 357, iv. 56, vi. 466; bled for influenza, ix. 317; bled in arm and foot, ix. 547; bleeding from breast not attributed to gout, ix. 547, 560, 567, 570, 607; bleeding resisted for fear of gout, viii. 188, 190; can neither walk nor stand for ten minutes, viii. 430; cold, i. 369, ii. 94, 98, 119, 321, 372, iii. 460-1, iv. 216, v. 58, vi. 173, vii. 450, viii. 188, 190; cold fingers, iii. 326; convulsion in eye and cheek, viii. 280; convulsion in left eye, viii. 430; cough, ix. 547, 567, 574, 580, 582, 585, 595, 597, 599, 621-2, 636, 643, 650, 652, 656, 662; cough diminishes, ix. 592; damp or cold feet, avoided, viii. 79; damp weather affects, vi. 117; delirium, ix. 664; does not decline, ix. 197; English sojourn would have been made difficult by, viii. 180, 182, 221; ephemera, i. 369; épuisement, iii. 252, 477, iv. 101; excuses him from Mozzi's wedding banquet, ix. 535; exhausted, ix. 658, 661, 662; false rumours about, i. 249, 286; feet bled and put in hot water to induce gout to relieve rheumatism in head, viii. 457; feet left weak by gout, ix. 61; fever, i. 48, 59, 66, 88, 89, 340-1, ii. 37, 38, 60, 94, 98, 117, 132, 294, 300, 321, 471, iii. 8, 9, 29, 252, 357, 369, 382, 461, vi. 313, 432, 466; fever gone, ix. 607, 658; Gatti advises treatment for, vii. 468; gout, iv. 335, vi. 114, 116, 117, 266, 313, 317, 322, 323, 335, vii. 38, 47, 231, 239, 243, 443, 448, 450-1, 458, 464, 467-8, 476, 480, viii. 58, 66, 80, 289, 290-1, 296-7, 299, 302, 304, 307, 311, 344, 404, 425, 430, 462, ix. 100, 144, 149, 341, 360, 550, 551, 560, 574, 580, 593, 595, 599; gout attributed to nerves, vi. 116, 117; gout discredited by HW, vii. 241; gout in head, ix. 176; gout not definitely suffered by, for some time, ix. 425; gout warded off by use of fur and flannel bags, ix. 248; gout will not be bad for, since it came so late, viii. 494; HW alarmed by, ix. 610; HW charmed with good accounts of, ix. 201; HW pleased with state of, ix. 185; HW recommends sea air for, viii. 311, 318, ix. 49; HW's compared to, viii. 532; HW surprised to hear that gout was not ailment of, ix. 561; Hamilton gives good account of, ix. 432; hands shaky, viii. 434, ix. 10, 168, 197, 201, 550;

[Mann, Sir Horace (1706–86), *continued*]
headache, i. 87, 317, 369, ii. 92, 98, 99, 109, 122, 269, 294, 299, 343, 486, 560, iii. 95, 143, iv. 350, 450, v. 123, 358, 362, 370, 377, 386, 464, vi. 117, viii. 188, 190, 532, ix. 128, 425; headache probably caused by snuff, iv. 376–7, 389; headaches cease with warm weather, ix. 441; headaches may be periodical, v. 370; headaches probably constitutional, v. 386; headaches to be eased by masses in Chute's chapel, iv. 485; herpes, vi. 466; hot water on feet resisted for fear of gout, viii. 190; hurt by standing long, ix. 301; influenza, ix. 314, 317; influenza, ending in gout, ix. 321; knee sinews contracted from lying in bed, ix. 599; lame, viii. 322, 337; languid in the morning, ix. 540; legs weak, ix. 425; Mann, Horace II, alarmed about, ix. 546; naturally weak constitution, vi. 459; nerves, ix. 45, 49; nerves agitated, iv. 377; nerves cannot be restored by air or water, ix. 61; nerves feeble, viii. 430; nerves shattered, ix. 500; nerves weak, v. 281–2, ix. 643, 656; nerves 'wore out,' iv. 537; nervousness prevents, from writing, ix. 143; not very well, iv. 404; numb fingers, ii. 128; ordered to stay in bed, ix. 555, 556; out of order, i. 21, viii. 425; pain, ix. 30; pain in breast, iii. 8, 207, iv. 335; pain in head and breast, iv. 225; pain in right hand, ix. 100; pain in stomach, vi. 468–9; piles, i. 30, 48, 52, 55, 59, 66–7, 69, 74, 77–8, 86, 88, 89, 94, 340–1, 349, 360, 365, 369, 381, iv. 334; Pisa baths improve, iii. 486–7, iv. 84, 85; pulse good, i. 372; recovers from verdigris, viii. 8, 15; rheumatism, v. 359, 369, ix. 493–4, 497, 500; rheumatism believed to be gout in head, viii. 479; rheumatism in head, viii. 457, 458, 463, 479; rheumatism in the loins, vi. 15; sleeps well when not coughing, ix. 567; stiff or weak knees, vi. 327; suffering, ix. 663; swollen ankles, viii. 280, 304; swollen feet, viii. 79, ix. 593; tender feet require frequent rest, viii. 518; toothache, iv. 87; trembling hand, ix. 197, 201, 550; trembling hand and weak head, ix. 168; unconscious, ix. 663; used as excuse to avoid Leghorn visitors, iv. 85; voyage to Naples, with coffin by his side, necessitated by, viii. 180; warm weather will reestablish, viii. 304, 311; weak feet, vi. 335; weakness, ix. 585, 646; weakness in the wrist, iv. 401; weather falsely blamed for low state of, ix. 567; well, ix. 312
hospitality of, too indiscriminate, iv. 87
hours of, i. 104
house and garden of: 'all south' vi. 77; full of company on Saturday night, ix. 70
house of: aired after Mrs Goldsworthy's departure, i. 395; another house under same roof taken by, ix. 431; at Pisa, arrangements at, for D. of Gloucester's occupancy, vii.

342, 348, 394–5; at Pisa, Beaufort, Ds of, borrows, vii. 372; at Pisa, secured, vii. 254; bath built in groundfloor room of, iv. 357; bedchamber temporarily has Bianca Cappello portrait, iv. 398; bedroom floors of, covered with mats, ii. 358; bedroom in, hung with design of HW's urn for Galfridus Mann, v. 253; Braitwitz lives two courts away from, ii. 353; Bute offered use of apartment in, vii. 96; carpets in, ii. 109; chimneys stopped up, in warm weather, iii. 391; cleaned for D. of York, vi. 180; Conway's apartment in, to be occupied by Sir James Gray, iv. 370; Conway's great antechamber in, becomes assembly room, iv. 292; cracks in, i. 381, 402; dark room in, occupied by HW's 'Old Barni,' iv. 370; Drummond describes, iv. 427; English have free access to, but foreigners are denied during Mann's illness, ix. 592; furniture of, taken to Pisa for D. of Gloucester's use, vii. 342; gallery made in garden into which ground rooms enter, iii. 115; garden front of, to be rebuilt, i. 381; gates, i. 104; Goldsworthy family to have, except for two rooms, i. 306, 381; Gray's rooms in, become ante-chambers, iv. 275; 'great room' in, hung with copies by Astley, iv. 313; HW longs to be at, i. 27; HW's apartment at, occupied by Conway, iv. 292; HW's apartment at, occupied by Mrs Goldsworthy, i. 314; HW's apartment at, to be occupied by Thomas Pitt, v. 543, 545; hall in, concert performed in, ii. 12, 29; hall turned into great room, with chimney, iv. 275; inner room to contain pedigree, iv. 205; in Via Bardi, *see* Ambrogi, Casa; in Via di Santo Spirito, ii. 561, iii. 317; 'little,' on the Arno, *see* Ambrogi, Casa; loggia in, i. 30; Mann prepares, for D. of York, vi. 165–6, 170, 180; Mann renews lease for, viii. 289; near Mme Salins', iv. 75; new great room in, hung with green and pictures, iv. 275; next garden to, to be scene of bell-raising, ii. 227; old (or 'other') apartment near the Gallery, *see* Ambrogi, Casa; paper procured for, iv. 362, 367; red room of, cups in, i. 52; red room of, HW occupies, iv. 275; red room of, Mann dines in, i. 369; Rinuccini 'neighbour' of, i. 137; smoke pervades, ii. 358; Stormont to occupy apartment in, vii. 2; summer apartment may be occupied by D. of York, vi. 236; terreno elegantly furnished, iv. 427; terreno, formerly occupied by HW, i. 72, 74; terreno, hall in, scene of opera rehearsal, ii. 294; terreno, Mann to be driven out of by cold weather, i. 118; terreno, Mann to delay quitting, i. 151; terreno, newly fitted up for Mann's occupancy, i. 72; terreno, not yet occupied, ii. 462; terreno, occupied too soon, i. 454; terreno, painted in fresco, iii. 490; terreno still too cold to be occupied, ix. 585; terreno, to

be used for *conversazioni*, ii. 281; warm and carpeted, ii. 109; windows broken by wind, iv. 25; windows towards garden made into doors, i. 499; winter apartment of, still used in June, iv. 69; winter bed-chamber becomes closet, iv. 275

ideas of, outrun his hand, ix. 46

letter of, of 31 March 1752, Mann keeps copy of, vii. 51

letters of: avoid delicate political subjects, vii. 71; dates of, mentioned by Mann to HW, ix. 180; HW gets, with difficulty, in Paris, vii. 134; HW leaves, at SH, vii. 73; HW tells Mann to write by proxy, when ill, ix. 602, 611; HW to receive, from England, when he is in Paris, vi. 548; long, ii. 560; long continuance of, would never have been predicted, ix. 556; Mann apologizes for handwriting in, v. 281–2; Mann obeys HW in not writing, to Paris, vii. 139; mere narratives of events in Rome-Florence area, ix. 464; must have been brought by east wind, ix. 319; politics never mentioned in, ix. 464; sent loose, ix. 272; sometimes dictated to a secretary, ix. 585; water-soaked, i. 334

life in England would be unsuitable to, viii. 166

list of English visitors to Florence should have been kept by, viii. 204

long life of, would not have been predicted in his youth, ix. 556

Mann, Horace II, calls, 'greatest friend that a man ever was happy with,' ix. 546

MS account of Tuscany by, vii. 27–8, ix. 230

ministerial privileges of, concessions constantly made in, iv. 205

morning *tête-à-têtes* sap the strength of, ix. 644

motto sought for, iv. 475, 480, 482, 487

nephew resembles, v. 409

Patch should make drawing of, vii. 267

———'s *Masaccio* dedicated to, x. 45

pension might be expected by, on retirement, viii. 160

portrait of: by Astley, iv. 309, 313, vii. 267; by Maron, sent to Edward Louisa Mann, vii. 565; HW asks name of painter of, viii. 28; HW sees, at Croft's, viii. 27; in Bath robes, should be sent to Linton, vii. 48; in Bath robes, to be done for Edward Louisa Mann, vii. 155; Mann explains circumstances of painting of, viii. 31–2; Mann sheds tears over HW's reactions to, viii. 31; painted by HW's advice, viii. 31; will go to Linton, viii. 27; Zoffany's, in painting of Tribune, unrecognizable to HW, viii. 527, 529; Zoffany's, said to be a good likeness, viii. 529; Zoffany to insert, in view of the Tribuna, vii. 519

promotion sought by, iv. 24–5, v. 453–5

promotion sought by, on arrival of new Court, vi. 318–22, 329, 341, 346, 349–51, 352–3, 355–6, 358

recall of, to England, seems possible, v. 115

reflections by, *see* Bereavement; Grief; Independent principles; Love; Lower classes; Moderation, political; Money; Nuns; Princes; Religion; Royal Connoisseurs; Satire; Slaughter; Superstitions; Treaties; Tyranny; Vanity; Young people

sepulchral urn of: HW offers to undertake, ix. 670, 671; Mann, Horace II, to bring dimensions for, to HW, ix. 678; to be designed and inscribed by HW, ix. 668

slowness of, in sending bills for commissions, iv. 587

social diversions of, iv. 115

strangers must be entertained by, and presented at Court, ix. 340–1

successor to, appointed, ix. 675–6

Thursday nights of, *see under* Thursday night

travelling boys met by, but not by HW, viii. 283

twin brother of, iii. 442n, iv. 522n

vanity of, satisfied by his Bath investiture, vii. 63

'Viceroy of the Mediterranean,' v. 326

vigilance and activity of, praised by HW, ix. 322

will of, executed in 1742, ii. 93

will of (last): Florentine furniture ordered to be sold for servants' benefit, ix. 669–70; HW left Poussin pictures in, ix. 664–5; Italian, Horace Mann II executor of, ix. 669; sepulchral urn mentioned in, ix. 668

Mann, Sir Horace (1744–1814), 2d Bt, 1786; M.P. Maidstone 1774–84, Sandwich 1790–1807:

Abano baths to be visited by, in hot months, viii. 108

absence of, from Parliament, may be resented by his constituents, viii. 146, 240

accounts received by, of Edward Louisa Mann's illness, viii. 145

affairs of, need attention, viii. 240

affliction of, still great, viii. 398

apprehensions of: about wife, may not be fulfilled, viii. 227; about wife's health, not lessened, viii. 233

attorney of, *see* Hull

Barcelona visited by, viii. 239

Bath order installation attended by, as uncle's proxy, vii. 327, 346, 350, 356, 359, 362, 366, 371, 379, 383, 388, 407–8, 410–11, 414–15, 417

Berlin visited by, viii. 389

better informed than HW, by being in Parliament and in the world, ix. 209

Borromean Islands to be visited by, viii. 129, ix. 586

Bourne visited by, ix. 659

brother-in-law of, ix. 475n

[Mann, Sir Horace (1744–1814), *continued*]
cabinet appointments will be interesting to, ix. 392
Cambridge attended by, under Bishop Keene, v. 409
campaign of, in Kent, unknown to HW, ix. 297
Campbell reproved by, for delay in binding Galluzzi's history, ix. 192
Carmarthen's correspondence with, ix. 667, 671–3, 675–6
Carpenter, Lady Almeria, angry at slight from, ix. 638, 674
case of books for, contained portrait of Lord Clinton, ix. 240, 304, 504
Challis's treatment from Edward Louisa Mann will shock, viii. 285
children and Parliament impel, to hasten home, viii. 530
children in country visited by, ix. 229, 539
children left happy by, ix. 662
children of, vii. 408
china may be taken by, to HW, ix. 598
constituents of: must be entertained when he is in England, viii. 363, 429; promised that he will be in England for opening of Parliament, viii. 396; refuse to let him resign his Parliamentary seat, viii. 281
Cottesmore visited by, ix. 222, 234, 461–2, 546–7, 678
could gallop from Naples to Florence in a few days, viii. 170
Cox Heath camp visited by, with James Mann II and Mary Mann II, ix. 320
Craven, Bns, quarrels with, ix. 615, 616
cricket match attended by, ix. 312
cricket match delays, on journey to Florence, viii. 506
cricket said to be ruining, vii. 495
Croft tells HW about, viii. 60
Damer, Mrs, and Caroline Campbell say that they are kindly treated by, ix. 623
Damer, Mrs, escorted by, at Florence, ix. 627
daughter's unfortunate attachment opposed by, ix. 268, 405, 414, 421, 423, 431
daughter the only child of, vii. 101
Deal representatives ask, to inquire in Parliament about Dutch ships, ix. 222
death of William Douglas will distress, ix. 604
departure of, from Italy, delayed by weather, ix. 203–4
diet of, vegetables and water, viii. 353
Duane consulted by letter from, about Linton mortgages, Sussex estate, and Tortola lands, viii. 181
East Kent place rented by, viii. 169
Elliot talks to, of Frederick II, viii. 389
England reached by, ix. 210, 539
England should be visited by, on account of Edward Louisa Mann's death, viii. 225
England to be visited by, in autumn of

1778, to prepare himself for Parliament, viii. 363
envoy's duties resigned by, to Udny, ix. 676
estate of, goes to Foote's sons, viii. 240, 257
evidence collected by, for possible Parliamentary inquiry, ix. 222–3, 234
executor of Mann's Italian will, ix. 669
expenses of Bath knighthood of, must be paid by Mann, vii. 411
expensive living of, viii. 523
fashionable follies avoided by, viii. 131
father probably resembled by, more strongly after being with Mann, viii. 413
father resembled by, v. 409, vi. 56, viii. 27, 91, 96–7, 104–5
Fawkener's arrival not awaited by, ix. 675–6
felucca from Genoa may transport, viii. 94
finances of, disordered, vi. 563, vii. 172, 506, viii. 36
Florence may be visited by: in spring of 1775, viii. 27, 54, 60, 115; in spring of 1776, viii. 136, 181; in spring of 1777, viii. 247, 251, 275, 286; in spring of 1778, viii. 337, 381; in spring of 1779, viii. 409; in 1781, viii. 184; in spring of 1783, ix. 367, 373, 378–9, 399; soon, ix. 475, 484, 550, 659; till he is old enough to wed, vi. 228, 237–8
Florence may have been left by, before return of courier from England, ix. 200
Florence reached by, viii. 96, 101, 131, 298, 300, 398, 517, ix. 404, 498, 662
Florence to be discussed by HW and, ix. 200
Florence too dangerous a place for, v. 415
Florentine journey as little regarded by, as trip to the races, ix. 373
Florentine stay of: prolonged, viii. 136, ix. 514; to end after Holy Week, ix. 672
Foote may send Edward Louisa Mann's will to, viii. 166
——'s letter to, forwarded by Mann to Naples, viii. 166
—— to stay at Linton until return of, to England, viii. 169, 180
Fox, C.J., does not acknowledge letters delivered by, ix. 461
fox-hunting of, prevented by gout, ix. 551
fox-hunting parties probably attended by, ix. 548
Fox's Martyrs mentions, ix. 505
Galluzzi history's delay explained by, ix. 192
Galluzzi's history sent to, ix. 205
Geneva to be visited by, on way to England, viii. 405, 409
Genoa visited by, ix. 628, 637, 638
George III presented by, with Batoni's portrait of D. of York, ix. 673, 676
—— should receive Galluzzi's history through, ix. 94
——'s levee and Drawing-Room to be attended by, ix. 659

Germany to be visited by, viii. 363, 374, 381

Gloucester, Ds of, to give audience to, viii. 163

Gloucester, D. and Ds of, and Lady Almeria Carpenter receive, cordially at Rome, ix. 674

Gloucester, D. and Ds of, awaited by, at Florence, ix. 676-7

—— rebuff, at Genoa, ix. 628, 637, 638

Gloucester House often visited by, ix. 247

goes abroad, viii. 36

good-hearted, but volatile and precipitate, ix. 297

Gordon's trial may be described by, to Mann, ix. 119

gun held by, for four hours, ix. 671

HW admires behaviour of, ix. 615

HW and Edward Louisa Mann think, is more prudent, vii. 506

HW and Mrs Noel uneasy at non-appearance of, in England, ix. 208

HW approves of, viii. 265-6, 282, ix. 49, 476, 582-3, 595, 618

HW approves of Mann's remarks about, viii. 54

HW asked by, for list of pamphlets for Mann, viii. 451

HW asks, to write to Mann, ix. 146, 221, 222, 257, 348

HW asks uncle about, vi. 568

HW called on by: at Berkeley Square, viii. 529, 538; at SH, viii. 490, ix. 370, 417; at SH, and extends dinner invitation, viii. 497; in Arlington St, vii. 547, viii. 423

HW condoles with Mann for losing, ix. 624, 629

HW did not expect apology from, for not informing him of departure, ix. 200-1

HW does not encourage, in opinions conformable to his own, if disagreeable to Mann, ix. 259, 268

HW expects, to come to town for Queen's birthday, ix. 236

HW explains to, his conduct with E. of Orford, vii. 549

HW glad that Mann will entertain, viii. 71

HW grieved that Mann is losing, ix. 624

HW has seen: not as often as Mann could wish, ix. 465; only thrice since his return, viii. 458; only twice since his arrival, viii. 455

HW hears news of, from Hon. Juliana Howe, ix. 320

HW hears nothing from, about proxy for K.B. installation, vii. 350, 359

HW hopes: has reached Florence, ix. 191; is reassured about his wife, viii. 205

HW hopes that son may be born to, viii. 144, 317

HW ignorant as to whether he has set out for Italy, ix. 187

HW impatient to see, viii. 422, ix. 629

HW informs, that Galluzzi's history has been delivered, ix. 193

HW kind to, in illness, ix. 560

HW knew how much Mann would enjoy, viii. 317

HW lives in a different world from, viii. 458

HW meets, at Ds of Montrose's, viii. 463

HW might delegate to, the task of conveying intelligence to Mann, ix. 65

HW neglected by, vii. 340, 364

HW not neglected by, ix. 197

HW pleased by Mann's satisfaction with, viii. 109, 144

HW pleased with, vi. 196, vii. 408, 547, viii. 27, 37, 54, 265-6

HW prepares Mann to welcome, at Florence, vi. 237-8, viii. 91

HW receives from, Italian poem to Mrs Montagu on Shakespeare, viii. 536

HW receives Mozzi's and Mann's letters through, ix. 421

HW's account of, pleases Mann, vii. 385, 554

HW's advice sought by, concerning proposed Parliamentary inquiry, ix. 222-3, 234, 251

HW's approval of daughter's marriage pleases, ix. 592

HW's correspondence with, vii. 366, 368, 369, viii. 77-8, 82, 532, ix. 196-7, 198, 200, 222-3, 234, 461-2, 494, 550-1, 574-5, 582, 584, 606-7, 608, 609, 659, 662, 663-85

HW sees; vi. 56; at Gloucester House, ix. 247; at Linton, v. 129; in London, ix. 461; on arrival, ix. 635

HW sends bootikins through, to Mann, viii. 463

HW sends letters through, to Mann, viii. 501, 517, ix. 378-9, 395, 484, 495, 498, 564, 580

HW sends Windham to replace, at Florence, viii. 524

HW's health reported by, as perfect, ix. 425

HW's health will be reported by, to Mann, viii. 433-4

HW's letter must be explained by, to Mann, ix. 380, 573

HW's letters to Mann taken back by, from Florence to England, viii. 100, 165, 247-8, 250, 379, 381, 409, 413, 493, 522, 530, ix. 198, 380, 411, 417, 419, 487, 498, 521, 540, 621, 668, 678, x. 36-7

HW's neglect from, distresses Mann, vii. 353, 357

HW's nephews excelled by, ix. 583

HW sorry at Mann's displeasure with, vii. 418

HW sorry that Mann is losing, viii. 342

HW sorry that return of, is delayed, viii. 387

[Mann, Sir Horace (1744-1814), *continued*]
HW's print considered by, a perfect likeness, ix. 10
HW's sets of Galluzzi's history sent to, for HW, ix. 181-2, 187-8, 192, 193, 197, 205
HW sure that he and Mann will not be disappointed in, ix. 519
HW surprised at stand by, against administration, viii. 451-2
HW surprised that Mann's promotion is not mentioned by, ix. 247
HW tells: not to be considerate in his suit against E. of Orford, viii. 82; not to use strong wines for gout, viii. 423
HW tells Mann not to preach to, viii. 481
HW to ask, about china vases sent by Mann, ix. 635
HW to be seen by, before departure, ix. 551, 659
HW to breakfast with, viii. 493
HW to entertain, at dinner, at SH, viii. 490
HW to give Orford's mourning ring to, for Mann, ix. 124
HW told by: of constant journals written to Mann, ix. 57; of faithful dispatches of political news to Mann, ix. 470; that Mrs Damer is going to Rome, ix. 213; that Mann complains of silence, ix. 30
HW to receive respects of, viii. 115, 298, 313, 398, 518, ix. 397, 406, 514
HW to see, vii. 366
HW to send *Mysterious Mother* to Mann through, viii. 481
HW to show Mann's letter to, ix. 45, 49
HW to teach use of bootikins to, viii. 479
HW to urge uncle to press decision of, vii. 364
HW wants: to bring back his letters, ix. 395, 487; to live at Florence instead of spending another year at Cambridge, v. 409; to send accounts of Mann's health, ix. 610
HW wants specimen of Tuscan porcelain to be brought by, ix. 591
HW wants to pay, for *Illustri fatti Farnesiani*, ix. 422, 459
HW will ask, to send Mann any news of importance, ix. 257
HW will be glad to see, viii. 413, 415
HW will be told by, of scene at James Mann's deathbed, viii. 271
HW wishes Mann had been visited by, viii. 54
HW would not have advised Mann's breaking Linton entail for daughters of, viii. 266
HW would prefer a letter from, to one written with difficulty by Mann, ix. 608
habits of, abstemious in diet, viii. 429-30
health of: breaks blood vessel, ix. 353; gout, viii. 318, 423, 429-30, ix. 197, 367, 406, 448, 461, 547, 551, 560, 598, 671; gout

cavalierly treated, ix. 406; influenza, ix. 290
holidays spent by, in country, viii. 477
hops on one foot, viii. 318, 429
House of Commons should be quitted by, viii. 452, ix. 465
Hull employed by, viii. 78, 258
—— sent by, to HW, viii. 78
—— writes to, about new grant for Tortola lands, viii. 200
Hull (nephew) sent by, to HW, viii. 258
—— to meet, at Lyon, viii. 258, 259, 265
hurries home to daughters, viii. 530
impatient to leave Nice for Florence, viii. 353
impatient to see Mann, ix. 567
inconsolable, viii. 369
in country, ix. 367
indefatigable rider, viii. 170
independence of, from political parties, a financial disadvantage, ix. 291
indiscreet, vii. 172, viii. 249
inheritance of, large, v. 50
Italian heat dreaded by, ix. 405
Italian tour benefits, ix. 540
Italy to be revisited by, ix. 678
itinerary of: may have been upset by weather and wife's health, viii. 225; on Mediterranean cruise, viii. 222, 225, 239; through northern Italy to Rome and Naples, viii. 118
Joseph II's arrival will hardly compensate Mann for loss of, viii. 109
Kentish electors of, will be angry at his absence, viii. 225, 240
Kentish opposition led by, against Mahon, ix. 32
Kent visited by, to support Marsham against Mahon, ix. 490
Leghorn visited by, viii. 94, 292
Leghorn would be first destination of, if wife died on shipboard, viii. 238
Leopold and Maria Louisa receive, with respect, ix. 666
(?) Leopold discusses Parliamentary freedom with, ix. 58
—— thanks, for fund for servants' benefit, ix. 670
Lerici visited by, to go to Nice, ix. 203-4, 210
letters of, short, ix. 268
Linton entail cut off by, viii. 257
Linton entail not doubted by, vii. 408
Linton to go to, vii. 172
London house of, rented, ix. 484, 488, 504
London to be visited by: before leaving for Florence, ix. 659; quite constantly, viii. 433-4; soon, ix. 116
London visited by, ix. 448
London will be visited by, for daughters' sake, ix. 363
London will not be revisited by, unless HW wants to see him, ix. 494

Lyon visited by, viii. 265, ix. 421
Maidstone borough abandoned by, ix. 488
Maidstone electors may carouse with, at Linton, viii. 381, 398
Maidstone meeting participated in by, ix. 290
Maidstone to be visited by, to settle constituents' subscription, viii. 513
Malta visited by, viii. 233
Mann advises: to be cautious during Gordon riots, ix. 64; to quit Parliament, ix. 474
Mann and wife of, try to curb his political rashness, viii. 457
Mann aroused by, to contest Edward Louisa Mann's will, viii. 181
—— asked by, to be godfather to his second child, vii. 354
—— asks: to inquire constantly about HW's health, viii. 425, 428; to send him *Mysterious Mother*, viii. 470
—— assisted by, in entertaining visitors, ix. 592
—— awaits news from, about English politics, ix. 388
—— called 'greatest friend' by, ix. 546
—— can be better informed by, than by HW, viii. 428
—— can easily be patient to, viii. 60
—— can tell, to write to HW, ix. 584
—— considers, too young to come to Florence, v. 47-8
—— counsels moderation to, ix. 268
—— does not want to relinquish Linton entirely to, viii. 240
—— dreads return of, to England so late in season, ix. 204, 207
—— expects, at Florence, viii. 289, ix. 182
—— fears early return of, to England, ix. 193
—— feels, should not now leave England, viii. 505
—— gets letters of recommendation for friends of, vii. 354
—— gives, use of Linton, viii. 180
—— grieves because HW is so seldom seen by, ix. 304
—— had better lodge, in Florence, viii. 60
—— has had no answer to his reproof of, viii. 477
—— has not biased conduct of, ix. 268
—— has not heard of intention of, to visit him, viii. 32
—— hears from, often, but his letters do not equal HW's, ix. 76
—— hopes for safe arrival of, at Dover, ix. 207
—— hopes he has prevented, from leaving England, viii. 505, 509, 513
—— instructs, to inform him of HW's health, ix. 351
—— invites, to Florence at HW's implied wish, viii. 64, 68, 78, 79
—— learns politics from, viii. 108
—— lives with, on easy footing, viii. 146
—— loved by, as much as his father, viii. 423
—— made happy by visit of, ix. 198
—— makes Linton over to, in return for annuity, viii. 257, 259
—— may be pained by stand of, against administration, viii. 452
—— may be visited by, now that daughter is married, ix. 649, 655
—— may consider, as a son, ix. 610
—— may have sent *Florence Miscellany* to HW through, ix. 633-4
—— may miss news because of absence of, from London, ix. 363
—— might be revisited by, at Florence, for a few days, to discuss Edward Louisa Mann's will, viii. 166
—— never urges, to talk about his finances, viii. 523
—— not told by, of his (or his sister's) marriages, vii. 354
—— pleased by description of, v. 142
—— pleased by inheritance of, v. 72
—— pleased with, viii. 96-7, 104, 108, 131, 167
—— prepares his house to receive, viii. 72, 84, ix. 431
—— promises Linton to, viii. 170
—— receives Burke's speech through, ix. 31
—— receives hopeful accounts from, of wife, viii. 281
—— receives regular accounts from, of House of Commons, ix. 475
—— regrets departure of, from Florence, ix. 523
—— rejects promise by, that he would never accept Linton during the former's lifetime, viii. 259
—— relieved to find that Linton will be secured to, viii. 166
—— resembled by, v. 409, viii. 423
——'s affection for, prompts him to break Linton entail, viii. 271
—— said by, to have been cheated out of snuff-box from Catherine II, ix. 84
——'s apology to Murray to be conveyed by, from HW, ix. 358
——'s appearance will be described by, ix. 523
——'s body to be sent to Linton by, ix. 665
——'s correspondence from, will be interrupted by Parliament attendance, viii. 425
——'s correspondence with, vi. 228, 476, vii. 354, 407, 408, 410, 414, viii. 64, 68, 129, 163, 172, 220, 239, 246-7, 251, 265, 281, 344, 389, 396, 425, 457, 458, 477, 505, 509, 512, 513, 517, 530, ix. 10, 57, 64, 76, 226, 239, 241, 248, 255, 268, 290, 302, 395, 421, 547-8, 550, 551, 560, 569, 635
——'s devotion from, ix. 610, 659

[Mann, Sir Horace (1744–1814), *continued*]

—— sends a servant to, at Leghorn, viii. 94

—— sends Newenham's letter through, to C.J. Fox, ix. 443

—— sends print of Old Pretender's marriage through, ix. 448

——'s esteem for, equal to Mann's affection for Galfridus Mann, viii. 167

——'s furniture and plate to be sold by, ix. 669, 678

——'s great confidence in, viii. 259

——'s health alarms, ix. 546–7

——'s health will be described by, to HW, ix. 621

—— should be able to control, in Florence, v. 420

—— should have been told by, about activity in Parliament, viii. 542

—— should not cede his estate to, viii. 249

—— shudders at danger of, viii. 541

——'s illness detains, at Florence, ix. 607

——'s letter to HW brought by, viii. 446, ix. 203, 370, 521, 524, 540

——'s liking for, should bring him to England, viii. 155

—— soon to be revisited by, at Florence, viii. 490

—— sorry that HW does not see, more often, viii. 477

——'s physician reassures, ix. 607

——'s poor health hastens departure of, to Italy, ix. 547

——'s respects to be conveyed by, to D. of Gloucester, through Col. Heywood, viii. 163

——'s servant conveys to, a letter to HW, viii. 446

——'s servants forbidden by, to attend amusements, ix. 670

——'s servants made by, to form fund for families' benefit, ix. 666, 669–70

——'s servants retained by, ix. 667

——'s servant writes letter to, ix. 570

——'s uneasiness about returning to England witnessed by, viii. 182

—— supposes, is now in England, viii. 418

—— suspects, may be coming to Italy, against his advice, ix. 319

—— tells: not to return to Florence until he can bring his family, viii. 170; to pay respects to D. and Ds of Gloucester at Rome, viii. 131; to write often to HW, ix. 664

—— to be visited by: in a year, vi. 56; in spring, viii. 78, 79; until winter drives him to Nice, viii. 312

—— to consult, before answering Foote's questions about Linton, viii. 169

—— to cut off Linton entail to help daughters of, viii. 225, 240, 257

—— to disguise his unwillingness to entertain, viii. 68

—— told by, before death that his remains would be taken to England, ix. 668

—— to receive news of Murray's court martial through, ix. 373

—— to tell, to placate Edward Louisa Mann, viii. 37

—— urged by: to accompany them to Rome and Naples, viii. 129; to go with him to Naples, viii. 131–2

—— walks with, in garden by moonlight before supper, viii. 517

—— wants, to be educated in Florence, v. 41

—— wants baronetcy chiefly for the benefit of, iv. 462

—— will be well advised by, from England, viii. 176

—— will have heard all the news from, ix. 502

—— will hear from, about common debates in Parliament, ix. 97

—— will hear more details from, than from HW, viii. 497

—— will soon be visited by, ix. 482

—— will tell: HW's feelings about law suit with E. of Orford, viii. 84; of Orford's suit with creditors, viii. 246

—— wishes: were at House of Commons, viii. 146; would consult HW on political matters, ix. 291

—— withholds news of his ill health from, ix. 659

—— writes to, of Tylney's death, ix. 533

Mann, Edward Louisa, breaks promises to, viii. 181, 276

—— cannot be depended upon by, viii. 131

—— corresponds with, vii. 346, 366, 379

—— deprived by, of financial guardianship, viii. 36–7

—— does not mention, in will, viii. 160

—— does not notify, of chance to be Mann's proxy, vii. 366

—— excludes: from James Mann's bedchamber, viii. 271–2; from will and induces James Mann to do so, viii. 225

—— flattered by marriage prospects of, vi. 242

—— hints about, v. 129

—— may be glad of an excuse to disinherit, vii. 76, 80

—— may merely have sought to alarm, vi. 576, vii. 76, viii. 155, 172

—— might have left Linton to, viii. 259

—— no longer complains about, vii. 172, 506

—— objects to expense of knighthood for, vii. 390

—— predicts future of, v. 142

—— prefers Sir William Boothby to, as proxy, vii. 371, 385, 389–90

—— probably has not left anything to, viii. 154

—— refuses permission to, to live at Linton, viii. 169–70

—— reports misconduct of, vi. 563, vii. 172, 506, viii. 36

—— sees, and sends him to HW, vii. 408

—— to consider, as son, vii. 113

—— to manage affairs of, to repay loans, vi. 576

—— to press, for decision, vii. 364

—— urged Mann to consider welfare of, and said he would do the same, viii. 271

—— worries, by asserting right to will Linton estate, viii. 146

Mann, James, should have left money to, vi. 241

—— should inherit estate of, if he dies childless, v. 61

Mann, James II, accompanies, to Florence, ix. 580

Mann family should have considered, as their chief heir, viii. 258

marriage of: vi. 242, 300; considered too expensive by uncle, viii. 304–5; not announced to uncle, vii. 354; planned, vi. 196; uncles approve of, vi. 245–6

Marsham a friend of, ix. 490

—— more prudent than, ix. 290

Marsham family's treatment of, makes him leave Parliament, ix. 465

Mediterranean voyage for wife recommended to, viii. 203

Merry's reasons for retirement to Florence are known to, ix. 522

Milan visited by, viii. 129

Montpellier visited by, viii. 246–7

Montrose, D. and Ds of, friends of, ix. 562

Montroses pitied by, ix. 677

mother benefits, by accepting jointure, v. 41

mother's temper not inherited by, v. 129

Murray could be told by, of Mann's sympathy, ix. 349

—— to be called on by, to satisfy him about Mann's letters, ix. 370–1

Mysterious Mother read by, on journey, viii. 517

Mysterious Mother sent through, to Mann, viii. 470

Naples visited by, viii. 131, 163, 181, 188, 225

neither ill nor on his way to Florence, ix. 319

Newenham's letter delivered by, to C.J. Fox, ix. 456

newspapers say, is ruining himself at cricket, vii. 495

Nice visited by, viii. 64, 77–8, 79, 82, 84, 247, 251, 281, 286, 305–6, 312, 337, 344, 346, 353, 369, 381, 530, ix. 431, 551

Noel, Mrs, source of information about, ix. 187, 200–1, 208, 210, 312, 319, 448

offer of resignation printed by, for circulation, viii. 275

opposition expected by, at next election, ix. 291

optimism of, about England's future, viii. 518

Orford, E. of, resists paying father's debts to, ix. 148, 155, 158

——'s bond turned over by, to Hull, viii. 78

—— sued by, viii. 82, 84

Ostend visited by, viii. 517

out of town, viii. 532–3, ix. 350, 354, 482

Parliamentary inquiry perhaps to be moved by, ix. 222–3, 234, 251

Parliamentary reelection of, ix. 86

Parliamentary representation reform opposed by, ix. 399, 404

Parliamentary seat may be resigned by, viii. 275, ix. 461

Parliamentary speech of: badly reported in *Public Advertiser,* viii. 450, 451–2; condemned by Mann, viii. 457

Parliament attendance impossible for, ix. 367

Parliament entered by, viii. 54

Parliament entered by, under illusions, viii. 518, ix. 560

Parliament faithfully attended by, viii. 477

Parliament's renunciation by: caused by rift with Romney family, ix. 465; leaves him free to follow his own inclinations, ix. 523; pleases him, ix. 505, 560

Perpignan visited by, viii. 246

Pisa's festivities to be seen by, ix. 581

Pitt does not answer letters of, ix. 678

——'s reform motion would have been opposed by, in Parliament, ix. 404

Pitt, Mrs William Augustus, writes about, ix. 320

political rôle of, an active one, ix. 45

portmanteau not yet unpacked by, ix. 417

Poussin paintings taken by, from their frames, to send to HW, ix. 668

Powys, a near relative of, may make him imprudent, viii. 429

prudence acquired by, viii. 423, 429

punctuality and 'flying,' two qualities of, ix. 208

rapid travelling of, ix. 399, 417, 629

remarriage might be considered by, viii. 358, 379, 523, 530

remarriage of, unlikely, ix. 592

Rome visited by, viii. 131, 140, 144–5, 146, 163, 181, ix. 673–5

rumoured lost on packet-boat, ix. 210

Rutlandshire visited by, from Kent, ix. 222

salary quarrel of, with secretary of state's office, ix. 671–3, 674, 675–6, 678

Schio visited by, viii. 122

servants of, to be lodged by (?) Rinuccini, viii. 72

Shelburne praises Mann to, ix. 271

sons cannot be expected by, in lifetime of present wife, viii. 257

[Mann, Sir Horace (1744–1814), *continued*]
southern France visited by, viii. 60
SH may be visited by, to see HW, ix. 154,
659
to return to England before Parliament
meets, ix. 200
Toulouse visited by, viii. 239, 251
Turin to be visited by, viii. 129
uncles fear, will become a fine gentleman,
v. 409
'unconnected' Member of Parliament, ix.
223
Valdagno journey of, prolonged by heat,
viii. 118
Van Dyck's alleged painting sent to: in
case of books left unopened in his London
house, ix. 504; to be sent to E. of Orford,
ix. 501
Vienna and Germany to be visited by, viii.
374
votes with the Court, viii. 455
Walpole, Sir Robert, disparaged by, vii. 340
Westminster election interests, ix. 505
wife believed by, to be in less danger, viii.
191
wife may embark with, viii. 203, 214, 220
wife of, vii. 101n
wife's death leaves, incapable of writing,
viii. 356
wife's death should be a relief to, viii. 358
wife's health considered better by, viii. 275
wife's health thought by, to have gained
much at Nice, viii. 286
wife's illness depresses, viii. 203, 353
wife's illness might be caught by, viii. 190,
199
wife's illness prevents, from seeing about
his and Mann's affairs, viii. 188
wife's loss felt by, as guardian to daughter,
ix. 405
wife's poor health compels, to take her out
of England, viii. 77
wife still mourned by, though her name is
never mentioned, viii. 523
wife to be brought by, to dine with HW at
SH, vii. 408
wife to be overtaken by, at Marseille, and
taken to Nice, viii. 265
winds detain, at Nice, ix. 404
York races might be visited by, ix. 373
Zoffany's picture of Mann declared by, to
be a good likeness, viii. 529
Mann, James (d. 1764), brother of Horace
Mann:
business absorbs, v. 158
Covent Garden playhouse mob engulfs, in
attempt to see Karl Wilhelm Ferdinand, vi.
199
Cumberland, D. of, favours, v. 50
death of, vi. 225–6
estate of, larger than expected, vi. 226,
viii. 225–6

Foote family unduly benefited by will of,
viii. 225, 257
Fox's vases and Hertford's liqueurs to be
procured by, on arrival, v. 139
George III's accession must make, too busy
to write, vi. 464
'good creature,' vi. 25
HW called on by: at Arlington St, v. 418;
at SH, iv. 456
HW calls on, to ask about Edward Louisa
Mann's commission for picture for Royston,
v. 540
HW consults, about payment to Sisson, v.
384
HW contrasts Galfridus Mann with, vi. 133
HW does not rebuke, vi. 49
HW fears that death of, will upset Mann,
vi. 237
HW finds, as uncommunicative as Mann
does, vi. 196
HW gives bills of lading to, v. 538
HW had better give bill of lading to, v.
164
HW happy that Mann is relieved about, vi.
147
HW hopes to aid, v. 79
HW scolds, for not writing to Mann, v.
384, vi. 42, 133, 144
HW sees, iv. 523
HW sends books to Mann by means of, v.
120, 125, 214, 289, 339, 472
HW sends fans through, to Mann, v. 462,
472
HW sends to, on false news of brother's
death, v. 555
HW's financial transactions with, on Mann's
account, v. 293, 348, 414, 491, 525, vi. 9,
25, 35
HW talks with, about nephew, v. 409
HW to be told by: of Royston's commission
to Mann to get paintings, v. 532; of ship's
departure, v. 554
HW to instruct, to treat with Sisson, v. 414
Handelians better known to, than to HW,
vi. 49
Handel's oratorios to be selected by order
of, for Mann, vi. 49
health of, flux, vi. 219, 227–8, 231
Hertford's drams puzzle, v. 156
(?) Houghton visited by, iii. 510
Linton entailed upon, vii. 51, 112
lives in the wrong world to collect information, v. 178
Mann asks HW to investigate silence of,
vi. 124–5
—— asks HW to send pamphlets and
prints through, v. 90
—— does not trust, to answer question
about Sisson, v. 414
—— does not want HW to scold, vi. 50
—— fears, does not want to be bothered
with commissions, vi. 20
—— has not heard from: for four posts,

v. 158; for several mails, v. 168; for six months, but writes to him by every post, v. 380; more than twice a year, v. 35; since brother's death, v. 41, 42, 49–50; since last November, vi. 122–3, 124–5, 133
—— hears from, about niece's health, v. 503
—— hopes, has sent separate bill of lading for Santini's watch, v. 322
—— neglected by will of, v. 226, 235, viii. 167, 170, 266
—— receives promises of amendment from, vi. 41, 141–2, 144
—— receives remittances from, vi. 41
—— recommends, to HW, v. 72
——'s affairs to be managed by, v. 41, 47
——'s correspondence with, v. 41, 60, 72, 107, 418–19, vi. 35, 41, 133, 141–2, 144, 147
——'s intention to stay in Italy misinterpreted by, v. 175
——'s music to be forwarded by, vi. 73
——'s relations with, vi. 231, 234
——'s shipments of wine to Fox go through, v. 156
—— to leave bijoux to, ii. 93
—— to receive particulars from, about machine, v. 418–19
—— will probably be content with, vi. 133
Mann, Edward Louisa, does not surprise HW by his misconduct at deathbed of, viii. 276
—— induces, to exclude Horace Mann II and leave money to the Footes, viii. 225–6
Mann, Galfridus, better placed than, to collect information, v. 178
—— makes, his executor, v. 34
——'s delicacy of friendship not shared by, vi. 25
—— seen weekly by, iv. 523
——'s estate keeps, busy, v. 72
——'s kindness to, v. 33
Mann, Horace II, excluded from bedchamber of, though on good terms with him, viii. 271–2
——'s estate should be inherited by, v. 61
——'s marriage plans reported by, to HW, vi. 196
—— will tell HW about deathbed scene of, viii. 271
money not remitted by, vi. 125
payment to be the only function of, in executing Mann's commissions, vi. 25
regimental clothier, v. 50n
'very weak,' viii. 266
'very worthy man,' v. 35
watch received by, for shipment to Mann, v. 313
wealth and bequests of, vi. 226
will of: Footes benefited by, vi. 234, viii. 225, 271; Mann slighted by, vi. 226, 235, viii. 167, 170, 266; Mann, Edward Louisa, dictated and drew up, vi. 240–1, viii. 225, 271; Mann, Edward Louisa, regrets Footes'

large share in, viii. 226, 271–2; Torriano's caveat against, vi. 240, 241, 242, 245, 247, viii. 271
Mann, James II (b. ca 1761), illegitimate son of Edward Louisa Mann:
about three years old, vi. 247
arrived in England, ix. 635
Bentley's bond might have gone to, viii. 277
Borromean Islands to be visited by, ix. 586
china may be taken by, to HW, ix. 598
Coxheath visited by, ix. 320
Croft increases fortune of, ix. 580–1
—— praises, to HW, ix. 595
Damer, Mrs, escorted by, at Florence, ix. 627
delicate and has ugly swelling at throat, vii. 100
father may disinherit nephew to aid, vii. 76, 80, viii. 154–5
father may try to legitimate, vi. 242
father's bequest to, viii. 160, 168
father's fondness for, alarms uncle, vi. 568
father to provide for, vi. **240**
friend fails to join, at Nice, for Italian tour, ix. 580
HW admires behaviour of, ix. 615
HW condoles with Mann for losing, ix. 629
HW does not know, ix. 583
HW expects soon to hear of marriage of, ix. 649
HW grieved that Mann is losing, ix. 624
HW hopes for arrival of, ix. 635
HW praises, for staying with Mann, ix. 618
HW thinks, has died, vi. 242
HW would never attack, to get back his father's money, viii. 286
Lombardy to be toured by, before returning to Florence, ix. 598
Mann, Horace II, brings, to Florence to meet Mann, ix. 580
Mann, Lucy, to wed, ix. 580
marriage of: ix. 655; HW approves of, ix. 582–3; HW's approval of, pleases father-in-law and Mann, ix. 592
Rome and Naples to be visited by, instead of seeing Battle of the Bridge at Pisa, ix. 581
Rome visited by, ix. 586, 592
said to be sickly, viii. 159
Mann, John; Mann's grandfather:
(?) death of, while Mann is at Paris, ix. 2
estate lost by, iv. 78
Mann, John (?1707–1778), Clerk of the Rates in the Customs:
death of, viii. 358
HW and Sir Edward Walpole employ, in Customs House, viii. 358
Mann never heard of, viii. 368
Mann, Robert, probably recommended, viii. 358
Sims to succeed, viii. 368

Mann, Lucy (ca 1766–1816), m. (1786) James Mann II:

consumption might be caught by, from mother, viii. 189, 199, 206

father fears unfortunate attachment by, ix. 268, 405, 414, 421, 423, 431

father hurries home to, viii. 530

father joins, in Kent, ix. 539

father leaves, happy, ix. 662

father's only child, vii. 101

father visits, in country, ix. 229

father will come to London for the sake of, ix. 363

HW would not have advised Mann to break Linton entail for sake of, viii. 266

late passion of, an obstacle to an ambitious marriage, ix. 580

living in 1772, vii. 408

lover of: is from insane family, ix. 423–4; obliged by his father to cease his courtship, ix. 448; see also Marsham, Rev. Hon. Jacob

Mann must leave his money to, viii. 225

—— wishes to secure Linton to, viii. 240, 257, 266

marriage of: ix. 655; HW approves of, ix. 582–3; HW's approval of, pleases her father and Mann, ix. 592; to take place, ix. 580

mother's attention absorbed by, viii. 97, 105

mother's violent cough revealed by, viii. 346

prospective mother-in-law of, seen by HW 'in her moods,' ix. 424

Romney family's attitude in affair of, impels father to leave Parliament, ix. 465

spirits of, good, ix. 448

Mann, Lady Lucy. See Noel, Lady Lucy (d. 1778)

Mann, Mary (ca. 1718–78), m. (ca 1744) Benjamin Hatley Foote:

(?) Amorevoli wants introduction to, i. 101

(?) Arrigoni 'master' of, ii. 12

father saves portion for, ii. 308

HW admires singing of, i. 166, vi. 304

HW praises, vi. 304, viii. 155, 266

HW sees: at Linton, v. 129; at Cts of Ailesbury's concert, vi. 506; at opera with Cts of Ailesbury, vi. 304

husband of, viii. 205n

in love, ii. 367

Linton entailed upon, vii. 51, 112

London visited by, for opera, i. 359

Mann may offend, by breaking Linton entail, viii. 257

—— should be impatient to see, viii. 160

—— to leave bijoux to, ii. 93

Mann, Edward Louisa, establishes, at Linton, v. 129

Mann, James, makes, residuary legatee, vi. 226, 234, 240–1, viii. 225–6, 257, 271

marriage of, planned, ii. 354, 366–7

marriage probably preferred by, to life with father, ii. 354

musical accomplishments of, i. 166, 359, iii. 316, vi. 304

nieces and their husbands summoned by, for reading of brother's will, viii. 158–9

settles in London, vi. 304

sings, i. 359

sons of, to inherit Galfridus Mann's estate after Horace Mann II, viii. 225, 257

Walpole, Lady Mary, visited by, at Richmond, i. 359

Westmorland friend of, vi. 72

Westmorland, Cts of, friend of, viii. 401

—— visits, vi. 72

Mann, Mary (d. 1815–1818), illegitimate daughter of Edward Louisa Mann, m. (1789) Christopher Nevile:

Bentley's bond might have gone to, viii. 277

Coxheath visited by, ix. 320

Croft may want to marry one of his relatives to, viii. 159

—— urges father to make liberal provision for, viii. 159

father leaves Sussex estate to, viii. 168, 173, 176

father may disinherit nephew to aid, vii. 76, 80, viii. 154–5

father may try to get fortune for, at expense of other heirs, vii. 101

father saddles Linton with annuity to, viii. 160, 168, 176

father's bequest to, viii. 160, 168

father's fondness for, alarms uncle, vi. 568

fathers' letter transcribed by, vii. 408

father to provide for, vi. **240**

father tries to marry his nephew to, vii. 100–1, 112

HW calls, 'infanta,' vi. 247

HW hears, is great favourite, vi. 242

HW would never attack, to get back her father's money, viii. 286

Tortola lands mistakenly left to, viii. 168, 202, 219–20, 264

Mann, Robert (d. 1752), of Linton, Kent; Horace Mann's father:

avaricious, ii. 326

Chute and HW sure that estate of, is entailed, ix. 101

Cicero bust to be sent to, by Mann, iv. 86

copy of pedigree wished by, iv. 205

Customs place granted to, x. 52–3

daughter of, i. 166n

daughter probably married to escape from, ii. 354

daughters' portions saved by, ii. 308

Day partner of, i. 49, viii. 183

—— persuades, to add Mann's portion to that of Galfridus Mann, viii. 183

——'s treachery later known to, viii. 183

death of, iv. 302n

dying, but wants roast beef, iv. 301

English public losses usually shared by, iii. 405

HW and Horatio Walpole (1678–1757) 'bait,' to aid Mann, ii. 308

HW outraged by letter of, to Mann, ii. 326

HW praises Mann's letter to, ii. 140, 152
HW talks with, ii. 244–5
HW will not provoke anger of, against Mann, iv. 138
health of: bad, ii. 308; recovered, ii. 189
intemperance the failing of, iv. 301
law suit of, over estate, ii. 307–8
Mann abused by, to Galfridus Mann, ii. 190
—— borrows from, ii. 17, 517
—— curious about ancestry of, iv. 78
—— fears that HW's severity may enrage, ii. 273
—— has few expectations from, ii. 517
—— indifferent about entail of estate of, vii. 112
—— receives disquieting hints from, iv. 129
—— says that he will bequeath his debts to, ii. 93
——'s correspondence with, ii. 120, 140, 152, 189–90, 244–5, 307–8, 326, 338, 553
——'s financial relations with, i. 27, ii. 17, 152, 190, 307–8, 517, iv. 307
——'s letter enrages, ii. 189–90
—— the second son of, ii. 332
—— to be left a miserable pension by, ii. 152
Mann, John, probably recommended by, for Customs House post, viii. 358
'old cross man', ii. 332
paternal tyranny of, ii. 120
Pelham's retirement from paymastership may injure, ii. 313
——'s successor not likely to dismiss, ii. 326
position lost by, ii. 479, 496
position may be lost by, ii. 307, 326
Richecourt says, will be demolished for shady conduct, ii. 67
sons on bad terms with, ii. 273
Sussex estate bought by, and assigned to Edward Louisa Mann, viii. 168, 173, 176
temper of, will grow worse, ii. 479
Torriano's quarrel with, vi. 245
Walpole, Sir Robert, called on by, ii. 244
—— may intercede with, i. 27
will of: bequests to sons in, ix. 301–2, 306–8, v. 61; declared invalid by Edward Louisa Mann, viii. 146; Mann's letter from Edward Louisa Mann about, iv. 306–8, vii. 51, 71, 79, 112, 129, viii. 147, 154, 165; Mann, Galfridus, ordered by, to pay annuity to Mann in case of Mann's retirement from Florence, iv. 301–2, 307, v. 61, vii. 51, 112, viii. 167, 172–3, 183–4; Mann, Galfridus, writes about, vi. 564, vii. 51, 129; said to have entailed Linton, vi. 564, 576, vii. 76; son-in-law may have been influenced by, iv. 308; Torriano family omitted from, vii. 51, 112; will probably not be changed in Mann's favour, iv. 129
Winnington dismisses, ii. 479
——'s dismissal of, violates promise to Sir Robert Walpole, ii. 496–7

Mann, Robert jr (d. 1755):
death of, contributed to Mann's fortune, viii. 183
Linton estate entailed upon, vii. 51, 112
Mann to leave bijoux to, ii. **93**
Mann, Mrs Robert. See Guise, Eleanor
Mann, Sarah (1740–61):
Bath visited by, for health, v. 503
death of, from consumption, v. 499, 503
father's legacy to, v. 34
father's resemblance to, makes her his favourite, v. 499
Mann estate should not be entailed upon, v. 61
mother benefits, by accepting jointure, v. 41
obstacle to parents' separation, v. **29**
Mann, Sarah (d. 1775), illegitimate daughter of Edward Louisa Mann, m. Charles Rivington:
death of, viii. 101
father may disinherit nephew to aid, vii. 76, 80
father's fondness for, alarms uncle, vi. 568
father to provide for, vi. **240**
Mann, Thomas (d. 1741):
death of, i. 49
HW knew, at Eton, i. 49
Mann family:
coat of arms of, ii. 184, iv. 482, 487
estates of, in Tortola, see under Tortola
fortunes of, involved in those of E. of Orford, vii. 496
Gainsborough family's relation with, vi. 242
HW had hoped to repay, by restoring E. of Orford's finances, vii. 549
Linton the seat of, viii. 154n
Mann's neglect from, regretted by HW, viii. 176
—— wants to know more about history of, iv. 78
name of, less impressive than that of Guise family, iv. 415–16
Orford, E. of, would please HW by paying debts to, ix. 148
pedigree of, iv. 13, 31, 64–5, 77–8, 88, 96, 129, 138, 150, 166–7, 180, 193, 194, 197, 205
pew of, in Linton church, v. 250
Richecourt disparages, iv. 64n
Walpole, Sir Robert, owed the gratitude of, despite his and his son's unpaid debts, viii. 292
Walpole family always revered by, vii. 353
Walpole family's goodness to, i. 348
Walpole family should always be treated by, with delicacy, viii. 78
Mannelli, Ottavio Francesco (1710–67):
Grifoni, Signora, abandoned by, iii. 358
—— attended by, ii. 65
—— awaited by, i. 202, 218
—— has, as cicisbeo, iii. 308n
marriage of, iii. 308

[Mannelli, Ottavia Francesco, *continued*]
Pandolfini's correspondence with, iii. 369
Pecori's rupture with the Parigi arranged by, i. **111**

Manners, Lady Catherine (ca 1701–80), **m.** (1726) Henry Pelham:
brag to be played by, out of town to avoid earthquake, iv. 137
brother of, iv. 183
death of, ix. 20
Esher not visited by, after sons' deaths, i. **398n**
Greenwich Hospital post might be given to, x. 10
(?) HW mentions, iv. 441
matrons consulted by, about daughter's lost earrings, iv. 114
miscarriage of, i. 398
Newcastle, Ds of, accuses, of making Pelham conceal Greenwich Park affair, x. 10
Nugent talks with, at masquerade, iv. 124
son born to, could disinherit Lincoln, ii. 245
Walpole, Horatio (1678–1757), wants orange flower water for, iii. 330
Wilmot saves, by lancing, v. 369

Manners, Charles, (1754–87), styled Lord Roos 1760–70 and M. of Granby 1770–9; 4th **D.** of Rutland, 1779; M.P.:
brother of, ix. 278
marriage of, viii. 54n, **120**–1, 148

Manners, Lady Frances (d. 1769), m. (1732) Hon. Richard Arundell:
brag to be played by, out of town to avoid earthquake, iv. 137

Manners, John (1696–1779), 3d D. of Rutland:
becomes Master of the Horse so that Talbot may become Lord Steward, v. 489
daughter of, v. 362, viii. 463n
death of, viii. 482
Frederick P. of Wales, has, in his suite, iv. 183
grandson of, viii. 120n
health of, voids stones, iv. 418
Hertford succeeds, as Master of the Horse, vi. 450
Knight of the Garter for over fifty years, viii. 482
Mastership of the Horse may go to, iv. 183
mistress of, viii. 15
Privy Seal promised to, iv. 418
regiment raised by, iii. 128
resignation of, expected, v. 98
sister of, i. 184n, 398n, iv. 114n, 183, ix. 20n
son's Irish post will please, vi. 131
son's marriage may be stopped by, because of dowry difficulties, iv. 91, 183
to be Master of the Horse, iv. 470

Manners, John (1721–70), styled M. of Granby:
anxiety over military campaign of, v. 316
army command and ordnance post resigned

by, reserving only regiment of Blues, vii. 174–5
becomes commander-in-chief, vi. 449
character of, shrinks from vacillations, vii. 168
commended for conduct in German battle, vi. 47
Constable a friend of, vii. 244
Conway succeeds: as Col. of the Blues, vii. 246; as Master of the Ordnance, vii. 179; in command of army in Germany, v. 554
death of, deprives Pitt of support, vii. 246
dismissal of officers for Parliamentary conduct opposed by, vi. 274
Ewer proposed by, for Armagh archbishopric, vi. 275–6
—— tutor to, vi. 275
expected from Germany, vi. 104
Ferdinand said to have been directed by, v. 314–15
generosity and hard drinking of, vi. 131n
honours offered to, vi. 104
Irish post to go to, vi. 131
Le Fevre's testimonials sent to, vii. 244
London mob's hero, v. 315
ministers no longer propose, as captain-general, vi. 302
minority joined by, in House of Commons, vii. 168
Ordnance resigned by, vii. 179
political failure of, vii. 216
resignation of: rumoured, vii. 170; weakens Court party, vii. 182
Seymour, Lady Frances, to wed, iv. 91, 183
Soubise cannonades army of, vi. 86
successful in skirmishes, v. 549
wife of, iv. 10n
Winchilsea tries to tie up wife's dowry from, iv. 183

Manners, Lady Lucy (ca 1717–88), m. (1742) William Graham, 2d E. Graham, 1731; 2d D. of Montrose, 1742:
HW and Horace Mann II friends of, ix. 562
HW and Horace Mann II meet at house of, viii. 463
HW learns news of Horace Mann II at house of, ix. 320
HW often sees Mrs Graeme at house of, ix. 595
health of, paralytic, ix. 562n, 604n
house of, Twickenham Park, ix. 187
maid from Richmond wants to stay in town to see, v. 535
Mann, Horace II, pities, ix. 677
Mann, Lady Lucy, related to, viii. 463n
mother tells, to put down gossip to fill country letters, ii. 129–30
Noel, Mrs, a constant visitor at house of, ix. 187
—— to come to town with, ix. 208
Robinson entertains, i. **184**
son's marriage alleviates miseries of, ix. 562, 604

Manners, Lady Rachel (d. 1740):
  death of, v. 362
Manners, Lord Robert (ca 1717–82), M.P.:
  death of, after naval battle in West Indies,
  ix. 278, 281, 282
  distinguished at Tuscan court because of
  beauty of sister-in-law, Ds of Rutland, ix.
  282
  poem on, Mann sends, to HW, ix. 636
Manners, Lord William (1697–1772); M.P.:
  best known in groom-porter's annals, iv. 418
  Gower's dismissal demanded by, iv. 418
Manners. See under Whitehead, Paul
Manners. See Etiquette
Manners family:
  Newcastle intimidated by, into substituting
  Rutland for Gower, iv. 418
Mannetti. See Manetti
Mannheim:
  Charles Albert's letter from, i. 352
Manningtree, Essex:
  Mistley near, iii. 494n
Mannito, Bp of. See Attems, Karl Michael,
  Graf von
Man of Taste. See under Bramston
Man-of-war; men-of-war:
  at Leghorn, ii. 145, v. 197
  bills of lading not given by captains of, ii.
  234
  Choiseul might have forced Holland to
  give, for attack on England, vii. 269
  commanders of, should insure merchant
  ships under their protection, v. 415
  Conway not taken by, to Leghorn, iv. 280
  Dutch: Feilding brings, to Plymouth, ix.
  3–4; to be in small squadrons, v. 269; unmolested by British officer, ix. 222
  England's, unequipped, viii. 392
  English: at Leghorn, prefer preying on
  enemy's ships to protecting their own, v.
  524; captures Pope's vessel, i. 8, 16; chased
  into Plymouth by French and Spanish fleet,
  viii. 506; Feilding chases Dutch with, ix. 3;
  in the Downs, iii. 103; Leghorn reached by,
  from Gibraltar, vi. 12; Mathews refuses to
  take, to Giogo, ii. 296; said to be conveying French troops from Dunkirk to Sweden,
  vii. 466; seize English ships carrying Tuscan
  flag, v. 269–70, 273–4; ship convoyed by,
  from Leghorn to Gibraltar, v. 132; stop
  French Levant trade, v. 282
  English capture, from Calais to California,
  iv. 500
  French: at Villafranca, v. 264; Boscawen
  captures, v. 511; pursued in Mediterranean
  by English fleet, v. 249
  French assemble, at Dunkirk, iii. 103
  from Leghorn to England, lacking, ii. 106
  from Plymouth, to join Norris, ii. 393
  gun barrels to be transported by, ii. 325,
  329
  HW wants eagle sent by, iii. 210, 230
  hurricane destroys whole crews of, ix. 109

  Keppel captain of, iv. 459n
  lost, with officers and men, in attack on
  Charleston, viii. 236
  Mann prefers not to ship eagle by, iii. 216
  —— to have eagle shipped on, iii. 220
  —— to ship HW's eagle in, iii. 122, 246
  Martinique fleet convoyed by, iii. 186
  Moore sends, to intercept Dutch convoy,
  vi. 71
  Rowley sends, to England, iii. 110
  Russian, will cause Turks to murder Christians if they threaten Smyrna, vii. 235
  Spanish: captured, i. 175; English take
  escaped English vessel from, near Gibraltar,
  viii. 306–7; off Gorgona, i. 182
  spoil brought by, from St Eustatius, ix. 152
  statue may not travel on, ii. 178
  Turkish, Russians pursue, vii. 235
  two, England loses, ix. 326
  unsuitable to convey art objects, iii. 13, 246
  Walpole, Sir Robert, wants Domenichino
  painting shipped by, ii. 79, 89, 123, 144
  See also Ship of the line; Ship of war
Mansell, Thomas (1719–44), 2d Bn Mansell:
  Clephane accompanies, i. 63, 70
  testoons named testicles, by, i. 4
Mansfeld und Fondi, Heinrich Franz (1712–
  after 1780), Fürst von; Bavarian minister at
  Rome:
  Old Pretender called on by, i. 445
Mansfield, Bn. See Murray, Hon. William
  (1705–93)
Mansfield, E. of. See Murray, David (1727–96);
  Murray, Hon. William (1705–93)
Mansfield, Lord Chief Justice. See Murray,
  Hon. William
Mansfield, James (1734–1821), Kt, 1804; M.P.;
  barrister:
  counsel for Ds of Kingston, viii. 192–3, 196
Mansion House:
  Lord Mayor's dinner at, vii. 200
Mantilla:
  Mann wins, at lottery for Mme Vitelli, ii.
  340, 351
Mantle:
  Charlotte's, of violet-coloured velvet, lined
  with ermine, v. 529
  Elijah's, viii. 455
  Leopold's, viii. 515
Mantua ('Mantova'):
  Anson's victory reported in letters to, iii.
  415
  artillery goes to Modena from, i. 464
  Brown awaits artillery from, iii. 236
  ——'s troops arrive at, iii. 220
  couriers from, prevented from reaching
  Florence, iii. 156
  duke of, might be defied by Venice, iv. 409
  gazette of, see Gazzetta di Mantova
  German troops reach Italy through, iii. 267
  HW's letter comes by way of, iii. 348
  Jews of, buy Francis III's furniture, ii. 323

[Mantua, continued]
Joseph II to receive Ferdinand I and Maria Carolina at, ix. 586
Leopold to go to, ix. 586
lies from, i. 417
Lobkowitz to garrison, ii. 513
Mann inquires about postal delays at, ii. 233
—— sends Giuseppe to, with letters, iii. 99
post to Florence may come by way of, iii. 190
Te Deum sung in, for Daun's defeat, v. 463
visitors to: Ferdinand, vii. 446–7; Huntingdon, vii. 446–7, 452; Joseph II, vii. 137, 140; Maria Carolina, vii. 17; Maria Ricciarda Beatrice, vii. 446–7; Paoli, vii. 137, 140; Parma, D. of, vii. 17
Mantua Gazette. See Gazzetta di Mantova
Mantua-maker; mantua-makers:
fashions invented by, ix. 541
George III's coronation will be food for, v. 513
Manufacturers:
English: should not let the country gentlemen turn them against America, viii. 132; Wall probably tries to lure, into Spanish service, iv. 170–1
Manure:
Germans no good as, in England, v. 5
Manuscripts:
export of, from Tuscany, forbidden, iv. 465
Manvers, E. of. *See* Medows (later Pierrepont), Charles (1737–1816)
Manzoli. *See* Manzuoli
Manzuoli, Giovanni ('Panone'); lemonade vendor:
coffee-house of, *see* Pannoni's
Manzuoli, Giovanni (ca 1725–after 1780); opera singer:
applause for, excessive, vi. 265
best singer in Italy, v. 128
Disfatta di Dario, La, has, in chief rôle, v. 128
Foote, Mrs, likes, vi. 304
HW hears, vi. 264, 265
Mann instrumental in sending, to England, vi. 273
—— recommends, to Ds of Grafton, vi. 273
mourning rules prevent Maria Louisa from hearing, vi. 340
second opera at great theatre to be improved by, vi. 477
York, D. of, hears, at Vct Fordwich's, vi. 223
Map; maps:
American: defective, iv. 497; HW cannot remember, viii. 98
Anville, J.-B. Bourguignon d', maker of, viii. 29
Brown, Sir Robert, makes, of London bylanes, ix. 609n
Conway asks Lloyd about, vii. 421–2

from England, Mann gives to Francis II, ix. 282
HW gives, to Sir William Hamilton for delivery to Mann, vii. 431
HW hopes to find positive directions about, from Mann, vii. 425
La Condamine walks London streets with, vi. 146
Mann wants, for Mormorai from England, vii. 411, 413, 418, 421–2, 427
of Rome and papal states, iv. 459
Popple's, iv. 497
size of, too small for good maps, vii. 421
Stosch's: bought by Frederick II, ix. 651; catalogue of, printed by Natter, v. 192; Valenti makes offer for, v. 186, 192
Mar, Cts of. *See* Pierrepont, Lady Frances (d. 1761)
Mar, E. of. *See* Erskine, John (1675–1732)
Mara, Mme. *See* Schmeling, Gertrud Elisabeth
Marátha state, in India:
European plunderers properly scourged by, viii. 516
Hornby's army captured by, viii. 509–10
Marattas. *See* Marátha
Maratti, Carlo (1625–1713), painter:
Cipriani's paintings to replace those by, at Houghton, ix. 316
Guise owns miniature by, ii. 162
Mengs deemed equal to, iv. 352
Orford, E. of, complained of having too many pictures by, ix. 418
paintings by: Arnaldi owns, i. 56, v. 208, 478–9; Frederick II buys, v. 479; HW buys, x. 7; Hoare rejects, as damaged, v. 479; sold at Furnese's auction, v. 172; with self-portrait and figure of Pallavicini, bought by Mann from Arnaldi for Hoare, v. 208, 478–9
Maratts. *See* Marátha
Marbeuf, Louis-Charles-René (1712–86), Comte de:
communication between Bastia and San Fiorenzo wished by, vii. 6
Jesuits may be admitted by, to Corsica, vi. 526–7
Jesuits permitted by, to visit shore in small groups, vi. 532
Paoli's ultimatum from, vii. 46
troops of, ordered out of Corsica to accommodate Jesuits, vi. 535–6
Marble:
black, Morpheus statue in, iii. 561
Damer, Mrs, begins bust in, ix. 184
dogs modelled in, ix. 576
fragment of, in Stosch's collection, v. 192
HW able to stamp on his hearth of, with gouty feet, viii. 71, 80
Hoare models Ganymede in, iv. 86
John the Baptist's head in, x. 56
Mann obtains, from Siena, iii. 423
pavement of, iv. 54
polished, HW mentions, iv. 427

statues in Florentine Tribune are of various shades of, viii. 527

urn of, for Galfridus Mann's memorial, v. 250

white, eagle and pedestal of, iii. 122

Marble Hill, Middlesex:
HW dines at, with Buckinghamshire, vii. 316

Suffolk, Cts of, said to have bequeathed, to E. of Buckinghamshire, vi. 544

Marc Antonio. See Antoniazzo

Marcel (d. 1759), dancing master:
(?) teaches dancing though helpless, iv. 444

March, E. of. See Douglas, William (1725–1810); Mortimer, Roger (?1287–1330)

March:
HW's reflections on weather of, ix. 562

Marchais, Bn de. See Binet, Gérard (ca 1711–80)

Marche, Comte de la. See Bourbon, Louis-François-Joseph de

Marche, Comtesse de la. See Fortunata Maria

'Marchesa, the little.' See Dini, Giovanna

Marchesi or Marchesini, Luigi Lodovico (1754–1829), male soprano:
Cholmondeley may hear, at Florence, ix. 426

England to be visited by, ix. 435

Mann praises, though many prefer Paccherotti, ix. 462

—— takes Morice to theatre at Florence to hear, ix. 435

Marchmont, E. of. See Hume-Campbell, Alexander (1675–1740); Hume-Campbell, Hugh (1708–94)

Marciana:
English outrages at, ii. 28, 47, 59, 195
Piombino, Ps of, owns, ii. 28

Marcinforte. See Manciforte

Marcolini, Contessa. See Ferretti di Castelferretti, Francesca

Marcus Agrippa. See under Agrippa

Marcus Antonius. See Antonius, Marcus

Mardi Gras:
ball after midnight on, i. 311
Florentine archbishop alters, to Mardi Maigre, iv. 219–20

Mare:
Loreto visit makes, pregnant, iv. 437

Maréchal de Belle-Isle, Le, French frigate:
Thurot's ship, v. 372, 376

Maréchaux de France:
Louis XV spurns plea of, then reconsiders, vii. 283–4
Maillebois sentenced by, vii. 283

Marefoschi, Mario (1714–80), cardinal, 1770:
(?) Jesuits opposed by, x. 49
villa of, at Macerata, used by Young Pretender and bride, vii. 406

Maremma, the, in Tuscany:
drainage projects for, viii. 343
Siena's air rendered unwholesome by, viii. 130

Margaret (ca 1282–1317) of France, m. (1299) Edward I of England:
Pomfrets descended from, iv. 180

Margaret (?1430–82), of Anjou, m. (1445) Henry VI, K. of England:
Augusta, Ps of Wales, compared with, vi. 53

Margaret (1480–1530) of Austria; m. 1 (1497) John, P. of Aragon; m. 2 (1501) Philibert, D. of Savoy; Governess of Holland, 1507:
father desires prayers of, ix. 468

Margate:
Morice's heavy luggage left at, ix. 88

Marguerite (1492–1549), of Valois, m. 1 (1509) Charles, D. of Alençon; m. 2 (1527) Henri d'Albret, K. of Navarre:
portrait of, said to be in Vyne chapel window, iv. 485n

Marguerite-Louise (1645–1721), m. (1661) Cosimo III, Grand Duke of Tuscany:
Galluzzi mentions, often, ix. 434
——'s account of, read by HW, ix. 214
prints of, sent to HW by Mann, ix. 434, 444, 473

Marguetel de St-Denis de St-Évremond, Charles de (1613–1703), writer; diplomatist:
HW quotes, ii. 498

Mari, Lorenzo, Doge of Genoa 1744–6:
(?) follies of, iii. 76

Mari, Stefano; commissary; governor of Bastia:
garrison led by, to Calvi, iii. 162

Mari, Marchese Stefano (d. 1748), Spanish ambassador to Venice; Vice-Adm.:
HW promises black spaniel to, at Genoa, ii. 293
house to be prepared by, for Don Philip, i. 389
Venice left by, to meet Don Philip, i. 226

Maria, Santa:
St Antonio faction opposed to, in Pisa, iv. 473, ix. 582

Maria I (1734–1816), m. (1760) Pedro III; Q. of Portugal 1777–1816:
Cumberland, D. of, mentioned as possible husband for, v. 341–2
Spain seizes island from, viii. 309–10
uncle attacks, without regard for her misfortunes, vi. 49, viii. 309–10
uncle's marriage to, v. 422

Maria Amalia (1724–60) of Saxony, m. (1738) Charles, K. of Naples; K. of Spain, 1759, as Charles III:
alarmed, i. 501, ii. 3
Albertini told by, to thank George II for promotion for Gray, v. 160
Capona abbess dines with, weekly, iv. 429
daughter born to, ii. 223, 478
death of, v. 441
Gaeta the refuge of, ii. 420, 435, 438
Gray complimented by, v. 160
Gregori the confidant of, v. 330
HW scolds Mann for tenderness to, ii. 518
husband rewards, for son's birth, iii. 423

[Maria Amalia, *continued*]
Long not to frighten, ii. 474n
Naples to be abandoned by, i. 101
Palazzo Farnese at Rome prepared for, ii. 435, 438
pregnant, ii. 474n
Rome to be visited by: for *anno santo*, iv. 43; from Gaeta, ii. 435, 438
Sersali will please, iv. 429
Spain disliked by, as refuge, ii. 3
to return to Naples, ii. 519
Vienna's mourning for, v. 462
Maria Amalia (1746–1804), m. (1769) Ferdinand, D. of Parma:
'Amazon,' ix. 301
Coke, Lady Mary, cannot get admittance to, vii. 535, 539
Du Tillot and Llano expelled by, to displeasure of France and Spain, vii. 445–6
Du Tillot's punishment desired by, vii. 325
France and Spain complain of extravagance of, vii. 412
HW pities, vii. 452
HW regrets Mann's fatigue caused by attending, ix. 307
horse races liked by, ix. 301
Leopold and Maria Louisa escort, on Bologna road to Naples for carnival, ix. 2
Leopold visited by, at Florence, ix. 307n
mother does not permit, to marry Ferdinand of Parma till his quarrel with Clement XIV is settled, vii. 518
mother gets French ladies to educate, iv. 326, 334
mother wants Leopold to advise, on economy, vii. 412
stables visited by, in preference to Palazzo Pitti, ix. 301
visit of, to Florence, retards post, ix. 301
Maria Amalia (1780–98), Archduchess:
living, ix. 549
Maria Anna (1718–44), Archduchess; m. (1744) Prince Charles (Alexander) of Lorraine:
Brussels to be visited by, ii. 331
Charles, P., to marry, ii. 330
death of, ii. 540, 550
father said to have left Flanders to, ii. 331
Patapan to marry, i. 76
(?) Theodore of Corsica said to be about to marry, ii. 208
to retire, with her mother, to Hungary, i. 143
Maria Anna (1738–89), Archduchess:
mother gets French ladies to educate, iv. 326, 334
Maria Anna (1770–1809), Archduchess; abbess of Prague:
Gloucester, D. and Ds of, see, at Poggio Imperiale, viii. 297
(?) grandmother to meet, at Gorizia, viii. 191
living, ix. 549

Maria Anna (1693–1751), of Neuberg, m. (1719) Ferdinand Maria of Bavaria:
Electress's bequest to, ii. 171
Maria Anna (1693–1762) of Sulzbach; Carmelite nun:
Electress's bequest to, ii. 171
Maria Anna Charlotte Amalie (1722–90), of Sulzbach, m. (1742) Klemens, D. of Bavaria:
Electress's bequest to, ii. 171
Maria Anna Francesca Josepha (b. 1736), of Portugal:
uncle attacks, without regard for her misfortunes, vi. 49
Maria Anna Giosefa Antoinetta (1683–1754), m. (1708) João V, K. of Portugal:
Florence in mourning for, iv. 451
Maria Anna Vittoria (1718–81), m. (1732) José Manoel, K. of Portugal 1750–77:
brother attacks, without regard for her misfortunes, vi. 49
Charles III might shelter, v. 560
Portuguese conspiracy ascribed to, v. 342
Maria Antonia (1724–80) of Bavaria, m. (1747) Friedrich Christian, Elector of Saxony, 1763:
Gloucester, D. of, hears defence from, of Ds of Kingston, viii. 25
incognito well preserved by, viii. 164
Kingston, Ds of, friend of, viii. 7, 25, 31
Maria Louisa told by, to entertain Ds of Kingston, viii. 40–1
Maria Antonia Ferdinanda (1729–85), m. (1750) Victor Amadeus III, K. of Sardinia, 1773:
death of, ix. 608
mother said to be resembled by, vii. 465
Spain said to be making family compact with, vii. 465
Viviani instructs, ii. 129
wedding of, iv. 159
Maria Carolina (1752–1814), m. (1768) Ferdinand, K. of Naples; K. of Two Sicilies, 1815:
Albani, and Clement XIII not to be visited by, at Rome, vii. 2
Borghese entertains, at villa, vii. 23
cardinals refuse to wait on, unless wearing frocks, vii. 18, 26
Clement XIII thanked by, through Schwarzenberg, vii. 23
Coke, Lady Mary, may become angry with, vii. 547
detained in Piombino channel by bad navigation, ix. 581
eats off her knees, at supper at Caserta, vii. 191
father's annual requiem attended by, at Florence, ix. 600
Ferdinand of Parma visits, at Mantua, vii. 17
Florentine visits of, vii. 2, 11, 15, ix. 583, 585–7, 589, 593–4, 598, 602
Gatti's letter from, urges him to inoculate her family, viii. 330

HW does not care a straw about, ix. 602
homage of Roman subjects received by, at Marino, vii. 23
itinerary of: from Florence, ix. 586; from Florence to Naples, vii. 17; from Modena to Florence, Leghorn, and Naples, ix. 593-4
Joseph II to receive, at Mantua, ix. 586
Leghorn visited by, ix. 581, 600
Leopold and Maria Louisa may be glad to be rid of, ix. 600
Leopold and Maria Louisa to accompany, to Naples, vii. 2, 11
Leopold and Maria Louisa to live quietly with, at Poggio Imperiale, ix. 598
Leopold and Maria Louisa to meet, at Pistoia, and take her to Poggio a Caiano and Poggio Imperiale, ix. 594
Leopold entertains, at Florence, vii. 17
—— to meet, at Bologna, vii. 15
Mann's gala liveries made for reception of, vii. 60
Mantua visited by, vii. 17
Marino visited by, vii. 18, 23, 26
Pisa welcomes, with festivities, ix. 581
pregnant, ix. 599
receptions for, all along route, vii. 23
repose preferred by, ix. 600
Rome to be avoided by, vii. 2, 17
Rome visited by, vii. 23-4, 26
to embark at Leghorn for Naples, ix. 600
Maria Christine (1742-98), m. (1766) Albrecht Kasimir August, D. of Saxe-Teschen:
birth of, i. 433
Gloucester, D. and Ds of, meet, at public places only, viii. 190
mother gets French ladies to educate, iv. 326, 334
Maria Clementina (1777-1801), Archduchess; m. (1797) Francis I, K. of the Two Sicilies:
Gloucester, D. and Ds of, see, at Poggio Imperiale, viii. 297
living, ix. 549
Maria Clementina (Sobieska) (1702-35), m. (1719) James Francis Edward Stuart, the 'Old Pretender'; 'Santa Sobieski':
husband gets money from lands of, in Poland, vi. 387
husband receives inspiration from ghost of, iv. 147
son inherits share of jewels of, ix. 525
Maria Elisabeth Auguste (1721-94) of Sulzbach. m. (1742) Karl Theodor, Elector Palatine:
Electress's bequest to, ii. 171
Maria Elizabeth (1680-1741), 'Archduchess of Brussels':
mourning for, at Florence, i. 193
Maria Elizabeth (1743-1808), Archduchess; Abbess of Innsbruck, 1781:
birth of, to be celebrated by opera in Florence, ii. 294
mother gets French ladies to educate, iv. 326, 334

Maria Francesca Dorothea Josepha (1739-71), of Portugal:
uncle attacks, without regard for her misfortunes, vi. 49
Maria Francisca Benedetta (1746-1829), m. (1777) José Francisco Xavier, P. of Beira:
uncle attacks, without regard for her misfortunes, vi. 49
Maria Franziska Dorothea (1724-94), m. (1746) Friedrich Michael, Pfalzgraf von Zweibrucken-Birkenfeld:
Electress's bequest to, ii. 171
María Isabel (1743-9), Ps, of Naples:
birth of, ii. 223
Gaeta the refuge of, ii. 420
Maria Isabella (1741-63) of Parma, m. (1760) Archduke Joseph, later Joseph II:
death of, vi. 194
France favours match of, v. 323
Maria Josefa (1699-1757), m. (1719) Frederick Augustus III, K. of Poland:
Frederick II would live in Dresden if it were evacuated by, v. 15
Maria Josefa (1739-67), of Bavaria, m. (1765) Joseph II, Holy Roman Emperor:
death of, from smallpox, vi. 526
Florence has galas despite mourning for, vi. 532
Maria Theresa sorry that she arranged fruitless marriage of, with Joseph II, vi. 481
Maria Josefa (1744-1801), of Naples:
birth of, ii. 478
father would like to marry, to Joseph II, v. 323
Maria Josefa (1751-67), Archduchess:
Albani's villa to be visited by, for one day, vi. 556
death of, vi. 561
Florence prepares to receive, vi. 525, 533, 556
Florentine visitors disappointed at not seeing, vi. 564
health of, smallpox, vi. 558, 561
Joseph II to escort, to Florence, vi. 533, 548, 556
Leopold to be visited by, in Florence, vi. 492
luggage of, to be stopped at Florence from going to Naples, vi. 558
mother gets French ladies to educate, iv. 326, 334
mother removes Jesuit confessor of, vi. 519
Neapolitans to receive, vi. 556
Rome to be visited by, vi. 556
Tuscan Court must be in gala for wedding of, vi. 556
Maria Louisa (1745-92), m. (1765) Leopold, Grand Duke of Tuscany 1765-90; Holy Roman Emperor (as Leopold II) 1790-2:
accoucheur accompanies, on travels, vii. 220
affability of, Medicean, vi. 390
alarm of, at Duomo fire may have ended her pregnancy, vi. 367

[Maria Louisa, *continued*]

Albani and Clement XIII not to be visited by, at Rome, vii. 2

Albany, Cts of, protected by official of, from husband, ix. 101

Albizzi, Mme degli, *grande maitresse* to, vii. 253

always pregnant during Carnivals, vii. 171

arrival of, in Florence, vi. 337

bal masqué and supper to be given by, at great theatre, for D. and Ds of Cumberland, ix. 644–5

Beaufort, Ds of, befriended by, vii. 372

birthday of: celebrated at Florence, vii. 253; gala for, vii. 352; to pass as that of St Leopold, vi. 371

Borghese entertains, at villa, vii. 23

Botta's taste will probably not be approved by, vi. 335

Carducci, Mme, represents, at reception, vi. 491

carnival enjoyed by: though only as a spectator, vii. 189; to fullest extent, vi. 491

carried to Poggio Imperiale, vii. 111

casino added to Pitti palace for women of, vi. 258, 291

Castello visited by, ix. 203, ix. 644

chambellans give festival for, after daughter's birth, vi. 491

character of, praised by Mann, vii. 372

Charlotte's rival in fertility, ix. 425

childbed to be abandoned by, vii. 1

childbirths and miscarriages of, ix. 548–9

child expected by, in April, vii. 91

children of, may lure her back to Florence, vii. 72

churching ceremony for, elaborate, vi. 486

Clement XIII thanked by, through Schwarzenberg, vii. 23

Clive's gift to Q. Charlotte, makes, jealous, vi. 547

cockades given to, at Leghorn, vi. 423

Coke, Lady Mary, coldly received by, vii. 535

Corsini major-domo to, vii. 294

Court procedure of, vi. 367

Cowper, Huntingdon, and Ds of Beaufort often with, vii. 429

Cowper's burletta not attended by, for fear of reprimand from Vienna, vi. 393

Cumberland, D. and Ds of, to be received by, ix. 644–5

Damer, Mrs, declines being presented to, ix. 203

dances at all the theatres, vi. 491

dancing prevented by pregnancy of, vii. 171

daughter born to, vi. 481

decisions to be made by, about entrance ceremonies at Florence, vi. 334

diamonds the passion of, vi. 547

distinction made by, between old and new nobility, vi. 360n

dogs brought by, from Spain, vi. 330

English to be learned by, vi. 438

father-in-law's annual requiem attended by, at Florence, ix. 600

father loves, ix. 43

father's letters to: about destruction of floating batteries, ix. (?) 324, 329; about his pacific intentions towards England, viii. 476; about Spain's opposition to French policy, viii. 375; contradicted by her brothers, ix. 32–3; deceptive, viii. 498, ix. 334; delivered by Spanish Minister, ix. 334; freely written on international affairs, viii. 467

father's sanity worried about by, vi. 438

Ferdinand and Maria Amalia of Parma escorted by, on Bologna road to Naples for Carnival, ix. 2

Ferdinand of Naples and Maria Carolina to be met by, at Postoia, and taken to Poggio a Caiano and Poggio Imperiale, ix. 594

Ferdinand of Naples and Maria Carolina to live quietly with, at Poggio Imperiale, ix. 598

Ferdinand of Naples and Maria Carolina will relieve, by their departure, ix. 600

Ferdinand of Naples to entertain, on her name's day, on shipboard at Leghorn, ix. 600

Florence prepares for, vi. 206, 255, 258, 273, 290–1, 327, 333–5

Florence to be revisited by, before Holy Week, viii. 453–4

Florentine ladies (first-class) presented to, vi. 347, 350–1, 583–4

Florentine public entry of, vi. 424

foreign ministers play ombre with, ix. 51

Frascati visited by, vii. 23

fruitfulness of, will endear her to Viennese Court, vii. 214

Gatti receives chaise and courier from, for trip to Naples, vii. 330

Genoa to be visited by, vi. 255

German physician overdoses, vi. 459–60

Gloucester, D. and Ds of, received by, despite previous intention not to see the Ds, viii. 297–8

Gloucester, D. of, arouses concern of, vii. 335

—— attends theatre, concert and dinner with, at Florence, vii. 405

—— congratulated by, on recovery, vii. 342

—— exchanges civilities with, at Pisa, vii. 352, 355–6

—— hoped to compliment, on mother-in-law's name-day, vii. 332

—— inquires about health of, after childbed, viii. 291

—— invites, to dine on shipboard and attend a *bal masqué* at Leghorn, vii. 353

—— plays loo with, vii. 352

—— to be attentively but tactfully welcomed by, vii. 348

Grande Maîtress not to tell, of approach of spaniel puppies, vii. 54

Guasco often spoken to, by, vi. 531

HW does not care a straw about royal visitors to, ix. 602

HW fears that Ferdinand's and Maria Carolina's visit to, may inconvenience Mann, ix. 583

HW's procurement of spaniel puppies for Mann to give to, vi. 438, 470, 519, 534, 546, vii. 40, 50, 54, 56, 72

harlequin comedies enjoyed by, vi. 412

health of: bled, vi. 430; miscarriage, vii. 458; overdosed by German doctor, vi. 459–60; possible miscarriage, vii. 111

Hervey, Mrs, plays whist with, vi. 430

House of Austria gets many heirs from, vii. 171, 214

husband and Joseph II to hurry back for delivery of, vii. 108

husband cannot eat in chamber with, because male servants are not admitted, vi. 529

husband followed by, in coach to Florence, vi. 427

husband leaves, to attend balls, vi. 486

impatient for delivery, that she may spend Ascension at Venice on way to Vienna, vii. 205

Innsbruck to be visited by, via Genoa, vi. 255

itinerary of, from Florence to Naples, vii. 17

Jesuit confessor still employed by, vi. 519

jewels brought by, from Spain, vi. 481

Joseph II received by, in Boboli gardens, vii. 108

—— sends honours to, ix. 128

——'s simplicity copied by, vii. 220

Kingston, Ds of, to be entertained by, at Electress of Saxony's recommendation, viii. 40–1

Leghorn ceremony missed by, vi. 557

Leghorn visited by, vi. 423, ix. 600

letters to, tell of floating batteries at Gibraltar, ix. 324

limited amusements of, during mourning period, vi. 340, 354

Llano communicates Charles III's instructions to, vii. 446

Lorenzi's treatment by France considered by, to be typical French ingratitude, vi. 430

Mann and P. of Mecklenburg entertained by, at Poggio Imperiale, vi. 438

Mann asked by: (?) about Ds of Cumberland, vii. 501–2; about spaniels, vi. 519, 546

—— gives black spaniel to, vii. 56

—— has had no instructions about his behaviour to, vi. 319

—— invited by, to dinner, vi. 390

—— persuades, to urge father to cease supporting France against England, ix. 43

—— plays whist with, vi. 430

—— presents young Chernyshev to, ix. 84

—— recommends Carmelite friar to, as English teacher, vi. 438

——'s dispatch approved by, ix. 43

—— tells: of diamonds brought to Q. Charlotte through Clive, vi. 547; of spaniels' approach, vii. 72

—— to house-break puppies for, vii. 72

—— told by: of Cumberland's negotiations in Madrid, ix. 82; that Vienna may not let her and Leopold attend theatre, vi. 407

—— would be embarrassed to answer, about peace treaty, ix. 383

Mann, Horace II, received by, with marks of respect, ix. 666

Maria Carolina to be accompanied by, to Naples, vii. 2, 11

Marino visited by, vii. 23

Maron summoned to paint, viii. 31

marriage of, vi. 123, 125, 319, 321, 343n

Maximilian to visit quietly, in country, viii. 123

minchiate played by, vi. 340

miscarriage feared by, ix. 301

miscarriage of, from too much Carnival frivolity, vii. 458

mother-in-law gives diamond buttons to, vi. 481

mother-in-law promised to recommend Lady Mary Coke to, vii. 535

mother-in-law to be visited by, vii. 214

mother-in-law to meet, with children at Gorizia, viii. 191

mourning rules prevent, from hearing Manzuoli, vi. 340

Murray, Capt., to be presented to, vi. 350

nousvoullone insult, by avoiding her reception, vi. 357, 467

Order of La Croix étoilée conferred upon, ix. 128

Order of St Catherine of Russia declined by, ix. 128

Orlov gives Turkish girls to, vii. 228

physician may be chosen by, from Cocchi's disciples, vi. 460

Pisa baths to be visited by, for health, vii. 108

Pisa hated by, vii. 72, 342

Pisa visited by, vi. 422, ix. 425

Pitt, Anne, told by, of father's remarks on Spanish policy, viii. 375

Pitt, Mrs George, asked by, to dance a minuet, vii. 456

Poggio a Caiano visited by, vii. 342

Poggio Imperiale visited by, vi. 424, 427, 526, vii. 112, 449

Pratolino visited by, vi. 337, 350

pregnancy of: cannot be announced soon, due to Madrid and Vienna etiquette, vi. 427, may prevent her return to Florence for carnival, vii. 262; obliges her to travel slowly, viii. 240; suspected, vi. 529, vii. 11

pregnant, vi. 423, 424, 427, 430, 477–8, 529, 581, vii. 108, 171, 205, 220, 429, ix. 425

[Maria Louisa *continued*]
prophecies of her father's doom alarm, viii. 50
repose preferred by, ix. 600
retires to Poggio Imperiale with only two servants, vii. 449
returns to Florence from Vienna, but still in retirement, viii. 250
Riccardi, Marchesa, and Mme Antinori attend, from Bolsano, vi. 334
Rome not to be visited by, vii. 2, 17
Rome visited by, vii. 23
secluded at Poggio Imperiale, vi. 526
sentiments little disguised by, ix. 383
son born to, ix. 548–9
Stuart, Charlotte, not yet received by, ix. 537
Sudley, Vcts, plays whist with, when she feels like it, vii. 203
supper guests of, not restricted, vii. 191
supper taken by, at 9 P.M., vi. 354
theatre may be attended by, despite pregnancy, vi. 477–8
theatres attended in mask nightly, despite pregnancy, vi. 581
Thurn, Comtesse, accompanies, on travels, vii. 220
—— receives picture and diamond bracelet from, vii. 253
travels *en bourgeois*, vii. 220
Vienna to be visited by, vii. 220, viii. 240, 409
Vienna to be visited by, when well enough to travel, vii. 214
visitors received by, at bedside after childbirth, viii. 297
Zoffany makes Mann appear before, to be painted, viii. 540
—— should have put, in painting of Tribune, viii. 539
Mariani, Conde de (d. 1744), Spanish Lt-Gen.: capture of, ii. 489, 491
Gages may be succeeded by, ii. 135
Marianne. See under Marivaux
Maria Ricciarda Beatrice (1750–1829) of Este, m. (1771) Archduke Ferdinand of Austria; D. of Modena, 1803:
Florentine entertainments for, ix. 50
Francis III sends, to Milan for education, vi. 171–2
Huntingdon favoured by, at Mantua, vii. 446–7
Leopold engaged to, iv. **393–4**, 396, 400
—— not to marry, now that he is to have Tuscany, vi. **125–6**
Modena duchy may be inherited by, iv. 400
Simonetti, Mme, makes plans at Vienna for, vi. 201
—— may educate, vi. 172
Maria Sofia (1759–1828) of Württemburg, m. (1776) Paul I, Emperor of Russia, 1801:
Florence to be visited by, ix. 250–1

Maria Teresa Felicità (1726–54) d'Este, m. (1744) Louis-Jean-Marie de Bourbon, Duc de Penthièvre:
at Paris, ii. 378
HW hospitably treated by, i. **44**
husband mourns, iv. 466
mother shows Florentine sights to, ii. 227–8
Orléans, Duchesse d', fond of, ii. 385
pleated tresses of, worn in husband's bosom, iv. 466
Young Pretender may wed, ii. 378, 385
Maria Theresa (1717–80), m. (1736) Francis, D. of Lorraine; Grand Duke of Tuscany 1737–65; Holy Roman Emperor 1745–65; she was Queen of Hungary 1740–80; 'Empress-Queen':
acquisitive, vii. 562
affairs of, in Lombardy, i. 427
Aix peace preliminaries win consent of, iii. 488
Aix treaty preparations said to be halted by, iii. 495–6
Aix treaty rejected by, iii. 479–81
Albani dismissed from meddling with affairs of, at Rome, iii. 475
—— minister of, at Rome, ii. 467n
alliance formed by, against Frederick II, v. 564
allies of, rumoured to be forcing her to make peace, ii. 241
army of: absorbed in fighting Frederick II, v. 90; in Lombardy, estimated, i. 291; Neapolitans defeated by, ii. 489; near Rome, ii. 473; protects Tuscany, ii. 353; told to stop hostilities, iii. 488; too weak to fight both Spain and Naples, ii. 390; *see also* Austria: army of
Aulic council persuaded by, to fine Frankfurt, v. 28
Austrian defeat supposedly misrepresented to, to avoid upsetting her pregnancy, i. 465
ballad ridicules alleged English betrayal of, i. 188
Bartolommei sent by, to Turin, i. 196
Bavarian-French army opposes, i. 194
Benedict XIV asks about Parma claims of, i. 201
—— may quarrel with, over her general's seizure of Gonzaga's abbeys, ii. 55–6
—— persuaded by, to appoint Attems to Aquileia, iv. 160–1
——'s correspondence with, ii. 55
—— tells, not to attack Venice, iv. 177
Berrue received by, i. 205
birthday of, to be celebrated in Florence, vi. 232
Botta expected by, to be influential at Florence, vi. 448
—— explains ceremonial of, vi. 378
—— says that Peter III will never join Frederick II against, vi. 41
Bourbon family pact should alarm, v. 565
Braitwitz calls, 'potence,' ii. 524n

Brown bribed by, with *toison* and diamond pictures, v. 72
Carteret supposed to be the chief English supporter of, ii. 557
Catherine II called 'ma vilaine sœur' by, ix. 128
—— given ultimatum from, vii. 310
Charles III asks, for another bride for Ferdinand, vi. 564
—— sends message to, about Parma, vii. 446
Charles Emmanuel III blames, for wanting to capture Naples, ii. 461
—— friendly to, i. 291
—— may be weaned from alliance with, i. 312
—— said to have signed treaty with, i. 342
——'s alliance with, i. 350
——'s negotiations with, awaited by Traun, ii. 263
——'s retreat might be against interests of, ii. 142
——'s treaty with, gives him towns, i. 379
—— to get cessions from, by Aix treaty, iii. 481
—— wants army of, at Bologna, ii. 461
child born to, i. 433
children reassembled by, vii. 214
Choiseul settles boundary disputes with, vii. 143
——'s fall may displease, vii. 259
Coke, Lady Mary, formerly adored, vii. 530, 539, 544
—— imagines herself persecuted by, vii. 535, 542–3, 544–5, 547, 552–3
coronation of, as Q. of Hungary, i. 100
Corsican policy of, ii. 157
Corsican rebels falsely encouraged by, iii. 276
Craon, Princesse de, honoured by, at Frankfurt and Innsbruck, vi. 537
—— represents, at ceremony of the *doti*, ii. 196
Cristiani may be assigned by, to Francis I to rule Tuscany, iv. 335
Dalmatia confiscated by, viii. 11–12
daughter disregards instructions of, vii. 321
daughter's Jesuit confessor removed by, vi. 519
Daun should be exchanged by, for Wolfes and Loudons, v. 428
—— tells, to pray for victory, v. 435
death of, ix. 102, 103, 104, 107
Deskford favours, i. 371
edict of, to Neapolitans, ii. 454, 461
Elector Palatine's troops may be given to, iii. 41
Electress leaves jewels to, ii. 171
—— receives Hungary water from, by Ginori, ii. 139
Elizabeth of Russia compared with, vi. 1
England and Sardinia sign treaty with, ii. 311

England's denial of demands by, may bring war, v. 28
England's instant aid to, ix. 389
England's pensioner, vi. 483
England would like to massacre, iv. 578
English alliance may be repudiated by, if Mathews does not send aid to her army, ii. 447
English ambassador of, said to oppose Sir Robert Walpole, i. 325–6
English fleet cannot be expected to do much without troops from, iii. 121
English fleet's refusal to fight Naples angers, ii. 390
English fleet to defend Italian possessions of, i. 259
English fleet would endanger, by attacking Naples, ii. 390
English internal divisions favoured by, v. 538
English ministry will not fortify towns of, iii. 69
English naval help promised to, at Worms treaty, ii. 470
English reverses may please bigotry of, iii. 118–19
English subsidy for, voted, i. 390
English support of, said to depend on Sir Robert Walpole's fall, i. 326
English troops wanted by, at Mainz, ii. 102
faints at Loudon's defeat, v. 435
Ferdinand of Parma's correspondence with, vi. 379
fête for delivery of, avoided by Princesse de Craon, ii. 302
Flanders has few towns still controlled by, iii. 209
Flanders to be retained by, by Aix treaty, iii. 481
Florentine celebration of coronation of, i. 100
Florentine followers of, predict Modena's surrender, i. 443
Florentine post no step to preferment with, iii. 23
Florentine soldiers intend to bring Frederick II a captive to, v. 179
Forrester brings English money to, ii. 107
—— given jewelled snuff-box by, ii. 107
——'s officer receives diamond ring from, ii. 107
France allowed by, to occupy Flemish towns, v. 117
France may be aroused by threats of, to Venice, iv. 176
France may be joined by, in attack on England from Flanders, v. 18–19
France must borrow exclusion from, for Conclave, v. 216
France's alliance with: probably desired by her, i. 144; probably motivated by wish to regain Italian and Silesian losses,

[Maria Theresa, *continued*]

iv. 576; to crush Frederick II, v. 564; will make England continue war in Germany, v. 456; will provoke Germany, iv. 589

France's distress probably will not move, v. 369

France should not continue a disastrous war for the sake of, v. 502

France supposedly courted by, during her English alliance, i. 160

France takes advantage of animosity of, towards Frederick II, v. 107

France tells, that she must make peace with Prussia, v. 498

Francis III may aid, i. 432

——'s stipulations from, ii. 127

Frederick II antagonized by, i. 208

—— endangers position of, ii. 511

—— makes peace with, i. 456

—— may make peace with, by George II's mediation, i. 76, 87

—— might have forced, to make peace, v. 107

—— might reduce, too quickly, v. 211

—— prevents, from reinforcing her armies in Italy, ii. 502

—— said to have made peace with, vi. 118

——'s becoming D. of Burgundy may displease, iii. 238

——'s demand treated by, as an insult, v. 564

——'s destruction prayed for by, v. 176

(?) —— sends troops to Bohemia as auxiliaries to, i. 206, 215

——'s enlarged army must discourage, from further warfare, v. 502

——'s escape from, vi. 119–20

——'s peace terms may be forced upon, i. 144, 154, 168

——'s peace with, iii. 194

——'s peace with, doubted in Florence, i. 472, 483

——'s quarrel with, pleases HW, v. 2

——'s retreat from Bohemia permits, to dispense with French aid, v. 229

——'s victories disappoint, v. 94

—— unlikely to appease, except by restoring Silesia, v. 15

—— upsets 'pacific' schemes of, iv. 589

—— will be opposed by, to the last, to regain Silesia, v. 502

freemasons suppressed by, at Benedict XIV's instigation, ii. 208

French ambassador rebuked by, for American-French alliance, viii. 395–6

French counsels prevail with, vii. 137

French domination of councils of, v. 28

French ladies brought by, to educate her daughters, iv. 326, 334

French marriage for daughter planned by, vii. 137

French tributes to Frederick II's heroism would displease, v. 142

gala for: at opera, ii. 322; not celebrated by Princesse de Craon, ii. 324

Galluzzi's history may be suppressed by bigotry of, ix. 80

——'s history published after death of, ix. 87n

——'s history would cause, to shudder in her grave, ix. 238

Gatti rewarded by, for inoculating her grandsons, viii. 7

generals of, advise English against engaging the French, ii. 250

Genoa and Spain may be left to mercy of, by peace treaty, iii. 219

Genoa campaign to be ordered by, iii. 437

Genoa may declare war on, iii. 58

Genoa sues to, for peace, iii. 305

Genoese and Levantine offensives planned by, iii. 478

Genoese populace may avenge quarrel of, iii. 505

George II orders his fleet to protect dominions of, i. 281

——'s aid to, disparaged by Richecourt's party, i. 371

——'s ally, ii. 301

——'s negotiations with, demanded by Pulteney for examination, i. 250

—— to aid, i. 376

German affairs of, favourable, ii. 108

Germany will be embroiled by, in civil war, v. 28

Giustiniani's panegyrics to, rewarded, vi. 465

Gorizia trip to meet Leopold and his family cancelled by, because of age and ill health, viii. 191, 200–1

grandson wanted by, to make up for barren daughter-in-law, vi. 481

HW and Mann know more about, than about each other's friends, vii. 260

HW calls: 'Juno,' vii. 547; 'Tisiphone,' v. 498

HW hopes Joseph II will not be murdered by, vii. 145

HW sneers at piety of, vii. 437

HW was visiting Mann at time of accession of, to throne, ix. 103

HW would force, to make peace, v. 285

halting of war with Prussia the last and best act of, ix. 104

Hamerani's medal for election of husband of, iii. 184

Hanover troops to be paid by, iii. 17

health drunk to, at Leghorn, iii. 152

health of, smallpox, vi. 525, 532, 561

Holland to aid, with troops, i. 476

Hungarians to assist, v. 176

husband jealously kept by, iv. 177–8, vi. 404

husband may aid, with merely a few troops, v. 175

husband not permitted by, to join army, ii. 310

husband not to be estranged from, by France, i. 152

husband ordered by, to return to Vienna, i. 316

husband's art collection never visited by, for fear of nudes, vi. 291

husband's good sense may be overborne by vengeance of, v. 108

husband's separation from his advisors wished by, i. 328

husband to be welcomed by, with carrousel by her ladies, ii. 99

husband would want to keep Tuscany in case of death of, iv. 178

hussars of, pursue Spaniards, ii. 199

Hyndford secured Silesia to Frederick II instead of to, ii. 89

Ingenhousz's letter and present from, vii. 123

inoculation still opposed by, despite deaths from smallpox, vi. 561

intrigues of minister of, i. 360

Italian conquests preferred by, to Flemish towns, iii. 495–6

Italian subjects of, more rigorous in judging the Byng case because she has joined England's enemies, v. 69

James ordered to leave Vienna by order of, v. 462

Jesuits must be dealt with by, vii. 473

Jesuits protected by, vi. 519

Joseph II, after death of, will electrify Europe, viii. 38

—— asks approval of, to prolong stay at Florence, vii. 111–12

—— confirms ministers of, ix. 107

—— loaded by, with debts, ix. 107

—— may be impatient to rule estates of, vi. 395

——'s anti-French bias curbed by, vii. 154

——'s heir eagerly awaited by, vii. 2

——'s second wife chosen by, vi. 481

——'s war with Frederick II halted by, ix. 104

—— will not again allow, to get him a wife, vii. 123

Kaunitz could hardly justify war expenses of, in trying to regain Silesia, v. 519

Kingston, Ds of, would be worse treated by, than Lady Mary Coke was, vii. 559

Kloster-Zeven convention will prevent English hostilities with, v. 138

knights of Malta forbidden by, to fight Turks, v. 505

ladies of, not permitted to wear rouge in mourning period, vi. 354

Late Gallant Exploits satirizes George II's desertion of, i. 188

Lee refused audience by, viii. 390, 395–6

Leopold and Maria Louisa to visit, at Vienna, vii. 214

Leopold may visit, in Vienna during war, viii. 389

—— might infer adverse influence upon, from cancellation of Gorizia trip, viii. 201

—— receives trunk-load of medicines from, vi. 459

—— told by, to go to Parma to lecture his sister on economy, vii. 411–13

Lestock ordered to defend dominions of, i. 405

letter-envelope of, sent by Du Tillot to Florence, vi. 379

Liechtenstein's announcement might not have been approved by, v. 446

Lobkowitz ordered by, to retire to Lombardy, ii. 508

——'s army under, reinforced, ii. 336

—— sent by, to St Petersburg, vii. 310

—— should no longer command armies of, ii. 519

Lombard possessions of, may be invaded by Spaniards, ii. 76

Lorraine adherents in Florence expect, to execute Kaunitz's plans, v. 360–1

Louis XV asked by, for ladies to educate her daughters, iv. 326

lovers surprised by, v. 258

manifest of, see under edict of

Mann, as Sir Robert Walpole's tool, supposed to be hostile to, ii. 363

—— earns gratitude of, ii. 471

—— misrepresented as hostile to, i. 126

—— reported by Richecourt to be hostile to, ii. 67

—— represented as hostile to, ii. 476

——'s preservation of army of, acknowledged by her general and ministers, ii. 476

—— told by Albani of gratitude of, ii. 460–1

—— would have given part of his Leghorn toasts to, iii. 151

Maria I receives treatment similar to that of, viii. 310

Maria Amalia as generous as, vii. 412

—— not allowed by, to wed Ferdinand of Parma till quarrel with Clement XIV is settled, vii. 518

Maria Louisa receives diamond buttons from, on daughter's birth, vi. 481

maritime power of, established at Trieste, iv. 98, 102

Mathews blames, for not assisting Charles Emmanuel III, ii. 346

—— differs with, over Neapolitan war, ii. 370

—— unmoved by entreaties of followers of, to send ships against Naples, ii. 460

Maximilian Joseph concludes treaty with,

[Maria Theresa, *continued*]

regaining Bavaria and renouncing imperial claims, iii. 37

——'s peace with, will release troops for Italy, iii. 41

medal of, sent by Mann to HW, ii. 471, 477

medals of, v. 202

Mellini becomes minister plenipotentiary of, at Rome, iii. 475

Metastasio said to be dismissed by, at husband's order, iv. 163–4, 177–8

Milan exchange will consolidate husband's possessions with those of, i. 290

Mill, Col., in service of, iii. 407

millions of lives sacrificed by, vi. 81

minister of: negotiates with Williams, iv. 186–7; will outrank husband's envoy, iv. 29

ministers of, monopolize passports, v. 482

Modena administered in name of, i. 489

money lost by, in campaigns, v. 176, vi. 52

money sought by, at any interest, v. 102

name day of: ii. 322, 324, iii. 439, vii. 332, 334; Du Châtelet celebrates, by ball at Leghorn, ii. 78; Richecourt gives dinner on, v. 9

Naples coveted by, ii. 390

Neapolitan-Spanish alliance against, ii. 43

nudes not permitted by, in pictures, vi. 246, 291

nuncio may be dismissed by, from Vienna if Valenti is still supported by Benedict XIV, ii. 56

order of, *see* Maria Theresa, Order of

order of *La Croix Étoilée* presented by, to Mrs Swinburne, ix. 128

Order of St Stephen of Hungary worn by, as Roi d'Hongrie, ix. 128

Pallaviccini said to be authorized by, to treat with Genoese mob, iii. 359

Paris, Abp of, asked by, for nuns to start a convent, iv. 333–4

Parliament votes money for, i. 390

peace mediation may be attempted by, viii. 519

Peace of Paris ignores, vi. 95

peace rumours about, iii. 219

peace said to be wanted by, vi. 51

Peter III's abdication must please, vi. 60

—— said to be fighting for, vi. 2, 19

——'s assurances to, vi. 10

picture of, delivered by Richecourt to Hyndford, ii. 107

Pironi, consul of, at Ancona, ii. 253, 257

Poland to be partitioned by, vii. 419, 439

Pompadour, Marquise de, corresponds with, v. 258

Pontano has patent of protection from, ii. 56

Prague's loss grieves, i. 226

Pressburg predicted as residence of, i. 143

Pressburg visited by, i. 205

Prussia and Russia threaten, with war unless she consents to Poland's partition, vii. 439

Prussian minister at Venice speaks insolently of, i. 483

Prussian peace with, rumoured, i. 134

Prussians defeated by troops of, in Moravia, i. 372

Queensberry, Ds of, jokingly proposes to be lady of the Bedchamber to, ii. 136

rage of, will end only in death, vi. 23

Regency council receives honours from, i. 40

religious devotion of, iv. 421, vi. 2, ix. 80, 87n, 238

Richecourt condemns Sir Robert Walpole's neglect of, i. 367

—— reflects the insolence of, iv. 586

—— told by, that religious devotion is necessary for promotion, iv. 421

Robinson persuades, to give up all Silesia to Frederick II, ii. 108

Roman representative of, tells Mann of Young Pretender's flight, ii. 373

Romans acclaim, ii. 447

Rosenberg's debts not paid by, vii. 220

——'s debts paid by, in Denmark and Spain but not in Tuscany, vii. 294

ruins herself in presents to army, v. 332

Silesia lost by, because she would not give up part of it, ii. 521

Silesia may be obtained by, at expense of English and Dutch alliance, iii. 238

Silesian ambitions of, will provoke Germany, iv. 588–9

Silesia the cause of great expenditures by, v. 176, vi. 52

Simonetti, Cts, caressed by, in Vienna, vi. 126

son of, to marry Modenese princess, vi. 126

Spanish army may be resisted by troops of, in Lombardy, i. 266

successes of, i. 466

Theodore of Corsica said to be promised sister by, in secret treaty, ii. 208

Traun might be retained by, if Charles Emmanuel III and George II interceded for him, ii. 285

—— remonstrates with, for impossible orders, ii. 128

Trieste to be port of, iv. 98, 102

troops may be wanted by, from Tuscany, v. 175

troops of: in motion, vii. 292; may be stationed in Tuscany, iv. 320; may join German ones, ii. 98; said to be ordered to Italy, ii. 302; sent to Lombardy, v. 271; to join Sardinians, i. 424; to march through Lombardy towards the Tyrol and Bavaria, i. 154; *see also* Austria, army of; Maria Theresa: army of

troops, supplies and money lacking to, v. 2

Turkish threat to, will disappear if Sultana produces an heir, v. 494

Tuscan aid wanted by, ii. 359

Tuscan troops to take oath to, at Linz, v. 180

Tuscany will be lost by, because she did not respect Neapolitan neutrality, ii. 521

Uguccioni hopes for preferment through, ii. 455

Valenti will be blamed by, for Pontano's arrest, ii. 56

varnished case made by, for pocket flask, ii. 139

Venice's quarrel with, iv. 160–1, 173, 189–91

victories of: exaggerated in England, i. 404; please HW, i. 356

Wachtendonck commands troops of, at Leghorn, i. 467n

——'s cousin maid of honour to, i. 490

Walpole, Sir Robert, initiated English efforts to help, ii. 126

—— known to favour, ii. 382

—— thought to be hostile to, i. 404, 406, ii. 5, 126

war unlikely to be stopped by, v. 389

will of, said to favour Leopold, ix. 107

Worms treaty to be observed by, iii. 481

Wraxall's comments on, may offend Joseph II, ix. 138

Young Pretender's landing in Scotland may disconcert allies of, iii. 89

——'s rumoured departure known to, ii. 374

Maria Theresa (1726–46), m. (1745) Louis, Dauphin of France:

Châteauroux, Duchesse de, recommends laundresses to, ii. 523

Viviani instructs, ii. 129

Maria Theresa (1767–1827) of Tuscany, Archduchess; m. (1787) Anton, K. of Saxony:

Albizzi, Mme degli, to be grande maîtresse to, vi. 481

birth of, vi. 481, 491

Compton, Lady Elizabeth, plays with, vii. 372

Gloucester, D. and Ds of, see, at Poggio Imperiale, viii. 297

grandmother to meet, at Gorizia, viii. 191

inoculation of, viii. 7

living, ix. 549

Maron summoned to paint, viii. 31

mother impatient to see, vii. 72

Maria Theresa (1772–1807) of Naples, m. (1790) Francis II, Emperor:

inoculated, viii. 330

Maria Theresa, Order of:

Guasco receives, vi. 530

Kinský brings, to Leopold from Vienna, vi. 362

Maria Theresa, ship:

restoration of, v. 285

Maricone, Bartolommeo:

Braitwitz's correspondence with, i. 305, 308–9

Marie-Adélaïde (1732–1800), 4th dau. of Louis XV; 'Madame Adélaïde':

Beauvilliers scratched by, from party list, vii. 115–16

(?) Chartres, D. of, said to marry, i. 126–7

Du Barry, Comtesse, to be presented to, vii. 78

expense of coffee and rouge for, iv. 500

father nursed by, although she had never had smallpox, viii. 1–2

health of, smallpox, viii. 13, 19

La Vauguyon repulsed by, for suggesting that she receive Comtesse du Barry, vii. 87

Marie-Antoinette governed by, vii. 321

mother not addressed by, across father at dinner, iv. 340

Savoy, D. of, said to marry, iii. 218–19

Stanislas I visited by, vi. 403

Marie-Adélaïde-Clotilde-Xavière of France (1759–1802), m. (1775) Charles Emmanuel IV, P. of Piedmont, K. of Sardinia, 1796:

marriage of, planned, vii. 465

Marie à la Coque. See Alacoque, Marie

Marie-Antoinette (1755–93), of Austria; m. (1770) Louis XVI (Dauphin), K. of France, 1774:

Albany, Cts of, receives gracious letter from, ix. 150

Astley protected by, ix. 451

Austrian-Dutch quarrel discussed by, ix. 561

Choiseul will be upheld by, ix. 291

Clermont, Cts of, much noticed by, at Paris, ix. 357n

daughter born to, viii. 470

Du Barry, Comtesse, ignored by, despite mother's instructions, vii. 321

English newspapers banned in France because of scandal about, ix. 557

family of, may instruct her, viii. 18

HW expected to rave over, in Paris, vii. 312

influence of: gains ground, ix. 212; HW wonders about, viii. 3; will be for peace, viii. 17

Louis XVI's aunts govern, vii. 321

——'s match with, planned, vi. 404, vii. 54, 137

Malesherbes incited by Maurepas and Vergennes to ask, to dismiss Guines, viii. 207–8

Polignac, Duchesse de, favourite of, ix. 357n, 409

pregnant for first time, viii. 393n

Rohan pretended to buy necklace for, ix. 639

—— said to have forged the signature of, ix. 603

[Marie-Antoinette, *continued*]
Starhemberg's recall implies rupture of match for, vi. 404
Tessé has coaches and horses of, in Florence, viii. 353
—— Master of the Horse to, viii. 353
vivacity of, penetrates to England, viii. 86
Marie-Catherine-Sophie-Félicité (Leszczyńska) (1703–68), m. (1725) Louis XV, K. of France:
Carteret, Bns, compared to, ii. 501
Craon, Princesse de, might become stepmother of, iv. 132
daughters do not speak to, across Louis XV at dinner, iv. 340
father's bequest to, vi. 403
father's witticism on fatal nightgown given by, vi. 403
finances of, i. **127**
Gevaudan beast in antechamber of, vi. 289n
Louis XV at first prefers, to mistresses, vii. 87
—— gives Trianon to, i. 127
—— makes Mme de Pompadour *dame du palais* to, iv. 530
—— openly kept mistresses in lifetime of, vii. 78–9
Metz visited by, ii. 502
mourning for, at French Court, vii. 78–9
Stafford would please, i. 135
Talmond, Princesse de, in entourage of, iv. 44
triumphal entry of, into Paris, ii. 524
ugly, vii. 87
Walpole, Bns, talks with, vii. 435
Marie-Christine (1735–82), Ps, Abbess of Remiremont:
Stanislas I pays for journey of, to see her sister, vi. 403
Marie (1573–1642) de Médicis, m. (1600) Henri IV, K. of France:
Sforza, Duchessa, tries to buy Francavilla statues for, v. 480, vi. 583, ix. 657
Marie-Josèphe (1731–67), of Saxony, m. (1747) Louis, Dauphin of France:
daughter born to, iv. 191
Louis XV urged by, to save her father, v. 5
sister comes to see, vi. 403
Marie-Joséphine-Louise (1753–1810), of Savoy; m. (1771) Louis-Stanislas-Xavier, Comte de Provence, later Louis XVIII:
HW not expected to rave over, in Paris, vii. 312
sister of, vii. 465
very ugly, vii. 312n
Marie Louise, English ship:
French ship said to be disabled by, during Young Pretender's invasion voyage, iii. 88
Marie-Thérèse (1756–1805), m. (1773) Charles, Comte d'Artois, later Charles X:

Broglie was to have escorted, to Paris, vii. 521
marriage of, planned, vii. 465
Marie-Thérèse-Charlotte (1778–1851), m. (1799) Louis-Antoine de Bourbon, Duc d'Angoulême:
birth of, viii. 470
Marie-Thérèse-Félicité (d'Este). *See* Maria Teresa Felicità
Marie-Zéphirine (1750–5), of France:
birth of, iv. 191
Marigny, Marquis de. *See* Poisson, Abel-François
Marine belt:
invention of, vi. 332
Marines:
English: Mathews ready to debark, ii. 312; Mathews to land, in Tuscany in case of invasion, ii. 26; Palliser's removal as general of, asked, viii. 446
French, Kearnie, officer of, marries Lady Betty Brownlow, ii. 117
Mill to command, iii. 407
Marino:
Leopold, Maria Carolina, and Maria Louisa visit, vii. 17–18, 23
Lobkowitz marches to, ii. 447
Maria Carolina receives homage of Roman subjects at, vii. 23
Marius, Caius (157–86 B.C.), Roman general:
HW cites quotation about Cæsar and, viii. 28
statue of, in Pomfret collection, iv. 390
Marivaux, Pierre Carlet de Chamblain de (1688–1763), dramatist:
HW commissions Churchills to have portrait of, painted by Liotard, iv. 324–5
Liotard intimate with, iv. 325
Marianne by, iv. 362
picture of, Liotard delivers, to HW, iv. 362
Market:
at Covent Garden, v. 294
Market town:
apothecary's wife in, iii. 234
Markham, William (1719–1807), Bp of Chester 1771–7; Abp of York 1777–1807:
afterwards Abp of York, viii. 217n
dismissed as preceptor to George IV, viii. 217
Mann attributes cabals to, viii. 225
Marlay. *See* Marley
Marlborough, Ds of. *See* Churchill, Henrietta (ca 1671–1733); Jennings, Sarah (1660–1744); Russell, Lady Caroline (1743–1811); Trevor, Hon. Elizabeth (d. 1761)
Marlborough, D. of. *See* Churchill, John (1650–1722); Spencer, Charles (1706–58); Spencer, George (1739–1817)
Marlborough, Wilts:
Pitt visits, vi. 488

Marlborough, English ship:
at Port Mahon, i. 285
Cornwall captain of, ii. 415
French and Spanish chase, into Plymouth, viii. 506
Marlborough Fort, xebec. *See Malborough Fort*
Marley, Thomas (d. 1784), army officer: wounded, v. 516
Marli. *See* Marly
Marlow, William (1740–1813), artist:
Canaletto's views copied by, vii. 299
Scott's pupil, vii. 299
Marly:
Du Barry, Mme, at, vii. 115
machine at, HW not fit to be entrusted with, v. 354
Maron, Anton von (1733–1808), artist:
Mann's portrait by, vii. **565**, viii. 27, 31–2
Mengs' brother-in-law, vii. 565, viii. 31
summoned from Rome to Florence to paint Maria Louisa and Maria Theresa, viii. 31
Marque, letters of. *See* Letters of marque
Marriage; marriages:
boys perform, when under age, and are sent abroad to ripen, vi. 159
clandestine, Parliamentary bill to prevent, iv. 383, 441, vi. 294
clergymen most apt to be faithful in, ix. 424
Cocchi's treatise on, banned, vi. 204
HW considers duty in, ill-performed when prompted only by periodic obligation, ix. 426
state of, in England and Italy, ii. 199
witnesses not required for, by English law, vii. 484
Marriot, Mrs—(d. 1714), 'housekeeper' of Windsor Castle ca 1684–ca 1697:
Verrio paints, as a Fury, iv. 212
Marriot, Anne (1697–1750), housekeeper of Windsor Castle:
death of, iv. 212
Marroni, Tuscan officer:
(?) Montemar to be attended by, i. 228
Marrow-bones:
in Arlington St, ii. 96
London streets full of, i. 196
Mars:
HW's name for Guadagni, iv. 41
Mars, English prison ship:
escapes to Ireland, ix. 152
Mars, French ship:
Jacobites escape in, to France, iii. 254, 270
Marseille:
Ædes Walpolianæ delayed at, iv. 68
Austrians and Sardinians threaten, iii. 323
bark reaches Leghorn from, i. 179, 407–8
Conway and Cts of Ailesbury may meet at, iv. 285
Cumberland, D. of, probably to embark to, from Leghorn, ix. 645

English invasion might threaten, v. 223
English seizures of ships will ruin, ii. 448
French couriers go by way of, ii. 75
Giberne and Hoare to go home by way of, iv. 86
HW may step from, to Leghorn, on marine belt, vi. 333
Jew receives letter from, about sea battles, ii. 410
letters from, received at Leghorn, viii. 461
Levant ships bound for, captured by privateers, viii. 437
Mann, Horace II, to overtake Lady Lucy Mann at, viii. 265
Mathews threatens, ii. 463
Orford, Cts of, to reach, in Spry's ship, vii. 2
Osborne's fleet menaces, v. 135
passage from, uncertain in winter, ii. 84
Prince George captured by French privateer near, v. 414
protected by *cordon* from fatal malady in Languedoc, ix. 304
Prussian privateer ordered to carry his prize to, v. 350
ship from: reaches Leghorn with Louisbourg news, v. 242; to pursue Wright, v. 21
Spanish expedition reported at, i. 179
Stormont to visit, vii. 25
tartans escape to, ii. 455
Townshend may command squadron off, iii. 376
trade at, interrupted, v. 123
Veers deceives bankers of, iii. 507
Villars' country house between Aix and, vi. 553
visitors to: Holland, vi. 467; York, D. of, vi. 553
Walpole, Sir Robert, might go to Italy through, ii. 202, 212
Marseilles, —— (dancer). *See* Marcel
Marshal, Lord. *See* Keith, George
Marshall, Samuel (ca 1740–95), naval officer:
despairs in storm, ix. 115
Marshal of Conclave. *See* Chigi
Marsham, Hon. Charles (1744–1811), 3d Bn Romney; cr (1801) E. of Romney; M.P.:
conduct of, more prudent than Horace Mann II's, ix. **290**
Mahon drops opposition to, ix. 490, 494
—— opposes, in Kent election, ix. 490
Mann, Horace II, a friend of, ix. 490
Marsham, Rev. Hon. Jacob (1759–1840):
father obliges, to cease courting Miss Mann, ix. 448
Mann, Lucy, attached to, ix. 268, 405, 414, 421, 423, 431
Marsham, Robert (1712–93), 2d Bn Romney, 1724:
lives opposite HW in Arlington St, vii. 286
maid awakes, with news of HW's house being broken into, vii. 286

[Marsham, Robert, *continued*]
president of the Society of Arts and Sciences, x. 48
Shipley lives near, in Kent, x. 48
son obliged by, to cease his courtship, ix. 448
Marsham family:
insanity in, ix. 423–4
Marsilly, Abbé de:
(?) La Condamine questions, at Damiens' execution, vi. 147
Marsorio:
Pasquin's dialogue with, iv. 189
Marteaux, Ensign:
captured at Velletri, ii. 492
Martelli, Signora. *See* Tempi, Maria Maddalena
Martelli, Camilla (d. 1590), m. Cosimo I, Grand Duke of Tuscany; formerly his mistress:
HW desires picture of, ix. 214
HW finds print of, by Allegrini, ix. 226
Pius V said to have forced Cosimo I to wed, viii. 16
print of, in Mann's possession, too large for post, ix. 230
second wife of Cosimo I, ix. 214, 230
Martelli, Francesco, Chute's servant:
Capezzoli sought by, vii. 569
(?) Chute's death reported by, viii. 211
earthquake predicted by, iv. 119, 143
English earthquake preferred by, to Leghorn one, iv. 130
Martenico; Martenique. *See* Martinique
Martial (Marcus Valerius Martialis) (A.D. 43–104), Roman poet:
Patapan throws, into fire, ii. 339
Martin, Charles, painter and duellist:
(?) Mann sends letter to HW through, i. 6
Philipps accompanied by, i. 81
Martin, Samuel (1714–88), M.P.:
Augusta, Ps of Wales's treasurer, vi. 183n
West succeeded by, as secretary of the Treasury, v. 25
West Indian, vi. 183n
Wilkes chats with, in Paris, vi. 198
——'s duel with, vi. 183, 192
Martin, William (ca 1696–1756), Capt.; Admiral:
Brindisi may be visited by, to fetch Spanish artillery, ii. 27
Catalogue of French Books, A, mentions, ii. 52
death of, v. 3
HW receives copy by Giberne of letter of, ii. 39, 42, 43, 62
Leghorn may be destination of, ii. 27
Mann knew, in Italy, v. 3, 121
—— quotes, ii. 100
——'s advice awaited by, ii. 38
——'s correspondence with, ii. 39, 42–3
——'s restraint of, irritates English captains, ii. 100

Mathews joined by, ii. 398
—— recalls squadron of, ii. 38
Naples threatened by, ii. 15–16, 26, 27, 38, 39, 42–3, 47, 52, vii. 506
orange trees auctioned on lawn of, v. 121
Salas's letter to, ii. 43
Tuscany to be protected by squadron under, from invasion, ii. 26
Vernon to be succeeded by, iii. 188
Martin, William (d. 1766), Lt and Capt.:
ship of, sinks, iii. 269
Martinelli, Vincenzio (1702–85), Florentine writer:
bed-ridden and sinking into imbecility, ix. 554
Orford, E. of, to receive letter of, forwarded by Mann to HW, ix. 554–5
Martini, ——:
French affectations of, iv. 103
Goodwin, Mrs, asks, about Florentine finance, iv. 103
Martini, Padre Giovanni Battista (1706–84), composer:
Mann sends to HW, index to book by, v. 496
Martinique ('Martinica'; 'Martinico'):
Albemarle's expedition may go to, vi. 7
Beckford clamours for retention of, vi. 39
Byron blockades Estaing at, viii. 456
—— does not conquer, viii. 475
—— may starve, viii. 466
—— said to have captured, viii. 461
capture of: Albemarle will be encouraged by, vi. 15–16; does not hasten peace, vi. 23; English casualties at, slight, vi. 43; expected, vi. 29–30; justifies deferring peace treaty, vi. 99; Monckton responsible for, vi. 15–16; prisoners from, conducted to France, vi. 32; will release Albemarle for further conquests, vi. 21–2
English invasion threatens, v. 277, 279, 282, 297, 534, vi. 13
English success at, iii. 190
Estaing strips, of provisions, viii. 530–1
fleet of: Boscawen to intercept, iv. 579; captured, iii. 487; defeated by Townsend in West Indies, iii. 186; France said to await, before declaring war, iv. 491
hurricane ravages, viii. 530
Mann reminds Botta of false rumours about, vi. 89
Moore's squadron to fight Bompart's at, v. 297
Martyr, Justin. *See* Justin Martyr
Martyr; martyrs:
ridiculousness of, HW's reflections on, iv. 555
Martyrs of Mr Fox, The. See Fox's Martyrs
Mary, Virgin:
Fuentes vows to, never to visit public places, v. 428
HW jokes about, to Chute, i. 257

Italian painter includes, in Trinity, vii. 459

Levis depicted as meeting, iv. 88

Mirepoix, Duchesse de, entitled to uphold the train of, iv. 92

Stuart family's loyalty to, satirized, vi. 227

Wilkes's irreverent mention of, vi. 184

York, Cardinal, to celebrate first Mass on birthday of, iii. 500

See also Madonna

Mary (Tudor) (1516–58), Q. of England 1553–8:

HW ridicules alleged virtues of reign of, ix. 605

Mary (1658–1718) of Modena, m. (1673) James II, K. of England 1685–8:

maid of honour to, later at Reggio, i. 44

Mary (Stuart) (1542–87), Q. of Scots, m. 1 (1558) François II, K. of France; m. 2 (1565) Henry Stewart, E. of Darnley; m. 3 (1567) James Hepburn, 4th E. of Bothwell:

George III's death would have led to long minority like that of, vi. 42

masqueraders costumed as, i. 338

picture of, HW gives, to Mme Grifoni, i. 415

Mary (1723–72), Ps, dau. of George II, m. (1740) Friedrich II, Elector of Hesse-Cassel:

death of, vii. 375

Delorain, Cts of, governess of, ii. 82n

England to be visited by, iii. 295

George II's bequests to, v. 450

HW played with, in childhood, at Leicester House, ix. 647

husband's quarrel with, iii. 80, 295

Orford, Cts of, fondles children of, iii. 70

—— well received by, iii. 80

son born to, i. 255

Mary (1776–1857), Ps, dau. of George III, m. (1816) William Frederick, D. of Gloucester:

father requests provision for, viii. 371

inoculation of, ix. 406

Mary, Cts of Pomfret's servant:

Barney knew, i. 101

Scully's lawsuit with, i. 101–3

Mary, English ship:

Leghorn to be defended by, ii. 38

Marz, Maj. —— (d. 1743):

killed at Campo Santo, ii. 164

Marzo, Tuscan officer:

(?) Montemar to be attended by, i. 228

Marzocco, Tuscan fort:

quarantine for plague-stricken crew established at, i. 105

Marzolin cheese. *See under* Cheese

Masaccio (Tommaso Guidi) (1401–ca 1428), painter:

Bartolommeo, Fra, inferior to, vii. 362, 371, 469

paintings of, hardly known out of Florence, before Patch's prints, ix. 280

Patch's engravings from frescoes of, vii. 266–7, 275–7, 287–8, 315, 362, 371, 422, 465, 469, ix. 280, x. 45; HW to show to Reynolds, vii. 267; Mann sends, to HW, vii. 266

——'s rescue of designs of, providential, vii. 287

Raphael's precursor, vii. 267, x. 45

Masaniello (Tommaso Aniello) (1620–47), demagogue:

ghost of: Mann should appeal to, vii. 5; may alarm Neapolitan Court, i. 501

Wilkes compared with, vii. 5, 317, viii. 535–6

Maschere, Villa delle, Gerini's villa:

HW has print of, vi. 202

Modena, Ps of, stays at, vi. 202

Masetti, Caterina (1713–90), m. (1733) Conte Agnolo Galli:

death of, falsely reported by Cerretesi to HW, ii. 166, 186

Goldsworthy, Mrs, helped by, i. 350–1

HW's correspondence with, i. 435–6

HW sends pins and fans to, i. 193, 239, 416, 422

Mann's social relations with, i. 239, 350, ii. 29

marital relations of, i. 57, ii. 46, 186, iv. 147

Maynard talks French with, ii. 372

Montemar does not write to, ii. 46, 62

—— said to have proposed minchiate game to, i. 193

——'s former mistress, i. 193n

opera box of, iii. 505

pregnancies to be avoided by, ii. 186

pregnancy of, attributed by husband to Montemar or Don Philip, ii. 46

screams through her nose, i. 239

senator who was cicisbeo to, dies, iv. 336

son born to, i. 56–7

(?) Stosch subject of joke by, i. 445

Masham, Bns; Masham, Mrs. *See* Winnington, Henrietta

Masin, ——, Ensign:

captured at Velletri, ii. 492

Masiniello. *See* Masaniello

Mask; masks:

balls in, for Archduke and Archduchess of Milan, at Florentine theatres, ix. 50

Barretts miss, at Florence, iv. 92

begin to appear on Florentine streets, ii. 139

Botta forbids, in hopes of Dresden victory, v. 435

Craon, Princesse de, to have worn, to theatre, iii. 8

Electress's hostility to, ii. 178

Eleonora, Ps, wears, i. 77

'Fiscal' asks Regency council to forbid, ii. 372

Florentine, at Carnival, i. 311, iii. 207, 364, iv. 464

[Mask; masks, *continued*]

Florentine opera somnolent except for, iii. 439

Florentines dread a prohibition of, ii. 369

Florentines mad with, iii. 207

forbidden, in Florence, i. 284

gay, at Florentine carnival, iii. 364

Grifoni, Signora, wears, i. 294

guests at Stanley's fête champêtre not to wear, viii. 14

HW adopts, to avoid dancing, i. 77

HW shuns, at Reggio, i. 46

in opera, in London, i. 302

lack of, prevents balls in theatre, iv. 219

Leopold amuses himself with, at Florentine theatre in Carnevalino, viii. 343

—— enjoys, vi. 477, 486, 491

—— permits, vi. 491

Mann indifferent to, iv. 404

Maria Louisa attends theatre in, vi. 581

mob demands removal of, vii. 194

not permitted in theatres, ii. 139

of wax, covers Clement XIV's disfigured face, viii. 43

on Cellini's bell, vii. 383

optional, at Pisa ball, ix. 581

other topics excluded by, iv. 464

permitted at Florence: i. 291, ii. 113, 364, 435, vi. 559; at opera while Caffarelli remains, iii. 439; on St John's Eve, ii. 435, 462, iii. 8; without opera, iii. 8

pleasures of, i. 304

popularity of, crowds Florentine theatres, ii. 372

rank obscured by use of, iv. 219

Richecourt forbids, iv. 216, 219

——'s orders about, iii. 8

theatres crowded with, ii. 391

Venetian, Leopold wears, vi. 491

Venice's, i. 77

See also Masquerade

Mason, John (d. 1781):

Clinton's messenger, captured by Americans, ix. 135

Mason, Mrs John. *See* Finch, Elizabeth

Mason, Rev. William (1725–97), poet:

Gray's works edited by, vii. 442n

Masones de Lima y Sotomayor, Don Jaime, Marqués de Sotomayor; Spanish army officer and diplomatist:

Tencin's complaints of, iv. 28

Masons. *See* Freemasonry

Mason-Villiers, George (1751–1800), styled Vct Villiers, 1st E. of Grandison, 1782, M.P.:

marriage of, vii. 381

marriage of, planned, vii. **323**

Masque:

Congreve's, iii. 45

Masque. *See also* Mask

Masquerade; masquerades:

at Ranelagh, i. 487, 495, iii. 414, iv. 46, 57, 70, vii. 58, viii. 103

at Pantheon, viii. 103

at Richmond House, vi. 148

at Soho, HW attends, vii. 193

at Stanley's fête champêtre, viii. 14

Capello, Signora, gives, iii. 17–18

Christian VII to give, at Ranelagh, vii. 58

Cornelys, Theresa, gives, vii. 271

England has not had, since Lisbon earthquake, iv. 539, vi. 17, 49, vii. 58

English: dissipates political clouds, vii. 201; more sprightly than Florentine ones, iv. 464

English bishops associate, with earthquakes, iv. 539, 548, vii. 58

Florentine, not prevented by earthquakes, iv. 548

George II and Elizabeth Chudleigh to open, iv. 122

HW and Lincoln attend, from Ds of Richmond's, ii. 167

HW attends, dressed as old woman, i. 359

HW's former passion for, vii. 193

HW's trunk of costumes for, vii. 193

HW to attend, ii. 149

Hamilton falls in love with Elizabeth Gunning at, iv. 302

in Florence, ii. 386

in London, i. 331

jubilee: at Ranelagh, iv. 46, 57, 70; for Elizabeth Chudleigh, iv. 57, 70

Norfolk, Ds of, gives, i. 331, 338–9, 343, 368, 370

Northumberland will open his gallery with, iv. 507

numerous in London, iii. 464, iv. 71, viii. 102–3

officers give, for Friedrich Wilhelm, iii. 265

on bridge at Florence, i. 97

Parliament and war do not disturb, iv. 469

politics replaced by, vii. 476

Queensberry, Ds of, gives, iii. 464, 469, 471

Savoir Vivre club to give, viii. 103

subscription: at Haymarket, iii. 483; at Ranelagh, iv. 47, 59; House of Commons fairly adjourns for, vii. 192–3

to be held on the Thames, viii. 86

Mass; masses:

commander-in-chief at Genoa will not stir until he hears, v. 329

Craon, Princesse de, attends, ii. 115

downfall of, might be engineered by Old Pretender, v. 8

Dumesnil says, privately in Volterra cathedral, iii. 493

Egizziello has, performed for his recovery, i. 472

for destruction of Polish dissidents, vi. 577

Jesuits again permitted to say, viii. 106

Jesuits forbidden to say, vii. 507

requiem, Angiola Lucchi arranges, for lover's repose, iv. 254

Riccardi orders, to get fair weather for garden party, v. 435
said at Vienna, for all those killed in a campaign, v. 333
said for Wachtendonck's recovery, iii. 110
York, Cardinal, to celebrate, for his father, iii. 500
Massa, Ds of. *See* Gonzaga, Riccarda (1698–1768)
Massa, D. of. *See* Cybo, Alderano (1690–1731)
Massa, Ps of. *See* Cybo, Anna Matilde; Cybo, Maria Theresia
Massa, Vincenzio (b. ca 1744); monk of the Carmine:
  (?) Clement XIV's relative, vii. 118
Massa:
  Albani prince to wed princess of, iii. 475
  claims to, i. 34–5, 47
  Hercules III to take refuge in, ii. 223
  Modena, Ps of, retires to, iv. 201
  Modenese court may move to, i. 425
  Montemar visits, ii. 59
  small yield of, i. 47
  Spaniards at, i. 314, 323
  visitors to, Modena, P. and Ps of, vi. 144
  Young Pretender at, ii. 376, 388
Massaccio. *See* Masaccio
Massachusetts:
  assembly of: passes act regarded as illegal, vi. 507; said to have usurped Parliament's powers, vi. 507
  assembly's act rejected by Privy Council and examined by House of Lords, vi. 520
  rebellion in, vii. 550–1, viii. 63, *see also under* Boston
Masserano, Principe di. *See* Ferrero di Biella, Vittorio Filippo (1713–77)
Massesi, Matteo:
  Paoli forgives betrayal by, vii. 68
Mass-houses:
  burned in Edinburgh, viii. 439
Massimo, Marchesa. *See* Savelli, Barbara
Massingham, Norfolk:
  living of, vii. 510
Mast; masts:
  cabin-boys at top of, iv. 210
  France needs, for navy, ix. 4
  ship loses, in approaching Leghorn, iii. 235
Master builders:
  fires should be responsibility of, during construction, iv. 185
Master General of the Ordnance:
  Richmond resigns as, ix. 392
  See also Townshend, George (1724–1807)
Master of Ceremonies, Tuscan. *See* Baldocci, Nunziato
Master of the Buckhounds:
  Halifax succeeds Jenison as, ii. 551
  Orford, 2d E. of, is, iii. 496, iv. 233n
  place of, sinks, under 2d E. of Orford, iii. 496

Master of the Great Wardrobe. *See under* Great Wardrobe
Master of the Horse:
  Bloodworth is, to Augusta, Ps of Wales, iv. 245
  Caroline's: Pomfret buys post of, i. 276; Pomfret is, i. 165n, 276
  Charlotte's: aspirants to, vii. 176; Beaufort resigns as, vii. 174; De la Warr succeeds Ancaster as, vi. 473; Harcourt is, v. 517; Waldegrave becomes, vii. 180
  George II consults Augusta, Ps of Wales, about, iv. 245
  George II's: aspirants for, after D. of Richmond's death, iv. 182–3, 202; Bedford may become, iv. 235; Gower succeeds, Dorset as, v. 104; Hartington to be, iv. 258; Richmond is, i. 319, 338n; Rutland may become, iv. 470; Sandwich may become, iv. 217
  George III's: Ancaster becomes, vi. 473; Ancaster's death leaves vacancy in, viii. 407; Bristol, E. of, said to become, vi. 453; Hertford succeeds Rutland as, vi. 450; Huntingdon becomes, v. 13; Huntingdon remains as, iv. 452; Mann asks about Huntingdon's shift from, v. 500; Marlborough to be, vi. 130; Pembroke resents denial of, viii. 435; Rutland becomes, v. 489
  Marie-Antoinette's, Tessé is, vii. 353
  Middlesex to be, to Frederick, P. of Wales, iii. 370
Master of the Household:
  Frederick, P. of Wales's, Gage is, i. 252n
  Harris, John, is, to George II, iv. 418n
Master of the Jewel Office:
  Lyttelton succeeds Breadalbane as, v. 25
Master of the Mint. *See* Arundel, Hon. Richard (d. 1758); Chetwynd, Hon. William (1684–1770)
Master of the Ordnance:
  Conway succeeds Granby as, without accepting salary, vii. 179
  Marlborough becomes, iv. 517
  Richmond becomes, ix. 262
  —— resigns as, ix. 392
  ——'s willingness to retain trifling post of, shows his disinterestedness, ix. 296
  Townshend is, ix. 53
Master of the Rolls:
  Norton succeeds Clarke as, vi. 263
  Strange, Sir John, is, i. 494n
  See also Fortescue, William (1687–1749); Sewell, Sir Thomas (ca 1710–84); Strange, Sir John (1696–1754)
Masucci, Agostino (1691–1758), painter:
  'Aurora' copied by, for Northumberland, iv. 352, 490, v. 88
  print from drawing by, of Old Pretender's marriage, ix. 448
Masulipatam:
  Clive said to have captured, v. 378

Mat; mats:
Mann's bedroom floor covered with, ii. 358
Matallana, Marqués de. *See* Torres y Morales, Rodrigo (ca 1687–1755)
Match:
of bomb, v. 155
Materassi, Pier Maria; Medici servant:
(?) son of, ii. 39
Mathematics:
Albany, Cts of, studies, ix. 106
HW belittles advantages of, v. 409
HW does not know Latin terms in, v. 353
Mozzi's work in, vii. 155, ix. 130
St-Germain said to understand, x. 20
Sanderson discourages HW from studying, at Cambridge, v. 353
Mather, Roger (ca 1719–68), D.D., public orator of Oxford, 1749–60:
Pomfret, Cts of, praised by, iv. 579
Mathew, Francis (1738 *or* 1744–1806), cr. (1783) Bn Landaff, (1793) E. of Landaff; Irish M.P.:
peerage of, ix. 433
Mathews *or* Matthews, David (fl. 1769–84), Mayor of New York 1776–84:
arrest of, viii. 230
Mathews, Thomas (1676–1751), naval officer:
agitation of, ii. 205
Albani asks Mann to ask, for help, ii. 453
——, Lobkowitz, and Thun suspect friendship of, to Austria, ii. 476
—— sends compliments to, ii. 491
Austrian and Sardinian lack of cooperation infuriates, ii. 228–9
Austrian ministers ask Mann to ask, for help, ii. 452
Benedict XIV receives protest from, ii. 300–1
——'s reception of Spanish xebecs will enrage, ii. 291
—— to have been punished by, ii. 314
Bradshaw from ship of, ii. 146
Carteret and Newcastle displease, ii. 346
Carteret neglects, ii. 395
Charles of Naples's message from, ii. 461
——'s treatment from, unjustifiable, ii. 195
Charles Emmanuel III wanted by, to coop up Spaniards in Tuscany, ii. 108
Chute and Whithed laugh at, ii. 279
Civita Vecchia to have been demolished by bomb ships of, ii. 314
clothes prepared by, ii. 360
cockade of, ii. 522, 544
Cornish seeks, at Roses and Hyères, ii. 415
couriers to be sent by, to London and Vienna, ii. 325
court martial of, iii. 33, 321, 327–8
Court may be attacked by, at Toulon, ii. 443
crew of, disturb Roman Catholic church ceremonies on Italian island, and hang crucifix on monkey's neck, ii. 79n
departure of, threatened, ii. 346

diamond-studded sword given to, by Hungary and Sardinia, ii. 370
Domenichino painting might be sent to England by, ii. 144
England hears little of, ii. 293
England probably reached by, ii. 514
England receives news from, of sea battle, ii. 423
English captain questions wisdom of, in sending so many ships to Leghorn, ii. 106
English captains advise, to buy Mann's coffee pot, ii. 472
English merchants at Leghorn protected by, ii. 92
English ships at Leghorn told by, to await Mann's orders, ii. 59, 67
fleet of: at Hyères, ii. 370, 395–6; not to be separated, ii. 447
fleet soon to be left by, ii. 477
Fogliani's opinion of, wanted by Mann, ii. 215
Francis I's insistence on Tuscan neutrality enrages, ii. 339, 361
French and Spanish fleets awaited by, ii. 106
French coasts blockaded by ships of, ii. 411
French fleet must be pursued by, to Brest, ii. 423
French Levant ships to be seized by, ii. 453
French to be attacked by, ii. 296
Genoa may be attacked by, ii. 229
George II puts, in command of Mediterranean fleet, i. **405**
Goldsworthy's dispatches alarm, ii. 107
Grenville told by Mann not to execute orders of, ii. 27
HW attributes Mann's illness to tiring qualities of, ii. 60–1
HW has not yet seen, but will thank him and inquire about cases, ii. 522
HW impressed by Mann's negotiations with, ii. 467
HW's shipments to be forwarded by, ii. 325, 445, 496, 514, 522
HW surprised at use of 'His Holiness' in dispatches by, ii. 317
health of: bowel pains from gravel, ii. 215
Hyères to be visited by, ii. 360, 420
investigation into naval action of, iii. 25
Italians call, 'furibondo,' ii. 46, 60n., and *passim*
Italian terror of fleet of, ii. 205
Leghorn cannot be defended by, alone, ii. 77
Leghorn ships ordered by, to await Mann's commands, ii. 59, 67
Lestock sends complaints against, ii. 432
letters of, confused, iii. 47
Lobkowitz and Mann unaware of plans of, to make descents, ii. 484
Lobkowitz asks, for loan of ships, ii. 438, 470, 471

—— not to receive ships from, ii. 443
—— to receive remonstrances of, against Neapolitan expedition, ii. 444
Long's instructions from, ii. 473
Mann and Villettes may summon, ii. 16
Mann awaits approval of, ii. 471
—— gets excuse from, for not blockading xebecs in Civita Vecchia, ii. 300
—— gives cheese and citrons to, ii. 195
—— harassed by, ii. 205, 293
—— has to defend, against Richecourt, ii. 328–9
—— not surprised that orders by, were confused, iii. 47
—— overwhelmed by ignorance of, ii. 342
—— pleases, by remonstrating for English captains, ii. 309
—— requested by, to consult Long at Leghorn, ii. 469
——'s arguments against Papal recognition of Young Pretender should be reinforced by squadron of, vi. 386
—— saves Civita Vecchia from fury of, vi. 386
——'s correspondence with, ii. 26, 27, 37, 77, 92, 152, 188, 195, 215, 256–7, 279, 284, 287, 296, 299, 325, 328, 443, 445, 453, 461
——'s dispatch of ships to Nettuno may not be approved by, ii. 461
—— sells HW's coffee pot to, ii. 472
—— sends 'sweetmeats' to, ii. 195
——'s instructions from, read aloud at war council, ii. 484
——'s letter to HW to be forwarded by, ii. 471, 477
——'s packet sent by, to HW, ii. 518
——'s passports alone respected by, ii. 46
——'s sending ships to Nettuno approved by, ii. 476
——'s shipments to HW to be traced by, ii. 477
—— supposed to have influence with, ii. 476
—— told by: of delays in shipping HW's things, ii. 445; that Osborne took HW's cases to England, ii. 514; that Theodore of Corsica deceived English ministers, ii. 221–2
—— writes to, about Theodore of Corsica, ii. 188
Maria Theresa blamed by, for not assisting Charles Emmanuel III, ii. 346
—— differs with, over Neapolitan war, ii. 370
——'s followers' entreaties fail to induce, to send ships against Naples, ii. 460
—— wants, to aid her army, ii. 447
marines of, i. 26, 312
Marseille and Toulon threatened by, ii. 463
Martin joins, ii. 398
—— sent by, against Naples, ii. 15

——'s squadron recalled by, ii. 38
may be on man of war at Leghorn, ii. 145
Montallegre and consul present horse to, ii. 453
Murray fears that Mann may tell, to intercept Young Pretender, ii. 419
Naples threatened by part of fleet of, ii. 15
Navarro attacked by, ii. 413
Nettuno fleet augmented by, ii. 476
Newcastle's silence disgusts, ii. 361
news of battle awaited from, ii. 403, 410
Nuremberg visited by, while awaiting passports, ii. 517
Old Pretender's letters intercepted by, ii. 280
plague may be brought by, ii. 279
Port Mahon visited by, ii. 420
prize-taking said to be preferred by, to helping Austrian army, ii. 452
Prole may be dismissed by, ii. 309
Protestantism of, ridiculed by HW, ii. 79
protest of, forwarded to Rome, ii. 300–1
quarantine difficulties complained of, by, ii. 300
quarantine irks, ii. 279
refuses to take men of war to the Giogo, ii. 296
Regency council asks Mann to ask, to guard against plague, ii. 256–7
reinforcements expected by, ii. 106
resignation of, announced, ii. 215
retirement no longer intended by, ii. 336
Richecourt arouses threats from, ii. 309
Scottish officer comments on, iii. 25
ship sent by, to Leghorn with letters for Mann, ii. 26, 37
ships expected by, from Adriatic, Genoa and Minorca, ii. 395–6
ships recalled to England from, ii. 458
Spanish advance on Nice to be forestalled by, ii. 312
Spanish fleet at Majorca eludes, ii. 244
Spanish invasion of Tuscany to be repelled by, ii. 26, 37–8
spelling mistakes of, ii. 215, 301
Susa entertains, at Villefranche, ii. 360
tartans blockaded by, at Marseille, ii. 455
tastes of, in eating and amusement, ridiculed by HW, ii. 79
Theodore of Corsica causes confusion to, ii. 188, 194
——'s installation desired by, ii. 229
Tories oppose, for opposing them in Monmouthshire election, iii. 33
Toulon approached by, ii. 443, 447
Toulon battle of, ii. 402, 403, 410, 413–15
Toulon fleet bottled up by squadron of, ii. 15
Toulon fleet must be withstood by, ii. 384
Toulon fleet should be defeated by, before it joins Brest fleet, ii. 393
Townshend to excel, iii. 253

[Mathews, Thomas, *continued*]
Traun and Charles Emmanuel III urged by, to coop up Spaniards in Tuscany, ii. 108
Turin conferences attended by, ii. 370
Turin court to have been dazzled by, ii. 215
Turin visit planned by, ii. 360
Tuscan situation not understood by, ii. 98
Tuscany's defence rests upon, ii. 296
Vado visited by, ii. 438
Vernon may succeed, ii. 312
Villefranche to be left by, ii. 360
Villettes's dealings with, ii. 26, 37, 240, 271, 455, 529
Walpole, Sir Robert, esteemed by, ii. 153
Wentworth from ship of, ii. 146
Winchilsea directs, to send shipments to Sir Robert Walpole, ii. 144, 330
wounded, ii. 415
xebecs elude, ii. 287, 296
Mathurā, India:
(?) temple at, viii. 433
Matignon, Marquise de. *See* Brenne de Bourbon, Edmée-Charlotte de (ca 1700–56)
Matilde (1046–1115), Cts of Tuscany:
Pope receives patrimony of, v. 562
Matilde (1729–1803) d'Este, Ps of Modena:
Novellara duchy may be given to, iii. 335
Young Pretender may wed, iii. 335
Matos, João de, Portuguese Jesuit:
Portugal does not release, v. 341
Matrimony. *See* Marriage
Mattei, Girolamo (d. 1753), Duca di Giove:
(?) Valle gives statue mould to, vi. 115
Mattei, Livia. *See* Livia
Mattei, Villa:
eagle at, seen by Chute, iii. 121
Matter:
HW condemns modern deification of, vi. 410
Matthew, St:
in Correggio painting, i. 167
Matthew, Mrs George. *See* Brownlow, Isabella
Matthew, Sir Tobie (1577–1655), Kt, 1623; M.P.; courtier:
letters by, quoted, iii. 243–4
Matthews. *See* Mathew; Mathews; Matthew
Mattos. *See* Matos
Mattresses:
Joseph II rides in wagon full of, vii. 108
Maubeuge:
siege of, rumoured, ii. 500
Maudlin College. *See* Magdalen College
Mauduit, Isaac. *See* Mauduit, Israel
Mauduit, Israel (1708–87), woolen-draper:
Considerations on the Present German War, v. 458, 469, 472
Maule, Hon. John (1706–81), M.P.:
Argyll's friend, iii. 107
Edinburgh magistrates search house of, for arms, iii. 107

Maule, William (1700–82), cr. (1743) E. of Panmure; M.P.; army officer:
brother of, iii. 107
mission of, to Gibraltar, to punish Fowke and Stuart, iv. 562
troops raised by, to oppose Young Pretender, iii. **103**
Mauleverer, Lady. *See* Slingsby, Barbara (ca 1669–1721)
Maupeou, René-Nicolas-Charles-Augustin de (1714–92), Chancellor:
abhorred, vii. 265
Aiguillon opposes, vii. 453
—— tries to keep, from reconciling the Princes of the Blood, vii. 399
banished, viii. 34–5
Choiseul tells, to name new controller, vii. 164
Clement XIV's death supposed to have been partly caused by, viii. 50
clergy and Princesse Louise cultivated by, vii. 398
Conti's report to, vii. 298
credit of: advances vii. 265; declines, vii. 398
English-Spanish war averted by, vii. 304
epigram on award to, of cordon bleu, vii. 259
France banishes, while England elects his counterpart, viii. 134
French people curse, vii. 320
French people may dispatch, vii. 304
Fuentes ignores, vii. 321
HW abhorred, viii. 35
HW hopes for fall of, viii. 12–13
law courts suppressed by, vii. 317
Louis XV advised by, to remove Choiseul to make parliaments submit, vii. 259
Louis XV and Comtesse du Barry almost alone with, at Versailles, vii. 298
Louis XV often met by, in Princesse Louise's cell at St-Denis, vii. 321
—— would not imitate conduct of, vii. 359
Louis XVI said to like, viii. 1
Parliament de Paris attacks declaration of, against arrêt of 1762, vii. 398
prime minister cannot be made by, vii. 268
retires amid curses of his people, viii. 36
SH makes HW pity, vii. 315
Maupertuis. *See* Moreau de Maupertuis
Maurepas, Comte de. *See* Phélypeaux, Jean-Frédéric
Mauri, Joseph, cadet:
captured at Velletri, ii. 493
Maurice (1567–1625) of Nassau, P. of Orange, 1618; Stadholder of Netherlands 1587–1625:
illegitimate descendants of, viii. 360
Mauritius:
French retain, v. 523
Mauvillain, Hannah (ca 1710–82), m. (1743) Andrew Stone:
Mann's errand for, ii. 330

Mawkin:
mob carries, i. 391

Mawson, Matthias (1683–1770), Bp of Llandaff 1738, of Chichester 1740, of Ely 1754:
Pembroke's conversation with, about Hounslow postmaster, iv. 109

Maxen:
battle at, v. 354

Maximilian I (1459–1519), Holy Roman Emperor 1493–1519:
daughter's prayers desired by, ix. 468
money lacked by, to become cardinal by bribing Pope and Sacred College, ix. 468
wants to become pope and saint, ix. 468

Maximilian (1774–8), Archduke:
death of, ix. 549
Gloucester, D. and Ds of, see, at Poggio Imperiale, viii. 297

Maximilian Franz (1756–1801), Archduke; Elector of Cologne and Bp of Münster, 1784:
Florence to be visited by, ix. 367
Frederick II forbids Elector of Cologne to give succession to, ix. 81
Ingenhousz inoculates, vii. 91, 123
Leopold accompanied by, to Pisa, Leghorn and Lucca, viii. 129–30
—— and Maria Louisa to be visited by, in country, viii. 123
—— escorts, to Florence from Rome, viii. 123
—— to meet, at Venice, and escort him to Tuscany, viii. 95
Pius VI might demand price for making, Bp of Münster, ix. 80

Maximilian Friedrich (1708–84), Graf Königsegg-Rothenfels; Abp and Elector of Cologne, 1761; P.-Bp of Münster, 1762:
Frederick II's letter to, ix. 81

Maximilian Joseph I (1727–77), Elector of Bavaria 1745–77:
Austrian succession may be claimed by, iii. 5
declares neutrality, v. 102
English favoured by, iii. 5
French sympathies of, iii. 24
Kingston, Ds of, claims to have received title from, viii. 404
neutrality treaty of, iii. 34, 37, 39, 41
sent to Vienna and Dresden, x. 10

Maxwell, Robert (ca 1720–79), 2d Bn Farnham, 1759; cr. (1760) Vct Farnham and (1763) E. of Farnham; M.P.:
HW mentions, iv. 441

May day:
milkmaids dance with garlands on, ix. 274–5
milkmaids' garlands on, will have to be of ivy and holly, due to poor weather, ix. 639

Mayence. *See* Mainz
Mayerne. *See* Mayne

Mayfair Chapel:
Hamilton marries Elizabeth Gunning at, iv. 303
sermon at, on Frederick, P. of Wales, iv. 241, 243–4

Maynard, Vcts. *See* Parsons, Anne (ca 1735–ca 1814)

Maynard, Charles (1752–1824), 2d Vct Maynard, 1775:
suicide of, at Naples, falsely rumoured, viii. 435, 451

Maynard, Sir William (1721–72), 4th Bt; M.P.:
brutality of, iii. 331
Chute dislikes, ii. 439–40
Craon, Princesse de, drops, ii. 440
Craons introduced to, by Mann, ii. 371
Craons to entertain, ii. 372
Florence to be visited by, ii. 367
Galli, Mme, and Mme Suares talk French with, ii. 372
HW apologizes for, ii. 451, iii. 5
HW never saw, ii. 451
HW recommends, to Mann, to be introduced to Craons, ii. 367
HW's letter to, transmitted by Selwyn, ii. 371
Italian not spoken by, ii. 372
Jacobite, ii. 451, v. 550n, ix. 40n
Mann promises to look after, ii. 371–2
——'s civilities to (on HW's recommendation), rudely requited, v. 550n
Mirepoix, Mme de, gives letter of introduction to, for Craon, ii. 371
quarrels with everybody at Florence, ii. 439–40
Selwyn, George, friend of, ii. 451
Selwyn, John, asked HW to recommend, to Mann, ii. 451

Maynards:
tragedy acted by, iii. 439

Mayne, Perry (ca 1700–61), naval officer:
Willes sends summons to, iii. 328

Mayne. *See also* Main

Maynon d'Invault, Étienne (1721–1801), controller-general:
Choiseul's favourite, vii. 164, 169
resignation of, vii. 164, 169

Mayoli. *See* Majoli, Clemente

'Mayoress, Lady.' *See* Lady Mayoress

Mayor of London. *See* Lord Mayor of London

Mayor's wife:
country church visited by, during recitation of Creed, i. 3

Maypole:
dancing around, at jubilee-masquerade at Ranelagh, iv. 47

Mazarin, Jules (1602–61), cardinal:
Pitt's name for Granville, x. 10

Mazucci. *See* Masucci
Mazulipatam. *See* Masulipatam

Mazzei, Filippo (1730–1816), Italian merchant; American diplomat:
Florentine who has lived in England, v. 492
goes to England as merchant for Florentine produce, v. 495
Mann recommends, to HW, v. 492
—— sends letter through, to HW, v. 495
music book to be taken by, to England, v. 492, 495
prank by, offends Florentine priests, v. 495
Mazzinghi, Abate (d. ca 1771), Florentine seminarist:
Ferdinand of Naples tosses, in blanket, vii. 254
Mazzuchelli, Conte Giovanni Maria (1707–65), scholar, collector:
Museum Mazzuchelianum: published at Venice, vi. 14; Walpole, Sir Robert, to be described in, vi. 15, 24, 25–7, 35
Mazzuoli *or* Mazzoli, banker at Rome:
Compagni and Libri fail to give orders to, i. 11
Parker's dealings with, for HW, x. 5
Mccartney. *See* Macartney
Mccintosh clan. *See* MacIntosh
McDonald:
Henry Benedict (Stuart) said to have assumed name of, iii. 189
See also Macdonald
McDonald clan:
Glenbucket wants to transplant, to the McPhersons, x. 31
Mcintosk. *See* MacIntosh
'McKay, Lord.' *See* Prévost, Jacques
Mckinsy. *See* Stuart-Mackenzie
Mclean. *See* Maclaine
McPherson clan:
Glenbucket wants to transplant McDonalds to, x. 31
Mead, Dr Richard (1673–1754), M.D., physician; collector:
bankruptcy of: Cocchi would have been involved in, iv. 189; family deny, iv. 185
Beaufort's potency examined at house of, ii. **185**
Cocchi helped by, with subscriptions for his book, iv. 179
collection of: HW to buy bronzes and vases at sale of, iv. 470; said to be on sale for debts, iv. 165; sold, iv. 185n
nerves treated by, iv. 389
Patch lived with, vii. 275
seraglio kept by, iv. 165
Meade, Sir John (1744–1800), 4th Bt, cr. (1766) Vct Clanwilliam and (1776) E. of Clanwilliam:
heiress married by, viii. 544
mistress unfaithful to, viii. 544
rival fatally castrated by, viii. 544
Meadows. *See* Medows
Meanness:
pride the counter-poison to, ix. 655

Measles:
occurrences of, i. 343, 352, 381, 416, 445, ii. 121
oranges cause, i. 352
prevalent in Florence, i. 381
Meat:
Catholics avoid, on Friday, i. 254
Clement XIII allows Spaniards to eat, 4 days a week in Lent, vi. 5
—— might allow, in Lent during fish shortage, vi. 101
cold, country ladies stock up with, after Session, ii. 498
for breakfast, vi. 202
Genoese lack, iii. 352
Mann avoids over-eating, i. 78
newspaper squib warns English butchers against Roman Catholic avoidance of, on fast days, iii. 129
pies of, iv. 219
Pius VI allows Roman Catholics to eat, in Lent, ix. 17, 21
price of, in Italy, will rise because it is eaten in Lent, ix. 17
roasted by means of burning-glass, v. 121
salt, Leghorn supplied with, i. 193
scanty at Leghorn, i. 304
Meath, Bp of. *See* Smyth, Arthur (1706–71)
Mechanics:
HW ignorant in, v. 354
Mechel, Laurence, Lt:
captured at Velletri, ii. 492
'Mecklemburg King at Arms':
HW calls himself, v. 532
Mecklenburg:
Bernstorff's estate in, vii. 43
Dalton draws Q. Charlotte's picture at, v. 525
Mecklenburg-Strelitz, Ds of. *See* Elizabeth (1713–61) of Saxe-Hildburghausen
Mecklenburg-Strelitz, D. of. *See* Adolf Friedrich IV (1738–94); Karl II (1741–1816); Karl Ludwig (1708–52)
Mecklenburg-Strelitz, P. of. *See* Georg August (b. 1748)
Medal; medals:
Albani's, coveted by Mann for HW, ii. 477
brass, Mann receives, from Rome, ii. 45
Clement XIV strikes, on reconciliation with Portugal, vii. 221
Cocchi and Craon do not discuss, i. 342
Cocchi instructs Conway about, iv. 297
——'s, seen by Huntingdon, iv. 457
—— suggests design for, ii. 471–2
Elizabeth's, on Armada's defeat, v. 357
Florentine export of, forbidden, iv. 465
for Francis I's election, sent by Mann to HW, iii. 184, 185, 203
French would make, if even one ship returned safely to port, v. 357
George II should have, for his victories, v. 212

George III collects, v. 231, 238, 449, 478
gold: antique, Duane sells, to Hunter, ix. 572n; Benedict XIV gives, to Lobkowitz, ii. 447; HW buys, i. 24; Mann to buy, i. 24; Winckelmann said to have left, to Wilkes, vii. 113
Greek, of silver, Stosch secures, through Albani and Mann, from deceased Roman collector, ii. 478
HW leaves, at Florence, i. 11–12
HW may have trouble with, at customs, i. 64
HW's: almost stopped at Calais customs, i. 142; of Caesar, x. 7; of Coliseum, x. 7; of gold, x. 7; of Sabina, x. 7; of the Bridge, i. 12; of Trajan's father, x. 7; of Trajan's forum, x. 7; of Vitellius, x. 7
HW's collection of, untouched by housebreakers, vii. 284–5
HW thanks Mann for, ii. 518, v. 203–4, 215, 222, 233
Hamerani's: for Francis I's election, done for Albani, iii. 184; of Benedict XIV, x. 5; of Pretender's sons, i. 18, 19, 218, x. 3
in Florence gallery, remain as before, ix. 170
lack of, for collectors, in Florence, vi. 115
Leopold orders, to commemorate Moroccan ambassador's reception, viii. 469
Louis XV has, struck for Siamese ambassador's reception, viii. 469
Mann sends, to HW, ii. 406, 424, v. 272, viii. 478
—— sends, to HW through Wills, v. 209, 215, 233, 242
modern, Bute orders Dalton to buy, for George III, v. 478
of Argyll, v. 202, 233
of Benedict XIV: HW has not acknowledged receipt of, v. 299; HW wants, v. 203; Mann awaits, from Rome, v. 231; Mann will send, to HW, v. 242; Mann writes to Rome about, v. 215
of Benedict XIV and Clement XIII, sent by Mann to HW, v. 272, 278
of Cardinal York, wanted by HW, v. 487
of Charles II, ii. 424n
of Cocchi, v. 202
of Francis I, i. 380, 401, ii. 272, iii. 184
of Galla Placidia, offered by Stosch to HW, iv. 53, 70
of Maria Theresa, ii. 471–2, 477, iii. 184
of Moroccan ambassador's reception by Leopold: HW receives, viii. 500; Mann sends, to HW by Gascoigne, viii. 478; Mann to send, to HW, viii. 469–70; miserable performance, viii. 478
of rhinoceros, iv. 128
Old Pretender coins, v. 45
on submission of Genoa to Louis XIV, iii. 313
Oxford's, sell for high prices, i. 374
Pomfret, Cts of, and HW collect, i. 4

Roman, of great brass, HW exchanges for Cellini's bell, vii. 383
satirical: of George II and Sir Robert Walpole, i. 229; of Sir Robert Walpole, i. 189, 229, 426, ii. 45, v. 202
silver, ii. 406, 424, 478, v. 189, 201–2, 203; Benedict XIV gives, to Lobkowitz's staff, ii. 477
Stosch carries, from Rome for HW, i. 416
—— collects intaglii like, v. 186
——'s: bawdy, v. 160, 189; bought by Dalton for George III, v. 231, 478; desired by HW, v. 178, 189, 201; HW insists on paying for, v. 215; HW thanks Mann for, v. 203; Mann to send, to HW, v. 201–2; prices of, v. 218, 227; sent by Albani, ii. 478
Taylor honoured by, ii. 272
Medaliuncino:
of Alexander Severus, vii. 383
Medallions:
Cellini's, of the Medici, ix. 215
HW's, of Antinous, x. 7
Medallist:
may be Siries's grandson, viii. 500
Medici, royal and ducal members of family of, see under their first names
Medici, Alessandro Marzio de' (d. 1630), Bp of Fiesole 1596–1605; Abp of Florence 1605–30:
Dudley brings suit in court of, ix. 225
Medici, Filippo Antonio (b. 1687), impresario for little theatre:
accademia begun by, ii. **178**
Electress not related to, ii. 178
Regency council to receive a caution from, unknown to accademici, ii. 445
theatre denied to, by accademici, ii. 439
Medici, Francesco Maria de' (1660–1711), cardinal 1686–1709:
wife of, ii. 39–40, 62n, 177
Medici, Giovanni Gastone de'. See Giovanni Gastone
Medici, Giulio de'. See Clement VII
Medici, Giuseppe de' (d. 1743), Principe d'Ottajano:
death of: at Leghorn, ii. 173; expected, ii. 160
Electress leaves ring to, ii. 173
Sani accompanied by, to Leghorn, ii. 160
valet of, sent to Naples, i. **238**
Medici, Maria Maddalena de' (d. 1785), m. (1749) Marchese Giovanni Corsi:
Acciaioli, Mme, invites, to meet Ds of Grafton, vi. 28
Cowper kept by, in Florence, v. 415, vi. 361
Maria Louisa met by, at Bolsano, vi. 334
marriage of, iv. 95
'sweet,' vi. 28
Medici, Niccolò Giuseppe de' (1663–1749), of Via Larga:
commissary at Prato, ii. **170**
Electress calls, her nearest relative, ii. 170
——'s legacy to, ii. 170, 176–7

Medici, Ottajaro *or* Ottaviano de'. *See* Medici, Giuseppe de'

Medici, Balì Tommaso Gaetano (1676–1749):
(?) Lisbon earthquake injures, iv. 519
(?) Niccolini partner of, iv. 519

Medici, Palazzo, on Trinità del Monte in Rome, Franchini's house:
Roman mob visits, iii. 114

Medici, Villa, at Fiesole:
Orford, Cts of, alters, as home for her old age, viii. 244
—— anxious to see repairs at, viii. 305
—— buys, vii. 463–4, 468
—— confined at, by snow, viii. 344
—— leases, and then buys it, viii. 190
—— makes, accessible by coach, viii. 190
—— makes new road to, viii. 260
—— refits and ornaments, viii. 260
—— to live at, in autumn and winter, viii. 322

Medici, Villa, at Rome:
Leopold takes art objects from, to Florence, ix. 531n

Medici family:
Allegrini's heads of, ix. 226
allodials of, i. 238
arms of: on HW's china, ix. 591; to adorn Bianca Cappello's portrait, iv. 407, 415
art treasures of, the only reason for their being remembered in Florence, ix. 93
bastards of, in hospital, ii. 39–40
Cellini's medallions of, ix. 215
chapel of, ii. 160, 171–2
Charles VIII gives *fleur-de-lis* to arms of, iv. 415
collection of: assembled and augmented by Leopold, ix. 530–1; Cellini's chest from, vii. 407; dispersion of, prevented by Act of Accession, iv. 465–6; Uffizi represents, vi. 71
Court economy practised by, vi. 154
drainage project found impracticable by, viii. 343
eccentricities of, ii. 176–7
Electress excludes Bianca Cappello's portrait from those of grand duchesses of, iv. 399, 414, v. 561
—— is last of, iii. 370n, v. 561n
export of antiquities never forbidden by, iv. 465–6
fleur-de-lis on Cappello arms probably derived from, iv. 407
Galluzzi's history of, should make them shudder in tombs, ix. 202
gold foot given by, to Uffizi, ix. 65
grand dukes of, seldom made noteworthy achievements, v. 284
guardaroba of, sold by Leopold, vii. 407, ix. 531
HW thanks Mann for prints of, ix. 245
HW to imitate, i. 505
HW wants Mann to send historical tracts about, v. 278, 284

HW wishes Mann would get his Bath ribbon from, vii. 47
HW wishes popes were extinct like, ix. 224
history of: Cocchi intended doing, v. 284; discouraged by Lorraine regime, v. 284; HW thinks of writing, v. 278; should be written, v. 291; *see also under* Galluzzi, Riguccio
Joseph II may try to regain property taken from, by the church, ix. 595
larger proportion of good and great members, than in most families, ix. 223
Leopold allows history of, to be published now that it is extinct, ix. 87n
Leopold's and Maria Louisa's affability reminiscent of, vi. 390
manuscripts about, in peoples' hands, mostly vulgar and obscene, v. 284
Maria Theresa's dislike of nudes would not suit taste of, vi. 246
medals of, Dalton buys, from Stosch collection, for George III, v. 231
prints of: bill of lading for, v. 533, 538; HW's not to be broken up, ix. 434; HW to have complete set of, v. 533, 561; Mann sends, to HW, iv. 414; sent to George III by Mann, vii. 37, ix. 230
Stosch collection had tracts about, v. 278, 284
Stuart family history may be written like that of, ix. 538
successors of: 'Goths,' vii. 407; melt art objects for metal to avoid shame of selling them, vii. 427
tax collectors of, lenient, vi. 255
tombs of, in San Lorenzo, ix. 202
visiting princes fêted by, in former days, ix. 589

Medicine:
and politics, HW's reflections on, v. 377–8
Cocchi's book on Greek surgeons, iv. 34, 179, 189, 437–8
—— stops Barrett from taking drugs and, iv. 94–5
Craon, Princesse de, takes, ii. 98
diseases, French prisoners afflicted with, ix. 207
HW compares, to lotteries, ix. 428
Irish priest studies, i. 142
Leopold takes, frequently, vi. 459
Maria Theresa gives trunkload of, to Leopold, vi. 459
Montaigne's *Journal du voyage* much concerned with, viii. 16
newspaper advertisements for quack cures in, for impotency and barrenness, ii. 561
sleeping in damp air thought to be injurious, vi. 457
strong, England overdoes, iv. 543
See also Abscess; Ague; Amputation; Antimonial medicine; Apoplexy; Apothecary; Arm; Asafœtida; Asthma; Bark;

Bleeding; Blindness; Blister; Blistering; Blood, spitting of; Blood vessel; Boils; Bootikins; Brain, inflammation of; Breast, inflammation of; Cancer; Carbuncular state of blood; Castration; Cataracts; Cauterizing; Chalkstones; *Chaud d'eau;* Clap, the; Cold; Colic; Confectio Raleana; Consumption; Convulsions; Couching; Cough; Cresta; Cutaneous disorders; Deafness; Delirium; Dentistry; Diabetes; Diarrhoea; Discharge from legs; Disorder in legs; Disorder in stomach and bowels; Dissection; Distempers; Douche; Dropsy; Dropsy in the stomach; Dysentery; Emaciation; Ephemera; Epidemic; Epidemic disorder; Epileptic fits; Eruptions, Erysipelas; Eyes; Eye-waters; Fainting; Female indisposition; Fever; Fire, internal; Fistula; Fit; Fits apoplectic; Flannel; Flux, bloody; Flux of water; Fumigations; Hare: skins of; Hartshorn; Headache; Heart; Hellebore; Herpes; Hiccup; Hip; Humour in the ears; Humour in the face; Humour in the knee; Humour on the breast; Hydrophobia; Hypochondria; Impostumation; Indigestion; Inflammation in the face; Inflammation of the bowels; Inflammation of the brain; Inflammation of the eyes; Influenza; Inoculation; Insanity; Insomnia; Iron-pear-tree-water; Issue of blood; Itch; James's Powders; Jaundice; Keysar's pills; Kneepan; Lancet; Lancing; Laudanum; Lavendar drops; Lazarettos; Leeches; Lethargy, apoplectic; Limewater; Lock-jaw; Malaria; Mange; Measles; Melancholia; Mercurial unctions; Miscarriage; Mortification in the legs; Murrain; Nerves; Nervous disorders; Nose-bleed; Oculist; Ointments; Opiates; Oppression on the breast; Page-surgeon; Pain in back; Pain in bowels; Pain in breast; Pain in hands; Pain in head and breast; Palsy; Paralysis; Paralytic disorder; Parotides; Perspiration; Physic; *Piaga aperta;* Piles; Plague, the; Plaster; Pleurisy; Polypus; Pores; Potency; Powder, red; Pox; Ptisan; Pulse; Purblindness; Purging; Quack; Quarantine; Quicksilver; Quinsy; Rheumatism; Rhubarb; Rupture; Sage; St Anthony's Fire; Salivation; Scarlet fever; Scrofula; Scurvy; Senapisms; Shivering fits; Shortness of breath; Shoulder; Skin diseases; Smallpox; Soap; Sore; Sore leg; Sore mouth; Sore throat; Spleen; Sponging; Starving; Stone; Styptic; Suffocation; Sulphur; Surfeit water; Surgeon; Surgical instruments; Swelling; Swollen ankles; Swollen legs; Syringe; Syringe-baths; Tapping; Tar water; Thrush; Tooth; Tooth-ache; Trepanning; Ulcer; Unctions; Urine, suppression of; Venereal disease; Vinegar; Vomiting; Water in the stomach; Weakness on the breast; Wen; Worming; Wrist; Yellow fever

Medina Sidonia, D. of. *See* Alcántura Guzman Pacheco y Silva, Don Pedro

Mediterranean Sea:
  Boscawen's fleet in, superior to French, v. 297
  Bourbons control, vii. 36
  Brest fleet thought to be headed for, ii. 393
  Byng sails to, iv. 538
  Camilly to bring ships to, from Brest, ii. 443
  cruise on: planned for Lady Lucy Mann, viii. 203, 214, 220, 222, 225, 233, 239; recovery of Percy brothers attributed to, viii. 203
  Danish, Russian, and Swedish fleets expected in, ix. 59–60
  Dutch ships in, few, ix. 112
  Dutch war begun in, ix. 120
  Elphinston's division only partly assembled in, vii. 185
  enemy fleet might impound English in, ix. 201
  England expects news of sea battle in, ii. 539
  England might have mastery of, with fleet of proper size, iv. 565, 566–7
  England needs port on, iv. 553, 574
  England's post through, 'out of repair,' ix. 191
  England supplied Leghorn with fish when in control of, ix. 211
  England will regret her loss of, through not aiding Paoli, vii. 125
  English actions in, not blamed on Sir Robert Walpole, ii. 205
  English fleet from, arrives safely, viii. 391
  English fleet in: can injure French trade, v. 122–3; pursues French men-of-war, v. 249; Vernon unpopular with, ii. 312; would endanger Austrian possessions if it attacked Naples, ii. 390
  English fleet needed in, to protect Gibraltar and Minorca, iv. 545
  English fleet patrols French coast of, i. 407–8
  English fleet to go to, iv. 538, v. 58, 197, vii. 174
  English invasion might threaten France from, v. 223
  English loss of Minorca disgraces her in, iv. 583
  English merchant ships in, could be captured by frigates at Corsica, vi. 157, viii. 352, 375, 397
  English ministry should have thought of fleets for, instead of local politics, iv. 578
  English naval investigation concerning, iii. 12, 25, 32–4, 47
  English naval strength in, promised by Saunders, v. 97

[Mediterranean Sea, *continued*]
English privateers capture Dutch merchant ships in, ix. 120
English privateers in, few, v. 20–1, ix. 112
English ship of the line to enter, with D. of York, vi. 260, 267
France's seizure of Corsica will mean control of, vi. 157, vii. 27, 36, 38, 47
French fleet moved from, to Rochefort, iii. 78
French may exclude English trade from, iv. 581
French merchant ships captured in, worth less than 3 English vessels, v. 414–15
French ports on, expect English attack, v. 134
French ships dominate, v. 20, 101, 264, viii. 352, 375, 397–8, 466
George II does not send army to, iii. 121
—— wants invincible fleet in, i. 405
Gibraltar's retention safeguards, ix. 357
Hawke may be expelled from, by Toulon fleet, iv. 587
Howe appointed commander in, vii. 250
Italy hopes to see free navigation restored in, ix. 17
Leghorn to eclipse other seaports of, iv. 102
Louis XV to expel English from, iv. 588
Mann threatens to resign his naval command in, iii. 236
—— 'viceroy' of, v. 326
Minorca more useful than Gibraltar as British base in, iv. 574
pirates inhabit islands in, ix. 493
Rodney's victory eases situation in, ix. 21
Rowley once commanded fleet in, vi. 581
Russia has no trade in, ix. 61, 84
Russian fleet coming to, ix. 59–60
Russian fleet sails from England to, vii. 151, 157
Russian fleet's disasters in, vii. 202
Russian fleet supposedly in, ix. 187
Russian war ships in, few, viii. 114
shipments from, again reach England, v. 118
Villafranca and Nice the last ports available to England in, iv. 575
war preparations in, vii. 38
William IV sails to, and may visit Leghorn, ix. 590
winds in, delay post, i. 393
York, D. of, to tour, with Augustus Hervey, vi. 154
—— unlikely to go to, again, vi. 270
Medley, Henry (d. 1747), naval officer:
at Gibraltar, iii. 146
captures proclaimed by, iii. 384
convoy sent by, to Adriatic, iii. 220
Corsican chiefs to receive letter from, iii. 216
death of, rumoured, iii. 433
fleet of, reaches Villefranche, iii. 334

French boats to be intercepted by, iii. 378
Genoa to be blockaded by, iii. 352, 384–5
Genoese cannon may obstruct, iii. 385
Genoese convoys elude, iii. 410
Gorsegno tells Mann to tell, of English captain's treachery, iii. 150
ill, iii. 432–3
Mann entrusted by, with direction of English fleet, iii. 235
——'s correspondence with, iii. 410
—— sends ship to, iii. 206
Port Mahon still the station of, iii. 216
Rowley succeeded by, iii. **132,** 146
Schulenburg to be assisted by, against Genoa, iii. 385
secretary of, ill, iii. 433
ship sent by, from Port Mahon to Leghorn, iii. 192
ships sent by, to Adriatic, to escort Germans from Trieste, iii. 220
squadron of, tempest encountered by, ii. 556
Townshend cannot remain with, iii. 374
—— discusses court martial with, iii. 359–60
——'s disgrace explained by, iii. 324–5
Vado house occupied by, iii. 432
Medows (later Pierrepont), Charles Pierrepont (1737–1816), cr. (1796) Vct Newark and (1806) E. Manvers; M.P.; naval officer:
Bristol, E. of, said to be sued by, for income of Kingston estate, viii. 227
Hermione prize to be shared by, vi. **45**
Mann's particular friend, vi. 45
uncle's estate may be intercepted by, viii. 56
uncle should have been permitted to leave most of his estates to, viii. 31
uncle's wealth may be deserved by, viii. 30
uncle's will disputed by, viii. 21
Medows, Edward (d. 1813), naval Capt.:
Bristol, E. of, said to be sued by, for income of uncle's estate, viii. 227
uncle's estate may be intercepted by, viii. 56
uncle should have been permitted to leave most of his estates to, viii. 31
uncle's wealth may be deserved by, viii. 30
uncle's will to be contested by, viii. **21**
Medows, Evelyn Philip (1736–1826):
Bristol, E. of, said to be sued by, for income of Kingston estate, viii. 227
uncle's estate may be intercepted by, viii. 56
uncle should have been permitted to leave most of his estates to, viii. 31
uncle's wealth may be deserved by, viii. 30
uncle's will disputed by, viii. **21**
Medows, Lady Frances. *See* Pierrepont, Lady Frances (b. 1713)
Medows, Sir Philip (d. 1757), Bt:
grandsons of, viii. **227n**

INDEX

Medows, Philip (1708–81):
Bristol, E. of, sued by, viii. 227
sons of, viii. 227n
Medows, Thomas (ca 1749–80):
Bristol, E. of, said to be sued by, for income of uncle's estate, viii. 227
uncle's estate may be intercepted by, viii. 56
uncle should have been permitted to leave most of his estates to, viii. 31
uncle's wealth may be deserved by, viii. 30
uncle's will to be contested by, viii. **21**
Medows, Sir William (1739–1813), K.B., 1792; army officer:
Bristol, E. of, said to be sued by, for income of uncle's estate, viii. 227
uncle's estate may be intercepted by, viii. 56
uncle should have been permitted to leave most of his estates to, viii. 31
uncle's wealth may be deserved by, viii. 30
uncle's will to be contested by, viii. **21**
Medrano, Jean Antoine, Brigadier:
captured at Velletri, ii. 494
Medusa:
gem of, not stolen, iii. 350
Meek. *See* Mick
Meer, Vander. *See* Montvandermeer
Meerman, Gerard (1722–71), scholar; Dutch deputy to England, 1759:
English mission of, v. 290
Meeting-house:
Presbyterian, Roman Catholics said to have destroyed, ix. 56
Megæra (one of the Furies):
East India Company should be corrected by, vii. 442
Meget, Meggit, Meggitt, *or* Meghitt, Florentine innkeeper:
Cumberland, D. and Ds of, stay at inn of, ix. 644
Megliorucci. *See* Migliorucci
Meguire. *See* McGuire
Mehemmed Pāshā Karamānlī (d. 1754), Dey of Tripoli 1745–54:
French threaten, iv. 319–20
Mehr:
battle of, v. 228, 234
Melancholia:
occurrences of, ii. 89
Melcombe, Bn. *See* Bubb Dodington, George (1691–1762)
Meldola, Principe di. *See* Pamfili, Camillo (1675–1747)
Meleager, intaglio of:
Stosch's: ii. 369; Duncannon may buy, iv. 159; HW wants, i. 213; Stosch receives offer for, i. 264; Stosch's only first-class one, v. 151
Mellini, Mario (1667–1756), cardinal, 1747:
dying, iv. 463–4

Maria Theresa's minister plenipotentiary at Rome, iii. 475
Mellish, William (ca 1710–91), M.P.; politician:
HW mentions, ii. 374
Parliamentary debates by: on amendment to the Address, x. 23; on privately-raised regiments, x. 18
voting of, i. 243
Mello e Castro, Martinho (1716–95), Conde de Galvas, Portuguese diplomatist:
Theodore seeks, v. 45
Melon seeds:
HW mentions, i. 42
HW receives, i. 45
HW wants, iv. 170
Hartington asks HW to write to Mann for, ii. 384
—— has not received, ii. 496
——'s, shipped from Leghorn, ii. 428
Hervey to convey to HW, i. 34
Mann sends, to Sir Robert Walpole, i. 34, 38
Melville, Vct. *See* Dundas, Henry (1742–1811)
Memel:
Prussian troops at, prepare against Russians, v. 72
Mémoire justificatif:
English, against France: Mann to give, to Barbantane, viii. 531; Young Pretender approves of, viii. 531
Mémoire pour le Comte de Cagliostro:
Fitzgerald's case relieved by, ix. 631
Mémoires de Grammont. See under Hamilton, Anthony
Mémoires politiques et militaires . . . de Noailles. See under Millot, Claude-François-Xavier
Memoir of the Revolution in Bengal. See under Campbell, John (1708–75)
Memoirs:
of Louis XIV's minority, v. 13
Memoirs of a Woman of Pleasure. See Cleland, John: *Fanny Hill*
Memoirs of Martin Scriblerus. See under Swift, Jonathan
Memorial; memorials:
Mann's expense allowance for, ii. 516
Memorial of the E—— of S——. See under Dalrymple, John (1673–1747)
Memphis:
probably stared at its own downfall, viii. 228
Menagerie:
Francis I's, iv. 463
Mendes da Costa, Mrs. *See* Salvador, ——
Mendip, Bn. *See* Ellis, Welbore
Mengden, Dorothea von, m. Ernst, Graf von Münnich:
exiled, vi. 11
Mengozzi, Bernardo, Bargello of Cortona:
house of, menaced, iv. 423

Mengs, Anton Raphael (1728–79), painter:
HW does not know, iv. 352
Mann engages, to copy 'School of Athens'
for D. of Northumberland, iv. 352, 490,
507n, v. 88
Maron brother-in-law of, vii. 565, viii. 31
Rome visited by, to work for K. of Poland,
iv. 330–1
Titian's alleged painting doubted by, iv.
331
Williams recommends, to Mann, iv. 330–1,
352
—— thinks, equal to Carlo Maratti, iv. 352
Menil, Du. See Dumesnil
Menin:
French besiege, ii. 448
French capture, ii. 456
Mentz, Col. See Menzel, Johann Daniel von
Mentz. See Mainz; Mengs
Menxe. See Mengs
Menzel, Friedrich Wilhelm (ca 1724–96),
Elector of Saxony's secretary:
Frederick II bribes, to copy Brühl's dis-
patches, v. 5n
Menzel, Johann Daniel von (d. 1744), Col.:
Catalogue of French Books, A, satirizes, ii.
53
Mercer:
Rudd, Mrs, pays, for brocaded silk, viii.
153
Merchant; merchants:
Dutch, at Leghorn, vi. 418, 423
English: at Leghorn, see Leghorn: English
merchants at; at Messina, ii. 257; at
Naples, fear retaliation for Marciana out-
rage, ii. 28; in India, vi. 211–12; may
beget gentlemen, vi. 483; prepare to leave
Genoa, iii. 10; should not let country
gentlemen turn them, against America, viii.
132; should resent Corsican seizure by
France, viii. 477
English, in London: are loyal, ii. 408;
Dingley carries address from, vii. 98; dissatisfied with Aix treaty, iii. 511; HW
cares more for human life than for interests of, vi. 39; Halifax popular with,
vi. 43; mob attacks, when presenting address, vii. 98; petitions from, i. 211, 295,
344, 353; resent anti-plague measures, ii.
282; subscribe for raising troops, iii. 106;
West Indian, Keppel declines invitation
from, viii. 449
French: at Leghorn, vi. 418, 423; at
Plymouth, has concealed weapons, ii. 402;
implicated in plot in England, ii. 426
Genoese foreign, flee to Leghorn, iii. 338
Tuscan, names of, on bill of lading, v. 269
Merchantmen (merchant ships):
Dutch, see Holland: merchant ships of
English, see England: merchant ships of
French, see France: merchant ships of
Mercure de France, La:
Cours de l'Europe satirizes, i. 177

Mercury:
gesse of, Mann to get, for Sir George
Lyttelton, iv. 539, 547, 554
Mercury (chemical). See Quicksilver
'Mercury and Battus.' See under Fernandi,
Francesco
Mercury and Cupid. See under Prior, Matthew
Mercy-Argenteau, Florimond-Claude-Charles
(1727–94), Comte de; Austrian ambassador
to France 1766–90:
Austrian-Dutch quarrel discussed by, at
Paris, ix. 561
Meredith, Mary (ca 1738–1807), m. 1 (1752)
Laurence Shirley, 4th E. Ferrers; m. 2
(1769) Lord Frederick Campbell:
Campbell, Lord Frederick, marries, v.
396n
husband accuses, of snaring him into mar-
riage, v. 395
husband separated from, by Act of Par-
liament, v. 367, 396
husband's sanity attested by, v. 399
husband tries to murder, v. 183–4, 396
Johnson pays money to, v. 396
mother-in-law's letter to, v. 399
pretty but without fortune, v. 367, 395
Meredith, Sir William (ca 1725–90), 3d Bt;
M.P.:
Clive driven by, out of House of Commons, vii. 490–1
Ferrers's courage expected by, to fail, v.
399
North saved by, from mob, vii. 290
sister of, v. 395
Meredith family:
Ferrers's deathbed paper attacks, v. 398
Merenda:
Riccardi gives, in garden, v. 435
Merlin, John Joseph (1735–1803), mechanic:
(?) chair made by, for Mann's use in gout
attacks, viii. 346, 404, 462
Merlin, British ship:
loss of, viii. 339
Merlo, ——, Capt.:
militia commanded by, at San Remo, iii.
124
San Carlo defended by, on Danube, iii.
124
Mermaid, English ship:
Michael captain of, iii. 410
Mermaid; mermaids:
Townshend's pun on, v. 66
Virgil mentions, v. 213
Merry, Robert (1755–98), Capt.:
Arno Miscellany poems written by, ix.
517n, 522, 633, x. 46
Elogy of James Cook and Robert Manners
translations by, ix. 635–6
Florence Miscellany has contributions by,
ix. 633
Mann, Horace II, knows reasons for retire-
ment by, to Florence, ix. 522

sold out of Horse Guards and retired to Florence, ix. 517n, 522, x. 46

Meschersky. *See* Meshcherskiĭ

Meshcherskiĭ, Prince Alexander *or* Prince Platon Stepanovich (1713–99):
(?) Chernyshev recommends, to Mann, ix. 84

Mesman, Daniel (d. 1794), silk-weaver:
(?) Florence visited by, with Giles, his brother-in-law, viii. 243–4

Mesmene. *See* Mesman

Mesnil. *See* Dumesnil

Mesnildot. *See* Du Mesnildot

Messalina (Valeria Messalina) (ca 22–48 A.D.), m. Emperor Claudius:
bigamy of, like Ds of Kingston's, viii. 333
Bocchineri, Mme, the successor of, iv. 449

Messenger; messengers:
Clinton's, delivered to Congress, ix. 135
Conway sends, to HW, v. 119, vii. 284
English, from Hanover to Spain, iv. 498
George III's, v. 513
Gloucester, D. of, sends, to England, to announce his recovery, vii. 336
Gray, Sir James, receives ensigns of Order of the Bath through, v. 507, vii. 14
Mann sends dispatches to Murray and HW's letter by, viii. 437
Northampton to be told by, of uncle's death, v. 272
Pitt sends, to Sir Richard Lyttelton, v. 507–8
private, Leopold receives, from Vienna, every fortnight, ix. 44
San Severino's, from England to Naples, v. 453, 455
to Stuart-Mackenzie, not arrived, v. 511
Wallmoden sends, to summon servants from Rome, vi. 357
See also Baisly, ——; Butson, John Joseph; Collins, George; Cox, Samuel; Crew, Samuel; Dawson, John; Frediani, Lorenzo; Haite, Richard William; Hunter, William; Money, John; Moss, James; Otto, Henry; Potter, Hanbury (d. 1800); Sarti, Matteo; Staley, Andrew; Whittam, William; *see also under* Courier

Messenger's house:
Pitt carried to, from Parliament, viii. 371

Messenger-sloop:
Rodney's, possibly captured, ix. 17

Messiano:
earthquake account mentions, ix. 376

Messina:
earthquake at: ix. 374–6; ceases, ix. 383; less severe than at first represented, ix. 391; news about, reaches England, ix. 388
English merchants at, safe from plague, ii. 257
governor of, *see* Grimau y Corbera, Don José
plague at, ii. 252, 256, 257, 261–2, 269–70, 274, 282–3
volcano alleged at, ix. 374

Messini, colour-maker:
pastels the specialty of, iii. 369
Raphael's picture of angels copied by, for Garney, iv. 145

Metaphysics:
Walpole, Bns, fond of discussing, ii. 555

Metastasio, Pietro (Pietro Bonaventura Trapassi) (1698–1782), poet and dramatist; 'Mestastagio':
Allessandro nell' Indie, Tesi's part in, ii. 353
Demetrio: Mann and Chute see, at Suares villa, i. 120; Suares, Mme, performed for Modenese princess, i. 104; Suares girls to act, for Modenese princess, i. 99, 101
dénouement not divulged by, vii. 281
Francis I said to have dismissed, making him insane, iv. 163–4
imitation of, suppressed in Italy, viii. 65
Maria Theresa's relations with, iv. 177–8
Olimpiade, L' by, i. 401, iii. 70, 95, 149, vi. 558
Temistocle by, ii. 180

Meteors:
England has, ix. 427

Methodism:
adherents of, iii. 250, iv. 52
Barrett-Lennard, Mrs, prevented by, from going to opera on Sunday, iv. 86
big sinners wanted by, iv. 52–3
England famous for, iv. 70
English visitors to Florence cannot define, iv. 70
HW explains, iv. 81–2
Kilmorey, Vcts, not quite a convert to, iv. 271
popularity of, iv. 41, 52
shopkeepers and women of fashion attracted by, iv. 82
Smythe an adherent of, vii. 248
Townshend, Vcts, makes witticism on, iv. 52

Methodist; Methodists:
Cock Lane Ghost used by, on incredulous mob, vi. 8
Cornwallis will not attract, as Oglethorpe did, iv. 40–1
early, wear hair long and lank about their shoulders, ix. 11
Ferrers gives no opportunity to, v. 398, 399
Fuentes unlikely to become, v. 428
HW glad that Wilkes has not joined, vii. 87
holy days revived by, vi. 17
Huntingdon, Cts of, patroness of, iv. 271, viii. 401n
—— 'primate' of, viii. 90
—— 'Queen of,' iv. 33
—— 'St Theresa' of, v. 398
Kidgell an adherent of, vi. 187
modern, are not anti-Catholic, ix. 11
mysteries, hymns, and canticles of, iv. 271

[Methodist; Methodists, *continued*]
religious sentences scribbled by, on walls, iv. 82
Richardson's novels are romances spiritualized by, vi. 271
'seminary' of, in Welsh mountains, attended by Lady Gertrude Hotham and Cts of Huntingdon, viii. 90–1
Shirley, Lady Fanny, becomes, when no longer admired, iv. 52, viii. 401
Sunday card-playing avoided by, iv. 34
Sunday opera-going repugnant to, iv. 86
Venetian gondoliers would be made by, to sing hymns, iv. 177
Methodist minister:
Indian convert of, in America prefers rum to sacrament, i. 477
Methuen, Sir Paul (ca 1672–1757), K.B., 1725; diplomatist; collector; M.P.:
Grifoni, Mme, might exchange presents with, ii. 366
Lee proposed by, i. 243
Methuselah:
HW appears, to young persons, vi. 485
HW as old as, vi. 304
HW as wrinkled as, viii. 176
HW is, in constitution, ix. 22
HW is skeleton of, viii. 527
HW not yet as old as, ix. 559
HW older than, ix. 635
HW resembles, vi. 341, viii. 228
HW's and Mann's only topics of conversation are modern counterparts of, viii. 283
HW's life seems as long as that of, vi. 415
Metz:
execution at, of officers of Piedmont regiment, v. 382
Louis XV's escape from death at, ii. 502–3, 504–5
'Meursius.' See Chorier, Nicolas
Meusnier de Querlon, Anne-Gabriel (1702–80), litterateur:
note by, in Montaigne's *Journal du voyage*, viii. 16
Mexborough, E. of. See Savil, John (1719–78)
Mexicans:
ghosts of, must insult those of European usurpers, ix. 109
Mexico:
Englishman's life worth more than conquest of, v. 558
gulf of, England now has a foothold on, vi. 106
new Virgil may be produced by, viii. 62
revolts in, rumoured, viii. 384
St-Germain said to have married heiress in, iii. 182
viceroy of, *see* Montserrat, Joaquin, Marqués de Cruillas
Mezzi pauli (coins):
Dumesnil scatters, to mob, iii. 493

Mezzotints:
prices of, vii. 211
Mi:
song says, is no longer a note in music, vi. 334
Micchiate. *See* Minchiate
Michael, Capt. of the *Mermaid:*
Anson's victory reported by, iii. 410
Michelangelo Buonarroti (1475–1564), sculptor and painter:
Medici chapel of, at Florence, ii. 160
Michelets. *See* Miquelets
Micheli. *See* Michieli
Michelozzi, Villa:
Francavilla group at, desired by Mann, v. 480
Michieli, Antonio, Venetian ambassador to Spain 1740–4:
(?) news from, of galleons, i. 84
Michieli, Mme Chiara:
Montagu, Lady Mary Wortley, corresponds with, iv. 279
Michieli, Romano (ca 1575–ca 1660), composer:
Musica vaga ed artificiosa, Mann to send, to Hawkins, v. 467; unobtainable, v. 477, 482, 492
Mick, ——, English ship's surgeon:
Gloucester, D. of, attended by, vii. 337, 342, 393
Midas:
barber of, HW alludes to fable of, vi. 74
Middlesex, Cts of. See Boyle, Hon. Grace
Middlesex, E. of. See Sackville, Charles
Middlesex:
Cooke M.P. for, iv. 223, 235, vii. 7
election for: ii. 25, vii. 6, 73, 78, 97, 104, 110, 167, 186, 208–9, 215, viii. 47; at Brentford, Wilkes and Townshend contend for, viii. 47; Court candidates elected by, iii. 425; Court defeated in, iv. 131; discussed in Parliament, vii. 182; Mann dreads, vii. 147; might be reversed, vii. 186; Pitt discusses, till nobody will answer him, vii. 208–9; Pitt proposes that House of Lords investigate, vii. 167; settled, vii. 215; Townsend refuses to pay tax in protest against, vii. 346; Wilkes's examination deferred until after, vii. 73–4; Wilkes wins, vii. 7, 97, 104–5, viii. 51; wrecked by Proctor's mob, vii. 78
electors of, Wilkes's letter to, vii. 213
Mann not to consult map of, v. 284
—— surprised that House of Commons' decision is not obeyed by, vii. 119
nominations for election of members for, to be held at Guildhall, viii. 48
Parliamentary seat for, vacated by Smithson's accession to peerage, iv. 125
petition from: freeholders sign, vii. 114; Mann has seen, vii. 130; presented, vii. 120
second election must be held for, vii. 30

sheriffs of, summon Wilkes, vii. 475
Wilkes in political control of, vii. 45
—— will be able to name his successor for, vii. 82
Middleton, Rev. Conyers (1683–1750), HW's correspondent:
Ashton attacks, iv. 164, 215
Bolingbroke, Vcts, compliments, iv. 136
Cooke attacks, in sermon, iv. 185–6
death of, iv. 167
Examination of the Lord Bishop of London's Discourses: HW gives, to Galfridus Mann, iv. 185; Mann and Cocchi want, iv. 179; Sherlock attacked in, iv. 134
Germana quædam antiquitatis eruditæ monumenta, HW to give, to Mann, ii. 465
HW accused of bringing, to write Sir Robert Walpole's life, iv. 215
Italian antique collection of, purchased by HW, ii. 465, 478
marriage of, iv. 167
Montfort brings, to Houghton, iv. 215
papers of, might be suppressed by clergy, iv. 215–16
Thirlby's quarrel with, iv. 215
works of, Mann lends, to Firmian, v. 340
Middleton, Mrs Conyers. See Powell, Anne (d. 1760)
Middleton, Lady Mary. See Mackenzie, Lady Mary
Middleton, Sir William (ca 1700–57), 3d Bt; M.P.:
voted for, as commissioner, i. 437
Middleton, Sir William (1738–95), 5th Bt, 1768; M.P.; army officer:
death of, in battle, falsely rumoured, vi. 47
Midhurst, Sussex:
Somerset, D. of, leaves borough of, to Bootle, iv. 11
Midshipman:
Harvey was, ix. 12
'Migas Frias':
Portuguese king's attempted assassination by, vii. 166
Migazzi zu Wall und Sonnenthurn, Christoph Bartholomaüs Anton von (1714–1803), cardinal, 1761; Francis I's minister to Rome:
Dumesnil's consecration opposed by, iii. 492
Kaunitz's downfall said to be hastened by, vi. 51
Regency notified by, of Dumesnil's escape from Rome, iii. 493
Migliorucci, Conte Jacopo Antonio (b. 1717):
England visited by, to strip cousin of estate, iv. 266
rogueries committed by, with lawyers in Florence, iv. 266
Mignanelli, Prudenza (ca 1691–1775), m. (1715) Tomasso Soderini:
(?) Niccolini, Mme, serves, ii. 251
'Mignon.' See Filippo; Ubaldo

Mignonne, La, French frigate:
engineers captured by, viii. 477
Mignot, Mme:
sempstress, iv. 132
Mignot, Marie (d. 1711), m. 1 Pierre de Portes; m. 2 (1653) François de l'Hôpital, Maréchal de France; m. 3 (1672) John II (Kasimir), K. of Poland:
Craon, Princesse de, compared with, iv. 131
marriages of, iv. 132
Milan:
abbeys at, seized from Gonzaga by Maria Theresa's general, ii. 55
Austrian appendage, ix. 505
Austrian army sends courier from, i. 427
Austrians order artillery carriages from, iii. 406
Austrians under Schulenburg diverted to, by Gages's feint, iii. 119
Bavarian elector may give, to Don Philip, i. 290
Bellardire's press at, ii. 421
Castiglione, Contessa, lured from, for Ds of Kingston's trial, viii. 192, 196
castle of: Maria Theresa gives, to Charles Emmanuel III, i. 379; to be besieged by Spaniards, iii. 220, 225
Charles Emmanuel III's designs on, vi. 55
Chute and Whithed to visit, iii. 257
Coke, Lady Mary, wants to avoid, vii. 543
courier from, to Rome, ii. 515
Cumberland, D. and Ds of, set up pretensions at, vii. 543
English to winter at, iv. 336
female nobility of, complain of D. and Ds of Cumberland, vii. 559
France, Sardinia, and Spain may divide, vii. 469
Francis I may exchange, for Tuscany, i. 290
Francis III sends grand-daughter to, for education, vi. 171–2
—— to administer duchy of, for Leopold, iv. 393
Genoese senators to go to, iii. 316
governor of, see Firmian
Lobkowitz to garrison, ii. 513
—— to visit, ii. 555
Lorrainers may go to, i. 380
Molinari or Mulinari from, ii. 29, 138
Pallavicini exposes, to Spaniards, iii. 120
Simonetti, Cts, from, vi. 135
Spaniards may take, i. 198
Victor Amadeus III covets, vii. 469
Villars puns on name of, iv. 159
visitors to: Beauchamp, Vct, vi. 319; Bruce, iv. 336; Cowper, ix. 641; Cumberland, Ds of, vii. 500, 505, 511, 519, 543, 553, 559; Cumberland, D. of, vii. 505, 511, 513, 519, 525, 543, 553, 559, 566; Ferdinand of Naples, ix. 586; Gloucester, Ds of, ix. 628, 632, 641; Gloucester, D. of, vii. 331,

[Milan, *continued*]
ix. 628, 632, Hillsborough, vi. 430; Joseph
II, vi. 556, vii. 331; Leopold, vii. 331;
Mann, Horace II, viii. 129; Maria Caro-
lina, ix. 586; Orford, Cts of, vii. 135;
York, D. of, vi. 193, 204, 244

Milan's Register. See under Millan, John

Milbanke, Acclom (ca 1731–66), army officer;
youngest son of Sir Ralph:
father leaves little to, iv. 172

Milbanke, Edward (ca 1725–84):
father leaves little to, iv. 172

Milbanke, Rev. Francis (ca 1728–69):
father leaves little to, iv. 172

Milbanke, John (ca 1725–1806):
Acciaioli, Mme, accompanied by, iv. 158,
284
bear tournament won by, at Hanover, iv.
200
Delaval's relative, iv. 55
HW called on by, iv. 207
HW has not seen, iv. 200
HW sees, iv. 225
HW's opinion of, iv. 225
leaves Florence, iv. 171–2
Mann accompanied by, in riding parties,
iv. 172
—— hopes that Pelham's family will aid,
iv. 171–2, 180
—— praises, iv. 55, 171–2, 195
—— regularly entertains, at supper, iv.
115
—— resembles, iv. 225
——'s arrears solicited by, at Hanover, iv.
195
—— thanks HW for attentions to, iv. 211
Newcastle House the abode of, iv. 207
Pisa baths visited by, iv. 158

Milbanke, Mark (ca 1722–1805), Adm.:
father leaves little to, iv. 172

Milbanke, Sir Ralph (ca 1688–1748), 4th Bt,
1705:
children of, left poorly provided for, iv.
171–2

Milborne Port, Somerset:
Luttrell attacks North over purchase of
borough of, ix. 29

Mild Arcadians ever Blooming. See under
Swift, Jonathan

Mildmay, Benjamin (1672–1756), cr. (1730)
E. Fitzwalter; treasurer of the Household:
diet of, iv. 518–19
dying, iv. 518

Mildmay, Letitia (1694–1749), m. (1706)
Humphrey Mildmay:
death of: Anthony Chute grieved by, iv.
102; John Chute may find, a great misfortune, iv. 96

Mileto:
earthquake account mentions, ix. 376

Miliary fever. See under Fever

Milico. See Millico

Military Discipline. See under Bland

Militia:
American colonel of, testifies that he
ordered his men to fire on British troops,
viii. 112
at San Remo, iii. 124
Botta's poor opinion of, v. 307
Buckinghamshire, vi. 138
Cambridgeshire, Montfort to lead, v. 312
Del Monti's, to assemble at Prato, ii. 85
difficulties in raising, in Tuscany, i. 288
English: bill for doubling, passed by Commons but defeated in House of Lords,
viii. 497; deficiencies in, iii. 166; difficulties faced in organization of, v. 312; elections invalid if supervised by, i. 252;
English prisoners released by, iii. 204; half
of England playing the fool in, v. 363;
invalids numerous in, iii. 166; members of
Parliament train, viii. 384; new-raised, may
prevent invasion, v. 307, 311–12, 347;
Northumberland colliers fight, v. 491; officers of, cannot be major-generals, viii.
372; Opposition wants, perpetual, v. 552;
ordered to march, v. 293–4; Shaftesbury
colonel of, v. 300; to take the field, viii.
367; Townshend, George, the restorer of,
v. 552; unrest among, v. 154
Ferrara may be garrisoned by, i. 380
Francis I orders Braitwitz to increase, i.
288
HW not to lead, from Twickenham, v.
300, 307, viii. 98
HW one of few Englishmen who are not
in army or, v. 344
Norfolk: at Portsmouth, v. 300; led by
Windham as lieutenant under E. of Orford, ix. 11n; Orford, E. of, distributes
onions to, ix. 11; Orford, E. of, plagues,
viii. 451; Orford, E. of, thanked by Hull
mayor for children propagated there by,
ix. 355; Orford, E. of, to command, viii.
372; secretary of, at Houghton, reads
Statius aloud, viii. 295; Windham resigns
from, because of Orford's trouble-making,
ix. 11n
of Cumberland and Westmorland, iii. 159
Papal, ordered to mobilize, ii. 444
Pitt calls, impractical, x. 15
regiments to be raised from, in Tuscany,
i. 123, 156, 214, 266, 288

Militia Bill. See under Parliament: acts of

Milk:
ass's, vi. 348
Chute lives on, ii. 132
diet of, Cocchi recommends, iv. 543
English dare not use, iii. 174
Mann serves coffee with, i. 33
Pitt, Anne, takes, with chocolate for
breakfast, vii. 567
price of, rises, vi. 49
woman's: Gloucester, D. of, takes, viii.
321; used in cases of consumption, viii. 321

Milkmaids:
dance with garlands on May 1, ix. 274–5
Mayday garlands of, will have to be of
holly and ivy, due to bad weather, ix. 639
Mill, James, army officer:
East India Company's former employee,
vi. 548
English trip considered too dangerous for,
iii. 454
famous in England as a projector, iii. 454
Florence visited by, iii. **407**
HW knows nothing about, iii. 421, 435
Indian scheme of, iv. 43, 97, vi. 548
Leghorn and Pisa visited by, iii. 407, iv.
98
Leopold still pays salary to, vi. 548
London familiar to, iii. 407
Mann describes, iii. 407, 454
—— supposed by, to be ignorant of ships'
prizes, iii. 441
marines to be commanded by, iii. 407
misinformed about opposition to peace
treaty, iv. 43
prizes from captured ships to be supervised by, in England, iii. 441
Richecourt involved in affairs of, iii.
427–8, iv. 98
servants kept by, iii. 407
ships' prizes shared by, iii. 441
sister-in-law of, iii. 427
Toussaint confers with, in Florence, iv.
97–8
—— quashes scheme of, to destroy East
India Company, iv. 101–2
—— recommends, iii. 407
uniform of, iii. 407
unknown in England, iii. 460
Vienna visited by, iii. 454
Mill; mills:
Florentine, fail because of low water, ix.
318
Millan, John (ca 1701–82), bookseller; author:
Millan's Universal Register: HW sends,
vi. 49; Mann wants, vi. 36
Millar, Andrew (1707–68), bookseller:
Bower does not patronize, iv. 533
——'s alleged perfidy proclaimed by, iv.
533
Milleleva:
HW wins, at faro, like Catherine of
Braganza, iii. 494
Miller, Lady. *See* Riggs, Anne (1741–81)
Miller, James (1706–44), rector of Upcerne:
Are These Things So: Crudeli to have
translated, i. 387–8, 424, ii. 11; not Pope's,
i. 409–10
Miller, John, printer of the *London Even-
ing Post:*
arrest of, vii. 280
Miller, Sir John (d. 1798), cr. (1778) Bt;
M.P.:

academy established by, at Batheaston,
viii. 197
children left by, with mother-in-law in
France, viii. 197
HW used to know, at Bath, viii. 197
Italy visited by, for virtu, viii. 197
Miller, Mrs John. *See* Riggs, Anne (1741–81)
Miller, Sir John Edward Augustus Riggs
(1770–1825), 2d Bt, 1798:
grandmother takes care of, viii. 197
Milles, ——, Lady Astley's sister:
Rome visited by, ix. 480
Milles, Anne (d. 1792), m. (1759) Sir Edward
Astley, 4th Bt:
Rome visited by, ix. 480
son's capture by pirates distresses, ix. 480
Milliary fever. *See under* Fever
Millico, Giuseppe (1730–1802), castrato
singer:
Davis, Miss, envied by, vii. 547
HW to hear, at opera, vii. 403
'Millimant, Mrs.' *See under* Congreve, Wil-
liam: *Way of the World*
Millot, Claude-François-Xavier (1726–85),
abbé:
*Mémoires politiques et militaires . . . de
Noailles,* viii. 391
Mills, Col. *See* Mill, James
Milltown, E. of. *See* Leeson, Joseph (1711–
83)
Milton, Bn. *See* Damer, Joseph (1718–98)
Milton, Bns. *See* Sackville, Lady Caroline
(1718–75)
Milton, Vct. *See* Damer, Hon. George (1746–
1808)
Milton, John (1608–74), poet:
epics of, not surpassed in HW's time, ii.
124
'Il Penseroso' quoted by Burke, ix. 684
Paradise Lost: Du Boccage, Mme, trans-
lates, iv. 142; HW paraphrases lines from,
ix. 616; Morris's essay on wit quotes, ii.
464; quotation from, about moon, vi. 382;
Vallombrosa mentioned in, iv. 317
Mina; Minas. *See* La Mina
Mince pies:
HW dislikes, ii. 367
Minchiate:
Leopold and Maria Louisa play, vi. 340
Montemar hopes to play, ii. 193
played at Casa Craon, iii. 477
played in Mann's garden, i. 483
Mindelheim:
Marlborough prefers English title to prin-
cipality of, viii. 360
Minden:
battle of: v. 314; Sackville disgraced at,
v. 320n, viii. 187n
Mindleheim. *See* Mindelheim
Mine; mines:
at Minorca: French, ineffective, iv. 572;
not sprung, iv. 584
coal, *see* Coal mines

[Mine; mines, *continued*]
French threaten to blow up, under Namur and Bergen-op-Zoom, iii. 482
iron: near Porto Longone, vii. 131; *see also under* Iron
lead, on Powis estate, iii. 468
Miner; miners:
York Buildings Co. settles, at Strontian, x. 31
Mineral water:
Mann, Galfridus, mistakes cobalt and zinc for, ii. 216
Minerbetti, Signora. *See* Acciaioli, Clarice (b. 1727)
Minerbetti, Maria Teresa (1751–1820), m. (1771) Niccolò Santini:
HW uses greatest speed to get fans to, vii. 309
Santini to wed, vii. 294–5, 306
Minerbetti di Calenzano, Anna Maria (ca 1684–1749), m. (1699) Lorenzo Ginori:
Chute and Whithed to call on, i. 161
Minerva:
Catherine II called, viii. 333
Minerva, Ds of Kingston's ship:
plunder sent in, viii. 59–60
Minerva, English war ship:
in danger, v. 350
Minerva, French war ship:
in Mediterranean, v. 249
Mingotti, Signora. *See* Valentini, Regina
Miniatures:
Cooper's, of Cromwell, v. 173
HW's: cabinet for, ii. 277; of Digby family, vii. 267; untouched by housebreakers, vii. 284; Zincke's, of Cowley, vi. 523
Maratti's, ii. 162
Oxford, E. of, has, i. 358
Strange's coloured drawings more delicate than, vi. 108
Zincke's, of Cts of Orford, ix. 501, 504
See also Enamel
Minister; ministers (cabinet):
change of, HW would not benefit by, ix. 260
English, beg not to be tried, viii. 387
excused from returning calls, viii. 228
HW compares lot of, to that of generals, ix. 255
lucre buys, viii. 493
Minister; ministers (foreign):
from Austria to Breda conference, *see* Harrach, Ferdinand Bonaventura (1708–78)
from Austria to Denmark, *see* Khevenhüller, Johann Josef (1706–76)
from Austria to England, *see* Barbiano di Belgioioso, Lodovico Carlo Maria (1728–1801), Conte di; Kageneck, (?) Johann Friedrich (1741–1800), Nay, Louis-Hyacinthe de (d. 1752), Comte de Richecourt; Wasner, Johann Ignaz (ca 1688–1767), Freiherr von

from Austria to Holland, *see* Reischach, Judas Thaddäus (1696–1782), Freiherr von
from Austria to Poland, *see* Khevenhüller, Johann Josef (1706–76)
from Austria to Rome, *see* Albani, Alessandro (1692–1779); Mellini, Mario (1677–1756); Thun, Josef Maria von (d. 1763)
from Austria to Russia, *see* Lobkowitz, Joseph Maria Karl (1725–1802)
from Austria to the Imperial Diet, *see* Khevenhüller, Johann Josef (1706–76)
from Austria to Tuscany, *see* Wilczek, Johann (1738–1819)
from Bavaria to England, *see* Haszlang, Josef Xaver (ca 1700–83), Freiherr von
from Bavaria to Rome, *see* Mansfeld und Fondi, Heinrich Franz (1712–after 1780), Fürst von; Scarlatti, Pompeo (fl. 1742–65)
from Denmark to Naples, *see* Osten, Greve Adolph Siegfried von der (1726–97)
from England to Austria, *see* Keith, Robert (d. 1774); Keith, Sir Robert Murray (1730–95); Robinson, Sir Thomas (1695–1770), Bn Grantham; Robinson, Thomas (1738–86), Bn Grantham
from England to Brussels: Hanger, Hon. William, may be, viii. 236; *see also* Gordon, Sir William (1726–98)
from England to Denmark, *see* Keith, Sir Robert Murray (1730–95)
from England to diet at Ratisbon, *see* Trevor, Hon. John (1749–1824)
from England to Hanover, *see* Leheup, Isaac (ca 1686–1747)
from England to Holland, *see* Montagu, John (1718–92), 4th E. of Sandwich; Yorke, Hon. Joseph (1724–92)
from England to Naples, *see* Hamilton, Sir William (1730–1803)
from England to Portugal, *see* Walpole, Hon. Robert (1736–1810)
from England to Prussia: Frederick II said to want Villiers as, iv. 541; *see also* Legge, Henry Bilson (1708–64)
from England to Russia, *see* Keith, Robert (d. 1774)
from England to Sardinia: Northington may succeed Mount Stuart as, ix. 336, 354; *see also* Hervey, George William (1721–75), E. of Bristol; Lynch, Sir William (ca 1730–85); Pitt, George (1721–1803), Bn Rivers; Villettes, Arthur (ca 1702–76)
from England to Saxony, *see* Keith, Sir Robert Murray (1730–95); Villiers, Thomas; Williams, Sir Charles Hanbury (1708–59)
from England to Spain: HW thinks that Mann should be, v. 166; *see also* Hervey, George William (1721–75), E. of Bristol
from England to Sweden, *see* Poyntz, Stephen (1685–1750)
from England to Switzerland (Grison Leagues), *see* Burnaby, John (d. 1779);

Colebrooke, Robert (1718–84); Villettes, Arthur (ca 1702–76)
from England to Turkey, see Porter, Sir James (1710–86)
from England to Tuscany: George II needs, because of English at Leghorn, i. 215; see also Fane, Charles (d. 1766); Mann, Sir Horatio (1706–86)
from England to Venice, see Compton, Charles (1737–63), E. of Northampton; Darcy, Robert (1718–78), E. of Holdernesse; Gray, Sir James (ca 1708–73)
from France to Austria, Vienna expects, i. 151
from France to Denmark, see Blosset, Paul (1728–after 1780), Marquis de
from France to England, see Batailhe de Francès, Jacques (ca 1724–88); Chavignard de Chavigny, Théodore (ca 1688–1771); Gérard de Rayneval, Joseph-Matthias (1746–1812); Moustier Éléonore-François-Élie de (1751–1817)
from France to Hanover, see Bussy, François de (1699–1780)
from France to Parma, see Du Tillot, Guillaume-Léon (1711–74)
from France to Portugal, see Clermont, Jean-Baptiste-Charles-François (1728–92), Chevalier de
from France to Prussia, see Mancini-Mazarini, Louis-Barbon-Jules (1716–98), Duc de Nivernais; Valory, Guy-Louis-Henry (ca 1691–1774)
from France to Rome, see Bouchard d'Esparbez de Lussan, Henri-Joseph (1714–88), Marquis d'Aubeterre; Guérin de Tencin, Pierre (1679–1758)
from France to Tuscany: is a plenipotentiary, vii. 293; see also Puget, Joseph-Pierre-Balthazar-Hilaire de (1725–ca 1800), Marquis de Barbantane
from Genoa to England: see Ageno, Francesco Maria; Celesia, Pietro Paolo (d. 1806); Gastaldi, Giambattista (fl. 1728–55)
from Genoa to France, see Sorba, Agostino Paolo Domenico (1715–71), Marchese
from Genoa to Naples, see Casale, Scipione Giuseppe (d. 1765)
from Hanover to England, see Münchhausen, Gerlach Adolf (1688–1770), Freiherr von
from Hesse to England, see Alt, Justus Heinrich (d. 1768)
from Holland to England, see Boreel, Jacob (1711–78); Hop, Hendrik (1686–1761)
from Hungary to England, see Wasner, Johann Ignaz (ca 1688–1767), Freiherr von
from Hungary to Rome, see Albani, Alessandro (1692–1779); Mellini, Mario (1677–1756)
from Hungary to Sardinia, see Bartolommei, Ferdinando (1678–1748); Kaunitz, Wenceslas Anton (1711–94)

from Lucca to Florence, see Santini, Niccolò (1729–1812), Marchese
from Mantua to Venice, see Valenti, Silvio (1690–1756)
from Modena to England, see Grossatesta, Abate Antonio (d. 1761)
from Modena to France, see Cioia de Forges, Bernardo, Conte
from Naples to Holland, see Fogliani d'Aragona, Giovanni (1697–1780), Marchese
from Naples to Rome, see Orsini, Domenico Amadeo (1719–89)
from Naples to Saxony, see Malaspina Azzolini (1697–1774)
from Naples to Tuscany, see Viviani, Luigi (1709–80)
from Poland to Rome, see Antici, Tommaso (1731–1812)
from Portugal to England, see Mello e Castro, Martinho (1716–95), Conde de Galvas
from Portugal to Rome, see Almada de Mendonça, Francisco de (fl. 1756–70)
from Prussia to England, see Knyphausen, Dodo Heinrich (1729–89), Freiherr von; Maltzan, Joachim Karl (1733–1817), Graf von
from Prussia to Venice, see Cataneo, Giovanni
from Russia to England, see Golitsyn, Prince Alexander Mikhailovich (b. 1723); Simolin, Ivan Matveevich (1720–ca 1800)
from Russia to Prussia, see Gross, Heinrich (d. 1765), Freiherr von
from Russia to Rome, see Benislawski, Jan (1735–1814)
from Russia to Turkey, see Obreskov, Alexei Mikhailovich (1719–87)
from Sardinia to England, see Osorio-Alarcon, Cavaliere Giuseppe (ca 1697–1763); Sallier della Tour, Francesco Giuseppe (1726–1800); Viry, Francesco Giuseppe (d. 1766), Conte di
from Sardinia to France, see Solaro di Breglio, Roberto Ignazio (d. 1765)
from Sardinia to Rome, see Balbis-Simeone di Rivera, Giovanni Battista (d. 1777), Conte
from Sardinia to Spain, see Osorio-Alarcon, Cavaliere Giuseppe (ca 1697–1763)
from Saxony to England, see Brühl, Hans Moritz (1736–1809); Flemming, Carl Georg Friedrich (1706–67)
from Saxony to Tuscany, see Agdollo, Gregorio (fl. 1741)
from Spain to England, see Abreu y Bertodano, Felix de (fl. 1754–60)
from Spain to Parma, see Revilla, Marqués
from Spain to Rome, see Azpuru y Jiménez, Tomás (1713–72); Clemente de Arostegui, Alfonso (fl. 1747–70); Moñino y Redondo, José (1728–1809), Conde de Floridablanca

[Minister; ministers, *continued*]

from Spain to Tuscany, *see* Ascanio, Père Salvator Maria (ca 1655–1741); Moñino, Francesco; Viviani, Luigi (1709–80)

from the Empire to England, *see* Colloredo, Karl Octav (1723–86), Graf von

from the Empire to Prussia, *see* Portugal, Anton von (d. 1769), Graf von Puebla

from the Empire to Venice, *see* Durazzo, Giacomo (1718–95)

from Tripoli to Holland, *see* Sidi Mahmud Aga

from Tuscany to Austria, *see* Bartolommei, Marchese Ferdinando (1678–1748)

from Tuscany to England, *see* Pucci, Domenico (1718–83); Pucci, Vincenzo (ca 1675–1757)

from Tuscany to France, *see* Choiseul, François-Joseph de (d. 1769), Marquis de Stainville

from Tuscany to Rome, *see* Franchini Taviani, Abate Giulio (d. 1759); Migazzi, Christoph Bartholomaüs Anton von (1714–1803); Poirot, Domenico Matteo di (d. 1775), Barone di Saint-Odile

from Tuscany to Sardinia, *see* Bartolommei, Ferdinando (1678–1748)

in Italy, do not allow sbirri near their embassies, ii. 467n

Maria Theresa's: monopolize passports, v. 482; will outrank her husband's envoy, iv. 29

See also Ambassador; Envoy; Resident

'Ministerial':

synonymous with 'patriot,' though formerly its opposite, v. 277

Minister of finance:

Nivernais to succeed Maurepas as, ix. 212

Minister of Marine, French. *See* Ministre de la Marine

Minister Plenipotentiary:

French court uses, when there is no ambassador, vi. 356

Mann made, ix. 246, 248–9, 257

—— needs to be, to restore his finances, vii. 293

Murray's appointment as, may lead to Mann's, vi. 356

next rank above that of Resident, vi. 355

Tuscany might not be worthy of, vii. 293

Ministre de la guerre:

Belle-Isle is, v. 187

Ministre de la Marine:

Du Châtelet to succeed Praslin as, vii. 258

See also Berryer; Sartine

Minnib. *See* Ibrahim Minnib

Minorca:

alarm for, over, viii. 380–1

Algerian vessels assist English in, ix. 205

Anstruther ill-treats Erskine in, iv. 229–30

Blakeney blocks roads and removes cattle at, iv. 567

——'s duties at, performed by others, iv. 583–4

Byng may not attempt relief of, iv. 560–2

—— may not be in time to prevent French attack upon, iv. 545

—— might have reached, before its surrender, iv. 577

can be saved only by fleet from England, ix. 197, 199

capture of: may upset English-Italian negotiations, iv. 576; over-shadowed by ministerial change, ix. 263, 275; political effect of, v. 12, 19; reported, iv. 571–2, ix. 243, 257, 263, 269

castle at. *See* St Philip's Castle

Catherine II would probably not accept, ix. 187

Charles III calls, nest of Jews and rabble, ix. 189

Conway's exile in, iv. 316

—— to join regiment at, iv. 264

—— will probably visit, before going to Florence, iv. 274, 278

Corsica more strategically placed than, for English base, v. 37

court martial to result from, ix. 196

court of admiralty at, accused by Charles III of condoning piracy, ix. 189

dispatches from, sent by Mann to London, ix. 144

Draper accuses Murray of losing, vi. 383n

Duncan clergyman at, iv. 584

enemy vessels cruise between Leghorn and, ix. 205

England exercised about defenceless state of, iv. 554–5

England may have ceded, to Russia, ix. 187

England may yet save, iv. 570

England unconcerned about, ix. 196

England will not be willing to lose, ix. 197

England would not exchange Carrickfergus for, v. 371

English attack expected at, iv. 587, v. 134

English credit declines after capture of, iv. 587

English engineers on way to, in Venetian vessel, captured by French, viii. 476–7

English fleet needed for protection of, iv. 545

English prisoners from, may be sent by French to Gibraltar, iv. 581

English resentment at loss of, iv. 577–8, 585

enormous sums thrown away on, ix. 303

females of, embark for Leghorn, viii. 453, ix. 179, 180

fleet nearly a month on passage from Cadiz to, ix. 190

Florentine communication with, cut off, ix. 59

France and Spain may attack, ix. 48, 139

France bides her time after conquest of, iv. 585

France may borrow Spanish fleet to besiege, viii. 437, 443, 467

France may give: to Spain, iv. 545, 572, 575, ix. 180; to Spain, in return for San Domingo, ix. 180

France must protect her forces on, iv. 559

France to restore, to England, v. 526

French and Spanish fleet lands troops on, ix. 178, 180, 182

French and Spanish fleet threatens, ix. 173-4

French and Spanish fleet to obstruct aid to, ix. 181

French and Spanish troops on: said to be sickly, ix. 197; should be bottled up by English fleet, ix. 205

French expected to besiege, in spring of 1779, viii. 437, 443, 467, 468-9

French expect English attempt to recapture, iv. 587

French expedition sets out for, iv. 545

French intend to besiege, iv. 552, viii. 504

French may cut communications of, with Leghorn, viii. 443

French may not think of, viii. 448

French may reinforce, iv. 588

French not thought to be ready to attack, iv. 549, 552

garrison at: destitute of provisions, ix. 198; drop in at Leghorn from Spain, where they were prisoners, ix. 430; sally made by, ix. 205; to be furnished with men and supplies by Mann, ix. 199-200; weak, though fortification strong, ix. 174

Gibraltar less useful than, iv. 574

Gibraltar will be forgotten like, in subsequent events, ix. 347

Governor of, see Blakeney, William (1672-1761); Murray, Gen. James (?1719-94)

HW expects, to be taken, ix. 185, 187, 201

HW expects Gibraltar to fall like, ix. 310

HW hopes that Cape Breton's capture may lead to English control over, v. 233

HW reconciled to loss of, ix. 362

HW thinks it would be folly to send fleet to relieve, ix. 201

Haddock's expedition to, i. 17

Hawke approaches, iv. 581

Irish provisions for, missing, viii. 380

Leghorn cut off from, ix. 429-30

Mann fears England's incapacity to save, ix. 188

——'s conduct about, approved by George III, ix. 229

——'s courier from, ix. 228

—— sends ships to, ix. 204, 207, 234, 249

——'s zeal in affairs in, applauded by HW, ix. 218

—— writes to Boothby and Hervey at, vi. 166

Mann, Horace II and Lady Lucy, to sail to, viii. 222, 225

Mathews expects ships from, ii. 398

Murray alarmed for safety of, viii. 380, 468

—— sends his wife and children to Leghorn from, ix. 179, 180

—— sends Sturt as courier from, ix. 42

—— the governor of, ix. 213n, 263n

—— to defend, to last extremity, ix. 174, 178-9

news of: can come only through Mann, ix. 191; comes only from Spain, ix. 205

newspapers blame danger of, on English ministry, viii. 468

officers from, report to Mann, ix. 269

Oswego more important than, v. 14

Parliamentary investigation of loss of, v. 55-6, 76-7, 85-6, 95

Pringle hostage for transports in attack on, ix. 309

privateers from, oppose French privateers in Mediterranean, viii. 466

Rainsford sent to, but in vain, ix. 271

refugees from, in Florence, describe surrender, iv. 583, ix. 269

Richelieu's landing at, iv. 567

Russian war ships cannot be received at, for fear of Spanish attack, viii. 114

St Philip's castle at, see under St Philip's

separation of combined fleet will give English fleet chance to relieve, ix. 197

siege of: Draper's harsh expressions to Murray during, ix. 361; not yet begun, ix. 196; rumoured in England, ix. 48, 59; Udny's accounts relating to, examined by Mann, ix. 303, 429-30

Spain is resolved to have, ix. 180

Spain may attack, viii. 114

Spain unlikely to capture, viii. 119

Spanish troops on Majorca may threaten, vii. 261

supplies for, gathered at Leghorn, viii. 375, 429-30

Sutherland leaves, for England, after rift with Murray, ix. 81

Udny to collect Tuscan provisions for, viii. 380

value of merchandise taken at, said by Crillon to be equal to that taken at St Eustatius by English, ix. 189-90

See also Port Mahon; St Philip's Castle

Minorum Conventialium (Franciscan order): Clement XIV a member of, vii. 117

Mint, Master of the. See Master of the Mint

Mint, Tuscan:
Florentine church plate sent to, vi. 476
Florentine plate may have to be carried to, i. 239

Mintz. See Mainz

Minucci, Christian Adam Ossalko (ca 1673-1758), Graf; Bavarian general:
Austrians capture, ii. 230, 234

Minuet; minuets:
Anson, Bns, dances, at Sandwich's ball, iv. 121
Astley dances, on galloping horses, ix. 451
at Robinson's ball, i. 184
people over 50 should not dance, i. 184, iv. 106
Pitt, Mrs George, dances, in Florentine theatre, vii. 456
Villars dances, supported by aides-de-camp, iv. 159
'Minutes of the office':
Mann receives, with gazettes, iv. 467
Miquelets:
Hussars skirmish with, i. 432
in Ponte Molle battle, ii. 531
Spanish and Austrian, skirmish with Tuscan pickets, ii. 100
Miracles:
Catherine, St, produces, by her relics, iv. 430
Mann no longer believes in, ii. 477
Sobieski, Ps, performs, v. 424, ix. 106
Miranda:
Spaniards besiege, vi. 38
surrender of, may disconcert English measures to aid Portugal, vi. 41
Mirandola:
Austrian artillery from, ii. 163
Francis III fortifies, iv. 45
ill provided, iii. 156
Montemar's failure to relieve, said to anger Spanish queen, ii. 6
Sardinians to besiege, i. 465
Spaniards besiege, i. 489
surrender of, i. 500
Mirepoix, Duc, Maréchal and Marquis de. See Lévis de Lomagne, Gaston-Charles-Pierre de
Mirepoix, Duchesse and Maréchale and Marquise de. See Beauvau-Craon, Anne-Marguerite-Gabrielle de (1707–91)
Mirepoix, Casa:
HW intends to be intimate at, iv. 68
Mirepoix family:
Lorenzi amuses, iv. 106
Mir Jafar (1691–1765), Nawab of Bengal 1757–60, 1763–5:
made king by the English, v. 279
Miro, Maj. Joseph:
captured at Velletri, ii. 493
Mirror; mirrors:
chamber of, in Richelieu's garden pavilion, vii. 329
chimney-piece polished like, iv. 398
HW thinks that self-knowledge should be aided by, ix. 539–40
in cabinet of every Paris hotel, vii. 312
over George Pitt's ballroom fireplace, Coventry stands in front of, iv. 367
See also Looking-glass; Pocket-glass
Misantropo. See under Rucellai

Miscarriage:
Grifoni, Mme, escapes, at ball, ii. 65
—— recovers from, ii. 100
Maria Louisa fears, ix. 301
—— may have had, vii. 111
occurrences of, iii. 447, iv. 42, 122, v. 42, vi. 498, vii. 101, 458, ix. 549
Mischief:
HW considers, a natural appetite, viii. 516
Miserere:
to be sung in London, ii. 211
Miséricorde, La, convent in Paris:
Walkinshaw, Mrs, at, x. 47
Misers:
HW gives instances of, ix. 609
Missal:
Dumesnil's secretary turns pages of, iii. 493
Mississippi Bubble:
French footman wins fortune in, iv. 195
Miss Lucy in Town. See under Fielding, Henry
Misson, François-Maximilien (ca 1650–1722), traveller:
HW does not imitate, vi. 343
Mistley, Essex:
HW writes from, iii. 494, iv. 271, 490
Rigby's seat, iv. 490n
Mistresses, royal:
longevity of, HW's reflections on, vi. 324
Mistress of the Robes:
Ancaster, Ds of, becomes, to Q. Charlotte, v. 518
Hamilton, Lady Archibald, is, to Augusta, Ps of Wales, iii. 62, 361n
Middlesex, Cts of, is, to Augusta, Ps of Wales, iii. 62
Suffolk, Cts of, was, to Q. Caroline, vi. 543n
Mitchell, Sir Andrew (1708–71), K.B., 1765; British minister and envoy to Prussia 1756–71; M.P.:
Bath knighthood promised to, vi. 323
becomes K.B., vi. 380, 383
Frederick II's health and spirits praised by, v. 90
later commissary at Antwerp, iv. 209n
Mann's claim to be K.B. probably antedates that of, vi. 338
Quin's witticism to, at supper, iv. 209–10
Tweeddale's secretary, iv. 209
Mithridate. See under Racine, Jean
Mitres:
Clement XIV to bestow, upon bishops, viii. 39
Mittens:
cotton, Craon wears indoors in winter, ii. 109
Mob. See under names of cities, such as London; see also Gordon Riots; Riot
'Mobocracy':
England called, by Dr Stevens, v. 138
Mocoa:
patch box of, i. 414

Mode. *See* Fashion

Model; models:

Breton's, for Wolfe's tomb, v. 421–2

in terracotta of Henley bridge keystones, exhibited at Royal Academy, ix. 576

of kittens, in terracotta by Mrs Damer, ix. 576

Proctor's, in terracotta, of Ixion, ix. 577

Sisson's, for machine for raising water, *see under* Sisson

terracotta, of Livia statue, ii. 178–9, 190, 197, 200, 210, 560, vi. 111

wax, by Cellini, ix. 215n

Modena, Bp of. *See* Sabbatini, Giuliano (1685–1767)

Modena, Ds of. *See* Charlotte Aglaé (1700–61); Cybo, Maria Theresia (1725–90); Maria Ricciarda Beatrice (1750–1829)

Modena, D. of. *See* Ferdinand Karl Anton Joseph (1754–1806); Francis III (1698–1780); Hercules III (1727-1803)

Modena, Ps of. *See* Amalia (1699–1778); Benedetta Ernestina (1697–1777); Felicità (1726–54); Matilde (1729–1803)

Modena:

Amalia to return to, i. 99

Austria's treaty with, iv. 393, 395–6, 400

Beauchamp to go to, vi. 336

Brown awaits artillery from, iii. 236

cannon firing at, said to be heard by Mme Sarrazin, i. 443

castle of, ill provided, iii. 156

Charles Emmanuel III and Maria Theresa administer, i. 489

citadel of: desires truce, i. 464; Gages expected to write from, ii. 196; surrenders, i. 465

courier leaves Bologna for, iii. 156

court of, moves to Sassuola on way to Genoa or Massa, i. 425

ducal family flees from, i. 442

Elizabeth Farnese expects conquest of, ii. 196

Ferrara may be seized by, vii. 35, 45

Firmian at, vi. 126

Florentine in service of, i. 47

Francis III's return to, iv. 76

——'s revenues from, seized, i. 464

—— to bring Duchess to, iv. 45

—— to regain, by Aix treaty, iii. 481

Frederick Augustus II will never relinquish pictures from, iv. 76

Germans to defend, against Spaniards, i. 379

Giovanardi lives near, i. 54

HW contrasts Newmarket with, ii. 315

HW met Francis III near, i. 43–7, vi. 144

HW prefers Canterbury to, i. 142

HW's quinsy said to be at, v. 369

Jesuits take refuge in, vii. 494

Leopold tours Tuscany in the direction of, viii. 343

Lobkowitz near, iii. 30, 35

—— to garrison, ii. 513

Lucca's new road to, iv. 514

Maria Ricciarda Beatrice may inherit duchy of, iv. 400

Montemar may relieve siege of, i. 443, 455

——'s loss of, said to enrage Spanish queen, ii. 6

——'s troops to reunite at, i. 226

new road to Pistoia from, ix. 594

Penthièvre to visit, iv. 466

princess of, may wed Young Pretender, ii. 378, 385

Pucci, Mme, may be affected by fall of, ii. 31

—— receives HW's silks at, ii. 112

—— stays near, ii. 54

—— writes from, i. 158

Richecourt has no news from, i. 432

Sardinian troops enter, i. 442

secretary of state of, *see* Sabbatini, Giuliano (1685–1767)

Spaniards and Neapolitans may march to, iii. 65

Spaniards may be opposed in, i. 379, 424

Spaniards may conquer, iii. 22, 30

Spaniards prevent couriers from crossing, iii. 156

Spaniards will easily restore Francis III to, iii. 156

Spanish Court expected Montemar to relieve, i. 501

visitors to: Ferdinand of Naples and Maria Carolina, ix. 594; (?) Richecourt, i. 195; Young Pretender, vii. 318

Modena collection:

Venetian Court buys, for K. of Poland, iii. 392

Modern languages. *See under* Language

Moders, Mary (ca 1634–73), m. 1 John Stedman; m. 2 (1663) John Carleton; 'German princess':

Vane, Lady, comparable to, i. 459

Mogg, Thomas (d. 1756), Capt.:

news of sea engagement brought by, ii. 404

Mognino. *See* Moñino

Mogul, Great. *See* Muhammed Shah (d. 1748); Shah Alam (1728–1806)

Mogul Tales:

HW's anecdotes reminiscent of, ix. 118

Mohammed (ca 1710–90), ben Abdallah, Emperor of Morocco 1757–90:

ambassador of, presents Leopold with horse mounted only by, viii. 469

increased revenue demanded by, vii. 30

Mohammedan; Mohammedans:

England may adopt customs of, iv. 494

Hervey, Bp, would enfranchise, if there were any in Ireland, ix. 530

Polish Catholics invited to become, vii. 81

Mohammedanism:

Clive's associate expresses concern for, vii. 381

senility of, ix. 48

Mohilov, Bp coadjutor of, *see* Benislawski, Jan

Mohilov:
Joseph II satisfied by his reception at, ix. 72

Mohun, Charles (1677–1712), 4th Bn Mohun:
Hamilton, D., killed by, in duel, x. 45

Moira, Cts of. *See* Hastings, Lady Elizabeth (1731–1808)

Moira, E. of. *See* Rawdon, Sir John (1720–93)

Moldau, river:
Prussians throw ammunition into, ii. 543

Moldavangi Ali Pascha, Grand Vizir (1769) of Turkey:
fights Russians, vii. 160

Moldavia:
Russian defeats in, vii. 148
Russians take, from Turks, vii. 154–5

Mole:
at Leghorn, i. 303, ii. 27, ix. 581
at Naples, vi. 6

Molenist:
Damiens may have been instigated by, v. 48

Molesworth, Vcts. *See* Usher, Mary Jenney

Molesworth, Hon. Charlotte (b. 1755):
birth of, vi. 140

Molesworth, Hon. Coote (ca 1697–1782), M.D.:
escapes fire at sister-in-law's house, vi. 139, 140
sister-in-law persuades her husband to give annuity to, vi. 140

Molesworth, Mrs Coote. *See* Palmer, Mary

Molesworth, Hon. Elizabeth (1751–1835), m. James Stewart:
escapes fire in Upper Brook St, vi. 139–40
refuses to eat, vi. 146
sister visited by, vi. 145
uncle sees leap of, vi. 139

Molesworth, Frances (b. 1756–62, d. 1829), m. (1785) Hon. John Jeffreys Pratt, styled Vct Bayham, 1786; 2d E. Camden, 1794; cr. (1812) M. Camden:
Lucan family accompanied by, to Florence, viii. 417
Mann receives sooty drawings from, viii. 462
—— saw, with her aunt and cousin, ix. 620
marriage of, ix. 620
Shelburne rejected by, viii. 417

Molesworth, Hon. Henrietta (1745–1813) m. (1774) Rt Hon. John Staples:
escapes fire in Upper Brook St, vi. 139
Grosvenor, Lady, visited by, vi. 145–6
leg of, cut off, vi. 139, 145

Molesworth, Hon. Louisa (1749–1824), m. 1 (1769) William Brabazon Ponsonby cr. (1806) Bn Ponsonby; m. 2 (1823) William Fitzwilliam, 4th E. Fitzwilliam, 1756:
escapes fire in Upper Brook St, vi. 140

Molesworth, Hon. Mary, m. (1736) Robert Rochfort, cr. (1738) Bn and (1751) Vct Belfield, and (1756) E. of Belvidere:
beauty of, ii. 220
Rochfort's affair with, ii. 220

Molesworth, Hon. Mary (b. 1744):
birth of, vi. 140

Molesworth, Hon. Mary (1747–63):
burnt in fire at house in Upper Brook St, vi. 138, 145

Molesworth, Hon. Melesina (1746–63):
burnt in fire at house in Upper Brook St, vi. 138, 145

Molesworth, Richard (ca 1680–1758), 3d Vct Molesworth, 1726; M.P.:
daughter of, ii. 220
widow of, vi. 140
wife persuades, to give annuity to brother, vi. 140

Molesworth, Richard Nassau (1748–93), 4th Vct Molesworth, 1758:
Westminster schoolboy, vi. 140

Molière (Jean-Baptiste Poquelin) (1622–73), dramatist:
Amphitryon, HW alludes to Cardinal and D. of York as characters in, vi. 257
Bourgeois Gentilhomme, Le: Mamamouchi in, compared to Newcastle, iv. 72; *New Ode, A,* alludes to, ii. 52
Malade imaginaire, Le, physician in, iii. 256
Tartuffe: banned by Abp of Paris, ii. 63; *Don Pilogio* imitates, ii. 41

Molina, José de (b. 1710), Spanish military governor of Rio Grande de S. Pedro:
death of, rumoured, viii. 223

Molinari, Marchese —— (b. ca 1724):
Milanese, ii. 29, 138
rich, ii. 29, 138
rich uncle of, vice-legate of Bologna, ii. 138
size of, ii. 29, 138
Suares, Vittoria, wooed by, ii. 29, 138

Molinari, Giovanni Carlo (ca 1717–63); Abp of Damascus, legate of Bologna, 1741; nuncio at Brussels, 1753:
nephew of, ii. 138

Molini, (?) Dr:
Gloucester, D. of, attended by, at Leghorn, vii. 394

Molini, Giuseppe:
(?) printer of *Il Conclave,* viii. 70

Mollwitz, battle of:
Frederick II runs away from, ii. 505, v. 5n

Molly. *See* Mann, Mary; Shadwell, Molly

Molo di Gaeta:
Orford, Cts of, ill at, viii. 312, 317

Molone [? Maloney *or* Malone], ——, merchant at Cadiz:
ship of, v. 269

Molowitz; Molwitz. *See* Mollwitz

Molyneux, Sir Francis (before 1737–1812), Kt, 1765; 7th Bt, 1781; gentleman usher of the Black Rod, 1765:

Kingston, Ds of, threatens, by showing him pistol-mark, viii. 198

Molza, Mme (b. ca 1657), Mary of Modena's attendant:
(?) Modena, Ds of, discusses Old Pretender's legitimacy with, i. 44

Momo:
lansquenet resembled by, i. 194
played, i. 194, 218

Monaco, P. of. See Honoré III (1720–95)

Monaco:
situation of, awkward, vi. 555
York, D. of, dies at, vi. 553–4, 555, vii. 345

Monarchs:
crimes of, HW's reflections on, vii. 292
HW's reflections on, vi. 254, ix. 336
See also Crown; King; Prince; Royalty

Monastery. See Convent

Monastic orders:
two, reported to have been forbidden by Joseph II to receive new members, ix. 283

Moncastello. See Montcastello; Pavon e Moncastello

Monck, Christopher (1653–88), 2d D. of Albemarle:
widow of, ix. 564n

Monckton, John (1695–1751), cr. (1727) Vct Galway; M.P.:
brag to be played by, out of town to avoid earthquake, iv. 137

Monckton, Robert (1726–82); army officer; M.P.:
Martinique conquered by, vi. 15–16, 21, 29–30
wounded at Quebec, v. 338

Monckton, William (? 1725–72), 6th Vct Galway, 1751; M.P.:
brother of, vi. 15n

Mondo della luna, Il. See under Galuppi, Baldassare

Mondovi:
Maillebois and Don Philip may march by, iii. 58

Money, John (fl. 1734–59), King's messenger:
Genoa visited by, with dispatches for Rowley, iii. 12
HW reassures Mann about, i. 152
Mann sends, to Hanover instead of England, i. 113, 115, 208
—— sends letters by, to HW, i. 115, 144
Turin visited by, iii. 12
Walpole, Lady, to receive leases from, i. 108, 113, 115
Walpole, Sir Robert, orders, to find HW, i. 108, 115

Money, John (1752–1817), aeronaut; army officer:
(?) Orford encourages balloon ascent of, ix. 596

Money:
Mann's reflections about, vi. 353
pleasure does not recognize want of, ix. 243

See also Riches; Wealth

'Mongibel, Bn de':
Mann may receive title of, ii. 484

Monimo. See Moñino

Moñino, Don Francisco, Spanish envoy to Tuscany 1782–4:
brother said to tell state secrets to, ix. 416–17
Charles III declared by, to be able to have Gibraltar when he pleases, ix. 416
Crillon writes to, ix. 340
Mann calls, poor senseless creature, ix. 416
—— told by, of French victory, ix. 393
Maria Louisa receives letters through, ix. 334
receives letters about Gibraltar, ix. 324, (?) 334
Spanish gazette published by, in Italian, ix. 329
Tuscan court always attended by, at Pisa, ix. 334, 548

Moñino y Redondo, José (1728–1808), cr. (1773) Conde de Floridablanca; Spanish ambassador to Rome 1772–6; prime minister 1777–92:
brother said to hear state secrets from, ix. 416–17
Clement XIV expects, vii. 413
—— threatened by, for not expelling Jesuits, vii. 428, 430
—— told by, that Jesuits' total suppression alone can satisfy Charles III, vii. 446
Charles III told by, of Pius VI's intention to release Jesuits, viii. 115
France cannot seduce, against Spanish interests, viii. 478
friends who knew, at Rome, inform Mann of his character, viii. 478

Monitor:
Russians will not waste time writing, vi. 60
Shebbeare the author of, v. 39

Monk; monks. See Convent

Monkey:
element of, in human composition, vii. 192, 194, 201
Mathew's crew hang crucifix on neck of, ii. 79n

Monmouth, D. of. See Scott, James

Monmouth, English ship:
Foudroyant fired on by, v. 193
French ships pursued by, iii. 411

Monmouth, Battle of:
Mann praises Clinton's conduct of, viii. 408
—— to consider, an English victory, viii. 405–6

Monmouthshire:
Mathews opposes Tories in election in, iii. 33
Morgan remains lord lieutenant of, vii. 174

Monmouth's Rebellion:
Scrope participates in, i. 457n

Monpellier. See Montpellier

Monreale, Bp of. *See* Testa, Francesco Maria (d. 1773)

Monreale:
York, Cardinal, may succeed Acquaviva as archbishop of, iii. 416–17

Monro, Dr James (1680–1752), physician:
Bedlam physician, ii. 224n
English army needs, ii. 224
epigram by, on Hulse and Cheselden, i. 168
'mad doctor,' iii. 191, 196
son of, iii. 191, 196
Walpole, Sir Robert, friend of, iii. 210

Monro, Dr John (1715–91), physician:
Bedlam physician, ix. 11n
Bouverie accompanied by, at Rome, iii. 191, 196
Ferrers's lunacy attested by, v. 397
Florence visited by, on way from Rome to England, iii. 400
George III should make, Groom of the Bedchamber, ix. 11
HW tells, to quit E. of Orford when it is safe, viii. 368
Old Pretender entertains, after being congratulated by him at St Apostoli, iii. 191, 196
Orford, E. of, praises, to Martha Turk, viii. 372
——'s condition diagnosed by, viii. 316
——'s letter to Withers brought by, to HW, iii. 367
——'s recovery reported by, viii. 367
pension of, said to be withdrawn, iii. 400
travelling physician, iii. 196, 210, 400
Walpole, Sir Robert, has, made travelling physician, iii. 210

Monro; Monroe. *See also* Monro; Munro

Monroe clan:
Young Pretender to be opposed by, iii. 105

Mons:
capture of, iii. 275
French to besiege, ii. 417
Ostend more important than, iii. 69

Monseme, ——, Capt.:
captured at Velletri, ii. 491

Monsignore:
HW's conversation with, at Conclave, i. 29

Monson, John (1727–74), 2d Bn Monson, 1748:
brother of, iv. 36
resigns, as chief justice in eyre, vi. 471

Monson, Hon. Lewis. *See* Watson, Hon. Lewis

Mont, Du. *See* Du Mont

Montagne. *See* Montaigne

Montagu, Bn. *See* Brudenell, John (1735–70)

Montagu, Ds of. *See* Cavendish, Lady Elizabeth (1654–1734); Churchill, Lady Mary (1689–1751); Montagu, Lady Mary (ca 1711–75)

Montagu, D. of. *See* Brudenell, George (1712–90)

Montagu, Augusta (d. 1849), m. (1789) Francesco Giuseppe Maria Enrico di Viry, Conte di Viry:
Sandwich's child by Martha Ray, viii. 459

Montagu, Basil (1770–1851), legal writer:
Sandwich's child by Martha Ray, viii. 459

Montagu, Lady Caroline (1736–1818), m. (1775) Capt. Charles Herbert:
Charlotte's bridesmaid, v. 529

Montagu, Charles (1661–1715), cr. (1700) Bn Halifax and (1714) E. of Halifax; statesman:
poem by, on Battle of the Boyne, quoted by HW, ii. 266
Pope satirizes contribution by, to Dryden's monument, v. 140

Montagu, Charles (d. 1777); Lt-Gen.:
made K.B., vii. 272

Montagu, Edward (d. 1745), Lt-Col.:
killed at Fontenoy, iii. 43

Montagu, Mrs Edward. *See* Robinson, Elizabeth

Montagu, Sir Edward Hussey. *See* Hussey, Edward

Montagu, Edward Wortley. *See* Wortley Montagu, Edward

Montagu, Lady Elizabeth (1743–1827), m. (1767) Henry Scott, 3d D. of Buccleuch:
mother's bequest to, viii. 99

Montagu, Frederick (1733–1800), M.P.:
lord of the Treasury, ix. 392

Montagu, George (ca 1684–1739), 2d Bn Halifax, cr. (1715) E. of Halifax:
spaniels, black, scarce after death of, ii. 293

Montagu, George (1712–90), *see* Brudenell, George

Montagu, George (ca 1713–80), M.P.; HW's correspondent:
Barrett-Lennards know HW through, iv. 78
Barrett-Lennard to receive compliments of, iv. 87
Parliamentary vote by, on privately-raised regiments, x. 19

Montagu (after 1741, Montagu-Dunk), George (1716–71), 2d E. of Halifax, 1739:
additional salary of, turned over to D. of Leeds, v. 489
agrees with rest of Cabinet Council, vi. 295
Bedford, D. of, may be succeeded by, in plantations, iv. 259
—— presents ultimatum of, to George III, vi. 307
Bute affronted by opposition of, to Regency Bill, vi. 299–300
——'s removal demanded by, vi. 168
Conway opposed by, vi. 507
—— succeeds, as secretary of state, vi. 310
death of, vii. 310, 313
dismissed, vi. 310

Dupplin does not yet succeed, as lord of Trade, v. 104, 111

English diplomats in Italy ordered by, to welcome Vorontsov, vi. 173

Éon arrested for misbehaviour at house of, vi. 190, 217

first lord of the Admiralty, vi. 42, 91

Frederick, P. of Wales, dismisses, ii. 551

—— makes, lord of the Bedchamber, ii. 159

George II attended by, at St James's Palace, i. 338

George III and D. of Cumberland unite in hating, vi. 364

George III arrogantly treated by, vi. 309

—— dismisses, but has to recall him, vi. 302

—— forced by, at Q. Charlotte's house, to propose omission of mother's name from Regency Bill, vi. 297n

—— orders, to move a Regency Bill similar to Richmond's, vi. 297

—— probably influenced by, to exclude Ps of Wales from Regency, vi. 297

—— treats, coldly, vi. 307

Grenville cannot be succeeded by, as manager of House of Commons, vi. 91

—— succeeded by, as secretary of state, vi. 91

—— succeeds, as first lord of the Admiralty, vi. 91

HW mentions, iv. 292

health of, recovering from great crisis, vii. 304

Holdernesse not to be superior to, iv. 249

—— to be replaced by, in secretary's office, iv. 346

Irish lord lieutenancy of, v. 485, 489, vi. 42

Jenison succeeded by, as Master of the Buckhounds, ii. 551

Mann's report to, about Damer's and Gascoigne's escapade, vi. 287

—— writes to, asking for promotion, vi. 318–19, 320–1

motion on Regency Bill proposed by, in House of Lords, vi. 297n

Nova Scotia to be colonized by, iv. 40

Opposition joined by, ii. 159

Parliamentary motion against Hanover troops advocated by, ii. 159, 356

Pitt proscribes, vi. 161

—— refuses to make, secretary of state for West Indies, v. 104

plantations to be taken from, and put under Board of Trade, iv. 259

popular with merchants, vi. 43

privately-raised regiments defended by, iii. 154

regiment raised by, iii. 128

ribbon of, to go to Bp of Osnaburgh, vii. 313

Sandwich opposes, over Turnpike Bill, iv. 121

—— succeeded by, as secretary of state, vii. 268

Sandys succeeds, in Board of Trade, v. 489

sent to the devil, vi. 312

speech of, Raymond answers, i. **230**, 263

Suffolk may succeed, as secretary of state, vii. 304, 310

Talbot to succeed, in Board of Trade, v. 486

Temple reconciled with, vi. 304

to be K.G., vi. 227

Walpole, Sir Robert, 'cut' by, at House of Lords, i. 338

West Indian department disjoined to accommodate, v. 488

Wilkes complains to, vi. 138

Montagu, George (1737–88), 4th D. of Manchester, 1762; ambassador to France, 1783; M.P.:

Paris post to be assumed by, ix. 398

Montagu, Lady Isabella (d. 1786), m. 1 (1723) William Montagu, 2d D. of Manchester; m. 2 (1743) Edward Hussey, cr. (1762) Bn Beaulieu and (1784) E. of Beaulieu:

father's bequest to, iv. 80

Montagu, John (1690–1749), 2d D. of Montagu, 1709:

daughter of, viii. 99n

death of, iv. 79

estate and will of, iv. 80

Fox attacks raising of regiments by, iii. 153–4

Frederick, P. of Wales, offends, i. **391**

mother-in-law's will bound by, with *Old Woman's Will*, ii. 566

opera announced by, ii. 104

pensions paid by, iv. 79

regiment of, to be headed by Sandwich, iii. 176

regiments raised by, iii. 128, x. 13, 16

troop of horse raised by, iii. 110

Walpole, Sir Robert, wants to make, generalissimo, iv. 79

witticism by, on opera bass, ii. 342

Montagu, John (1718–92), 4th E. of Sandwich, 1729; politician:

able, but obstinate, peevish, and intractable, ix. 276

address against use of Hanoverian troops seconded by, ii. 158

Admiralty abilities of, vii. 263, 350

Admiralty first lord, iii. 464, vii. 263

Admiralty lord, ii. 550, 561, iii. 176, 388

agrees with rest of Cabinet Council, vi. 295

ambassador to Holland, iii. 289, 294, 341, 351, 422

attacked both by Opposition and Court, ix. 221

[Montagu, John (1718–92), *continued*]

ball given by, for D. of Cumberland, iv. 121

Barré attacks, in Parliamentary speech, vi. 283–4, 286

Beauclerk resigns from pique against, iv. 135

Bedford, D. of, and D. of Cumberland seek support of, iv. 113

Bedford, D. of, governed by, through the Ds, iv. 120

—— hunts and gambles with, iv. 113

—— may be abandoned by, iv. 305

—— may be succeeded by, as secretary of state, iv. 217, 235

—— 'protector' of, iv. 144

—— presents ultimatum of, to George III, vi. 307

Breda visited by, iii. 351

Bute affronted by opposition of, to Regency Bill, vi. 299–300

Chesterfield may be succeeded by, as secretary of state, iii. 413

Churchill does not satirize correctly, vi. 261

coffee-girl's affair with, vi. 284

colonelcy of regiment added by, to his posts as lord of the Admiralty, lt-col. to Bedford, and aide-de-camp to Richmond, iii. 176

Cumberland, D. of, supports, iv. 113, 201

cunning preferred by, to prudence, viii. 435

Dayrolles resident to Holland under, iii. 403, 422

dice carried by, iv. 113

dismissed as secretary of state, iv. 258, 266, vi. 310

docks visited by, with Anson and Beauclerk, iv. 80

Fane gives annuity to, iv. 258, 266

first lord of Admiralty, viii. 435n, 438n

fleet said to be detained by, at Portsmouth, to divert George III and Charlotte, viii. 377

foes of, numerous, but friends not lacking, ix. 238

Fox, C.J., attacks, in Parliament, ix. 244

—— demands removal of, viii. 460

Frederick, P. of Wales, hates, for slurs on Hanover, iv. 217

George III and D. of Cumberland unite in hating, vi. 364

George III arrogantly treated by, vi. 309

—— dismisses, but has to recall him, vi. 302

—— may still support, viii. 449

—— possibly forced by, at Q. Charlotte's house, to propose omission of mother's name from Regency Bill, vi. 297n

—— probably influenced by, to exclude Ps of Wales from Regency, vi. 297

—— treats, coldly, vi. 307

Gower's daughter given by, to Col. Waldegrave, iv. 258

—— seeks support of, iv. 113

——'s quarrel with, iv. 258

Grafton called to order by, i. 231–2, 263

—— succeeds, as secretary of state, vi. 310

HW describes character of, iii. 361, viii. 435

HW jokes about asking, to defend Tuscany, ii. 561

HW mentions, iv. 292

Halifax opposed by, over Turnpike Bill, iv. 121

Hardwicke's contest with, over Cambridge high stewardship, vi. 219

Hawke succeeded by, as first lord of Admiralty, vii. 263

hooted off the stage, with Scott, vi. 410

Huntingdonshire boroughs of, iii. 413

Jacobite healths proposed by, iii. 388

Keene repairs omissions of, in Spanish treaty at Aix, iv. 198

Kempenfelt dispatched by, with only fourteen ships, ix. 221

Keppel's court martial will be regretted by, viii. 435

——'s enemy, viii. 438n

——'s persecution by, disgraces the Court, viii. 447

libels written by, vi. 323

Mann facilitates marriage of, iii. 351

—— neglected by, iii. 351, 361

—— once knew, well, viii. 435

——'s correspondence with, i. ?382, ?396, iii. 12, 351, 363, 373, 375, vi. 318–19, 321–2

——'s friendship with, i. 230–1, ii. 561, iii. 294, 373, v. 77, vi. 103, 112, 159, vii. 350

——'s protector, viii. 160

Marlborough and Pembroke declare against, viii. 435

Mastership of the Horse may go to, iv. 217

Mirepoix's promotion may depend on, iv. 29

Montagu's regiment to be headed by, iii. 176

naval disaster may cause downfall of, ix. 221

Navy Bill proposed by, iv. 33

Newcastle, D. of, hates, iv. 120

Niccolini a friend of, iv. 217

—— correctly describes unpopularity of, iv. 225

Nugent attacks, in Parliament over Westminster scrutiny, iv. 123

Parliamentary attacks upon, iv. 123, vi. 283–4, viii. 445, ix. 244

Parliamentary inquiry into conduct of, killed by vote of approbation, ix. 243

Parliamentary motion against Hanover troops advocated by, ii. 356

Parliamentary motion for removal of, defeated, viii. 464

Parry's cause to be Eton fellow deserted by, iv. 121
'Patriot,' iv. 198
Pitt hates, iv. 38
—— jealous of, iv. 38, 138
—— proscribes, vi. 161
——'s speech ridiculed by, as nonsense, vii. 167
—— supports Newcastle against, iv. 222
postmaster, vi. 569, 571
precedence disputed by ladies at ball given by, iv. 121, 144
profane conversation of, drives harlequins from club at Drury Lane Theatre, vi. 185
prosecution of, in House of Commons, will probably lead to nothing, ix. 241
Ray, Martha, mistress of, viii. 459
recall of, from Holland, rumoured, iii. 303
reprieved by Parliamentary recess, ix. 222
Rockingham attacks, in House of Lords, ix. 221
Sackville's principal enemy, ix. 238
St-Séverin tells, that French are ready to sign Aix treaty, iii. 482
secretary of state, vi. 159, 167
secretary of state's post to be resigned by, vii. 263
Selwyn's witticism on, at tennis game, iv. 155
sent to the devil, vi. 312
Seymour half-brother of, iv. 217
Skrine, Mrs, bestowed by, on the public, vi. 402
Spanish post rumoured for, vi. 103, 112
Suffolk may be succeeded by, as secretary of state, viii. 450
talents of, fit him to be head of the marine, vii. 350
Temple reconciled with, vi. 304
tie wig worn by, ii. 561
Townshend (Capt.)'s court martial caused by, iii. 332, 361, 373
Townshend (Lord)'s caricature of, v. 77
treaty with Saxony defended by, in Parliament, iv. 300
tricky, vi. 382
universally hated, iv. 201
unpopular, iv. 138
Waldegrave's marriage arranged by, iv. 258
Weymouth succeeded by, as secretary of state, but in northern province, vii. 255
wife separated from, because of her insanity, vi. 312n
wife's fortune and insanity will be useful to, vi. 396
wife's treatment from, iv. 258
Wilkes has, summoned to bar of House of Commons, vii. 73, 77
—— reads Essay on Woman to, vi. 185
——'s Essay on Woman denounced by, in House of Lords, vi. 184
will return, even if has to marry his wife, vi. 312

Wortley Montagu's bequest to, v. 473
Yonge succeeded by, as vice-treasurer of Ireland, iv. 518
Montagu (before 1749, Brudenell), John (1735–70), styled Bn Montagu 1735–62, M. of Monthermer 1766–70; cr (1762) Bn Montagu:
peerage granted to, vi. 31
Montagu, John (b. and d. 1742):
birth of, ii. 130
Montagu, John (b. ca 1771), naval capt:
Sandwich's child by Martha Ray, viii. 459
Montagu, Lady Mary (ca 1711–75), m. (1730) George Brudenell, 4th E. of Cardigan; cr. (1776) D. of Montagu:
bequests of, to daughter and husband, viii. 99
death of, viii. 98–9
death of, afflicts Anne Pitt, viii. 105
father's bequest to, iv. 80
yacht awaits at Calais the return of, from Spa, i. 141
Montagu, Lady Mary Wortley. See Pierrepont, Lady Mary (1689–1762)
Montagu, Ralph (1638–1709), 3d Bn Montagu; cr. (1705) D. of Montagu:
death of, ix. 564n
wife married by, as Emperor of China, ix. 564
wife produced by, at Westminster Hall, ix. 564n
Montagu, Robert (ca 1710–62), 3d D. of Manchester; M.P.:
chamberlain to Q. Charlotte, v. 517
daughter of, v. 530
George III does not retain, in Bedchamber, v. 460
men presented by, to Q. Charlotte, v. 531
Montagu, Robert (1763–1830), Adm., 1810:
Sandwich's child by Martha Ray, viii. 459
Montagu, William:
Sandwich's child by Martha Ray, viii. 459
Montagu House:
Albemarle, Ds of, confined at, ix. 564n
Montaigne, Michel Eyquem de (1533–92), philosopher:
HW paraphrases, vii. 529
Journal du voyage: editor of, see Meusnier de Querlon; HW's opinion of, viii. 16–17
Mont Albano:
garrison of, iii. 323
Montale:
Spaniards stationed near, iii. 30
Montallegre, Duca di. See Guzmann, José Joaquín
Montcalm de St-Véran, Louis-Joseph (1712–59), Marquis de:
alleged victory by, v. 344
death of, v. 338
English to be driven by, from Louisbourg, v. 229–30
Mont Castello:
Spaniards force Charles Emmanuel III to abandon, iii. 120

Monte Albano:
   road to, ii. 532
Monteallegri. *See* Montallegre
Monte Cassino:
   Charles of Naples may visit, ii. 447
Monte Cavallo:
   Clement XIV and D. of Gloucester talk
   in garden of, vii. 389
   popes abandon St Peter's for, in summer,
   viii. 344
   York, D. of, visits, vi. 228–9
Montecuccoli, (?) Raimondo:
   HW mentions, i. 42
   HW sees, at Reggio, i. 44–5
Monte di Pietà:
   at Leghorn, Leghorn houses to be repaired
   with money from, i. 304
   at Rome: Kingston, Ds of, takes treasure
   from, viii. 404; Old Pretender said to
   deposit jewels at, iii. 94, 96
Monte di Santa Maria:
   Benedict XIV disputes control of, with
   Francis I, iv. 428
   Del Monte family hold, as imperial fief, iv.
   422, 428, 437
Montefiascone:
   Inquisition officers sent to, to examine the
   Madonna de Valentano, viii. 30, 39–40, 42
Monte Guffone, villa:
   Mann visits, iv. 160
Monteleone:
   earthquake account mentions, ix. 376
Montemar, Duque de. *See* Carrillo de Al-
   bornoz, Don José
Montenegro:
   Dolgorukov's conduct in, disapproved by
   Catherine II, vii. 160
Monte Rosi:
   Austrian army at, ii. 525, 534
Monte Rosso:
   Young Pretender at, ii. 388
Monte Rotondo:
   Atrisco to attack, ii. 443
   Lobkowitz's troops rendezvous at, ii. 443
   —— to approach Naples through, by Bene-
   dict XIV's permission, ii. 437
Montesquieu, Baron de. *See* Secondat, Charles
   de (1689–1755)
Montesquiou-Fézensac, Anne-Élisabeth-Pierre
   de (1764–1834), Baron de Montesquiou; cr.
   (1809) Comte de Montesquiou-Fézensac:
   SH visited by, ix. 423
Monteynard, Louis-Francois (b. 1716), Mar-
   quis de; minister of war:
   French drag out, to fill government, vii.
   264
   Louis XV first consents to plea of, then
   punishes him, vii. 284
   Maillebois aided by, vii. 283
   resignation of, rumoured, vii. 284
Montezuma II (d. 1520), Emperor of Mexico:
   ghost of, should not complain now, vi. 49

Montezuma. *See* Motezuma
Montfort, Bn. *See* Bromley, Henry (1705–
   55); Bromley, Thomas (1733–99)
Montforts:
   scene of, reenacted, vi. 303
Montgomerie, Alexander (1723–69), 10th E.
   of Eglintoun, 1729:
   Florence visited by, ii. 479
   George III adds, to Bedchamber, v. 460
   Maclaine robs, iv. 168
   Mann entertains, iv. 426
   Ramsay communicates Jacobite sympathies
   to, as his tutor, iii. 112–13
Montgomery, Richard (1738–75), American
   army officer:
   Carleton said to be defeated and St John's
   captured by, viii. 156–7, 161
   death of, in attack on Quebec, viii. 185
   Irishman, viii. 158
Monthermer, M. of. *See* Montagu, John
   (1735–70)
Monthly Review:
   Mann wants, vi. 36, 49
Monti, Filippo Maria (1675–1754), cardinal,
   1743:
   Young Pretender's departure from Rome
   described by, ii. 418–19
Monticelli, Angelo Maria (ca 1710–64), singer:
   admired, i. 190, 211
   Calais visited by, i. 141
   Conway, Bns, to have, sing at assembly, i.
   334
   elephant to have been ridden by, i. 358
   Frederick, P. of Wales, sends for, i. 279
   HW accuses Lady Mary Walpole of loving,
   i. 487
   HW has, sing at entertainment, i. 274
   HW's witticism on Lady Rich's desertion
   by, ii. 481
   HW travels with, i. 141
   Holdernesse entertains, ii. 131
   ill, i. 190
   London opera retains, i. 191, 358
   Middlesex sued by, for salary, iv. 4
   salary of, i. 191
   sings in the Olimpiade, i. 401
   to sing, at opera, i. 185
   Townshend, Vcts, to entertain, i. 211
   Walpole, Sir Robert, often dines with, i.
   487
   yacht visited by, i. 141
Montini, ——:
   executed at Naples for treason, ii. 271
Montmorency, Duchesse de. *See* Diane (1538–
   1619)
Montmorency, Marie-Anne-Philippine Thérèse de (d. 1797), m. (1747) Charles-Joseph,
   Duc de Boufflers:
   inoculation of, unsuccessful, vi. 357–8
Montmorency:
   aucune a more impressive name than, vii.
   435

Montmorency family:
  genealogy of, merely proves their long vassalage, vi. 483
Montmorency-Luxembourg, Charles-François-Frédéric de (d. 1764), Duc de Luxembourg:
  Coventry rudely thanks, for summoning wife's coach, iv. 338
Montopoli:
  Barrett-Lennards invite Mann to, iv. 194
Montpellier:
  Brownlow, Lady Betty, married at, to marine officer, ii. 116–17
  HW visits, i. 103, 119, 127, 132
  Mann, Horace II and Lady Lucy, visit, viii. 246–7
Montpensier, D. of:
  HW dreams of capture of, v. 212
Montrath. See Mountrath
Montreal:
  American capture of, expected, viii. 157
  Byron captures ships destined for, v. 440
  English capture of, v. 416, 421, 437, 440, 445
  French proclaimed English repulse at, vi. 21, 89
Montreal, British ship:
  Joseph II boards, vii. 108
  York's body to go in, to England, vi. 554
Mont Reale. See Monreale
Montrose, Ds of. See Manners, Lady Lucy
Montrose, D. and M. of. See Graham, James (1682–1742)
Montrose, D. of. See Graham, James (1755–1836); Graham, William (1712–90)
Montrose:
  Soleil bound towards, iii. 173
Montroth. See Mountrath
Montserrat, Joaquin, Marqués de Cruillas; viceroy of Mexico 1761–6:
  wealth of, disregarded, vi. 89
Montvandermeer, Capt. Davide:
  made Baron for bringing rhinoceros, iv. 127–8
Monzone, Conte di. See Cioia de Forges, Bernardo
Moon:
  Europeans would reduce, to a province, ix. 451
  Galileo's retort about, iv. 149–50
  London bonfires eclipse, v. 314
  March, Sersali's remark about malignity of, iv. 429
  Milton's lines on, vi. 382
  travellers to, would instantly hunt for gold, ix. 545
Moonlight:
  Mann and Horace Mann II walk in garden by, before supper, viii. 517
Moore, Arthur (ca 1666–1730), economist and politician:
  coffin of, chained to whore's in St Giles's vault, iv. 181

Craggs's remark to, on entering coach, iv. 181
  footman's livery formerly worn by, iv. 181
Moore, Edward (1712–57), dramatist:
  Foundling, The: controversy over, iii. 469; successful, iii. 465
Moore, Commodore Sir John (d. 1779), cr. (1766) Bt:
  member of Byng court martial, v. 63, 64, 65
  men of war dispatched by, to intercept Dutch convoy, vi. 71
  squadron of, to fight Bompart's at Martinique, v. 297
Moorfields:
  Gordon, Lord George, appropriate to, ix. 23
Moors:
  England should send, to invade Spain, vi. 100
Morant, Philip (1700–70), historian:
  Tapestry Hangings of the House of Lords, ii. 127
Morat. See Maratti, Carlo
Moravia:
  Austrian victory in, i. 372
  Braitwitz may be sent to, i. 407
  Daun retires into, v. 95
  Frederick II recalls outposts from, vi. 63
  priests said to be ill-treated in, i. 445
Moravian; Moravians:
  colony of, in London, iv. 359
  Reus is, iv. 359
Morawska, Countess. See Radziwill, Teofila Konstancia
Moray, E. of. See Stuart, James (ca 1708–67)
Mordaunt, Anna Maria (d. 1771), m. (1733) Stephen Poyntz:
  Croxall writes The Fair Circassian for, iv. 208n, vi. 163n
  French royal family kiss, vi. 164
  husband ruined by, in marrying off her poor cousins, iv. 208
  maid of honour to Q. Caroline, iv. 208n, vi. 163n
  Spa to be visited by, vi. 164
  Victoire, Mme, cured by, in Paris, with Mrs Stephens' medicine, vi. 163–4
Mordaunt, Charles (ca 1658–1735), 3d E. of Peterborough:
  army hunted by, in Spain in Q. Anne's War, ii. 180, viii. 482
  Pope celebrates, viii. 112n
  witticism by, on being shown the Sainte Ampoulle at Rheims, viii. 112–13
Mordaunt, Sir Charles (? 1697–1778), 6th Bt, 1721; M.P.:
  voted for, as commissioner, i. 438
Mordaunt, Sir John (1697–1780), K.B., 1749; army officer, M.P.:
  acquittal of, v. 165, 174, 177
  arrest of, v. 163

[Mordaunt, Sir John, *continued*]
clamour against, for failure of Rochefort expedition, v. **143**
George II receives, badly, v. 143–4
inquiry demanded by, v. 145, 154–5
Kingston's lieutenant-colonel, x. 14
Parliamentary debates by: against Scotch bill, iv. 311, x. 31, 32, 33; on privately-raised regiments, x. 14, 18
Mordaunt, Hon. John (?1709–67), Lt-Col.:
Pembroke, Cts of, marries, i. 495n
Morden, William. *See* Harbord, Sir William
More, ——, capt. of British merchant ship:
Estaing's probable loss conjectured by, viii. 545
More, ?Robert (1703–80), M.P.:
HW mentions, i. 123
More. *See also* Moore
Morea:
Greek inhabitants of, support Russian incasion, vii. 204
Greeks in, vii. 235
Russian fleet reaches coast of, vii. 204–5
Russians abandon, for lack of Greek assistance, vii. 226, 235
Russians to distribute arms to people of, vii. 202
Russian victory repairs disgrace of leaving, vii. 235
Turks and Russians haggle over villages in, vii. 224
Moreau de Maupertuis, Pierre-Louis (1698–1759), mathematician and astronomer:
Catalogue of French Books, A, satirizes, ii. 52
Moreau de Séchelles, Jean (1690–1760), controller general of finances:
French finances and navy to be rehabilitated by, iv. 500
Morehead, Mrs ——:
Florence to be visited by, iii. 477
Hunt accompanies, to Paris, iii. 477
—— leaves estate to, iii. 477
Mann entertains, iii. 489
—— talks to, at Mrs Strode's, iii. 477
passes in France and Lorraine for a lady of condition, iii. 489
weeds worn by, for Hunt, iii. 477
Morelle, Mrs, governess to Molesworth family:
death of, in fire, vi. 138, 140
Morelli Adimari, Signora. *See* Franchini, Agnese
Morello cherries. *See under* Cherries
Moretti, Gaspero:
Albani recommends, to Mann, iv. 37, 46
England to be visited by, on business, iv. 37
Mann recommends, to Whithed, iv. 46
—— writes letter of introduction for, to HW, iv. 37, 46
Roman merchant, iv. 46

Morgan, David *or* Thomas David (d. 1746), barrister:
execution of, iii. 287
Morgan, Thomas (1727–71) of Tredegar; M.P.:
Beaufort tries to wrest lieutenancy of Welsh counties from, vii. 174
Whig enemy of Beaufort family, vii. 174
Morice, Humphrey (1723–85); M.P.:
Bath visited by, for gout, ix. 191, 195, 202, 213, 216, 220, 235
Brown, Lady, leaves estate to, ix. 246
cameo sent through, by Mann, to HW, ix. 51, 56, 65, 88, 89, 94
Chiswick Grove bought by, from Grantham, ix. 298n
Chiswick visited by, ix. 266
Chute's friend, v. **389,** 442
—— to be approached by, about Sophia Lucchi, vi. 266
Clerk of the Green Cloth, v. 389
comes to town and can attend to business, ix. 266
comptroller of the Household, vi. 103, 113
confined in the country, ix. 97
crutches used by, ix. 435
disapproves of delaying tactics of lawyers, ix. 202
Duane recommended by, to take his place in Mozzi affair, ix. 298, 303
England revisited by, ix. 51, 56, 87
Florence to be visited by, on way to Naples for health, v. 389
Florence visited by, v. 389, 442, vi. 28, 29, 36, vii. 113, ix. 51
France left by, vii. 147
German mud-baths to be visited by, ix. 307
going abroad for health, ix. 297–8, 303
HW agrees with, in Mozzi-Orford affairs, ix. 164
HW agrees with advice of, about choosing Handelian oratorios, vi. 41–2
HW and, to take care of Mozzi's affairs, ix. 162, 230
HW dines with, at Chiswick, ix. 298
HW encloses letter to, to Mann, ix. 432, 434
HW has not seen, ix. 97, 176
HW insists he had written to Mann about, v. 450
HW mentions, in postscript, v. 457
HW receives copy of paper sent by Sharpe to, ix. 186
HW receives report from, on Mozzi's affairs, ix. 191
HW recommends, to Mann, v. 389
HW's collaborator in Mozzi's business, ix. 172
HW's correspondence with, ix. 286, 289, 297–8, 432, 434, 435
HW will advise, to consult Duane, ix. 217
HW willing to deal with, if permitted to act like gentleman, ix. 158

health of: bad, ix. 265; better, ix. 435; gout, ix. 51, 97, 184, 202, 213; gout confines, at Paris, ix. 74; loses use of legs and feet, ix. 298; melancholy account of, ix. 202; not in danger, but weakened by overbathing, ix. 220; not likely to recover, ix. 216; not so bad as Lucas reported, ix. 217; relapse, ix. 289; unable to come to town, ix. 246; worse, ix. 297–8

heavy luggage left by, at Margate, ix. 88

Lausanne visited by, ix. 432

lives near SH, ix. 159

Lucas replies to scolding by, for his delay, ix. 286

Mann advises Mozzi to write to, about intended gift to Duane, ix. 524

—— asks to be remembered to, ix. 182

—— discusses HW and Chute with, v. 442, vi. 39

—— entertains, at dinners, ix. 435

—— sends compliments to, ix. 171

—— sends letter through, to HW, vii. 140–1, 146, 147

—— thinks Mozzi should not write to, ix. 171

—— told by, to ask HW to get advice in selecting oratorios, vi. 36

—— wants to congratulate, on being Comptroller of the Household, vi. 113

Mozzi advised by: to name Duane referee, ix. 298; to sell his rights, ix. 286

—— begs HW and, to conclude affairs, ix. 190

—— cannot be aided by, ix. 247

—— commissions, to handle affairs in England, ix. 157–8

—— confers with, ix. 434–5

—— hopes to see, at Cambrai, ix. 303

—— pleased to have assistance of HW and, ix. 181

——'s affairs delayed by illness of, ix. 216–17

—— says that division of money held by Hoare was opposed by, ix. 426

——'s correspondence with, ix. 168, 230, 304

—— should have younger assistants than HW and, ix. 344

—— to accept decision of HW and, ix. 162, 169

—— told by, not to come to England, ix. 435

Naples to be visited by, v. 389, ix. 289, 432, 435

Naples visited by, when ill with gout, ix. 51

Orford thinks HW and, will differ, ix. 164

Paris visited by, vii. 140–1, 146, ix. 74

Petraia palm tree praised by, vi. 29

privateer avoided by, ix. 89

Rome to be visited by, ix. 435

Sharpe advises, to call for papers, ix. 289

—— sends papers to, ix. 184

Tissot regulates motions of, ix. 435

withdrawal of, causes Mozzi to decide on English trip, ix. 303

writing-box of, ix. 94

Morice, Sir William (?1707–50), 3d Bt, 1726; M.P.:

heir of, v. 389

Morice family:

Launceston a borough of, iv. 113

Morin-Dumesnil, Anne-Louise (1729–1823), m. Jean-Baptiste-Jacques Élie de Beaumont:

Lettres du Marquis de Roselle, HW recommends, vi. 271

Morison, William (d. 1772):

(?) HW talks to, ii. 294

Morley, J.:

Rawdon promised money by, for Wallingford election, i. 400

Mormorai, Antonio (ca 1712–84), senator:

(?) Mann seeks maps for, vii. 411, 413, 418, 427, 431

Moro, Dr Bartolomeo, Lady Mary Wortley Montagu's secretary

Montagu, Lady Mary Wortley accompanied by, vi. 3

Morocco, Emperor of. See Mohammed (ca 1710–90) ben Abdallah

Morocco:

ambassadors from and to, see under Ambassador

slaves of, viii. 469

Moroni, Pietro Celestino, Col. in Spanish service:

Riva, Maria da, marries, ii. 86

Morosini, Cavaliere Francesco (fl. 1744–85), Venetian ambassador to England:

Venice sends, to England, v. 508

Morpheus:

gesso of: at Leghorn awaiting shipment, ii. 329; Mann may not send, to HW, ii. 303; to be sent to England, ii. 178

HW receives, preferring it in plaster to black marble original, ii. 561

Mann has, copied in gesso for HW, ii. 153

Morphews. See Morpheus

Morphy, Marie-Louise (ca 1738–1815), m. 1 (1755) Jacques de Beaufranchet d'Ayat; m. 2 (ca 1759) François-Nicolas Le Normant, cr. (1765) Comte de Flaghac; m. 3 (before 1798) Louis-Philippe Dumont (divorced, 1798); Louis XV's mistress:

(?) Pompadour, Mme de, provides, as Louis XV's mistress, v. 542

Morray. See Moray

Morres, Hervey Redmond (ca 1743–97), 2d Vct Mountmorres, 1766:

defeated as Wilkes's candidate for Westminster, viii. 52

Morrice. See Morice

Morris, Corbyn (d. 1779):
Essay towards Fixing the True Standards of Wit, ii. 464
Morris, John (d. 1776), naval Capt.:
killed in Charleston attempt, viii. 236
Morris, Mary (d. 1742):
death of, i. 504
Morrison, George (ca 1704–99), army officer:
accompanies D. of York's body to England, vi. 554
York, D. of, taken by, to Monaco, vi. 553
Morrison, William (d. ?1772), secretary to the opera:
HW talks to, of opera expenses, ii. 294
Mortars:
batteries of, surrounding St Philip's, ix. 233
Schulenburg obtains, to subdue Genoa, iii. 367
Spaniards to receive, from Naples by Adriatic, iii. 30
Wade demands, for Ostend, iii. 69
Mortgage; mortgages:
German, George II's money in, v. 450
Houghton estate overwhelmed by, vii. 510, 515
on Linton: declared illegal, viii. 258; HW believes falsely imposed, viii. 176, 187; Mann, Horace II, consults Duane about, viii. 181
Mortification in the legs:
occurrences of, ix. 394
Mortimer, Roger de (1287–1330), 8th Bn, cr. (1328) E. of March:
Bute compared with, vi. 53
Morton, E. of. See Douglas, James (ca 1702–68)
Morton, John (ca 1420–1500), Abp of Canterbury 1486–1500; cardinal, 1493:
painting of, in Pomfret's collection, iv. 390
Mosaic:
HW's table of, x. 7
picture in: given to D. of Cumberland, at Rome, vii. 566; given to D. of York, at Rome, vi. 229, 232
Mosca, Agapeto (1678–1760), cardinal, 1732:
Albani faction tries to elect, v. 207
Moscow, Metropolitan of. See Levshin, Petr Georgievich
Moscow:
Joseph II to visit, ix. 72
Moses:
animals preserved and distinguished by, iv. 71
Bolingbroke writes Craftsman against, iv. 454
Moslem:
HW asks if Wilkes becomes, vi. 290
Mosques:
Turks insist upon retaining, vii. 469–70
Mosquito Coast:
English capture fort on, viii. 543–4

Moss, James (d. 1758), King's messenger:
(?) Giberne sends letter through, i. 454
Mann receives instructions by, i. 405
—— sends letter by, i. 408, 412
'Most Noble She-Witch, The,' by HW:
text of, x. 9
Mostyn, John (1709–79), Gen., 1772; M.P.:
garrulity of, iv. 4
Pomfret challenges, in bed, for having laughed at him at Court, ix. 96
Rich, Lady, and, i. 139
Mostyn, Savage (?1713–57), naval officer; M.P.:
Admiralty post for, v. 73
Motezuma (opera). See under Bottarelli, Giovan Gualberto; Sacchini Antonio
Mothe-Fénelon, de la. See La Mothe-Fénelon
Motier, Du. See Du Motier
'Motion, The':
Gravelot's print of, ii. 21
Motte, la. See La Motte
Motto; mottoes:
for pictures, Uguccioni provides, for Cts of Pomfret, ii. 545
Holland's, iii. 397, 411
in fireworks, ii. 242
Mann seeks, iv. 475, 480, 482, 487
Walpole family's, v. 167
Mouchy, Duc de. See Noailles, Philippe de (1715–94)
Moulsey, Middlesex:
Windham and Sadler make balloon ascent from, ix. 579
Mount:
for fan, see under Fan
temple on, at Ranelagh, iv. 47
Mount Edgcumbe, Cts of. See Gilbert, Emma (1729–1807); Hobart, Lady Sophia (1768–1806)
Mount Edgcumbe, E. of. See Edgcumbe, George (1720–95); Edgcumbe, Richard (1764–1839)
Mount Edgcumbe, Vct. See Edgcumbe, George (1720–95)
Mount Edgcumbe, Vcts. See Gilbert, Emma (1729–1807)
Mount Edgcumbe, Cornwall:
HW visits, iii. 92, 101
Mountford. See Montfort
Mountjoy, Vcts. See Boyle, Anne (d. 1741)
Mountmorres, Vct. See Morres, Hervey Redmond (ca 1743–97)
Mountnorris, E. of. See Annesley, Arthur (1744–1816); Annesley, George (1771–1844)
Mountrath, E. of. See Coote, Algernon (1689–1744); Coote, Charles Henry (ca 1725–1802)
Mount Stewart. See Mount Stuart
Mount Stewart of Wortley, Bns. See Wortley Montagu, Mary
Mount Stuart, Vct. See Stuart, John (1744–1814)
Mount Stuart, Vcts. See Windsor, Hon. Charlotte Jane (1746–1800)

Mourning:
Ancaster, Ds of, tells Lady Anna Horatia Waldegrave to wear, viii. 494
black coat a sign of, iv. 175
black wax used on letters during, i. 164
Craon, Princesse de, finds, painful to her eyes, ii. 228
—— gets, vi. 536
Florence has gala in spite of, vi. 532
Florentine theatres closed because of, ii. 559, vi. 340
for Archduchess of Brussels, i. 193, 433
for Empress Dowager, iv. 211
for Francis I, vi. 337, 340, 347, 354
for George II, v. 462
for Madame Royale, ii. 558–9, iii. 1, 8, 14, iv. 211
for Marie Leszczyńska, vii. 78
for Princess Eleonora, i. 433
HW orders, for Cts of Orford, ix. 123
HW's waistcoat cannot be worn by Mann because of, i. 433
HW to get, for Q. of Denmark, viii. 104
London may assume, for Pitt's resignation, v. 540
observances during, i. 122–3
on Electress's death, ii. 175, 190–1, 206
Orford, Cts of, may wear, iii. 37, 42, 47, 49, 53
rings for, out of fashion among people of rank, ix. 124
rouge forbidden to Viennese ladies during, vi. 354
servants want to wear, v. 165
Vienna to regulate, for Tuscan court, vi. 337, 340, 354
See also Weepers
Mourning Bride, The. See under Congreve, William
Mourning ring. See under Ring
Mouse:
God compared to, ii. 79
time's womb will not bring forth, viii. 356
Moustier, Éléonore-François-Élie (1751–1817), Comte (Marquis, 1801) de; army officer; minister to England, 1783:
English mission of, ix. 363
Moysey, Dr Abel (1715–80), physician:
daughter implored by, not to marry Hervey, vii. 93
Moysey, Mary, m. Rev. John Richards of Long Bredy House, Dorset:
Hervey in love with, vii. 193
Moyston. See Mostyn
Moyzer, Col. [? John (b. ca 1660)]:
Mann receives, at Galfridus Mann's recommendation, i. 408
Mozzi (or Mozzi del Garbo), Signora. See Barbolani da Montanto, Isabella; Bartolini Salimbeni, Maria Luisa (1766–1813)
Mozzi, Giulio Giuseppe (1730–1813), cavaliere; mathematician:
affair of, over E. of Orford's claims against

Cts of Orford's estate: ix. 167, 439–41, 444–7, 448, 504, 509–11; claims and counter-claims in, ix. 169, 335; compromise suggested in, ix. 335, 471–3, 478–9; delayed, ix. 150, 168, 191, 215–17, 397; Duane accepts arbitration in, ix. 330; Duane allows some of Lucas's claims in, ix. 414; Duane and Lucas dispute about, ix. 397–8; Duane writes to HW about, ix. 447; HW and Morice joint referees in, ix. 161–2, 181, 230; HW attempts to conclude, ix. 505–6; HW confers with Duane, Lucas, and Sharpe about, ix. 419, 429, 439–41, 444–7, 471–2; HW declines acting as sole arbiter for, ix. 216, 265–6, 304; HW disagrees about harm to Orford from delay in, ix. 265–6; HW's delay in, caused by Lucas, ix. 172, 200; HW's note from Lucas about concluding, ix. 510; HW's tenderness for Mozzi prevents his withdrawing from, ix. 328; HW thanked by Orford for concluding, ix. 516; HW wants Camden as referee in, ix. 216; less involved than Chancery suit would be, ix. 397; Morice wants HW to write to Florence about, ix. 432; Mozzi impatient to conclude, ix. 190, 200, 202, 345, 421; Mozzi wants to end HW's vexation in, ix. 345; must rest until he goes to England, ix. 304; Sharpe and Duane too much for Lucas in, ix. 410
age of, past 50, ix. 535
ancestral town house of, partly purchased by Cts of Orford, viii. 260
appearance of, fallen off, vii. 237
beauty of, is his attraction for Cts of Orford, ix. 130
bride not taken home by, till two days after wedding, ix. 535, 539
Carder, Mrs, persuades, not to accept compromise, ix. 419
—— sends letter to, ix. 168
—— to be paid by, ix. 512
—— urges, to come to England, ix. 435
caveat's removal demanded by, ix. 504, 509
claim of, against Cts of Orford's landed estate, explained by Mann, ix. 168–9
Corsini and Strozzi matches available to, ix. 130, 498
could foil Lucas only by another like him, ix. 298
courier perhaps sent by, ix. 121
decency and civility will be of no use to, ix. 328
desires only what Cts of Orford's will entitles him to, ix. 162
disinterestedness of, communicated to HW by Mann, ix. 324
Duane approved by, as referee, ix. 229–30
—— gets carte blanche from, ix. 412
—— is sent Guercino painting and Florentine prints by, ix. 524, 568, 571–2

[Mozzi, Giulio Giuseppe, *continued*]
—— neglects, ix. 371, 390
Duane, Orford, and Sharpe to be paid by, through Hoare, ix. 492
Duane recommended to, by Morice, ix. 298, 303
——'s correspondence with, ix. 304, 315, 328, 333, 390, 391, 514–15, 524
——'s decision approved by, ix. 478
—— should be employed by, ix. 216–17
English journey contemplated by, ix. 144, 217, 220, 230–1, 235, 265, 289, 298, 300, 307, 315, 319, 320, 322, 328, 330, 341, 390, 391, 396, 404, 431, 496, 516
English might dislike, for getting old lady's inheritance away from her son, ix. 396, 404
family of, ancient, ix. 130
family to be protected by, from future claims, ix. 466
fears of: of irritating Sharpe, ix. 341; that Sharpe may not produce papers favouring him, ix. 333
finances of, not poor for Florence, ix. 130
Florence admires, for devotion to Cts of Orford, ix. 396
(?) Gem, Dr, reports about, vii. 158
Geoffrin, Mme, called on by, at Paris, vii. 141–2
glad to escape from Lucas and Sharpe, ix. 161
HW advises: not to be sanguine, ix. 266; to come to England, ix. 217, 220, 235, 265, 289, 298, 320, 328, 330; to offer or accept compromise, ix. 320; to put himself in Duane's hands, ix. 320; to sell claim to rich lawyer, ix. 328
HW agrees with Morice in affairs of, ix. 164
HW and Morice authorized by, to employ chamber counsel, ix. 232
HW asked by, to conceal doubts of Sharpe, ix. 341
HW asks Mann to inform, of E. of Orford's inherited wealth, ix. 126
HW, as Orford's nominee, cannot altogether favour, ix. 462
HW, as referee, favoured, ix. 516
HW asserts that he is not partial to, ix. 445
HW condemns Sharpe and Lucas for forcing, to come to England, ix. 315
HW dares not write letters to, for fear of being put in his power, ix. 265
HW declines to tell Morice how to advise, ix. 298
HW desires list from, of demands Cts of Orford might have had on son, ix. 158
HW does not wish to favour, ix. 216
HW earns gratitude of, by trouble with Lucas, ix. 404
HW expects Orford to accommodate, ix. 184

HW has saved, from Chancery suit, ix. 448
HW hopes Duane will be accepted by, as referee, ix. 216
HW hopes Duane will prevent injustice to, ix. 350
HW meets, when he calls on Hollands at Holland House, vii. 229–30
HW not an enemy of, ix. 158
HW proposes to obey commands of, ix. 350
HW's and Duane's letters from, will end their arbitrage, ix. 462
HW's conferences with Lucas please, ix. 156
HW's connection with, might jeopardize claim to impartiality, ix. 235
HW's correspondence with, ix. 417, 421, 426, 470, 477, 519
HW's letter raises hopes of, ix. 417
HW's relations with Duane over affair of, ix. 320, 330, 333, 334, 335, 344, 371, 391, 404, 419, 421–2, 439–41, 444–7, 448, 465–6, 471–3, 477–8, 495, 516, 519
HW's relations with Lucas over affair of, ix. 124, 126, 131, 143, 147–8, 154–5, 156, 157–8, 166, 167, 172, 176, 184, 186, 195, 213, 215–17, 235, 266, 286, 315, 331, 404, 419, 421–2, 427, 439–41, 444–7, 448, 471–3, 477–8, 495, 505–6, 509, 515, 516, 519
HW thanked by, ix. 190, 229, 230, 341, 345, 431, 521
HW to act as counsel for, though not partial to him, ix. 158
HW to favour, as much as equity will allow, ix. 166
HW to tell Duane and Sharpe of resolution of, ix. 466
HW unable to make a report to, ix. 347
HW unable to tell, what Orford's demands are, ix. 176
health of: fever, ix. 322; nervous disorder, vii. 155, 237; 'out of order,' ix. 300; spits blood, ix. 322
Hoare authorized by, to pay E. of Orford, ix. 498, 504, 509, 511, 521, 540
——'s bank informs, of balance due to Lady Orford, ix. 130
house of, viii. 260, 322, 330
houses of pleasure attended by, vii. 158
Huntingdon knows, v. 70
indolent and peaceable, averse to going to law, ix. 341
lawyer consulted by, about interest on jointure arrears, ix. 456
lawyers probably suggested Orford's claims on, ix. 186
less than £4000 to be received by, ix. 515n
London lawyers complicate case of, ix. 397–8
Lucas and Sharpe suspected by, of wishing him to go to law, ix. 322

Lucas complains of being blamed by, for delay, ix. 213–14

—— demands back interest from, ix. 637

—— expects to get five or six thousand pounds from, ix. 286

—— gives gout as excuse for delaying business of, ix. 195

——'s negotiations with Sharpe displease, ix. 492

—— suspicious of reasonableness of, ix. 298

—— wishes to get something from, ix. 143

Mann alarms, by threat that HW may quit arbitrage, ix. 469

—— always visited by, after arrival of post, ix. 404, 465

—— asks HW not to forget, ix. 283

—— calls, 'Gloria in Excelsis,' v. 70

—— communicates HW's news to, ix. 319, 396, 426, 456, 469, 478

—— declines invitation to wedding banquet of, ix. 535

—— dissuades: from bribing Lucas, ix. 200; from setting out for England, ix. 200; from writing to HW or Morice, ix. 171

—— gets letters from, on Cts of Orford's illness, viii. 312, ix. 112, 113

—— has conference with, ix. 229–30

—— not to alarm, by account of HW's dissatisfaction with Lucas, ix. 509

—— receives letter from, and sends it to HW, ix. 231–2, 235

—— shown Cts of Orford's writing-box by, ix. 114

—— to inquire of, about Orford deeds, ix. 160

—— told by, of Cts of Orford's heart palpitation, ix. 102

marriage of: prevented by affair with Cts of Orford, ix. 130; takes place, ix. 535; to girl of 17, to take place, ix. 498, 512, 527; unhappy, ix. 568, 571

mathematician, vii. 155, 237, ix. 130

money left in London by Cts of Orford should be divided by, with E. of Orford, Sharpe thinks, ix. 154–5

money wanted by, to invest in French funds, ix. 477

Morice advises: to name Duane referee, ix. 298; to sell his rights, ix. 286

—— cannot assist, ix. 247

—— commissioned by, to handle affairs in England, ix. 157–8

—— confers with, ix. 434–5

—— informs, of intention of going abroad, ix. 303

—— is HW's fellow-labourer in affairs of, ix. 171, 172

—— may be informed by, of intended gift to Duane, ix. 524

—— perhaps to be seen by, at Cambrai, ix. 303

——'s and HW's decision to be accepted by, ix. 162

——'s correspondence with, ix. 168, 230, 304

——'s withdrawal causes determination of, to go to England, ix. 303

—— tells, not to come to England, ix. 435

mother of, wants him to marry, ix. 130

oath to be administered to, by Mann and Palombo, ix. 167

obliged but not consoled by HW's news, ix. 292

Orford, Cts of, accompanied by: at Calais, vii. 158; at Naples, vii. 155; in London, vii. 229–30; to Paris, vii. 141–2, 155, 158

—— attended by, while pleading bad health, vii. 158

—— buys house next to that of, viii. 260, 322, 330

—— did not confide English affairs to, ix. 129

—— enriches, vii. 158

—— leaves everything to, ix. 114, 122n, 168–9

—— leaves paintings to, ix. 524

—— left by, because of his family affairs, viii. 145

—— may be abandoned by, unless she foresakes Naples, vii. 559, viii. 305

—— nearly discards, for lack of sexual prowess, v. 70

—— not expected by, to die, ix. 129

—— said to have deposited sums in French funds in name of, ix. 113

——'s effects expected by, from Naples, ix. 160

—— sends, as messenger to Mann, vii. 464

——'s furniture listed by, ix. 163, 169

——'s papers received by, from Naples, ix. 162

—— the obstacle to marriage of, ix. 130

—— to recombine next-door house with that of, viii. 330

—— turned back by, at Calais, to keep her from meeting her son, vii. 158

—— will probably leave Italian property to, ix. 113

Orford, E. of, answers offer of, ix. 495

—— approves mother's disposition in favour of, ix. 168, 181

—— offers to assist, in tossing Lucas in a blanket, ix. 322, 328

—— pleased by conduct of, ix. 156

—— presented by, with Clinton's portrait, ix. 298n

——'s correspondence with, ix. 176, 186, 300, 301–2, 306–7, 319, 322, 328, 330

——'s creditors should get money returned by, ix. 440, 441, 446

——'s creditor told by Lucas that money would come from, ix. 286, 439

——'s demands on: at last received, ix. 333; awaited impatiently, ix. 161; counter-claims against, ix. 166, 333; delayed in transmission, ix. 172, 191; should be

[Mozzi, Giulio Giuseppe, *continued*]
moderate, ix. 147; to be met, ix. 144, 161, 163
—— sent list by, of things taken to Italy by Cts of Orford, ix. 151, 156
—— should not give mother's portrait to, ix. 501-2
——'s lawyers irritated by, ix. 216
——'s lawyers may be quickened by, ix. 307
——'s opinion of, improved by Mrs Carder, ix. 168
——'s proceeding against, called by HW 'unjust, nugatory, and insulting,' ix. 328
——'s release to, ix. 466, 498, 521, 527
—— to be paid by, through Hoare, ix. 492
Orford deeds unknown to, ix. 160
Orford papers sent to England by, ix. 161
Pisa baths visited by, ix. 421
'poor emaciated low-spirited knight of St Stephen, who is said to be a *savant*,' vii. 141
Pratolino cannot be the night lodging of, viii. 23
Richecourt compared with, ix. 122, 130
safer in HW's hands than in Sharpe's, ix. 158
sculptor does hideous bust of Cts of Orford for, ix. 504-5
Sharpe advises, to divide sum equally with E. of Orford, ix. 419
Sharpe assures, that Orford will act honourably, ix. 144
—— employed by, ix. 160
—— informs, of Duane's death, ix. 568
—— is surprised at being employed by, because of connection with Orford, ix. 320, 333
—— less zealous for, ix. 200
—— mistakenly trusted by, and is his enemy, ix. 172
—— must be retained by, despite bad conduct, ix. 181
—— neglects, ix. 390
—— not a friend to, ix. 320
—— not answered by, ix. 419, 459
—— notifies, of Hoare's acceptance of order to pay E. of Orford and withdrawal of caveat, ix. 511
—— offers to collect rents for, at salary, ix. 492-3
—— receives power of attorney from, ix. 137, 144
—— reports to, on Cts of Orford's affairs, ix. 144-5
——'s correspondence with, ix. 137, 156, 166, 168-9, 216, 289, 315, 324, 333, 412, 465, 471, 478, 479, 492, 500, 504, 524
——'s duplicity angers, ix. 333
—— thinks, should divide Cts of Orford's money in Hoare's hands with E. of Orford, ix. 157, 160, 217, 335, 426
—— thinks Cts of Orford should not have left so much to, ix. 161-2
—— to receive from, copy of paper signed by Yorke, ix. 169
—— urges, to come to England, ix. 435
—— wishes to evade claim of, against deficiencies in Cts of Orford's jointure, ix. 172
should have younger assistants than Morice and HW, ix. 344
Skrine wanted by E. of Orford to assist in affair of, ix. 158, 162, 163-4, 166
submissions of, have worked against him, ix. 298
trunks unpacked by, ix. 435
verses by, on Buondelmonte's death, v. 70-1, 79
Zincke's portrait of Cts of Orford may be sent to, or copied in oils, ix. 501
Mozzi family:
Mozzi the only male of, ix. 130
—— wants to protect, from claims by Cts of Orford's estate, ix. 466
Mud-baths:
Morice to visit, in Germany, ix. 307
Mud Island. *See* Fort Mifflin
Muff; muffs:
French army does not have, v. 435
grey, Nugent has, i. 165
HW sends, to Pandolfini, i. 42, 45, 47, 52
spy hanged in, iii. 201
Muffeteens:
velvet, Montagu, Lady Mary Wortley, wears, vi. 3
Mufti:
of Algiers, viii. 122
Mufti of Turkey. *See* Durrisade Mustafa Efendi
Mugello, the:
San Martino fortress at, iii. 11
Muhammad 'Ali Khān (1717-95), Nawab of Arcot and of the Carnatic; Wālājah, 1765:
Benfield said to be agent for, ix. 117
Muhammed-ben-Othman (ca 1710-91), Dey of Algiers, 1766-91:
O'Reilly's attack awaited by, ix. 416
reward offered by, for Spanish heads, viii. 122
Muhammed Shah (d. 1748), Mogul Emperor ('Great Mogul') 1719-48:
Francis I's designs on treasure of, foiled by Mann, iv. 401, vi. 547
Muhemed Ben Milas, (b. ca 1721) Moroccan ambassador to Tuscany:
medal of Leopold's reception of, viii. 469, 478, 500
Muhsinzade Mehmet Pasha (1707-74), Grand Vizir 1771-4 of Turkey:
Rumiantsev cuts off retreat of, viii. 33
—— to attack, at Schuma, viii. 29
treaty signed by, viii. 33, 40
Mule; mules:
Beauchamp may get, for lack of horses, vi. 336

caravan of, turned back by *Nonsuch*, iii. 51
convoy of, ii. 460
HW and Spence count, on road to Genoa, i. 91
Richecourt procures, iii. 11
——'s litter carried by, v. 80
Three Princes of Serendip mentions, iv. 408
'Muley.' *See* Russell, John, 4th D. of Bedford
Mulgrave, Bn. *See* Phipps, Constantine (1722–75); Phipps, Constantine John (1744–92)
Mulgrave, Bns. *See* Hervey, Hon. Lepell
Mulinari. *See* Molinari
Müller, John Sebastian (1715–ca 1785), engraver:
plates engraved by, for *Designs by Mr R. Bentley for Six Poems by Mr T. Gray*, iv. 368n
Mulloy, Terence, sergeant:
rebels repelled by, iii. 105
Mummius, Lucius (fl. 154–142 B.C.), consul; Roman general:
sailors told by, to replace any lost statues, iii. 264
Mun, Comtesse de. *See* Helvétius, Élisabeth-Charlotte
Muncaster, Bn. *See* Pennington, John
Münchhausen, Freiherrin von. *See* Wangenheim, Wilhelmina Sophia von
Münchhausen, Gerlach Adolf (1688–1770), Freiherr von; Hanoverian statesman:
Cumberland, D. of, rebukes, v. 145
dinner given by, iv. 125
Mann forwards letter through, iii. 99
Munib. *See* Ibrahim Minnib
Munich:
Austrian army threatens, i. 289
court of, Suares family may seek, i. 161
Cowper's installation notice from, ix. 568
Niccolini may be at, iv. 2, 7
Munich, von. *See* Münnich
Munichausen. *See* Münchhausen, Gerlach Adolf
Münnich, Grafin von. *See* Mengden, Dorothea von
Münnich, Burchard Christoph von (1693–1767), field marshal:
banished, vi. 11
Catalogue of New French Books, A, satirizes, ii. 53
HW curious about fate of, vi. 59
Münnich, Ernst, Graf von; head steward of Catherine II's household:
banished, vi. 11
Münnich, Ernst Gustav (d. 1812), Maj.-Gen.; or Johann Gottlieb:
Elizabeth of Russia banishes family of, vi. 11
Florence visited by, vi. 11

Munro, ——:
Mann writes to, at Birmingham about double silver-plated dish-covers, viii. 32
Munro, Sir Hector (ca 1726–1805), K.B., 1779; army officer; M.P.:
glory of, in East Indies, ix. 282
Munro, Sir Robert (ca 1684–1746), 6th Bt, 1729; M.P.; army officer:
Highland regiment commanded by, ii. 237
killed at Falkirk, iii. 204
Munro. *See also* Monro
Munster, Bns de. *See* Pratt, Caroline (d. 1805)
Münster, Bp of. See Klemens August (1700–61); Königseck-Rotenfels, Maximilian Friedrich von (d. 1784); Maximilian Franz (1756–1801)
Münster, Ds of. *See* Schulenburg, Ermengarde Melusina von der
Münster:
Abreu congratulates Alt on capture of, v. 315–16
Frederick II tells chapter of, not to admit Maximilian as canon of, ix. 80
Munter, Mme. *See* Poll, Margarethe Cornelia van de
Müntz, Johann Heinrich (1727–98), painter:
Bentley finds, in Jersey, v. 239
description published by, of encaustic method of painting, v. 239n
HW keeps, in house, iv. **554**, v. 120, 239
landscape genius of, v. 239
Swiss engineer in the French service, v. 239
Munzell. *See* Muzell
Muratori, Lodovico Antonio (1672–1750), historian:
Annals of Italy, HW quotes, ix. 491
Della pubblica felicità oggetto di buoni principi trattato, Florentines disappointed by, iv. 117
Francis III's librarian, i. **324**, iv. 117
——'s rights to Ferrara investigated by, i. 324
Murder:
English law for immediate execution after conviction for, iv. 317
Murderer; murderers:
bodies of, delivered to surgeons, v. 388
property of, goes to county sheriff, v. 398
Muri, Ab[1], (?) Mann's physician:
(?) Cocchi recommends, ix. 270
(?) Mann kept in bed by, ix. 555, 556
(?) Mann permitted by, to see Hollands, vi. 467
(?) Mann's ailment called gout by, viii. **479**
(?) Mann told by, that chalkstones are painful, ix. 626
(?) Mann, Horace II, reassured by, ix. 607
Muriccioli, the, at Florence:
Bosville, Mrs, misbehaves upon, ii. 286

Murphy, Arthur (1727–1805), writer; actor:
No One's Enemy but his Own, vi. 199
Pitt, Elizabeth, offers letters to, for the
Test, v. 46
Murphy. See also Morphy
Murrain:
cold weather may hamper, iii. 174
English cattle struck by, iii. 174
physicians call, infectious disease from
abroad, not caused by poisoned pools, iii.
174
'Murray':
Bute's pseudonym, vii. 91, 96
Murray, Lady. See Baillie, Grizel (ca 1691–
1759)
Murray, ——, British agent in Corsica:
Paoli tells, of his needs, vii. 46
Murray, Hon. Alexander (1712–78); cr. (1759)
E. of Westminster (Jacobite):
brother of, iv. 223
brother tries to put, in custody of Serjeant-
at-Arms, iv. 249
counsel desired by, at bar of House of
Commons, iv. 224–5
flees to France, iv. 286
House of Commons sentences, to Newgate,
iv. 225, 227, 234
Philipps moves King's Bench to produce,
iv. 249
sentences resumed against, by House of
Commons, iv. 286
Westminster high bailiff names, iv. 224
Westminster petition instigated by, iv. 223
Murray, Alexander, army officer:
Allen's death blamed upon, vii. 20
Murray, Lady Anne. See Mackenzie, Lady
Anne
Murray, Cordelia (b. 1781) m. (1803) Rev.
Henry Hodges:
escapes from Minorca to Leghorn, ix. 179,
180
father recommends, to Mann, ix. 349
father seeks pension for the sake of, ix.
364
Murray, David (ca 1689–1748), 6th Vct
Stormont:
brother of, i. 250n
Murray, David (1727–96), 7th Vct Stormont,
1748; 2d E. of Mansfield, 1793:
Boulogne visited by, on way to England,
viii. 365
character of, will be forgotten because he
is a Scot and Mansfield's nephew, viii. 526
Conway lives with, at Rome, iv. 296, 298
——'s friend, vii. 18, viii. 526
courier from, leaves Paris before horses
are stopped by Louis XV's death, viii. 1
dirge by, on P. of Wales's death, iv. 261
Florence left by, vii. 24
Francis I's decision about converted Protestant girls to be contested by, vi. 250
French embargo delays, viii. 365

Fullarton lately secretary to, at Paris, ix.
31
Gordon rioters assault, ix. 53
HW's danger alarms, vii. 15
HW thanks, for messages, vii. 22
HW to receive compliments of, vii. 15
HW wants Mann to describe, iv. 291
Holland may have to be route of, home to
England, viii. 366
Huntingdon's friend, iv. 457, vi. 113
itinerary of, from Florence to Vienna, vii.
18, 24–5
Langlois secretary to, ix. 246
Louis XV's illness said to have caused a
request to, to fetch Sutton, viii. 2
Mann and Lorenzi entertained by, iv. 285
Mann notified by, of order to quit Paris,
viii. 373
—— praises, iv. 285, 291, 297, 457, vi. 113
—— recommends, to Albani, iv. 298
——'s MS account of Tuscany praised by,
vii. 27–8
—— suspects, to be author of letters on
Poland, vii. 502–3
—— talks with, about HW and Conway,
vii. 18
—— told by: about Ferdinand of Naples,
vii. 17; that Americans are much reduced,
viii. 306
—— visited by, vii. 2, 11, 15, 18, 22, 24
melancholy of, impairs his health, vii. 18
Orléans, Duc d', said to have quarrelled
with, viii. 50
President of the Council, ix. 391
recalled, from Paris embassy, viii. 364, 373
Rome visited by, iv. 298, vii. 2
Russian war plans revealed by, vii. 438–9
Scottish post for, viii. 179
Suffolk, E. of, succeeded by, as secretary of
state, viii. 525–6
valet-de-chambre of, reports that Frederick
II approaches Dresden, v. 2
Viennese post to go to, vi. 130
virtu absorbs, iv. 298
Yorke may replace, at Paris, viii. 179
Murray, Elizabeth Mary (1783–5):
birth of, expected, ix. 364
Murray, Fanny (ca 1729–78), m. (1757) David
Ross; courtesan:
Wilkes's Essay on Woman dedicated to, vi.
184
Murray, Frances Cairnes (ca 1734–1820), m.
(1752) William Henry Fortescue, cr. (1770)
Bn and (1776) Vct Clermont, and (1777)
E. of Clermont:
Marie-Antoinette notices, at Paris, ix. 357n
Murray, Lord George (1694–1760):
Old Pretender visited by, iii. 379
Venice visited by, iii. 379
Young Pretender joined by, iii. 104
Murray, George (1741–97), naval officer;
M.P.:
Mann presents, at Court, vi. 350

Murray, James (1690–1764), 2d D. of Atholl, 1724:
brother of, iii. 104, 106n, 254n
London visited by, iii. **102**
troops cannot be raised by, iii. 102
wife separated from, iii. 106
Young Pretender at house of, iii. 106
Murray, Hon. James (ca 1690–1770), cr. (1721) titular E. of Dunbar:
about to leave Rome for Avignon, iii. 378
Acquaviva will not give passports to English without recommendation from, iii. 15
Avignon may be visited by, iii. 376, 378
brother of, i. 250n, iii. 283
Chute and Whithed maligned by, iii. 136
Del Monti's account of Young Pretender's departure distributed by, at Rome, ii. 418
English Jacobite visitors to Rome court, iii. 136
HW asks about rôle of, in Old Pretender's quarrel with sons, iv. 345
Johnson, Murray, and Stone accused of toasting, iv. 361
lies told by, about Young Pretender's prospects, iii. 311
Old Pretender said by, to be offended at Chute and Whithed, iii. 136
——'s intrigues with, i. **18**
——'s prime minister, i. 250n
Petroni assembly harangued by, iii. 218
probably no longer a Jacobite, vii. 328
Rivera persuaded by, that Charles Emmanuel III should support Young Pretender, iii. 142
Rome probably left by, iii. 143
Spanish naval operations reported by, to HW, i. 20
Young Pretender's absence from Scotland admitted by, iii. 145
—— said to have left Rome with, i. 113
——'s escape from Rome facilitated by, ii. 377
——'s invasion asserted by, iii. 93–4
Murray, Hon. James (ca 1719–94), army officer; governor of Canada and of Minorca:
arrested, ix. 361
capitulation of, criticized by military people, ix. 269
cheerfulness of, based on vain hope of reinforcement, ix. 233
Collet informs, of enemy's approach, ix. 349
conduct at Minorca given favourable construction by, at home, ix. 200
Conway procures mitigation of apology by, to Draper, ix. 364
Corsicans at Leghorn cannot aid, ix. 196
court martial of: details of, to be carried to Mann by Horace Mann II, ix. 373; Draper demands, ix. 308–9, 327, 342; finished but not announced, ix. 355, 358;

interrupted by Draper's illness, ix. 342; Mann awaits news of, ix. 360; Mann receives accounts of first three sittings of, ix. 348; Mann regrets being quoted to support the charge, ix. 348; order of, to apologize to Draper, refused, ix. 361; sentence of, published in newspapers though affair is not concluded, ix. 361
Crillon attempts to bribe, unsuccessfully, ix. 207–8, 213, 229, 263n
—— lends apartment to, ix. 269
—— praises, ix. 189, 263–4
——'s attack surprises, ix. 198
——'s relations with, ix. 229, 263–4, 269
Draper accuses, of losing Minorca, vi. 383n
—— has more partisans than, among officers, ix. 269
—— provoked by bad treatment by, ix. 360
——'s complaint against, rejected by Judge Advocate, ix. 308–9
——'s harsh expressions to, during Minorcan siege, ix. 361
——'s quarrel with, ix. 269, 271, 327, 342
enemy preparations to attack St Philip's described by, ix. 233–4
England the destination of, ix. 269
Florentine communication with, cut off, ix. 59
French defeat, in Canada, v. 416, 421, 422
French feared by, to cut Minorca-Leghorn communications, viii. 443
French strongly resisted by, ix. 207
George III excuses, from reprimand, ix. 364
Greeks (independent) do not aid, ix. 196–7
grieved by reports in gazettes, ix. 269
HW never saw, iv. 354
health of, much indisposed, ix. 269
Hillsborough's dispatches from, ix. 136, 207, 233
Leghorn visited by, ix. 269
letters reach Florence from, ix. 196
Mann can send communications of, by cipher, viii. 469, ix. 42
—— does not wish to accuse, of neglect, ix. 200
—— has no news from, ix. 192, 196
—— ordered to supply Udny with everything required by, ix. 429
——'s apology to, to be conveyed by Horace Mann II, ix. 358, 370–1
——'s correspondence with, viii. **380**, ix. 348–9
—— sends communications of, to England, viii. 380, 437, 443, 457
——'s letter criticizing, produced by Draper, ix. 354n
—— unsure of guilt of, ix. 360
—— visited by, ix. 268–9
—— wishes, could be informed of his sympathy, ix. 349

[Murray, Hon. James, *continued*]

Mann, Horace II, could inform, of Mann's sympathy, ix. 349

Minorcan castle's siege expected by, to last long, ix. 229

Minorcan castle to be defended by, to last extremity, ix. 174, 179, 190

Minorcan attempt by French feared by, viii. 380, 437, 468, ix. 59

more men needed by, to defend Minorca, ix. 174

no assistance can be obtained for, except from England, ix. 197

pension asked by, for children's sake, ix. 364

privateers of, successful, viii. 437

sails with family from Leghorn to Antibes, ix. 271

Sturt dispatched by, as courier, ix. 42

Sutherland's rift with, ix. 81

Udny forwards dispatches of, ix. 233

—— unable to aid, ix. 197

Weymouth tells, to send his secrets to Mann to be ciphered and sent by post, ix. 42

wife and children of: escape from Minorca to Leghorn, ix. 179, 180; pension for, ix. 364; recommended to Mann, ix. 349

Murray, James (1734–94), army officer; M.P.:

Gordon, Lord George, denounced by, ix. 55

Murray, Mrs James. *See* Whitham, Anne

Murray, James Patrick (1782–1834), army officer:

father seeks pension for the sake of, ix. 364

Murray, John (1685–1752), 2d E. of Dunmore, 1710; army officer:

brother of, iii. 104

Cumberland, D. of, served by, iii. **20**

Plymouth position granted to, iii. 62

Murray, John, Lt-Col.:

(?) Guise advised by, to retire, i. 485

Murray, John (ca 1714–75), English resident at Venice; ambassador to Turkey:

coronation probably not to be celebrated by, v. 542

courier from India sent on by, to England, v. 523

Grenville may be succeeded by, at Constantinople, vi. 356

HW knew, in England, v. 562

HW might be helped by, to get Zanetti's tiger gem, v. 562, vi. 14, 116

Lind chaplain to, at Constantinople, vii. 565

——'s quarrel with, vii. 565

Mann corresponds with, vi. 14, 116

of Isle of Man, v. 562n

Paduan opera attended by company of English in uniform from Venice, led by, v. 512–13

Sultan might lock up, vii. 479

Murray, Sir John (1718–77), of Broughton; titular 7th Bt, 1770; secretary to Young Pretender 1745–6:

capture of, iii. **274**

confessions by, iii. 288

Mann anxious to hear disclosures of, iii. 303

—— astonished by silencing of, iii. 391

testimony of, at Lovat's trial, iii. 381

Murray, John (1729–74), 3d D. of Atholl, 1764; M.P.:

brother of, vi. 350

drowned, vii. 56

Murray, John (1730–1809), styled Vct Fincastle 1752–6; 4th E. of Dunmore, 1756; colonial gov.:

Congressman and old cannon captured by, in fight with Americans, viii. 157

protest by, vi. 7

troops of, desert, viii. 88

Murray, Maria, m. Thomas Pitt sr:

jointure of, v. 517

Murray, Hon. Marjory (d. before 1770), m. (1715) Hon. John Hay, cr. (1718) titular E. and (1727) titular D. of Inverness; old Pretender's mistress:

Albano visited by, i. 28

Murray, Patrick (1703–78), 5th Bn Elibank, 1736:

brother of, iv. 223

brother repulses effort of, to put him in custody of Serjeant-at-Arms, iv. 249

Cromarty's financial relations with, iii. **284**

Cumberland to sue, iii. 284

Jacobite, iii. 284

Westminster petition instigated by, iv. 223

Murray, William (1689–1746), styled M. of Tullibardine 1709–46; cr. (1717) Jacobite D. of Rannoch:

brother receives word from, iii. **106**

brother's house prepared by, for Young Pretender, iii. 106

brought to London, iii. 272

capture of, iii. 254

dies in Tower, after being captured after Culloden battle, iii. 106n

foreign reinforcements necessary to success of, iii. 131

outlawed, iii. 106n

Murray, Hon. William (1696–1756), 3d E. of Dunmore, 1752:

Young Pretender joined by, iii. 104

Murray, Hon. William (1705–93), cr. (1756) Bn Mansfield, (1776) E. of Mansfield; lord chief justice; M.P.:

attorney-general, i. 344n, iv. 453

attorney-general rebuked by, for not taking out *capias utlegatum* for Wilkes, vii. 12

Balmerinoch's conversation with, iii. 283, 303

brother of, i. **250n**, iii. 283, vii. 328n

Byng reinvestigation opposed by, in House of Lords, v. 64–5

chief justice, iv. 557, v. 64, 99, viii. 134

cowed, iv. 453

Dividend Bill discussed by, vi. 534

Duke of Newcastle's Letter . . . to Monsieur Michell, v. 281, 286

elections held invalid by, if soldiers called in, i. 252

Exchequer seal to be carried by, v. 99

Frederick, P. of Wales, thinks, is a Jacobite, iv. 364

—— trusts, iv. 364

frightened out of speaker's chair, vii. 247

Gordon rioters burn house of, ix. 57

HW asks Mann for Roman gossip about, iv. 360

Harcourt's appointment regarded by, as a cipher, iv. 345

Hayter urged by, to promote Stone, iv. 345

innocence asserted by, in fine speech, iv. 361

Johnson and Stone contemporary with, iv. 345

Junius paper will discourage, vii. 247

Kingston, Ds of, wished by, to have private hearing in chamber of Parliament, viii. 150

Lloyd debates with, on Westminster election, i. 250

lord chancellor's post declined by, vii. 174

Lovat's trial conducted by, as solicitor-general, iii. 379–80

Massachusetts Bay assembly's act rejected by, vi. 520

Maupeou's counterpart, is now chief justice, viii. 134

may be lord chief justice, iv. 557

nephew of, iv. 261, 411n, viii. 526

Newcastle, D. of, cannot spare, from House of Commons, iv. 557

——'s scheme considered hopeless by, v. 99

North Briton threatens, for persecuting Wilkes, vii. 28

Parliamentary brilliance of, at expense of law practice, ii. 383–4

Parliament avoided by, to keep from discussing Ps of Wales as possible regent, vi. 297

Parliament may prosecute, vii. 256, 268, 282

Pelham may be succeeded by, as prime minister, iv. 411–12, 419

——'s protégé, ii. 384

Pitt answers, ii. 123

——'s speech answered by, vii. 167

Pope's friend, i. 250n, 344n

Pratt and Henley handle, roughly, vi. 520

Pratt's rift with, over *habeas corpus*, v. 205

proclamation drawn up by, about seizure of prize ships, v. 281

Prussian memorial answered by, iv. 362, 365

Ravensworth accuses, of toasting Old Pretender and Dunbar, iv. 360, 364, 367

rebel lords tried by, iii. 283

Royal Marriage Bill written by, vii. 390

Ryder succeeded by, as attorney-general, iv. 453n

Scottish origins of, a disadvantage, iv. 412

Sewell, Master of the Rolls, mistaken for, vi. 464

Shippen enraged by apostasy of, ii. 123

solicitor-general, i. 250n, 344n, 494, ii. 118, iii. 283, 379, iv. 345, 411n

speaks for first time, in House of Commons, ii. 123

speech by: against prerogative, cowed by Pratt and Pitt, vi. 464; at Wilkes's trial, vii. 29; in House of Lords on Massachusetts Bay act, vi. 520; in Parliament on Denbighshire election, i. 344; in Parliament on Westminster election, i. 250

Stone and Scott countenanced by, in dispute over George III's tutorship, iv. 323

Strange succeeded by, as solicitor-general, i. 494, ii. 118

Townshend's treachery betrayed by, vi. 552

unpopularity of, vii. 256

Whigs disown, iv. 345

Wilkes abuses, in speech, viii. 13

Wilkes's hearing adjourned by, vii. 19

'Muscovita,' opera singer:

Clive, Mrs, mimics, i. 435

Middlesex's mistress, i. 191n

opera directors retain, to please Middlesex, i. 358

salary of, i. 191

Muscovy. *See* Russia

Museum Florentinum:

Antinori, Buondelmonte, and Pini concerned in, ii. 390–1

Buondelmonte gives, to Kaunitz, i. 49

directors of, send commission through HW to English bookseller, ii. 390

Dodsley answers publishers of, ii. 417

HW receives, ii. 560

price of, ii. 330

Walpole, Sir Robert, to receive three last volumes of, ii. 329–30

Museum Mazzuchelianum. See under Gaetani, Pier Antonio; Mazzuchelli, Conte Giovanni Maria

Musgrave, George (?1740–1824), M. P.:

(?) Chute asks HW to recommend, to Mann, vii. 375

(?) Florence to be visited by, vii. 375

(?) Graves to accompany, vii. 375

(?) HW knows, slightly, vii. 375

Mushrooms:

Kensington Palace floor produces crop of, iv. 88

Music:

at Ranelagh: ends at 10 P.M., viii. 310;
not heard by late arrivals, viii. 310, ix.
317

at Villa Patrizzi, i. 25

bad, in new opera at Florence, i. 79

band of: Kingston, Ds of, said to take,
with her, viii. 556, 564, 567; Mann to have
been serenaded by, i. 104

Bayreuth, Margravine of, composes, iv. 478

Bingham, Hon. Lavinia and Hon. Margaret,
study, viii. 462

books on, wanted by HW for Hawkins and
sought by Mann, v. 466–7, 477, 482, 491,
492

church, used by opera performers for dance
music, iii. 369

English dislike, in opera, i. 190

expense of, for *Don Pilogio*, ii. 41

festival of, at Worcester, iv. 338

Gluck to play, on drinking-glasses, iii. 234

Grafton, Ds of, studies, vi. 29

HW has little knowledge of, vi. 42

HW wants Mann to get, for Elizabeth
Rich, i. 166, 301–2

Hamilton, Lady, proficient in, x. 46

Hawkins writes history of, v. 466–7

hazard and racing eclipse, vii. 570–1

Mann discusses, with Margravine of Bayreuth, iv. 478

—— has, performed in his garden, i. 112,
483, ii. 1, iii. 277

—— orders, from HW, for Mme Branchi,
on Ds of Grafton's account, vi. 35–6, 42,
50, 73

—— to procure, from England, for Accademia, ii. 13, 91

—— to send: to D. of York, vi. 390; to
HW, i. 240, 263, ii. 13

Martini's book on, v. 492, 495–6

'mi' no longer a note in, vi. 334

Norfolk heiress tries to display talents for,
ii. 316–17

Pandolfini promoter of, ii. 150

Pomfret, Cts of, makes ridiculous pose
when hearing, iv. 584

Richecourt has concert of, after dinner, iv.
478

rustic, at Ranelagh jubilee-masquerade, iv.
47

St-Germain's talent for, x. 20

Walpole, Sir Edward, makes witticism
about modern miracles in, ix. 577

water: concert of, at D. of Richmond's
fireworks, iv. 56; gondola for, at Ranelagh,
iv. 47

See also Airs; Andante; Ballad; Barcaroles;
Cantata; Catch; Cembali; Concert; Con-
certo; Contralto; Drums; Farces; Fiddler;
Flute; Guitars, Harpsichord; Hautboy;
Horns; Horns, French; Jigs; Kettle-drums;
'Long Live George the King'; *Miserere;* 'Old
Sir Simon the King'; Opera; Opera singer;

Oratorio; Orchestra; Organ; Overture; Pipe;
Pipera; Serenade; Singer; Singing; Sonata;
Tabor; Trumpets; Tympani; Violins; *see
also under names of composers*

Musical clock. *See* Clock

Musica vaga ed artificiosa. See under Micheli,
Romano

Musicians:

at Florence, mostly illiterate, v. 482

Lucca may import, from Genoa, vi. 222

Walpole, Sir Robert, despises, i. 487

Musin Pushkin, Alexei Semenovich (1732–
1817), Russian ambassador to England
1766–73:

Chesterfield compliments Catherine II
through, vii. 376

Cony consults, about sale of Houghton
pictures, x. 55

Muskerry, Vcts. *See* Burgh, Lady Margaret de
(d. 1698)

Musket; muskets:

ammunition for, i. 66

Birmingham hopes to make, for American
war, viii. 77

Francis III orders, i. 324

soldier must shoulder, when presenting
message, iii. 439

Young Pretender tries to take, to Scotland,
iii. 87

Musket balls:

lead coffins melted for, iv. 428

Musquito. *See* Mosquito

Mustafa III (1717–73), Sultan of Turkey
1757–73:

acquisition or loss of acres by, inconsequential, vii. 420

campaign must be attempted by, vii. 310–
11

France arms, against Catherine II, vii. 338

HW prefers, to Catherine II, vii. 195

ignorant of weak army, and rejects peace
offers, vii. 173

might lock up Murray, vii. 479

Polish Catholics invited by, to turn Mohammedan, vii. 81

Russians will probably give a good account of, vii. 81

undisturbed by impending Russian invasion,
vii. 205

wants peace, vii. 470

Mustard pot:

served as *hors d'œuvres*, iii. 357

Muti, Palazzo. *See* Santi Apostoli, Palazzo

Mutineers:

saying by, in Tacitus, iv. 125

Mutiny:

of French troops, v. 336

of Scottish regiment, ix. 362

Mutiny Bill. *See under* Parliament: acts of

Mutton:

Clement XIII might allow, in Lent, if
fish is scarce, vi. 101

Muy, Comte de. *See* Félix, Louis-Nicolas-Victor de (1711–75)

Muzell, Heinrich Wilhelm (1723–82), called Baron Stosch, 1757:
Bath visited by, v. 461
Berlin's capture would have distressed, v. 446
burgundy sent by, to Mann, v. 424, 427, 491
cameos sent by, to France, v. 201, 434
England probably to be left by, because of expense, v. 503
England to be visited by, to sell collection, v. 380, 427
English address of, unknown to Mann, v. 415
English to be learned by, at Yorkshire clergyman's, v. 427
Florence reached by, v. 557
France too poor to buy collection of, v. 434
Frederick II gives annuity to, ix. 651
Frederick Augustus of Poland might buy collection of, v. 434
Gordon, D. of, not to have, as travelling companion, v. 503, 512
Guise to entertain, at dinner, v. 429
HW calls, 'Stoschino,' v. 384
HW comes to London to see, v. 426–7, 433
HW dines with, at SH, v. 427, 433
HW has not yet heard of, v. 418, 420, 473
HW may buy medals from, v. 186, 192, 201–2, 215, 384
HW may get, to identify Castiglione painting, v. 522
HW pays, for Mann's burgundy, v. 427, 491
HW promises to receive, well, v. 384
HW's correspondence with, v. 440, 461, 527
HW's letters to Mann taken by, back to England, v. 413, 427, x. 36
HW to receive respects of, v. 557
health of: fever, v. 433; ill, v. 459
Italy to be visited by, v. 527
Knyphausen says, is expected in London, v. 474
letter to, about Zorndorf battle, v. 241
London to be visited by, v. 461
Mann encloses letter for, v. 415, 424, 454, 473, 477, 509, 522
—— praises, v. 380
—— promised by, a copy of *Œuvres du philosophe de Sans-Souci*, v. 413
——'s correspondence with, v. 424, 433, 464, 503, 512, 522, 527
—— will advise, to distribute catalogues of uncle's collection, v. 151
map collection of: Benedict XIV may buy, v. 186–7, 192, 434; Ferdinand VI and José Manoel might buy, v. 434; Frederick II gives annuity to buy, ix. 651
military career of, v. 149, 380, 434

Montagu, Lady Mary Wortley, scolds HW through, v. 458
Northumberland, D. of, might have, as son's travelling companion, v. 512, 514
Paris visited by, v. 424
sails for Spain, v. 527
Salisbury visited by, v. 433, 440, 459
Sardinian court might buy collection of, v. 434
uncle adopts, as his heir, v. **149**, 151, 380
uncle recalls, from army, v. 149, 434
uncle's collection may be sold by, in England, v. 380, 427
uncle's collection of intaglios to be sold by, intact, v. 186
uncle's collection unlikely to be sold by, in England, v. 512
uncle's obscene prints and drawings may be sold by, to Frederick II, v. 202
Wanstead to be visited by, v. 427
wants position as travelling companion, v. 434, 440, 503, 512

Myddelton, John (1685–1747), M.P.:
high sheriff related to, i. 344

Myddelton, William (d. ?1745):
related to M.P., i. 344
sentenced to Newgate, i. 344

'Myra, old':
HW refers to Pitt as, v. 168

Mysterious Mother, by HW:
Beauclerk, Lady Diana, illustrates, viii. 524
HW blushes at Mann's praises of, viii. 524
HW never published, nor contemplated a stage performance, viii. 524
HW sends, to Mann, viii. 481, 494
Hamilton has copy of, viii. 470
Mann knows Italian incident similar to plot of, viii. 517
—— praises, viii. 517
—— wants, viii. 470
Mann, Horace II, reads, on journey, viii. 517
—— to bring, to Mann, viii. 470, 481
subject of, disgusting, viii. 481

Mystery:
Methodists', iv. 271
unskilfulness the source of, in art, v. 561
'wisdom of blockheads,' v. 466

Mytilene:
Turkish ships near, vii. 235

Nabob; nabobs:
attacked, in Parliament, vii. 483
Bombay governor seeks to install, at Poona, viii. 509
England dethrones, in India, vii. 240
English: boroughs contested by, v. 484; cannot plunder India's climate, vii. 305; do not profess religion as an excuse for plundering, ix. 400; England filled with, vii. 499; Fox's reform schemes opposed by, ix. 484; France dreads, vii. 476; House of

[Nabob; nabobs, *continued*]
Commons to investigate riches of, ix. 277;
Mackheath the begetter of, vii. 524; ought
to be imprisoned like French swindlers, ix.
604; will not be able to oppress newly-
discovered stars, ix. 614
Francis I schemes to dethrone, vi. 547
Lyttelton at disadvantage because he is
not, vii. 511
Rumbold may have to disgorge million
acquired as, ix. 274, 277
St James's St thronged with, v. 518
Nabob of Bengal. *See* Mir Jafar (1691–1765);
Najam-du-Dowla (ca 1747–66)
Nádasdy, Franz Leopold (1708–83), Graf; Gen.
Major, 1741; Gen. of cavalry, 1754:
Hungarians to be commanded by, v. 176
Spaniards pursued by, iii. 244
Nadasti. *See* Nádasdy
Nâdir-Chah, Thamasp Kouli-Khan Vély-Nea-
men (1688–1747), Persian emperor:
HW compares Clive with, viii. 60
HW's letter under name of, ii. 167–8, 188
(?) HW's term for Rumbold, ix. 545
merchant's wife might claim to be married
to, vii. 550
Mill compared with, iv. **102**
Nag. *See* Horse
Nail; nails:
price of, rises, v. 536
San Donato's, cures hydrophobia, iv. 509
sold for coronation constructions, v. 536
Nain jaune, Le. See under Le Jumel de
Barneville, Marie-Catherine, Baronne d'Aul-
noy
Nairne ('Nairn'), William Murray (ca 1757–
1830), Lord Nairne (restored, 1824):
Scotchman, ix. 536
Stuart, Charlotte, has, as equerry, ix. 536
Najam-ud-Dowlah (ca 1747–66), Nabob (Na-
wab) of Bengal:
Clive makes, nabob of Bengal, vi. 416
Namur:
French threaten to explode mines under
forts of, iii. 482
Ostend more important than, iii. 69
Namur, ship:
captain of, ii. 415
'Nana':
Chute's name for Lady Caroline Peter-
sham, iv. 140
Nancy ('Nanci'):
Churchill's letter from, vi. 324
Churchills to settle at, vi. 244
Craon, Princesse de, returns to, vi. 536
HW will visit, if Princesse de Craon be-
comes queen, iv. 132
Pitt, Anne, to visit, for health, viii. 131
Stanislas I gives apartment at, to Princesse
de Craon, iv. 116
Nantes:
Jacobite refugees land at, iii. 270

Napier, Bns. *See* Clavering, Maria Margaret
(ca 1756–1821)
Napier, Hon. George (1751–1804), army offi-
cer:
marriage of, v. 530n
Napier, Lady Sarah. *See* Lennox, Lady Sarah
(1745–1826)
Napkin; napkins:
Coventry uses, to wipe off wife's rouge, iv.
338
Fermor lacks, iii. 148
George II has, prepared for Flemish trip,
ii. 69
hot, HW tells Mann to dry his feet with,
after using bootikins, viii. 494
Napkin-cap:
Kilmarnock wears, at execution, iii. 300
Naples, Abp of. *See* Sersali
Naples, K. of. *See* Charles III (1716–88);
Ferdinand (1751–1825)
Naples, Q. of. *See* Maria Amalia (1724–60);
Maria Carolina (1752–1814)
Naples:
Acquaviva refuses to shut off Roman communications with, ii. 270
agent from, at Florence, *see* Vernaccini,
Francesco
ambassadors from and to, *see under* Ambassador
antiquities restored at, v. 344
army of: assembled in Garigliano and Pescara, iii. 345; at Aquila, ii. 325; at Rome,
ii. 532; called 'Ligur-Napolispani,' iii. 82;
called 'Napolispani,' i. 427; England demands withdrawal of, from Lombardy, ii.
16; French crossing of the Var would encourage, iii. 378; Garfagnano may be invaded by, iii. 65; Genoa may be approached by, iii. 378; Lobkowitz may be
pursued by, ii. 508; Lombardy may be invaded by, iii. 237, 364, 367, 378, 402; may
invade Papal states, ii. 295–6, 443–4,
364; Modena threatened by, iii. 65; near
Presidii, ii. 546; near Rome, ii. 546;
Orbetello the theatre of, iii. 378; Parma
may be the objective of, iii. 65; 'patrimoine
de St-Pierre' reached by, ii. 546; Pescara
the theatre of, iii. 345; reach Porta del
Popolo at Rome, iii. 144; reduced, i. 464;
Rochester to blockade, ii. 453; Romagna
to be vacated by, ii. 43; Ronciglione the
theatre of, ii. 527; San Germano the station
of, iii. 378; Spaniards separated from, ii.
66; to advance if Don Philip succeeds, ii.
312; Tuscany may be invaded by, ii. 295–6,
iii. 364; Tuscany traversed by, to join
Gages, iii. 65; Val Montone the station of,
ii. 447; Velletri fortified by, ii. 454
Austrian possessions would be endangered
if English fleet attacked, ii. 390
Austrians complain that the English prevented their conquest of, iii. 423
Austrians threaten, ii. 271, 336, 405, 419–

20, 434–5, 437, 443–4, 451, 454, 473–6, 502, 508, iii. 41, 298, 306, 323–4, 423

Austrian threat to, displeases Charles Emmanuel III, ii. 444

authorities of, demand secret conference with Charles, v. 330

barks from, captured by English, iii. 56

Benedict XIV may be intimidated by troops of, iii. 144

Benevento to be seized by, vii. 24

Boufflers tells the Genoese to expect help from, iii. 406

Braitwitz accompanied to, by Marchesa Vitelli, iv. 399

bread shortage at, vi. 223

Byng's conversation with Bucareli reported to, iv. 566

Caffarelli-Egizziello feud does not disturb festivities at, iii. 452

cantata to be given by, iii. 437–8, 452

cardinals of, see under Cardinal

Castro and Ronciglione to be seized by, vii. 36

Castropignano leads Neapolitan troops back to, ii. 3, 7, 16

Catalogue of French Books, A, satirizes neutrality of, ii. 52

cavalry of, iii. 297

Changuion to be chargé d'affaires at, vi. 112

Charles III assembles troops on borders of, to enforce neutrality, v. 271

—— behaved better at, than in Spain, v. 560

—— does not trust inhabitants of, ii. 446

—— hates England ever since he was at, vii. 349–50

—— less likely to be bullied than when at, vi. 70

—— liked Sir James Gray when at, v. 556, 560n

—— must want English approval of his disposal of, v. 347

—— notifies, of his intentions about his sons, v. 270, 322–3, 324–6, 335

—— not to leave, iii. 15

—— to return to, ii. 519

—— unlikely to let France and Vienna seize, v. 280

—— will not relinquish, to brother, v. 264, 270

—— withdraws troops from confines of, v. 275

Charles, P., may get, as reward, ii. 336

Charles Emmanuel III blames Maria Theresa for wanting to capture, ii. 461

—— hoped by, to be bribed by Spain, i. 145, 291

—— to share invasion of, ii. 3

Chute to buy Pergolesi's Olimpiade at, iii. 149

climate of, no longer considered good for consumptives, iv. 536

Coke, Lady Mary, may have trouble at, vii. 547

consuls of, impertinent, iii. 90

convoys of, in Papal ports, should be burned, ii. 453

Conway may visit, iv. 293, 296, 304

corn shortage in, vi. 229

Corsican relations with, ii. 156

couriers from and to, see under Courier

Court of: alarmed, i. 501, ii. 3, 13; Albertini tells, of Gray's impending transfer, v. 159; assures Sir James Gray of Spain's sincerity, v. 551, 555; at Caserta, iv. 429; congratulates Sir James Gray on supposed appointment, v. 174; differs from court of Rome over cardinals' costume, vii. 18; disavows Orsini's homage to Young Pretender, vi. 399; English leave Florence to see, vii. 18; gives Hamilton a copy of letter to Orsini, vi. 399; induced by Frescobaldi to banish Marchesa Vitelli, iv. 399; Masaniello's ghost may alarm, i. 501; may flee from plague to Aquila, ii. 302; may flee to Rome, ii. 3, 13; Maynard, Vcts, distributes James's powders at, viii. 451; supplies amusements, viii. 280–1; to make plans according to Spanish campaign in Savoy, ii. 302; would reject Sir James Gray if it knew his low birth, iv. 415–16

Del Monte said to have fled to, iv. 437

drought at, viii. 479

earthquake damage in, less than was represented, ix. 391

earthquake victims to be relieved by ships from, ix. 375

embarkations from, iii. 55

England said to want attack upon, ii. 364

England's commercial treaty with, iv. 458

English dames at, astonish HW, v. 554

English envoy to, see under Envoy

English fleet should attack, i. 291, 306, 311

English fleet should not attack, ii. 390

English fleet unable to interrupt Genoese commerce with, iii. 207

English fleet under Martin threatens, ii. 15, 26, 32, 39, 42–3, 47

English fleet was destined for, vi. 95

English merchants at, fear retaliation, ii. 28

English negotiations with, may be upset by Minorca's capture, iv. 576

English squadron before, would encourage inhabitants to revolt, ii. 460

English squadron diverted from, to protect Tuscany, ii. 37–8

English to crowd to, for Maria Carolina's reception, vii. 2

English to leave, for Florence, after festivals, vii. 3

English visitors disappointed by lack of shows at, for carnival, vi. 491–2

English visitors seek passports for, iii. 15

envoys from and to, see under Envoy

[Naples, *continued*]

famine in, vi. 206, 216, 223, 229

Ferdinand of Naples and Maria Carolina to sail to, from Leghorn, ix. 594, 600

fishermen of, to be lured to Leghorn, iv. 217

footmen from, i. 421, vi. 32

Francis I may get, instead of Tuscany, ii. 331, 336

—— may invade, ii. 3

French-American treaty to be brought to, by extraordinary courier, viii. 369

Frenchmen at, will exclude Guasco, vi. 575

French send courier to, to announce Corsican successes, iii. 437

French-Spanish alliance deemed ill-judged by, v. 555

friar appeases mob at, viii. 541

Gages advised by, to await Spanish orders after Charles Albert's death, iii. 7–8, 10

—— may be reinforced by troops of, ii. 405

—— prevents Lobkowitz from inciting people of, ii. 471

——'s army covers, ii. 542

—— to be reinforced from, iii. 15

Gatti to reach, from Florence in less than 60 hours, viii. 330

Genoa not admitted by, as an ally, iii. 237

Genoese uprising encouraged by, iii. 364

German dukedom refused by gentleman of, unless his footman was also made a duke, vi. 32

Gray, Sir James, indispensable at, v. 166

—— to go to, iv. 409

HW admires opera plans for, iii. 442

HW discourages Mann from trying to go to, vi. 111

HW's health would not be suited by, vi. 116

HW to procure snuff-box at, for Mann, i. 26, 29

HW wishes to visit, to avoid heat, i. 22, 26

Hamilton, Lady, dies at, ix. 321, x. 46

Hamilton, Sir William, about to return to, vii. 431, viii. 321

—— brings alleged Correggio painting from, x. 46

—— in a hurry to reach, vi. 260

—— minister at, viii. 241n, ix. 459n, x. 46

——'s letter from, vi. 354

—— to succeed Sir James Gray at, vi. 243

Hamiltons leave, to visit England, vii. 339

Hamiltons to go to, vii. 448

Hervey, Bn, tries to quiet creditors at, ix. 652

honorary titles of, suggested for Mann, ii. 484

honours profusely distributed at, vi. 32

horse from: for Kaunitz, i. 49; for Mathews, ii. 453; for P. of Wales, ii. 200

inhabitants of, not really so eager to revolt, ii. 471, 474, 484

Inquisition's hold upon, to be broken by Maria Theresa, ii. 454

insurrection at, during eruption of Vesuvius, viii. 529

Italy will not be upset by succession of, v. 280

Jesuits' hoards may be seized by troops of, vii. 36

Jesuits may be banished from, vi. 565

Joseph II to visit, vi. 556

Leopold and Maria Louisa to escort Ferdinand and Maria Amalia of Parma to, for Carnival, ix. 2

Leopold II's possible loss of grand ducal title enrages, vi. 330

letters from: of Ferdinand's cruelty to Florentines, vii. 254; to army, captured with courier, ii. 85–6

Liechtenstein, P., to attack, iii. 323–4

Lobkowitz threatens, ii. 271, 405, 419–20, 434–5, 437, 443, 473–6, 512–13

Long to send ships to attack, ii. 470–6

Lunardi the secretary from, in London, ix. 528n, 543

Macdonald probably from, iii. 116

Malta to be starved by, iv. 405

Mann has received no account from, of Messina earthquake, ix. 374

—— hears from, of Mrs Garrick's accident, vi. 203

—— hopes that Francis I instead of P. Charles may take, ii. 336

—— might succeed Sir James Gray as minister to, v. 150, 556, vi. 107, 111, 114–15

—— receives sketch from, of Vesuvius eruption, viii. 514

—— rumoured to be taking message to, ii. 243

—— said by HW to be agent for conquest of, ii. 466

—— sent to, in ship, with coffin by his side, viii. 180

——'s presents to Stone from, ii. 115, 330, 445, 496

Mann, Galfridus, might go to, for health, iv. 526, 536

Mann, Horace II, could gallop to Florence from, in a few days, viii. 170

—— urges Mann to accompany him and Lady Lucy to, viii. 129, 131–2

Mann, James II, to visit, ix. 581

Mann, Lady Lucy, may be completely cured by winter at, viii. 136

Maria Amalia to return to, ii. 519

Maria Carolina's itinerary to, vii. 17–18, ix. 593–4, 600

—— to be accompanied to, by Leopold and Maria Louisa, vii. 2, 11, 17–18

Maria Josefa's entry into, planned, vi. 556

——'s luggage on way to, vi. 558

Maria Theresa covets, ii. 390

—— does not respect neutrality of, ii. 521

——'s edict to inhabitants of, ii. 454, 461

Martin may be summoned from, to protect Tuscany, ii. 27

——'s letter about his ultimatum to, iii. 42–3

Mass sent from, for Egizziello, i. 472

Mathews and Maria Theresa differ over war against, ii. 370

Mathews said to prefer prize-taking to capture of, ii. 452–3

Maynard said to have shot himself at, viii. 435

Maynard, Vcts, shunned at, by Cts of Berkeley and Cts of Orford, viii. 451

Medici, Ottaviano de', sends valet to, i. 238

messenger from: to Turin, iv. 576; travels slowly in chaise, iv. 581

ministers from and to, see under Minister

mole of, fortified, vi. 6

Montemar may retire to, ii. 2, 16

——'s army may be depleted by withdrawal of troops of, ii. 27

Montini's execution at, ii. 271

Morice to write from, to HW, ix. 435

Mountrath fails to get passports for, iii. 15

Mozzi expects Cts of Orford's effects from, ix. 160

—— receives Cts of Orford's papers from, ix. 162

Neapolitan troops recalled to, from Viterbo, iii. 237

neutrality of: Charles III proclaims, v. 271; Frederick II must be encouraged by, v. 271; HW enjoys Mann's accounts of, ii. 68; predicted by Sir James Gray, vi. 5, 12; Tanucci proclaims, vi. 5–6

Orbetello ruled by governor from, ii. 287

Orford, Cts of, has great effects at, ix. 113, 114

—— has town and country houses at, vii. 2

—— may be abandoned by Mozzi unless she leaves, vii. 559, viii. 305

—— may have bought estate at, viii. 187

—— relinquishes trip to, viii. 70, 83, ix. 107, 112

Otranto in kingdom of, vii. 107

Pallavicini formerly nuncio at, vii. 118

people of, demand secret conference with Charles III, v. 330

Philip, Don, may be promoted to, from Parma, v. 264, 330

—— may visit, i. 323, iii. 144

—— to be escorted by galleys of, i. 362

Philip Anton's sanity to be judged at, v. 322–5

Pironi said to have dispersed seditious papers at, ii. 253–4

Pitture antiche di Ercolano expected from, vi. 533

prince of, loves Bettina, i. 421

princess of, born, ii. 478

provisions hoarded in, against plague, ii. 288

public amusements at, bad, viii. 280

Putello loses voice at, iii. 355

religious credulity in, ii. 305, iv. 429

revolt might take place in, ii. 460

Rinuccini's uncle dies in, iv. 336

riots in, over food shortage, vi. 206

Russian fleet may be excluded from ports of, ix. 616n

Salas at, i. 215

San Severino's couriers from and to, v. 330, 453, 455, 477

serenade at, iii. 439

Sersale to go to, iv. 429

ships of, preyed on by English in Adriatic, iii. 231

ships sent from, with supplies to Genoa, iii. 236

Shuttleworth escapes to, iii. 77

Sicilian rebellion disturbs, viii. 39

Sicily isolated from, because of plague, ii. 252

snuff-boxes of, i. 26, 29, ii. 115, 330, 445, 496

soldiers and artillery at, i. 154

Spain exchanges couriers with, weekly, vi. 349

Spain not to sing Te Deums for victories in, ii. 486

Spain orders, despite Tanucci's hatred of Tuscany, to grant food to Tuscany, vi. 448

Spain sends troops to, iii. 367

Spain threatens nobles of, with confiscation of feudi if they celebrate Francis I's election, iii. 184

Spaniards may invade Lombardy from, iii. 367

Spaniards may not be received at, ii. 413

Spaniards may retire to, ii. 325, 397–8, 413

Spaniards to receive artillery from, by Adriatic, iii. 30

Spanish army may be cut off from, i. 500

Spanish expedition may join troops from, i. 198

Spanish fleet at, for Charles III's departure, v. 324, 333

Spanish troops from: reach Aquila, i. 265; to join those from Arezzo and Orbetello, i. 350

Spanish troops in, may embark, iii. 410

Spanish troops to go to, v. 335

Squillace unpopular at, v. 330

Stanley puts off visiting, vi. 326–7

Strange copies pictures at, vi. 108

—— looks in vain for art purchases at, vi. 115

Tanucci unpopular in, v. 330

[Naples, *continued*]
Thorold dies at, vi. 380
transports from, escape, iii. 82
troops said to advance from, towards Rome, i. 110
Tuscan regency gets memorial from, on allodials, ii. 177
Tuscany seeks loan from Jews at, vi. 448
Tuscany stops intercourse with, for fear of plague, ii. 270
Tylney defers visit to, viii. 145
——'s house in, viii. 280–1
——'s possessions at, to be sold for servants' benefit, ix. 534
—— to give public ball at, viii. 281
—— to visit, viii. 251
valuables of: at Palazzo Farnese, ii. 435; stored at Rome and Malta, ii. 501
Velletri gate faces, ii. 488
Vesuvius's eruption at, viii. 514, 541
viceroy for, ii. 420
Viennese Court wants to conquer, ii. 390
visitors to: Allens, iii. 477; Astrua, iii. 438; Babbi, iii. 438; Barrett-Lennards, iv. 92, 105; Beaufort, Ds of, vii. 449; Beauvau, i. 11, 16; Berkeley, Cts of, viii. 451; Bridgwater, Ds of, v. 550; Bulstrode, i. 11; Bute, vii. 91, 96; Caffarelli, iii. 438, 439; Carlisle, Cts of, vii. 449; Chartres, Duc de, ix. 417; Chartres, Duchesse de, viii. 222; Cholmondeley, ix. 324, 346; Chute, iii. 149, 171; Corsi, vi. 202; Cumberland, D. and Ds of, ix. 618, 628; Damer, Mrs, ix. 184, 645; Denis, iii. 439; Dicks, viii. 251; Doria, iii. 345; Duclos, vi. 531; Duncan, Sir William, viii. 41, 50; Egerton, Miss, v. 550; Egizziello, iii. 438; Eyles-Stiles, Mary, v. 550; Eyles-Stiles, Lady and Miss, v. 550; Ferrers, Cts, ix. 645; Firmian, v. 340; Floyd, viii. 508; Gatti, viii. 330; Gloucester, D. and Ds of, ix. 675; Gloucester, D. of, vii. 336, 342, 370, 374, 375, 377, 384, 405; Grafton, Ds of, v. 550; Hartington, i. 16; Hertford's valet-de-chambre, vii. 56; Hervey, Bn and Bns, ix. 651; Hervey, Mr and Mrs Frederick, vi. 398; Hillsborough, vi. 429; Hillsborough, Cts of, vi. 398; Hobart, iii. 408; Holland, vi. 503; Karl Wilhelm Ferdinand, vi. 458; Kingston, Ds of, viii. 220; Lyttelton, Sir Richard, v. 545; Macdonald, vi. 407; Mann, Horace II and Lady Lucy, viii. 115, 118, 129, 131–2, 136, 163, 166, 170, 181, 188, 225, 246; Maria Louisa, vii. 111; Maynard, vii. 435; Maynard, Vcts, viii. 451; Montagu, Lady Mary Wortley, i. 92; Morice, v. 389, ix. 51, 289, 432, 435; Mozzi, vii. 155; Northampton, Cts of, vi. 132, 142; Orford, Cts of, iv. 476, 499, 505, v. 550, vii. 2, 155, 464, 468, 472, 478, 486, 512, 525, 529, 531, 537, 559, viii. 9, 57, 82, 164, 220, 244, 251, 260, 304, 312, 317, 322, 451, 467, 479; Paul I, ix. 250; Pitt, Anne, viii. 344; Pitt, Mrs George, vii. 447; Pitt, Thomas, v. 545; Pitt, Thomas II, viii. 486; Rinuccini, iii. 8; Robinson, Mrs, v. 550; Roxburghe, v. 550; Rumbold family, ix. 651; Smyth, i. 16; Stanhope, Lady, v. 550; Stanhope, Sir William, v. 550, vi. 292, 418; Strange, vi. 108; Strathmore, v. 564; Stuart-Mackenzies, viii. 337; Tesi, iii. 438; (?) Vierpyl, iii. 100–1; Vorontsov, iii. 184; Whithed, iii. 171; Wilkes, vi. 281, 292, 305; Worsley, iii. 476–7
Viviani was mere chargé d'affaires from, vi. 349
water sold on streets of, during drought, viii. 479
Wortley Montagu may embark from, for Egypt, vi. 77
Wright hopes for post at, vi. 500
York, D. of, considers visiting, vi. 204, 224, 229
Napoli di Romania (Gulf of Argolis):
Russian fleet in gulf of, vii. 226
Turks attack Elphinston's squadron in harbour of, vii. 234
'Napolispani':
new word in Florence, for Spanish-Neapolitan troops, i. 427
Nappa, Niccola, Neapolitan courier:
news of Tylney's death taken by, to England by way of Florence, ix. 533
Nardi (singer):
Middlesex's mistress, iii. 293
Violette quarrels with, iii. 293
See also Narni
Nardini, Pietro (1722–93), Leghorn violinist:
Karl Wilhelm Ferdinand invites, to Germany, vi. 537
Narni, ——:
England visited by, iii. 455
Valenti dances with, in Florentine opera, iii. 455
see also Nardi
Naseby:
battle of, HW does not need to write about, vii. 224
Nassau, P. *See* Clavering-Cowper, George Nassau
Nassau, Jan Nicolas Floris (1709–82), Rijksgraaf van; Heer van Ouwerkerk:
Cowper not allowed by, to use Auverquerque title, viii. 370
Nassau, Hon. Richard Savage (1723–80), M.P.:
George III omits, from Bedchamber, v. 460
Nassau, ship:
African conquest by, v. 212
expected at Mahon, i. 285
Charles Emmanuel III to be aided by, iii. 313
Nassau d'Auverquerque, Henry (ca 1672–1754), cr. (1698) E. of Grantham:
Cowper sends for plate and jewels of, vii. 449
daughter of, viii. 360n, ix. 78n

Morice bought Grove of, at Chiswick, ix. 298n

Tyrawley comments on tiptoe walk of, ii. **104**

William III compels, to take name of Auverquerque instead of Nassau, viii. 360

—— does not allow, to use Nassau arms, viii. 370

Nassau de Zuylestein, William Henry (1717–81), 4th E. of Rochford, 1738:

Allen recommended by, as Mann's proxy, vii. 326–7, 362n, 379

ambassador at Turin, iv. 58

death of, ix. 191

Dick awaits word from, before accepting Order of St Anne, viii. 85

Florence to be visited by, iv. 376

former secretary of state and K.G., ix. 191n

French embassy hinted for, iv. 420, 426

gaiety of, iv. 76

HW might borrow suppressed satire on the Conclave from, viii. 65

HW's dealings with, about proxy for Mann's K.B. installation, vii. 341, 350, 362, 371, 408

HW's opinion of, iv. 58

hopes of, to get post nearer England, iv. 463

Irish pension awarded to, v. 460

Mann asks that proper answer be given to, vii. 358

—— encloses letter to, viii. 44

—— entertains, at Florence, iv. 378

—— not told by, how to treat D. of Gloucester, viii. 129

—— receives circular letter from, vii. 262, 478

——'s correspondence with, iv. 420, vi. 369, vii. 293, 326–7, 332

—— sends copy of papal bull to, vii. 507

—— sends suppressed satire on the Conclave to, viii. 65

——'s red ribbon may be sent through, vii. 14

——'s relations with, probably good, vii. 255

—— to entertain, in Florence, iv. 370

—— wants to notify, that Cowper's Florentine match is off, vii. 457

marriage of, i. **431**

Paris post expected by, iv. 467

Paris post to be accepted by, vi. 420

Sayre committed by, viii. 138n

secretary of state, vii. 62, viii. 138n

secretary of state for southern province, vii. 255

Spanish post desired by, v. 166

Strange should have told, of D. of Gloucester's health, viii. 136

to be Groom of the Stole, iv. 460, 469

to be prosecuted instead of Sayre, viii. 138–9

Turin the post of, iv. 58, 420, 426

Villettes to meet, at Paris, iv. 76

Weymouth succeeds, as secretary of state for southern province, viii. 142

wife no longer confines affections of, iv. 378

wife of, iv. 58n, v. 57n

Nassau family:

arms of, William III does not let Grantham and Rochford use, viii. 370

Grantham is of illegitimate branch of, ix. 78n

illegitimate branches of, viii. 360

princes of, object to Cowper's bearing their name or arms, viii. 370

Nassau-Siegen, Karl Heinrich Nicolaus Otto (1745–1808), P. of:

army of, should have been destroyed, viii. 487

HW calls, 'roi d'Yvetot,' viii. 472

HW hopes that attack on Ireland will be led by, viii. 480

Jersey attack led by, viii. 471

kingdom of Jersey promised to, viii. **471**

Nassau-Usingen, Friedrich August (1738–1816), P. of; D. of Nassau-Usingen, 1806:

(?) descended from royalty, vi. 291

(?) Mann attends, in Florence, vi. 291

Nassau van Zuylestein, William Henry van (1649–1708), cr. (1695) E. of Rochford:

William III compels, to call himself Zuylestein, not Nassau, viii. 360

—— does not allow, to use Nassau arms, viii. 370

Natalia, Russian frigate:

shipwrecked, ix. 2

National debt. *See under* Debt

Natolia. *See* Anatolia

Natter, Johann Lorenz (1705–63), German medallist and gem-engraver:

catalogue of Stosch's maps printed by, in Holland, v. 192

Stosch's correspondence with, iii. 243

Natural children:

HW's reflections on, viii. 159

Naturalization of the Jews. *See under* Jews

Naumachias:

HW does not object to royalty playing at, ix. 583

Navarre, Q. of. *See* Marguerite (1492–1549) of Valois

Navarro, Juan José (1687–1772), cr. (1744) Marqués de la Victoria; naval officer:

Mathews attacks, ii. 413

ship of, ii. 404

Navigation:

improved by Europe, ix. 141

Naviglio, the:

Lobkowitz stationed near, iii. 30

Navy, English:

Anson builds up, iv. 483

Dutch prizes taken by, repaid through wreck of Indiaman, ix. 134

French navy compared with, v. 101

[Navy, English, *continued*]
French surprised by strength and spirit of, iv. 483
half-pay captains of, seek pay increase, vii. 462
House of Commons should resist corruption in, x. 15
investigation into: occupies Parliament, iii. 12, 25, 32–4, 47; proposed in Parliament, ii. 399, 427
never so formidable, vii. 156
officer of, known by Charles Emmanuel III to be disloyal, iii. 147, 150
officers' conduct in, greatly criticized, v. 69
officers' court martial in, iii. 33
Pelham proposes reduction of, iv. 223
Pitt's demand for increase of, defeated by House of Commons, iii. 168–9
press warrants issued for, viii. 252
promotion system in, ii. 507, 509
strengthened, viii. 252–3
strength of, at Plymouth and Portsmouth, and Thames estuary, vii. 40
swinging is the exercise of, ii. 558
treasurer of: Bubb Dodington succeeds Grenville as, iv. 517; Bubb Dodington removed as, v. 18; Bubb Dodington resigns as, iv. 39, 54–5; Clutterbuck becomes, i. 391; Ellis is, ix. 241n; Grenville dismissed as, iv. 512, 517; Grenville succeeds Bubb Dodington as, v. 25; Hardwicke wants Anson to be, v. 93; Howe becomes, vi. 443; Howe will be disgusted at loss of post as, viii. 309; Legge is, iv. 39, 417n; Lyttelton covets, iv. 39; Onslow resigns as, i. 391; Rushout to be, ii. 350, 356; Townshend, Charles, becomes, ix. 392; Walpole, Sir Robert, becomes, vi. 26
Navy Bill. *See under* Parliament: acts of
Navy Board. *See* Admiralty
Nawab of Bengal. *See* Mir Jafar (1691–1765); Najam-ud-Dowla (ca 1747–66)
Nay, —— de, m. (?1731) François-Hyacinthe, Comte de la Tour en Voivre de Savonnières:
arrived from Lorraine, iv. **451**
father carries, to Grand Ducal palaces, iv. 451
(?) father has, in house, iv. 476
husband of, injured in coach accident, v. 442
(?) Mann entertains at dinner with Lady Orford, iv. 480
(?) Orford, Cts of, gives jewels to, iv. 499, 505, ix. 144
Nay, Charles de (d. 1789), called Comte de Richecourt:
Constantinople visited by, iv. 255
England visited by, iv. **90**
father talks with, of Cts of Orford's marriage, iv. 255
Orford, Cts of, brings up, 'by hand,' iv. 90

Nay, Emmanuel-François-Joseph-Ignace de (1694–1759), Comte de Richecourt; Marchese di Treschietto:
abbé-secretary of, *see* Niccoli
académie de belles lettres given by, in honour of Margravine of Bayreuth, iv. 476–8
Aigle, Comte d', pseudonym of, i. 195
Albani does not trust, iii. 2
—— sends compliments to, ii. 491
Alberti chosen by, for Tuscan Council, iv. 220
Algerine-Tuscan treaty negotiated by, iv. 472
allowance of, increased, iv. 392
ancestry of, ignoble, iv. 197, ix. 130
apartment of, in Palazzo Vecchio, i. 224, 283, iii. 97, 101, 385
appearance of, neither young nor handsome, ix. 130
Archinto entertained by, with story of Wachtendonck and Ps Triulzi, i. 489–90
—— often sees, at Florence and Leghorn, i. 490
assemblies of, every Thursday night at the Imperialino, iv. 446
audiences discontinued by, iv. 192
Austrian successes may make, impertinent, i. 477
authority of: confirmed, iv. 146; greatly increased by presidency of all councils, iv. 392, 395; reestablished, iv. 355; triumphant, ii. 122, iv. 210; unchallenged, iv. 77
Baden baths may be visited by, i. 95
Bagard hoped to supplant, i. 368, 406
ball given by, iv. 432
Bartolommei accused by, to Francis I, of Spanish leanings, i. 406
Bayreuth, Margrave and Margravine of, entertained by, iv. 476–9
Betange the enemy of, i. ?368, 490
Biglia entertained by, iv. 446
Borgherini, Mme, told by, about husband's fate, iii. 473
Botta compared with, v. 178
——'s appointment would displease, iii. 23
Braitwitz attributes orders to, ii. 120
—— avoids council meetings to escape affronts from, ii. 66
—— consulted by, about storing jewels, ii. 285
—— enemy of, i. 406, 490
—— to be supplied by, with money, ii. 66
brother of, i. 107, iv. 90n
brother's correspondence with, iv. 270, 271n, 277
brother's death afflicts, iv. 335
Careggi and Imperialino used by, iv. 116
Careggi the villa of, iii. 97
Careggi visited by, for health, iii. 402
Charles, P., may supplant, ii. 310
coach of, often waits at Mrs Richmond's door, iii. 97, 101

Cocchi abandons, ii. 133
—— conveys Mann's apologies to, i. 394
—— might have had ennoblement through, iv. 204
—— ordered to insert praises of, in book on Pisa baths, iv. 158
—— receives offer of hospital post through, i. 57
——'s defence of HW might offend, i. 448
——'s loyalty to Mann offends, ii. 133
commissary-general's post coveted by, iv. 295, 320
Conway and Mann called on, iv. 295
Corsi christening attended by, iv. 432
Councils of Finance and War headed by, iv. 392
courier robbed by Spaniards of money from, ii. 516
courier sent by, to Vienna, i. 314
Craon and Regency desired by, to disavow his enmity to Ginori, ii. 216
Craon converted by, in Regency Council discussion, iv. 14
—— discusses, with Mann, i. 326
—— employs, despite wife's warning, iv. 220
—— may be succeeded by, iv. 29
—— ordered to collaborate with, i. 407, 490
—— refuses request of, for certificate about Ginori, ii. 216
——'s departure opposed by, for fear of getting Stampa, iv. 24
——'s enemy, i. 327, 407
—— superseded by, v. 178n
—— to give news of Campo Santo to, ii. 165
Craon, Princesse de, calls, 'cet homme-là,' iv. 197
—— may yet triumph over, iv. 326
—— not yet permitted by, to resume faro, iii. 501
Craons mortified by, i. 189n
daughter lives with, iv. 476
daughter of, iv. 499, v. 442
daughter of, receives jewels from Cts of Orford, iv. 499, 505, ix. 144
daughter's death not yet told to, v. 42
daughter taken by, to all the Grand Duke's houses, iv. 451
departure of, expected, iii. 48
dinner given by: on Francis I's birthday, iv. 295, v. 9; on Maria Theresa's birthday, v. 9
does not retire, despite ill health, v. 21
Dumesnil, Alexandre, exchanges couriers with, i. 236
—— friend of, i. 225, 490
Dumesnil, Joseph, disregards advice of, iii. 491
economy the object of ministry of, iv. 472
edict against export of antiquities probably made by, to get Stosch's collection, iv. 465

Electress blames, for bad relations with Vienna, iv. 268
—— called on by, ii. 10–12
——'s estate estimated by, ii. 176
——'s treatment by, i. 225
Eleonora said to be with, i. 120
enemies of, dispersed, i. 406
England openly hated by, iv. 581
English at Leghorn claimed by, to be Francis I's subjects, iv. 266, 275–6
English earthquake known to, iv. 143
English excluded from dinners of, on holidays, v. 9
English fleet enrages, ii. 325, 328–9
English 'piracies' will be criticized by, to Mann, iv. 494
English relations with Tuscany may be guided by, through Chesterfield, i. 387
English superiority to French fleets denied by, iv. 472
entertainments forbidden by, iv. 146
epigrams on, iv. 268, 272
exposure of, threatened, i. 223
Ferreri's case opposed by, in Regency council, ii. 10, 31
fief obtained by, iii. 385, 394
Florence dull enough to give no pleasure to, iv. 401
Florence expects, iii. 394
Florence left by, i. 95, 97, 116; secretly, v. 80–1
Florentine 'chief minister,' i. 409n
Florentine children call, 'Pilate,' v. 85
Florentine clocks put on French time by order of, iv. 26
Florentine correspondence of, i. 120
Florentine money collected by, for deposit at Leghorn, i. 427–8
Florentines believe that Francis I's order for carnival was countermanded by, iii. 8
Florentines disciplined by, about masks and operas, iii. 8, 14, iv. 216, 219
Florentines fear return of, iii. 354
Florentine's remark on 'eternal' ministry of, iv. 268
Florentines resent rule of, ii. 352, iii. 8, iv. 77
Florentines terrified of, ii. 145
Florentines to blame for their subservience to, v. 148
Fogliani tells, to accept Viviani as minister, iv. 350–1
Francis I approves of conduct of, in the case of Leghorn suicide, iv. 14
—— grants fief and title to, iii. 385, 394
—— grants permission to, to visit Vienna when he pleases, iv. 392
—— ignores accusations against, iv. 335
—— impersonated by, at Corsi christening, iv. 432
—— influenced by, against Lucca, iv. 521–2
—— may make, minister to Ratisbon, iii. 49

[Nay, Emmanuel de ('Richecourt'), *cont.*]
—— might be persuaded by, to ask Carteret to oust Mann, ii. 362–3
—— receives courier from, i. 235
—— receives excuses from, iv. 162
——'s accountings with, ii. 201
—— said by, to need his assistance to become Emperor, iii. 7
——'s favourite minister favours, i. 189n
——'s plans withheld by, from Mann, ii. 3
——'s prime minister at Florence, iv. 586n, ix. 122n
——'s representative at Electress's death, ii. 171
—— temporarily disgraces, i. 490
—— to be prejudiced by, against Regency, i. 282
Frederick II is Mann's retort to insults of, v. 1–2
French naval superiority over England asserted by, iv. 472
French tax-farmers turned away by, iv. 327
friend of, sees Craon's letters to Francis I, i. 327
Gages's advance alarms, iii. 11, 40
Gavi friend of, i. 217, 490
——'s thefts may involve, i. 217, 224, 239
—— to prepare lodgings for, ii. 309
'gentleman of the old palace,' iv. 465
George II receives complaints from, *via* Vienna, ii. 328
——'s aid to Maria Theresa disparaged by party of, i. 371
——'s orders interpreted by, i. 288
Ginori made governor of Leghorn by, iii. 322
—— opposes, iii. 322–3, iv. 77, 463, 473, v. 81
—— ordered by, to seize Englishman's effects, iv. 1
——'s funeral forbidden by, v. 81
——'s plan for Leghorn suburb preferred to that of, iv. 217
——'s Spanish connections hinted by, to Francis I, i. 395
——'s Vienna mission instigated by, i. 395, 406, 490, ii. 122
goes into the country, ii. 309
gout thought by, to be cure for headache, iv. 79
Grand Prior di Perugia, iii. 394
HW admires Mann's treatment of, ii. 30–1, iv. 272, v. 19
HW amazed at subservience of, to Rome, iv. 448
HW distrusts Lady Orford's influence over, ii. 140
HW mentions, i. 43
HW pities, in his misery, v. 55
HW pities the Florentines for enduring, iii. 331
HW prefers, to Richmond as spy on Bns Walpole, ii. 31

HW said to have procured downfall of, i. 97–8
HW's opinion of, i. 25
HW wishes Mann good riddance of, iv. 342
HW wishes that Mann could triumph over, v. 347
HW would like to insult, iii. 128
health of: apoplexy, iv. 444, 445; 'attacks,' iv. 476; fever, iii. 402; gout, iii. 402; letters boast of improvement in, v. 85; stroke of palsy, v. 15, 21, 27, 29, 42–3; too ill to attend Regency council, ii. 66
hoards of, sought in Bns Walpole's cases, i. 224
Holy Week devotions of, iii. 31
house of, near Cts of Orford's, iv. 480
house to be taken by at Padua, i. 217, 235
Imperialino used by, iv. 116, 446
insincere, iv. 68
Juvrecourt, Comtesse de, friendly with, iii. 452, 457
Karl Friedrich of Baden-Durlach entertained by, iv. 148
law made by, requiring export license for art objects, iv. 465, v. 208
leave of absence probably granted to, when not desired, i. 134
Lee's correspondence with, about pilots, i. 455–6
Leghorn visited by, to christen ships, iv. 162
letters opened by, at Florentine post office, iii. 362
levee of, English colony boycotts, v. 9
Lorenzi disputes with, over citizenship of French at Leghorn, iv. 266–7
—— hears consolatory remarks from, on child's death, iv. 306
—— shows Maillebois's letter to, iii. 89
—— warns Mann against, ii. 362
Lorraine, Primate of, steps on toes of, to stop story, i. 490
Lorraine faction no longer protected by, v. 125
Lorraine may not be reached by, alive, v. 85
'Lorrainer and chief minister at Florence,' i. 409n
Lorrainer and Francis I's prime minister at Florence, ix. 122n
Lorraine's recovery expected by, to bring invasion of Tuscany, ii. 285
Lorraine the destination of, v. 62, 80
'low Lorrainer,' i. 189n
Lucca persecuted by, iv. 521
Lucca visited by, i. 468
Mann called on by, ii. 132–3, iv. 68
—— calls on, ii. 364, iii. 80, iv. 295
—— complains to, about sbirri, ii. 467
—— consults with, about defence of Tuscany by English fleet, ii. 27
—— dines with, iii. 450–1

—— disputes with, over privileges, iv. 146

—— entertained by, iv. 446, 476–9

—— entertains, at dinner, iv. 273

—— explains English affairs to, ii. 4–5, 10–11

—— forces, to submit in dispute over Leghorn factory, iv. 522

—— forgets that HW knew, ix. 140

—— forwards letter to, for Cts of Orford, iii. 51

—— frightens, with story of Zenón's application for passport, ii. 253

—— happy to be rid of, iii. 369

—— hears discussion by, of Hanover-Hessian quarrel and Cts of Orford's letter, iii. 80

—— hears Don Philip's plans from, i. 323

—— invited by, to dinner, i. 41

—— loses favour of, by hostility of Cts of Orford, iii. 452

—— misrepresented by, to Francis I, ii. 67

—— mistakenly occupies theatre box of, i. 394

—— need not fear malice of, ii. 384

—— never discusses the Leghorn suicide with, iv. 14

—— not invited to public dinner of, iv. 295

—— now treated politely by, ii. 67

—— overwhelmed by folly of, ii. 342

—— presents foreign visitors to, iv. 327

—— receives visit of condolence from, on Sir Robert Walpole's death, iii. 37

—— represented by, as hostile to Maria Theresa, ii. 476

—— resorts to snuff to appear nonchalant before, iv. 392

——'s complaints about, to England, iv. 310, 313

——'s correspondence with, iv. 2, 14

——'s curt call, unaccompanied by English visitors, disconcerts, v. 9

—— sees, but without discussing Cts of Orford, iii. 54

——'s family disparaged by, iv. 64n

——'s memorial to, about citizenship of English at Leghorn, iv. 275–6

——'s Pisa visit ingratiates himself with, iii. 487, iv. 84

——'s privileges disregarded by, iv. 205

——'s quarrel with, over citizenship of English at Leghorn, iv. 266, 275–6

—— supposed by, to be ignorant of ships' prizes, iii. 441

—— talks with, about Lady Orford's affairs, iii. 50

—— tells, to urge Lady Orford to sign papers, ii. 487

—— thanked by, for copy of speech, i. 38–9

—— to be ousted by, ii. 381

—— to denounce 'Onslow' to, iii. 506

—— to entertain, at dinner, iii. 501

—— to give compliments to, on Joseph II's birthday, iv. 129

—— told by: about Leopold's piles, i. 60; (?) that Frederick II must be punished, iv. 589; that gout will cure pain in breast, iv. 335; that he will be shifted to Genoa, iv. 270, 271n, 273, 280, 354

—— translates parts of Ædes Walpolianæ to, iv. 68

Marchese di Treschietto, iii. 385, 394

Maria Theresa's insolence reflected by, iv. 586

——'s treatment from Sir Robert Walpole condemned by, i. 367

—— tells, in Vienna, that religious devotion is necessary for promotion, iv. 421

Maricone encloses letter to, i. 309

Mathews's disputes with, ii. 309, 328

Mill involves, in his affairs, iii. 427

mob feared by, v. 80–1

Modena said to be visited by, i. 195

Modenese news unknown to, i. 432

money disbursed by, for military camp at San Martino, ii. 76

money-raising occupies, ii. 222

money wanted by, to take to Vienna, iv. 488

Mozzi said to be less creditable than, ix. 122, 130

mules procured by, iii. 11

mural crown should be flaunted before, by Mann, v. 347

Niccoli, Abbé, bribes, to continue salary after dismissal, on orders from Vienna, iv. 335

—— undersecretary to, i. 107, 224, iii. 42, 49

Niccolini entertained by, iv. 217

——'s banishment perhaps arranged by, iv. 2, 7–8, 117

——'s friendship with Frederick, P. of Wales, offends, iii. 441

——'s relations with, iv. 77, 146

old ladies excluded from party by, iv. 148

opera box of, Mann changes to, i. 240, ii. 128–9

Orford, Cts of (Bns Walpole), appears only at house of, ii. 122

—— assisted by, in journey, iii. 54

—— attends, with ptisan, ii. 67

—— awaited by, to marry him, iv. 268

—— corresponds with, iii. 64, 80, 97, iv. 143

—— encouraged by, to visit England, i. 426

—— encouraged by success of, ii. 122

—— entertains, on Thursdays, ii. 4

—— given servant by, iii. 50

—— goes to festine to meet, ii. 439

—— great admirer of, i. 360, 367, 409n

—— impelled by departure of, to leave Florence, i. 107

—— incites, to oust Mann, ii. 362–3

[Nay, Emmanuel de ('Richecourt'), *cont.*]
—— incites misbehaviour of, iv. 313
—— influences against England, ii. 329
—— lent money by, i. 461
—— lost by, iv. 272
—— may be followed by, to Venice, iii. 47
—— may have been entrusted by, with Hanoverian negotiation, iii. 70
—— may have courted Toussaint through, ii. 210
—— may receive chariot from, i. 53–4
—— may tempt, by her wealth, iv. 439
—— might be encouraged by, to seek bank credit, i. 422
—— more highly regarded by, after gift of jewels, iv. 505
—— not to accompany, to country, ii. 314
—— not to be relied upon by, i. 409
—— not to follow, to Vienna, i. 89, 95
—— not to marry, iv. 239
—— persuaded by, to sign papers, ii. 487
—— prejudices, against Mann, iii. 452
—— prepares lodgings for, ii. 309
—— probably foresaw departure of, iii. 49
—— repulsed by, at Imperialino, i. 34, 45, 53
—— said to be provided by, with apartment in his country house, iii. 80
—— soothes fears of, ii. 520
—— 's quarrels avenged by, ii. 10
—— subject of jokes by, iv. 444
—— supposed to have had two daughters by, ix. 122, 130
—— to have access to, by door into palace corridor, ii. 391
—— to join, at Verona, for return to Florence, i. 107
—— told not to interrupt Holy Week devotions of, iii. 31
—— unlikely to trouble, iv. 480
—— visits, ii. 364
—— will await return of, from Vienna, iii. 144
—— will not please, by her return, iv. 476
—— would not have left, had he shown more prowess, iv. 395
Orford, E. of, wants proof of wife's intrigue with, iii. 200
Padua visited by, i. 217, 224, 235, ii. 216
papal court opposed to, iv. 334
paper by English at Leghorn ridiculed by, to Mann, iv. 267
Petraia visited by, iv. 15
pies of fat or meat forbidden by, in theatre, iv. 219
Pisa baths patronized by, iii. 487
Pisa baths visited by, iv. 162, 252, 480
Plombières baths to be visited by, in litter, v. 62
prayer for, to Virgin: Mann sends, to HW, v. 60, 79; suppressed, v. 60
priest's epigram on, iv. 268, 272

reasons given for departure of, from Florence, i. 97–8
recovers from Cts of Orford's influence, iv. 68
Regency council blamed by, for publishing Mann's assurances from George II, i. 282
Regency council influenced by, against Mann, iv. 205
Regency council neglected since departure of, v. 112
Regency council overborne by, ii. 328
Regency council's president, iv. 392
Regency council's writings against, during his Padua visit to be disavowed, ii. 216
return of, to Florence: i. 235–6, 264, 468, iii. 394, 402, iv. 392; may re-establish him, iii. 219; threatened, i. 120
Richmond, Mrs, advised by, to quit house, iii. 238
—— may be kept by, in old palace, iii. 101
—— not evicted from her house for fear of offending, iii. 192
—— often called on by, iii. 80, 97, 101
—— supplies place of Cts of Orford in coach of, iii. 75, 101
—— suspected of writing to, iii. 290
—— visits, at Careggi, iii. 97, 101
Ridolfi disliked by, ii. 139
Rinuccini ascribes disgrace of, to Sir Robert Walpole, i. 108
(?) ——'s attestations against, i. 490
Rucellai fears to offend, ii. 133
St John's Day to have been made festive by, ii. 462
St Odile the antagonist of, iv. 305, 308
Santi Apostoli preferred by, to St James's, iii. 441
Sardinian treaty pressed by, iii. 6
Sassi approaches Frederick Augustus II through, i. 149
Savoy, D. of, may be preceded by, iv. 295
secretary of, *see* Niccoli
seditious billets annoy, iv. 252
Seymour complimented by, on Sandwich's alleged appointments, iv. 217
Shirley may cause Cts of Orford to forget, iii. 385
'simplicity' of, i. 24–5
son-in-law follows, to Lorraine, v. 80
son of, iv. 90
son talks with, of Cts of Orford's marriage, iv. 255
Sortes Virgilianæ for, i. 108
Spanish consul's complaints belittled by, ii. 542
Spanish depredations at Florence feared by, ii. 295
Stainville's appointment feared by, iv. 45, 84, 162, 192, 197
Stampa disputes with, over chairs and stools, iv. 320

—— may be succeeded by, as commissary for Italy, iv. 295, 320

——'s arrival dreaded by, iv. 24

Stosch's collection may be incorporated by edict of, iv. 465, 475

Suares, Bp, persecuted by, ii. 40

—— suspects that his niece is to be married to, ii. 40

subordinates of, servile to him though enjoying rebuffs to him from Vienna, iv. 284

Switzerland said to be visited by, i. 125, 134

tax farmers upheld by, iii. 23

Tesi reveals amours of, i. 45

—— scolded by Juvrecourt for applying to, ii. 368-9

Tornaquinci abuses, to Mann, iv. 267

—— submits to, iv. 146

Toussaint may get application from, ii. 363

—— reconciles, with Francis I, i. 490

——'s arrival a surprise to, iv. 97

——'s creature, i. 189n

treasures of, stored at Venice despite his talk of neutrality, ii. 513

Turin said to be visited by, i. 195

Tuscan discontent muzzled by, iv. 77

Tuscan disloyalty attributed to dislike of, iii. 11

Tuscan government may be taken away from, ii. 309-10

Tuscan money carried away by, iii. 115, iv. 488

Tuscan neutrality may be endangered by Spaniards' interception of letters of, ii. 516

Tuscan neutrality proclaimed by, ii. 513

Tuscany kept by, from being ruled by Ps Charlotte, iv. 355

Uguccioni hopes for preferment through, ii. 455

Vaughan would have been sentenced by, for similar insult, iv. 144

Venice visited by, incognito, i. 195

'viceroy of Jerusalem,' i. 97, 120

Vienna intrigues of, iii. 322

Vienna trip denied to, iv. 252

Vienna visited by, iii. 192, iv. 327, 334, 335, 421, 488, v. 80

Viennese influence of, said to decline, iii. 219, iv. 463

Viennese summons to, i. 89, 95

villa of, see Careggi

Wachtendonck may have procured disgrace of, i. 106, 107, 490

—— said to have frightened, from Florence by challenging him to a duel, i. 467-8

——'s cousin disgraces, with Francis I, i. 490

Walpole, Sir Robert, subject of insulting remarks by, i. 406, ii. 4

Walpole family disparaged by, i. 387, 393-4, 406

Wasner instigated by, to plead for Bns Walpole, ii. 194

witticism about, as 'father of the poor,' v. 81

witticisms against, would be punished, iv. 144

Young Pretender's arrest displeases, iv. 15, 22

——'s landing in Scotland announced to, iii. 86, 89

Nay, Louise-Charlotte de (1729-57), Richecourt's daughter, m. Conte Francesco di Thurn:

death of, from smallpox after miscarriage, v. 42-3

(?) father has, in house, iv. 476

(?) Mann entertains, at dinner, with Lady Orford, iv. 480

(?) Orford, Cts of, gives jewels to, iv. 499, 505, ix. 144

Nay, Louis (or Henri)-Hyacinthe de (d. 1752), Comte de Richecourt; Austrian and Tuscan diplomatist:

Berlin, visited by, on mission, ii. 107

brother probably hears of English earthquake through, iv. 143

brother told by, that Mann will be shifted to Genoa, iv. 270, 271n, 277

death of, iv. 335

England visited by, iv. 90, 270

English ministers confer with, about Mann and probably about Corsica, iv. 275, 277

health of, gout, iv. 335

itinerary of, to England, iv. 45

Maria Theresa's picture carried by, to Lord Hyndford, ii. 107

marriage of, iv. 45

minister to England, iv. 271n

of Turin, iv. 45

Naylor, Francis. See Hare-Naylor

Nebuchadnezzar (d. 562 B.C.), K. of Babylon ?604-562 B.C.:

would enjoy opulence in England, ix. 321

Neckar, river:

Charles's army on, ii. 267

Necker, Jacques (1732-1804), statesman:

appointment of, as comptroller of finances, viii. 254-5

fall of, expected to benefit England, ix. 159

Protestant, ix. 21

Protestant and former Genevan, viii. 254

Protestant, reformer, and of no birth, ix. 159

Roman Catholic Church opposed by, ix. 21

Necklace; necklaces:

Charlotte's, of diamonds, v. 529

diamond, Cowper gives, to wife, viii. 232

Mann distributes, among Suares family, i. 484

[Necklace; necklaces, *continued*]
    pearl, ii. 291
    Rohan pretended to buy, for Marie-An-
    toinette, ix. 639
Nectarine:
    blooms in December, iv. 16
Needham, 'Mother' Elizabeth (d. 1731), pro-
curess:
    Clement XIII might echo deathbed utter-
    ance of, vii. 32
    (?) Pomfret, Cts of, called 'sister' of, i.
    132–3
Needham, Father John Turberville (1731–
81), scientific writer; F.R.S.:
    counterpart of, may find that Hindustan
    was settled by Londoners, vii. 551
    'Jesuit,' vii. 551
Needham, Thomas (1703–68), 9th Vct Kil-
morey:
    Florence visited by, iv. 271, 278
    Nightingale family to separate from, iv.
    278
    wife mentions *gentil uomo* of, iv. 298
Needle:
    Pitt, Mrs, threads, by candlelight, vii. 456
Negro; Negroes:
    French cooks might be replaced by, as
    butchers, viii. 21
    HW distressed by sale of, iv. 126
    HW's sympathy for, vii. 452
    Montesquieu attacks sale of, into slavery,
    iv. 126
    mutiny of, in Brazil, vii. 452
    Portuguese call, 'disaffected,' vii. 452, 462
    Usher's, suspected of starting fire, vi. 141
    See also Gardiner, Charlotte; Sessaracoa,
    William Ansah
Negroni, Andrea (1710–89), cardinal, 1763:
    exclusion of, revoked by French, Neapoli-
    tan, and Spanish ministers, vii. 35–6
Negroni brothers:
    one of, refuses to sell Villa Negroni, viii.
    31
Negroni family:
    Clement XIV may negotiate with, at Genoa
    for villa for Ds of Kingston, viii. 6–7
    Kingston, Ds of, sends courier to, about
    purchase of villa, vii. 567
Negroni, Villa, at Rome:
    Clement XIV offers to be Ds of Kingston's
    agent in procuring, viii. 6–7
    hurricane uproots trees at, iv. 69
    Kingston, Ds of, may buy, vii. 566–7, viii.
    6–7, 14
    one of Negroni brothers refuses to sell,
    viii. 31
    Sixtus V's casino at, viii. 7
    ——'s villa, vii. 567, viii. 14, 31
Negropont:
    Russian fleet batters castle of, vii. 331
Neiberg. *See* Neipperg
Neipperg, Marie Wilhelmine Josephe (1738–
75), Gräfin; m. (1755) Fürst Johann Adam
Joseph Auersperg:

Guadagni's favour with, vii. 279
Neipperg, Wilhelm Reinhard (1684–1774),
Graf; field marshal:
    Daun's orders from, v. 96
    French forces considered inferior by, ii.
    250
    Königseck visited by, i. **205**
Neisse:
    Frederick II to relieve, v. 254, 257
Nemi, Duca di. *See* Braschi-Onesti, Luigi
Nemi:
    Austrians at, ii. 454, 473, 488
    letter from camp at, ii. 488
Nenny, Cornelius, Freiherr von, Austrian
cabinet secretary:
    toison d'or brought by, from Vienna, vii. 1
'Nephew, our.' *See* Frederick II
Nepotism:
    HW's witticism on, viii. 71
Neptune:
    French medals would depict, with Louis
    XV, v. 357
    Maria Theresa's medal includes, v. 202
'Neptune.' *See* King, John (ca 1753–1823):
    Letters of Neptune and Gracchus; see also
    Mathews, Thomas
Neptune, English man of war:
    expected at Port Mahon, i. 285
Neptune, English merchant ship:
    nearly captured, ii. 354
Neptune, Spanish galleon:
    in Spanish fleet, i. 286
Neri, Pompeo (1707–76), Abbé; scholar and
politician:
    Craon expects resignation of, i. 236
    (?) Gondi, Mme, courted by, at opera, ii.
    86
    (?) —— turns off, i. **136**
    new Regency member, v. 125
    pale, ii. 86
Néricault, Philippe (1680–1754), called Des-
touches:
    Rucellai translates version by, of Addi-
    son's *Drummer,* iv. 118, 151
Nerli, (?) Francesco:
    Gabburri, Mme, to make, her cicisbeo, i.
    150
Nero (Nero Claudius Cæsar Drusus Germani-
cus) (37–68), Roman emperor 54–68:
    Dauphin's comment on, v. 44
    Labour in Vain mentions, ii. 18
    Maupeou would have restored, viii. 35
    Rome the soil of, viii. 154
Nero, del. *See* Del Nero
Nerves:
    agitation of, iv. 377
    cold baths for, i. 452
    English suffer from, i. 452
    fashionable in England when cured at
    Bath, iv. 389
    Florence's sunshine and cool pure night
    air will rehabilitate, ix. 646
    gouty complaints attributed to, vi. 116, 117

HW's: ix. 201, 539; affected by damp, viii.
289; alarmable, viii. 272; shattered, ix. 49;
Tunbridge trip considered for, i. 452
hot baths too relaxing for, viii. 280
Mann's: cannot be cured by air or water,
ix. 61; interfere with his writing, ix.
45–6, 49, 143–4; shattered, ix. 500; 'wore
out,' by writing, iv. 537
Mead and Thompson cure, iv. 389
Pitt, Anne, suffers from weakness of, viii. 6
waters supposed to cure, iv. 389
weakness of, v. 281–2, viii. 6, 430, ix.
643, 656
Nervous disorder; nervous disorders:
occurrences of, vi. 74, vii. 155
Nesbitt, Dorothy (d. 1779), m. (1757) George
Parker, 2d E. of Macclesfield:
marriage of, to former paramour, vi. 211
Nesi, Francesco Maria (d. after 1800), Mann's
surgeon:
(?) Mann informed by, about HW's gout,
ix. 626
(?) Mann's foot treated by, viii. **79**
(?) Mann's rheumatism thought by, to be
gout, viii. 479
Nestor:
HW will not hobble like, to siege of Troy,
ix. 296
Net:
gold, for horse, ii. 69
Nettles:
Houghton overgrown with, vii. 510
Nettuno:
Mann sends ships under Long to, ii. 460,
475, 476
oats brought to, by ship, ii. 453
Neufchâtel:
Lucan to leave son at, to study, viii. 462
Neuhoff, Theodore (1694–1756), Baron de;
self-styled K. of Corsica:
act of insolvency benefits, v. 45, 140, 148
Carteret claimed by, as friend, ii. 187,
194, 210, 233, iv. 164, 385
—— discovers deception of, ii. 216
—— tells, of Bns Walpole's application,
ii. 194
—— urged by, to send Mann a courier,
ii. 190
Charles Emmanuel III cheated by, iv. 386
coins of, v. 45, 140
Corsican coasts skirted by, ii. 174
Corsicans and English did not want to
reinstate, iv. 386
creditors lure, from privileged place, iv.
164
death of, v. 39–40, 45
edict of, sent to HW by Mann, ii. 151,
155–8
England may acquire Corsica by paying
debts of, v. 59
England visited by, ii. 192, iv. 40
English fleet neglects, despite alleged
orders by George II, Newcastle, and
Carteret, ii. 188

English ministers deceived by, ii. 222
English newspapers wanted by, in Tuscany, iv. 378
George II may receive letter from, iii. 132
German gazette mentions, ii. 221
Goldsworthy conceals Leghorn visit of, ii.
145, 166, 187
—— ill-treats, ii. 188
HW erects monument to, in St Anne's
churchyard, v. 140, 148
HW promotes subscription for, iv. 373–4,
385
HW's inscription for: v. 40n, 140; Mann
asks about translation of, v. 197; Mann
translates, into Italian, v. 148; translation
of, pleases HW, v. 204
HW to meet, at Lady Schaub's, iv. 40
handwriting of, illegible, ii. 205
Hogarth to depict, at HW's request, iv.
164
imprisoned for debt, iv. 164, 373
kingdom to be occupied by, ii. 150–1
King's Bench prison confines, iv. 164, v.
140
Leghorn Corsicans expect, ii. 145
Leghorn near the station of, iii. 132
life of, see History of Theodore I; Life
and History of Theodore I
Mann accused by, of mishandling his
funds, v. 378–9
—— consults with, in Florence, ii. 187,
190, 194
—— less fit to write about, than are Mrs
Behn or Mrs Haywood, ii. 249
—— not a friend of, iv. 378
—— receives frequent communications
from, ii. 187–8, 190, 205, 216
—— refuses to lend money to, iv. 29
——'s letters mis-used by, in Tuscany, iv.
378
—— urged by, to find him a villa to hide
in, ii. 217
—— wants Sir Robert Walpole's report
on, ii. 190
Maria Theresa's alleged treaty with, ii.
208
marriage not immediately contemplated
by, ii. 207–8
Mathews confused about, ii. 194–5
—— wants to install, ii. 229
not Mann's friend, iv. 378–9
Old Bailey visited by, to benefit by insolvency act, v. 45
Portuguese minister called on by, v. 45
release of, from prison, v. 45, 140, 148
Rowley not seen by, iii. 132
rumoured to be on man of war at Leghorn, ii. 145
sails from Leghorn, ii. 174
secretary of, betrays him to Mann, iv. 379
Stanhope, Lady Lucy, receives addresses
of, ii. 192, 207, 221, **229**
transports of, dispersed, ii. 174

[Neuhoff, Theodore, *continued*]
Walpole, Sir Robert, claimed by, as friend, ii. 187, 233
—— denies having had connections with, ii. 210, 225, 233
—— knows nothing of Carteret's connections with, ii. 210, 225
World prints HW's paper in behalf of, iv. 373–4, 385
Yarmouth, Cts of, said to be niece of, ii. 187, 216
Young Pretender's will said to imitate that of, ix. 395
Neupergh. *See* Newburgh
Neuremberg. *See* Nuremberg
Neuschattel. *See* Neufchâtel
Neutrality, armed:
means no good to anybody, ix. 327
Nevile, Mrs Christopher. *See* Mann, Mary (d. between 1815 and 1818)
Nevill, Hon. Catherina (1728–?62):
to be Maid of Honour, iii. 63
Nevill, George (1727–85), 15th Bn Abergavenny; cr. (1784) E. of Abergavenny:
Cornbury visited by, with Selwyn and Mrs Frere, iv. 182
mother of, iv. 182
Oxford servant's death attributed to, iii. 387
Westminster Abbey visited by, with Selwyn, iv. 181
wife of, iv. 180n
Neville, ——, Lt; engineer:
captured by the French, viii. 477
Neville, Cosmus Henry Joseph Migliorucci (b. 1716):
(?) Florence visited by, vii. 64
Florentine cousin tries to cheat, iv. 266
Neville, Richard Neville Aldworth (1717–93), M.P.:
(?) Florence visited by, vii. 64
match of, at Geneva, iv. 7
Nevill family:
genealogy of, brings them no advantages, iv. 408
New and Easy etc. cioè Nuova e facile grammatica. See under Barker, Edward
Newark, Vct. *See* Medows (later Pierrepont), Charles Pierrepont (1737–1816)
Newburgh, Cts of. *See* Livingstone, Charlotte Maria
Newburgh, E. of. *See* Radcliffe, James Bartholomew
Newcastle, English ship:
Fox captain of, ii. 152, 182
Leghorn visited by, ii. 182
Mann sends, to cruise, ii. 460
ordered to England, iii. 12
prize brought by, to Leghorn, ii. 448
Suckling on board, ii. 152, 182
Newcastle estate:
entail of, cut off, i. 209–10

Newcastle House:
Bedford and Rockingham factions meet at, vi. 541–2
Milbanke and Thomas Pelham lived at, iv. 207
Newcastle, D. of, quits, because 2 servants die of sore throats, v. 312–13
Newcastle-under-Line *or* Lyne, D. of. *See* Fiennes Clinton, Henry (1720–94); Pelham Clinton, Lord Thomas (1752–95); Pelham Holles, Thomas (1693–1768)
Newcastle-under-Line *or* Lyne:
duchy of: Lincoln to inherit, v. 18, 26; the only dukedom bestowed by George II, v. 26
Newcastle-upon-Tyne, Ds of. *See* Godolphin, Lady Henrietta (d. 1776)
Newcastle-upon-Tyne, D. of. *See* Cavendish, Henry (1630–91); Holles, John (1662–1711); Pelham Holles, Thomas (1693–1768)
Newcastle-upon-Tyne, Northumberland:
Chute and Whithed call, 'Carbonari,' iii. 143
coal from, pun on, v. 460
colliers of, said to feed their children with fire shovels, iv. 450
Wade and Edinburgh provost meet at, iii. 175–6
Wade marches from, iii. 165
—— stays at, iii. 159
—— to march from, iii. 153
Newdigate, Sir Roger (1719–1806), 5th Bt, 1734; M.P.:
HW and Sir Robert Walpole meet, in Grosvenor Square, ii. 25
Pitt answers, in Parliamentary debate, x. 10
Rome visited by, viii. 144
Tories accompany, to Brentford election, ii. 25
Young Pretender would formerly have been mourned by, viii. 144
New England:
Cape Breton said to be taken by troops of, iv. 474
England may be conquered in, vii. 551
forces of: may attack Quebec after Burgoyne's defeat, viii. 342; may join Washington to besiege Clinton, viii. 342
Newenham, Sir Edward (1732–1814), Kt, 1763; Irish politician:
Mann's turbulent letter from, sent to Horace Mann II to be shown to C. J. Fox, ix. 443, 456
New Forest, Hants:
Gloucester, D. and Ds of, go to lodge in, viii. 360
Newfoundland:
capture of, by the French, vi. 52, 69
England will give fishing rights on, to France, v. 526
English recovery of, pleases Leghorn, vi. 100

Farinelli said to have escaped to, ii. 119
French ship with supplies for, captured, vi. 82
Italy gets fish from, vi. 100–1
ship from, reaches Leghorn, viii. 246
Newgate Prison:
Ayliffe committed to, vii. 74
criminal in, confesses robbing gentleman's scrutore, iv. 215
Denbighshire high sheriff sent to, i. 344
Franklin in, vi. 188
Gibson and Murray sentenced to, iv. 225, 227
mercer promises to send silk to, for Mrs Rudd, viii. 153
murderers of turnkey at, executed, iv. 312
Paxton released from, i. 502
—— to be sent to, i. 397, 400n
Russell's levee in, vii. 82
visitors throng to, iv. 199
Wilkes dates addresses to constituents from, vii. 82
—— should have gone to, vi. 198
New Holland:
unexploited because it has no wealth, ix. 545
New Jersey:
American army in, estimated, viii. 339
Washington said to have retired to, viii. 338
New Lesson for Pope. See Roome, Edward: Dean Jonathan's Parody
Newmarket, Suffolk:
bank bill discarded at, iv. 53
Chartres, Duc de, to visit, viii. 186
denizens of, disregard monarchs, vii. 497
Fox, C.J., the first figure at, ix. 154
French visitors flock to, ix. 409
HW contrasts houses of, with Modena's and Parma's, ii. 315
HW preferred to discuss, rather than politics, ix. 483
HW sells race-horses at, vii. 497
inn of, ii. 315, 332
London deserted because of, ix. 639
Londoners flock to, vii. 401
music eclipsed by, vii. 570–1
'never-to-be-violated festival of,' ix. 264
Orford, E. of, at inn on road to, vii. 460
—— has farm near, vii. 495
——'s bets at, vii. 503
Panton was horse jockey of, viii. 499
people will stay in London till it is fashionable to go to, ix. 105
politics slacken during season at, ix. 398
Pulteney contributes paper on, to The World, iv. 374
races at: forfeits prepaid at, iii. 318; to begin, vii. 99, viii. 20; trial of horses for, v. 490
visitors from, expected at Houghton, ii. 70
visitors to: Cumberland, D. of, iv. 373, vi.

288, 297; Fox, C.J., vii. 400; Grosvenor, v. 490; HW, ii. 315; Ponsonby, v. 7; Selwyn, v. 7; Walker, iii. 511n
younger generation goes to, in England, viii. 89
Newnham, Nathaniel (ca 1741–1809), M.P.; lord mayor of London 1780–90:
Rodney not given banquet by, ix. 343
New North St, Red Lion Square, London:
Suckling's address, viii. 209
New Ode, A. See under Williams, Sir Charles Hanbury
New Park, Richmond. See Richmond: New Park
Newport, Bn. See Jocelyn, Robert (ca 1688–1756)
Newry:
Bedford, D. of, to join army at, v. 373
Newsham, Mrs John. See Craggs, Anna
Newsham Craggs, James (1715–69), M.P.:
(?) mother of, i. 165, 254
Newspaper; newspapers:
cardinals' creations to be announced in, ii. 302
English: abound in scurrilities on young, handsome women, viii. 267, ix. 364, 584; Adam offended by version in, of Fox's speech, viii. 538; advertisements in, of sexual stimulants, iii. 561; American news in, viii. 220; announce patrols in Scotland, iv. 35; anonymous letters in, replace pamphlets, vi. 169n; at Dover inn, ii. 315; Bristol's posts announced in, vi. 453; Chartres's indecent buttons attacked in, ix. 409; Chesterfield's speech in, iii. 52; Choiseul's disgrace reported in, vii. 62; circulated over Europe, ix. 146; Conway credited by, with great commissions, viii. 33; Corsican news in, v. 140; Cumberland, D. of, called 'royal idiot' by, vii. 230; describe press gangs, vii. 239; detestable for lies, blunders, scandal, and factious letters, ix. 297; Doctors Commons a fit topic for lies of, viii. 427; East India Company denounced in, vii. 457; Egmont's pamphlet much advertised in, iv. 43; Elba affair mentioned in, ii. 47; Elizabeth of Russia's answer in, v. 368; English expedition to Naples mentioned in, ii. 47; escape of Frenchmen from Prague reported in, ii. 68–9; follies and lies in, ix. 530; foolish, brutal or scandalous, HW calls, ix. 146–7; former pamphleteers now write letters in, ix. 451; Fox's Martyrs advertised in, ix. 505; France bans, because of scandal about Marie-Antoinette, ix. 557; Franklin must comment upon, to French ministers, viii. 465; 'French disease' a term used in, vi. 175; full of invasion from France, v. 293; full of lies, but give main outline of events, vii. 536; George II's trip to Flanders announced in, ii. 48; George III's coronation will fill, v. 515; Gloucester,

[Newspaper; newspapers, *continued*]

D. of, called 'D. of Lancaster' in, vi. 264; Gloucester, D. of, said by, to have died, ix. 623; Gray's death in, vii. 319; HW calls, drag-nets, ix. 146; HW can only re-echo, ix. 212; HW does not wish to write more than is in, ix. 295; HW knows only what is told by, ix. 336; HW never hears of events until they are in, ix. 116; HW reads about sweepstakes in, vii. 497; HW reads in, of raising Gibraltar siege, ix. 331; HW said by, to have palsy, vi. 461; HW's American knowledge limited to reports in, viii. 38; HW's letters can give less news than, viii. 204; HW's letters often anticipated by, viii. 370, 385; HW's outlines will help Mann understand, ix. 273, 281; HW's reflections on worthlessness of, vi. 325, vii. 53, 432, viii. 232, 412, 512, ix. 363-4, 557, 584, 619, 623; Hall's deposition in, v. 377; Hanoverian neutrality the topic of, i. 187; hard pressed for news in a peaceable autumn, ix. 607; Hardwicke lauded by, iii. 293; heralds advertise in, for peeresses' names and addresses, v. 535; Hertford, Cts of, said by, to have died, vi. 468; Hertford, E. of, said by, to be K.G., vi. 325; horse races and casualties the staple of, iv. 321; Howe attacked by, vii. 270, ix. 439n; Irish wonders reported by, ix. 607; Jamaica fleet's arrival in, ix. 302; Karl Wilhelm Ferdinand said by, to be at Florence, vi. 463; Keppel's account criticized by, viii. 402-3; Lincoln's affair in, vii. 368; London riots in, vii. 305, viii. 117; Luttrells' articles in, viii. 77; Mann avidly reads about England in, vi. 123; Mann can get details from, ix. 79; Mann can learn more from, than from HW, viii. 428; Mann credited by, with sending news of Toulon fleet's sailing, viii. 376, 380; Mann finds HW's letters more hopeful than, viii. 388; Mann reads about Hastings' trial in, ix. 651; Mann reads inconclusive accounts in, of new administration, ix. 299; Mann receives arrears of, viii. 434; Mann sends, to Anne Pitt, viii. 233; Mann sends, to HW, i. 84; Mann's recall from Florence rumoured in, vi. 315; Mann would not trust accounts in, without HW's authority, viii. 270; Mann, Horace II, said by, to be ruining himself at cricket, vii. 495; Maria Theresa's treaty with Theodore printed in, ii. 208; Maurepas's death reported in, ix. 212; military suppression of Gordon riots attacked in, ix. 77; Minorca's danger blamed by, on English ministry, viii. 468; minute records of events printed in, ix. 363; more communicative, ix. 503; Murray's sentence published in, ix. 361; no event escapes notice of, ix. 527; odes on Pulteney frequent in, ii. 90; Orford's arrival noticed in, iv. 251; Oudh too inconsequential to be noticed in, ix. 13; Parliamentary debates so fully printed in, that HW could merely send extracts, ix. 464; Parliamentary members instructed through, by constituents, i. 392; Pembroke's discovery reported in, vi. 19; phrase used in, ii. 277; poem on Pope's death in, ii. 467; political letters in, HW rarely reads, ix. 503; Portsmouth mutiny described in, ix. 362; Pozzolini's arrival in England announced in, ix. 344; Prevereau forwards, to Mann, i. 421-2; Pucci's recall announced by, v. 108; Regency members listed in, ii. 218; report in, that combined fleet is at Brest, ix. 186; Russian victories reported in, vii. 231; Sandwich said by to keep fleet at Portsmouth, viii. 377; Scots attacked in, vii. 419; severe upon Anglo-Spanish peace, vii. 274; Smith probably shows, to HW, i. 84; squib in, about possible conquest of England, iii. 129; stocks, horse races, and ship arrivals staple of, vi. 174; testimonials in, to quacks, v. 132; Theodore of Corsica wants, iv. 378; Thurot discussed by, v. 381-2; Tory, satirizes ministry, ii. 33; Townshend's and Wilkes's memorials in, vii. 339; verses in, on Berkeley and tarwater, ii. 505; Walpole, Sir Robert, said by, to be recovered from indisposition, ii. 140; Walpole, Sir Robert, subject of exaggerated reports in, i. 165; war council announced in, v. 163; weekly, abuse Bute, vi. 42; writers in, purvey rubbish, ix. 146; York, Cardinal, said by, to have died, vii. 432; young Englishmen's follies reported in, vii. 506

English evening, Ds of Marlborough's will in, ii. 528

English morning, daily, page of political invective always to be found in, viii. 451

explanations always given by, though they may be false or incorrect, ix. 459

foreign: copy each other, ii. 213; Jacobite encouragement reported in, ii. 426; Repnin's mission to England announced in, viii. 487; Walpole, Horatio (1678-1757), credited by, with Parliamentary motion, ii. 427

HW will publish, when he starts inventing news, iii. 484

Italian, report Irish and Scotch encouragement of French invasion, ii. 415

Mann makes, from Italian MS newspapers, i. 156, 158

See also Gazette; Periodical; Press

Newton, Sir Isaac (1642-1727), Kt, 1705; philosopher:

gravitation theory of, once fashionable, iv. 154

HW invokes spirit of, v. 407

Halley's comet foretold by, v. 294

Orford, Cts of, and Cts of Pomfret should

have studied St Chrysostom instead of, iv. 555

Orford, Cts of, discusses, with Andrási, ii. 555

prediction by, of alteration in English climate, iv. 119

white said by, to be offensive to eyesight, ii. 228

Newton, Thomas (1704–82), Bp of Bristol, 1761:

Armagh archbishopric declined by, vi. 275

New Year's Day:

London empty around, iii. 455

Mann performs ceremonies of, at Leopold's palace, viii. 346

—— sends greetings on, to HW, iv. 210

storm on, considered a bad omen, viii. 431

New York, mayor of. See Mathews, David

New York:

Americans might recapture, viii. 347, 348, ix. 311

Carleton later commander at, viii. 215n

Charleston's surrender rumoured at, viii. 500

Clinton captures fort near, viii. 500

—— may have abandoned, viii. 416

——'s army reaches, viii. 405, 408

conflagration in, viii. 256

Cornwallis trying to scramble to, ix. 194

defenders of, not numerous, viii. 342, 347

English army finds no plenty in, viii. 406

English army in, small, viii. 336

English evacuate Philadelphia for, viii. 393

English occupy, viii. 255–6, 265, 336

Estaing blockades English fleet at, viii. 406, 410

——'s fleet might be attracted towards, viii. 408

Europe may have to take its laws from, viii. 229

events may be expected in, viii. 206

Fort William Henry's capture exposes, v. 144

gazette from, the only American news in England for a month, viii. 338

Howe, Sir William, and brother to attack, viii. 242–3

Howe, Sir William, draws lines between King's Bridge and, viii. 261

—— lands at Staten Island in face of, viii. 229, 241

—— leaves Halifax for, viii. 229

—— might abandon Philadelphia to save, viii. 342

—— said to have been repulsed at, viii. 216

——'s victory at, rumoured at Leghorn, viii. 246

—— takes possession of, viii. 255, 265

La Fayette said to expect capture of, ix. 70

letters from, say nothing of colonial revolt, ix. 321

mob in, said to have seized cargoes of

ships that were bringing supplies to Gage, viii. 111

news does not come from, viii. 252

new Xenophon may be produced by, viii. 62

'opulent and proud colony,' with factions, v. 144

province of, better disposed towards England, viii. 85

tea duty resisted by, viii. 13

New York Gazette:

Howe's alleged victory in, viii. 334, 338

New Zealand:

unexploited because it has no wealth, ix. 545

Niagara:

English capture of, v. 326, 333

Nicastro:

earthquake account mentions, ix. 375

Niccoli, Abbé Raimondo (d. 1780); Tuscan agent and chargé d' affaires at Paris 1767–80; ? Richecourt's undersecretary:

clothes of, unsuitable for England, iii. 49

Franklin knows, viii. 362

Italian maid brought by, from England, iii. 290

Leopold told by dispatch from, about high price of food, viii. 106

maid seduced by, iii. 224, 238

Mann told by, of American-French treaty, viii. 363, 369

misdeed of, discovered in Vienna, iv. 335

nephew of, acts as his substitute at Paris, viii. 363

Orford, Cts of, accompanied by, to England, iii. 42, 46, 49, 224, 238, iv. 335

—— gives bed to, i. 107

—— has cases arranged by, i. 224

—— sends news by, iii. 290

Richecourt bribed by, to continue salary, iv. 335

(?) —— orders, to give up opera box, i. 394

——'s undersecretary, iii. 42, 49

—— told to dismiss, iv. 335

(?) Tuscany ruled by, v. 62

Niccolina. See Nicolina

Niccolini, Mme ——:

Soderini, Mme, served by, ii. 251

Vernacci cicisbeo to, ii. 251

Niccolini, Marchesa. See Riccardi, Giulia Maria

Niccolini, Signorita ——:

about to be married, v. 343

watch from Paris for, v. 343

Niccolini, Agata (1741–55):

death of, iv. 519

Niccolini, Abbé Antonio (1701–69), Marchese di Ponsacco:

Aix-la-Chapelle to be visited by, iii. 485

Albani's letter about Austro-Sardinian treaty shown by, i. 342

[Niccolini, Abbé Antonio, *continued*]
Augsburg and Munich may be visited by, iv. 2, 7
ball to be given by, for D. of York, vi. 171
banishment order fails to reach, iv. 7
Barrett-Lennards entertained by, with Signora Capello, Mann, Rinuccini, and Stanhope, iv. 174
Botta told by, of Mann's coming promotion, vi. 318
Bubb Dodington accompanied by, iii. 420
Carlisle and Duncannon told by, about Riccardi's collection, iii. 361
Chute's witticism on banishment of, iv. 3–4
Cunningham tells, of Mann's coming promotion, vi. 317
Delci, Contessa, niece of, ii. 60, 85
England not to be revisited by, now that P. of Wales is dead, iv. 285
England pleases, iii. 339
England praised by, iv. 285
England visited by, iii. 72, 308, 329, 331, 348, 362, 369, 382, 387, 398, 436
English Court unlikely to complain about, to Viennese Court which would not listen, iv. 19
English government subject of lectures by, in Florence, iv. 145–6
English honours proclaimed by, iii. 369
English tour of, iii. 398
Florence dreads return of, iii. 369, iv. 117
Francis I banishes, from Tuscany, iv. 2, 7
Frederick, P. of Wales, accompanied by, to Cliveden, iii. 436
—— befriends, iii. 348, 362, iv. 2
—— tells: about Sandwich, iv. 217; that Murray is a Jacobite, iv. 364
George II's death may benefit, iii. 414
Guasco and Cerati indulge with, in mutual praise, vi. 531
HW entertains, on fast day, iii. 331
HW forwards letter to, iii. 372, 449
HW never sees, iii. 449
HW's inscription for bas relief of Benedict XIV translated by, v. 126–7
health of, fever, iv. 145–6
Kilmorey, Vcts, calls, 'my lord,' iv. 298
knighthood may be acquired by, iii. 414
Lovat's execution attended by, iii. 387
——'s trial shocks, iii. 382
Mann asked by, about George II giving Hanover to D. of Cumberland, i. 328
—— forwards letter to, through HW, iii. 385, 408, 445, 449
—— gives: copy of HW's inscription for Benedict XIV, v. 113; copy of HW's inscription for Theodore of Corsica, v. 148
—— said to have been ordered to complain about, to Regency, iv. 7
—— shows HW's verses to, ii. 372

—— tells Botta and, about insignificance of Carrickfergus raid, v. 381
—— to be aided by, in getting news of Lady Mary Wortley Montagu, iv. 285
—— to thank, for attentions to D. of York, vi. 179
nephew of, iv. 428, vi. 220
O'Kelly may be accuser of, iv. 2
Orford, Cts of, expected by, to return to Florence, iii. 394
—— may see, iii. 353, 362
—— not reliably discussed by, iii. 398
—— to have her jewels sold by, i. **95**, 134–5, 217
Padua may be visited by, iv. 24
Pandolfini's answer from, iv. 24
—— to notify, of banishment, iv. 2
Passionei invites, to Rome, v. 127
Pomfret, Cts of, corresponds with, i. 240, ii. 558
—— gives books to, ii. 126–7
—— may introduce, as a genius, iii. 353
—— sees, often, iii. 362
religion alone keeps, from becoming English, iii. 436
Riccardi can arrange sale of gems through, iii. 373
Richecourt angered by friendship of, with Frederick, P. of Wales, iii. 441
—— announces pardon of, to family, iv. 117
—— hates, iv. 7
—— prepares letter to procure banishment of, iv. 2
——'s relations with, iv. 146
—— still believed to have instigated banishment of, iv. 117
—— told by, that Sandwich is not to be congratulated on his alleged appointments, iv. 217
Sandwich's unpopularity correctly described by, iv. 225
satiric print or drawing of, vi. 531
still in exile, iv. 77
Tuscan ministry allegedly abused by, iv. 4
Venice visited by, iv. 24
Vienna probably visited by, iv. 7
York, Cardinal, talks with, in Florence, vi. 256
Niccolini, Luigi (1713–82), Lisbon merchant: losses of, in earthquake, iv. 519
Niccolini, Maria Lucrezia (d. 1778), m. (1742) Lodovico Pannocchieschi d'Elci:
crooked, ii. 85
Dal Borgo entertains, ii. 85
English riding habit worn by, ii. 85
marriage of, ii. **60**
Niccolini's niece, ii. 60
——'s 'sister,' ii. 85
Niccols. *See* Nicholls
Niccolucci, Stefano, Electress's doorkeeper: (?) Dumesnil asks, for admittance, i. 236
Niccotina. *See* Nicolina

Nice:
  Butler may go to Genoa or, ix. 303
  Charles Emmanuel III has smallpox at,
    iii. 334
  —— to attack, iii. 313
  —— to resist Spanish invasion through, ii.
    395
  Cornish puts in at, ii. 415
  English travellers swarm in, ix. 618
  French and Spaniards try to pass through,
    ii. 461
  Holland, Bn, increases reputation of, vii. 2
  —— to visit, vi. 561
  improper place to spend hot months, viii.
    286
  letters reach Florence from, iii. 344
  Leutrum to invade, iii. 432
  Maillebois may have to retire to, iii. 237
  Mann, Horace II, detained at, viii. 369, ix.
    404
  —— prevented from embarking for, ix. 203
  —— thinks of moving his family to, to
    break daughter's attachment, ix. 431
  Mathews to forestall Spanish advance on,
    ii. 312
  one of England's last available ports, iv.
    575
  Orford, Cts of, may spend winter at, vii.
    2
  Philip, Don, has not started from, iii. 36
  —— makes, his headquarters, iii. 432
  —— may enter, ii. 271
  —— may have to fight his way through,
    i. 408
  —— to command Spanish army in, ii. 547
  rendezvous for commissioners exchanging
    territory in Italy, iii. 508
  Sardinians covet, ii. 448
  sea engagement not reported at, ii. 403
  Spanish troops arrive at, iii. 9
  valley of, provides no forage, iii. 51
  Villettes receives letter from, ii. 413
  visitors to: Beauvau, ii. 448; Bristol, E. of,
    viii. 167, 203; Mann, Horace II, viii. 369,
    381, 530, 404, 551, 569; Mann, Horace II
    and Lady Lucy, viii. 64, 77–8, 79, 82, 84,
    247, 251, 265, 281, 286, 305–6, 312, 331,
    337, 344, 346, 353, 356; Mann, James II,
    ix. 580; Pembroke, E. and Cts of, and
    family, ix. 493, 497n
Nicholls, Rev. Norton (ca 1742–1809):
  Florence visited by, vii. 397, 446
  Gray's friend, vii. 397, 442n
  HW knows and likes, vii. 403
  HW's letters might be brought back to
    him by, vii. 442
  Huntingdon accompanied by, to Florence,
    vii. 397
  Mann knows and likes, vii. 446
  —— never mentions, though HW expected
    them to be congenial, vii. 442
Nichols. See also Nicholls; Nicoll; Nicols
Nickson, Christiana (1732–88), m. (1751) John

Hely Hutchinson; cr. (1783) Bns Donogh-
    more, s.j.:
  peerage of, ix. 433
Nicoli. See Niccoli
Nicolina or Niccotina, Signora, actress:
  HW praises, iv. 410
Nicoll, Lady. See Blundell, Elizabeth (d.
    1743)
Nicoll, Margaret (ca 1735–68), m. (1753)
    James Brydges, styled M. of Carnarvon;
    3d D. of Chandos, 1771:
  affair of: breaks HW's relations with uncle,
    iv. 425; narrative of, might have been sent
    to Mann by Brand, iv. 435; narrative of,
    should stay unpublished, iv. 278; spoiled
    by lawyers and HW's uncle, iv. 273; un-
    known to Mann, iv. 431
  Chute tries to marry, to E. of Orford, iv.
    256–7, 262
  fortune of, iv. 238, 256, v. 285, viii. 301
  HW would have enriched nephew by
    marrying her to, v. 285
  marriage of, iv. 238n
  Orford, E. of, refuses to marry, iv. 257,
    265, viii. 301
  Walpole, Horace (1678–1757), keeps E. of
    Orford from marrying, vii. 367
  Whithed to have married, iv. 238, 256
Nicoll, Mary (d. 1765), m. Leake Okeover:
  niece ill-treated by, iv. 256
Nicoll, W., bookseller:
  prosecuted, vii. 29
Nicols, ——, under-sheriff of London;
  Ferrers attended by, v. 399
Niece. See Nice
Nieuport:
  communication with, re-opened, ii. 416
  France may use, as Dunkirk's substitute,
    v. 527
  Maria Theresa gives, to the French, v. 117
Night-cap; night-caps:
  Balmerinoch dons, for execution, iii. 302
  men wear, at Reggio fair, vi. 148
Night-gown:
  Gloucester, D. of, wears, when receiving
    Count Thurn, vii. 352
  long, HW wears, at Florence, i. 105
  Lorraine, Primate of, wears, i. 12, 17
  of gold brocade, Bootle wears, at breakfast,
    iv. 184
  Stanislas I's, catches on fire, vi. 402, 403
Nightingale, Elizabeth (d. 1755), m. (1754)
    Wilmot Vaughan, 4th Vct Lisburne, 1766:
  chaperon will be needed by, iv. 278
  Florence visited by, iv. 271
  Mann describes, iv. 271
  Methodism familiar to, iv. 271
  Rome to be visited by, iv. 278
Nightingale, Joseph Gascoigne (d. 1752):
  Florence visited by, iv. 271
  Rome to be visited by, iv. 278
Nightingale, Washington (d. 1754):
  Florence visited by, iv. 271
  Rome to be visited by, iv. 278

Nightingale:
HW has not yet heard, in May, vii. 213
Nigroni, Mme, Mme Grimaldi's sister; Genoese:
Grifoni, Mme, entertains, i. 151
Nigroni. *See also* Negroni
'Nikin.' *See* Bosville, Godfrey
Nimeguen:
Cuyp's view of, vii. 569
Nîmes:
Maison Carrée, Chute recommends, to HW, i. 121
Nineteenth century:
HW expects new era in, ix. 237
Nineveh:
London compared to, iv. 469, vii. 133
Ninnin, ——, French physician:
Wilkes's certificate signed by, vi. 198
'Niobe, St:'
Guido painting to eclipse, i. 162
See also under Reni, Guido
Niobe:
(?) Damer, Mrs, begins bust of, ix. 184
Leopold disperses group of, in Uffizi, ix. 170–1, 530–1
sculpture of family of: bad placing of, will be described to HW by Mrs Damer, ix. 203; HW suggests adorning, with rouge, ix. 178; spoiled by division, ix. 177–8
Nischandschi Mohammed Emin Pascha (ca 1723–69), Turkish Grand Vizir 1768–9:
sacrificed to mob, vii. 160
Nitre:
Bey's son makes gunpowder of, at Tunis, iv. 319
Nivernais, Duc de. *See* Mancini-Mazarini, Louis-Jules-Barbon (1716–98)
Nivernais, Duchesse de. *See* Brancas, Marie-Thérèse de (1716–82); Phélypeaux de Pontchartrain, Hélène-Angélique-Françoise (1715–82)
Nivernois. *See* Nivernais
Noah:
animals preserved and distinguished by, iv. 71
Noailles, Adrien-Maurice (1678–1766), Duc de; Maréchal de France:
Broglie joins, ii. 267
Louis XV accompanied by, to Valenciennes, ii. 441
Mémoires by, *see under* Millot, C.-F.-X.
not wounded, ii. 265
rashness of, ii. **224**
reported to be wounded at Dettingen, ii. 260, 265
Noailles, Adrienne-Catherine de (1741–1814), m. (1755) René-Mans de Froulay, Comte de Tessé:
HW has seen, in England, viii. 353
Pitt, Anne, recommends, to Mann, viii. 353
Noailles, Emmanuel-Marie-Louis (1743–1822),

Marquis de; French ambassador to England:
American-French treaty to be avowed by, to England, viii. 369
arrives in England, viii. 253
HW not consoled by appointment of, as ambassador to England, viii. 208
Thamas Kouli Can the subject of vain rescue efforts of, viii. 366
Weymouth told by, of American-French treaty, viii. 363–4
Noailles, Jean-Louis-François-Paul de (1739–1824), Comte d'Ayen; Duc d'Ayen, 1766; Duc de Noailles, 1793:
(?) HW mentions, vi. 239
Noailles, Philippe de (1715–94), Comte de Noailles; later Duc de Mouchy and Maréchal de France:
son of, vi. 341n
Noailles, Philippe-Louis-Marc-Antoine de (1752–1819), Prince de Poix:
marriage of, vi. 341n
Nobili:
second rank of Tuscan nobility, iv. 192
society of, plays acted by, in Florence, at smallest theatre, vi. 393
Nobility:
thinking is equal to a headache to, vi. 415
Noel, Mrs ——, near relation of Lady Lucy Mann:
HW informed by, of Horace Mann II's movements, ix. 201
HW often sees, at Twickenham Park, ix. **187, 312**
HW thinks, would have given him news of Horace Mann II, ix. 319
HW told by: about lover of Lucy Mann, ix. 423; of Horace Mann II's daughter's ruptured match, ix. 448
HW to write to, about Horace Mann II, ix. 208
knows nothing of Horace Mann II, ix. 319
Mann, Horace II, expected by, ix. 210
—— not seen by, ix. 187, 312
Mann, Lady Lucy, closely related to, ix. 187
Twickenham Park to be visited by, ix. 319
uneasy at not seeing Horace Mann II, ix. 208
Noel, Edward (1715–74), 6th Bt, 1733; 9th Bn Wentworth, 1745; cr. (1762) Vct Wentworth:
viscounty granted to, vi. 31
Noel, Henry (1743–98), 6th E. of Gainsborough, 1759:
Mann, Edward Louisa, to advise, to check brother-in-law's expenses, vi. 305
Noel, Mrs, in constant correspondence with family of, ix. 187
sister of, vi. 196, vii. 101n, viii. 6on
Noel, Mrs John-Perrot. *See* Amphlett, Margaret

Noel, Juliana (1672–1750), m. (1688) Charles Boyle, 2d E. of Burlington:
husband's gift to Mrs Bracegirdle referred by her to, ix. 74
Noel, Lady Lucy (d. 1778), m. (1765) Horace Mann II, Kt, 1772; 2d Bt, 1786:
Abano baths to be visited by, in hot months, viii. 108
Barcelona-Perpignan-Montpellier trip survived by, viii. 246–7
Barcelona visited by, viii. 239
body of: may reach Linton as husband carouses with electors, viii. 363, 381, 398; on board ship at Gibraltar, viii. 398
burletta attended by, at Florence, viii. 105
childbearing unlikely for, viii. 131, 257, 304, 331, 349, 353
children of, vii. 408
daughter absorbs attention of, viii. 97, 105
death of: viii. 356; HW gets Mann's announcement of, viii. 364; on shipboard, would make husband sail to Leghorn, viii. 238; reported in England, viii. 357
diet of, very small, viii. 322
family of, demands attention, viii. 60
Florentine visits of, viii. 60, 78, 79, 96–7, 115, 136, 145, 181, 247, 251, 275, 286, 289, 298, 312, 337
gay and lively, viii. 298
HW glad that Mann will entertain, viii. 71
HW hopes that son may be born to, viii. 144, 317
HW sorry that Mann is losing, viii. 342
HW to receive compliments of, viii. 313
health of: accounts of, hopeful, viii. 281; accounts of, very bad, viii. 206, 220, 222; allows her to associate with ladies and attend burletta, viii. 105; amusements prevented by, viii. 97; bad, viii. 73, 77; better, viii. 108, 115, 129, 131, 136, 140, 144, 260; better, according to husband but not to others, viii. 275; better than expected, viii. 251, 298; cold, viii. 145; cold weather's onset affects, viii. 337; consumption no longer the diagnosis for, viii. 214, 220; cough revealed by maid and child, viii. 346; dropsy in the breast, viii. 214, 220; feeble and languorous, viii. 330–1; fever, inflammation, and cough, viii. 190; Florentine air may improve, viii. 84, 101; Gloucester, Ds of, writes about, to HW, viii. 191; great amendment in, viii. 306; HW considers hopeful, since she has survived so long, viii. 242, 255; HW hopes, is not in danger, viii. 196, 205, 227; HW hopes that journey will benefit, viii. 250; HW pleased by Mann's account of, viii. 144, 261, 282, 300, 311, 317; heat impairs, more than cold, viii. 305; hectic fever and cough, viii. 199; husband despairs over, viii. 203, 353; husband thinks, has gained much at Nice, viii. 286; illness delays her departure for

Rome, viii. 146; improving but still weak, viii. 304; laudanum prescribed by physician of, to make her sleep, viii. 199; lungs may be affected, viii. 199; Mediterranean cruise recommended for, viii. 203; miscarries frequently, viii. 101; much out of order, viii. 346; much worse, viii. 265; Naples rehabilitates, viii. 181; neither better nor worse than when she left Naples, viii. 246; not worse, viii. 239; pleuritic inflammatory fever, viii. 188; Porto Ferrajo water does not improve, viii. 318, 322; Puzzuolo and Portici do not benefit, viii. 190, 203; sea voyage may not help, viii. 220, 233; tolerable and unaffected by heat, viii. 318; tolerably well, viii. 292, 344; Valdagno waters agree with, viii. 122–3; visible decay, viii. 353; winter at Naples may completely restore, viii. 136; worse, viii. 220
husband feels loss of, as guardian to his daughter, ix. 405
husband's conduct to, admired by HW, viii. 282
husband's devotion to, viii. 97
husband's political rashness condemned by, viii. 457
husband still mourns, though never mentioning her name, viii. 523
husband to bring, to dine with HW at SH, vii. 408
husband to overtake, at Marseille and take her to Nice, viii. 265
impatient to leave Nice for Florence, viii. 353
itinerary of: may have been upset by health and weather, viii. 225; on Mediterranean cruise, viii. 222, 225, 233, 239
Leghorn reached by, viii. 292
Malta visited by, viii. 233
Mann had better lodge, in Florence, viii. 60
—— lives with, on easy footing, viii. 146
—— not sorry to have known, viii. 369
—— pleased with, viii. 97, 155
—— prepares his house to receive, viii. 72
——'s liking for, should bring him to England, viii. 155
—— to be visited by: in spring, viii. 78, 79; until cold weather drives her to Nice, viii. 312
—— to disguise his unwillingness to entertain, viii. 68
—— urged to accompany, to Naples, viii. 129, 131–2
—— will be glad to see, viii. 32
Mann, Edward Louisa, to advise, to check husband's expenses, viii. 305
marriage of: vi. 300; planned, vi. 196
Marseille to be visited by, viii. 265
Mediterranean cruise of, viii. 203, 214, 220, 222, 225, 233, 239
Montpellier visited by, viii. 246–7
Montrose, Ds of, related to, viii. 463n

[Noel, Lady Lucy, *continued*]
Naples improves health of, viii. 181
Naples may have to be summer home of, viii. 188
Naples to be winter home of, viii. 115, 131, 136
Neapolitan dances and amusements shared by, viii. 181
Nice visited by, viii. 73, 77–8, 79, 82, 247, 251, 265, 281, 286, 305, 312, 331, 337, 344, 346, 353
Noel, Mrs, a near relation of, ix. 187
Portici visited by, viii. 203
pregnant, vii. 408
Puzzuolo visited by, viii. 190, 203
Rome visited by, viii. 129, 131, 140, 146, 181
Schio visited by, viii. 122
southern France visited by, viii. 60
Toulouse visited by, viii. 239, 251
Valdagno waters may benefit, viii. 115, 118, 122–3
Noel, Thomas (d. 1756); naval Capt.:
Edgcumbe sends, to Villefranche and Toulon to spy on French, iv. 536
Severn commanded by, iv. 27
Noel, Hon. William (1695–1762), M. P.:
named in Secret Committee lists, i. 385
Noia, Duca di. *See* Carafa, Pompeio
Nolle prosequi:
Kingston, Ds of, asks George III for, viii. 151, 162
Nomis, Marchesa. *See* Botnmar, Sofia Eleonora Dorotea
Nomis, Giorgio Luigi (1719–89), Abate, Cavaliere, and Marchese:
Franchini challenges, ii. **110**–11
Franchini, Agnese, jilted by, ii. 110
HW shocked by story of, ii. 136
Harrington asks Mann to help, ii. 110
Nonjuror:
Holdsworth is, iii. 139n
Nonsense:
Charles II's witticism about, vi. 57, viii. 52
HW likes both sense and, vi. 271
one, as good as another, vi. 73
Nonsuch, English ship:
involved in Mediterranean war, iii. 207, 235, 269
mule caravan turned back by, iii. 51
No One's Enemy But His Own. See under Murphy, Arthur
Norfolk, Ds of. *See* Blount, Mary
Norfolk, D. of. *See* Howard, Charles (1720–86); Howard, Charles (1746–1815); Howard, Edward (1686–1777)
Norfolk:
'barren land,' ii. 24
Bedingfield 'a most bigoted Papist' in, iv. 532
Davis lacks dialect of, iii. 348
HW compares, to Siberia, i. 495, ii. 68
HW prefers St James's Palace to, ii. 218

HW tired of hearing about, ii. 236, 237–8
HW to visit, i. 495, ii. 237, 496; *see also under* Houghton
heiress of, displays musical talents at Houghton, ii. 316–17
Hobart from, iii. 63
Leicester's son not to introduce a third heiress into, iii. 27
Leneve family ancient in, v. 353n
Militia Bill opposed by, v. 138
militia of: at Hull, ix. 355; at Portsmouth, v. 300; Windham lieutenant-colonel of, under E. of Orford, ix. 11n; Windham resigns from, because of trouble made by E. of Orford, ix. 11n
Orford, E. of, at inn on road to, vii. 460
Patapan a foreign curiosity to, ii. 299
periwigs thought in, to be fashionable, ii. 318
Walpole, Sir Robert, to retire to, ii. 458
Windham a gentleman of, viii. 521, 524
young gentleman of, lost at sea, v. 206
Norfolk, duchy of:
descent of, vi. 483–4, 485
Norfolk St, London:
Patch, James, lives in, vii. 276
Normandy:
English invasion skirts, v. 220
St Lazare said to be in, iii. 86–7
Normant, Le. *See* Le Normant
Normanton:
Heathcote may get peerage of, iv. 81
Norris, Harry (d. 1764), naval officer:
member of Byng court martial, v. 63, **64**
Norris, Sir John (ca 1670–1749), Kt, 1705; admiral; M.P.:
Admiralty disappointment of, makes him resign all positions, i. 364
Brest fleet escapes from, ii. 407
Brest fleet may be pursued by, ii. 400
Charles of Naples guards against, i. 145–6
Dunkirk transports to be burned by, ii. 402
fleet of, at Portsmouth, ii. 393
French fleet said to be defeated by, ii. 420
Mann inquires about, i. 194
men-of-war from Plymouth to join, ii. 393
nicknamed 'Foul-weather Jack,' ii. 423n
return to England requested by, ii. 423
sailors of, condemn ingratitude of Lisbon people, i. 456
Norris, Richard (fl. 1735–44); naval Capt.:
England may be visited by, to stand trial, iii. 55
Spanish galleys attacked by, i. **471**
tartans captured by, ii. 455
Norsa, Miss —— (sister of Hannah Norsa):
marriage of, expected, iii. 419
Norsa, Hannah (d. 1785):
father of, iii. 284
Jewess, ii. 249n
Orford's mistress, ii. **249**, iii. 284, 419
Rich intimate with, iii. 419

singer, ii. 249n
Walpole, Lady Maria, not to be contaminated by, ii. 249
Norsa, 'Isaachar':
HW sees, at trial of rebel lords, iii. 284–5
tavern-keeper, iii. 284
North, Hon. Brownlow (1741–1820), Bp of Lichfield 1771–4, of Worcester 1774–81, of Winchester 1781–1820:
brother gives Worcester bishopric to, viii. 63
North, Hon. Dorothy (d. 1698), m. 1 (1625) Richard Lennard, 13th Bn Dacre; m. 2 (1650) Chaloner Chute:
Germain, Lady Elizabeth, mentions, to Chute, iii. 372
North, Francis (1704–90), 7th Bn North, 1734; cr. (1752) E. of Guilford:
earldom for, iv. 203
George II notified by, of son's death, iv. 233
George III's governor, iv. 203, 246
pension of, may revert, to son, vi. 552, 561
son of, vi. 552n
North, Frederick (1732–92), styled Lord North; 2d E. of Guilford, 1790; prime minister:
Adam attacks, in speeches, viii. 537
administration of: Americans ill-disposed towards, viii. 143; Americans provoked not intimidated by, viii. 137; American treaty not arranged by, ix. 259; Camden may be dismissed by, vii. 168; cared for nothing but their own power, ix. 276; Cornwallis's defeat has not further weakened, in House of Commons, ix. 212; disgraced, extremely angry, ix. 264; dissolution of, announced by North, ix. 258; fall of, unexpected, ix. 263; foreigners wonder why military defeats have not overthrown, ix. 255, 268; four wars provoked by, all unsuccessful, viii. 490, ix. 267–8; HW does not expect immediate change in, ix. 251–2; HW sees no prospect of victories to improve situation of, ix. 244, 255; has majority in Ireland, vii. 530; Ireland mismanaged by, ix. 267; Keppel refuses to serve under, viii. 449; Lord Mayor's committal offered by, ix. 290–1; Minorca's danger blamed upon, viii. 468; Murray's letters to, sent by Mann to England, ix. 233; must fall, ix. 19; no longer gives up America as lost, viii. 348; Opposition honester but not abler than, viii. 448; Opposition will blame St Eustatius's loss on, ix. 236; Parliament grants requests of, viii. 142; peace not sought by, though they bungled war, ix. 276; reported victory strengthens position of, ix. 253; Richmond, D. of, defeats, over India House, vii. 546; Rigby, Thurlow, and Weymouth might wreck, to satisfy Opposition, viii. 447; sinking, ix. 244; Spanish war not blamed upon, viii. 492; split by

faction, ix. 259; unashamed though all at variance, ix. 218; waste and negligence of, ix. 267
Banbury's representative, viii. 187
Barré attacks, in speech, vii. 186
brother given Worcester bishopric by, viii. 63
Cabinet Council's authorization to order magistrates to keep peace forgotten by, ix. 53
Chancellor cannot be made by, vii. 268
East India Company defeats, at India House, in bargain, ix. 18
flippancies of, severely handled by successors, ix. 285
Fox, C.J., attacks, in House of Commons, viii. 139
—— begins coalition with, ix. 369
—— dismissed for disrespect to, vii. 557
—— unites with, to defeat Shelburne, ix. 369–70, 372, 377, 379
Garter to be conferred upon, vii. 391, 415
George III acts revengefully towards, ix. 488
George III and D. of Portland differ from, about cabinet post, ix. 379
George III asks for seals of, as secretary of state, ix. 460
(?) —— does not easily stomach, as minister, ix. 418n
—— not treated by, with great gratitude, ix. 381
—— orders, to form new administration headed by D. of Portland, ix. 379–80, 387
—— tells D. of Portland through, that his arrangement is accepted, ix. 390–1
—— tries to detach, from alliance with C.J. Fox, ix. 378
(?) George IV's establishment urged by, ix. 418n
Gordon rioters told by, that religious laws would be considered, ix. 54
Gower's defeat of militia bill resented by, viii. 497
HW considers, a dexterous politician but fatal minister and selfish man, ix. 381
HW credits, with good answer to London's remonstrance, vii. 197
HW does not read of reception of, at Oxford, vii. 497
HW forwards Mann's letter to, viii. 268
HW hopes, will not retire, vii. 490
HW praises, vii. 186, 197, 199, 217, ix. 275
HW submits question of Mann's place in Customs House to, viii. 177–8
health of, fever, ix. 97
highwayman wounds postilion of, viii. 47
House of Commons tears Shelburne and, from power, in one year, ix. 402n
House of Commons told by, about government loan, viii. 448
ingratitude of, ix. 218

[North, Frederick, continued]

lacking in temper, feeling, activity, and good breeding, ix. 275

Luttrell accuses, of buying a borough, ix. 29

Mann grateful to, for letting Suckling be deputy in his place, viii. 184

——'s correspondence with, over Tortola grant, viii. 264, 281

mob assaults house of, vii. 305

mob attacks, and tears his chariot to pieces, vii. 291

most popular man in England, ix. 381

Norton accuses, in Parliament, of breach of promise, ix. 27

Opposition defeats, in Parliament, vii. 461–2

Parliamentary majority of, ix. 466

Parliamentary speech of: cool after escape from mob, vii. 290; praised by HW, vii. 186; prudent, vii. 248

Parliamentary support of, unsure, ix. 379

Parliamentary victory of: over disenfranchisement of revenue officers, ix. 37–8; over St Vincent, vii. 462

peace terms of, for America, viii. 348, 354, 358–9

pension reversion not given to, vi. 552, 561

Pitt, Thomas, denounces, for England's decline, ix. 35

Portland, D. of, proposed by, as first lord of the Treasury, ix. 377, 379

—— resigns Treasury post immediately on dismissal of, ix. 460n

prime minister, vii. 182

refuses to become prime minister again, ix. 372

regulating bill for East India Co. promoted by, vii. 490

resignation of, expected, ix. 256

reversion of father's pension accepted by, vi. 552

Royal Marriage Bill disliked but supported by, vii. 390

rumoured attempt to terrify, from keeping office, viii. 533–4

second reading of Burke's bill of reformation deferred by, ix. 20

secretary of state, vi. 552, ix. 391, 460

sensible and moderate, offending nobody, vii. 217

taxes to be laid by, before House of Commons, ix. 254

temper and prudence of, prevail over rash counsel, vii. 199, 203

Thurlow's dismissal demanded by, ix. 381

Tories may regret following, against Shelburne, ix. 379

windows of, broken by mob, viii. 442

wit and good humour of, ix. 275

witticism by, on cuckolds, ix. 246

Northampton, Cts of. See Somerset, Lady Anne (1741–63)

Northampton, E. of. See Compton, Charles (1737–63); Compton, Hon. George (1692–1758); Compton, James (1687–1754); Compton, Spencer (1738–96); Howard, Henry (1540–1614)

Northamptonshire:

Bedfordshire clashes with, over Turnpike Bill, iv. 112

Powys is M.P. for, ix. 475n

Spencer disappointed by moderate petition from, ix. 10

'North and Grey, Miss.' See Scotland

North Berwick:

Bury lands at, iii. 247

North Briton. See under Wilkes, John

North Carolina. See under Carolina

Northey, William (ca 1721–70), M.P.:

George III appoints, to Bedchamber, v. 460

Parliamentary debate by, on Scotch Bill, x. 32

Tory, v. 460

'North Indies':

England may become, v. 306

Northington, E. of. See Henley, Robert (1747–86)

Northumberland, Cts of. See Seymour, Lady Elizabeth (1716–76)

Northumberland, Ds of. See Burrell, Frances Julia (1752–1822); Seymour, Lady Elizabeth (1716–76)

Northumberland, D. of. See Dudley, Sir Robert (1573–1649); Percy, Hugh (1742–1817); Smithson, Sir Hugh (1715–86)

Northumberland, E. of. See Smithson, Sir Hugh (1715–86)

Northumberland:

colliers at, fight militia at Hexham, v. 491

Grafton, Ds of, visits father in, vi. 80

Northumberland, earldom of:

descent of, iv. 81

Somerset, D. of, wants Sir Charles Wyndham to have, iv. 12

Northumberland House, in the Strand:

gallery at: HW sees, by candlelight, v. 88; Northumberland, D. of, gets paintings copied for, iv. 507n; Northumberland, D. of, sends drawing of, to Mann, v. 209

Northumberlands build at, iv. 341

'Northumberland rout':

Mann's assembly compared to, by Vcts Spencer, vi. 180

Norton, Sir Fletcher (1716–89), Kt, 1762; cr. (1782) Bn Grantley; politician and lawyer, M.P.:

attorney-general, vi. 209, 227

Clarke to be succeeded by, as Master of the Rolls, vi. 263

complains that he was dismissed without notice, ix. 95

dismissed, as attorney-general, vi. 323

George III orders, to prosecute d'Éon, vi. 227

HW describes, vii. 176

Horne Tooke accused of attacking, vii. 555

House of Commons passes vote of thanks to, ix. 100

illness of, adjourns House of Commons, ix. 18, 38, 40–1

imprudence of, weakens Opposition, ix. 28

Keppel answers oration by, in House of Commons, viii. 445

lord chancellor's post not desired by, vii. 179–80

mercenaries will support, in Parliament, ix. 27

ministry's champion, vi. 209

mob breaks windows of, vii. 305

North accused by, in Parliament, of breach of promise, ix. 27

peerage obtained by, vi. 263n, ix. 264

resignation said to be contemplated by, ix. 38

solicitor-general, vi. **189**

Speaker of House of Commons, vi. 263n, vii. 176, 179, 305

tooth of, pulled, ix. 40

to return to House of Commons, ix. 41

treachery of, vi. 283

Wilkes's authorship of North Briton not proved by, vi. 189

Wilkes writes refusal to, vii. 281

Yorke's promotion opposed by, vii. 176

Norton, Richard (d. 1732):
estate of, left by Whithed to Thistlethwayte, iv. 238

will of, set aside for insanity, iv. 237n

Norway:
Caroline Matilda may be sent to, vii. 387

Norwich, Bp of. See Hayter, Thomas (1702–62)

Norwich, E. of. See Goring, George (1585–1663)

Norwich, Norfolk:
Beevor summoned from, to Eriswell, viii. 293, 294

election expense at, v. 56

French may be rumoured to occupy, v. 326

geese and turkeys to race from, to London, v. 7

Windham M.P. for, viii. 524n, ix. 579

Nose:
blowing of, considered disrespectful to D. of Cumberland, iii. 464

Curzon's, drips, iv. 12

Gondi, Mme, loses, ii. 87

Nose-bleed:
occurrences of, viii. 145

Nosegays:
macaronies', vii. 467

of holly and ivy for Christmas, ix. 639

Notary public:
at Rome, x. 5

Florentine: declaration by, ix. 120; Mann,

Horace II, derided by, for drawing up deed for servants' benefit, ix. 670

Kingston, Ds of, must execute order attested by, to have furniture and jewels released from Rome, viii. 83–4

'Notte, La.' See under Allegri, Antonio

Nottingham, English ship:
French ships pursued by, iii. 411

Nottingham ale. See under Ale

Nottinghamshire:
Belle-Isle may be sent to, like Tallard, ii. 563, iii. 18

Nourmanzor, Sultan:
Persian tale about, vii. 152

Nourse, (?) Charles (d. 1741):
suicide of, after Windsor refuses to duel with him for slandering Shuttleworth, i. 248

'Nousvoullone':
Florentine name for nobles raised by Francis I, vi. 351, 360n

HW's philosophy of indifference would be good for, vi. 360

Maria Louisa insulted by small attendance at her reception for, vi. 357, 467

——'s birthday to be celebrated by, vi. 371

Nouvelle Héloïse, La. See under Rousseau, Jean-Jacques

Nova Progenies. See Williams, Sir Charles Hanbury: New Ode

Nova Scotia:
Brest fleet probably goes to, iv. 538

Cornwallis governor of, iii. 177n

Halifax to colonize, under Cornwallis, iv. 40–1

Novati, Marchese (d. 1748), army officer:
capture or death of, rumoured, ii. 489

Florence visited by, ii. **514**

Perknlö assisted by, iii. 271

Novellara, Ricciarda di. See Gonzaga, Ricciarda

Novellara:
Francis III may give duchy of, to daughter, iii. 335

Novelle letterarie. See under Lami

Novena:
opera promoters dread, ii. 295

Novgorod, Abp of. See Sechenov, Daniil Andreievich

Novi, governor of. See Lomellini, Bortolommeo

Novi:
Botta approaches, iii. 297

French retire near, iii. 231

Gages tries to pass by, iii. 58

joint Spanish armies to cross Genoese state at, iii. 36

Lomellini denies entrance to, to Austrians, iii. 67

Maillebois near, iii. 237

Schulenburg occupies, before the Genoese do, iii. 58

Novogorod. See Novgorod

Nuestra Señora del Cabadonga; Spanish ship:
Anson takes, to Portsmouth, ii. 463
HW needs to capture, to defray expenses,
v. 561
Nugent, Cts. *See* Drax, Elizabeth
Nugent, Lady Louisa (ca 1757–1841), m.
(1784) Eliab Harvey, K.C.B., 1815:
father disowns, viii. 418, 422n
Florence visited by, viii. 417–18
Nugent calls, 'Chance,' viii. 417
Nugent, Lady Mary Elizabeth (d. 1812), m.
(1775) George Grenville (later Nugent-
Temple-Grenville), 2d E. Temple, 1779;
cr. (1784) M. of Buckingham; she was cr.
(1800) Bns Nugent, s.j.:
Temple marries, viii. 422n
Nugent, Robert (1709–88), cr. (1767) Vct
Clare, (1776) E. Nugent; M. P.:
'bashful,' i. 254
Berkeley, Cts of, jokes about, with Lucan,
viii. 418
bill against clandestine marriages opposed
by, iv. 383
bishops accused by, in Parliament, i. 431
Cobham's wager with, about spitting in
Hervey's hat, iv. 123–4, x. 29–30
converted Irish Catholic, i. 255, 431
daughters of, by Cts of Berkeley, viii. 422n
faction of P. of Wales led by, iv. 32
first lord of trade, vi. 473
HW coins 'nugentize' from fortune-hunt-
ing marriages of, ii. 481
HW mentions, ii. 374
HW quotes, on 'jurisdictions,' iii. 396
'indifferent speaker' in Parliament, i. 431
Leveson-Gower insults, at masquerade, iv.
124
Mann compares, with town bull, i. 322
Mountjoy, Lady, pays, i. 271
—— said to be wife of, i. 271n
Nugent, Lady Louisa, called 'Chance' by,
viii. 417
Parliamentary speeches by: on privately-
raised regiments, x. 13, 17; repeated to
wife on road, i. 271
Parliamentary vote by, on privately-raised
regiments, x. 19
Pelham, Lady Catherine, talks to, at
masquerade, iv. 124
Pelham's 'humble servant,' iv. 32
Pitt and Fox opposed by, iv. 454
poet, Patriot, author, and lord of the
Treasury, i. 254n
Sandwich attacked by, in Parliament, iv.
124
sick in the night, i. 271
Townshend, Vcts, jokes about gray muff
and ugly wife of, i. 165
Treasury post given to, i. 254n, v. 24
Walpole, Sir Robert, refuses to hear
charge of bigamy against, i. 271n
wife of, 'old she-goat,' i. 271
wife parts from, viii. 451n

wife tells Chesterfield to urge, to speak
in Parliament, i. 254–5
wit attributed to, i. 271
Nugent, Mrs Robert. *See* Craggs, Anna
Numero Due, Russian war ship:
dismasted, vii. 202
Nun; nuns:
confirmation of, attended by Mann, ii. 45
disguised to visit bagnios, iv. 464
elopement of, from Venice, i. 86
Ferdinando, P., gets picture from, i. 199
Finch, Lady Isabella, wears costume of, i.
495
Louis XV influenced by, vii. 414
Mann does not think Joseph II should
turn, out of nunneries, ix. 239
—— thinks, should be allowed to die off,
and not become burden to society, ix. 239
return of, to families, would cause derangement because of disposal of fortunes,
ix. 239
Saliciennes' convent to be staffed by, iv.
333–4
Nunciata. *See* Annunziata
Nunciature:
Venetians shut up, iv. 173
Nuncio; nuncios:
at Brussels, *see* Crivelli, Ignazio Michele
(1698–1768); Molinari, Giovanni Carlo (ca
1717–63); Tempi, Luca Melchior (1688–
1762)
at Cologne, *see* Crivelli, Ignazio Michele
(1698–1768); Tempi, Luca Melchior (1688–
1762)
at Florence, *see* Archinto, Alberigo (1698–
1758); Biglia, Antonio (ca 1708–55); Borromeo, Vitaliano (1720–93); Crivelli, Carlo
(1736–1818); Manciforte Sperelli, Giovanni
Ottavio (1730–81); Onorati, Bernardino (fl.
1759–67)
at Frankfort, *see* Doria, Giorgio (1708–59);
Stoppani, Giovanni Francesco (1695–1775)
at Henry VII's marriage, *see* Pasarella,
Jacopo (d. 1495)
at Lisbon, *see* Acciaioli, Filippo (1700–
66); Tempi, Luca Melchior (1688–1762)
at Paris, *see* Crescenzi, Marcello (1694–
1768); Durini, Carlo Francesco (1693–
1769); Giraud, Bernardino (1721–82)
at Venice, *see* Caracciolo, Martino Innico
(d. 1754)
at Vienna, *see* Crivelli, Ignazio Michele
(1698–1768); Paolucci, Camillo (1692–1763)
at Warsaw: Brühl's son excluded as, vi.
192; *see also* Durini, Angelo Maria (1725–
96)
Clement XIII notifies, of quarrel with
Genoa, v. 405, 411
Pallavicini formerly was, at Spain and
Naples, vii. 118
shifting of, ii. 288
Nuneham, Vct. *See* Harcourt, George Simon
(1736–1809)

Nuneham Courtenay, Oxon:
HW to visit, ix. 428
Harcourt dies at, viii. 328
——'s seat in Oxfordshire, ix. 428n
Nunnery. *See* Convent
Nunziata. *See* Annunziata
Nuremberg:
Aulic Council issues decree against, for
Prussian recruiting, v. 29
Frederick II's troops approach, v. 102
Holdernesse intercepted near, by hussars,
ii. 517
Mathews waits at, for passports, ii. 517
Nurse:
godparent might give money to, at child's
christening, viii. 199
Louis XV's, ii. 544
Pope's, *see* Beach, Mary
Nursery:
two-coloured brocatelle suitable for furni-
ture of, v. 468
Nuthall, Thomas (d. 1775), lawyer:
treachery of, iv. 273
Nutini, Florentine silk merchant:
bankruptcy of, i. 62
Nutmeg:
Holland to bewail loss of Ceylon monopoly
of, ix. 283
Nuvulloni. *See* Nousvoullone
'Nykin.' *See* Bosville, Godfrey
Nymph; nymphs:
Lyttelton retires with, to Epsom, viii. 537
Nymphenburg, Treaty of:
rumoured, i. 182–3

Oakhampton. *See* Okehampton
Oaks:
Northington's, cut down, vii. 368
Oaks, The, Epsom; Stanley's seat:
Stanley, Bn, to entertain fiancée at, viii. 14
Oakum:
sailor mends wooden leg with, viii. 283–4
Oat; oats:
HW tired of talk about, at Houghton, vii.
122
ship brings, to Fiumicino and Nettuno, ii.
453
Oaths:
Ciudadela magistrates give, on surrender,
iv. 552
Russian troops take, upon their sabres, v.
255
Oberg, Christian Ludwig von (1689–1778),
Hanoverian Maj.-Gen.:
Soubise defeats, v. 251
Obernam, Capt.; Austrian officer:
Lobkowitz sends, to Mann, ii. 484
O'Birne:
Harvey gambles with, at the *Cocoa Tree*,
ix. 12
Irish gamester, ix. 12

Oblivion:
HW to anticipate, ix. 542
Obreskov, Alexei Mikhailovich (1719–87),
Russian minister to Turkey 1751–68:
release of, vii. 308
O'Brien, Daniel (1683–1759), cr. (1726) Bn
Castle Lyons, (1746) E. of Lismore (Jaco-
bite peerage):
France honours, iv. 27
Old Pretender dismisses, at son's request,
iv. 45
wife of, banished, iv. 27–8, 45
O'Brien, Henry (1688–1741), 7th E. of
Thomond:
wife's nephew inherits estate of, iv. 24n
O'Brien, Margaret Josepha (living, 1763), m.
(1735) Daniel O'Brien, cr. (1726) Bn Castle
Lyons, (1746) E. of Lismore:
banished from Paris, iv. 27–8, 45
Tencin's secrets disclosed by, to Spain, iv.
28
O'Brien, Lady Susan. *See* Fox-Strangways,
Lady Susan (1743–1827)
O'Brien, William (ca. 1700–1777), 4th E. of
Inchiquin, 1719; M.P.:
Frederick, P. of Wales, appoints, ii. 551
O'Brien, William (d. 1815), actor and play-
wright:
marriage of, vi. 219
O'Brien. *See also* Wyndham-O'Brien
O'Brien de Clare, Laure (ca 1696–1781), m.
(1720) Claude-Charles le Tonnelier, Comte
de Breteuil:
son of, vi. 385
*Observations on a Pamphlet entitled Thoughts
on the Cause of the Present Discontents.
See under* Sawbridge, Catherine
Observations on Civil Liberty. See under
Price, Richard
*Observations on the Diseases of the Army.
See under,* Pringle, Sir John
Occhiali, Gaspar. *See* Wittel, Gaspar Adriaensz
van
Ocean:
HW calls, England's 'capital,' ix. 277
See also Sea
'Octavia and Cleopatra':
meeting of, iv. 201
Octavius, P. (1779–83):
birth of, viii. 454
death of: ix. 403; has not checked inocu-
lation in England, ix. 413, 420, 422; not
imputed to inoculation since he recovered
from smallpox, ix. 413
Leyden gazette attributes death of, to
inoculation, ix. 405–6, 412n
parents devoted to, ix. 403
Octavius Cæsar. *See* Augustus
Oculist. *See* Ilmer (b. ca 1720); Taylor, John
(1703–72)
Ode; odes:
English poets pour forth, ix. 612
in *Arno Miscellany*, ix. 507

[Ode; odes, *continued*]

West's, on Q. Caroline, i. 468n

Williams's: mentions Finches, v. 345n; to Pulteney, ii. 73–5, 90–1, 319–21, 334

Ode on a Distant Prospect of Eton College. *See under* Gray, Thomas

Oder river:

Frederick II said to be driven across, v. 241

Russians may cross, v. 308

Odes. See under Gray, Thomas

Odescalchi, Livio (1725–1805), Duca di Bracciano:

Gloucester, D. of, entertained by, at Rome, vii. 388–9

Ode . . . to the Earl of Bath, An. See under Williams, Sir Charles Hanbury

Odiarne, Wentworth (d. 1762), serjeant at arms to House of Commons:

Lever committed to, i. 251, 272–3

Murray in custody of, iv. 249

Paxton committed to, i. 397

O'Donell, Charles, Lt:

captured at Velletri, ii. 492

O'Donell, Joseph, Ensign:

captured at Velletri, ii. 492

O'Donell. *See also* O'Donnell; Oionell

Odongir, ——, volunteer:

captured at Velletri, ii. 493

O'Donnell, Mrs ——:

Frenchwoman, married to Irish officer, ix. 536

Stuart, Charlotte, accompanied by, to Florence, ix. 522, 536

O'Donnell, Colombe-Hycinthe (ca 1725–89), Chevalier; Comte; Irish officer in French service:

(?) wife of, ix. 536

O'Donnell. *See also* O'Donell; Oionell

O'Dunne, Comte. *See* Dunn, James

O'Dunne, Comtesse. *See* Parsons, Sarah

Odysseus. *See* Ulysses

Œdipus. See under Dryden, John

Œiras, Conde de. *See* Carvalho e Mello, Sebastião-José de (1699–1782)

Œuvres du philosophe de Sans-Souci:

Frederick II disowns, v. 413

Muzell promises to get copy of, for Mann, v. 413

See also under Frederick II

Œyras. *See* Œiras

'Office of the Madonna.' *See under* Pergolesi, Giovanni Battista

Officer; officers:

ball given by, in honour of Francis I's election, iii. 115

belts of, ii. 261

Dutch, may lead German-Swiss regiment in America, iv. 531

English army: Dettingen casualties of, ii. 258–61; dismissal of, for Parliamentary conduct, vi. 274; Edgcumbe brings, to Florence, iv. 536; from Minorca, report its

fall, ix. 269; in Flanders, Olimphant's alleged letter to, iii. 170; Lincoln's insult from, i. 411–12; of privately raised regiments, iii. 158, x. 14–19; on way to Flanders, i. 410, ii. 179; Parliament examines list of, at Port Mahon, i. 300; pretend zeal for active service, i. 410; Vernon hated by, ii. 251

English half-pay: attentive to HW, i. 270–1; Maclaine quarrels with, iv. 169

English militia, cannot be major-generals, viii. 372

English naval: bribed to let artillery pass, iii. 147; conduct of, greatly criticized, v. 69; court martial for, iii. 33; recalled from Mediterranean for examination, iii. 12; Vernon revered by, ii. 151

Florentine, horses bought by, at low prices, v. 179

Florentine gendarme: offers to fight San Vitali, ii. 368; sbirri at odds with, i. 225

Forrester's, ii. 107

France sends: to America, viii. 309; to Poland, vii. 338

Franchini driven into retirement by, ii. 111

Francis I's, said to debauch Spanish deserters, i. 349

French: captured by Murray, ix. 207; French losses at Assietta admitted by, iii. 427; Genoese orchestra composed of, iii. 505; HW may send watch to Mann through, v. 306; in Corsica, vii. 37, 124; may have to rejoin regiments, viii. 357; prevent paper on Louis XV, vii. 231; punishment of, for undivulged crime, v. 382; said to arouse Irish unrest, vi. 24; shoot holes in hats to show off at balls, iv. 159; wounded or killed at Dettingen, ii. 258, 261

German, will not serve with Vane unless he fights duel, i. 486

Hessian, challenges Hampshire justice to duel, iv. 563

Irish: Craon, Princesse de, accompanied by, vi. 536; in French service, vii. 402; in French service, brings news of French mobilization, viii. 357

Lorraine, *see under* Lorraine

of Swiss Guards, i. 236

Östergötland's, delivers HW's letter to Ds of Gloucester, viii. 247

Piedmont, in Reggio, i. 46

Portuguese, prosecuted for not paying taxes, vii. 166

Prussian: Berlin approached by, with message, v. 242; Berrue talks with, i. 206

Russian: Chernyshev recommends, to Mann, ix. 84; Orlov promotes, viii. 84; Orlov receives dispatches through, vii. 444; Orlov's, sail from Kronstadt, vii. 222; reaches Florence from Leghorn, vii. 235; tells Mann about arrival of Houghton collection, ix. 2; Spiridorf's, Orlov notified by, vii. 162

Spanish: at Bologna, ii. 154; bring horses to Orbetello, i. 214; deposit effects in banks and convents, i. 427; letters from, to Prato and Pistoia, i. 238; Montemar's mismanagement enrages, i. 262; Philip V notifies, of Montemar's dismissal, ii. 59

Offley, (?) John (ca 1717–84), M.P.:
mob knocks down, iv. 156

Of the Use and Abuse of Parliaments. See under Ralph, James

Ogden, James (d. 1781):
Clinton's messenger, captured by Americans, ix. 135

Ogilvie, David (1725–1803), styled Bn Ogilvie 1731–83; titular E. of Airlie, 1761:
capture of, rumoured, iii. 254
death of, rumoured, iii. 248

Ogilvy, Alexander (1718–46), 6th Bn Banff, 1738; Capt.:
Spanish register ship captured by, i. 377

Ogilvy, James (ca 1714–70), styled Lord Deskford, 1730; 6th E. of Findlater, 1764:
Albani called on by HW and, at Conclave door, i. 9
HW and Coke claimed by, as friends, i. 371
HW congratulated by, i. 320
HW gives Mann's packet to, i. 24
HW receives letter for, i. 26
HW's and Mann's old acquaintance, vii. 312
letter from, containing equivocal observations, i. 371
Santo Buono talks with, about Porto Bello, i. 7
son of, vii. 312

Ogilvy, James (1750–1811), styled Lord Deskford 1764–70; 7th E. of Findlater, 1770:
Bute's daughter to marry, vii. 312

Ogle, Cts of. *See* Percy, Lady Elizabeth (ca 1667–1722)

Ogle, Miss [?Catherine (d. 1790)]:
Damer, Mrs, teaches, ix. 577
models, ix. 577

Ogle, Sir Chaloner (ca 1680–1750), Kt, 1723; naval officer; M.P.:
American news comes from, i. 35
Frye prosecutes, iii. 328
Santiago attack advised by, i. 175

Oglethorpe, James Edward (1696–1785), Gen.; founder of Georgia:
fox-hunters converted by, into hussars, iii. 127
hussars to be commanded by, ii. 409
Methodists follow, to Georgia, iv. 41
neighbour challenged by, for trespassing, ix. 570
rebels pursued by, iii. 185–6
teeth of, gone, ix. 570
trial of, for cowardice, iii. 320–1
vigour of, at '95,' ix. 570

O'Hara, Charles (ca 1740–1802), Gen.:
father of, ii. 104n

O'Hara, Eugene, Ensign:
captured at Velletri, ii. 492

O'Hara, James (1690–1773), 2d Bn Tyrawley, 1724; diplomatist:
comment by, on fog, whist, and House of Commons, ii. 148
comments of, on Grantham and Pulteney, ii. **104**
English troops in Portugal to be commanded by, vi. 43
HW might ask, about Correggio painting, ii. 373
Jefferies not told by, of succour intended for St Philip's, v. 3
Lippe-Bückeburg's appointment sends, home in disgust, vi. 48
Lisbon post to go to, vi. 7
mission of, to Gibraltar, to punish Fowke and Stuart, iv. 562
Pope mentions seraglio of, ii. 104n
Portugal the residence of, for 15 years, ii. 148
Portuguese forces said to be commanded by, vi. 34
returns from Portugal, with scorn for 'war' there, vi. 70
Spanish post might go to, v. 166
wigs of, from Paris, v. 191
witticism by, to HW, on Col. Caesar and Margaret Woffington, v. 157
wives and children brought to England by, from Portugal, ii. 104

O'Hara, James (d. 1769), Capt.:
father of, ii. 104n

Ohio River:
England can compensate Frederick II with lands on, v. 326
HW would prefer SH to lands on, v. 306
Hillsborough opposes plan for settlements on, vii. 424
Parliamentary campaign eclipses events on, iv. 455
Popple's map omits, iv. 497

Oil:
Del Montes steal, iv. 428
England could have grown olives for, in hot summer, viii. 407
Florentine: cost of, in London, i. 240; Mazzei to sell, in England, v. 495
Genoese have, iii. 352
Lucca gives, to D. of York, vi. 221

Oilcloth:
picture on, advertises sights, iv. 40

Oilskin:
bootikins made of, vii. 464, viii. 494
HW's letters wrapped in, iv. 23

Ointment; ointments:
for wounds, i. 97
maids leave, at Mann's house, i. 395
of sulphur and hellebore, vii. 460

Oionell, Jean, Ensign:
captured at Velletri, ii. 492

Oiseau, L', French ship:
English ships pursue, v. 303
Glasgow's engagement with, v. 292
in Mediterranean, v. 249
Sardinian port sought by, v. 292
Okehampton, Devon, borough:
Lyttelton not elected at, iv. 39
—— steals, from Thomas Pitt, iv. 39
O'Kelly, (?) William (d. 1767), Freiherr;
Irish officer in Austrian service:
(?) gone into the country, i. **67**
Mill's substitute for English trip from
Vienna, iii. 454
Niccolini probably accused by, iv. 2
secret projects of, in England, iv. 2
O'Kelly, (?) Mrs William:
(?) gone into the country, i. 67
Okeover, Mrs. *See* Nicoll, Mary
Okeover, Leake (1701–63):
Fleet Prison confinement of, iv. 257
Nicoll, Margaret, maintained by, iv. 256–7
Old age. *See* Age, old; Youth and old age
Old Bailey, the:
Derwentwater to be tried at, iii. 180–1
felons at, deny their crimes, vii. 195
Rudd, Mrs, tried at, viii. 153
streetwalkers at, known under aliases, vii.
520
Theodore of Corsica visits, v. 45
trial at, for counterfeiting, iii. 242
Old Coachman, The. See under Williams,
Sir Charles Hanbury
Old England:
Mann receives issues of, ii. 411
readers of, condemn Londoners' lack of
modesty, ii. 316
Oldfield, Anne (1683–1730), actress:
chair conveys, from theatre, i. **435**
Cibber's expression on, in preface to *Pro-
voked Husband,* vii. 132n
granddaughter of, ii. 481
older generation can talk of, vii. 351
'Old Man of the Mountain':
Mann must think HW is, ix. 540
Old Palace. *See* Palazzo Vecchio
'Old Palace, gentleman of.' *See* Nay, Em-
manuel de, Comte de Richecourt
Old people:
HW calls, censors of modes, ix. 641
HW's reflections on, ix. 298, 308, 332
See also under Woman
Old Sir Simon the King:
tune of, i. 292
Old Woman's Will of Ratcliffe Highway:
Montagu binds, with mother-in-law's will,
ii. 566
Olimphant, Col. [?Laurence Oliphant (ca
1692–1767) of Gask; cr. (1760) Lord Oli-
phant (Jacobite)]:
alleged letter from, to officer in Flanders,
iii. 170
Olimpiade, The, opera. *See under* Metas-
tasio, Pietro; Pergolesi, Giovanni Battista;
Traetta, Tommaso

Oliver, Richard (1735–84), alderman; M.P.:
at liberty when Parliament is prorogued,
vii. 303
House of Commons sentences, to the
Tower, vii. 288
House of Commons to examine, vii. 283
printer released by, vii. **280**
Oliver, William (1695–1764), physician:
(?) Granville, Cts, attended by, iii. 133
Oliver Cromwell. See under Crébillon,
Prosper Jolyot de
Olive trees:
Spaniards cut down, ii. 344
Tuscan, warriors hang their arms on, vii.
159
Olivier, Francis, courier:
letters between London and Florence
carried by, ix. 196, 197, 198
returns to Florence, ix. 208
Olmutz:
Frederick II besieges, v. 204
—— forced to raise siege of, v. 224
—— leaves, v. 237
——'s outposts approached, vi. 63
—— wastes time at, v. 225
Olympiade. See Olimpiade
O'Mahony. *See* Mahony
Omai:
Conway breakfasts with, viii. 175
ice called 'stone-water' by, viii. 175
learns to skate, viii. 175
native of Otaheite, viii. 175
Ombre:
Craon, Princesse de, addicted to, ii. 101
foreign ministers play, at Tuscan Court,
with Maria Louisa and Archduchess of
Milan, ix. 51
Mann hopes to have honour of playing,
with Maria Louisa, ix. 301
played, i. 416
Omelet:
Cori eats, on Friday, i. 254
Omiah. *See* Omai
Omoa, Honduras:
capture of, viii. 543
'Omphale':
HW's name for Cts of Orford, iv. 439
O'Neal, Mrs. *See* Cameron, Jeanie
Oneglia:
Spaniards occupy, ii. 454, 559
Spaniards retire from, ii. 461
'O'Neil, King':
title of, to Irish throne, v. 371
Oneille. *See* Oneglia
Onel, Capt. Felix:
captured at Velletri, ii. 492
Onesti. *See* Braschi Onesti
Oniglia. *See* Oneglia
Onions:
Orford, E. of, distributes, to militia, ix. 11
—— fond of, ix. 11
Onorati, Bernardino; titular Abp of Sida;
nuncio at Florence 1759–66; at Venice,
1767:

Botta takes precedence of, vi. **44**
Leopold's relations with, vi. 319
Mann debates with, over Young Pretender, vi. 384
Mann preceded only by, vi. 349
Mann to thank, for attentions to, D. of York, vi. 179
told to give D. of York invitation to Rome, vi. 171
Onslow, Arthur (1691–1768), speaker of the House of Commons 1728–61; M.P.:
Barnard humiliated by, over trade bills, iv. 135
bill against clandestine marriages opposed by, iv. 383
Byng's expulsion from House of Commons demanded by, v. 63
chair of, ii. 191
Clutterbuck might succeed, i. 391n
Coke's retort to, about Taaffe and Wortley Montagu belonging to Parliament and not to White's, iv. 289
death of, painful, vii. 585
German treaties opposed by, iv. 501
Grenville, George, said to succeed, as Speaker of House of Commons, v. 491
HW addresses, x. 25
HW and Tonson meet at house of, iv. 165
HW mentions, ii. 519
HW referred by, to journals of House of Commons, iv. 139
impostor pretends to be son of, iii. 505–7, 510n
Liddell and Talbot named by, to Secret Committee list, i. 386, 391
Murray's insubordination provokes storm from, iv. 225
Navy post resigned by, i. 391
Parliamentary triumph over ministers hailed by, ii. 540
pompous speeches made by, iii. 412
son and nephew of, vii. 279
Speaker of the House of Commons, i. **219**, iii. 446
speech by, on Regency Bill, iv. 257
Strange wants to exempt, from place tax, v. 199
Walpole party might have been supported by vote of, i. 251
Onslow, Denzil (ca 1698–1765); M. P.:
Selwyn succeeds, as paymaster of the Board of Works, iv. 518
Onslow, George (1731–92), M.P.:
mob mistakes Sulivan for, vii. 288
printers of House of Commons debates arrested at request of, because speeches abuse him, vii. **279**–80
Onslow, George (1731–1814), cr. (1776) Bn Cranley; 4th Bn Onslow, 1776; cr. (1801) E. of Onslow; M.P.:
printers of House of Commons debates arrested at request of, because speeches abuse him, vii. 279–80

Onslow, Richard (ca 1697–1760), M.P.; army officer:
death of, dissolves Lord Charles Hay's court martial, v. 385
Onslow, Richard (1713–76), 3d Bn Onslow, 1740; M.P.:
red ribbon conferred on, iv. 311
'Onslow, Richard'. *See* Veers, Daniel
On the Death of Richard West, Esq. See under Ashton, Thomas
Opalinska, Katharina (1680–1747), m. (1698) Stanislas I (Leszczyński), K. of Poland:
apartment of, iv. 116
Opera; operas:
Alexander costumed in plumes in, viii. 222
Bayreuth, Margravine of, composes, iv. 478
German princes waste money on, viii. 186
Methodists do not attend, on Sunday, iv. 86
omitted in jubilee year in Papal States, iv. 83
politics less dignified than, v. 542
Rolli composer of, ii. 468n
Russel's puppet-show burlesques Italian, iii. 28
St-Germain composes songs for, x. 20
Spanish expedition in Italy has, ii. 228
Walpole, Bns, prefers tragedies to, ii. 128
Opera, English, in London:
admission price to, ix. 646
Ailesbury, Cts of, attends, vi. 304
Amorevoli not to sing in, i. 185, 190, ii. 342
Amorevoli retained by, i. 170, 211, 358, 478, ii. 32
Arenberg attends, ii. 137
at Haymarket, eclipsed by those at playhouses, iv. 410
at little theatre in Haymarket, v. 506
attendants at, hired from Bear Garden, i. 166
Auretti popular in, ii. 131
bankers usually recruit singers for, i. 191
Banks, Margaret, attends, iii. 234
Barbarina to be retained by, i. 358, ii. 31, 131
bass in, Montagu's witticism on, ii. 342
begins after George II's birthday, i. 165, 170
begins with pasticcio, ii. 96
benefit performance, ix. 134
Bettina dances in, i. 256, 421
Buckingham, Ds of, attends, i. 254
Chiaretta may not appear in, ii. 31–2
Christian VII sees *Buona figluola* at, vii. 42–3
Churchill, Lady Mary (Lady Mary Walpole), attends, i. 359, ii. 180–1, 196, v. 278
Chute and Whithed attend with Lord Hervey, iii. 372
comic, Paganini popular in, v. 491
comic operas the best at, vii. 82
'consumptive,' iii. 464
Conway a director of, i. 190

[Opera, English, *continued*]
Cori prompter at, i. 254n
Cornelys, Theresa, has Guadagni open in, vii. 271
crowded on Saturdays but not on Tuesdays, i. 256
dancers in: capital, ix. 243; Sodi pleases as much as Faussan in, ii. 104
dances in: charming, i. 302; church music used for, iii. 369; mended, iii. 454; on French system, i. 166, iii. 369; unpopular, i. 190, 197
Dashwood, Lady, attends, iii. 224
Davies, Cecilia, succeeds in, vii. 547, 570–1
deteriorated, ii. 342
Dilettanti solicit subscriptions for, ii. 211
directors of: i. 190–1; enrage HW, ii. 293–4; fear that Amorevoli may not return, i. 478; hire Fumagalli and Visconti, i. 421; replace Visconti by Fumagalli, i. 398, 423; retain Muscovita to please Middlesex, i. 358; ruin it by importing abbés and mistresses, ii. 210–11; spend money, i. 166
Dorset asks George II not to subscribe to, ii. 226
elephant breaks stage in, i. 358
Elisi has not appeared in, v. 459
English fondness for, on eve of war, iv. 469
'English' when given at play-houses, iv. 410
expense of, i. 166, 191, 216, 240, ii. 226, 293
Farinelli in, i. 190, 478
Faussans in, i. 358
five a week, iv. 410
Foote, Mrs (Mary Mann) attends, i. 359, vi. 304
Francis III attends, iv. 57
Frederick, P. of Wales, and George II to attend, on different nights, i. 186
Frederick, P. of Wales, sponsors, iii. 342
French system imitated in, i. 166
Galuppi's *Scipione* in, i. 358
Garrick, Mrs, danced at, iv. 74n
George II's quarrel with son suggested by, ii. 104
Gluck's operas flourish at, iii. 234
HW as a child saw almost the first, ix. 558
HW a subscriber to, i. 358, ii. 293–4
HW attends, i. 412, ii. 137, 180–1, iii. 224, iv. 57, vi. 264, 304, vii. 403
HW attends, only once in 1786, ix. 648
HW doubts reopening of, iii. 442
HW has heard Rubinelli at, ix. 648
HW hears Allegranti in, ix. 242–3
HW's box at, York, D. of, visits, vi. 264
HW tired of defraying expenses of, ii. 293–4
Handel sets up oratorios to oppose, ii. 180
Harmonic Meetings given in, vii. 271
hissing popular at, ii. 131
horses in, slow, iii. 369–70

Hume-Campbell prides himself on not attending, iv. 5
in decline, v. 363
Karl Wilhelm Ferdinand and Ps Augusta to attend, vi. 197
Lincoln's scuffle with drunken officer at, i. 411–12
London takes to, when given at playhouse, iv. 410
Mancini's performance at, ii. 342
Middlesex and Holdernesse the managers of, ii. 110
Middlesex does not pay performers of, iii. 370
—'s mismanagement of, iii. 226, 293
—— sponsors, iii. 342
—'s wife's fortune may be spent on, ii. 501
—— the contribution of, to politics, ii. 365
Millico sings in, vii. 403
miserable, ii. 104
mob may silence, i. 166
Monticelli retained by, i. 185, 190, 211, 358, 401
Muscovita retained in, by Middlesex, i. 358
music unpopular in, i. 190
officials give, for Friedrich Wilhelm, iii. 265
Olimpiade, The, given in, i. 401
omitted because of actors' illnesses, i. 190
Orford, Cts of, attends, iii. 224, 234
Pacchierotti admired in, ix. 243
Pescetti's, shows Venetians with gondolas and masks, i. 302
popular, i. 211, 331
popular when prices are equal to those of plays, iv. 410
races eclipse, vii. 570–1
Reginello acts in, iii. 370
Rubinelli's voice better at Handel jubilee than at, ix. 648
season for, almost over, i. 421, 434
serenata at, iv. 49
serious operas seldom played in, vi. 484
subscription for, i. 358
Tavistock, Marchioness, attends, with D. and Ds of Bedford at time of husband's accident, vi. 498
unfrequented, ii. 119, iii. 342, vii. 547
Vanneschi's, ii. 198
—— the manager of, through Lord Middlesex, i. 191, 216
—— to be discarded by, i. 358
Vauxhall eclipses, i. 421
Vestris benefit eclipses opera for hurricane sufferers in, ix. 134
Viscontina in, i. 190
would be thought magnificent at Florence, i. 208
Opera, French, at Paris:
Cornbury and Fontenelle converse at, iv. 213–14
English opera imitates, i. 165–6, iii. 369
HW first sees, in Paris, ii. 495

HW would like Elizabeth of Russia's amours to be made into, ii. 495
heroines of, quaver, ii. 495
Maurepas applauded at, viii. 61
Opera, Genoese:
French exclude Genoese from, and act all parts, iii. 505
Opera, Lucchese:
Vaneschi cheats Middlesex and Raymond at, i. 216
Opera, Neapolitan:
glorious, iii. 442
plans for cantata at, iii. 437–8
Opera, Paduan:
Murray takes English visitors to, from Venice, v. 512–13
Opera, Reggio:
HW attends, i. 39–40, 47
Opera, Roman:
Friedrich II of Hesse visited by D. of Gloucester in box at, viii. 275
Opera, Tuscan:
accademici deny use of theatre for, for St John's day, ii. 439
advantages (social) of, iii. 311
Amorevoli in, i. 80, 81
Andreone acts in, iii. 455
Astrua in, iii. 438
Babbi in, iii. 438
at Leghorn: Babbi hired for, for carnival, ii. 525–6; Braitwitz takes Mann to Francis I's box in, i. 259; Goldsworthy, Mrs, receives Mann at, i. 260; opera to be given at, for carnival, vi. 354; restored, iii. 1; Sani sings in, ii. 160
bad: at beginning of carnival, i. 284, ii. 128, 555, iii. 454, iv. 115, 210–11; at great theatre, ii. 555, iv. 357; for St John's Day, i. 79–80
Bagnano not to give, in Via del Cucumero, i. 56
Barlocci sings in, ii. 302
Barrett-Lennard, Mrs, will not attend, on Sunday, iv. 86
Barrett-Lennards miss, iv. 92
Bernacchi chief actor in, i. 239
Botta wants, in autumn at Florentine great theatre, vi. 166
boxes at, see under Teatro della Pergola; Theatre: Florentine
Caffarelli sings in, iii. 437, 439
Chimenti not worth hearing in, ii. 361
Chute and Whithed at, ii. 322
Chute attends, in chair, ii. 386
clergyman, English, does not attend, on Sunday, ii. 162–3
Craon attends, iii. 440
Craon, Princesse de, attends, i. 40, 83, ii. 302, iii. 357, 439–40
—— offended by incidents at, iii. 439–40
dance in, represents siege of Vienna, ix. 360
dances in, i. 48, ii. 322, iii. 355–6, 454–5

dances in, unsuccessful, ii. 361, iv. 357
Du Châtelet attends, iii. 439
Egizziello (Gizziello) singer at, i. 56, 449, 454, ii. 1, 12, iii. 438
Electress's courtiers attend, ii. 160
——'s death cuts, short, ii. 163
Elisi shines in, iv. 86
Elmi and Turcotti women impresarie for, i. 80
Estevenon attends, i. 217
Feroni, Mme, attends, i. 81
Forbes and Laurence attend, iii. 192
for Joseph II, vi. 564
for Maria Elizabeth's birth, ii. 294, 302
for Maria Theresa's coronation celebrations, i. 100, 101
for Maria Theresa's name day, ii. 322, vi. 558–9
for St John's day, i. 449, 463, ii. 435, 445
for the Carnival, iii. 355–6
fourth, recently begun, iii. 439–40
Francis I's box at, i. 60, 83
frequented, iii. 207
Gabburri, Mme, attends, in Mann's box, i. 136
Galli, Mme, has box at, iii. 505
gay, at carnival, iii. 364
Gloucester, D. of, hears Tenducci in, vii. 353
gossip lacking at, iii. 439
Gray, Sir James, lured from Venice by, iii. 433
Grifoni, Mme, attends, i. 48, 51, 78, ii. 54
HW admires accounts of, iii. 442
histrioni take place of, ii. 462
illumination after, unfrequented, ii. 303
illumination at, ii. 322
impresario of, dies, but wife goes on singing, iv. 298
Incontri, Abp, dislikes mingling of sexes in, ii. 41
in morning, at end of carnival, iii. 465
intermezzi bad in, iv. 210–11
in Via del Cocomero, see Teatro del Cocomero
in Via della Pergola, see Teatro della Pergola
last night of, i. 304
last of season, ii. 60
Leopold regulates, vi. 559
Lorraine faction impresarii for, ii. 555
Lucchi, Angiola, appears in, ii. 368
Mann and Chute avoid, i. 269
Mann attends, i. 69, 74, 81, 104, 106, 136, ii. 12, 29, 54, 60, 307, iii. 354–6, 357, 505
—— cannot attend: because of cold, ii. 322; because of gout, ix. 360
—— has rehearsal for, in his terreno hall, ii. 294
—— indifferent to, iv. 404
—— prefers HW's letters to, iv. 15
Mann's boxes at, see under Teatro della

[Opera, Tuscan, *continued*]
Pergola: Mann's box at; Theatre: Florentine, Mann's boxes at
——'s spirits not raised by, ii. 307
—— to attend, with special chairs, i. 69
—— to take Bns Lucan to, viii. 418
masks alone keep audience from slumbering at, iii. 439
masks permitted at, while Caffarelli remains, iii. 439
Medici, Filippo de', impresario for, ii. 439
Modenese princess attends, i. 60, 69, 99, 101
Modenese princess gives money to, i. 65
Narni and Valenti dance in, iii. 455
Neri courts Mme Gondi at, ii. 86
Orford, Cts of, supports, ii. 555
Philipps attends, in Mann's box, i. 81
Pinacci roars in, ii. 361
planned for Maria Josefa, vi. 525
prices of tickets for, vii. 458
promoters of, dread Novena, ii. 295
resumed, in Florence, ii. 1
Riccardi disputes with Mann at, about 'Onslow,' iii. 505
Richecourt's orders about, iii. 8
Ridolfi produces, with Bernacchi and Bagnolese, i. 239–40
—— will lose by, i. 284, ii. 128
Rosenberg regulates, vi. 559
Sade attends, i. 283
Salimbeni in, i. 79, 81
Santarelli's performance in, ii. 353, 361
Santi Barbieri sings in, ii. 302
Sauveterre dances in, ii. 361, iii. 355–6
—— directs, ii. 303
—— hissed by pit at, from respect to Denis, iii. 439
second one: at great theatre, vi. 477; to begin, iii. 437
Serristori, Andrea, attends, i. 136
singers' box at, i. 60
Suares, Francesco, attends, i. 81, 149
Suares, Mme, attends, i. 81, ii. 29, iii. 311
supper after, avoided, ii. 303
Tesi insulted at, ii. 368
—— may be in, iii. 438
——'s: promoted by Mme Suares, ii. 280–1; rehearsal at Mann's house, ii. 294; successful, ii. 302; unsuccessful, ii. 361
——'s costume for, ii. 353, 361
——'s fee for singing in, ii. 281
——'s ostentation ruins, ii. 361
unfrequented, i. 284, ii. 128, iv. 115, 357
Visconti sings in, iii. 437
visitors prefer, to seeing Mann, i. 97
weddings interfere with, ii. 59–60
worst ever, ii. 128, iii. 207
Opera books:
Italian, call plot of opera the *argomento*, vii. 281
Opera girl:
Vernon spends money on, i. 126
Opera house, Florentine. *See* Teatro degl'

Intrepidi; Teatro del Cocomero; Teatro della Pergola
Opera house, London. *See* Haymarket
Opera singer:
fee of, ii. 281
French, seem comic to HW, ii. 495–6
hussars frighten, into a fever at Bologna, ii. 302
See also Singer
Opera ticket:
Wrey gives, to Margaret Banks, iii. 234
Opiates:
Walpole, Sir Robert, takes, iii. 16
Opium:
Godschall's dullness suggests addiction to, i. 295
Oppidans. *See under* Eton
Oppido:
earthquake account mentions, ix. 376
Oppression on the breast:
occurrences of, ii. 139, 172, vi. 42, ix. 280
Orange, House of:
Cowper's claim to Nassau title opposed by, ix. 78n
minorities prevalent in, iv. 279
See also Nassau family
Orange, P. of. *See* Frederick Heinrik (1584–1647) William I (1533–84); William IV (1711–51); William V (1748–1806)
Orange; oranges:
Brown, Sir Robert, saves money by not having, on his sideboard, ix. 609
China, measles caused by, i. 352
climate of India suitable for ripening, to shaddocks, ix. 153
Du Barry, Comtesse, tosses, vii. 85
Orange flowers:
Guimar, Mlle, to have, outside dining room windows, vii. 323
Mann sends, dried, to Horatio Walpole (1678–1757), iv. 255
price of, in Florence, ii. 230
Orange flower water:
distilled, Mann uses, against Cocchi's advice, vi. 469
English seek, from Florence, iii. 330
HW will be able to send, if warm weather continues, iv. 131
Mann gets, from Malta, iii. 330
—— sends, to Horatio Walpole (1678–1757), iii. 330, iv. 255
Orange tree; orange trees:
at Ranelagh, iv. 47
HW to protect, at SH, v. 361, 369
in Mann's garden, i. 104, 499
Lorenzi praises colour scheme of, v. 501
Mann's, in bloom, ii. 230
Martin's, sold at auction, v. 121
Stanley buys, around London, for fête champêtre, viii. 14
Oratorio; oratorios:
Granville, Cts, attends, ii. 537
HW attends, ii. 537
Handel sets up, to oppose operas, ii. 180

Handel's: HW asks if Mann has received, vi. 73; Mann wants, for Mme Branchi, vi. 35, 36, 41–2; Mann, James, to have, selected, vi. 49
poor singers of, ii. 180, 186
popularity of, ii. 180, 186
Oratory, private:
Giovanni Gastone has, in Palazzo Pitti, iv. 489
Orbetello:
air of, bad, ii. 16
Modena, Ds of, not to visit, ii. 222, 223
Montemar may leave garrison at, ii. 27
—— may visit, i. 198, 204, 206, 214, ii. 7, 16, 27
—— sends courier from, i. 226
Neapolitan governor repels Spanish xebecs from, ii. 287
Neapolitan troops at, iii. 378
Philip, Don, may land at, i. 389
Sienese approach route covered by, i. 289
Spaniards prefer Foligno to, as headquarters, ii. 27
Spanish army leaves garrison at, i. 289
Spanish army to leave, for Foligno, i. 265
Spanish baggage approaches, ii. 243, 253
Spanish invalids may embark at, iii. 55
Spanish officers buy horses at, for baggage, i. 214
Spanish troops at, i. 154, 178, 179, 192, 197, 204, 206, 262, 289, 350
Orchestra:
at Genoa, entirely composed of French officers, iii. 505
Florentines expect Mann to have, to celebrate George III's coronation, v. 533
for fête champêtre in Boboli amphitheatre, ix. 586
See also Music: band of
'Orco,' Cardinal di:
Romans' name for Cardinal York, iii. 428
Ord, Robert (1700–78), M.P.:
Sandys' secretary, ii. 320n
Williams, Sir Charles Hanbury, satirizes, ii. 320
Order of La Croix étoilée. See Croix étoilée, Order of the
Order of Malta. See St John of Jerusalem, Knights of
Order of Maria Theresa. See Maria Theresa, Order of
Order of St Anne. See St Anne, Order of
Order of St Catherine. See Saint Catherine, Order of
Order of St Stephen. See St Stephen, Order of
Order of the Bath. See Bath, Order of the
Order of the Garter. See Garter, Order of the
Order of the Thistle. See Thistle, Order of the
Ordnance, Master of. See Master of the Ordnance
Ordnance:
Argyll restored to post in, i. 345

Granby resigns post in, vii. 170, 175
lieutenant-general of: Conway content with salary of, vi. 560; Townshend succeeded by Conway as, vi. 549
Pelham procures, for D. of Cumberland, iv. 120
O'Reilly, Alexander (1725–94), Conde de O'Reilly, Spanish army officer:
honour lost by, in previous attack on Algiers, ix. 416
Spanish attack on Algiers to be led by, ix. 416
Spanish fleet led by, against Algiers, viii. 121–2
Orestes:
HW and Mann compared to Pylades and, vi. 274, vii. 309, viii. 283, ix. 5, 9, 312, 615
Orford, Cts of. See Rolle, Margaret (1709–81)
Orford, E. of. See Russell, Edward (1653–1727); Walpole, George (1730–91); Walpole, Horatio (1717–97); Walpole, Horatio (1723–1809); Walpole, Horatio (1752–1822); Walpole, Horatio (1783–1858); Walpole, Sir Robert (1676–1745); Walpole, Robert (1701–51)
Orford, title of:
creation of, i. 318
Sandys enraged at Sir Robert Walpole for taking, i. 333
Orford estate:
entail of, Walpole, Horatio (1678–1757) defrauds brother's descendants of, vii. 367
Organ:
Young buys, iv. 331
Organist:
at Aschaffenburg, ii. 342
Orlandi, Casimirro, Florentine postmaster:
(?) Vorontsov consorts with, v. 249
Orlandi, Pellegrino Antonio (1660–1727):
Abcedario pittorico, L.: Dobson article in, amuses HW, ii. 312; Sassoferrato not included in, ii. 93–4
Orlandini, Mme —— (? née Butler):
Albany, Cts of, breakfasts with, ix. 101
Orlandini del Beccuto, Giulio Ranieri (1699–1782), Priore:
ball to be given by, for Tempi's wedding, ii. 435, 438
'Orlando Furioso':
Stair compared with, ii. 48
Orlaw. See Orlov
Orléans, Bp of. See Gérente de la Bruyère, Louis-Sextius de (d. 1788)
Orléans, Duc d'. See Bourbon, Louis de (1703–52); Bourbon, Louis-Philippe de (1725–85); Bourbon, Louis-Philippe-Joseph de (1747–93); Bourbon, Philippe de (1674–1723); Gaston-Jean-Baptiste (1608–60)
Orléans, Duchesse d'. See Bourbon, Françoise-Marie de (d. 1749); Bourbon, Louise-Marie-Adélaide de (1753–1821); Isabella (1387–1410) of Valois

Orléans family:
Barbantane, Marquise de, dismissed by, vii. 480
Orlov ('Orloff'; 'Orlow'), Alexeĭ Grigor'evich (1737–1808); Gen.:
agent in St Petersburg revolution, vii. 185
Catherine II's accomplice in murder, vii. 207
—— 's favourite, vii. 149
—— warned by, vi. **64**
Constantinople's capture by, would be known in Paris before Florence, vii. 311
courier brings peace treaty to, at Florence, viii. 40
courier from Venice tells, that Russian fleet reaches coast of Morea, vii. 204
determined to sail, vii. 309
Dick receives black boy from, vii. 228
—— receives letters from, about Russo-Turkish battle, vii. 232
—— receives Order of St Anne from, viii. 84, 96
Dick, Lady, receives Turkish girls from, vii. 228
Dolgoruky accompanied by, to Florence, vii. 191
English intervention against France must please, in Greek islands, vii. 478
English visit of, thought by French to be for intrigue, ix. 61
fleet of, repaired at Leghorn, goes to Aegean Sea, vii. 307
Florence visited by, vii. 149, 185, viii. 113
HW does not believe denial by, of Peter III's murder, vii. 195, 207
Leopold receives Egyptian horse from, vii. 228
Mann often sees, in Florence, but cannot easily talk with him, vii. 185
—— receives black boy from, vii. 228
—— repulses hints by, of giving him Russian honours, viii. 84
—— rides with, in coach, viii. 84
Maria Louisa receives Turkish girls from, vii. 228
messenger from St Petersburg tells, of Russian victories, vii. 160
officers of guards regiment of, sail from Cronstadt, vii. 222
officers promoted by, viii. 84
peace terms unknown to, viii. 33
returns to St Petersburg, after closing accounts with Dick and Rutherfurd, viii. 114
Rumiantsev's operations reported to, at Florence, viii. 29
Russian fleet commanded by, as Lord Admiral, vii. 234
Russian fleet found by, in gulf of Napoli di Romania, vii. 226
Russian officer and courier sent by, from Leghorn with dispatches for Russian Court, vii. 235
Russian officer carries dispatches to, through Florence to Greek Islands, vii. 444
Russian ships at Leghorn to fetch, vii. 191
Russians not permitted by, to land on Chios, vii. 233
Rutherfurd made agent for Russian fleet by, vii. 161, viii. 114
St Petersburg courier awaited by, at Florence, viii. 33
scourge of the Turks at sea, viii. 14
Orlov, Count Fedor Grigor'evich (1741–96):
Catherine II's favourite, vii. 149
escapes burning ship, vii. 227, 233
Florence visited by, vii. 149
Orlov, Grigoriĭ Grigor'evich (1734–83), Count:
Catherine II may discard, as favourite, while he is at Congress of Fokshani, vii. 441
—— put on her throne by, viii. 114
—— 's favourite lover, vii. **75n**, viii. 143n
dances and loves of, gigantic, viii. 143
diamonds carried by, viii. 114, 143
displaced as favourite but not as courtier, vii. 444
England to be visited by, viii. 113
England visited by, viii. 143
Florence visited by, viii. 95, 113
nonsense talked by, viii. 144
Spa to be visited by, for health, viii. 113
two men fill place of, with Catherine II, viii. 143
youthful prowess of, proved by loads of diamonds, viii. 114
Orme, Capt. Robert (d. 1790), Braddock's aide-de camp:
reward offered by, for Braddock's rescue, iv. 495
Townshend family do not consent to marriage of, to Lady Audrey Townshend, iv. 495n
Ormea, Marchese d'. See Ferrero di Roasio, Carlo Vincenzo (1680–1745)
Ormolu:
inventor of, see Boulton, Matthew
popularity of, in England, vii. 211–12
teakettle of, sold at auction, vii. 212
Ormond, D. of. See Butler, Charles (1671–1758); Butler, James (1665–1745)
Ormond, House of:
'heiress of ninety-nine' the sole survivor of, v. 261
Or moulu. See Ormolu
Ormuzd:
Ahriman gets the better of, by turns, vii. 192
Ornaments:
French, excel English, ix. 635
'Orondates', character in La Calprenède's *Cassandre*:
HW's name for George II, iv. 213, 218
Oroonko. See under Amis, Aphra; Southerne, Thomas
Orozmades. *See* Ormuzd

Orpheus:
bear would be tolerated by, if it danced to
his music, iv. 427
Orpheus and Eurydice:
pun on, at London theatre, i. 172
Orrery, Cts of. *See* Hamilton, Margaret
(1710–58)
Orrery, E. of. *See* Boyle, Hon. Hamilton
(1730–64); Boyle, John (1707–62)
Orsi, Donato, Florentine banker:
(?) Cholmondeley's credit with, ix. 314
(?) Cowper notifies, of consignment of plate,
ix. 661
Orford, Cts of, shows account to, ix. 113
Orsi, Giusto, Florentine banker:
(?) Cholmondeley's credit with, ix. 314
(?) Cowper notifies, of consignment of
plate, ix. 661
Orsi (pro-Spanish Florentine faction):
Ascanio's death depresses, i. 87
Austrian defeat encourages, i. 433
Cartagena victory confuses, i. 68
Castellar talks with member of, about
Spanish plans, i. 349
English-Spanish peace wished by, i. 263
Francis I disliked by, ii. 2
——'s retreat from Prague proclaimed by,
i. 488–9
Galli belongs to, ii. 46
Mann asked by, about fleets, i. 39
——'s reports not believed by, iii. 198
Modena's resistance predicted by, i. 443
Montemar's conquest of Lombardy hoped
by, i. 481
Philip, Don, wanted by, as Grand Duke of
Tuscany, i. 68n
report circulated by, that Maria Theresa's
allies may make her conclude peace, ii. 241
Spanish and Neapolitan defeat expected by,
i. 427
Te Deum avoided by, ii. 241
Tencin's supplanting Fleury wished by, i.
481
Volterra exile predicted for, because of
their indiscreet talk, ii. 46
Orsini, Domenico Amadeo (1719–89), cardinal,
1743; Neapolitan minister at Rome:
announcement by, at Conclave door, vii. 90
audience with Clement XIII demanded by,
to protest against treatment of Parma, vii.
15–16
Clement XIII sought by, vii. 10
—— told by, to discard Torreggiani, vii.
35
confers with French and Spanish ministers,
vii. 10
Ferdinand of Naples orders, to rebuke
Neapolitan cardinals, vii. 26
Jesuits' suppression again demanded by, vii.
214
Neapolitan Court disavows homage of, to
Young Pretender, vi. 399

Young Pretender given royal honours by,
vi. **392**
Orsini, Eleonora (d. 1634), m. (1592) Alessandro Attendolo Sforza, Duca di Segni:
letters of, about Francavilla statues, sent
by Mann to HW, v. 480, 497, vi. 583, 587,
ix. 657
Orsolene, convent of:
Albany, Cts of, retires to, ix. 106
Sobieski, Ps, fled to, from husband's tyr-
anny, ix. 106
Orvilliers, Comte d'. *See* Guillouet, Louis
(1708–92)
Osborn, Peter (d. 1754), naval Capt.:
Craon comments on, ii. 477
entertained at Florence, ii. 98, 99
Goldsworthy's correspondence with, ii. 28
HW's cases said to have been conveyed by,
ii. 477, 514
Lestock conveyed by, to England, ii. 477,
514
Mann may be visited by, ii. 67
Marciana and Porto Longone devastated
by, ii. **28, 59**
Osborne, Lady Anne (d. 1722), m. 1 Robert
Coke; m. 2 Col. Horace Walpole:
Leneve, Isabella, and Dorothy Walpole
brought up by, v. 353n
Osborne, Francis Godolphin (1751–99), styled
M. of Carmarthen 1761–89; 5th D. of
Leeds, 1789:
Cowper notified by, of George III's permis-
sion to accept Order of St Hubert, ix. 470
estate of, settled on children by first wife,
ix. 75n
foreigners talk of ignorance of, ix. 486
Godolphin's bequest to, ix. 583
Mann, Horace II, gets letter from, asking
him to be chargé d'affaires after uncle's
death, ix. 666–7
—— rejects salary offer from, ix. 672–3
—— told by, of successor's appointment,
ix. 675–6
Paris post assigned to, ix. 363
secretary of state, ix. 583
Waldegrave, Lady Elizabeth Laura, fails
to marry, ix. 75
Osborne, Lord Francis Godolphin (1777–
1850), cr. (1832) Bn Godolphin:
Godolphin's bequest to, ix. 583
Osborne, Henry (ca 1698–1771), naval Capt.;
Adm., 1757:
Byng's friend, v. 191
courier of, does not feel earthquake, v. 133
Dick visited by, at Leghorn, v. 123
fleet of, harasses French Mediterranean
coast, v. 135
French ships fight with fleet of, v. 188, 191
health of: apoplexy, v. 197; eye lost, v.
197
Hervey with, at Gibraltar, v. 197
Mann induces, to send courier to England,
v. 122

[Osborne, Henry, continued]
—— obtains provisions for fleet of, at Leghorn, v. 114
——'s correspondence with, v. 197
Osborne, Peregrine (1659–1729), 2d D. of Leeds:
Gates's mother housekeeper to, ix. 92n
Osborne, Peter. See Osborn, Peter
Osborne, Thomas (1713–89), 4th D. of Leeds, 1731:
becomes Cabinet Councillor, v. 489
George II makes, K.G., iv. 71, 72
Grenville succeeds, as Cofferer, v. 489
Halifax's former salary turned over to, v. 489
Lyttelton succeeded by, as Cofferer, iv. 517
Mastership of the Horse may go to, iv. 182–3
may become George III's governor, iv. 345
resignation of, expected, v. 98
Sandys succeeded by, as chief justice in eyre, v. 489
—— succeeds, as chief justice in eyre, iv. 518
son of, ix. 75n, 363n, 486n, 583n
Oslenghi, Roman courier:
Young Pretender to be notified by, of father's death, vi. 383
Osnabrück ('Osnaburg'), Bp of. See Frederick Augustus (1763–1827); Klemens August (1700–61)
Osnabrück:
Conway and Lady Ailesbury to spend winter at, v. 554
Osorio-Alarcon, Cavaliere Giuseppe (ca 1697–1763), Sardinian ambassador to England 1730–43:
Charles Emmanuel III shocked by news from, iii. 258
—— to tell, to write to George II or Newcastle about disloyal English officer, iii. 147, 150
fashionable in England, i. 186
first minister of Sardinia, after being minister to England, ii. 342n
Gorsegno's correspondence with, iii. 87, 95, 150
HW discusses Hanoverians with, ii. 342–3
HW knows, i. 186
Macartney, Miss, pursued by, i. 186
Mann told by, of Newcastle's appointment, iv. 421–2
Ossa:
Parlement de Paris relieved of, vii. 265
Ossegovich, Basile or Basilio (d. 1784), Slavonian sailor:
Great Duchess of Tuscany seized by, ix. 479–81
Osservazioni per ben regolare il coro. See under Adami, Andrea
Ossorio. See Osorio
Ossory. See Upper Ossory

Ossun, Pierre-Paul (1713–88), Marquis d'; French ambassador to Naples and Spain:
Charles III reassured by, v. 275
may get French cabinet post, vii. 264
Ostein, Johann Friedrich Karl von (d. 1763), Abp and Elector of Mainz 1743–63:
Frankfort fine to be levied by, v. 28–9
subsidies for, iii. 229
Osten, Greve Adolph Siegfried von der (1726–97), Danish ambassador to Naples 1768–70:
Danish revolution involves, vii. 380
Ostend:
boisterous weather at, may have detailed Mann's courier, ix. 334
convenient for invasion of England, iii. 88
East India Company buys tea at, ix. 577–8
English send troops to, ii. 457, iii. 78
fortifications of, weak, iii. 69
France may offer, to Holland, iii. 88
France may use, as Dunkirk's substitute, v. 527
French embark Fitzjames's regiment at, iii. 208
French progress in Flanders reported from, iii. 67
French threaten, ii. 456–7, iii. 69, 92, 96
Joseph II should keep, open, so that HW and Mann can correspond, ix. 105
Leyden gazetteer gets news from more accessible port than, vii. 110
Mann hopes English will give, to Dutch, ii. 290
Mann, Horace II, rumoured lost on packet-boat from, ix. 210
Maria Theresa gives, to the French, v. 117
Morice sends valuables back to, on sighting a privateer, ix. 89
passage to, from England, makes post to Italy irregular, vii. 541, viii. 141 ix. 383
Riccardi's jewels may be sent through, to Brussels, iii. 94
Thurot said to have put in at, v. 349
visitors to, Horace Mann II, viii. 517
Wade demands artillery for, iii. 69
Young Pretender said to have landed at, iii. 311
Ostentation:
HW averse to, vi. 480
Östergötland, D. of. See Fredrik Adolf (1750–1803)
Ostermann, Heinrich Johann Friedrich (1679–1747), Graf von:
Catalogue of French Books, A, satirizes, ii. 53
Ost Frize. See East Friesland
Ostrogothia. See Östergötland
Oswald, George (d. 1742), Sir Robert Walpole's steward:
HW's art shipments sent to, x. 6
HW's correspondence with, i. 6
Mann's correspondence with, i. 108, 113
—— sends bill of lading for HW's cases to, i. 31

——'s parcels mistakenly addressed by, to Goldsworthy, i. 302

Mann, Galfridus, to be paid by, at Sir Robert Walpole's order, i. 228

—— to tell, of HW's illness, ii. 51

melon seeds desired by, for Sir Robert Walpole, i. 34

Oswald, James (1715–69), M.P.; commissioner of trade and plantations; lord of the Treasury:

commissioner of trade and plantations, i. 299n

Walpole party voted against by, i. 299

Oswego:

capture of v. 14

more important than Minorca, v. 14

prisoners from, forwarded from Quebec to Plymouth, v. 18

Otaheite. See Tahiti

Othello. See under Shakespeare, William

Otranto:

Bute would have written from, to HW, vii. 103, 107n

in Naples, not Sicily, vii. 107

'Otranto':

HW's name for SH, vii. 350

Ottajano ('Ottajaro'), Principe d'. See Medici, Giuseppe de

Otter, sloop:

shipwrecked, i. 298

Otto, Henry (fl. 1759–74), King's messenger:

Pitt sends, to Lyttelton, v. 507

Ottoman Empire. See Turkey

Oudh, Province of, in India:

army, revenue, and population of, ix. 13

England acquires, ix. 13

Ouwerkerk, Heer van. See Nassau, Jan Nicolas Floris, Rÿksgraaf van

Ouwerkerk, Mevrouw van. See Testas, Maria Anna

Ovada:

Maillebois near, iii. 258

'Overkirk, P. and Ps':

Cowpers to become, viii. 353

Overkirk: Overquerque. See Auverquerque; Ouwerkerk

Overture; overtures:

audience bawls for, at theatre, viii. 348

Handel's, see under Handel

Ovid (Publius Ovidius Naso) (43 B.C.–A.D. ca 18), Roman poet:

Ars amatoria, HW quotes, i. 466, ii. 74

Metamorphosis: Cambridge cooks to surpass transformations of, iv. 71; Fox family's political shift reminiscent of, ix. 11

Owyhees (Hawaians):

unexploited because they have no wealth, ix. 545

Ox; oxen:

artillery conveyed by, ii. 530

Clinton captures, viii. 419

Doria wounded by, v. 386

live, Bruce breakfasts on, with Abyssinian maids, viii. 21

Mann obtains, for British fleet, v. 114

Tuscan regency begrudges, for Austrian artillery, ii. 541

Oxenden, Sir George (1694–1775), 5th Bt, 1720; M.P.:

Orford, Cts of, had affair with, iii. 5

son of, iii. 5

Oxenden, Sir Henry (1721–1803), 6th Bt, 1775:

Florence to be visited by, with introductory letter from HW to Mann, iii. 5

Fortini's affair with, iii. 374

lame, iii. 232

Mann entertains, and accompanies him to Mme Grifoni's, iii. 232

—— not to worry about HW's recommendation of, iii. 250

—— receives HW's letter through, iii. 232

——'s coach to be used by, in Siena, iii. 232

Siena may be visited by, to learn Italian, iii. 232

Oxford, Bp of. See Butler, John (1717–1802); Hough, John (1651–1743); Parker, Samuel (d. 1688); Potter, John (?1674–1747); Secker, Thomas (1693–1768)

Oxford, Cts of. See Holles, Henrietta Cavendish (1694–1755)

Oxford, E. of. See Harley, Edward (ca 1699–1755); Harley, Edward (1726–90); Harley, Robert (1661–1724)

Oxford, Oxon:

Cerretesi taken to, by Venetians, ii. 166

Christian VII gives masquerade tickets to, vii. 58

college servant dies at, iii. 387

Corporation of, House of Commons punishes, vi. 584

dirges at, on P. of Wales's death, iv. 261

Fitzpatrick's balloon ascent from, ix. 591

Francis III receives degree at, iv. 57

HW does not read of North's reception at, vii. 497

Paoli visits, vii. 150

Parliament to chastise, iv. 50

Pomfret, Cts of, wants to be buried at, vi. 562

Radcliffe Camera opened at, iv. 50

riots at, iv. 6, 50

Secker becomes bishop of, i. 451n

singers from, to sing Miserere, ii. 211

Oxford, English ship:

at Mahon, i. 285

Mathews sends, to seize xebecs, ii. 300

Oxford, English transport ship:

Americans capture, viii. 229

Oxford Road, London:

Pantheon erected in, vii. 210, 298

Oxfordshire:

election in, iv. 435, 469

Jacobites of, v. 531

[Oxfordshire, *continued*]
jailor in, suggests hanging a prisoner ahead of time, iii. 418
Nuneham in, ix. 428n
Oxford University:
Bonus employed by, to repair Guise's pictures, v. 429
chancellor's post at, will be bone of contention, vi. 72
Christian VII fortunate in not having tutor from, vii. 40
Croxall attends, iv. 208n
HW quotes language of, ix. 454
HW will not give his collection to, iv. 471
king may nominate chancellor of, iv. 18
Phelps fellow at, iii. 196
Phipps studies at, ii. 185
Pomfret, Cts of, presents husband's collection of statues to, iv. 390n, 470, 579, v. 562n
public act at: iv. 71; Pomfret, Cts of, lauded by, iv. 579, 584
public orator of, *see* Mather, Roger
scholars of, condemned for treason, iv. 6
vice-chancellor of, *see* Huddesford, George (ca 1699–1776); Purnell, John (ca 1708–64)
Westmorland chancellor of, v. 531, vi. 72
Young Pretender's health no longer drunk by, vii. 329
Oynhausen, Georg Ludwig (d. 1759), Graf von; Maj.-Gen.:
brother sends, on embassy, iii. 64
Kendal, Ds of, aunt of, iii. 64
Oyster; oysters:
Fitzwalter consumes 14 barrels of, weekly, iv. 518–19
Vorontsov's soul little more animated than, v. 247
Oziozi society:
Arno Miscellany written by, x. 46

'P——, Mother.' *See* Jeffreys, Hon. Henrietta, Cts of Pomfret
Pacchierotti, Gasparo (1740–1821), male soprano:
Mann has not heard, ix. 426
many prefer, to Marchesi, ix. 426
much admired in London, ix. 243
Pace, the:
Spaniards to pass, i. 342
Packet; packets:
Mann's expense allowance for, ii. 516
Packet-boat; packet-boats:
at Ostend, delays English post, vii. 541
Carteret detains, at Harwich, iii. 213
delays of, frequent in winter, iii. 453
detained at Flushing, for fear of the French, v. 465, 474
English: captured or delayed by French, iii. 430, v. 75, 84, 168, 541, viii. 302, 504; privateer carries, to Dunkirk, viii. 302; stopped, ii. 401

English capture, from Lisbon, iv. 320
Flushing the worst port for, v. 141, 464
French must have captured or delayed, iii. 430
HW's letter lost on, v. 186
mail thrown from, into sea, v. 168, 541, viii. 504
Mann, Horace II, rumoured lost on, ix. 210
pass between England and France despite undeclared war, viii. 399
Port Mahon, Tuscan government almost destroys, viii. 416
post delayed by: to England, i. 476, v. 75, 84, 465, 474; to Italy, iii. 196, 430, 453, v. 141, 464, vii. 541, viii. 504
winds prevent, from reaching Holland, iii. 196
Packing cases:
expense of, i. 130, x. 4
Pad; pads:
Mann's great-great-grandmother famous for breaking, iv. 13
Paddington, London:
hanging prevalent in, iv. 65
Townshend, Vcts, takes villa at, near Tyburn, vi. 165
Paderborn:
Ferdinand retires to, v. 498
Padlock:
Bird puts, on park gate, iv. 323
Padona. *See* Padua
Padri di famiglie:
Florentine, ask Leopold to curb extravagance in ladies' dress, ix. 175
Padroni:
of barks, vi. 546
Padua:
Abano near, viii. 9
couriers from Lombardy and Germany do not pass through, viii. 136
Eleonora's death announced from, i. 362
—— visits, i. 74
lady of, i. 74
letters from, reach Florence on Wednesdays only, viii. 136
Mann's letters from, about D. of Gloucester's health, viii. 144
Marlborough takes house at, v. 512
Niccolini may live at, iv. 24
opera at, will detain English, v. 512
visitors to: Gloucester, Ds of, viii. 144; Gloucester, D. of, viii. 135, 144, 314; Marlborough, D. of, v. 512–13; Murray, v. 512–13; Niccoli, i. 224; Orford, Cts of (Bns Walpole), i. 217, 224, 235; Pitt, Anne, viii. 22; Richecourt, i. 217, 224, 235, ii. 216
Paganini, Giuditta. *See* Giuditta
Paganini, Maria Angela (fl. 1743–?60), opera singer:
popular in comic opera in London, v. 459
Paganini, Rosa, m. (?) Francesco Sauveterre:
HW mentions, i. 42
Rangoni pursued by, i. 45

Page, William (d. 1758), highwayman:
Ferrers appears against, at Hertford assizes, v. 184
Page. *See under* Servant
Pageants:
HW's news will all be of, v. 515
Page-surgeon, D. of Gloucester's. *See* Bryant, Robert (d. 1788); Charlton, John
Paglio. *See* Palio
Paglioni. *See* Pallione
Pail:
HW uses, full of cold water, to dip his head in, v. 168
Pain:
absence of, the pleasure of age, viii. 327
HW's reflections on advantages of, vii. 462–3
Paine. *See* Payne
Pain in back:
Philipps has, i. 67
Pain in bowels:
occurrences of, iii. 192
Pain in breast:
gout supposed to cure, iv. 335
occurrences of, iii. 8, 207, iv. 225, 335, vi. 110, viii. 210
remedy for, hot sponge, iii. 8
Pain in hands:
occurrences of, ix. 100
Pain in head:
occurrences of, iv. 225
See also Headache
Pain in stomach:
Bath waters do not remove, from HW, vi. 461
occurrences of, vi. 110, 450, 454–5, 461, 468, viii. 68
Paint; paints:
for china, *see* Cobalt; Zinc
Francis III uses, on face, iv. 75
Mann to send, to Sir Edward and (?) Mary Walpole, iii. 368–9
Sturgis promises, to academician, i. 462
Painters:
English, do animals and landscapes well, viii. 93
engravers' prices exceed those formerly charged by, ix. 532
HW hears from, at Rome, about Old Pretender's movements, i. 15
modern, heads by, crowd Uffizi, ix. 170
Painting; paintings:
Anson's, of sea victory, iv. 38
exhibitions of, in London, vii. 210–11
HW eschews tawdry use of, at SH, iv. 382
HW's knowledge of, v. 368
high price of, in England, vii. 210–12, 466
historical, West imitates Poussin in, vii. 210–11
in oil, and washed drawings, Pars does, viii. 135, 144
Proctor's prize in, ix. 577
Walpole, Sir Edward, makes witticism about modern miracles in, ix. 577

See also Landscape; Picture; Portrait; Seascape, *and under names of collectors and painters*
Paisley, Bn. *See* Hamilton, James
Palace; palaces:
little princes specialize in, in Italy, ix. 587, 589
plan of, bought by HW, x. 4
Soubise can build, free of cost, v. 178
'Palace, old.' *See* Palazzo Vecchio
'Palace, the.' *See* Pitti, Palazzo
Palace Yard, Westminster:
HW sleeps in, on night before George III's coronation, v. 534
Palafox y Mendoza, Juan de (1600–59), Bp of Puebla:
Clement XIV to resume attempt to canonize, vii. 123–4
Jesuits delay canonization of, vii. 124
Palais Royal, at Paris:
La Frenaye's shop at, i. 98–9
Santini's watch would discredit performances of, v. 322
Palatine, Elector. *See* Elector Palatine
Palavicini. *See* Pallavicini
Palazza Madama, at Rome:
Francis I sells, to the French, iv. 264
Palazzi, Conte Ugolino (b. ca 1715):
Montagu, Lady Mary Wortley, at Brescia with, iv. 235, 272, 279, 281
Palazzo Pitti. *See* Pitti, Palazzo
Palazzo Vecchio:
corridor from, to Pitti Palace, ii. 391
English sculptor at Florence makes chimney-pieces for, ix. 93
fireworks at, i. 100
'gentleman of,' *see* Nay, Emmanuel de, Comte de Richecourt
gold from furnishings at, made into plate for Leopold, ix. 231
Niccoli visits, daily, iv. 335
Orford, Cts of, visits, i. 283
poor girls given a dinner and ball at, after marriage, vi. 491
Richecourt may keep Mrs Richmond in, iii. 97, 101
——'s apartment in, i. 224, 283, ii. 391, iii. 385
sales from, ix. 230–1
Siries, Louis, at, i. 213, iv. 475n, viii. 500
Paleotti, Adelaide (d. 1726), m. 1 Alessandro Roffeni; m. 2 (1705) Charles Talbot, 12th E. of Shrewsbury, cr. (1694) D. of Shrewsbury:
silver tube used by, to ventilate bed, iv. 203
Palermo:
Mann, Horace II and Lady Lucy, to sail to, viii. 222, 225
Messina plague described in letters from, ii. 269
Palestina:
earthquake damages, ix. 376

Palestine:
Russia unlikely to take, from Turkey, vii. 194–5
See also Holy Land
Palestrina, Principe di. *See* Colonna Barberini, Carlo
Palestrina:
HW and Gray visit, i. 26
Pálffy, Maria Anna (1716–73), Cts, m. (1739) Gerolamo Luigi Malabaila di Canale, Conte di Canale; Maria Theresa's maid of honour; Wachtendonck's 'cousin':
Richecourt's recall procured by, i. 490
Palfrey:
Clement XIII unlikely to be assisted to, by Joseph II, vi. 555
Palgrave, Rev. William (ca 1735–99), fellow of Pembroke College, Cambridge:
Gray's friend, vi. 272
Mann asked by, to ask HW for Bn Herbert of Cherbury's *Life*, vi. 273
Palhava brothers. *See* Antonio (1714–1800); José (1720–after 1777)
Palifox. *See* Palafox y Mendoza
Palio:
Francis I's horse wins, i. 79, 456
Mann and guests attend, ii. 251
Palio dei Cocchi. *See* Corso dei Cocchi
Palisser. *See* Palliser
Pall:
made at Monaco for D. of York, vi. 554
Pallas, English frigate:
Thurot pursued by, v. 376
Pallavicini, Gian Luca (1697–1773), Austrian army officer; governor of Lombardy:
artillery carriages sent by, from Milan, iii. 406
Batthyáni and Schulenburg refuse to serve under, iii. 50
Maria Theresa said to authorize, to treat with Genoese mob, iii. 359
Maricone advised by, to report Spanish fleet's arrival, i. 309
Milan exposed by retreat of, iii. 120
regiment of, reinforces Lobkowitz, iii. 30
Spaniards escape from, iii. 244
Pallavicini, Lazzaro Opizio (1719–85), cardinal, 1766:
Clement XIV's secretary of state, vii. 118
former nuncio to Spain and Naples, vii. 118
York, Cardinal, asked by, about Young Pretender, vii. 324
Pallavicino, Marchese (?) Nicolò Maria:
Maratti's painting includes, v. 208, 231, 478–9
Pallazi *or* Pallazio, (?) Roman art dealer:
attestation fee to, x. 4
medals, pictures, and urn bought from, by HW, x. 7
Pallio. *See* Palio
Pallione:
Guido's painting of, *see under* Guido Reni

Palliser, Sir Hugh (1723–96), cr. (1773) Bt; Adm.; M.P.:
Admiralty and Parliamentary posts vacated by, viii. 444
Admiralty reached by, after escape from Portsmouth, viii. 442
coat of, pulled by mob, viii. 442
court martial of: begins, viii. 459; demanded by, of Admiralty, viii. 444; ends in acquittal, viii. 474–5; expected to end in acquittal, viii. 464; Mann interested in, viii. 478; oblivion preferable to, viii. 453
furniture of, removed, viii. 442
Greenwich Hospital appointment of, not censured by Parliament, ix. 118
House of Commons may ask George III to remove, as General of the Marines and Governor of Scarborough, viii. 446
Keppel risks reputation to save that of, viii. 474
——'s court martial caused by, viii. 427
——'s court martial will probably be regretted by, viii. 435
——'s quarrel with: rumoured, viii. **406**; to be investigated again, ix. 103
——'s signals disobeyed by, because of rotten mast, viii. 474
Mann not solicitous for fate of, viii. 434
mob breaks into house of, despite soldiers and constables, viii. 442
Pall Mall, London:
house in, Cts of Orford's claim to money from sale of, ix. 162–3
looking-glasses sought in shops of, iv. 141
mail from France robbed in, ix. 619
St Alban's tavern near, iv. 50
Pallon grosso:
English travellers to introduce, at home, i. 132
Ferdinand of Naples enjoys, ix. 600
public game performed outside Florentine walls, ix. 600
Pallucci, Natalis Joseph (1719–97), Florentine physician and surgeon:
Young Pretender treated by, ix. **394**
(?) ——'s approaching apoplexy predicted by, ix. 245
Palma città:
earthquake account mentions, ix. 376
Palmer, ——, glazier:
HW calls on, to pay bill and complain about it, iv. 391, 396, 401
HW mentions, iv. 326
silk waistcoat and wife's and son's portraits owned by, iv. 396
Palmer, Mary, m. Hon. Dr Coote Molesworth:
escapes fire at sister-in-law's house, vi. 139
Palmerston, Vct. *See* Temple, Henry (ca 1673–1757); Temple, Henry (1739–1802)
Palmieri, Villa (Villa de Tre Visi), near Fiesole:
Cowper gives concert at, vii. 64

farces performed at, vii. 325–6
HW has picture of, iv. 191
Mann rides from, on horseback, iv. 191
Palm tree; palm trees:
at Petraia, astonishes Morice by its size, vi. 29
Johnson says that Palmyra is an Irish bog planted with, ix. 638
state coach adorned with, vi. 104
Palmyra:
effects of, imitated in modern landscape, v. 418
Johnson says, is a bog in Ireland, ix. 638
London may resemble, vii. 569
ruins of, *see under* Wood, Robert
St Paul's will resemble ruins of, viii. 62
Paloma, La, ship:
in Spanish fleet, i. 286
Palombo, Domenico, Mann's secretary:
'does not love trouble,' i. 38
French not familiar to, iv. 329
George II's speech copied by, i. 38
greenhouse collapse in Mann's garden first discovered by, iv. 94
HW may remember, iv. 465, vi. 466
Hollands receive messages through, from Mann, vi. 466
Lami's request to, vi. 13, 24
Lucchese secretary tells, of lack of news, iv. 465
Mann quotes, i. 240, 432
—— 's correspondence with abbé in Rome kept from, i. 114
—— sends message by, i. 342
—— 's letters copied by, i. 97, iv. 275
—— supposes, to be faithful, iv. 275
—— told by, of edict against export of antiquities, iv. 465
—— wishes to replace, i. 157–8, 172, 189
office letters copied by, in Mann's letter-book, iv. 275
paper carried by, in hat, iv. 465
'sedate,' vi. 466
solemn and stupid as ever, vi. 13
spelling of, bad, ii. 240
Voltaire's epistle copied by, iv. 329
wages and duties of, i. 157–8
Palsy:
Bath, Cts of, attributes paralytic stroke to, v. 232, 234
gout may turn into, viii. 67, ix. 402
newspapers attribute, to HW, vi. 461
occurrences of, ii. 225
stroke of, *see* Stroke, paralytic
treatment for, bleeding and blisters, v. 15
Palude Pontine. *See* Pontine marshes
Palzig:
battle of, v. 316
Pam:
HW will build altar to, vi. 17
Pamfili, Benedetto (1675–1760), Duca di San Martino; Principe di Valmontone, Meldola, and San Martino, 1747:

belly of, large, iii. 445
clothes of, iii. 445
Doria has former palace of, vii. 109
Florence visited by, iii. 444
parsimony of, iii. 445
Pisa the home of, iii. 445
Pamfili, Camillo (ca 1673–1747), Principe di Meldola:
brother is heir to fortune of, iii. 444–5
Doria has former palace of, vii. 109
Pamphlet; pamphlets:
anti-Jesuit, v. 383
Egmont's, iv. 43
HW has no taste for, ix. 503
HW sends, to Mann, ii. 31, 89, 353–4, v. 90, 554
Mann, Horace II, seeks list of, from HW for Mann, viii. 451
on Ireland, ix. 11
on Maclaine, iv. 188
scarcer, now that anonymous letters can be printed in newspapers, vi. 169n, viii. 451
Pamphleteers:
now writers of letters to newspapers, viii. 451
Pan:
earthen, Clement XIV's bowels put in, thereby breaking it, viii. 43
Panama:
Anson captures ship off coast of, ii. 478
Panaro, river:
almost dry, i. 464
Austrian army nearer, i. 432–3, 464
campaign to reopen on, ii. 45
Charles Emmanuel III may cross, i. 472
—— 's troops await his permission to cross, ii. 197
—— tries to bridge, i. 449
Gages crosses, iii. 35
—— to reopen the campaign on, ii. 55
German cavalry crosses, ii. 197
Lobkowitz crosses, iii. 30
—— retires to, iii. 22
Montemar approaches, i. 427
—— said to have crossed, i. 455
Sardinian troops near, i. 424, 432–3
skirmishes near, i. 432
Spaniards blow up bridges over, after retreat, ii. 154, 161
Spaniards cross, ii. 151, iii. 30
Spaniards cross, at Bondeno, i. 464, 472
Spaniards may return to, ii. 76
Spaniards watched by Austrians and Sardinians near, i. 489
Spanish army retreats from, ii. 196
Spanish retreat from, ii. 163
Traun does not dare to leave, ii. 76
—— does not expect to cross, ii. 66
—— on other side of, ii. 154
'Pancake, John.' *See* Panciatichi, Giovanni
Panchaud, Isaac (1726–89), Paris banker:
bankruptcy of, over East India stock, vii.

Panciatichi, Signora. *See* Corsi, Giulia (d. 1744)

Panciatichi, Bandino (1719–61):
health of, smallpox, i. 148, 150, 416
house of, not good for ball, i. 122
Rinuccini discusses Albizzi's fistula with, in Mann's presence, i. 481
son born to, ii. 121
wedding feast of, i. 416
wedding night of, i. 150, 169
wife's present from, on birth of heir, ii. 121

Panciatichi, Giovanni Gualberto (1721–50), 'young Panciattici'; 'Giovannino':
darkened but enlivened, iii. 371
England to be visited by, iii. 308
English visit improves the mind but ruins the constitution of, iv. 117
fashionable at The Hague, iii. 371
Franchi, Cocchi, and French and German surgeons attend, iv. 36
Grifoni, Mme, attended by, i. 37
HW's civilities to, in England, deeply appreciated, iv. 36
health of: fever, iv. 36; humour in the knee, iv. 36; knee-pan broken, i. 202; measles, i. 381, 416
London visited by, iii. 371
Lovat's execution attended by, iii. 387
Malta knight, i. 381, ii. 121
Mann calls on, iv. 36
Parigi receives settlement from, i. 111
Paris visited by, iv. 36
sister-in-law's present from, on birth of heir, ii. 121
Suares, Teresa, may be married by, ii. 197
to leave England, iii. 435
Vitelli, Mme, abandoned by, ii. 197, 333
—— deserted by, for the Parigi, i. 111
—— pursued by, ii. 520

Panciatichi, Niccolò (1742–1811):
birth of, ii. 121
Electress godmother to, ii. 121
Mann attends christening of, ii. 121

Panciatichi family:
HW hopes that Onslow affair discredited English knowledge of, iii. 510

'Pancrazio, Signor':
Pertici acts, iv. 357

'Pandæmonium, The.' *See under* Williams, Sir Charles Hanbury

Pandolfini, Mme. *See* Bardi, Maria Costanza

Pandolfini, Elisabetta (d. 1750), m. (1737) Giuseppe Maria Gabburri:
(?) Libri to be cicisbeo of, i. 150
(?) Nerli may be cicisbeo of, i. 150
(?) opera attended by, in Mann's box, i. 136
(?) returns to Spain and husband, ii. 46
(?) Ricasolis entertain, i. 136
(?) Serristori, Andrea, dismissed by, i. 136, 150

Pandolfini, Conte Ferdinando (1716–80); Col. of militia; Gen.:
Albizzi, Marchesa degli, attended by, i. 33
—— brings, to Mann's concert, ii. 12
—— cicisbea of, ii. 12, 29
—— deprived of company of, i. 156
—— quarrels with, ii. 369
—— would enjoy telling Buckingham's story to, ii. 307
brother of, breaks with the Ginori, i. 52
Feroni, Mme, entertains, i. 33
HW mentions, i. 42
HW sends muff and tippet to, i. 45, 47, 52
(?) hæmorrhoid operation avoided by, i. 59
Mann called on by, i. 52
—— discusses HW with, i. 33
—— to entertain, at dinner, iii. 501
militia regiment of, at Leghorn, i. 156, 266, 288
sings, at Mann's entertainment, ii. 12, 29

Pandolfini, Conte Roberto (1705–83):
becomes Count and secretary of Regency, iii. 501
Capponi, Abbé, lives with, ii. 149–50
English visit of: iii. 72, 308, 329, 331, 348, 353–4, 435, 501; ruins his mind and constitution, iv. 117
Eszterházys entertained by, at dinner, iv. 350
Ginori, Signora, has affair with, i. 52, 111
HW entertains, on fast day, iii. 331
HW knew, in England, iii. 501
HW's friend, iii. 72
Harrach accompanies, from England, iii. 435
health of: (?) hæmorrhoids, i. 59; ill, iii. 353–4, iv. 2
Mannelli's correspondence with, iii. 369
Mann to entertain, at dinner, iii. 501
mother's dowry must be equalled by wife of, i. 137–8
Niccolini receives letter of banishment from, iv. 2, 24
promoter of music, ii. 150
put to bed, iii. 348
Suares, Teresa, might marry, i. 137–8, 171, 202

Pandolfini family:
HW hopes that Onslow affair discredited English knowledge of, iii. 510

Pandours ('Panduri'):
left at Prague to annoy the French, ii. 58
to be placed outside of Vienna, i. 144

Panin, Nikita Ivanovich (1718–83), governor of Paul I:
(?) in power, vi. 59

Panmure, E. of. *See* Maule, William

Pannilini, Porzia (b. 1729), m. (1746) Giovanni Sansedoni:
York, D. of, entertained by, vi. 224

Pannini, Giovanni Paolo (1691 or 2–1765), painter:
pictures by, bought by HW, x. 7
Pannocchieschi d'Elci, Marchese Lodovico (1706–88):
HW civil to, in England, ii. 459
HW met, at Mme Grifoni's, ii. 459
Mann to attend ball given by, ii. 60
Niccolini's relative married by, ii. **60**, 85
Pannoni's coffee-house, at Florence ('Pannonia'):
abbés spread false reports in, ii. 557
Cerretesi's English notes to entertain, i. 503
Florentine coffee-house, i. 97n, 503n, iii. 460n
Florentine nobility meet at, i. 503n, iv. 496
gazettes print news worthy of gossipers at, i. 417
gossip at: about Mann and Niccolini, iv. 7; more enduring than that of London, iii. 460
gossiping material lacking at, iii. 439
HW says that England could be routed by a detachment from, iv. 496
Richecourt's departure discussed at, i. 97
scandal banished from, iii. 476
Sturgis avoids, i. 462
See also under Manzuoli, Giovanni
'Panone.' See Manzuoli, Giovanni
Pantagruel. See under Rabelais, François
Pantheon, London:
almost finished, vii. 298
erected in Oxford Road, vii. 210
HW describes, as 'new winter Ranelagh.' vii. 210, 298
HW takes Guines and Lévis to, vii. 298
Lunardi's exhibitions at, ix. 543
masquerade to be held at, viii. 103
subscription ball to be held at, viii. 481
Pantheon, Rome:
cupola to be added to, v. 37
frieze of, Greek buildings at Paris said to be copied from, vii. 158
HW dislikes, v. 31
London Pantheon's dome resembles that of, vii. 298
said to have fallen down, v. 31, 37
'Pantheon chapel':
HW's name for SH cabinet, vi. 523
Panther, ship:
at Port Mahon, i. 285
Pantins. See Puppet shows
Pantolomina:
Sauveterre and 'Spaccatavola' compared with, iii. 356
Pantomime; pantomimes:
Fleetwood supports, ii. 538
London tries to expel, from theatres, ii. 538
Panton, Mary (d. 1793), m. (1750) Peregrine Bertie, 3d D. of Ancaster:
first lady of the Bedchamber and Mistress of the Robes to Q. Charlotte, v. **518**

Florence visited by, ix. 618n
French prefer, to other English duchesses, vi. 155
HW ridicules, v. 156
never sober, viii. 499
Paris visited by, vi. 155
son's bequest to, viii. 494
Waldegrave, Lady Anna Horatia, told by: that son would have married her, viii. 494; to wear mourning, viii. 494
Panton, Thomas (ca 1697–1782):
daughter of, v. 156n, viii. 499
'disreputable horse jock of Newmarket,' viii. 499
Pantoufles:
HW's 'high historical,' iv. 503
Paoli, Fra. See Scarpi, Paolo
Paoli, Clemente (1715–93), Corsican general:
Leghorn visited by, vii. **130**
prays at Vallombrosa, vii. 159
prays for enemies, before shooting them with perfect aim, vii. 130, 159
retreat sought by, at Vallombrosa or La Verna, vii. 130
Paoli, Pasquale (1725–1807), Corsican patriot:
alleged French negotiations with, fabricated to discredit him, vii. 37–8
Bath and Oxford visited by, vii. 150
Caprara may be taken from, vii. 46
Choiseul's perfidy can be exposed by his own letters to, vii. 154
Cocchi with, vii. 68
Corsican independence still awaited by, vii. 130
defeat of, is England's disgrace, vii. 125
dressed in scarlet and gold, vii. 150
Du Barry, Comtesse, might save, vii. 75, 81, 87, 90–1, 124
England approves of, vii. 145
England expects, to hold out in Corsican fastnesses, vii. 121
England may some day espouse the cause of, vii. 159
England pensions, ix. 242n
England visited by, vii. 139, 142, 150
England will be glad of diverting news of, vii. 121
English supporters of, demand help for Corsica, vii. 31
followers of, near Leghorn and Florence, vii. 159
France said to resent English visit of, vii. 139–40
Franco-Genoese treaty over Corsica dooms, vii. 27
French decry, as a coward, vii. 142
French defeated by, vii. 75
French invasion-threats alarm, vii. 96
French offers rejected by, vii. 36
French say, acquired a fortune on the continent, vii. 142
French slander, vii. 154
French try to take Corsica from, vii. 45–7

[Paoli, Pasquale, *continued*]
George III and Charlotte notice, vii. 150
HW sees, at Court, vii. 150, 159
HW suggests, as fit company for Benedict
Arnold, ix. 242
Joseph II confers with, at Mantua, vii.
137, 140
——'s letter about, quoted by Beauvau to
HW, vii. 142, 154
—— writes about, to Leopold, vii. 137, 154
Leghorn visited by, vii. 130
Leopold talks with, at Florence, vii. 130,
136–7
letter of, enclosed by Mann to HW, vii. 68
life of, in danger, vii. 81
Louis XV's expulsion of Comtesse du
Barry would undo, vii. 90–1
Macaulay, Mrs, does not blight English
visit of, vii. 150
Mann should persuade Joseph II to rescue,
vii. 107
——'s letters from, probably intercepted,
vii. 150
—— told by, that Corsicans will submit
to France unless aided by England, vii.
51–2
—— to write to, vii. 159
Marbeuf's ultimatum to, vii. 46
Pembroke may escort to, London, vii. 138
plot against, discovered, vii. 68
troops of, to occupy ports evacuated by
the French, vi. 536
Versailles said to be visited by, for peerage and pension, vii. 31
Viennese mob tries to honour, vii. 140
Paolucci, Camillo (1692–1763), cardinal,
1743; nuncio to Vienna 1738–46:
Benedict XIV gets information from, i.
465
Maria Theresa may dismiss, from Vienna
if Valenti is still supported by Benedict
XIV, ii. 56
Papacy:
now a mere gouty chair, vi. 254
Papal states:
Alfieri banished from, ix. 397
ambassadors from and to Holy See at, *see
under* Ambassador
armies in, ii. 473
Del Monte family invades, iv. 423, 428–9,
442, 445, 446
food shortage in, acute, vi. 453
French ships in, should be burned, ii.
453
grain not to be exported by, to other
parts of Italy, till French and Spanish
wants are filled, vii. 430
incident similar to plot of *Mysterious
Mother* occurred in, viii. 517
Jesuits' colleges in, seized, vii. 504
Jesuits excluded from, vi. 517
Jesuits to be distributed in, vii. 473
Jesuit wealth in, vii. 517

map of, Newcastle asks Mann to procure,
iv. 459
Montemar may pass through, i. 226, 229,
261, 342
Neapolitan convoys in ports of, should be
burned by English, ii. 453
Neapolitans may invade, ii. 295–6, 443–4,
iii. 364
opera omitted in, in jubilee year, iv. 83
ports of, neutral, ii. 301
recalcitrant Jesuits to be banished from,
vii. 507
Sardinians ask leave to pass through, i.
472, 482
seamen of, fear enslavement by Turkish
pirates, i. 16
secretary of state for, *see* Secretary of
State, Papal
ship of: carried to Spezia, i. 16; from
Pesaro, i. 8
ships of, destroyed by Colville, iii. 246
Spaniards may invade, ii. 444
Spanish troops pass through, i. 323
Traun to march through, to Bologna, i.
350
Ubaldini, Cts, banished from, iii. 497
Young Pretender to be offered residence
in, iv. 22
Paparini. *See* Paperini
Papa Silvia:
Spaniards at, ii. 531
Paper:
carta cerulea, ix. 88, 93
Florentine, ix. 507
foolscap, HW jokes about, ii. 204
furniture: Florence should manufacture,
iv. 362; HW and Conway buy, for Mann,
iv. 362
gilt: chimney sweepers wear crowns of, on
May 1, ix. 275; HW writes on, to Mann, ii.
204
HW changes size of, for letters, i. 426, 502
India: at Cornbury, iv. 182; HW seems to
be made of, viii. 66
scraps of, with holy words, made into
soup, iv. 430
Uguccioni's poems will provide pastry
shops with, ii. 554
wall, *see* Wallpaper
wet brown: HW compares Mann to, ii.
467, iii. 61n, 127, viii. 66, 521, ix. 656;
HW has iron stamina in case of, like
Mann's, viii. 521
windows of, at Florence, viii. 232
Paperhangers:
HW scolds, at SH, iv. 371
Paperini, ——, Florentine publisher:
Lunario per la Toscana: earthquake to
be indicated in, iv. 143; HW to consult,
i. 155; Roman hurricane described by, iv.
69
Paperini, Giuseppe, Florentine postmaster:
(?) Vorontsov consorts with, v. 249

Papio, Jean, Capt.:
  captured at Velletri, ii. 494
Paraclete:
  HW names SH hall after, iv. 372
Paradise Lost. See under Milton, John
Paradis terrestre (?by HW):
  Mann's opinion of, i. 108
Paraguay:
  Portugal and Spain to exchange territories in, v. 341
Parallèle de la conduite. See under La Ville, Abbé Jean-Ignace de
Parallel in the Manner of Plutarch, A. See under Spence, Joseph
Paralysis:
  Acquaviva's eyesight threatened by, iii. 136
  occurrences of, iv. 463, vi. 211, vii. 175, ix. 562n, 604n
  See also Palsy; Stroke, paralytic
Paralytic disorder:
  HW said by gazetteer to have, vi. 459, 468
Paralytic stroke. *See under* Stroke
Parchment; parchments:
  deed on, iv. 547
  éloges of the deceased written on, in Italy, to be put into tombs, v. 170
  petitions inscribed upon, ix. 34
Parc-Royal, Hôtel du, at Paris:
  Beaufort's ball at, vi. 365
  HW at, vi. 365
  HW confined by gout in bedchamber of, vi. 348
Pardaillan de Gondrin, Antoine-François de (1709–41), Marquis d'Antin:
  death of, reported, i. 46
  fleet of, disappears, i. 36
Pardo:
  Elizabeth of Spain wins 'battle' of, ii. 195
Parents:
  HW never counsels sons to go against inclinations of, ix. 259
  trials of, HW's reflections on, ix. 414
Parere (medical opinion):
  Cocchi's, iii. 329
Parigi, (?) Maddalena (d ?1774), opera singer:
  Panciatichi, Giovanni, makes settlement on, i. 111
  Pecori deserts the Pepi for, i. 111, 136
  Pepi to shoot, for giving disease to Pecori, i. 136–7, 144, iii. 136
  Tesi's 'creature,' ii. 302
  Vitelli, Mme, jealous of Giovanni Panciatichi's attentions to, i. 136
Paris, Abp of. *See* Beaumont de Péréfixe, Hardouin de (1605–71); Beaumont du Repaire, Christophe de (1703–81)
Paris:
  Albany, Cts of, may be at, viii. 102
  Albemarle dies at, iv. 459–60
  —— retires from, with Mlle Gaucher, iv. 156
  ——'s entertainments at, iv. 156

  architecture of, *see under* Architecture
  Artois to return to, *colle trombe in sacco,* ix. 334
  Aubeterre would be disavowed by, if he upheld Young Pretender, ix. 526
  Austrian and Russian peace delegates to reside at, v. 498
  bankers in, lend to Veers, iii. 507, 510n
  Barbantane supposed to have sent Mann snuff-box from, ix. 206
  barbarity of, vi. 421
  Beaufort gives ball at, vi. 365
  Benedictines at, petition parliament to doff habits and rules, vi. 325
  Boisgelin recalled to, vii. 330
  Boufflers, Comtesse de, will not return to, till HW is gone, vi. 554
  Broglie, Comte de, banished from, vii. 521
  Broglie, Maréchal de, has partisans at, to enjoy defeat of Estrées and Soubise, vi. 50–1
  Busoni banker at, ix. 113
  Campoflorido, Ps, avoids, because it lacks macaroni, ii. 315
  Carmarthen appointed to embassy at, ix. 363
  Caylus discovers encaustic method at, v. 239
  change in English ministry called *malheureux pour la France* in, ix. 287
  civil war may arise in, v. 435
  Conclave sends courier to, to complain of Bourbon cardinals, viii. 79
  Constantinople news would reach, before it reached Florence, vii. 311
  courier escorts Stuart to, ix. 513
  courier, couriers, from: about peace, vi. 65, 105; outruns one from Rome, vi. 407; reaches Florence after departure of courier from Rome, vi. 405; with news of Lestock's raid, iii. 330
  courier sent to, for copy of dispatch stolen from French mail, ix. 619
  Cowper's valet-de-chambre goes through, without stopping for HW's letter, vi. 380
  Craon and Richecourt hear news from, of Young Pretender, iii. 86–7
  Craon gets condolences from, by post, i. 463
  Dorset inefficient as ambassador at, ix. 486
  Du Barry, Comtesse, rumoured at, to have died, viii. 18
  —— the only topic in, vii. 133
  Du Deffand, Marquise, dies at, ix. 90
  embassy at, will probably cease at Albemarle's death, iv. 460
  England's ultimatum sent to, for peace, ix. 342
  English allowed to go to, despite undeclared war, viii. 399
  English army expected to capture, iii. 91, v. 228, 352
  English visitors at: on way to Rome, iv.

[Paris, continued]

82; return, vi. 175; spend large sums there since the peace, vi. 152; swarm, vi. 365

fireworks at: on the peace, vi. 163; produce accidents, iv. 48, vii. 217-18; to celebrate 'victories' over English and Hessians, v. 246

Fontenelle's opera revived at, iv. 213

Forbes challenges Wilkes in, vi. 162

foreigner at, wears orders of different countries, viii. 360-1, ix. 572

Francis I sends courier to, i. 216

French noblemen exiled to, vii. 298

from Peru to, French are defeated, v. 352

Fronsac brings news of St Philip's surrender to, iv. 572

Fullarton lately Stormont's secretary at, ix. 31

funeral orations at, vi. 403-4

Galluzzi's history being translated at, ix. 238

Gatti lived long at, viii. 67n

gazette extract from, v. 344

Gem attended Charlotte Stuart at, ix. 516, x. 47

—— English physician at, ix. 516

Genoa's courier to, iv. 588

George II's death reported from, iv. 388

Grecian buildings in, vii. 158

Grimaldi receives cordon bleu at, v. 560

HW cannot spend winter in, though he wants to, viii. 117

HW drops correspondence with Bns Craven at, ix. 615

HW knew Gatti in, vi. 342, vii. 468

HW likes, as little as London, vi. 451

HW may not like, now that Hertford has left, vi. 492

HW might amuse himself in, with bull Unigenitus, iv. 337

HW might prefer Bath, Tunbridge Wells, or Italy to, vi. 492

HW not to go beyond, vi. 332

HW orders clothes at, i. 176

HW receives letter from, vii. 568

HW saw Lettere pittoriche at, vii. 266

HW's 'dear old friend at,' see Vichy-Champrond, Marie de, Marquise du Deffand

HW sends letter by way of, vi. 294, 301, 308, viii. 137

HW's first visit to opera at, ii. 495

HW's letter from: about D. of York's death, may have miscarried, vi. 560; not to be specifically answered by Mann, viii. 127; received by Mann, viii. 130

HW's services at, to Lady Mary Coke, viii. 179

HW's visit to, may be prevented by Parliamentary session, vi. 247

HW tells Mann not to write to him at, vi. 411, 548, vii. 134, 139, 311, viii. 128

HW to revisit: i. 127, vi. 135, 152, 175,

247, 270-1, 285, 289, 484, 544, vii. 128-9, 133-4, 304, 311, viii. 120; as 'the way of all flesh,' vi. 152; to see Mme du Deffand, vi. 484, vii. 311, viii. 120; when Parliament rises, vi. 285

HW tried to see little of, on first visit, vi. 175

HW would like to be at, when Pitt returned to power, vi. 441

HW writes from, i. 124-7, vi. 340-4, 347-8, 358-60, 363-6, 371-3, 380-3, 394-7, 400-5, 409-11, 550-5, viii. 123-7, 132-4

Harcourt to get embassy at, vii. 65-6

headdress from, for Mme Grifoni, i. 239

Hertford's embassy to, iv. 467-8, vi. 130, 135, 175, 315-16, 341

——'s resignation disrupts HW's plans to go to, vi. 316

Hervey, Bp, ejected from, ix. 454

Holland said to have sent Wassenaer to, with peace terms, iii. 216

Honoré III probably notifies, of D. of York's illness, vi. 556

hôtels of, all look alike, vii. 312

Hume-Rousseau quarrel famous in, vi. 465

iron wig brought from, by Wortley Montagu, iv. 226

Italy used to get ton from, ix. 495

Jacobite emissary at, ii. 426

James II said to have deposited funds at Hôtel de Ville in, vi. 385

Jersey, Cts of, to visit, ix. 411

Jersey attack announced by post from, viii. 471

Julienne's sale at, vi. 523

Kingston, Ds of, summoned to, to meet agents of Ecclesiastical Court, viii. 83

—— to rent palace at, viii. 242

letters from: about French invasion of Jersey, viii. 471; about Mme du Barry, vii. 151; about peace negotiations, vi. 86; about storm-wrecked English fleet, viii. 436-7; bewail French situation, viii. 466; encourage Lorenzi, vi. 370; lament Laeffeld battle, iii. 426; says France will defend Holland against Austria, ix. 545; speak of breakup of French camps, viii. 413; to Florence, should take 9 or 10 days, vi. 352; to Rome about new schemes of Young Pretender, iii. 451

Liotard's prices higher in England than in, iv. 362

London compared with, vii. 121

Lorenzi says that his clothes come from, v. 501

Lorenzi, Comtesse de, follows styles of, v. 501

Louis XVI invites D. and Ds of Gloucester to, viii. 125

Louisbourg news at, v. 230, 234-5

Maillebois posts Louis XV's reprimand to, vii. 284

Manchester, D. of, takes embassy at, ix. 398

Mann encloses letter to Stanley at, vi. 340

—— sends iris roots for, vii. 333

——'s letter probably detained at, by Thompson, ii. 412

—— tries to get gossip from, about visit of Cts of Coventry and Lady Caroline Petersham, iv. 333

—— would learn news of peace from, before HW could send it, ix. 347

Marie Leszczyńska's triumphal entry into, ii. 524

Mauduit's *Considerations* appear at, v. 469

Medina Sidonia, D. of, dies on way to, viii. 440

mendicants at, ii. 72

Mercy-Argenteau and Starhemberg make statements at, about Austrian-Dutch quarrel, ix. 561

Mirepoix family seldom at, iv. 87

mob of, tramples old woman for cheering Louis XV, v. 56

Modena, Ds of, to stay at, ii. 222

Niccoli is Tuscan agent at, viii. 362

nuncio at, *see under* Nuncio

O'Brien, Mrs, banished from, iv. 27–8, 45

opera at, *see under* Opera

Panchaud a banker in, vii. 133

Papal election to be influenced from, i. 21

Parliamentary opposition goes to, viii. 262

Parliament of Paris' retirement causes loss of money by, vii. 322

Patapan barks at Frenchmen in, ii. 221

post from, i. 463, vi. 352, 353

president's family from, argue over dinner course, vi. 163

Presle's collection at, x. 46

provinces gayer than, viii. 498

public opinion and religion in, governed by fashion, vi. 412

rainwater from, iii. 414

reports of Wilkes's trial sent to, vii. 12

Richmond's embassy to, vi. 323, 341, 369

riots at: over children being sent to the colonies, iv. 170; over corn prices, viii. 101–2

Rochford and Villettes to meet at, iv. 76

Rochford's possible embassy to, iv. 420, 426, 467, vi. 420

Rohan, Cardinal de, imprisoned at, ix. 603

rouge fashionable at, ii. 220

Rousseau's possible opinion of, viii. 62

royal academy of, Sloane's museum offered to, iv. 358

Selwin banker at, i. 93, x. 29

Seymour's visit to, might be caused by Young Pretender's wife, viii. 102

snow in, vi. 396

Sorba, Genoese minister to, v. 509, vii. 363

——'s birth and death at, vii. 363

Stafford, E. and Cts of, to live half-time at, ii. 277

Stainville envoy at, iv. 29

Stanley's missions to, v. 504, 514, vi. 300

Stormont ordered to quit, viii. 373

——'s courier leaves, viii. 1

Stuart, Charlotte, brings new modes from, ix. 535

—— educated in convent at, ix. 512, x. 47

—— registered at, as Ds of Albany, ix. 513, 516n, 521–2

surgeons of, fail to cure Panciatichi's knee, iv. 36

surgeon would never leave, for private service, i. 81

Sutton rumoured to be at, viii. 2

toys from, at Leghorn fair, vi. 423

travelling time from, to Florence, vi. 352

Tyrawley's wigs from, v. 191

visitors to: Albany, Cts of, vii. 398; Ancaster, Ds of, vi. 155; Anhalt-Zerbst, Ps of, vi. 65; Astley, ix. 451; Baillie, Griselda, ix. 2; Barré, vi. 365; Bath, E. of, iv. 155, vi. 343n; Beauchamp, vi. 344; Bedford, Ds of, vi. 78, 105; Bedford, D. of, vi. 69–70, 90, 92–3; Bridgwater, Ds of, vi. 155; Burdett, iv. 20; Carlisle, vi. 554; Churchills, iv. 324–5, 339; Clermont, E. and Cts of, ix. 357n; Clinton, Bn, iv. 429; Coke, Lady Mary, vi. 94, vii. 568, viii. 179; Cornbury, iii. 188n, iv. 213–14; Coventry, Cts of, iv. 324, 333, 337–9, 376; Coventry, E. of, iv. 337–9, 376; Crébillons, iv. 325; Douglas, Ds of, vi. 155; Elcho, iii. 272; Estaing, viii. 545; Felicità d'Este, ii. 378; Fitzherbert, ix. 311; Forbes, vi. 162; Franchini, Abbé, ii. 131; Grenville, Thomas, ix. 279; Guasco, vi. 529; HW, i. 124–7, 131, 164, 176, ii. 495, vi. 332–3, 340–4, 347–8, 358–60, 363–6, 370, 371–3, 380–3, 394–7, 400–5, 409–11, 434, 441, 524, 548, 550–5, vii. 133, 139, 141–5, 157, 158, 266, 311, 319, 320–3, 330–1, 398, 524, viii. 116–17, 123–7, 132–4, 179, ix. 516, 558; Hamilton, Ds of, vi. 155; Hamilton, Lady Archibald, iii. 361n; Holland, Bn, vi. 163, 554; Holland, Bns, vi. 163; Hunt, iii. 477; Izard, viii. 102; Joseph II, viii. 281, 298, 367; Karl Alexander, iv. 376; Karl Wilhelm Ferdinand, vi. 414; Kingston, Ds of, viii. 88, 242; Lincoln, i. 165; Lorenzi, Chevalier de, iv. 542; Lorraine, Duchesse de, ii. 298n; Macdonald, Sir James, vi. 343; Magnan, iii. 564; Mann, ix. 2; Martin, vi. 198; Montfort, iv. 155–6; Morehead, Mrs, iii. 477; Morice, vii. 140, 146, ix. 74; Mozzi, vii. 141–2; Orford, Cts of, iv. 335, vii. 120, 141–2, 230; Oswald, ix. 279; Panciatichi, iv. 36; Pars, viii. 144; Parsons family, i. 185; Penn, Mrs, iv. 20; Petersham, Lady Caroline, iv. 324, 333, 337–9; Poyntz, Mrs, vi. 163–4; Richmond, Ds of, vi. 155; Richmond, D. of, vi. 163, 364; Salm, Ps of, vii. 398; Selwyn, vi. 105, 163; Sempill, ii. 426; Stanley, v. 504, 514, vi.

[Paris, *continued*]
300, 327, 340; Taaffe, iii. 450n, iv. 287-8, v. 473n; Van Hoey, iii. 264; Veers, iii. 507; Vernon, Lady Harriet, viii. 242; Voltaire, viii. 356; Walpole, Hon. Robert, vii. 141; Wilkes, vi. 162, 198, 282, 365, vii. 28; Wortley Montagu, iii. 450n, iv. 287-8, v. 473n; Wrottesley, vi. 554; York, D. of, vi. 245, 550, 558; Young Pretender, ii. 389, 394, iv. 8, 15, 44, vii. 398
  vivacity uncommon in, except among rash young men, viii. 498
  Waldegrave's embassy to, iii. 564
  Walkinshaw, Mrs, in convent at, x. 47
  watches from, for Riccardi and Niccolini girls, v. 343
  witticism at, about d'Estaing, viii. 450
  Yorke may replace Stormont at, viii. 179
  Young Pretender collects volunteers from, iii. 87
  —— may enter French army at, ii. 378
  —— probably visits Princesse de Talmond at, iv. 44
  ——'s arrest at, iv. 8, 15
  ——'s disappearance reported from, iii. 367
  —— sends Stuart to, to fetch daughter, ix. 513
  ——'s income rumoured at, vii. 402
  ——'s non-recognition from Clement XIII variously interpreted at, vi. 394
Paris, Parlement de. *See* Parliament of Paris
Paris, Peace Treaty of (1763):
  concluding, vi. 116
  couriers announce, vi. 105
  deferred, vi. 99-100
  definitive treaty for, awaited, vi. 118
  English negotiators for, v. 504, 514, vi. 69-70, 86, 90, 92-3, 300
  English victories sacrificed by delegates to, vi. 401
  in progress, vi. 52, 60, 65
  opposed, vi. 89, 91, 95
  Pompadour, Marquise de, buys English stocks to profit by rise at news of, ix. 357
  Pynsent lived to see, vi. 277, 284
  said to be broken off, vi. 81
  signing and terms of, vi. 95-6
  stocks rise and fall according to expectation of, vi. 38, 81
Paris, Peace Treaty of (1783):
  England's ultimatum about, ix. 342
  English negotiators for, ix. 279, 311
  Gibraltar's defence may influence, ix. 352
  ignominious, but hardly mentioned after Parliament's approval, ix. 373-4
  in progress, ix. 279, 311
  not yet concluded, ix. 354, 355
  preliminaries for, ix. 356-7, 362
  signed, ix. 426-7
  to be adhered to, despite English political shift, ix. 372
  unpopular in England, ix. 362, 366-7

Park, English:
  Cascines reminiscent of, vii. 6
Parker, Dorothea (d. 1768), m. Robert Gates:
  intimate with Lady Walpole's woman, ix. 92n
  son of, ix. 92n
Parker, George (ca 1697-1764), 2d E. of Macclesfield, 1732; M.P.:
  chairman of trustees of Sloane's museum, iv. **359**
  death of, vi. 211
  Grenville succeeds, as teller of the Exchequer, vi. 211
  HW to send papers to, iv. 557
  longitude investigated by, iv. 359
  mistress marries, vi. 211
Parker, Sir Hyde (1714-82), 5th Bt, 1782; naval officer:
  French transports defeated by, ix. **21**
  George III thanks, for doubtful victory over Dutch, ix. 176-7
  St Eustatius convoy should have been protected by, ix. 159-60
Parker, John (ca 1730-ca 1765), painter; art agent:
  (?) Pulteney warned against, iv. 174
Parker, Capt. John, of *Fort St Philip*:
  Mann commissions, ix. 249
  Minorcan news brought by, ix. **196**
Parker, Mark (ca 1698-1775); papal naval captain; art dealer:
  Compagni and Libri to pay money to, i. **81-2**
  Cybo's collection known to, ii. 236
  expenses of, over statue, ii. 178
  HW's correspondence with, i. 291, x. 3-5
  HW's views of Rome billed by, i. 81-2
  HW's views of Rome sent by, to Howe, i. 395
  Lanfranco painting may be owned by, ii. 275
  list of pictures owned by, forwarded to HW, ii. 243
  Mann pays, ii. 214
  —— regrets not having bought collection of, for Sir Robert Walpole, ii. 273
  ——'s correspondence with, about 'views' and statue for HW, i. 81-2, 268, 291, 317, ii. 56, 133, 152, 161, 177-8, 190, 197, 236, 239-40
  prices of, excessive, ii. 296
  (?) Pulteney warned against, iv. 174
  Raphael painting bought by, from Cybo collection, ii. 239-40
  statue procured through, by HW, i. 82, 212, 268, 291, 317, ii. 56, 133, 152, 161, 177-8, 190, 197, x. 5
  Valle does not trust, ii. 152
  —— to be threatened by, i. 317
Parker, Sir Peter (?1721-1811), Kt, 1772; cr. (1783) Bt; naval officer; M.P.:
  Charleston expedition of, fails, viii. 236
  said to be wounded in 6 places, viii. 236

Parker, Samuel (1640–88), Bp of Oxford 1686–8:
conversion of, from Presbyterianism, iv. 188
James II's master of Magdalen College, iv. 188
Park Place, Berks; Conway's seat:
Conway and Cts of Ailesbury buy, iv. 316–17
—— in bed at, ix. 115
——'s seat, ix. 428n, 576n
—— visits, in winter, vi. 413
Henley near, ix. 428n, 576n
previous owners of, iv. 316–17
'Sabine Farm,' vi. 413
visitors to: HW, vi. 263, vii. 339, ix. 119, 428, 659; Hamilton, Sir William and Lady, vii. 339
Parlements, French. See Parliament of Paris; Parliaments, French
Parliament:
accuracy of reports of speeches in, ix. 58
acts and bills of: act for abolishing sinecures, ix. 273; Act of Insolvency, v. 45, 140, 148; Act of Settlement, iii. 142; against arming without authority, iii. 102n; American acts, viii. 77; American trade restriction bill, viii. 158; army supply bills, iii. 4–5; Bill of Pains and Penalties, i. 330; Bill of Rights, vii. 114, 209; Bribery Bill, vi. 584–5; Cambric Bill, ii. 192; Clandestine Marriages Act, iv. 383, vi. 294; Contractor's Bill, ix. 28, 38–9, 47; Correspondence with the Pretender Bill, ii. 440; Defence by Counsel Bill, iii. 396; Detention of Suspected Persons Bill, ii. 408; East India Co. Dividend Bill, vi. 513, 534; East India Judicature Bill, vii. 399; Election Laws Bill, i. 484; Excise Bill on cider, see under Cider Tax; Exclusion Bill, iv. 222; Ferrers' separation bill, v. 184, 367, 396; Gin Act, iv. 48; Gold Coin Act, vii. 498; Grafton's divorce bill, vii. 99; HW imitates language of, ix. 358; habeas corpus extension, v. 182, 199, 205; habeas corpus suspension, ii. 408; Hanover troops, see under Hanover; Indemnity Bill, i. 425, 428–9, 436–7, 448, 454; India Bills, ix. 448–9, 451–2, 457, 458n, 459, 484–5, 488, 490–1; Jacobites restored by, to forfeited Scottish estates, ix. 520; make war but cannot repeal it, viii. 355; Marriage Act, see Clandestine Marriages Act, Royal Marriage Act; Massachusetts Bay Act, vii. 568; Militia Bills, v. 137, 552, viii. 497; Murder, Preventing, Act, iv. 317, v. 388; Mutiny Bill, iv. 33, 38, 51, 54, 112, 229; Navy Bill, iv. 33, 38, 54, v. 182; Northumberland procures, for erection of powder mills, vii. 365; Pension Bill, i. 392; Place Bill, i. 295–6, 391–2, 431, ii. 19; Players of Interludes Act, vii. 271; private bills, iv. 50; Quaker Bill, iii. 503n; Quebec Government Bill, viii. 13; Quieting Bill, viii. 542; Regency

Bill, iv. 239–40, 247, 249, 257, 263, 434, vi. 294–9; regulation of the King's civil establishments, ix. 20, 26–7, 28; Riot Act, i. 252; Royal Marriage Bill, vii. 390, 396, 398, ix. 629; Scottish Bills, iii. 388, 396, iv. 310, x. 31–3; Septennial Act, i. 386; Somerset, D of, disinherits son by, ii. 523; Stamp Act, vi. 401–2, 408, 409–10, 494, viii. 208, ix. 213, 252, 279; Trade Bills, iv. 135; Triennial Act, i. 392; Turnpike Bills, iv. 112, 120–1, vii. 455; Wrought Silks and Velvets Bill, vi. 301
addresses may be procured by, on national disgraces, viii. 132
addresses to George II from, ii. 418
adjournments of: delay conclusion of Wilkes controversies, vi. 200; during Gordon riots, ix. 67, 76; expected, iv. 554, ix. 167; for re-elections, vi. 31; for three weeks, vi. 194, 200, 455; in summer of 1778, to be short, viii. 384; over Christmas holidays, ii. 366, 552, iii. 194, 455, iv. 409, v. 35, 558, vi. 194, 200, 478, viii. 341, ix. 103, 116, 222; over Easter holidays, iii. 234, iv. 240, v. 75, viii. 458, ix. 30–1, 264; to see Othello, iv. 231; to settle things, i. 319
administration change depends on next meeting of, ix. 462
African Company's slave trade discussed in, iv. 126
agenda of, vii. 66, ix. 562, 563, 566
Aix treaty debated in, iv. 3
allusions to, often obscure to HW, ix. 612
Almack's club resembled by, viii. 81
America and India absorb attention of, viii. 46
America may receive virtual declaration of war from, viii. 75
American agitation in, must be intense, viii. 87
American disputes should be laid before, vi. 390, 407, 408
American negotiations proposed in, viii. 141–2, 354, 355, 358–9
American subjection upheld in, by Pitt's followers alone, viii. 371
American war eagerly promoted by, viii. 81, 85
animosity in, viii. 434
annuity settled by, on Earldom of Chatham, viii. 382
'archiepiscopal seat of folly and knavery,' viii. 284
army officers who are members of: have not left, ii. 203; may get leave to come home on 'private affairs' to 'drop in' at House of Commons, ii. 97; nearly all return to England, ii. 102
army's disgust may be felt in, v. 252
associations seek to reform, ix. 29
Austria promised support by, i. 133
Aylett committed to Newgate by, vii. 74

[Parliament, *continued*]

balls and masquerades not disturbed by, iv. 469

battles no longer fought in, v. 344

Belloni avenges himself on, iii. 77

Benfield said to have bribed members of, for Nawab of Arcot, ix. 117

bills for reform of: mentioned, ix. 272; resisted by Lord Chancellor Thurlow, ix. 273

bills in, the proving-ground for ministerial leaders, x. 27

Birmingham petitions, to enforce American acts, viii. 77

bishops accused in, by Nugent, i. 431

Bostonians will not drink tea with, vii. 550

Buckingham grand jury thanks, for lowering land tax, vi. 494–5

Burgoyne's surrender arouses no consternation in, viii. 341

Burke's reform bill in: has clause cashiering the King's Household, ix. 28; resisted by Lord North, ix. 20; would annihilate Board of Trade, ix. 26–7

business of: deferred till after the holidays, iv. 240; left off, ix. 146

Byng cannot be tried until meeting of, v. 3

campaign in: almost over, iv. 538–9; heat of, viii. 349; opens warmly, iv. 455

cannot do worse than it did last year, viii. 133

Caribs unrepresented in, vii. 462

chamber of, Mansfield wants Ds of Kingston to have private hearing in, viii. 150

change in, since Cromwell's day, iv. 339

Chavigny's observation about, vi. 294

Cholmondeley to travel before opening of, vii. 316

Christmas not to disperse, from London, viii. 542–3

church more fashionable than, iv. 357–8

clergy's adherence to Thirty-nine Articles to be debated in, vii. 366

common business alone transacted by, viii. 67

condemned by Abp of Florence to pay large sum to Northumberland, ix. 225

confusion in, ix. 66

Constitutional Queries subject of motions in, iv. 222

convention with Frederick II to be considered by, v. 190

Cornwallis's surrender makes no impression on, ix. 218

county associations send petitions to, ix. 6

Court must resist dissolution of, vii. 151

Court party prevails in, ix. 482, 502

Court wins victory in, over new-raised regiments, ix. 34

Crébillon may dedicate *Oliver Cromwell* to, iv. 339

crowd at opening of, greater than at Coronation, vi. 104

debates in: on West Indian regiment, iv. 531; over burning of queries, iv. 222; over foreign situation, viii. 341

deep game must be played by, viii. 61

dissolution of: iii. 412, 418, 421, vi. 587, vii. 5, viii. 44, ix. 481–2; blamed by Cts of Orford for mismanagement of her boroughs, viii. 57, 66–7; by Pitt or Rockingham, would leave Wilkes to control the next one, vii. 181; Court must resist, vii. 151; Dunning seeks to delay, ix. 41; expected, iv. 187, 337, ix. 465, 467, 474; George II's speech on, iii. 418; irregular, viii. 44; Mann hopes for, ii. 4; not surprising, ix. 85–6; rumoured, ix. 461; threatened, vii. 176, 182, 186, 188; will empty London and send HW to SH, ix. 461

does nothing for want of an Opposition, vii. 454

Dunning seeks to prevent prorogation or dissolution of, until petitions are satisfied, ix. 41

East India Company settles affairs with, vi. 478–9

East India Company to be regulated by, vii. 442

East Indian squadron to be voted funds by, iv. 410

ending of: ii. 440; pleases Mann, ii. 14; pleases Sir Robert Walpole, i. 502; to precipitate politics, vi. 219

English counties and towns send petitions to, ix. 6, 10

English diversions undisturbed by, iv. 469

English extravagance cannot be curbed by, viii. 231

English-German negotiations may not please, iv. 493

English mistakes authorized by, viii. 474

factions will not arise till next session of, v. 504

fate of leaders of, compared to that of generals, ix. 255

first session of, apt to be dull, iv. 456

Fox, C.J., the first figure in, ix. 154

French aid to America discussed in, viii. 254

French insult to be communicated to, by ministry, vi. 364

French invasion set after assembling of, i. 160

French parliaments resembled by, iv. 286–7

galleries for members of, at fireworks, iv. 48

Garrick's family not to be provided for by, viii. 435

George II adjourns, i. 319

—— receives loyal address from, ii. 430

—— said to be urged by, to give Hanover to D. of Cumberland, i. 328

——'s message to, incites resolution to aid Lisbon sufferers, iv. 520

—— tells: of Drummond's proposal to exchange prisoners, iii. 187; of invasion threats, ii. 399

—— to address, i. 220, ii. 429

—— to be addressed by, about court martial for naval officers, iii. 33

George III may denounce son to, if he weds Mrs Fitzherbert, ix. 629

——'s address to, vi. 274

——'s messages to, about French notification, viii. 374

——'s speech at opening of: ix. 352; disordered by Cornwallis's defeat, ix. 209; unpromising, viii. 423

——'s sudden visit to, vii. 303

Gordon rioters assault members of, ix. 53-4

Gower and Weymouth resign on eve of, viii. 533-4

Grenville's friends avoid, vii. 248, 251

—— tired of, vi. 520

Guines astonished by uproar in, vii. 256-7

HW does not heed debates in, about war and generals' conduct, viii. 485

HW may delay letter for session of, ix. 427

HW's quitting of, called taking up his 'freedom,' viii. 46

HW wants act by, about master builders' fire liability, iv. 185

HW will regret ending of, ii. 186

Hamilton's Etruscan vases bought by, x. 46

Hanover's safety insured by, i. 46

harmony of, about war, pleases Mann, v. 263

Holland may ask, to make war on America, viii. 77

House of Commons: address against Hanover troops proposed in, ii. 355; address against rank for officers of privately-raised regiments carried in, iii. 154, 158; address in, scarcely opposed, iv. 286, ix. 437; address moved in, i. 375-6, ii. 351, 399; address of, almost thanks Hanover troops, v. 30-1; address of, on accommodation with America, passed unanimously, ix. 352; adjourned, i. 484, vi. 508, vii. 292; adjourned because of Norton's illness, ix. 18, 38, 40-1; adjourned to choose a Speaker, vii. 176; adjourns for subscription masquerade, vii. 193; adjourns to see Othello, iv. 231; admirals' and generals' conduct examined by, viii. 481; ailments of, compared to HW's gout, ix. 402; amendment to Address debated in, iii. 188, x. 22-4; America to be discussed by, day and night, vi. 513; approach to, through Westminster Hall, i. 300; army and navy corruption should be resisted by, x. 15; army increase voted by, i. 410; army in Flanders discussed in, ii. 123, 382-3; army remit-

tances examined in, ii. 191; army unanimity discussed in, x. 10; army voted on by, i. 343; as acquisitive as if composed of Catherine II, Frederick II, and Maria Theresa, viii. 562; authority of, must not be weakened by the Crown or mob, vii. 181; bar of, prisoners to kneel at, iv. 224; bar of, Wilkes has March, Sandwich, and Temple summoned to, vii. 73-4, 77; bar of, Wilkes to be heard at, vii. 73, 78; Barré and Saville leave, in rage, vii. 289, 291; Bavarian treaty to be ratified in, iv. 212; Beckford conducts Chatham's business in, vi. 506-7; becomes a mere war office, v. 344; Bedfords do not want Conway to lead, vi. 542, 570; Bedford's followers desert, vi. 464; bill passed in, absolving Keppel and Norris from oath of secrecy about Byng trial, v. 63-4; bribery and corruption investigated by, vii. 584; Buckingham assizes cause of controversy in, iii. 470-1, x. 25-8; Buckinghamshire petition committee not chosen by, ix. 572; Bunbury fails to make motion in, against German war, vi. 7-8; Burgoyne discussed in, viii. 383; Burke attacks, vii. 170, 184; Burke defends himself in, for restoring dismissed men to Pay Office, ix. 407-8; Byng may have to face, iv. 578, v. 55; Byng's court martial discussed in, v. 63-5; call of, i. 440, v. 35; Camden's expulsion weakens Court party in, vii. 182; Carteret might be sent to Tower by, iii. 213; Carteret's ministry has majority in, ii. 96; chairman of, ix. 35; Chairman of the Committee on Privileges and Elections chosen by, i. 220, 242, 250; changes in, rumoured at Florence, iii. 325; chaos in, iii. 202; Chippenham election decided in, i. 318-19; Clavering's motion to ask George III to lay London's remonstrance before, vii. 198; clerk of, see Dyson, Jeremiah (1722-66), Hatsell, John (1743-1820), Ley, John (ca 1732-1814); clerks forced by, to sit in empty walls, ix. 572-3; Clive exonerated by, vii. 484-5, 562; Clive names 10 members to, viii. 61; coffee-girl attends in Speaker's chambers at, vi. 284; coffee-house resembled by, v. 52; Coke sits 22 hours in, i. 383; committee of, examines Independents, iii. 387-8; committees formed in, on riots, vii. 291, 297, 303; composition of, uncertain, ii. 327; contested elections reviewed by, viii. 67; Conway and C.J. Fox attack Court party in, viii. 139; Conway-Grenville debate in, vi. 274; Conway moves address to George III in, ix. 244, 251-2, 259; Conway opposed by D. of Bedford as leader of, vi. 542, 570; Conway's colleagues should protect HW from long sessions in, vi. 317; Conway's distinction in, iv. 265; Conway's membership in, impediment to his going to Scotland,

[Parliament, *continued*]

iii. 204; Conway to remain as leader of, vi. 571; Cornish and Scottish vote in, overturns Sir Robert Walpole, i. 346n; Cornish election (Bossiney) settled by, i. 233, 247, 263; Cornwall becomes Speaker of, ix. 95; Cornwallis's surrender has not further weakened administration supporters in, ix. 212; Corsica noticed by, vii. 66, 69; country gentlemen desert, vi. 520; country gentlemen in, oppose land tax, vi. 487; country gentlemen in, probably bribe their constituencies to present anti-American addresses, viii. 132; Court party wins in, ii. 96, vi. 109, vii. 168, 194; Court puts Luttrell in, in Wilkes's place, vii. 344, 346; Crowle calls, *brutum fulmen,* iv. 224; Cumberland, D. of, exposed by, iv. 33; Cust resigns as Speaker of, vii. 175; *Daily Advertiser* advertisement said to be condemned by, iii. 353, 362; Deal representatives ask Horace Mann II to inquire in, about Dutch ships, ix. 222–3; debate in, over abolition of Thirty-Nine Articles, vii. 376; debates in, of little consequence because of unshaken majority, ix. 153; De Grey cannot be spared from, vii. 175; Denbighshire election settled by, i. 343–4, ii. 394, 401; division in, advocated by Jacobites and opposed by Patriots, i. 231; Dowdeswell and George Grenville amuse, with squabble, vi. 566; Dunning denounces Crown influence in, ix. 35–6; Dunning deserts minority in, vii. 168; Dunning moves *by authority* for adjournment of, ix. 262; Easter adjournment impossible for, ix. 572; East India Company enrages, by voting irregular dividend, vi. 513; East India Company examined by, vi. 493, 495–7, 504, vii. 392, 399, 401, 451–2, 490; Egmont, and Opposition walk out of, on Mutiny Bill, iv. 112; elections embroil, iv. 469; elections for, iv. 388, 456, v. 484; election voting in, requries 100 members, viii. 273; English-Spanish negotiations to be discussed in, v. 553; *Essay on Woman* discussed in, vi. 181–5, 186–8; Exchequer house has door to, i. 299–300; excise discussed in, i. 458; Fortrose a member of, iii. 233; Fordwich, Vct, loses seat in, by staying in Florence, v. 543; Fox, C.J., attacks Sandwich in, viii. 460, ix. 244; Fox, C.J., compliments Conway on triumphs in, ix. 251–2; Fox, C.J., has majority in, ix. 449, 466; Fox, C.J., may be carried to, in procession, ix. 563; Fox, C.J., might by violence provoke Tories of, against North and Fox, ix. 379; Fox, C.J., proposes India bill in, ix. 448–9; Fox, C.J., shines in, vii. 188, ix. 154, 437; Fox, Henry, and Pitt have daily altercations in, v. 65; Fox, Henry, becomes manager of, for Bute, vi. 92; Fox, Henry, defers motion in, on continuing term of privately-raised regiments,

iii. 209; Fox, Henry, persuaded by Carteret to be leader of, iv. 502; Fox, Henry, refuses secretaryship of state because he cannot have control of, iv. 417; Fox, Henry, should manage, more easily, vi. 112; Fox, Henry, to preside at Cockpit on eve of session of, iv. 503; Fox, Henry, vacates seat in, vi. 101; Fullarton's regiment discussed in, ix. 34; Gage preserved from arrest by membership in, i. 255n; Gage's son to enter, i. 255; generals at bar of, say that America cannot be conquered, viii. 474; George II and Sir Robert Walpole said to dread changes in, i. 203; George II does not go to, v. 345; George II notifies, of sending Hessians to Scotland, iii. 188; George II tells Pulteney to quit, i. 494; George II voted money by, for Maria Theresa, i. 390; George II wants, to tell him not to give rank to officers of privately-raised regiments, iii. 154; George II wants to prorogue, iv. 469; George III hissed by mob on way to, vii. 291; George III recommends increased pensions for his brothers, and dowry for his sister to, vi. 425; George III's speech to, v. 344–5; George III visits, and announces its dissolution, ix. 481; George III visits, for bill for D. of Grafton's divorce, vii. 99; German war unpopular with, v. 553; Gibson and Murray sentenced by, iv. 224–5; Gordon, Lord George, a candidate for, ix. 183, 187; Gordon attends, wearing blister and flannel, i. 298; Granby deserts to minority in, vii. 168; Granville ministry not permitted by, iii. 212; Great Seal cast used for death-warrant of, ix. 481; Grenville, George, defeated in, vi. 381–2; Grenville, George, proposes election bill in, viii. 45, 273; Grenville, George, said to succeed Onslow as speaker of, v. 491; Grenville, George, to be manager but not speaker of, v. 541; Grenville, George, was manager of, for Bute, vi. 91; HW absent from, during re-election, v. 63; HW attends constantly, but never stays long, i. 344; HW avoids, v. 344; HW calls, 'Sanhedrin,' vii. 555; HW calls, 'Temple of Virtue' and 'Temple of Concord,' viii. 341; HW calls, 'that scold,' vi. 316; HW dines after leaving, ii. 351; HW dreads entering, i. 109, 176; HW fatigued by attendance at, i. 294, ii. 381, v. 28, vi. 506; HW glad to be rid of, vi. 316; HW glad to have forsaken, vi. 570, vii. 66, 128–9, 351, viii. 46, 101, 284, ix. 476; HW goes to, to hear C.J. Fox, vii. 399–400; HW has seen no member of, ix. 578; HW kept busy by, ii. 381, 392, iv. 30, 522; HW leaves, before vote, in order not to vote against Henry Fox, v. 86; HW looks back on career in, ix. 558; HW paraphrases Bible verse to apply to, ix. 262; HW resolves never to set foot in, vii. 399–400; HW's aversion to, vi. 348, viii. 101;

HW's election to, i. 73, 84; HW's health impaired by attendance at, vi. 285, viii. 146; HW's motion in, for the Address, iv. 227; HW's refusal to return to, alienates his friends, vi. 359; HW 'stewing' in, vi. 514; HW's voting in, iii. 154, iv. 126, x. 19; HW to forsake, vi. 522; HW would feel gout if he returned to, vii. 66; Hanover troops debated in, ii. 123, 180, 382, iii. 241; Hartington and Wyndham move for address of loyalty to George II from, ii. 399; Hartington sits 22 hours in, i. 383; Hastings's trial at, ix. 630, 639, 642, 651, 653; Hay not permitted by George III to become member of, v. 73; Hedon election in, i. 355; Hertford may have six sons in, ix. 488; Hervey not to attend, till majority is certain, i. 275; Hickey and Reynolds punished by, vi. 584; Hood to have replaced Rodney in, ix. 284-5; Horne Tooke summoned before, for attacking Norton, vii. 555; House of Lords agrees to resolutions of, vi. 187; House of Lords asked by, for peers to appear at their bar, vii. 73-4, 77; Hume-Campbell again frequents, iv. 111; imperialistic, vii. 562; India's affairs examined by, see under East India Company; Ireland considered by, ix. 583; Ireland's independence signed by, ix. 279-80; Jacobites expect, to thwart George II and Sir Robert Walpole, i. 203; Jacobites in, instructed to oppose Sir Robert Walpole, i. 232n; Jacobites in, oppose suspension of habeas corpus, iii. 138-9; Jacobites incite instructions to members of, v. 12, 19; Jacobites want division in, i. 231; Jacobites will try to buy seats in, iv. 131; Johnstone abuses Germain in, vii. 255-6; journals of, consulted by HW, iv. 139; keyhole of, stopped, i. 300; King's Bench remands prisoner committed by, iv. 249-50; late servility of, to Crown, ix. 273; Lee opposes Pitt in, iii. 241; London and Westminster members of, vote for address, ii. 125; London city's quarrel with, over Wilkes, vii. 196-7, 198, 199-200, 279-81, 288-9; long session in, i. 294, 383; Lord Mayor summoned by, vii. 281, 288; Lords told by, to 'withdraw,' i. 431; Macartney to enter, vi. 586; Mackreth a member of, viii. 53n, 60; Madrid treaty to be ratified in, iv. 212; Manchester counsel heard by, against taxes, ix. 573; Mann asks how often Wilkes can be chosen for, and rejected, vii. 96, 110; Mann fears that HW's health may suffer from late hours of, ii. 114, 395; Mann hopes that Wilkes will never sit in, vii. 96; Mann pleased by HW's release from, iv. 42; Mann pleased by Opposition's defeat in, vi. 111-12; Mann pleased by Wilkes's expulsion from, vii. 88; Mann surprised that Middlesex does not obey decision of, vii. 119; Mann wishes that

HW's moderation and prudence could be felt in, vii. 184; Mann, Horace II, advised by Mann to quit, ix. 474; Mann, Horace II, an 'unconnected' member of, ix. 223; Mann, Horace II, as member of, is better informed than HW, ix. 209, 236; Mann, Horace II, attends, viii. 425, 477; Mann, Horace II, entered, under illusions, viii. 518, ix. 560; Mann, Horace II, enters, viii. 54; Mann, Horace II, hurries back to, viii. 363, 396, 530, ix. 200; Mann, Horace II, is asked to institute inquiry at, ix. 222-3, 234; Mann, Horace II, may cause resentment in constituents by his absence from, viii. 146; Mann, Horace II, not at, viii. 146, ix. 367; Mann, Horace II, offers to resign from, viii. 275, 281; Mann, Horace II, reelected to, ix. 86; Mann, Horace II, retires from, ix. 461, 465, 476, 488, 505, 523; Mann, Horace II, sends regular accounts of, to Mann, ix. 475; Mann, Horace II, should quit, if he votes against Mann's wishes, viii. 452; Mann, Horace II, to report news of, to uncle, viii. 532, 542; Mann, Horace II, votes for Court party in, viii. 455; Mann, Horace II, would never benefit by seat in, ix. 465; Mansfield will not express opinion to, about Ps of Wales as possible Regency member, vi. 297; Marchmont's peerage stops his career in, iii. 5; Mediterranean naval investigation by, iii. 12, 25, 32-3, 47; members of, consider themselves superior to titular lords, vi. 482; members of, divide with every new minister, iii. 4; members of, go to political dinners at taverns, i. 243; members of, instructed by constituents through newspapers, i. 392; members of, meet at Cockpit to hear George II's speech, ii. 103; members of, speculate in East India Company stock, vi. 498; members of, superior to Tuscan nobles, vi. 483; mercenaries will support Norton in, ix. 27; merchants' petition discussed in, i. 353-4; Meredith and C.J. Fox drive Clive out of, vii. 490-1; Middlesex election discussed by, vii. 181-2; Middlesex sheriffs summon Wilkes as member of, vii. 475; Middlesex will be enraged by performance of, in rejecting Wilkes and electing Luttrell, vii. 105; millions voted by, v. 256; ministries not over-turned by, v. 261; ministry defeated in, over land tax, vi. 487-8; ministry without influence in, v. 57; Minorca's loss investigated by, v. 56, 76-7, 85-6, 95; minutes of, see Votes of; money to be raised by, iv. 212; Murray, Alexander, sentenced by, iv. 286; Murray, William, cannot be spared from, iv. 557; Murray, William, successful in, ii. 383-4; nabobs called to account by, ix. 277; naval augmentation defeated in, iii. 168; naval captains' petition to, for increased half-pay, vii. 462; naval investigation proposed in,

[Parliament, *continued*]

ii. 399-400, 427; Newcastle, D. of, has devotion from, v. 11; newly-raised regiments and county and town petitions considered in, ix. 34; North and C.J. Fox have majority in, ix. 466; North and Shelburne torn from power by, in a year, ix. 402n; North announces resignation in, ix. 258-9; North defeated in, on revenue question, vii. 461-2; North's fever will probably postpone first debate in, ix. 97; North's victory in, over St Vincent, vii. 462; North tells, about government loan, viii. 448; North to lay taxes before, ix. 254-5; North wins victory in, over disenfranchisement of revenue officers, ix. 37-8; Norton attacks North in, ix. 27; Norton becomes Speaker of, vi. 263n, vii. 176, 179-80; Norton thanked by vote of, ix. 100; Norton to return to, ix. 41; nothing but jobs in, ix. 140; not in mood to be dallied with, ix. 261-2; not well attended, iii. 138, 272, viii. 148, 273, ix. 572-3, 583; Nugent attacks Sandwich in, iv. 123, 124; Nugent, Mrs, wants her husband to speak in, i. 254-5; officers' dismissal for conduct in, opposed by Granby, vi. 274; Old Pretender hopes, will lack spirit, i. 202; Oliver sentenced by, to Tower, vii. 288; Onslow demands Byng's expulsion from, v. 63; Onslow, Speaker of, i. 219-20, iii. 446; opening session of, discusses George III's complaint against Wilkes for *North Briton*, vi. 181-2; Opposition has best speakers of, vi. 208; Opposition has majority in, ix. 471n; Opposition in, alarms Mann, i. 133; Opposition in, humbled, ix. 449, 451; Opposition in, strengthened by faction in ministry, ix. 259; Opposition in, to oppose George II's speech, ii. 102; Opposition in, will decry North's taxes, ix. 255; Opposition in, will have no effect, iv. 513; Orford, Cts of, corresponds with HW about members of, viii. 534; outside pressure may force, to bow to Pitt, v. 13; Oxford corporation punished by, vi. 584; Palliser resigns seat in, viii. 444; Palliser's removal may be asked by, in petition to George III, viii. 446; parties in, almost equally balanced, ix. 256; path to, from Change Alley, vi. 498; peace articles may be resented by, ix. 362; peace with Spain declared in, vii. 268; Pelham absent from, i. 484; Pelham has majorities in, iii. 202; Pelham ministry triumphant in, iii. 458; Pelham ministry unpopular in, 4; Pelham mortified by speeches in, iv. 257; Pelham visits, just before death, iv. 413; Philipps's committal wanted by, iv. 250; Pitt asks D. of Newcastle not to meddle in, v. 91; Pitt attacks Carteret in, ii. 383; Pitt attends, only twice in winter, v. 182; Pitt holds, *in commendam*, v. 56; Pitt may lose control of,

vi. 501; Pitt must manage, vi. 490; Pitt probably controls better, in absentia, v. 58; Pitt's absence from, encourages Charles Townshend, vi. 492-3; Pitt's burial to be attended by, viii. 379; Pitt's demand for increased navy defeated in, iii. 168-9; Pitt's departure from, disliked, vi. 443; Pitt's expression in, about Clive, vi. 176, 243n, vii. 381n, 387; Pitt still unable to attend, v. 33, 35; Pitt tells Beckford to lay plans before, for East India Company, vi. 493; Pitt the meteor of, though some Tories oppose him, iii. 202; Pitt voted a funeral and monument by, at public expense, viii. 379; Pitt, William II, behaves well in, ix. 437; Pitt, William II, defeated in, over fortification plan, ix. 629-30; Pitt, William II's, Irish propositions in, *see under* Parliament: Irish propositions; Pitt, William II's, motion for reform of, defeated, ix. 401-2, 404-5; Pitt William II, supported by George III against majority in, ix. 471n; Pitt, William II, wounds, in way which may be fatal to Constitution, ix. 484-5; place tax debated in, v. 199; Powys may be successful in, ix. 474; printers of debates in, arrested, vii. 280; printing of Secret Committee report not decided by, i. 475-6; privately-raised regiments discussed in, iii. 154-5, x. 13-19; Pulteney kept from, by daughter's illness, i. 363; Pulteney leads Patriots in, i. 231; Pulteney leaves, ii. 23; Pulteney quells disputes in, i. 355; Pulteney's motion for examination of foreign negotiations defeated in, i. 250-1; quarrel with House of Lords vainly provoked in, vii. 256; reform in, *see* Parliament: reform of representation in; Rockingham ministry to include members of, vi. 311; Rockingham ministry triumphant in, vi. 381; royal household members of, have not yet kissed hands, iv. 247; Rumbold to be squeezed by, ix. 277; Rushout leads Carteret's party in, iii. 212; Sackville (Germain), does not attend, v. 345; Sackville tells, that America must give unlimited submission, viii. 282n; Sandwich's prosecution in, ix. 243; Sandys, 1st Bn, considers, unfair tribunal, iii. 25-6; Sandys, 2d Bn, vacates seat in, vii. 206; Saturday sessions may be introduced at, i. 247; Saville attacks, vii. 169-70, 184; Sayre said to have planned seizure of George III on way to, viii. 138; Scottish bill debated in, x. 31-3; Scottish election decided in, i. 294; Scottish members of, i. 496; Seaforth election debated in, iii. 449; seamen to be voted by, for American war, viii. 127; seat in, unprofitable, iv. 11, ix. 465; seat in, vacated for Robinson, iv. 17; Secret Committee again proposed in, and defeated, ii. 117-18; Secret Committee proposed in, against Sir Robert Walpole, i. 297, 355,

364, 375, 379, 383–6, 388, 425, 475–6, 484; sensible members of, probably disgusted by Opposition orators, ix. 57; Shelburne defeated in, ix. 368; sits eternally, though half empty, viii. 148; sits for 22 hours, i. 383; Smithson vacates seat in, iv. 125; Somerset, Lord Noel, leads Jacobites in, i. 231; Speaker of, see Cornwall, Charles Wolfran; Norton, Sir Fletcher; Onslow, Arthur; Speaker's chair in, Mansfield frightened out of, vii. 247; Speaker's chamber in, used by HW for writing letter, i. 246; Speaker's chambers at, crowded for voting Secret Committee lists, i. 383; Speaker's chamber visitors locked out by under-doorkeeper, i. 244–5; Speaker's mace, vii. 175–6, viii. 356; Speaker's speeches in, hint at Sir Robert Walpole's impeachment, i. 354–5; spirit of, shows Constitution is not quite gone, ix. 262; Stanhope, Sir William, too deaf to hear debates in, vi. 183; Taaffe and Wortley Montagu belong to, iii. 450n, iv. 289; taxes considered by, ix. 583; taxes debated in, iii. 458; taxes should be heaped by, on those who present flattering addresses, viii. 133–4; toast drunk in, i. 354; too small to vote on election, viii. 273; Tories avoid voting in, ii. 383, ix. 19; Tories in, oppose subsidiary treaties, iv. 300; Tory side of, popular, iii. 4; Townsend blames arbitrary conduct of, on Ps of Wales, vii. 289; treaty with Saxony opposed in, by Cobham and old Horace Walpole, iv. 299–300; two prime ministers overturned by, in one year, ix. 402; Tyrawley comments on, ii. 148; vacillations of, over prerogative and petitions, ix. 66–7; *Votes* of, seen by Mann, iv. 304, v. 58, 163, vi. 406; voting in, about naval questions, viii. 449; wainscot of, ix. 35; Walpole, Horatio (1678–1757), cannot be spared by, iii. 469; Walpole, Horatio (1678–1757) shocks Mann by opposition in, iv. 304; Walpole, Horatio (1678–1757), told by, to withdraw, i. 431; Walpole, Sir Robert, hurries HW to, ii. 394; Walpole, Sir Robert, manages, against Dr Sacheverel, vi. 26; Walpole, Sir Robert, member of, from 1700 on, vi. 26; Walpole, Sir Robert, the only K.G. in, since Q. Elizabeth's day, vii. 391; Walpole, Sir Robert, to have been removed from George II's councils by motion of, i. 83, 142, 232n; Wareham election discussed in, iii. 458; war inquiry started and halted by, viii. 474; warmth in, rekindles, ix. 212; warrants, general, debated by, vi. 274–5, 283; Weobly election contested in, iv. 31; Westminster election examined by, i. 220, 233, 246, 247, 250–2, 272–3, 298, 322, iv. 107–8, 113, 122–3, 156, 223–4, ix. 502, 565; Whig union saves Pelham's mastery of, ii. 118; Whithed enters, iii. 446–7; Wilkes dull in, vi. 136; Wilkes expelled by, vi. 181–5,

186–8, 199, 207, vii. 86, 316–17; Wilkes fails to appear before, vi. 198; Wilkes prints manifestos against, but hopes to re-enter it, vii. 205–6; Wilkes rejected by, vii. 97; Wilkes's appearance before, prevented by members' fears, vii. 303; Wilkes's examination by, vii. 73–4, 82, 84; Wilkes's friends in, petition against Luttrell, vii. 114–15; Wilkes's papers illegally seized according to opposition in, vi. 207–8; Wilkes summoned by, but refuses unless he can occupy his seat, vii. 281; Wilkes wants more equal representation in, viii. 187; Wilkes will be harmless in, vii. 8; Wilkes will control, vii. 181; Worms treaty to be discussed in, ii. 383; Wortley Montagu enters, iii. 450; Wynn, Sir W. Williams, enters, ii. 344; Yorke brothers stay away from, viii. 178; Young Pretender's Scottish scheme depends on, i. 202; see also under Parliament: acts and bills; speeches

House of Lords: address against Hanoverian troops proposed in, ii. 158; address against Massachusetts act considered by, vi. 507; address in, almost ruined by clause of thanks for Hanoverian troops, v. 30; address of, on accommodation with America, passed unanimously, ix. 352; address to George II debated in, ii. 230–1; address to George II not made by, ii. 409; address to George III voted in, against London's remonstrances, vii. 200; adjourns, out of respect for Lord Chatham, viii. 371; antiquated and idle, ix. 153; Argyll does not attend, i. 338, ii. 159; aristocratic tendencies of, at end of George II's reign, vii. 164; army should not include too many from, x. 13; Bedford asks, to investigate toasts to Old Pretender, iv. 365–6, 375; Bedford attends, i. 338; Bedford makes motion in, against German war, vi. 7, 15; Bell may be huzzahed by mob on way to, i. 503; Berkshire attends, i. 338; bills defeated in, i. 391–2, v. 182, ix. 38, 47, 459; bishops and Scottish peers in, considered household 'troops,' ix. 368; Buckingham assizes controversy may go to, iii. 470; Byng court martial called to bar of, v. 65; Chesterfield attends, i. 338; Commons' resolutions on Wilkes agreed to by, vi. 187; controversy to be expected in, ix. 398; crowds from Charing Cross to, v. 389; Cumberland, Henry, D. of, votes in, vi. 521; Cumberland, William, D. of, enters, i. 398; Cumberland, William, D. of, leads minority in, vi. 187; Cumberland, William, D. of, votes in, iv. 38; Dashwood to enter, vi. 130; divorce case in, ix. 228; divorce should not be granted by, after proof of collusion, viii. 227; Douglas case to be tried before, vii. 83; *Essay on Woman*, examined by, vi. 195, 199; Ferrers's paper

[Parliament, *continued*]

attacks, v. 398–9; Ferrers's separation trial at, v. 184, 396; Ferrers, Cts, testifies to, that husband is sane, v. 399; Frederick, P. of Wales, attends, iv. 232; Frederick, P. of Wales's party suffers rift in, iv. 38; George II's bills passed in, iv. 232; George II's speech debated in, i. 230; George III goes to prorogue, vii. 115; George III humbles, vi. 97; George III wants India Bill defeated in, ix. 458n; Gloucester, D. of, votes in, vi. 521; Grafton and Lyttelton attack Court party in, viii. 139; Grenville's death keeps Chatham and Temple from, vii. 248; HW calls, 'Temple of Honour,' viii. 341; HW listens to speeches in, ii. 356; *habeas corpus* extension to be defeated in, v. 199, 205–6; Halifax attends, i. 338; Halifax proposes adjournment of, before Bute's or Ps of Wales's friends come, vi. 297n; Halifax proposes motion in, on Regency Bill, vi. 297; Hanoverian troops not debated in, by Tories, ii. 141; Hardwicke attacks Henry Fox in, iv. 383; House of Commons asks, for peers to appear at their bar, vii. 73–4, 77; House of Commons provoked to quarrel with, vii. 256; House of Commons tells members of, to 'withdraw,' i. 431; inactive, iv. 111; Ireland's independence signed by, ix. 279–80; Irish bankruptcy tried by, v. 65; Italians ignorant of founding of, ii. 126; Kingston, Ds of, petitions, for her trial, viii. 143, 149–50; Kingston, Ds of, says, acknowledges her to be Countess, viii. 220; Kingston, Ds of, tried by, viii. 191–3, 195–6, 198–9; Lyttelton attacks Court party in, viii. 139, 534; Mann shocked by mob's treatment of member of, vi. 112; Marchmont to succeed Crawford in, iv. 110–11; Marlborough moves for address of loyalty to George II from, ii. 399; Massachusetts assembly's act examined by, vi. 507, 520; ministry's majority in, dwindles, vi. 525; motion in, against use of Hanover troops, ii. 356; naval investigation proposed in, ii. 400; Newcastle, D. of, and Hardwicke formerly treated subserviently in, vi. 109–10; Newcastle avoids voting in, vi. 508; no division in, ii. 351, vi. 109; Northington and Camden clash in, with Mansfield, vi. 520; nothing passes in, ix. 140; Opposition in, only 'dignified ciphers,' ix. 295; Opposition withdraws from, vii. 256; Pitt (Chatham) appears in, vii. 167, viii. 14, 308; Pitt (Chatham) forsakes, vii. 194, 199–200, 256; Pitt (Chatham) has little influence in, v. 205–6, vii. 186; Pitt (Chatham) proposes, should investigate Middlesex election, vii. 167; Pitt (Chatham)'s motion in, vii. 180, viii. 75; Pitt (Chatham) visits, for last time, viii. 370–1; Pitt (Chatham) wants Temple to stay in, v. 485; Port Mahon officers' lists examined by, i. 300; princes' pensions delayed in, by Con-

way, vi. 425; printer taken up by, for printing Weymouth's letter, vii. 77; Pulteney enters, as E. of Bath, i. 485n, ii. 23; Ravensworth makes motion in, for Hanover troops, iv. 526; rebel lords tried by, iii. 280–7; Richmond defends Sir Robert Walpole in, i. 330; Rockingham attacks Sandwich in, ix. 221; Rockingham makes motion in, vii. 180; Rockingham ministry triumphant in, vi. 381; Rockingham speaks in, only by necessity, ix. 288; Sandwich denounces *Essay on Woman* in, vi. 184; Sandys's entrance into, satirized by HW, ii. 257–8; Sandys succeeds Hardwicke as Speaker of, v. 25; Secret Committee may be hampered by, i. 400; Shelburne defeated in, ix. 368; Shelburne opposes loan in, ix. 402; Shelburne ridiculous in, ix. 407; Stanhope, 2d E., moves address in, ii. 158, 178; Suffolk urges, to ask George III to reward Harley, vii. 21; tapestry in, of Armada's destruction, ii. 126–7, vii. 242; taxes called heavy in, ii. 158; Temple assembles, without giving reason, vi. 507; Temple does not attend, vii. 251; Temple proposes first minister in, v. 546; Temple to stay in, v. 485; Thurlow resists Parliamentary reform in, ix. 273; Thurlow ridiculous in, ix. 407; treaty with Saxony debated in, iv. 300; twelve peerages conferred to alter, ix. 605; uproar in, brings Chatham's secession, vii. 256; Walpole, Sir Robert, sends proxy to, ii. 159; Walpole, Sir Robert, to enter, i. 319; 325, 333, 335, 338; weaver's relief bill thrown out of, by D. of Bedford, vi. 301; weavers surround, vi. 301; Wilkes not to be heard by, vii. 77; Wilkes's writs of error to be argued before, vii. 81; York, D. of, speaks but does not vote in, vi. 521

'important' issues in, soon forgotten, ix. 365

India discussed in, vii. 490, viii. 46, ix. 159; *see also* acts of: India bill; East India Company, etc.

India's plunder winked at by, viii. 231

infirm, ix. 565

inquiry in: about Dutch ships at Deal, proposed by Horace Mann II, but dropped on HW's advice, ix. 222–3, 234; about war conduct, viii. 348, 351

invalids brought to, i. 298

Ireland defies, ix. 681

Ireland receives concessions from, viii. 542

Irish deliberations deferred by adjournment of, iv. 409

Irish propositions considered by, ix. 564–5, 578, 589, 596

Jacobites prefer invasion to disputes in, ii. 417

Jacobites to make attempt after meeting of, i. 160

Jews give money to, v. 341

jokes while provoking a civil war, viii. 133

Keppel-Palliser affair again to be examined by, ix. 103

lack of opposition in, results in lack of interest, viii. 278

Lestock vindicated by, iii. 33

list of, newspapers could avoid errors by consulting, vi. 325

London does not throng to see, iii. 118

London not to be vacated by, at Christmas, viii. 542-3

London's remonstrances to, vii. 196-8, ix. 218

London will be empty till meeting of, ix. 105

Lucas tends E. of Orford's boroughs in case of dissolution of, ix. 462

mad woman presents her speech at opening of, as Q. Elizabeth, viii. 361

Mann awaits new system for, v. 492-3

—— calls, 'great seat of discord,' viii. 39

—— expects to hear echoes from, of victory at Gibraltar, ix. 340

—— fails to understand debates in, iv. 54

—— fears for HW's health at, vi. 469, 532

—— glad that HW is not in, during riots, vii. 300

—— hopes that Wilkes and Lord Mayor will be humbled by, vii. 296

—— impatient to see opening addresses of, vii. 253

—— indignant at anti-administration agitation in, vii. 203

Mann, Horace II, discusses, with Grand Duke, ix. 58

Mansfield to be baited by, vii. 268

masquerades undisturbed by, iv. 469

Massachusetts, assembly said to have usurped powers of, vi. 507

members of: avoid arrest for debt, iii. 418; mostly frozen in the country, viii. 175; paid for secret services, ix. 605; rapacious, vi. 395; though unable to raise money for war, prey upon government, viii. 465; tired or absent, vi. 519-20; to return for trials of rebel lords, iii. 273; turn to army instead of horseracing, viii. 384; see also Parliament: House of Commons: members of

ministry's requests granted by, viii. 142

mob tries to take Wilkes from prison and put him in, vii. 20

more confined to personalities than to divisions, ix. 98

Morgan more powerful in, than D. of Beaufort, vii. 174

motions in, over Falkland Islands, vii. 251

navy strengthened soon after meeting of, viii. 252

new, but little changed, ix. 95

Newcastle ministry will have to explain loss of Minorca to, iv. 578

Newcastle, D. of, will be deserted by, v. 93

new parties in, iv. 509-10

newspapers give such full accounts of de-

bates in, that HW can merely send extracts, ix. 464

North and Fox not sure of following of, ix. 379

Norton leaves estate to, for use of the poor, iv. 237n

nothing likely to be decided by, viii. 254

nothing settled about, v. 244

not yet prorogued, but languishing, vi. 23

Onslow hails triumph of, over ministers, ii. 540

opposition but no division at meeting of, on the Address, iv. 100

opposition in: abandons it for Paris and country, viii. 262; address on George II's speech to be opposed by, ii. 102; admits total defeat, ix. 488; Aix treaty to be attacked by, iv. 30; alarms Mann, iii. 372, v. 552; American sovereignty acknowledged by all but Pitt's followers in, viii. 371; American war should have been opposed by, more strongly, viii. 491; awaits move by opponents, i. 168; awaits its opening, vi. 559; Baltimore leads, iii. 360; Barré dismissed for joining, vi. 189; Bathurst prominent in, iv. 32; Bedford faction one that does not support, vi. 382; Bubb Dodington ineffective as leader of, iv. 51, 96; Burke and Fox only efficient members of, ix. 295; Bute opposed by, vi. 52-3, 508; checked a little, ix. 28, 30; Chesterfield included in, i. 232n, ii. 102; county associations eclipse, in power, ix. 29; Cumberland, Henry, D of, joins, viii. 74, ix. 140; Cumberland, Henry, D. of, slighted by, because of marriage, vii. 434; Cumberland, William, D. of, in relation to, iv. 300, v. 145, vi. 310; Dashwood supports, i. 247; defeat of, will enhance Bedford's reputation, vi. 172; defeats Shelburne, ix. 368, 369, 371-2, 402; demolishes Westminster scrutiny, ix. 562; did not start county committees, ix. 30; disjointed, ix. 437; does not lurk at Knightsbridge, vii. 461-2; Earle opposed by, as chairman of Committee, i. 220, 242; East India Company examination disappoints, vi. 506; Eden deserts, ix. 623-4; finds its warnings unheeded, viii. 491-2; Fountain the meeting place of, i. 429n; Fox, C.J., shines in, ix. 212; Frederick, P. of Wales, forms, iii. 360, 372, iv. 30, v. 145; Frederick, P. of Wales, recruits members for, iii. 449; George II and D. of Newcastle may join in suppressing, iv. 513; George II's speech to be opposed by, ii. 102; Gower joins, ii. 159; Grafton will probably head, vi. 109; Grenville, George, odious in, vi. 483; Halifax joins, ii. 159; Hardwicke approaches, slowly, vi. 109; has majority in House of Commons, ix. 471n; Hastings opposed by, ix. 630; honester but not abler than administration, viii. 448; inactive, except on Indian affairs, ix. 623;

[Parliament, *continued*]

ineffectual in both houses, i. 241; invigo-
rated by hope, ix. 19; Keppel a member
of, viii. 263; lacking, viii. 278; ix. 386; led
by George III's own servants, vi. 7; Lee,
George, wanted by, as chairman of Committee of Elections, i. 220, 242–3; liberty
of the press opposed and then abused by,
vi. 315; Lord Mayor gives dinner for, vii.
200; Lyttelton included in, ii. 102; Mann
used to be terrified by, iv. 43; meeting of,
at St Alban's Tavern, iv. 50, v. 552; might
profit by resentment against Keppel's persecution, viii. 447; Mutiny Bill opposed by,
iv. 112; Newcastle joins, vi. 98; Newcastle
may chastise, iv. 513; Newcastle not to
join, vi. 464; North's peace terms virtually
acknowledge arguments of, viii. 354; Norton's impudence weakens, ix. 28; not
unanimous, ix. 47; not very able, viii. 447;
now includes powerful men, iv. 516; perpetual militia demanded by, v. 552; petitions encourage, ix. 29; Pitt (Chatham)
encourages, to form ministry, vi. 310; Pitt
(Chatham) leads, ii. 102, iv. 516, v. 552,
viii. 341; Pitt (Chatham) not to join, vi.
78; Pitt, William II, shines in, ix. 212, 407;
Potter aids, iii. 449, iv. 32; Powys tries to
reconcile William Pitt II with, ix. 475n;
prepares address, viii. 254; proposes amendment to Address, viii. 534; Pulteney persuades Frederick, P. of Wales, to form, iii.
229; punctilious, ix. 275; Quarendon supports, i. 247; quelled, ix. 556; quiet, viii.
546; recovers spirit, ix. 218; refuses to be
led by Bubb Dodington, iv. 96; Rigby
might wreck administration to satisfy, viii.
447; Rockingham declares against, though
opposing, vi. 549; Rockingham does not
come to London to lead, viii. 546; Rockingham not to join, vi. 464; St Alban's
tavern the rendezvous of, iv. 50, v. 552;
Sandwich attacked by, ix. 221; Shelburne
dismissed for joining, vi. 189; sold for
pensions, vi. 274; stays away, viii. 273; successful not because of abilities but because
of reverses in war, ix. 244; Temple, 1st E.,
does not attract followers into, vi. 382;
Temple, 1st E., to be nominal head of, vi.
549; Temple, 2d E., supports D. of Richmond at meeting of, ix. 295; Thurlow
might have wrecked administration to satisfy, viii. 447; too dull to produce ballads
or epigrams, vi. 110; Tories dislike, iii.
370; Townshend to have betrayed administration to, vi. 552; two, at same time, vi.
483; upholds clause in Burke's bill, ix. 26;
Wasner said to work with, i. 325–6; weak
in numbers, ix. 295; Weymouth might wreck
administration to satisfy, viii. 447; will be
strengthened, iii. 449; will impute shame of
St Eustatius's loss to ministry, ix. 236; wins
victory, ix. 251–2

orators in, should speak by inch of candle
or by hour-glass, ix. 58
ousted ministers do not propose divisions
in, ix. 407
Oxford to be chastised by, iv. 50
Palliser's appointment not censured by, ix.
118
Peace of Aix not brought before, iii. 464,
iv. 30
Peace of Aix probably will be approved
by, iv. 27
Peace of Paris (1763) probably will not be
made until meeting of, vi. 78
Peace of Paris (1783) hardly mentioned
after its approval by, ix. 374
Peace of Paris (1783) preliminaries awaited
by, ix. 352, 356, 357
peace proposals to be passed by, viii. 359
petitions attack, vii. 133
petitions to, i. 232–3, 295, 344, ix. 29; *see
also under* Parliament: House of Commons
Pitt (Chatham) attacks, for taxing America,
vi. 395–6
—— may lead George III's forces in, viii.
350
——'s adulation from, a farce, viii. 415
——'s burial poorly attended by members
of, viii. 393, 415
——'s death during session of, lucky for his
family, viii. 389
——'s debts to be paid by allotment by,
viii. 382
—— the meteor of, iii. 202
—— will be buried by, in Westminster
Abbey or St Paul's, viii. 382
prerogative subject of vacillation by, ix. 66
prorogation of: i. 484, 503, ii. 211, 227, iv.
135, 212, 410–11, 435, v. 290, 294, 409, 491,
vi. 227, 285, 424, 533, 537, vii. 115, 214,
308, 416, viii. 34, 497, ix. 295, 418, 519;
expected, iii. 29, 35, vi. 519–20, viii. 483;
may quell tumults, vii. 301; produces few
changes, viii. 386; sudden, vii. 303; Walpole, Sir Robert, may be saved by, ii. 4, 9;
wanted by George II, iv. 469; will be brief,
viii. 14; will make HW's letters less frequent, viii. 385
quartering of government places might be
attacked in, viii. 276
quiet: v. 267; during Easter and Newmarket season, ix. 398
recess of, *see* Parliament: adjournments of
reform of representation in: begun, ix. 273;
deferred, ix. 573; feared by Mann to be
unconstitutional, ix. 49; HW opposes, ix.
399, 541–2; not genuinely admired in
England, ix. 273–4; opposed by Rockingham and Cavendishes, and backed by Shelburne and Fox, ix. 29–30; Pitt's motion for,
ix. 399, 401, 405; Quintuple Alliance seeks,
ix. 401–2; repulsed, ix. 406; to be discussed,
ix. 566; Wilkes wants, viii. 187; would have

been opposed by Horace Mann II, ix. 399, 404

Regency Act not passed by, before George III's recovery, ix. 682–4

Regency may be established by, iv. 239

rising of, *see* Parliament: prorogation of

Rochefort inquiry might be brought into, v. 165

Rome gets news of, through Goddard, i. 368–9

Rowley to allay fears of, ii. 526

Sackville (Germain)'s resignation to be announced to, ix. 236

—— will probably attempt revenge after meeting of, v. 328

sailors' petition to, vii. 21

Sandwich, E. of, attacked in, iv. 123, 124, viii. 445, 460, 464, ix. 221, 244

—— receives vote of approbation in, ix. 243

satires on neutrality to be commented upon in, i. 189

Saxon treaty debated in, iv. 299–300

serene, iii. 341–2

session of: awaited with suspense, viii. 71; begins, i. 160, 170, 171, 211, 335, ii. 327, 349, 429, 526, 529, 537, 556, 561, 564, iii. 134, 138, 446, 511, iv. 3, 221, 280, 286, 434, 506, v. 7, 30, 39, 158, 263, 344, 452, 562, vi. 101, 104, 463, 478, 573, vii. 61, 66, 150, 167, 172, 219, 245, 247, 248, 316, 326, 368, 442, viii. 61, 133, 252, 423, 529, 532–3, ix. 209, 236, 319, 351; country ladies lay in supplies after, ii. 498; ended, ii. 341, iii. 107, v. 12, 153, ix. 321, 341; has lasted a week, vi. 565; imprudent to postpone, vii. 150; may be violent, ii. 511; may end unexpectedly, from weariness, ix. 47; may prevent HW's Paris visit, vi. 247; not to begin till after Christmas, vi. 169, 256, vii. 150, 520, ix. 103, 519–20, 608; should have novelty because of new administration, ix. 95; to begin and then adjourn for re-elections, v. 22; to begin in October, ix. 596; to end before ministry changes, iv. 212; will revive set of poets, ix. 612

Shelburne administration should give novelty to, ix. 95

—— defeated in, ix. 368, 369, 371–2, 402

sheriffs examined by, for failure to burn *North Briton*, vi. 188

sits only on necessary business, ix. 506

Sloane's museum offered to, iv. 358

sold and despised, vii. 499

speeches in, by: Adam, William, viii. 537; Baltimore, 5th Bn, x. 14, 18; Barnard, Sir John, iv. 257, x. 10; Barré, Isaac, vii. 186, 248; Barrington, Lord, x. 13, 14, 15, 16, 17, 18; Bathurst, x. 17; Bedford, D. of, iv. 310, vi. 463–4; Bennet, x. 17; Bladen, x. 14; Boone, x. 15; Bubb Dodington, i. 354, x. 14, 23; Burke, Edmund, vii. 170, 184, 248, ix. 31, 408; Calvert, x. 23; Camden,

Earl, vi. 520; Campbell, Gen., x. 18, 31; Carew, x. 23; Carteret, John (Lord Granville), ii. 158; Cholmondeley, George, E. of, ii. 230; Cholmondeley, Richard, i. 296; Chute, Francis, i. 234, 297; Coke, Edward, Viscount, i. 298, x. 23, 32; Conway, Henry Seymour, vi. 208, 274, viii. 139, x. 15; Cornbury, Lord, x. 22, 24; Cotes, x. 18; Cotton, Sir John, i. 355, x. 15; Danvers, x. 15; Dashwood, i. 298, x. 15, 18; Doneraile, Lord, i. 354, x. 14; Dowdeswell, vi. 556; Dunning, ix. 35–6; Egmont, E. of, iv. 51, 222; Erskine, iv. 229–30; Fazakerley, x. 16; Fox, Charles J., viii. 139, ix. 244; Fox, Henry (Lord Holland), i. 297, 355, x. 15, 16, 17, 24; Grafton, D. of, viii. 139; Grenville, George, i. 297, vi. 274, 382, 444–5, 464, 496, 566, x. 19, 23; HW, i. 376–7, 404, ii. 406; Halifax, George, E. of, i. 230, ii. 356; Henley, Robert (Lord Northington), vi. 520; Hervey, John, Bn, ii. 159; Hillsborough, x. 14, 22, 32, 33; Hume Campbell, x. 24; Keppel, Augustus, viii. 445; Knight, x. 23; Lee, Sir George, iii. 470, x. 16, 17, 18; Legge, x. 18, 23, 32; Lyttelton, George, Bn, viii. 139, x. 18; Lyttelton, Richard, iv. 33; Mann, Horace II, viii. 451–2, 457, 458; Mellish, x. 18, 23; Mordaunt, x. 14, 18, 31, 32, 33; Murray, William (E. of Mansfield), i. 123, vi. 520, vii. 167; Newcastle, D. of, x. 10; Newdigate, x. 10; North, Frederick, Bn, vii. 186, 248, 290; Northey, x. 32; Norton, Sir Fletcher (Bn Grantley), viii. 445; Nugent, x. 13, 17; Pelham, Henry, iii. 470–1, iv. 300, x. 10, 14, 16, 17, 18, 22, 24; Philipps, Sir J., x. 13, 14, 16; Pitt, Thomas, ix. 35; Pitt, William (E. of Chatham), i. 297, ii. 383, iii. 4–5, 168, 370, iv. 453, v. 256–7, 344–5, 547, vi. 208, vii. 167, 180, viii. 371, x. 10, 14, 15, 17, 18, 24; Pomfret, E. of, iv. 470; Potter, iii. 470; Prowse, x. 23; Raymond, ii. 230; Robinson, x. 32, 33; Rockingham, M. of, vii. 180, ix. 221; Rushout, x. 17, 18; Ryder, i. 297, x. 18, 23, 31, 33; Sackville, Lord George (Lord Germain), vi. 208; Sandwich, John, E. of, ii. 158, 230–1, 356, iv. 300, vii. 167; Saville, vii. 169–70, 184; Stanhope, Earl, ii. 158; Strange, Lord, x. 10, 14, 16, 17, 18, 23, 24; Sydenham, x. 23, 31; Temple, George, 2d E., ix. 437; Temple, Richard, 1st E., iv. 257, vi. 464, viii. 362; Thornton, x. 32; Townshend, Charles, vi. 208, 493–4, 512; Tracy, x. 31; Vernon, ii. 206; Vyner, x. 15, 31, 32; Waller, Edmund, i. 354–5; Walpole, Horatio (1st Bn Walpole of Wolterton), ii. 467, iii. 168–9, x. 18; Walpole, Sir Robert (E. of Orford), ii. 409; White, x. 18; Wilkes, John, viii. 304; Willes, John, iii. 471; Williams Wynn, x. 17; Winnington, i. 484, x. 16, 17, 18, 22, 23; Wraxall, ix. 137–8; Yonge, i. 297, x. 13, 14, 15, 16, 17, 18; York, Edward, D. of,

[Parliament, *continued*]
vi. 521; Yorke, Charles, vi. 208; Yorke, Philip, E. of Hardwicke, iv. 383
Stair said to have obeyed, in defiance of George II, ii. 289
Stamp Act repealed by, vi. 400–1, 404–5, 408, 409–10
supporters of Bill of Rights decrease in, vii. 209
too corrupt to be a court of correction, ix. 400
Tories avoid voting in, ix. 19
treasurer and pensions indispensable to, ix. 97
turnpike bill would upset, more than India or West Indies do, vii. 455
unable to raise money for American war, viii. 465
unanimity of: iv. 286; makes it unsensational, viii. 85
unshaken, viii. 426
'venal and false,' vi. 382
vote of, will not clear Cornwallis in his conduct toward loyalist Americans, ix. 211
Wales, Ps of, stigmatized by act of, vi. 396
Walpole, Sir Robert, accused of bribing, ix. 605
—— attends opening of, from St James's, viii. 361
Westminster's remonstrance to, ix. 218
Wilkes recommends purchase by, of Houghton collection, viii. 304
will probably meet again under gloomy circumstances, viii. 432
winter is equivalent to, in HW's opinion, ix. 358
wit suggests that voting in, should precede debates, viii. 533
wives of members of, revive in London, vi. 451
young members of, should not endanger England just to show off their talents, v. 565
Young Pretender threatens attendants at, iii. 138
Parliament, Irish:
acts of, money bills, vii. 155–6, 163, 166, 359
adjourned, and to be prorogued, iv. 409–10
Boyle, the Speaker, heads faction in, against Dorset, iv. 316, 401–2
Bristol, E. of, to attend sessions of, vi. 450
Egmont spoke in, iv. 31
George III may receive protest from, against new board, vii. 380
—— might prorogue, vii. 359
Hervey, Bp, urges admittance of Roman Catholics to, ix. 438n
House of Commons of, broken into by mob, in protest against failure to pass Protecting Duties, ix. 491
incendiary delegates repulsed by, with resolutions of loyalty, ix. 452–3

Lord Lieutenant prorogues, vii. 166, 170
political turmoil in, iv. 315
proceeds heavily, iv. 432
prorogation of, deferred till passing of money bills, vii. 155–6, 163, 166
Roman Catholics should not vote for members of, ix. 529
speaker of, *see* Boyle, Hon. Henry (1682–1764); Ponsonby, John (1713–89)
Stewart to enter, vii. 4
Stone brings Cunningham into, iv. 316
treated like a French parliament, iv. 432, 440
troop bill passed and money bill rejected by, iv. 155–6
Parliament, Scottish:
Young Pretender calls, iii. 118
Parliamentary Spy:
Wales, Ps of, denounced by, vii. 196
Parliament of Bordeaux. *See* Bordeaux, Parliament of
Parliament of Brittany. *See* Brittany, Parliament of
Parliament of Dijon. *See* Dijon, Parliament of
Parliament of Douai. *See* Douai, Parliament of
Parliament of Grenoble. *See* Grenoble, Parliament of
Parliament of Paris:
arrêt of, rebukes Clement XIII, vii. 4, 10
banished, iv. 440, vii. 270, 322
Barbantane dislikes behaviour of, vii. 278
Beauvau opposed fate of, vii. 322
Benedictines and Cordeliers ask permission of, to doff habits and rules, vi. 325
cabals of, may injure the cause of inoculation, vi. 153
Louis XV's tyranny opposed by, vi. 153
new: appointed, vii. 270; Louis XVI angry with, viii. 102; Maupeou's declaration against arrêt of 1762 attacked by, vii. 398; members of, urged by wives to resign, vii. 303; Orléans and Chartres refuse to salute, viii. 26
old: restoration of, viii. 55, 61; restoration of, expected, viii. 19, 25, 35
Paris loses money by retirement of, vii. 322
parliaments may imitate suspension of, vii. 259
Parma defended by, against Rome, vii. 4
quits its functions, vii. 259
resolutions of, against Jesuits, vi. 519
restoration of, iv. 440
Versailles to compromise with, vii. 265
Wilkes must fight, to retrieve honour, vi. 198
Young Pretender wants daughter registered by, as Ds of Albany, ix. 513, 516n
Parliament of Rennes. *See* Brittany, Parliament of
Parliament of Toulouse. *See* Toulouse, Parliament of

Parliaments, French:
Aiguillon detested by, vii. 259
brochures of, less illuminating than HW's letters, vii. 331
Chauvelin denounces Jesuits to, vi. 514
Choiseul said to give clandestine support to, vii. 259
Dauphin would crush, v. 44
English Parliament resembles, iv. 287
Irish parliament treated like, iv. 440
king's formula when turning over, to his chancellor, vi. 244
Louis XV forbids, to dispute his acts, vi. 415n
——'s dispute with, iv. 293, vi. 412, vii. 317
——'s temporizing to govern, iv. 440
—— survives rage of, vii. 329
Machault leads faction of, v. 56
mutinous, vii. 270
Parliament of Paris may be imitated by, vii. 259
proceed heavily, iv. 432
reform of, vii. 320
remonstrances of, hushed by bribery, vii. 320
struggles of, merely bring on despotism, vii. 376
war with England repugnant to, vii. 253
Parma, Ds of. See Elizabeth (1727–59) of France; Maria Amalia (1746–1804) of Austria
Parma, D. of. See Ferdinand-Marie-Philippe-Louis (1751–1802); Philip, Don (1720–65)
Parma:
Acquaviva asks Benedict XIV for, for Don Philip, i. 201
arrêt of 1762 caused by excommunication of, vii. 398–9
Aubeterre and Orsini protest to Clement XIII against treatment of, vii. 15–16
Austria may have designs upon, vi. 379
battle expected near, iii. 236
besieged, iii. 231, 236
Boisgelin recalled to Paris because of court squabble at, vii. 330
Braitwitz's letter from, ii. 161, 163–4
Brown blockades, iii. 236
Castellar evacuates, iii. 244
—— occupies, iii. 236
castle of, captured, iii. 245
Castro and Ronciglione to be seized by, vii. 24
Charles III sends message about, to Joseph II and Maria Theresa, and recalls his minister, vii. 446
Charles Emmanuel III and Mann might appear before, v. 266
Clement XIII's brief against, vi. 582, vii. 26, 38
——'s death puts a stop to his opposition to, vii. 88
——'s quarrel with, vii. 10

Clement XIV resigns pretensions to, vii. 518
Coke, Lady Mary, wants to avoid, vii. 543
convent at, Correggio painting in church of San Antonio Abbate at, i. 167, 196, 199, 268, ii. 323, 337, 351, 355, 370, 373
duke of, may be preceded by Richecourt, iv. 295
Du Tillot and Llano dismissed from, vii. 445
Elizabeth Farnese might have bought, ii. 345
Ferdinand of Naples to visit, ix. 586–7
Fiorenzuola near, iii. 47
France sends couriers to, about Louis XV's escape from assassin, v. 48
HW contrasts Newmarket with, ii. 315
HW prefers Canterbury to, i. 142
hussars at, ii. 338
Illustri fatti Farnesiani may be found at, ix. 403, 411–12
Joseph II wants, as fief of Empire, vi. 395
Leopold's letter rejected by, vi. 378–9
—— told by mother to go to, to lecture his sister, vii. 411–12
Liechtenstein awaits cannon from, iii. 258
Llano goes to, vii. 325, 445, 518–19
Lobkowitz's army near, iii. 36–7, 40, 50
Maria Theresa gives, to Charles Emmanuel III, i. 379
Parliament of Paris defends, against Rome, vii. 4
Philip, Don, disliked by people of, iv. 45
—— may be transferred from, to Naples, v. 264
—— to bring Duchess to, iv. 45
—— to receive, by Aix treaty, iii. 481
Revilla formerly Spanish minister at, vi. 330
—— returns to, vii. 518–19
revolution at, vii. 444–6
Sanvitale, Cts, detains Strathmore at, vi. 88
Spain ends dissension in, by removing Du Tillot, vii. 324–5
Spaniards and Neapolitans may march to, iii. 65
Spaniards escape from, iii. 244
Spaniards may take, i. 198, 204, 214, ii. 454, iii. 22
Spanish weekly couriers to avoid, vii. 446
visitors to: Coke, Lady Mary, vii. 535, 539; Gustav III, ix. 499; Strathmore, v. 524, vi. 23, 88; York, D. of, vi. 232, 241
Parnassus:
Pope's house carved out of, v. 417
Paroli:
at faro, viii. 370
Paros:
Orlov writes from, vii. 226
Russian fleet sails to, vii. 226
Russian fleet winters at, vii. 307
Russian frigates from, reach Leghorn, vii. 326

Parotides:
swelling of, i. 52
Parrots:
Craon, Princesse de, has, ii. 78
ships' language might be repeated by, in polite circles, vii. 66
Parry, Rev. Mr (?) Gregory (1717–85):
Sandwich deserts the cause of, for Eton fellowship, iv. 121
Pars, William (1742–82), draughtsman:
death of, at Rome, viii. 173, x. 48
HW gives, a letter of recommendation to Sir William Hamilton, viii. 135
HW has, do washed drawings of SH, viii. 135, 144
HW recommends, to Mann, viii. 134–5, 144, 173
HW's account of, x. 48
HW wants view of Fiesole done by, viii. 135
Mann to recommend, to Cardinal Albani, and at Rome, viii. 135
not yet appeared at Florence, viii. 173, 189, 232
oil paintings and portraits now done by, viii. 135, 144
Palmerston has volume of washed drawings done by, viii. 135, x. 48
—— the patron of, viii. 135
portmanteau lost by, between Calais and Paris, viii. 144, x. 48
Rome to be visited by, for study, viii. 144
Parson:
popular, Charles II's witticism about, vi. 57, viii. 52
See also Clergyman
Parsons, Anne (d. 1769), m. (1754) Sir John Hinde Cotton, 4th Bt:
Robinson entertains, i. 185
Parsons, Anne ('Nancy,' 'Mrs Haughton' or 'Houghton') (ca 1735–ca 1814), m. 1 —— Horton; m. 2 (1776) Charles, 2d Vct Maynard:
Berkeley, Cts of, and Cts of Orford the only people who do not call on, viii. 451
Cumberland, Ds of, mistaken for, vii. 344
Dorset as badly off as if he had married, viii. 435
Grafton's and Dorset's mistress, vii. 344, viii. 435n
James's powder dispensed by, at Court of Naples, viii. 451
Parsons, Elizabeth (1749–1807):
Cock Lane Ghost an imposture by, vi. 8
Parsons, Humphrey (ca 1676–1741), lord mayor of London, 1730, 1740:
brewer, i. 185n, vi. 7
daughter of, iv. 9, vi. 7
George II notices, i. 185n
Jacobite, often in France, i. 185n
Jacobite Lord Mayor of London, vi. 7n
Parsons, John:
Robinson entertains, i. 185

Parsons, Sarah, m. James Dunn, called Jacques, Comte O'Dunne:
husband of, iv. 9, vi. 7
Robinson entertains, i. 185
Parsons, William (d. 1807), poet:
Florence Miscellany has poems by, ix. 633
Parsons family:
Paris visited by, i. 185
Robinson entertains, i. 185
Partridge; partridges:
campaign opened for, with waste of gun-power, ix. 188
covey of, Russian army compared to, v. 237
English politicians kill, in summer vacation, ix. 596
Ferdinand of Naples rises at 2 A.M. to catch, when leaving roosts, ix. 600
soldier shoots at, ii. 286
Partridge-net:
Prussian troops caught as if by, v. 354
Pasarella, Jacopo (d. 1495), Bp of Imola 1479–88; Bp of Rimini 1488–95:
figure of, in Gossaert's painting, iv. 390n
Innocent VIII's nuncio at Henry VII's marriage, iv. 390n
Pasetti, Capt. ——:
Albani sends, to Mann, iii. 2, 7
Pasquale, (?) Gaetano (ca 1700–45), Livornese physician:
English not known by, ii. 11
satire 'translated' by, ii. 11
Sturgis's death not expected by, ii. 198–9
Pasquali, Mme. See Capponi, Elisabetta (1729–1800)
Pasquali, Cosimo (1716–82), senator, 'eldest Pasquale':
marriage of, planned, iii. 438
Pasquali, Giovanni Battista (fl. 1738–73), Venetian bookseller and printer:
seeks music books wanted by HW, v. 477, 482
Pasquier, Étienne (1529–1615):
Recherches de la France: English credit mentioned by, iv. 48–9; HW mentions, iii. 486
'Pasquin':
Benedict XIV attacked by, iv. 189
HW wants epigrams by, about Clement XIII, v. 491
York, Cardinal, satirized by, v. 259
Pasquinade; pasquinades:
HW likes, iv. 199
in Ireland, on Sackville family and Stone, iv. 316
in style of Forum, i. 351, 372
Passau, Bp of. See Thun, Josef Maria von (d. 1763)
Passau:
Bavarian Elector said to have entered, i. 108
Passeck, Peter Bogdanovich (1736–1804), Capt.-Lt:
arrest of, vi. 64

'Pass eldest.' *See under* Loo

Passion; passions:
HW says: 'embrace their opposites,' when carried too far, iv. 449; form airy balloons, ix. 532

Passionei, Domenico (1682–1761), cardinal, 1738:
Almada directed by, v. 383
anti-Jesuit champion, v. 475
Benedict XIV consults, about Young Pretender, iv. 22
Niccolini invited by, to Rome, v. 127
—— reproved by, for not giving him HW's inscription on Benedict XIV, v. 127
permission of, necessary for copying Vatican MSS, v. 170

Passion play:
Leopold stops theatre manager from presenting, in Lent, vii. 459

Passport; passports:
Acquaviva obtains, for Young Pretender, ii. 378, 388
—— withholds, from English visitors, iii. 15
Agdollo carries, i. 149
Belloni procures, from Acquaviva for Shuttleworth, iii. 77
Boothby to get, at Venice, v. 482
French: Lorenzi may obtain, from France for Thomas Pitt, v. 524; Pitt, Thomas, fails to get, for French journey, v. 543, 545, 550; Strathmore obtains, vi. 22–3; Young Pretender travels with, vi. 389
George II's, to be treated with respect, iii. 384
La Ensenada seeks, for furniture, ii. 253
Maillebois receives, iii. 231
Mann makes out, ii. 46
—— procures, for Cholmondeley's journey through France, ix. 348
Maria Theresa's ministers monopolize, v. 482
Mathews awaits, at Nuremberg, ii. 517
Modena, Ds of, wants, for Tuscany, ii. 223
Montemar and Castellara want, ii. 44
Mountrath fails to get, for Naples, iii. 15
Tuscan, declared invalid, v. 482

Pastel; pastels:
Chute's and Whithed's portraits in, ii. 243, viii. 222
Mann to send, to HW's cousin, iii. 368–9

Pastilles:
burned in churches, v. 554
Florentine, in cakes or drops, v. 565
HW obtains, from Mann, v. 554, 565

Pastoral:
in *Arno Miscellany*, ix. 507

Pastor se torna Aprile, Il:
Mann sends, to HW, i. 181, 212
Rich, Elizabeth, wants, i. 166

Pastry shops:
Uguccioni's poems will provide paper for, ii. 554

Pasty:
venison, HW tries, for gout cure, vi. 322

Patagonia:
Byron discovers giants in, vi. 421
ladies' promenade suggests, ix. 174

Patapan (d. 1745), HW's dog:
barks at Frenchmen in Paris, ii. 221
beauty of, i. 352, 452
death of, iii. 39, 59
HW accompanied by: at Downing St, i. 495; at Houghton, ii. 36, 299, 498; to New Park, ii. 136; while writing letter, ii. 36
HW's joke about, i. 76
Houghton visitors curious about, ii. 299
Italy not regretted by, i. 143
Mann and Chute to visualize, in HW's room at Houghton, ii. 17, 36, 60
Mann asks about, i. 41, 53, 56, ii. 243, 264
—— jokes about, ii. 174
Martial thrown by, into fire, ii. 339
Patapan, 'Miss,' 'corresponds' with, ii. 530
pointer shakes and bruises, ii. 71
rainbow ribbon tied around neck of, ii. 317
Roman, ii. 220
Rosette the successor of, vii. 200
Walpole, Sir Robert, amused by, ii. 71, 299
Whithed's puppy had, as godfather. ii. 333
Wootton to paint, ii. 221, 243
wormed, ii. 317

Patapan, 'Miss,' friend of HW's dog:
Patapan's 'correspondence' with, ii. 530

Patapanino, Pettapanino (Patapan's puppy):
Eleonora called godmother of, i. 149
HW sends, to Florence, i. 112

Patch, James (d. 1791), surgeon:
brother's engravings distributed by, vii. **276**
brother to send case to, vii. 447
HW receives, kindly, vii. 301
HW receives Patch's engravings and Donatello bas-relief from, vii. 459
HW to talk to, about subscription for brother's engravings, vii. 288
surgeon in Norfolk St, vii. 276

Patch, Thomas (d. 1782), painter:
Beauchamp has picture by, x. 45
brother to receive case from, vii. 447
career of, vii. 275–6, x. 45
caricatures and conversation pieces of, vii. 275
caricatures by, vii. 5, 267, 422, 427, 429, x. 45
dies of apoplexy, ix. 272, 280
English in Florence caricatured by, vii. 5, x. 45
English painter at Florence, vii. 287n, x. 45
Florentine baptistery doors engraved by, vii. 429–30, 435
Florentine landscapes by, sent to HW, vii. 287–8, 301, 333, 360, 362

[Patch, Thomas, *continued*]
Giotto's paintings engraved by, vii. 459, 465
HW's account of, x. 45
HW's criticism of his engravings approved by, vii. 371, 468–9
HW's dedication from, in book of engravings, vii. 371–2, 382, 465
HW wants drawing by, of Mann, vii. 267
HW will aid subscription of, vii. 288, 435
Hawkwood's portrait engraved by, vii. 428
Italian painter told by, that Madonna is not member of the Trinity, vii. 459
Mann sends tabernacle through, vii. 447
——'s house visited by, daily, vii. 275
Masaccio's frescoes engraved by, vii. 267–8, 276, 287, 315, 362, 371, 422, 465, 469, ix. 280, x. 45
Mead, Dalton, and Vernet aid, vii. 275
Michelangelo pictures engraved by, vii. 276
paintings by Andrea del Sarto engraved by, vii. 276
paintings of Fra Bartolommeo engraved by, vii. 268, 276, 362, 371, 459, 465, 468–9
Piccolomini aids, when expelled from Rome for religion, vii. 275
Poussin pictures sought by, for Lowther, v. 209
Rome visited by, vii. 390
'Sterne and Death' by, vii. 5, 27, 33, 37
Patch; patches:
HW would not put, on St Ethelburgh's statue, v. 471
Patch box. *See under* box
Patent:
for fish supply, vii. 448
for Customs place, viii. 178, x. 52–4
pension deduction for, iv. 204
Patent place:
Sackville's, in Ireland, v. 328
Pateras:
on eagle's pedestal, iii. 122
Paterson, John (?1705–89), M.P.:
London election candidate, vii. 5
Paterson. *See also* Patterson; Pattinson
'Patience,' Catherine of Aragon's maid in waiting:
Catherine attended by, in *Henry VIII*, ii. 537
Patience:
'desperate substitute to hope,' viii. 178
HW cultivates, viii. 178, 342
Patino, Don Lucas Fernando (ca 1701–51), 2d Marqués de Castelar, 1733; Spanish army officer:
Gages may permit capture of, iii. 237
Montemar wants passport for, through Tuscany, ii. 44
Orso talks with, about Spanish plans, i. 349
Parma occupied by, iii. 236, 245
Philip, Don, arranges troop passage with, iii. 51

Spanish agent at Florence told by, to threaten Regency with blockade unless deserters were returned, i. **349**
Patinson. *See* Pattinson
Patmos, Isle of:
HW jokes about, i. 495
Patriarchate:
of Venice, to be transferred, iv. 206
Patriarch of Lisbon. *See* Saldanha, Francisco de
'Patrimoine de St-Pierre,' near Rome:
Spaniards and Neapolitans at, ii. 546
Patrimonio, Corsica:
capture of, vii. 46
Patriot; Patriots (political faction):
Bedford formerly associated with, iv. 72
Bolingbroke's letters on spirit of, iv. 59–62
Chesterfield and Pitt to receive legacies as, ii. 540
Country Girl, The, satirizes, ii. 23
Coventry of the 'breed' of, iv. 302
Cox belongs to, iv. 156
dismissal of, from St James's used to turn them toward Albano, vi. 257
dismissal of Hanover troops discredits, iii. 17
Earle satirizes, i. 243
English losses attributed to, iii. 255
first ministers used to be attacked, not proposed by, v. 546–7
Frederick, P. of Wales, builds up Opposition after the desertion of, iv. 30
George II expected by Carteret to reward, ii. 81
—— wins over, by giving them places, iii. 229
Glover's *Leonidas* praised by, ii. 124n
HW pleased by dissension among, iv. 61, 65–6
Houghton lantern excites wit of, iv. 163
House of Commons's keyhole stopped by, i. 300
in Florence, pretends to know all English politics, iv. 227
Jacobites join, in opposing Sir Robert Walpole, vi. 93
Labour in Vain satirizes, ii. 18
'ministerial' synonymous with, though formerly its opposite, v. 277
mutual accusations by, iv. 65–6
no less harmful than the Stuarts to England, iii. 456
Parliamentary division opposed by, i. 231
Pelham must bring in, ii. 537
privately-raised regiments opposed by, iii. 154
Pulteney (E. of Bath) abused by, iv. 31
—— leads, in Parliament, i. 231
——'s period with, iv. 257
——'s treatment of, satirized, ii. 91
ruinous activity of, ii. 425
Sandwich an adherent of, iv. 198

Walpole, Sir Robert, blames, i. 232
—— cannot conciliate, i. 330–1
wives of, attend Court in Queen Anne dresses, ii. 95
See also Whig-Patriots
Patriotism:
HW's reflections on, ii. 423
modern, political moderation incompatible with, ix. 50
power and prostitution inevitably succeed, v. 546
Patriots are Come, The. See under Hervey, John (1696–1743)
Patrizi, Villa, Rome:
Charles of Naples at, ii. 532
entertainment at, i. 25
Patrizii:
first rank of Tuscan nobility, iv. 192
old Florentine noble families called, vi. 350–1
Pattens:
Bracegirdle, Anne, wears, i. 435
lowest Englishwomen tramp in, viii. 126
Patterson, Mrs, Lady Molesworth's maid:
dies in fire, vi. 138
Patterson. *See also* Paterson; Pattinson
Pattinson, Thomas, deputy mayor of Carlisle:
boastful letter of, about repulsing rebels, nullified by his surrender, iii. 165–6
Paul, St (d. ?A.D. 67):
Bolingbroke writes *Craftsman* against, iv. 454
Paul III (Alexander Farnese) (1468–1549), pope 1534–49:
medal of, v. 201
Paul V (Camillo Borghese) (1552–1621), pope 1605–21:
supposed opulence of England did not weigh with, to induce him to grant dispensation to James I, ix. 224, 226
Venetians quarrel with, iv. 198
Paul I (1754–1801), Emperor of Russia, 1796:
birth of, iv. 457
Florence to be visited by, ix. 250–1
HW hopes, will be childless so that his family's history may be published, ix. 87
impostor claims to be father of, vii. 547
mother confers Order of St Anne in name of, viii. 84
mother has, inoculated, vii. 76
mother may poison, vi. 253, vii. 236
mother might give Turkey to, vii. 236
Naples left by, sooner than expected, ix. 250
Peter III disowns, vi. 57, 75, vii. 215
Rome visited by, ix. 250
Paul, George (d. 1755), LL.D.; King's Advocate:
Duke of Newcastle's Letter attributed to, v. 281
Paul; pauls (Italian coins):
worth of, i. 227
Paulin, Comte de. *See* La Tour du Pin-Gouvernet, Jean-Frédéric de

Paulis, Giacinto de:
Theodore of Corsica calls, traitor, ii. 156
Paulmy, Marquis de. *See* Voyer, Marc-Antoine-René de
Paulo, Don. *See* Borghese, Paolo
Paulone. *See* Paulin
Pavement:
marble, Mann has, made for Bubb Dodington, iv. 54, 253
Pavia:
Botta's nephew from, vi. 14
—— to retire to, vi. 448, 454
Charles Emmanuel III and Lobkowitz to join at, iii. 55
Philip, Don, retires to, iii. 231
Spaniards may invade, iii. 41
Pavilion:
Mann uses, to mean 'flag,' v. 270, 277–8
Richelieu's, *see Pavillon d'Hanovre*
Pavilions, The, near Hampton Court; D. of Gloucester's seat:
HW calls on D. and Ds of Gloucester at, vii. 433
Pavillon d'Hanovre:
HW visits and describes, vii. 329
Richelieu's garden pavilion called, v. 172n, vii. 329
Pavonarius, Frederick (d. 1783), page:
(?) Wales, P. of, attended by, iv. 232
Pavon e Moncastello:
Charles Emmanuel III and Austrians near, iii. 84
Pawnbroker:
Jewish, Mme Suares rents her own jewels from, i. 137
Maclaine takes waistcoat to, iv. 168
Pawning:
of jewels, i. 137, 484, iii. 181
of Whithed's clothes, ii. 4
Paxton, Nicholas (d. 1744), solicitor to the Treasury:
Fitzwilliam kisses, at Chelsea in HW's presence after release from Newgate, i. 502
Florentines call, Sir Robert Walpole's secretary, i. 417
Newgate may be the prison of, i. 397, 400n
Secret Committee causes loss of place by, i. 502
Secret Committee examines, about money given at Limerick's election, i. 397
Secret Committee report exposes, i. 425
Payba, Abraham (?d. 1776), *alias* James Roberts:
Taaffe and Wortley Montagu arrested in Paris for cheating, iii. 450n, iv. 288, v. 473n
Payerback; Payersberg. *See* Poymont
Paymaster of Chelsea Hospital:
Pelham's resignation as, ii. 313
Paymaster of the Board of Works:
Gilmour succeeds Brown as, i. 493
Selwyn succeeds Onslow as, iv. 518

Paymaster of the Land Forces:
Burke becomes, ix. 392
Fox, Henry, is, v. 74, 92, 99, 103, vi. 92, 134
George II appoints Pitt as, iv. 138
—— insists on Fox's retention as, v. 99
joint: Darlington and Dupplin become, iv. 517; Potter succeeds Darlington as, v. 25
Leicester's witticism on Pitt's appointment as, iii. 286
Pelham retires as, ii. 313
Pitt is, iii. 256, 286, iv. 138, 512, 517
salary of, vi. 440
Townshend, Charles, not to be, vi. 440
—— succeeds Henry Fox as, vi. 302, 304
Walpole, Sir Robert, is, vi. 26
Winnington is, i. 172n, ii. 350, 356, iii. 211
Paymaster of the Marines:
Pitt, John, to become, v. 26
See also Williams, Sir Charles Hanbury
Paymaster of the Pensions:
Gage succeeds Compton as, iv. 517
Jeffries said to succeed Stewart as, i. 495
See also Hooper, Edward; Keene, Benjamin
Payne, Ralph (1739–1807), cr. (1795) Bn Lavington; M.P.:
made K.B., vii. 272
West Indian, vii. 272
Pay Office:
Burke restores Bembridge and Powell to, ix. 407–8
—— succeeds Barré in, ix. 407
Powell dismissed from, for deficiency in accounts, ix. 407
—— placed in, by Holland, ix. 407
Pazzi, St Maria Maddalena de' (1566–1607), nun:
painting by, ii. 171, 207
Peace:
HW prefers, to doctrines, ix. 39–40
HW's reflections on, viii. 393
not so catching as war, ix. 188
victory less desirable than, vi. 85
Peace in Europe, serenata:
performed at London opera, iv. 49
Wall's witticism at, iv. 51–2
Peach; peaches:
stewed, Mann eats, at dinner, i. 104
Peach colour:
fades rapidly, v. 471
Peachey, James (1723–1808), 4th Bt, 1765; cr. (1794) Bn Selsey, M.P.:
George III's groom, iv. 247
Peacocks:
York, D. of, receives, at Rome, vi. 228
'Peak, Sir James of the.' See James of the Peak
Pear; pears:
HW eats, for supper, vi. 110
HW should not eat, cold, vi. 114
Pearce, Zachary (1690–1774), Bp of Bangor, 1748; of Rochester, 1756:

Faction Detected attributed to, ii. 319
Ferrers declines services of, v. 398
Pulteney makes, dean, ii. 319
—— supplies, with material, ii. 319
Pearl; pearls:
Charlotte's mantle fastened with, v. 529
Clive may not again return with, vi. 243
necklace of, ii. 291
Waldegrave, Cts, wears, vii. 193
wedding gown trimmed with, vii. 93
Pearse. See Pearce
Pearson. See Pierson
Pear tree. See Iron-pear-tree-water
Peas:
frost said to have killed, in England, vii. 200
Goldsworthy makes profit by sale of, to English ships, ii. 107
Pecari; Peccori. See Pecori
Péché-mortel:
HW wants to loll in, ii. 315
Mann not familiar with, ii. 332
Pecori, Contessa. See Berzichelli, Maria Leopolda (1704–82); Suares de la Concha, Maria Teresa (1728–1809)
Pecori, Antonfrancesco (1682–1743), Conte:
death of, ii. 150
marries to spite nephew, ii. 150
Pecori, Bernardo (1720–63), Conte:
Chesupiades shared by, ii. 345
Mann describes, iii. 145
Parigi, the, rival of the Pepi with, i. 111, 136, 444, iii. 136
Pepi cicisbea to, ii. 150
——'s engagement with, broken, i. 111, 136
—— to shoot Parigi for giving disease to, i. 444, iii. 136
—— tries to kill, i. 136
Suares, Teresa, to marry, iii. 136, 145
uncle marries to displease, ii. 150
wife said to arouse jealousy of, iii. 311
Pedestal:
for Boccapadugli eagle, see under Eagle: Boccapadugli
for bust of Vespasian, see under Vespasian
Montfort will need, to lead Cambridgeshire militia, v. 312
of buried column, used as rubbish for foundation of arch, v. 343
Pedigree; pedigrees:
Chesterfield's of Stanhope family, iv. 181, 195
Italians hang, in conspicuous places, iv. 205
Mann's, see Mann family: pedigree of
of Vere family, iv. 181
Pomfret, Cts of, devises scheme for, iv. 180–1, 194
Pedro III (1717–86), K. consort of Portugal 1777–86:
niece's marriage to, v. 422

Peer:
trial of, more interesting than a coronation, v. 535
Peerage. See under Collins, Arthur
Peerage; peerages:
Bouverie gets, by bribery, iii. 419
Clinton barony's descent, ix. 165
conferred upon: Anson, iii. 414; Archer, iii. 419; Bagot, ix. 86; Bateman, viii. 227; Beauclerk, Lord Vere, iv. 135; Bessborough, iv. 66; Blakeney, v. 24, 52; Brooke, i. 391n; Brudenell, ix. 86; Bubb Dodington, v. 490; Bute, Cts of, v. 490; Carpenter, v. 490; Conway, Francis, iv. 135; Courtenay, vi. 31; Curzon, v. 484, 490; Damer, vi. 31; De Grey, ix. 86; De la Warr, v. 490; Duncombe, iii. 419; Dunning, ix. 264; Edgcumbe, i. 399n; Edward Augustus, P., v. 389; Egmont, vi. 32; Fauconberg, iv. 563; Fitzroy, ix. 86; Fitzwilliam, i. 399, iii. 296; Fox, Lady Georgiana, vi. 31; Fox, Henry, iv. 502n, vi. 129; Fox-Lane, vi. 31; Gage, ix. 86; Garth-Turnour, v. 490; Grosvenor, v. 490; Harrington, i. 333; Henley, v. 389; Herbert, ix. 86; Hillsborough, i. 436n, iv. 26; Hobart, iii. 296, 307; Hunsdon, ix. 166; Ilchester, iv. 563; Irby, v. 490; Keppel, ix. 264; Kildare, iii. 371, v. 485; Liddell, iii. 419; Ligonier, vi. 449–50; Lyttelton, v. 18, 24, 26; Norton, ix. 264; Phipps, vi. 548; Pitt, vi. 442–3; Pitt, Lady Hester, v. 541; Rawdon, iv. 135–6; Robinson, v. 490; Rolle, iii. 419; Sandys, i. 249n, ii. 142, 357–8, 365; Shelburne, ix. 542; Spencer, v. 490; Talbot, v. 489, 490, ix. 86; Temple, ix. 542; Vernon, vi. 31; Vesey, iv. 136; Walpole, Horatio (1678–1757), iv. 556, 563; Walpole, Sir Robert, i. 318, 319, vi. 27; Wentworth, vi. 31; Wyndham-O'Brien, v. 24, 26
creation of, to convert House of Lords, ix. 605
Fox, Henry, wants, for wife, v. 75
HW's comments on new members of, viii. 227
Heathcote has promise of, iv. 81
Irish, newly created: HW only saw one third of, ix. 433; HW ridicules, v. 24, viii. 227
Lowther to receive, vii. 58
Mann expects, to be given to Sir James Gray, vi. 469
new creations for, viii. 205
Northumberland and Somerset titles perpetuated in, iv. 81
Paoli said to get, from France, vii. 31
Pitt's, disliked by London, vi. 442–3
Ryder almost gets, iv. 557
Sackville to receive, ix. 237, 241
Saye and Sele descent, ix. 165
Peeresses:
English, travel as much as their eldest sons, ix. 649

heralds advertise for names and addresses of, v. 535
Peers, Col. Newsham (d. 1743):
killed at Dettingen, ii. 258
Peggi, Pier Francesco (1688–1780), Canon, 1710:
Benedict XIV's letter to, v. 126, 196
Peirse, Henry (?1754–1824), M.P.:
(?) Gabrielli, Caterina, kept by, viii. 148–9
Peking:
HW's friend at, *see Letter from Xo Ho*
HW speculates about Rousseau's opinion of, viii. 62
Peleus et Thétis. See under Le Bovier de Fontenelle
Pelham, Bns. *See* Frankland, Anne (ca 1734–1813)
Pelham, Lady Catherine. *See* Manners, Lady Catherine (ca 1701–80)
Pelham, Catherine (1727–60), m. (1744) Henry Fiennes-Clinton, 9th E. of Lincoln; 2d D. of Newcastle-under-Lyne, 1768:
Capello, Signora, does not invite, iii. 18
death of, v. 428
marriage of, ii. **245**, 277, 483, v. 18n
Sandwich's ball not attended by, iv. 121
Pelham, Dorothy:
death of, from fever and sore throat, v. 362
Pelham, Frances (1728–1804):
Bower's theory about earthquake known to, iv. 157
cousin has hardly seen, iv. 180
cousin should go to England to wed, iv. 115, 129, 172–3
cousin's marriage to, will make him the chief Pelham heir, iv. 173
earrings lost by, in hackney chair, iv. **114**, 129
Pelham, Henrietta (1730–68), m. 1 (1748) Hon. Richard Temple, m. 2 (1753) George Nevill, Bn Abergavenny:
brother to seek, at Hanover, iv. 172, 180
second marriage of, iv. 180n
Sussex visited by, iv. 180
Pelham, Hon. Henry (1695–1754), prime minister; M.P.:
absent from Parliament, i. 484
address of thanks proposed by, iii. 188
Admiralty and Navy Bill opposed by, iv. 38
Arlington St house of, opposite HW's, ii. 231, v. 167n
Augusta, Ps of Wales, made regent by, iv. 249
Barnard defends discipleship of, to Granville, x. 10
—— influences, iv. 111
Beauclerk's peerage requested by, iv. 135
Bedford, D. of, aided by, iii. 154, iv. 120
—— to punish, iv. 38
bishops flock to house of, ii. 231
Bower consulted by, about earthquake, iv. 157

[Pelham, Hon. Henry, *continued*]

Burdett promises to present Castle-Durrow and Rodney to, iv. 20

Cabinet Council to resist removal by, ii. 537

Carteret and Newcastle might be warned by, not to trust Richecourt's insinuations against Mann, ii. 363

Carteret arouses jealousy of, ii. 535

—— betrays, into losing sugar tax, vi. 489

—— makes Admiralty appointments unbeknownst to, ii. 349

—— opposes, about privately-raised regiments, iii. 158

—— reconciled with, ii. 349

——'s failure to form new ministry strengthens, iii. 213

——'s vengeance might be feared by, iii. 17

Chancellor of the Exchequer, iv. 114n, 180n, 233n

Chesterfield, Pitt, 'Patriots,' and Tories to be brought in by, ii. 537

Chesterfield's witticism on, iv. 214

children of, die of fever and sore throat, i. 399, v. 362

Clutterbuck infuses scruples into, i. 391n

Cockpit meeting to be presided over by, ii. 103

Cumberland, D. of, gets ordnance from, iv. 120

——'s quarrel with Newcastle calmed by, iv. 120

Custom House place secured by, for E. of Lincoln and son, iv. 18

daughter of, iv. 121n, 180n, v. 18n, 428n

death of, iv. 411–14, 419, ix. 288

distribution of patronage difficult for, ii. 550

Egmont formerly preferred Fox to, iv. 224

—— helped by, in Weobly election contest, iv. 31

——'s pamphlet attacks, iv. 32

——'s party heaps incense on, iv. 224

Euston visited by, ii. 254

Exchequer auditorship controlled by, iv. 233n

Exchequer resigned to, by Sandys, ii. 350, 356

faction of, unpopular in House of Commons, iii. 4

far from rich, iv. 413

first Lord of the Treasury, ii. 299, iv. 233n, ix. 20n

Fox and his friends courted by, ii. 451

Fox may succeed, as prime minister, iv. 411, 419

Fraigneau tells, about George I's intentions for Bolingbroke, iv. 452

Frederick, P. of Wales's adherents bribed by, iv. 30

——'s opposition shows strength of, iii. 158–9

—— speaks to, at Carlton House, i. 337

—— toasts Fox for opposing, iii. 161

Garter might be expected by, iv. 84

George II approached by, about Berlin post for Sir James Gray, iii. 444

—— asks Winnington to recall, to ministry, iii. 212

—— on distant terms with, ii. 552

—— permitted by, to choose Admiralty candidate, iv. 17

—— sick of timidity and compromises of, iii. 212

—— to remove, to make room for Carteret, v. 100n

—— will hardly speak to, iii. 159

Gower in the hands of, iv. 258

Grafton to head dependents of, iv. 120

Granville, Cts, distresses, by assembly, ii. 562

Gray, Sir James, promised Berlin post by, iii. 444, 453

Grodno's diet breakup would disturb, ii. 562

Gunnings eclipse, iv. 260

HW's unfavourable opinion of, justified by Bubb Dodington's diary, ix. 503

HW to speak to, about Mann, ii. 382

Harcourt a creature of, iv. 246

Hardwicke bows to, at trial of rebel lords, iii. 280

—— discusses retirement with, iv. 202

Harrington sacrificed by, v. 100n

Hartington the favourite of, iv. 74n

health of, iv. 413

Hervey hated by, i. 430

House of Commons mortifies, iv. 257

House of Commons visited by, just before death, iv. 413

interest reduction planned by, iv. 111

Jackson may apply to, for Leghorn post, i. 409, 430

Lee and Potter speak against, iii. 470

Legge courts, iii. 458

lenient measures preferred by, vii. 86

levee of, ii. 231, iii. 20

Leveson family subject of invectives by, iv. 201

Lincoln to inherit property of, ii. 245

Lovat calls to, at trial, iii. 347

Mann fears that Robert Mann may be injured by retirement of, from paymastership, ii. 313

—— surprised at news of, ii. 557

ministry of: Conway may be prevented by, from going to Scotland, iii. 204; follies involve, iv. 74n; George II forced by, to assign Beefeaters to Falmouth, iii. 397; has seen its best days, iii. 17; Mann glad that Granville's association with, did not wreck it, iii. 225; Maria Theresa's towns will not be fortified by, iii. 69; Scottish taxes of, iv. 310–11; triumphant in Parliament,

iii. 458; Williams, Sir C.H., disliked by, iii. 16

Murray a protégé of, ii. 384

—— may succeed, as prime minister, ii. 411, 419

naval reduction proposed by, opposed by Pitt faction, iv. 223

Newcastle jealous of, i. 430

—— links, in 'passion' against Harrington, x. 10

Nugent attached to, iv. 32

old politicians hate Egmont because of, iv. 32

Onslow's election as Speaker moved by, i. 219

Orford's death would vacate place in gift of, iv. 233

overshoots himself, iv. 259

Parliamentary debates by: on amendment to the Address, x. 22, 24; on privately-raised regiments, x. 16, 17, 18; on Scotch bill, x. 33; on unanimity on the Army, x. 10

Parliamentary majorities commanded by, iii. 202

Parliamentary motion's alteration suggested by, i. 354

Patriots' dismissal of Hanover troops discredits, after his attack on Whigs for similar acts, iii. 17

peace may be restored by, in absence of George II and Newcastle, iv. 143

peace will secure position of, iii. 5

Pitt and Fox injure, in their strife, iv. 230

Pitt attacks, iii. 169

—— bullies and flatters, iii. 155

—— cannot be got by, into place, iii. 159

—— courted by, ii. 327

—— faction flatters, despite disagreement, iv. 224

—— may succeed, as prime minister, iv. 411, 419

—— might get concessions from, iv. 223

—— praises, x. 10

political situation of, resembles that of 1765, vi. 303

Prowse favours, iv. 32

pusillanimity of, iv. 483

regent, ii. 209

resignation proposed by, iii. 105

resigns, as first lord of the Treasury, iii. 211

Richmonds friendly with, ii. 451

Rutland wanted by, as Master of the Horse, iv. 183

sacrifice of political embroils, iv. 39

sacrifices all to jealousy and ambition, ii. 535, 537

Scarborough visited by, to cure scurvy, iv. 413

successor of: not likely to dismiss Robert Mann, ii. 326; unfit for post, iv. 431

supporters of, may overturn him, iii. 6

Townshend, Vcts, hates followers of, ii. 497

Treasury to be headed by, ii. 147, 265, 277, 299, 313

treaty with Saxony defended by, in Parliament, iv. 300

Trevor related to, i. 366

Walpole, Sir Robert, asks, to secure pension, i. 229n, ii. 465-6

—— had, as friend and pupil, i. 229n

—— not to be replaced by, i. 319

—— said to be ungratefully treated by, iii. 471

—— visited by, at Houghton, ii. 245, 248, 254

war opposed by, iii. 448

West secretary to, as Chancellor of the Exchequer, iv. 371n

wife of, iv. 114n, ix. 20n

wife said to keep, from revealing Greenwich Park affair, x. 10

Williams's candidacy for K.B. opposed by, ii. 451

Pelham, Henry (ca 1736-9):
death of, i. 399, v. 362, 369

Pelham, James (ca 1683-1761), M.P.; Col.:
Pelham, Thomas, corresponds with, iv. 172, 195

Pelham, Louisa or Lucy (ca 1728-40):
death of, v. 362

Pelham, Lucy (d. 1736), m. (1717) Henry Clinton, 7th E. of Lincoln:
husband's death a blow never surmounted by, v. 93

'Treaty, the' said to cast aspersions upon, v. 93

Pelham, Lucy. See Pelham, Louisa

Pelham, Thomas (1728-1805), Bn Pelham, 1768; cr. (1801) E. of Chichester:
Acciaioli, Mme, has affair with, iv. 115-16, 129, 158, 172, 180, 284

—— visited by, in the country, iv. 115-16

Acciaioli family likes, iv. 115-16, 172

becomes lord of the Admiralty, v. 490

chief justice in eyre, vii. 562

Customs reversion to go to, v. 26

family of, use subterfuges to lure him home, iv. 180

George II commends dancing of, iv. 200

HW called on by, iv. 207

HW calls on, iv. 200

HW's opinion of, iv. 225

heir should be produced by, for D. œ Newcastle, iv. 116

leaves Florence, iv. 171

Mann accompanied by, in riding parties iv. 172

—— assured by, of receiving baronetcy, iv. 462

—— entertains, regularly at supper, iv. 115

—— might be aided by, in case of recall from Florence, v. 129

[Pelham, Thomas, *continued*]
—— might be helped by, to become K.B.,
vi. 381
——'s arrears solicited by, at Hanover, iv.
173, 195
——'s friend, v. 490, vi. 32, vii. 562
—— should seek intercession of, for himself not Milbanke, iv. 180
——'s 'little waxen friend,' v. 26
——'s opinion of, iv. 171
—— thanks HW for civilities to, iv. 211
—— thinks of joining, in Hanover, iv. 150
Mann, Galfridus, to press, about Mann's
affairs, iv. 211
marriage of, to Frances Pelham, will make
him chief Pelham heir, iv. 172–3
Newcastle, D. of, to be approached by,
about Mann's arrears, iv. 173
Newcastle House the abode of, iv. 207
Pelham, Frances, should marry, iv. 115,
129, 180
Pelham, Col. James, told by, to intercede
with D. of Newcastle for Mann's salary
arrears, iv. 195
Pisa baths visited by, iv. 158
reversion of Newcastle's new peerage to
go to, vi. 32
sister will not be found by, in Hanover,
iv. 180
(?) Stone advises, about Mann's salary arrears, iv. 195
to be master of the Great Wardrobe, viii.
142
Pelham, Thomas (1729–39):
death of, i. 399, v. 362, 369
Pelham, Mrs Thomas. *See* Frankland, Anne
(ca 1734–1813)
Pelham Clinton, Lady Catherine Fiennes
(1776–1804), m. (1800) William Pleydell-
Bouverie styled Vct Folkestone, 1779; 3d
E. of Radnor, 1828:
Clinton barony to revert to, HW thinks,
ix. 165
Pelham Clinton, Henry Fiennes (1750–78),
styled Bn Clinton 1752–68 and E. of Lincoln 1768–78; M.P.:
Chamberlayne accompanies, vii. 224
cheated and poxed, vii. 378
death of, viii. 420
English at Florence have not gambled
heavily since affair of, vii. 536
Florence visited by, on way from Rome
to England, viii. 252
France visited by, for health, viii. 420
HW recommends, to Mann, vii. **223**, 228
Seymour-Conway, Lady Frances, marries,
viii. 71, 420
story about, repeated from Tuscany and
printed in newspapers, vii. 368
Pelham Clinton, Lord John (1755–81), M.P.:
Mann to present, at Tuscan Court, viii.
251

Pelham Clinton, Lord Thomas (1752–95),
styled E. of Lincoln 1779–94; 3d D. of
Newcastle-under-Lyne, 1794; M.P.:
elected for Westminster, by Ds of North-
umberland's efforts, viii. 52
HW intended to recommend, to Mann,
viii. 263
Pelham faction:
Capello, Signora, excludes, iii. 18
resignations expected from, v. 98
Pelham family:
HW never loved, vi. 109
HW predicts that rule of, will end in
October, v. 93
Legge ingratiates himself with, iii. 458
Milbanke should be aided by, iv. 171
no less harmful than the Stuarts to Eng-
land, iii. 456
Pelham, Thomas, will be chief heir to, if
he marries Frances Pelham, iv. 172–3
Pelham Holles, Thomas (1693–1768), cr.
(1715) D. of Newcastle-upon-Tyne, (1756)
D. of Newcastle-under-Lyne; statesman:
absurdity of, vi. 102–3
alleged disinterestedness of, v. 26
ambition of, to be prime minister, ii. 535
Augusta, Ps of Wales, made regent by, iv.
249
authority of, established, iv. 425
Bath, E. of, Carteret, Furnese, and Limerick entertained by, i. 503, ii. 20–1
Bath, E. of, frightens, at Lovat's trial, iii.
347
Bath visited by, vi. 566–7
Beauclerk's peerage requested by, iv. 135
Bedford, D. of, about to clash with, over
Turnpike Bill, iv. 112
—— embraced and then avoided by, iv.
201
—— given aid by, iv. 120
——'s breach with, iv. 38
Bedford faction and Rockingham to be
reconciled by, vi. 549
Bedford House visited by, to unite Bedford and Rockingham factions, vi. 566
bishops avoid, after fall, although he
appointed most of them, vi. 36–7, 323–4
Bolingbroke may be aped by, vi. 442
Botta believes, must return to the government, vi. 44
Brussels dinner party with Botta involves,
in question of precedence, vi. 44
Burdett promises to present Castle-Durrow
and Rodney to, iv. 20
Bute advised by, to be secretary of state,
v. 488
Bute and Hardwicke join, against Pitt, v.
539n
Bute and Temple meet, at Bute's Garter
installation, vi. 79
Bute's dismissal of, implies certainty of
peace, vi. 38

Byng's courage compared to timidity of, v. 67

cabinet and Parliament will oppose, v. 93

Cabinet Council place may be kept by, vi. 79

Cambridge clergy ungrateful to, vi. 38

Cambridge college head might be recommended by, for K.B., vi. 332

Cambridge to celebrate installation of, as chancellor, iv. 71, 83

Cambridge turned half Jacobite by ordinances of, iv. 346–7

caricature of, in 'The Treaty,' v. 93

Carteret arouses jealousy of, ii. 535

—— calls, to witness that Sir Robert Walpole aided Hanover troops measure, ii. 382

—— makes Admiralty appointments unbeknownst to, ii. 349

—— mediates between Fox and, iv. 502

—— never writes to, ii. 382

—— reconciled with, ii. 349

—— said to leave in place, but without power, ii. 82

——'s discomfiture at rebels' progress enjoyed by, iii. 109

——'s letter with Dettingen news copied by, ii. 258

——'s union with, i. 301

——'s vengeance might be feared by, iii. 17

—— told by, about venison, i. 506

Charlotte's retiring-room at Westminster Abbey occupied by, v. 535

Chesterfield and Fox discuss downfall of, iv. 502

Chesterfield may arouse jealousy of, iii. 413

——'s witticism on, iv. 214

Chloé, French cook of, i. 485n

Claremont to be retreat of, for a few days, v. 92

clergy patronized by, vi. 323–4

clerks and tide-waiters restored by, to offices, vi. 323

Conway's friends led by, towards Bedford faction, vi. 533

—— to be entertained by, at dinner at Clarement, vi. 332

credit of, decays, iv. 505

Cumberland, D. of, at odds with, iv. 120

death of, vii. 70

dessert designed by, iv. 126

Devonshire leaves Bath after fall of, vi. 96

—— replaces, as prime minister, v. 24

dukedom of, entailed on E. of Lincoln, v. 18, 26

dupes must be reemployed by, iv. 518

Dupplin a follower of, v. 74

Egmont continues to support, in Parliament, iv. 31

——'s pamphlet attacks, iv. 32

English success attributed by HW to loss by, of absolute power, v. 499

exchange of provinces by, as secretary of state, iii. 463

extravagance of, at elections, satirized in ballad, ii. 82

faction of, iii. 4, v. 27

Fane offended by letter of, vii. 550

followers of: weary of following, vi. 444; will desert to George III and D. of Cumberland, v. 93; would find no room if Winchilsea and Fox remained, v. 99

folly of, complicates debate over Regency Bill, vi. 299

Fox allowed no scope by, v. 6

Fox and his friends courted by, ii. 451

Fox disliked by, iv. 412

—— may receive trifle from, v. 91

—— offends, v. 17

—— persuaded by, to lead House of Commons, iv. 502

—— proposes no cordiality to, iv. 502

—— ridicules jealousy of, of Granvilles' assemblies, ii. 562

——'s alliance with, marred by squabbles, iv. 516

——'s negotiations with, broken off, v. 73

——'s rupture with, iv. 417

——'s unpopularity terrifies, v. 76

—— unlikely to be conciliated by, v. 93

Frederick, P. of Wales's adherents bribed by, iv. 30

—— speaks to, at Carlton House, i. 337

'frisking while his grave is digging,' vi. 102

friends of, dismissed from government, vi. 109

gazette money summoned by, iv. 270

geographical ignorance of, iii. 485

George II abuses Pitt and the Grenvilles to, iv. 223

—— alarmed by, over fate of German treaties, iv. 501

George II and Pitt reconciled by, iv. 138

George II called on by, at Kensington, v. 93, 97

—— calls, 'puppy,' ii. 535

—— feels, has broken faith with him, v. 97, 99

—— given consent of, to be sole minister, with Fox as paymaster, v. 92

—— may join, in suppressing opposition, iv. 513

—— on distant terms with, ii. 552

—— sees, while excluding Holdernesse, iv. 346

——'s relations with, v. 76

—— tired by, iii. 212

—— to be accompanied by, to Hanover, iv. 39, 143

—— to be entertained by, at Claremont, iv. 72

—— told by, of Mann's hint of Dashwood's treachery, i. 412

[Pelham Holles, Thomas, *continued*]
—— to remove, to make room for Carteret, v. 100n
—— wants, to resume Seals, v. 76
George III grants less power to, than his predecessors did, vi. 36
—— to be appeased by, v. 76
German measures must be taken by, to regain George II's favour, v. 93
Germany and Holland to be visited by, iii. 484–5
'gives everything,' v. 257
Goldsworthy probably sent Roman letter to, iii. 226
Gower in the hands of, iv. 258
Grafton intruded upon by, on sickbed, v. 78–9
—— to head dependents of, iv. 120
Granville, Cts, distresses, by her assemblies, ii. 562
Gray, Sir James, promised Berlin post by, iii. 444, 453
Grodno diet's breakup would disturb, ii. 562
Gunnings eclipse, iv. 260
HW calls: 'Duke Trinculo,' iv. 502; 'Lepidus,' v. 79; 'Lindamira,' iv. 214n; 'Mamamouchi,' iv. 72; 'old busy sinner,' vi. 508
HW did not admire, vii. 265
HW lacks ambition of, vi. 38
HW lacks persistence of, vi. 570
HW's unfavourable opinion, justified by Bubb Dodington's diary, ix. 503
'Hanoverizes,' iv. 39
Hanover to be visited by, iii. 484–5, 490, iv. 39, 143
Harcourt a creature of, iv. 246
—— told by, that Bp Hayter must be dismissed, iv. 343
Hardinge, Mrs, makes witticism about George III's choice of, v. 460
Hardwicke prevents, from joining Fox, v. 87
——'s alliance with, may cause trouble, vi. 107
—— to succeed, as High Steward of Cambridge, iv. 19
—— upheld by, at rebels' trial, iii. 286
Harrington and Holdernesse abandon George II's favour to please, v. 100
Harrington and Pelham attacked by, x. 10
Harrington may quarrel with, iii. 326
health of: out of danger, vi. 579; stroke of the palsy, vii. 70
Hervey hated by, i. 430
Holland journey of, delayed, iii. 484–5
House of Commons devoted to, v. 11
House of Lords formerly subservient to, vi. 109–10
intrigues of, vi. 566–7
Jackson hopes to get Leghorn post through, i. 218, 409, 430

—— proposes letter of thanks to, from Leghorn merchants, i. 260
Jones secretary to, v. 26
Keene the tool of, at Cambridge, iv. 346
Lee courted by, iv. 245
Legge courts, iii. 458
—— frowned upon by, though formerly his protégé, iv. 493
—— replaced by, in Treasury, v. 103
Leicester's witticism to, at rebels' trial, iii. 286
levee of, iv. 20, vi. 37
Lincoln liked by, i. 210
—— to inherit property of, ii. 245
London approves of, iv. 493
Mann advises Townshend to write to, iii. 375
—— asked by, for information about Young Pretender, i. 159, 160, 203
—— delays writing to, i. 265, ii. 374
—— doubtful about his favour with, ii. 115–16, iii. 383–4
—— encloses letter to, iii. 99
—— fails to understand how Treasury can be headed by, iv. 422
—— informs, of Young Pretender's departure, ii. 375, 376, 380
—— in letter to, contradicts *London Gazette* report, ii. 205–6
—— kept waiting for credentials by servants of, i. 24
—— may send HW's coffee-pot to, ii. 115–16, 137
—— ordered by, to send duplicate dispatches to Hanover, ii. 229
—— prepares, to expect few letters, i. 97
——'s baronetcy delayed by, iv. 458, 467
—— scolded by, for not asking for salary until too late, v. 483
——'s correspondence with, i. 97, 203, 311, 315, 341, 369, ii. 190, 374, 375, 376, 379, 380, 392, 411, 412, 420, 488, 516–17, 557, iii. 56, 99, 158, 474, iv. 195, 467, v. 483
—— seeks salary arrears from, ii. 516–17, iii. 56, 338, 474, iv. 195–6, v. 483
—— sends Benedict XIV's speech to, iii. 422
—— sends Charles of Naples's manifesto to, ii. 420
—— sends duplicates of dispatches for, to HW, ii. 488
—— sends duplicates of his letters to, i. 311
—— sends medals to, i. 218
——'s inquiries about Theodore of Corsica unanswered by, ii. 205
——'s information sent to, about Young Pretender being an impersonator: iii. 141, 198; discussed with Horatio Walpole (1678–1757), iii. 172
—— surprised at news about, i. 361, ii. 557, v. 106
—— thinks of seeing, in Hanover, iv. 151

—— told by, to assure Francis I of continued English support, ii. 557

—— told by HW and Galfridus Mann not to give presents to, ii. 137, 151–2

—— to send Roman account of rebels' successes to, iii. 158

—— wants Sir Robert Walpole to write to, ii. 517

—— wonders how his conduct impresses, i. 119

—— would like hint conveyed to, about measures in case of his recall from Tuscany, v. 115

Manners family intimidates, into substituting Rutland for Gower, iv. 418

Mansfield upheld by, against Pratt, v. 205

Mathews displeased by, ii. 346, 361

may be Lord Treasurer, iv. 412

may hope to return to power under George IV, vi. 442

ministry of: Byng quarrels with, v. 3; Byng said to have compassion of, v. 63; cannot endure at same time with two others, v. 465; Fox and Mansfield and Waldegrave consider, hopeless, v. 99; has seen its best days, iii. 17; Mirepoix complains to, of attack on French ships, iv. 489; Parliament will expect explanation of Minorca's loss from, iv. 578

Murray cannot be spared by, from House of Commons, iv. 557

Newcastle House left by, from fear of contagious sore throat, v. 312–13

new ministers entertained by, at Claremont, i. 503, ii. 20

niece's marriage to Lincoln to please, ii. 277

northern province of state department coveted by, iii. 326

Northington abuses, vi. 109

office-seekers and clergy patronized by, vi. 323–4

Old Coachman, The, mentions, ii. 20

Opposition joined by, vi. 98

Opposition may be chastised by, iv. 513

Opposition not to be joined by, vi. 464

Osorio to write to, about disloyal English officer, iii. 147

overshoots himself, iv. 259

Parliamentary voting avoided by, vi. 508

Parliament will desert, v. 93

party of, lies quiet, v. 34

peerage granted to, vi. 32

Pelham arouses jealousy of, i. 430

—— attacked by, x. 10

—— might warn, not to trust Richecourt's insinuations against Mann, ii. 363

Pelham, Thomas, should produce heir to, iv. 116

—— to approach, about Mann's arrears, iv. 151, 173, 195

Pitt and Fox contend over, v. 79

Pitt and Fox fail to terrify, iv. 454

Pitt and friends to avoid provoking, v. 77

Pitt and Legge oppose, iv. 509

Pitt asks, not to meddle in House of Commons or state department, but stick to Treasury, v. 91

—— attacks, vi. 395

—— breaks with, iv. 453

—— confers with, v. 97, vi. 160

—— connection denied by, v. 74

—— content to manage the war under, v. 448

—— demands exclusion of, v. 11

—— given overtures from, v. 23

—— not chosen by, for colleague, iv. 248

—— praises, iv. 222

—— proposes government posts for, vi. 161

—— refuses to join, vi. 78

—— said to reject overtures of, vi. 93

——'s appointments opposed by, vi. 442

——'s coalition with, v. 103–4

——'s demands rejected by, and conferences broken off, v. 91, 92

——'s friends want union with, v. 87

—— supports, against Sandwich and the Bedfords, iv. 222

—— unlikely to get along with, v. 99–100

—— upsets power of, iv. 230

Pitt faction mutinous against, iv. 248

Pitt faction not to provoke, v. 77

policy of, becomes very military, iii. 464

political situation in 1765 like that of era of, vi. 303

politics said to be renounced by, vi. 579, vii. 70

Port Mahon officers' list discussed by, in House of Lords, i. 300

Pratt's rift with, v. 205

pretends to be willing to retire, v. 448

Prevereau in office of, i. 98

private resentment should be stifled by, v. 28

Pulteney parodies speech of, to Regency, in ballad, iii. 106

pusillanimity abandoned by, iv. 483

resignation of, as prime minister, v. 11, 17, vi. 36

resigns as secretary of state, iii. 211

Richecourt's attempts to oust Mann would not please, ii. 363

Richmond may influence, against Mann, i. 334

Richmonds friendly with, ii. 451

Rockingham ministry's resignation delayed by, vi. 432

Rutland substituted for Gower by, iv. 418

Rutland wanted by, as Master of the Horse, iv. 183

sacrifices all to jealousy and ambition, ii. 535, 537

St-Germain's retort to, x. 20, 21

Sainthill and Cholwick recommended by, to Mann, i. 483

Sandwich opposed by, iv. 120, 222

[Pelham Holles, Thomas, *continued*]
Seaforth election disturbed by, iii. 449
Shebbeare's letter to, v. 87
Shelley nephew of, iv. 26
Somerset succeeded by, as Chancellor of Cambridge, iv. 9–10
Stone, Andrew, consulted by, iii. 347
—— secretary to, i. 6, ii. 137n, iii. 347n, vii. 538n
Stone, George, brother of favourite of, iv. 505
Stosch might have written to, about Mann's illness, i. 51
stronger than ever, iv. 510
supporters of, may overturn him, iii. 6
Sussex men kissed by, in army review, iii. 495
Sussex post might be begged by, v. 499
Taaffe attends, at Lewes races, iv. 289
Talbot advises, on Pitt's resignation, v. 540
——'s witticism about, vi. 79
Theodore of Corsica claims that aid was promised him by, ii. 188
——'s speculations told to, ii. 234
Thompson forwards Mann's packet to, ii. 397
Townshend and Tories do not push Port Mahon investigation for fear of reuniting, with Fox. v. 56
transport hired by, to hold his travelling furniture, iii. 484
Treasury post taken by, iv. 417, 422
Trevor related to, i. 366
Vane paid by, to cut off entail of Newcastle estate, i. 209–10
venison procured by, from New Park, i. 506
Violette's performances concern the politics of, iv. 74n
vote lost through ill-treatment by, i. 243
Waldegrave said to be favourite of, iv. 505
Walpole, Horatio (1678–1757), approaches, about Mann's salary arrears, iii. 474
—— asks, to stifle rumour of sham Pretender, iii. 174, 199
Walpole, Sir Robert, arouses jealousy of, ii. 535
—— hears complaints of, about HW's attending Granvilles' assembly, ii. 562
—— kept ignorant of foreign affairs by, ii. 30
—— makes witticisms about dinner guests of, i. 506
—— receives Dettingen news from, ii. 258
—— said to have been betrayed by, ii. 82
'whets his busy blunted sting,' vi. 505
wife frightened by, with account of D. of Grafton, v. 79
Williams's candidacy for K.B. opposed by, ii. 451
witticism on George III's being the only surviving member of the government brought in by, vi. 110
yacht of, iii. 484
Young Pretender's declaration burned by order of, at Royal Exchange, iii. 161
Pelican; pelicans (artillery shot):
Guise at Cartagena says, would make a pelican pie, i. 485, iv. 450
Pelion:
Parliament of Paris relieved of, vii. 265
Pellegrini, Ignazio (b. ca 1716, d. after 1777), army officer:
Pitti palace altered by, vi. 258–9, 291
Pembroke, Cts of. *See* Fitzwilliam, Hon. Mary (d. 1769); Howe, Hon. Mary (d. 1749); Slingsby, Barbara (ca 1669–1721); Spencer, Lady Elizabeth (1737–1831)
Pembroke, E. of. *See* Herbert, George Augustus (1759–1827); Herbert, Henry (ca 1689–1750); Herbert, Henry (1734–94); Herbert, Thomas (1656–1733)
Pembroke, ship:
arrival of, in England, ii. 267
at Leghorn, i. 455
at Port Mahon, i. 285
HW's shipment goes by, ii. 214–15, 234, 250
Lee captain of, ii. 234
quarantine might be performed by, ii. 275, 282
Pembrokeshire:
Picton Castle in, iii. 310n
Pen. *See* Penn
Pen; pens:
HW to send, to Mme Galli, i. 193
Mann can hardly hold, because of bitter cold, vi. 385
Penancoët de Kéroualle, Louise-Renée de (1649–1734), cr. (1673) Ds of Portsmouth:
Yarmouth, Cts of, the successor of, iv. 90
Penaro. *See* Panaro
Pen-box (*pennino*):
set with brilliants, i. 64–5
Pencil:
HW inserts words in, in blank, viii. 209
silver, i. 194
Penelope. See under Galuppi, Baldassare; Rolli, Paolo Antonio
Penelope:
HW to imitate patience of, vii. 365
Lyttelton describes his first wife under name of, v. 409
web of HW's health unravelled like, viii. 148
Penkethman. *See* Pinkethman
Penn, Lady Juliana. *See* Fermor, Lady Juliana
Penn, Richard (?1734–1811), colonist; M.P.:
Mann wants to know about mediation attempts of, in America, viii. 128
Penn, Thomas (1702–75):
Fermor, Lady Juliana, marries, iii. 565n, iv. 97, 248

Pennsylvania's 'sovereign,' iv. 248
pistol wounds, in post-chaise accident, iv. 248
Penn, William (1703–47), Quaker:
wife of, iv. 20
Penn, Mrs William. *See* Vaux, Ann
Pennant, Richard (d. 1808), cr. (1783) Bn Penrhyn; M.P.:
peerage of, ix. 433
Pennée. *See* Penny
Pennington, John (1737–1813), cr. (1783) Bn Muncaster; M.P.:
peerage of, ix. 433
Pennino, Del. *See* Del Pennino
Pennsylvania:
Germans and Swiss in, may form regiment, iv. 531
'sovereign' of, iv. 248
Penny, Edward (1714–91), painter; 'Pennée':
Chute told by, of Domenichino sibyl at Bologna, i. 267–8
Creti's pupil talks with, ii. 334
Mann employs, to secure Domenichino painting at Bologna for HW, i. **226**, 227–8, 241, 257, 267, ii. 334
—— receives 'Magdalen' by Torri from, i. 268
——'s correspondence with, i. 227, 257, 268
(?) —— to seek Correggio painting through, i. 199
Penny:
silver, small size of, ix. 15
Penrhyn, Bn. *See* Pennant, Richard
Penrith, Cumberland:
rebels said to have reached, iii. 165
Pensacola, Florida:
taken by Spaniards, ix. 172
Penshurst, Kent:
Chute and HW make Perry vacate his dressing-room at, iv. 389
Pension; pensions:
Acton's, from Tuscan grand dukes, vi. 548
Albany, Cts of, gets: from Cardinal York, ix. 150; from French Court, ix. 150, 536; from popes, ix. 107
Amherst refuses, vii. 44
Arundel gets, on Ireland, iv. 517
Cameron, Jeanie, seeks, from Young Pretender, vi. 453
Charles III grants, to expelled Jesuits, vi. 516
Charles Emmanuel III said to continue, to Modenese princesses, ii. 223
Choiseul's, for relinquishing Swiss guards, vii. 363
Cocchi's, iv. 204
——'s widow's, v. 194
Cowper gives, to aunt's old friend, vii. 416
Craon's, iv. 25–6
Cybo's, i. 47
deduction from, for patent, iv. 204
Dorset, D. of, rejects, v. 104, 109

Electress's, to servants, Serristori, and Mme Uguccioni, taxed, iii. 23–4
English Opposition sold for, vi. 274
Ferdinand's, v. 491
Finch, Hon. William, said to receive, vi. 311
for Dukes of Gloucester, Cumberland, and York, vi. 424–5, 428
Francis I and Leopold pay, to East India Company employees, vi. 548
friends of Gascoigne and Damer give, to wife of man injured by them, vi. 286
George II gives: to Carteret, ii. 556; to Cts of Albemarle, iv. 460, 467
George III's, Saville demands list of, ix. 18
granted to persuade office-holders to accept salaries, vii. 247
Guilford's, North to have reversion of, vi. 552
Hamilton, Lady Archibald, receives, iii. 62, 361
—— refuses, iii. 361
heralds get, for registering the nobility, v. 535
Hertford, Cts of, resigns, as lady of the Bedchamber, i. 346
Hume Campbell accepts, iv. 5
Irish unrest over, v. 154
Jenison's, ii. 551
Jesuits', vii. 191, 508
Kilmarnock's, iii. 283–4
Lami's, vi. 13
Ligonier's, vi. 450
Lorenzi's, disappoints him, vi. 346, 351, 356, 370–1
Louis XVI gives, to Cts of Albany, ix. 150
Lowther's, from Tuscany, vi. 548
Magnan's, iii. 564
Mann should expect, on retirement, viii. 160
Massa duchess and princesses have, i. 47
Mill receives, from Tuscany, vi. 548
Monro's, iii. 400
Montagu, D. of, pays, iv. 79
Murray seeks, for children, ix. 364
North does not get, vi. 561
Northington's, vi. 443, 571
O'Brien, Mrs, loses, iv. 28
Old Pretender's: from France and Spain, vi. 387; son secures reversion of, v. 391, vi. 368
Paoli's, vii. 31, ix. 242n
Parliament cannot do without, ix. 97
Pitt gets dispensation for, from Common Council, v. 546
—— must regret acceptance of, vi. 277
——'s, v. 548, viii. 389
Porter's, viii. 160
Rantzau dismissed with, vii. 426
Razumovskiǐ gets, from Catherine II, vi. 456
Robinson's, on Ireland, iv. 502
Rochford gets, on Ireland, v. 460

[Pension; pensions, *continued*]
　Roman proconsuls', ix. 118
　satirized in *Labour in Vain*, ii. 20
　Scottish and Cornish outcry against, i. 347
　Stanhope's, ii. 178
　Stanislas I's, vi. 403
　Stosch's, i. 212n, iv. 53
　Tabuerniga brothers', i. 278
　Thurn, Comtesse, receives, vii. 253
　Torreggiani's, from Jesuits, v. 425
　Torrington may receive, iii. 155
　Walkinshaw, Mrs, gets, x. 47
　Walpole, Sir Robert, secures, after first refusing it, i. 329n, ii. 465
　York, Cardinal gives: to Cts of Albany, ix. 150; to Jesuits, vii. 191
　—— receives, v. 391, 392
　Young Pretender assured of, by Clement XIII, vi. 368
　——'s, Pius VI to give half of, to Cts of Albany, ix. 107
　—— to receive, from Spain, iii. 392
　See also Annuity
Pension Bill. *See under* Parliament: acts of
Pensioners. *See* Yeomen of the Guard
Pensions, Paymaster of the. *See* Paymaster of the Pensions
Penthièvre, Duc de. *See* Bourbon, Louis-Jean-Marie de (1725–93)
Penthièvre, Duchesse de. *See* Maria Teresa Felicità (1726–54)
Pentolino (pot):
　Walpole, Bns, takes ptisan in, to Richecourt, ii. 67
Pepi, Signora. *See* Macinghi, Ottavia (1717–77)
Pepi, Francesco Gaspero (1708–64):
　Florence, Abp of, does not permit, to let *Don Pilogio* be acted, ii. **41, 63**
　wife goes home to, i. 137
　wife's child attributed by, to Suares, ii. 345
Pepi, Maria Giulia Gaspera (b. 1743):
　birth of, ii. 345
'Pepin, le roi.' *See* 'Le roi Pepin'
Pepper:
　England will get, from Ceylon conquest, ix. 277
　French will be unable to get, for ragoûts, v. 523
　Holland to bewail loss of Ceylon monopoly of, ix. 283
Peppercorn:
　HW's letters as worthless as, ix. 530, 576
Perceval, John (1683–1748), 1st E. of Egmont:
　death of, iv. 31
Perceval, John (1711–70), styled Vct Perceval 1733–48; 2d E. of Egmont, 1748; M.P.:
　Admiralty headed by, vi. 167
　Craftsman prints work of, iv. 31
　death of, expected, vii. 247
　election of, at Westminster, i. **253, 272,** iv. 31

Examination of the Principles of Conduct of the Two Brothers published by, iv. **32,** 43
Faction Detected: antagonizes Pitts and Lytteltons, iv. 31; Mann wants to see, ii. 334; Mann, Galfridus, mentions, ii. 334; meeting described in, i. 335n; Williams's verses mention, ii. 320
Fox formerly preferred by, to Pelham, iv. 224
—— handles, severely, iv. 224
Frederick, P. of Wales, favours, iv. 31
—— makes, lord of the Bedchamber, iv. 32
——'s faction summoned by, for postmortem conference, iv. 239–40
—— warned by, against cold, iv. 232
Genealogical History of the House of Yvery, A, by, i. 272n, iv. 31
HW mentions, iv. 292
HW's opinion of, iv. 31–2
House of Commons left by, on Mutiny Bill, iv. 112
Jacobites to be united by, with P. of Wales's party, iv. 50
Mann shocked by behaviour of, iv. 244
—— wishes to see pamphlets by, ii. 334, iv. 43
may become secretary of state, vi. 159
Mutiny Bill opposed by, iv. 51
newspapers advertise pamphlet of, iv. 43
old politicians hate, on account of Pelham and Sir Robert Walpole, iv. 32
opposition assembly addressed by, at St Alban's Tavern, iv. 50
Parliament threatened by, with long sitting, iv. 50
party of, heaps incense on Pelham and Pitt, iv. **224**
peerage granted to, vi. 32
Pelham helps, in Weobly election contest, iv. **31**
Pelhams assisted by, in Parliament, iv. 31
Pitt's oratory compared to that of, iv. 32
porter at house of, disparages political guests, i. 301
Saunders succeeds, in Admiralty, vi. 449
Secret Committee called by, 'of Accusation,' i. 297
speech by: in Irish Parliament, iv. 31; on burning *Constitutional Queries*, iv. 222
Strange clashes with, iv. **32**
title of, may indicate descent from Cts of Holland, vi. 32
Vandeput's petition presented by, iv. 224
William's epigram on, iv. 51
Percy, Cts. *See* Stuart, Lady Anne (1746–ca 1819)
Percy, Lady. *See* Burrell, Frances Julia (1752–1822)
Percy, Lady Algernon. *See* Burrell, Isabella Susanna (1750–1812)

Percy, Lord Algernon (1750–1830), 2d Bn
Lovaine, 1786; cr. (1790) E. of Beverley:
HW does not know, and only saw him
once, ix. 422
health of: flimsy, v. 514–15; Mediterranean
cruise restores, viii. 203
Illustri fatti Farnesiani sent from Leghorn
in case belonging to, ix. 420, 448, 459
Mann entertains, at Florence, ix. 420
—— to be accompanied by, at investiture,
vii. 60
marriage of, viii. 499
Percy, Lady Elizabeth (1667–1722), m. 1
(1679) Henry Cavendish, styled E. of Ogle;
m. 2 (1681) Thomas Thynne; m. 3 (1682)
Charles Seymour, 6th D. of Somerset:
Northumberland title descends through, vii.
365n
settlement by, of her estate, iv. 11n
Percy, Lady Elizabeth Anne Frances (1744–
61):
death of, v. 515
Percy, Hugh (1742–1817), styled Bn Warkworth 1750–66, E. of Percy, 1766; 2d D.
of Northumberland, 1786:
accommodation with America may be
brought by, viii. 313, 315
English troops reinforced by, at battle of
Lexington, viii. 110
health of: Mediterranean cruise restores,
viii. 203; miserable constitution, v. 514–15
Howe disgusts, viii. 309
marriage of, vi. 302n
Muzell might be travelling companion to,
v. 512
predictions ascribed to, viii. 315
returns to England, viii. 309
Westminster election won by, viii. 52
Percy, Thomas (1729–1811), Bp of Dromore,
1782:
Reliques of Ancient English Poetry, 'Chevy
Chase' in, vii. 264
Percy family:
estate of, settled, iii. 11–12
title of, goes to coachman's grandson, iv.
124–5
Péréfixe. *See* Beaumont de Péréfixe
*Peregrinaggio di tre giovani figluoli. See
under* Christoforo ('Armeno')
Perelli, Tommaso (1704–83), Professor of Astronomy at University of Pisa 1739–80:
English understood by, v. 390
financial backers of, angry at him for expense, v. 430
letter of, to Sisson: HW delivers to Sisson, v. 354, 359–60; Mann sends, to HW,
v. 348
machine for raising water sent to, by
Sisson, v. 406
Pisa visited by, v. 390
professor of astronomy, v. 348
Sisson says, has description of drawing, v.
407

——'s letter to, v. 414
——'s plan praised by, v. 430, 432–3
——'s plan to be sent to, v. 390
witticism by, about the Host being carried
everywhere during epidemic, vi. 511–12
Peretti, Felice. *See* Sixtus V
Pérez de Alderete, Juan Manuel (1705–86),
Spanish naval officer:
(?) tender of, captured, i. 381
Perfumes:
Mann sends, to HW, ii. 201
silver trunk for, vii. 407, x. 56
See also Essences
Pergama, Bp of. *See* Attems, Charles-Mi-
chel d'
Pergola, Via della, Florence:
theatre in, *see* Teatro della Pergola
Pergolesi, Giovanni Battista (1710–36), com-
poser:
Olimpiade: Chute promises to get, at
Naples, iii. 149; HW mentions, iii. 70;
Mann seeks, for Lady Maria Walpole, iii.
95; Monticelli sings in, i. 401
Serva padrona, La: Mann has Chute send,
to Leghorn to be sent to HW, i. 262, 263;
Rich, Elizabeth, wants, i. 166
Virgin of the Seven Sorrows, office of, i.
166, 408
'Pericles':
Lyttelton uses name of, for Pitt, v. 409
Periodicals. *See* Magazines; Newspapers
Periwig:
Balmerinoch doffs, at execution, iii. 302
Charlotte will wear, if George III prefers
it, v. 529
'Permaloso':
Huntingdon's favourite word, v. 545
Pernklö, Johann Leopold (1700–46), Freiherr
von Schönreuth, called 'Bernklau'; Gen.:
Charles Emmanuel III joined by, at the
Trebbia, iii. 269
Elector Palatine's troops may be given by,
to Maria Theresa, iii. 41
successes of infantry under, at Piacenza, iii.
271
Peroz, Admiral. *See* Pérez
Perpignan:
Mann, Horace II and Lady Lucy, visit, viii.
246
Perrière, La. *See* La Perrière
Perroni, Cts. *See* Zambecarri, ——
Perroni, Lodovico (d. 1757), Conte; (?) Hun-
garian consul at Ancona:
(?) Spaniards accuse, of circulating seditious
papers at Naples, ii. 253–4
(?) Spaniards capture, ii. 253
(?) Spaniards confine, in Rimini prison, ii.
253, 257
Perry, Micajah (d. 1753), M.P.; alderman;
lord mayor:
Scrope almost fights duel with, i. 458
Perry, William (d. 1757) of Penshurst:
Florence visited by, iv. 379

[Perry, William, *continued*]
　HW and Chute drive, from dressing-room at Penshurst, iv. 389
　Mann likes, because he claims to know HW, iv. 379
　marriage of, iv. 389n
　obesity of, diminishes after leaving England, iv. 379
Perry, Mrs William. *See* Sidney, Elizabeth
Persecution:
　politics as well as religion thrive on, vii. 87
Perseus:
　statue of, in Florentine loggia, vi. 123
Persia:
　Erekle II pretender to throne of, iv. 401n
　etiquette in, vii. 550
　sultana of, Ds of Richmond dressed as, vi. 148
Persian Tale; Persian Tales:
　HW tells, about Sultan Nourmanzor, vii. 152-3, 162
　See also Arabian Nights; Arabian tales; Pétis de la Croix, François, *Persian and Turkish Tales*
Perspiration:
　bootikins induce, viii. 280
　checking of, for medicinal purposes, iii. 250
　Franklin walks naked about room at night to bring on, viii. 430
　HW tells Mann not to check, for gout, ix. 595
　Mann attributes Princesse de Craon's ailments to checking of, by heavy clothing, ii. 110
Perth, D. of. *See* Drummond, James (1713-46); Drummond, Lord John (1714-47)
Perth:
　Stormont, Vcts, aids rebels in, iii. 283
　Young Pretender's forces at, iii. 105, 107, 167, 208, 283
Pertici, Signora. *See* Isola, Anna
Pertici, Pietro, 'buffo man'; comedian:
　burletta of, to rival Tesi's opera, ii. 294
　English theatre engagement wanted by, ii. 198
　Garrick admires acting of, in burlettas, iv. 4, 357
　HW praises, ii. 198, iv. 41
　Smith tries to hire, for English performances, ii. 198
Pertusati, Conte, Austrian general:
　wounded at Campo Santo, ii. 164
Peru:
　Englishman's life worth more than conquest of, v. 558
　from Paris to, French are defeated, v. 352
　'king of,' crowned at Quito, vi. 426
　masters of, supposedly generous, viii. 413
　Spaniards in, outdone by English in India, vii. 387, 396-7
　viceroy of, *see* Amat y Junient Planella Aimeric y Saint Pau, Manuel de

Perugia:
　Lobkowitz at, ii. 529
　Richecourt grand prior of, iii. 394
　Spanish army active at, ii. 42, 76, 542, iii. 7, 10
Pérusseau *or* Perussault, Sylvain (ca 1678-1753), Louis XV's confessor:
　(?) Louis XV's lessons from, vi. 415
　Pompadour, Marquise de, retires in order to appease, iv. 236
Peruvians:
　ghosts of, must insult European usurpers, ix. 109
Peruzzi Leopolda. *See* Berzichelli, Maria Leopolda
Perversion, sexual:
　instances of, ii. 369, iv. 41, 53
　scandal about, among Irish rulers, iv. 316
　verses on, ii. 369, iv. 316
　Winstanley's joke on, iv. 317-18
Pesaro, Francesco (1739-1819), Venetian diplomatist:
　(?) Mann told by, of Greek refugees in Venice, vii. 226
Pesaro:
　Lobkowitz may shut Spaniards up in, ii. 405
　—— retreats to, ii. 542
　Montemar visits, i. 323, 342, 350
　Pope's ship from, i. 8
　Spaniards at, i. 323, 342, 350, 379, ii. 76, 335, 339, 412, 419
　Spaniards may retire to, ii. 174
　Spanish barks may escape to, ii. 288
　Velluti to visit, i. 323
Pescara:
　Austrians hope to capture, ii. 460
　Neapolitan troops assembled in, iii. 345
Pescetti, Giovanni Battista (ca 1704-ca 1766), composer:
　Polidoro by, i. 302
Pesciolini. *See* Venerosi Pesciolini
Pestalozzi, Giuseppe (ca 1683-1751), Barone; Gen.:
　capture of, ii. 460, 478
Pesters, Nikolaas de, Cts of Denbigh's nephew:
　Fontenoy accounts of, agree with HW's, iii. 56
　in Dutch service in Flanders, iii. 56
　(?) Lobkowitz's retreat described by, ii. 529
　Mann's old friend, ii. 514, iii. 56
Pestilence. *See* Plague
Pet. *See* Pett
Pet en l'air (dressing-gown):
　eccentric Englishwoman attends assembly in, at Florence, viii. 260
　Montagu, Lady Mary Wortley, wears riding coat as, vi. 3
　verses about, ii. 369
Peter, St (d. ?A.D. 67):
　HW imagines Cts of Bath's squabble with, ii. 8

Joseph II might dethrone, vii. 117
Kingston, Ds of, secures her treasures under key of, viii. 234
Matilda gives patrimony to, vi. 562
patrimony of, iv. 459
popes the successors of, i. 204, v. 291
Westminster Abbey dedicated to, viii. 382n
Peter I (1672–1725) (the Great), Emperor of Russia 1682–1725:
Catherine II has celebration at tomb of, vii. 249
Russians taught by, to read, vi. 71
Stanislas I profited by wars of, vi. 404
Peter III (1728–62), Emperor of Russia, 1762:
abdication of, vi. 58, 74
Austrian and Prussian adherents contend for favour of, vi. 14
Austrians rejoice in any misfortunes of, vi. 52
Bologna Gazette's report about, vi. 19
Botta says, will never join Frederick II against Maria Theresa, vi. 40–1
Catherine II deprives Frederick II of friendship of, vii. 145
—— dethrones, vi. 54, 56–60, 61–2, 81, vii. 329
——'s execution never intended by, vii. 207
——'s manifesto on death of, vi. 64, 74–6, 570n
—— weeps for, and wants to go to his funeral, vi. 71
—— would have been divorced by, vi. 57
—— would have been imprisoned by, vi. 68, vii. 215
China, Emperor of, reminds Catherine II of murder of, vii. 116, viii. 333
Colberg inhabitants generously treated by, vi. 22
Colberg's conquest may induce, to keep a foothold in Pomerania, vi. 10–11
death of: asserted by Russians to have been non-violent, vii. 215; attributed by Orlov to despair and drink, vii. 185; preferable to exile in Siberia, vi. 68
embarkation attempt of, at Cronstadt, vi. 58
English revolutions pale beside murder of, vi. 91
Frederick II object of enthusiasm of, vi. 16, 54, 61, vii. 145
—— said to be likely to get aid from, vi. 19
—— the only beneficiary of, so far, vi. 23
German campaign will reveal allegiance of, vi. 40
ghost of, should hail Russian fleet from dome at Constantinople, vii. 195
HW curious about fate of, vi. 59–60
impostor claims to be, vii. 547
Ivan VI to have been made heir to, vi. 57
leniency of, augurs well, vi. 22
Maria Theresa's assurances from, vi. 10
mistress of, is Vorontsov's niece, vi. 55

mistress said to have received Order of St Catherine from, vi. 58
mistress to have been married by, vii. 215
murder of, makes past crimes seem more credible, vi. 65
nobles to erect statue to, in gratitude for freedom, vi. 22
Orlov's denial of murder of, not believed by HW, vii. 195
proclaimed czar at army in Pomerania, vi. 1
Prussia liked by, vi. 7
Pugachev impersonates, vii. 547
Razumovskiĭ forced into conspiracy against, vi. 456
said to be impotent, vi. 57
son born to, iv. 457
son said to have been repudiated by, vi. 57, 75, vii. 215
Voltaire will probably claim that Catherine II did not murder, vi. 253
Vorontsov may be banished by, vi. 11
Vorontsov, Elizabeth, tells sister of intention of, to imprison Catherine II, vi. 68
Vorontsov, Mme, attracts, vi. 173
Peterborough, Bp of. See Hinchliffe, John (1731–94); Terrick, Richard (1710–77); Thomas, John (1696–1781)
Peterborough, E. of. See Mordaunt, Charles (ca 1658–1735)
Peterborough collection:
Germain, Lady Elizabeth, disperses natural philosophy part of, vii. 286
Peterhoff:
Catherine II at, when told that Peter III may kill her, vi. 57
Peter Leopold. See Leopold II
Peters, ——, 'Russia merchant':
Cony gets introduction to Musin-Pushkin from, x. 55
Petersberg; Petersbourgh; Petersburgh. See St Petersburg
Petersham, Vct. See Stanhope, William (1719–79)
Petersham, Vcts; Petersham, Lady Caroline. See Fitzroy, Lady Caroline
Petersham Lodge, Richmond, Harrington's seat:
Ligonier and Harrington play whist at, iii. 166
Pétis de la Croix, François (1653–1713):
Persian and Turkish Tales, iv. 347
Petition; petitions:
answer to, should have been more prudent, vii. 197
Birmingham's, for enforcement of American acts, viii. 77
Buckinghamshire's, ix. 572
bluster about, ends, vii. 168
Cornish, i. 233
counties and towns send, to Parliament, ix. 6, 10, 12, 18, 29, 34, 41

[Petition; petitions, *continued*]
Dunning seeks to prevent Parliament's dissolution or prorogation until demands of, are satisfied, ix. 41
elections will produce, vii. 66
fashionable in Dec. 1779, ix. 66
Fox, Henry, said to be made ill by, vii. 152
Frederick's and Hume's, i. 318
half-pay naval captains', vii. 462
Heathcote proposes, at meeting, iii. 107
Kirkwall and Westminster present, against C.J. Fox, ix. 488n
livery of London's, vii. 132
London's, hasten Bute's downfall, vi. 129
Mann distrusts, ix. 23
merchants', i. 295, 353
Middlesex freeholders', vii. 114, 120, 130
Northamptonshire's, ix. 10
on Hedon election, i. 234n
Opposition encouraged by, ix. 29
Parliamentary vacillation over, vii. 223
Parliament's postponement encourages, vii. 150
Parliament to receive, i. 232–3, 295, 343–4
presented in House of Commons, ix. 34
Protestant Association's, carried to Parliament, ix. 52–3
sailors', to Parliament, vii. 21
Scottish, vii. 151
supporters of Bill of Rights present, vii. 114
undertakers for, in English counties, vii. 163
Westminster, i. 232–3, 298, iv. 223–4, 235
Wiltshire and Worcester and Yorkshire to present, vii. 132
Petra, Vincenzo (1662–1747), cardinal, 1724:
Louis XV wants French candidate elected by, i. 20–1
Petraia:
Barbantane on way to, vi. 537
cannon at Modena may be audible at, i. 443
Craon at, i. 95, 100, 109, 122, 443, 463, ii. 1, 17, iii. 498
—— rented, iv. 116
——'s summer residence, i. 390n
Craon, Princesse de, at, i. 109, 443, 463, 481, ii. 1, iii. 407, 500, iv. 14, vi. 29, 536, vii. 296
—— passes summers at, vi. 224–5
Craons invite Mann, Chute, and Whithed to visit, i. 443
destitute of necessary furniture, vi. 536
Francis I gave life use of, to Princesse de Craon, vii. 296
—— owns, i. 390n
furniture supplied to, by Craons, iv. 116
George II's condition discussed at, i. 390
Grafton, Ds of, to visit, on horseback, vi. 29
HW's favourite, vi. 224

HW's 'sweet,' vi. 29
Mann might pick up news at, i. 116
—— takes D. of York to, vi. 224–5
Morice astonished at size of palm tree at, vi. 29
Rosenberg drives Princesse de Craon from, vii. 296
terrace of, has large palm tree, vi. 29
Tuscan court prefers Lappeggi to, vi. 412
visitors to: Beauvau, iii. 500; (?) Chute, i. 443, ii. 1; HW, vi. 29, 224; Mann, i. 443, 463, 481, ii. 1, iii. 498, 500, vi. 537; Morice, vi. 29; Richecourt, iv. 15; Whithed, i. 443, ii. 1
water at, bad, i. 481
Wilczek occupies, vii. 296
Petrarch (Francesco Petrarca) (1304–74), poet:
notes by, on Vatican MS, v. 169
Petrignani, Giacomo, officer of Corsican recruits for Minorca:
sails to Minorca, ix. 199
Petrillo, ——:
Tesi's dependant, i. 130
Walsegg insults, at burletta, i. 130
Petroni, Count Alessandro (ca 1704–71), Papal official:
assembly of: attended by Giuseppe, Riviera, and Whithed, iii. 85; Dunbar harangues, iii. 218
HW ushered about by, in Rome, at Albani's request, i. 9
Pett, Robert (d. 1776), Capt.:
Mann meets, at Leghorn, ii. 509
Walpole family favours, ii. 509
Pettalazzi. *See* Pestalozzi
'Pettapanino' (Patapan's puppy):
HW's joke about, i. 112
'Pettegola.' *See* Vanbrugh, Philippia
Petticoat:
dimity, vi. 3
Petticoat, under. *See* Underpetticoat
Petty, Henry (1675–1751), 1st E. of Shelburne; M.P.:
Fox, Lady Caroline, gets legacy from, iv. 248
Petty, William (1737–1805), styled Vct Fitzmaurice; 2d E. of Shelburne, n.c., 1761; cr. (1784) M. of Lansdowne; prime minister 1782–3:
administration of: begins, ix. 293–4, 299; HW hopes, will be pacific, ix. 337; will give Parliament novelty, vi. 336
Barré friend of, vii. 65
Bedford faction objects to, vi. 571
Board of Trade to be headed by, vi. 130
breach between Rockingham Whigs and those of, not healed when they took office, ix. 294
Cavendish, Lord John, declines to serve under, ix. 293
Charlotte's house visited by, for conference on new ministry, ix. 260–1
Cholmondeley not preferred by, ix. 319

Dick to carry letters from, to Italy, vii. 55
dismissed for joining opposition, vi. 189
Dunning friend of, ix. 262
Florence visited by, ix. 271
Fox, C.J., bluntly announces his resignation to, ix. 393
—— quarrels with, ix. 320
Fullarton's duel with, ix. 31, 37
Garter given to, ix. 273
George III confers with, ix. 260
—— persuaded by, to ask Victor Amadeus III to pardon Viry, viii. 328n
——'s negotiations with, without Rockingham's consent, ix. 372n
——'s wish to patch up administration seconded by, ix. 379
goes abroad, vii. 263
HW always civilly treated by, ix. 310
HW calls: 'ridiculous,' ix. 407, 437; 'the minister paramount,' ix. 296
HW condemns faults of, ix. 372, 380-1, 402, 407
Hervey, Bp, rejects offer of, to go to Versailles as peace delegate, ix. 454
Hillsborough may succeed, as secretary of state, vi. 569
House of Commons tears North and, from power, in one year, ix. 402n
in the country, ix. 437
loan opposed by, in House of Lords, ix. 402
Mann praised by, ix. 271
—— sends courier to, vii. 51, 60, 71
——'s letters from: convey George III's approbation, vi. 500-1; do not mention MS account of Tuscany, vii. 27-8; on assuming secretary of state's office, vi. 447; show continuance as secretary of state, vi. 581
——'s MS account of Tuscany sent to, through Capt. Steward for George III, vii. 27-8
——'s 'master' and friend, ix. 271
(?) —— thinks new ministry might be headed by, ix. 553-4
Mann, Horace II, acquainted with, ix. 271
marquessate conferred upon, ix. 542
marriage plans of, announced, vi. 275
may consider himself Pitt's political heir, viii. 379
may resign America in secretary of state's office, vi. 569
ministers may be opposed by, over peace treaties, ix. 428
ministry formed by, would fail, HW thinks, ix. 260
Molesworth, Frances, rejects, viii. 417
North and C.J. Fox unite to defeat, in Parliament, ix. 368, 372
Parliamentary reforms backed by, ix. 30
Pitt complains of removal of, vii. 61
—— proscribes, vi. 161
popularity falsely vaunted by, ix. 402

Pratt's and James Grenville's continuance will place, in awkward position, vii. 65
predecessors severely handled by, for their flippancies, ix. 285
prime ministry alone would satisfy, viii. 493
protest by, vi. 7
recent Irish earl and more recent English baron, ix. 273
'reciprocity' a favourite term of, much used and ridiculed at time of peace with America, ix. 519n
resignation of: as first lord of trade, vi. 167; as prime minister, ix. 377; as secretary of state, vii. 62
Rockingham's appointment as prime minister negotiated by, ix. 260-1
rumoured as Rockingham's successor, ix. 289
secretary of state, vi. 439, 443, 571, ix. 262, 319
secretary of state's position coveted by, vi. 159
Sydney may be succeeded by, as Home Secretary, ix. 487
system of, for numbering letters, vi. 563
Tories may regret following North against, ix. 379
Viry, Contessa di, friend of, viii. 328n
Weymouth succeeds, as secretary of state, vii. 62
wife of, dies, vii. 263
witticism by, about D. of Dorset's ignorance, ix. 487
'Petulant.' See under Congreve, William: Way of the World
Pew:
Mann family's, at Linton, v. 250
Pewter:
alms-boxes of, v. 238
English bury, on approach of rebel army, iii. 173
shillings counterfeited from, iii. 242
Pewterer. See Cleeve, Bourchier
Pewter mines:
cobalt and zinc by-products of, ii. 323
Pfützchner, Charles de (d. ca 1766), Bn; 'Fishner':
Craon's correspondence with, i. 287, 472
Dumesnil accuses, of heresy for frequenting Mass, iii. 491
Khevenhüller's progress into Bavaria reported by, i. 288
Phaeton (carriage):
Craon, Princesse de, uses, i. 83
horses of, in English opera, iii. 370
Pharoah. See Faro
Pharisee; pharisees:
HW confesses that he is, vii. 528
See also under Bible
Pharsalia. See under Lucan
Pharsalia and Philippi. See under Holdsworth, Edward

Pheasants:
campaign opened for, with waste of gun-powder, ix. 188
Chinese: Mann sends, to Leopold, vi. 368; price of, at auction of stuffed birds, vii. 210
Ferdinand of Naples rises at 2 A.M. to catch, when leaving roosts, ix. 600
gold, sold at Covent Garden market, v. 294
Phelipps or Phillipps, Ann, m. John Horner: (?) HW mentions, i. 475
Phelps, Richard (ca 1720–71), diplomatist:
Bouverie accompanied by, at Rome iii. 191, 196
—— pays travelling expenses of, iii. 196
Conway's friend, v. 113
fellow at Oxford, iii. 196
Florence hurriedly visited by, on way to England, v. 113
Grevilles accompanied by, to Italy, v. 124
Italy often visited by, as tutor or governor, v. 124
Mann has known, for years, v. 113
—— sends HW's letters back to England by, v. 113, 118, 124, x. 36
Old Pretender entertains, after being con-gratulated by him, iii. 191, 196
Sicily secretly visited by, v. 124
to be secretary at embassy in Spain, vi. 112
Phélypeaux, Jean-Frédéric (1701–81), Comte de Maurepas, minister de marine:
death of, reported in papers, ix. 212
disgrace of, will benefit England, iv. 51
does not gain ground, viii. 13
French navy promoted by, iv. 51
invasion not abetted by, ii. 415
Malesherbes incited by, to ask Marie-Antoinette to dismiss Guines, viii. 207
mob applauds, at opera, for restoring par-liament, viii. 61
naval funds for, diverted to Prussia, iv. 51
Nivernais, brother-in-law of, is expected to succeed him, as minister of finance, ix. 212
quotes from Racine, on Cornwallis's sur-render, ix. 211
Turgot makes, jealous, viii. 207
younger minister than, would declare war at once on England, viii. 300
Phélypeaux, Louis (1705–77), Comte de St-Florentin; Duc de la Vrillière, 1770; states-man:
hand of, cut off by bursting gun, vi. 342
likely to fall, viii. 12
Sabatin, Mme, mistress of, vii. 339
secretary of state, vi. 342
Phélypeaux de Pontchartrain, Hélène-Angél-ique-Françoise (1715–82), m. (1730) Louis-Jules-Barbon Mancini-Mazarini, Duc de Nivernais:
Borghese, Ps, acts as hostess for, iv. 285–6
Philadelphia:
England and Europe may have to take laws from, viii. 229

English army under Howe captures and occupies, viii. 281, 282, 336, 338–9, 342, 348, 352, 361–2, 393
Franklin boasts, will be starved into sur-render, viii. 361–2
—— might abandon, to save New York, viii. 342
Washington said to have foiled Howe's attempt to capture, viii. 327
'Philander':
Tankerville's and Rochefort's nom-de-plume, ii. 220
Philibert, Philipp (d. 1753), Freiherr von; Austrian Gen.:
Leghorn may be commanded by, i. 406–7
Toussaint's father-in-law, i. 406
Philibert, French ship of India Company:
captured off Cape Finisterre, iii. 410
Philip II (1527–98), K. of Spain, 1556–98:
Holland could not be conquered by, viii. 127
Popes bullied, ii. 344
Philip V (1683–1746), K. of Spain 1700–46:
army of, Electress's jewels endangered by, i. 241–2
army officers notified by, of Montemar's dismissal, ii. 59
Catalogue of French Books, A, satirizes, ii. 54
death of: iii. 277–8; England disappointed by results of, vi. 1; falsely rumoured, iii. 19, 25; Tabuerniga returns to Spain after, i. 277n
Haddock intercepts packet for, i. 53
Louis XV said to influence, about Papal election, i. 20–1
Neapolitan alliance with, ii. 43
sea victory attributed to, ii. 413
Silva consul of, iii. 57
son dislikes policies of, iii. 278
Viviani wants to be minister of, to Francis I, ii. 129
Philip, 'Don' (1720–65), D. of Parma 1749–65:
Acquaviva may lend Caprarola palace to, i. 389
Aix to be visited by, i. 361–2
Aix treaty had destined Neapolitan crown for, v. 330
Albenga reached by, iii. 58
Antibes to be visited by, i. 362, 380, 388–9, ii. 395, iii. 313–14
army of: advances to join other Spanish army, iii. 36, 47; has not started from Nice, iii. 36
baggage of, at Barcelona, i. 182
Bavarian elector may give Milan to, i. 290
Beauvau to join, iii. 54
brother cannot set up, iii. 432
brother to be met by, at Lerici, v. 280
brother will not relinquish Naples to, v. 264, 270
Castel Ceriolo e St Giuliano captured by, iii. 84

Castellar arranges troop passage for, iii. 51
Catalogue of French Books, A, satirizes, ii. 53
Chambéry may be station of, ii. 513
Charles Emmanuel III may be persuaded by, to permit Spanish invasion, i. 323
—— threatened by, with retaliations in Piedmont for English bombardment of Genoese coast, iii. 121
—— to expel, from Savoy, ii. 65
—— to resist, at Nice, ii. 395
—— wants to transfer, to Naples, v. 264
Coni and Demont may be approached by, through Mondovi, iii. 58
Cuneo's resistance may force back, to Savoy, ii. 513
daughter's letters from, vi. 313
death of, vi. 313, 364
England may acknowledge, i. 196
English fleet impedes, i. 405, 408, iii. 51
flees to Sestri, iii. 304
France will lose face by abandoning interests of, v. 323
Francis III given equal rank with, in army, ii. 235
—— prevented by Charles Emmanuel III from joining, ii. 322
—— sells Guastalla allodials to, vi. 144
—— vies with, iv. 45
French and other galleys to escort, i. 362
French may join, in Savoy, ii. 295
Gages may join army to that of, ii. 556, iii. 2, 36
Galli thinks of asking, to be godfather, ii. 46
Genoese house prepared for, i. 389, ii. 454, 554
HW did not know, vi. 325
Henry Benedict (Stuart) may join, iii. 99
'horridly French,' iv. 45
Italy to be invaded by, i. 195, 215, 350, 380, 388–9
La Ensenada secretary of state to, ii. 253
letters for, from Naples, v. 280
Lombardy to be domain of, i. 427
Mann praises generosity and civility of, vi. 314, 325
Mari to attend, i. 226
—— to prepare house for, i. 389
may have to fight his way through Nice, i. 408
Montemar's actions to be guided by acts of army of, ii. 27
——'s preference of Charles of Naples to, said to irritate their mother, ii. 5
—— to obtain Tuscan conquests for, ii. 16
mother might have bought Parma Placentia for, ii. 345
mother seeks title for, i. 389
Naples may be visited by, i. 323
Naples may be winter home of, iii. 144
news of: awaited, iii. 267; from Rome, i. 389

Nice may be entered by, i. 408, ii. 271
Nice the headquarters of, iii. 36, 432
Orbetello may be visited by, i. 389
Parma and Placentia asked for, by Acquaviva, of Benedict XIV, i. 201
Parma and Placentia assigned to, by Aix treaty, iii. 481
Parmesans dislike, iv. 45
Pavia the refuge of, iii. 231
poor, iv. 45
reigned virtuously, with absolute power, vi. 404
retreat of, to Venice alleged, iii. 269
Savoy invasion of, angers Charles Emmanuel III, ii. 58–9
Savoy rule of, ended, ii. 95
servants quartered by, on chief families, iv. 45
soldiers desert, iv. 45
Spanish army to be commanded by, at Nice, ii. 547
Spanish convoy to include, i. 215, 323
Spanish invasion of Tuscany and Neapolitan advance depend on success of, ii. 312
Spanish party at Florence want, i. 68n, iii. 498
Spanish plan to instate, in Maria Theresa's dominions, ii. 43
title of D. of Savoy taken by, ii. 65
Tuscan title may be given to, i. 380, 389
Tuscany to be seized by, i. 196
wife of, iv. 147–8
York, D. of, to be entertained by, vi. 232
Young Pretender expected by Amelot to assist, ii. 415
Philip Anton (1747–77), D. of Calabria:
birth of, iii. **423**
cantata for, iii. 437–8
death of, viii. 330
father sets aside, for imbecility, v. 322–3, 329, 333, 337, 347, vi. 570
medical commission examines, v. 322–3, 324–5, 329
miracle might restore, v. 329, 333
Philippi. *See under* Virgil
Philipps, Sir Erasmus (1699–1743), 5th Bt, 1737; M.P.:
arrives at Florence, i. **67**
Craon avoided by, i. 81
death of, ii. 343–4
HW exchanges compliments with, i. 81
health of: pain in back, i. 67; recovered, i. 81
lean, i. 121
leaves Florence for Turin, i. 138
Mann avoided by, i. 80–1
—— entertains, i. 70
—— exchanges calls with, i. 67
—— meets, at Franceschi's sale, i. 121
Martin accompanies, i. 81
servant of, i. 67
Wright friend of, i. 423

Philipps, Sir John (1700–64), 6th Bt, 1743;
M.P.:
afterwards lord of trade and baronet, i.
384n
Commissioner of Trade, ii. 551
HW mentions, i. 418
HW's cousin, iii. 27, iv. 249
House of Commons would like to commit,
iv. 250
Jacobite, iii. 168, 310n
King's Bench moved by, to produce Mur-
ray, iv. 249
named in Secret Committee lists, i. 384
not elected as commissioner to examine
accounts, i. 438
Parliamentary debate by, on privately-raised
regiments, x. 13, 14, 16
resigns, iii. 27–8
Vernon complains to, about provisions, iii.
168
Philipps family:
Picton Castle the home of, iii. 310n
Philips, Con. See Phillips, Teresia Constantia
Philipson. See Phillipson
Phillips, Mrs. See Amis, Judith
Phillips, Teresia Constantia (1709–65), cour-
tesan; m. (1723) Henry Muilman:
HW would not distinguish between Cath-
erine II and, viii. 35
Phillips. See also Phelipps; Philipps
Phillipson, John (1698–1756), M.P.:
Admiralty post lost by, ii. 550
Carteret appoints, to Admiralty, ii. 349
not of the Carteret or Pulteney factions, ii.
551
Surveyor of the Roads, iii. 34
Phillis, servant maid:
fights Downing St fire, i. 496
Philosopher; philosophers:
always affect to act in character, vi. 151
ambassador should be, v. 335
deathbed affectations of, vi. 551
French: affectations of, vi. 271; Catherine
II and Frederick II receive incense from,
ix. 39; Catherine II charms, vi. 570; Frenchmen become, while Englishmen dance, viii.
112; merely bring on despotism, vii. 376;
'solemn, arrogant, and dictatorial,' viii. 498
greatest of actors, v. 335
HW does not want to be taken for, vi.
271
HW thinks that systems of, are as foolish
as simpletons' collections, ix. 604
in great countries, are usually those who
have no philosophy, ix. 105
motives of, for travel, viii. 186
predictions of, invalidated by unforeseen
events, ix. 369
Philosopher's stone:
discoveries made when in search of, iv. 415
Philosophes. See Philosophers: French
*Philosophical Reflections . . . Concerning
. . . Tar Water. See* Berkeley, George
(1685–1753): *Siris*

Philosophical Transactions:
Grand Lama's letter printed in, ix. 15
Philosophy:
excusable when exertion is in vain, viii.
378
HW defines, as presence of mind, v. 335
HW despises affectation of, vi. 451
HW's, *see under* HW
Mann's, will keep loss of Bath ribbon from
making him unhappy, vi. 407
—— unable to accept HW's, vi. 376, 381
materialist, HW condemns, vi. 410
Philosophy of Earthquakes. See under Stuke-
ley, William
Phipps, Constantine (1722–75), cr. (1767) Bn
Mulgrave:
Bristol's brother-in-law, vi. 548
made Irish baron, vi. 548
marriage of, ii. 185
Oxford attended by, ii. 185
wife, of, i. **274n**
Phipps, Mrs Constantine. *See* Hervey, Hon.
Lepell
Phipps, Constantine John (1744–92), 2d Bn
Mulgrave, 1775; M.P.:
returns from unsuccessful design against
Flushing, ix. 167
Phoenix:
HW mentions, ix. 599
Wilkes compared to, viii. 45
Phoenix, English ship:
involved in war, iii. 313
Physic:
degree in, HW scoffs at, ix. 316
HW does not believe in, vi. 257
HW does not understand, iv. 440
HW knows no more of, than a physician
does, v. 368
professor of, refuses to aid Gray, vii. 329
Physic garden:
at Chelsea, ii. 250
Physician; physicians:
at Florence, for the insane, ix. 270
at Pisa: Orford, Cts of, not hopefully
regarded by, ix. 112; supplies drugs for
D. of Gloucester, vii. 369
at Valdagno, promises a complete recovery
to Lady Lucy Mann, viii. 122
Beelzebub the devil's name as, viii. 71
bootikins at first praised but later condemned by, viii. 70–1
bootikins decried by, vii. 76
Campbell, Lady William, accompanied by,
at Florence, ix. 271
Carteret's, order him to Spa, iii. 26
Charles Emmanuel III sends, to Hercules,
III, i. 489
Chute's aversion to, viii. 210
Clement XIV's, forbid his *villeggiatura,*
viii. 39
——'s, *see also* Adinolfi, Pasquale
Clive's, prescribes laudanum, viii. 60, 68
commit more deaths than soldiers, ix. 342

Dalkeith's, iv. 138
English weather benefits, ix. 582
fever and sore throat baffling to, v. 362
'flying gout' a term showing ignorance of, vi. 114
from Rome, attends Cts of Orford, viii. 312
from York, joins rebels, iii. 180
George III's, HW cannot consult, ix. 413
German: fears Leopold's exposure to small-pox, vi. 559; Maria Louisa overdosed by, vi. 459-60
Gloucester's: fear effects of autumn campaign, viii. 401; give contradictory statements, viii. 76; prevent him from going to Rome, vii. 357
grave faces and tied wigs of, viii. 71
HW agrees with, about warm weather helping Mann, viii. 311
HW disparages knowledge of, v. 368, vi. 110, viii. 76, ix. 441
HW''s life invaded by, vii. 497
Italian: HW has less faith in, than in English ones, viii. 206, 281; HW has no opinion of, viii. 432; Mann tells Rainsford to consult, vii. 393; take gloomy view of D. of Gloucester's illness, vii. 337, 341
James's powders not prescribed by, for Waldegrave, till too late, vi. 127
Jesuits' fate should be shared by, vii. 76
Mann quite ready to distrust, viii. 83
——'s: believes his rheumatism to be gout in the head, viii. 479; feeds him ice creams and uses bleedings and senapisms, ix. 560; gives him false encouragement, ix. 567; Mann tells, that he must get well to entertain Hollands, vi. 467; orders him to stay in bed, ix. 555, 556; reassures Horace Mann II, ix. 607; tells him that chalkstones are painful, ix. 626; see also Muri
—— suggests, for Lady William Campbell, ix. 270
Maria Louisa may choose, vi. 460
Marlborough, Ds of, repulses, i. 235
Mozzi invites, to houses of pleasure, vii. 158
murrain explained by, iii. 174
Northampton, Cts of, attended by, vi. 142
not needed for gout, vii. 451
old Greek, Cocchi to edit works of, iv. 34
Orford, Cts of, and Mozzi accompanied by, vii. 158
Orford, 2d E. of, rejects, iv. 233
Orford, 3d E. of, has no opinion of, viii. 294
—— wished by, to be secluded, vii. 482
Pelham sons neglected by, v. 369
Pitt (Chatham) told by, not to go to Parliament, viii. 370
Pius VI's, consider his illness serious, viii. 461
quack, fee of, vii. 251
Rome should not be prescribed by, vii. 451
stuffed birds bought by, vii. 210

Young Pretender's, consider him to be in great danger, ix. 394, 467; see also Pallucci, Natalis Joseph
See also Doctor; Medicine; Quack
Piacenza ('Placentia'; 'Plaisance'):
capture of, prematurely reported, iii. 291
Charles Emmanuel III at, i. 392
—— insists on evacuation of, iii. 279
French and Spaniards said to have escaped from, iii. 275
Gages at, iii. 253
garrison of, escapes battle, iii. 279
lists of casualties and captures at, iii. 266-7, 270-1
Maillebois joins Spaniards at, iii. 266
Maria Theresa gives, to Charles Emmanuel III, i. 379
Philip, Don, seeks, i. 201
—— to receive, iii. 481
second battle of, iii. 302-3
Spaniards and French cannot hold, iii. 268
Spaniards bombarded by Austrians at, iii. 276
Spaniards may take, i. 198, 204-5, 214
Spaniards prevent couriers from crossing, iii. 156
Spaniards retire to defences of, iii. 266
Spanish army at, iii. 258, 262
Piaga aperta:
Tencin has, i. 481
Piantanida:
Lenten concerts arranged by, iii. 374
Piazza del Grand Duca:
Craon, Princesse de, not well received in, i. 178-9
impostor would not have succeeded at, iv. 29
Piazza della Signoria, Florence:
'festa degli omaggi' in, ii. 251
Piazza di Santo Spirito, Florence:
cocchiata begins at, ii. 485
Piccadilly, London:
butcher in, rents lodging to Giustinianis, vii. 287
highwayman attacks post-chaise in, iv. 188
mob takes possession of, vii. 6
White Horse Cellar in, place of stage-coaches' departure, v. 313
Williams, White Horse innkeeper in, denounces Independents, iii. 387n
Piccenza. See Piacenza
Piccini, Niccolò (1728-1800):
Cecchina ossia la buona figliuola by: Christian VII sees, played by Lovatini and Guadagni, vii. 42; George III and Charlotte praise, vi. 474; HW praises, vi. 473-4; second part of, not so popular as the first, vi. 484
Piccolomini, Eneo Silvio (1708-68), cardinal, 1766; governor of Rome, 1761.
(?) Chute and Whithed would like to send Young Pretender's limb to, iii. 318

[Piccolomini, Eneo Silvio, *continued*]
edict of, declares narrative to be false, vi. 328
Gascoigne and Hon. George Damer protected by, from consequences of drunken brawl, vi. 286
Patch aided by, when Governor of Rome, vii. 275
Piccolomini, Ottavio Eneo Giuseppe (1698–1757), Gen.:
advantageous situation of, will keep Frederick II in winter quarters, v. 15
Gavi to surrender to, iii. 315
too strongly entrenched to be attacked, v. 5
Piccolomini, Senatore Cavaliere Priore Tommaso (d. 1784), Tuscan minister for foreign affairs 1771–84:
government post given to, vii. 294
HW hopes that letters are not opened by, vii. 38
Mann notifies, of English manifesto, ix. 112
Pickets:
Tuscan, ii. 100
Pickle:
Corsican questions to be preserved in, vii. 128
Pico, Lodovico (1668–1743), cardinal, 1712:
death of, ii. 288
Picquet (game). *See* Piquet
Picquet de la Motte, Toussaint-Guillaume (1720–91), Comte de la Motte Picquet; French naval officer:
English convoy captured by, ix. 152, 159–60
Pictet, Marc (1693–1768), treasurer of Geneva:
(?) Veers forges signature of of, iii. 507
Picton Castle, Pembroke:
Philipps's home, iii. 310n
Pictures:
Callot's, i. 118
export of, forbidden, iv. 465–6
George III likes, v. 449, 451–2
HW's, Mann packs in case, to be sent to England, ii. 152
Leopold buys, of Gaddi family, ix. 170
See also Landscape; Painting; Portrait; Print; Seascape
Piddletown, Dorset:
not an old Rolle estate, ix. 148
Orford, E. of, may sell, ix. 148
——'s seat at, ix. 227
Pie:
chicken, Mann's English guest prefers, to beef, ii. 162
macaroni, refused admittance to Florentine theatre, iv. 219
mince, ii. 367
of fat or meat, forbidden in theatre, iv. 219
'pelican,' i. 485, iv. 450
rebel, Townshend, Vcts, fears to encounter, iii. 302, viii. 21

Pièce:
for Genoese opera, read by Mann, iii. 505
Piedmont, Ps of. *See* Marie-Adélaïde-Clotilde-Xavière (1759–1802) of France
Piedmont:
Alfieri from, ix. 538n
army of, Wentworth said to favour, iii. 451
Beauvau said to be in, iii. 70
Broglie family from, vii. 521
—— was to have fetched Comtesse d'Artois from, vii. 521
French attempts upon, ii. 504–5, iii. 417, 426–7, 436
Genoa campaign to follow campaign in, iii. 437
Guasco from, vi. 529
Lobkowitz to send regiment to, ii. 512
officers of, in Reggio, i. 46
Philip, Don, threatens to burn places in, iii. 121
Richecourt, Cts, from, iv. 90n
troops from: cross the Var, iii. 335–6; officers of, executed at Metz, v. 382–3; retreat towards Ventimiglia, iii. 409
Piercy. *See* Percy
Pier glasses:
St John offers, to Mann, i. 283, 292
Pieri, Pietro Maria (1676–1743), cardinal, 1734:
death of, ii. 150
Pierot. *See* Pierrot
Pierpoint. *See* Pierrepont
Pierre, François-Joachim de (1715–94), Cardinal de Bernis:
circular letter of, Mann sends, to HW, v. 218
Clement XIV's negotiations with, over Jesuits, vii. 414
conclave attendance in hot months feared by, viii. 461–2
dismissal of, v. 262–3, 265
embonpoint of, extraordinary, viii. 462
Gloucester, D. of, entertained at dinner by, vii. 389
Gustav III discouraged by, at Rome, from aiding Young Pretender, ix. 475
Jesuits' suppression again demanded by, vii. 214
lavish expenditure of, vii. 389
Louis XVI is said to have recalled, ix. 222
Mann, Horace II, to dine with, at Rome, ix. 675
may be fetched back to France to become prime minister, viii. 10
may get French cabinet post, vii. 264
Pompadour, Marquise de, advances, to be a cardinal, v. 242
—— overturns, because of insults, vii. 144
publishes erroneous news of French victory, ix. 127
Santacroce, Principessa di, maintained by, ix. 675
satire on, v. 265

Young Pretender's journey discussed by, vii. 324

Pierre d'Arena:
Spaniards reach, iii. 47

Pierrepont, Lady Caroline (d. 1753), m. (1749) Thomas Brand:
marriage and death of, iv. 434–5

Pierrepont, Charles. See Medows, Charles

Pierrepont, Lady Evelyn (1691–1727), m. (1712) John Leveson-Gower, 2d Bn Gower, cr. (1746) E. Gower:
relatives of, iv. 281n

Pierrepont, Evelyn (ca 1665–1726), 1st D. of Kingston-upon-Hull:
daughters of, iv. 281n, 434n

Pierrepont, Evelyn (1711–73), 2d D. of Kingston-upon-Hull, 1726:
Chudleigh, Miss, to marry, vii. 93
death of, leaving all to his 'wife,' vii. 520
Hervey said to have connived at marriage of, for money, viii. 192n
losses of, by fires at Lincoln's Inn and Thoresby, iv. 321
marriage of, iv. 213n
mob pelts, by mistake for D. of Bedford, vii. 99
Mordaunt, Lt-Col. to, x. 14
nephews hope to intercept estate of, viii. 56
nephews may deserve wealth of, viii. 30
nephews of, viii. 227n
nephews sue E. of Bristol for estate of, viii. 227
relatives of, might be aided by Bp of Derry in proving his marriage invalid, viii. 55–6
wedding coach, favours, and liveries of, covered with mud, vii. 99
widow reminded of, in Florence Cascines, viii. 6
wife may swoon at name of, viii. 187
wife said to terrify, with pistol, viii. 198
wife should have divorced former husband before marrying, viii. 88–9
wife should have permitted, to leave most of his estates to his family, viii. 31
will of: vii. 520; lawyers may try to break, despite aliases, viii. 30; nephews dispute, viii. 20–1; widow wins Chancery case in regard to, viii. 118

Pierrepont, Lady Frances (d. 1761), m. 1714) John Erskine, 22d E. of Mar:
Bedford, D. of, lends house to, iv. 281
daughter tends, iv. 281
insane, iv. 281
sister ill-treats, iv. 281
sister's letters to, iv. 281

Pierrepont, Lady Frances (1713–95), m. (1734) Philip Medows:
sons of, viii. 227n

Pierrepont, Lady Mary (1689–1762), m. (1712) Edward Wortley-Montagu:
appearance, avarice, and costume of, vi. 3

arrival of, in England, rumoured, v. 540
avarice of, v. 472–3
Barnett takes, on shipboard at Genoa, v. 473
Bedford House entertainment attended by, vi. 17
Birtles disliked by, i. 98, 103–4
Brescia official entertains, at dinner, iv. 279
Buondelmonte incited by, to satirize English at Florence, i. 92
château of, a mere hovel, vii. 315
clothes of, coarse and unclean, ii. 306, vi. 3
costume of, at Bedford House, vi. 17
death and will of, vi. 72
death of, expected, vi. 76
dirt of, should make her stay in quarantine, v. 540
doge to reconciled by, with George II, i. 98
eclogues of: praised by Chute, iii. 450; printed, iii. 449
England to be visited by, v. 545
England will probably be revisited by, v. 472
English consul at Venice insulted by, i. 98
English reputation at Florence lowered by, ii. 309
Epistle from Arthur Gray: iii. 450; Murray, Lady, mentioned in, v. 301n
false emeralds would still be fobbed off by, despite husband's death, v. 483
Firmian may be asked by, for book, v. 447
Florence visited by, i. 91–2
Florentines hear boasts of, vii. 315
Genoa visited by, i. 91–2, 138, v. 473
Genoese supported by, in dispute with English captain, i. 92, 104
HW calls on, vi. 3
HW's account of, diverts Mann, vi. 13
HW to call on, i. 92
HW to send Catalogue of the Royal and Noble Authors to, v. 458, 472
half-sister of, iv. 434
Hamilton, Ds of, calls on, vi. 4
health of, cancer of the breast, vi. 56
letters of: copied at Venice, vi. 141; from Constantinople, vi. 85n; to her sister, seen by HW, iv. 281
Lincoln to call on, i. 91
Mann asked by, for Catalogue of the Royal and Noble Authors, v. 447
—— to get news of, through Niccolini, iv. 285
manuscripts of: given to clergyman in Holland, vi. 84; HW would like to see, vi. 84; volumes of prose and verse bequeathed to daughter, vi. 84
Marlborough, Ds of, discusses Bns Sundon with, i. 276–7
memoirs of, compared with Mme del Pozzo's, vi. 84
Micheli, Mme, told by, that Palazzo stops their correspondence iv. 279

[Pierrepont, Lady Mary, *continued*]
Muzell brings HW a scolding from, v. 458
Naples visited by, i. 91–2
nieces of, iv. 281
not yet arrived, v. 560
Palazzo, Count, said to have imprisoned, at Brescia, iv. 235, 272, 279, 281
Pitt, George, admired by, in Italy, i. 468n
—— known by, iv. 58
Pomfret, Cts of, forced to air the bedchamber of, iii. 72
Pomfret, E. of, host to, while she tries to play joke on him, i. 92
Pope satirizes, iv. 282, v. 472n
Raper brings diamond crochette to, i. 138
Rémond de St Mard almost cheated by, iv. 281–2
—— lover of, iv. 281–2
republics preferred by, i. 98
ring given by, to Barnard, v. 473
Rome visited by, i. 91–2
secretary of, *see* Moro, Dr Bartolomeo
Simonetti, Cts, compared with, vi. 148
sister ill-treated by, iv. 281
son left one guinea by, vi. 81
son not supplied by, iv. 235
son of, iv. 226
son's conversation with, at Geneva, ii. 567
tedious in her narrations, vi. 17
Townshend, Charles, exaggerates quantity of MSS of, vi. 85–6
Townshend, Vcts, imitates ogling of, i. 468
Turin visited and abused by, i. 91
Venetian doge and senate assured by, that she will reconcile them with George II, i. 98
Venice visited by, i. 91–2, 98
verses by, on shipboard, v. 473
Walpole, Sir Robert, sent letter by, i. 98
witticism by, about Adam, iv. 282
Wrottesley, Lady Mary, confused with, v. 540
Pierrot:
Harlequin's dialogue with, ii. 501
Piers, Lt Riccarde:
captured at Velletri, ii. 492
Piers. *See also* Peers; Peirse
Pierson, James Bradshaw (1741–ca 1818), collector:
Duncombe buys a Guido from paintings brought by, mostly from Venice, vii. 569–70
marriage of, vii. 569–70
Pierson, Mrs James Bradshaw. *See* Giacomazzi, Teresa
'Pietra; 'Pietraccia.' *See* Stone, Andrew
Pietraja. *See* Petraia
Pietra Mala:
Botta to meet Leopold at, vi. 334
Modena, Ps of, entertained at, by Botta's delegates, vi. 202
Pietra Santa:
Spaniards to cross, iii. 35
Spanish army crosses Tuscany at, iii. 40

Pig:
HW might have promoted interests of Ds of Newcastle's, iv. 83
Newcastle, Ds of, brings, from Hanover, iv. 72
Pigeon:
Irishman's saying about, viii. 64
Pignatelli de Aragón, Juan Joaquín Atanasio (1724–76), Conde de Fuentes:
arrival of, in England, v. 417
Charles III's declaration delivered by, to foreign ministers in England, v. 559
Du Barry, Comtesse, refused homage by, vii. 321, 338
French declaration opposed by, vii. 322
leaves for Spain, v. 558
Maupeou ignored by, vii. 321
out-of-town invitations declined by, ungraciously, v. 417
public places avoided by, according to vow, v. 428
Toison d'Or conferred on, v. 560
Tylney's ball not attended by, v. 417
Pignatelli d'Egmont, Casimir (1727–1801), Comte d'Egmont:
father-in-law sends, to Madrid, iv. 572
Pignotti, Abbate Lorenzo (1739–1812), M.D., poet and scientist:
Roberto Manners, ix. 636
Shakespear, viii. 536
Pigot, George (1719–77), cr. (1766) Bn Pigot:
East India Company in London votes to restore, after his illegal imprisonment, viii. 288
Pigot, Hugh, (1722–92), Adm.; M.P.:
news of schooner taken by, should not have been put in gazette, ix. 318
Pigot, Mrs Hugh. *See* Le Neve, Elizabeth
Pigott, Mrs John. *See* Brownlow, Mary
Pigott, Margaret (ca 1714–88), m. Edward Riggs:
Millers leave children with, in France, viii. 197
Millers live with, at Batheaston, viii. 197
rough English humourist, viii. 197
Pigtail Tobacco. *See under* Tobacco
'Pigwiggin.' *See* Walpole, Horatio (1723–1809)
'Pigwigginhood':
Astley draws pictures of, iv. 341
Pike, Lt Edward (d. 1776):
killed in expedition against Charleston, viii. 237
'Pilate':
Florentine children's name for Richecourt, v. 85
Pilâtre ['Pilatrier'] de Rosier, Jean-François (1754–85), aeronaut:
balloon ascent of, ix. 450
death of: chills but does not stop rage for balloons, ix. 596; in balloon accident, ix. 590; lamented by Mann, ix. 593
Piles. *See* Hæmorrhoids.
Pilgrims:

masqueraders costumed as, i. 339, 343, 368, 370

Pilkington, Mrs. *See* Lewen, Lætitia van (1712–50)

Pill box:
Mann sends cameo in, to HW, ix. 650

Pillory:
Shebbeare may be punished by, v. 39
—— will end in, v. 87
Wilkes threatened with, vi. 183
—— unlikely to be put in, vii. 30

Pillow, pillows:
Craon, Princesse de, has all sizes of, i. 481
Walpole, Sir Robert, snores upon, i. 171

Pilot, pilots:
English seek, at Leghorn for Adriatic, i. 455–6
of barge, Ferdinand of Naples reprimands, ix. 581

Pilsen:
Austrians advance on, ii. 58

Pin; pins:
Galli, Mme, to have, i. 239
HW sends, to Mme Galli, i. 416, 422

Pinacci, Angela (fl. 1757–92), m. (1757) Casimiro Branchi; singer:
'divine singer,' vi. 35
Grafton, Ds of, charmed by, vi. 35
Mann wants Handel's oratorios for, vi. 35–6
—— wants music for, on Ds of Grafton's account, vi. 50

Pinacci, Giovanni Battista (b. 1696), singer:
roars, ii. 361

Pindar (?518–ca 448 B.C.), poet:
seal may depict, iii. 483

'Pindar, Peter.' *See* Wolcot, Dr John

Pine, John, printer:
Tapestry Hangings of the House of Lords, ii. 126–7

Pine; pines:
Florentine commissary has, cut down in Lucca, iv. 514
hurricane uproots, at Villa Negrone, iv. 69

Pineapple; pineapples:
Botta's room hot enough to produce, v. 370
Italians first see, in England, iii. 331
Pomfret pedigree depicts, iv. 180–1
sold at Covent Garden market, v. 294
Taaffe brings, to Marquise de Pompadour, iv. 289
Young Pretender first tastes, at Blair Atholl, iii. 106

Pini, (?) Alessandro:
Museum Florentinum directed by, ii. 390–1

Pinkethman, William (fl. 1692–1724), actor:
acts in *Dioclesian*, ii. 565
HW did not admire, vii. 265
petition of, in *Spectator*, ii. 565

Pinot Duclos, Charles (1704–72):
La Chalotais receives offers through, vii. 207
Montesquieu's letters infuriate, vi. 531

——'s *Lettres familières* to be taken by, to France, vi. 531
Pisa visited by, vi. 531
secretary of Académie des Sciences, vi. 531

Pinsent. *See* Pynsent

Pinto, Don Tommaso:
Neapolitan physician, v. 325

Pinto de Fonseca, Emmanuel (1681–1773), Grand Master of the Order of the Knights of St John of Jerusalem:
does not declare war on England for affair of *La Rose*, v. 335
Rohan, Prince Camille de, sent by, with galleys, to Leopold II, vi. 556

Pioche de la Vergne, Marie-Madeleine (1634–93), m. (1655) Francois, Comte de la Fayette; novelist:
memoirs of, HW quotes, iii. 5

Piombanti, Teresa (ca 1711–after 1774), m. (ca 1734) Antonio Cocchi:
pension of, v. 194

Piombino, P. of. *See* Boncompagni, Gaetano (1707–77)

Piombino, Ps of. *See* Boncompagni, Maria (1686–1745)

Piombino, straits of:
English ships cruise in, iii. 235–6
Ferdinand and Maria Carolina detained in, ix. 581
Mann hopes to capture prizes in, iii. 236
Neapolitans intercept grain ships in, vi. 206

Piovene, Conte Agostino:
Tamerlano by, ii. 280–2, 294
Tamerlano, *Giramondo* may surpass, ii. 294

Piozzi, Mrs. *See* Salusbury, Hester Lynch

Piozzi, Gabriel (1740–1809), musician:
Florence visited by, with wife, ix. 611n
Italian fiddler, ix. 633n
Mann cannot invite, with Italian nobility, ix. 633n

Pipe:
country fellows walk down lanes holding, in mouths, v. 417
Stanislas I smokes, iv. 26

Pipe (musical instrument):
people dance to, around maypole, iv. 47

Piperno:
Austrian hussars capture convoy near, ii. 460

Pipers:
Northumberland, Ds of, has, iv. 341

Piquet:
Ferrers plays, with warders, v. 397
Florentine society's chief diversion, iv. 115
played, i. 61–2

Piquet. *See also* Picquet de la Motte

Piracy:
more practicable than victory, ix. 108

Piranesi, Giovanni Battista (1720–78), engraver and architect:
Cumberland, D. of, receives works of, at Rome, vii. 576

Pirate; pirates:
Mann calls Algerians, ix. 270
—— grants commissions to foreign officers to protect them against being treated as, ix. 199, 249
Mediterranean islands inhabited by, ix. 493
Slavonian sailors become, after seizing *Great Duchess of Tuscany,* ix. 479–81
Turkish, Pope's seamen fear enslavement by, i. 15–16
Pironi. *See* Perroni
Pisa, Abp of. *See* Guidi, Paolo Francisco Salvatico (1694–1778)
Pisa:
abbey of, Leopold suppresses, without consulting Rome, vii. 504
Austrian troops encamped at, iii. 254
balls at: vii. 262, ix. 581; end at Leopold's retirement, vii. 171
baths of: Barrett-Lennards do not ask Mann to go to, iv. 194; Cocchi advises Mann to visit, iii. 477; Cocchi's book on, *see* Cocchi, Antonio, *Dei Bagni di Pisa;* Craon asks Cocchi about, i. 342; cutaneous disorders thought to be cured by, viii. 83; HW hopes that Mann will enjoy his visit to, iv. 91; Leopold and Maria Louisa to visit, vii. 108; Mann and Barrett-Lennards visit, iv. 84, 85; Mann prefers, to all places in Tuscany, iv. 158; Mann to see Pelham and Milbanke at, iv. 158; Orford, Cts of, may go to, viii. 83; Pitt, Anne, not benefited by, vii. 567; Richecourt to visit, iv. 252; Richecourt visits, iv. 480; York, D. of, may visit, vi. 236; Young Pretender to visit, vii. 226
Battle of the Bridge at: ix. 582; Leopold may defer, till Ferdinand of Naples's visit, ix. 569; Mann not to attend triennial celebration of, iv. 473; popular with the Pisans, ix. 569; preferable to Scheldt invasion, ix. 583; Regency may forbid, iv. 473; scaffolds for, viii. 188; too violent to please Leopold, vi. 515
burletta to be held at, vi. 424
Capitolo, the, at, iii. 238, 245
Capponi to visit, with troops, ii. 85
cavaliere of, sent to Volterra for indiscreet talk about Spaniards, ii. 46
certificate of Cts of Orford's death to be procured from, ix. 114
chapter at, Ginori presides over, iv. 473
Chute might land at Leghorn to make acquaintances at, iv. 114
climate and weather of, vii. 71–2, 80, 94, 149–50
courier from, tells Mann of Cts of Orford's illness, ix. 113
Court's stay at, will be expensive for Mann, vii. 55, 64, 80
death of Cts of Orford reported from, ix. 129
Empoli on way to, ii. 54

English absurd at, iv. 352
Englishmen at, send home story about Lincoln, vii. 368
Ferdinand of Naples and Maria Carolina welcomed at, with festivities, ix. 581–2
floods averted from, vii. 378
Florentine nobility despise, as provincial, vii. 80
foreign ministers (except Spanish) no longer need to attend Court at, ix. 548
galley slaves escape from, iv. 206
Gloucester, D. of, may visit, vii. 336, 342, 347
—— to stay at Mann's house at, vii. 347
Gustav III coolly received at, ix. 458
HW never saw, vii. 79
illumination at, i. 66
Joseph II may visit, ix. 350, 352, 367, 457, 468
Karl Wilhelm Ferdinand to visit, vi. 458
Leghorn residents flee to, i. 303
Leghorn visitors at, inconvenience Mann, iii. 487, iv. 85, 91
Leopold has more liberty at, vii. 278
—— loves place but not inhabitants of, vii. 254
—— may conduct Joseph II to, ix. 367, 468
—— passes winter of 1782–3 at, ix. 421
——'s statue may be erected in, vii. 95
—— to return from, ix. 393
—— to return to, in Sept. 1783 for ten months, ix. 421
—— to spend winter of 1783–4 at, but without his own or foreign ministers, ix. 425
—— to stay at Leghorn and, till February, vii. 71–2
—— to visit, vi. 453, vii. 336–7, 342, 348
lodgings at, awaited by Mann and Barrett-Lennards, iv. 84
Mann and Barrett-Lennards postpone departure for, iv. 86
Mann benefited by baths of, iii. 486–7, iv. 84, 85
——'s coolness from D. of Gloucester at, viii. 247, 296–7
—— secures house in, vii. 254
—— sees *Giuoco del Ponte* at, for first time, v. 499
—— sends furniture to, for D. of Gloucester's use, vii. 342
——'s expenses at, will be ruinous, vii. 150
——'s finances will be ruined by sojourns at, vii. 254, 278, 293
——'s house at: arrangements at, for D. of Gloucester's occupancy, vii. 394, 397; Beaufort, Ds of, borrows, vii. 372
——'s occupations at, iv. 91–2
——'s sojourn at, better than being at a military camp, vii. 88
——'s visit to, makes him want a villa, iv. 25

——'s winters at, very expensive, vii. 129
—— to avoid visit to, viii. 188
—— to entertain lady from, ii. 353
—— to go to, from Leghorn, vii. 337
—— to prepare to go to, vii. 64
—— to return to Florence to make preparations for visit to, vii. 337
—— to visit, vii. 149
—— to visit, with Tuscan Court, vi. 511
—— to visit baths of, iii. 477
—— writes from, vii. 153, 159, 171, 184, 260, 273, 277, 347, 351, 355, 356, 369
Maria Louisa does not enjoy, vii. 72, 342
—— to have child at, ix. 425
ministers found removal to, expensive, ix. 548
Modenese princess distributes presents at, i. 70
noble English couple at, iv. 352
Orford, Cts of, defers visit to, ix. 107
—— dies at, ix. 112, 113–14, 195
palace at, Rosenberg to examine, vii. 253
Pamfili loves lady of, iii. 445
people of, unworthy of Leopold's favour, vii. 95
physician at: not hopeful about Cts of Orford, ix. 112; supplies drugs for D. of Gloucester, vii. 369
Pitt, Anne, astonishes HW by visit to, viii. 194
—— to visit, vii. 557
price at, of apartment, vii. 55
prices at, higher than at Florence, vii. 278
pumps at baths of, ix. 442
report from, that Austrian-Dutch quarrel is not healed, ix. 561
Richecourt patronizes baths of, iii. 487
riot at, iv. 473
Roccettini convent at, suppressed, vii. 504
Russians at, rejoice over peace with Turkey, viii. 84
Russians spend lavishly at, viii. 95
St Ranieri celebration at, ii. 455
scaffold at, for Battle of the Bridge, drives Anne Pitt away, viii. 188
shows at, for Tuscan Court, uninteresting, vi. 515
snow in, in late March, vii. 294
Suares, Mme, conducts lady from, ii. 353
Teatro dei Ravvivati at, new, vii. 353
theatre at: impresario of, has burletta performed by bad company, vii. 171; Mann to attend, vii. 72; new, vii. 353
troops may be sent to, ii. 77
Tuscan court at, ix. 436, 548
Tuscan court gives weekly ball and supper at, vii. 171, 191, 262
Tuscan court goes to, vi. 511, vii. 149, 352, ix. 334
Tuscan court returns to, from Leghorn, vii. 80
Tuscan court to visit, vi. 417, vii. 325, viii. 188
university of, Gualtieri a professor of, ii. 88
visitors to: Acciaioli, Mme, iv. 158; Barbantane, Marquis de, vii. 480; Barbantane family, vii. 480; Barrett-Lennards, iv. 91–2; Beaufort, Ds of, vii. 372, 397; Benedict XIV's niece, iii. 487; Bouverie, i. 67; Chute, ii. 455; Clephane, i. 67; Compton, Lady Elizabeth, vii. 372, 397; Corks, iv. 451; Corsini, P. and Ps, vi. 424; Davison, iii. 407; Dick, Sir John, vii. 395; Dick, Sir John, and Lady, vii. 262, 395; Duclos, vi. 531; Eszterházys, iv. 351; Fuller, i. 67; Gloucester, D. of, vii. 352–3, 355–6, 356–8, 392–6, 404–7, 502, viii. 247; Grifoni, Mme, i. 33; Gustav III, ix. 442, 458; Hervey, vi. 430; Heywood, vii. 394; Joseph II and Leopold, vii. 108–9, viii. 129; Leopold II, vi. 422, 515, vii. 185, ix. 383; Liechtenstein, P. of, vi. 154; Mann, iii. 486–7, 494, 500, iv. 25, 91, 158, v. 499, 503, vi. 422–3, 427, 514, 515, 531, vii. 67–8, 71–2, 79–80, 88–92, 94–7, 117–20, 153–5, 260–2, 269–73, 277–9, 347–9, 351–4, 355–6, 356–8, 369–72, 392–7, 404–7; Mann, Horace II, ix. 581; Maria Louisa, vi. 423; Milbanke, iv. 158; Mill, iii. 407; Mozzi, ix. 421; Orford, Cts of, viii. 105, ix. 112, 113; Pelham, iv. 158; Perelli, v. 390; Pitt, Anne, vii. 564, 567, viii. 188; (?) Pratt, Caroline, iv. 91; Rena, Mme, vii. 119; Richecourt, iv. 162; Rinuccini, iii. 245; Smollett, vii. 189; Somerset, Lady Mary Isabella, vii. 372, 397; Stampa, iv. 24; Suares family, iii. 238; Sudleys, vii. 203; Trapp, i. 67; Vorontsov family, vi. 202–3, 204–5; Whithed, ii. 455; York, Cardinal, iv. 164, 250, (?) 256; York, D. of, vi. 220, 223
Vorontsov family returns to Florence from, vi. 204
York, D. of, entertained at park near, vi. 221
Young Pretender quits, for Siena, vii. 318
Pisa, University of:
Sapienza court of, prepared for ball, ix. 581
Pisa Forest:
does from, eaten by Leghorn slaves, iv. 83
Pisani, Luigi (1663–1741), Doge of Venice 1735–41:
burial of, i. 75
Montagu, Lady Mary Wortley, promises to reconcile, with George II, i. 98
Pistoia ('Pistoja'):
Braitwitz to make, his headquarters, ii. 98
German troops reach Bagni della Porretta near, ii. 98
Grifoni, Mme, visits, i. 100
gun barrels from, ii. 329
gun barrels to be made at, ii. 242
iron worker at, leaves for Seravezza, ii. 242

[Pistoia, *continued*]

Leopold and Maria Louisa to meet Ferdinand of Naples and Maria Carolina at, ix. 594

letters to, from Spanish officers, i. 238

Modenese princess visits, i. 100

new road from Modena to, ix. 594

post-house outside walls of, vi. 222

Te Deum sung at, v. 112

Tuscan troops to go to, ii. 98, 100

visitors to: Serristori, iv. 442; Suares 'Cecco,' i. 103; York, D. of, vi. 222

York, D. of, and Mann greeted by governor of, but do not enter town, vi. 222

Pistol; pistols:

Acquaviva's guard armed with, iii. 113

Adam and Fullarton use the same, for their duels, ix. 37

Chudleigh, Mrs, threatened with, by footpads, viii. 198

Damer's suicide with, viii. 234–5

duel fought with, iv. 364

extra, Maclaine carries, iv. 184

Ferrers carries, to bed, v. 396

—— pulls, against robber, vi. 184

Flobert guards mistress's house with, v. 386

Fortescue said to have killed himself with, vi. 333

Gascoigne discharges, without bullets, at Roman populace, vi. 287

HW cannot fire, ix. 570

Kingston, Ds of, said to terrify husband with, viii. 198

Nourse proposes duel with, i. 248

Penn's, goes off accidentally, iv. 248

Pepi takes, in pockets, i. 136

Spanish agent at Florence buys, for Montemar, i. 207

Wright's, confiscated, i. 449

See also Gun; Weapon

Pistoles, Spanish:

English feluccas capture, ii. 116

Pistro:

Mann surprised by accounts of, ii. 381

Pitaval. *See* Gayot de Pitaval

Pitch:

Southwark magazines of, ix. 577

Pitigliano, governor of. *See* Borghesi, Domenico Antonio

Pitonessa:

imprisoned, together with her confessor, for publishing their dreams, viii. 30

Pitt, Amelia, m. (1761) Dr William Spry:

brother gives portion to, v. 365

Pitt, Anne (1712–81):

Abano baths to be visited by, viii. 9, 22, 105, 108, 220

Abano visited by, viii. 220, 233

Abano waters benefit, viii. 22, 233

artistic talents of, vii. 457

ball of, described by HW, viii. 16

brother mourned by, on her return to England, viii. 415

brother's talents and ambition shared by, viii. 379

Butes' calamity will distress, viii. 378

Chesterfield's witticism to, on Pitt's intention to speak in a horizontal posture, vii. 177

Craon, Princesse de, resembles, viii. 6

Cumberland, Ds of, may be subject of liberties taken by, vii. 558n

curiosities eagerly pursued by, in Rome, viii. 105

death of Ds of Montagu afflicts, viii. 105

dies in madhouse, ix. 127

dismissal of, as Augusta, Ps of Wales's Privy Purse, vii. 558

England expects, daily, viii. 401

England reached by, viii. 411

English people would be found by, to be as mad as herself, viii. 349

Florence left by, viii. 9

Florence left by, for Bologna, viii. 381

French female servant nursed by, at Rome, viii. 344, 353

French sojourn of, adds to her *ton*, viii. 6

Geneva visited by, viii. 118, 131

HW asks about, viii. 227

HW attends 'fairy entertainment' of, viii. 8

HW calls house of, 'Pittsburgh,' and 'Temple' of Vesta, viii. 15

HW esteemed by, vii. 567

HW glad that Mann's verdigris was mentioned by, viii. 15

HW not sorry that Mann has been forsaken by, viii. 17

HW often mentioned by, vii. 456

HW recommends, to Mann, vii. 557–8

HW's compliments to be conveyed to, by Mann, viii. 233

HW tells Mann to beware of, viii. 3

HW thanked by, for Mann's civilities to her, viii. 3

health of: Abano waters benefit, viii. 233; better, viii. 374; Pisa baths might benefit, viii. 188; relapse in, compels her to return to Abano despite hot weather, viii. 22; weak and emaciated, viii. 9; weak nerves, viii. 6

Holland, Bns, reported by, to be wounded by sons' ingratitude, viii. 30

insanity of, vii. 558n

Italy may be winter home of, for fear of English journey, viii. 381

Kingston, Ds of, believed by, to enjoy her trial, viii. 199

—— blamed by, for mentioning Augusta, Ps of Wales, viii. 203

—— does not see, but exchanges messages with her, viii. 7

Knightsbridge house of, viii. 15

Lorraine visited by, viii. 188, 131

Mann charmed with, viii. 6

—— exchanges affectionate letters with, viii. 233

—— exchanges kind messages with, viii. 188

—— may tell, about her brother's alliance with Temple, viii. 14

—— receives notes from, viii. 6

——'s correspondence with, vii. 564, viii. 22, 131, 405

—— sends newspapers to, viii. 233

——'s house occupied by, vii. 567

——'s regard for, vii. 567

—— to ask, if Mme Grifoni is still beautiful, viii. 17

—— told by, of C.J. Fox's ingratitude to mother, viii. 22

—— to tell: about neighbour's elopement, viii. 15; that English ladies weep no more, viii. 112

Maria Louisa tells, of father's remarks on Spanish policy, viii. 375

milk and chocolate taken by, for breakfast, vii. 567

Nancy to be visited by, viii. 131

Naples to be visited by, viii. 344

neighbours of, at Knightsbridge, viii. 15

nephew gives sad account of, viii. 431, 462

once sprightly, viii. 462

Padua visited by, viii. 22

perches contrived by, for guests at overcrowded party, viii. 8

Pisa visited by, vii. 557, 564, 567, viii. 188, 194

Pius VI might make, Ps Fossani, viii. 360

privy purse to Augusta, Ps of Wales, vii. 451n, 558n

Provence visited by, viii. 194

Rome visited by, viii. 105, 344, 357–8, 374

Tessés recommended by, to Mann, viii. 353

troop movements detain, at Trent, viii. 389

wild, and may be confined, viii. 421

witticism by: about Bp Hervey's title, viii. 430–1, 462; about Ds of Kingston, viii. 6

Pitt, Hon. Anne (1772–1864), m. (1792) William Wyndham Grenville, cr (1790) Bn Grenville:

father to take, to Italy, viii. 411

Pitt, Christian (d. 1761), m. (1760) Thomas Saunders:

brother gives portion to, v. 365

death of, vi. 2

Pitt, Elizabeth 'Villiers' (1712–70), m. (1761) John Hanham (or Hannam):

Augusta, Ps of Wales, has, as maid of honour, iv. 507n

brother attacked by, iv. 507n

brother's affair with, iv. 411

brother's kindness to, ill requited, v. 46

calls herself by her middle name, iv. **406**

conversion of, to Roman Catholicism, iv. 507n

Cork, Cts of, to shun, despite former intimacy, iv. 452

England revisited by, v. 46

Florence visited by, iv. 406, 410–11, 416

Germany to be the wedding-place, and Holland the winter residence of, iv. 499

HW considers, 'a dangerous inmate,' iv. 507

HW warns Mann against, iv. 410–11

Mann has no connection with, iv. 452

—— hears bad accounts of, iv. 416

marriage of, iv. 507n

Popish chapel the resort of, v. 46

Preston accompanies, perhaps to marry her, iv. 499

Prujean writes letter to, iv. 499

Prujean, Mrs, quarrels with, about religion, iv. 499

pseudonym of, iv. 507n

religion changed by, iv. 416

returns from Italy, iv. 507n

Talbot's mistress, iv. 507n

Test given brother's letters by, to prove that he cheated her, v. 46

Warren a friend of, iv. 499

writings of, iv. 507n

Pitt, George (1721–1803), cr. (1776) Bn Rivers; M.P.:

brutal and half mad, vii. 451

Chatham's distant relative, vi. 572n

Churchill entertained by, at ball, iv. 367

Coventrys entertained by, at ball, iv. 367

daughter of, ix. 538n, x. 48

Fermor, Lady Charlotte, loved by, i. **468n**

—— renounced by, ii. 103

George III appoints, to Bedchamber, v. 460

Graftons' house at Turin to be taken by, vi. 2

HW entertained by, at ball, iv. 367

handsome, i. 468n

Holdernesse entertained by, at ball, iv. 367

Holdsworth tutor to, iii. 139n

Italy to be visited by, iv. 58

Lincoln to entertain, i. 468

Mann may remember, v. 460

—— remembers, iv. 58

minister to Turin, vi. 2n

Montagu, Lady Mary Wortley, admires, in Italy, i. 468n

—— knows, iv. 58

Spanish post may be offered to, vi. 500

Stratfieldsaye residence of, i. 468

Tory, v. 460

Townshend, Vcts, ogles, i. 468n

Turin post to go to, v. 548, vi. 2n

uncle of, iii. 458

wife ill-treated by, vii. 451

wife loves, iv. 58

Pitt, George (1751–1828), 2d Bn Rivers, 1803:

mother cannot communicate with, vii. 451

Pitt, Mrs George. *See* Atkins, Penelope (d. 1795)

Pitt, Lady Harriot (1758–86), m. (1785) Hon. Edward James Eliot:
mother puts, under uncles' protection, vii. 74

Pitt, Lady Hester (1755–80), m. (1774) Charles Stanhope, styled Vct Mahon, later 3d E. Stanhope:
marriage of, viii. 67
mother puts, under uncles' protection, vii. 74

Pitt, Hon. James Charles (1761–1800):
father attended by, viii. 371
mother puts, under uncles' protection, vii. 74

Pitt, John (? 1706–87), M.P.:
Admiralty post temporarily given to, v. 25–6
Commissioner of Trade, ii. **551**
dismissed from Board of Trade, iv. 517
Drax contests Wareham election with, iii. 458–9
Jacobite, iii. 458
Lord of Trade, iii. 458n
to be Paymaster of the Marines, v. 26

Pitt, John (1756–1835), 2d E. of Chatham, 1778:
father attended by, viii. 371
Mann hears, is to be envoy to Berlin, ix. 314
mother puts, under uncles' protection, vii. 74
pension reversion for, viii. 389

Pitt, Louisa (ca 1756–91), m. (1773) Peter Beckford:
mother cannot communicate with, vii. 451

Pitt, Marcia Lucy (1756–1822), m. James Lane-Fox:
mother cannot communicate with, vii. 451

Pitt, Hon. Penelope (b. 1749), m. 1 (1766) Edward, 2d Vct Ligonier; m. 2 (1784) Capt. Smith:
husband divorces, because of affair with Alfieri, vii. 451n, ix. 538n, x. 48

Pitt, Thomas (ca 1705–61), M.P.:
Cornish boroughs managed by, i. **346n**
death of: probably mentioned in letters forwarded by Mann, v. 524; soon after second marriage, v. 517
jointure given by, to second wife, v. 517
Lyttelton steals Okehampton borough from, iv. 39
Opposition assembly addressed by, at St Alban's Tavern, iv. 50
sister's affair with, iv. 411
son cuts off entail to pay debts of, v. 365
son of, v. 364n
Waldegrave replaces, as Warden of the Stannaries, iv. 246–7

Pitt, Thomas (1737–93), cr. (1784) Bn Camelford:
Dagge praises, v. 365

draws Gothic ornaments for HW's cabinet and gallery ornaments, vi. 25
entail cut off by, to pay father's debts and sisters' portions, v. 365
father of, dies, v. 517
foreign tours of, reveal England's waning prestige, ix. 35
French passport for, v. 524
French passport not received by, v. 543, 545, 550
Granada and Italy to be visited by, with Strathmore, v. 364
HW calls on, and is called on by him, v. 558
HW delivers Mann's letter to, vi. 2
HW gives letter of introduction to, to Mann, v. 365
HW's apartment in Mann's house may be occupied by, v. 543, 545
HW sends messages to, v. 505
HW's relations with, cool since George Grenville's rule, viii. 411
HW undeceived by mourning feigned by, for detested uncle, viii. 415
health of, crippled knees, viii. 411
house called by, Palazzo Pitti, vi. 33
house taken by, at Twickenham, vi. 18, 25
Italy to be visited by, with family, viii. 411
itinerary of, from Rome, v. 543, 545
Kinnoull accompanied by, to Lisbon, v. 364
letters from, enclosed by Mann, v. 543
(?) Lyttelton's ill temper not to be mentioned to, vi. 251
Mann forwards letters probably about death of father of, v. 524
—— greets, on arrival in Florence from Leghorn, v. 500
(?) —— hears sad account from, of aunt, viii. 431, 462
—— impatient for arrival of, v. 380
—— may arrange for return of, to England, v. 524
—— sends remembrances to, vi. 46, 69
—— sends word to, that Strathmore returns to England, vi. 22–3
—— takes, to Uffizi gallery, v. 500
—— to take, to burletta, v. 501
—— visited by, v. 550
Mann, Horace II, quotes letter of, about his salary, ix. 672–3
Naples to be visited by, v. 545
Naples visited by, viii. 486
Parliamentary speech of, denounces North for England's declining prestige, ix. 35
probably on way back from Rome, v. 543
San Casciano baths visited by, with Sir Richard Lyttelton, v. 524
sets out for Germany, v. 550
Strathmore awaits, v. 524
—— calls on, at Twickenham, vi. 152
—— friend of, v. 543

——'s conduct will surprise, vi. 45

—— separates from, in Spain, v. 501

Sunning Hill visited by, to drink waters for health, vi. 73

swears by uncle's ghost, despite previous dislike, viii. 412

Venice to be visited by, to attend Ascension celebrations, v. 500

Venice visited by, v. 512

wife sends courier to, viii. 486

Pitt, Thomas (1775–1804), 2d Bn Camelford, 1793:

father to take, to Italy, viii. 411

Pitt, Mrs Thomas. *See* Murray, Maria; Wilkinson, Anne (1738–1803)

Pitt, William (1708–78), cr. (1766) E. of Chatham; M.P.; prime minister:

achievements of, in opposition, surpass his former efforts, iv. 516

Addington attends, vi. 505

—— forbids, to transact any business, vi. 505

administration declined by, vi. 541

Admiralty and Navy Bill opposed by, iv. 38

Admiralty board selected by, v. 104

Africa's conqueror, v. 541

alone politically, vii. 264

Alt congratulated by, on Russian defeat, v. 316

amendment proposed by, to address, vii. 167

American sovereignty upheld in Parliament by followers of, viii. 371

Americans the chief supporters of, vi. 396

America said by, to be conquered in Germany, vii. 551, 187

appears in House of Lords, viii. 13

appointment not given to, ii. 551

appointments by, opposed by Newcastle, vi. 442

army appropriation bill to be supported by, iii. 4

assertion by, that English troops would never be sent to Germany, vii. 258

at end of his reckoning, vii. 270

attorney-general to be a follower of, v. 110

Barnard compared with, vi. 84

Bath, Exeter, London, Worcester, and Yarmouth give freedom of city to, v. 87

Bath visited by, v. 540, vi. 425, 449, 461, 462, 472, 479, 483, 488, 492, 567

Beckford confers with, vi. 160

—— desired by, to lay reorganization plan for East India Company before House of Commons, vi. 493

—— friend of, vi. 39n, viii. 132

Beckford's, Granby's, and Grenville's deaths to deprive, of support, vii. 246

Beckford transacts business of, in Parliament, vi. 506–7

becomes Lord Privy Seal and E. of Chatham, vi. 442

bedchamber post to Frederick, P. of Wales, resigned by, in friendship to Lyttelton, iii. 27

Bedford, D. of, no longer wants return of. vi. 167

——'s adherents opposed by, vi. 308

——'s demands rejected by, vi. 472

——'s Irish post instigated by Fox to spite, v. 31

—— speaks like, iv. 310

—— to punish, iv. 38

Bedfords forsaken by, iv. 138

big words used by, vii. 163

Blackfriars Bridge has inscription in honour of, v. 449

blazing meteor, successful in war but not in peace, ix. 275

Bolingbroke's *Letters* formerly read by, iv. 59

—— wanes in esteem of, iv. 59

Botta to write to, v. 180

Bristol friend of, vii. 65

——'s recall wished by, v. 536–7

brother of, v. 517n

Buckingham House visited by, in chair, vi. 159

budget opened by, in private, vi. 439

burial of, poorly attended by Parliament members despite their affected concern, viii. 393

Bute could have been deposed earlier by, vi. 129

—— does not relinquish keys to, vi. 130

—— may be approached closer by, vi. 490

Bute, Newcastle, and Parliamentary oppression of America all attacked by, vi. 395–6

Bute's alliance may cause unpopularity of, vi. 433

——'s alliance with, vi. 473

——'s chief rival at George II's death, vii. 152

—— sends for, vi. 159–60

——'s friendship with, would please George III but alienate the people, vi. 440

Canada and Cabinet Council to be conquered by, v. 290

Canada's conqueror, v. 541

cannon sent by, against St Malo but not Rochefort, v. 213

career of, ended, viii. 376

caricature of, in 'The Turnstile,' v. 93

(?) Caroline, Q., connected with, i. 146

Carteret abused by, in Parliament, ii. 383

Charles III, Louis XV, and Great Mogul threatened by, vi. 276

Charles III's declaration against, v. 559

Chesterfield's witticism on intention of, to speak in a horizontal posture, vii. 177

Choiseul probably dreads, vii. 134

Churchill could now attack, vi. 304

—— longed to satirize, vi. 261

[Pitt, William (1708–78), *continued*]

Clive called 'heaven-born' by, vii. 381n, 387

—— called 'heaven-born hero' by, vi. 176, 243

——'s father makes offer to, v. 404

complains of Shelburne's removal, vii. 61–2

concessions might be obtained by, from Pelham, iv. 223

content to manage war under D. of Newcastle, v. 448

Continental entanglements disliked by, iii. 168

Conway displeases, over East India Company affair, vi. 509

——'s speech praised by, x. 15

—— urged by, to stay in office, vi. 472

Cornbury joined by, in opposing George II's use of Hessian troops, iii. 188

Court supports, vi. 497

Court would not get much quarter from, vi. 102

Cumberland, D. of, confers with, vi. 102

—— sent to, vi. 302

—— wanted by, as army leader, vi. 161

daughter of, marries, viii. 67

death of: viii. 379; during Parliament session, lucky for family, viii. 388–9; makes him seem indispensable, viii. 382

defeat of, in absence, over question of land tax reduction, vi. 488

departure of, from House of Commons, disliked, vi. 440

designs of, on secretary of state, iv. 223

Despenser the only friend to ask about health of, on his return to Parliament, viii. 393

despotism of, based on his popularity, vii. 100

Devonshire, D. of, urges, to become minister, v. 11

——'s favour to, disgusts Fox, v. 31

dismissed: as Paymaster, iv. 512, 517; as secretary of state, v. 74

does not appear, vii. 115

Du Barry, Comtesse, may anticipate, in saving Paoli, vii. 75

eastern monarchs and Borealian electors attend, in his Sabine farm, v. 518

East India Company 'begot' by, vii. 400

East India Company crisis will be weathered by, vi. 496

East India Company's restrictions from, opposed by Conway at Charles Townshend's instigation, vi. 493

Edgcumbe removed by, without telling Conway, vi. 470–1

Edinburgh may give freedom to, v. 87

Egmont's oratory compared to that of, iv. 32

——'s party heaps incense on, iv. 224

England brought to glory under, vii. 82

England can still conquer, even without, vi. 82

England now lacks, viii. 485

England owes its security to, v. 261

England's dependence upon sole abilities of, alarms Mann, v. 84

England will clamour for return of, at first calamity, v. 558

England would prefer, to Bute, in victory or defeat, vi. 47–8

English disgraces must be removed by, v. 31

English expedition a sacrifice to vainglorious whims of, v. 244

English ignoramuses mistake Frederick II for, v. 237–8

English troops said by, never to be used in Germany, vii. 258

epigram on Bath's and London's gifts to, v. 87

faction of: v. 27; does not resign, iii. 27; Lyttelton, George, abandons, iv. 512; only Whigs that do not vote with Court, ii. 118; Pelham flattered by, iv. 224; Regency Bill opposed by, iv. 248; to avoid provoking D. of Newcastle in order to lay Minorcan blame on Fox, v. 77

family attend, at messenger's house, viii. 371

followers of: alone acknowledge American sovereignty in Parliament, viii. 371; would find no places if Winchilsea and Fox remained, v. 99

foreigners should be made to think that all English soldiers and sailors inherit cloak of, ix. 15

foreigners watch, making speech at 5 A.M., vi. 209

fortune still constant to, even though he sees no one, vi. 508–9

Fox is expected to unite with, and then attack, iv. 453

—— may be succeeded by, as secretary of state, v. 6–7, 11

—— not to be joined by, in ministry, v. 11

—— proscribed by, vi. 161

——'s breach with, widens, v. 34

——'s daily altercations with, in House of Commons, v. 65

——'s rivalry with, iv. 230

France and Spain will be humbled by England during rule of, vi. 441

France dreaded crutch of, to the last, viii. 379

France must be tied up by next treaty of, v. 338

France no longer opposed by crutch of, viii. 381

Frederick II and P. Ferdinand the heroes of, vi. 440–1

Frederick, P. of Wales, calls Elizabeth Chudleigh better candidate than, for secretary at war, iii. 175

—— hates, since Carteret's fall, iii. 175
—— may dismiss, ii. 118
——'s follower, ii. 102
—— warns, ii. 102
French declaration sent by, to Mann, to be communicated to Regency, v. 502–3
French expeditions of, unsuccessful, vii. 186
French fear of, discovered by HW at Paris, vi. 441
French fear wild beast of Gevaudan as much as, vi. 289
French invasion expected by, v. 299
French puzzled by refusal of, to lead administration, vi. 342
friends of: advocate firmness, vi. 513; want union with D. of Newcastle, v. 86–7
further legacies may be sought by, ii. 541
Garrick equivalent to, in HW's opinion, vii. 41
—— less attentive than, to worldly riches, viii. 435
genius of, still constant, vi. 463
George II abuses, to D. of Newcastle, iv. 223
—— cannot place, in power, iii. 159
—— confers with, once, v. 43
—— dislikes, iv. 412, v. 473
—— enjoys defeat of, iv. 223
—— laughed at by, for liking military shows, v. 238
—— makes, Paymaster, iv. 138
—— pleased by, in the Closet, v. 31
—— receives Shah Goest from, v. 378
—— reconciled with, by D. of Newcastle, iv. 138
—— rejects, as secretary at war, at Pulteney's instigation, iii. 209, 211
George III and royal family eclipsed by, at Lord Mayor's dinner, v. 547
George III arranges ministry with, vi. 439
—— asked by, to dismiss peace supporters, vi. 160–1
—— confers with, vii. 132
—— does not consult, on Bute's appointment as secretary of state, v. 487–8
—— favours, v. 93n
—— has to summon, to ministry, vi. 302
—— notified by, of willingness to continue, v. 448
——'s conference with, variously reported, vi. 168
—— sends for, vi. 432
—— sends Grafton to ask, for interview, vi. 307
——'s forces may be led by, in Parliament, viii. 350
——'s levee attended by, vi. 161
——'s rebuke to, about proposing his friends, vi. 161
—— summons Temple, at desire of, vi. 435
—— treats, firmly, vi. 495

—— tries to appease, by Grenville's appointment and restoration of West Indies department, v. 488
—— will support, after loss of land tax, vi. 489
—— would not send for, a third time, vi. 419
German subsidy advocated by, v. 65
German treaties opposed by, iv. 501
German war supported by reputation of, v. 549
Germany must be conquered by, since Frederick II is unlikely to do so, v. 354
gout and smell of war will bring back, to the stage, vii. 70
government leadership offered to, vi. 159
government may be led by, vii. 182
government offers waived by, v. 540
Gower sent by, with overtures to D. of Bedford, vi. 472
Grafton hears complaints of, vii. 61
—— unable to see, vi. 436
'Great Commoner' a common term for, vi. 425n
Grenville and Temple reconciled with, vii. 74
Grenville may have underhand dealings with, vi. 91
——'s death keeps, from House of Lords, vii. 248
—— would have Exchequer post according to demands of, v. 92
Grenvilles condescendingly treated by, vi. 419
Grenvilles driven by, iii. 194
Grenvilles the only allies of, iii. 169
'grey-headed experience' boasted of by, iii. 169
Grub Street papers about, printed in Vienna Court gazette, vi. 178
HW ascribes English victories to, v. 347
HW calls: 'Demosthenes,' v. 365, vii. 163; 'Gorgon', iv. 454; 'Hannibal,' vi. 211; 'old Myra,' vii. 168
HW compares: to Cæsar, vii. 82; to Dr Rock, v. 547; to Fabius, v. 337
HW disillusioned by acceptance by, of peerage and gifts, v. 541
HW hints to Choiseul's friends that Wilkes might bring, back to power, vii. 143
HW more interested in, than in his son, ix. 487
HW predicts new administration by, vi. 308
HW quotes, vi. 1
HW's appraisal of, viii. 415
HW saw whole career of, ix. 559
HW's opinion of, v. 541, 547
HW's speech praised by, i. 377
HW undeceived by mourning feigned for, by nephew, viii. 415
habeas corpus voting shunned by, ii. 408–9

[Pitt, William (1708–78), *continued*]

Halifax proscribed by, vi. 161

Hampden covets office of, iv. 224

——'s quarrel with, iv. 224, 235

Hanoverian troop bill supported by, iii. 241

harangues in House of Commons, v. 547

Hardinge, Mrs, makes witticism about George III's choice of, v. 459–60

Hardwicke alarmed at popularity of, v. 87

—— and D. of Newcastle join Bute against, v. 539n

Hartington opposes, iv. 222

'has kicked and cuffed,' vi. 416

haughtiness pushed too far by, vi. 419

Hay loses seat in service of, v. 73

health and spirits of, good, vi. 462

health but not popularity regained by, vi. 552

health of: apoplectic fit, viii. 371; as bad as his situation, v. 67; better, vi. 559; better, but unlikely to recover, viii. 378; cannot yet walk, v. 39; eyesight affected by gout, v. 484; fat and well, vii. 132; fever, vi. 436; fever, symptomatic, vi. 505; gout, v. 22, 31, 33, 35, 39, 43, 52, 171, 177–8, 198, 261, 286, 374, 484, 518, vi. 101, 208, 211, 277, 284, 298, 449, 479, 501, 521, 578, vii. 70, 74, 194, 199, viii. 126; ill, vi. 488; mental derangement rumoured, vi. 505; mental disorder still suspected, vi. 513; poor, iv. 412; sleepless for 14 nights, v. 484

Hillsborough has no connection with, vi. 439

Holdernesse to be attacked by, over release of Hanoverian soldier at Maidstone, v. 34

House of Commons defeats demand of, for increased navy, iii. 168–9

House of Commons held by, *in commendam*, v. 56

House of Commons may be snatched from leadership of, vi. 501

House of Commons must be managed by, vi. 490

House of Commons probably better controlled by, in absentia, v. 58

House of Commons to attend burial of, viii. 379

House of Commons votes funeral and monument to, at public expense, viii. 379

House of Lords little influenced by, v. 205–6

House of Lords not attended by, vii. 194, 199–200

House of Lords visited by, against physician's wish, probably for last time, viii. 371

House of Lords will be as little impressed by, as France was by his coastal attacks, vii. 186

hunts, vii. 387

India's 'conqueror,' v. 541

Lee opposes, in Parliament, iii. 241

—— resigns post from resentment towards, v. 104

Legge avoids dispute with, iv. 453

—— ignored by, vi. 161

—— would have peerage and Admiralty according to demands of, v. 92

Leicester House said to countenance, v. 13

Leicester's witticism on appointment of, as paymaster, iii. 286

likes to bid on others' haughtiness, v. 536

London Common Council gives freedom of city to, v. 77

London Common Council receives letter from, explaining his acceptance of pension, v. 546

London dislikes acceptance by, of peerage, vi. 442–3

London lured by, with hope of Spanish plunder, v. 549

London's policy towards, v. 90

Lord Mayor's dinner attended by, in chariot and pair, v. 547

Louis XV almost tossed in a blanket by, vi. 276

Lyttelton calls, 'Pericles,' v. 408–9

—— related to, vi. 251

——'s friendship with, iii. 27

—— to receive messenger from, with offer of Turin post, v. 507–8

Lytteltons and Grenvilles driven by, iii. 194

Lytteltons and Grenvilles only allies of, iii. 169

Mann expects, as new superior, v. 16

—— favourably mentioned by, to Wood, vi. 469

—— informs, of Old Pretender's ill health, v. 390

—— must be haughty now that he represents, vi. 441

—— not likely to be opposed by, vi. 433

—— receives letter by order of, v. 381

—— receives letter from, on death of George II, v. 453, 455

——'s correspondence with, v. 36

——'s credentials from, v. 463–4

——'s obligation to, stressed by Chute, v. 338

——'s political remarks should first be authorized by, v. 465–6

——'s truculence to Tuscan Court would be backed by, vi. 483

—— to inform, of Botta's reception of George III's letter, v. 464

—— will think HW has succeeded, v. 539

—— would be surprised to find, secretary of state, iv. 235

Mann, Galfridus, favoured by, v. 166

Mansfield's prosecution dropped by, vii. 282

——'s speech cowed by sight of, vi. 464

Marlborough visited by, vi. 488

Marlborough, Ds of, leaves legacy to, as 'patriot', ii. 540, vi. 277

Masserano frightened by return of, vi. 441

Maurepas to be frowned on by, in the other world, ix. 212

may become secretary at war, iii. 155

may be sent for, after debate over Regency Bill, vi. 300

may emerge with Wilkes, vii. 82

'meteor' of House of Commons, iii. 202

Middlesex election discussed by, till nobody will answer him, vii. 208–9

Middlesex election heated and reheated by, vii. 215

Middlesex election referred by, to House of Lords, vii. 167

military men may be preferred by, vi. 439

military success due to, v. 277

ministers, Opposition, Wilkes and London abused by, vii. 251

ministry might engage Paoli against, vii. 145

ministry of, cannot endure at same time with two others, v. 465

miscarriages and derision suffered by, vii. 216

mob cheers, vi. 405

mob have not put, into St James's Palace, v. 541

mob ill-treats, vi. 449

Mogul frightened by, vi. 276

money and people both impossible to raise by, vii. 218

motion by, in House of Lords, vii. 180, viii. 75

Murray answered by, in House of Commons, ii. 123

nation may call for, vii. 100

naval investigation supported by, in Parliament, ii. 399

naval reduction opposed by, iv. 223

nephew of, v. 364–5

nephew swears by ghost of, despite previous dislike, vii. 412

Newcastle, D. of, abandoned by, iv. 453

—— and Fox opposed by, iv. 509–10

Newcastle, D. of, asked by, not to meddle in House of Commons or state department, v. 91

—— confers with, vi. 160

—— denies connection with, v. 74

—— does not choose, as colleague, iv. 248

—— not to be joined by, vi. 78

—— rejects demands of, and breaks off conferences, v. 92

—— resumes conference with, v. 97

—— said to have rejected extravagant terms of, v. 91

——'s coalition with, v. 103–5

——'s exclusion demanded by, v. 11

——'s overtures rejected by, v. 23, vi. 93

—— supported by, against Sandwich and the Bedfords, iv. 222

—— unlikely to get along with, v. 99–100

—— upset by, iv. 230

new Opposition led by, v. 552

nominee for secretaryship, iv. 202

not yet in place, iii. 202

Nugent opposes, iv. 454

Opposition encouraged by, to form ministry, vi. 310

Opposition led by, in Parliament, viii. 341

Opposition not to be joined by, vi. 78

Parliamentary appearance again made by, viii. 308

Parliamentary attendance still impossible for, v. 33, 35

Parliamentary Opposition to be led by, ii. 102

Parliamentary speeches by: i. **297**; alarms House of Commons, iv. 453; implies world conquest, v. 344–5; not up to his old style, vii. 167; on amendment to the Address, x. 24; on privately-raised regiments, x. 14, 15, 17, 18; on Secret Committee, iii. 370; on seizure of Wilkes's papers, vi. 208; on unanimity on the Army, x. 10; Parliament swayed by, v. 256–7; praising Newcastle, and reversing stand on Spanish war, iv. 222

Parliamentary vote by, on privately-raised regiments, x. 19

Parliament attacked by, for taxing America, vi. 395–6

Parliament attended by, only twice in winter, v. 182

Parliament begins without, vi. 101

Parliament may be forced by outside pressure to bow to, v. 13

Parliament's adulation of, a farce, viii. 415

Parliament's dissolution by, would leave Wilkes in control, vii. 181

Parliament to pay debts of, viii. 382

Parliament will bury, in either Westminster Abbey or St Paul's, viii. 382

paymaster, iii. 256, iv. 138, 406

peaceable and has reason to be pleased, vii. 65

peace made by, will be a good one, v. 355

Peace of Paris condemned by, vi. 95–6

Pelham attacked by, iii. 169

—— bullied and flattered by, iii. 155

—— courts, ii. 327

—— may be succeeded by, as prime minister, iv. 411, 419

—— must bring in, ii. 537

pension acceptance must be regretted by, vi. 277

pension of, v. 546, viii. 389

perpetual militia bill may be necessary to, v. 552

personally very expensive, viii. 389

Pitt, George, a distant relative of, vi. 572n

[Pitt, William (1708–78), *continued*]

Pitt, Mrs George, visited by, at Wandsworth Hill, vi. 572

political prospects of, on becoming secretary of state, v. 17

popularity of, even in illness, would have made new ministry difficult, viii. 381

Potter, Thomas, may rival, iii. 449

Pratt named by, for lord chancellor, vi. 161

privately-raised regiments defended by, iii. 154, x. 14–19

Privy Seal to be taken by, vi. 442

Pynsent's bequest to, vi. 276–7, 284

——'s bequest to, equalled only in England, vi. 280–1

Queensberry friend of, iii. 175

Queensberry, Ds of, governs, iii. 195

Reading visited by, vi. 490, 572

recovery of, would quash opposition, vi. 506

Regency Bill opposed by, vi. 298

resignation of, v. 537, vii. 61

resignation of, will make Spain bolder, v. 538, 539

resignation threatened by, v. 30–1

restoration of: in sight, v. 557–8; rumoured, viii. 366

Robinson attacked by, iv. 453

Rockingham called on by, though he was formerly ejected from the house, vii. 181

Rockingham ministry charged by, with perfidy, vi. 425

Rockingham ministry favoured by, vi. 382

Rockingham must aid, vii. 246

——'s coolness with, viii. 350

——'s faction deserts, vii. 199

rumour of acceptance by, of administration. vi. 410

'Sabine farm' of, v. 518

St Malo's capture never intended by, v. 213

Sandwich arouses jealousy of, iv. 138

—— hated by, iv. 38

—— opposed by, iv. 222

—— proscribed by, vi. 161

Scrope almost fights with, i. 458

Seals to be taken by, v. 22

seat of, *see* Hayes

secession from Parliamentary majority threatened but retracted by, v. 86

secession of, in House of Lords, vii. 256

second son, ix. 487n

second son of, in opposition, a proof that eloquence has not degenerated, ix. 212

secretary at war application of, rejected, ii. 552

secretary at war's post coveted by, iii. 168

secretaryship of state accepted by, for southern province, v. 17

secretaryship of state expected by, v. 12

secretaryship of state expected for, iv. 461

secretaryship of state for West Indies not permitted by, v. 104

secretaryship of state goes to, v. 103

Shelburne may consider himself political heir to, viii. 379

—— proscribed by, vi. 161

sister attacks, iv. 507n

sister mourns for, viii. 415

sister of, iv. 406, vii. 451n, viii. 194n

sister of, resembles him, vii. 557, viii. 379

sister sends letters of, to the *Test* to show that he cheated her, v. 46

situation of, unchanged, vi. 543

Somersetshire man at Bath calls, 'your Majesty,' vi. 425–6

son compared with, ix. 407, 449, 452, 487

Spanish negotiations wanted by, to be discussed in House, v. 553

Spanish war should be avoided by, v. 544

Spencer, Hon. John, leaves reversion of estate to, vi. 277

Stanley recalled by, v. 536

Stuart Mackenzie asks Mann about chances of help from, vi. 469

success of, probably unexpected by him, viii. 388

sun of, broke forth after Seven Years' War, viii. 356

Talbot's advice to D. of Newcastle on resignation of, v. 540

Temple again unites with, viii. 14

—— demands equal power with, vi. 538

—— deplores violence of, vii. 167

—— enjoys reflected glory of, viii. 517

—— made by, to refuse Irish post and stay in House of Lords, v. 485

—— may be proposed by, for Treasury post, vi. 433

—— offended at promise of, to aid Bute's friends, vi. 436

—— quarrels with, vii. 263

——'s consent needed by, to join administration, vi. 307–8

——'s demand for George Grenville refused by, vi. 436

——'s treachery disappoints, vi. 309–10

—— urges, to retain his place, v. 346

—— would have Irish post and blue ribbon according to demands of, v. 92

Test, The, attacks, v. 38

third expedition planned by, v. 243

Tories abandon, v. 553

Tories hate, iv. 510

Tories support, in attempt to oust Hessian troops, v. 33–4

Townshend, Charles, encouraged by absence of, from House of Commons, vi. 492–3

—— half-ally of, v. 553

—— rejected by, as Chancellor of the Exchequer, vi. 442

—— resents being made Chancellor of the Exchequer by, vi. 493

—— told by, to become Chancellor of the Exchequer, not Paymaster, vi. 439–40

Turin candidate to be proposed by, to George III, v. 507–8

Turkey would oblige, by impertinence, v. 537

turns against Rockingham ministry, vi. 413

venal, v. 541

verses by, to Garrick, disclaim ambition, vii. 387

vice-treasury of Ireland granted to, iii. 241

victory does not resign with, vi. 15

voted for, as commissioner, i. 437–8

Wales, Ps of, denounced by, as 'secret influence,' vii. 195

Walpole, Sir Edward, calls on, iii. 371

Walpole, Horatio (1678–1757), debates with, iii. 168–9

—— thanks, iii. 371

Walpole, Sir Robert, acquitted by, in speech, iii. 370

war hints will certainly cure, vii. 32

war talk revives, vii. 156

war would restore faculties of, vii. 78

Westminster scrutiny investigation demanded by, iv. 123

Weymouth said to be in league with, vii. 259

Whigs may detain Hessian troops to thwart, v. 33–4

Widdrington resembled by, vii. 264

wife of, said to think him imbecile, vii. 74

Wilkes quarrels with, in print, vii. 163

Williams's witticism on resignation of, iii. 27

Winchilsea will not act with, v. 99

Winnington answers charges of, against Carteret, ii. 351

——'s witticism on resignation of, iii. 27

——'s witticism on turncoat politics of, ii. 540

Wood to mention to, Mann's request for promotion, v. 483

Pitt, William (1759–1806), prime minister; M.P.:

behaviour of, in House of Commons, praised, ix. 437

burnt in effigy, ix. 604

Charlotte, Q., protects, ix. 680, 683

father attended by, viii. 371

father compared with, ix. 407, 449, 452, 487

foreign ministers proclaim C.J. Fox as superior to, ix. 486

fortification plan of, adopted to please D. of Richmond, but defeated, ix. 629–30

Fox, C.J., compared with, ix. 407, 452, 487

—— loved and courted, ix. 452

—— reported to be succeeded by, as secretary of state, at age of 22, ix. 295

——'s opposition makes success of, remarkable, ix. 407

George III abuses, while raving, ix. 685

—— alienated by, from sons, ix. 680

——averse to, before insanity, ix. 680–1

——'s offer of prime ministry said to be rejected by, ix. 377, 379

—— supports, against majority in House of Commons, ix. 471n

George IV and D. of York averse to, ix. 683

government to be assumed by, ix. 683

Grattan opposes Irish plan of, ix. 589

HW calls, 'our young Cicero,' ix. 278

HW cites, to show that eloquence has not degenerated, ix. 212

HW more interested in father of, than in the son, ix. 487

HW's poor opinion of, ix. 566

Hastings opposed by, ix. 653

House of Commons wounded by, in way which may be fatal to the Constitution, ix. 484

India bill not opposed by, despite boast, ix. 451

indiscreet, ix. 683

Ireland promised equal trade by, ix. 564–5

Irish courtiers fly in the face of, ix. 681

Irish propositions of: Grattan opposes, ix. 589; will be passed by House of Commons, ix. 578

Mann's opinion of, ix. 405

Mann, Horace II, gets no answer from letters to, ix. 678

—— pleased by rejection of Parliamentary reform motion of, ix. 405

may become first lord of the Treasury, ix. 460

mother puts, under uncles' protection, vii. 74

new party may be formed by, ix. 380

Parliamentary reform motion of: defeated, ix. 401–2, 405; to be moved, ix. 399

position of, conspicuous, ix. 314

Powys alienated by rejection by, of reconciliation attempt, ix. 475n

second son of a second son, ix. 487n

shines in Parliament through ill supported, ix. 407

Temple, E., is expected to be secretary of state with, ix. 295

Versailles cabinet upholds, ix. 485

Westminster nominates, for Parliament, ix. 278

youths attached to, ix. 380

Pitt, William Augustus (ca 1728–1809), Gen.; K.B.; M.P.:

at camp at Cox Heath, ix. 320

wife of, v. 245, ix. 320

Pitt, Mrs William Augustus. See Howe, Mary

Pitt family:

army increase opposed by, in Parliament, i. 410

Egmont's Faction Detected never forgotten by, iv. 31

Pitt's death during Parliament session lucky for, viii. 388

Secret Committee not attended by, i. 366

Pitti, Cavaliere:
Del Vernaccia, Mme, attended by, ii. 112
Rinaldi's duel with, prevented, i. 111–12
sale of effects of, i. 53
Pitti, Nerozzo, Capt. in Tuscan army:
Franchini tells lies about, v. 510–1
Pitti, Palazzo:
apartment and guardhouse added to, vi. 258, 290–1
approaches to, levelled, vi. 124
architect alters additions to, vi. 291
Boboli amphitheatre faces back of, ix. 586
Botta changes pictures and furniture in, vi. 206
—— furnishes apartment in, for Leopold, vi. 157
—— lowers place before, after first raising it, vi. 290
—— plans guardhouses for, vi. 124
—— prepares, for Leopold II, vi. 123
—— rearranges pictures in, according to gilding of frames, vi. 246, 291
——'s discourse about his alterations at, vi. 178–9
Calvin's and Luther's portraits expelled from, vi. 179, 246, 291
casino at, vi. 258, 290–1
Charles III shoots at tapestry in, vii. 237–8
church to be added to, vi. 258
Cocchi and Mann visit, to see cenacolo, iv. 489
corridor from, to old palace, ii. 391
Cosimo III's travels said to be preserved in, ix. 97
dinner served at great hall in, vi. 367
English houses cost more than, viii. 93
Fox permitted to visit most sacred parts of, in sedan chair, vi. 528
Francis I has not as yet stripped, iii. 82–3
Francis III covets furniture of, ii. 323
Giovanni Gastone's oratory in, iv. 489
gold taken from furnishings in, made into plate for Leopold II, ix. 231
Grand Maîtresse's apartment in, drawing rooms held in, vi. 368
guards at, doubled, i. 238
(?) HW has seen Craon receive homage at, for Francis I, vi. 427
hailstorm damages, vi. 77
heating arrangements at, vi. 291
kitchenware from, sold, i. 53
Leopold's aversion to, vii. 253
Mann escorts Karl Alexander to, iv. 376
—— must not apologize for writing so much about alterations in, vi. 303
—— performs New Year's ceremonies at, viii. 346
Maria Amelia prefers stables to, ix. 301
Modena, Ds of, shows, to daughter, ii. 227–8
pictures in, rearranged by Botta, vi. 178–9, 246, 291

Pietro da Cortona's ceiling at, cleaned, v. 556
Pitt, Thomas, names his house after, vi. 33
posterity will be indifferent to revolutions in, vi. 303
refurnished for Leopold, v. 556–7
Richecourt fears that the Spaniards may rob, ii. 295
stoves installed in, vi. 576
Titian painting banished from state apartment in, vi. 179
treasures of, not removed, i. 380
Walpole, Bns, takes Franceschi's house near, ii. 391
Walpole, Sir Robert, would enjoy, ii. 212
Zoffany had right to take down any painting in, viii. 540
Pitti Gaddi family:
collection of: Mann sends catalogues of, to England, viii. 80; to be sold, viii. 80
Leopold buys bust and pictures of, ix. 170
Pitti Gaddi. See also Gaddi, Gaspero
Pitti Palace. See Pitti, Palazzo
'Pittsburgh':
HW's name for Anne Pitt's house, viii. 15
Pitture antiche di Ercolano, Le:
Albani might procure, for HW, v. 262
await shipment at Leghorn, v. 318–19
Charles III does not distribute, generously, v. 142
—— hedges publication of, with precautions, vi. 457
—— restricts new volume of, that recipients may not sell their copies, vi. 35
expected at Leghorn from Naples, vi. 533
HW has only first volume and catalogue of, vi. 452
HW receives, v. 363, vi. 568
HW sees copy of, v. 291
HW thanks Mann for, v. 327
HW thanks Mann for his trouble over, v. 278
HW wants copy of royal edition of, v. 131, 262
HW wants later volumes of, if printed, v. 363
HW wants new volume of, vi. 25
HW wants other volumes of, vi. 422, 452
HW would exchange SH imprints for, v. 131, 262
Hamilton might be jealous of Mann over, vi. 547
Mann, gets, and will get further volumes too, vi. 547
—— has long tried to get new volumes of, vi. 35
—— has never ceased trying to get, for HW, v. 272
—— hopes, is on way to England, vi. 533
—— obtains, for HW, vi. 457

—— sends bill of lading for, to HW, v. 324, vi. 547, 557, 559, 561, 562

—— sends bill of lading for 5th volume of, vii. 109

—— sends second bill of lading for, to HW, vi. 559

—— should have bought, from Viviani instead of waiting for Sir James Gray, v. 299

—— to get, for HW, v. 142

prints in, flatter the originals, v. 379

remaining volumes of, said to have gone to Leghorn, vi. 477

unlikely to be completed after Charles III's departure for Spain, v. 363

Pius V (Antonio, later Michele Ghislieri) (1504–72), pope 1566–72; saint:

Cosimo I said to have been forced by, to wed Camilla Martelli, viii. 16

Pius VI (Giovanni Angelo Braschi) (1717–99), pope 1775–99:

Albany, Cts of, invited by, to convent at Rome, ix. 106

Alfieri imposes upon, ix. 397

antidotes said to be taken by, against poison, viii. 467

blessings distributed by, ix. 283

Bologna's dispute with, ix. 85

bulls of, have blunted horns, ix. 85

Butta su used by, for couvre salope, viii. 107

Canadian adherents of, joined American colonists, viii. 161

cardinals' hats sold by, ix. 568

cardinals' promotion postponed by, to save money for his family, ix. 568

cardinals to be created by, in bedchamber, viii. 477

cardinals to be made by, viii. 479

Catherine II asks, to reestablish Jesuits in Russia, ix. 389

ceremony for, of taking possession, viii. 131, 136, 145

Cesena, Bp of, ordered by, to reward girls, viii. 107

Charles III may be persuaded by, to admit Jesuits, viii. 106

clergy regulated by edicts of, viii. 107

consistory appointed by, to communicate Joseph II's reply to request to visit him, ix. 239

Cowper might get cardinal's hat from, ix. 572

—— should ask, for bishopric for one of his sons, ix. 606

despised at Rome, ix. 383

education of, not so polite as his predecessor's, viii. 275

Falconieri, Ps, appointed by, to wait on Ds of Gloucester, viii. 164

family of, might be provided for by wealth from suppressed convents, ix. 594

Florentine carnival not suppressed in compliment to, ix. 243

French not spoken by, viii. 275

(?) Friedrich II of Hesse visits, by back stairs, viii. 275

Gloucester, D. and Ds of, courteously treated by, viii. 174

—— shown attentions by, viii. 190

Gloucester, D. of, pleases, by giving surgical instruments to hospital at Rome, viii. 129

Gordon, Lord George, would be sent to devil by, ix. 131

Gordon rioters plunder more Protestants than followers of, ix. 61

grandmother of, consumed by internal fire, viii. 467

HW calls: 'Madam of Babylon,' viii. 162; 'Pontifex Maximus,' ix. 589; 'your holy neighbour,' ix. 544

HW expects Mann to tell him of lamentations of, ix. 243

HW inquires about return of, after visiting Joseph II, to Italy, ix. 275

HW mentions, ix. 272

HW prefers, to Joseph II, ix. 596

HW wonders whether, will be most afraid of France, Spain, or poison, ix. 86

health of: better, viii. 470; illness considered serious, viii. 461; much better, viii. 479; rheumatism, viii. 467; very ill, viii. 467

Hervey, Bp, urges, to put Irish bishops on footing with Gallican church, viii. 430

illness of, concealed at Rome, viii. 467

indifference of, to earthquake, ix. 383, 391

Jesuits at Castel St Angelo might have been released by, had not Charles III intervened, viii. 115

Jesuits released by, viii. 99

Joseph II consents to receive, but visit will be futile, ix. 245

—— humbles, ix. 400

—— said to wall up doors at time of visit of, ix. 275

——'s attack on Holland instead of one on church property, probably pleases, ix. 544

Kingston, Ds of, can get her treasures from, only when her authorization is proved not to be a forced one, viii. 234

—— cannot be cleansed by, with all the holy water in the Tiber, viii. 126

—— entrusted, with her treasure, viii. 123

—— friend of, viii. 175

—— gets promise from, never to give up her treasure without well-authenticated order, viii. 167

—— may find her valuables appropriated by, viii. 162

—— may fly to, for dispensation, viii. 123

—— may prove an embarrassment to, by leaving treasure in his custody, viii. 167

[Pius VI, *continued*]
—— may revisit Rome, under protection of, viii. 123
—— told by, that her jewels and furniture will be kept for her at Rome, viii. 83–4
—— will shock, by her trial, viii. 149
leave asked by, of Joseph II, to pay him visit in Vienna, ix. 238–9
Leopold II does not compliment, with suppression of carnival, ix. 243
Lepri gives wealth to, ix. 384–5
——'s donation to, declared invalid, ix. 587, 589
Mann gets weekly bulletin of illness of, viii. 461, 467
—— informs, of Rodney's victory, ix. 24
—— might have to demand Ds of Kingston's treasures from, viii. 191
Marie-Antoinette's daughter disappoints, viii. 470
meat will be less permitted by, if Necker roots out the monks, ix. 21
Messini earthquake attributed by, to suppression of Inquisition in Sicily, ix. 383
nephew of, in France, might receive rich benefice on Dauphin's birth, viii. 470
Orford, Cts of, carried in litter of, viii. 317
Pitt, Anne, might be made Ps Fossani by, viii. 360
pompous, simple, and at heart a Jesuit, viii. 106
Pontine marsh drainage project of, viii. 343, 379, ix. 383
priests' costume regulated by, forbidding powdered hair, viii. 107
Rohan's censure by, imprudent, ix. 658
Roman Catholics permitted by, to eat meat in Lent because of fish shortage, ix. 17, 24
Roman governor's proposal to close theatres and stop carnival rejected by, ix. 383
Rome crowded with strangers to see ceremony of *possesso* of, viii. 145
Russian minister asks, to reestablish Jesuits in Russia, ix. 389–90
St Peter's to be provided with new sacristy built by, viii. 343, ix. 383–4
Scottish Presbyterians forswear, tooth and nail, viii. 475
Sforza Cesarini will dispute Lepri inheritance with, ix. 385
simple man, viii. 115
Stuart, Charlotte, receives congratulatory answer from, ix. 550
suppression of Galluzzi's history might have been demanded by, as price for making Maximilian Bp of Münster, ix. 80
uncle ordered by, to reward pretty and virtuous girls, viii. 107
unpopularity of, ix. 587–8
Venetians threatened by, with interdiction, viii. 189
Vienna to be visited by, ix. 250

Vienna visit of: a farce to balance tragic wars, ix. 283; disapproved by cardinals, ix. 250; does not interrupt Joseph II's suppression of convents, ix. 283; expensive, humiliating, and useless, ix. 384
York, Cardinal, persuades, to banish Alfieri, ix. 397
—— will not be permitted by, to assume crown, ix. 526
Young Pretender given allowance by, but not recognized as king, viii. 244
—— never permitted by, to assume crown, ix. 526
——'s pension from, partly granted to Cts of Albany, ix. 107
—— though denied royal status, is allowed by, to make his daughter a duchess, ix. 552–3
Pizzighettone:
Lobkowitz to garrison, ii. 513
Maria Theresa gives, to Charles Emmanuel III, i. 379
Pizzo:
earthquake account mentions, ix. 376
Place Bill. *See under* Parliament: acts of
Place d'Espagne, Naples:
Pontano lives in, ii. 56
Placentia. *See* Piacenza
Place Tax. *See under* Tax
Plague:
at Danzig, ix. 422
at Messina, ii. 252, 256, 261–2, 269–70, 274
at Reggio, ii. 282, 288, 301–2
at Smyrna, x. 48
Egyptian, ix. 582
English naval captains seize vessels, regardless of fear of, ii. 256
Florentines guard against, ii. 252, 288
French ship brings, to Leghorn, i. 105, vii. 24
HW hears, is spreading, ii. 294
HW wants to hear about, ii. 284
in Bengal, vii. 282
in Calabria, ii. 270, 282–3, 288
in Hungary, ii. 122
in London when HW was a child, ix. 423
in Sicily, ii. 283
Italian, HW does not like, v. 369
Leghorn alarmed by arrival of, in ship from Algiers, i. 105
Leghorn repels ship because of, ii. 262
London merchants object to precautions about, ii. 282
Mathews may bring, ii. 279
Neapolitan court may flee from, to Aquila, ii. 302
Neapolitans hoard provisions against, ii. 288
Neapolitans mass troops on borders, under pretence of guarding against, ii. 295–6
Orlov fears, on Chios, vii. 233
quarantine forty days for, ii. 275
rumour of, in London, v. 427

Tuscan precautions against, ii. 270, 285
Tuscan quarantines against, futile, ii. 295
Tuscany mobilizes under pretence of guarding against, ii. 285
vinegar used to prevent, ii. 270
Plaid:
offensive to England, iii. 471
Queensberry, D. of, dressed in, iii. 471
Scotch, nightcap of, iii. 302
suppression of, in Scotland, x. 32
waistcoat of, Frederick, P. of Wales, wears, iv. 131
Plaisance. See Piacenza
Plaisanteri, the:
Alberoni's lands in, seized by Traun, ii. 199
Plans, Elevations, and Sections . . . of Houghton. See under Ware, Isaac
Plant; plants:
Mann sends, to Bubb Dodington, iv. 253
See also Auriculas
Plantagenet family:
Huntingdon and Ds of Beaufort represent, in Florence, vii. 406
Plantagenets:
scene of, reenacted, vi. 303
Plantations:
Board of Trade to control, iv. 259
Plaster:
HW prefers Morpheus statue in, ii. 561
Plaster, medicinal:
applications of, v. 78
quack, cancer supposed to be cured by, iv. 291
Plasterers:
HW hurries, at SH, iv. 371
Plaster of Paris:
Zoffany depicts statues in Tribune as if they were casts in, viii. 527
Plata, La. See La Plata
Plate:
Botta prepares, for Leopold II, vi. 123
carried abroad by Cts of Orford, ix. 158
cases of, (?) Cowper to send, to banker at Florence, ix. 661
chest of, Young Pretender's staff bring to him, from Rome, ii. 433–4
church, in Florence: may be sacrificed to import food, vi. 447, 448; sent to the mint without Clement XIII's permission, vi. 475–6
Cowper to have, fetched from England to Florence, vii. 449
Craon may pawn, ii. 134
Craon, Princesse de, sends, by sea to Leghorn, vi. 536
Fane's, i. 135, ii. 472
Fermor lacks, iii. 148
Florentine, may have to be carried to mint, i. 239
Franceschi's, sold, i. 122
Frederick II gives, to Hyndford, ii. 89, 107
George III gives, to godchildren, viii. 206

gold, for Leopold II's household, made from furnishings in Palazzo Vecchio, ix. 231
HW's, at Arlington St, untouched by housebreakers, vii. 285
Jesuits', seized, vii. 506
Lepri gives, to Pius VI, ix. 384
Mann buys, vi. 357
—— pawns, for Theodore of Corsica, iv. 378–9
——'s, Horace Mann II to sell, to settle estate, ix. 678
—— to buy, ii. 472
Old Pretender's, vi. 385
Orford, Cts of, had: list of, sent to England by Mozzi, ix. 163; Orford's claims for, on mother, ix. 158, 169; Orford, Cts of, exchanged, in England for small set taken to Italy, ix. 144
Rinuccini leaves piece of, to daughter-in-law, iii. 461
Rosenberg's not sold for debt, vii. 294
set of, Du Quesne has, on shipboard, v. 255
Seymour, Lady Frances, buys, iv. 183
silver-gilt, (?) travelling, Tencin gives, to Young Pretender, i. 114
Stuart Mackenzie gets, for Spanish embassy, v. 508
Tylney's, at Naples, to be sold for servants' benefit, ix. 534
Young Pretender receives, ix. 525
Plate-covers. See Dish-covers
Plates:
copper, of Hancarville's book, vii. 448–9
Mann lacks, for 16, iv. 387
—— to buy, ii. 472
of Chelsea china, vi. 121–2
'Platon, Father.' See Levshin, Petr Georgievich
Platz, ——, Gen.:
Artimiso attacked by, ii. 488
Leutrum joined by, iii. 227
Plautus:
Amphitryon, (?) Mann paraphrases, i. 120
Play; plays:
fashionable in London, iii. 342
fashionable people act, in England, viii. 86
more dignified than politics, v. 542
numerous in London, iii. 464
officers give, for Friedrich Wilhelm, iii. 265
opera prices made equal to those of, in London, iv. 410
politics less dignified than, v. 542
Portici, Signora, considers, inferior to burlettas, iv. 357
strolling companies act, in barns, viii. 371
Suares family give, for Modenese princess, i. 65, 99, 100, 104
unfashionable in London, ii. 119
See also Comedy; Theatre; Tragedy
Players. See Actors
Playhouse. See Theatre

Pleasure:
    English make a business of, ix. 110
    Londoners in pursuit of, ignore want of
        money and weight of taxes, ix. 243
Pléiade, the, French ship:
    English ships pursue, v. 303
    escape of, v. 188
Plenipotentiary:
    Hamilton becomes, vii. 293
    Mann wants to be, vii. 293
    Stuart Mackenzie becomes, v. 471–2
Pleurisy:
    Italians get, in cold spell, iv. 143
    occurrences of, iv. 232, 244, vi. 560
Pleuritic inflammatory fever. *See under* Fever
Pleydell, John Cleeve (ca 1736–1816), army
    officer; equerry to the D. of Gloucester:
    Gloucester, D. of, accompanied by, viii. 311
    Udny gets letter from, viii. 311
Plimouth. *See* Plymouth
Pliny (Caius Plinius Cæcilius Secundus) the
    younger (?62–ca 113), orator and states-
    man:
    Damer, Mrs, writes Latin like, ix. 184
    English architecture as classic as villas of,
        vii. 313
    Epistles of, Cork translates, iv. 454n
Plombières:
    Richecourt to take baths at, v. 62
Plover's eggs:
    HW receives, from Lord Orford, ix. 143
Plum; plums:
    cake of, i. 263
Plumard de Dangeul, René-Joseph (b. 1722),
    maître des comptes:
    HW takes, in coach, to Cts of Hertford,
        vii. 6
Plumber. *See* Plumer
Plume; plumes:
    Alexander wears, in opera, viii. 222
    American, Mann should flaunt, before
        Richecourt, v. 347
    Chartres, Duchesse de, wears, viii. 222
    HW mentions, iv. 375
    ladies covered with, in England, viii. 86
    Mann should not be paid with, vi. 226
Plumer, Anne (1690–1776), m. (1711) James
    Hamilton, 7th E. of Abercorn:
    auction attended by, i. 477–8
    Devonshire, Ds of, talks to, of 'ugly
        women,' i. 478
    ugly, i. 478
Plumer, Walter (? 1682–1746), M.P.:
    witticism by, on Pulteney's Treasury ap-
        pointments, ii. 350
Plum porridge:
    out of fashion among people of rank, ix.
        124
Plumptre, John (1679–1751), M.P.:
    named in Secret Committee lists, i. 384
Plumptre, Russell (1709–93), Regius Professor
    of Physic at Cambridge:
    Gray not aided by, vii. 329

Plunket, William, journeyman apothecary:
    Maclaine's accomplice, iv. 168
Plutarch (? 46–ca 120), Greek essayist and
    biographer:
    Pitt will look well in future editions of,
        v. 558
'Pluto, iron':
    Burke's term for Thurlow, ix. 684
Plutus:
    Clive compared to, vii. 381
Plymouth, E. of. *See* Windsor, Other Hick-
    man (1751–99)
Plymouth:
    Conway driven to, by storm, ix. 115
    Dunmore succeeds Churchill as governor of,
        iii. 62
    English men of war chased into, viii. 506
    English naval strength at, vii. 40
    English prisoners from Oswego and Quebec
        arrive at, v. 18
    Feilding brings captured Dutch convoy to,
        ix. 3
    fortications at, strengthened, ix. 183
    French and Spanish fleet approaches, viii.
        506, ix. 183
    French and Spanish fleets disappear from,
        viii. 511
    French merchant at, has concealed weapons,
        ii. 402
    French prisoners from Jersey arrive at, ix.
        115
    Goldsworthy, Mrs, to visit her father at,
        ii. 158
    Keppel returns to, viii. 400
    men of war from, to join Norris, ii. 393
Plymouth, ship:
    at Port Mahon, i. 285
Po, river:
    Charles Emmanuel III on other side of,
        iii. 156
    English ships to guard mouth of, i. 455
    Gages recrosses, iii. 291
    German troops oppose Spaniards at, iii. 267
    Lobkowitz builds bridges across, iii. 41
    overflows, iii. 163, v. 510
    Patapan not to drown in, i. 56
    Spaniards control, iii. 276
Pocket; pockets:
    coat, *canonici* and *abbés* forbidden to wear,
        v. 224
    in abbé's costume, i. 136
    Louis XV carries bread in, iv. 340
    Sandwich carries dice in, iv. 113
Pocket book:
    Cerretesi enters descriptions in, i. 503
    Craon wants, i. 194
    Craon, Princesse de, shows, to Electress, i.
        424
    Ferrers sends, by Vaillant, to Mrs Clifford,
        v. 402
    Nugent's payments from Lady Mountjoy
        revealed by, i. 271
    Rudd, Mrs, pulls out, viii. 153

sardonyx: Craon receives, from HW, i. 414;
HW to send, to Craon, i. 222
Pocket glass:
Coventry, Cts of, looks at, in last illness,
v. 451
old women should carry, to remind them
of their own death's heads, ix. 584
See also Mirror
Poder, Spanish ship:
capture of, ii. 414
in Spanish fleet, i. 286
sunk, ii. 417
Poellnitz, Bns von. *See* Stuart, Lady Anne
(1746–ca 1819)
Poet; poets:
English, epigrams poured forth by, ix. 612
Florentine, derided by HW, ix. 612
insipid, HW's reflections on, iii. 27–8
Poet laureate:
Cibber recommends Jones as, iv. 214
Poetry:
Albany, Cts of, reads, ix. 106
gone to bed, or into prose, vii. 212
HW's knowledge of, v. 368
Lucan, Bns, has turn for, viii. 475
Poggio a Caiano:
Cappello, Bianca, and Francesco I die at,
vii. 296
Cowper to be entertained at, vii. 296
HW has print of, vi. 222
Leopold and Maria Louisa to take Ferdi-
nand of Naples and Maria Carolina to,
for hunting, ix. 594
Tuscan Court moves to, vii. 296
Tuscan Court to visit, to hear Cowper's
farces, vii. 325–6
York, D. of, eats dinner at, prepared by,
Mann's servants, vi. 222
Poggio Imperiale:
Botta's French horns at, announce Peter
III's overturn, vi. 63
Craon not allowed to sleep at, viii. 23
Craon, Princesse de, obtains apartment at,
for herself only, viii. 23
—— pays court at, to Leopold, vi. 536
Craons play cards at, viii. 23
Electress hoped to live at, iv. 414–15
enlarged and redecorated since HW saw it,
but façade towards avenue is still ugly,
ix. 598
enlarged but not yet completed, vii. 296
Ferdinand of Naples and Maria Carolina
live quietly at, with Leopold and Maria
Louisa, ix. 598
furniture at, iv. 116
Gloucester, D. and Ds of, see all Leopold's
family at, viii. 297
guards dismissed from, by Joseph II's request, vii. 112
HW's favourite palace, vi. 41
hangings at, Bianca Cappello's portrait in,
iv. 414–15
Joseph II expected at, viii. 108

Joseph II, Leopold, and Maria Louisa at,
vii. 111–12
Leopold and family move to, from Castello,
ix. 421
Leopold and Maria Louisa retire to, with
two servants only, vii. 449
Leopold and Maria Louisa stay shut up
in, during mourning, vi. 526
Leopold and Maria Louisa to take Ferdinand of Naples and Maria Carolina to,
ix. 594
Leopold and Maria Louisa visit, vi. 424,
427
Leopold lives at, like a country gentleman,
ix. 498–9
—— met by people in lanes and roads
near, vii. 122
—— must have, as summer residence, vii.
296
Mann's and P. of Mecklenburg's entertainment at Court at, more flattering than if
in Florence, vi. 438
Mann sends news of Clinton's success to,
ix. 71
—— visits Botta at, vi. 40–1
Maria Amelia is lodged at, ix. 301
Paul I and wife to be lodged at, ix. 250–1
Tuscan Court in retreat at, while princes
are inoculated, viii. 7
Pointer; pointers:
HW does not turn, to grass, vii. 497
Patapan shaken and bruised by, ii. 71
Poirot, Domenico Matteo de (d. 1775), Barone
di Saint-Odile, 1752; Tuscan minister to
Rome 1752–74:
Clement XIII does not summon, because
he does not wait in Torreggiani's ante-
chamber, vi. 573
Florence to be visited by, on way to settle
Tuscan disputes with Benedict XIV at
Rome, iv. 305
minister to Rome, to aggrandize priests and
inquisition, iv. 308
Regency council to be joined by, in Flor-
ence, iv. 305–6
Richecourt bars visitors from, iv. 308
——'s antagonist, in Vienna, iv. 305, 308
Valenti asked by, about Benedict XIV's
claim to Monte Santa Maria, iv. 428
Poison:
Clement XIV and his confectioner said to
have died of, viii. 42–4, 49–50
in 'vipers' of the Church, ix. 245
Pius VI may fear France or Spain more
than, viii. 86
Poisson, Abel-François (1727–81), Seigneur de
Vandières; Marquis de Marigny:
Argenson asked by, for *cordon bleu*, iv. 228
brother of Mme de Pompadour, iv. 227
Frenchman seeks, in church of San Lorenzo,
iv. 228
Le Blanc accompanies, in Florence, iv. 228
Leghorn visited by, iv. 236

[Poisson, Abel-François, *continued*]
nickname of, iv. 228
Rena captivates, v. 162
Poisson, Jeanne-Antoinette (1721–64), m.
(1741) Charles-Guillaume Le Normand
d'Étiolles; Marquise de Pompadour:
Bernis and Choiseul advanced by, v. 242
Bernis fell because of insults to, vii. 144
brother of, iv. 227, v. 162
cameos made popular by, v. 201
death of, expected, vi. 212
devotional turn of, iv. 530
Durini refuses to visit, v. 216
English stocks bought by, to profit by
Peace of Paris, ix. 357
engraving done by, v. 201
eye said to be lost by, vi. 30
fireworks given by, iv. 338
German studied by, v. 514
Guerchy, Comtesse de, may be successor
to, vi. 239
HW calls, 'Bathsheba,' vi. 4
jubilee said to be observed by, at Ca-
pucines', iv. 236
Louis XV influenced by love of, for peace,
iv. 530
—— makes, *dame du palais* to his wife, iv.
530
—— mismanaged by, vi. 30
—— provided by, with Irish mistress after
her own physical inadequacy, iv. 542
—— said to be abandoned by, iv. 236
—— said to be separated from, iv. 530, 542
——'s expenses not all caused by, iv. 500
——'s mistress, vi. 212
Maria Theresa's correspondence with, v.
258
Matignon, Mme de, said to have been introduced by, to Louis XV, vi. 4
rouge may be abandoned by, iv. 530
Souvré's witticism when at home of, v. 514
Taaffe brings turtles and pineapples to, in
post-chaise, iv. 289
Yarmouth, Cts of, the counterpart of, iv.
91
Poitiers:
HW fancies himself at, v. 212
Poix, P. de. *See* Noailles, Philippe-Louis-
Marc-Antoine de (1752–1819)
Poix, Princesse de. *See* Beauvau, Anne-Louise-
Marie de (1750–1833)
Poland, K. of. *See* Frederick Augustus I
(1670–1733); Frederick Augustus II (1696–
1763); John II (Kasimir) (1609–72); John
(Sobieski) (1629–96)
Poland, Q. of. *See* Maria Josefa (1699–1757);
Opalinska, Katharina (1680–1747)
Poland:
acquisitiveness and cupidity of, i. 168
Austria and Russia may dismember Turkey
in fashion of, ix. 399
Austrian claims on Dalmatia as clear as
those upon, viii. 11–12

Austrians march into, vii. 145
Brühl's son excluded as nuncio to, vi. 192
Catherine II and Joseph II to meet in, ix.
61
Catherine II asked by, to restore Biron to
Courland, vi. 118–19
—— to visit her acquisitions in, ix. 44
Catholics of, Turkish Grand Signor invites,
to turn Mohammedan, vii. 81
Choiseul might espouse quarrel of, viii. 11
confederates of: Jablonowsky, Ps, sent by,
to England, as ambassadress, vii. 319; Louis
XV and French ministers vainly encourage,
vii. 331; Talmond, Princesse de, emissary
of, vii. 319; Turks unable to aid, vii. 319;
Young Pretender may be invited by, vii.
318
dissidents in: Clement XIII cannot persuade Catholic princes to crusade against,
vi. 574; Clement XIII orders mass and
procession for destruction of, vi. 577; have
not a cheeseparing left, vii. 328; Louis XVI
might want to destroy, viii. 11
English fleet should come to aid of, vii.
475
France and Spain may be inspired by
partition of, to divide Milan with Sardinia,
vii. 469
France sends officers to, vii. 338
France turns, against Catherine II, vii. 338
Frederick II defeats Russians in, v. 237
—— drives Russians into, v. 246–7
—— quarters, vii. 437
—— said to receive assurances from, ii. 512
—— the pickpocket of, viii. 55
—— to meet Catherine II and Joseph II
in, ix. 44
—— to review troops in area newly-ac-
quired from, viii. 18
Holland might be divided like, ix. 539
Joseph II said to have reported disturbances in, to Leopold, ix. 44
—— to visit his acquisitions in, ix. 44
king chosen for, vi. 248
king's death may cause war in, vi. 177
letter from, reveals Russian news, i. 20
Mann suspects authorship of English letters
about, vii. 502–3
Maria Theresa's reasons for reluctantly consenting to partition of, vii. 439
ministers from and to, *see under* Minister
news must be sought in, vii. 505
nobility cause of ruin of, vii. 436
nuncio to, expelled, vi. 192
Old Pretender's revenue from wife's lands
in, vi. 387
partition of: ix. 613n; accomplished in
short time, ix. 201; dialogue satirizes, vii.
556; HW ridicules, viii. 55; impudent force
the cause of, viii. 365; Joseph II's invasion
of Venice made credible by, viii. 37–8;
Mann enjoys dialogue about, vii. 564;

Maria I might accede to, viii. 310; said to be planned, vii. 419
prime minister of, *see* Brühl, Heinrich
ruby supposedly pawned by, to Prince James Sobieski, ix. 525
Stanislas I not reelected by, vi. 402
Stanislas II king of, vi. 253
Talmond, Princesse de, from, iv. 44
Turkish sultan withdraws protection from, viii. 40
Voltaire lauds ravagers of, vii. 515
wars in, out of England's reach, vii. 432
Young Pretender may have gone to be king of, vii. 324
—— may marry in, iv. 44
—— said to have joined Catholics and Dissidents in, vii. 337
——'s alleged journey to, reported to Stanislas II, vii. 352
Polastron, Gabrielle-Yolande-Claude-Martine de (ca 1749–93), m. (1767) Armand-Jules-François, Comte (Duc, 1780) de Polignac:
Clermont's letter from, ix. 356–7
Devonshire, Ds of, exchanges presents with, ix. 427
husband of, ix. 409
Marie-Antoinette's favourite, ix. 357n, 409
Polcevera, valley of:
Genoese mob joined by people of, iii. 343
Pole, William de la (1396–1450), 4th E. of Suffolk, cr. (1448) D. of Suffolk:
Bute compared with, vi. 53
Pole; poles:
green, Mann's garden lamps suspended from, ii. 479
Poli, Anna Teresa (Sister Maria Teresa) of Valentano:
Clement XIV's death foretold by, viii. 30, 41–2
prosecution of, viii. 30, 41–2
Police:
English, riots a disgrace to, vii. 13
Polidoro. *See under* Pescetti, Giovanni Battista
Polignac, Comtesse and Duchesse de. *See* Polastron, Gabrielle-Yolande-Claude-Martine de (ca 1749–93)
Polignac, Marquise de. *See* Rioult de Douilly, Marie (1712–84)
Polignac, Armand-Jules-François (1745–1817), Comte and (1780) Duc de:
England visited by, ix. 408–9
Polish language:
St-Germain understands, x. 20
Polish Partition, The. See under Lind, John
Politicians:
arts of, less effective than chance, ix. 248
Politics:
assemblies, balls, operas, and plays more dignified than, v. 542
balls and masquerades replace, in England, vii. 476
English absorption in, vii. 157–8

English credulity about, ii. 305
English indifference to, iv. 260
English ladies addicted to, ix. 476, 483, 495
ephemeral character of, ix. 604
HW adopts from no side, and preaches to nobody, viii. 351
HW compares, with stage, vii. 41
HW considers, a farce except when war is involved, ix. 365
HW continues to avoid, vii. 145, 570, 579
HW glad to have forsaken, vii. 128–9
HW glad to quit, vi. 572
HW hates, vi. 550
HW is done with, ix. 309
HW preferred Newmarket to, as topic at White's, ix. 483
HW retreats from, vi. 300, 304, 308–9, 316, 348, 359–60, 365, 436
HW sick of, viii. 117
HW's mind worn out by, vi. 316
HW's reflections on inability to decide merits of, in heat of events, ix. 142
HW tells Mann not to mention, except to ministers, ix. 459
HW tired of witnessing, vi. 110
Mann's letters avoid subjects of, vii. 71
moderation in, incompatible with modern patriotism, ix. 50
never end, ix. 370
people forced by, into alliance with their enemies, vii. 145
piddling, HW's aversion to, vii. 420
vanity of, HW's reflections on, iii. 4
Poll, Jan van de (?1721–?1801), Dutch deputy to England, 1759:
English mission of, v. 290–1
Poll, Margarethe Cornelia van de (1726–93), m. 1 (1743) Cornelis Munter; m. 2 (1754) Pierre-Chrysostome d'Usson de Bonac, Comte d'Usson:
London visited by, vi. 135
Pollard, Arthur (d. 1754), English consul at Aleppo, 1745–53:
Rena persuades, to spend fortune, v. 162
Pollington, Vct. *See* Savile, Sir John (1719–78)
Pöllnitz, Bns. *See* Stuart, Lady Anne
Pöllnitz, Karl Ludwig, Freiherr von (1692–1775), memoir-writer:
HW does not imitate, vi. 343
writings of, vi. 343n
'Polly Peachum.' *See* Gay, John: *Beggar's Opera*
Polnitz. *See* Pöllnitz
Polonaise; polonaises:
Florentine ladies dress in, ix. 175
Mann ignorant about, i. 152
Polviglio:
Uguccioni gives, to Granvilles, ii. 553–4
Polybius (d. ?122 B.C.), Greek historian:
Histories, Demetrius described by, ii. 422
Polycarpe, Joseph:
(?) José Manoel attacked by, v. 250

Polypus:
occurrence of, viii. 211
Pomatums:
Mann sends, to HW, vii. 407
Pombal, Marqués de. See Carvalho e Melo, Sebastião-José de (1699–1782)
Pomerania:
Calmucks wanted to set fire to villages of, vi. 14
Frederick II drives Russians into, v. 246–7
Peter III may be induced to keep a foothold in, vi. 10–11
—— proclaimed czar in, vi. 1
Pomeroy, Arthur (1723–98), cr. (1783) Bn, and (1791) Vct Harberton:
peerage of, ix. 433
Pomfret Cts of. See Jeffreys, Hon. Henrietta Louisa (d. 1761)
Pomfret, E. of. See Fermor, George (1722–85); Fermor, Thomas (1698–1752)
Pomfret family. See Fermor family
Pompadour, Marquise de. See Poisson, Jeanne-Antoinette
Pompeiata:
Cornelys, Theresa, sang under the name of, vii. 271
Pompey, (?) Mann's dog:
Patapan's 'correspondence' said to excite, ii. 530
Pompons:
mahonnoises replace, in France, v. 52
Ponce de Guerrero, Don Manuel, 4th Conde de Selva Florida:
Peruvians hail, as king, vi. 426
Ponce de Léon y Spinola, Don Joaquín (d. 1743), Duque de Arcos y Maqueda:
wounded, ii. 154
Pond:
of goldfish, at SH, iv. 188
Pondicherry:
Boscawen's fleet sent to, iv. 113
capture of, v. 515
courier carries news of capture of, through Turkey to Italy, v. 523
earlier peace would have spared France the loss of, v. 534
English capture of, viii. 454
Mann will read about, in gazette, v. 516
reduction of, known to Florence, viii. 461
war extends from, to Canada, v. 290
Poniatowski, Stanislas (1732–98). See Stanislas II
Poniatowski, P. Stanislas (1754–1833):
Lind tutor to, vii. 564–5
Ponsonby, Bns. See Molesworth, Hon. Louisa (1749–1824)
Ponsonby, Brabazon (1679–1758), 2d Vct Duncannon, cr. (1739) E. of Bessborough:
Devonshire obtains peerage for, iv. 66
nominated lord justice in Ireland, iv. 426
Ponsonby, Hon. Caroline (d. 1756):
death of, v. 362
Ponsonby, Lady Catherine (1742–89), m.

(1763) Hon. Aubrey Beauclerk, 2d Bn Vere, 1781; 5th D. of St Albans, 1787:
HW thinks Mann has seen, with husband, ix. 191
health of, fever and sore throat, v. 362
Ponsonby, Lady Charlotte (1747–1822), m. (1770) William Fitzwilliam, 4th E. Fitzwilliam:
Fitzwilliam to wed, vii. 213
Ponsonby, Hon. Henry (d. 1745), Maj.-Gen.:
killed at Fontenoy, iii. 42–3
Ponsonby, Hon. Henry (d. ? ca 1756):
death of, v. 362
Ponsonby, John (1713–89), Irish speaker 1756–71:
Selwyn's witticism about gambling of, at Newmarket, v. 7
Ponsonby, Hon. John (d. ca 1756):
death of, v. 362
Ponsonby, William (1704–93), styled Vct Duncannon; 2d E. of Bessborough, 1758:
Admiralty post given to, iii. 256, iv. 157
Admiralty post taken from, v. 25
daughter of, vii. 213
Gray, Sir James, hoped to supplant, as secretary to Ireland, iii. 472
HW to receive answer from, to Riccardi's offer, iii. 387
health of, fever and sore throat, v. 362
Mann buys marble fragment for, from Stosch's collection, v. 192
—— expects Riccardi's offer to be rejected by, iii. 392
—— sends gladiator intaglio to, iv. 159
Mann, Galfridus, procures seeds for, iv. 25
marriage of, iv. 66
postmaster, vi. 311
resignation of, as Joint Postmaster-General, vi. 97, 471
Riccardi's jewelry may be bought by, iii. 361, 372–3, 382, 398
Stosch corresponds with, about Meleager, iv. 159
—— gives or sells intaglio of Gladiator to, for procuring arrears of his pension, i. 212, iv. 157, 159, v. 151
——'s affairs executed by, iv. 70
Treasury post goes to, v. 24
Vere, Bns, the daughter of, ix. 191n
Ponsonby, Hon. William (d. ? ca 1756):
death of, v. 362
Pontano, Don Cicio, Neapolitan abbé:
Acquaviva orders seizure of papers and arrest of, on suspicion of treasonable correspondence, despite Maria Theresa's patent of protection, ii. 55–6
Place d'Espagne, residence of, ii. 56
Thun claims, ii. 56
Pont-de-Beauvoisin:
Young Pretender said to be banished to, with Sheridan and Stafford, iv. 9
Ponte a Santa Trinità:
Azzi attacked on, by coachmen, i. 488

Bosville, Mrs, misbehaves upon, ii. 286
cocchiata moves to, ii. 485
frequented, i. 473
HW prowls about, after supper, i. 473
Henley bridge excelled only by, ix. 613
ladies to walk in Mann's garden instead of, i. 498
Mann frequents, i. 77
masquerades on, at night, i. 97
people prefer, to seeing Mann, i. 97
Vincent calls, unsuitable for duel, ii. 111
whimsical dresses worn by Florentine ladies on, ix. 174
Ponte della Madelena (at Naples):
San Gennaro's relative harangues mob at, viii. 541
Ponte del Reno:
Charles Emmanuel III and Traun at, i. 500
Pontefract:
HW uses, for 'Pomfret,' i. 339
Ponte Molle:
hussars demolish part of, ii. 444
Lobkowitz's army at, ii. 531
Ponte Vecchio:
Riccardi must have bought his jewels on, iii. 73
Strozzi, Principessa, seeks stolen jewels on, iii. 350
York, D. of, looks forward to walking on, vi. 236
Pontifex Maximus:
HW's 's term for Pius VI, ix. 589
Wilkes more conspicuous than, viii. 48
Pontine marshes:
drainage project not needed for, in drought of 1779, viii. 479
Pius VI's drainage project for: expensive failure, ix. 383, 588; may fail from lack of declivity, viii. 479; Romans failed to do it, viii. 343–4
Pontius Pilate (fl. A.D. 26):
Benedict XIV's witticism about, v. 37
Pontneuf, at Paris:
threatening verses posted at, iv. 287
Pontoise:
French parliament may be exiled to, iv. 293
Pontremoli:
Fivizano near, iii. 35
Lobkowitz sends Gorani to, iii. 36
Spanish army threatens approach from, to Tuscany, i. 289
Spanish troops approach, iii. 245
Traun's troops must enter Tuscany through, ii. 76
Ponzio, Pietro, Benedict XIV's surgeon:
Benedict XIV's witticism to, on use of syringe, v. 37
Poona. *See* Puna
Pope, Alexander (ca 1642–1717), 'hatter;' father of the poet:
son of, satirized in *New Lesson for Pope*, ii. 34

Pope, Alexander (1688–1744), poet:
Are These Things So?: attributed to, i. 387; not written by, i. 410
Atterbury's witticism on, iv. 66
Bolingbroke and Swift admired by, ix. 6
Bolingbroke persuaded by friends of, to pay for printing of book, iv. 66
——'s *Letters* printed and altered by, iv. 61
Burlington, Cts of, said to have been furnished by, with inscription for her daughter's picture, ii. 482
—— talks with, at Chiswick, ii. 449
Cibber attacks, ii. 8
——'s quarrel with, satirized in *New Lesson for Pope*, ii. 34–6
death of, iii. 229
Dunciad, The: HW quotes, i. 451; HW transcribes, for Mann, i. 403; Mallet subject of sonnet affixed to, iv. 62; *Rolliad* compared with, ix. 612
Epistle to Cobham, HW quotes, viii. 301
Essay on Criticism, HW quotes, ii. 129
Essay on Man: HW quotes, ii. 36; Warburton's notes to, vi. 184; Wilkes's parody of, vi. 184–5
faults of, iv. 65–6
Frederick, P. of Wales, talks with, i. 143
friends of, publish pamphlets against Bolingbroke, iv. 65
garden of: art and deception used in design of, to make it appear larger, ix. 177; 'improved' by Stanhope, ix. 177–8
HW and Mrs Spence discuss, iv. 189
HW disclaims authorship of verses on, ii. 505
HW quotes, ii. 129, viii. 301
HW quotes lines from English newspaper on death of, ii. 467–8
Halifax's contribution toward Dryden's monument satirized by, v. 140
health of, dropsy, ii. 449
Imitations of Horace: Kinnoull and Tyrawley satirized in, ii. 104; Wortley Montagu and wife satirized in, v. 472n
Lyttelton a friend of, iv. 61
Mallet's relations with, iv. 62
Mann dislikes, i. 403
Marchmont a 'hero' of, iv. 5
Monro mentions, in epigram on doctors, i. 168
Montagu, Lady Mary Wortley, satirized by, iv. 282, v. 472n
Murray's friendship with, i. 250n, 344n
New Lesson for Pope satirizes, ii. 34–6
nurse of, *see* Beach, Mary
out of his senses, ii. 449
Oxford a friend of, iv. 61
Peterborough celebrated by, viii. 112
Prologue to the Satires, HW quotes, iv. 189, ix. 321
Queensberry, Ds of, mentioned in letters of, iii. 195n

[Pope, Alexander, *continued*]

Rape of the Lock, The, Bonducci's translation of, i. 64

Rolli's epitaph on, quoted by HW, ii. 468, 485

Satires of Dr Donne Versified, Janssen's cheating of Bedford hinted at in, ii. 124n

Spence defends, in pamphlet, iv. 62n

Stanhope alters house and garden of, v. 417

Suffolk, Cts of, often mentioned by, vi. 544

Swift urged by, to burn history of Anne's reign, v. 184

Three Hours after Marriage, fails on stage, ii. 34

Walpole, Bns, commends satire supposedly by, i. 491

Walpole, Sir Robert, never reviled by, ix. 6–7

Warburton to defend, iv. 62

Pope, Mrs Alexander. *See* Turner, Edith (1642–1733)

Pope, Dramley, Leghorn merchant:

dishonesty of, i. 68

failure of, results in tea shortage, i. 59

Rome the refuge of, i. 68

'Pope':

Walpole, Sir Robert, and Bns Sundon joke about, i. 278

Pope; Popes:

ease of governing astonishes, after accession, v. 10

election of, *see* Conclave; Election: papal

England, having taken over authority of, has their excuse for tyranny and rapine, ix. 642

Galluzzi consulted Leopold II concerning publication of infamy of, ix. 238

—— exposes iniquity of, ix. 80, 202, 224, 238

HW wishes, were extinct like Medici, so that their true history could be published, ix. 224

illegitimate children no longer begotten by, vi. 254

imperial fiefs usurped by, may be coveted by Joseph II, ix. 224

Joseph II may dethrone, vii. 117

later history of, as dull as that of later Byzantine emperors, viii. 48

Maximilian I lacks bribe-money to become, ix. 468

Monte Cavallo the summer home of, viii. 344

office of, compared by Mann to doge's, i. 87

old saying about thinking no more of, vii. 128

Philip II bullied by, ii. 344

quotation from, about ease of governing, iv. 425

ring of, v. 52

rose-water baptism case to be settled by, i. 62–3

ship of, captured by English, i. 8, 15–16

state of, *see* Papal states

Stosch's medals of, v. 231

succession of rascals, HW calls, ix. 224

testoons of, i. 4

whole world claimed by, as heirs of Christ, ix. 642

See also Benedict XIV (1675–1758); Clement VII (d. 1534); Clement XI (1649–1721); Clement XII (1652–1740); Clement XIII (1693–1769); Clement XIV (1705–74); Gregory XIII (1502–85); Innocent VIII (1432–92); Innocent X (1572–1655); Julius III (1487–1555); Paul III (1468–1549); Paul V (1552–1621); Pius V (1504–72); Pius VI (1717–99); Sixtus V (1521–90)

'Pope Joan':

brought to bed, vi. 450

Walpole, Sir Robert, calls Bns Sundon, i. 278

Popery:

totters, though bolstered up by England, ix. 237

See also Roman Catholic Church

Pop-gun; pop-guns:

Abercrombie might be terrified by child with, v. 56

citadels not captured by, vi. 116

HW may mount, in castle battlements, v. 311

Popple, Henry (d. 1743), F.R.S.:

map of, omits Ohio River, iv. 497

Porcelain:

HW compares varieties of, ix. 635

HW's collection of, ix. 591

HW's folly in collecting, ix. 604

Tuscan: HW wants Horace Mann II to bring him specimen of, ix. 590–1; *see also* under China factory: Tuscan

See also China

Porchester, Bn. *See* Herbert, Henry (1741–1811)

Porci, Ciccio. *See* Cicciaporci, F.

Porcia, Leandro (1673–1740), cardinal, 1728:

Conclave abandoned by, after quarrel with Benedictines, i. 22

Pordenone, Giovanni de' Sacchis (1484–1539), called:

alleged painting by, vi. 291

Pores:

Mann attributes Princesse de Craon's ailments to checking of perspiration in, by heavy clothing, ii. 109–10

Pornography:

earthquake said to be a judgment against, iv. 133–4

See also Chorier, Nicolas; Cleland, John; Gervais de la Touche, Jean-Charles; Godart de Beauchamps, Pierre-François

Porphyria. *See* George III: health of: 'insanity'

Porphyry:
tables of, x. 7
Porpora, Niccolò Antonio (1686–1767), composer:
Temistocle, by, ii. 180
Porridge, plum. *See* Plum porridge
Port:
Fitzwalter consumes 24 bottles of, weekly, iv. 518–19
Pembroke, E. of, makes his own, ix. 497
Wilkes's ghost laid in a sea of, vii. 5
Porta al Prato ('Cascine Gate'):
Corsini's house near, i. 101
Porta del Popolo, at Rome:
Neapolitan troops reach, iii. 144
Porta di Bacco:
church to be erected near, vi. 258
Porta di San Gallo:
Florentines frequent, ii. 445
Portarlington, Cts of. *See* Stuart, Lady Caroline
Porta San Gallo:
arch at, Viviani displays, to San Severino, iv. 369
deserters attack, iv. 424
Florentines flock to, ii. 445
Grafton, Ds of, declines to visit, vi. 29
Karl Alexander received by ladies at, iv. 376
Porte, La. *See* La Porte
Porte-dieu:
Guasco serves as, in French church, vi. 529–30
Porteous, John (d. 1736):
affair of, iv. 230
Porter, David (ca 1747–1819), master chimney sweeper:
(?) benevolent efforts proposed by, in letter sent by HW to Horace Mann II, ix. 353
Porter, Sir James (1710–86), ambassador at Constantinople 1746–62; minister plenipotentiary at Brussels 1763–5; Kt, 1763:
former minister at Constantinople, viii. 160
Frederick II will be the only possible protector of, v. 248
pension of, viii. 160
Vorontsov displeased by conduct of, at Constantinople, v. 247–8
Porter, Mary (d. 1765), actress:
benefit for, i. 336
Porter (beverage):
Ferrers obtains, from brother, v. 397
Porter; porters:
expense of, i. 130
Mann entrusts letter to, v. 461
Richecourt's litter carried by, v. 80
See also under Servants
Porter's lodge:
Houghton lantern compared to, iv. 163n
Portes, Mme de. *See* Mignot, Marie *or* Claudine-Françoise

Portes, Pierre de:
marriage of, iv. 132
Port-holes:
left open, on French ship, v. 357
Portia. *See* Porcia
Portici:
Ferdinand of Naples tosses Florentines in blanket at, vii. 254
Mann, Lady Lucy, not benefited by air of, viii. 203
Portier des Chartreux, Le. See under Gervaise de la Touche, Jean-Charles
Portland, Cts of. *See* Temple, Jane Martha (1672–1751)
Portland, Ds of. *See* Cavendish, Lady Dorothy (1750–94); Harley, Margaret Cavendish (1715–85)
Portland, D. of. *See* Bentinck, William (1709–62); Bentinck, William Henry Cavendish (1738–1809)
Portland:
English fleet near, v. 232
Portland, English war ship:
in danger, v. 350
Port l'Orient:
Sinclair bungles, iii. 456
Port Mahon:
Ailesbury, Cts of, may be at, iv. 285
air of, considered bad, iv. 293
Beauvau behaves well at, iv. 579
Blakeney ennobled for loss of, v. 52
Byng said to have captured, v. 15
Colvill takes HW's eagle to, iii. 268
Conway does not wish to take wife to, iv. 293
—— may have lost weight at, iv. 313
Dartmouth at, i. 285
Edgcumbe escapes from harbour of, iv. 559
endangered, iv. 538, viii. 490
England must be anxious over, iv. 558
English fleet at, iii. 9
Englishman and wife come to Florence from, iii. 304
English ships at, listed, i. 285–6
English ships take French prizes to, ii. 438
English ship takes Venetian prize to, iii. 81
English troops from, ii. 312
French announce intention of attacking, iv. 541
French capture, v. 135
French may intend to attack, iv. 537
garrison of, weak, viii. 375, 380
Gloucester, D. of, to visit, vii. 294
governor of, prepares for French attack, iv. 528–9
HW's shipments delayed at, ii. 445
Haddock advised at, of Spanish fleet's arrival, i. 306
—— anchors fleet at, i. 314
—— at, i. 267, 290

[Port Mahon, *continued*]
House of Lords examines list of officers at, i. 300
Leghorn might be exchanged for, by England, i. 267
Leghorn supplies to replace missing ones from Ireland for, viii. 375
Lestock to visit, i. 290
Mann ignorant of Conway's departure from, iv. 290
—— may send Domenichino painting to Anstruther at, ii. 144
—— should plan secret expedition against, v. 239
——'s ship from Leghorn to visit, iii. 206
—— to write to, about pedestal for eagle, iii. 427
Mann, Horace II and Lady Lucy, to visit, viii. 233
man-of-war may leave HW's shipment at, iii. 216
Mathews at, ii. 420
Medley sends ship from, to Leghorn, iii. 192
—— still at, iii. 216
news from, that Elphinston's division is at Gibraltar, vii. 162
old tar's letter about captures of, v. 51–2
packet-boat of, *see Earl of Besborough*
Parliamentary investigation of fall of, languidly pursued, v. 55–6
Postillion obliged to refit at, iii. 235
Richelieu captures town of, iv. 552
Rowley at, iii. 146
—— may leave, ii. 555
Russian ships at, vii. 162, 172, 189, 192
sea captain formerly of, talks to Mann after Algiers visit, ix. 416
Severn to stop at, iv. 27
ship from: reaches Leghorn, i. 314; visits Leghorn in search of Rowley, iii. 132
Spanish artillery diverted from, to Genoa, ii. 257
Spanish expedition against, from Cadiz, would have little chance of success, ix. 59
Spiridorf at, vii. 162, 185
Stanhope captures, v. 52
Te Deums sung at, for Spanish landing on Minorca, ix. 189
Toulon squadron might have been bound for, viii. 375
Townshend leaves Corsica for, iv. 385
—— pretends to be driven to, iv. 274
—— puts in at, for repairs, iii. 207
—— to be court-martialled at, iii. 324
—— writes from, to Mann, iii. 216
Villettes arrives at, iii. 81
visitors to: Arbuthnot, iv. 284; Conway, iv. 284–5
Windham hopes for loss of, to embarrass the government, ix. 50
York, D. of, to visit, vi. 179

Portmanteau; portmanteaus:
embroidered, HW jokes about laurels kept in, ii. 61
French mail carried in, ix. 619
HW uses, for blankets, ii. 315
Mann, Horace II, has not yet unpacked, ix. 417
Pars loses, viii. 144
Portmore, E. of. *See* Colyear, Charles (1700–85)
Porto Bello:
American war may produce successor to, iv. 449
capture of, not believed at Rome, i. 29
news of, reaches HW at Rome, i. 5
(?) Old Pretender's movements may be influenced by capture of, i. 23–4
Pulteney's letter to Vernon on capture of, iii. 459
Santo Buono pronounces, impregnable, i. 7
Porto Ferrajo:
capable of receiving a large fleet, v. 36
Francis I tells Braitwitz to defend, i. 229
frigate sails from, to pursue pirates, ix. 480
grenadiers relegated to, viii. 8–9
Mann, Lady Lucy, not improved by water of, viii. 322
—— takes waters of, in hopes of getting a son, viii. 318
next best port to Leghorn, v. 59
Townshend driven from, by storm, iii. 206–7
tunny fish caught near fortress of, vii. 131
Tuscan Court at, vii. 131
Wright's prizes take refuge in, v. 69
Porto Ferraro:
garrison at, iii. 11
procaccia banished to, iv. 447
Porto Longone:
boats at, ready to follow Capt. Wright, v. 69
Charles of Naples owns, ii. 28
iron mines near, vii. 131
Leopold not to visit, vii. 131
Mann hopes that troops may be prevented from reaching, iii. 410
Marciana near, ii. 28
Osborne devastates, ii. 28
soldiers at, i. 154
Spanish possession, vii. 131
Porto Rico:
capture of, not believed at Rome, i. 29
Dutch ship captured on way from, i. 53
Porto San Stefano:
Jesuits remain before, vi. 532
Spaniards arrive at, i. 197
Porto Spezia, Spezie *or* Spezza. *See* Spezia
Portraits:
English, HW collects, vii. 423, ix. 448
Portsmouth, Ds of. *See* Penancoët de Kéroualle, Louise-Renée de (ca 1647–1734)
Portsmouth, E. of. *See* Wallop, John

Portsmouth:
accident at, shocks Mann, vii. 228
alleged attempt to set fire to, viii. 273
Anson takes Acapulco ship to, ii. 463
Cherbourg cannon brought from, v. 238
Conway embarks at, for Jersey, ix. 111, 115
——'s expedition disembarks at, v. 143
——'s groom refuses to go to, to see his horses embarked, v. 155
English expedition sails from, v. 210
English naval strength at, vii. 40
fire at, v. 419–20
French may attack, viii. 500
George III to visit, to see the fleet, vii. 491, 497
Hardy at, viii. 511, 516
—— dies at, ix. 48
Jersey may be relieved by force from, ix. 111
Keppel revisits, viii. 420
——'s court martial at, viii. 433, 435, 438
Norris at, ii. 393
Orford, E. of, takes Norfolk militia to, v. 300
Palliser escapes from, viii. 442
—— returns to, despite rotten mast, viii. 474
Sandwich, E. of, said to have detained fleet at, to divert George III and Charlotte, viii. 377
Scottish regiment mutinies at, ix. 362
secret expedition beats about near, v. 461
ships in port at, ix. 221
storm at, ix. 115
Portugal, K. of. See Henry I (1512–80); João V (1689–1750); José Manoel (1714–77); Pedro III (1717–86); Sebastian (1554–78)
Portugal, Princes (bastard) of. See Antonio (1714–1800); José (1720–after 1777)
Portugal, Q. of. See Maria I (1734–1816); Maria Anna Josephine Antoinette (1683–1754); Maria Anna Vittoria (1718–81)
Portugal, Anton von (d. 1769), Graf von Puebla, imperial minister, plenipotentiary to Prussia:
Williams negotiates with, iv. 186–7
Portugal:
Acciaioli expelled by, v. 422, 475
animosity of, towards Spain may make up for military deficiencies, vi. 41
arms of, removed from Almada's door in Rome, v. 426
banker from, see Rosa, Lopez
Boscawen to ask pardon of, for La Clue's defeat in Portuguese waters, v. 35
Braganza, D. of, of illegitimate branch of royal family of, vi. 174
Catherine II's manifestos illiterate enough to be from, vi. 71
Clement XIII's death may keep, in the Church, vi. 331

——'s quarrel with, v. 422–4, 425–6, 428, 436–7
Clement XIV detaches, from Franco-Spanish cabal, vii. 221
conspiracy in: v. 264–5, 267, 275–6; said to be fabricated to discredit the Jesuits, v. 342; to be subject of book printed at Rome, v. 275
Correggio painting might be sold to, ii. 373
Corsini the Protector of, v. 423
Cours de l'Europe satirizes, i. 177
England recommends Jews to, v. 341
England should send aid to, to humble Spain, vi. 100
England to send troops to aid, vi. 23
English destroy French ships on coast of, v. 334
English fleet returns safely from, viii. 412
English leaders divided over question of aiding, vi. 30–1
English plans to aid, may be disconcerted, vi. 41
English-Spanish war fought in, vi. 34–5, 43
Fane said to be appointed ambassador to, i. 135
Ferdinand VI kind to, iv. 512
France tempts Charles III into designs on, vi. 99
general of, cowardly, vi. 94
Guy Fawkes Day might be imitated by, v. 477
havocked world for gold, ix. 142
hostilities in, almost the only sign of war in Europe, vi. 40
island of, seized by Spain, viii. 309–10
Jesuits' attempt in, v. 267
Jesuits from, reach Genoa, v. 348
Jesuits mortified by, v. 217
Jesuits' part in conspiracy in, unconcealed, v. 275–6
Jesuits precipitate Clement XIII's rupture with, v. 425–6
Jesuits probably did not promote assassination plot in, vii. 173
Jesuits' suppression determined by, vii. 136, x. 49
Judaistic tendencies of, v. 430
Kinnoull to beg pardon of, for English violation of neutrality, v. 352
Lippe to command troops of, vi. 43
ministers from and to, see under Minister
officer of, prosecuted for not paying taxes, vii. 166
patriarch of, might appease his king by curtailing Rome's power, v. 348–9
Peace of Paris saves, vi. 95
Pulteney on way home from, vi. 121
relation from, of negro mutiny in Brazil, vii. 452
religion used by, as an excuse for plunder, ix. 400
Riccardi's jewels to be sold in, iii. 349

[Portugal, *continued*]

Rome's quarrel with, over Jesuits, v. 475–7

royal family of: may have to live at Somerset House, vi. 38, 95; might be sheltered by Charles III, v. 560

secretary of war of, *see* Secretary at War, Portuguese

Spain continues conquest of, vi. 78

Spain disappointed in not getting, vi. 95

Spain has not enslaved, vi. 1

Spain may attack, viii. 253

Spain may be unable to conquer or keep, vi. 51

Spain may push conquest of, to exchange it for Havana, vi. 99–100

Spain more interested in conquest of, than in Havana's loss, vi. 48, 51, 92

Spain's campaign in, fails to live up to boastful manifestos, vi. 66

Spain's preoccupation with, pleases HW, vi. 31

Spain's success in, vi. 48, 51, 94

Spain threatens to invade, if it does not declare war on England, v. 559

Spain to exchange territories with, in Paraguay, v. 341

Spanish attack upon, reported, vi. 34

Spanish conquest of, would make France more insolent, vi. 76

Spanish settlement at Rio Grande attacked by, viii. 223–4

Tyrawley returns from, with wives and children, ii. 104

—— said to command forces of, vi. 34

—— says that war in, is scheme to get English money, vi. 70

—— spends 15 years in, ii. 148

—— to command English troops in, vi. 43

war in, seems more interesting than that in Germany, vi. 41

Portuguese, the:

rebellious Negroes of, called 'disaffected,' vii. 452, 462

Portuguese banker at Rome. *See* Rosa, Lopez

Portuguese Hospital at Rome:

Almada fixes notice at, v. 423

Portuguese language:

(?) St-Germain's native tongue, x. 20

Porus:

Alexander did not despoil, after victory, ix. 545

——'s plea for seizing wealth of, ix. 642

Possesso, Papal:

Pius VI to celebrate, viii. 131, 136

Post; posts:

'actually setting out,' from Florence, v. 342

arrival of: expected in Florence with impatience, ix. 302; in Florence, from Leghorn, Reggio, Bologna, i. 47; with alarming news of French and Spanish fleets, ix. 173

binding removed, to enable book to be sent by, i. 64

courier forgets English mail, ix. 366

Crew slower than, ii. 272

day of departure of, from Florence, iv. 85

delay of: ii. 233, 343, 352, iii. 360, 362, 365, 405, 430, v. 270, vii. 378; by bad weather, iii. 333, 360, iv. 467, viii. 433; by floods, iii. 135; by Maria Amalia's visit, ix. 299; by winds in Mediterranean, i. 393; facilitates false rumours by England's enemies in Italy, iii. 362–3; from England, vii. 110; from Florence, vii. 537; from France by snow, i. 207; in reaching Florence, vii. 203; makes 3 or 4 arrive together, viii. 513; probably caused by bad weather, v. 369

delays of: always at most critical junctures, v. 543, ix. 492; could be endured by long-lived patriarchs, vii. 240; in winter, vii. 273–4

Dutch, i. 84

Dutch route longer than French, ii. 92

Dutch route more hazardous than French, ii. 102

Dutch route not yet followed by, ii. 437

English: Ostend packet-boat often delays, vii. 541; to Italy, goes by way of Flushing, v. 215

English merchants at Leghorn receive, regularly, ii. 442–3

English visitors at Florence assemble on arrival of, v. 445

expected at Houghton, ii. 247, 259

expense of sending watch from England by, would be heavy, v. 322

floods retard, iii. 135

for Germany, awaits letter from Leghorn, vii. 232

four mails from England, arrive together at Florence, v. 410, ix. 399, 553

France establishes, for men supposed to be fighting in England, v. 326

French capture fishing-boat carrying, to England, iii. 143, 146

French mail robbed in Pall Mall, ix. 619

from Bologna to Florence, i. 32, 47

from England: not expected till next day, viii. 495; reaches Florence twice a week except sometimes in winter, viii. 368; retarded, viii. 461

from England through Mediterranean, 'out of repair,' ix. 191

from England to Italy, becomes irregular, viii. 140–1

from Genoa, delayed by weather, iii. 360

from Holland, i. 84

from Leghorn, i. 47, iii. 22, ix. 313

from Paris, i. 463; announces Jersey attack, viii. 471; to Florence, vi. 352

from Rome, viii. 250

from Venice to Florence, i. 88, iii. 439

German: arrives March 9, ix. 383; English letters come by, to Italy, ix. 383; fails to bring mail from London to Italy, ix. 192;

mails brought from England to Florence by, ix. 205

German prince may stop, v. 452

HW awaits eagerly, from England, i. 32

HW colours some things, when writing by, lest foreigners read them, viii. 493

HW does not like to send his predictions through, viii. 364

HW's letters may be read at every post-house in, viii. 427

HW's new footman puts letter in, by mistake, ix. 118

HW would not trust secrets to, ix. 185

hour of departure of, at Florence, vii. 515

interrupted by capture of packet boat, iii. 133

irregular in France, i. 103

irregular in winter, i. 213, 286

irregularity of, i. 476, ix. 567

irregularity of, aggravated by bad weather, v. 141

lack of privacy of: i. 265, 382–3, 396, 421–2, 453–4, 476, ii. 362, vi. 373, 570, vii. 455, 537, viii. 364, 427, 493, 507, ix. 15, 89, 185, 257; HW hopes, does not prevail in Tuscany, viii. 38; Leopold opens all letters before delivery, ix. 412n, 566n

leaves London on Friday, vii. 500

letter from London reaches Florence in 16 days, vi. 499

letters from Venice and Padua reach Florence on Wednesdays only, viii. 136

Leyden route retards, iii. 257

liberty of, now enjoyed by HW, vi. 309

Lorenzi demands unfranked letters from Genoa, vi. 347

—— forbids Genoese postmaster to send him unfranked letters, vi. 362

mail packets thrown overboard when ships are taken, v. 168, ix. 339

mails from England and Holland lacking in Italy, ix. 388

Mann awaits eagerly, from HW, i. 32

—— does not believe that HW's letters have been opened by, vii. 542

—— hurries letter to catch, viii. 89

—— wants Sisson's plan sent by, v. 375, 379

Mantua route of, ii. 233, iii. 190

medal too heavy to send by, viii. 470

missing, from England, v. 406

packet-boats delayed in carrying, v. 464, 465

penny, paper distributed by, iv. 222

Pergolesi's Olimpiade too big for, iii. 95

Preverau blamed for delay in, ii. 233, 442–3, 448

price of, ix. 608

print of Camilla Martelli too large for, ix. 230

scissors not safe to send by, i. 98–9

slower in November than in summer, vi. 265

stopped between Bologna and Florence, iii. 462

three mails arrive together in Florence, viii. 513, ix. 317, 521

three mails from Italy reported lost, viii. 468

through Germany, to England, v. 134

through Holland, interrupted by French, iii. 146

time of: between England and Florence, discussed by Mann, ix. 313; between Paris and Florence, vi. 352; from London to Florence, vi. 499, vii. 541–2

Van Heck to forward, from Leyden, iii. 145–6

Venice or Mantua routes of, to Florence, iii. 190

Weymouth tells Murray to send his secrets by, in cipher, ix. 42

See also Mail; Post day

Postage:

HW may not think Mann's letter worth, viii. 463

Mann's expense allowance for, ii. 516

Trigge may demand, as Mann's messenger, viii. 380

Post-chaise; post-chaises:

Gloucester, D. of, travels in, viii. 314

HW glad he is finished with, i. 142

HW's, will not take him to Florence, vi. 116

Hamilton, Ds of, enters, at Yorkshire inn, iv. 317

highwayman attacks, in Piccadilly, iv. 188

hired, Palliser reaches Admiralty in, viii. 442

Modena, Ds of, travels in, ii. 227

Modena, Ps of, sees Florence from, vi. 202

Parliament's dissolution causes flurry of, viii. 45

Pembroke nearly destroys, iv. 109

Penn wounded by overturn of, iv. 248

Pomfret, Cts of, has, in Italy, iii. 390

Taaffe carries turtles and pineapples in, iv. 289

visible from SH, iv. 380, ix. 532

warm, HW will be comfortable in, if he goes to Italy, vi. 339–40

York, D. of, goes in, to Marseille, vi. 553

Post day; post days:

foreign, from London, Tuesday and Friday, ix. 255

in Florence: arrives Wednesdays and Saturdays, v. 168, ix. 302; from Venice and Padua, viii. 136

Mann dreads, iii. 54, 56

——'s porter repels visitors on, iii. 59

—— writes three days before, ix. 238

Poster:

oilcloth, to advertise sights, iv. 40

Posterity:

eighteenth-century England will be lightly regarded by, viii. 266

[Posterity, *continued*]
England will be ridiculed by, for idolizing
Dr Johnson, ix. 638
Fearne's remark about, v. 61
HW cannot predict opinions of, when he
knows so little of actions of his own time,
ix. 63–4
HW's letters must be limited to events of
interest to, viii. 450–1
HW's reflections on, vi. 303
newspaper writers have no mercy on, ix.
116
younger generation seems to HW to be, ix.
109
Post horse. *See under* Horse
Post-house; post-houses:
at Pistoia, vi. 222
Florentine, hours of departure from, vii.
515
HW and Spence regret interruption of
mule-counting by stops at, i. 91
Leopold and Maria Louisa have servant
to announce them at, vii. 220
letters at, are addressed to Ricci in cipher,
vii. 517
Mann to have Young Pretender watched
at, i. 13
Modena, Ds of, borrows post chaise at, ii.
227
Postiglione, Il (ship). See *Il Postiglione*
Postilion, Spanish register ship:
capture of, iii. 81–2
Postilion; postilions:
Albemarle bows to, iv. 270
Electress's, separated from coachman, iii.
369–70
HW's letter about victory might be pre-
ceded by, blowing horns, viii. 338
Liechtenstein preceded by, v. 445
Mann fears, have been frozen, v. 369
North's wounded by highwayman, viii. 47
officer accompanied by, when bearing mes-
sage to Berlin, v. 242
stumbling horse of, may delay mail, vii.
274
Vitelli, Mme, orders, to pass Mme Grifoni's
coach, i. 37
Werpup's death blamed upon, vi. 306
Postillion, English xebec:
Genoese vessels damage, iii. 235
Port Mahon visited by, for refitting, iii.
235
Townshend leaves, off Corsica, iii. 207
Postmark:
of Leghorn, on letter, i. 47
Postmaster; postmasters:
at Florence, *see* Gazzeri, Giovan Battista;
Giusti, Tommaso; Orlandi, Casimirro;
Paperini, Giuseppe
at Hounslow, iv. 109
French, at Genoa, *see* Regny
French and Italian, dispute, vi. 358
HW does not wish to be intelligible to,
ix. 245

HW fears less, than irresponsible young
Englishmen, v. 374–5
HW implores, not to peek into his mail,
vi. 373
Mann to get horses from, to attend Court
to Pisa and Leghorn, vi. 417
rupture between, on route from France to
Tuscany, vi. 347
Postmaster General:
Bessborough and Grantham succeed Hyde
and Trevor as, vi. 311
Bessborough, E. of, resigns as, vi. 97, 471
Fawkener does not become, iii. 26
—— is, iii. 456n
Hillsborough and Despenser become, vi.
473
Sandwich may become, vi. 569, 571
See also, Eyles, Sir John (d. 1745); Fawkener, Sir Everard (1684–1758)
Post obits:
misery caused by, iv. 242
Post office; post offices:
Euston's tenant threatened with dismissal
from, ii. 255
Florentine: Leopold opens letters from, ix.
412n, 566; Richecourt opens letters at,
ii. 362
foreign: HW cannot write freely when his
letter must pass through so many, viii.
507; HW does not want to announce
England's difficulties to, vii. 455; HW does
not want to entertain, with bad news, ix.
89; HW does not want to test the credulity
of, ix. 15; not likely to be friendly to
English letters, viii. 518–19; will learn
nothing new from HW's letters, ix. 105
French, German, and Tuscan, HW cannot
write freely by, ix. 564
HW-Mann correspondence unequalled in
annals of, ix. 520
HW's letter returned to him by, ix. 118
letter must have stayed a week at, ix. 395
Post-road:
Mann, Horace II, unable to travel over,
because of bad weather, ix. 204
Pot; pots:
auriculas in, at Ranelagh, iv. 47
brass, sold in Florence, i. 53
pewter, used as alms-boxes, v. 238
'Potences, deux':
Braitwitz's, ii. 524
Potency:
Beaufort's, examined by physicians and
surgeons, ii. 185
Potion:
Young Pretender accuses wife of giving
him, to make him impotent, ix. 102
Potosi:
Spain digs for weath of, vii. 561–2
whichever party in England had wealth
of, would be victorious, ix. 256
Potter, John (?1674–1747), Bp of Oxford
1715–37, Abp of Canterbury 1737–47:

George II said to have been promised by, that prayers would be said for him, iii. 149

Gibson supplanted by, as candidate for archbishopric, iii. 503n

son of, iii. 449, vi. 184

Thuanus quoted by, to Sir Robert Walpole, i. 301

Potter, Thomas (? 1718–59), politician; wit; M.P.:

Augusta, Ps of Wales, has, as secretary, iii. **449n**

Cholmondeley succeeded by, as joint vice-treasurer of Ireland, v. 109

Cresset succeeds, as secretary to the Ps of Wales, iv. 247

Darlington succeeded by, as joint paymaster, v. 25

Frederick, P. of Wales, recruits, as promising Opposition member, iii. 449

health of, bad constitution, iv. 32

Opposition aided by, iv. 32

Opposition assembly addressed by, at St Alban's Tavern, iv. 50

son of Abp of Canterbury, vi. 184n

speech by, against Pelham over Buckingham assizes, iii. 470

speeches by, iii. 449n

Wilkes's *Essay on Woman* said to have originated with, vi. 184

Pouch:

leather, countrymen carry money in, ii. 148

Poulett, Hon. Anne (1711–85), M.P.:

(?) Florence visited by, iv. 387

Poulett, John (ca 1668–1743), 4th Bn Poulett; cr. (1706) E. Poulett:

death of, ii. 245

Poulett, John (1708–64), 2d E. Poulett, 1743:

Bedchamber resigned by, iv. 469–70

Poulett, Hon. Vere (1710–88), 3d E. Poulett, 1764; M.P.:

(?) Florence visited by, iv. 387

Poulett. *See also* Powlett

Poulterers:

Irish peerage includes, v. 24

Poultney. *See* Pulteney

Pounds:

Mann wants price in, instead of guineas, v. 303

Poussin (originally Dughet), Gaspard (1615–75), painter:

landscapes by: HW may remember, v. 231; Mann buys, for Hoare, v. 231, 479; Mann leaves, to HW, ix. 664–5, 668; Mann may get, for Hoare, v. 208–9; Mann, Horace II takes, from bad frames, ix. 668; sold at Furnese's auction, v. 172; to go to England on same ship with Mann's body, ix. 668

Whithed collects paintings by, iv. 142

Poussin, Nicolas (1594–1655), painter:

painting portrays, v. 208–9

West imitates, in historical painting, vii. 210–11

Williams buys painting by, vii. 466

Pover, Diego, Lt:

captured at Velletri, ii. 492

Powder:

Beaufort, Ds of, now wears, in her hair, viii. 54

canonici and *abbés* forbidden to wear, v. 224

Coventry, Cts of, cannot use, in France, iv. 338

Du Barry, Comtesse, flings, in Louis XV's face, vii. 85

French opera singers omit, if they represent widows, witches, or distressed ladies, ii. 496

Hare-Naylor would have used, in hair, had he known his father was to remarry, ii. 64

Pius VI forbids priests to wear, in hair, viii. 107

red, used for wounds, i. 94

wig covered with, vii. 258

See also Gunpowder

Powder-mills:

earthquake ascribed to explosion at, iv. 131

explosion of, near Twickenham, vii. 365

Northumberland gets Parliamentary act for erection of, vii. 365–6

—— pretends, will be corn mills, vii. 365–6

Powell, Anne (d. 1760), m. 1—Wilkins; m. 2 (1747) Rev. Dr Conyers Middleton:

Gordon, Mrs, has, as companion, iv. 167

husband's creditors threaten, with seizure of his papers, iv. 216

Powell, John (d. 1783):

Burke restores, to Pay Office, ix. 407–8

Pay Office employs, as Holland's tool, ix. 407

suicide of, after second dismissal from Pay Office, ix. 407–8

Powell, William (1735–69):

Garrick may be eclipsed by, vi. 176

Ladbroke's former clerk, vi. 176

Mann will not mention, to Garrick, vi. 180

Power of attorney. *See* Attorney, power of

Powis, Cts of. *See* Herbert, Barbara Antonia (1735–86); Herbert, Lady Henrietta Antonia (1758–1830)

Powis, E. of. *See* Herbert, George Edward Henry Arthur (1755–1801); Herbert, Henry Arthur (ca 1703–72)

Powis, M. of. *See* Herbert, William (ca 1698–1748)

Powis, Thomas. *See* Powys

Powlett, Charles (1685–1754), 3d D. of Bolton:

Cabinet Council's move to oust Carteret not aided by, ii. 535–6

Carteret, Bns, escorted by, ii. 501

[Powlett, Charles (1685–1754), *continued*]
Colonel of the Blues, iv. 207
Granville's friend, iv. 207
Granville, Cts. attended by, ii. 537
Irish preferment promised to, ii. 535–6
Isle of Wight to be commanded by, supposedly in place of Beefeaters, i. 457
sister-in-law of, iv. 231n

Powlett, Charles (ca 1718–65), 5th D. of Bolton, 1759; M.P.:
red ribbon vacated by, may make room for Mann, vi. 312
suicide of, vi. 312

Powlett, Charles, illegitimate son of D. of Bolton:
mother leaves fortune away from, v. 365

Powlett, Harry (1720–94), 6th D. of Bolton, 1765:
ball by, for D. and Ds of Gloucester, to be attended by HW, ix. 22
Mann disobeyed by, ii. (?) 287–8, 301
mission of, to Civita Vecchia, ii. **301**

Powlett, Henrietta (d. 1753), m. (1741) Robert Colebrooke:
Robinson entertains, i. 185

Powlett, Horatio Armand:
mother leaves fortune away from, v. 365

Powlett, Lady Nassau. *See* Tufton, Lady Isabella

Powlett, Lord Nassau (1698–1741):
wife of, iv. 231n

Powlett, Percy:
mother leaves fortune away from, v. 365

Powlett family:
madness in, vi. 312

Pownall, Commander Philemon, Capt., 1771:
Sawyer's prize money shared by, vi. 45
——'s sister weds, vi. 45

Pownall, Mrs Philemon. *See* Majendie, ——

Pownall, Mrs Thomas. *See* Churchill, Harriet

Powys, Thomas (1743–1800), cr. (1797) Bn Lilford; 'Powis'; M.P.:
Foote, Mrs summons, to reading of Edward Louisa Mann's will, viii. 159
Mann's 'half-nephew,' ix. 474
Mann, Horace II, brother-in-law of, ix. 475n
—— may be made imprudent by, viii. **429**
M.P. for Northamptonshire, ix. 475n
Pitt, William II, forfeits good will of, in reconciliation attempt, ix. 475n
political career open to, ix. 474
speeches of, acrimonious, viii. 429

Powys, Mrs Thomas. *See* Mann, Eleanor (1747–1823)

Pox:
Chute unwittingly discusses, with Mme Sarrazin, i. 498
occurrences of, i. 480, vii. 278

Poymont, Josef von (d. 1743), Graf von Payersberg:
Spaniards capture, ii. 153–4

wounded at Campo Santo, ii. 164

Poyntz, Charles (1735–1809), D. D.:
Cumberland, D. of, has, educated abroad, iv. 208

Poyntz, Margaret Georgiana (1737–1814), m. (1755) Hon. John Spencer, cr. (1761) Bn and (1765) E. Spencer:
Bologna visited by, vi. 173
Mann gives assembly for, vi. 180
(?) son's match disapproved by, ix. 104
Spa benefits, vi. 173
York, D. of, sups with, and gives her presents, vi. 228

Poyntz, Stephen (1685–1750), D. of Cumberland's treasurer and former governor:
brother and wife ruin, iv. 207–8
character of, iv. 208
Cumberland, D. of, aids family of, iv. 208
—— had, as governor, iv. 207–8, vi. 163n
——'s treasurer and former governor, iii. 242n
minister to Sweden, iv. 208n
Primate of Scotland's baggage discovered by, iii. 242
Townshend's sons tutored by, iv. 208n

Poyntz, Mrs Stephen. *See* Mordaunt, Anna Maria

Poyntz, William (d. 1748), receiver-general of the Excise:
brother ruined by, iv. 208
devout, iv. 208

Poyntz, William (ca 1734–1809), son of Stephen Poyntz:
Cumberland, D. of, has, educated abroad, iv. 208

Pozzo. *See* Dal Pozzo

Pozzolini, Pietro, Mann's servant:
arrival of, in England, reported to Mann by HW, ix. 344
detained in England before starting back to Italy, ix. 350, 351
Mann sends packets to England by, ix. 207, 325, 329, 334

Praetorian guard:
constitution could be overthrown by, vii. 304

Prague:
Austrian battle with Bavarian-French army expected at, i. 194
battle of, England hears of, v. 91–2
Beauvau said to have escaped from, ii. 68–9
Belle-Isle ill at, ii. 108
Braitwitz alludes to capture of, i. 259
capture of: by Austrians, reported, i. 466, 472, 481; by French, i. 221, 226; by Prussians, ii. 511; Craon, Princesse de, anxious for, ii. 1–2; England hears no news of, ii. 32; English fear, will not take place, ii. 47; expected, i. 472, ii. 58
Charles, P., approaches, i. 464–5
—— forced to conciliate townspeople of, ii. 512

coronation at, ii. 240, 241–2, vi. 324
Czaslau near, i. 433
Daun's army relieves, v. 116
English army not to attack, ii. 202
escape of Frenchmen from, reported in English newspapers, ii. 68–9
Francis I or P. Charles may capture, i. 472, ii. 58
Francis I's visit to, causes dissension, ii. 2
—— to destroy French army at, i. 481
Frederick II captures, ii. 511
—— fails to take, v. 106–7
—— menaces, ii. 499, v. 95, 102, vi. 63
French-Bavarian army driven back to, i. 205
futile attacks on, fashionable, ii. 202–3
Joseph II crowned at, as K. of Romans, vi. 324
news of capture of, premature, i. 488
Prussians evacuate, ii. 543
siege of: changed to blockade, ii. 61; HW and Sir Robert Walpole laugh at raising of, ii. 68; raised, ii. 58, v. 109, 112; Te Deums sung for raising of, v. 112, 114
Vienna conceals disaster at, v. 242
visitors to, Craon, Princesse de, vi. 324
Praitenstain, ——, Capt. (d. 1743):
killed at Campo Santo, ii. 164
Prantner, ——, Capt. (d. 1743):
killed at Campo Santo, ii. 164
Prat, Mrs:
Mann attends, ii. 65
Prati della Masone, near Bologna:
Spaniards encamp near, i. 424
Prati della Sala:
Montemar encamps at, i. 427
Prato:
Bocchineri, Mme, relegated to, by Regency, iv. 447
Braitwitz to visit, ii. 134
Del Monte's militia to assemble at, ii. 85
English fleet could not have conquered, iii. 215
letters to, from Spanish officers, i. 238
Medici commissary of, ii. 170
Tuscan troops to go to, ii. 98, 100
Pratolino:
HW visits, i. 31
Leopold and Maria Louisa at, vi. 337, 350
Leopold to visit, vi. 334
Mann to take visitors to, i. 484
Mozzi not allowed to spend night at, viii. 23
Orford, Cts of, allowed by Leopold to use apartment in, during hot season, viii. 23
Pratt, Anna Maria (d. 1806), m. (1739) Thomas Barrett-Lennard, 17th Bn Dacre of the South, 1755:
brother of, viii. 103
Chute responsible for Mann's attentions to, iv. 173
daughter's death, iv. 92

Davis, Mrs, calls, 'Barrett's folks' iv. 174
Florentine amusements missed by, iv. 92
Giberne's prospects not to be told to, iv. 91
Goldsworthy, Mrs, will tire, iv. 93
HW does not know, iv. 100
HW entertains, at dinner, at SH, viii. 103
HW known by, through Montagu, iv. 78
HW pleased by Mann's liking for, iv. 96
HW sees Mann's partiality for, iv. 204
house taken by, at Florence, iv. 75
husband may not permit, to live in same house with Mann, iv. 194
Mann admits truth of HW's remarks about, iv. 180
—— asks, to live with him, iv. 159, 165
—— coolly treated by, iv. 173
—— declines to meet, at Montopoli, iv. 194
—— defends, from HW's charge of prudery, iv. 105
—— gets house for, in Florence, iv. 75
—— gives garden assembly for, iv. 174, 191
—— likes, for Chute's sake, iv. 84
—— may invite, to Fiesole, iv. 194
—— not invited by, to Pisa baths, iv. 194
——'s admiration for, iv. 94
—— said to be in love with, iv. 165n
——'s attentions to, iv. 94
—— scolds HW for disparaging, iv. 105
——'s devotion to, noticed by Mme Antinori, iv. 105
—— sees, daily, iv. 159
——'s hospitality to, praised by HW, iv. 87
——'s life after departure of, iv. 98
—— teaches Italian to, iv. 91–2
—— to accompany, to Pisa baths, iv. 84, 85, 86
—— to give conversazione for, iv. 75
Mann, Galfridus, urged by, to come to Italy, iv. 564
Naples to be visited by, iv. 92
Naples visited by, iv. 105
Niccolini entertains, at dinner, iv. 174
Pisa visited by, iv. 91–2
sister mourned by, iv. 92
spaniel bitch of, said to have miscarried, vi. 546
Sunday opera shunned by, iv. 86
Pratt, Caroline (d. 1805), m. Herbert, Bn de Munster:
(?) Mann teaches Italian to, iv. 91–2
(?) Pisa baths visited by, iv. 91
Pratt, Sir Charles (1714–94), Kt, 1761; cr. (1765) Bn and (1786) E. Camden; lord chancellor, 1766; M.P.:
dismissal of, imprudent, vii. 174
Dunning's friend, vii. 175
expulsion of, weakens court party in Parliament, vii. 182
former lord chancellor, viii. 103, ix. 440n

[Pratt, Sir Charles, *continued*]
George III insists on keeping, as Chancellor, vi. 538
Great Seal obtained by, vi. 442, 443
habeas corpus extension attacked by, v. 205
Mansfield roughly handled by, in House of Lords, vi. 520
——'s prosecution dropped by, vii. 282
——'s speech cowed by sight of, vi. 464
ministry may dismiss, vii. 168
opinion of, sought in affairs of Cts of Orford, and her son, ix. 125, 216, 230, 440
Pitt names, for lord chancellor, vi. 161
point laboured by, against the Court, in case of Middlesex election, vii. 167
political failure of, vii. 216
President of the Council, ix. 262
remains in place as lord chancellor, vii. 65
retired, and too old to think merely as lawyer, ix. 125
rift of, with Mansfield, Hardwicke, Newcastle, and Fox, v. 205
sister of, viii. 103
son of, ix. 620
Wilmot succeeds, as chief justice of Common Pleas, vi. 443
Pratt, Frances (d. 1749):
sister mourns, iv. 92
Pratt, Sir John (1657–1725), Kt; lord chief justice:
daughter of, iv. 87n
Pratt, Hon. John Jeffreys (1759–1840), styled Vct Bayham 1786–94; 2d E. Camden, 1794; cr. (1812) M. Camden:
marriage of, ix. 620
Pratt, Mrs John Jeffreys. *See* Molesworth, Frances (before 1766–1829)
Prawns:
eyes and tails of, v. 191
Prayer; prayers:
clergyman prefers, to be said by light of tallow candles instead of farthing ones, i. 85
Ferrers's, at execution, v. 401
for George II, iii. 149
for Richecourt, v. 79
for royal family, George III excludes all but his mother from, v. 449
HW's reflections on, vii. 145
ordered, for earthquake relief, i. 284
Thomas, Bp, reads, to George II, iv. 348
York, Cardinal, delays expedition with, iii. 509
Prayer-book:
Stafford has *Portier des Chartreux* bound like, i. 273–4
See also Book of Common Prayer
Preacher:
Charles II's witticism about, vi. 57, viii. 52
See also Clergyman

Precedence:
dispute over, at Sandwich's ball, iv. 121–2, 144
Mann's ideas about, iv. 144
Precipitate. *See* Powder, red
Prédiction. See under Voltaire
Predictions:
HW tells Mann not to trust his, viii. 379
unforeseen events invalidate, ix. 369
unreliability of, HW's reflections on, viii. 256
Preferment:
death follows after, vii. 313
Preising. *See* Preysing
Prenner, Giorgio Gasparo de (1721–66), engraver:
Illustri fatti Farnesiani engraved by, ix. 403
Preobazinsky Guards:
Catherine II proclaimed by, vi. 57–8
constitution could be overthrown by, vii. 304
Prerogative:
Parliamentary vacillation about, ix. 66
royal, Tories foster, viii. 492
Presbourg, Presburg. *See* Pressburg
Presbyterian; Presbyterians:
Charles I demands homage of, vii. 100
Dashwood, Lady, belongs to, iii. 224
HW jokes about, iii. 247
Kilmarnock belongs to, iii. 283
London has dullness of, iii. 189
meeting-house of, said to be destroyed by Roman Catholics, ix. 56
Roman Catholics oppose, ix. 64
Scottish: forswear the Pope, viii. 475; Gordon leads, against Roman Catholics, ix. 11
Presbyterian Church:
Charles II lectured by, vii. 386
Secker and Parker start as members of, iv. 188
Presidency, the:
Chesterfield's witticism on, iv. 214
President:
of Board of Trade, iv. 249
Président, French:
Louis XV compensates, for dog shot by Charolais, iv. 340
sister argues with, about names of dinner courses, vi. 163
President of the Council ('lord president'):
Bathurst succeeds Gower as, viii. 534
Bedford, D. of, becomes, vi. 130, 167
Camden becomes, ix. 262
Carteret (Granville) is, iv. 207, 258–9, vi. 569
Chesterfield declines to become, iv. 207
Dorset resigns as, iv. 202
Gower expected to resign as, viii. 526
—— is, viii. 497
—— may become, after Northington and Granville, vi. 569, 571

Hardwicke, may become, iv. 202
—— might consent to be, v. 92–3
Harrington is, i. 333
—— may become, iii. 327
Henley now is, vi. 500
—— succeeds Winchilsea as, vi. 443
—— to become, vi. 439
Pulteney, E. of Bath, becomes, ii. 556
Stormont becomes, ix. 391
vacancy for, iv. 202
See also Carteret, John (1690–1763); Compton, Spencer (ca 1674–1743); Henley, Robert (ca 1708–72); Leveson-Gower, Granville (1721–1803); Pulteney, William (1684–1764); Sackville, Lionel Cranfield (1688–1765); Stanhope, William (ca 1690–1756); Yorke, Philip (1690–1764)
Presidii, the:
embarkations from, iii. 55
Montemar may leave garrison at, ii. 27
Spaniards and Neapolitans near, ii. 546
Spaniards may retire to, ii. 325
Spanish expedition said to have reached, i. 192
Spanish troops in, ill equipped, i. 261–2
Spanish troops may go towards, iii. 410
Présomption punie, La:
Frederick II said to have written, ii. 337
Press:
liberty of: anonymous publications should be barred from, vii. 274; Mann thinks, is abused in England, vii. 189; Opposition abuses, after previously trying to suppress it, vi. 315
Pressburg:
Maria Theresa and Francis I said to be retiring to, i. 143
visitors to: Berrue, i. 205; Maria Theresa, i. 205
'Pressburg, Court of':
Montemar's name for Francis I, i. 261, 280
Press gangs:
English papers give account of, vii. 239
number of reprobates not thinned by, ix. 317
Press warrants:
England issues, to increase navy, viii. 252
Preston, Charles (ca 1735–1800), 5th Bt, 1779; M.P.; Maj.:
St John's surrendered by, viii. 157
Preston, Col. George (d. 1748), lt-gov. of Edinburgh Castle:
Edinburgh threatened with fire, unless rebels supply Edinburgh Castle, iii. 126
Preston, William, jr:
business at Leghorn relinquished by, iv. 499
Germany to be wedding-place and Holland the winter residence of, iv. 499
Pitt, Elizabeth, accompanies, and may become his wife, iv. 499
Preston:
Durand sends express to Ligonier at, iii. 166

few Highlanders consented to go to, iii. 107
rebels expected at, iii. 173
Prestonpans:
battle of, Young Pretender defeats Cope at, iii. 116–17, 198
Culloden battle not to be named for, iii. 247
English dragoons flee at, iii. 117, 203
near Edinburgh, iii. 116n
Pretender, the Old. *See* James Francis Edward (Stuart)
Pretender, the Young. *See* Charles Edward (Stuart)
Pretorian Palace:
at Cortona, iv. 423
Prevereau, Daniel (d. 1746) first clerk in the D. of Newcastle's office:
HW's and Mann's letters to go through, i. **98,** 280, 421–2, 425 (?)
Mann receives newspapers through, i. 421–2
——'s order to send letters through Holland neglected by, ii. 418
—— writes to, about sending mail, ii. 443
Mann, Galfridus, to complain to, about mail, ii. 448
packet to be forwarded by, to Mann, ii. 411
postal packets irregularly sent by officials of, ii. 233
Prévost *or* Prevost, Jacques *or* James (1725–75), styled McKay; Maj.-Gen., 1762:
Cumberland, D. of, left by, to visit Swiss family, vii. 553–4
English authorities probably disapprove of, vii. 554
Mann to be informed by, of D. of Cumberland's requirements, vii. 525–6
Preysing, Johann Carl Joseph (ca 1689–1771), Graf von; Bavarian Maj.-Gen.:
captured by Austrians, ii. 234
Price, ——:
Mann mistakes Giles's name for, viii. 260, 266, 271
Price, ——, London lawyer:
Cony consults, about Houghton pictures, x. 55
Price, (?Richard) (d. 1759), Lt:
killed, v. 351
Price, Richard (1723–91), D. D., dissenting clergyman:
Observations on Civil Liberty, copy of, supposedly found in lodgings of Bristol incendiary, viii. 274
Price; prices:
Albano painting, x. 7
Allectus medal, gold, i. 378
apartment, for coronation, v. 536
apartment rent, at Pisa, vii. 55
art collections, vi. 107, 115, ix. 93–4, *see also* Painting
art export license, at Rome, x. 4
artillery, ii. 457

[Price; prices, *continued*]
  at brothel, viii. 413
  balloon sightseers' admission, ix. 528
  bank construction, vii. 210
  book publication, iv. 31
  boutonnière of roses, vii. 210
  bread, v. 520, vi. 450, 455
  burgundy, v. 491
  busts, at Rome, x. 4, 7
  cameo, x. 5
  Canaletto copies, vii. 298–9
  Carlo Maratti miniature, ii. 162
  casing art objects, x. 4
  chair frames, v. 556–7
  chariot, i. 53–4
  china, Chelsea, vi. 122
  Chinese pheasant, vii. 210
  coal, ix. 274
  cocchiata, at Florence, vi. 158
  concert in London, ix. 646
  Correggio copy, x. 7
  Cortona painting, x. 7
  cracked jar, iv. 155
  criminals' capture or murder, iv. 446
  custom house export duty, at Rome, x. 5
  damask, v. 447
  dentistry, iv. 291–2
  deserters, ii. 243, iii. 23
  diamond buttons, vi. 481
  diamond earrings, ix. 148
  dinners, i. 506
  Domenichino painting, i. 226–7, 241
  eagle, iii. 66, 121–2
  election expense, iv. 435–6
  electrical instruments, iv. 331
  embassy entrance expenses, v. 508
  English satiric prints, ix. 496
  engravers', exceed those of former great painters, ix. 532
  exhibition entrance fee, vii. 211
  fans, vii. 294–5, 302
  fête champêtre, viii. 14
  Florence oil, in London, i. 240
  for ball, at Florence, iv. 276
  for making a saint, iii. 171
  Francavilla's statues, vi. 583
  Fumagalli's travelling allowance, ii. 96
  funeral at Rome, v. 391
  Gabburri's drawings, ii. 338
  gesse figures, iii. 47–8
  gladiator intaglio, i. 212, v. 151
  glazier's daily pay, iv. 396
  grain from abroad, for Florence, ix. 314
  HW does not understand, vii. 122
  Hermaphrodite, i. 213
  historical paintings by Benjamin West, vii. 210–11
  horses, at Florence, v. 179
  Houghton collection, viii. 427, 434, 440–1, 502, ix. 316
  house construction, iv. 217
  house rent at Turin, v. 175
  Illustri fatti Farnesiani, ix. 465

Imperiali painting, x. 7
Indiaman, ix. 134–5
intaglio, iii. 476, 483, 489, iv. 159
ivory carving, x. 7
ladies' ribbons, ii. 281
linen, i. 53
Liotard's portraits, iv. 324–5, 362
lodging, in London, vii. 287
London Pantheon's construction, vii. 210, 298
machine for raising water, v. 419
Maratti painting, x. 7
masquerade tickets, iii. 483
medals, i. 378, v. 201–2, 203, x. 5, 7
mezzotints, vii. 211
model of water-raising machine, v. 407
Museum Florentinum, ii. 330
notary public, at Rome, x. 5
Occhiali paintings, x. 8
opera singer's fee, ii. 281
operas popular when made equal with plays in, iv. 410
opera tickets, vii. 458
orange flowers, ii. 230
organ, iv. 331
ormolu teakettle, vii. 211–12
painting of marriage of Henry VII, iv. 390n
paintings, iv. 142, v. 172–3, 200, 208–9, v. 478–9, vi. 466, 569–70, x. 7, 8; *see also under names of artists*
Palazza Madama, iv. 264
Pallione copy, ii. 334
Pannini paintings, x. 7
Pantheon entrance fee in London, ix. 543
passport, in Florence, v. 482
pistols, i. 207
post, ix. 608
princedom in Holy Roman Empire, viii. 370
prints, in England, vii. 465, ix. 496
prostitutes, viii. 234, 413
quack physician's fee, vii. 251
race horse, vii. 497
Ranelagh admission, i. 401, 434
Raphael painting, ii. 239
rent of house in St James's Square, ix. 455
rent of jewels, v. 536
repairs to Villa Salviati, v. 310, 373
Riccardi's collection of jewels, iii. 73, 74
——'s rings, iii. 372, 398
roses, vii. 210
Sardinian deserters, i. 500
scaffold for coronation, v. 536
seals by Costanzi, x. 8
ship, ii. 521
shipping charges, x. 4, 5
silk hangings, v. 468
silver plate, ii. 472
state coach, vi. 104
statue model, ii. 179
statue of 'Livia,' ii. 177, x. 5
statues, v. 480

Stosch's library, v. 284
——'s map collection, v. 186–7, 192
straw, vii. 323
stuffed birds, vii. 210
table: ancient mosaic, x. 7, granite, x. 7;
oriental alabaster, x. 7; porphyry, x. 7;
scagliola, ii. 87, 106
theatre admission, in Florence, iv. 357
Tortola lands, viii. 264–5
two days' food, in France, viii. 106
urns, x. 8
vases: x. 7; Etruscan, vii. 211
ventletrap, v. 173
'views,' i. 81
Viviani landscapes, x. 7
Viviani's, for book on Herculaneum, vi. 299
watch, iv. 57, v. 295–6
watch-seals, v. 296
wig, i. 506, ix. 609n
window repairs in Florence, iv. 25
wine, vii. 302
Zoffany painting, viii. 540
Pridden, J., bookseller:
prosecuted, vii. 29
Pridden, Sally (1690–1724), alias Sally Salis-
bury; courtesan:
Finch stabbed by, iii. 389
Pride:
arrogance is a declaration of, ix. 636
HW considers, a less heinous sin, ix. 655
HW determined to preserve, vii. 528
HW's reflections on national, as similar to
that of family, ix. 133
Prideaux, George (d. 1784):
HW discusses Italy and Stosch with, i. 378,
404
Mann quotes, i. 491
Prideaux, Humphrey (1648–1724), orientalist;
Dean of Norwich 1702–24:
grandson of, i. 378n
Prideaux, Humphrey (d. 1793), of Prideaux
Place, Cornwall:
HW discusses Italy and Stosch with, i. 378,
404
Mann forwards letters of, to Rome, i. 491
son of, i. 491
Prie. See Priero
Priero, Marchese di. See Turinetti, Ercole
(1717–81); Turinetti, Giovanni Antonio
(1687–1757)
Priest; priests:
despotism supported by, vii. 376
HW satirizes, viii. 71
may be laid aside, in new era, ix. 237
religious fashions invented by, ix. 541
See also Clergy
See also under Church of England; Church
of Scotland, Roman Catholic Church
Prince; princes:
fame earned by, with buckets of blood, viii.
367
Galluzzi's history reveals, in horrid light,
ix. 202

German, enjoy hunting, ix. 364
gradations of entertainment of, in Italy,
England, and France, ix. 587, 589
HW prefers churchmen's artful conquests
to the forcible ones of, ix. 596
HW's reflections on, viii. 140
HW to judge, at their burials and not at
their coronations, viii. 310
Mann's reflections on responsibilities of, ix.
314
ministers hoodwink, to increase their own
power, viii. 140
See also Crown; King; Monarch; Royalty
Prince, young, in Tuscany:
Mann's letter from Gustav III described
by, ix. 499
Prince Ferdinand, Prussian privateer:
Tuscan vessel seized by, v. 330, 349
Prince Frederick, packet boat:
capture of, v. 168
Prince George, English ship:
capture of, viii. 504
catastrophe of, v. 206
French privateer captures, off Marseille, v.
414
India ship captured by, v. 524
operates as privateer, v. 524
plies between London and Leghorn, v. 414
Prince of Orange, packet boat:
capture of, v. 451, viii. 302
Prince of Piedmont, English victualling ship:
(?) loss of, viii. 236
Prince of Wales, English ship:
French capture, v. 414–15
Princes of the Blood Royal, French:
Aiguillon tries to reconcile, to spite Mau-
peou, vii. 399
French court excludes, vii. 298
Louis XV not endangered by opposition of,
vii. 320
prevented from volunteering, ii. 62
Princess, German, Narrative of. See under
Moders, Mary
Princess Amelia, English ship:
involved in war, ii. 393
Princess Louisa, English ship:
Michael receives news from lieutenant of,
iii. 410
Watson captain of, iii. 410
Princess Royal. See Anne (1709–59), of Eng-
land
Prince William, British war ship:
escapes to Ireland, ix. 152
Pringle, Henry, army officer:
Amherst to be informed by, of Murray's
conduct, ix. 200
hostage for transport vessels, in attack on
Minorca, ix. 309
Mann cites authority of, in representing
need for assistance in Minorca, ix. 199
St Philip's Castle to carry, to Minorca, ix.
199

[Pringle, Henry, *continued*]
presence of, needed for trial of Draper's complaint against Murray, ix. 309
Pringle, Sir John (1707–82), cr. (1766) Bt; physician:
Cocchi wants medical description by, of Galfridus Mann's case, iv. 544, 554, v. 36
Cumberland, D. of, discusses Galfridus Mann's illness with, iv. 529
—— has, as his physician, iv. 525, 529
HW interviews, about Galfridus Mann, iv. 554
HW's gout wrongly diagnosed by, vi. 454, 459
HW to send news from, to Mann, iv. 559
Mann, Galfridus, consults, iv. 523, 525, 529, 540, 543, 544, 551, 554, 559, v. 36
(?) *Observations on the Diseases of the Army*, sent by Conway to Cocchi, iv. 544
Orford, Cts of, wants, to examine her son, vii. 488
Print; prints:
Albani's collection of, bought by George III, vi. 107, 115
Allegrini's, of Camilla Martelli, ix. 226, 230
Antoniazzo's, after Raphael, vii. 432
at SH, iv. 380
Cardigan invents frames for, iv. 381
Chute collects, ii. 284
English, of criminals, iv. 199
Faber's, of Lady Burlington's portrait of Lady Euston, ii. 482
Florentine, Mozzi sends, to Duane, ix. 568
for *Description of SH*, HW dissatisfied with, ix. 531–2
Gerini's, ii. 477
Gravelot's, of the 'Motion,' ii. 21
HW collects, of persons mentioned in Mme de Sévigné's letters, ix. 433–4
HW has: of Camilla Martelli, ix. 226; of Maschere, vi. 202; of Poggio a Caiano, vi. 222
HW passes time with, viii. 91
HW probably has, of Guido's Magdalen, v. 532–3
HW to send, to Mann through James Mann, v. 90
HW wants: of Cardinal York, v. 467, 487; of Young Pretender, vii. 422
high price of, in England, vii. 466
Illustri fatti Farnesiani contains, ix. 403
in *Pitture antiche di Ercolano*, v. 379
Jackson's, iv. 380–1
Mann sends, to HW, ii. 201
—— sends, to HW, of Cardinal York, v. 495
obscene, from China, v. 202
of Bianca Cappello, Electress burns, v. 561n
of Catherine II, HW has, vii. 242–3
of Charles I's sufferings, i. 358
of eagle, iv. 485, 489, v. 461, 470
of English portraits: HW has collected, for over 30 years, vii. 211; vogue for, vii. 211
of George III and Charlotte, v. 554
of HW: HW sends, to Mann, v. 407–8, 446; Mann keeps, and Horace Mann II considers it a perfect likeness, ix. 10
of Knight of the Bath, Mann wants, vii. 155
of Lady Euston from Cts of Burlington's portrait, ii. 482
of Maclaine, iv. 184, 188
of Marguerite-Louise, Grand Ds of Tuscany, ix. 434, 444, 473
of Maschere, vi. 202
of Medici: bill of lading for, v. 533, 538; engraved, v. 533; HW receives rest of, v. 561; HW's set of, not to be broken up, ix. 434; HW thanks Mann for, ix. 245; Mann sends, to HW, iv. 414
of Old Pretender's marriage, Mann sends, through Horace Mann II to HW, ix. 448
of Rome, York, D. of receives, vi. 229, 232–3
of Saxe and Lowendal, published in Holland, iii. 395–6
of SH, do not do it justice, ix. 531–2
of Townshend, Vcts, ii. 482
of Vallombrosa, iv. 317, 320, 329
of wives of the Medici, Mann may send, to England, ix. 230
of Young Pretender and wife, Mann to send to Rome for, vii. 427, 429
Oxford, E. of, collects, from book frontispieces, i. 357–8
Patch's: after Andrea del Sarto, vii. 275; after Fra Bartolommeo, vii. 275, 362, 371, 465, 468–9; after Giotto, vii. 465; after Masaccio, vii. 267, 276–7, 287–8, 315–16, 422, 465, 468–9, ix. 280; after Michelangelo, vii. 276; of Florentine baptistery, vii. 429–30, 435; of Sir John Hawkwood, vii. 428; received by HW, vii. 459
Pompadour, Mme de, makes, v. 201
Raphael's, vii. 432
rolls of, in HW's exchequer chest, vii. 285
satiric: in Florence, of three abbés' mutual admiration, vi. 531; of Boswell, Johnson, and Mrs Piozzi, ix. 641; of Elizabeth Chudleigh and Ps of Wales, v. 487; of Westminster election, ix. 496; price of, ix. 496
Stephens's: HW gets, vii. 435; Mann does not know, vii. 427; not to be had in Rome, vii. 429
Stosch's, obscene, v. 189, 202
Townshend's caricatures, v. 77–8, 90
to Waller's works, vii. 248
two-penny, at Dover inn, ii. 315
Venetian, by Jackson, iv. 380–1
Printer; printers:
English, absorbed in politics, vii. 157
Francklin was, of *Craftsman*, iv. 374
French officers threaten, for considering paper on Louis XV, vii. 230–1

George III's proclamation for arrest of, vii. 280

HW's, see Kirgate, Thomas; Robinson, William

House of Lords takes up, for illegally printing Weymouth's letter, vii. 77

Lord Mayor releases, vii. 280

of *The Champion*, may be prosecuted by Sir Robert Walpole for mentioning his natural daughter, ii. 33

of Tory newspaper, ii. 33

Print-shops:

satiric prints of Boswell, Johnson, and Mrs Piozzi in, ix. 641

Prior, Matthew (1664–1721), poet:

Dorset said to be brother of, iv. 62–3

Jacobites send, to persuade Dorset to give up Dover Castle, iv. 62–3

Mercury and Cupid, HW quotes, ii. 204

Queensberry, Ds of, celebrated by, in poem, iii. 195n

—— was goddess in days of, vii. 299

Prior, the:

(?) Craon, Princesse de, in love with, i. 17

Prison; prisons:

alms-boxes at, v. 238

Caffarelli enjoys, iii. 438

footman committed to, for getting bastard, ix. 355

Gordon rioters demolish, and release inmates, ix. 61

Hanoverian soldier delivered from, v. 12

Spanish, condemned men from, to be used in storming St Philip's, ix. 180

Prisoner; prisoners:

Austrian, Frederick II interrogates, v. 258

cartel for exchange of, iii. 187, 202, 205

Cumberland, D. of, takes, iii. 273–4

Curzay's magnanimity to, iv. 206

English: Aiguillon's courtesy to, v. 251, 255; French conceal, v. 368; French treat, cruelly, v. 21; French treat, well, v. 251; from Minorca, French may send, to Gibraltar, iv. 581; from Minorca, sent to Spain, ix. 430; from Oswego and Quebec, v. 18; in Scotland, released, iii. 204–5

English captain brings, to Leghorn, ii. 354

exchange of: in Irish fashion, v. 504; suggested, iii. 187, 202

French: Derwentwater to be treated as, iii. 180; English magnanimity to, v. 367–8; Frederick II hears complaints from, v. 180; in Hungary may rebel, ii. 446; taken at Minorca, ix. 207; taken on Jersey, ix. 115

parole of, iii. 204–5

Spain releases Minorca's garrison after taking them as, ix. 430

Spanish, Gibraltar garrison may get the itch from, ix. 59

Wright treats, gently, v. 21

Pritchard, Mrs. See Vaughan, Hannah (1711–68)

Privateer; privateers:

American: English and Scottish coasts infested by, viii. 315–16; plunders Selkirk's house and attacks Whitehaven, viii. 377–8

captured on way to Scotland, or lost on Dutch coast, iii. 173

crew of, imprisoned, viii. 302

Dunmore captures cannon of, viii. 157

Dutch war delights, ix. 108

England better than France at war of, viii. 448

England's only success is with, viii. 472

English: capture French transports, iii. 230; capture supply ships for Brest fleet, iii. 230; contraband articles to be distinguished by, v. 285–6; in Mediterranean, Dutch merchant ships sought by, ix. 120; Lorenzi accuses Mann of justifying, v. 356; not numerous in Mediterranean, ix. 112; to capture unescorted vessels, v. 269

English packet boat carried by, to Dunkirk, viii. 302

fortune-seekers may well turn into, viii. 465

French: at Corsica, intimidate Leghorn's shipping, viii. 437; at Corsica, ruin Leghorn's trade, viii. 476–7; between Corsica and Leghorn, iv. 577; capture English merchant ships, iii. 229; capture English merchant ships in Mediterranean, v. 69; captures English merchant ship off Leghorn, v. 264; dominate the Mediterranean, v. 20; English merchant ships pass by Corsica to escape, vi. 157; French consul at Leghorn warns, when vessels leave, viii. 476–7; French Court encourages, viii. 398; Mediterranean Sea will soon swarm with, viii. 397–8; off Corsica, blockade Leghorn, viii. 437, 508–9; prevented Leghorn commerce, v.115; swarm on Dutch coast to intercept George II's jewels, v. 465; triumph in the Mediterranean, viii. 466

from Jersey, prey on French, viii. 472

from Minorca, oppose French privateers in Mediterranean, viii. 466

HW's letters might be intercepted by, viii. 507

Hunter, Elizabeth, brought back by, only to be released by her father, vi. 24

Hunter's obligations to, vi. 16

Mann's courier liable to be taken by, ix. 218

Morice sends valuables back to Ostend on sighting, ix. 89

Murray's, take Levant ships bound for Marseille, viii. 437

Pembroke and Elizabeth Hunter brought back by, vi. 16

Prince George operates as, v. 524

prizes taken by, iii. 441

Prussia borrows, from England, v. 335

Prussian, see *Prince Ferdinand*

Rullecourt said to be acting as, ix. 127

Russia tells England to curb, ix. 39

[Privateer; privateers, *continued*]
Spanish, i. 153
Sturt subjected to quarantine because he travelled in, from Minorca to Leghorn, ix. 42
Tuscany almost ready to fight England because of rage at, v. 335
vessels for relief of St Philip's watched by, ix. 205
Privateering:
Londoners uphold, v. 549
Privileged place:
Théodore lured from, and arrested by creditors, iv. 164
Privy Council:
Cabinet Council almost as large as, v. 489
causes heard by, in afternoon only, vi. 443
disputes in, over trial of Oxford vice-chancellor, iv. 18
Dutch ship restored by, v. 285, 287-8
Florentine Regency attentive to resolutions of, about Dutch prizes, v. 287
George II welcomed by members of, ii. 340-1
George III sees, v. 443
——'s household may be chosen by, iv. 570
——'s marriage discussed by, v. 513
Grenville said to be head of, iv. 216
Lee a member of, i. 242n
lord president of, *see under* President of the Council
Massachusetts assembly's act rejected by, vi. 520
Santiago attack to be decided by, i. 175
Wade's answer to Drummond approved by, iii. 202
Privy Councillor:
Anson, Hyndford, and Robinson become, iv. 135
Harley becomes, vii. 32
Privy Purse:
Augusta, Ps of Wales's, Anne Pitt was, vii. 451n, 558n
George II buys watch from, iv. 57
Privy seal, lord. *See* Lord privy seal
Privy Seal:
Bristol receives, vii. 65
—— transferred from, vii. 173
Cholmondeley receives, ii. 356
Gower may resign, ii. 159
—— prevented by gout from taking, i. 478
—— resigns, iv. 417
—— rumoured to obtain, vi. 130
—— succeeds Hervey in, i. 492, ii. 70, 89
Grafton and Weymouth may fight for, vii. 310
Grafton obtains, vii. 314
HW does not know destination of, vii. 62
Hardwicke might accept, v. 92-3
Hervey takes, to Ickworth, i. 457
Pitt to take, vi. 442
Pulteney's aspirations for, ii. 70, 89
——'s intrigues to get refusal of, ii. 231

Rutland has the promise of, iv. 417-18
Scottish, Stuart Mackenzie restored to, vi. 444, 453
Temple resigns, v. 345-6
Prize; prizes:
Proctor gains, in drawing, painting and sculpture, ix. 577
Prize-fighting:
Mathews's taste for, ridiculed by HW, ii. 79
Prize money:
English seamen eager for, vii. 242
Prize ships:
Cocceji's article on seizure of, v. 281
Dutch: Florentine Regency heeds Privy Council's resolutions about, v. 287; taken by English navy, ix. 134
English captains at Leghorn share, with Townshend, iii. 277
English captains prefer, to artillery, iii. 100
English proclamation on seizure of, v. 281
English ships capture, viii. 420
Evening Post mentions, iii. 441
French: England captures many of, viii. 472; English ships take, to Genoa, Port Mahon, and Leghorn, ii. 438
Jersey advertises sale of, viii. 472
Leopard's, iii. 245-6
Mann hopes for capture of, at Piombino, iii. 236
Mathews prefers capture of, to aiding Austrian army, ii. 452-3
Newcastle, The, brings, to Leghorn, ii. 448
privateers capture, iii. 441
regulations for English ships taking, iv. 54
richness of, England's only consolation for war, viii. 422
St Stephen knights to win, from Turks, vi. 259
Venetian, English ship takes, to Port Mahon, iii. 81
Walpole, Sir Robert, opposes giving, entirely to captors, v. 415
—— would have regulated taking of, iv. 54
Wright's, at Porto Ferrajo, v. 69
Proby, Charles (1725-99) naval officer:
Gibraltar visited by, vii. 261
son of, receives greatest part of Jermy's fortune, ix. 206
Proby, John (1720-72), cr. (1752) Bn Carysfort:
Admiralty post for, v. 73
Proby-Jermy, Henry Francis (b. ca 1769):
Jermy leaves fortune to, ix. 206
Procaccia (carrier):
Bocchineri, Mme, has affair with, iv. 447
books sent by, i. 64
fanali to be carried by, i. 77
fee to, x. 4
melon seeds sent by, i. 34
model of statue to go by, ii. 200
Penny to send pictures by, i. 241
Regency banishes, to Porto Ferraro, iv. 447

Procession; processions:
   ennobled Florentines rank as nobles only
   in, until third generation, viii. 227
   for destruction of Polish dissidents, vi. 577
   for Frederick II's birthday, v. 171
   religious, for Wachtendonck's recovery, i.
   105
*Procession and Ceremonies . . . of the . . .
Order of the Bath:*
   (?) Pomfret, Cts of, sends, to Niccolini, ii.
   126–7
Proconsuls:
   Roman, pensioned by tributary sovereigns,
   ix. 118
Proctor, Thomas, (1753–94), painter and
sculptor:
   HW praises, ix. 577
   prizes gained by, in drawing, painting,
   and sculpture, ix. 577
Proctor, Sir William Beauchamp (1722–73),
cr. (1745), Bt; K.B., 1761; M.P.:
   coach of, torn to pieces by mob, vii. 6
   K.B. predicted for, iv. 136
   may be prosecuted for hiring mob at
   Brentford, vii. 79
   Middlesex candidate, vii. 6
   mob of, wrecks Middlesex elections, vii. 78
Procuratore di San Marco:
   election of, at Venice, i. 75, 77
   Venice to send, to England, to congratulate
   George III, v. 508–9
Procureur-général:
   La Chalotais offered reversion of place of,
   vii. 207
Prodromo. See under Baiardi, Ottavio Antonio
Professor:
   Genevan, makes witticism on Mountrath,
   iv. 103
   of anatomy, Cocchi's salary as, v. 194
Projectors:
   little regarded in England, iii. 460
Prole, (?) Capt. Henry, Mrs Bosville's lover:
   Bosville tells wife to follow, ii. 286
   Bosville, Mrs. to join, ii. 309
   (?) Bosvilles accompanied by, ii. 251
   Mann induces, to leave town, ii. 286
   Mathews may dismiss, ii. 309
Prologue to the Satires. See under Pope,
Alexander
Prompter:
   Holdernesse entertains, ii. 130–1
Propagation:
   HW's reflections on, viii. 393
Prophecy:
   folly of, HW's reflections on, vi. 572
Prophet; prophets:
   HW a gazeteer with no attempt to be, vii.
   86
   religious, made predictions after the events,
   not before, ix. 37
Prosperity:
   dangers of, to nations, HW's reflections on,
   viii. 378

Protecting duties:
   Irish mob insults Irish House of Commons
   for not passing, ix. 491
Protector. *See* Cromwell, Oliver; Seymour, Edward (ca 1500–52)
Protectors:
   of glass, for candles, i. 59
Protestant; Protestants:
   Albany, Cts of, probably is not, vii. 402
   cabals of, iv. 542
   Clarendon swings between Catholicism and,
   ix. 224
   divines of, join plot against Bower, iv.
   531
   English, Rome's changed attitude to,
   pleases HW, vi. 177
   Florentine lady's family rejects marriage
   proposal because her children would be,
   vii. 449
   French: Dutens is, ix. 625n; ready to join
   a French Pretender, iii. 309–10
   French invade Ireland in part most dominated by, v. 381
   Fuentes unlikely to become, v. 428
   Gordon rioters do more damage to, than
   to Roman Catholics, ix. 61
   Hungarian, Frederick II writes about, to
   Bp of Breslau, iv. 269
   Irish area controlled by, is short of ammunition, v. 373
   Necker given post in spite of being, viii.
   254–5, ix. 21, 159
   Norfolk dukedom's heir converted to being,
   vii. 485
   prejudices of, not preferred by HW to
   Catholic practices, ii. 79
   reverses may invigorate, iii. 118
   ridicule by, of Catholic customs deplored
   by Mann, ii. 59
   Roman Catholic fasting in Italy upset by,
   ix. 21
   Tuscan priests induce, to escape from
   parents and change religion, vi. 249
   Young Pretender said to have become, iv.
   333, vi. 324–5, 368, vii. 402–3
   ——'s wife probably is not, vii. 402
Protestant Association:
   petition of, carried to Parliament by Lord
   George Gordon and his rioters, ix. 52–3
Protestantism:
   Gordon, Lord George, sets fire to London
   in defence of, ix. 131
   Mathews's ridiculed by HW, ii. 79
   senility of, ix. 48
Proteus:
   gout compared with, viii. 67
   HW compares himself to, vii. 537
Provençal language:
   Richard I's poem in, v. 156–7, 186
   Sainte-Palaye interprets, v. 186
Provence, Comtesse de. *See* Marie-Joséphine-
   Louise

Provence:
advances in, iii. 352
Austrians about to invade, iii. 333
Austrians blame their defeat in, upon the English, iii. 423
Botta responsible for failure of expedition to, iii. 364
Brown to invade, iii. 323
Charles Emmanuel III's attack on, facilitated by Savona's capture, iii. 352
Crescimbeni's book on poets of, v. 157
embargo on coast of, ii. 360
expedition withdrawn from, iii. 363, 364
French army quiet in, iii. 374
French have no troops in, v. 223
French preparations in, vigorous, iv. 540-1
French troops in, iii. 334
French troops said to be withdrawn from, iii. 405
French troops withdrawn from Spanish army in, iii. 8
Genoa tries to exclude provisions from coast of, iii. 344
HW foresees failure of expedition to, iii. 367
Mann hopes that Austria will invade, iii. 306
Pitt, Anne, visits, viii. 194
provisions sent from Leghorn for expedition to, iii. 352
trade in, interrupted, v. 123
troops from, said to be shifted to Flanders, iii. 405
Proverb:
about cost of gold, vii. 152-3
Irish, about Gunnings' luck, iv. 358
Italian, Mann quotes, vi. 112-13
Latin, HW quotes, vii. 208
Providence, American sloop:
Glasgow's battle with, viii. 216
Provoked Husband. See under Cibber, Colley; Vanbrugh, Sir John
Provost. *See* Prevost
Provvidenza, Russian war ship:
at Leghorn, vii. 192
Prowse, Thomas (ca 1707-67), M.P.:
named in Secret Committee lists, i. 385
Parliamentary debate by, on amendment to the Address, x. 23
Pelham favoured by, iv. 32
Tories led by, iv. 32
Proxy:
HW consults Cts of Holdernesse about Mann's duties as, viii. 209
Mann asks about his duties as, at baptism, viii. 199
——'s, for Bath installation, *see under* Bath, Order of the: installation of
——'s function as, prominently mentioned in gazettes, viii. 238
—— thanks HW for instructions about, viii. 219

Prudence:
HW considers, out of fashion in England, viii. 433
Prujean, (?) Anne (d. before 1774), wife of (?) Francis Prujean:
Pitt, Elizabeth Villiers, quarrels with, about religion, iv. 499
Prujean, (?) Francis (d. 1780) of Sutton Gate, Hornchurch, Essex:
Pitt, Elizabeth Villiers, receives letter from, iv. 499
Warren a friend of, iv. 499
Prussia, K. of. *See* Frederick II (1712-86); Frederick William I (1688-1740)
Prussia:
army of: ammunition discarded by, ii. 543; at Königsberg prepares against Russians, v. 72; Austrians defeat, in Moravia, i. 372; Charles, P., intercepts retreat of, v. 109; defeated on the Rhine, v. 456; deserters in, ii. 547; Dresden to be retained by, v. 355; Richelieu compelled by, to fight in winter, v. 176; Russian battle with, expected in Saxony, v. 72; Saxe-Weissenfels opposes, iii. 61-2
Austria and Russia may be joined by, against Turkey, ix. 359, 436
Austrian-Dutch war may be joined by, ix. 544
Austria's war with, *see* War, Austrian-Prussian
Cameron supposedly commissioned from, iv. 384
(?) Charles Albert allied with, at France's instigation to attack Hanover, ii. 396
Conway visits, to see its army, viii. 38
courier from, v. 452
Cours de l'Europe satirizes, i. 177
Danish conspiracy may be instigated by, vii. 426
East Friesland claimed by, ii. 449-50
Elizabeth of Russia drinks destruction to, v. 255
England may substitute for Austria as ally, iii. 238
England promised aid by, iv. 523
England's alliance with, uncertain, iv. 571
England's reply to, iv. 362
England's sole ally, v. 84
England's subsidy to, Bunbury to oppose, vi. 8
English capture ships of, iv. 348
English feel, is almost part of England, v. 171
English privateers borrowed by, v. 335
English relations with, iii. 448
English treaty with, alarms French sympathizers, iv. 528
envoys from and to, *see under* Envoy
Florentines do not favour, v. 9
France may aid Turkey against, ix. 360
France tells Austria and Russia to make peace with, v. 497-8

Frankfurt and Nuremberg to be punished for recruiting for, v. 28–9
French naval funds diverted to, iv. 51
George II does not negotiate peace with, ii. 4–5
——'s negotiations with, demanded by Pulteney for examination, i. 250
Hanover may be attacked by, i. 202, 208, 316, iv. 501, vii. 401
Holland might be divided by, ix. 539
Hungarian insurgents annihilate regiments of, iii. 62
Joseph II does not start war with, viii. 367
—— may fight with, viii. 364–5
Kunersdorf falsely reported to be victory for, v. 331
Legge mismanages affair of, iv. 39
manifesto of: Mansfield's answer to, v. 286; stops payment on Silesian loan, iv. 348
Mann hopes that peace has been made with, iii. 95
Maria Theresa said to have made peace with, i. 134
——'s peace with, iii. 194
—— threatened with war by, unless she consents to Poland's partition, vii. 439
memorial of, Mansfield answers, iv. 362, 365
military action expected in, v. 71–2
ministers from and to, see under Minister
must be contemptuous of western European warfare, ix. 201
Muzell (Stosch) a Baron of, v. 380
officer of, i. 206
Peter III likes, vi. 7
Prague evacuated by, ii. 543
princes of the Empire want Austrian power offset by, viii. 450
princess of, may wed D. of Cumberland, ii. 62
privateer of, v. 330, 349
Russia forbidden by, to aid England, ix. 39
Russian army again marching towards, v. 172
Russian impostor may be sponsored by, vii. 546–7
Russia's campaign against, v. 72
Russia to sent troops against, v. 176
Saltykov's action in taking back oath of allegiance for, is disavowed, vi. 75–6
Stosch from, i. 164n
Swedish interference by, vii. 439
troops of, at Memel, prepare against Russians, v. 72
Viennese court organizes Europe to destroy, v. 15
Young Pretender to be rescued by, iii. 311
Prydden. See Pridden
Prynne, William (1600–69), Puritan agitator:
London mobs reminiscent of, vii. 19
Ptisan:
Walpole, Bns, takes, to Richecourt, ii. 66–7

Ptolemy (Claudius Ptolemæus) (fl. 127–141 or 151), astronomer and geographer:
geography of, iv. 501
Public:
interested only in what is before its eyes, ix. 331
Public Advertiser:
HW reads in, that Horace Mann II spoke for the Court, viii. 450
HW's undrained field described in, ix. 146
Norton attacked in, vii. 555
Public house; public houses:
Cholmondeley's regiment not allowed by, to pay, ii. 408
country magistrates refuse to billet foreign troops in, v. 13
English, in Florence, Young Pretender asks permission to use, viii. 137
Mann looks for Lady William Campbell in, ix. 272
Publicola, Scipio (d. 1747), Principe di Santa Croce; Charles VI's ambassador extraordinary to the Conclave of 1740:
cantata and ball given by, i. 20
Craon, Princesse de, met by, i. 3
Craon receives toison d'or from, i. 20
Pucci, Mme. See Degli Albizzi, Caterina (d. 1750); Valvasone Maria Cristina di (d. 1747)
Pucci, Domenico (1718–83), Tuscan agent in London:
(?) Acciaioli, Signora, cicisbea to, iv. 284
anxious to return to Florence, v. 180–1
Botta botches credentials of, v. 197
Francis I orders Botta to accredit, as minister to England, v. 180
letter of, from London to Florence, mentions no Vienna orders, v. 116
Lottinger appointed as successor to, vi. 345
Pucci, Lorenzo Orazio (1694–1764), senator, 1736:
(?) wife of, ii. 122
Pucci, Luisa Ninfa (d. 1743), m. (1720) Francesco Gaetano Giucciardini:
death of, ii. 138
Pucci, Vincenzo (ca 1675–1757), Tuscan agent in England, 1713–57:
Carteret's retirement predicted by, ii. 557
case of Leghorn suicide to be pressed by, at English Court, iv. 14
Culloden news announced by, in Florence, iii. 257
death of, v. 111, 175
French declaration of war against England sent by, to Florence, ii. 442
George II's Hanover trip discussed by, ii. 213
——'s sending for Sir Robert Walpole reported by, ii. 553
HW avoids, i. 186
HW's dealings with, over Riccardi's gems, iii. 74, 331, 392, 398, 411, 420
letters of, Lorenzi probably told by, of Mann's baronetcy, iv. 467

[Pucci, Vincenzo, *continued*]
London papers announce recall of, v. 108
Mann embarrassed by, ii. 342
—— encloses letter to, i. 307
—— to answer ill-worded remonstrance by, ii. 325
nephew of, says he is ill, v. 116
recall of, implied by his name, joined to Colloredo's in foreign gazettes, v. 113–14
resident in London for fifty years, v. 108n
Riccardi's correspondence with, about gems, iii. 372, 411
Tornaquinci hears from, of English earthquake, iv. 143
Pucelle. See under Voltaire
Pudding; puddings:
Goldsworthy, Charles, to eat, i. 351
Mann lives upon, i. 57
Mathews's taste for, ridiculed by HW, ii. 79
Puddletown. *See* Piddletown
Puebla, Graf von. *See* Portugal, Anton von
Puerto Rico. *See* Porto Rico
Pufendorf, Samuel (1632–94), Freiherr von; German jurist and authority on national and international law:
Mann 'laying in such bales of,' v. 286
Turks will be taught to read, vii. 88
'Pug.' *See* Lombard, Marie-Magdelaine
Pug (monkey):
crucifix tied around neck of, ii. 59
HW probably uglier than, viii. 433
Indian temple enshrines, viii. 433
Pugachev ('Pugatsheff'), Emel'yan Ivanovich (ca 1726 or 41–75):
Catherine II defeats, viii. 3
may have contributed to Russo-Turkish peace, viii. 35
Peter III impersonated by, vii. 547
Puget, Henriette de, m. (1775) Jacques-Anne-Joseph de Prestre, Marquis de Vauban:
Pisa visited by, vii. 480
Puget, Hilarion-Paul-François Bienvenu de (1754–1828), Marquis de Barbantane:
Pisa visited by, vii. 480
Puget, Joseph-Pierre-Balthazar-Hilaire de (1725–ca 1800), Marquis de Barbantane, French envoy to Tuscany 1766–84:
Boufflers, Comtesse de, much connected with, vi. 434
Choiseul's disgrace shocks, vii. 261
Craon, Princesse de, complains to, vi. 537
English victories give Mann right to hold his head to, viii. 545, ix. 17, 92
family of, all at Pisa baths, vii. 480
French capture of Jersey wrongly reported by, ix. 127
French defeat excused by, ix. 127–8
French weekly courier takes letters for, vii. 14
HW glad to be able to dispel the visions of, ix. 73
La Fayette's alleged letter exhibited by, in Florence, ix. 70

Mann announces English victories to, ix. 24, 70–1
—— argues with, vii. 278
—— asked by, for English *Mémoire justificatif*, viii. 531
—— assured by: that Jesuits caused French food riots, viii. 118; that Louis XV will not take Comtesse du Barry, vii. 90
—— entertains, at dinner, vi. 482
—— forbears to send letters through, to HW, vii. 317–18
—— hears from, about Duclos's rage over Montesquieu letters, vi. 531
—— hopes to have chance to tease, ix. 9
—— often talks with, but does not exchange visits, viii. 531
—— on good terms with, vii. 261
—— saucily treated by, but avenged by Court and town, ix. 9
—— sends compliments to, vii. 141
—— shown Parliament of Paris's anti-Jesuit resolutions by, vi. 519
——'s letter from, about *La Belle Perle*, quoted, viii. 394–5
—— told by: of way to forward letter to HW, vi. 557; that wife corresponds with Hume, vi. 562–3
monarchical leanings of, vii. 278
plenipotentiary, vii. 293
Rosenberg alone called on by, on coming to Florence, vi. 481
secretary and valet of, *see* Billerey
snuff-box to have been sent to Mann by, probably forgotten, ix. 206
Tavistock recommends, to Mann, vi. 482
Thurn's letter from, by courier, about Toulon fleet, viii. 394–5
to be French minister at Florence, vi. 445–6
Tuscan titles not acknowledged by, vi. 481
wife of, can forward letters to Hume, vi. 557
Young Pretender gets, to ask Mann for use of English public house in Florence, viii. 136–7
—— tells, how Mann spoiled his scheme, ix. 526
Pugi:
Craon, Princesse de, entertains, i. 413–14
Puisieux, Marquis de. *See* Brulart, Louis-Philogène (1702–70)
Pulse:
Albemarle's, felt by his mother, iv. 460
Cocchi's, irregular, v. 152
Pulteney, Anna Maria (1727–42):
death of, i. 363, 366
Pulteney, Anne (1663–1746), m. 1 (1694) Charles Fitzroy, 1st D. of Cleveland; m. 2 (1733) Philip Southcote:
grandson of, vi. 560n
Pulteney, Frances (1725–82), m. (1760) William Johnstone, later Sir William Pulteney:
pregnant, fat, and not young, vi. 561
Pulteney's bequest to, vi. 560

Pulteney, Gen. Harry (1686–1767); M.P.:
death and bequests of, vi. 560–1
Pulteney, Henrietta Laura (1766–1808), cr.
(1792) Bns and (1803) Cts of Bath; m.
(1794) Sir James Murray-Pulteney, Bt:
Pulteney's estate may go to, vi. 561
Pulteney, William (1684–1764), cr. (1742) E.
of Bath:
address against use of Hanoverian troops
discussed by, ii. 158–9
address to the King proposed by, in Parliament, i. 375–6
Argyll retorts to, about Scottish taxes, iv.
310–11
—— scolds, i. 335
Arlington St house of, ii. 231
army increases supported by, in Parliament,
i. 410
ballads satirize, ii. 18–20, 22–4, 49, 71–5,
83, 90–1, 99
Bath visited by, ii. 24, 89
Bathurst's quarrel with, iv. 38
bill proposed by, on returning officers and
regulating elections, i. 484
Bootle's connection with, ii. 72
bribery practised by, though he talks
against corruption, i. 355
Cabinet Council's move to oust Carteret
not helped by, ii. 535–6
'Caleb,' nickname for, ii. 20
Carteret disowns connections with, iv. 259
—— said to tell George II to grant demands of, ii. 83
——'s friend, iii. 167
Chancellor of Exchequer, iii. 211
chancellorship of the Exchequer predicted
for, by Gage, ii. 296
change in ministry must meet approval of,
ii. 147
Churchill's promise held by, about Hedon
election, i. 220–1
—— talks with, i. 331
Cleveland, Ds of, said to be aunt of, vi.
560n
Colman recommended by, to brother, for
Bradford estate, vi. 560
Craftsman never written by, iv. 374
creditor of, points to him in church during
sermon on avarice, iii. 53, 59
Cumberland, D. of, may be injured by,
iii. 347
Danvers's witticism on, i. 232
daughter of, dies, i. 363, 366
daughter's illness keeps, from Parliament,
i. 363
deserted, ii. 89
disinterestedness of, doubtful, considering
his greedy followers, ii. 72
dodges responsibilities of opposing rebels,
iii. 167
Doneraile held by, to voting promise, i.
251
Douglas an intimate friend of, iv. 533

earldom may be postponed by, to stay in
House of Commons, i. 484–5
earldom of Bath granted to, i. 467
epigram on riding accident of, i. 437
faction of, ii. 550–1
followers of: ii. 72n; desert to Carteret,
Sandys, and Wilmington, ii. 74
'Fountain' meeting attended by, i. 335
'Fountain' meeting avoided by, i. 436
'Fountain' speeches of, satirized, ii. 91
Frederick, P. of Wales, captured by, from
Carteret, iii. 229
—— may deal with, secretly, iv. 30
—— persuaded by: to make a new opposition, iii. 229; to write to George II, i. 337,
367
French praise, vi. 343
Furnese a friend of, v. 172n
—— given position by, ii. 72
Garter may be requested by, ii. 245
George II denies having offered Privy Seal
to, ii. 231
—— insists on resignation of, from House
of Commons, before granting places to his
followers, i. 494
—— instigated by, to refuse Pitt, iii. 209,
211
—— receives, iv. 80
——'s appointment of Edgcumbe displeases,
ii. 9
——'s negotiations with Maria Theresa,
France, Prussia, and Holland, demanded
by, for discussion, i. 250
——'s reply to, admired by Mann, ii. 42
—— told by, that House of Commons will
not permit new ministry, iii. 212
—— vainly asked by, for Hill's dismissal,
ii. 24–5
government places dispensed by, i. 492–4
Gower joins, at Bath, ii. 89
—— may be succeeded by, as lord privy
seal, ii. 96
Granville, Cts, entertains, ii. 527
Gybbon appointed by, ii. 72
HW calls, 'mean exploded miser,' ix. 8
HW expects more from paper by, than
from Chesterfield's, iv. 374
HW satirizes, ii. 357–8
HW would never pride himself on being
richer than, v. 57
Hanover troops debate not joined by, ii.
356
Hedon a borough of, i. 234n, iii. 342
Hedon election concerns, i. 220, 355
Hedon loss causes, to rave, iii. 371
Hervey friendly with, at Bath, ii. 89
—— lives with, i. 275
high bailiff's censure carried by, i. 251
Hill opposes, at Hedon, ii. 24–5
Hooke governs, iv. 533
House of Lords appeases, by passing Place
Bill, i. 431
impartiality professed by, i. 454

[Pulteney, William (1684–1764), *continued*]
increase of taxes and stocks attributed to, ii. 91
Indemnity Bill dispute fomented by, i. 429
legatee of many estates, vi. 277
Leicester's servants receive paltry gratuity from, at Holkham, iii. 443
Limerick aided by, ii. 72n
list demanded by, of opposing Hedon electors, iii. 342
lord president, ii. 556
Lovat's trial arouses activity of, iii. 347
Mann asks about 'disgusts' of, i. 454, 476
Marlborough, Ds of, describes intrigue of, to get refusal of Privy Seal, ii. 231
money contributed by, for raising regiment, v. 311
money for Maria Theresa's aid proposed by, i. 390
name of, stricken from Council book, vi. 96
Newcastle entertains, at Claremont, i. 503, ii. 20
——'s speech to the Regency parodied by, in a ballad, iii. 106
new ministry wrecked by association with, iii. 212
odes on, frequent in newspapers, ii. 90
Orford, Cts of, may intercede with, for Mann, iii. 310
Orford's coachman drives, home from New Park, i. 503, ii. 22
paper on Newmarket contributed by, to *The World*, iv. 374
Paris visited by, iv. 155, vi. 343n
Parliamentary disputes quelled by, i. 355
Parliamentary motion by, for examination of foreign negotiations, i. 250
party betrayed by, i. 329n
patent of Bath earldom trampled by, on entering House of Lords, i. 485n
Patriot days of, iv. 257
Patriots abuse, iv. 31
Patriots led by, in Parliament, i. 231
Pearce made Dean of Winchester by, ii. 319
Pitt as venal as, v. 541
pretends to join Tories, and Whigs, ii. 49–50
Privy Seal aspirations of, ii. 70, 89, 231
Privy Seal may be refused by, ii. 159
refuses to be lord chancellor, ii. 72
Regency Bill defended by, iv. 257
regent, ii. 209
Richecourt astonished at conduct of, ii. 10
riding accident of, i. 437
Rushout's valet sent by, to Hanau, ii. 299
Rushout to be representative of, i. 333
Sackvilles not to vote for, i. 221
Sandys's advancement by, satirized, ii. 91
Scrope examined by, i. 458
Secret Committee motion not introduced by, i. 375
Secret Committee proposed by, i. 297–8

son of, dies, vi. 121
son's bequests scornfully ignored by, vi. 146
Spa to be visited by, iv. 80
Stafford formerly the creature of, iv. 9
Townshend, Vcts, ridicules, ii. 277
Treasury and Exchequer posts given to, iii. 211
Treasury appointees of, called 'dishclouts,' ii. 350
Treasury post coveted but not accepted by, iii. 212
Treasury post coveted by, ii. 265
Treasury post not thought appropriate for, ii. 277
Treasury post refused by, ii. 72
Treasury post requested by, through Rushout's valet, ii. 299
triumph of, over Sir Robert Walpole, satirized, ii. 91
Tyrawley's comment on, ii. 104
'unresolved,' ii. 327–8
Vane receives position through, ii. 72
—— 'toad-eater' to, i. 487
Vernon's correspondence with, iii. 459–60
virtue vaunted by, ix. 8
Walpole, Bns, turns against, ii. 99
Walpole, Sir Robert, answers speech of, i. 231–2
—— attacks, i. 297
—— excluded, ix. 605
—— jokes about, ii. 25
—— might have been executed by, iv. 65
—— not openly demanded by, for impeachment, i. 328–9, 336
—— persuades George II to insist that House of Lords be entered by, i. 485n
wealth of, has no heir, vi. 121
Westminster petition presented by, i. 232–3
whisk played by, at Richmond Green, iv. 63–4
White's Club member, iv. 63
wife of; iv. 496; said to receive bribes for posts he hands out, ii. 72–3
Williams, Sir Charles Hanbury, satirizes, in ode, ii. 319–21
'Will' the nickname of, vi. 277
Winchilsea called on by, iii. 53
World contributions by, iv. 374, 395n
Pulteney, Sir William (1729–1805). *See* Johnstone, William
Pulteney, William (ca 1731–63), styled Vct Pulteney; M.P.:
death of, at Madrid on return from Portugal, vi. 121
father scorns bequests of, to cousins, vi. 146
father's only child after death of sister, i. 366
Florence visited by, iv. 174
HW told by, about Bower's persecutors, iv. 533
Jacobite antiquary recommended to, in Rome, iv. 174

Leicester's servants receive paltry gratuity from, at Holkham, iii. 443
political parties shunned by, iv. 174
regiment may be raised by, for Col. Craufurd, v. 311
Pulteney, Mrs William. *See* Gumley, Anna Maria
Pulteney family:
Granville, Cts, entertains, ii. 527
Hooke governs, iv. 533
parsimony of, iii. 443
Pumps:
at Pisa baths, Gustav III exercises broken arm upon, ix. 442
Pun; puns:
Churchill translates, from jest-books, ii. 131, 307
HW's, on Man-n, viii. 144
on Eurydice, i. 171–2
on Fordyce, vii. 418
on Lady Sandys, iii. 28
on Milan, iv. 159
on Radclyffe, iii. 380
Townshend's, on 'mermaid,' v. 66
Whithed's, on Spain and Young Pretender, iii. 97
Winnington's, on Walpole, Horatio (1678–1757), iii. 28
Puna:
Bombay governor seeks to install new governor at, viii. 509
Punch:
at Cambridge banquet, iv. 83
English visitors at Tuscan Court always get a bowl of, vi. 430
George I and Sir Robert Walpole consume, at New Park, iv. 455
Leopold's comptroller serves, to Cowper and Tylney, vi. 379
Londoners to drink, to celebrate Cherbourg capture, v. 227
Pupilli:
Del Benino put under, by wife, i. 122
Puppet show:
in Corso de' Tintori, i. 202
last trumpet would be ascribed to, by London club-men, iv. 131
Patagonian, Mann calls promenade of ladies, ix. 174
Russel's, iii. 28
vogue for, in France, iv. 483
Purbeck, Vcts. *See* Burgh, Lady Margaret de (d. 1698)
Purblindness:
occurrences of, v. 443
Purgatory:
Riccardi has masses said for souls in, v. 435
Purging:
instances of, iii. 250, iv. 175
Purnell, John (ca 1708–1764), warden of New College 1740–64; vice-chancellor of Oxford (1747–50):

may be tried for treason, iv. 6
Privy Council disputes over trial of, iv. 18
Purses:
Maclaine's lodgings contain, iv. 169
Pushkin. *See* Musin Pushkin
Putello, ——:
Ulysses acted by, in opera, iii. 355
voice lost by, at Naples, iii. 355
Putnam, Maj.-Gen. Israel (1718–90):
Long Island defeat of, viii. 249
Putney, London:
bowling-green at, Maclaine and officer quarrel at, iv. 168–9
Lorenzi visits Mirepoix at, iv. 87
Putrid fever. *See under* Fever
Puzzuolo:
Mann, Lady Lucy, not benefited by air of, viii. 203
—— was to have been taken to, to breathe sulphur, viii. 190
Pylades:
HW and Mann compared to Orestes and, vi. 274, vii. 309, viii. 283, ix. 5, 9, 312, 615
Pym, John (1584–1643), Parliamentary statesman:
perishes before his cause succeeds, vii. 200
Pym, Priscilla (1724–71), m. (1742) Robert Marsham, 2d Bn Romney:
HW has seen, 'in her moods,' ix. 424
Pynsent, Sir William (ca 1679–1765), 2d Bt; M.P.:
generosity of, unequalled outside England, vi. 280–1
housekeeper of, keeps will, vi. 276–7
old Whig baronet, vi. 284
Pitt's bequest from, vi. 276–7, 284
Utrecht treaty opposed by, vi. 277, 284
'Pyrenees, our':
HW's term for English Channel, ix. 590
Pyrmont:
Conway to have visited, v. 549
Pyrrhus (ca 318–272 B.C.), king of Epirus:
'victories' of, i. 233
Pythagoras (582–ca 507 B. C.), Greek philosopher:
diet of, ii. 567
HW almost thinks he equals, ix. 559

Quack; quacks:
HW considers Le Fevre to be, vii. 251
HW prefers, to doctors, v. 378
Mann averse to, v. 386
testimonials to, in newspapers, v. 132
Thompson called, iii. 249
See also Rock, Dr Richard; Ward, Joshua; *see also under* Physician
Quack oculist. *See under* Oculist
Quack remedies:
plaster for cancers, iv. 291
Quadrille:
Florentine society's chief diversion, iv. 115
HW pities Mme Sarrazin's craving for, ii. 148

[Quadrille, *continued*]
    Mann gets up party of, for Stanley, vi. 326
    médiateur: Craon plays, incessantly, ii.
    101; played, ii. 122, 329; Sarrazin, Mme,
    forces Mann, Chute, and Whithed to play,
    ii. 132, 148; Sarrazin, Mme, languishes for,
    ii. 329
    played, i. 483
    Sarrazin, Mme, will not be able to afford,
    ii. 361–2
Quadruple alliance:
    HW's name for authors of *Florence Mis-
    cellany,* ix. 635
    Old Pretender's claims rejected by terms
    of, iii. 481–2
Quail:
    Old Pretender's sons pretend to shoot, i.
    13
Quaker; Quakers:
    doffs hat to Karl Wilhelm Ferdinand at
    Chelmsford, vi. 197
    old, Fordyce's request for a loan refused
    by, vii. 418
    Penn an adherent of, iv. 20
    Provence, Comte de, and Comte d'Artois
    entertain, with his hat on, viii. 53
    shipowner, tells his captain to shed no
    blood, v. 264
Quaker Bill. *See under* Parliament, Acts of
Quakerism:
    HW has, in his composition, ix. 40
Quaker meeting:
    Dashkov, Ps, attends, vii. 249
Quarantine:
    Admiralty excuses the *Pembroke* from, ii.
    282
    at Leghorn, lasts 25 days, ix. 42
    Cellini's chest performs, vii. 421
    couriers perform, ii. 297
    Florentine courier would have to perform,
    before reaching Genoa, ii. 375, 376
    for plague-stricken crew, i. 105
    HW's difficulties with, over Domenichino
    painting, ii. 291
    HW's present to Mann has to go through,
    ii. 406
    iris roots detained in, vii. 362
    Lanfranco picture cannot come from Rome
    because of, ii. 297
    length of, 40 days, ii. 275
    letters from Rome delayed because of, ii.
    282
    letters received by sea at Leghorn subject
    to, viii. 461
    Mann not to bother with shipments
    during, ii. 318
    Mathews complains of difficulties of, ii.
    279, 300
    Montagu, Lady Mary Wortley, should be
    in, for dirt, v. 540
    on Venetian borders, ii. 122
    Pembroke, The, to perform, ii. 275, 282
    ship from England performs, at Leghorn,
    vi. 108–9

    Tuscan, creates only confusion and taxes,
    ii. 295
Quaratesi, Giovanni Francesco (1696–1761),
    senator, 1736:
    annuity to be paid to, as Electress's ex-
    ecutor, ii. 168–9
Quarendon, Vct. *See* Lee, George Henry
Quaresima:
    beginning of, i. 316
Quarries:
    Vanbrugh 'dealt in,' viii. 93
Quartering of government places:
    Parliament might complain about, viii.
    276–7
Quarterings, armorial:
    HW collects, at SH, iv. 372
Quartermaster:
    Wade captures, on way to Carlisle, iii. 167
Quarter sessions:
    Byron's murder of Chaworth worthy to be
    tried in, vi. 284
Quay. *See* Du Quesne
Que. *See* Kew
Quebec:
    American campaigns depend on capture
    of, v. 335
    Amherst covets coal mines of, vii. 49
    campaign in, said to be a ruse to divert
    Russians from Frederick II, v. 335–6
    capture of, v. 337
    capture of, expected, v. 301, 327, viii.
    157, 161, 175, 194, 205, 347
    Carleton must retire to, viii. 263
    —— repulses Americans at, viii. 215
    —— sends news from, viii. 339–40
    England would not exchange Carrickfergus
    for, v. 371
    expedition to, v. 266–7
    French Court receives news of loss of, v.
    357
    French may recapture, v. 416
    French victory at, alleged, v. 342–3, 344,
    vi. 21–2
    garrison of, slender, viii. 347
    HW prepares Mann for probable English
    defeat at, v. 335–6
    Lorenzi stresses possible recapture of, v.
    421
    Mann hopes for onslaught upon, v. 270
    —— pleased by French disappointment at,
    v. 426
    —— reminds Botta of false rumours about,
    vi. 89
    ——'s joy over capture of, v. 342
    Montgomery's attack on, said to have
    failed, viii. 185
    New England forces may attack, viii. 342
    provisions at, too scanty for English pris-
    oners, v. 18
    saved, v. 419
    surrenders to Townshend, vi. 16
    Vaudreuil hopes to regain, v. 357–8, 421
    well victualled and defended, v. 336

Queen Anne's War:
    joke in, about Peterborough hunting in Spain for his army, ii. 180, viii. 482
Queensberry, Ds of. *See* Hyde, Lady Catharine
Queensberry, D. of. *See* Douglas, Charles (1698–1778); Douglas, William (1725–1810)
Quelen de Stuer de Caussade, Antoine-Paul-Jacques de (1706–72), Duc de la Vauguyon:
    Adélaïde, Mme, repulses, for suggesting that she receive Comtesse du Barry, vii. 87
    Dauphin's governor, vii. 87
    Du Barry, Comtesse, aided by, vii. 87
    Jesuits' friend, vii. 87, 94
Queries. See Constitutional Queries
Querini, Angelo Maria (1680–1755), cardinal, 1727:
    Benedict XIV and Ricci at odds with, iv. 464
    Berlin Catholic church receives ornaments from, iv. 329
    death of, iv. 463–4
    Venice tells, to suppress writings about quarrel with Benedict XIV, iv. 190
    Voltaire's epistle to, iv. 329
Querini, Tommaso, Procuratore di San Marco; Venetian ambassador extraordinary to England:
    Venice sends, to England, v. 508–9
Querlon. *See* Meusnier de Querlon
Quero, American ship:
    Lexington news reaches England by, viii. 109–10
Quesne, Du. *See* Du Quesne
Quiberon:
    English expedition to, iii. 327
Quiberon Bay:
    battle of, v. 350–2, 356–7, 358
    Hawke enjoys himself in, v. 355
Quicksilver (mercury):
    Cocchi disapproves of, as a medicine, iv. 543
    English capture, from Spaniards, and refuse bribe to relinquish it, viii. 543
    Mann, Galfridus, takes, iv. 523, 527, 537, 543, 551
    unctions of, ii. 87
Quieras, valley of:
    French to invade Piedmont by, iii. 417
Quieta non movere:
    Walpole, Sir Robert, has, as maxim, iv. 409, vi. 111, vii. 289, 304, 359, ix. 434, 506, 529, 541, 603
Quiete, Conservatorio delle:
    Electress at, i. 65
    —— leaves, i. 83
    —— not to visit, i. 428
Quieting Bill. *See under* Parliament, Acts of
Quill. *See* Goose quill
Quilt:
    HW throws, from bed, viii. 442
Quin, James (1693–1766), actor:
    Barry vainly urges, to play ghost in *Hamlet,* iv. 209

Mitchell sups with, iv. 209
    plays acted by, iii. 342
    witticism by, to Mitchell, about cabin-boys doing nothing, iv. 209–10
Quinsy:
    HW has, i. 51–2, 54–5, 66, v. 369
Quintuple Alliance:
    Parliamentary reform sought by, ix. 401
Quinze:
    Gloucester, D. of, plays, with Cholmondeley, as his favourite game, vii. 356
    played by men at Stanhope's, iii. 485
Quinzevingts:
    Hénault's *Abrégé* treats, iv. 107
Quirinal, Rome:
    Benedict XIV receives Charles of Naples at coffee-house at, ii. 533
Quirini. *See* Querini
Quistello:
    Broglie loses breeches at, i. 465
Quito:
    'King of Peru' crowned at, vi. 426
Quit-rent:
    monthly, HW's term for his letters to Mann, ix. 530
Quivers:
    at SH, iv. 381
Quixote, Don:
    costume of, at masquerade, i. 339
Quota; quotas:
    Colloredo demands, from George II, v. 18
    England should demand, of Austria against France, v. 28

R., J. *See* Richardson, Joseph
Rabbits:
    German princes hunt, ix. 364
'Rabbit-woman.' *See* Tofts, Mary
Rabelais, François (ca 1494–1553), writer:
    Fais ce que voudras the motto of, ix. 22
    Gargantua, newspapers would inspire histories as fabulous as, viii. 412
    Lyttelton's *Dialogues of the Dead* mention, v. 408
    Pantagruel: HW alludes to, i. 339; Lyttelton prefers dissertation on Hippocrates to, v. 408
Rabutin, Roger de (1618–93), Comte de Bussy:
    lady's cosmetics satirized by, iv. 150
Rabutin-Chantal, Marie de (1626–96), m. (1644) Henri, Marquis de Sévigné:
    Craon, Princesse de, would tell Sade to read letters of, to her, iv. 387
    daughter receives pearl necklace from, ii. 291
    HW admires letters of, iv. 90
    HW quotes, ii. 291
    HW's collection of letters of, iv. 382, 387
    HW's letters not to be compared with those of, iv. 90
    letters of, HW collects portrait prints of all people mentioned in, ix. 433–4

[Rabutin-Chantal, Marie de, *continued*]
Mann enjoys HW's letters as much as her daughter's were enjoyed by, iv. 83–4
—— quotes, iv. 84
Montagu, Lady Mary Wortley, compared to, as a letter-writer, iv. 282
Raby:
Wentworth takes title of, enraging Vane, i. 333n
Raccolta di lettere sulla pittura, scultura, ed architettura. See under Bottari, Giovanni Gaetano
Race; races:
at Derby, Huntingdon, Stafford, and Warwick, v. 427
at Florence, on St John's Day, i. 78–9, 454
at Leghorn, for Tuscan court, vi. 418, 423
at Lewes, iii. 495, iv. 289
at Newmarket, *see under* Newmarket
at York, vii. 48, ix. 373
English newspapers concerned about, vi. 174
geese versus turkeys, v. 7
HW will not attend, at Windsor, iii. 298
macaronies run, in Kensington Gardens, vii. 491
Mann, Horace II, regards Florentine trip as lightly as trip to, ix. 373
Montfort places bets at, iv. 74
music eclipsed by, vii. 571
Welsh, Williams attends, ii. 305
See also Chariot race
Race horse. *See under* Horse
Racine, Jean (1639–99), dramatist:
Bajazet, Belle-Isle's letter reminds HW of passage in, v. 321
Mithridate, Maurepas quotes from, on Cornwallis's surrender, ix. 211
Rackstrow, (?) Benjamin (d. 1772):
waxworks of, vi. 135
Radcliffe Camera:
King's speech at opening of, iv. 50
Radclyffe, Charles (1693–1746), titular 5th E. of Derwentwater:
captured on board the *Soleil*, iii. 173
execution of, expected, iii. 341
Mann wants, executed, iii. 353
Old Bailey trial proving his condemnation in 1715 will send, to Tyburn, iii. 180–1
Tower of London reached by, after narrow escape from mob, iii. 180
Radclyffe, James (1689–1716), 3d E. of Derwentwater:
brother of, iii. 173, 341
Radclyffe, James Bartholomew (1725–86), styled Vct Kynnaird 1725–55; 3d E. of Newburgh, 1755:
captured on board the *Soleil*, iii. 173
Dettingen battle preferred by, to English mob, iii. 180
London mob nearly tears, to pieces, iii. 180
release of, iii. 241

Richmond entertains, as a relation, iii. 241
to be treated as a French prisoner, iii. 180
York, Cardinal, thought to be, iii. 177, 180, 241
Radclyffe family:
Lovat's pun on name of, iii. 380
Radicofani:
Orford, Cts of, carried to, in Pius VI's litter, viii. 317
Young Pretender at, ii. 388
Radishes:
white, served as hors d'œuvre, iii. 357
Radix de Sainte-Foy, Claude-Pierre-Maximilien (b. ca 1735), French diplomatist:
(?) Éon prints letters by, vi. 217–18
Radnor, E. of. *See* Bouverie, William (1725–76); Robartes, John (1686–1757)
Radziwill, Teofila Konstancia (1738–80), m. (1764) Count Ignacy Morawski:
Young Pretender might wed, iv. 35, 44
Raffaello Sanzio (1483–1520), painter:
angels painted by, Mann has copy of, by Messini, iv. 145
Bartolommeo's paintings once regarded by HW as equal to those of, vii. 465
—— the 'parent' of, vii. 267
Cellini's chest said to be copied from print by, vii. 432
——'s chest worthy of, vii. 425
copy of painting by, v. 200
'Doctors' equals any paintings in Italy but those of, vii. 570
Madonna della Seggiola copied by Strange, v. 470
Mann thinks Flemish painters inferior to, iv. 398
Masaccio's designs the precursors of, vii. 266–7, x. 45
paintings by: Beaufort may buy, ii. 273; Gaven's price for, ii. 273; in Cybo collection, ii. 235; Mann to get copies of, iv. 328–9, 490, v. 88; of Christ and the doctors, Charles Emmanuel III would have bought, from D. of Massa for Marlborough, ii. 235–6; Parker buys, from Cybo collection, ii. 239; Portland, Ds of, buys, v. 200n; 'School of Athens' copied by Mengs, iv. 490, v. 88; Walpole, Sir Robert, refuses to buy, without seeing it, ii. 254; Walpole, Sir Robert, wants further information about, ii. 250
Raimondi's print after, vii. 432
(?) self-portrait by, copied Strange, v. 470
Vatican loggias painted by, vii. 298
Raffle:
of china, won by Mme Pucci, i. 159
See also Lottery
Raffle-picture:
HW sees, at Wolterton, ii. 47
Raffron du Trouillet, Nicolas (1723–1801), tutor; Revolutionary official:
Boufflers accompanied by, at Florence, vi. 474

Raftor, Catherine (1711–85), m. (1732) George Clive; actress:
Muscovita mimicked by, in *Miss Lucy in Town*, i. 435
voice of, inadequate, ii. 180

Ragley, Warwickshire, Hertford's seat:
HW to visit: iv. 265, v. 128, 226; with Conway, v. 226, 228; with Ds of Grafton, v. 427

Ragoût:
French will be unable to get pepper for, v. 523

Raimondi, Marcantonio (1480–ca 1534), engraver:
Raphael's 'Judgment of Paris' engraved by, vii. 432

Rainford. *See* Rainsford

Rainham. *See* Raynham

Rainsford, Charles (1728–1809), army officer; D. of Gloucester's equerry; M.P.:
Dick's letter from, about D. of Gloucester's marriage, vii. 437
Gloucester, D. of, accompanied by, to Florence, vii. 353
—— declares marriage to, at Florence, vii. 484
letter from Mann to HW carried by, ix. 271
Mann consulted by, concerning assistance for St Philip's, ix. 233
—— gets express from, about D. of Gloucester's lodging, vii. 333
—— tells, to consult Italian physicians about D. of Gloucester, vii. 393
—— told by, of Charlton's despair over D. of Gloucester, vii. 335
Minorcan mission of, unsuccessful, ix. 271

Rajadhi Rajasingha, K. of Ceylon, 1781–98:
England may bully, ix. 277

Rajahs:
sons of, in India, called 'rajah-pouts,' ix. 609n

Raleigh, Sir Walter (? 1552–1618):
cordial of, *see* Confectio Raleana

Rall, Johann Gottlieb (*after* 1717–76), Hessian colonel:
Hessians' defeat blamed upon, vii. 285

Ralph, James (ca 1705–62):
Of the Use and Abuse of Parliaments, ii. 464
Remembrancer by, attacks D. of Cumberland and Hawley, iv. 73
Remembrancer prepared by, in case George III is not K.G., iv. 73

Ramillies, English ship:
(?) sunk in storm, ix. 326

Ramsay, ——:
Florence visited by, ii. 479

Ramsay, Allan (1686–1758), poet:
son of, ix. 517n, 540n

Ramsay, Allan (1713–84), painter:
Arno Miscellany has poems by, ix. 517n, x. 46

Arno Miscellany sent by, from Florence for HW, ix. 517n, 633
bad poet and great scribbler, ix. 540
death of: at Dover on return to England, ix. 517n, 522; on way to meet daughter and son-in-law, ix. 522
HW surprised that *Arno Miscellany* should be joined by, ix. 540
Italy visited by, for health, ix. 517n, 522
Mann promised by, that copies of *Arno Miscellany* will be sent to England, ix. 523
political essays and other things written by, ix. 540n
sister to distribute *Arno Miscellany* for, ix. 523, x. 46
well known by pen and pencil, ix. 522

Ramsay, Amelia (1755–1813), m. (1779) Gen. Sir Archibald Campbell, K.C.B., 1785:
father dies on way to meet, ix. 522
returns from Jamaica, ix. 522–3

Ramsay, Catherine (before 1725–after 1798), Allan Ramsay's sister:
Arno Miscellany distributed by, ix. 523, x. 46

Ramsay, Michael (fl. 1727–64), Lord Eglintoun's tutor:
Eglintoun derives Jacobite sympathies from, iii. 112–13

Ramsden, Sir John (1699–1769), 3d Bt; M.P.:
named in Secret Committee lists, i. 384

Ram's heads:
on eagle's pedestal, iii. 122

Ranby, John (1703–73), principal sergeant-surgeon to George II:
letter of, about French officers wounded at Dettingen, ii. **260**
(?) HW mentions, iv. 375
Walpole, Sir Robert, attended by, ii. 538, x. 12

Ranelagh:
admission price to, i. 401, 434
Carteret, Bns, said to countenance, too much, ii. 501
Christian VII to give masquerade at, vii. 58
closed, iii. 308
Colisée the French counterpart of, viii. 242n
completion of, i. 401
cost of construction of, i. 434
fashionable hour at, is after music stops, viii. 310, ix. 317
full, ii. 8
George II enjoys masquerades at, i. 487, 495
German proprietor of, has influence with Cts of Yarmouth, iv. 46–7
HW breakfasts at, i. 401
HW prefers Vauxhall to, i. 434
HW to attend masquerade at, i. 487
inclement weather must curtail diversions at, iv. 69
jubilee-masquerade at, iv. 46, 57

[Ranelagh, *continued*]
masquerade at, i. 487, 495, iii. 414, viii. 103

new winter, in Oxford Road, *see* Pantheon, London

opening of, i. 434

Pantheon imitates, vii. 210

ridottos at, i. 434

subscription ball at, ii. 464

Venetian masquerade imitated at, iv. 46

visitors to: Augusta, Ps of Wales, i. 434; Burdett, iv. 21; Carterets, ii. 464; Carteret, Bns (Lady Sophia Fermor), ii. 483; Castle-Durrow, iv. 21; Christian VII, vii. 41; Cumberland, D. of, i. 434; Egremont, E. and Cts dowager of, ix. 68; Fermor, Lady Charlotte, i. 495; Fermor, Lady Sophia, i. 495, ii. 464, 483; Finch, Lady Isabella, i. 495; Frederick, P. of Wales, i. 434, iii. 414; George II, i. 487, 495, iii. 414; Gloucester, D. and Ds of, and family, ix. 68; HW, i. 434, 495, ii. 8, 464, iii. 414; Lincoln, ii. 483; Pomfret, Cts of, i. 495, ii. 464; Pomfret E. of, ii. 464; Tabuerniga, ii. 483; Waldegrave sisters, ix. 68; Walpole, Sir Robert, ii. 8

Ranger of the Parks:
Pomfret becomes, iv. 225–6

Rangerships:
Orford's, to be taken from him, ix. 266

Rangoni, Francesco Giovanni Maria (b. 1713), Marchese:
offers himself as cicisbeo, i. 46
Paganini, Rosa, and Giuditta pursue, i. 45

Rangoni, Lodovico (d. 1762), Marchese:
HW hears news from, i. 43

Rangoni, Vittoria, m. Federico Rossi, Conte di S. Secondo:
(?) husband's quarrels with, i. 123

Ranieri (? 1118–61), patron saint of Pisa:
festival of, ii. 455

Rantzau, Shack Carl (1717–89), Rigsgreve:
Christian VII closely guarded by, vii. 386
dismissed with pension, vii. 426

Rape of the Lock, The. See under Pope, Alexander

Rape of the Sabines:
in Florentine loggia, vi. 123–4

Raper, (?) Matthew (d. ? 1778):
diamond crochette carried by, from Turin to Lady Mary Wortley Montagu at Genoa, i. 138
dines often at Houghton, i. 138
Florence visited by, i. 138
Jackson's letter brought by, to Mann, i. 138

Raphael. *See* Raffaello Sanzio

Raphael ware:
HW's collection of, ix. 591

Rapin, Paul de (1661–1725), sieur de Thoyras:
Histoire d'Angleterre: Jeffreys called butcher in, iv. 194–5; Mann has copy of,

iv. 195; Pomfret, Cts of, objects to, iv. 194–5

Rasomoufski; Rasumofsky, Rasumowsky. *See* Razumovskiĭ

Rat; rats:
Lovat puns on Williamson's complaints about, iii. 380

Ratcliffe. *See* Radcliffe

Ratcliffe Library. *See* Radcliffe Camera

Ratisbon:
diet of; iv. 90; *mémoire* about, v. 102
England's seizure of Dutch contraband might be disapproved by, ix. 4
Francis I seeks votes at, after contemptuous treatment there, v. 90
Frederick II's troops approach, v. 102
HW as grave about SH as he could be about statecraft at, iv. 396
peace seldom enforced by conferences at, ix. 39
Richecourt may be minister to, iii. 49

Ravaillac, François (1578–1610), Henri IV's assassin:
Louis XV threatened with successors to, iv. 287, 387–8
renewal of age of, v. 48

Raven; ravens:
English compared to, v. 204

Ravenna:
Chute and Whithed to visit, iii. 48

Ravensworth, Bn. *See* Liddell, Sir Henry

Ravioli:
Chute eats, i. 218

Ravvivate, Teatro dei. *See under* Pisa

Rawdon, Bns. *See* Hastings, Lady Elizabeth (1731–1808)

Rawdon, Sir John (1720–93), cr. (1750) Bn Rawdon, (1762) E. of Moira:
expenses at Wallingford election revealed by, to Secret Committee, i. 400
kicked downstairs for not drinking Old Pretender's health, iv. 136
Mann remembers follies of, iv. 135–6
Naylor resembles, iv. 136
peerage given to, iv. 135–6

Rawlinson, Arthur (d. 1749), High Constable of Westminster 1737–42:
testimony against, about Westminster election, i. 246

Ray, Martha (ca 1745–79), Sandwich's mistress:
Hackman murders, viii. 459, 477

Raymond, Amy (ca 1700–89), m. (1723) Peter Burrell:
grandchildren's brilliant marriages witnessed by, viii. 499

Raymond, Robert (1673–1733), cr. (1731) Bn Raymond; M.P.:
lord chief justice, i. 438n

Raymond, Robert (ca 1717–56), 2d Bn Raymond, 1732:
epitaph by, on Indemnity Bill, i. 438, 455
father of, i. 438n

girl beats, ii. 322
 Halifax answered by, i. 230, 263
 Stosch receives offer from, for Meleager,
  i. 264
 Vaneschi cheats, at Lucca, i. **216**
Rayneval. *See* Gérard de Rayneval
Raynham:
 Leicester's son not to imitate marriage
  of heir of, iii. 27
Razors:
 Louis Siries makes, for Sultan of Turkey,
  iii. 437
Razumovskiĭ, Andreĭ Kirillovich (1752–1836),
  Fürst Rasumofsky:
 (?) Shuvalov accompanied by, at Florence,
  vi. 564–5
Razumovskiĭ, Kirill Grigor'evich (1728–1808),
  Grand Hetman of Little Russia:
 exiled and pensioned by mistress, vi. 456
 forced into conspiracy against Peter III,
  vi. 456
 HW refuses Shuvalov's invitation to meet,
  vi. 456
 (?) in power, vi. **59**
 Mann saw, in Florence, vi. 460
 (?) son of, vi. 564–5
Read, William, justice of the peace in
  Massachusetts:
 affidavit to, viii. 112
Reading, Berks:
 Pitt visits, vi. 490, 572
Reading:
 HW's, is just for his own amusement, ix.
  584
Real, Spanish ship:
 in Spanish fleet, i. 286
Reale accademia Ercolanese di Archaeologia:
 Antiquities of Herculaneum by, *see Pitture
  antiche di Ercolano*
*Real galleria di Firenze accresciuta, La. See
  under* Lanzi, Luigi Antonio
Real Felipe, Spanish ship:
 alleged destruction of, ii. 404
Reality:
 HW speculates on nature of, ix. 133
Re alla caccia, Il, opera:
 performed, vii. 171
Reaping:
 HW avoids, ii. 8
Reason:
 HW calls, charter obtained only by blood-
  shed, ix. 237
Rebellion of 1745:
 Walpole, Sir Robert, foresaw, viii. 356
'Rebel lords':
 Florence awaits news of trials of, iii. 293,
  298
 HW describes execution of, iii. 298–302
 Mann comments on execution of, iii. 311
 trial of: arouses Mann's sympathies, iii.
  303; described by HW, iii. 280–7; expected,
  iii. 271–2, 273

'Rebel pie':
 Townshend, Vcts, fears she will have to
  eat, iii. 302, vii. 21
Recanati:
 Austrians seize hospital at, ii. 419
Receipt to Make a Lord:
 HW quotes, from *Common Sense*, i. 469–70
 Mann dislikes, i. 491
Receiver of Rents:
 Cromarty was, iii. 284
Reception:
 Leopold to give, vi. 362
Recherches de la France. See under Pasquier,
  Étienne
'Recruiting Serjeant, The,' satiric print:
 Mann receives, v. 90
 Townshend publishes, v. 77
*Recueil d'estampes d'après les plus beaux
  tableaux:*
 Mann sends, to HW, ii. 181
Red Bank, New Jersey:
 capture of, viii. 352
Red Book:
 newspapers could have prevented errors
  by consulting, vi. 325
Redcoats:
 England's disputes should not be settled
  by, ix. 5
Red Lion Square, London:
 Suckling's address at New North St in,
  viii. 209
Redmond, Jean de (ca 1709–78), Lt-Gen.;
  chevalier:
 HW told by, of Young Pretender's alleged
  conversion, vii. 402
 Irish officer in French service, vii. 402
*Reflections on the Different Ideas of . . .
  Cruelty. See under* Bentley, Richard (1708–
  82)
Regalo:
 bringers of, receive money from Modenese
  princess, i. 64–5
Regan, Patrice, Ensign:
 captured at Velletri, ii. 492
Regatta; regattas:
 England transplants, viii. 112
 to be held on Thames, viii. 112
 Venice to give, for D. of York, vi. 241
Regency:
 Clive establishes, in Bengal for Najam-ud-
  Dowlah, vi. 416
Regency, Council of, in Tuscany:
 Alberti discloses letter of, about Mann's
  future promotion, vi. 317–18, 346
 Algerian war contemplated by, vi. 259
 Antinori, Chevalier, member of, iv. 124,
  350
 —— the sole functioning member of,
  now that Richecourt and Tornaquinci are
  incapacitated, v. 84–5, 90
 Austrian artillery permitted by, to pass
  through Tuscany, ii. 541

[Regency, Council of, *continued*]

author and publisher of sonetto banished by, iii. 499

'battle of the bridge' may be forbidden by, iv. 473

Benedict XIV's disputes over, iv. 305

Bocchineri complains to, of wife's affair with procaccia, iv. 447

Bosville, Mrs, might have been summoned before, ii. 286

Botta does not return visits from members of, v. 148

——'s circular letter to members of, announcing Peter III's overturn, vi. 63

—— to head, v. 107

Braitwitz avoids, to escape Richecourt's affronts, ii. 66

burletta dispute carried before, i. 163

Carteret never wrote to, ii. 382

Castellar tells, to give up deserters, i. 349

courier sent by, to Francis I, about Montemar's demands, i. 281

Craon head of, i. 189n, vii. 142n

—— to present demand to, for Electress's jewels, i. 242

delegate from, escorts Mann to Elizabeth Christina's requiem, iv. 227

Del Monte, Giambattista, excluded by, from Tuscany, iv. 422

Del Vernaccia appeals to, for wife's release, ii. 121–2

duel opposed by, iv. 363

Dumesnil's complaints disregarded by, iii. 491

each member of, has department, vii. 253

edict of, on Francis I's death, copied by Mann for Conway, vi. 329

English captains wish to 'kiss the hand' of, ii. 92–3, 99–100

English protection not welcomed by, for fear of antagonizing Spain, ii. 37–8

Ferrarini's case discussed by, ii. 10, 31

'Fiscal' asks, to forbid masks, ii. 372

Francis I names two new members to, v. 125

—— orders: to ask Naples to seize Del Monte, iv. 437; to have Te Deum sung, v. 112; to tell Mann that Tuscany will receive British fleet, v. 114

——'s correspondence with, about Spanish invasion, i. 206

——'s letter from, mentions Mann's coming promotion, vi. 317–18, 346

——'s message to Electress alarms, i. 236–8

——'s orders sought by, about Neapolitan cavalry, iii. 297–8

—— to receive news from, by courier, of Del Monte uprising, iv. 423

Francis III's intentions unknown to, i. 324

Gavi investigated by, i. 368

George II's protection of Tuscany known to, ii. 27, 38

Ginori may resign from, ii. 135

Goldsworthy says that Tuscan danger is belittled by, ii. 107

Haddock's letter to be communicated to, by Craon, i. 380

Hervey thanked by, iii. 473

Karl Alexander expected by, to call on them, iv. 376

Langlois supported by, in dispute with officer, iii. 366

Leghorn earthquakes to be assuaged by, i. 304

Leghorn governor asks, how to receive D. of York, vi. 166

Leghorn governor tells, of Saunders's approach, v. 507

Leghorn memorial to, iv. 267

Leopold II's arrival to be announced in notice by, vi. 330

Lobkowitz's discard of artillery disliked by, ii. 529

local affairs only, entrusted to, i. 134

Lorenzi asks, whether to celebrate wedding or funeral, iii. 14

—— urges, to expel English fleet from Leghorn, v. 274

Lucca punished by, for making new road, iv. 514–16, 521–2

Mann announces D. of York's changed plans to, vi. 245

—— asked by: to ask Mathews to guard against plague, ii. 256; to help Goldsworthy's difficulties, ii. 485

—— asks, to restore English brig, v. 334

—— assured by, of Francis I's intention to preserve Tuscan neutrality, v. 176

—— avoids dispute with, iv. 2

—— battles with, to stop French Levant trade, v. 282

—— complains to, of General's civilities to Cardinal York, vi. 250

—— disputes with, over seizure of English ships carrying Tuscan flag, v. 269, 273

—— negotiates with, about English interference with Tuscan trade, v. 269

—— persuades, to allow amusements at Leghorn, iii. 1

—— said to have been ordered to complain to, about Niccolini, iv. 7

——'s garden party considered by, as sufficient celebration, iii. 115

—— should have denounced *sonetto's* author to, iii. 498

——'s involved correspondence with, about capture of prizes, v. 288

—— takes Almada to members of, v. 436

—— to be asked by, for English aid, ii. 27

—— urges, to defend Leghorn, i. 259

—— writes to, defending Langlois, iii. 366

Maria Theresa honours members of, i. 40

Medici, Filippo, to give a caution to, ii. 445

meets on Thursdays, ii. 4, 17

members of, leave town on eve of St Charles's Day, iv. 451

Migazzi notifies, of Dumesnil's escape from Rome, iii. 493

Modena, Ds of, entertained by, ii. 228

Modenese princess ill-treated by, i. 60

Modenese princess refuses invitation of, i. 100

Montemar announces his intentions to, i. 261

—— answered by, i. 281

—— requests passports from, ii. 46

——'s demands considered by, i. 226

Naples presents memorial to, on allodials, ii. 177

Neapolitan cavalry seeks right of way from, iii. 297–8

Neapolitan minister to be told by, to have Del Monte seized, iv. 437

Niccolini's letter to be read in, iv. 24

opera attended by, in coronation rejoicings, i. 100

Pandolfini, Ferdinando, becomes secretary of, iii. 501

passports formerly issued by, v. 482

Pisa bridge battle may be forbidden by, iv. 473

Pitt sends French declaration to Mann, for transmission to, v. 502–3

Privy Council resolutions about Dutch prizes considered by, v. 287

procaccia banished by, iv. 447

public dispatch of, mentions Mann's rumoured promotion, vi. 346

Richecourt blames, i. 282

—— converts Craon to his opinion of Leghorn suicide, at meeting of, iv. 14

—— influences, to curtail Mann's privileges, iv. 205

—— overbears, ii. 328

—— president of, iv. 392

—— seeks to discredit, i. 282

—— too ill to attend, ii. 66

—— wants, to disavow his enmity to Ginori, ii. 216

Rinuccini a member of, iii. 251

St-Odile to join, iv. 305–6

Serristori appointed by, as attendant to Modenese princess, i. 64

Te Deum for Maria Theresa's coronation attended by, i. 100

Tornaquinci a member of, v. 62

Tuscan general honours Cardinal York without approval of, vi. 250, 256

Uffizi fire combatted by, vi. 68

Vernaccini presents Neapolitan memorial to, on allodials, ii. 177

Vienna neglects, v. 107

Walpole, Bns, subjected to search of her cases by order of, i. 224, 283

Warren examined by, i. 223

Regency, Dutch:
may terminate with William IV's death, iv. 279

Regency, English:
bill regulating, iv. 247, 248

Bristow and Frankland not discarded by, iv. 156–7

Cumberland, D. of, dominates, iv. 491

—— in, iv. 483

—— to head, iv. 125

for George II's Hanover trip, ii. 209, 218

for George II's trip to Flanders, disputed over, ii. 61

Frederick, P. of Wales, not included by, ii. 218

George II does not want Frederick, P. of Wales, in, ii. 25

George III's plans for, vi. 294–8

Mann hopes, will be unnecessary, iv. 254

Newcastle's speech to, parodied, iii. 106

no law for, vi. 42

Parliament may establish, with Ps of Wales as head, iv. 239

Pelhams establish Augusta, Ps of Wales, at head of, iv. 249

Sandwich's membership in, ridiculed by Selwyn, iv. 155

Spanish commerce discussed by, during George II's absence in Hanover, iii. 504

suspended on George III's recovery, ix. 682

Young Pretender's departure need not at once be told to, i. 114

See also Regents, English

Regency, Irish:
Dorset family wants to make Stone sole member of, iv. 316

George IV to receive, ix. 681–2

Irish Catholics considered by, too dangerous for army, ii. 566

members of, have aides-de-camp, iv. 316

Regency Act. See under Parliament, Acts of

Regensburg, Bp of. See Johann Theodor (1703–63); Klemens August (1700–61); Klemens Wenzel (1739–1812)

Regensburg, bishopric of:
Saxony covets, vi. 119

Regent:
Ireland chooses, in defiance of Parliament, ix. 681

Regent of France. See Bourbon, Philippe de (1674–1723)

Regents, English:
at their country seats in crisis, iii. 79

come to town, to quell invasion, iii. 90

Mann wonders about reaction of, to term 'His Holiness,' ii. 301

Newcastle's speech to, parodied by Pulteney, iii. 106

timidity of, ii. 282

Reggio:
earthquake account mentions, ix. 376

fair at, HW sees Cts Simonetti at, vi. 135, 148

gambling at, i. 46

HW prefers Canterbury to, i. 142

[Reggio, *continued*]
HW sees Forni and Montecuculi at, i. 44
Mary of Modena's maid of honour at, i. 43-4
melon seeds sent to, i. 34
plague at, ii. 282, 288, 301-2
post from, to Florence, i. 47
Rivalta at, i. 44
secrecy at, i. 43
Tesi brings fashion from, i. 110
visitors to: Fermor, Lady Sophia, i. 46; Gray, i. 82; HW, i. 34, 37, 41-7, 51, 57, 59, 61; Hervey, i. 45; Piedmont officers, i. 46; Pucci, Mme, i. 46
York, D. of, to visit, vi. 232
Reggio e Branciforte, Don Luigi (d. 1757), Principe di Catena; di Iaci; di Campofiorito, 1696; Duca di Valverde; Spanish diplomatist:
Wright captures baggage of, iii. 383
Reggio e Branciforte, Don Michele, Knight of Malta:
Neapolitan regency headed by, ii. 420
Reghelini di Scio, Dr Giovanni (fl. 1764):
(?) Northampton, Cts of, accompanied by, vi. 142
Regicides:
portraits of, at Cornbury, iv. 182
Regiment; regiments:
Bedford raises, iii. 128
—— to lead, in person, iii. 160
—— to raise, iii. 110
Bury colonel of, iv. 459n
Capponi's, i. 156, 198, 214, 266, 288
Charles III raises, ii. 542
Cholmondeley raises, ii. 128
——'s, ii. 408
Churchill's, acquired by Cobham, iii. 62
Clerici's, iii. 30
Conway awaits, vi. 559-60
—— receives, iii. 240
——'s: in Ireland, iv. 316, 372; in Minorca, iv. 264
De la Warr's, i. 353
Del Monte's, i. 123, 156, 473-4
Derby raises, iii. 128
disbanded, mutinous spirit of, disappears, ix. 406
Englishmen busy raising, iii. 126, 128, v. 363
Fitzjames's, iii. 208-9
Floyd to rejoin, viii. 508
for West Indies, debated in Parliament, iv. 531
Fox, Henry Edward, takes, to America, viii. 5
French army officers may be summoned to rejoin, viii. 357
Fullarton's, ix. 34
George II assigns, to Drumlanrig, iii. 420
German, in French service, v. 149
Gower prevented from leading, by gout, iii. 161

——'s, mutinies, iii. 209
Halifax raises, iii. 128
Herbert raises, iii. 128
Hertford not to resign, i. 345
Highland, mutinies, ii. 236-7
Honywood's, ii. 260-1
Irish, said to have been sent to Scotland, iii. 170
Kildare offers to raise, iii. 99, 155
Lobkowitz to send, to Piedmont, ii. 512
Lorraine, iii. 457n
Malpas accompanies, to Ireland, vi. 210
Malton raises, iii. 128
Montagu raises, iii. 128
——'s, to be headed by Sandwich, iii. 176
newly-raised, Court wins victory over, in Parliament, ix. 34
of dragoons, *see under* Dragoons
of Gardes Vallonnes, ii. 154
of horse, to be formed from militia, i. 123
of militia, to be raised, i. 156, 214, 266, 288
ordered to America, viii. 74
Orlov's, of guards, vii. 222
Pallavicini's, reinforces Lobkowitz, iii. 30
Pembroke urged not to resign, iv. 109
Pennsylvania's Germans and Swiss may form, iv. 531
Piedmont, v. 382-3
Pringle's, at Minorca, ix. 199
privately-raised: Carteret opposes Pelham over, iii. 158; Jacobites and Patriots oppose, iii. 154; motion to continue term of, deferred by Fox, iii. 209; Parliament discusses, x. 31-3
private raising of, irritates regular army, iii. 153-4
Prussian, annihilated by Hungarian insurgents, iii. 62
Pulteney may raise, for Craufurd, v. 311
Rutland raises, iii. 128
Sandwich colonel of, iii. 176
Scottish, destined for India, ix. 362
Scottish Lords to raise, iii. 167
Swiss servants in London to form, ii. 409
Townshend may raise, ii. 566
Westmorland may get, i. 353
Reginello. *See* La Reginella
Register ship:
Spanish: Banff captures, i. 377; Edgcumbe captures, iii. 82; English capture, i. 175, 208
See also Hermione; Postilion
Regnier, Claude-Louis-François de (1715-67), Comte de Guerchy; French ambassador to England:
Bedford, Ds of, complimented by, on fender at Woburn, vi. 218
death of, v. 551
Éon affair makes, ridiculous, vi. 273
—— robs, while his secretary, vi. 191, 217
expected in London, vi. **175**

foreign ministers complain to George III in behalf of, vi. 227

gone for the summer months, vi. 248

HW mentions, vi. 239

Nivernais and Praslin disparage, in letters, vi. 218

reception of, in France, freezing, v. 551

Vergy accuses, of hiring him to cut d'Éon's throat, vi. 262

Regny, François (d. 1779), French consul at Genoa 1756–75; directeur de la poste at Genoa ca 1740–51:

Lorenzi forbids, to forward unfranked mail to him, v. 362

Mann's English correspondence forwarded to, i. 103

Rehearsal, The. See under Villiers, George (1628–87), 2d E. of Buckingham

Rehearsal:

for Handel's jubilee, ix. 647

Reims. See Rheims

Richenbach:

battle of, vi. 70

Richenberg, Bohemia:

battle of, v. 88

Rein; reins:

Electress's, has long traces, iii. 370

Reiner Joseph Johann Michael Heronymus (1783–1853), archduke:

living, ix. 549

mother expects birth of, to be at Pisa, ix. 425

Reischach 'Reiscack', Judas Thaddäus (1696–1782), Freiherr von; Austrian envoy to Holland:

daughter of, vi. 398

Reischach, Maria Gabriele von (d. 1815), m. 1 (1765) Franz, Graf Thurn-Valsassina; m. 2 (1767) Anton, Graf Thurn-Valsassina:

Albizzi, Mme degli, succeeds, as Maria Louisa's grande maîtresse, vii. 253

apartment of, vi. **368**

Grande Maîtresse at Tuscan court, vi. 398

left at Vienna, vii. 253

Leopold and Maria Louisa accompanied by, on travels, vii. 220

Leopold and Maria Louisa reward, on her retirement, vii. 253

Mann tells, of approach of spaniel puppies, vii. 54

marriage of, vi. 398

menservants forbidden by, to enter Maria Louisa's chamber, vi. 529

Reissin, Jean, Lt:

captured at Velletri, ii. 492

Relatio Caroli Alberti Cardinalis Cavalchini. See under Cavalchini, Carlo Alberto

Relation de la maladie du jésuite Berthier. See under Voltaire

Relativism:

HW speculates on size of sublunary objects, ix. 133

Relics:

at St Peter's, i. 4

at Wachtendonck's bedside, i. 109–10

Madonna, painted in pulverized martyrs' bones, iv. 489

Mann ridicules, iv 430

Religion:

Catherine II and Joseph II lack, ix. 400

controversies over, have died down, iii. 229

English nabobs do not use, as excuse for plunder, ix. 400

epigram about disgrace to, in Ireland, iv. 316

Ferrers's opinions about, v. 400–1

HW's ideas about, iv. 81–2

HW's philosophy of, viii. 516

HW's reflections on old women's pretence of, ix. 584

Indians', ix. 438

HW thinks that modes in, are like ladies' fashions, ix. 541

inactivity of, HW considers, a sign of the world's senility, ix. 48

Leghorn church attendance, i. 260

Mann's reflections on, iv. 378

massacres committed by, in one age; philosophy in another, ix. 400

Neapolitan credulity about, ii. 305

Spaniards and Portuguese used, as an excuse for plunder, ix. 400

Uguccioni might change, to get English preferment, ii. 554

used as an excuse for war, vi. 39

Voltaire softens expressions about, in La Pucelle, iv. 548

women take to, on losing charms, iv. 378, ix. 584

See also Absolution; Altar; Altar-piece; Augustinian fathers; Baptism; Benediction; Bible, the; Canticles; Capuchins; Carmelites; Carmes; Chapel; Chaplain; Churching; Churchmen; Church of England; Churchwardens; Clergy; Clergyman; Communion; Confession; Confessors; Confirmation; Consistory; Copes; Cordeliers; Creed; Crucifix; Dominican order; Excommunication; Extreme unction; Fast days; Fasting; Friars; Gallican church; Good Friday; Grace; Greek Orthodox Church; Holy Week; Host, the; Hymns; Jansenism; Jesuit; Lent; Litany; Lutheran; Mass; Masshouses; Meeting-house; Methodism; Methodist; Miracles; Missal; Molenist; Mosque; Nonjuror; Nun; Prayer; Presbyterians; Priest; Processions; Relics; Requiem; Roman Catholic Church; Rosary; Sacrament; Sacrilege; Sacristy; Sermon; Subdeacon; Templar; Ten Commandments; Tenebrae; Theologian; Thirty-nine Articles; Transubstantiation; Trinity, doctrine of the; Unigenitas; Vestments; Viaticum

Reliques of Ancient English Poetry. *See under* Percy, Thomas

Remarks of a Persian Traveller. *See under* Magnan

Remarks on the Life and Writings of Jonathan Swift. *See under* Boyle, John (1707–62)

Remembrancer, The. *See under* Ralph, James

Remer, T.G.:
Serendipity, x. 34

Remiencourt, Marquis de. *See* Boufflers, Louis-François de

Remiremont, Abbess of. *See* Marie-Christine (1735–82)

Rémond de St Mard, Toussaint (1682–1757):
Montagu, Lady Mary Wortley, has, as lover, iv. 281–2
—— tries to cheat, iv. 281–2

Rena, Contessa:
'Contessa' not used by, in Italy, vii. 119
Englishmen and valets knew, at Florence, v. 162
Florence sends, to England, v. 156
Florentine wine merchant's wife, and Pembroke's and March's former mistress, vii. 106n
HW asks about, 'antique as she is,' v. 156
HW asks Mann to befriend, vii. 106–7
HW visited by, at SH, vii. 107
Machault and Marigny lovers of, v. 162
Mann calls on, at Pisa, vii. 119
—— to entertain, at dinner in Florence, vii. 119, 124
Pembroke buys from, v. 156
Pollard relieved by, of large sums, v. 162
title assumed by, in travels, v. 162
Tuscan Court must exclude, vii. 119

Renel, Marquise de. *See* Rohan-Chabot, Marie-Sylvie de (1729–1807)

Renelaugh. *See* Ranelagh

Renfrew, Count:
Young Pretender's pseudonym, vii. 225–6

Reni, Guido. *See* Guido

Reno, the:
Montemar passes, i. 427

Renzi, Bernardina, of Valentano:
Clement XIV's death prophesied by, viii. 41

Repas:
Mann must give, vi. 355

Repeater; repeating watch. *See under* Watch

Repnin, Prince Nikolaï Vasil'evich (1734–1801), Russian army officer and diplomatist:
Kücük Kainardje Treaty signed by, viii. 40
newspapers announce mission of, to England to make peace, viii. 487

Repulin Bacha, Turkish ship:
Russians capture, vii. 228, 235

Requiem:
annual, for Francis I at Florence, ix. 600
for Elizabeth Christina, iv. 227

Resident; residents:

from England to Holland, *see* Dayrolles, Solomon (1709–86)
from England to Tuscany, *see* Colman, Francis (d. 1733); Fane, Charles (d. 1766); Mann, Sir Horatio (1706–86)
from England to Venice, *see* Murray, John (d. 1775); Strange, John (1732–99); Wright, Sir James (d. 1803)
from Genoa to England, *see* Zuccato, Giovanni Girolamo
from Tuscany to England, *see* Pucci, Domenico (1718–83); Pucci, Vincenzo (ca 1675–1757); Salvetti Antelminelli, Giovanni (b. ca 1634)
from Venice to England, Almódovar claims to be, viii. 413
Mann's salary as, ii. 516
minister plenipotentiary next rank above that of, vi. 356

Resolution, English ship:
lost at Quiberon Bay, v. 351

Resurrexit:
on Henri IV's statue, a compliment to Louis XVI, viii. 19, 36

Retirement:
HW's reflections on pleasures of, vii. 315
Mann's aversion to, viii. 166

Reusz zu Ebersdorf, Heinrich XXVIII (1726–97), Graf:
Moravian, iv. 359
Sloane Museum trustee, iv. 359

Revelations, Book of. *See under* Bible

Revenge, English war ship:
French ship taken by, v. 192–3
involved in war, iii. 313
men from, lose arms, ii. 189
St Isidore pursued by, ii. 189

Revenge, The. *See under* Young, Edward

Revenue officer; revenue officers:
disenfranchisement of, proposed in Parliament, ix. 38
Gates's father was, ix. 92n

Revest. *See* Du Revest

Revett. *See* Rivett

Review of the Late Motion:
publication of, advertised in *Common Sense,* i. 83

Reviews, military:
English royal family like, i. 410
George II enjoys, i. 450–1, ii. 84

Revilla, Marqués, Spanish minister to Parma:
Charles III recalls, from Parma, vii. 446
Dresden visited by, vi. 303
Parma formerly the post of, vi. 330
return of, to Parma, vii. 518
Spanish minister to Tuscany, vi. 330

Revolution; revolutions:
HW expects, with new impostures replacing old, ix. 237
HW regards, as one of the many passing scenes in which he is little concerned, ix. 387

Revolution, American. *See under* America; War: American-English

Révolutions d'Angleterre:
HW's letters compose, in imitation of Vertot, vi. 158
Revolutions of England. See under Dorléans, Pierre-Joseph
Rey, Jacob. *See* King, John (ca 1753–1823)
Reynolds, John:
imprisoned for election corruption, vi. 584
Reynolds, Sir Joshua (1723–92), Kt, 1769; painter:
colours of, as impermanent as crayons, viii. 93
England's best painter, vii. 267
HW considers, a great painter, viii. 93
HW's portrait by: HW sends prints of, to Mann, v. 407–8; Mann impatient for, v. 414; Mann receives and frames, v. 446
HW to show miniatures and Masaccio's heads to, vii. 267
Reynolds, William (ca 1699–1784), page:
(?) Wales, P. of, attended by, iv. 232
'Rezzonica, Signora':
Pasquin might allude to, v. 491
Rezzonico, Cardinal. *See* Clement XIII
Rezzonico, Abbondio (1742–1810), senator:
Roman populace threatens, vi. 229
state visitors welcomed by, vii. 23
uncle starved by, vi. 380
Rezzonico, Carlo (1693–1769). *See* Clement XIII
Rezzonico, Carlo (1724–99), cardinal, 1758:
French and Spanish declarations to, about Young Pretender, vi. 399
Roman populace threatens, vi. 229
uncle starved by, vi. 380
Rezzonico, Giovanni Battista (1740–83), cardinal, 1770:
Roman populace threatens, vi. 229
state visitors welcomed by, vii. 23
uncle starved by, vi. 380
Rezzonico, Luigi (1726–ca 86), Gonfaloniere:
Roman populace threatens, vi. 229
uncle starved by, vi. 380
Rheims:
Peterborough's witticism when shown the Sainte Ampoulle at, viii. 112–13
Rheumatic fever. *See under* Fever
Rheumatism:
cold weather causes, ix. 493–4
HW prefers gout to, ix. 497
HW's, may be caused by damps at SH, vi. 450, 456
HW thinks he may have, vi. 450
in arm, occurrences of, ix. 432
in head, occurrences of, viii. 457, 458, 479
in loins, occurrences of, vi. 15
Mann prefers, to gout, ix. 500
——'s, believed to be gout in head, viii. 479
occurrences of, ii. 401, 520, iii. 234, 249, v. 359, 369, 443, vi. 15, 413, vii. 59, 462, viii. 457, 458, 467, ix. 115, 166, 494, 497, 500, 570

occurrences of inflammatory, iii. 249
treatment for: bleeding, iii. 250; bootikins, viii. 463; hare skins, ii. 520
Rhine, the:
Broglie retires towards, ii. 99
Charles, P., might cross, ii. 297, 311, 457
——'s crossing of: ii. 466, 478, 505; fruitless, ii. 481
Clermont about to cross, v. 193
English army crosses, ii. 209
English may cross, ii. 290, 293
English victory over French unprecedented, when on other side of, ii. 218
Ferdinand crosses, v. 211
French army on the, estimated, v. 271
French said to have crossed, i. 121
French should not have been allowed to cross, v. 264
French troops withdrawn to, from Provence, iii. 8
Mann hopes that Conway will drive French across, v. 493
Prussian defeat on, v. 456
Young Pretender may make campaign towards, ii. 434
Rhinoceros:
Italian head-dress imitates, iv. 147–8
medal of, struck off, iv. 128
shields made from hides of, iv. 381
Vandermeer brings, to Rome and Florence, iv. 127
Rhode Island:
Americans quit, viii. 419
English capture of, viii. 273
Estaing may attack, viii. 410, 416
Howe makes progress in conquering, viii. 281
Rodney finds, too strongly fortified, ix. 99
Rhubarb:
Lyttelton takes, viii. 537
'Rhubarb, Miss':
HW's name for physician's daughter, vii. 93
Rialto. *See under* Venice
Riazan and Murom, Bp of. *See* Sechanov, Daniil Andreievich
Ribbon; ribbons:
black, chaplain wears, across forehead, viii. 539
blue: footmen's gallery in Drury Lane strung with, iv. 231; in 'The Turnstile,' v. 93; of Garter Order, *see* Garter, Order of Carteret, Bns, wears, ii. 501
Catherine, St, causes miracles by, iv. 430
French embroidered, cockades of, vi. 423
George II distributes, iv. 311
green, of Thistle order, *see* Thistle, Order of the
horses bedecked with, v. 399
ladies', cost of, ii. 281
of knighthood, mad foreigner wears, at Paris, viii. 361, ix. 572
rainbow, around Patapan's neck, ii. 317

[Ribbon; ribbons, *continued*]
red, of Bath Order, *see* Bath, Order of the
washed, worn by humbler Florentine ladies,
ix. 175
watered light blue, Order of St Patrick to
wear, ix. 365
Ribera, José de (1590–1652), called Lo Spagnoletto:
Modena artists inferior to, ix. 247
Ricasoli, Baronessa. *See* Corsi, Teresa
Ricasoli, Barone Bindaccio:
festa given by, i. 136
Riccardi, Marchesa. *See* Gerini, Maria Mad-
dalena (1717–75)
Riccardi, Signora. *See* Strozzi, Teresa (1747–
1816)
Riccardi, —— (ca 1732–52), son of Vincenzo
Riccardi:
death of, iii. 336, 340
Riccardi, Bernardino (1708–76), Marchese di:
(?) father quarrels with, i. 147
Frescobaldi, Mme, dismisses, i. 136
(?) Grafton, Ds of, to receive letter from,
enclosed by Mann, vi. 108
Grifoni, Mme, replaces Mme Frescobaldi in
affections of, iii. 358
Mann discusses *Demetrio* with, i. **120**
Ricasolis entertain, i. 136
Riccardi, Cosimo:
ball forbidden by, i. 122
Carteret wedding shocks, by its simplicity,
ii. 445–6
curiosity of, about pregnancies and christen-
ings, vi. 8
father's gallery spoiled by candles with
rock-crystal lustres provided by, vi. 157–8
financial arrangements of, with estranged
relatives, i. 147
gossip loved by, ii. 358n
granddaughter of, iii. 350
granddaughter of, to be entertained, i. 122
granddaughter's death said to afflict, ii.
405
health of, apoplectic fit, iv. 192
Lami librarian to, v. 476, vi. 13
Mann constantly asked by, about Adolf
Fredrik's marrying Ps Amelia, ii. 304
—— plagued by inquiries from, ii. 289
son-in-law's death expected by, ii. 289
sons and daughter told by, of recent fit,
iv. 192
souls in purgatory reproached by, for not
giving him good weather for garden party,
in return for masses, i. 499, v. 435
Riccardi, Francesco (1648–1719), Tuscan ambassador to Rome:
(?) Giordano paints gallery for, vi. 157
Riccardi, Giulia Maria (1737–70), m. (1759)
Marchese Lorenzo Niccolini:
approaching marriage of, v. 343
Riccardi, Giuseppe Luigi (1744–98):
ball given by, for Archduke and Archduchess from Milan, ix. 50–1
(?) wedding dinner for, vi. 458

Riccardi, Laura (1699–1777), m. (1718) Marchese Antonio Corsi:
daughter instructed by, about marriage, i.
150
daughter's present from, on birth of heir,
ii. 121
father tells, of recent fit, iv. 192
husband of, i. **137n**
Riccardi, Vincenzo Maria (1704–52), Marchese:
Antinori, Mme, entertains, at villa, iii. 411
Carlisle and Duncannon interested in buying gems of, iii. 361, 372, 382, 387, 398
death of, iv. 336, 340
England formerly the diplomatic post of,
iii. 506, v. 464
father quarrels with, i. 147
father tells, of recent fit, iv. 192
festa to be given by, for niece, i. 122
Galli, Contessa, mourns, iv. 336
HW asked by, to send gems to Tempi, iii.
259
HW decides to keep rings of, iii. 398
HW has no time to deal with, iii. 104
HW loses catalogue of jewels sent by, iii.
73
HW receives letter from, asking him to sell
gems, iii. 28–9, 73
HW refuses to forward gems of, to Lisbon,
iii. 273
HW's correspondence with, iii. 28–9, 73–4,
331
HW's message makes, inquisitive about his
gems, iii. 408
HW tells, through Mann, that he cannot
sell his jewels for him, iii. 73–4
HW to receive letter from, iii. 94
HW would like to buy rings from, iii.
331–2
Lorenzi entertained by, i. 147
Mann awaits HW's instructions before seeing, iii. 392
—— concludes deal with, for rings for HW,
iii. 411
—— confers with, on sale of jewels, iii.
372–3
—— disputes with, at opera, over 'Onslow,'
iii. 506
—— not invited by, i. 147, 164
—— pays, for HW's rings, iii. 433
—— plagued by inquiries from, ii. 289
—— tells HW's instructions to, iii. 94
—— to pay, for HW's rings, iii. 420, 427,
435
'Onslow' accepted by, iii. 505, 506
Pucci's correspondence with, about sale of
gems, iii. 372
Tempi receives list from, of gems to be
sold in Portugal, iii. 349
Whithed attends festino of, i. 146
Riccardi family:
debts of, iv. 336
Mann does not want, at great assemblies,
ii. 284
wedding in, Lorenzi's greatest treat, iv. 92

Riccasoli. *See* Ricasoli

Ricci, Francesco (1679–1755), cardinal, 1743; commissary; governor of Rome 1741–3:
death of, iv. 464
denies having Pontano arrested, ii. 56
receives Pontano's sequestered papers, ii. 56
sent to Civita Vecchia to adjudge *Sea Horse*'s capture, i. 8

Ricci, Lorenzo (1703–75), general of the Jesuits:
Clement XIII said to have been urged by, to repel Jesuit refugees, vi. 527
——'s retort to complaints of, v. **230**
Clement XIV receives, coldly, vii. 135
——'s orders annulled by counter-briefs of, vii. 517
death of, viii. 147
dismissal of, to be decreed, vii. 473
imprisoned and examined daily, vii. 513
Jesuits' revenues should be used by, to support refugees, vi. 527
Jesuits suffer from inflexibility of, vi. 535
(?) York, D. of, asked by, for aid for American Jesuits, vi. 233

Ricci, Sebastiano (1659–1734), painter:
Smith has paintings by, ii. 465

Ricci family:
Bonaventuri murdered by, at Francesco I's instigation, iv. 414

Ricciarelli, (?) Giuseppe, opera singer:
Vaneschi disputes with, iv. 557

Riccio rapito, il. See under Bonducci, Andrea

Rice, ——:
Richecourt, Cts, has, as lover, iv. 90

Rice, ——, of Spittle Square, Bishopsgate St:
HW mentions, iv. 397

Rice, Lady Cecil. *See* Talbot, Lady Cecil (1735–93)

Rice, George (ca 1724–91), M.P.:
becomes lord of Trade, v. 489
marriage of, ix. 86n

Rich, Lady. *See* Griffith, Elizabeth

Rich, Edward Henry (1699–1721), 7th E. of Warwick:
Warner, Betty, seduced by, ii. 540

Rich, Elizabeth (ca 1716–95), m. (1749) Sir George Lyttelton, 5th Bt, 1751; cr. (1756) Bn Lyttelton:
HW admires singing of, i. 166
HW asks Mann to get music for, i. 166

Rich, Henry (1590–1649), 1st E. of Holland:
buried in Kensington Church, iv. 182
Henrietta Maria loved by, iii. **397**
Holland House owned by, iii. 397
motto of, interpreted by HW, iii. 397, 411
portrait of, at Cornbury, iv. 182

Rich, John (1691 *or* 2–1761), 'harlequin':
Horton, Mrs, and Miss Norsa intimate with, iii. 419

Rich, Sir Robert (1685–1768), 4th Bt, 1706:
Augusta mistakes, for Sir Robert Walpole, at Leicester House, ii. 219

daughter of, i. **166n**
Flanders visited by, i. 486
son of, iii. 248
son's quarrel to be adjusted by, i. 486

Rich, Sir Robert (1717–85), 5th Bt, 1768:
father to settle quarrel of, i. 486
Vane's quarrel with, i. 486
wounded, iii. 248

Richard I (1157–99), K. of England 1189–99:
HW seeks poems by, v. 156–7
HW thanks Mann for investigation about, v. 178
HW wants another copy of poem by, v. 178
Mann will seek poems of, v. 162
poem by: HW thanks Mann for second copy of, v. 189; in San Lorenzo library, Mann to send copy of, to HW, v. 169
Provençal poem by, copied by young Cocchi, v. 186

Richard II (1367–1400), K. of England 1377–99:
alleged Grand Justiciary of, iv. 64–5

Richard III (1452–85), K. of England 1483–85:
Catherine II's crimes may make HW believe Lancastrian histories about, vi. 253
HW later publishes *Historic Doubts* on, vi. 253n
HW's vindication of, to be told to Young Pretender, ix. 104
HW to write verses on, i. 234
Robinson resembles, v. 120

Richard III. See under Shakespeare, William

Richard (1473–83), cr. (1474) D. of York:
room of, in Tower of London, jokingly desired by HW, i. 233–4

Richard, ——, financier:
dismissal of, iv. 327

Richard, Abbé Jérôme:
Description de l'Italie, HW reads, ix. 97

Richard de Tarascon, Provençal poet:
poem by, v. 169–70

Richards, Mrs John. *See* Moysey, Mary

Richardson, Francis, adjutant of the Guards:
Sayre denounced by, viii. 138

Richardson, Joseph (d. 1766), clerk in the secretary of state's office:
Mann's dispatches acknowledged by, ii. 290

Richardson, Samuel (1689–1761), novelist:
Clarissa, HW dislikes, vi. 271
novels of: dull, vi. 555; French adopt, vi. 555
printer, not bookseller, vi. 271n
Sir Charles Grandison, HW dislikes, vi. 271

Richauts de Tarascon. *See* Richard de Tarascon

Richauts de Verberil. *See* Rigaut de Barbezieu

'Richcourt, Lady.' *See* Rolle, Margaret

Richecourt, Comte de. *See* Nay, Charles de (d. 1789); Nay, Emmanuel-François-Joseph-Ignace de (1694–1759); Nay, Louis-Hyacinthe de (d. 1752)

Richecourt, Comtesse:
England visited by, iv. 90
Florence visited by, iv. 365
HW describes, iv. 90
itinerary of, to England, iv. 45
Mann entertains, iv. 365
Piedmontese, iv. 90n
Rice lover of, iv. 90
stays worn by, in England, iv. 365
Richelieu, Cardinal. *See* Du Plessis, Armand-Jean
Richelieu, Duc and Maréchal de. *See* Vignerot du Plessis, Louis-François-Armand
'Richelieu, M. de':
Mann mistakes, for P. de Guise, iii. 426
Riches:
HW's reflections on futility of, ix. 583
See also Money; Wealth
Richie, Robert, English consul at Venice ca 1776–ca 1790:
Mann seldom gets news from, about D. of Gloucester, viii. 329
Richmond, Ds of. *See* Bruce, Lady Mary (1740–96); Brudenell, Anne (d. 1722); Cadogan, Lady Sarah (1706–51)
Richmond, D. of. *See* Lennox, Charles (1672–1723); Lennox, Charles (1701–50); Lennox, Charles (1735–1806)
Richmond, Mrs ——:
English only spoken by, iii. 97
English only understood well by, iii. 97
English washerwoman refuses proposals of, iii. 46
furniture moved by, from Florence, iii. 252
furniture removed by, iii. 290
HW prefers Richecourt to, as spy on Bns Walpole, iv. 31
house retained by, against law, iii. 238
leaves Florence, for England, iii. 304
Mann might have hired, to spy on Bns Walpole, ii. 14
Orford, Cts of, does not tell, whether to renew lease on Florentine house or to go to England, iii. 101
—— escorted only part way by, to Bologna, iii. 49
—— expected by, iii. 252
—— orders, to return to England, iii. 290
—— to be accompanied by, iii. 46
—— to be accompanied by, only to Bologna, iii. 49
—— writes to, about son, iii. 192
Richecourt advises, to quit house, iii. 238
Richecourt and Lady Orford leave, to renew lease on Florentine house, iii. 97, 101
Richecourt calls on, constantly, iii. 97, 101
—— may get letters from, iii. 290
—— may keep, in old palace, iii. 101
—— often sees, iii. 80
——'s coach waits at door of, iii. 97, 101
——'s friendship with, prevents her eviction from house at Florence, iii. 192

—— visited by: at Careggi, iii. 97, 101; in his coach, iii. 75, 101
things taken by, to Lappeggi, iii. 238
Richmond, Surrey:
Augusta, Ps of Wales, visits George III at, vii. 345
Baker, Dr, physician at, iv. 523
Croft calls on Edward Louisa Mann at, vii. 379, 383
floods between HW and, viii. 47
HW calls on Edward Louisa Mann at, viii. 36
HW takes Galfridus Mann to, iv. 63
HW to visit, i. 358
maid from, wants to see Ds of Montrose in coronation robes, v. 535
Mann, Edward Louisa, at, vii. 379, 383, (?) 506, viii. 36
—— ill at, vii. 340
—— too ill to be moved to, viii. 165
Mann, Galfridus, ill at, iv. 520, 522, v. 27
—— persuaded by friends at, to take tarwater, v. 30
—— still at, iv. 549
—— visited at, by Edward Louisa Mann and lawyer, v. 33
New Park: Amelia, Ps, closes, to public, iv. 322; Amelia, Ps, did not expect reversion of, iv. 29; Amelia, Ps, succeeds Orford as Ranger of, iv. 322; Amelia, Ps, to succeed Orford as Ranger of, iv. 233; Amelia, Ps, visits, ii. 449; Caroline given ground at, by Bird, iv. 29; George I orders Sir Robert Walpole to have New Lodge in, finished, iv. 455; George I shoots and dines at, with Sir Robert Walpole, iv. 455; HW's terrace overlooks, vi. 16; HW takes Rinuccini to, iii. 308; HW to go to, ii. 136; innkeeper at gate of, i. 503; Mann, Mrs Galfridus, robbed in, ix. 343–4; ministers' servants disappear at inn at gate of, i. 503; Newcastle procures venison from, i. 506; Orford ranger of, i. 503n, iv. 233n; Orford, Cts of, takes villa in, iii. 309; Patapan to go to, ii. 136; rangership of, George II tells Orford that reversion of, goes to Ps Amelia, iv. 125; SH overlooks, iii. 414; tickets not granted for, at breeding-time, iv. 323; visitors to inn at gate of, i. 503, ii. 20; Walpole, Hon. George, visits, in holidays, ii. 70; Walpole, Horatio (1678–1757) puts horses to graze in, ii. 70; Walpole, Sir Robert, at, ii. 136; Walpole, Sir Robert, catches cold at, while fishing, ii. 449; Walpole, Sir Robert, hunts in, on Saturdays, i. 247; Walpole, Sir Robert, ranger of, iv. 455; Walpole, Sir Robert, returns from, ii. 430; Walpole, Sir Robert, stores pictures at, ii. 249
Robinson's letter mentions, v. 121
SH faces towards, ix. 532
Thames difficult to cross at, vii. 47, 73
visitors to: Mann, Mary, i. 359; Walpole,

Lady Mary i. 330, 359; Walpole, Sir Robert, i. 164, 330, 333, 335, 358
Richmond Gardens:
HW takes Rinuccini to, iii. 308
Richmond Green:
Montfort gets parsons to play cricket at, iv. 74
visitors to: Bath, iv. 63, 64; Lonsdale, iv. 63; whisk-players from White's Club, iv. 63
Richmond Hill:
Fiesole higher than, ix. 532
view of, from SH, iv. 16, 380
Richmond House:
masquerade and fireworks at, vi. 148
Richmond Park. See Richmond: New Park
Richter, Ferdinand (b. 1693), painter:
'one-eyed German,' vii. 28
portrait by, of Mme Grifoni, i. 44, vii. 28
Ricouart, Antoine de (ca 1713–82), Comte d'Hérouville de Claye:
made director of troops, vii. 283
Riding:
Astley establishes amphitheatre for, in Southwark, ix. 451n
Leopold's only amusement, vi. 353–4
Mann's, iv. 143, 191, v. 58
Mann, Galfridus, accustomed to, iv. 549, 554
—— uses, to cure cold, iv. 520
Mann, Horace II, fond of, viii. 170
Riding coat. See under Coat
Riding habit:
English, Contessa Delci wears, ii. 85
Riding parties:
Mann's, Milbanke and Pelham share, iv. 172
Ridolfi, Giuseppe (1694–1756), Marchese; impresario:
Andromache staged by, ii. 128
Bagnolesi's costume for Iphiginia pleases, ii. 134
impresario of opera, i. 239, 284
Mann attends ball given by, ii. 60
—— entertains, i. 104
—— mistakenly given Richecourt's theatre box by, i. 394
Richecourt dislikes, ii. 139
Ridolfi, Palazzo; Cts of Pomfret's house at Florence:
HW saw fanali at, i. 59
Ridotto; ridottos:
Arthur postpones, because of earthquake, iv. 135
at Ranelagh, i. 434
deserted, after earthequake, iv. 131
English fondness for, on eve of war, iv. 469
HW to attend, i. 378
officers give, for Friedrich Wilhelm, iii. 265
Shaw, Elizabeth, said to have flirted at, with Stuart-Mackenzie, iii. 27
Rienzi, Cola di (1313–54), demagogue:
Wilkes's success would astonish, viii. 536
—— the counterpart of, vii. 8

Rieti, Bp of. See Clarelli, (?) Girolamo
Rifier, Capt., Lobkowitz's adjutant:
Lobkowitz sends, to Mann, ii. 519
Riga:
Anne of Mecklenburg dies at, i. 256n
Russian troops approach, v. 72
Rigadoon:
older generation could talk of, vii. 351
Rigaud, Louis-Philippe de (ca 1691–1763), called the Comte de Vaudreuil:
Young Pretender arrested by, iv. 9
Rigaud, Louis-Philippe de (1724–1802), Marquis de Vaudreuil:
Elliot's ship engaged with, ix. 220
Rigaud, Pierre-François de (1704–78), Marquis de Vaudreuil-Cavagnal, Governor of Canada:
alleged victory of, at Quebec, v. 344
Quebec's recapture predicted by, v. 357
Quebec to be recaptured by, according to French reports, v. 421
Rigaut de Barbezieu (fl. 1175–1215), Provençal poet:
poem by, v. 169–70
Rigby, Richard (1722–88), politician; M.P.:
administration might have been wrecked by, to satisfy Opposition, viii. 447
any post will be accepted by, vi. 569
Bedford House visited by, iv. 135
HW designs Chinese drawing-room for, in Essex, iv. 166
HW mentions, ii. 374
HW visits, at Mistley, iii. 494
lord of Trade, iv. 517
Mistley the seat of, iv. 490
Orford and George III bet against, v. 531
Parliamentary vote by, on privately-raised regiments, x. 19
watchman's earthquake warning feigned by, iv. 135
Riggs, Mrs. See Pigott, Margaret (ca 1714–88)
Riggs, Anne (1741–81), m. (1765) Sir John Miller, cr. (1778) Bt:
academy of, at Batheaston, viii. 197
HW used to know, at Bath, viii. 197
Italy visited by, viii. 197
Letters from Italy, Mann mentioned in, viii. 197, 203–4
Mann remembers little about, viii. 204
Riggs-Miller, Sir John Edward Augustus (1770–1825), 2d Bt:
parents leave, with grandmother in France, viii. 197
Righelini. See Reghelini
Right of Search:
English obstinacy in denying, to Spain, iii. 255
Rihm, Suzanne-Dorothée (ca 1741–1810), dancer:
Etiolles forbidden to keep, iv. 340
Rimini, Bp of. See Pasarella, Jacopo (d. 1495)
Rimini:
Austrians at, ii. 335
La Cattolica near, ii. 58

[Rimini, *continued*]
  Lobkowitz at, ii. 330, 331, 339
  Montemar may fortify himself at, ii. 2
  ——'s headquarters, i. 379
  Pironi imprisoned at, ii. 253, 257
  Spaniards abandon, ii. 16, 331
  Spaniards at, ii. 13
  Spaniards expected to settle at, ii. 199
  Spaniards quiet at, i. 379
  Spanish army at, diminished by desertion, ii. 216
  Spanish artillery sent towards, iii. 35–6
  Spanish barks may escape to, ii. 288
  Spanish forces at, increase, ii. 243
  visitors to, Modena, D. and Ds of, ii. 222
Rinaldi, Signora. *See* Arnaldi, Teresa Maria
Rinaldi, Margherita (1712–90), m. (1731) Duca Alamanno Salviati:
  Craons entertain, i. 217–18
Rinaldi Generotti, Francesco Maria (1715–84), Balì di Cortona:
  ball given by, at villa, ii. 84–5
  Pitti's duel with, prevented, i. 111–12
Rinaldo:
  Richelieu compared to, vii. 329
Rinaldo. See under Handel, George Frideric; Sacchini, Antonio
Rinfreschi:
  consumption of, at Mann's cocchiata, ii. 1
Ring; rings:
  cameo, iii. 332
  diamond: Electress leaves, to P. Ottajano de' Medici, ii. 173; given by Maria Theresa to Forrester's officer, ii. 107; Mirepoix, Duchesse de, has, iv. 107; mourning, Chute receives from cousin, v. 52
  Electress leaves, to Old Pretender, ii. 171
  'emerald,' Montagu, Lady Mary Wortley, gives, to Barnard, v. 473
  gold, English soldier cuts, from old woman's finger, in France, v. 221
  HW mistakes cameo for, ix. 88, 89
  HW will choose any additional, iii. 420
  HW would like to buy, from Riccardi, iii. 331–2
  Mann left legacies for, by Jermy and Cts of Orford, ix. 206
  mourning: HW and Sir Edward Walpole to receive, from E. of Orford, ix. 124; Orford has probably forgotten to send, to Mann, ix. 206; out of fashion among people of rank, ix. 124
  of bed-curtain, Hamilton uses, as wedding ring, iv. 303
  pope's, v. 52
  Riccardi does not want to sell, to HW, iii. 349
  —— offers, at high price to HW, iii. 372–3
  ——'s: HW decides to take, iii. 398; Mann and Riccardi settle for, iii. 411; Mann to pay for, for HW, iii. 420, 427, 433, 435; Riccardi accepts HW's offer for, iii. 411
  Strozzi, Principessa, loses, iii. 349–50
  See also Cameo; Intaglio

Ring box. *See* Box
Rinuccini, Marchesa. *See* Aldobrandini, Maria Camilla (1718–83); Guicciardini, Vittoria (1697–1753)
Rinuccini, Marchese Alessandro (1685–1758):
  death of, at Naples, iv. 336
Rinuccini, Carlo (1679–1748), Marchese:
  Albani's arrangement with, over Electress's rights to church lands, ii. 169
  Albizzi cousin to, i. 481–2
  (?) Capello, Signora, formerly loved by, iv. 174–5
  council formed by, i. 178
  death and will of, iii. 461–2
  dictatorship given to, iii. 245
  Du Châtelet to turn Leghorn keys over to, i. 199
  Electress leaves annuity and silver framed glasses to, ii. 169
  envoy in England, iii. 308n
  festa di cuoco to be given by, i. 137
  Giovanni Gastone de' Medici's prime minister, iii. 308n
  hangings of brocatelle at house of: HW dislikes, v. 497, 501; HW remembers, v. 471; Mann sends pattern of, to HW, v. 481
  legacies of, iii. 461–2
  Mann hears from, of Sir Robert Walpole's supposed trip to Italy, i. 426
  —— hears news from, of Fane, i. 135
  —— hears rumour from, of English-French war, ii. 44
  ——'s neighbour, i. 137, 481
  —— talks politics to, in Florence, iii. 308
  —— talks with, i. 108
  —— thanked by, for HW's attentions to his son, iii. 322, 349
  —— to be entertained by, i. 137
  —— told by, of French-Spanish rifts, ii. 416
  Mathews's treaty commented upon by, ii. 455
  '(?) my cautious neighbour,' i. 490
  Panciatichi discusses Albizzi's fistula with, in Mann's presence, i. 481–2
  piles feared by, i. 112
  Pisa visited by, iii. 245
  Regency member, iii. 251
  (?) Richecourt may avenge attestations of, against him, i. 490
  ——'s disgrace attributed by, to Sir Robert Walpole, i. 108
  ——'s opposition to Mann discussed by, with Braitwitz and Tornaquinci, ii. 10
  son of, iii. 251
  three-coloured brocatelle the whim of, v. 468
Rinuccini, Carlo Maria Giuseppe (1742–90):
  birth and baptism of, i. 473
  plays acted by, iv. 336
Rinuccini, Mme 'Flora.' *See* Aldobrandini, Camilla
Rinuccini, Folco (1719–60):
  charities of, at father's death, iii. 461

departure of, iii. 348
Electress leaves annuity and china to, ii. **169**
England hated by, iii. 329, 339
father not regretted by, iii. 461
Francis I's gentleman of the bedchamber, iii. 251
greatest man in Florence, iv. 336
HW's dinner declined by, iii. 331
HW takes, sightseeing in London, iii. 308
HW tells Mann not to apologize for introduction for, iii. 331
income of, iv. 336
Mann explains to HW his recommendation for, iii. 321
—— hopes to disprove accusations of low birth from, iv. 24
—— recommends, to HW, iii. 251
——'s correspondence with, iii. 322
Naples visited by, iv. 8
Niccolini entertains, at dinner, iv. 174-5
——'s affair discussed by, in letter, iv. 7-8
plays acted by children of, iv. 336
return of, to Florence expected, iii. 339
uncle of, dies in Naples, iv. 336
wife thanks Mann for HW's attentions to, iii. 349
Rinuccini, Mme Folco. See Aldobrandini, Camilla (1718-83)
Rinuccini, Giovanni (1743-1801):
plays acted by, iv. 336
Rinuccini, Maria Teresa (d. before 1765), m. (1711) Francesco Gioacchino Buondelmonti:
brother's legacy to, iii. 461
Rinuccini, Maria Virginia (d. 1751), m. (1706) Barone Cerbone del Nero:
brother's legacy to, iii. 461
Rinuccini family:
HW hopes that 'Onslow' affair discredited English knowledge of, iii. 510
Mann avoids house of, v. 468
Serristori chief follower of, i. 473
Rio Grande de S. Pedro, governor of. See Molina, José de
Rio Grande de S. Pedro, Brazil:
Portuguese attack on Spanish settlement at, viii. 223-4
Riot; riots:
at Oxford, iv. 50
at Paris, iv. 170, viii. 101-2
English, frighten Mann, vii. 15
HW's reflections on, vii. 21-2
in Boston, vii. 39
in Edinburgh, over Catholic toleration, viii. 438-9
in England, over price of bread, vi. 455
in France, over corn, viii. 105-6
in London: vi. 187-8, 200, vii. 25, 98-9, 290-2; against French actors, iv. 99-100; at Keppel's acquittal, viii. 438; at time of Keppel's banquet, viii. 449; by coal-heavers, vii. 33-4, 39; by glaziers and tallow chandlers, vii. 200; Mann pleased by punishment

of ringleaders of, vii. 49; Mann shudders at, vii. 25-6, 49, 110-11, 147; newspapers print insolence from, vii. 305; reported by Leyden gazette, vii. 110; see also Gordon Riots
Neapolitan, vi. 206
over Westminster election, ix. 489
Parliamentary committees on, vii. 291-2, 297
Riot Act. See under Parliament: acts of
Rioult de Douilly, Marie (1712-84), m. François-Francillon, Marquis de Polignac:
French court banishes, iv. 354
Rioult de Douilly, Nicolas-Marie-Séraphin (1706-66), Marquis de Curzay:
Antibes to be the prison of, iv. 354
arrest of, iv. 353-4
French commandant of Corsica, iv. 206
Lorenzi hears from, about Genoese compliance, iv. 277
magnanimity of, to returning prisoner, iv. 206
Ripalta:
Austrians capture Spaniards at, iii. 262
Ripperda, Jean-Guillaume (1690-1737), Bn de:
HW asks if Wilkes imitates, by becoming Moslem, vi. 290
Riva, Maria da (b. ca 1703), nun:
Benedict XIV permits transfer of, to Ferrara convent, ii. 86
Froullay debauches, ii. 86
Spanish colonel married by, ii. 86
Rivalta, palace of the Dukes of Modena:
HW sups at, i. 44
visitors to, d'Ormea, i. 424
Rivarola, Col. or Count (?) Domenico (d. before 1754):
Bastia captured by, iii. 162
circular letter of, to Corsicans, iii. 162-3
Corsican revolt not procured by, iii. 157
Corsicans will not permit, to hoist Sardinian flag, iii. 171
English fleet awaited by, iii. 162
French and Genoese force, to retreat, iii. 437
letter of, about capture of Bastia, iii. 162
Townshend not assisted by, iii. 157
—— to land, on Corsica, iii. 162-3
Rivera. See Balbis-Simeone de Rivera
Rivers, Bn. See Pitt, George (1721-1803); Pitt, George (1751-1828)
Rivers, Bns. See Atkins, Penelope (d. 1795)
Rivett, Thomas (ca 1713-63), M.P.:
Stanhope defeated by, in Derby election, iv. 19
Riviera, Domenico (1671-1752), cardinal, 1733:
Giuseppe talks to, about Young Pretender at Petroni's assembly, iii. **85**
HW to help Chute confute, iii. 176
Old Pretender confers with, iii. 85
—— secured promotion of, iii. 176n

Riviera, the:
English bombardment of, might cause insurrection, iii. 121
Riviera di Levante:
Maria Theresa plans offensive against, iii. 478
Riviera di Ponente:
Austria expects Charles Emmanuel III to defend, iii. 478
Charles Emmanuel III's troops at, iii. 344
French and Spaniards plunder, iii. 306
Genoa tries to exclude provisions from coast of, iii. 344
Townshend to send ships to, iii. 292
Riversdale, Bn. See Tonson, William
Rivington, Charles (1754–1831), printer:
wife of, dies, viii. 101
Rivington, Mrs Charles. See Mann, Sarah (d. 1775)
Rizzio or Riccio, David (ca 1533–66), secretary to Mary, Q. of Scots:
Metastasio compared with, iv. 163–4
Struensee shares fate of, vii. 409
Road; roads:
English: highwaymen infest, viii. 47; rain makes impassable, iv. 506, 522–3
Francis I permits Lucca to build, iv. 514
Francis III makes, i. 323
Italian, spoiled by rain, viii. 145
present age prefers riding about streets to riding on, ix. 317
See also Post Road; Turnpike road
Roast Beef:
singers of, ii. 180
'Roast Beef of Old England.' See under Hogarth, William
Robartes, John (1686–1757), 4th E. of Radnor:
Chinese summerhouse of, iv. 382
Mann, Galfridus, seen by, v. 1
Mann brothers entertained by, at dinner, iv. 456
Mann's friend, v. 1n
Twickenham residence of, v. 1n
Robber; robbers:
numerous in England, ix. 497
Robbery; robberies:
continues in England, iv. 199
English, terrify Mann, iv. 127
HW's in Hyde Park, iv. 99, 101, 106, 112
in New Park, of Mrs Mann, ix. 343–4
'Robbing Peter to pay Paul':
dispute over Pitt's grave recalls, viii. 382
Robe; robes:
Bristol sighs for, vi. 549
Dumesnil's, held up by his secretary, iii. 493
earl's, given to Hunsdon by Q. Elizabeth on his death-bed, ix. 166
not worn in English costumes, i. 170
Vaillant wears, as sheriff at Ferrers's execution, v. 400
velvet, red, and ermine, Ds of Buckingham wears, i. 253–4

white and silver, Charlotte's bridesmaids wear, v. 530
Robert, ——, Lt:
captured at Velletri, ii. 491
Robert Manners. See under Merry, Robert
Roberto Manners. See under Pignotti Lorenzo
Robins:
HW jokes about, i. 234
Robinson, Capt. ——:
Mann not readily obeyed by, ii. 507
Robinson, Lady. See Howard, Lady Elizabeth (d. 1739)
Robinson, Mrs ——:
Naples visited by, v. 550
Robinson, Elizabeth (1720–1800), m. (1742) Edward Montagu:
Essay on . . . Shakespear, Mrs Piozzi condemns Boswell's account of Johnson's disparagement of, ix. 634, 640
Pignotti's poem to, on Shakespeare, viii. 536
Voltaire's attack on Shakespeare at Académie française heard by Suard and, viii. 267
Robinson, Luke (d. 1773), M.P.:
Chute, Francis, allied with, in disputing Hedon with Pulteney, i. 234n
—— colleague of, iii. 371
Hedon election disputed by, i. 234n
Hedon election granted to, iii. 371
Hedon election won by, iii. 342
Hedon seat lost by, i. 234n, 355
lawyer, i. 234n
Walpole, Sir Robert, object of sacrifices of, iii. 371
Robinson, Palmes [?Palmer (d. 1790)]:
Pomfret said by, never to get as far as Hyde Park for duels, ix. 96
Robinson, Richard (ca 1708–94), cr. (1777) Bn Rokeby; Bp of Killala, 1752; of Leighlin and Ferns, 1759; of Kildare, 1761; Abp of Armagh:
Northumberland induces appointment of, as Abp of Armagh, vi. 276
Robinson, Sir Thomas (1695–1770), cr. (1761) Bn Grantham; diplomatist:
ambassador at Vienna and Madrid, and secretary of state, ix. 296n
death of, leaves K.B. vacancy, vii. 240
English minister at Vienna, i. 497n
former minister at Vienna, iv. 417n
Fox and Pitt attack, iv. 453
Frederick II's camp again visited by, i. 134
Great Wardrobe to be resumed by, iv. 502
Hanover gets courier from, ii. 234
health of, scurvy, vii. 240
Lord of Trade, iv. 17
Maclaine robs, iv. 168
Maria Theresa persuaded by, to give up all Silesia to Frederick II, ii. 107–8
Master of the Great Wardrobe, iv. 417n
nominee for secretaryship, iv. 202
Parliamentary debate by, on Scotch Bill, x. 32, 33
Parliamentary seat created for, iv. 17

peace efforts of: believed to be fruitless, i.
121; ill-rewarded, iv. 17; unsuccessful, i.
121
peerage granted to, v. 490
pension of, iv. 502
postmaster, vi. 311
red ribbon awarded to, for procuring Prussian peace, i. 496–7
return of, to Frederick II's camp, i. 134
secretary of state, i. 497n, iv. 417
secretaryship of state may go to, v. 92
son of, v. 436
Stanhope persuaded by, to 'improve' Pope's
garden, ix. 177
Suares recommended by, for preferment, ii.
455
Vienna visited by, iv. 202
Robinson, Sir Thomas (? 1702–77), cr. (1731)
Bt:
ball given by: for Richmond's daughter, i.
174, 183–5; for second time, i. 221–2
Barbados post taken by, i. 301, viii. 282n
becomes privy councillor, iv. 135
death of, viii. 282
guests of: Ancram, Cts of, i. 184; Bennet,
Lady Camilla, i. 184; Churchill, Charles,
i. 222; Churchill, Harriet, i. 184; Cole-
brooke, Mrs, i. 185; Conway, i. 221; Euston,
Cts of, i. 184; Fermor, Lady Sophia, i. 184,
221; Fitzroy, Lady Caroline, i. 184, 221;
Hardwicke, i. 174; Holdernesse, i. 184,
222; Lennox, Ladies Georgiana and Emilia
Mary, i. 184; Lincoln, i. 222; Manners,
Lady Lucy, i. 184; Parsons family, i. 184;
Richmonds, i. 184; Schaub, Lady, i. 185;
Sutton, Lord Robert, i. 222
Lincoln wants house of, i. 301
Mann delighted by ball of, i. 208
Mann remembers, viii. 282
second wife of, viii. 282n
Walpole, Sir Robert, does not attend ball
of, i. 185
Robinson, Thomas (1738–86), 2d Bn Grantham, 1770:
ambassador at Vienna and Madrid, and
secretary of state, ix. 296n
becomes secretary of state, ix. 296
Etruscan vases said by, to have been discovered, v. 561
Mann enjoys meeting, at Florence, v. 436
—— receives letter of congratulation from,
ix. 344
——'s dispatch to, ix. 326
——'s old acquaintance, ix. 296
—— wants to know opinion of, about
Mediterranean affairs, viii. 437, 453
painter at Florence misinforms, about Etruscan vases, vi. 6
stays in Spain despite war declaration, viii.
487
Robinson, William, HW's printer 1757–9:
Garrick comments on appearance of, v. 120
HW finds letter by, v. 120–1

HW keeps, at SH, v. 120
(?) HW mentions, v. 160
Mann enjoys letter of, v. 125
Robinson, William (ca 1720–75), architect:
HW mentions, iv. 375
Robinson, William, deputy to House of Bur-
gesses:
(?) capture of, rumoured, viii. 157
Robsart, Sir Terry:
HW's ancestor, iv. 381n
K.G., iv. 381n
SH trophies supposedly belonged to, iv. 381
Robuste, French war ship:
in Vilaine river, v. 351
Rocca d'Arazzo, Conte di. *See* Cacherano
d'Osasco, Giuseppe Ottaviano
Roccella:
earthquake account mentions, ix. 376
Roccettini:
convent of, at Pisa, suppressed, vii. 504
Rochambaut, Rochambeau, Rochambeure,
Comte de. *See* Vimeur, Jean-Baptiste-Dona-
tien de
Rochechouart, Diane-Adélaïde de (d. 1794),
m. (1751) Louis-Marie-Florent, Comte (1777,
Duc) du Châtelet:
HW admires, vii. 127–8
to come to England for autumn, vi. 586
Rochechouart, Jean-François-Joseph de (1708–
77), cardinal, 1761:
Florence to be visited by, vi. 28
Roche de Kerandraon. *See* La Roche de Ker-
andraon
Rochefort, Comtesse de. *See* Brancas, Marie-
Thérèse de (1716–82)
Rochefort:
English expedition against, v. 117n, 119,
134–5, 137, 143, 153
English objective in France should be as
important as, v. 223
French fleet preparing to leave, ii. 360
French Mediterranean fleet moved to, iii.
78
French ships from, captured by English, iii.
411
inquiry into English attack upon, v. 145,
154–5, 158, 160–1, 163, 164–5
Pitt sends no cannon against, v. 213
Rochefoucauld. *See* La Rochefoucauld
Rochelle, La. *See* La Rochelle
Rocheouart. *See* Rochechouart
Rochester, Bp of. *See* Atterbury, Francis
(1662–1732); Pearce, Zachary (1690–1774);
Thomas, John (1712–93); Wilcocks, Joseph
(1673–1756)
Rochester, E. of. *See* Wilmot, John
Rochester, ship:
in danger, v. 350
Neapolitan troops to be blockaded by, ii.
453
(?) oats transported by, ii. 453
Rochford, Cts of. *See* Young, Lucy (ca 1723–
73)

Rochford, E. of. *See* Nassau de Zuylestein, William Henry (1717–81); Nassau van Zuylestein, William Henry (1645–1709)

Rochford. *See also* Rochefort; Rochfort

Rochfort, Arthur (1711–?72), M.P.:
sister-in-law's intrigue with, ii. 220

Rochfort, Lady Jane (1737–1828), m. 1 (1754) Brinsley Butler, 2d E. of Lanesborough; m. 2 (ca 1785) John King:
King takes, to Leghorn, ix. 601
refuses Leghorn merchants' offer of separation from King, ix. 601

Rochfort, Mrs John Staunton. *See* Mann, Harriet

Rochfort, Robert (1708–74), cr. (1738) Bn and (1751) Vct Belfield, (1756) E. of Belvidere; M.P.:
wife's intrigue with brother of, ii. 220

Rochfort, *See also* Rochefort

Rock, Dr Richard (fl. 1731–69), quack doctor:
Pitt compared with, v. 547
testimonials from patients of, v. 132

Rock crystal:
lustres of, vi. 157
vase of: sent by Mann to HW, ix. 65, 165, 169, x. 56; sold from Tribune at Uffizi, ix. 65

Rockets:
at D. of Richmond's fireworks, iv. 56
at peace celebration, iv. 47
for Rodney, disturb HW's sleep, ix. 281

Rockingham:
earldom of, extinct, iii. 244

Rockingham, E. of. *See* Watson, Lewis (ca 1714–45); Watson, Thomas (ca 1715–46)

Rockingham, Marchioness of. *See* Finch, Lady Mary (d. 1761)

Rockingham, M. of. *See* Watson-Wentworth, Charles (1730–82); Watson-Wentworth, Thomas (1693–1750)

Rockingham faction. *See under* Watson-Wentworth, Charles, M. of Rockingham

Rockingham family:
credit lost by, in its counties, ix. 488

Rocque, La. *See* La Rocque de Varengeville; Rocca d'Arazzo

Rode, La. *See* Sénezergues de la Rode

Rodet, Marie-Thérèse (1699–1777), m. (1713) François Geoffrin:
Guasco protected by, from her friends' resentment, vi. 575
—— punished by, for indiscretion, vi. 529
HW hears wise observation by, about England, vi. 343
HW might hint to, that there is corn in Genoa and Leghorn, viii. 106
HW well treated by, in Paris, vi. 524
Hervey, Bns, fond of, vi. 524
Montesquieu's *Lettres* will hurt, vi. 523–4
Orford, Cts of, and Cavalier Mozzi call on, in Paris, vii. 141–2

Rodi, Abp of. *See* Dugnani, Antonio

Rodney, George Brydges (1719–92), Adm. cr. (1782) Bn Rodney:

Admiralty recalls, ix. 278, 282
Boyle-Walsingham said to have joined, ix. 79
Burdett cheats, iv. 20–1
Clevland's letter from, in *London Gazette*, v. 309
Common Council gives banquet for, ix. 343
convoy of, captured by French, ix. 159
Dutch settlements 'stifled' by, ix. 150
English reputation retrieved by, at sea, ix. 32
fleet of: coming from Martinique, meets French squadron, vi. 32; probably exceeded by French and Spanish ones, ix. 73
French fleet eludes, ix. 311
Havre-de-Grâce burnt by, v. 305
Havre governor summoned by, to deliver all flat-bottomed boats, v. 310
Hood to have replaced, in Parliament, ix. 284
in port, ix. 221
London illuminated for, ix. 280
Lord Mayor and aldermen refuse to give banquet for, ix. 343
loss of English fleets from East and West Indies will depress, ix. 83
Mann hopes, will not let laurels wither, ix. 291
Martinique conquest due to, v. 21
messenger-sloop of, ix. 17
no news from, ix. 291, 318
parades through London with window-breaking rabble, ix. 343
Pitt nominated by Westminster to replace, ix. 278
recall of, regretted by Mann, despite probable reinstatement, ix. 282
Rhode Island too strongly fortified by, ix. 99
St Eustatius conquered by, ix. 139
St Eustatius plundered by, ix. 194n, 278
victory of: at Cape St Vincent, over Lángara, ix. 16, 17, 21, 24; at the Saintes, over French, ix. 277–8, 281; should give England an advantage in peace treaty, ix. 352
West Indies supposed to be destination of, ix. 24, 99

Rodriguez, P.F. Antonio Giuseppe:
(?) Almada's secretary, v. 430, 476

Rodt, Franz Conrad von (1706–75), cardinal, 1756:
cardinals await, v. 215

Roebuck, fire ship:
at Port Mahon, i. 285

Roffeni, Signora. *See* Paleotti, Adelaide

Rogers, Mrs John. *See* Mann, Eleanor

Rohan, Bailli de:
Mann invited by, to Leghorn celebration, vi. 557
—— visited by, vi. 557

Rohan, Cardinal de. *See* Rohan-Guéménée, Louis-René-Édouard

Rohan, Duc de. *See* Rohan-Chabot, Louis-Antoine-Auguste de (1733–1807)

Rohan, Armand-Gaston-Maximilien de (1674–1749), cardinal, 1712; Bp of Strasbourg: château of, occupied by Hussars, ii. 293
pope to be chosen from faction of, i. 20–1
Rohan, P. Camille de. *See* Rohan, Eugène-Hercule-Camille de
Rohan, Charles de (1715–87), P. de Soubise; Maréchal de France:
Broglie's forces blame defeat on, v. 519
defeat of: v. 153, 515; would vindicate Broglie, vi. 50–1
detained until Contades defeats P. Ferdinand, v. 254
epigram on, v. 178
Estrées and Broglie compared with, vi. 47
Ferdinand may be overcome by army of, v. 229
—— must be dislodged by, or retreat will be necessary, vi. 50
Frederick II defeats, at Rossbach, v. 153
—— had expected to outwit, v. 136–7
Granby's army cannonaded by that of, vi. 86
HW mentions, v. 168
Hanover invaded by, after defeating the Hessians, v. 226–7
Hanover may be taken by, v. 251
Hesse invaded by, v. 229
Isenburg and Oberg defeated by, v. 251
mistress of, vii. 322
Richelieu must aid, v. 158
——'s army an aid to tactics of, v. 146
Rohan, Eugène-Hercule-Camille de (1737–after 1791), called P. Camille de Rohan-Rochefort:
Leopold invited by, to supper and illumination at Leghorn, vi. 556
Pinto de Fonseca sends, with galleys, to Leopold II, vi. 556
Rohan, Henri-Louis-Marie de (1745–1808), styled P. de Guéménée:
flees France because of swindling, ix. 604
Florence lately visited by, ix. 513
uncle's friendship with Charlotte Stuart described by, ix. 513
Rohan-Chabot, Guy-Auguste de (1683–1760), Comte de Chabot:
marriage of, ii. 429–30
Rohan-Chabot, Louis-Antoine-Auguste de (1733–1807), Comte and (1775) Duc de Chabot; Duc de Rohan, 1791:
sister of, vi. 341–2n
Rohan-Chabot, Marie-Sylvie de (1729–1807), m. 1 (1749) Jean-Baptiste-Louis de Clermont d'Amboise, Marquis de Renel; m. 2 (1764) Charles-Just de Beauvau, P. de Beauvau:
Choiseul braves Comtesse du Barry to please, vii. 264
——'s violence against Comtesse du Barry incited by, vii. 144
marriage of, vi. 342n
sister-in-law at odds with, vii. 144

Rohan family:
should not suffer for Cardinal de Rohan's folly, ix. 654
Rohan-Guéménée, Ferdinand-Maximilien-Mériadec de (1738–1813), Abp of Bordeaux 1770–81; of Cambrai 1781–1801:
Stuart, Charlotte, often visits, ix. 513
Rohan-Guéménée, Louis-René-Édouard (1734–1803), Cardinal-Prince de:
conversation about, ix. 639
imprisoned in Bastille for forging Marie-Antoinette's signature to get diamonds, ix. 603
insufficiently punished, ix. 654
Pius VI and cardinals censure, for preferring French tribunal to that of a consistory, ix. 658
very gallant, ix. 603
Rohan-Montauban, Louise-Julie-Constance de (1734–1815), m. (1748) Charles-Louis de Lorraine, Comte de Brionne:
Coventry, Cts of, eclipsed by, iv. 337–8
'Roi de Garbe.' *See under* La Fontaine, Jean de
'Roi d'Yvetot':
Nassau-Siegen called, by HW, viii. 472
Rokeby, Bn. *See* Robinson, Richard (ca 1708–94)
Rokeby, Yorks:
Robinson of, viii. 282n
Roland, —— (d. 1752):
death of, iv. 306
Roland, Francesco Orlando (1754–1823):
birth of, iv. 437
Roland, Jacques (d. 1784), Chevalier de Lorenzi:
boastfulness of, iv. 584
brother has not heard from, vi. 369
brother's correspondence with, iv. 98, vi. 362
brother's dismissal a great surprise to, vi. 362
brother told by: of false rumour of promotion, vi. 356; of HW's civilities, iv. 92
Chute told by, of plan to land at Bristol, iv. 114
costume of, frock in morning, iv. 285
England praised by, iv. 285
England to be visited by, with Mirepoix, iv. 67, 68
English events will be described by, in letters, iv. 100
Florence seldom visited by, iv. 68
Florence visited by, vi. 557
HW entertains, at SH, iv. 89
HW has not met, iv. 67, 68
HW met, at Florence, iv. 87
HW's civilities to, pleasing, iv. 92, 98
HW's letters should not be entrusted to, vi. 362
HW's letter to Mann enclosed by, to brother, vi. 358
HW to entertain, at SH, iv. 87

[Roland, Jacques, *continued*]

HW told by: about dispute between French and Italian postmasters, vi. 358; that letters should be franked to Genoa, vi. 347

health of, gout, vi. 557

iricisms of, vi. 106–7, 117

long in the French service, iv. 67, 68

Louis XV thought by, not to be separated from Mme de Pompadour, iv. 542

Mann asked by, to give HW his compliments, vi. 557

—— called on by, in Florence, iv. 584

—— meets, at Stormont's, iv. 285

Mirepoix, Duchesse de, hears absurd comments of, on sapphire and Lincoln's gesse, iv. 106–7

Mirepoix family amused by absurdities of, iv. 106

Mirepoix visited by at Putney, iv. 87

Paris visited by, iv. 542

Schutz mistaken by, for Chute, iv. 89–90

venison compared by, to beef, iv. 89

Yarmouth, Cts of, and Lady Middlesex subjects of inquiry by, iv. 96–7

Roland, Luigi *or* Louis (d. 1766), Conte Lorenzi:

Agdollo advised by, i. 149

allowance to, for ball, iv. 276

Amelot's correspondence with, ii. 415

ball to be given by, for D. of Burgundy's birth, iv. 276

ball would have been given by, if Dauphiness had a son, iv. 191–2

Bavarian-French alliance may embroil, i. 119

Botta and Vienna Court reprimand, for embroiling them about Leghorn, v. 475

Botta called on by, with book on Kloster-Zeven Convention, v. 235

—— criticizes, for attentions to Wilkes, vi. 282

—— may be informed by, of English secret expedition, v. 446

——'s circular letter to, on Peter III's overturn, vi. 63

bread given by, to Florentine poor, iii. 14

brother astonished at dismissal of, vi. 362

brother has not written to, vi. 369

brother of, vi. 347n

brother of, to go to England, iv. 67, 68

brother's correspondence with, iv. 98, vi. 362

brother sends HW's letter through, to Mann, vi. 358

brother tells false rumour to, of increased rank and salary, vi. 356

Cartagena victory contradicted by news of, from Barcelona, v. 193

Chauvelin tells, of Curzay's arrest, iv. 354

Chavigny assures, that Louisbourg will be saved, v. 234–5

Choiseul may be ashamed of his treatment of, vi. 371

—— notifies, that he must yield post to a Frenchman, vi. 346, 351

Chute's dispute with, over yellow and green colours for chariot, v. 501

—— to receive compliments of, iv. 89

clothes of, in bad taste, though said to come from Paris, v. 501

Craon, Princesse de, takes, through Corso in phaeton, i. 83

crime of degraded army officers guessed by, v. 383

Curzay's correspondence with, iv. 277

daughter's illness was to have been described by, to La Condamine, vi. 153

Dauphin's marriage celebrated by, with Te Deum instead of ball, iii. 14

——'s wedding to be celebrated by, ii. 559

death of, vi. 430

Dettingen slain estimated by, ii. 269

dispatches of, discuss the whole state of Europe, v. 475

Elizabeth Christina's requiem avoided by, out of jealousy of Mann's rank, iv. 227

English damage to French flat-bottomed boats denied by, v. 309

English victory announced by, v. 356

Éon's book desired by, vi. 230

Feroni, Mme, entertains, i. 317

Fleury sent cedrati by, i. 317

Florentine baptisms and weddings the greatest events for, iv. 92

Florentine by birth, but employed by France, ii. 466

Florentine Regency asked by, whether he should celebrate Dauphin's wedding or mourn for Madame Royale, iii. 14

France's treatment of, considered ungrateful by Maria Louisa, vi. 430

Francis I's demand for Electress's jewels told to, i. 238

franking of mail at Genoa demanded by, vi. 347

French court corresponds heavily with, v. 356

French court may order, into mourning, ii. 175

French letters tell, that Dunkirk will not be demolished, vi. 118

Frenchmen presented by, to Mann at assembly, iv. 489

French minister at Florence, though a Florentine, v. 362n

Genoese postmaster forbidden by, to send him unfranked letters, vi. 362

'great abbé at Rome' corresponds with, i. 206–7

Grotius tortured by, to draw up remonstrances, v. 274–5

HW grieved by Mann's enmity with, v. 362

HW liked by, i. 326

HW refuses to be introduced by, to La Condamine, vi. 149, 151

HW sorry for, vi. 440
HW's regard for, iv. 87
HW thanked by, for civilities to brother, iv. 92, 98
HW to receive compliments of, vi. 369
HW wanted by, to meet La Condamine, vi. 149
Havana's capture not expected by, vi. 88–9
health of, weak constitution and lame leg, iv. 192
house of, too small for festino, ii. 559
La Condamine's letter from, forwarded by Mann, vi. 149
Lally said by, to be Irish, v. 523
lame, i. 119, 206, 326, v. 274
letters from Paris encourage, vi. 370–1
low credentials of, exclude him from Chambellan's ante-chamber, vi. 346
Maillebois informs, of Young Pretender's landing, iii. 87
——'s correspondence with, iii. 334
manifesto will probably be sent by, on capture of English brig, v. 334
Mann accused by, of justifying English privateers, v. 356
—— called on by, vi. 369
—— does not talk to, ii. 484–5
—— hears from: about travelling time from Paris, vi. 352; that Spaniards may take Lombardy and exchange it for Tuscany, i. 206
—— hears of Richecourt from, i. 98
—— hears story from of French abbé's irregular baptism, i. 62
—— hears Viennese gossip from, i. 325–6
—— not allowed to enter house of, iv. 584
—— not supposed to speak to, except at accidental meetings, ii. 559
——'s 'civil whisper' with, ii. 466
——'s conferences with Botta invented by, v. 356
—— sends letter through, i. 422
——'s friendship with: cooled by political disputes, ii. 438; will be interrupted by war, iv. 485
——'s regard for, iv. 67
——'s trick on Niccolini pleases, ii. 372
—— told by, of baronetcy and of Hertford's embassy, iv. 467
—— warned by, against Richecourt, ii. 362
—— whispers with, about Toussaint's intrigues, iv. 98
—— will not tell, of brother's iricisms, iv. 117
marriage of, to take place, iv. 191–2
matrimonial prospects of, amuse HW, iv. 197
ministerial gazette of, announces d'Éon's new book, vi. 272
Modena, Ds of, meets, at dinner, ii. 228
mourning for Electress prescribed to, by French Court, ii. 206

'my little lame brother,' vi. 118
never out of Tuscany, iv. 96
Newfoundland's capture the boast of, vi. 69
Orford, Cts of, clears out Florentine house for, iii. 385
—— hoped by, to pay him rent, iii. 238
—— permitted by, to retain house, iii. 238
passport for France may be granted through, to Thomas Pitt, v. 524
pension of: disappointing, vi. 351, 356, 360; may be raised, vi. 370–1; vaguely promised, vi. 346
permission asked by, to attend meeting of kings at Lyon, v. 283
Praslin tells, of dismissal, vi. 356
Pucci probably writes to, of Mann's baronetcy, iv. 467
Quebec's possible recapture stressed by, v. 421
Regency urged by, to expel English fleet from Leghorn, v. 274
Riccardi entertains, i. 147
Richecourt's dispute with, over citizenship of French at Leghorn, iv. 266–7
—— shown by, Maillebois's letter to him, iii. 86–7
—— tries to console, for child's death, iv. 306
St-Aignan gives presents to, i. 95–6
secretary of, replaced, i. 157
son born to, iv. 437
son of, dies, iv. 306
successor of, may have new title, vi. 346, 355–6
Te Deum given by, for Dauphin's wedding, iii. 14
Tencin's correspondence with, i. 62, (?) 206–7
wax torches in three windows of, iii. 14
Wilkes brings letters of recommendation to, from Paris, vi. 282
will be *ministre de famille* at Leopold II's wedding, vi. 319
[?Roland de] Lorenzi, Luisa Elisabetta, m. Senatore Conte Cavalieri Balì Federigo Barbolani:
smallpox attack of, after inoculation, vi. 153
Role, Roles. *See* Rolle
Roll; rolls:
hot, English supposed by Maréchale de Villars to like, vi. 105, 113
Rolle, Mr. *See* Rolle-Walter, John
Rolle, Lady Arabella. *See* Clinton, Lady Arabella
Rolle, Henry (1708–50), cr (1748) Bn Rolle; M.P.:
peerage granted to, iii. 419
Rolle, Margaret (1709–81), m. 1 (1724) Robert Walpole, cr. (1723) Bn Walpole, 2d E. of Orford, 1745; m. 2 (1751) Hon. Sewallis Shirley; Bns Clinton, s.j., 1760:

[Rolle, Margaret, *continued*]

abbé-secretary of, gets maid with child, iii. 224, 238

academy of savants to be collected by, iv. 476

affairs closely tended by, iv. 433

affairs of, Sharpe reports to Mozzi about, ix. 144

Aix visited by, vii. 155, 161

Albani answers letter of, announcing her trip to England, iii. 51

allowance of: may be doubled, iii. 210; rumoured to be increased, ii. 122; to be demanded, iii. 104

altered since fall from horse, ii. 364

amorousness of, HW jokes about, ii. 306

ancestry of, ix. 501n

Andreasi discusses Newton and Voltaire with, ii. 555

appearance of, iii. 224, vii. 230, viii. 255, 312, 318, 374

appears only at Richecourt's house, ii. 122

Ashburton borough assigned by, to HW's care, vii. 548

Atri, Duchesse d', talks with, ix. 130

attendants forbidden by, to write to Mann, viii. 467

attentive to small expenses, ix. 129

Banks, Margaret, thanked by, with card after conversation at opera, iii. 234

(?) Barbarigo's affair with, i. 196

Blair's talk with, iii. 99, 119

boroughs lost by, from not trusting HW, viii. 308

boroughs of, should have been more completely entrusted to her agents, viii. 67

Buondelmonte receives letter from, from The Hague, iii. 101

burial of, ix. 114, 195

Busoni invests money for, in French funds, ix. 113

bust of, done by sculptor for Mozzi, ix. 504

Calais twice visited by, but she returns to Paris, vii. 141, 155, 218, ix. 641

Callington borough, promised by, to Sir William Hamilton, vii. 548, 557, viii. 52

Callington borough subject of correspondence by, with HW, vii. 545–6, 547, 548

Camden's opinion sought in affairs of, ix. 230, 440

Carder, Mrs, brought by, from England, ix. 151, 169

—— poorly recompensed by, in will, ix. 122

Carteret expected by, to vex Sir Robert Walpole, i. 461

——'s conversation with, i. 441

——'s coolness puts off English journey of, ii. 4

—— tells Theodore of Corsica about application of, ii. 194

'case' of, containing claims on son, probably drawn by Sharpe, ix. 162

cases of, searched by order of Regency council, i. 224–5, 283

chambermaid of, iii. 224, 238

Chesterfield receives letter from, iii. 60–1

—— ridicules mistakes in letter of, to him, iii. 70

—— unable and unwilling to aid, i. 409

—— would never satisfy, iv. 439

claim of, on money arising from sale of Pall Mall house, ix. 162–3

Clinton an ancestor of, ix. 298n

Clinton, Bns, in her own right, ix. 195

Clinton barony improperly represented on proposed monument for, ix. 226–7

Clinton barony inherited by, ii. 126, 143n, v. 385, ix. 151, 157

Clinton barony may be secured by, through Chesterfield, i. 360–1, 367, 389–90, 406

Clinton portrait brought by, from England, ix. 240

coachman robs, iii. 88

coach ordered by, to be made, iii. 59

Cocchi contradicts, about HW, i. 448

—— rebuked by, for not congratulating her on Sir Robert Walpole's retirement, i. 371

——'s defence of Sir Robert Walpole may offend, ii. 133

Caffarelli's affair with, i. 448

Compagni and Libri approached by, for credit in England, i. 422, 461

complexion blistered by, in Richecourt's absence, iii. 31

Conti, Abbate, to rent apartment to, i. 217

cook of, ii. 4

Cork, Cts of, to dine with, iv. 480

country house in England to be visited by, after trip to Wanstead House, vii. 120

courier accompanies, iii. 48

Court of Chancery would not entrust son to, unless she lived in England, vii. 481, 510

Cox courier to, ii. 516

——'s difficulties with, do not surprise HW, ii. 505–6

—— sent by HW with papers for, ii. 486

Craon invites, only on most public occasions, i. 462

Craon family stories exhumed by, i. 327

Craon tells Mann that Francis I would expel, from Florence if Sir Robert Walpole wished it, i. 326

Crew detained by, ii. 272

Cumberland, D. of, angers, by German campaign, v. 96

Dashwood forces wife to consort with, iii. 224

death of: at Pisa, ix. 113–14, 120–1, 195; benefits her son, ix. 125–6; might have prevented sale of Houghton collection, ix. 108, 121; perhaps reported by courier, ix.

121; premature report of, justified by event, ix. 129; rumoured in England, ix. 119, 120–1; wished by Mann and Chute, i. 432

declaration of, accompanying will, shows 'extensive intention' in favour of Mozzi, ix. 169

deeds may have been left by, with elder Sharpe, ix. 160

Del Monte's affair with, i. 448

Denbigh, Cts of, to be visited by, iii. 61

Devonshire estates of, subject of queries, ix. 414

Devonshire estate visited by, ix. 224

(?) Diharce writes to, that she will soon see him in Italy, iv. 421

dined out shortly before death, ix. 129

dress of, English, iii. 111

education of, poor, ix. 121

effects of, at Florence and Naples, ix. 113, 114

elbow broken by, in fall from horse, ii. 314

Electress's funeral attended by, ii. 173

England disgusts, iii. 210

England reached by, iii. 104

England's revenues may satisfy spite of, iii. 118–19

England to be visited by: i. 367, 422, 426, 441, iii. 54, 60, vii. 2, 218; for two months, viii. 2, 121; in spring, iv. 342, vii. 152, 155, 161; to settle her affairs, vii. 113

England visited by, with kisses and embraces, vii. 224

English agents' letters disregarded by, ix. 129

English journey repugnant to, vii. 464, 468, 472, 481, 486, 488, 493

English might forget son's alienation from, ix. 396

English news dispensed by, i. 406

English politics meddled in by, iii. 224

English relations with Tuscany might be guided by, through Chesterfield, i. 387

English reputation at Florence lowered by, ii. 309

English servants not brought by, to England, iii. 61

English trip of, may be put off, i. 460–1

English visit of: deferred, vii. 135, 141, 155, 218, ix. 641; would be unwise, iii. 38–9

English winters dreaded by, vii. 155

entourage of, for English trip, iii. 49, 50

epitaph for, at Leghorn, to be in English, ix. 195

Essex discussed by, ii. 114

estate and jointure retained by, iv. 439

estate of: cannot be settled in Florence, ix. 128; son intends to give, to Rolles, ix. 148, 156

estate said to have been bought by, viii. 187

estate to be reclaimed by, i. 406, 424

exercises much, viii. 488

expects congratulations on father-in-law's retirement, i. 371

festine attended by, to meet Richecourt, ii. 439

Fiesole to be visited by: in autumn and winter, viii. 322, 330 to see remodelled house, viii. 305

Fiesole villa (Villa Medici) of: bought, vii. 190, 463, 468; improved, viii. 190, 260; leased and then bought, viii. 190; snow confines her at, viii. 347; used for autumn and winter, viii. 322

finances of: improved (?) by Sturgis's death, ii. 217; mistaken notions concerning, ix. 130

fines on renewal of leases were paid to, instead of to son, ix. 335

Florence may not be revisited by, iii. 263, iv. 342

Florence not now to be visited by, iv. 97

Florence reached by, i. 283, viii. 19, 317

Florence to be left by, iii. 46

Florence to be revisited by, i. 264, iii. 59, 252, 394, iv. 392–3, 421, 476, vii. 113, viii. 9, 12

Florence visited by: vii. 120; because of sale of her Fiesole villa, vii. 463

Florentine and Leghorn gossip about HW and, i. 146

Florentine and Lorraine people told by, that she would return after recovering English estates, iii. 75

Florentine banker sees account of, ix. 113

Florentine half-house bought by, viii. 260

Florentine house of, Richecourt's Italian secretary lives in, i. 224

Florentine house sought by, vii. 468

Florentines and 'Pannonian' abbés too much influenced by, ii. 557

Florentines hear from, of her intention to return, iii. 144

Florentines might hear London gossip from, iii. 502

forsaken by the world, iii. 502

Fortescue, William, related to, ii. 236n

frailties not disguised by, ix. 122

France and Italy to be visited by, iv. 439

Franceschi's house near Pitti Palace taken by, ii. 391

France to be visited by, vii. 2

Francis I's courier escorts, iii. 50

furniture of: Gavi to have, iii. 290; listed by Mozzi, ix. 169; may be removed from Naples, viii. 467; moved to country, iii. 252; stored in Richecourt's apartment, iii. 385

Geoffrin, Mme, called on by, at Paris, vii. 141

George II barely speaks to, at Court, iii. 111

[Rolle, Margaret, *continued*]

—— did not regard with any special favour in Hanover, iii. 11

—— graciously receives, at Hanover, iii. 72, 80

—— said to have been applied to by, through Hanover, ii. 194

——'s disavowal of civility to, iii. 144

Givrecourt, Comtesse de, may supplant, in Richecourt's affections, iii. 452, 457

Gloucester, D. and Ds of, graciously receive, at Rome, viii. 164, 170, 222

Gloucester, D. of, not liked by, when he was at Florence, viii. 175

Goldsworthy, Mrs, told by, of Haddock's rumoured recall, i. 361

Gray's *Odes* sent to, by post, v. 163

HW 'amused' by, with words, viii. 311

HW amused by expectations of, on Sir Robert Walpole's death, iii. 53

HW and Sir Edward Walpole not paid their legacies after death of, ix. 315–16

HW and Sir Edward Walpole want, to look after her son, vii. 471, 476, 481, 485

HW approves of Mann's being on good terms with, iv. 490

HW became referee in dispute about estate of, only to save her honour from public courts, ix. 445

HW calls: mad, ii. 140; 'Omphale,' iv. 439

HW confirms prophecy of, about his getting Tesi a dog, ii. 350–1

HW curious about audience of, with D. of Gloucester, viii. 175

HW disparaged by, i. 448

HW does not understand politics of, iv. 510

HW explains claim of, to Clinton barony, ii. 143–4

HW fears showing prejudice against, ix. 216

HW had not met, for at least 16 years, vii. 231

HW has money paid to banker of, vii. 498

HW knows little of, iii. 362

HW meets: at Cts of Pomfret's, ii. 364; at Florence, iii. 111; at Vcts Townshend's, twice, iii. 111; when she calls on Hollands at Holland House, vii. 229–30, 231–2

HW must have written authorization from, vii. 496, 501, 505, 510, 523

HW not concerned in business affairs of, ix. 125

HW pities son for behaviour of, iv. 439

HW pleased that Mann did not force, to discuss her son, viii. 320

HW prefers Richecourt to Richmond as spy upon, ii. 31

HW reassures Mann about, i. 439–40

HW said to dislike Richecourt's affair with, i. 97–8

HW's attitude towards, vii. 121, 551, viii. 316, ix. 124, 195, 445

HW scorns claim of, to jointure arrears, vii. 519

HW's correspondence with, over son, vii. 470, 472, 476, 478, 485, 486, 487–8, 492, 496, 505, 509–10, 512, 514, 515–16, 517, 519, 523, 525, 529, 531–2, 534, 537, 541, 544, 545, 548, 551, 552, 557, 558–9, 560, 563, viii. 52, 57, 58, 61, 66, 70, 91–2, 105, 292

HW's lack of confidence from, will be regretted by her, viii. 316–17

HW's motives should not be distrusted by, viii. 91–2

HW tells, that he will never again manage her son's affairs, viii. 53

HW tells Sharpe to tell, of her son's latest insanity, viii. 292

HW to tell schemes of, to husband, i. 389–90

HW wants Mann to urge, to come to England, vii. 467, 471, 472, 476–7, 478, 481–2, 488–9

HW wants to keep son on good terms with, vii. 557, viii. 17

HW will probably be relieved of correspondence with, viii. 57–8

HW wished by, to resume managing her son's affairs, viii. 305

HW writes to, through Mann, to ask favour for Boone, viii. 82, 105, 292

habits of, procrastinatory, vii. 545

Haddock's return wished by, i. 423

Hague, The, to be first stop of, on way to England, iii. 49

Hague, The, visited by, iii. 75, 101

Hamilton, Sir William, deals with, about Callington borough, vii. 548, 557, viii. 52

—— forwards letters by, vii. 558

Hanover left by, iii. 92

Hanover receives, well, iii. 69–70

Hanover visit of, suspected by Mann to be a scheme concealed by Richecourt, iii. 97

health of: amazingly recovered, due to Fiesole air, viii. 346–7; asthma, iv. 433, vii. 83, 230, viii. 244, ix. 112; bled, ix. 102, 112; bled by having foot lanced, viii. 79; blisters applied to, ix. 113; cold, vii. 512; convulsed and cannot swallow water, ix. 102; cough, viii. 467; elbow 'put out', ii. 314; emaciated, ix. 112; emaciated and weak, viii. 312, 318; erysipelas, viii. 244, 255, ix. 112; face frequently red, viii. 255; fall from horse, ii. 314, 364; fever, viii. 312; foot injury, vii. 464, viii. 79; HW hears, is bad, vii. 505, 512; HW learns nothing about, vii. 230; habitual disorder, described by Mann, ix. 112; heart palpitations, ix. 102; humour in the ears, viii. 83; in bad state, viii. 467; indisposed, due to air of Florence, viii. 79; inflammation in the face, viii. 83; pale and haggard, ii. 153; past re-

covery, ix. 113; perfect, vii. 525; quite rosy, viii. 374; recovered, viii. 251, 322; recovered except for cough, viii. 487–8; relapses of usual disorder, ix. 107; rides every morning, vii. 512; suffocation relieved by bleeding, ix. 112; teeth missing, vii. 230; thighs rubbed, ii. 153; very ill, viii. 316; vomits, ii. 153; well but much decayed, viii. 330

Herrenhausen daily visited by, iii. 80
Hesse, Ps of, receives, favourably, iii. 80
Hesse-Cassel visited by, iii. 70
Hoare custodian of money of, in London, ix. 113, 114, 123, 130, 131, 143, 157, 160, 217, 335, 426
Hobart ousted by, iii. 290
——'s friendship with, iii. 252
Holland, Bns, called on by, vii. 229–30
Holland visited by, iii. 252
Houghton mortgaged to, vii. 510
household of, starts arriving in Florence, viii. 312
housekeeping of, ii. 4
house next to Mozzi's to be recombined with it by, viii. 330
house of: at Naples, vii. 2; at New Park, Richmond, iii. 309; at Stanhoe, ii. 249; at Venice, iii. 50; in Florence, leased from Lorenzi, iii. 61, 75, 238, 385; in Florence, 'little,' i. 71; in Florence, next to Mozzi, viii. 322, 330; in Florence, two, vii. 2; in London, iii. 309, ix. 162–3; outside Florence, near Richecourt's reoccupied by her, iv. 479–80; Palazzo Franceschi, ii. 391; recommended by Rucellai, i. 107; Villa Medici, see under Medici, Villa; Villa Salviati, v. 310
houses stripped of furniture and plate by, ix. 144
house taken by, at Padua, i. 235
house to be changed by, ii. 217
husband expected by, to write to her, iii. 37
husband gives allowance to, iii. 88, 224
husband fees lawyers in preparation for visit from, iii. 61
husband gives in to, too much, iii. 219
husband has substitute for, ii. 249
husband may be forced by, to give back her estate to her, iii. 49
husband said to have written to, iii. 47, 49
husband's allowance to, reduced, iii. 88
husband's death would not frighten, iv. 233
husband settles affairs with, iii. 348
husband's harsh letter cherished by, iii. 50
husband should lock up, iii. 192
husband's intercourse with, restricted after son's birth, iii. 203
husband's separation and negotiations with, iii. 111, 202, 290, iv. 547–8, 568–9
husband wants proof of infidelity of, with Richecourt, iii. 200

husband will lose property to, if he divorces her, iii. 88
improved except in appearance, vii. 230, 237
income of, insufficient for life in England, iii. 348
intrigues of, i. 326
Italy not to be revisited by, iii. 290
Italy to be revisited by, vii. 113, 141, 224
itinerary of, from Florence to England, vii. 2, 120
Jermy, Mrs, should be imitated by, ii. 311
jewels of: carried abroad, ix. 144, 158; claimed to be at her disposal, ix. 162; diamond earrings, not permitted by Sir Robert Walpole to be carried abroad, ix. 148; few given her by husband, ix. 148; given to Richecourt's daughter, iv. 499, 505, ix. 144; husband receives demand from her for, after he takes them, ix. 162; husband retains most of, when she goes abroad, ix. 472; mother's diamonds, ix. 148; Niccolini gets, i. 95, 134–5, 217; son's right to, ix. 169; Tylney buys, ix. 144
jewels taken from, by husband, demanded by her, ix. 162
jointure of: arrears in, not mentioned, ix. 144; arrears of interest on, computed, ix. 440, 445, 456; deficiencies should be made good, ix. 172; deficiency being examined by Orford and Lucas, ix. 176; deficiency estimated, ix. 412; deficient, according to 'case' drawn by Sharpe, ix. 162; farm to be rented for, viii. 308; HW not allowed to raise, ix. 140; in arrears, vii. 512; should be sacrificed to son instead of demanding arrears, iv. 486
laudaunum or liquor may be taken by, i. 89–90
lawyers may be consulted by, viii. 91
learned ladies considered ridiculous by, iv. 584
leases not signed by, until her allowance is on its way, ii. 39
leases received by, ii. 39, 272
leases signed by, i. 115
leases to be received by, i. 108, 115
Leghorn correspondence of, to see if her allowance is paid, ii. 39, 272
Leghorn merchants tell lies to, i. 462
legs soaked by, in hot water, ii. 153
Leheup's remark about his not calling on, iii. 111–12
Leicester not to let his son marry an heiress like, iii. 27
letters of, intercepted by husband, iv. 247–8
letters of credit on Augsburg taken by, iii. 49
letters to, Mann sends HW copies of, ix. 171
Lichfield, E. of, connected with, ii. 210
——'s earldom will please, ii. 188

[Rolle, Margaret, *continued*]

London cannot be endured by, even for one night, vii. 492

London house of, rented, iii. 309

London to be visited by, vii. 120

Lorenzi hopes for rent from, iii. 238

—— permits, to retain house, iii. 238

—— to inhabit house of, after Hobart's departure, iii. 385

Lorraine faction knows plans of, iii. 75

(?) Louis XV's amours known to, when in France, iv. 542

Lucas and Sharpe seek agreement on estate of, ix. 150

Lyon visited by, vii. 152

Mackreth said to have lent money to, viii. 53

Maffei praises, i. 150

maître d'hôtel of, *see* Waters, Charles

Mann approves of George II's disavowal of civilities to, iii. 144

—— asked by, to get satisfaction for her affronts, i. 283

—— asks HW about calling on, iii. 232

—— blamed for not inviting, to cocchiata, ii. 4

—— called on by, i. 317

—— calls on, at villa near Florence, vii. 492

—— conceals contents of HW's letter from, viii. 19

—— confers with, about HW and her son, vii. 501, 503, 515–16, 517, viii. 17, 57, 61

—— congratulates, on becoming unmarried, iv. 548

—— described by, to HW, vii. 231–2

—— discusses, with Richecourt, ii. 11

—— discusses son's situation with, vii. 468

—— disliked by: iii. 119, 139; for preventing Crudeli from translating 'Pope's' satire, i. 491

—— does not want, back in Florence, iii. 172, 232, 305, 323, iv. 335

—— entertains, at dinner, iv. 480

—— expects English stay of, to end soon, iii. 219

—— forwards letter to, iii. 51, vii. 531

—— hopes that husband is not worried by, iii. 132

—— hopes that husband will not divorce, iii. 80

—— ignorant of estates and marriage settlement of, ix. 129

—— informs, of son's relapse but she does not discuss it, viii. 318

—— inherits legacy from, ix. 124, 206

—— inquires about, iii. 59

—— may be summoned by, to bury Sturgis, ii. 198

—— mentions election to, viii. 59

—— might have hired Mrs Richmond to spy upon, ii. 14

—— need not fear malice of, ii. 382

—— never mentions her son to, viii. 23, 353

—— not to complain about son to, viii. 47

—— not to prod, into writing to HW, viii. 91–2

—— not to read HW's letter to, vii. 499

—— not to tell, that her son has broken with HW, viii. 17

—— pities, iv. 444

—— pleased by Carteret's conduct to, i. 460

—— pleased by Sir Robert Walpole's opinion of, ii. 4

—— praised by, at Hanover, iii. 99

—— reassured about, ii. 196

—— represented by, as hostile to Maria Theresa, ii. 476

——'s cold greetings to, ii. 364

——'s conversation with Rucellai 'impeached' by, i. 30

——'s correspondence with, over HW and her son's situation, vii. 472, 476, 478, 486, 531–2, 534, 541, 544, 545, 552, 558–9, viii. 305

—— sees: frequently, viii. 330; often, in bed, viii. 318

——'s letters about departure of, may be retarded, iii. 64

——'s letters from, conceal her poor health, viii. 467

——'s letters possibly detained until after the departure of, iii. 75

——'s motives for being on good terms with, iv. 487

—— suspected by, of tampering with her mail, iii. 172

—— suspects, of tampering with his letters, i. 361, 422

——'s veracity questioned by, i. 406

—— tells, of son's recovery, viii. 376

—— thinks, is moving, i. 95

—— to deliver in person HW's letter to, viii. 52

—— to notify, of son's recovery, viii. 368

—— urges HW to send, to Venice, iii. 369

—— will no longer try to bow to, ii. 173

—— will not mention son to, since she never asks about him, viii. 353

Mann, Galfridus, to convey news of, to HW, iii. 54

—— writes Mann about, iii. 200

marriage of: ix. 121; arranged by Sir Robert Walpole, ix. 156–7; settlements for, ix. 129–30, 440n

Mary of Hesse's children fondled by, iii. 70

Maynard, Vcts, shunned by, at Naples, viii. 451

metaphysics discussed by, ii. 555

Milan visited by, vii. 135

Molo di Gaetà visited by, viii. 312, 317

money taken away by, from country seats, ix. 496

monument for: arms improperly represented in design for, ix. 226–7; design for, made by sculptor ignorant in heraldry, ix. 239–40; design for, sent to son, ix. 350; HW asks if son has paid Mann for, ix. 427; HW says, will be ugly but not costly, ix. 226; inscription to be in Italian, ix. 219; makes a noble figure, ix. 436; Mann sends to Orford the design of, ix. 345; might contain name of Sewallis Shirley, ix. 227; Orford has paid Mann for, ix. 436; Orford's orders and Mann's response, ix. 219; planned by son, ix. 206; son may forget, ix. 213; to be superintended by Mann, ix. 195–6

mother accused by, of 'selling' her to Sir Robert Walpole, iv. 439

mother and stepfather of, i. 486

mother gives allowance to, iii. 224

mother, husband, and son all wounded by misconduct of, iii. 38–9

mother leaves nothing to, iv. 418

mother offers house to, iii. 104

mother receives, coolly, iii. 139

mother's diamonds went to, ix. 148

mother told by: of approaching visit, iii. 60; that Orford is best and HW worst of family, iii. 139

mourning for father-in-law may be worn by, iii. 37, 42, 47, 49, 53

Mozzi accompanies: at Holland House, vii. 229–30; at Naples, vii. 155; to Paris, vii. 141–2, 155

—— cannot be given a bed by, while at Pratolino, vii. 23

—— chosen by, for his beauty, ix. 130

—— desired by Sharpe to make list of belongings of, ix. 151

—— enriches himself from, vii. 158

—— expects effects of, from Naples, ix. 160

—— finds it easier to be a gallant to, than to marry a young wife, ix. 571

—— leaves, because of his family affairs, viii. 145

—— may abandon, unless she leaves Naples, viii. 305

—— may forsake, if she stays away from Florence, vii. 559

—— might be unpopular in England for getting inheritance from, away from her son, ix. 396, 404

—— nearly discarded by, for lack of sexual prowess, v. 70

——'s claims against landed estate of, requested by Sharpe, ix. 168

—— sends Orford list of family things taken to Italy by, ix. 156

—— sends to England list and valuation of plate and jewels of, ix. 163

—— sent by, to Mann, vii. 464

——'s family abuse, for obstructing his marriage, ix. 130

—— to send HW list of possible demands of, on son, ix. 158

—— turns back, at Calais, to keep from meeting her son, vii. 158

—— wants release from son of, for acting as her executor, ix. 466, 498

—— will probably inherit Florentine town house and villa from, viii. 260

—— will probably inherit Italian property of, ix. 113

Naples left by, vii. 512, viii. 220, 312, 317, 479

Naples may be visited by, viii. 82

Naples may be summer residence of, vii. 559

Naples may be visited by, in winter, iv. 476, vii. 2

Naples not to be visited by, iv. 505

Naples not to be visited by, till following winter, viii. 83

Naples to be left by, vii. 2, 478, 487

Naples to be left by, for Florence, because of disappointment over a house, viii. 9

Naples to be visited by, iv. 499, v. 550, vii. 155, 525, 529, 531, viii. 57, 70, 164, 251

Naples to be visited by, probably to get her furniture away, vii. 464, 468, 472

Naples visit deferred by, because of Mozzi's absence, viii. 145

Naples visited by, vii. 537, 559, viii. 260

Naples visit of: for last time, viii. 467; given up, ix. 107; impossible, viii. 70; in autumn, prevented by illness, ix. 112

Neapolitan estate might be the one bought by, viii. 187

Neapolitan friends of, press her to stay there, viii. 305

Neapolitan houses of, vii. 2

Neapolitan journeys may be too much for, viii. 244, 322

nerves of, unshaken by son's calamities, viii. 293

never travels in hot weather, viii. 467

new affluence of, will make her more impudent on her return to Florence, iii. 238

New Park house taken by, iii. 309

news sent by, through Niccoli, iii. 290

Newton studied by, iv. 555

Niccoli accompanies, to England, iii. 42, 46, 50, 54, 290, iv. 335

—— ordered by, to send her clothes, i. 223–4

—— receives furniture from, i. 107

Niccolini knows little about, iii. 398

—— may see, in London, iii. 353, 362

—— predicts return of, to Florence, iii. 394

—— to get jewels of, for debt payment, i. 95

[Rolle, Margaret, *continued*]

—— to sell jewels of, i. 134–5, 217

Nice or Naples may be winter resort of, vii. 2

nothing can be said about, if she says nothing about son, viii. 327

offers to take bootikins to Mann, vii. 231

Old Pretender's boys fussed over by, iii. 70

opera attended by, in London, with Lady Dashwood, iii. 224

opera supported by, in Florence, ii. 555

Orange, Ps of, to be visited by, iii. 49

Orford family deeds supposed to have been taken to Italy by, ix. 160

Orford family said to have given nothing to, ix. 130

Oxenden lover of, iii. 5

Padua visited by, i. 217, 224, 235

paintings inherited from, by Mozzi, ix. 524

Palazzo Vecchio visited by, i. 283

papers of, from Naples, received by Mozzi, ix. 162

Paris to be visited by, vii. 120, 230

Paris visited by, iv. 335, vii. 141–2

Parliament's dissolution blamed by, for mismanagement of her boroughs, viii. 57, 67

passes her time between Florence and Fiesole, viii. 488

physician from Rome attends at Molo di Gaetà, viii. 312

Pisa baths may be visited by, vii. 83, ix. 107

Pisa baths visited by, viii. 105

Pisa visited by, ix. 112–13

plate and jewels of, right of disposal claimed, ix. 163

plate carried by, to Italy, ix. 144, 169

Podestà of Verona's son has affair with, i. 196

politics and 'metaphidgets' of, iv. 504

Pomfret, Cts of, entertains, ii. 364

—— receives letter from, iii. 61

—— takes, to Court, after Cts of Yarmouth refuses to do so, iii. 111

Pratolino apartment occupied by, with Leopold's consent in hot season, viii. 23

pregnancy of, suspected, ii. 153

pretensions of, to learning, ix. 122

property of, may not escape English lawyers, ix. 131

prudence of, iv. 481

public and private calamities do not disturb tranquillity of, viii. 488

Pulteney might be influenced by, iii. 310

—— opposed by, ii. 99

quack oculist patronized by, ii. 272

Radicofani visited by, in Pius VI's litter, viii. 317

rent arrears due at death of, ix. 511–12

rents of estates of, collected by son, ix. 144

Richecourt accompanied by, at Padua, i. 217, 224, 235

—— admired by, i. 360, 367

—— discusses with his son the marriage of, iv. 255

—— assists, in journey, iii. 54

—— attended by, in illness with home-made ptisan, ii. 66–7

—— avenges quarrels of, ii. 10

—— constantly hears from, iii. 97

—— does not discuss, with Mann, iii. 54

—— encourages, to visit England, i. 426

—— entertained by, on Thursdays, ii. 4

—— forbids, to interrupt his devotions, iii. 31

—— gives attendants to, iii. 49–50

—— had expected to marry, iv. 255, 268

—— has chariot made for, i. 53–4

—— incited by, to oust Mann, ii. 362

—— influenced by: ii. 140; against England, ii. 329

—— jokes about, iv. 444

—— lends money to, i. 461

—— loses, iv. 272

—— may be tempted by wealth of, iv. 439

—— may follow, to Venice, iii. 47

—— may have entrusted, with Hanoverian negotiation, iii. 70

—— might dress, as a man to answer his duel challenge, i. 468

—— might encourage, to seek bank credit, i. 422–3

—— not to be accompanied by, to country, ii. 314

—— not to be followed by, to Vienna, i. 89, 95

—— not to be married by, iv. 239

—— not to rely on, i. 409

—— persuades, to sign papers, ii. 487

—— prejudiced by, against Mann, iii. 452

—— probably does not hear from, iv. 143

—— receives letter from, from Hanover, iii. 80

—— recovers from influence of, iv. 68

——'s access to, by door into palace corridor, ii. 391

——'s affair with: i. 90, 409n; said by Rinuccini to have displeased Sir Robert Walpole, i. 108

—— said to be preparing apartment for, in his country house, iii. 80

—— said to have received letters from, from England, iii. 64

——'s daughter dines with, iv. 480

——'s daughter receives gifts from, iv. 499, 505, ix. 144

——'s 'deary,' ii. 12

——'s departure impels, to leave Florence, i. 107

——'s departure probably foreseen by, iii. 49

——'s disgrace attributed by, to Wachtendonck, i. 107

——'s fears soothed by, ii. 520

——'s house near that of, iv. 480

——'s lodgings to be prepared by, ii. 309

——'s misbehaviour incited by, iv. 313

——'s opinion of, rises after gift of jewels, iv. 505

——'s return from Vienna will be awaited by, iii. 144

——'s rudeness to, i. 34, 53

——'s son brought up by, iv. 90

——'s success encourages, ii. 122

—— supposedly father of two daughters by, ix. 122, 130

—— to join, at Verona, for return to Florence, i. 107

—— to repeat Mann's conversation to, ii. 12

—— unlikely to be troubled by, iv. 480

—— visited by, ii. 364

—— will not be pleased by return of, iv. 476

—— would not have been left by, had he shown more prowess, iv. 395

Richmond, Mrs, escorts, only part way to Bologna, iii. 50

—— expects, iii. 252

—— hears from, about meeting with son, iii. 192

—— not told by, whether to go to England or to renew lease on Florentine house, iii. 101

—— ordered by, to return to England, iii. 290

—— replaces, in Richecourt's coach, iii. 75, 101

—— to accompany: iii. 46; only to Bologna and then await her return to Florence, iii. 49–50

—— to vacate Florentine house of, iii. 192, 238

—— wonders whether to renew lease on Florentine house of, iii. 97

rides horseback, ii. 314, 364, vii. 512

Rolle family to receive estate of, ix. 148

Rome visited by, vii. 478, 492, viii. 164, 170, 222, 304, 317, 318

Rucellai's affair with, i. 54

——'s defence of, silenced, i. 448

—— second in affections of, i. 71

—— supervises making of bed of, i. 107

Salimbeni assisted by, in road accident, i. 116

Salo visited by, i. 196, 217

Salviati villa may be taken by, v. 310

satire by Crudeli liked by, i. 424, 491, ii. 11

scandal exhausted by, iii. 229

scandals concerning, would be revived if will is contested, ix. 124

scientific folly of, worse than religious folly, iv. 555

Scott, Lady Isabella, receives letter from, iii. 61

Scully's renting of Florentine house at Mann's expense for Walpole family asserted by, ii. 14

servant dismissed by, under suspicion of being Mann's spy, ii. 14

servants of, unaware of postal hours, vii. 515

Sharpe corresponds with, about her son, vii. 464, 472, 476, 477, 486, 491, 492, 493, 496, 501, 503, 509, 514, 516, 525, 537, 548, viii. 47, 57, 304, 305, 317, 318

—— disappointed at not receiving legacy from, ix. 320, 328

—— handles English affairs of, ix. 160

—— has confidence of, vii. 477

—— may be consulted by, viii. 91

—— mistakenly trusted by, ix. 172

—— no longer entitled to salary paid him by, ix. 496

—— offered a borough by, for his nephew, viii. 52

—— should produce counter-demands in favour of, ix. 333

——'s letters probably never opened by, viii. 318

——'s letter to, forwarded by Mann, viii. 304

——'s salary from, ix. 492

—— thinks: should have left son funds in England, ix. 157; should not have left so much to Mozzi, ix. 162

—— threatens, because of failure to send him order for money, ix. 129

—— wants English funds of, divided by Mozzi with E. of Orford, ix. 155, 157, 160, 217, 335, 426

—— wants HW to aid in letting jointure farm of, viii. 308

—— was lawyer of, ix. 320

—— will tell, of her son's neglect of boroughs, viii. 47

Shirley, Sewallis, discarded by, iv. 438–9, 476, 479

—— disparaged by, iv. 476, 479, 481, 487

—— engages affections of, iii. 309, iv. 143

—— given separate maintenance by, iv. 547, 568

—— may eclipse Richecourt in the favour of, iii. 385

—— might yet make, pregnant, iv. 250, 254–5

—— probably accompanies, iv. 143

——'s death leaves, free to wed a third time, vi. 366

—— sends dunning letters to, iv. 479

—— slave to jealousy of, iv. 433

——'s marriage with, iv. 239, 255

——'s name omitted from monument of, ix. 227

——'s separation from, iv. 444

—— to marry, iv. 239, 250

Shirley arms worn by, but not to be used on monument, ix. 240

[Rolle, Margaret, *continued*]

Smollett's *Adventures of Peregrine Pickle* includes Lady Vane's mention of, i. 459n

snow confines, at Fiesole, viii. 347

snow turns back, at Siena, from trip to Naples, viii. 70

snuff-box with cipher of, supposed to have been sent to Mann by Barbantane, ix. 206

son apparently the object of concern by, iv. 479, 481, 486

son approves disposition of, in favour of Mozzi, ix. 168, 181

son avoids, vii. 224

son cannot well be disinherited by, iv. 433

son collects rents on estates of, ix. 144

son does not pay uncles' fortunes after death of, ix. 316

son expresses regard for memory of, ix. 168

son given power over her boroughs by, viii. 46

son inherits barony of Clinton from, ix. 165

son inherits estate and jointure of, ix. 125

son left by, to care of HW and Sir Edward Walpole, vii. 464, 491, 492, 496, 514

son liked by, though she robs him, iv. 247

son may be taken by, to Italy, iv. 247

son may meet, in England, vii. 121

son neglects, during lifetime, but is now to honour, with monument, ix. 195

son never inspired tenderness in, viii. 376

son never the subject of inquiries by, viii. 322, 347, 374

son not to be rescued by, from scoundrels, vii. 58

son not to repay Mackreth until death of, viii. 53

son pretends that Mackreth borrowed money from, viii. 53n

son resembles, i. 450

son's claims against estate of, ix. 143, 158

son's condition may not be known to, viii. 330

son's correspondence with, vii. 559, 560, 563, viii. 541–2

son's demands on estate of, ix. 412

son's dismissal of HW will offend, viii. 4

son sees, iii. 192, vii. 230

son's estate ruined by, iv. 239

son should not give portrait of, to Mozzi, ix. 501

son's ingratitude to her and HW condemned by, viii. 57

son's letter to be brought by, to Mann to be deciphered, viii. 541–2

son slights, iv. 482

son's neglect of, did not exceed hers for him, ix. 195

son's paternity doubted by HW, ix. 132

son's recovery feared by, to be transitory, viii. 376

son too far away to be aided by, vii. 460

son welcomes delay in settling affairs of, ix. 247

Spry, Commodore, to take, in ship from Naples to Marseille, vii. 2

Stephan accompanies, to England, iii. 46, 50

steward of, Lucas pretends to have found paper of, ix. 440

'Stitara,' the signature of, iv. 248

Sturgis bores, ii. 198

—— housed by, i. 70–1

—— incited by, to tell lies at coffeehouse, i. 406, 462

——'s affair with, i. (?) 90, 461

——'s clothes found in effects of, i. 224

——'s death affects, ii. 199

—— sent by, to Leghorn, i. 95

sums in French funds said to be deposited by, in Mozzi's name, ix. 113

taxes disliked by, iv. 504–5

Tesi told by, that HW will forget to send her a dog, ii. 334

testamentary powers not claimed by, over landed estates in England, ix. 121

Theodore of Corsica's account of, confirms his connection with Carteret, ii. 210

tomb of, see *under* monument for

Toussaint said to be courted by, through Richecourt, ii. 210, 363

Townshend, Vcts, chief companion of, iii. 119

—— protects, iii. 111

—— receives letter from, iii. 60

tragedies preferred by, to operas, ii. 128

Turin to be visited by, vii. 120

Tuscany unlikely to be again the residence of, vii. 2

Tylney buys jewels from, ix. 144

——'s house in Florence occupied by, in winter, vii. 468

Uguccioni gets recommendation from, for Guise and Valtravers, iv. 393

—— may be asked by, to get her a house, iv. 393

——'s affair with, i. 448

—— says that house has been taken by, in Florence, iii. 61, 75

'universally lamented' according to son's epitaph for, ix. 195

unpopular during English visit, iii. 111

Vane, Vcts, emulates adventures of, i. 459

Venetian costume and conversation of, i. 317

Venetian visit of, i. 107, 115, 125, 134

Venice may become residence of, iii. 47, 50

veracity of, defective, ix. 140

Verona to be visited by, i. 107, 134

Verona visited by, i. 150

Vienna may be visited by, i. 125, iii. 48

villa of, at Fiesole, see Medici, Villa

Villa Salviati may be taken by, v. 310

vivacity of, uncommon for one of her age, vii. 512

Wachtendonck disparaged by, i. 107

Walpole, Hon. Robert, seen by, in Paris, vii. 141

Walpole, Sir Robert, disparaged by, i. 387, 406, 423, 448

—— expected by: to be beheaded, i. 444; to flee to Florence, i. 450n, ii. 14

—— indifferent to actions of, i. 326

—— knows infidelities of, i. 425

—— pleases, by his disgrace, i. 360, 367, 393–4

—— rents jewels for, for George II's coronation, v. 536

—— said to enrich, by his death, iii. 37

—— said to have 'bought,' iv. 439

—— should not by his death encourage, to go to England, iii. 38, 46, 49

Walpole family jewels the responsibility of, ix. 144

Walpole family now mentioned by, with regard, iv. 479, 481, 486

Walpole family pictures not valued by, enough to take them to Italy, ix. 227

Walpole name to be abandoned by, i. 367, 406, 423–4, ii. 126

Walter related to, iv. 393

Wasner instigated by Richecourt to plead for, ii. 194

whist played by, iii. 111

will of: caveat against, ix. 124, 126, 137, 143, 167, 195, 493, 504, 509; codicil not valid in England, ix. 121; contest concerns what she had no right to dispose of, ix. 144; deposited at Florentine archivio in 1773, ix. 114; droll and illiterate, ix. 121–2; Florentine lawyers allowed, to be valid, ix. 137; HW condemns Lucas for advising Orford to contest, ix. 315, 510; in her writing-box, ix. 114; intention of testator evident in, ix. 137; Mann consults lawyer about, ix. 120; Mann sends copy of, to HW, ix. 114; Mozzi desires only what is justly his by, ix. 162; Mozzi entitled to make additional claims under, ix. 168–9; Mozzi to deposit, in archivio, ix. 114; Mozzi to inherit everything by, ix. 114; probate received by HW, ix. 123; sent to son, ix. 121, 136; servants neglected in, ix. 122; Sharpe disapproves of, ix. 134–5, 162; son and alleged daughters not named in, ix. 122; son may remove caveat against, ix. 493; son not to contest, ix. 124, 172; son's business with Mozzi to be settled by probate of, ix. 167; son should not have contested, ix. 217; son's name omitted from, ix. 120; tenants withhold rent until caveat is withdrawn from, ix. 493; to be proved in England, ix. 167; trumpery understanding shown in, ix. 140; validity of, doubted, ix. 123

Wood hears plans and complaints of, iv. 476

Wray at Exeter receives letter from, iii. 284

—— cousin to, iii. 238

—— lived with, at Florence, iii. 238

—— lodged by, in London, iii. 284

writing box of, brought to Mann by Mozzi, ix. 114

(?) Yorke's opinion on case of, ix. 162, 186

Young Pretender said to be friend of, iii. 70, 310

Zincke's portrait of: on snuffbox, for her husband, ix. 501; son to do with, as he pleases, ix. 504

Rolle, Samuel (1646–1717), of Heanton Satchville, M.P.:

wife of, iv. 418n

Rolle, Mrs Samuel. See Tuckfield, Margaret

Rolle family:

arms of, to be on Cts of Orford's monument, ix. 240

Clinton title may come to, ii. 143n; see also under Clinton, Barony of

estate of, inherited by Orford, with power to cut off entail, ix. 164n

estate of Cts of Orford to be given to, ix. 148, 156

insanity in, vii. 495

Orford to sell old estate of, ix. 148

Rolle Walter, John (?1714–79), M.P.:

Mann told by, of Lady Orford's plans, iv. 393

Rolli, Paolo Antonio (1687–1767), poet:

excessive charges by, i. 191

lines by, on Pope's death, ii. 468, 485

operas composed and translations made by, ii. 468n

Penelope by, i. 256

Rolliad, The:

group of poets compose, ix. 612

Rolls, Master of. See Master of the Rolls

Rolt, Richard (?1725–70):

Crawford's life written by, iv. 110n

Rolt. See also Bayntun Rolt

Romagna, Priore di. See Ximenes d'Aragona, Ferdinando

Romagna, the:

epidemic in, v. 359

Leopold tours Tuscany in direction of, viii. 343

Neapolitans to retire from, ii. 43

taxes at, ii. 344

Romain, Pierre-Ange (ca 1761–85), attorney, aeronaut:

death of, ix. 590

Romana, the. See Romani

Roman cabinet:

HW's, at Arlington St, vii. 285

Roman Catholic Church:

Anglican bishop pleads for toleration of, in Ireland, while Joseph II suppresses convents, ix. 439

Anglican bishop to urge Pius VI to give autonomy to Irish bishops of, viii. 430

Anglican divines as absurd as those of, iv. 186

[Roman Catholic Church, *continued*]

Argenson deems Louis XV's devotion to, necessary for monarchy, v. 48

Arundell and Booth adherents of, v. 339

Bedingfield the most bigoted member of, in Norfolk, iv. 532

Benedict XIV tells princes of, not to disturb *anno santo*, iv. 98

Berlin church of, receives ornaments from Querini, iv. 329

bishop of, appointed for Corsica, *see* Crescenzi de Angelis, Cesare

bishops of, Clement XIV to bestow mitres on, viii. 39

Bower deserts from, and writes against it, iv. 157

—'s alleged conversion to, iv. 532–4

Brownlow, Lady Betty, joins, ii. 117

cattle murrain attributed to poisoning of pools by, iii. 174

chapel of, in London, Elizabeth Pitt frequents, v. 46

chapels of, in London, destroyed by Gordon rioters, ix. 54–5, 56

Choiseul annihilates power of, vii. 130

Clarendon swung between Protestantism and, ix. 224

Clement XIII cannot persuade princes of, to crusade against Polish dissidents, vi. 574

— orders women to cover their faces in, v. 292

—'s death may keep France and Portugal in, vi. 331

— would sacrifice, to his brief, vii. 16

Clement XIV's murder may become the destruction of, viii. 51

clergy of: Anglican clergy as absurd as, iv. 186; benediction *in articulo mortis* almost never given by, when recovery seems possible, vi. 14; continue in sickroom after death of patient, v. 391; Cosimo III impoverished his subjects to enrich, ix. 223–4; Duke of Burgundy called a pretender by, iv. 287; epigram by, on Richecourt, iv. 268, 272, finesse and jealousy of, traditional, viii. 497; gendarmes preserved by, from mob, i. 79; Henry Benedict (Stuart) joins, ii. 499–500, 501; high headdresses condemned by, ix. 183; interpret earthquake as a judgment, iv. 150; Irish, i. 142, iii. 12; licentiousness of, to be curbed, iv. 458; Louis XV's relations with, iv. 199, 206, 294, vii. 399; Louise, Princesse, at centre of intrigues of, vii. 398; Maupeou cultivates, vii. 398; Mazzei's prank offends, v. 495; Pius VI forbids, to powder hair, viii. 107; Protestant girls induced by, to forsake parents and change religion, vi. 249–50; riots incited by, viii. 102; Wachtendonck's deathbed dominated by, i. 109–10

Cocchi's treatise on matrimony banned by, vi. 204

Crawford's French servant has rites of, before going to save his master, iv. 110

declining, ix. 541, 603

donations and decretals formerly forged by, ix. 603

Duane an adherent of, ix. 216

duellers excommunicated by, iv. 364

Edinburgh riots against, viii. 439

Elizabeth, Q., excommunicated by, vi. 177, 390

end will be obtained by, in time, viii. 106–7

England's lenity to members of, may make it renounce Young Pretender, vi. 369, 386

English adherents of, persecuted by Bp of London, vi. 394–5

English bishops favour toleration of, ix. 66

English legislation for, shows vacillation, ix. 66–7

English members of: circulate story about Young Pretender's not being in Scotland in person, iii. 172, 198–9; publish mournful letters about Jesuits, vii. 524; send contributions to Young Pretender, iii. 176

English newspaper squib warns English butchers against fasting practices of, iii. 129

Fitzherbert, Mrs, a member of, ix. 628

Florentine jurisdizione defends Francis I against encroachments of, iii. 491

Florentine members of, told by confessors: to hate the English, iii. 196–7; to pray for the Young Pretender's success, iii. 112

French clergy of, at odds with Louis XV, iv. 199, 287, 294

Friday fasting in, i. 254, iii. 129

Friedrich II of Hesse converted to, viii. 274–5

Gage a former member of, i. 255

Garrick married in chapel of, iv. 74

Giberne's love affair with Italian girl stopped by, iv. 128–9

girl of, Irish priest escorts, to England, i. 142

Gordon, Lord George, leads Scottish Presbyterians against, ix. 11

— persecutes, ix. 131; *see also* Gordon Riots

Gordon family formerly belonged to, ix. 11

Gordon rioters plunder more Protestants than adherents of, ix. 61

HW averse to tolerating, because it is itself so intolerant, ix. 541

HW calls: 'Madame of Babylon,' viii. 255; 'Old Mother Babylon,' vi. 420; 'Whore of Babylon,' vii. 81

HW despises, for abandoning Young Pretender when his family sacrificed all for her sake, viii. 255

HW reproduces chapel of, v. 306, vi. 136

Hervey, Bp, may expect to be admitted into, ix. 454

— urges admittance of, to seats in Parliament, ix. 438n

—— urges enfranchisement of, in Ireland, ix. 529

Hooke a convert to, iv. 533

Howard family's relations with, vii. 485

Howe, Lady, converted to, because it is more entertaining, iv. 378, 416, viii. 107–8

ingratitude of, to benefactors, viii. 4

intercourse with heretics disapproved by, iv. 128–9

Irish adherents of: civilized by landlords despite resistance, x. 32; considered too dangerous for English army, ii. 566; forbidden to carry swords, iv. 289; France might get secret agents from, iv. 491; landowners fear to enfranchise, ix. 529, 541; might have to supply rebel army in Wales, iii. 160; said to stop supplies to Young Pretender because he renounced church, vii. 402; should not vote for Irish parliament members, ix. 529

Irish and Scottish members of, said to encourage French invasion, ii. 415

Irish bishops of, might be put on footing of Gallican church, viii. 430

Irish member of, more dangerous (to England) than a Spanish grandee, iv. 171

Irish priests of, i. 142, iii. 116, v. 202; interpret for English naval captains, iii. 12

Italian members of: permitted by Pius VI to eat meat in Lent because of fish shortage, ix. 17, 21; usually include Madonna in Trinity, vii. 459

Jesuits the janizaries of, vii. 214

Jesuits to be under control of bishops of, vii. 473

jewels stolen out of, by soldier, ix. 499

Joseph II may press claims against, for its usurpations from the Medici, ix. 595

—— will not squander lands of, on courtiers, ix. 544

jubilee observances by, iv. 82–3

Lancashire members of, threaten loyal citizens, iii. 172

Lenten fasting of, upset by Protestant Necker and Protestant English fishmongers, ix. 21

London members of, expected to rise up, iii. 138, 171–2

Louis XV's quarrel with, iv. 199, 287, 294

Louis XVI may become a champion of, in Poland, viii. 11

Maguire deserts, i. 420

Mann delighted at exposure of villainy of, iv. 542

Mathews's crew disturbs ceremonies of, on Italian island, and hangs crucifix on monkey's neck, ii. 59, 79n

medal for St Bartholomew Massacre suppressed by, v. 201

members of, hope for Young Pretender's success, iii. 131

Methodists, modern, not opposed to, ix. 11

miracles adduced as proofs of, ii. 305–6

Miserere of to be sung in London, ii. 211

misfortunes of, vi. 324–5

Necker resists, ix. 21

—— will shock, by holding office in France while a Protestant, viii. 254–5

Norfolk, Ds of, fears that rebellion may injure, iii. 176

Norfolk dukedom's heir, though a member of, attends masquerade dressed as a cardinal, vii. 194

Nugent a former member of, i. 255, 431

passion play as Lenten devotion in, vii. 459

Pitt, Elizabeth, converted to, iv. 416, 507n

Pius VI probably pleased that Joseph II attacks Holland instead of property of, ix. 544

Polish adherents of, invited to turn Mohammedan, vii. 81

political interference of, in England, enrages Mann, ii. 428

Powis a member of, iii. 467

Presbyterian meeting-house said to be destroyed by, ix. 56

Presbyterians oppose, ix. 64

Protestant prejudices not preferred to practices of, by HW, ii. 79

Protestant ridicule of customs of, deplored by Mann, ii. 59

religion of, forces its adherents to hate Turkey and England, ii. 428

Rohan's disgrace will not prop, ix. 603

said to be waning in England, ix. 66

St-Germain possibly trained for, x. 20

St John wants to unite, with Church of England, iii. 358

Scotland not to tolerate, viii. 439

Scottish colonization barred to members of, x. 33

senility of, ix. 48

SH cabinet modelled upon chapel of, v. 306, vi. 136

suppression of Lombard convents disgorges wealth of, ix. 594

Taaffe forsakes, to fight duel, iv. 289

Thorold renounces, to get inheritance, vi. 380

treaties made by, with intention of breaking them, vi. 574

Turenne's conversion to, viii. 255

Turkey regarded by, as Christianity's bulwark against Russia, vii. 140

Tuscan clergy of, to have their licentiousness curbed by nuncio's edicts, iv. 458

Tuscan friars of, forbidden to go out alone, iv. 458

vipers of, have more than metaphoric poison, ix. 245

Wall an adherent of, v. 347n

wealth formerly bequeathed to, ix. 214

Winnington jokes about, to Stafford, ii. 283

women take to, in old age for entertainment, iv. 378, 416, viii. 107–8

Young Pretender said to have joined Polish members of, vii. 337

[Roman Catholic Church, *continued*]
— said to have renounced, iv. 333, vi. 324, 368, 379–80, vii. 402
——'s alleged renunciation of, a false rumour, vi. 379–80
See also Clergy; Priests
Romances:
HW to read, on his return to SH, viii. 117
Roman Empire:
British Empire compared with, vi. 513, vii. 32
Roman History. See under Hooke, Nathaniel (d. 1763)
Romani, Angela, opera singer:
(?) Albergotti jealous of applause for, i. 162
Roman medals. *See under* Medal
Romans, ancient:
effeminate because they went into winter quarters, ix. 105
English magnanimity to prisoners should shame, v. 367
HW calls London rabble, ix. 343
havocked world for glory, ix. 142
only once suffered a second army to be taken, ix. 210
sometimes had sense, ix. 337
Romans, King of:
Francis II may become, ix. 613n, 661
Joseph II's election and coronation as, vi. 324
——'s election as, expected, iv. 294
Roman sailor:
Corinthian statues belittled by, iii. 264
Romanzov; Romanzow. *See* Rumiantsev
Rome:
Acciaiolis leave, iii. 407
account from, of Acciaioli's expulsion, v. 476
accounts from, of D. and Ds of Gloucester, favourable, viii. 181
accounts printed at, of rebels' success in Scotland, iii. 158
Acquaviva omnipotent at, ii. 55
— sends recruits from, to Spanish army, ii. 542
Admiralty appointments to please, i. 355
agents to and from, *see under* Agent
air of, determined by D. of Gloucester to be favourable to his health, viii. 130
Albani introduces Chute and Whithed to society in, iii. 59
——'s circular letter to foreign ministers at, vi. 76
——'s villa surpasses all sights of, vi. 229
Albany, Cts of, called a prisoner at, by HW, ix. 115
— discourages Gustav III at, ix. 475
— protected at, by brother-in-law, ix. 108n
— to occupy convent at, ix. 106
Almada's absence from, required by Clement XIII's advisors, v. 425
——'s house in, v. 426

'almost reduced to her own bawdy-house,' vii. 81
altar, sepulchral, may be bought at, iv. 325
ambassadors from and to Holy See at, *see under* Ambassador
ancient: Brutus and, ii. 19; consuls of, receive Gauls in Forum, iv. 469; copper dish of, i. 374; Corinthian statues belittled by sailors of, iii. 264; defeats of, were not reflected by stock exchange, v. 558; duels not customary in senate of, ix. 31; eagles of, vi. 404, vii. 32; England compared with, vii. 212; England excels, in eloquence and extravagance, vii. 400; fathers of families rewarded by, despite devastation of other lands, viii. 393; history of, before Republic's fall, compared to modern England, ix. 118; matrons of, addicted to mysteries, iv. 41; medals of, vii. 383; Pontine marshes not drained by, viii. 344; probably stared at its own downfall, viii. 228; proconsuls of, pensioned by tributary sovereigns, ix. 118; senate of, appears to barbarian ambassadors like an assembly of kings, vii. 562; senator of, ii. 221, vi. 499, viii. 186
anno santo to draw visitors to, iv. 43
antiques not to be exported from, ii. 161
antiquities restored at, v. 344
architecture of, *see under* Architecture
armies near, ii. 531–4
Ashburnham shuns, for fear of imprisonment, iii. 454
assemblies at, attended by D. of Gloucester, viii. 163
Atrisco's approach terrifies, ii. 444
Aubeterre learns little at, vii. 158
Austrian party at, iii. 114
Balhaldies and Bandini leave, ii. 380
balls postponed at, till after Easter, vii. 95
Barbarini palace at, v. 533
Basquiat former secretary of Swedish legation at, vii. 439
Batoni's portrait of D. of York to come from, vi. 255
Bavarian representative at, calls on Old Pretender, i. 445
Bayreuth, Margrave and Margravine of, not to change religion at, iv. 479
Benedict XIV closes borders of, ii. 270
— furbishes up churches and theatres at, iv. 98
— might prevent eagle from leaving, iii. 149
— to return to, and hold congregation of cardinals, iii. 416
Bernis publishes at, mistaken news of French victory, ix. 127
book on Portuguese conspiracy printed in, v. 275
Bottari at, vii. 469
Bourbon ministers at: begin to press Clement XIV to dissolve Jesuits, vii. 214; treat Almada with contempt, vii. 221

Bouverie, Clephane, Fuller and Trap to visit, i. 154

Braitwitz's retirement will not please, because of scarcity of hard-working people, iii. 3

Brand to visit, iv. 434, 456

Breton designs bas relief at, for Wolfe's tomb, v. 436

Bridgwater to visit, iv. 451

bust of Vespasian considered the fourth or fifth in, vi. 523

Bute to return to, iv. 96

caballing expected at, over papal election, v. 197

Capello's departure from, iv. 173, 176, 177

cardinals at; see under Cardinal

Carlisle, Cts of, to stay at, 'for the air,' vii. 447

carnival dull at, viii. 280

Catherine II sends minister to, ix. 389

Charles of Naples (Charles III of Spain) marches to, ii. 525

—'s edict brought to, vii. 10

— to make pilgrimage to, ii. 519

— to visit, for *anno santo*, iv. 43

Chartres, Duchesse de, visits, for five days, viii. 222

Cholmondeley's portrait to be painted at, vii. 349, 357, 371

— to visit, ix. 324

Chute asserts at, that Young Pretender is not really in Scotland, iii. 198

— to spread reports in, about English zeal, iii. 128

Clark avoids, iii. 454

Clement XIII puts, in a bustle, v. 230

—'s quarrel with Genoa forgotten at, v. 422

Clement XIV invites D. of Gloucester to, vii. 343, 348

—'s death at: not discussed, viii. 50; shocks people, viii. 49; the only recent crime, viii. 154

—'s nephew a fiddler at, vii. 117

— well received on return to, vii. 526

Coke, Lady Mary, may have trouble at, vii. 547

— should visit Young Pretender's court at, vii. 550

Conclaves at, see under Conclave

confusion at, vii. 35–6

convent at, Wortley Montagu's daughter said to be at, vi. 113

Conway to visit, iv. 293, 295–6

Cope's defeat predicted at, iii. 142

corn shortage at, vi. 223, 229, 446

Corsi prevented from going to, ii. 121

corso at, i. 3, iii. 358

courier from: ii. 477, iv. 42; awaited by Mann, iii. 501; Paris courier outruns, vi. 405, 407; seeks Young Pretender, vi. 383, 387; to Florence prevented by floods, iii. 131

courier from Naples to stop at, v. 463

couriers from: forbidden, ii. 525; to Vienna, iii. 158

couriers sent to, about Dumesnil's arrest, iii. 493

courier to: from France, iii. 150, 218, 253, 257, viii. 10; from Milan, ii. 515; spreads reports of Young Pretender's successes, iii. 197

courier to Old Pretender walks about streets of, iii. 89

Cours de l'Europe, Les, satirizes, i. 177

Court of: Acciaioli's expulsion from Lisbon published by, v. 476; Choiseul tells Aubeterre to treat, with a high hand, vi. 384; claims Monte Santa Maria, iv. 428; dislikes Leopold's letter, vi. 378; England obliges, by lenity to Roman Catholics, vi. 369; Francis III disgusted by, vii. 45; Galluzzi's history unfavourable to, ix. 87n; George III acknowledged by, vi. 389–90; may placate England by refusing to acknowledge Young Pretender, vi. 369; Neapolitan court differs with, over cardinals' costume, vii. 18; opposed to Richecourt, iv. 334; shocked by narrative about Fiore case, vi. 328; tries to destroy Gregory XIII medal, v. 201

Cowpers to visit, viii. 251

Craon, Princesse de, dislikes fleeing to, i. 178

Crescimbeni's blunder about Richard I's letter at, v. 178

crimes no longer characteristic of, vi. 254, viii. 154

Cumberland, D. and Ds of, may be ill received at, vii. 502

Cumberland, D. of, and D. of Gloucester did not make good impressions at, viii. 123

Damer, Mrs, to visit, ix. 213

Damer's and Gascoigne's fray with coachman at, vi. 286, 300n

Dashwood's hatred of George II exposed in letters from, i. 417

degradation of, ix. 589

Del Anima church at, vii. 36

Dick, Sir John and Lady, to spend winter at, viii. 240, 251

Doria said to have sent peace news to, i. 134

Dumesnil escapes from, iii. 493

Dunbar about to leave, iii. 378

— may have left, iii. 143

— slanders Chute and Whithed to, iii. 136

eagle found at, iii. 66, 79, 121–2, 197, 420

edict to be published by, for Del Montes' arrest or death, iv. 446

Electress's money at, to be used to finish chapel, ii. 113

—'s will deposited at, ii. 168

enamellers of, v. 313

England's enemies at, distort news, iii. 158, 217, 362

[Rome, *continued*]

England will allow, to starve, vi. 462

English at: arrive at Florence, vii. 296, viii. 214, ix. 672; attentive to D. and Ds of Gloucester, viii. 190; believe in Young Pretender's success, iii. 191; crowd from Florence, viii. 131; play faro, i. 29; see design for Wolfe's tomb, v. 436

English crowd to, for jubilee, iv. 82–3, 98

English-French war expected at, i. 24

English Jacobites at: call on Dunbar, iii. 136; court Old Pretender's sons when forbidden to see himself, iii. 112, 136; make junkets after Falkirk news, iii. 218; might molest Chute and Whithed, iii. 113; more confident than those in England, iii. 139;

English news echoed from, to Florence, ii. 368–9, iii. 217

English visit, for Holy Week, vi. 492, ix. 672

experience of, in maintaining dignity in difficult circumstances, vi. 236

famine threatens, vi. 446, 448

faro suppressed at, i. 29

fishermen of, to be lured to Leghorn, iv. 217

floods in, iv. 77, vii. 378

Florentine intercourse with, cut off, ii. 525

foreign ministers at: dispatch couriers to their courts, vii. 16; report Pius VI's illness to their courts, viii. 468

fountains the only water supply of, viii. 479

France has little influence at, v. 220

French couriers to and from, iv. 42, 147, vii. 10, 14, 16

funeral price at, v. 391

Gages's plans reported from, iii. 556

Galluzzi's history may be suppressed by, ix. 59, 80

——'s history not controverted in, ix. 238

—— treats Court of, unfavourably, ix. 80, 87n

Gascoigne and Hon. George Damer have drunken riot with coachman at, vi. 286

Genoese quarrel with Clement XIII causes commotion in, v. 394

George II's illness rumoured at, iii. 377

George III indebted to, for hospitality to D. of Cumberland, vii. 566

——'s art purchases at, vi. 115

German cardinals not at, vii. 95

Giustiniani's palace at, vii. 287

glory of, family pride on large scale, ix. 133

Gloucester, D. and Ds of, leave, for the summer, viii. 290

—— may visit, viii. 298, 312, ix. 618, 624

—— not pleased with all the great ladies at, viii. 247

—— pleased with, viii. 186

—— probably already on way to, viii. 144

—— to spend winter at, viii. 82

—— urged by HW not to go to, viii. 125

Gloucester, D. of, able to set out for, viii. 141

—— approaches, though he seemed averse to revisiting it, viii. 129

—— has more faith than most people in air of, viii. 84

—— house kept for at, viii. 312

—— in no condition to go to, vii. 370

—— insults, vii. 566

—— may be unable to set out to, viii. 140

—— may deter Ds of Kingston from visiting, viii. 220

—— may not be well received at, viii. 123

—— may visit, vii. 384, viii. 117, 130

—— plumper in England than at, viii. 332

—— prevented by physicians from going to, vii. 357

—— to spend winter at, viii. 117

—— writes from, to Mann, viii. 291

gossip of, i. 24

Gothic remains probably non-existent at, iv. 372

government of, in state of confusion, ix. 588

governor of, *see* Buondelmonte, Filippo (1691–1741); Caprara, Cornelio (1703–65); Piccolomini, Eneo Silvio (1709–68); Ricci, Francesco (1679–1755); Spinelli, Ferdinando Maria (1728–95)

Gower jokingly said to await dispensation from, i. 494

Grafton, Ds of, to visit, v. 554

Graftons take other road to, v. 565

'great abbé' at, *see* Guerin de Tencin, Pierre

great ladies of: are proud and saucy, viii. 123; ignore Ds of Kingston, viii. 95; offended by Ds of Gloucester's postponed reception, viii. 164

HW asks Mann for gossip in, about Murray and Stone, iv. 360

HW calls: 'Babylon,' vii. 212; 'Catholic dunghill,' vi. 237; 'Madame of Babylon,' viii. 255; 'old Mother Babylon,' vi. 420

HW expects Lady Mary Coke to have trouble at, vii. 547

HW pleased by changed attitude of, to English Protestants, vi. 177

HW's statue at, i. 212, ii. 161–2, 177–9

HW's views of, *see under* Locatelli

HW wants altar from, to use as pedestal, v. 461

Hamilton buys Cignani painting at, v. 208

Henry Benedict (Stuart) said to leave, i. 13, ii. 436, iii. 98–9

Hervey, Bp, sends speech to agent at, ix. 443, 459n

holy days cancelled at, vi. 17

hospital at, receives surgical instruments from D. of Gloucester, viii. 129

house in, falls, vi. 17

hurricane at, iv. 69–70, 77

Illustri fatti Farnesiani may be scarce at, ix. 403

'inexhaustible,' i. 22

inoculation not used in, vi. 150

Irish priest at, does medal, v. 202

Jacobite antiquarian at, iv. 174

Jacobites at: call Falkirk a victory, iii. 214; depress Mann, iii. 182

Jerusalem's recovery dubious at downfall of, vii. 195

Jesuit refugees too numerous for, vi. 516

Jesuits' College at, Jesuits' correspondence about Gunpowder Plot said to be found at, vii. 517–18, 532, 539n, ix. 458

Jesuits flock to, viii. 43

Jesuits' silver weighed at, vii. 512–13

Jesuits' suppression planned at, vii. 135

Jesuits to be expelled from, vii. 473

Jesuits' vast wealth at, vi. 527

Jesuits' war at, uninteresting to HW, v. 491

João V may visit, iv. 43

José Manoel may precipitate revolt by withdrawing subjects from, v. 430

Joseph II acclaimed at, as 'king,' vii. 103

Joseph II and Maria Josefa to visit, vi. 556

Karl Friedrich's reception at, amuses England, iv. 155

Kingston, Ds of, leaves jewels and furniture at, viii. 83–4, 123, 162n, 203, 398, 404, 409

—— may not visit, while D. and Ds of Gloucester are there, viii. 220

lady from, *see* Savelli, Barbara

Laocoön duplicate at, vi. 71

Leicester to obtain statues from, iv. 104

Leopold opposes dictates of, ix. 81

—— suppresses Pisa abbey without consulting, vii. 504

letters from: about Old Pretender's health, v. 392, 406; delayed because of quarantine, ii. 282; expected at Florence, iii. 13; from St Thomas Aquinas's, Piazza Navona, iii. 227–8; last, iii. 143; say that Spanish progress is arrested, iii. 8–9; tell of Benedict XIV's stand about Monte Santa Maria, iv. 428; to Goldsworthy, iii. 226

letters to: from France and Germany, ask about Clement XIV's health, viii. 43–4; from Paris, about Young Pretender, iii. 451

Lobkowitz and Maria Theresa acclaimed at, ii. 446–7

Lobkowitz's army approaching, ii. 531–4

—— sends stores and women to, for safety, ii. 447

London compared with, viii. 228

Louis XV avoids break with, vii. 518

lower classes at, disarmed for fear of bread riots, vi. 229

Lucan, Bn or Bns, gets sarcophagus at, viii. 462

Mann afraid to inquire at, about Gloucester family, viii. 181

—— alarmed by reports from, of Young Pretender's Scottish invasion, iii. 130–1

—— awaits Benedict XIV's medals from, v. 231

—— buys *Illustri fatti Farnesiani* at, ix. 412, 417

—— denies having visited, iv. 473

—— forwards letter received from, i. 31

—— gets altar at, for HW, iv. 365

—— gets news from: of Scottish emissaries, i. 145; of Young Pretender's departure, i. 113

—— has not heard from, about pedestal for Vespasian bust, v. 482

—— hears from: about Lanfranco, ii. 296–7; of Clement XIII's reception of Young Pretender, vi. 517

—— hears nothing from, i. 119

—— hears nothing from, about Lanfranco picture, ii. 290

—— may have to wait at, i. 196

—— misled by reports from, i. 118

—— not to spread news at, of Edinburgh troubles, iii. 129

—— offers to send Young Pretender's acquaintances at, to England to identify him, iii. 141

—— plans Sir Robert Walpole's visit to, ii. 211–13

—— prevented Young Pretender's coronation at, vii. 329

—— receives account through, of Russo-Turkish naval battle, vii. 226–7

—— rumoured to be visiting, iv. 470

——'s abbé at, i. 3, 113, 114, 145, ii. 466, 485, iii. 140

——'s art advisers at, are Chambers and Vierpyl, iv. 391–2

—— sends sketch of eagle's pedestal to, iv. 333

——'s friends at, warn him about Young Pretender, iii. 368

——'s information about Young Pretender all comes from, iii. 86

——'s letters limited to area of Florence and, ix. 464

——'s 'neighbour at,' *see* James Francis

——'s spy at, an abbé, i. 113, iii. 140

—— tells architect to get Gothic ornaments at, iv. 368–9

—— tells Horace Mann II to pay respects to D. and Ds of Gloucester at, viii. 163

—— to get copies of paintings at, iv. 328–9

—— to inquire at, about mould of Livia statue, vi. 98

—— to recommend Pars at, viii. 135, 144

—— to send English propaganda to, ii. 259, 427, iii. 205, 298, vi. 386–7

—— unable to go to, to investigate rumours, i. 116

—— would like to send Irish epigram to, iv. 318

—— writes to: about Lanfranco, ii. 275; about pedestal, v. 470; for antique sepulchral urn, iv. 333; for medals of Benedict

[Rome, *continued*]

XIV, v. 215; for prints of Young Pretender and wife, vii. 427, 429

Mann, Horace II and Lady Lucy, to go to, viii. 118, 129, 131, 140, 145, 146, 181

Mann, Horace II and Lady Lucy, urge Mann to accompany them to, viii. 129

many at, think Pius VI will pay visit to Joseph II, ix. 239

map of, Cumberland, D. of, asks Mann to procure, iv. 459

Maria Amalia to visit, ii. 435, 438, iv. 43

Maria Carolina, Leopold, and Maria Louisa not to enter, vii. 2, 17

Maria Carolina's subjects at, pay homage to her at Marino, vii. 23

——'s visit to, forbidden but will be forgiven, vii. 26

Maria Josefa to visit, vi. 556

Maria Theresa acclaimed at, ii. 447

——'s affairs at, no longer managed by Albani, iii. 475

——'s representative at, tells Mann of Young Pretender's flight, ii. 373

Mathews's protest forwarded to, ii. 301

medals procured from estate of deceased collector at, ii. 478

medals sent from, to Mann, ii. 45

medals sent to, from England, i. 229

ministers from and to Holy See, at, *see under* Minister

mob in: Austrian in sympathies, i. 114; bread thrown by, into Clement XIII's coach, vi. 446; celebrates Francis I's election, iii. 113

Modenese rulers may take refuge at, i. 489

Moniño's friends during stay at, inform Mann of his character, viii. 478

Monti's account of Young Pretender's departure from, ii. 418–19

Moretti a merchant in, iv. 46

Murray's promotion may be rumoured from, to Mann, ii. 118

Naples and Tuscany might be shut off from, ii. 270

narrative burned at, by hangman, vi. 328

Neapolitan court may flee to, i. 501, ii. 3, 13

Neapolitan court quarrels with, over cardinals' costume, vii. 18

Neapolitan troops reach Porta del Popolo at, iii. 144

Necker's appointment in France may cause comment in, viii. 255

nobility of: attentive to D. and Ds of Gloucester, viii. 190; entertain Joseph II and Leopold, vii. 108–9; prepare festivals for Leopold, vii. 95; said to be jealous of Young Pretender, vi. 394; to give tragedy at Frascati, iv. 481; York, Cardinal, despised by, ix. 397

O'Brien leaves, iv. 45

Old Pretender acknowledged at, by ambassadors of George II's allies, ii. 428

—— at, receives English news from Goddard, i. 368

—— joined at, by Cardinal York, iv. 354

—— languishes forgotten at, vi. 106

—— may leave, iii. 94, 96, 99, 135, 141–2

——'s burial eagerly awaited at, so that theatres may reopen, vi. 385

——'s condition reported from, v. 391, vi. 379

——'s court troublesome and expensive to, vi. 369

——'s faction at, iii. 400

——'s funeral still expected by, v. 412

——'s furniture brought from, to Florence by son, ix. 525

——'s Herrenhausen, iv. 341

——'s high spirits reported from, i. 306

——'s property in, left to Cardinal York, vi. 387

——'s underling and Bandini leave, for Tuscany, ii. 379–80

—— thought by, to be last English king to cure King's Evil, v. 392

old princesses of, offended by Clement XIV's exclusion, vii. 431

old saying about pope of, vii. 128

old senators at, keep Adonis wigs with their robes for days of ceremony, viii. 32

Orford, Cts of, ill at, viii. 317–18

—— to visit, vii. 478, viii. 222, 304

Ormond sends courier to, iii. 85

Palazza Madama at, iv. 264

Paris letters in, quoted about new attempt by Young Pretender, iii. 451

Paris nuncio writes to, iii. 399

Parlement de Paris defends Parma against, vii. 4

Parliament's disapprobation of peace treaty attributed by, to Young Pretender, iv. 27

Pars dies at, x. 48

—— to study in, viii. 144

pasquinades at, on imperial election, i. 351

Passionei invites Niccolini to, v. 127

Patch studied under Vernet at, vii. 275

pedestal to have been sent from, v. 521

Philip, Don, may stay near, ii. 389

physician from, attends Cts of Orford, viii. 312

physicians should not prescribe air of, vii. 451

Piccolomini to obtain act of oblivion so that Damer and Gascoigne may return to, vi. 287

Pitt, Anne, nurses French female servant at, viii. 344, 353

Pius VI and Cardinal York invite Cts of Albany to convent at, ix. 106

Pius VI may not be applauded at, upon return from Vienna, ix. 283

——'s illness concealed at, viii. 467–8

——'s *possesso* draws crowds to, viii. 131, 136, 145

——'s unpopularity at, ix. 383, 587–8

——'s visit to Vienna disapproved by, ix. 250

Pontine drainage expensive to, ix. 383, 588

Porta Angelica: road to, ii. 532; Spaniards fear to seize, ii. 533

Porta del Popolo: Lobkowitz's army passes near, ii. 531; Neapolitan troops at, iii. 144; road to, ii. 532; Young Pretender's escape by, ii. 388

Porta San Giovanni: Lobkowitz's army passes near, ii. 531; Young Pretender escapes through, ii. 387, 388

Portugal's quarrel with, over Jesuits, v. 423–6, 475–7

Portuguese banker at, *see* Rosa, Lopez

Portuguese Hospital at, v. 423

Portuguese representatives threaten to leave, v. 423, 425–6

post from, brings Ds of Gloucester's letter to Mann, viii. 250

Prideaux's letters forwarded to, by Mann, ii. 491

Priero to leave, after arrival of Viennese couriers, iii. 158

princes and princesses of, act at Frascati, iv. 481

prints of, given to D. of York, vi. 229, 232–3

rebels' executions have no effect at, iii. 311

reports fabricated at, iii. 155–6

rhinoceros goes to jubilee at, iv. 127

Richard I's poem not at, v. 169, 178

Richecourt's persecutions from, iv. 334

——'s subservience to, iv. 448

Rienzi a demagogue of, vii. 8n

rumour from, of Austrian-Prussian peace, i. 134

St-Aignan enters, i. 12

sainthood delayed by cabals at, vii. 124

St Peter's day to be celebrated at, ii. 462

Santa Croce entertains people of, i. 20

Santo Spirito hospital in, viii. 129

satires at, about Conclave, v. 217

seal cut at, iii. 9

searchers prevent antiques from leaving, ii. 161–2

Secret Committee defeat disheartens Jacobites at, i. 388

sede vacante at, compared to English change of administration, ix. 377–8

senate of, *see under* Senate

sepulchral altar bought in, iv. 365

silver scarce in, i. 4

Skrine's letter from important personage in, vi. 447

snow cuts off, from Florence, ix. 470

'soil of Neros and Borgias,' viii. 154

Spain lowers revenue of, by buying nomination to benefices, v. 349

Spain said by, to be about to aid Young Pretender, iii. 335

Spaniards and Neapolitans near, ii. 546

Spaniards chase people back to, ii. 532

Spanish army reported from, to be advancing, iii. 15

Spanish cardinals arrive at, vii. 113

Spanish success alarms, ii. 460

Stephens's prints not to be found at, vii. 429

Stoppani sends Falkirk news to, by courier, iii. 214

Stormont to visit, iv. 296

Stosch carries medals from, i. 416

—— driven from, i. 164n

—— manages English secret service in, v. 149–50

——'s agent at, dies, ii. 380–1

Strange copies pictures at, vi. 108

—— looks in vain for art purchases at, vi. 115

Strozzi, Principessa, loses museum articles from cabinet in, iii. 350

Stuart family must resent D. of York's welcome at, vi. 237

Tencin visits Old Pretender at, i. 481

Tissot advises Cts of Carlisle to fix at, vii. 447

Titchfield does not see, v. 543, 550–1

Trasteverini at, *see under* Trasteverini

troops said to advance towards, from Naples, i. 110

Tuscan agreement with, iv. 420

Tuscan measures against authority of, vii. 504

Tuscany not yet severely treated by, iv. 458

Tuscany stops intercourse with, for fear of plague, ii. 270

Veers sets out for, iii. 506, 510n

Venice's quarrel with, iv. 173, 189–91, v. 219–20, 230, vii. 56

Vernon's victory depreciated at, i. 7

Verskovis returns to, iii. 420–1

'views' of, *see under* Locatelli, Andrea

visitors to: Astley, Lady, ix. 480; Astley, Sir Jacob Henry, ix. 480; Bagot, vi. 142; Beauvau, i. 16, 22–3; Bouverie, iii. 191, 196, 400; Brand, iv. 471; Bulstrode, i. 11, ?14; Bute, vii. 83, 91; Cameron, Jeanie, vi. 453; Carlisle, Cts of, vii. 447; Carpenter, Lady Almeria ix. 674; Charles of Naples, ii. 533; Chute, iii. 48–210; Clephane, i. 317; Cologne, Elector of, iv. 508; Conway, iv. 297, 299, 304; Cowper, viii. 94, 251; Cowper, Lady, viii. 94, 251; Craon, i. 9, 11, 16, 20, 21; Craon, Princesse de, i. 3, 9, 10, 16, 28, iii. 358; Cumberland, D. and Ds of, vii. 559, 564, 565–6; Damer, Mrs, ix. 645, 646, 650; Damer, Hon. George, vi. 286, 300n; Damer, Hon. John, vi. 300n; Deskford, i. 7, 9, 24; Dumesnil, iii. 491–3; Englebert, i. 13, 15, 17, 19; Francis III, ii. 532; Friedrich II of Hesse, viii. 274–5; Gages, ii. 532; Gascoigne, vi. 286; German baron, iv. 546; Giles, viii. 243; Gloucester, D. and Ds of, viii. 82, 129, 130, 144, 163–4, 170–1, 174–5, 181, 184, 186, 190,

[Rome, *continued*]

201, 214, 222, 247–8, 252, 291, ix. 618, 624, 674; Gloucester, D. of, vii. 140, 141, 357, 370, 384, 396–7, 405, 566, viii. 129, 290; Grafton, Ds of, vi. 12, 17, 22; Grafton, D. of, vi. 12, 20; Gustav III, ix. 475; HW, i. 2–31, x. 3–8; Hamilton, Sir William and Lady, vii. 448, viii. 337; Hartington, i. 7–8, 16, 23; Hervey, Bn, ix. 651; Hervey, Bp, viii. 430, ix. 651; Hillsborough, vi. 429; Hobart, iii. 421; Holland, Bn and Bns, vi. 467; Holt, iii. 191, 196, 400; Jablonowsky, Ps, vii. 319; Joseph II, vii. 103, 109, ix. 468; Karl Wilhelm Ferdinand, vi. 458; Kilmorey, Vcts, v. 406; Kingston, Ds of, vii. 559, 564, 566–7, viii. 79, 83–4, 123, 162n, 203, 398, 404, 409; Leopold, vii. 23, 91, 95, 103, 108–9; Lincoln, elder E. of, i. 31, 41; Lincoln, younger E. of, viii. 252; Lockart, iv. 78; Lorraine, Primate of, i. 12, 17, 22; Lucans, viii. 462; Lyttelton, Sir Richard, iv. 12; Macdonald, Sir James, vi. 447; Macgregor, ii. 379–80; Mann, Horace II, viii. 140, 163, 181, ix. 673–5; Mann, James II, ix. 581, 586, 592; Mann, Lady Lucy, viii. 140, 181; Maria Carolina, vii. 23; Maria Louisa, vii. 23; Maximilian, viii. 123; Mengs, iv. 331; Milles, Miss, ix. 480; Monro, iii. 191, 196, 400; Montagu, Lady Mary Wortley, i. 92; Montemar, i. 281; Morice, ix. 435; Newdigate, viii. 144; Nightingale family, iv. 278; Northampton, Cts of, vi. 142; Northington, ix. 652; Orford, Cts of, vii. 492, viii. 164, 170–1, 175, 222, 312; Pars, x. 48; Patch, vii. 390; Paul I, ix. 250; Phelps, iii. 191, 196; Pitt, Anne, viii. 105, 337–8, 344, 353, 374; Pitt, Mrs George, vii. 447; Pitt, Thomas, v. 543, 545; Pomfrets, i. 35; Pope, i. 68; Righellini, vi. 142; Rochechouart, vi. 28; Roxburghe, v. 550; St-Aignan, i. 12, 81; St John, vi. 231; St John, Vcts, iv. 23; St-Odile, iv. 305; Scott, Arthur, iii. 461; Shrewsbury, E. of, i. 4; Skrine, Mrs, vi. 398; Smyth, i. 10, 14, 15, 16, 23, 25; Stanley, vi. 327; Stephens, vii. 427–8; Stormont, iv. 298, vii. 2; Strange, v. 470, vi. 108, 115; Strathmore, v. 543, 564; Stuart, Charlotte, x. 47; Taylor, iv. 458, 461; Thun, i. 282; Trigge, viii. 380; Trumbull, iii. 232; Tylney, viii. 251; Vance, Abbé de, i. 63; Walkinshaw, Clementina, x. 47; Walpole, Horatio (1723–1809), iii. 232, 238–9; Werpup, vi. 306; Whithed, iii. 48–210; Wilkes, vi. 290, 292; Wortley Montagu, vi. 76–7; Wyseman, i. 15, 18, 21, 23; York, D. of, vi. 171, 177, 180, 204, 223, 224, 226–34, 257n, 325, 384

Wallmoden summons servants from, vi. 357
—— to return by way of, vi. 362
Walpole, Sir Robert, might visit, ii. 202, 211–13
Walpole family not likely to be a good recommendation at, iv. 461

Warsaw's courier to, vi. 119
washerwoman at, i. 461
William Frederick christened at, viii. 181
——'s birth at, viii. 178
Wilton does statue at, iv. 397
Wolfe's monument designed at, by Breton, v. 421–2, 428
York, Cardinal, called 'Cardinal di Orco' at, iii. 428
—— called *Sua Eminenza Reale* at, viii. 480
—— carries brother through, in coach, vi. 392
—— does not tell father about D. of York's visit to, vi. 256, 257
—— expected to return to, i. 18
—— may leave, iii. 96
—— receives courier at, with news of brother's illness, ix. 394, 467
—— returns to, ii. 354
—— will not return to, except on independent footing, iv. 332
Young Pretender brings bride to, vii. 406
—— brings companions to, from France, vii. 351
—— called P. of Wales at, vi. 389, 406
—— can exist decently only at, vi. 394
—— drinks and quarrels at, vii. 351
—— driven from, by Clement XIII's non-recognition, viii. 244
—— leaves, ii. 373–81, 384–9, 419, 421–2, iii. 98, vii. 242
—— less dangerous at Avignon than at, iv. 27
—— may leave, i. 13, 14, 113, 116, 159, ii. 101, 373, vi. 393
—— may visit, to make public confession of faith, iv. 333
—— no more a king at, than in London, vi. 399
—— pursued to, by Clementina Walkinshaw, x. 47
—— ridiculed on his return to, vii. 343
—— said by, to be still in Scotland, iii. 311
——'s alleged conversion not known at, vi. 336
——'s alleged success celebrated at, iii. 257
——'s apartment at, prepared by Jews, vi. 379
——'s attendants return to, from Siena, vii. 318–19
——'s aversion to, iv. 15
——'s Bavarian alliance rumoured from, ii. 396
——'s cause seems more favourable at, than in Scotland, iii. 140
—— sends 'Lockat' to, iv. 27
——'s French trip may be financed by, ii. 101
——'s house at, shorn of English arms, vi. 408
——'s illness announced to his wife and brother at, ix. 394

——'s ingratitude from, despised by HW, viii. 255

——'s marriage negotiations discussed in, iv. 35

——'s negotiations about returning to, vi. 368, 384–90

——'s plans announced in, iii. 509

——'s recognition at, as king, prevented, vi. 374, 383–5, 388–9, 405–6, 408, viii. 244

——'s return to, expected, i. 18

——'s second expedition rumoured at, iii. 330, 335

——'s Spanish negotiations discussed in, iii. 97, 140, 330, 335

——'s speeches repeated at, iii. 170

——'s staff leave, to join him, ii. 433–4

——'s success proclaimed at, iii. 140–1, 257

——'s treatment by, does not interest HW, vi. 397, 405–6

——'s 'valet' arrives at, iii. 312

——'s whereabouts announced to, from Paris, iii. 399

——'s whereabouts unknown at, v. 59

—— to be induced by, to leave Avignon, iv. 22

—— to make, his family residence, ix. 627

—— wants permission to return to, vi. 368, 374

Zoffany to go to, vii. 430

Rome Gate, at Florence:
Spaniards to pass, i. 342

Rominagrobis. See under La Fontaine

Romney, Bn. See Marsham, Hon. Charles (1744–1811); Marsham, Robert (1717–93)

Romney, Bns. See Pym, Priscilla (1724–71)

Romney, E. of. See Marsham, Hon. Charles (1744–1811)

Romney, ship:
Grenville commands, ii. 26, 27
Mathews sends, to Leghorn with letters to Mann, ii. 26, 37

Romney family:
Mann, Horace II, decides to leave Parliament because of treatment by, ix. 465

Romulus:
Nassau-Siegen, P. of, imitates, viii. 472
younger generation knows, better than George II, vii. 350

Ronchetti, Elisabetta, opera singer:
(?) performs at Florence, ii. 462

Ronciglione:
Damer and Gascoigne at, vi. 286
Farnese allodial pawned to Pope, i. 204
Leopold, Maria Carolina, and Maria Louisa to visit, vii. 17
Naples and Spain may seize, vii. 10, 24, 36, 45, 413
Parma may gain, vii. 24
Spaniards and Neapolitans at, ii. 527
Spaniards may take winter quarters at, i. 204

Rondeau (platform):
architect adds, to Pitti Palace for military parades, vi. 291

Ronquillo, Don Pedro (1630–91), Spanish ambassador to England 1680–91:
unburied, vi. 216, 230

Roome, Edward (d. 1729):
Blast Upon Blast or Dean Jonathan's Parody: Chute has already seen, ii. 60; Fielding said to have written, ii. 34; HW transcribes, ii. 34–6

Roos, Lord. See Manners, Charles (1754–87)

Roos. See also Ros

Roots:
Hume-Campbell lives on, iv. 5

Rope:
Ferrers's executioners fight over, v. 403
Violante descends St Martin's steeple by, ix. 450

Rope-dancing:
Astley established amphitheatre for, at Southwark, ix. 451n

Roque, La. See La Rocque de Varengeville; Rocca d'Arazzo

Roquefeuille, Jeanne-Thérèse de (d. 1725), m. (1704) Ferdinand, Marquis de Lunati-Visconti:
Leopold makes advances to, iv. 351

Ros or Roos, Bns. See Boyle, Charlotte (1769–1831)

Rosa, Lopez (fl. 1740), Portuguese banker at Rome:
ship belonging to, captured by English, i. 8, 15–16

Rosa, Salvator (1615–73), painter:
Beauclerk, Lady Diana, equals, viii. 524
HW prefers, to modern artists, ix. 247

Rosach. See Rossbach

Rosamond. See under Addison, Joseph; Arne, Thomas Augustine

Rosamouski. See Razumovskiĭ

Rosario, El (galleon):
in Spanish fleet, i. 286

Rosarno:
earthquake damages, ix. 376

Rosary:
Almada and secretary say, v. 430

Rosciad. See under Churchill, Charles (d. 1764)

Rose; roses:
boutonnière of, costs half a guinea, vii. 210
essence of, scarce, ii. 214
from Damascus, HW mentions, v. 113
of India, to be Mann's title, viii. 454
worm-eaten in Florence in 1742, ii. 214

Rose, La. See La Rose

Rosenberg-Orsini, Franz Xaver Wolf (1723–96), Graf (Fürst, 1790), Tuscan war and finance minister 1766–71:
Barbantane calls on, vi. 481
Botta to be replaced by, as major-domo and first minister, vi. 447–8, 453–4
Craon, Princesse de, driven by, from Petraia, vii. 296
dinner to be given by, vii. 64
effects of, to be sold to pay debts, vii. 294

[Rosenberg-Orsini, Franz Xaver Wolf, *cont.*]
employments abandoned by, vii. 253
English visit of, results in love of liberty
of the press, vi. 530
Florence left by, vii. 294
Florentines hope, will become Grand Chambellan, vi. 400
Guasco favoured by, vi. 530–1
Joseph II and Maria Theresa refuse to
pay large debts of, vii. 220, 294
Joseph II's relations with Leopold to be
settled by, on visit to Florence from Vienna,
vi. **393**–4
Leopold accompanied by, vii. 253
—— decides with, about festivities, vi. 559
——'s exposure to smallpox feared by, vi.
559
—— should not be encouraged by, to hate
Florence, vii. 94–5
—— tells, of print satirizing three abbés'
mutual admiration, vi. 531
Mann and Dicks to dine with, vii. 59
Mann jokes with, about publications of
Guasco, Niccolini, and Cerati, vi. 530–1
—— told by, of Leopold's congratulations
on Bath ribbon, vii. 9
Maria Theresa paid debts of, in Denmark
and Spain but not in Tuscany, vii. 294
Montesquieu's letters printed in Tuscany
by favour of, vi. 530
opera regulated by, vi. 559
Pisa palace to be inspected by, vii. 253
resignation of, vii. 220
Vienna visited by, to get his debts paid,
vii. 220
wants to become a foreign minister, vii.
220
Roses (place):
Cornish, Capt., looks for Mathews at, ii.
415
Rosette, HW's spaniel:
HW saved by, from chimney fire, vii. 200–1
tanned black, vii. 200
Rose water:
baptism with, i. 62–3
Rosewood:
cabinet of, ii. 277
Rosier. *See* Pilâtre de Rosier, Jean-François
Rosina. *See* Paganini, Rosa
Rosnay, Comte de. *See* L'Hôpital, François de
Ross, Mrs. *See* Foote, Catharine (ca 1758–
1808); Murray, Fanny (ca 1729–78)
Ross, Hon. Charles (1721–45), M.P.; army
officer:
HW mentions, ii. 374
killed at Fontenoy, ii. 244n, iii. 43
story told by, in Parliament, ii. 355
votes against his party, i. **244**
Walpole, Sir Robert, saves, from going to
West Indies, i. 244
Ross, David (1728–90), actor:
Murray, Fanny, marries, vi. 184n

Ross, George (1681–1754), 13th Lord Ross of
Halkhead; commissioner of customs:
son of, i. 244n
Ross, Sir John Lockhart (1721–90), 6th Bt,
1778; Rear-Adm., 1779; Vice-Adm., 1787:
England supposed to be destination of, ix.
24–5
Rossbach:
battle of, v. 153, 158, 180
Rosset, Jean-André-Hercule de (1726–81),
called Chevalier *or* Commandeur de Fleury:
(?) HW to accompany, in London, vi. 135
Rossi, Signora. *See* Rangoni, Vittoria
Rossi, Federico, Conte di S. Secondo:
(?) wife's quarrels with, i. 123
Rossi, Giuseppe de, Papal physician, 1774–98:
Pius VI's illness considered by, to be seri-
ous, viii. 461
Rosslyn, E. of. *See* Wedderburn, Alexander
Rossmore, Bn. *See* Cunninghame, Robert
Rota:
Lepri, Marchesa, granted verdict by, against
Pius VI, ix. 587
Rotari, Pietro (1707–62), painter:
Catherine II's portrait by, vii. 242
Roth:
regiment or battalion of, ii. 164
Rottofreno:
battle of, iii. 291, 302
Rotunda, at Rome:
closed because of floods, vii. 378
Roucoux:
battle of, iii. 318
Rouge:
Amelia, Ps, compliments Duchesse de Mire-
poix on leaving off, iv. 89
cost of, ii. 281
Coventry wipes, from wife's face, iv. 338
Coventry, Cts of, cannot use, in France, iv.
338
expense of, to Mesdames de France, iv. 500
fashionable at Paris, ii. 220
Grafton, Ds of, does not use, vi. 80
HW suggests adorning sculptures of Niobe's
family with, ix. 178
HW would not put, on St Ethelburgh's
statue, v. 471
Hewet, Mrs, wears, viii. 204
Maria Theresa does not permit ladies to
wear, in mourning period, vi. 354
Pompadour, Marquise de, may abandon,
iv. 530
Rougham, Norfolk:
HW jokes about, ii. 238
Rouillé du Coudray, Antoine-Louis (ca 1689–
1761), Comte de Jouy, minister of marine,
1749–57:
mémoire of, to Fox, a partial war declara-
tion, iv. 524, 526
Roundhouse:
at St Margaret's church, v. 536
HW prefers confinement in, to supping
with his grandmother, iii. 27–8

women suffocated in, i. 503-5
Rousseau, Jean-Jacques (1712-78), philosopher:
answer by, to HW's letter, vi. 434
Boufflers, Comtesse de, the protectress of, vi. 434
—— writes to Trouillet about, vi. 475
HW quotes, about foretelling cities' fate, vii. 400, viii. 62
HW's letter to, in Frederick II's name, Conti and Comtesse de Boufflers angry at, vi. 434
Hume's quarrel with, vi. 434, 465, 475
Nouvelle Héloïse, La, Voltaire said to ridicule, v. 514
Rout; routs:
Mann gives, for Vorontsovs, vi. 193
—— has, during Lent, vii. 458
Roverisi, Conte:
San Remo deputy, iii. 123
Roviglia. See Revilla
Rowe, Nicholas (1674-1718), dramatist:
Fair Penitent: D. of York, Delavals, and Lady Stanhope act, vi. 521; HW quotes, from Horatio in, vii. 181
Tamerlane: HW's epilogue to, praised by Mann, iii. 350-1; HW's epilogue to, sent to Mann, iii. 333; HW refers to Bajazet in, vii. 224
Rowley, Sir Joshua (1734-90), cr. (1786) Bt:
expected at Martinique, viii. 456
father leaves little to, vi. 578
nothing heard of, ix. 105-6
Rowley, Sir Joshua Ricketts (ca 1790-1857), 3d Bt, 1832:
heir of family, vi. 578
Rowley, Sir William (ca 1690-1768), K.B., 1753; Admiral:
Admiralty includes, iv. 259, v. 25, 73
Ambrose to be sent to England by, under arrest, iii. 55
Birtles told by, to leave Genoa when it aids Spanish army, iii. 65
Cadiz supposedly watched by, iii. 81
Charles Emmanuel III asks, to pacify Genoa, ii. 509
—— blames Corsican rebellion on instigation of, iii. 276
Cooper imitates conduct of, iii. 81
Court, M. de, attacked by, ii. 414
Craon, Princesse de, receives beer from, iii. 9
death of, makes vacancy in Bath order, vi. 578
D'Ormea's agreement with, iii. 10
Dutchman meets, near Alicante, ii. 525
English captains to be scolded by, for disobeying Mann, ii. 507
Finale scene of failure by, iii. 120
fleet at Genoa awaits orders from, iii. 76
fleet of: largely unfit for service, iii. 10; to be diminished through continuing to awe Genoa and protect Tuscany, iii. 12

Gardiner introduced by, to Mann, ii. 507, 543-4
Genoa said to have bribed, iii. 120
Genoa threatened by, iii. 12
Genoese assure, that they mobilize in self-defence, ii. 546-7, 554
Genoese coast to be patrolled by, with whole fleet, iii. 37
Gorsegno approves of Mann's telling, of English captain's disloyalty, iii. 146-7, 150
greatgrandson the chief heir of, vi. 578
leave of, to return home, brought in ship from Port Mahon, iii. 132
lieutenant of, to carry Mann's letter to HW, iii. 146
Mann has not heard from, iii. 120, 132
—— has seal made for, iii. 9
—— may send eagle with, to England, iii. 122
—— receives gifts from, iii. 9
——'s conference with, at Leghorn, ii. 503, 506-7, iii. 9
——'s correspondence with, iii. 29, 147, 150
——'s good relations with, ii. 506-7, iii. 9, vi. 581
—— tells, of English officer's suspected loyalty, iii. 146-7, 150
Medley may succeed, iii. 132, 146
men of war sent by, to England, iii. 110
Money brings dispatches to, iii. 12
Port Mahon may be left by, ii. 555
Port Mahon visited by, on way to England, iii. 146
San Remo destroyed by, iii. 120, 132
seal lost by, iii. 9
Spanish preparations for Genoese invasion reported to, iii. 555
Theodore of Corsica cannot get passage to, iii. 132
Townshend told by, to conquer Corsica, iii. 146
Walpole, Sir Robert, resembles, ii. 506
Walpole family esteemed by, ii. 507, 544
will of, vi. 578, 581
wounded, ii. 415
Rowley, Sir William (1761-1832), 2d Bt; M.P.:
grandfather leaves little to, vi. 578
Roxana:
strolling, HW's term for Bns Craven, ix. 633
Roxana. See under Lampugnani, Giovanni Battista
Roxburghe, D. and E. of. See Ker, John (ca 1680-1741)
Roxburghe, D. of. See Ker, John (1740-1804); Ker, Robert (ca 1709-55)
Royal Academy:
exhibit of: vii. 210-11; HW dines at, viii. 92-3
models of Henley bridge keystones and kittens exhibited at, by Mrs Damer, ix. 576

Royal Botanical Society, Florence:
Gualtieri a fellow of, ii. 88
Royal connoisseurs:
Mann's reflections on, iv. 398
Royal Constantinople, Turkish ship:
(?) destroyed, vii. 227
Royal Exchange:
Young Pretender's declaration burnt at,
iii. 161
Royal family, English:
Augusta, Ps of Wales, brings 'evil' into,
ix. 406, 412n
Flanders not to be destination of, ii. 32
lawyers to guard, at St James's Palace, in
George II's absence, iii. 180
military reviews loved by, i. 410
rebel lords' trial not attended by, iii. 280
red-eyed, i. 410
stupid questions asked by, of visitors, ii.
148
Royal Gardens:
Hervey surveyor of, i. 244n
Royal George, ship:
loss, of, learned in Florence, ix. 323
Royal Horse Guards. *See under* Blues, the
'Royal hunter':
Mann's term for Ferdinand, viii. 505
Royal Incorporated Society of Artists:
exhibit of, vii. 210–11
Royalists:
portraits of, at Cornbury, iv. 182
Royal Marriage Bill. *See under* Parliament:
acts of
Royal Oak, British ship:
expected at Port Mahon, i. 285
Howe to be joined by, viii. 411
involved in war, iii. 25
Royal Philip. See Real Felipe
Royal Society:
Albani recommends Fantoni to, vi. 527
Boščović's California trip approved by, vi.
527
Dick forwards Fantoni's credentials to, vi.
527
dissertation on *arbor vitæ* presented to, as
a joke, viii. 290
HW a member of, but attends no meetings,
viii. 284
HW compares French invasion to expedi-
tions by, iii. 327
HW's 'Most Noble She-Witch' mentions,
x. 9
Hamilton's account of Vesuvius for, x. 46
Hillsborough to recommend Fantoni to,
vi. 527
Karl Wilhelm Ferdinand made a member
of, vi. 199
Oxford, E. of, receives gifts from, i. 357
sailor's repair of broken wooden leg reported
to, viii. 283–4, 290
West treasurer to, iv. 371n
Wortley Montagu elected to, ix. 226

Royalty:
HW regards, as actors on a stage, ix. 552,
624
See also Crown; King; Monarch; Prince;
Royal family
Royston, Vct. *See* Yorke, Philip (1720–90)
Royston, Vcts. *See* Campbell, Jemima
Rozier. *See* Pilâtre de Rosier, Jean-François
Rubens, Peter Paul (1577–1640), painter:
Astley not to be compared to, iv. 341
Cipriani's paintings to replace those by,
at Houghton, ix. 316
Orford, E. of, complained of having too
many pictures by, ix. 418
Rubinelli, Giovanni Battista (1753–1829),
opera singer:
HW has heard, at London opera house,
ix. 646
HW hears, in Westminster Abbey at Han-
del's jubilee rehearsal, ix. 648
one song sung by, at Mrs Cosway's concert,
ix. 646
voice of, more distinct at Handel jubilee
than at opera, ix. 648
Ruby; rubies:
Clive may not again return with, vi. 243
England will get, from Ceylon conquest,
ix. 277
Poland pawns, to John Sobieski to be re-
deemed in a century, ix. 525
Rumbold carries off, from Mogul's golden
throne, ix. 545
York, Cardinal, does not trust brother with,
ix. 525
Ruby, French ship:
captured off Cape Finisterre, iii. 410
Rucellai, Senator Giulio (1702–78), head of
the Segretaria della Giurisdizione:
Cocchi receives warning from, to stop de-
fending Sir Robert Walpole in Bns Wal-
pole's presence, ii. 133
Dumesnil accuses, of heresy, iii. 491
—— seeks to remove, as auditor of the
Giurisdizione, iii. 490–1
Francis I orders Dumesnil to apologize to,
iii. 491
HW to show snuff-box to, i. 30
house recommended by, to Bns Walpole,
i. 107
Ligniville, Comtesse de, denounces works of,
iv. 118
Mann abandoned by, i. 71, 460, ii. 133, 148
—— silences defence of Bns Walpole by,
i. 448
Misantropo by, iv. 118
Suares, Bp, persecuted by, i. 40, 63
Tamburro notturno translated by, of Addi-
son's *Drummer,* iv. 118, 151
Walpole, Bns, favours, i. 54, 71, 448
—— has bed made by direction of, i. 107
Rudd, Mrs. *See* Young, Margaret Caroline
(ca 1745–79)

Rueil ('Ruel'), Aiguillon's seat:
Du Barry, Comtesse, retires to, viii. 2
Ruffec, Broglie's seat:
Broglie exiled to, vii. 521
'Ruffham, Ds of':
HW's nom-de-plume, ii. 238
Ruffham. See also Rougham
Ruffle; ruffles:
canonici and abbés forbidden to wear, v. 224
Hotham, Lady Gertrude, sets fire to, viii. 90
lady catches on fire from, vi. 403
Pitt, Mrs, mends, before attending ball, vii. 456
Ruffo, Tommaso (1663–1753), cardinal, 1706:
Benedict XIV consults, about Young Pretender, iv. 22
—— ridicules complaints of, at Castel Gandolfo, iii. 415–16
election of, to Papacy rumoured, i. 9, 16
Louis XV wants French candidate elected by, i. 21
Old Pretender wants Cardinal York to succeed, iv. 589
York, Cardinal, tries to take place next to, iii. 415
Rug coat. See under Coat, horseman's
Ruins of Baalbec. See under Wood, Robert
Ruins of Palmyra. See under Wood, Robert
Rule a Wife and Have a Wife. See under Fletcher, John (1579–1625)
Rullecourt, Bn de. See Macquart, Philippe-Charles-Félix
Rum:
for punch, at Cambridge banquet, iv. 83
Indian convert prefers, to Sacrament, i. 477
old, HW uses, to cure his eyes, v. 168
Rumbold, Lady; Rumbold, Mrs Thomas. See Law, Joanna (d. 1823)
Rumbold, Sir Thomas (1736–91), cr. (1779) Bt; Indian administrator; M.P.:
Dundas prosecutes, for corruption at Madras, ix. 400
former waiter at White's, ix. 141, 400
(?) HW calls, 'Thomas Kouli Kan,' ix. 545
HW mentions, ix. 272
Haidar Ali thinks he has as much right as, to Indian diamonds, ix. 141
House of Commons to investigate, ix. 277
Ireland reached by, on East India fleet, ix. 119
may have to disgorge million acquired as nabob, ix. 274
Mogul's crown jewels carried off by, ix. 545
tours Italy for son's health, ix. 651
trial of, discloses tyranny of East India Company, ix. 400
wealth of, ix. 119
Rumbold, William Richard (1760–86); Capt.; M.P.:
health not recovered by, at Naples, so he must return to England, ix. 651

Rumiantsev (later Rumiantsev-Zadunaĭskiĭ), Petr Alexandrovich (1725–96), Russian general:
Danube crossed by, to attack Grand Vizir at Schuma, viii. 29
Danube may be crossed by, with army, viii. 479
Danube said to have been crossed by, after defeat, viii. 504
Grand Vizir's retreat cut off by, viii. 33
Russian army commanded by, vii. 202
Running footman. See under Servants
Rupees:
lacks of, Alexander the Great did not carry off, ix. 545
Rumbold's sacks of, to be squeezed by House of Commons, ix. 277
Rupert, English ship:
involved in war, iii. 25
Rupture:
occurrences of, iv. 109
Ruremond. See Rémond
Rushout, Sir John (1685–1775), 4th Bt, 1711; M.P.:
Bubb Dodington replaces, as treasurer of the Navy, ii. 551
Carteret's party to be led by, in House of Commons, iii. 212
'dishclout,' ii. 350
lord of the Treasury, i. 332–3
named in Secret Committee lists, i. 385
Parliamentary debate by, on privately-raised regiments, x. 17
Pulteney's follower, i. 333, ii. 72n
Scrope defended by, i. 467
Secret Committee not attended by, i. 401
treasurer of Navy's post to go to, ii. 350, 356
valet of, sent to Hanau by Pulteney, ii. 299
Williams, Sir Charles Hanbury, satirizes, ii. 320
Wilmington and Compton outvoted by, ii. 50n
Ruspanti:
Medici, Giovanni Gastone di, employs, i. 273n
'Ruspantism':
Lorraine, Primate of, addicted to, i. 273
Ruspi (sequins):
Ruspanti receive, i. 273n
Russborough, Bn. See Leeson, Joseph (1711–83)
Russel, —— (d. ca 1745):
puppet-show by, burlesques Italian opera, iii. 28
Russell, Bns. See Wriothesley, Lady Rachel (ca 1637–1723)
Russell, Lady Caroline (1743–1811), m. (1762) George Spencer, 3d D. of Marlborough:
Charlotte's bridesmaid, v. 529
handsome, v. 530
Marlborough to wed, despite his dislike of her mother, vi. 73

[Russell, Lady Caroline, *continued*]
miscarriage of, at time of brother's accident, vi. 498

Russell, Edward (1652–1727), cr. (1697) E. of Orford:
great-niece of, i. 333

Russell, Lady Elizabeth (d. 1784), m. (1726) William Capell, 3d E. of Essex:
Euston's rudeness enrages, ii. 273

Russell, Francis (1739–67), styled M. of Tavistock; M.P.:
Barbantane recommended by, to Mann, vi. 482
death of, vi. 506
death of, expected after fall from horse, vi. 497
father goes to India House soon after death of, vi. 507
Keppel, Lady Elizabeth, to wed, vi. 243
Mann encloses letter to, vi. 482
—— praised in letters of, vi. 2
—— presents, to Botta, v. 564
—— told by, of Bunbury's chicken oratory, vi. 19
trepanned, vi. 497

Russell, Francis (1765–1802), styled Bn Russell, and (1767) M. of Tavistock; 5th D. of Bedford, 1771:
infant at time of father's death, vi. 498
minority of, will accumulate wealth, vii. 274

Russell, John (d. 1744), Capt.:
wounded, ii. 415

Russell, John (1710–71), 4th D. of Bedford; 'little Æolus':
Admiralty post of, ii. 550
agrees with rest of Cabinet Council, vi. 295
American colonies would be conquered by, vi. 401
Argyll accused by, of favouring Jacobites, iv. 310
——'s bill attacked by, in House of Lords, iv. 310–11
Brand's connections with, iv. 435
Bute affronted by opposition of, to Regency Bill, vi. 299–300
—— joins Grenville and, in wanting troops sent to America, vi. 401
Cape Breton's abandonment opposed by, iii. 255
Carmichael's appointment to Armagh archbishopric sought by, vi. 276
Carrickfergus's loss might be attributed to, v. 371
Carteret, Robert, wakens, after cropping horses' ears during visit, ii. 501
Cobhamite dismissal wished by, iii. 188–9
Conway opposed by, as leader of House of Commons, vi. 542, 570
——'s administration to be endured by, despite former opposition, vi. 571
Council presidency offered to, vi. 130

Cumberland, D. of, supports, iv. 113, 120, 201, 207, 224
—— visits, at Woburn, iv. 89
daughter-in-law accompanied by, to opera at time of her husband's accident, vi. 498
daughter of, v. 529–30, vi. 73n, 498n
death of, vii. 262
dismissed as lord president, vi. 310
England's victories over France sacrificed by, vi. 401
Exeter mob attacks, vii. 139
faction of: Anson deserts, iv. 135; attachments of, few, iv. 201; does not resign, iii. 27; fall of, may not take place, iv. 230; Fox enlists, iv. 502; Frederick, P. of Wales, may league with, iv. 230; George III's wish to patch up administration seconded by, ix. 379; Grafton ministry makes overtures to, through Rockingham, vi. 538; Grenville, George, deserted by, vi. 462, 463, 566; Grenville, George, not forsaken by, vi. 533; Grenville, George, will dampen rage of, vi. 549; HW frequents, iv. 207; House of Commons deserted by, vi. 464; London mob conjured up by, vii. 549; Newcastle at odds with, iv. 201; Newcastle to unite, with Rockingham faction, vi. 533, 565–6; not accommodated in ministry, vi. 449; Opposition supported only by, vi. 382; Pitt and Newcastle oppose, iv. 222; Pitt begins negotiations with, at Bath, vi. 472; Pitt detaches himself from, iv. 138; Pitt's defeat strengthens, iv. 223; Pitt, Elizabeth Villiers, once intimate with, iv. 416; quarrels with Rockingham faction, vi. 565–6; Rockingham faction meets, at Newcastle House, vi. 541–2; Rockingham negotiates with, at Woburn, vi. 538; Rockingham to be reconciled with, by D. of Newcastle, vi. 549; Shelburne opposed by, vi. 571; Shelburne's removal demanded by, vii. 61; Tavistock's death weakens, vi. 498; too shameless to be hypocrites, vi. 570; trifles to be conferred upon, vi. 572
Fane protégé of, i. 247
—— told by, that he cannot go to Spain, iv. 203
Fitzwilliam sent by, to drive French from Carrickfergus, v. 373
'Fountain' meeting attended by, i. 336
Fox attached to, iv. 224
Francis III entertained by, iv. 56–7
Garter may be conferred upon, i. 497
George II attended by, at St James's Palace, i. 338
—— makes, K.G., iv. 72
George III and D. of Cumberland unite in hating, vi. 364
George III arrogantly treated by, vi. 309
—— has to summon, to ministry, vi. 302
—— probably influenced by, to exclude Ps of Wales from regency, vi. 298

—— receives ultimatum from other ministers and, vi. 307

German war opposed by, in House of Lords, vi. 7

Gower breaks with, iv. 258

Grafton, D. of, disputes with, over turnpike road, iv. 549

—— offered allegiance of faction by, vi. 569

Grenville, George, confers with, vi. 569

Grenville faction's agent, at Newcastle House, vi. 541

HW calls, 'honest man,' iv. 203

HW describes, vi. 69–70

HW mentions, iv. 292

HW urges, to print grandmother's letters, iv. 283

Halifax may succeed: in Irish post, v. 485; in plantations post, iv. 259

health of: boils on the head, vi. 498; cataracts to be couched, vi. 567; gout, v. 198–9, vi. 498; loses speech and limbs, vii. 262; nearly blind, vi. 498, vii. 262; wounded by weavers, vi. 301

Holdernesse to succeed as secretary of state, iv. 259

house and family of, narrowly escape weavers, vi. 301

House of Lords attended by, i. 336, 338, iv. 300, vi. 7, 366, 463–4, 507

India House visited by, to vote, vi. 507

Ireland mismanaged by, v. 154, 371, 376–7

Irish popularity of, grows after gout confines him, v. 199

Irish post of: arranged, v. 31; relinquished, v. 484–5

Kildare's faction joined by, to please Fox, v. 154

Kinsale notified by, of invasion, v. 376

Kingston mistaken for, vii. 99

Legge courts, iii. 458

London leaders attacked by, for allowing riot in Wilkes's favour, vi. 188

lord lieutenancy of Ireland to go to, at Fox's instigation to spite Pitt, v. 31

Lovel calls, 'Muley,' i. 497

Mann asked by, to aid Megliorucci Nevil, iv. 265–6

—— corresponds with, about India, iv. 97–8, 101–2, vi. 547–8

——'s correspondence with, iii. 474, iv. 265–6

Mar, Cts of, and her daughter borrow house from, iv. 281

Massachusetts act opposed by motion of, vi. 507

Mastership of the Horse may go to, iv. 235

military books studied by, at Blandford, v. 373–4

Mirepoix, Duchesse de, gives precedence to, at Sandwich's ball, iv. 122

Morices opposed by, at Launceston election, iv. 113

Newcastle, D. of, about to clash with, over Turnpike Bill, iv. 112

—— embraces, iv. 201

——'s breach with, iv. 38, 222

Newcastle House meeting attended by, vi. 541–2

Newry to be visited by, to join army, v. 373

Niccolini's banishment discussed at office of, iv. 3

niece of, iv. 226n

Nivernais to meet, at Dover, vi. 55, 70

Opposition's defeat will enhance reputation of, vi. 172

Paris arrival of, coincides with Te Deum for French victory, vi. 90

Paris embassy of: arranged, vi. 69–70; followed by daughter's marriage, vi. 73

Parliamentary speech of, shows temper, vi. 463–4

Parliament asked by, to investigate Ravensworth's and Fawcett's charges about toasts to Old Pretender, iv. 366

Patriots formerly included, iv. 72

peace delegate to France, vi. 55, 69–70, 73, 86, 90, 92–3

Pelham aids, in defending privately-raised regiments, iii. 154

Pelham and Pitt enrage, over Navy Bill, iv. 38

Pelhams support, iv. 120

Pitt opposed to adherents of, vi. 308

—— rejects demands of, vi. 472

—— sends Gower to Woburn with overtures to, vi. 472

——'s return no longer wanted by, since Pitt ignores him, vi. 167

—— to be punished by, iv. 38

play by company of, could not be memorized by Shirley, iii. 309, iv. 395

plays acted by, at Woburn, iii. 309n

politicians of, say that he will soon recover from son's death, vi. 506

presidency of the Council to go to, vi. 130, 167

privately-raised regiments defended by, iii. 154

Purnell's trial urged by, iv. 18

rebel lords' right to counsel supported by, iii. 287

Regency Bill opposed by friends of, in House of Commons, vi. 299

regiment led by, in person, iii. 160–1

regiment raised by, iii. 110, 128

resigns, iv. 258

resigns Admiralty post, iii. 463–4

Sandwich abandons, iv. 305

—— 'espoused' by, iv. 113

—— governs, through wife, iv. 120

—— lieutenant-colonel to, iii. 176

—— may succeed, as secretary of state, iv. 217, 235

——'s protector, iv. 144

[Russell, John, D. of Bedford, *continued*]
Scottish peers insulted by letter of, asking them to vote for Turnpike Bill, iv. 124
secretary of state, iii. 463
sister of, iii. 189n
son of, vi. 2n
speaks like Pitt, iv. 310
Stair's discussion of Patinson with George II corrected by, at George II's levee, iii. 165
Stanley affected by dismissal of, vi. 326
—— to follow, vi. 92-3
Stone's overtures rejected by, v. 154
teeth and nails of, scanty, vi. 541
Temple may be connected with, vi. 308
——'s proposal answered by, v. 547
Thurot does not await army of, v. 376
treaty with Saxony opposed by, in Parliament, iv. 300
Trentham brother-in-law to, iv. 113n
Turnpike Bill of, iv. 112, 120
tutor of, supported by Sandwich for Eton fellowship, iv. 121
Vernon visits, at Woburn, iv. 301
Walpole, Sir Robert, 'cut' by, at House of Lords, i. 338
wealth of, brings him little happiness, vii. 274
weavers' relief opposed by, in House of Lords, vi. 301
Westminster election paid for by, iv. 112-13
Winchilsea succeeds, as lord president, vi. 310
Woburn would never be relinquished by, iii. 255
Yonge attacked by, i. 336
York, D. of, allies, with Bute and Grenville, vi. 402
Russell, Lord John (1766-1839), 6th D. of Bedford, 1802; M.P.:
infant at time of father's death, vi. 498
Russell, Lady Rachel (d. 1777), m. 1 (1722) Scroop Egerton, 4th E. of Bridgwater; cr. (1720) D. of Bridgwater; m. 2 (1745) Sir Richard Lyttelton:
children of, iii. 189
daughter of, iv. 226n
HW praises, v. 505-6
health of, gout, vi. 247
Lyttelton marries, iii. 189, iv. 33n
Naples visited by, v. 550
Paris visited by, vi. 155
Pitt, Thomas, leaves, at Leghorn, v. 501
Temple, Cts, entertains, at Stowe, vi. 247
Russell, Lady Rachel. *See also* Wriothesley, Lady Rachel (ca 1637-1732)
Russell, William (1639-83), styled Bn Russell:
levee of, in Newgate prison, vii. 82
widow of, iv. 282-3
Russell, Lord William (1767-1840), M.P.:
birth of, expected, vi. 498

Russell, Wriothesley (1708-32), 3d D. of Bedford:
Pope hints at Janssen's cheating, at White's, ii. 124n
Russell family:
credit lost by, in their own counties, ix. 488
Russia, Emperor of. *See* Ivan VI (1740-64); Paul I (1754-1801); Peter I (1672-1725); Peter III (1728-62)
Russia, Empress of. *See* Anne (1693-1740); Catherine II (1729-96); Elizabeth (1709-61), Maria Sofia (1759-1828)
Russia:
admiralty of, *see under* Admiralty
allies of, insist on conclusion of Turkish war, viii. 33
ambassadors from and to, *see under* Ambassador
'armed neutrality' of, ix. 160
army of: again marching towards Prussia, v. 172; Austrian savagery restrained by, v. 444; Azov seized by, vii. 116; Bender the theatre of, vii. 155, 160, 245; Berlin may be sacked by, v. 441; Berlin not captured by, v. 332; Choiseul impels Turks against, vii. 134, 143; covey of partridges resembles, v. 237; Danube crossed by, vii. 478-9; Danube must not be crossed by, vii. 310; Frederick II aided by, vi. 59, 62-3; Frederick II drives, into Pomerania and Poland, v. 246-7; Frederick II opposed by, v. 72, 229, 236, 237, 244, 246-7, 258, 317, 319, 327, 331, 419; gives and accepts no quarter, v. 255; halted by lack of men, money, and supplies, v. 78; horses, cattle, and camels captured by, vii. 160; inactive on the Danube, vii. 331; Moldavia the theatre of, vii. 148, 154-5; Oder may be crossed by, v. 308; Prussian troops at Memel prepare against, v. 72; retreats, v. 144; Riga approached by, v. 72; Rumiantsev commands, vii. 202; Silistria invaded by, vii. 479; Silistrian side of Danube might be taken by, viii. 29; take oaths on their sabres, v. 255; Turkish Grand Signor will probably be given a good account by, vii. 91; Turks defeated by, vii. 146; Wedell said to have defeated, v. 315
Austria and Prussia may join, against Turks, ix. 359, 436
bankrupt, v. 502
Buckinghamshire's failure in embassy to, vi. 205, 212
Catherine II cannot civilize, in one reign, ix. 389
—— may lend troops from, to England for American war, viii. 127
—— tells Frederick II to return troops of, vi. 59
—— wants Jesuits reestablished in, ix. 389-90

celebration in: for heir's birth, iv. 457–8; for Turkish defeat, vii. 249

Chinese dispute with, vii. 116, viii. 333

Choiseul's fall liked by, vii. 259

—— will be hurt by successes of, vii. 151, 154

Constantinople's capture delayed by, vii. 323

Court of, Orlov's dispatches to, vii. 235

Cracow incendiary removed by, vi. 574

Craons comment on news from, i. 20

crime now shifts to, vi. 253–4

Denmark's war with, see War, Danish-Russian

Dick honoured by, viii. 96

eagle of, turns vulture, viii. 55

England may be lent troops by, iii. 466, iv. 501, v. 54, viii. 127, 132, 138, 324

England may cede Georgia to, viii. 132, 138

England receives rescripts from, ix. 39, 118

England should not enhance the maritime power of, viii. 132

England's mediation offer rejected by, v. 53

England to be reconciled with, ix. 267

English sculptor at Florence makes chimneypieces for, ix. 93

English simpletons visit, vii. 195

European powers may not let England cede maritime post to, viii. 138

fleet of: agent for, see Rutherfurd, Robert; at Lemnos to starve Constantinople, vii. 245; at Port Mahon and Leghorn, vii. 191–2; coming to Mediterranean, ix. 59–61; Constantinople may be attacked by, but Louis XVI and Charles III are said to tell Ferdinand of Naples to keep it out of his ports, ix. 616n; Constantinople unlikely to be captured by, vii. 169; Danish officers leave, vii. 326; Dardanelles threatened by, vii. 161, 245, 331; direct passage to England from Leghorn must be made by, viii. 114; disasters to, in Mediterranean, vii. 202; Dolgorukov discusses arrangements for, vii. 160–1; England prevents French fleet from attacking, vii. 474, 478; expected at Leghorn, ix. 160, 415; expected in Mediterranean, ix. 59–60; France to aid, vii. 161; French merchant ships intercepted by, vii. 307; frigate of, injured, vii. 192; frigates of, reach Leghorn from Paros, vii. 326; gets provisions from Leghorn, vii. 172; Greek Islands the destination of, vii. 306; Greig to command, ix. 60; HW ridicules, as troop of schoolboys, vii. 187; in Ægean, vii. 212; Leghorn expenditure for, vii. 222, viii. 95, 114; Leghorn to be visited by, ix. 84; Malta may be station of, vii. 189; may appear at Leghorn or Cagliari, vii. 148; may pass Dardanelles but army must not

pass the Danube, vii. 310; off Chios, vii. 232–3; on Yorkshire coast, vii. 146; Orlov appoints English agent for, vii. 161; Orlov commands, vii. 234–5; Orlov finds, in gulf of Napoli di Romania, vii. 226; partly at Port Mahon, vii. 162, 172, 185, 189, 192; Peter III's ghost should hail, at Constantinople, vii. 195; reaches coast of Morea, vii. 204–5; repaired at Leghorn or wintered at Paros, vii. 307; said to be attacking Negropont castle, vii. 331; said to have returned, to North Sea, ix. 79; sails from Cronstadt, vii. 222; sails from England to Mediterranean, vii. 151, 159; slowness of, vii. 157, 185, 187, 224, 331; Spain may intercept, ix. 415; stalks in English Channel, ix. 77; still at Leghorn, vii. 308; supposedly in Mediterranean, ix. 187; to return to St Petersburg, viii. 84; Turkey might be frightened by, into peace, vii. 192; Turkey thinks England should have stopped, in English Channel, vii. 479; Turkey to be attacked by, vii. 148; Turkish fleet destroyed by, vii. 226–8, 232–3, 234–5, 236, 239; Turkish fleet said to have been burnt by, at Lemnos, vii. 319, 330

France incited Turkey against, vii. 307

France may aid Turkey against, ix. 360

Franco-Prussian peace negotiations denied by, v. 159

Frederick II may have provoked rebellion in, vii. 556

—— receives assurances from, ii. 512

—— removed by, from French alliance, iv. 524

——'s alleged alliance with, viii. 389

French illusions will be shattered by, viii. 498

German campaigns of, ridiculous, v. 312

German couriers to, v. 369

Greeks do not assist, vii. 222, 226

Greeks said to aid, vii. 204

Greeks to get arms from, vii. 202

Greeks will be sacrificed by, to Turkish vengeance, vii. 212

HW would be afraid to be in, vi. 65

Houghton pictures will be burnt at first insurrection in, viii. 441

impostor claims throne of, vii. 547, 556

instability of, feared in Florence, ix. 156

Kingston, Ds of, might send courier from, to husband, viii. 333

La Chétardie said to have been dismissed by, i. 20, ii. 466

long-boat of, sinks at Leghorn, ix. 493

Mann refuses honours from, viii. 96, ix. 84

Maria Theresa's alliance with, vi. 564

—— threatened with war by, unless she consents to Poland's partition, vii. 439

Mediterranean area does not trade with, ix. 61, 84

[Russia, *continued*]

minister of, released from Seven Towers, vii. 308–9

Minorca said to be ceded to, ix. 187

Morea abandoned by, vii. 226

must be contemptuous of Western warfare, ix. 201

news from, comes through Holland, i. 255–6

officers of, vii. 233, 444, ix. 2, 84

order of St Catherine of, *see under* St Catherine

Orléans may marry princess of, ii. 564

peace delegates of, at Paris, v. 498

peace negotiations for war of American Revolution may be aided by, viii. 523

Peter I teaches, to read, vi. 71

Pitt congratulates Alt on defeat of, v. 316

Pitti palace heated as if in, vi. 291

Poles may pray for success of rebellion in, vii. 556

Polish incendiaries removed by, vi. 574

Prussia forbids, to aid England, ix. 39

Quebec campaign might be said to be a stratagem to divert, from Frederick II, v. 336

revolution in: against Ivan VI, i. 255, 264; against Peter III, vi. 52–4, 56–62, 64–6, 68, 71, 74–6

Rome regards Turkey as Christianity's bulwark against, vii. 140

Rutherfurd and Dick the agents and commissaries of, at Leghorn, vii. 222, viii. 114, 453

ship of war of, ordered by Catherine II to take Ds of Kingston's treasure to Calais, but sails too soon from Leghorn, viii. 404, 409–10

Stanley to have post in, vi. 444

Stormont reveals war plans of, vii. 438–9

successes of: cannot be concealed, vii. 154; not followed up, vii. 331

Sweden's war with, *see* War, Swedish-Russian

Swedish interference by, vii. 439

Te Deums sung in, for Zorndorf 'victory,' v. 246

theatre head from, has translated *Hamlet*, vi. 426

topic of conversation in Florence, vii. 503

Turkey's grumblings against, more audible in England than in Italy, ix. 436

Turkey's negotiations with, vii. 224, 441, 469–70, viii. 40

Turkey's threat to, v. 247

Turkey's war with, *see under* War, Russian-Turkish

Turkey unlikely to cede Holy Land to, vii. 194

Turkish dismemberment may be plotted by, with Austria, ix. 399

Turkish invasion by, disliked by France, vii. 204–5

Turkish military chest captured by, vii. 479

Tuscany's connection with, ix. 128

vice chancellor of, *see* Vorontsov

victories of, not readily believed in by HW, vii. 231

Vorontsov afraid of revolutions in, vi. 202–3, 205

—— the 'soul' of the ministry of, v. 247

war extends from, to Senegal, v. 290

Williams leaves, v. 183

Zoffany may return to, viii. 92

See also Siberia; Tartary

Russian; Russians:

at Pisa: rejoice over end of Turkish war, viii. 84; spend lavishly, viii. 95

England may hire, for American war, viii. 127, 132, 138, 324

HW calls 'Vandals of the North,' ix. 146

kingdoms overrun in a few weeks by, ix. 146

Leghorn will regret loss of lavish expenditures by, viii. 95

Mann calls, 'horse-eaters,' v. 446

—— considered the protector of, in Florence, ix. 84

—— entertains, at dinner, vii. 161

Russian ladies:

Mann must entertain, in Florence, ix. 340–1

Russian language:

Kingston, Ds of, said to be learning, vii. 559

Latin as useless as, when addressing kings, vi. 84

Regent has his son study, iii. 564

Ruth:

HW compares Chute to, i. 209

Rutherford. *See* Rutherfurd

Rutherfurd, John (ca 1748–1834), M.P.:

laird of Scottish family, viii. 453

Rutherfurd, Robert (1719–94), cr. (ca 1775) Bn (Russian):

Catherine II makes, baron, and gives him jewelled box with her portrait, viii. 453

HW often meets, at Gloucester House and hears Mann's praises, viii. 445, 453

Leghorn the home of, during business career and service as Russian commissary, viii. 453

Mann visited by, viii. 289

Order of St Anne of Holstein rejected by, viii. 453

Orlov closes his accounts with, viii. 114

Russian agent at Leghorn, vii. **161,** 222

Rutland, Ds of. *See* Sherard, Hon. Lucy (ca 1685–1751); Somerset, Lady Mary Isabella 1756–1831)

Rutland, D. of. *See* Manners, Charles (1754–87); Manners, John (1696–1779)

Rutlandshire:

Mann, Horace II, in, ix. 222

Rutledge, Edward (1749–1800), member of Continental Congress:

Howe receives, viii. 270

Ryder, Sir Dudley (1691–1756), Kt, 1740; attorney-general; lord chief justice; M.P.:
attorney-general at Lovat's trial, iii. 380
death of, on eve of getting peerage, iv. 556, 557
Gower's conversation with, about Purnell's trial, iv. 18
Lee succeeded by, as lord chief justice, iv. 453n
lord chief justice, iii. 380n
Murray excels, iii. 380
—— succeeds, as attorney-general, iv. 453n
Parliamentary speech by, i. **297**
promotion of, to lord chancellor, suggested, iv. 202
Seymour, Sir Edward, confirmed by, in Somerset title, iv. 139
Ryder, Nathaniel (1735–1803), cr. (1776) Bn Harrowby:
peerage to go to, iv. 557
Rye, English ship:
African conquest by, v. 212
Rymer, Thomas (1641–1713), author and archæologist:
Fœdera by, reports Edward I's corpse being given a new cere-cloth yearly, viii. 4
Rysbrack, John Michael (1694–1770), sculptor:
Ganymede and statue model mended by, iii. 63
Ganymede statue to be mended by, ii. 561

Sabatier de Cabre, Honoré-Auguste (1737–1802), French chargé d'affairs in Russia:
appointment of, vii. 127
Sabatin, Mme. *See* Cusack, Marie-Madeleine de
Sabatina:
on Saturday nights, in Florence, i. 97
Sabbath. *See* Sunday
Sabbatini, Giuliano (1685–1767), Bp of Modena, secretary of state:
HW flattered by, iv. 57
Sabina:
medal (gold) of, bought by HW, x. 7
Sabine, Mrs. *See* Malyn, Elizabeth
'Sabine' (painting):
Mann to bequeath, to Sir Robert Walpole, ii. 93
'Sabine farm':
Pitt's, v. 518
Sables:
Montagu, Lady Mary Wortley, wears, vi. 17
Sabre; sabres:
Acquaviva's guard armed with, iii. 113
British sailor boards Spanish ship with, viii. 543
Russians take oaths upon, v. 255
Sacchetti family, of Rome:
Albano and Cortona pictures bought from, by HW, x. 7
Sacchi, Andrea (1599–1661), painter:
painting by: desired by Sir Robert Wal-

pole, v. 173; Spencer buys, at Furnese's auction, v. 172
Sacchini, Antonio (1734–86), composer:
Finto pazzo per amore, Il, performed by Lord Cowper's *troupe,* vii. 325
Motezuma, viii. 89
Rinaldo, ix. 134
Sacchis, Giovanni de'. *See* Pordenone
Sacco, Gioseffo Pompeo, prime minister of Parma 1772–3:
Llano replaced by, vii. 445
'Sacharissa.' *See* Sidney, Lady Dorothy (1617–84)
Sacheverell, Dr Henry (ca 1674–1724), political preacher:
Gunnings more famous than, iv. 312
life of, paralleled by modern occurrences, vi. 186
Walpole, Sir Robert, opposes, vi. 26
Wilkes and d'Éon compared with, vi. 263
Wilkes as dead as, vii. 360
Sachsen-Gotha. *See* Saxe-Gotha
Sachsen-Hildburghausen. *See* Saxe-Hildburghausen
Sachsen-Weissenfels, D. of. *See* Johann Adolf II
Sack; sacks:
black, Vitelli, Mme, to discard, ii. 334
'Nousvollone' expected to wear, at Court, vi. 357
Sackcloth:
HW asks if Vatican is hung with, ix. 237
Sackville, Lady Caroline (1718–75), m. (1742) Joseph Damer, cr. (1753) Bn Milton, (1792) E. of Dorchester:
death of, viii. 98
HW does not repeat Mann's compliments to, vi. 301
HW mentions, iv. 292
HW not to tell, about son's escapade, vi. 287, 300
HW's opinion of, iv. 179
Italians avoided by, because they seek whist games, iv. **175**
Mann's invitation refused by, iv. 175
—— thanked by, for civilities to son, vi. 284, 286
—— told by, about Elizabeth Pitt, iv. 416
Sackville, Charles (1638–1706) 6th E. of Dorset:
ballad by, v. 57
Sackville, Charles (1711–69), styled E. of Middlesex; 2d D. of Dorset, 1765; M.P.:
ambassador's post rumoured for, ii. 289, 346, 365
Constitutional Queries attributed to, iv. 235, 245
constitution and estate worn out by, vii. 83
death of, vii. 82–3
Dilettanti society led by, ii. 211
father made unhappy by, v. 321
father may stop opera subsidies of, ii. 225–6

[Sackville, Charles, *continued*]
father scolded about, by George II, i. **221**
Frederick, P. of Wales, to have, as Master of the Horse, iii. 370
George II discards, iv. 245
—— objects to, as Master of the Horse, iv. 245
HW has no interest with, ii. 210
Hume-Campbell counsel for, iv. 5
Kent lieutenancy may go to, vi. 375
Knole's trees sacrificed by, vii. 83
Mann's old acquaintance, iv. 235, vii. 82
—— told by, about Elizabeth Pitt, iv. 416
marriage of, ii. 481, 501, 523, 527
mistress might have been married by, vii. 83
Monticelli sues, for salary, iv. 4–5
Muscovita mistress to, i. 191
—— retained to please, i. 358
Nardi mistress of, iii. 293
opera deficits due to mismanagement of, ii. 210–11, 225–6, 293–4
opera director, i. **191**
opera house contributes, to politics, ii. 365
opera intrigues of, iii. 293–4
opera performers unpaid by, iii. 294, 370
operas sponsored by, iii. 342
royal children and P. of Wales entertained by, at masked ball, iii. 398
seldom sober in Italy, ii. 211
Treasury post of, ii. 365, iii. 370, 419
Vaneschi cheats: at Lucca, i. 216; in England, ii. 198
—— dominates, i. 191
—— the poet of, i. 200
verse written by, iv. 235
weeps over wife's miscarriage, iii. 447
wife of, iii. 62n
wife's fortune may be used by, for operas, ii. 501
Sackville, Lady George. *See* Sambrooke, Diana (d. 1778)
Sackville (later Sackville-Germain), Lord George (1716–85), cr. (1782) Vct Sackville; M.P.:
anxiety over military campaign of, v. 316
arrested, v. 374
Barrington succeeded by, as secretary at war, v. 104
Botta cannot understand why rank was retained by, after court martial, v. 411
Boyle affronts, iv. 316
Byng compared with, v. 320–1
Charlotte's birthday not to be attended by, ix. 236
Conway would be preferred by, as one of his judges, v. 366–7
Court attendance denied to, v. 403
court martial of, v. 328, 366–7, 374, 377, 384–5, 387
Cumberland, D. of, sends, to Saxe about Maestricht siege, iii. 481

Dartmouth succeeded by, as secretary of state for American province, viii. 142
death of, ix. 606
disgraced at Minden, v. 320n, viii. 187
East Grinstead's representative, viii. 187
Ellis succeeds, as secretary of state, ix. 241
English invasion of France led by, v. 204
English mob wants to tear, to pieces, v. 320
father disappointed in, v. 321
father scolded by George II about, i. 221
first 'tome' of, remembered, because of failure of second, ix. 237
Fox, C.J., debates with, in Parliament, viii. 341
George II does not accept, as secretary at war, v. 109
George III's court no longer countenances, v. 403
Germain name assumed by, on inheriting Lady Elizabeth Germain's estate, vii. 256n
goes to the country, v. 403
Grenville, James, succeeds, as vice-treasurer of Ireland, vi. 443
HW sends *Trial* of, to Mann, v. 407
Holdernesse and Ligonier inform, about court martial, v. 328
House of Commons told by, when secretary of state, that America must yield unlimited submission, viii. 282n
Howe said to object to, viii. 439
income of, reduced, v. 328
Ireland upset by, when secretary to his father, ix. 606
Johnstone's duel with, after abuse in House of Commons, vii. 256
Luttrell's quarrel with, viii. 383
Marlborough's command really under, v. 198
name of, stricken from council book, vi. 96
news about, awaited in Florence, v. 406
office of, as colonial secretary, not to be filled up, ix. 237
Parliamentary speech of, on seizure of Wilkes's papers, vi. 208
Parliament not attended by, v. 345
patent place (in Ireland) of, v. 328
peerage to be given to, ix. 237
resignation of: as minister of colonies, expected, ix. 236, 237; imminent, ix. 240; neither voluntary nor a disgrace, but the result of disagreement with colleagues, ix. 240–1
retirement of, welcomed by everybody, ix. 238
Rochefort inquiry conducted by, v. 155
Sandwich the principal enemy of, ix. 238
scandalous career of, iv. 315
secretaryship at war not to go to, v. 109
sentence of, v. 387, 403
Smith, aide-de-camp to, v. 211
spirited behaviour of, during trial, v. 387
Stone, Abp, friend of, iv. 315

Townshend proposed by, for Speaker, vii. 180

Townshend, Charles, resents appointment of, v. 104

unpopular, viii. 383

Viscountcy to be given to, ix. 241

Wilkes's witticism on American rôle and German failure of, viii. 187

windows of, broken by mob, viii. 442

Sackville, John Frederick (1745–99), 3d D. of Dorset, 1769:

Derby, Cts of, to wed, after her divorce, viii. 435

inefficient as English ambassador in France, ix. 486–7

Parsons, Anne, mistress of, vii. 344n, viii. 435n

Shelburne's witticism about, ix. 487

succeeds Vct Falmouth as captain of Yeomen of the Guard, ix. 241

Sackville, Lord John Philip (1713–65), M.P.:

father scolded by George II about, i. 221

Sackville, Lionel Cranfield (1688–1765), 7th E. of Dorset; cr. (1720) D. of Dorset:

again to be lord steward, iv. 470

Beauclerk, Lord Vere, owes appointment to, i. 356

Berkeley's influence upon, i. 221

Boyle's opposition to, in Irish Parliament, iv. 316, 402

Cinque Ports and Dover posts lost by, iv. 63

Cinque Ports to remain in custody of, v. 109

daughter imitates, iv. 179

daughter-in-law of, iii. 62n

daughter of, viii. 98n

death of, vi. 361

Devonshire succeeds, as lord steward, ii. 550

dismissions not executed by, in Ireland, iv. 410

George II asked by, not to subscribe to opera, ii. 226

—— scolds, about his sons, i. 221

Gower succeeds, as Master of the Horse, v. 104

Harrington replaced by, in Ireland, iv. 202

—— succeeded by, as lord president, ii. 550

Hartington succeeds, in Irish post, iv. 469

health of, infirm, v. 489

Holdernesse to inherit Cinque Ports post of, v. 489

Ireland or lord presidency to be offered to, iii. 327

Irish lord lieutenantcy seized by, iv. 207

Irish lord lieutenant, with son as secretary, ix. 606

Irish opposition to, because of son's scandal, iv. 315

Jacobites try, through Prior, to persuade, to give up Dover Castle, iv. 62–3

Kent lieutenancy held by, vi. 361

lord presidency vacated by, iv. 202

Middlesex's opera-subsidizing may be stopped by, ii. 226

pension offered to, v. 104, 109

Prior possibly brother of, iv. 63

son of, iii. 293n

sons of, make him unhappy, v. 321

Sackville family:

ballads and epigrams against, iv. 316

blood of, 'worst,' iii. 442

Hedon election concerns, i. 221

influence of, vast, iv. 316

Middlesex's opera transactions may ruin, ii. 226

——'s wedding not announced by, ii. 527

Sacrament; sacraments:

Balmerinoch takes, before execution, iii. 301

Clement XIII receives, vi. 331

Corsican rebels receive, from Clement XIII's bishop, v. 394

Electress takes, on deathbed, ii. 160, 173

English troops bicker over, with Flemish friars, ii. 30

exposed in churches for Wachtendonck's recovery, i. 105

exposure of, in Roman churches, v. 392

Indian convert prefers rum to, i. 477

Louis XV receives, ii. 503

Spanish officers take, i. 427

Vane, Vcts, 'comforted' by, i. 210, 240

Sacrilege:

HW's reflections on execution for, in Venice, i. 85

Sacristy:

Pius VI builds, at St Peter's, viii. 344, ix. 383–4

Saddle; saddles:

HW uses, for blankets, ii. 315

refugees from fire take, to Sir Robert Walpole's house, i. 496

Saddler's Company:

Frederick, P. of Wales, belongs to, i. 451n

Sadducees. See under Bible

Sade, Jean-Baptiste-François-Joseph (1701–67), Comte de:

capture of, iii. 18

Sade, Richard-Jean-Louis de, chevalier:

brother of, captured by Austrians, iii. 18

clothes pawned by, ii. 62, 318

Craon borrows from, ii. 38–9, 62

—— plays quadrille with, ii. 329

—— told by, that his cold house caused Mann's illness, ii. 110

Craon, Princesse de, entertains, i. 413

—— tells, to negotiate about etiquette with Modenese princess, i. 60

—— would tell, to read Mme de Sévigné's letters to her, iv. 387

Craons dissuaded by, from Leghorn trip, ii. 38

[Sade, Richard-Jean-Louis de, *continued*]
debts of, in Florence, i. 46
HW asks about, i. 402, ii. 318, iii. 18
Mann entertains, at dinner, ii. 17
—— serves chocolate to, i. 413
—— talks with, at opera, i. 283
—— tells, to distinguish between France and England, iii. 80
Modena, Ds of, asks HW about, i. 46
—— supplies, ii. 39
Orléans, Duchesse d', said by, to hate her daughter, ii. 386
Sadler, James (1753–1828):
balloon ascent made by, as Windham's pilot, ix. 579
missing, but is found, ix. 590, 591
Sage:
HW uses, for eyes, ii. 365
Sagunto:
regiment of, ii. 489
Said Effendi, Turkish ambassador to France:
English naval supremacy observed by, ii. 15
Sailing:
Orford, E. of, takes up, viii. 38
Sailor; sailors:
America recruits, viii. 81
at Villafranca, reports victory, i. 471
English: Anson's leadership not envied by, v. 223; coal-heavers feud with, in London, vii. 30, 33; Conway's arm almost rebroken by, ix. 115; crucifix hung by, on monkey's neck, ii. 59, 79n; Edgcumbe leaves, to strengthen St Philip's garrison, iv. 559; England enlists, viii. 81; enlist to capture prizes, vii. 242; Fermor might have to eat with, unless given money, iii. 148; generosity of, with captured Spanish booty, viii. 543; gentlemen disguised as, i. 211; Gray, Sir James, must be preceded by, to Spain, v. 560; Green aided by, vii. 39; Hood supported by, in election riot, ix. 489; impressment of, indicates war, viii. 262; Ireland contributes, ix. 285; Lisbon people blamed by, for ingratitude, i. 456; Mann disgusted with rudeness of, iii. 275; Mann opposes enlistment of, in Tuscan navy, iv. 472; Mann receives, and sends to Leghorn, i. 158; mends wooden leg, viii. 283–4, 290; merchant ships prevented by, from sailing, vii. 21; often tamper with wine shipments, v. 304; old, Boscawen gets letter from, about Port Mahon's capture, v. 52; Parliament petitioned by, vii. 21; Parliament to vote, for American war, viii. 127; received from West Indian and Mediterranean fleets, viii. 392; tosses sword to unarmed opponent, viii. 543; Wilkes's mob driven off by, vii. 21
English, Danish, French, and Swedish, on Prussian privateer, v. 349
French: France loses, in war with England, ix. 7; French navy lacks, v. 264; from

Languedoc for Toulon fleet, ii. 396; obtained from Corsica, vii. 47, 478
galley, i. 471
Jesuits disguised as, vi. 545
Leghorn hopes to convert fishermen into, iv. 217
Papal, fear enslavement by Turkish pirates, i. 16
Roman, Corinthian statues belittled by, iii. 264
Slavonian, seize *Great Duchess of Tuscany* and turn pirates, ix. 479–80
Saint; Saints:
corpse of, on board Spanish fleet at Algiers, viii. 122
long, in SH windows, iv. 372
Maximilian wants to become, ix. 468
price for making, iii. 171
Sobieski, Ps, aspires to be, v. 424, ix. 106
St-Aignan, Duc de. *See* Beauvilliers, Paul-Hippolyte de (1684–1776)
St Albans, Ds of. *See* Ponsonby, Lady Catherine (1742–89); Vere, Lady Diana de (d. 1742)
St Albans, D. of. *See* Beauclerk, Aubrey (1740–1802); Beauclerk, Charles (1670–1726); Beauclerk, Charles (1696–1751); Beauclerk, George (1730–86)
St Albans, Herts:
West, M.P. for, iv. 371n
St Alban's Tavern, near Pall Mall:
Jacobites meet at, with P. of Wales's party, iv. 50
new opposition forms in, v. 552–3
Townshend, Charles, attends assemblies at, v. 553
young men at, have street littered with straw, vii. 323
St Andrea, near Marciana:
barks pursued into, by Osborne, ii. 28
St Andrews, Holborn, London:
Barton rector of, iv. 155
St Andrew's Cross:
Young Pretender wears, vii. 225
St Andrew's Day:
Young Pretender celebrates, by drunkenness, ix. 100
St Angelo in Vado:
Clement XIV from, vii. 117
St Anne of Holstein, Order of:
Catherine II distributes, in son's name, viii. 84
conferred on Sir John Dick by Catherine II, viii. 84–5, 96
Dick assumes, when no longer degraded by being consul, viii. 96, 114, 239
Orlov delivers, to Dick, viii. 84, 96
Rutherfurd rejects, though Dick accepted it, viii. 453
St Anne's, Soho:
HW erects monument in, to Theodore of Corsica, v. 140, 148
rector of, *see* Squire, Samuel (1713–66)

St Anthony's fire. *See* Erysipelas

St Antonio. See *San Antonio*

'St Antonio Abate.' *See* Parma: convent at

St Apostoli. *See* Santi Apostoli

St Asaph, Bp of. *See* Hare, Francis (1671–1740); Maddox, Isaac (1697–1759)

St Asaph, Vct. *See* Ashburnham, George (1760–1830)

St Aubyn ('St Aubin'), Sir John (?1702–1744), 3d Bt; M.P.:
  named in secret Committee lists, i. 385
  Secret Committee seconded by, i. 364, 375

St Barnabas. *See* San Barnaba

St Bartholomew's Massacre:
  account of, supposedly found in lodgings of Bristol incendiary, viii. 274

St Botolph's, Bishopsgate:
  Ashton rector of, iv. 164n

St Caroline, ship:
  artillery brought by, to Italian coast from Barcelona, i. 286

St-Cast, Bay of:
  Aiguillon's supper for English prisoners after battle of, v. 251
  English embark at, v. 243

St Castaldo:
  Lobkowitz stationed near, iii. 30

St Catherine of Russia, Order of:
  declined by Maria Louisa, ix. 128
  Peter III said to have bestowed, on Vorontsov lady, who tried to resign it to Catherine II, vi. 58–9, 65

St-Chamans, Armand de (b. 1754), styled (1778) Marquis de Saint-Chamans:
  (?) SH visited by, ix. 423

St-Chamans, Auguste-Gabriel-Louis de (b. 1761), Vicomte de Saint-Chamans:
  (?) SH visited by, ix. 423

St Charles's Day. *See under* Borromeo, Carlo

St Christopher (St Kitt's):
  hurricane at, ix. 105
  lost, like Minorca, ix. 263
  reported to have been rescued by Hood, ix. 254, 257

St-Cloud:
  Coventry forsakes fête at, for Worcester music festival, iv. 338

St-Contest. *See* Barberie-de-St-Contest

St Crispino. *See* Crespino

St Croce. *See* Santa Croce

St Davids, Bp of. *See* Squire, Samuel (1713–66); Stuart, Hon. William (1755–1822); Trevor, Richard (1707–71); Willes, Edward (d. 1773)

St-Denis:
  Coke, Lady Mary, enters Louis XIV's vault at, viii. 14
  Louis XV and Maupeou visit Princess Louise's cell at, vii. 321

St Domingo, Spanish register ship:
  capture of, viii. 543

Sainte Ampoulle:
  Peterborough's witticism on seeing, at Reims, viii. 112–13

Sainte Anne, French ship:
  Holmes's squadron captures, v. 524

Sainte-Foy. *See* Radix de Sainte-Foy

Sainte-Marguerite (Lérins), Îles de:
  France offers, to Malta, iv. 406
  French bombard, and recapture it, iii. 406

Sainte-Marie, Dames de:
  Stuart, Charlotte, prefers Abp of Bordeaux's society to that of, ix. 513

Sainte-Palaye. *See* La Curne de Sainte-Palaye

St-Esprit, French ship:
  Jersey fights, possibly sinking it, iii. 82

St-Esprit, Ordre du:
  'cordon bleu' of: Grimaldi receives, at Paris, v. 560; mad foreigner forbidden to wear, at Paris, viii. 361, ix. 572; Maupeou receives, vii. 259; received by Bulkeley, ii. 429n; sought by Vandières, iv. 228

St Estevan, galleon:
  in Spanish fleet, i. 286

St Eustatia, Russian ship. *See* Evstafiĭ

St Eustatius:
  Dutch not to be comforted for loss of, ix. 152
  English fleet from, captured, ix. 152, 159
  French 'purchase' of, from Cockburn, ix. 235–6
  merchandise taken by British at, said to be equalled by that taken by Spanish at Minorca, ix. 189
  Rodney conquers, ix. 139, 141
  —— plunders, ix. 194n, 278

St-Évremond. *See* Marguetel de St-Denis de St-Évremond

St Firenzo. *See* San Fiorenzo

St-Florentin, Comte de. *See* Phélypeaux, Louis (1705–77)

St George's Day:
  Mann told not to wait for, before presenting his memorial to Senate, iv. 198

St George's Fields:
  Gordon rioters assemble in, ix. 53
  guards fire on mob in, vii. 20, 77, 98

St-Germain, Count (d. 1784), adventurer:
  description of, after his arrest and release, iii. 181–2
  Frederick, P. of Wales, curious about, iii. 182
  HW's accounts of, x. 20–1

St-Germain-en-Laye:
  French nobleman exiled to, vii. 298
  Magnan, Marquise de, from, ii. 548
  Marlborough implicated in schemes of, iv. 322
  pun on, x. 20, 21

St Germano. *See* San Germano

St Giles's:
  Selwyn finds Moore and his whore buried in vault of, iv. 181

Saint-Gilles, Mme de. *See* Coardi di Carpanetto, Caterina Maria Teresa

St Giorgio:
  earthquake account mentions, ix. 376

St Giorgio Gate, at Florence:
Spaniards to pass out by, i. 342
St Giovanni. *See* John the Baptist, St; St John's Day; San Giovanni
St Giuliano:
Philip, Don, captures, iii. 84
St Helena:
gentlewoman thinks London must be deserted when fleet is away, because China ships make such a difference at, ix. 110
St Helens, Bn. *See* Fitzherbert, Alleyne
Sainthill, Edward (d. 1782), of Bradninch, Devon:
Mann to take, to Pratolino, i. 484
Newcastle recommends, to Mann, i. 483
St-Honoré, Messrs de la rue. *See* Parliament of Paris
St Hubert, Order of, of Bavaria:
Cowper gets George III's permission to accept, from Karl Theodor, ix. 470
—— to be installed in, ix. 568
HW ridicules Cowper for accepting, ix. 572, 646
St Iago. *See* Santiago
St Isidore. *See* San Isidro
St James's Church:
Secker to preach at, about earthquakes, iv. 155
St James's Coffeehouse:
waiter at, says he could thrash Nivernais, vi. 84
Worsley, Lady, gallantries of, aired in, ix. 228
St James's Market:
HW will not sit in, to await French invaders, iv. 469
St James's Palace:
ball at, for Karl Wilhelm Ferdinand's wedding and Q. Charlotte's birthday, vi. 197, 199
Burdett meets Castle-Durrow at, iv. 20
Bute does not relinquish keys of, to Pitt, vi. 130
chapel of, Kingston, Ds of, screams in, viii. 150
Charlotte, Q., arrives at, v. 528
Christian VII at, vii. 41–2, 48
Dashwood, Catherine, at, as Charlotte's duenna, v. 531
foreigners think that riot may endanger, vi. 200
French mail robbed within call of guard of, ix. 619
George II arrives at, from abroad, ii. 340
—— keeps, mostly locked up, iv. 88
George III and brothers to live at, iv. 239
George III besieged at, by mob, vii. 98
—— excludes D. of Cumberland's followers from, vii. 358
—— to move to, v. 443
Grenville faction must divide spoils before storming, vi. 489
Grenville's friends point to, vii. 263

HW lives near, i. 279
HW prefers, to Norfolk, ii. 218
Jacobites entertained at, v. 409
Karl Wilhelm Ferdinand greets English soldier on way to, vi. 197
lawyers to guard Royal Family at, in George II's absence, iii. 180
Leicester House no longer at odds with, iv. 549
London Common Council's affront to, v. 77
Mann jokes about sending the Pope to, vi. 390
—— wants Genoese Doge and Senate to visit, iii. 76
—— wishes Francis III's pictures were at, iii. 314
merchants to present address at, vii. 98–9
ministers in control of, vi. 302
mob have not replaced George III by Pitt in, v. 541
Old Coachman, The, mentions, ii. 22
Orford, Cts of, may be lodged at, iii. 72
paintings from Arnaldi collection would be worthy of, v. 479
Patriots used to think of Albano when dismissed from, vi. 257
posterity will be indifferent to revolutions in, vi. 303
Princesses spend summer at, ii. 218
Richecourt prefers Santi Apostoli to, iii. 441
Secker seeks preferment from, iv. 187
Thatched House Tavern near, vii. 200
visitors to: Bedford, i. 338; Brunswick, P. and Ps of, vi. 342; Frederick, P. of Wales, ii. 340–1; Halifax, i. 338; Wales, Ps of, ii. 343
Walpole, Sir Robert, comes down from, for opening of Parliament, viii. 361
—— does not go to, i. 403
Wotton carries memorial from, to Venice, iv. 198
Young Pretender has not reached, iii. 125
St James's Park:
Downing St house of Sir Robert Walpole looks out upon, i. 478
Duck Island in, iv. 226
Éon talks to people in, vi. 239
Estaing's defeat hailed in, viii. 545
Frederick, P. of Wales, and D. of Cumberland, appear before mob in, iii. 288
Frederick, P. of Wales, sits under wall of, iv. 131
gates of, shut against mob, vii. 98
Godfrey, Mrs, seen in, in sedan chair, by HW, ix. 571
Mathews wears tricolour cockade in, ii. 522
mob pursues Waldegrave to, iv. 156
Orford to be removed as ranger of, ix. 266
Pelham walks in, just before death, iv. 413
sentinel in, accosted by mad parson, i. 197
St James's Square:
Hervey, Bp, rents house in, at high rate, ix. 455

St James's St, London:
club opened in, viii. 186
George II hates mob in, v. 63
Maclaine lodges in, iv. 168
nabobs and American chiefs fill, v. 518
White's (Arthur's) Club in, iv. 168, ix.
483n
St Jean. *See* St John, 'old'
St John, Vcts. *See* Clarke, Hester (1723-52)
St John, 'old' ——:
(?) Craons accompanied by, i. 414
HW and Princesse de Craon play faro
with, v. 533
Mann receives offer from, to preside over
cooks at coronation celebration, v. 533
suppers prepared by, for HW at Craon's,
v. 33
St John, Anne (d. ca 1742), m. (before
1728) Giuseppe Grisoni:
brother says that he hears from, from
heaven, iii. 84
St John, Frederick (1734-87), 2d Vct Bolingbroke, 1751:
brother of, vi. 553n
confined in madhouse, ix. 11
divorce of, vi. 567
Mann to entertain, at dinner, iv. **387**
wife of, vi. 148n, viii. 524n
St John, Hon. Henrietta (1699-1756), m.
(1727) Robert Knight, cr. (1745) Bn Luxborough and (1763) E. of Catherlough:
(?) affair of, i. 126
St John, Sir Henry (1652-1742), 4th Bt; cr.
(1716) Vct St John:
(?) auction of effects of, i. 477
Custom House place bought by, from Ds
of Kendal, for son, iv. 18
St John, Henry (1678-1751), cr. (1712) Vct
Bolingbroke:
Aix-la-Chapelle to be visited by, ii. 304
British isles 'sold' by, to France, ii. 247
character of, detestable, ix. 7
Chetwynd agent to, i. 356
——'s friend, ii. 191, vi. 544n
Cork's intimacy with, iv. 452
Cornbury's letter from, iv. 59
Craftsmen written by, against Moses and
St Paul, iv. 454
dying, iv. 291
faults of, iv. 66
Ferrers thinks that religious notions should
not have been published by, v. 401
forgotten, iii. 460
Fraigneau lived with, iv. 452
George I gives memorial of, to Sir Robert
Walpole, iv. 455
—— would have replaced Sir Robert Wal-
pole by, iv. 452, 455
George III's tutors governed by, after
Bolingbroke's own death, iv. 323
HW asks if Wilkes resembles, in courting
Old Pretender, vi. 290
HW calls: 'arch-fiend,' ix. 6; 'rascal,' ix. 7

health of: cancer, iv. 291; ill, iv. 225
*Letters on the Spirit of Patriotism, on the
Idea of a Patriot King, and on the State of
Parties at the Accession of King George the
First:* Dartmouth comments on, iv. 208; HW
discusses, iv. 59-62; Mann hopes to read,
iv. 76; Pope prints and alters, iv. 61; Wal-
pole, Horatio (1678-1757) to answer, iv. 62
Letter to Sir William Wyndham, iv. 452
Lyttelton a friend of, iv. 61
——'s letters from, iv. 59-60
—— tells, not to publish reflections against
Sir Robert Walpole, iv. 59
Mallet receives letters from, as bribe, iv.
62
Mann discusses, with E. of Cork, iv. 452,
454
—— hopes to get anecdotes about, from
Cork, iv. 452
Marlborough overborne by cabal of, ix.
605
metaphysical writings of, ruin his reputation in England, iv. 454-5
Mirepoix, Mme de, invites, with HW, to
dinner, iv. 225
Newcastle, D. of, may imitate, vi. 442
Pitt's respect for, declines, iv. 59
Pope an idolator of, ix. 6
—— persuades, to pay for printing of
book, iv. 65-6
——'s friends attack, in pamphlets, iv. 65
return of, unlucky, i. 134
Scott recommended by, as George III's
underpreceptor, iv. 203, 344
silver tubes used by, to ventilate bed, iv.
203
subordinates of, not as guilty as himself,
ix. 7-8
Swift's letters from, ix. 6-7
—— urged by, to burn history of Anne's
reign, v. 184
Vernon introduced by, to Duchesse du
Maine, i. 126
Walpole, Sir Robert, annihilated the falsely
boasted abilities of, ix. 7
—— excluded, ix. 605
—— treated ungratefully by, iv. 452
wife of, dies, iv. 136
St John, Hon. Henry (1738-1818) M.P.; D.
of York's groom of the Bedchamber:
accompanies D. of York's body to England,
vi. 554
expresses about D. of York's illness must
have been sent by, vi. 556
ill at Rome, vi. 231
Mann assured by, that D. of York remembers his request for Bath ribbon, vi. 390
—— informed by, that D. of York will
tour Germany and Italy, vi. 408
—— praises, vi. 223
——'s letter from, thanking him for attentions to D. of York, vi. 230

[St John, Hon. Henry, *continued*]
York, D. of, accompanied by, on Tuscan tour, vi. 220
—— has, as Groom of the Bedchamber, vi. 553n
—— sends message by, to Mann, vi. 417
—— taken by, to Monaco, vi. 553
—— wants to recommend, to George III, in dictated letter, vi. 553
St John, John (ca 1695–1748), 2d Vct St John:
death of, iv. 15, 18
father buys Custom House place for, iv. 18
widow mourns, iv. 23
St John, Oliver (ca 1691–1749), F.R.S.:
Carducci refuses to pay, iii. 84
confessor of, receives Latin letters, ii. 205
George II cursed by, iii. 191
Great News to the Listening Jews, by, i. 292
Horton's correspondence with, about converting Leghorn Jews, i. 292
madman in religion, i. 283
Mann harassed by, ii. 205
—— refuses money offered by, i. 292
—— refuses pier glasses offered by, i. 283, 292
—— saves library of, i. 283, 292
——'s letter from, about Carducci and testicles, iii. 84
—— urged by, to unite churches of England and Rome, iii. 358
poetry by, i. 292
sister communicates to, from heaven, iii. 84
St John, gates of. *See* Baptistery, at Florence: gates of
St John of Jerusalem, Knights of, (Knights of Malta):
Beauvau, Chevalier de, is, ii. 298n
cardinal honoured by presence of, in his antechamber, v. 380
France offers Îles de Ste-Marguerite to, iv. 406
Grand Master of, *see* Pinto de Fonseca, Manuel
Naples disputes with, iv. 405–6
wills of, invalid without permission of Order, i. 110
St John's, near Montreal:
Montgomery said to have captured, viii. 157, 161
St John's Day:
celebrations on, i. 78–80, 454, 456, 463
drawing of, sent to HW, ii. 181
eve of, Mann writes on, ii. 462
Florentine senators avoid, ii. 251
Gerini to return on, i. 68
HW's plans for, i. 29
Leopold to visit Florence on, vi. 427
Mann takes Mrs Bosville to, ii. 251
—— writes on, i. 69, 453

operas on, i. 79–80, 449, 454, 463, ii. 435, 439, 445
races held on, i. 79, 454, 456, ii. 251, 462
Richecourt's orders about celebration of, iii. 8
See also under John the Baptist, St; San Giovanni
St Joseph, Convent of, at Paris:
Orléans, Bp of, lodges Mlle Guimard in, vii. 324–5
St Joseph, Spanish register ship:
capture of, viii. 543
St Kitt's. *See* St Christopher
St Laurence, church of, at Florence. *See* San Lorenzo
St-Laurent:
French forces at, iii. 336
St Lawrence River:
English fleet said to be destroyed in, v. 344
English ships must quit, in winter, v. 357
St Lazare. *See* St Nazarre
St Lazaro. *See* San Lazaro
St Leger, Arthur Mohun (1718–50), 3d Vct Doneraile, 1734; M.P.:
Comptroller to the P. of Wales, iii. 388
Frederick, P. of Wales's lord of the Bedchamber, i. 251n
Kildare's proposals for raising regiment read by, iii. 155
Lyttelton plagued by, in Parliamentary committee, iii. 388
Parliamentary speeches by: hinting at impeachment, i. 354; on privately-raised regiments, x. 14
Parliamentary vote by, on privately-raised regiments, x. 19
Pulteney holds, to promise about Westminster election voting, i. 251
St Leger, Barry Matthew (b. 1733):
(?) dinner given by, iv. 260
(?) sharper ducked by, iv. 260
St Leger, Sir John (d. 1743), Kt, 1701:
(?) son of, iv. 260
St Leger, (?) John (1726–69):
Craon's letter to Mme de Mirepoix recommends, iv. 55–6, 64, 77
'romping greyhound puppy,' iv. 64
St Leger, John Hayes (1756–1800), army officer:
(?) arrest of, for riot, ix. 565
St Lorenzo. *See* San Lorenzo
St-Louis, Croix de. *See under* St-Louis, Ordre de
St-Louis, Ordre de:
Croix de: Beauvau wins, ii. 216; Louis XV said to have given, to Brown, iii. 217; Pilâtre de Rosier said to have carried, ix. 590
St Lucia:
capture of, viii. 447, 449, 454
epidemic in, attacks English forces, viii. 475
Estaing's failure to save, ridiculed at Paris, viii. 450

Saint-Lunaire Bay:
English land at, v. 243
Saint-Malo:
England threatened from, viii. 502
English burn vessels at, v. 212–13
English expedition against, v. 210–11, 212, 218, 223, 228, 243, 245
Marlborough abandons teaspoons in retreat from, v. 221
Paris fireworks to celebrate victory of, v. 246
Pitt never intended to capture, v. 213
quatrain on English attack on, v. 244
Walpole, Edward performs bravely at, v. 240
St Marco. See San Marco
St Margaret's Church, Westminster:
roundhouse at, scaffold from, to church, rented for Coronation, v. 536
St Mark's, Venice, library of:
Chute has seen, ii. 63
Houghton gallery ceiling copied from, ii. 63
St-Marsault. See Green de St-Marsault
St Martino. See San Martino
St Martin's Day:
Mann writes on, i. 178
St Martin's-in-the-Fields, Vicar of. See Pearce, Zachariah (1690–1774)
St Martin's-in-the-Fields, London:
parish of: said to include foreign areas, vii. 551, ix. 357–8, 642; Yonge promotes troop-raising by, x. 15
Thorold abjures Roman Catholicism in, vi. 380
Violante's descent from steeple of, ix. 450
Young Pretender's alleged conversion in, vi. 324, 368, 380
St Martin's Lane:
Strange probably lives in, viii. 24
St Martin's roundhouse, London:
women confined in, by drunken constables, i. 504
St Martin's summer:
Florentines prolong villegiatura till, iv. 451
St Mary Axe:
Hindustan may be peopled by colony from parish of, vii. 551
St Mary Isle, Kirkcudbright, Lord Selkirk's seat:
Jones plunders, viii. 377
St-Michel, Ordre de:
Pilâtre de Rosier expected, ix. 590
St-Nazaire:
Young Pretender embarks at, iii. 86
St-Odile, Barone di. See Poirot, Domenico Matteo
St-Omer:
actors send messenger to D. and Ds of Cumberland at, vii. 520
St Palais. See La Curne de Sainte-Palaye
St Patrick, Order of:
George III institutes, ix. 365
St-Paul, Curé of. See Gueret, N.P.

St Paul's, Covent Garden:
O'Brien marries Lady Susan Fox-Strangways in, vi. 219
St Paul's Cathedral, London:
Englishmen who never visited, go to see St Peter's at Rome, vii. 213
George II does not visit, on peace proclamation, iv. 46
Louisbourg standards carried to, v. 237, 238
Pitt may be buried in, viii. 382
Secker wants deanery of, iv. 187
traveller may view the ruins of, viii. 62
St Pelegrino:
Spaniards approach Lucca across mountains of, iii. 35
St Pelten. See Sankt Pölten
St Peter's, Rome:
canons of, to have apartments in new sacristy, viii. 344
chapter of, Clement XIV's body to be consigned to, viii. 43
English who never visited St Paul's go to see, vii. 213
HW and Princesse de Craon visit, to see relics, i. 4
Leopold, Maria Carolina, and Maria Louisa visit, vii. 23
mausoleum in, for Ps Sobieski, v. 391
Old Pretender's burial to be in, v. 391, 392, vi. 385
Pius VI builds costly new sacristy at, viii. 344, ix. 383–4
popes abandon, in summer, for Monte Cavallo, viii. 344
to be illuminated for D. of Cumberland, vii. 564
St Petersburg:
Buckinghamshire accepts post at, vi. 54
Catherine II's celebration at, over naval battle with Turks, vii. 249
———'s crimes at, vi. 65, 74, vii. 195, viii. 154
Czarina's burial at, should help England, vi. 1
'devil' rules at, vi. 570
East India Company's tyranny as bad as that of, ix. 400
Éon carries treaties from, vi. 217
from Cape of Good Hope to, French are defeated, v. 352
Hamlet acted in, in Russian translation, vi. 426
Houghton pictures arrive at, ix. 2
inundation at, viii. 332
Jesuits should start revolution in, vi. 514
Joseph II and Maria Theresa send Lobkowitz to, vii. 310
messenger from, to Orlov, vii. 160, viii. 33, 40
Munnich hopes to rejoin his family at, vi. 11
Orlov, Alexei, returns to, viii. 114
——— tells about revolution in, vii. 185

[St Petersburg, *continued*]
Orlov, Grigorii, supplanted at, vii. 441
peace expected by, vii. 438
Peter III's ghost should be heard in, vii. 195
Peterhoff near, vi. 57
report from, in *Bologna Gazette*, v. 247
royal academy of, Sloane's museum offered to, iv. 358
Russian fleet returns to, viii. 84
visitors to; Craven, Bns, ix. 632, 654; Joseph II, ix. 72; Kingston, Ds of, ix. 632; Lobkowitz, vii. 310
Vorontsovs' reasons for leaving, vi. 173
St Peter's Day:
HW's plans for, i. 29
opera arrangements on, i. 81
Roman celebrations for, ii. 462
St Philip's Castle, Minorca:
affairs at, proceeding favourably, ix. 219
Boyd passes from, v. 3
Byng does not reinforce, ix. 562, 566-7
cannon from Barcelona to attack, ix. 229
communication between England and, through Florence, ix. 192
Crillon hopes to starve, but dares not assault it, ix. 249-50
—— offers Murray bribe to let him take, ix. 207-8, 213n
defended as long as possible, ix. 269
Edgcumbe leaves sailors to strengthen garrison of, ix. 559
enemy preparations for attack upon, ix. 233-4
France and Spain complain to Leopold about supplies to, ix. 250
French about to attack, iv. 552
French and Spaniards to storm, using prisoners, ix. 180
frigates and privateers watch attempts to relieve, ix. 205
garrison at, worn out by fatigue and sickness, ix. 269
Mann grants commissions to foreign officers going to, ix. 249
—— sends Hillsborough accounts of expenditures for assistance to, ix. 204-5
——'s labours for relief of, rewarded, ix. 246
——'s ships reach, ix. 219
——'s zeal and prudence in assisting defence of, approved by George III, ix. 229
only a powerful fleet can be of assistance to, ix. 234
Murray and Draper to defend, ix. 190
Rainsford consults Mann about assistance for, ix. 233
siege of, in 1756: becomes a blockade, iv. 570, 582; French did not foresee difficulty of, iv. 567; surrender terminates, iv. 571-6, 578, 581-2
siege of, in 1781-2: expected to last long, ix. 229; may be retarded if Mann's vessels

arrive, ix. 249; successful sally of garrison in, against enemy, reported from Spain, ix. 205, 207; supplies sent to, from Leghorn, ix. 249-50
surprise prevented cattle being driven into, ix. 190, 198-9
See also Minorca; Port Mahon
St *Philip's Castle*, English brig:
captain of, brings news from Minorca, ix. 196
Mann sends, to Minorca, ix. 199, 204, 219, 249
Murray's dispatches come on, ix. 207
Pringle and officers sail in, to Minorca, ix. 199
'small scuttling vessel,' ix. 205
St Phillip's. *See* St Philip's
'St-Pierre, Patrimoine de." *See* Patrimoine St-Pierre:
La Touche should have been surrendered, with Martinique, vi. 29-30
St-Pierre, port of, near Sardinia:
Oiseau escapes to, v. 292
St Pierre d'Arena:
Townshend and Villettes visit Austrian camp at, iii. 312
St *Quintin*, ship:
captain of, *see* Barker, John
HW sends Giberne and box by, to Mann, i. 279, 302, 324, 325, 407
voyage of, i. 302, 394, 419
St Ranieri's Day:
Pisa to celebrate, ii. 455
St Remo. *See* San Remo
Saint-Rémy de Valois, Jeanne de (1756-91), m. (1780) Marc-Antoine-Nicolas, Comte de Lamotte:
Rohan suspected of giving diamond necklace to, ix. 603
St Rock. *See* San Roque
St-Séverin d'Aragon, Alphonse-Marie-Louis (1705-57), Comte de:
Sandwich, E. of, told by, that Aix treaty preliminaries can be signed, iii. 482
St Severins. *See* San Severino
St Sophia:
Catherine II would be detestable even when crowned in, vii. 208
St Stefano. *See* Porto San Stefano; San Stefano, Order of
St Stephen, Order of. *See* San Stefano, Order of
St Stephen of Hungary, Order of:
Maria Louisa receives, from Joseph II, ix. 128
St Stephen's Chapel, Westminster:
more rejoicing in, over one turncoat than over 99 just men, ix. 23
Parliamentary drama to be enacted in, ix. 10
to be pointed out in schoolboys' lesson, vii. 400

St Teresa's Day:
   opera on, ix. 558–9
   See also Maria Theresa: name-day of
St Thomas's Hospital, London:
   plague rumoured to be at, v. 427
St Tropez:
   Spanish galleys destroyed near, i. 471, 481
St Vincent, E. and Vct of. See Jervis, Capt.
   Sir John (1735–1823)
St Vincent:
   England's troubles with Caribs in, vii. 455,
   462, viii. 503
   French conquer, viii. 503
   North's victory in Parliament over, vii. 462
   secured, viii. 447
St Vincent. See also Cape St Vincent
St Vitali. See Sanvitale
Salary; salaries:
   Bengal governor's, vi. 540
   doge of Venice's, i. 75
   Dorset's, for Cinque Ports, v. 109
   Florentine hospital inspector's, i. 57
   Magnan's, ii. 548–9
Salas, Marchese di. See Guzmann, José Joa-
   quín
Saldanha, Francisco de (1723–76), cardinal,
   1756; Patriarch 1759–76 of Lisbon:
   Portugal to be preserved by, for the Church,
   vi. 331
Sales, Comte de (d. 1749), Charles Emmanuel
   III's illegitimate uncle:
   Lanze, Cardinal de, son of, v. 207
   Mann receives paper sent by, from Bologna,
   iii. 226
   niece recommended by, to Mann, iii. 499
Saliceti, Natale (d. 1789), papal physician:
   Clement XIV's autopsy by, viii. 42–3
   Pius VI's illness considered by, to be seri-
   ous, viii. 461
Saliciennes:
   convent of, iv. 333–4
Salignac, François-Louis de (1722–67), Che-
   valier, later Marquis, de la Mothe-Fénelon:
   captured at Dettingen, ii. 260
Salignac, Gabriel-Jacques de (1688–1746), Mar-
   quis de la Mothe-Fénelon:
   son of, ii. 260
Salimbeni, Felice (ca 1712–51), singer:
   Feroni, Mme, wants to hear, i. 81
   Mann entertains, i. 104
   —— expects to prefer, to Egiziello, i. 454
   opera ill-adapted to voice of, i. 79
   shoulder of, well set, and teeth fast, i. 132
   sings in Mann's garden, i. 240
   Suares, Mme, brings, to Mann, i. 101
   Suares girls sing with, i. 101
   Tedeschino imitates, i. 284
   Venetian airs sung by, to Mann, i. 101, 240
   Walpole, Bns, assists, in road accident, i.
   116
Salimbeni. See also Bartolini Salimbeni
Salins, Conte de. See Lamesan, Gaetano Carlo
Salins, Contessa de. See Kalnoki, Maria
   Caterina

Salis, Jérôme de (ca 1708–94), Count of the
   Holy Roman Empire; Reichsgraf von Salis-
   Soglio, 1748:
   Fane's news to be told by, ii. 269
   minister at Coire, ii. 215
Salisbury, Bp of. See Burnet, Gilbert (1643–
   1715); Douglas, John (1721–1807); Gilbert,
   John (1693–1761); Hoadly, Benjamin (1676–
   1761); Sherlock, Thomas (1678–1761);
   Thomas, John (1691–1766); Thomas, John
   (1696–1781)
Salisbury, Cts of. See Tufton, Lady Anne
   (1693–1757)
Salisbury, E. of. See Cecil, Robert (1563–
   1612)
Salisbury, Sally. See Pridden, Sally
Salisbury, Wilts:
   man from, killed in London accident, iii.
   386
   Muzell (Stosch) at, v. 433, 440, 459
Salisbury, ship:
   at Port Mahon, i. 285
   Leghorn to be defended by, ii. 38
   Townshend sends snuff-box in, to England,
   ii. 445
Salivation:
   applications of, iii. 248, iv. 175, 537, 543
   Cumberland, D. of, needs, iii. 483
Sallier de la Tour, Vittorio Amedeo (1726–
   1800), Marchese di Cordon; Sardinian en-
   voy to England 1774–84; to France 1788–
   ca 92:
   Gordon rioters break into house and chapel
   of, ix. 55
Sally, English merchant ship:
   capture of, v. 16
Salm, Ps of. See Hornes, Marie-Thérèse-
   Josèphe de
Salo:
   Walpole, Bns, at, i. 196, 217
Salt cellars:
   at Dover inn, ii. 315
   Mann's, acquired from Fane, ii. 472
   of Chelsea china, vi. 122
Salt fish. See under Fish
Salt meat. See under Meat
Salt provisions:
   Blakeney orders Dick to provide, for gar-
   rison, iv. 537
   puppies may get mange from, vii. 40
Salts:
   HW gets, for Giovanardi, i. 159, 416
Saltykov, Ekaterina Petrovna (1743–1817), m.
   Comte André Shuvalov
   England and Florence visited by, vi. 460
   Mann calls, 'pretty,' vi. 460
Salusbury, Hester Lynch (1741–1821), m. 1
   (1763) Henry Thrale; m. 2 (1784) Gabriel
   Piozzi:
   Anecdotes of the late Samuel Johnson: first
   impression of, sold out on publication day,
   ix. 640; HW criticizes, ix. 638; Mann would
   rather see Wolcot's satire than, ix. 643

[Salusbury, Hester Lynch, *continued*]
Boswell refutes, over opinion of Mrs Montagu's book, ix. 640
Florence visited by, with husband, ix. 611n
HW likes preface of, to *Florence Miscellany*, ix. **633–4**
HW ridicules, ix. 611–12
Mann's quarrel with, ix. 633n
Montagu, Mrs, gets letter from, disavowing Boswell, ix. 634
satiric prints of, ix. 641
Wolcot ridicules, ix. 638, 640–1, 643
Salute; salutes:
cannon at Monaco fire, for D. of York as for French marshal, vi. 554
English ships fire, at Leghorn, v. 123
to English ships, disputes over, vi. 156
Salvador, ——, m. (1760) Joshua Mendes da Costa:
(?) card sent by, to Q. Charlotte, vi. 72–3
Salvador, Sarah, m. Francis Daniel Salvador:
(?) card sent by, to Q. Charlotte, vi. 72–3
Salvator. *See* Rosa, Salvator
Salver; salvers:
Mann's, acquired from Fane, ii. 472
Skrine serves drinks on, iv. 145
Salvetti, Lino, chancellor of Volterra:
Dumesnil avoided by, iii. 493
Salvetti Antelminelli, Giovanni, Tuscan Resident at London 1657–80:
hesitant to report Cromwell's death, iv. 170
Salvi, Antonio, librettist:
Arminio (opera), Mann criticizes, i. 80
Salvi, Giovanni Battista (1609–85), called Sassoferrato, painter:
Abcedario pittorico does not include, ii. 94
Baldocci and Corsi have paintings by, ii. 94
Madonna paintings of, famous in Florence, ii. 94
Mann's Madonna by, sent to HW, ii. 94, 182, 214, 291, 292
name of, on back of alleged Domenichino painting, ii. 93, 162
Salviati, Duchessa. *See* Buoncompagni Anna Maria (1697–1752); Lante della Rovere, Maria Christina; Rinaldi, Margherita (1712–90)
Salviati, Marchese:
HW civil to, in England, ii. 459
Salviati, Antonio Maria (1693–1757), Duca di Giuliano-Salviati:
(?) Craon, Princesse de, entertains, iii. 145
Dumesnil escapes from Florence with horses and servants of, iii. 491
son of, v. 310
Salviati, Averardo (1721–83), Duca di Giuliano-Salviati:
(?) English visitors favoured by, vi. 379
Gloucester, D. of, sends message to, viii. **291**
Leopold to be entertained by, vii. 95

Tuscan court makes, Grand Chambellan, against his will, vi. 467
Villa Salviati may be rented by, to Cts of Orford, v. **310**
Salviati, Caterina Zephyrina, m. (1717) Fabrizzio Colonna, constable:
Craon, Princesse de, tired of entertaining, ii. 545
Salviati, Laura (1725–1802), m. (1742) Rodolfo Acquaviva, Duca d'Atri:
Orford, Cts of, talks with, ix. 130
Salviati family:
Tesi's banishment from Florence procured by, from Vienna, to protect Tempi and Corsi, ii. 520
Salviati Villa:
Orford, Cts of, may take, v. 310
Salvini, Rev. Gregorio:
Theodore calls, traitor, ii. 156
Salvini, Salvino (1667–1751), canon, antiquarian:
(?) Mann attributes saying to, vi. 511
Sal volatile:
HW's letter to act as, on Mann, ii. 117
Mann compares HW's letters to, iii. 182
Salzburg:
Bavarian elector said to have entered, i. 108
Sambrooke, Diana (ca 1731–78), m. (1754) Lord George Sackville:
income of, v. 328
Samminiati, Ascanio (b. 1678), senator:
annuity to be paid to, as Electress's executor, ii. 168–9
Samoggia:
Montemar encamps at, i. 427
Sampieri, Valerio, Bolognese collector:
collection of, v. 231, 478
Sampson, James (d. 1768), D. of Richmond's servant:
Conway's house robbed and set afire by, vi. 587–8, vii. 9
Samson. See under Handel, George Frederick
San Antonio, ship:
artillery brought by, to Italian coast from Barcelona, i. **286**
taken as prize, ii. 344
San Antonio Abbate, church of. *See under* Parma
San Barnaba, **Venice:**
Barnabotti of, i. 75
San Bruno:
earthquake account mentions, ix. **376**
San Carlo, ship:
Merlo defends, on Danube, iii. 124
San Casciano:
Almada leaves, v. 436
Corsini's villa at, occupied by Almada, v. 426
San Casciano dei Bagni:
Lyttelton, Sir Richard, and Thomas Pitt at, v. 524
'Sancho Panza.' *See under* Cervantes

Sancta Sophia. *See under* Constantinople

Sandershausen:
battle of, v. 227

Sanderson, Nicholas (1683–1739), LL.D., professor of mathematics at Cambridge:
HW's lack of mathematical capacity discerned by, v. 353, 359

Sandford, Francis (1630–94), Lancaster herald:
HW signs himself as, v. 532

San Domingo:
Albemarle may now capture, vi. 22
fleet of: captured by English, iii. 424, 427, 487; said to be destroyed by storm, viii. 531; unmolested by English, viii. 501; *see also* Domingo-men
France to have share in, with Spain, ix. 180
French reverses at, iii. 487–8

Sandwich, Cts of. *See* Fane, Hon. Dorothy (d. 1797)

Sandwich, E. of. *See* Montagu, John (1718–92); Montagu, John (1742–1814)

Sandys, Bns. *See* Tipping, Letitia

Sandys, Hon. Edwin (1726–97), 2d Bn Sandys, 1770; M.P.:
Admiralty post for, v. 73
succession of, to father's title vacates seat for Westminster, vii. 206

Sandys, Samuel (1695–1770), cr. (1743) Bn Sandys; M.P.:
Argyll scolds, i. 335
chancellor of the Exchequer, i. **249n**, 332, 335, ii. 51, 103, 118n, 350, 356
cofferer, i. 249n, ii. 350, 357, 365, 551
Dashwood allied with, i. 249
death of, from fractured skull, vii. 206
'dishclout,' ii. 350
dull, ii. 142
Earle's witticism on, i. 250
Exchequer acceptance defended by, i. 335
Exchequer resigned by, to Pelham, ii. 350, 356
'Fountain' meeting attended by, i. 335
HW called on by, iii. 25–6
HW's verses on appointment of, to House of Lords, ii. 357–8, 372
hackney coaches said to be hired to stand at door of, ii. 232
Halifax succeeded by, in Board of Trade, v. 489
Hardwicke succeeded by, as speaker of the House of Lords, v. 25
House of Commons considered an unfair tribunal by, iii. 26
Indemnity Bill opposed by, i. 437
justice in eyre, iv. 25, 518, v. 489
levee (pretended) of, ii. 232
Mann will be amused by reappearance of, iv. 518
Mediterranean naval investigation discussed by, iii. 25–6
New Ode, A, satirizes, ii. 50–1
Ord secretary to, ii. **320n**
Parliamentary debate **discusses, ii. 118**

Parliamentary motion by, for punishing sheriff, i. 294
peerage for, i. 249n, ii. 142, 357, **365**
Pulteney's protégé, ii. 91, 72n, **74**
reelection of, expected, i. 363
'republican,' i. 249n
Scrope defended by, i. 467
Secret Committee lists include, i. 385
Walpole, Sir Robert, enrages, by taking Orford title, i. 333
—— ordered by, to vacate Downing St house, i. 478, 495
Williams, Sir Charles Hanbury, satirizes, ii. 320
Wilmington and Compton outvoted by, ii. 50n
Wilmington offers Downing St house to, i. 478, 495
Worcester's instructions to, ii. 103

Sandys, Mrs Samuel. *See* Tipping, Letitia

Sandys, William (ca 1470–1540), cr. (1523) Bn Sandys:
Henry VIII's lord chamberlain, who 'built' chapel at the Vyne, iv. 485n

San Fernando, Spanish ship:
in Spanish fleet, i. 286

San Fernando de Omoa:
English capture, viii. **543**

San Fiorenzo, Corsica:
Corsican attack upon, fails, vii. 80
Marbeuf wants communication between Bastia and, vii. 46
rebels safe at, iii. 258
Rivarola may retire to, iii. 437

San Gennaro; San Gennore. *See under* Januarius, St

San Germano:
Neapolitan troops at, iii. **378**
Spaniards fortify, ii. 438

Sanges. *See* Castello di Sanges

San Gillio, Contessa di. *See* Coardi di Carpanetto, Caterina Maria Teresa

San Giorgio, Russian frigate:
arrives at Leghorn from Paros, vii. 326

San Giovacchino, Neapolitan ship:
Ferdinand of Naples sails in, to Leghorn, ix. 581

San Giovanni:
Spanish troops retire to, ii. 154

San Giovanni, Augustinian church at Leghorn:
falls in earthquake, i. 307

Sanhedrin:
HW's name for House of Commons, vii. 555

Sani, Agata (*or* Prudenza Sani Grandi), singer; 'Sani':
first singer in Leghorn opera, ii. 160
'Ottajano de' Medici' accompanies, to Leghorn, ii. 160
(?) 'vile herd,' i. **463**

San Isidore (*or Isidro,*) Spanish ship:
destruction of, ii. 189
in Spanish fleet, i. 286

Sanitary conveniences:
French indelicacy about, shocks Lady Mary Churchill, iv. 339
Hervey's behaviour in, amuses ladies, ii. 96
See also Bath; Close stool; Jordan; Urinal
Sankt Pölten:
Bavarian-French army at, i. 194
San Lazaro:
battle of, iii. 266–7, 271
HW hopes for Flemish victory similar to, iii. 274
San Lazzaro e Sant'Antonio, Tuscan ship:
seizure of, v. 269
San Lorenzo, Florentine church:
chapel of: Electress to be buried in, ii. 160; Electress to provide for completion of, ii. 113; left unfinished at Electress's death, ii. 172
Craon, Princesse de, walks to, from SS. Annunziata, ii. 196
Electress's funeral at, attended by Mann and Lady Walpole, ii. 173
Frenchman seeks Vandières in, iv. 228
Mann attends Elizabeth Christina's requiem in, iv. 227
pompous tombs of Medici in, ix. 202
San Lorenzo, convent of. See under Venice
San Lorenzo Library:
Richard I's poems in Provençal MS in, v. 156–7, 169, 186
San Luigi Gonzaga, Tuscan ship:
seizure of, v. 273–4
San Marco, convent of, at Florence:
Bartolommeo's picture in, vii. 276
Branchi's essences equal those of, ii. 177
San Marco, Venice. See St Mark's
San Marco, procuratore di. See Foscarini, Marco (1695–1763); Grimani, Pietro (ca 1677–1752); Morosini, Cavaliere Francesco (fl. 1744–85); Querini, Tommaso
San Marino:
Austrian archduke would not be sent to defend, v. 96
San Martino, Duca di. See Pamfili, Benedetto
San Martino:
Braitwitz to visit, i. 134
garrison for, iii. 11
Leghorn troops sent to, ii. 66, 76, 77
mountain fortress of Francis I, ii. 66
Traun orders Braitwitz to send troops to, ii. 85
San Martino:
villa of, iii. 123
San Mignati. See Samminiati
San Miniato:
Grifoni, Mme, visits, ii. 100
Suares, Bp, brought from, ii. 40
San Nicandro, Principe di:
(?) Neapolitan orders relating to, v. 325
Sanosino. See Bernardi, Francesco
San Paolo, Russian frigate:
arrives at Leghorn, from Paros, vii. 326

San Pasquale, Marchese di. See Würtz von Rudenz, Wolfgang Ignatz
San Pieri. See Sampieri
Sanremaschi family:
pro-Spanish, iii. 123
San Remo:
Francis I claims, as imperial fief, iv. 429
Genoese chastise, iv. 429
governor of, see Albero
letter about bombardment of, ii. 123–4
Rowley destroys, iii. 120–1, 123–4, 132
San Roque:
Spanish camp at: expensive and pestiferous, ix. 59; may be abandoned, ix. 72
San Rosori, near Leghorn:
hunt in woods of, vi. 220
San Secondo, Conte di. See Rossi, Federico
San Secondo, Contessa di. See Rangoni, Vittoria
Sansedoni, Signora. See Pannilini, Porzia; Venturi Gallerini, Ottavia
Sansedoni, Ballì Giovanni (b. 1711):
Bichi lives with, iv. 228
cats mistakenly forwarded by, i. 394
cold caught by, in churches, in jubilee, iv. 228
Craon, Princesse de, favours, iv. 228
lottery ticket investigated by, ii. 206
Mann to ask, for cats from Malta, i. 181, 212
—— wants sailor's report translated for, i. 471
Sanseverino, Don Domenico (1707–60), Neapolitan physician:
Neapolitan heir's incapacity certified by, v. 325
Sanseverino, Principessa di. See Carafa, ——
San Severino Albertini, Giovanni Battista, Principe di Cimitile; Neapolitan ambassador to England 1753–63:
Albani recommends to Mann, iv. 369
Ammon to accompany, to England, iv. 369
courier of, v. 330, 453, 455, 461, 463, 465, 477
George II to be thanked by, for promotion of Sir James Gray, v. 159
HW and Conway to welcome, in England, iv. 370, 372
Herculaneum book announced by, in England, v. 262, 272
letter to wife of, forwarded by Mann, v. 331
Mann entertains, at Florence, iv. 369
—— praises, iv. 369
Neapolitan envoy (ambassador) to England, iv. 369, 372n
new credentials of, in courier's pocket, v. 463
Sansidoni, Sansidonio. See Sansedoni
Sanson, Nicholas (1600–67):
geography of, iv. 501
Sansovino, Jacopo Tatti (1486–1570) called, Florentine sculptor:
Bacchus by, unhurt by Uffizi fire, vi. 67

San Spirito. *See* Santo Spirito

Sans Souci, philosopher of. *See* Frederick II

San Stefano, Order of:
capitolo of, iii. 238, 245, iv. 473
church of Pitti palace to be built by, from prizes from Turks, vi. 259
Mozzi belongs to, vii. 141

Santa Catarina, island of:
Spanish capture, from Portuguese, viii. 309

Santa Croce, Principe di. *See* Publicola, Scipio

Santa Croce, Principessa di. *See* Falconieri, Juliana; Vecchiarelli, Isabella

Santa Croce, church:
English cocchiata ends at, ii. 485
Pepi jokes about, to Abp of Florence, ii. 41
Rinuccini's funeral at, iii. 461

Santa Croce, convent of, at Florence:
Clement XIV was confrère of members of, vii. 118

Santa Croce, Place of, at Florence:
alleged flirtation in, i. 150
flooded, iii. 131

Santa Lucia, college of, at Bologna:
rector refuses to disband, without Clement XIV's order, vii. 487

Santa Margherita, church of:
Gavi flees to, i. 217, 223, 239

Santa Maria:
faction of, at Pisan Battle of the Bridge, ix. 582

Santa Maria, Forte:
reinforced by Genoa, i. 309

Santa Maria del Carmine, Florentine church:
Corsini's church, vii. 287n
crucifix of, v. 510
fire damages Masaccio's paintings in, vii. 276, 287

Santa Maria dell'Anima:
Albani has keys of, vii. 36

Santa Maria Novella, church of:
(?) gens d'armes take refuge in, i. 79

Santa Maria Novella, place of:
celebrations in, i. 79, 100, viii. 514

Santa Maria Nuova, bank of:
Electress deposits money at, ii. 169

Santarelli, Giuseppe (1710–90), singer:
inaudible, ii. **353**, 361
opera performance of, ii. (?) 302, 353

Santa Rosa, Spanish ship:
Grenville captures, iii. 403

Sante. *See* Solis y Sante

Santiago:
sea attack on, impracticable, i. 175

Santi Apostoli, Church of, at Rome:
catafalco prepared in, for Old Pretender, v. 392
Jacobites congratulate Old Pretender at door of, iii. 191, 196

Santi Apostoli, Palace of, at Rome (Palazzo Muti):
joy at, over Young Pretender's venture, iii. 85

Richecourt prefers, to St James's Palace, iii. 441
rumours at, iii. 362
Young Pretender called heir of, vi. 383–4

Santi Apostoli, Via de':
HW thinks, is Mann's street, vii. 107, 135

Santi Barbieri:
opera sung by, ii. 302

Santini, Marchesa. *See* Balbani, Lucrezia

Santini, Signora. *See* Minerbetti, Maria Teresa

Santini, Marchese Niccolò (1729–1812), Lucchese envoy to Tuscany 1758–1800:
becomes envoy to Tuscany, vi. 319, 352
delivers his credentials as envoy, vi. 353
Dick asked by, for fans for fiancée, vii. 295
HW's efforts to get a watch for Mann to send to, for sister-in-law, v. **293**, 295–6, 302, 303–4, 322, 330, 339, 340, 343, 355
honours at Lucca to be done by, to Joseph II and Leopold, viii. 130
Mann and Young Pretender invited by, to concert, vii. 229
Mann asks HW to get fans for bride of, vii. 295
ministerial dinner to be given by, vi. 355
to wed Signorita Minerbetti, Mann's cicisbea's daughter, vii. 295, 306
will give ball for D. of York, vi. 171

Santini, Marchese Paolino (1727–99):
brother of, vii. 306
HW bought watch for, vii. 306
heiress to marry, v. **293**

Santo Buono ('Santa Boni'), Principe di. *See* Caracciolo, Carmine Nicolo (1671–1726); Caracciolo, Marino (1696–1745)

Santo di Tito. *See* Tito, Santi di

'Santon Barsisa':
Hales called, iv. 347

Santo Spirito, convent:
bell installed in, ii. 227
Franchini, Ugo, may take refuge in, i. 65
lodge of, overlooks Mann's garden, iv. 446
nuncio lodges at, iv. 446

Santo Spirito, Priore di (d. 1766):
Church condemns, for giving plate to state, vi. 475

Santo Spirito, Via di:
HW's former residence in, ii. 561
Mann's house in, ii. 561n, iii. 317

Sanvitale, Cts. *See* Scotti, Costanza

Sanvitale, (?) Marchese Giacomantonio (1699–1780), Gran Conestabile:
family reduce, to short allowance, ii. 391
gendarme officer offers to fight, ii. 368
libels against, ii. 368, 391
Mann to be called on by, ii. 281
Niccolini may sell jewels to, for Tesi, i. 135
Tesi breaks with, ii. 391
—— receives presents from, i. **70**, ii. 263
——'s dismissal leaves, almost penniless, ii. 520
——'s dying lover, i. 70
——'s opera backed by, ii. **281**

[Sanvitali, (?) Marchese, *continued*]
theatre directors told by, to arrest the Tesi's insulter, ii. 368

San Vitali. *See* Sanvitale

Sanz, Frans:
captured at Velletri, ii. 493

Sanzilla, Thomas:
captured at Velletri, ii. 493

San Zirioco, Spanish ship:
Trial captures, iii. 134, 138, 149

Saorgio:
French repulsed at, ii. 461

Sapieha, Maria Anna (b. 1728), m. (1750) Prince Johann Cajetan Jablonowsky:
(?) Polish emissary to England, vii. 319
(?) Young Pretender's negotiations with, vii. 319

Saporiti, Giuseppe Maria (ca 1691–1767), Abp of Genoa:
Clement XIII's letter received by, v. 411

Sapphire:
Lorenzi's boast about, iv. 107

Saracin *or* Sarasin. *See* Sarrazin

Sarao. *See* Serao

Saratoga:
battle of, Washington would like to duplicate, viii. 408
Burgoyne's surrender at, viii. 340–1
capitulations at Yorktown and, erroneously said to have been signed on same day, ix. 212

Sarcophagus:
child's bones in, viii. 462
Lucan, Bn or Bns, gets, at Rome, for HW, viii. 462

Sardanapalus V (d. 625 B.C.), K. of Assyria:
reincarnation of, v. 7

Sardi, Giovanni Antonio:
San Remo deputy, iii. 123

Sardini, Giovanni Battista Domenico (fl. 1722–61), Lucchese emissary to Vienna:
Viennese mission of, v. 515

Sardinia, K. of. *See* Charles Emmanuel III (1701–73); Victor Amadeus II (1666–1732); Victor Amadeus III (1726–96)

Sardinia, Q. of. *See* Élisabeth-Thérèse (1711–41); Maria Antonia Ferdinanda (1729–85); Marie-Adélaïde-Clotilde-Xavière (1759–1802)

Sardinia:
ambassadors from and to, *see under* Ambassador
army of: Alessandria approached by, iii. 259; at Buon Porto, ii. 151; Austrian army meets, in Stura valley, iii. 431–2; Gages attacks, ii. 153; Gages defeats, iii. 119; Genoa thwarts, iii. 75; Genoa to blockade, iii. 344; Mann regrets having recommended Townshend to, iii. 169–70; Maria Theresa's troops to join, i. 424; Marseille threatened by, iii. 323; Mathews infuriated by failure of, to cooperate, ii. 229; Mirandola to be besieged by, i. 465; Nice should be taken by, ii. 448; Panaro the theatre of, i. 424,

432–3, 464, 489; Papal states may be traversed by, i. 342, 472, 482; Spaniards may be pursued by, ii. 200; threatens Antibes, iii. 323; Victor Amadeus III directs, iii. 344; Villafranca abandoned by, ii. 435–6
Austrian treaty with, i. 342, ii. 311
Charles of Naples alarmed by successes of, in Lombardy, iii. 237
Choiseul settles boundary disputes with, vii. 143
deserters from army of, i. 500–1
England asked by, to finance Corsican campaign, iv. 386
England hoped by, to produce vigorous war measures, iii. 441
England's treaties with, ii. 311
English minister to, instructs Mann to report on Spanish invasion, i. 265
envoys from and to, *see under* Envoy
France and Spain may be allied with, i. 85
France and Spain may divide Milan with, vii. 469
France may order, to restore territory to Austria, iv. 576
France's boundaries with, vii. 143
French negotiations with, iii. 230, 231
galleys of, at Leghorn, iii. 82
Gorsegno secretary of state of, iv. 386
grain not to be sent by, to Italy, till French and Spanish wants are filled, vii. 430
Mathews gets diamond-studded sword from, ii. 370
Oiseau escapes to a port in, v. 292
Spain fails to bribe, i. 145
Spain said to be making family compact with, vii. 465
Viry conspires to become prime minister of, viii. 328n
See also Turin: court of

Sardonyx:
pocket-book of, i. 222, 414

Sarmiento de Acuña, Diego (1567–1626), Conde de Gondomar; Spanish ambassador to England 1613–22:
Wall resembles, iv. 51–2

Sarrazin, Mme. *See* Vignolles, Maria Carlotta de

Sarrazin, Maria, m. Joseph-Claude de Juvrecourt:
husband of, i. **193n**
Mann may profit by Richecourt's friendship with, iii. 452
(?) mother to be cared for by, ii. 361
Orford, Cts of, may be supplanted by, in Richecourt's affections, iii. 452, 457

Sarti, Matteo, Florentine messenger:
Mann sends to England, with dispatches, viii. 443, 457

Sartine, Antoine-Raimond-Jean-Gualbert-Gabriel de (1729–1801), Comte d'Alby; lieutenant-general of police; minister of marine:

Brest visited by, to make Spanish admiral give precedence to French, viii. 528

Conti searched by, at the Temple, vii. 453

Sartorogo. *See* Saratoga

Sarzana:

Spaniards threaten, ii. 314

Sash:

black, Ferrers pinioned with, at execution, v. 402

Lippe-Bückeburg tears, from cowardly Portuguese general, vi. 94

Sassi, banker:

Agdollo's creditor, i. 148–9

Sassoferrato. *See* Salvi, Giovanni Battista

Sassoferrato:

town of, i. 94

Sassuolo, Francis III's villa:

Francis III reoccupies, iii. 30

Hercules of Modena confined at, vi. 171

Modena, P. and Ps of, visit, i. 489

Modenese court moves to, i. 425

Sas van Ghent:

French besiege, iii. 389

Satan:

Devil's name, as priest, viii. 71

Suares, Mme, 'bowed of,' iii. 226

Satin:

hangings based on ground of, v. 468

uniforms of, for *calcio* players at Leghorn, vi. 423

white: Chudleigh, Miss, has wedding gown of, vii. 93; Kingston, Ds of, has her attendants wear, at her trial, viii. 199

Satire; satires:

Mann's reflections on, vi. 272

modern, has no sting, viii. 62

on Conclave, *see under* Conclave

on Sir Robert Walpole, *see* Miller, James: *Are These Things So?*

Satires of Dr Donne Versified. See under Pope, Alexander

Saturday:

House of Commons may have sessions on, i. 247

Sauce:

'au bleu,' for large fish, iv. 228

Sauceboat; sauceboats:

Mann to buy, ii. 472

melted butter served in, vi. 105

of Chelsea china, vi. 122

Seymour, Lady Frances, orders, in vast numbers, iv. 183

Saucers:

for basins of Chelsea china, vi. 180

Saufterre. *See* Sauveterre

Saunders, Mr ——:

family deeds of, to be carried from Florence to England by courier, ix. 204

Saunders, Sir Charles (ca 1713–75), Rear-Adm., 1756; Vice-Adm., 1759; Adm., 1770; K.B.; M.P.:

Cadiz attack said to be planned by, vi. 12

death of, viii. 149

Dick told by, in letter, of possible visit, vi. 507

Egmont succeeded by, in Admiralty, vi. 449

French fleet to have been attacked by, vii. 475

Hawke followed by, in battle of Quiberon Bay, v. 351

—— succeeds, as first lord of Admiralty, vi. 471–2

Leghorn governor expects to receive, v. 507

made admiral, iv. **561–2**

Mann must get, to defeat French and Spanish fleets, vi. 48

—— receives letter from, promising English naval strength in Mediterranean, v. 97

mission of, to Gibraltar to punish Byng and West, iv. 561–2

near Cartagena, v. 197

resigns as first lord of the Admiralty, vi. 471

taciturn, viii. 149n

Toulon fleet pursued by, from Malta towards the Levant, v. 431

Saunders, Mrs Thomas. *See* Pitt, Christian

Saunderson, Edward (d. ?1755), High Sheriff of Surrey, 1752:

Richmond Park ticket refused by, iv. 322

Saunderson. *See also* Sanderson

Sausage, Bologna:

HW not to receive, ii. 386

Sauveterre, Mme. *See* Paganini, Rosa

Sauveterre ('Saufterre'; 'Sauvter'), Francesco; dancer:

Bologna performances of, i. **463**

dances, in Florentine theatre, ii. 303, 322, 361, iii. 355–6, 439

may come to Florence, i. 463

of French royal blood, ii. 303, iii. 355

Savannah, Georgia:

Estaing repulsed at, viii. 544, ix. 1

Savannerola. *See* Savonarola

Savelli, Barbara (ca 1750–1826), m. (1765) Francesco Camillo Massimo, Marchese di Roccasecca:

Santini and Mann entertain, vii. 229

Savile, Lady Dorothy (1699–1758), m. (1721) Richard Boyle, 3d E. of Burlington:

Euston quarrels with, i. **174**, ii. 482

Garrick, Mrs, may have been spoiled by, vi. 180

—— may receive fortune from, iv. 74

Hartington son-in-law of, iv. 74n

inscription by, on engravings of her portrait of her daughter, ii. 482

Pope's conversation with, at Chiswick, ii. 449

Savile, Sir George (1726–84), 8th Bt; M.P.:

chariot of, demolished, ix. 54

George III's pension list demanded by, to humour Yorkshire committee, ix. 18

House of Commons attacked by, vii. **169**–70, 184, 289, 291

[Savile, Sir George, *continued*]
witticism by, on Shelburne and C.J. Fox being wounded in their groins, ix. 37
Savile, Sir John (1719–78), K.B., 1749; cr. (1753) Vct Pollington, (1766) E. of Mexborough; M.P.:
Bath ribbon awarded to, iv. 40
Savoir vivre, club:
Lyttelton the leader of, viii. 103
masquerades and gambling of, viii. 103
Savona:
bark from, reaches Leghorn, iii. 434
Brown to receive captured cannon from, iii. 353, 358
Charles Emmanuel III captures, iii. 352
—— to besiege, iii. 313
Cooper bombards, iii. 81
Della Rocca to attack, iii. 344–5
French fail to surprise, iii. 476
governor of, sinks powder-laden bark, iii. 81
Jesuits in disguise rejected by, vi. 546
Maillebois may be attacked from, iii. 237
Young Pretender at, ii. 385
Savonarola, Girolamo Maria Francesco Matteo (1452–98), reformer:
medal struck in time of, v. 201
Savorgio. *See* Saorgio
Savoy, D. of. *See* Victor Amadeus II (1666–1732); Victor Amadeus III (1726–96)
Savoy:
Charles Emmanuel III to expel Don Philip from, ii. 65
Corsicans hate people of, iii. 171
Cours de l'Europe satirizes, i. 177
duke of, may be preceded by Richecourt, iv. 295
French may join Don Philip in, ii. 295
Philip, Don, invades, enraging Charles Emmanuel III, ii. 58–9
—— may retire to, ii. 513
—— no longer rules, ii. 95
Spain plunders, iii. 505
Spaniards from, awaited by D. of Modena, ii. 322
Spanish campaign in, will decide plans of Neapolitan Court, ii. 302
Sawbridge, Catherine (1731–91), m. 1 (1760) George Macaulay; m. 2 (1778) William Graham:
Burke's pamphlet attacked by, vii. 209
faction's 'brood-hen,' vii. 145
HW and Duc de la Rochefoucauld to dine with, vii. 92
Observations on a Pamphlet entitled Thoughts on the Cause of the Present Discontents, Burke attacked in, vii. 209
Paoli's English visit not blighted by, vii. 150
Sawbridge, John (1732–95), alderman, lord mayor, and sheriff of London; M.P.:
dying, vii. 263–4
George III disrespectfully treated by, vii. 196

London remonstrance avowed by, vii. 198
weavers pacified by, vii. 163
Sawdust:
scaffold sprinkled with, iii. 301
Sawyer, Edmund (ca 1687–1759), Master in Chancery:
fire at chambers of, iv. 321
Sawyer, Herbert (ca 1731–98), Capt., 1758; later Adm.:
Hermione captured by, vi. 44–5
Sawyers:
mob of, rises in London, vii. 21
Saxe, Hermann-Maurice (1696–1750), Comte de; Maréchal de France:
Aix treaty probably facilitated by fear of, of losing power, iii. 482–3
Belle-Isle's death does not distress, iii. 429
Cumberland, D. of, sends Sackville to, about Maestricht siege, iii. 481
death of: expected, iii. 39; helps England's chances, iv. 506
English army outnumbers that of, ii. 496
English army prevents, from preventing P. Charles's expulsion of Frederick II from Bohemia, ii. 526
English army to attack, ii. 481
France needs, to resist English invasion, v. 211
French invasion of England to be led by, ii. 402
print of, iii. 395–6
sieges started by, iii. 395
tapped three times since Fontenoy, iii. 91
Saxe-Gotha, Ds of. *See* Charlotte (1751–1827) of Saxe-Meiningen
Saxe-Gotha, D. and P. of. *See* Ernst (1745–1804); Friedrich III (1699–1772)
Saxe-Gotha, P. of. *See* August (1747–1806)
Saxe-Hildburghausen, Ds of. *See* Luise (1726–56) of Denmark
Saxe-Hildburghausen, Wilhelm (1702–87), D. of; Austrian field marshal:
Tesi's affair with, v. 194
Saxe-Teschen, Ds of. *See* Maria-Christine (1742–98)
Saxe-Teschen, D. of. *See* Albert (1738–1822)
Saxe-Weimar, Ds of. *See* Anna Amalie
Saxe-Weissenfels, D. of. *See* Johann Adolf II
Saxon china. *See under* China
Saxons:
Mann meets, in Florence, iv. 327
Saxony, Elector of. *See* Frederick Augustus II (1696–1763); Friedrich Christian (1722–63)
Saxony, Electress of. *See* Maria Antoinette (1724–80)
Saxony, Q. of. *See* Maria Theresa (1767–1827)
Saxony:
army of: Frederick II defeats, iii. 189; Hessians oppose, vi. 60; may join English, iii. 240, 255; surrenders to Frederick II, v. 14–15
bishoprics may be obtained by, vi. 119

Bohemian areas adjacent to, retained by Frederick II, v. 116
England's treaty with, iv. 299
Frederick II discovers treachery of, by bribing Menzel to copy Brühl's dispatches, v. 5
—— loses, v. 332
——'s alleged alliance with, viii. 389
—— should not pause in, v. 2
Frederick Augustus II allows no French provisions to cross, ii. 108
—— cuts off Maillebois's escape through, ii. 89
Ginori imports workmen from, to make china, ii. 184
HW imagines Frederick II bouncing into, ix. 190
Maria Theresa's alliance with, v. 564
ministers from and to, see under Minister
paste of, excels all other for porcelain, ix. 635
prime minister of, see Brühl
Prussian-Russian battle expected in, v. 72
Say, Charles Green (d. 1775), printer:
French officers threaten, vii. 231
Saye and Sele, barony of:
descent of barony of Clinton compared to that of, ix. 165
Sayre ('Sayer'), Stephen (1736–1818); sheriff of London, 1773:
arrest and former career of, viii. 138–9
Sbirri:
Benedict XIV's, ii. 56
Del Monte arrested by, at Cortona, iv. 422
—— pursued by, in Castello, iv. 442
Dumesnil (Alessandro)'s valet arrested by, i. 225
Dumesnil, Joseph, detained by, iii. 493
Florentine children whipped by, for taunts against Richecourt, v. 85
foreign ministers in Italy do not allow, in streets near their embassies, ii. 467n
Gavi's house searched by, i. 217, 223
Mann complains about, to Richecourt, ii. 467
Mary's effects inventoried by, i. 102
Pepi arrested by, i. 136–7
prohibited weapons seized by, from suspicious characters at night, i. 136
Richecourt's, obey his orders on St John's Day, iii. 8
satire on the Conclave sought by, at printers', viii. 70
sentenced to the galleys, after quarrel with grenadiers, viii. 8–9
Serchio river to be diverted by, iv. 514
See also 'Bargellos'
Scaffold; scaffolds:
collapse of, at Lovat's execution, iii. 386
for the Battle of the Bridge at Pisa, viii. 188
for execution of rebel lords, iii. 299–302
for Ferrers's execution, v. 402
for fireworks celebration, iv. 47
for seeing cocchiata, at Florence, vi. 158
hammering of, keeps HW awake on night before Coronation, v. 534
workmen fall off, at Kew, iv. 240
Scagliola:
box of pictures in, sent to Strafford, i. 396, ii. 13
HW orders tables of, for friend, iii. 414, 423, 427, 430, 510, iv. 23, 26–7, 37, 88, 93
HW's own table of: finished, ii. 87, 106; HW receives, ii. 291, 292; HW thanks Mann for his trouble in getting, (?)i. 24, ii. 105; HW to have, i. 36, 41, 58, 123, 482, 214; HW wants two more of, iv. 88, 93; Hugford begins, i. 58; Mann to send, ii. 152; price of, ii. 87, 106; spoiled, i. 199–200, 482
Hugford makes, iii. 430n
—— no longer makes, iv. 93
——'s pupils slow at making, iii. 423, iv. 93
tables of: made for Leeson, iii. 423; Mann's, take four years, iv. 93
Scaligero, Giulio Cesare (1484–1558), scholar and controversialist:
Grattan and Flood imitate acrimony of, ix. 438
Scaling-ladder; scaling-ladders:
British sailor boards Spanish ship with, viii. 543
Carlisle assaulted with, iii. 165
Scalping:
heroes would shrink from, v. 290
Scamozzi, Vincenzo (1552–1616), architect:
L'idea dell' architettura by, (?) bought by HW, x. 5
Scaramouches:
at Ranelagh jubilee-masquerade, iv. 47
Scarborough:
Palliser's removal as governor of, asked, viii. 446
visitors to: Pelham, Henry, iv. 413; Shirley, iv. 439
See also Scarbrough
Scarbrough, E. of. See Lumley, Richard (ca 1688–1740); Lumley-Saunderson, Richard (1725–82); Lumley-Saunderson, Thomas
Scarlatti, Alessandro (ca 1659–1725), composer:
Arminio in Germania by, i. 80
Scarlatti, Giovanna Barbera (1723–46), nun:
Craon attends vestimento of, i. 53
Scarlatti, Pompeo (fl. 1742–4), Imperial minister to Rome:
Old Pretender often sees, ii. 397
Scarlatti-Rondinelli, Elena Vittoria (ca 1728–82), m. (1740) Marchese Antonio Francesco Ximenes d'Aragona:
Mann intimate with, vii. 25
Scarlet fever:
drinking and rioting occasion, viii. 498
occurrences of, ii. 430, 431, 444, viii. 498
Scarlett, Edward, jun., optician:
(?) HW buys spectacles from, v. 131

Scarniccia, Capt. Pascal:
Malborough Fort commanded by, ix. 198
Mann commissions, ix. 249
(?) Mann receives news from, of Algiers, ix. 416
Scarperia:
Vitelli, Mme, and Mme and Ball Suares attend dinner at, in honour of Modenese princess, i. 56
Scarpi, Paolo (1552–1623), Venetian theologian:
Venice anti-papal since time of, vii. 56
Scarsdale, Bn. *See* Curzon, Sir Nathaniel (1727–1804)
Sceau:
French wounded left at, iii. 427
Sceptres:
kings and emperors must abandon, to others as actors abandon their stage properties, ix. 552
Schaffgotsch, Philipp Gotthard, Graf von (1716–95), Bp of Breslau 1748–95:
Frederick II's letter to, about Hungarian Protestants, iv. 269
Schairner, Col. (d. 1743):
killed at Campo Santo, ii. 164
Schaub, Lady. *See* Ligonier du Buisson, Marguerite de (d. 1793)
Schaub, Sir Luke (1690–1758), Kt, 1720; diplomatist:
auction of, v. 199–200
Frederick, P. of Wales, makes offer to, for pictures, v. 200
Houghton collection should bring three times as much as collection of, v. 208
remark by, on wife, i. 181
Spanish pictures cheaply bought by, v. 199–200
Schelde. *See* Scheldt
Scheldt ('Schelda;' 'Schelde'), river:
English army crosses, ii. 481
English make bridges across, ii. 448
Joseph II's quarrel with Holland over navigation of, ix. 530n, 543–4, 554
Pisa's Battle of the Bridge preferable to invasion of, ix. 583
Tuscany must be interested in, through Austrian connections, ix. 544
Schio, near Valdagno:
visitors to, Mann, Horace II, and Lady Lucy, viii. 122
Schleswig-Holstein-Augustenburg, Ds of. *See* Louisa Augusta (1771–1843) of Denmark
Schmeling, Gertrud Elisabeth (1749–1833), m. J. Mara; singer:
HW hears, at Westminster Abbey in Handel Jubilee rehearsal, ix. 648
not so much in fashion, ix. 648
Schmettau, Karl Christoph (1696–1775), Graf von; Prussian Lt-Gen.:
Dresden suburbs burned by, v. 257–8
Schomberg, Isaac (1714–80), physician:
Kingston, Ds of, subject of testimony by, at House of Lords, viii. 151

'School of Athens.' *See under* Raffaello Sanzio
Schooner:
news of Pigot's having taken, should not have been put in gazette, ix. 318
Schoppe, Kaspar (1576–1649), called Scioppius, Roman Catholic controversialist:
Grattan and Flood imitate acrimony of, ix. 438
Schoualoff; Schouvalow. *See* Shuvalov
Schröder, ——, George II's valet-de-chambre:
George II's death discovered by, v. 443
Schroeder, William; Hanoverian soldier:
arrest of, v. 12, 34
Schualow. *See* Shuvalov
Schulembourg. *See* Schulenburg
Schulenburg, Ermengarde Melusina (1667–1743), Bns von der, cr. (1716) Ds of Munster, (1719) Ds of Kendal; George I's mistress:
Bolingbroke favoured by, iv. 455
Chesterfield inherits nothing from, ii. 231
death of, ii. 231
George I said to be younger than, ii. 231
——'s drinking to be prevented by, iv. 455
——'s mistress, ix. 248n
HW sees George I going to supper with, ix. 248
nephew of, iii. 64
'niece' of, ii. 231, viii. 283n, 412n, ix. 248n
St John buys Custom House place from, iv. 18
Walpole, Sir Robert, hated by, iv. 455
wealth of, ii. 231
Yarmouth, Cts of, the counterpart of, iii. 419
Schulenburg, Georg Ludwig (d. 1759), Graf von Oynhausen; army officer:
brother sends, on embassy, iii. 64
Schulenburg, Ludwig Ferdinand (1700–54), Graf von Schulenburg und Oynhausen; Gen.:
army command assumed by, iii. 47
army command refused by, from dislike of Pallavicini, iii. 50–1
brother of, sent on embassy, iii. 64
Brown succeeds, in army command, iii. 393
Charles Emmanuel III grants requests of, iii. 367
(?) Estevenon accompanied by, to Florence, i. 200
(?) Faiola reconnoitred by, ii. 530–1
fall of, from horse, iii. 393
Gages deludes, into defending Milan, iii. 119
Genoa approached by army of, iii. 384
Genoa to be reduced by, iii. 367
Genoese message to, iii. 65
Genoese must be intimidated by, iii. 363
Lobkowitz replaced by, iii. 41, 50, 55, 58
Lomellini's letter denying entrance to, iii. 67
Medley to assist, against Genoa, iii. 384
Novi the station of, iii. 58

Spanish invalids will embarrass, iii. 55

Venice and Vienna visited by, iii. 50

Schulenburg, Petronille Melusine de (1693–1778), m. (1733) Philip Dormer Stanhope, 4th E. of Chesterfield; she was cr. (1722) Cts of Walsingham; s.j.:

'aunt' of, ii. 231n, viii. 283n, 412n, ix. 248n

death of, viii. 412

George I came over with, when she was not young, viii. 412

—— creates, Cts of Walsingham, viii. 412n

HW taken by, to kiss George I's hand, ix. 248

health of, stroke of palsy, viii. 283

mother of, dies, ii. 231

St-Germain intimate with, x. 21

Schulenburg-Oynhausen, Margarete Gertrud von (1698–1726), m. (1721) Albert Wolfgang, Graf von Lippe-Bückeburg:

son of, vi. 43n

Schuma. See Shulma

Schutz, Augustus (1690–1757), Baron of the Holy Roman Empire; Master of the Robes to George II:

Carteret said to leave, with George II to play cards with Cts of Delorain, ii. 82

(?) Lorenzi mistakes, for Chute, iv. 89

Schutz, George Augustus (1722–49), page:

(?) HW's letters conveyed by, to England, iv. 15, 23, 54, x. 36

(?) puny, iv. 15, 23

(?) St John, Vcts, escorted by, iv. 15, 23

Schutz, George Frederick (1724–1802):

George III's groom, iv. 247

(?) HW's letters conveyed by, to England, iv. 15, 23, 54, x. 36

(?) puny, iv. 15, 23

(?) St John, Vcts, escorted by, iv. 15, 23

Schuwalof. See Shuvalov

Schwartzenberg, Johann Nepomuk (1742–89), Prinz von; chamberlain:

Clement XIII thanked by, vii. 23

Schweidnitz:

Frederick II captures, v. 198, vi. 87

—— gets between Daun and, vi. 60

—— loses, vi. 544

—— said to have captured, v. 166

garrison of, defends itself with honour, vi. 87

Schwellenberg (or Schwellenbergen), Elizabeth Juliana (ca 1728–97), keeper of the Robes to Q. Charlotte:

Charlotte accompanied by, v. 530

Schwerin, Kurd Christoph (1684–1757), Graf von; Prussian general:

death of, v. 92, 95

Schwichelt, Ernst Otto (d. 1750), Baron von:

Frechapelle kills, in duel, iv. 184

Science:

HW implies that greed is the real motive of, ix. 545

HW's ignorance of, v. 368

Orford, Cts of, 'flings herself into arms of,' ix. 121

tediousness of, HW's reflections on, iv. 555

Scientific discoveries:

HW's reflections on, iv. 292

Scilla città:

earthquake account mentions, ix. 376

Scilly:

combined fleet appears off, ix. 182

Scimitar:

Mogul, through Clive, gives, to George III, vi. 540

Scio. See Chios

Scione:

harbour of, scene of Russo-Turkish naval battle, vii. 233

Scioppius. See Schoppe, Kaspar

Scipio, Publius Cornelius (?234–183 B.C.), 'Africanus':

breeches of, continent, viii. 426

Clodius must be discussed for want of, vii. 499

HW recommends good breeding of, ii. 518

military career of, unhampered by financial intrigues, v. 559

Roman enamellers might eclipse, v. 313

statues of, in Pomfret Collection, iv. 390

Scipione in Cartagine. See under Buranello; Galuppi, Baldassare

Scipioni, ——, Corsican murderer:

escape of, iv. 206

Scissors:

gold: Mann tells Lincoln to buy, at La Frenaye's, i. 99; ordered by Lincoln through HW and Mann in care of Charles Selwin, i. 93

mercer pretends not to have, viii. 153–4

street-criers advertise, v. 154

Sclavonians. See Slavonians

Sconces:

Electress leaves, to Rinuccini, ii. 169

Scot; Scots:

avarice of, HW hints at, v. 87

banknotes circulated by, vii. 418–19

Bute does not dare to promote, vi. 295

Danish and Russian fleets to be commanded by, ix. 60

Earle satirizes, i. 243

English enslavement planned by, viii. 448–9

English newspapers attack, vii. 419

Fox hated by, iv. 412

Gordon, Lord George, would have been martyrized by, ix. 131

Hamilton's marriage enrages, iv. 303

Junius papers attack, vii. 247–8

migrate to London and America, vii. 569

second sight of, purblind, viii. 356

Stormont will be disliked for being, viii. 526

Walpole, Sir Robert, to be defended by, i. 338

Scotland, Primate of, titular. See Macdonald, Hugh (1701–73)

Scotland, Q. of. *See* Mary (Stuart) (1542–87)
Scotland:
accounts of rebels' success in: printed at Rome, iii. 158; vary, iii. 108
ambassadors from and to, *see under* Ambassador
American independence caused by people of, viii. 378
American privateers infest coast of, viii. 315, 377–8
Anstruther unpopular in, iv. 230
Argyll's death leaves Bute the chief power in, v. 527n
——'s plan for colonizing forfeited estates in, iv. 310
bankers of, remit bills and draw cash from England, vii. 418–19
banks of, fail, vii. 418–19, 498
Belle-île no better than islands off coast of, v. 505
bills for control of, endangered in Parliament, iii. 388–9, 396, iv. 310–11
Brest fleet said to approach, ii. 404
Bute shows no favouritism to people of, v. 465
Cameron arrested in, iv. 373
Carlisle boasts of its superiority to, iii. 165
clans of: do not support George II, iii. 102; urged to revolt, ii. 402–3
(?) Common Council to summon members from, i. 329
Conway not prevented from going to, with D. of Cumberland, iii. 204
Corsican rebels swifter than those in, iii. 162
counties in, send petitions, vii. 151
Crawford was premier earl of, iv. 109–10n
Cumberland, D. of, hated by, iii. 288
—— may go to, iii. 193
——'s baggage returned from, iii. 242
——'s conduct in, investigated by Lyttelton, iv. 240
——'s return from, awaited, iii. 271
——'s stay in, prolonged, iii. 228
—— takes Fawkener to, as secretary, iii. 382n
—— to pacify, iii. 205, 257
Drummond, Lord John, reaches, iii. 187
—— said to escape from, iii. 270
Dutch troops to land in, iii. 103, 109
elections in, i. 294, x. 32–3
emigration from, to London and America, vii. 569
emissaries from, at Rome, i. 145
England, if armed, might have speedily crushed rebellion in, iii. 130
England said to be betrayed by Cornwall and, i. 346
English civil wars caused by, viii. 124
English prisoners in, released, iii. 204
English settlement in, proposed, x. 31–3
English severity said to have enraged, iii. 399–400

English union with, may be broken, i. 159, 160, 202, ix. 280, 310
English weather might make, more Arcadian, v. 267
Fitzjames captured on ship bound for, iii. 222
——'s regiment, to go to, iii. 208–9
Forbes from, vi. 162
Fordyce from, vii. 418
forfeited estates in: mortgaged, x. 31–3; restored, ix. 520; to be purchased, iv. 310
'45' has a different meaning for, than for Wilkes, vii. 30
France might recruit secret agents from, iv. 491
France said to have sent Irish regiment to, iii. 170
French expedition may be sailing to, v. 315
French fleet may attack, iii. 261
French invasion of, indicated by Don Giuseppe, iii. 85
French invasion said to be encouraged by, ii. 415
French will use troops from, iv. 508
gentlemen from, at Vienna, iii. 290
George II might give up, to keep Hanover, i. 202
—— would be joined by clans of, if his army were strong, iii. 130
Gordon, Lord George, might have started revolt in, ix. 64
Grosett from, ix. 410
HW denounces, as hotbed of traitors, ix. 62
Hawley condemned by jury of, iii. 241
—— sent to, with Wade's army, as military magistrate, iii. 193
heart of, unsafe for English messenger, iii. 247
Hessians to be sent to, iii. 188, 205
Highland chiefs of: Lovat's execution, an example to, iii. 386, 399; Scotch bills to humble, iii. 388–9
Highlanders of: *Caledonian Mercury*'s term for rebels, iii. 107; Carleton's, said to be cut to pieces by Montgomery, viii. 156; Charles II not accompanied by, to Worcester, iii. 107; Corsicans differ from, iii. 157; Edinburgh Castle garrison captures, iii. 133; must not suspect that Young Pretender is not in Scotland, iii. 198; not likely again to invade England, iii. 188; not to be defeated by unbuilt navy, iii. 168; Seaforth's, repel Jersey attack, viii. 472n; well trained by system of rotation, iii. 116; Young Pretender may not be followed by, to England, iii. 107, 137; Young Pretender's speeches to, iii. 170
Highlands of: colonization attempts in, x. 31–3; rebels may retreat to, iii. 137; regiment from, mutinies, ii. 236–7
Jacobite estates in: might be forfeited, iii.

247; mortgaged, x. 31–3; restored, ix. 520; to be purchased, iv. 310

Jacobites from: always provoke civil wars in England, viii. 124; betrayed, vii. 338; persuade Old Pretender that English union with, may be broken, i. 145, 159; restored to forfeited estates, ix. 520; said to have encouraged Louis XV, ii. 426

Keith may invade, iii. 261

Keppel, Laura, and Hon. George Fitzroy elope to, ix. 508

Kirk of, Charles II lectured by, on eve of battle of Worcester, vii. 386

Lorn in, vii. 7

Loudoun beats rebels in north of, iii. 153

Lovat's body not sent to, iii. 386

Mansfield's origins in, a disadvantage, iv. 412

marches of, London as lawless as, ix. 619–20

Marchmont had position in, iv. 5

mountains of, to be patrolled, iv. 35

Nairne from, ix. 536

nobility of: form theatre, iii. 468; to be humbled by Hawley, iii. 201

Old Pretender receives emissaries from, i. 145, 159

Parliamentary members from: criticize Lestock and Mathews, iii. 25; take refuge in Sir Robert Walpole's house, i. 496

peers of, HW considers, 'household troops,' in House of Lords, ix. 368; in danger of bankruptcy, vii. 426; oppose Turnpike Bill, iv. 124; to raise regiments in London, iii. 167–8

Porteous affair in, iv. 230

Presbyterians of: forswear the Pope, viii. 475; Gordon leads, against Roman Catholics, ix. 11

Pretenders may be joined by, i. 160

privateers captured on way to, iii. 173

Privy seal of: Stuart-Mackenzie restored as keeper of, vi. 444, 453; to appoint commissioners for colonization, x. 33

rebel clans of, unite to capture Inverness, iii. 221

rebellion in: may be prolonged, iii. 188, 228; may divert troops from Flanders, iii. 222; possible, ii. 237; precautions against, x. 31–3

rebels in, no more remote than Charles Emmanuel III's camp, iii. 190

rebels may retreat to, iii. 179

rebels may wait in, for French support, iii. 117

rebels on defensive in, iii. 201

rebels said to be about to recapture, iii. 235

regiment from, mutinies at Portsmouth, ix. 362

representative peer of, Marchmont to succeed Crawford as, iv. 110–11

Roman Catholicism not to be tolerated in, viii. 439, x. 33

Roman Catholics in, said to encourage French invasion, ii. 415

Rutherfurd of old family in, viii. 453

secretary from, may not be liked in Ireland, vi. 549

Sinclair from, iii. 456

soldier from, finds glove and meets Selwyn, ii. 524

Spanish ships leave for, iii. 134, 137–8

Stair to visit, ii. 494

Stone deals with place-seekers from, iv. 366

Stormont may have post in, viii. 179

——'s character will be forgotten since he is from, viii. 526

taxes not paid by, iv. 311

Thurot hovers over coast of, v. 352

——'s fleet destined for, v. 328

Townshend may raise regiment in, ii. 566

Tweeddale resigns as secretary of state for, iii. 195

—— secretary of state for, iv. 209

—— upholders of, to be defeated in national points, iv. 100

Wade to advance on, from Doncaster, iii. 137

Walpole, Sir Robert, overthrown by votes from, i. 346n

Wilkes hated by people of, vi. 189, vii. 6, 99, 317n

William III and Hamilton discuss, iii. 103

Young Pretender calls a Parliament in, iii. 118

—— joined by few people in, iii. 104

—— may go to, ii. 373, 375, 378–9, iv. 35

—— may wait in, for French support, iii. 117

—— said not really to be in, iii. 140–1, 172, 174, 198–9, 205, 227

—— said to be still in, iii. 270, 311

—— said to have escaped from, iii. 269–70

—— said to invade, iii. 85, 86–90, 93, 95, 96, 98, 99, 112

——'s flight from, reported, iii. 213–14

——'s projects with, not laid aside, i. 202

—— threatens to confiscate estates in, of loyal M.P.s, iii. 138

—— unlikely to invade, again, iv. 35

—— will conquer, iii. 103

Scott, Arthur (1718–56), Capt.:
Mann not readily obeyed by, ii. 507

——'s permission awaited by, ii. 453

Rome visited by, ii. 461

Scott, Lord Charles (1727–47):
death of, iv. 138

Oxford servant's death attributed to, iii. 387

Scott, Lady Frances (1750–1817), m. (1783) Archibald James Edward Douglas, cr. (1790) Bn Douglas:
birth of, iv. 138

Scott, Francis (1695–1751), 2d D. of Buccleuch:
  rebels camp at park of, iii. 152
  son of, iii. 468n, iv. 137n
Scott, Francis (1721–50), styled E. of Dal-
keith:
  Argyll refuses to sign marriage articles of,
    i. 479–**80n**
  death of, iv. 137
  smallpox fatal to family and, iv. 137–8
  wife of, iii. 468n
Scott, George Lewis (1708–80):
  Bolingbroke recommends, as George III's
    under-preceptor, iv. **203**, 344
  George III's sub-preceptor, iv. 246, 344
  Harcourt refuses to act with, iv. 343
  Hayter and Harcourt oppose, over George
    III's tutorship, iv. 323
Scott, Lady Isabella (d. 1748):
  Orford, Cts of, writes to, iii. 61
Scott, James (1649–85), D. of Monmouth and
Buccleuch:
  descendants of, to attend Ds of Bucking-
    ham's funeral, ii. 203
Scott, Rev. James (1733–1814), 'Anti-Sejanus;'
D.D.:
  hooted off the stage with Sandwich, vi. 410
Scott, John (1745–9), styled Lord Whit-
chester or Bn Scott of Whitchester:
  death of, iv. 137
Scott, Marjory (d. 1746), m. (1688) David
Murray, 5th Vct Stormont:
  Jacobites aided by, at Perth, iii. 283
Scott, Samuel (1710–72), artist:
  Marlow a pupil of, vii. 299
  seapiece by, iv. 38
Scotti, Costanza (ca 1736–94), m. (1756) Ales-
sandro Sanvitale:
  Mann to entertain, in garden, vi. 45
  Strathmore's affair with, vi. 45, 69, 88,
    145
Scott-Montagu, Mrs. See Douglas, Jane
Margaret
Scrafton, Luke (1732–?70), East India Com-
pany Official:
  ship of, lost, vii. 282
Screen: screens:
  Chinese, iv. 191, 193
  in HW's exchequer chest, vii. 285
  linen, taken by Princesse de Craon to
    opera, iii. 357
Scrine. See Skrine
Scrofula:
  Fitzgeralds said to have, iii. 241–2
  HW says that kings are the evil that they
    pretend to cure, ix. 423
  Romans believe that Old Pretender is last
    king of England who can cure, v. 392
  royal bastards may claim ability to heal,
    iii. 241
Scroll:
  dirty, Mann receives invitation in, ii. 113
Scrope, Mrs. See Long, Emma

Scrope, John (ca 1662–1752), judge; M.P.:
  death of, i. 458n
  George II and Sir Robert Walpole not to
    be betrayed by, i. 459
  Holland visited by, in disguise, i. 457n
  Monmouth's rebellion participated in by,
    i. 457n
  nephew's Treasury clerkship said by *Lon-
    don Evening Post* to be reward of silence
    of, before Secret Committee, ii. 33
  Perry and Pitt almost fought by, i. 458
  Pulteney examines, i. 458
  Rushout and Sandys defend, i. 467
  secretary to the Treasury, i. 457n, 467
  Secret Committee drops investigation of, i.
    467
  Secret Committee examines, i. **457–9**
  Tower not dreaded by, i. 458–9
Scrutiny:
  of Westminster election, iv. 108, 112–13,
    122–3, 223–4, ix. 565
Scrutore; scrutores:
  gentleman's, robbed while owner was with
    maid in garret, iv. 215
  Mann's, HW's letter lies unanswered in,
    ix. 429
  Volterra vases to adorn, i. 394–5
Scudamore, Charles. See Fitzroy, Charles (ca
  1707–82)
Scudamore, Hon. Frances (1711–50), m. 1
  (1729) Henry Somerset, 3d D. of Beaufort
  (divorced, 1744); m. 2 Charles Fitzroy:
  divorce of, i. 452–3, ii. 185, 199
  Fitzroy weds, i. 452n
  silver lace on gown of, i. 453
  Talbot's adultery with, i. 452n, 453, 486,
    ii. 199
Scudamore, James (ca 1678–1716), 3d Vct
Scudamore:
  daughter of, i. 452n
Scudéry, Madeleine de (1607–1701), novelist:
  Anson's sea-piece worthy of, iv. 38
  Artamène, ou le grand Cyrus, HW re-
    minded of, ii. **69**
  Clélie, old gentlewomen study no map
    but that of *tendre* in, ix. 530
  Ibraham, ou l'illustre Bassa, HW re-
    minded of, ii. 69
Scudo; scude:
  Florentine currency, ii. 348
Scully, ———, Irish tailor at Florence 1741–3:
  English naval captain lodges with Bos-
    villes to avoid expense of renting another
    room from, ii. 251
  English people lodge with, at Florence, i.
    450n
  house of, near Mann's, may receive over-
    flow of guests, ii. 212
  (?) Karl Friedrich lodges with, iv. 149
  Mann said to have persuaded, to take
    large house for Walpole family, i. 426,
    450, ii. 14

Mary's lawsuit with, to be decided by Mann, i. 101–2

Pomfret, Cts of, says that Mann split the fees of, i. 130

—— scolds, i. 102–3

Sculptor:
'drunken' English, at Florence, *see* Harwood, Francis
England has one or two, viii. 93
Florentine, would not understand English heraldry, ix. 227
'little English,' Chute to employ, to buy eagle, iii. 101

Sculpture:
at low ebb in England, iv. 86
Damer, Mrs, has taste and judgment in, ix. 203
—— has talent for, ix. 184
declining taste in, iv. 398
Mann gives Mrs Damer an antique foot, ix. 287
Proctor's prize in, ix. 577

Scurvy:
occurrences of, ii. 86–7, 289, iv. 413, vi. 154, 413, vii. 240, viii. 39
Orford's eruption might be caused by, vii. 460
treatment for, mercurial unctions, ii. 87

Scythes:
(?) HW mentions, iv. 441

Scythian Diana. *See under* Diana

Sea:
consumption thought to be cured by voyage on, viii. 220
English princesses and P. Alfred bathed in, ix. 413
Joseph II anxious to see, vi. 548
See also Ocean

Sea air:
Gloucester, D. of, may go to Bordeaux for, viii. 360
HW helped by, viii. 227, 272, 311, 318, ix. 49
HW recommends, to Mann, viii. 311, ix. 49
Mann glad that HW is helped by, viii. 318

Sea-bathing:
HW now neglects, ix. 49

Sea captain. *See* Captain

Seaford, English ship:
involved in war, iii. 207
sent to the Adriatic, iii. 220, 231, 235

Seaforth, E. of. *See* Mackenzie, Kenneth (1744–81); Mackenzie, William (d. 1740)

Seaforth:
election at, iii. 449
Potter's speech on election at, iii. 449n

Sea Horse, English vessel:
release of, i. 8

Seal; seals (of letters):
by Costanzi, x. 7
'flying,' ix. 176
HW changes, on his letters, i. 421

Mann opens, on Craon's letter to daughter, iv. 55–6
—— replaces Rowley's, which was lost, iii. 9
—— tells HW to put on inside of cover, i. 98
Mann, Galfridus, to have, cut for Mann, iv. 480
medal for Francis I's election under Mann's, iii. 185
on HW's letter, viii. 72
Waldegrave, Cts, gives her late husband's, to his brother, vi. 164

Seal, Privy. *See* Privy Seal

Seal, Tuscany's (official):
Leopold awaits, vi. 356

Seals (of lord chancellor; Great Seal):
De Grey cannot accept, vii. 175
Irish attorney-general thinks, should be set to Irish regency act, ix. 682
Mansfield refuses, vii. 174
must be put into commission, vii. 179
Pulteney refuses, ii. 72
Ryder may be promoted to, iv. 202
to be in commission if not given to a lord keeper, v. 18
Willes, Wilmot and Smythe succeed Hardwicke as commissioners of, vii. 25
Wilmot may receive, vii. 175, 179
Yorke's rejection and acceptance of, vii. 175, 178

Seals (of secretaries of state):
Egremont said to have refused, v. 76
—— said to receive, v. 72, 98
Fox accepts, iv. 502
George II wants Newcastle to resume, v. 76
Granville resigns, ii. 537
Hardwicke refuses, v. 92
Harrington receives, ii. 537
North declines, then accepts them, vi. 552
Pitt kisses hands for, v. 103
—— threatens to reject, v. 30
—— to take, v. 22
Weymouth resigns, vii. 255
See also Secretary of state

Seamen. *See* Sailor; sailors

Search, Right of. *See* Right of Search

Seascape:
painted for Anson, iv. 38

Seashore:
HW may go to, viii. 272

Seasons. See under Thomson, James

Sebastian (1554–78), K. of Portugal 1557–78:
uncle and successor of, ix. 482n

'*Se cerca, se dice*':
Mann's favourite song, in *Olimpiade*, sung by Monticelli, i. 401

Séchelles. *See* Moreau de Séchelles

Sechenov, Daniil Andreievich (1709–67), known as Dimitri; Bp of Nizhni Novgorod and Alatyr, 1742, of Riazan and Murom, 1752; Abp (1757) and Metro-

[Sechenov, Daniil Andreievich, *continued*]
politan (1762) of Novgorod and Velikie Luki:
Catherine II aided by, vi. 64
crimes of, vi. 66

Seckendorf, Friedrich Heinrich (1673–1763), Graf von; marshal:
Austrians fail to capture, ii. 230
Austrians formerly injured, ii. 230
Frederick II arrests, and sends to Magdeburg for giving plan to Vienna for seizure of Dresden and Leipzig, v. 266

Secker, Thomas (1693–1768), Bp of Bristol 1734–7, of Oxford 1737–58; Abp of Canterbury 1758–68:
Augusta, Ps, married by, to Karl Wilhelm Ferdinand, vi. 197
Canterbury archbishopric no longer expected by, iv. 187
death of, vii. 40
Frederick, P. of Wales, may be advised by, i. 451
——'s representative, in dealing with George II, i. 296n
—— talks with, i. 328–9
George II's message to Frederick, P. of Wales, jotted down by, i. **296**
HW satirizes, in verse, iv. 134
hypocrisy of, vii. 43
jesuitical and popish, iv. 133
Oxford bishopric given to, i. 451n
St Paul's deanery wanted by, iv. 187
sermon to be preached by, at St James's, about earthquakes, iv. 155
started as a Presbyterian, iv. 188
women told by, not to flee from London earthquake, iv. 133

Secondat, Charles de (1689–1755), Bn de Montesquieu:
Esprit des lois: Florentine opinion of, iv. 117; HW asks Mann's and Cocchi's opinion of, iv. 107; HW praises, iv. 126
Guasco publisher of letters of, vi. 575
Lettres familières: authenticity of, doubted, vi. 529, 530; Duclos takes, to France in rage, vi. 531; Galliani said to be editor of, vi. 524n; Guasco said to be editor of, vi. 529; HW thanks Mann for, vi. 523–4
satiric print or drawing of, vi. 531

Second courses:
misers should save money by not having, since they are seldom eaten, ix. 609

Secretary:
Almada's, v. 430, 476
Barbantane's, viii. 369
French, at Florence, Mann hears from, about Duc de Chartres, viii. 408–9
HW tells Mann to dictate a few lines to, instead of writing, ix. 602
HW uses, to spare his eyes, viii. 501
HW, when ill, usually employs, for letter-writing, ix. 354
Lorenzi's, replaced, i. 157

Mann dictates common letters to, ix. 585
—— grieved that HW is compelled to use, viii. 513
—— seeks, i. 156–8, 172, 189, 190, 207, 216, 246, 255, 257
——'s, *see* Giberne, Gabriel George; Gregori, Antonio; Palombo, Domenico
—— tells HW to have notes written by, about health when HW is unable to write, ix. 359

Richecourt's, *see* Niccoli

Secretary at War:
Barrington remains as, instead of Sackville, v. 109
—— to be, iv. 502
Fox appointed as, iii. 256
—— remains as, iv. 417
—— urged to remain as, iv. 39
Frederick, P. of Wales, prefers Elizabeth Chudleigh to Pitt as, iii. 175
George II rejects Pitt as, iii. 209, 211
—— rejects Sackville as, v. 109
Pitt covets post of, ii. 552, iii. 168
—— may become, iii. 155, 175
Sackville said to succeed Barrington as, v. 104
Townshend, Charles, replaces Barrington as, v. 490
—— to be, v. 486
Walpole, Sir Robert, was, vi. 26

Secretary at War, French. *See under* Secretary of State, French

Secretary at War, Portuguese:
'Migas Frias' applies to, vii. 166

Secretary at War, Tuscan:
Antinori was, vi. 124

Secretary of state:
aspirants to office of, iv. 461, vi. 159, 161
Barré praises present incumbents in office of, vi. 283
Bedford is, iii. 463
—— to be succeeded by Holdernesse as, iv. 258–9
Bute succeeds Holdernesse as, v. 487
Carmarthen is, ix. 583
changes in office of, iv. 259, 265
Chesterfield resigns as, iii. 463
circular letters by: about D. and Ds of Cumberland, vii. 543; on Grafton's resignation, vii. 190; usually sent to correspondents upon retirement, ix. 299
Conway changes departments in, vi. 427
—— refuses salary as, vi. 559
—— succeeds Halifax as, vi. 309
—— to resign as, vi. 571
—— was, ix. 129, 526
Dartmouth, 1st E. of, served as, under Q. Anne, iv. 208n
Dartmouth, 2d E. of, almost becomes, for America, which might have been separated from southern province, vi. 444
dissension in office of, iv. 38–9
Egmont may become, vi. 159

Egremont may be, v. 72, 75–6, 540, 541
—— might be succeeded as, by Bubb Dodington, vi. 17
Ellis to succeed Sackville as, ix. 241
fashionable to leave one's name with, when newly appointed, vi. 17
Fox, C.J., is, ix. 262, 391, 460
—— resigns seals of office as, ix. 293
Fox, Henry, may become, iv. 502, v. 6, 11
—— refuses to become, because he cannot have control of House of Commons, iv. 417
Gage predicts that Chesterfield and Carteret will be, i. 296
George II usually sees both, at once, iv. 346
—— wants D. of Newcastle to resume seals as, v. 76
Germain's declaration as, viii. 282n
—— succeeds Dartmouth as, for American province, viii. 142
Grafton succeeded by D. of Richmond as, vi. 419–20
—— succeeds Sandwich as, vi. 310
Grantham, 1st and 2d Bns, are, ix. 296n
Granville does not notify Italy of his becoming, iii. 213
—— is to be, i. 296, 333
green velvet bags used by, ii. 225, iv. 346
Grenville, George, becomes, vi. 37
HW implores, not to peek into his mail, vi. 373
Halifax prevents Holdernesse from being, iv. 249
—— succeeds Grenville as, vi. 91
—— succeeds Sandwich as, vii. 268
—— to replace Holdernesse as, iv. 346
Hanoverian soldier delivered from English prison by warrant of, iv. 12
Harrington resigns as, iii. 326
Hillsborough becomes, for America, vi. 569, 571
—— succeeds Weymouth as, viii. 534
—— to resign as, vii. 423
Holdernesse, Pitt, and Robinson are nominees for, iv. 202
Holdernesse becomes, v. 103
—— remains as, for northern province, v. 17
Lyttelton angered by failure to become, viii. 465
Mann hopes for instructions from a new, ix. 299
—— may be affected by changes in department of, iii. 338
—— 's ignorance of identity of, causes delay in letters, ix. 306
Newcastle and Harrington resign as, iii. 211
Newcastle changes provinces as, iii. 463
North and C.J. Fox asked by George III to turn in their seals as, ix. 460
North and C.J. Fox become, ix. 391

North succeeds Charles Townshend as, vi. 552
office of: Gloucester, D. of, to receive packets from, at Genoa, vii. 328; HW brings letter to, vi. 176; HW has barely time to send letter to, at 7 P.M., ix. 467; HW has no time to send letter to, v. 433; HW inquires about Mann's courier at, ix. 228; HW sends letter for Mann to, i. 359, iv. 165, ix. 326; HW sends to, for Mann's servant, ix. 215; HW's letter intercepted on way to, ix. 564; HW's letter to Mann must have stayed a week at, ix. 395; HW's letter to Mann sent through, delayed, ix. 179–80; HW's new footman puts letter in post instead of carrying it to, ix. 118; Larpent to have successor in, vii. 443–4; Mann asks about punctuality of people at, in forwarding letters, vii. 542; Mann sends weekly gazette under blank cover to, viii. 396; Mann still dictates and signs letters to, ix. 660; Mann, Horace II, quarrels with, over salary, ix. 671–3, 674, 675–6, 678; Murray's letter to Mann produced by, as evidence against him, ix. 349; sends Mann a full account of expulsion of Polish nuncio, vi. 192; Sneyd's continuance in, unknown to Mann, ix. 272
Pitt (Chatham) asks D. of Newcastle not to meddle in department of, v. 91
—— becomes, v. 103
—— becomes, for southern province, v. 17
—— does not permit formation of, for West Indies, v. 104
—— may become, iv. 461
—— may succeed Fox as, iv. 12
—— names himself and Charles Townshend for, vi. 161
—— 's designs on, iv. 223, 235
Pitt, William II, reported to become, ix. 295
Robinson becomes, i. 497n, iv. 417
—— may become, iv. 202
—— to be, v. 92
Rochford, acting as, commits Sayre to Tower, viii. 138n
—— becomes, vii. 62
—— becomes, for southern province, vii. 255
—— was, ix. 191n
Sackville's place as, for the colonies, not to be filled, ix. 237
—— 's resignation as, for the colonies, expected, ix. 236, 240–1
Sandwich becomes, vi. 159, 167
—— dismissed as, iv. 258
—— may succeed D. of Bedford as, iv. 217, 235
—— may succeed Suffolk as, viii. 450
—— succeeds Weymouth as, but in northern province, vii. 255
—— to resign as, vii. 263
Shelburne and C.J. Fox become, ix. 262

[Secretary of state, *continued*]

Shelburne becomes, vi. 439, 443, 447, ix. 262

—— may resign as, for America, vi. 569

—— may succeed Sydney as, for Home Affairs, ix. 487

—— remains as, vi. 571, 581

—— wants to be, vi. 159

Stormont succeeds Suffolk as, viii. 525

Suffolk may become, vii. 263

—— may succeed Halifax as, vii. 304, 310

——'s death leaves vacancy in, viii. 450

Sydney and Carmarthen are, ix. 583

Temple becomes, ix. 465

—— rumoured to become, ix. 295

Townshend, 2d Vct, was, ix. 423

Townshend, Thomas, is, ix. 355n

Tweeddale resigns as, for Scotland, iii. 195

—— was, for Scotland, iv. 209

vacancy in, unfilled, viii. 455

warrant from, for St-Germain's arrest, x. 21

Weymouth may become, vi. 570

—— succeeds Rochford as, for southern province, viii. 142

—— succeeds Shelburne as, vii. 62

—— to succeed Conway as, vi. 571, 578

Wilkes writes to, accusing them of robbing him, vi. 138

See also Seals (of secretaries of state)

Secretary of state, French:

Du Muy becomes, for war, vii. 258, viii. 17

——'s death leaves place of, for war, vacant, viii. 133

St-Contest succeeds Puisieux as, for, foreign affairs, to Nivernais's disappointment, iv. 286

St-Florentin is, vi. 342

Turgot replaces Boynes as, for the marine, viii. 26

Secretary of state, Papal. *See* Archinto, Alberigo; Pallavicini, Lazzaro Opizio; Torregiani, Luigi Maria; Valenti, Silvio

Secretary of state, Sardinian. *See* Del Carreto, Leopoldo, Marchese di Gorsegno

Secretary of state, Spanish:

Wall to succeed Carvajal as, for foreign affairs, iv. 426

Secretary of state, Tuscan:

HW hopes that letters are not opened by, viii. 38

See Degli Alberti, Giovan Vincenzo; Piccolomini, Tommaso; Tornaquinci, Giovanni Antonio

Secretary of the Latin briefs. *See* Giacomelli, Michelangelo

Secret Committee:

Bristow, Burrell, and Hanbury Williams to be examined by, i. 411

defeat of, i. 363-4, 379, 388

dissolution of: pleases Mann, ii. 14, 29; predicted, i. 438

Edgcumbe created a baron to prevent examination by, about Cornish boroughs, i. 399n

forgotten, i. 502, ii. 29

Labour in Vain satirizes, ii. 19

lists for, voted on, i. 383-6, 403

Lyttelton proposes, ii. 117

may consist of Sir Robert Walpole's friends, i. 375, 429

members absent from, i. 401

Paxton and Wendover borough exposed by, i. 425

Paxton examined by, i. 397, 502

Pitt discusses, in speech, iii. 370

proposed in Parliament, i. 297-300, 355, 375

Rawdon reveals Wallingford expenses to, i. 400

report expected from, i. 450, 467

report of, on Bristow, Burrell, Weymouth election, and secret service money, i. 475

Scrope examined by, i. 457-8

—— investigation dropped by, i. 467

——'s silence before, said by *London Evening Post* to be rewarded by giving Treasury clerkship to Fane, ii. 33

second attempt to form, expected, ii. 89

secret service money investigated by, i. 399, 475

Tilson's persecution by, causes his death, ii. 33

to investigate Q. Anne's last administration, vi. 26

voting for, attended by P. of Wales's friends, but not by Lytteltons and Pitts, i. 366

Walpole, Sir Robert, investigated by, vi. 27

—— not mentioned in report of, i. 425

——'s supporters in, support Indemnity Bill, i. 429

—— unharmed by, i. 419, 421

Weymouth customs officials examined by, i. 420

Secret expedition. *See under* Expedition

Secret service:

Mann's allowance for, v. 149

Secret Committee investigates money for, i. 399, 475

Stosch manages, at Rome, v. 149-50

Sedan. *See* Chair, sedan

Sedley, Catherine (1657–1717), m. (1696) Sir David Colyear, 2d Bt, cr. (1699) Bn Portmore and (1703) E. of Portmore; she was cr. (1686) Cts of Dorchester:

Selwyn, Mrs, told by, that Graham was Ds of Buckingham's father, ii. 193

Seeds:

HW receives, from Mann, for Galfridus Mann, ii. 560

ivy, v. 457, 466

Mann sends, to Galfridus Mann, ii. 330, 560

—— wants to send, to HW, iv. 25

Mann, Galfridus, gets, for Duncannon, Whithed, and others, iv. 25
melon, see Melon seeds
tea, see under Tea
Segni, Bp of. See Angelis, Cesare Crescenzi de
Segni, Duchessa di. See Orsini, Eleonora (d. 1634)
Segretario dell'ambasciate:
  York, Cardinal, to have, iii. 416
Seilern, Christian August (1717–1801), Graf; Austrian ambassador to England 1763–9:
  council considers complaint by, on mob stopping his coach, vii. 7
  Du Châtelet thrusts himself between Chernyshev and, at George III's birthday ball, vii. 125–6
  fierce and stiff, vii. 125
  HW to entertain at SH, vii. 311
Seine:
  Paris mob drowned in, vii. 218
Seinsheim, Adam Friedrich von (d. 1779), Bp of Würzburg 1755–79; of Bamberg 1757–79:
  Nuremberg to be punished by, v. 29
Seise. See Sezi
Seleucidæ:
  Russian crimes reminiscent of, vi. 54
Seleucus:
  Demetrius son of, ii. 421
Self-criticism:
  HW's reflections on, ii. 518
Self-knowledge:
  HW's reflections on prevalence of, despite maxim to the contrary, ix. 539–40
Self-love:
  HW's and La Rochefoucauld's reflections on, viii. 373
Selkirk, E. of. See Douglas, Dunbar (1722–99)
Selsey, Bn. See Peachey, James
Selva Florida, Conte de. See Ponce de Guerrero, Don Manuel
Selwin, Charles (ca 1716–94), banker at Paris:
  Conway to receive packet from, iv. 285
  HW sends presents through, i. 181, 183
  Hervey, Augustus, addressed in care of bank of, x. 29
  Lincoln orders gold scissors sent to, from Siries at Florence, i. 93
  Mann sends letter to HW at, i. 115
  Maynard receives letter through, ii. 371
  Veers forges signature of, iii. 507
Selwyn, Charles (1689–1749), Maj.; M.P.:
  'dirty pensioner,' iii. 25
  naval investigation proposed by, iii. 25
Selwyn, George Augustus (1719–91), wit; M.P.:
  anecdote of, about Paris president's family arguing about names of dinner courses, vi. 163
  Bedford, Ds of, accompanied by, to Paris, vi. 105

brother of, asked to recommend Maynard to Mann, iv. 451
  Cornbury visited by, with Abergavenny and Mrs Frere, iv. 182
  executions and corpses delight, iv. 181
  HW visited by, on 1 May 1782, ix. 274–5
  Mann has heard much of, without seeing him, vi. 105
  mother's witticism worthy of, vii. 94
  Onslow succeeded by, as paymaster of the Board of Works, iv. 518
  St Giles's vault visited by, iv. 181
  Scottish officer meets, on Bexley Heath, ii. 524
  Westminster Abbey visited by, with Abergavenny, iv. 181–2
  witticisms by: about Ponsonby 'passing the money bills' at Newmarket, iv. 7; on Chartres' display of horses' and dogs' copulations, ix. 409; on collar-day and May Day, ix. 275; on Cooke's sermon, iv. 186; on Duncan's marriage, viii. 49; on E. of Sandwich, iv. 155; on Leake, iv. 391; on Pitt's gout, v. 43; to D. of Richmond, when presented to Louis XV, vi. 163
Selwyn, Col. John (1688–1751), M.P.:
  Caroline's treasurer, iv. 114n, vii. 94n
  treasurer of George III's household, iv. 247
  Walpole, Sir Robert, advised by, to decline pension, i. 329, ii. 465
  wife of, iv. 114n, vii. 94n
Selwyn, John (ca 1709–51), George Selwyn's brother; M.P.:
  brother of, ii. 451
  HW asked by, to recommend Maynard at Florence, ii. 367, 451
  Parliamentary vote by, on privately-raised regiments, x. 19
  (?) Walpole, Sir Robert, advised by, to decline pension, ii. 465
Selwyn, Mrs John. See Farrington, Mary
Seminara città:
  earthquake account mentions, ix. 376
Semiramis, legendary Q. of Assyria:
  HW compares Catherine II to, vi. 71, 253
Sempill, Francis (d. 1748), styled Lord Sempill (Jacobite):
  agent of English Jacobites in Paris, ii. 426
Semplicetta pastorella:
  Mann sends, to HW, i. 181, 212
  Rich, Elizabeth, wants, i. 166
Senapisms:
  applied to Mann's feet, ix. 560
Senate:
  Genoese, see under Genoa
  of Bologna, vi. 236, ix. 85
  of Sweden, ii. 305
  Roman: conservatori represent, iii. 428; duels not prevalent in, ix. 31; York, Cardinal, receives visit of, iii. 428
  Venetian, see under Venice

Senator; senators:
    at Florence and Rome, keep Adonis wigs
        with robes of ceremony, viii. 32
    Florentine, St John celebration avoided by,
        ii. 251
'Senator of Rome, while Rome survives.'
    See under Addison, Joseph: Cato
Senegal:
    England to demand, from France, v. 526
    war extends from, to Russia, v. 290
Senesino. See Bernardi, Francesco
Sénezergues de la Rode, Étienne-Guillaume
    (1709–59), brigadier:
    wounded at Quebec, v. 338
Senhouse, Grace (ca 1695–1755), m. (1721)
    Richard Boyle, 2d Vct Shannon, 1699:
    daughter of, ii. 481
Seni. See Sani
Sens, Abp of. See Albert de Luynes, Paul d'
    (1703–88)
Sensidoni. See Sansedoni
Sensitive Plant:
    HW's nerves as tender as, viii. 272
Sentença que em 12 de Janeiro de 1759 se
    proferio:
    being printed at Rome, v. 275
Sentinel; sentinels:
    in Boboli Gardens, viii. 204
    in Germany, may be frozen, v. 369
    in London park, accosted by mad parson,
    i. 197
Septennial Act. See under Parliament: acts of
Sequins. See Ruspi; Zecchins
Serao, Francesco (1702–83), physician:
    Philip Anton's incapacity considered by, v.
    325, 329, 337
Seravalle. See Serravalle
Seravezza:
    iron worker goes to, from Pistoia, ii. 242
    Mann orders gun barrels from, ii. 243
Serbelloni, Fabrizio (1695–1775), cardinal,
    1753:
    Benedict XIV tells, to negotiate with
        Francis I about Monte Santa Maria, iv. 428
Serchio, river in Tuscany:
    Brunelleschi advises diversion of, in war-
        time, iv. 514
    Regency orders, to be diverted into Lucca,
    iv. 514–16, 521–2
Serenade; serenades:
    at Naples, iii. 439
    Mann avoids, i. 105
    on Lung'arno at Florence, i. 97, 105
    See also Cocchiata
Serenata:
    performed at London opera, iv. 49
'Serendip, Isle of':
    Ceylon called, in Arabian Nights, ix. 277
Serendipity:
    HW explains, iv. 407–8
    history of, x. 34–5
    Mann's explanation of, iv. 415

Sergeant:
    Cope's, see Molloy
    Walpole, Edward, restrained by, v. 240
Sergeant-at-arms. See Serjeant-at-arms
Sérieux, French ship:
    captured off Cape Finisterre, iii. 410
Serjeant-at-Arms. See Bonfoy, Nicholas (d.
    1775); Odiarne, Wentworth (d. 1762)
Serlupi-Crescenzi, Teresa (d. 1779), m. (1723)
    Antonfrancesco Acciaioli:
    Bolognetti, Contessa, to meet, ii. 65
    Loreto visited by, for daughter's wedding,
    ii. 65
    Mann takes Marchesa Bichi to call on, iii.
    407–8
    Rome left by, for Florence, iii. 408
Sermon; sermons:
    at Mayfair Chapel, on Frederick, P. of
        Wales, iv. 241, 243–4
    Churchill's, vi. 261–2
    city, in London, attended by Wilkes, vii.
    208
    Cooke's, against Middleton, iv. 185–6
    on earthquakes as judgments, iv. 133–4,
    154–5, 158
Sermoneta, Duca di. See Gaetani, Michel-
    angelo (ca 1689–1760)
Sermoneta-Gaetano, Duchessa di. See Corsini,
    Maria Teresa (b. 1732)
Sermon Preached by Order of her Imperial
    Majesty. See under Hinchliffe, John
Sermon prêché . . . sur la tombe de Pierre.
    See under Vorontsova, Ekaterina Roman-
    ovna
Serra, Angelina, m. —— Durazzo:
    daughter of, vi. 236
    York, D. of, attentive to, at Genoa, vi.
    201, 236, 251, 260, 267, 553
Serrao. See Serao
Serravalle:
    Austrians capture, iii. 297
    Spaniards capture, iii. 84
    Spaniards to retire through, iii. 292
Serristori, Mme. See Del Monte Santa Maria,
    Giovanna (b. 1684); Guadagni, Maria Mad-
    dalena Teresa (1719–97)
Serristori, Andrea (1716–95):
    Gabburri, Mme, dismisses, i. 136, 150
    Modenese princess gives cane and snuff-
        box to, i. 64, 70
    Regency appoints, to attend Modenese
        princess, i. 64
    (?) Ricasolis entertain, i. 136
Serristori, Anna Maria Luisa (1722–98), m.
    (1741) Cavaliere Anton Vincenzo Bartolini
    Baldelli:
    Bartolini to wed, i. 40, 53
Serristori, Anton Maria (1712–96); senator:
    Albizzi challenges, i. 381
    Antinori, Mme, attracts, i. 381
    —— has, as cicisbeo, iii. 322
    —— regains, after his marriage, iv. 95
    Guadagni, Maddalena, to wed, iii. 322

(?) Mann asked by, to get from **HW** a design of the machine for raising water, v. 348

Pistoia and Leghorn visited by, for affairs of his farm, iv. 442

sister of, to wed Bartolini, i. **40,** 53

Suares, 'Cecco,' rebuked by, i. 149

travel used by, to dissipate grief, iv. 442

wedding festivities for, expected, iii. 461

Serristori, Averardo (1675–1744), cavaliere:

(?) dies about a year after Electress, iii. 23

(?) Electress leaves money and silver to, ii. 169

(?) —— leaves pension to, iii. 23

Rinuccini's adherent, i. **473**

Sersale, Antonio (1702–75), cardinal, 1754:

archbishopric of Naples to go to, iv. 429

Benedict XIV told by, that the March moon caused Livizzani's death, iv. 429

Maria Amalia will enjoy, iv. 429

Sertor, Gaetano (fl. 1774–ca92); Abbé:

Conclave dell'anno 1774, Il, by, viii. 64–5, 69–70, 73

Servant; servants:

Albany, Cts of, maintained with, by Cardinal York, ix. 150

Americans carried on shoulders of, vii. 240–1

Angelelli's, sent to Young Pretender for message, vi. 374

Bessboroughs', die of fever and sore throat, v. 362

Bichi, Marchesa's, breaks leg, iii. 408

Braitwitz to give, to Mme Vitelli, ii. 334

Bristol collects, for Spanish embassy, v. 202

Burlington's, delivers letter and china to Mrs Bracegirdle, ix. 74

butler: Clement XIV's, dies of chocolate that poisoned his master, viii. 49; Hapsburgs originated in, iv. 409; Mann's, sends ices every day for D. and Ds of Cumberland's dessert, ix. 644; Mann's, *see also* Beaushini *or* Brianchini, Giuseppe

Catherine of Aragon attended only by, ii. 537

chambermaids: Coventry wishes to take, in vehicle, iv. 324; Eleonora, Ps, desires HW's room for, in Venice, i. 74; of Cts of Orford, Mann wishes abbé-secretary would marry, iii. 238

Chute's, *see* Martelli, Francesco

coachmen: at Rome, resents being treated as valet, vi. 286, 300n; Azzi mistreated by, at Florence, i. 488; Electress's, separated from postilion, iii. 370; Eleonora's, *see* Bacci, Lorenzo; Ferrers's, cries all the way, at execution, v. 399; Florentine, crack whips, i. 488; Frederick, P. of Wales's, *see* Biddel, Thomas; Bradshaw, Robert; Leopold's, is Clement XIV's near relation, vii. 118; ministers', tumbles off box, i. 503, ii. 21–2; Modenese princess gives money to, i. 65; Northumberland, D. of,

said to be descended from, iv. 124–5; old English, brought to Florence by eccentric Englishwoman, viii. 260; Orford, Cts of, robbed by, iii. 88; Orford's, i. 503, ii. 21–2 Coke, Lady Mary, dismisses, at Genoa, vii. 553

—— might have had to appear before public tribunals because of, vii. 535

confectioner, Clement XIII's, poisoned, viii. 43

cook-maid, St Albans's, has affair with her master, v. 172

cooks: Bns Walpole's, ii. 4; Craon's, asks guests if they stay to supper, ii. 122; Derby's, resents serving supper at 3 A.M., viii. 310; French, in Florence, iii. 356–7; French, may be replaced by Negro butchers, viii. 21; HW's, in Reggio, i. 57; Lovat's, poisons enemies, iii. 380; Mann's, i. 57, *see also* Bambi, Michele; Mann's, prepares dinners for D. and Ds of Cumberland, ix. 644; Newcastle's i. 485n, iv. 71; St John offers to preside over, at Mann's house, v. 533; to join Young Pretender in France, ii. 434

Corsini's body rescued by, vii. 276

Cowper's, Mann might have given tips to, at christening, viii. 219

Craon, Princesse de, attended by, ii. 196

Craons', i. 9; wait badly on dinner guests, v. 248

Crawford's: *see* Kopp

doorkeeper, Electress's, i. 236

doorkeeper, Mann's, *see* Bianchi, Antonio

drawers, *see* Waiters

Electress's, livery, taxed on Electress's pensions to them, iii. 23–4

——'s provision for, ii. 169

English, Orford, Cts of, does not take, to England, iii. 61

English gentlemen should never be unattended by, ii. 344

English liberality to, imitated by Duc and Duchesse de Mirepoix, iv. 89

fanciulla, Marchesa Gerini's, i. 41–2, 62

firearms learned by, viii. 512

Florentine, must be searched for brandmarks, iv. 144

footboy, HW's, always drunk, v. 300

footmen: Aiguillon, Duchesse d', has, open her coach door, vi. 163; Almódovar's, left by him at brothel door with flambeaux, viii. 413; Bettina's, from Naples, absconds after her illness, i. 421; Brown, Sir Robert, tells, to carry map of London by-lanes in his pocket, ix. 609n; carry effigy in chair, i. 391; Craggs and Moore start as, iv. 181; eccentric Englishwoman does not have, for her carriage, viii. 260; Fox's father served as, ii. 450; Frederick, P. of Wales's, ordered, to give letter to Harrington in Yonge's presence, iii. 175; French, carries his lady's goblet to every

[Servant; servants, *continued*]

dinner she attends, iv. 340; French, enters Lady Mary Churchill's bedroom, iv. 339–40; French, shows Lady Mary Churchill all sanitary conveniences, iv. 339; French, to join Young Pretender, ii. 434; French, wins fortune, but forgetfully climbs into back of coach, iv. 195; French running, father of Ps Eleonora's son, i. 39; gallery for, in Drury Lane Theatre, iv. 231; Giovanni Gastone's, *see* Giuliano; HW expects, only to execute errand, ix. 337; HW's, to accompany him to Houghton, ii. 498; HW's new, cannot read, ix. 118; HW's new, puts letter in post by mistake, ix. 118; HW's, *see also* Colomb, James; Sibley, James; James II's, becomes father of Sir James Gray, iv. 409; Molesworths', tries to save family, vi. 140; Neapolitan demands that dukedom be conferred upon his, vi. 32; Orford's, committed to prison by Bn Walpole for fathering illegitimate child, ix. 355; ride in back of coach, iv. 181, 195; Wasner's, delivers letter, iii. 29

Francis I's, in his livery, ii. 196

French female, dying of cancer at Rome and tended by Anne Pitt, viii. 344, 353

gardener, Northington's, disobeys order to cut trees, vii. 368

gentleman: Chute's, attends his death-bed, viii. 211; Kilmorey's, iv. 298; of D. of Grafton, v. 78

gentleman-usher, *see* Griffith

Giberne resents being, i. 454, 480

godparent might give money to, at christening, viii. 199, 219

governess, Molesworths', *see* Morelle, Mrs

groom-porter, Manners, Lord William, famous in annals of, iv. 418

grooms: Conway's, refuses to go with him, because wife not adequately protected in case of accident, v. 155; Ferrers's, *see* Williams, Peter; Orford's, gives him medical advice, vii. 460; Orford's, help wreck his estate, vii. 511

HW delivers Mann's letter to Horace Mann II's, viii. 512

HW's: at Berkeley Square, gets letter too late, ix. 57; at SH, listed, v. 300; brings letter from Mann, ix. 185; carry him to bed, vi. 316, ix. 347; dies, iii. 132; forced to display lights for Rodney, ix. 280, 343; frightened by earthquake, iv. 130; lop trees at SH, viii. 48; mistakes chimney-back for armour, iv. 396; run to light candles for mob, ix. 563; tell about mob's activities, viii. 442

HW's Swiss boy. *See* Louis

HW's upper, HW sends, to Arlington St from SH, vii. 284, *see also* Favre

Hewet's, interrupt his wife-beating, viii. 204

Holland's, tells HW of D. of Gloucester's death, vii. 343

housekeeper's typical legacy, iv. 11

housemaid, Townshend's, bears three children to him and inherits money, vi. 211

Jewesses', sent with card to Q. Charlotte, vi. 73

Joseph II attended by only one, vii. 112

kitchen boy, Mann's, wears tricolour cockade, ii. 544

Leicester's, at Holkham receive paltry gratuity from E. of Bath, iii. 443

Leopold and Maria Louisa take only two, at Poggio Imperiale, vii. 449

Leopold's and Maria Louisa's, while travelling, vii. 220

Lorraine officers', i. 162

Lovat's, imprisoned for marrying each other, iii. 380

Lucchese, attend D. of York in livery, vi. 222

maids: Albemarle, Ds of, pretends, are ladies of the bedchamber, ix. 564; at brothel, gets niggardly fee, viii. 413; captain of *Great Duchess of Tuscany* leaves, in pirates' clutches, ix. 480; Cornelys, Theresa, left by, because of excessive bedmaking, vii. 272; counterfeiter's, tried at Old Bailey, iii. 242–3; Craon, Princesse de, makes rooms odorous with, ii. 78; from Richmond, wants to stay in town to see Ds of Montrose, v. 535; Goldsworthy, Mrs, brings, to Mann's house, i. 306, 313, 395; HW's, at Arlington St, vii. 286, *see also* Mary; Mann, Lady Lucy, reveals extent of illness to, viii. 346; Maule's, reveals coats of arms, iii. 107; Molesworth', *see* Patterson, Mrs; Niccoli brings, from England, iii. 290; of Cts of Orford, seduced by abbé-secretary, iii. 224, 238; sleeps in garret when not in employer's bed, iv. 215

maître d'hôtel: of Cts of Orford, *see* Waters, Charles; Tencin's, *see* Goudine; Tylney's, made executor and residuary legatee, ix. 534

major-domo, Clement XIII's, gives presents to D. of York, vi. 229

male, not allowed in Maria Louisa's chamber, vi. 529

man, Goldsworthy, Mrs, brings, to Mann's, i. 313

Mann furnishes, to Lady Mary Coke, vii. 544–5

—— praises Conway and Cts of Ailesbury for refusing to suspect, of robbery, vii. 9

——'s: delivers letter to Horace Mann II in London, viii. 446; Florentine furniture to be sold for benefit of, ix. 669–70; frightened of thunder-storm, i. 117; Gloucester, D. of, dismisses, vii. 394; HW sends, to secretary of state's office for, ix. 215; honoured by carrying message to Mann from Leopold's son, ix. 282; Leopold II

exempts, from 8 per cent inheritance tax on legacies, ix. 666; Mann may have to take, to Leghorn for clothes, iv. 205; Mann's legacies and annuities to, ix. 667; Mann, Horace II, forbids amusements to, ix. 670; Mann, Horace II, forms fund for, for families' benefit, ix. 669–70; Mann, Horace II, retains, while still in Tuscany, ix. 667; Mann, Horace II, to sell furniture for benefit of, ix. 678; mourning clothes for Electress too expensive for, ii. 206; not told where Lady William Campbell is going, ix. 272; return of, to Florence, from London, delayed, viii. 450; sent on horseback to Castello, ix. 329; sent with message, i. 51; serve dinners out of town for D. of York, vi. 220, 222; suffer from influenza, ix. 304; to attend Ds of Gloucester at theatre with ice refreshments, viii. 291; tricolour cockades worn by, ii. 544; writes letter to Horace Mann II, ix. 570; see also Pozzolini, Pietro
—— sends, to Horace Mann II, viii. 94
——'s nephew's, may be lodged at neighbour's, viii. 72–3
Mann, Galfridus, has, cut his bread and butter, iv. 554
Mann, Horace II, tells, to tell Mann's servant of wife's death, viii. 356
may be put into mourning, on Electress's death, ii. 175
Mill's, iii. 407
ministers', made drunk at Claremont, i. 503
Modenese princess brings, on journey, vi. 201
Molesworth, Hon. Charlotte, probably learns of mother's death from, vi. 146
Montagu, Lady Mary Wortley, has only men as, vi. 3
Mount Stuart dismisses, ix. 345
Newcastle's: die of sore throat, v. 312; keep Mann waiting for credentials, i. 24
Norfolk's and Northumberland's, want to be stylish by wearing mourning for Ps Caroline, v. 165
nurse: Englishwoman brings, to Florence, for her child, viii. 260; Lorenzi's, causes child's death, iv. 306
Old Pretender dismisses, iii. 96
Orford's, persist in pilfering, vii. 521
Orford, Cts of, neglects, in will, ix. 122
Oxford college, Abergavenny and others said to have killed, iii. 387
pages: Botta's, to wear new liveries, vi. 330; Bristol to have for embassy, v. 202; carries Princesse de Craon's train, ii. 196; Charles III's, puts hooks in wigs, vii. 238; Craon, Princesse de, has, i. 414; Frederick, P. of Wales's, iv. 232; Karl Alexander does not bring, iv. 376; of Mme Pucci, i. 39, 42; York, D. of, leaves, at Florence, vi. 225
page-in-waiting, George III's, vi. 96

peeresses', exhibit their mistresses' costumes for coronation, v. 535
Philip, Don, quarters, on chief families, iv. 45
Philipps's, i. 67
pipers, Northumberland, Ds of, has, iv. 341
Pitt's, precede his chair to Buckingham House, vi. 159
Pomfret, Cts of, employs Mary as, i. 101
porter: Mann's, repels visitors on post days, iii. 59; Mann's, to open door at any hour of night for express from Leghorn, ix. 9; of Q. Elizabeth, De la Warr dresses as, iv. 49; Perceval's, i. 301; Sir Robert Walpole's, 'customers' of, now go to Carteret, ii. 96; Sir Robert Walpole's, HW tells, to shoo away the mob, ii. 96; Swiss, kept by Northumberlands, iv. 341
postilion: North's, wounded by highwayman, viii. 47; Werpup's, overturns chaise, vi. 306
Richecourt brings, for Tesi, ii. 263
—— gives, to Cts of Orford, iii. 49
Richmond's, see Sampson, James
Rinuccini's generosity to, in his will, iii. 462
running footman: Mann's, i. 81; Ps Eleonora's, i. 39
Salviati's, Dumesnil escapes with, iii. 491
scrub, given by Florentine Regency to Modenese princess, i. 60
secretary: Dumesnil's, assists him at Mass, iii. 493; HW's, see Kirgate, Thomas; Mann's, see Giberne, Gabriel George; Gregori, Antonio; Palombo, Domenico; Tylney's, made executor and residuary legatee, ix. 534
Shrewsbury's, i. 14
steward: Ferrers's, see Johnson, John (d. 1760); HW's life invaded by, vii. 497; Northampton's, to forward box of medals to HW, v. 272; of Cts of Orford, ix. 440; Orford's, see Withers, William; Talbot's, iii. 176
Strozzi's, ii. 146
Swiss, from London, to form a regiment, ii. 409
Townshend accompanied by, when raising mob, v. 138
Tripolitanian minister's, die of plague, vii. 24
Tylney's: have new laced clothes, vii. 60, 63–4; to get proceeds of sale of his Neapolitan possessions, ix. 534
unable to carry messages because of epidemic disorder, ii. 284
under-cooks, Young Pretender to be joined by, in France, ii. 434
valet-de-chambre: Acciaioli's, returns Clement XIII's letter, v. 340–1; Alexandre Dumesnil's, arrested, i. 225; Barbantane's, conveys threat to Leopold, viii. 505; Borghese's, drowns in Tiber, iii. 444; Cowper's,

[Servant; servants, *continued*]
hurries back to Florence with Conway's letter to Mann, vi. 374, 380; Cowper's, takes Mann's letter to HW, vi. 361, 366; discarded clothes the perquisite of, i. 158, 172; George II's, *see* Schröder; HW's, announces Chute's death, viii. 211; Hertford's, at Naples for health, brings Mann a black spaniel, vii. 56; Joseph Dumesnil's, proclaims him bishop, iii. 493; livery not worn by, i. 207; Lorenzi to have, as secretary, i. 157; Louis XVI's, *see* Binet, Gérard, Bn de Marchais; Mann's, *see* Galletti, Giuseppe; Giarlii, Giuseppe; Mann thinks St-Aignan's surgeon is, i. 81; Mann wants, out of livery, i. 207; Ottaviano de' Medici's, i. 238; Pomfret, Cts of, has Stephan as, iii. 46; Rushout's, ii. 299; Stormont's, v. 2; Tencin's, assists Old Pretender's sons to escape from Rome, iii. 98–9; Tornaquinci's, issues passports, v. 482; wages of, i. 157; Werpup's, killed by overturned chaise, vi. 306; Whithed's, *see* Ferreri; Young Pretender's, *see* Stewart, John (d. 1788) valet-de-place: coachman in Rome refuses to serve as, vi. 286; Rena well known to, v. 162
Veers's, stripped of lace liveries, iii. 507
Villettes's, takes news to England, iii. 431
Vitelli, Mme, solicitous about Braitwitz's health in presence of, ii. 353
waiter: Mackreth was, at White's, viii. 53n; Rumbold and Sykes formerly were, at tavern, ix. 141; Rumbold was, at White's, ix. 400
waiter at St James coffeehouse, says he could thrash Nivernais, vi. 84
waiters, wear brown frocks and blue aprons, iv. 209
waiting maid, *see* Patience
Wallmoden's, summoned from Rome, vi. 357
Walpole, Bns, dismisses, for being Mann's spy, ii. 14
washerwoman: at Rome, i. 461; Bootle's, told to tell him of George II's death, iv. 245, 254; English, at Florence, refuses Mrs Richmond's proposals, iii. 46
weeding-girl, Orford's, bears him a daughter, ix. 355
woman, Lady Walpole's, intimate with Mrs Gates, ix. 92n
women of fashion never give tips to, iv. 89
Worsley's, *see* Cardini
Wright's, i. 449
Yorke's, dies of sore throat, v. 312
Young Pretender's: aid him when he goes to theatre corridor to be sick, viii. 244; bring his effects, ii. 434; support him as he walks, ix. 442; *see also* Stewart, John
Young Pretender said to have left Rome with, i. 113
See also Barney, Tom; Chloé; Engelbert;

Favre; Ferrarini, Antonio; Giuseppe; Kopp; Martini, Francesco; Palombo; Phillis
Serva padrona. See under Pergolesi
Servetus, Michael (Miguel Serveto) (1511–53), Spanish physician and theologian:
Calvin burns, iv. 555
Servi, Via dei:
Florentines frequent, ii. 445
Sesostris:
HW's letter might have been written in time of, ix. 15
Vesuvius would have felled, viii. 515
Sessaracoa, William Ansah (b. ca 1721–living, 1752), African chief's son:
Oroonoko resembles story of, iv. 40
Sestorio, Giuseppe Maria, Genoese secretary of state:
Austrian-Genoese agreement signed by, iii. 316
Sestri:
Philip, Don, flees to, iii. 304
Spaniards at, iii. 40
Settees:
linen-covered, at SH, iv. 382, 387
Settimia. *See* Guadagni, Settimia
Settlement. *See under* Parliament: acts of
1739:
Mann's happiest year, because it brought him HW's friendship, ix. 9
1741. See under Williams, Sir Charles Hanbury
1770:
treads in footsteps of 1641, vii. 170
Seven Towers, prison at Constantinople:
Mann unlikely to be confined in, vii. 88, 92
Russian minister released from, vii. 308–9
Sultan may confine Murray in, vii. 479
Seven Years' War:
America makes, but peace will be made for Germany, v. 369
progress of, *see under* War
Severambians:
HW's letters discuss people as unknown as, v. 552
Severn, English war ship:
scagliola tables to be sent by, iv. 27
Sévigné, Marquise de. *See* Rabutin-Chantal, Marie de (1626–96)
Sévigné, Françoise-Marguerite de (1648–1705), m. (1669) François de Castellane-Adhémar de Monteil, Comte de Grignan:
mother admires letters of, iv. 84
mother gives pearl necklace to, ii. 291
Seville:
Charles III may settle at, vi. 415
Sèvres:
Spencer, Cts, gives piece of china from, to Mann, ix. 645
Sewell, Sir Thomas (ca 1710–84), Kt, 1764; Master of the Rolls; M.P.:
De Grey persuaded by, not to sign Wilkes's writ of error, vii. 12

insulted, by mistake for Mansfield, vi. 464

Seychelles. *See* Moreau de Séchelles

Seymour, Algernon (1684–1750), styled E. of Hertford 1684–1748; 7th D. of Somerset, 1748:
daughter and mother of, vii. 365n
death of, iv. 124
earldom wanted by, for son-in-law instead of daughter, iv. 81
estate settled on, iv. 10
father blames son's death on, ii. 522
father reconciled with, i. 364
father's bequest to, iv. 10
George II receives letter of resignation from, through Beauchamp, i. 346
Northumberland peerage for Sir Charles Wyndham opposed by, iv. 12
Northumberland title to go to daughter after death of, iv. 81
regiment not to be resigned by, i. **345–6**
Sturrock's correspondence with, ii. 544

Seymour, Berkeley (d. 1777):
Somerset dukedom claimed by, iv. 167

Seymour, Lady Caroline. *See* Cowper, Lady Caroline

Seymour, Caroline (b. 1755), m. (1775) William Danby:
Danby to wed, viii. 94

Seymour, Charles (1662–1748), 6th D. of Somerset:
Ancaster, D. of, sells house to, iv. 11
assets of, discovered, iv. 18
daughter of, iv. 183, v. 24n, 429n
daughter punished by, for letting him fall off a couch, iv. 18
death of, iv. 9
HW imagines presents that would be given by, according to Italian custom, ii. 141
Mann shocked by inhumanity of, ii. 544
Newcastle succeeds, as Chancellor of Cambridge, iv. 9–10
pride and tyranny of, iv. 18
settlements not divulged by, iv. 12
Seymour, Sir Edward, retorts to William III about, ii. 523
son blamed by, for grandson's death, ii. 522
son reconciled with, i. 364
will of, iv. 10–12, 18

Seymour, Lady Charlotte (1730–1805), m. (1750) Heneage Finch, styled Bn Gernsey; 3d E. of Aylesford, 1757:
father punishes, for letting him fall off a couch, iv. 18
father's bequest to, iv. 10, 18
money squandered by, iv. 183
uncle marries, to his relative, iv. 183

Seymour, Edward (ca 1500–52), cr. (1536) Vct Beauchamp, (1537) E. of Hertford, (1547) D. of Somerset; Protector:
Beauchamp title recreated for, to deprive son, iv. 138

France visited by, when 'son' was begotten, iv. 139
son by first wife disinherited by, in favour of son by second wife, ii. 523, iv. 138–9
wife repudiated by, iv. 139

Seymour, Sir Edward (1529–93), of Berry Pomeroy; Kt, 1547:
father disinherits, ii. 523, iv. 138
Hertford's alleged trial with, iv. 139

Seymour, Sir Edward (1537–1621), styled E. of Hertford 1547–52; cr. (1559) E. of Hertford:
father disinherits elder brothers in favour of, ii. 523
Seymour, Sir Edward, has trial with, iv. 139

Seymour, Sir Edward (ca 1563–1613), cr. (1611) Bt; of Berry Pomeroy:
Hertford's contest with, iv. 139

Seymour, Sir Edward (1633–1708) 4th Bt, Speaker:
William III receives retort from, about D. of Somerset, ii. 523

Seymour, Sir Edward (1695–1757), 6th Bt; 8th D. of Somerset, 1750:
Bruce's estate may be claimed by, iv. 331
Hertford title granted to Conway with consent of, iv. 167
Lord Chancellor refuses writ to, iv. 139
rival claimant opposes, iv. 167
Somerset title goes to, ii. **522**, iv. 124
Somerset title won by, after dispute, iv. 139

Seymour, Mrs Edward. *See* Fillol, Catherine

Seymour, Lady Elizabeth (1685–1734), m. (1707) Henry O'Brien, 7th E. of Thomond:
nephew of, v. 24n

Seymour, Lady Elizabeth (1716–76), m. (1740) Sir Hugh Smithson 4th Bt, 2d E. of Northumberland, 1750; cr. (1766) D. of Northumberland:
Bedchamber post to Q. Charlotte given to, v. 518
dying, viii. 99, 102
extravagant construction by, iv. 341
father wants title to go to husband instead of, iv. 81
HW does not know, well enough to recommend Muzell to her, v. 514
Jewesses' servant rebuked by, for improper delivery of card to Q. Charlotte, vi. 73
marriage of, vii. 365n
mob forces, to drink Wilkes's health, vii. 7
Northumberland title to go to, iv. 81
opera opened by, for Guadagni, vii. 271
Percy estate does not go to, iv. **11n**
pipers and Swiss porters kept by, iv. 341
subscription masquerade attended by, in fantastic head-dress, iv. 49–50
supper given by, for Cts of Yarmouth, v. 191
Westminster election won by, for her candidates, by daily attendance in Covent Garden, viii. 51–2

Seymour, Lady Frances (1728–60), m. (1750) John Manners, styled M. of Granby:
  death of, v. 429
  father leaves house to, hoping her mother can live with her, iv. 10–11
  father's bequest to, iv. 10, 18
  Granby to wed, iv. 91, 183
  money squandered by, iv. 183
Seymour, Francis (1697–1761), M.P.:
  son at Florence told by, of Sandwich's prospects, iv. 216–17
Seymour, George (1725–44), styled Vct Beauchamp:
  death of, ii. **510**, iv. 11n
  father sends, with letter to George II, i. 346
  Mann never saw, ii. 510
  Somerset blames death of, on Hertford, ii. 522
  Sturrock tutor to, ii. 544
Seymour, Lord Henry. See Seymour-Conway, Hon. Henry
Seymour, Henry (1729–1807), M.P.:
  Albany, Cts of, attached to, with husband's consent, viii. 94
  father tells, of Sandwich's prospects, iv. **216–17**
  Florence to have been summer resort of, but for daughter's engagement, viii. 94
  Florence visited by, iv. 216–17
  Sandwich's half-brother, iv. 217
  Young Pretender and wife must be followed by, to Paris, viii. 102
Seymour, Lady Hugh. See Waldegrave, Lady Anna Horatia
Seymour, Jane (1509?–37), m. (1536) Henry VIII of England:
  Richmond, Ds of, dresses as, i. 338
Seymour, Sir John (d. 1536), Kt:
  daughter-in-law's alleged relations with, iv. 139
Seymour, John (d. 1552):
  begotten while 'father' was in France, iv. 139
  father deprives, of title because of illegitimacy, iv. 139
  father disinherits, ii. **523,** iv. 138–9
Seymour, Dr John (d. ca 1749):
  Somerset dukedom said to be claimed by, iv. 167
Seymour, Lady Katherine (d. 1731), m. (1708) Sir William Wyndham, 3d Bt:
  Percy estate settled on children of, iv. 11n
  son of, v. 24n
Seymour-Conway, Lady Anna Horatia. See Waldegrave, Lady Anna Horatia
Seymour-Conway, Lady Elizabeth (1754–1825):
  more beautiful than elder sister, vii. 323
Seymour-Conway, Lady Frances (1751–1820), m. (1775) Henry Fiennes Pelham-Clinton, styled E. of Lincoln:
  daughter of, to inherit barony of Clinton, HW thinks, ix. 165

HW praises, viii. 71
  husband's body brought back to England by, viii. 420
  Lincoln, E. of, to marry, viii. 71
  more beautiful than elder sister, vii. **323**
Seymour-Conway (after 1807, Ingram-Seymour-Conway), Francis (1743–1822), styled Vct Beauchamp 1750–93; E. of Yarmouth, 1793; 2d M. of Hertford, 1794; M.P.:
  father's instructions awaited by, vi. 319, 327
  Florence visited by, from Milan, vi. 319
  HW hears Mann's praises from, in Paris, vi. 344
  HW shown Mann's letter by, vi. 495
  HW to tell, of Mann's readiness to oblige him, vii. 213
  horses obtained by, vi. 338
  itinerary of, from Florence, vi. 336, 344
  Macdonald a friend of, vi. 344
  Mann conceals false news of mother's death from, vi. 468
  —— congratulated by, on HW's recovery, vi. 466
  —— encloses letter to, vi. 470, 476, 486, 495
  —— praises, vi. 282
  —— procures Italian wine for, vii. 200, 204, 213, 215, 279, 302
  ——'s correspondence with, about Bath Knighthood, vi. 480, 486, 502
  —— tells, of father's Irish post, vi. 327
  —— to entertain, at dinner, vi. 327
  mules sought by, to facilitate departure from Florence, vi. 336
  Parliamentary membership expected for, ix. ix. 488
  Patch's painting owned by, x. 45
  uncle to receive letter from, through Mann, vi. 320
  wife's death distracts, vii. 381
  Wilkes asks, to deliver message to Mann, vi. **281–2**
  Windsor, Hon. Alice, to wed, vi. 480
Seymour-Conway (after 1794, Seymour), Hon. (Lord after 1793) George (1763–1848), M.P.:
  Parliamentary membership expected for, ix. 488
Seymour-Conway, Lady Gertrude (1750–93), m. (1772) George Mason-Villiers, styled Vct Villiers, 1st E. Grandison, 1782:
  marriage of, vii. 323, 381
Seymour-Conway, Hon. (after 1793 Lord) Henry (1746–1830), M.P.:
  abbreviated address by, on letter to T. Tighe, ix. 608
  Fox, Hon. Stephen and Lady Mary, accompanied by, in dressing-room, vii. **392**
  indolent and humorous, ix. 608
  Parliamentary membership expected for, ix. 488
Seymour-Conway, Hon. (after 1793, Lord) Hugh (1759–1801):
  HW praises, ix. 632

marriage of, results in HW's dining with George IV at Hertford's and at Leicester House, ix. 647
Parliamentary membership expected for, ix. 488
Waldegrave, Lady Anna Horatia, to marry, ix. 632
wife's relationship to, ix. 632n, 647
Seymour-Conway, Hon. (after 1793, Lord) Robert (1748–1831), M.P.; army officer:
Parliamentary membership expected for, ix. **488**
uncle's calmness admired by, ix. 115
Seymour-Conway, Hon. (after 1793, Lord) William (1760–1837), M.P.:
Parliamentary membership expected for, ix. 488
Seymour-Conway family:
daughters of, HW accompanies, to Soho masquerade ball, vii. 194
Seymour family:
Chute discovers scandal in, iv. 138–9
descent of titles of, ii. 523, iv. 138–9, 167
Sézanne:
French losses admitted at, by officers, iii. **427**
Sezi or Seise:
Spaniards arrive at, iii. 225–6
Sforza, Duchessa. See Orsini, Eleonora (d. 1634)
Sforza Cesarini ['Cetarini'] Marchese [?Francesco (1773–1816)]:
Lepri heiress engaged to, ix. 385
Pius VI will be opposed by, over Lepri donation, ix. 385
Shaddocks:
climate of India suitable for ripening oranges to, ix. 153
Shade:
green, for candle, ii. 228
Shadwell, Lady. See Binns, Ann (ca 1681–1777)
Shadwell, Miss —— (eldest):
costumed as Mary, Q. of Scots, at Ds of Norfolk's, i. 338
HW meets, at Court, i. 185
Shadwell, Catherine, m. (1737) Edward Allen:
Charles of Naples might seize, as hostage, iii. 57–8
Florence to be visited by, from Naples, on way to England, iii. 477
(?) HW meets, at Court, i. **185**
Shadwell, Sir John (1671–1747), Kt, 1715; physician:
HW meets, at Court, i. 185
widow of, viii. 282–3n
Shadwell, Molly:
called 'Mademoiselle Miss Molli' in Italy, i. 185n
HW meets, at Court, i. 185
Shadwell, Richard (d. 1785), clerk of secretary of state's office:

Larpent recommends, to handle Mann's affairs, vii. 443–4
Shaftesbury, E. of. See Cooper, Anthony Ashley (1621–83); Cooper, Anthony Ashley (1711–71)
Shag, scarlet:
under-petticoat lined with, ii. 333
Shah Alam (1728–1806), Mogul emperor, 1759:
George III and Charlotte get 'presents' from, through Clive, vi. 540, 547
(?) grandmother of, v. 378
Shah Goest, Indian animal:
Pitt gives, to George II, v. 378
Shakespear. See under Pignotti, Lorenzo
Shakespeare, William (1564–1616), dramatist:
'argosie' a word used by, ii. 202
Beauclerk, Lady Diana, does illustrations worthy of plays of, viii. 524
HW compares, with Correggio, vii. 350
HW's letter resembles historic plays of, ix. 68
Hamlet: 'Gertrude' in, should be counterpart of Catherine II, vi. 426; ghost in, wears scanty costume, iv. 209; grave of, iv. 240; HW quotes, vii. 345, viii. 366, ix. 48; keeper reads, to Ferrers, v. 408; Pulteney alludes to, i. 298; Russian translation of, performed in St Petersburg, vi. 426; soliloquy in, on Yorick's skull, ix. 7
Hanmer's edition of, ii. 566–7
Henry IV, lines from, repeated at Drury Lane, i. 336
Henry VIII, ii. 537
Julius Cæsar, HW quotes from, vi. 367
King Henry V, HW paraphrases, iv. 402
Macbeth: Selwyn quotes, in witticism on Lady Duncan, viii. 49; Stanislas I's situation reminiscent of scene in, vi. 253
Othello: Delaval family act, in Drury Lane, iv. 230–1; Hanmer's alteration of, ii. 567; Parliament adjourns to see, iv. 231
Pignotti's Shakespear on, to Mrs Montagu, viii. 536
Richard III, HW quotes, ii. 248, vii. 195
Tempest, The, HW alludes to, ii. 117
Theobald's edition of, iv. 215n
Voltaire attacked by Pignotti for pillaging and reviling, viii. 536
—— first praised and then disparaged, in France, viii. 267
worst plays of, like those of modern playwrights, but best ones far above theirs, viii. 415
Shakespeare traduit de l'anglois. See under Le Tourneur, Pierre-Prime-Félicien
Shannon, E. of. See Boyle, Henry (ca 1686–1764)
Shannon, Vct. See Boyle, Richard (1675–1740)
Shannon, Vcts. See Senhouse, Grace
Sharawaggi:
HW admires, iv. 127
Sharks:
Sloane's museum contains, iv. 358

Sharp, Samuel (ca 1700–78) surgeon; writer:
Hawkwood's picture in Florentine Duomo claimed by, as ancestral portrait, vii. 428
Sharpe, Horatio (1718–90), governor of Maryland:
(?) borough for, viii. 52
Sharpe, John (?1700–56), M.P.: lawyer:
(?) Orford, Cts of, may have left documents with, ix. 160
(?) —— receives documents from, iv. 547
Sharpe, Joshua (d. 1788), lawyer:
acts in concert with Lucas, ix. 328
agreement with Lucas on Cts of Orford's estate desired by, ix. 150
conduct of, shameful in disloyalty to clients, ix. 172
counter-demands against Orford should be produced by, ix. 333
courier may have reported Cts of Orford's death to, ix. 121
denies having objected to Duane, ix. 320
division of money held by Hoare may have been suggested by, ix. 426
Duane feared by, because of honesty and intelligence, ix. 217
—— finally approved by, ix. 315, 324
—— probably would not be approved by, ix. 304
——'s nomination disapproved by, ix. 217, 235
—— told, that he would accept no reward, ix. 519
—— will tell, of Orford's indecent letter to Mozzi, ix. 330
duplicity and dishonesty of, surprising to Mozzi, ix. 335
fire in Lincoln's Inn nearly destroys papers of, ix. 350–1
former opinion of, that Cts of Orford's jointure should be made good, will surprise him, ix. 172
gives opinion against Mozzi, before considering justice of Orford's claims, ix. 217
HW asks, to tell Cts of Orford of her son's latest insanity, viii. 292
HW calls, rogue and fool, ix. 315
HW complains of delays of, ix. 433
HW condemns, for forcing Mozzi to come to England, ix. 315
HW consults, about E. of Orford, vii. 496, 503, 545
HW does not wish treachery of, shifted to himself, ix. 289
HW, Duane, and Lucas confer with, about Mozzi's affairs, ix. 391, 419, 421, 439, 444, 448
HW glad to sow division between Lucas and, ix. 315
HW hears from, of Duane's apoplexy, ix. 495
HW hopes, will be afraid of Duane, ix. 331
HW impeded by difficulties from, viii. 308
HW not aided by, in keeping E. of Orford from letting a farm to a jockey, viii. 52

HW not allowed by, to raise Cts of Orford's jointure, ix. 140
HW not to be influenced by, ix. 172
HW praises, in Mozzi affair, ix. 410
HW receives copy of paper sent by, to Morice, ix. 186
HW reproached by, at the same time that he asks for aid, ix. 308
HW scolds, in letter, for asking him to take Mozzi's affair upon himself, ix. 315
HW's letter from: about Hoare's payment, ix. 509; laments E. of Orford's conduct, viii. 53; telling of reception of Mozzi's letter, ix. 500
HW's note of resentment to, ix. 509
HW's relations with, ix. 154–5, 172, 439–40, 444–7, 471–2, 477, 496
HW suspects collusion between Lucas and, ix. 286
HW told by, of Cts of Orford's habits, vii. 545
HW to tell, of Mozzi's resolution, ix. 466
HW urged by, to resume care of E. of Orford's affairs, vii. 308
HW writes to, complaining of delay, ix. 500
less zealous for Mozzi than Lucas appears to be for Orford, ix. 200
Lucas and, had settled on £6000 for Orford, HW thinks, ix. 335
Lucas scolded by, for his delay, ix. 286
——'s demands against Mozzi are sent to him by, ix. 333
——'s possible collusion with, ix. 150, 328, 492
——'s summary delivered to Duane by, ix. 335
—— told by, that Cts of Orford's money in England should be divided between Orford and Mozzi, ix. 160
Mann and secretary to receive legal instrument from, ix. 167
Mann censures, for treatment of Mozzi, ix. 161–2
—— does not trust, to convey Mozzi's letter to Duane, ix. 304
Morice advised by, to call for papers, ix. 289
—— receives papers from, ix. 184
Mozzi advised by, to divide sum with E. of Orford, ix. 419
—— asks HW to conceal doubts about, ix. 341
—— assured by, that Orford will act honourably, ix. 144
—— awaits letter from, ix. 479
—— claims he always answers letters of, ix. 465
—— complains to, ix. 289
—— desired by: to list Cts of Orford's things, ix. 151; to return release from E. of Orford to HW, ix. 527; to send him copy of paper signed by Yorke, ix. 169

—— employed, because of having been Cts of Orford's lawyer, ix. 320

—— fears, might secrete papers in his favour, ix. 333, 341

—— glad to escape from, ix. 161

—— has bad opinion of, but must retain him, ix. 181

—— may go to England unless prevented by, ix. 431

—— mistakenly employs, ix. 160, 172, 320

—— neglected by, ix. 390

—— safer in HW's hands than in those of, ix. 158

——'s claims against Cts of Orford's estate requested by, ix. 168

——'s correspondence with, ix. 144, 156, 166, 216, 300–1, 315, 324, 412, 459, 471, 478, 492, 500, 504, 511, 514, 524, 540

——'s employment of, surprises him, ix. 320

—— sends power of attorney to, ix. 137, 144

——'s relations with, ix. 181

——'s release as Cts of Orford's executor to be drawn up by, ix. 498

—— suspects Lucas and, of wishing him to go to law, ix. 322

—— to pay, through Hoare, ix. 492

—— urged by, to come to England, ix. 144, 435

Orford and Mozzi advised by, to divide money in Hoare's hands, ix. 154–5, 157, 160, 217, 335, 419, 426

Orford does not answer expresses from, about elections and boroughs, viii. 46

—— persuaded by, to reject Duane, ix. 265

—— to receive from, a letter from Mozzi, ix. 300–1

—— would probably be favoured by, ix. 421–2

Orford, Cts of, allowed salary to, as agent, ix. 492

—— can convey hint to HW through, vii. 514

—— corresponds with, about her son, vii. 464, 472, 476, 477, 486, 491, 492, 493, 496, 500–1, 503, 509, 514, 516, 525, 537, 548, viii. 46–7, 57, 304, 305, 317, 318

—— disappoints, by not leaving him a legacy, ix. 320, 328

—— had, as her lawyer, ix. 160, 320

—— has confidence in, vii. 477

—— may consult, vii. 537, viii. 91

—— mistakenly trusted, ix. 172

—— offers borough to, for his nephew, viii. 52

—— preferred by, to have left less to Mozzi, ix. 162

—— probably does not open letters of, viii. 318

—— refused to send order for money to, ix. 129

—— should have given fuller powers to, viii. 67

—— will be made by, to regret her want of confidence in HW, viii. 317

—— will be told by, of her son's neglect of boroughs, viii. 47

private expectations of, disappointed by Cts of Orford's will, ix. 162

probable author of Cts of Orford's 'case,' ix. 162

rent arrears to be collected by, ix. 511–12

rents not collected by, to earn salary, ix. 496

sale of E. of Orford's boroughs advised by, viii. 52

(?) Shirley has, send deed to Cts of Orford, iv. 547

Zincke's portrait of Cts of Orford sent by, to HW, ix. 501

Shaving:
Italian women perform, on their bodies, iii. 437

Shaw, Charles:
Customs place of, x. 52

Shaw, Elizabeth (d. 1788), m. (1747) William Byron, 5th Bn Byron:
Byron later marries, iii. 19n
Coke breaks with, on her flirtation at ridotto with Stuart-Mackenzie, iii. 27
—— rumoured to be marrying, iii. 19
fortune of, iii. 19

Shaw, James; deputy ranger of Richmond Park ca 1751–ca 1761:
Bird consulted by, in Ps Amelia's behalf, iv. 323

Shaw, Sir John (d. 1702), 2d Bt:
Customs place of, x. 52

Shaw, Peter (1694–1763), physician:
Newcastle, Ds of, attended by, v. 79

Sheba, Q. of:
Coke, Lady Mary, compared with, vii. 539

Shebbeare, Dr John (1709–88), political writer:
broken Jacobite physician, v. 87
career and writings of, v. 39n
HW's epigram on Hume-Campbell's attack from, v. 87
Hardwicke attacked by, v. 39
Letter to his Grace the D—— of N——, v. 87
Monitor, The, written by, v. 39

Sheene, Mrs Mary, (?) weeding-girl:
(?) Orford, E. of, begets daughter on, ix. 355

Sheep:
Blake might order, for supper at Almack's, viii. 21
Clinton captures, viii. 419
eaten at Cambridge banquet, iv. 83
England will tend, vii. 116
HW vends, vii. 497
Mann obtains, for British fleet, v. 114
Turkish, HW has, at SH, iii. 414
visible from SH, iv. 380, ix. 532

Sheerness:
George II delayed at, ii. 224

Sheet; sheets:
Benedict XIV's attendants carry off, before his death, v. 81
Strozzi's servants borrow, for him, ii. 146
white, Kingston, Ds of, may have to stand in, if condemned, viii. 162
Sheffield, Bn and E. of. *See* Baker-Holroyd, John
Sheffield, Charles (ca 1706–74), cr. (1755) Bt; D. of Buckingham's natural son:
Buckingham, Ds of, has law suit against, i. 254n
Cori accused of being in league with, i. 254
Sheffield, Edmund (1716–35), 2d D. of Buckingham, 1721:
burial of, ii. 193n
Sheffield, John (1647–1721), 1st D. of Buckingham, n.c.:
Ferrers imitates epitaph of, v. 408
HW attributes allusion to, in Pope's poem, v. 140
Sheffield natural son of, i. **254n**
Sheffield:
earldom of, rumoured for Horatio Walpole (1678–1757), i. 430, 469n
Shelburne, Cts of. *See* Carteret, Lady Sophia (1745–71)
Shelburne, E. of. *See* Petty, Henry (ca 1675–1750); Petty, William (1737–1805)
Sheldon, Father Henry (1686–1756), Jesuit:
Bower's alleged letters to, iv. 532, 580
Sheldonian Theatre, Oxford:
(?) box built in, for Cts of Pomfret, iv. 579
Shell; shells:
book of, HW will be glad to receive, from Mann, ii. 105
HW's cabinet of, vii. 285
Shell; shells (artillery):
magazine of, belonging to French, destroyed by Murray, ix. 207
Voyer and Paulin take, past Lyon, iv. 536
Shelley, Miss ?Catherine:
Constantinople to be visited by, with Cts of Pomfret, iv. 53
Florence to be visited by, iv. 70, 116
Mann advises a convent for, iv. 70
Pomfret, Cts of, tries to introduce, at rebels' trials, iii. **294**
Uguccioni expects to be in love with, iv. 70
Winnington calls, 'filial piety,' iv. 53
Shelley, J., printer:
prosecution of, threatened, ii. 33
Shelley, Sir John (1692–1771), 4th Bt, 1703; M.P.:
daughter of, iv. 53
(?) nose of, v. 4
Shelley, Sir John (?1730–83), 5th Bt, 1771; M.P.:
Arundel to be succeeded by, as Clerk of the Pipe, v. 26
Edgcumbe replaced by, as treasurer of the Household, vi. 470

Shelly. *See* Shelley
Shelvocke, George (d. 1760), secretary to post office:
HW's correspondence with, iv. 436
Shepherdesses:
at Ranelagh masquerade, i. 495
Sherard, Lady. *See* Sidney, Mary
Sherard, Hon. Lucy (ca 1685–1751), m. (1713) John Manners, 2d D. of Rutland:
daughter ordered by, to put down gossip to fill country letters, ii. 129–30
Sherbet:
Florentine nobility scramble for, at conversazioni, iv. 75
Mann serves, to visitors, before theatres open, ix. 585, 592
—— to serve jar of, to Mrs Damer, ix. 650
snow from Vallombrosa imported for, when ice fails, iv. 25
Sheridan, Michael:
arrival of, in Scotland, iii. 138
Young Pretender accompanied by to Pont-de-Beauvoisin, iv. **9**
Sheridan, Sir Thomas (ca 1672–1746), cr. (1726) Bt (Jacobite); Young Pretender's sub-tutor:
Excerpta said to be written by, ii. 419
Young Pretender to be joined by, ii. 433
Sheriff; sheriffs:
at trial of rebel lords, iii. 301
county, murderer's property goes to, v. 398
eat and drink on execution scaffold, v. 402–3
election of, London populace may win, from Court party, vii. 419
Ferrers attended by, v. 399–402, 408
high, of Denbighshire, i. 344
London's remonstrance presented by, to George III, vii. 196
Mann, Edward Louisa, gets exemption from being, viii. 146–7
of Berwickshire, *see* Home, David
of London, *see* Blachford, John (d. 1759); Blunt, Richard (d. 1763); Cockayne, Francis (d. 1767); Errington, George (d. 1769); Harley, Thomas (1730–1804); Sawbridge, John (1732–95); Townsend, James (1737–87); Vaillant, Paul (ca 1715–1802); Wilkes, John (1727–97)
of Middlesex, summon Wilkes, viii. 475
Parliament may punish, for remonstrance, vii. 197
picked by 'committees of council,' x. 26
robes of, worn by Vaillant, v. 400
Sayre was, under Wilkes, viii. 138
Wilkes becomes, vii. 317, 360
—— canvasses for, vii. 314
Sheriff's Account, The. See under Vaillant, Paul
Sheriff's officers:
Harley turns out, for not arresting Wilkes, vii. 13
Sherlock, Thomas (1678–1761), Bp of Bangor,

1728; of Salisbury, 1734; of London, 1748:
Canterbury see refused by, iii. 511
Chute and HW do not believe, iv. 137
futility of answering bigotry of, iv. 555
HW not to tell, about Voltaire's *Pucelle*, iv. 548
Letter to the Clergy and People of London by, on earthquake, iv. 133-4, 548
London bishopric accepted by, ii. **203n**, iii. 511
Master of the Temple, iv. 133n
Middleton's controversy with, iv. 134
——'s death will please, iv. 167
Pilkington, Mrs, draws picture of, in bawdy book, iv. 134
Regency bill obstructed by, iv. 248
York archbishopric refused by, ii. 203
Shields:
at SH, iv. 375, 381
Shift:
Montagu, Lady Mary Wortley, wears of coarse cloth, ii. 306
Shillings:
counterfeited, iii. 242-3
Shins:
Flobert breaks, at Carrickfergus, v. 386
Ship; ships:
Blake sinks, to see if man can live under water, viii. 20
English, *see* England: ships of
for Coromandel, bought in England, and turned into Tuscan navy, iv. 102, vi. 548
France has, built in Boston, viii. 386
French, *see* France: ships of
from Canada, at Bordeaux, v. 344
hulks used as prisons, ix. 316
Joseph II anxious to see, vi. 548
Kingston, Ds of, has, viii. 7
Mann orders, to be purchased, for relief of Minorcan garrison, ix. 199
——'s, for Minorca, *see* Dolphin; Fly; General Murray; Indian King; Malborough Fort; St Philip's Castle; Tartar
merchant, Holland must not send, under convoy, ix. 8-9
Neapolitan, *see under* Naples
Southwark fire destroys, ix. 577
Spanish, *see* Spain: ships of
victualling, England gets news by, viii. 327
See also Achilles; Actæon; Active; Æolus; Aigrette; Alarm; Alcmena; A Leon Franca; Alfred; Ambuscade; America; Andrea Doria; Ann; Anne; Appollon; Aquila; Ardent; Arethusa; Augusta; Augustus Cæsar; Aurora; Barfleur; Bark; Beaumont; Bedford; Belle Perle; Belle Poule, La; Bellona; Bellone; Blandford; Blonde; Bomb-ketch; Bomb-ship; Boreas; Bouffon; Brederode; Bretagne; Brig; Brilliant; Brilliante; Britannia; Bruna; Cabot; Cæsar; Cambridge; Capitan Hali Bey; Carvel; Carysfort; Centaur; César; Charité, La; Charlotte; Charmante; Charming Nancy; Chatham; Chester;

Colliers; *Columbus; Commandante; Conqueror; Conserva; Conte d'Urbeck; Crawford; Culloden; Cumberland;* Cutter; *Dartmouth; Diadème; Diamant; Diana; Dolphin;* Domingo-men; *Doutelle; Dragon; Duke; Duke of Cumberland; Dursley; Earl of Besborough; Elena Fortunata; Elisabeth; Elizabeth; Emerald; Esperance; Essex; Éveillé; Evstafii; Falkland; Fame; Familia Real;* Felucca; *Ferrytoat; Feversham;* Fireship; First-rates; Fishing-boats; *Florissant; Fly; Folkstone; Formidable; Foudroyant; Fox;* Frigate; Galleon; Galley; *General Barker; General Murray; Gentille; Glasgow; Gloire; Glorieux; Grafton; Gran Duca di Toscana; Grand Duchess of Tuscany; Great Duchess of Tuscany; Guarland; Guernsey;* Gunboats; Gunship; *Hampton Court; Hanover; Happy Jennet; Hardwick; Harwich; Hastings; Hazard; Hector; Helena; Hermione; Héros; Hibernia;* Hoy; *Hunter; Hyæna; Illarim; Il Postiglione; Inconstante, L'; Indian King; Inflexible; Invincible; Ipswich; Isabel; Isis;* Jamaica men; *Jason; Jersey; Junon; Kennington; Kingston; Lancaster; La Pace; La Santa Fortuna; Lemon; Lenox; Leopard; Licorne;* Lighters; *Lightning; Lion; Lively;* Longboat; *Louis; Lowestoft;* Mackerel-boat; *Malborough Fort; Maréchal de Belle-Isle; Maria Theresa; Marie-Louise; Marlborough; Mars; Mary;* Merchantmen; Merchant ship; *Merlin; Mermaid; Messenger-sloop; Mignonne La; Minerva; Monmouth; Montreal; Namur; Nassau; Natalia; Neptune; Newcastle; Nonsuch; Nottingham; Nuestra Senora; Numero Due; Oiseau; Otter; Oxford; Paerl; Pallas; Paloma; Panther; Pembroke; Philibert; Philip; Pléiade; Plymouth; Poder; Portland; Postilion; Postillion; Prince Ferdinand; Prince Frederick; Prince George; Prince of Orange; Prince of Piedmont; Prince of Wales; Princess Louisa; Prince William; Providence; Provvidenza; Quero; Ramillies; Real Filipe; Repulin Bacha, Resolution; Revenge; Robuste; Rochester; Roebuck; Romney; Rosario; Royal Constantinople; Royal George; Royal Oak; Royal Philip; Ruby; Rye; St Caroline; St Domingo; Ste Anne; St Esprit; St Estevan; St Joseph; St Philip's Castle; St Quintin; Salisbury; Sally; San Antonio; San Fernando; San Giorgio; San Giovacchino; San Isidro; San Lazzaro e Sant'Antonio; San Luigi Gonzaga; San Pablo; Santa Rosa; San Zirioco;* Schooner; *Seaford; Sea Horse; Sérieux; Severn;* Ship of the line; Ship of war; Sloop; Snow; *Sobervia; Soleil Royal; Somerset; Southampton; Spence; Speronara; Sphinx;* Store-ship; *Sukey; Sultan; Superbe; Surprize; Sutherland; Swiftsure;* Tartan; *Tartar;* Tender; *Teresa; Terpsichore; Thamas Kouli Kan; Thames; Thésée; Thétis; Theÿlinger; Thunder-Bomb; Tocha;*

[Ship; ships, *continued*]
Transport; *Trepid; Tre-Primati; Trial; Trident; Triton; Vengeance; Venus; Vespa; Vestale; Victory; Ville de Paris; Warwick; Wherry; William; William and Mary; Willingmi; Winchelsea; Worcester; Xavier; Xebec; Yacht; Yarmouth*

Ship of the line; ships of the line:
English: Hawke brings, towards Minorca, iv. 581; in English invasion of France, v. 204; put in commission, viii. 252; ready to sail to Mediterranean, vii. 474; York, D. of, to take, to Italy, vi. 260, 267; *see also* England: ship, ships of
French: at Gibraltar, viii. 541; Estaing's squadron to be reinforced by, viii. 397; from Brest, ix. 345; Guichen returns to Europe with, ix. 94; in French fleet at Minorca, iv. 558; in Toulon squadron, v. 431, vii. 474; *see also* France: ship, ships of
French and Spanish, threaten Minorca, ix. 173–4
Spanish: Rodney defeats, ix. 16; said to be bombarding Algiers, ix. 416; *see also* Spain: ship, ships of
Turkish, defeated by Russians, vii. 234; *see also* Russia: ship, ships of; Turkey: ship, ships of

Ship of war; ships of war:
English: at Leghorn, i. 455; to have access to Genoese and Corsican ports, iv. 588; *see also* England: ship, ships of
French: at Toulon, iv. 545; *see also* France: ship, ships of
Russian: leave Leghorn for Calais, without waiting for Ds of Kingston's treasure, viii. 404, 409–10; must sail direct from Leghorn to England, viii. 114; *see also* Russia: ship, ships of
Tuscan: at Leghorn, to be visited by Joseph II, vii. 108; rescue Tuscan prize from Prussian privateer, v. 349; *see also* Tuscany: ship, ships of

Shipley, ——, drawing master:
Romney, friend of, lives near him in Kent, x. 48
Society of Arts and Sciences 'invented' by, x. 48

Shippen, William (1673–1743), M.P.:
army proposals opposed by, i. 370
army voting opposed by, i. 343
Jacobites led by, in Parliament, i. 231
Murray's apostasy enrages, ii. 123
Walpole, Sir Robert, does not know price of, i. 343n

Shirley, Mrs. *See* Clarges, Anne (d. 1782)

Shirley, Lady Frances (ca 1706–78):
(?) Chesterfield's song about beauty of, viii. 401n
death of, viii. 401
Huntingdon, Cts of, heiress to, viii. 401
Methodism of, iv. 52, viii. 401

senses lost by, viii. 401
turns Methodist when no longer admired, iv. 52, viii. 401

Shirley, Laurence (1720–60), 4th E. Ferrers:
children of, v. 396, 397, 398
Cornwallis's correspondence with, v. 399
date of trial of, fixed, v. 385
excommunicated, and therefore unable to give evidence, v. 184
execution of, v. 394–403, 410–11
family said to have forced, to plead insanity, v. 396
foreigners cannot understand ignominious treatment of, v. 410–11
George II consents that India bonds of, go to mistress and Johnson family, v. 397–8
groom supposedly killed by, v. 395
HW sends *Trial* of, to Mann, v. 388, 407
hanging of, announced by cousin in circular letter, v. 406, ix. 658
Hertford assizes attended by, v. 184
House of Lords ties, to the peace, v. 184, 396
Huntingdon, Cts of, visits, in prison, v. 398
in Tower, v. 374
keeper of, reads *Hamlet* to him, v. 408
mistress of, *see* Clifford, Mrs
Monro affirms lunacy of, v. 397
mother of, seeks his pardon, v. 388, 397
piquet played by, with warders, v. 397
robber fought by, v. 184
steward murdered by, v. 367, 396
trial of, v. 388, 406
uncle of, iii. 309n
Whitefield tries to convert, v. 398
wife and mistress ill-treated by, v. 395–6
wife separated from, by Act of Parliament, v. 367, 396
wife's murder attempted by, v. 183, 396

Shirley, Lady Mary (1712–84), m. (1730) Thomas Needham, 9th Vct Kilmorey:
almost a Methodist, iv. 271
Cheroffini, Contessa, at Rome, called by, *più meretrice di me*, v. 406
cousin's hanging announced by, in circular letter, v. 406, ix. 658
Dick, Lady, called 'Dyke' by, in letter, to avoid indelicate word, ix. 108
Florence visited by, iv. 271
malapropisms of, to Niccolini and Salins, iv. 298
mother lived with, in France, iv. 298
Nightingale family to separate from, iv. 278
Nightingales' relationship to, iv. 271, 278
scandal whispered by, about George II's amours, iv. 278
Shirley's aunt, iv. 271
Taylor recommended by, to Albani, iv. 458

Shirley, Robert (1650–1717), 1st E. Ferrers:
son of, iv. 481n

Shirley, Robert (1723–87), 6th E. Ferrers, 1778:

family insanity attested by, v. 388
Shirley, Lady Selina (1707–91), m. (1728)
Theophilus Hastings, 9th E. of Huntingdon:
Cornwallis told by, to exclude Ferrers's mistress, v. 398
daughter not allowed by, to accept Bedchamber post, iv. 33–4
Ferrers's courage expected by, to fail, v. 399
—— visited by, in prison, v. 398
HW calls: 'Queen of the Methodists,' iv. 33; 'St Theresa of the Methodists,' v. 398
Methodist seminary in Welsh mountains attended by, viii. 90
Methodists' patroness, viii. 401n
Shirley, Lady Fanny, makes, her heir, viii. 401
sister less Methodist than, iv. 271
Whitefield sent by, to convert Ferrers, v. 398
Shirley, Hon. Sewallis (1709–65), M.P.:
Bedford's play could not be memorized by, iii. 309, iv. 395
death of, vi. 366
document in duplicate sent by, through Sharpe, to Cts of Orford, iv. 547–8
HW calls: 'Hercules,' iv. 439; 'Hornadatus,' iv. 248
Kilmorey, Vcts, aunt of, iv. 271
Mann pities, iv. 443–4
name of, might be placed on Cts of Orford's monument, ix. 227
Orford, Cts of, discards, iv. 438–9, 443–4, 476
—— disparages, iv. 476, 479, 481, 487
—— gives separate maintenance to, iv. 439, 547–8, 568–9
—— keeps, as a slave to her jealousy, iv. 433
—— may forsake Richecourt for, iii. 385
—— might be made pregnant by, iv. 254
—— picks up, iii. 309
—— probably does not write when accompanied by, iv. 143
—— receives dunning letters from, iv. 479
—— to wed, iv. 239, 250
picture of, perhaps being claimed by Orford, ix. 227
Scarborough visited by, iv. 439
Vane, Vcts, describes her affair with, iv. 439
Shirley, Hon. Walter (1725–86), divine:
brother prefers services of, v. 398
brother procures porter from, v. 397
family insanity attested by, v. 388
Shirley, Washington (1677–1729), 2d E. Ferrers:
daughter of, iv. 33n, v. 398n
Shirley family:
arms of, worn by Cts of Orford, but not to be used on monument, ix. 240
Ferrers said to have been forced by, to

plead insanity, v. 396
——'s scaffold decorated at expense of, v. 402
insanity of, v. 388, 397
Shirts:
Franceschi's, sold, i. 122
Strozzi's servants borrow, for him, ii. 146
Young Pretender said to want, at Albano, ii. 378
Shivering fit; shivering fits:
occurrences of, ii. 268, viii. 76
Shoe; shoes:
Coventry, Cts of, has, made at Worcester, iv. 324
Mann wears galoches over, viii. 79
red-heeled, 'exploded,' ii. 148
Young Pretender's forces repair, at Perth, iii. 105
Shoe-buckles:
English ladies' bosoms do not hang to, ix. 641
Wortley Montagu wears, of diamonds, with a frock, iv. 226
Shoemaker:
at Worcester, exhibits Cts of Coventry's shoe, iv. 324
Shooting:
Ferdinand of Naples enjoys, in Florentine cascines and woods, ix. 600
See also Hunting
Shooting season:
London deserted during, ix. 433
Shop; shops:
at Genoa, plundered, iii. 338
at Leghorn fair, vi. 423
at Ranelagh jubilee-masquerade, iv. 47
in London: full of favours, i. 196; looking-glass sought in, from Pall Mall to Cheapside, iv. 141
See also Apothecary's Shop; Pastry shops; Ponte Vecchio; Snuff shop; Upholsterer's shop
Shopkeepers:
Methodism attracts, iv. 82
Shore, Jane (d. ?1527), mistress of Edward IV:
'Blagrave,' Mrs, friend of, viii. 162
Shorter, Catherine (ca 1682–1737), m. (1700) Sir Robert Walpole, K.B., 1725; K.G., 1726; HW's mother:
apartment rented by, for George II's coronation, v. 536
Boothby-Skrymsher's mother a cousin of, v. 497
brother of, iv. 403
death of, one of HW's heaviest blows, vi. 226
enemies of, i. 403
engraving of, in Ædes Walpolianæ, iii. 511
HW seeks statue for tomb of, i. 212n
HW taken by, to see George I, ix. 248
husband's defeat cannot injure, i. 246
India ink obtained by, from China after

[Shorter, Catherine, *continued*]
  Sir Hans Sloane refused to give her any, i. 436
  marriage of, vi. 27
  monument of, in Westminster Abbey, vi. 98n; *see also* Livia, statue of
  nephew of, iv. 468n, viii. 71n
  Philipps a cousin to, iii. 310n
  son of, ix. 462n
  statue for monument of, *see* Livia, statue of
  woman of, intimate with Mrs Gates, ix. 92n
Shorter, Charlotte (d. 1734), m. (1716) Francis Seymour Conway, cr. (1703) Bn Conway:
  brother of, iv. 403n
  son of, iv. 468n
Shorter, Erasmus (d. 1753):
  death of, iv. 403, 436
  Mann disapproves of, for not making a will, iv. 404–5
  nephews and niece share estate of, iv. 403
Shortness of breath:
  occurrences of, iv. 523, v. 1, ix. 394
Short Treatise on the Game of Whist. See under Hoyle, Edmond
Shoulder:
  Salimbeni breaks, i. 116, 132
Shovels, fire:
  Newcastle colliers said to feed their children with, iv. 450
Shows:
  London full of, ix. 502
  See also Opera; Plays; Theatre
Shreeve, Edmund (d. 1779), captain of *Earl of Besborough*, packet boat:
  Tuscans want satisfaction from, viii. 417
Shrewsbury, Ds of. *See* Paleotti, Adelaide (d. 1726)
Shrewsbury, D. of. *See* Talbot, Charles (1660–1718)
Shrewsbury, E. of. *See* Talbot, Charles (1660–1718); Talbot, George (1719–87); Talbot, John (ca 1384–1453)
Shroud:
  Balmerinoch wears, iii. 299
Shrub; shrubs:
  English, are often in full leaf by the end of April, ix. 497
  in bloom in February, v. 268
  walks edged with, v. 417
Shrubberies:
  HW ridicules, v. 418
Shuckburgh, Richard (1728–72), Col.:
  Mann called on by, at Florence, iv. 160
  Orford said to have recommended, to Mann, iv. 160
  whist addict, iv. 160
Shuckburgh, Mrs Richard. *See* Hayward, Sarah
Shuja-ud-daulah ('Sujah Dowla') (ca 1731–75), nawab-vizir of Oudh 1754–75:
  Oudh belongs to, ix. 13

Shulma ('Schuma'):
  Danville's maps do not include, viii. 29
  Rumiantsev to attack Grand Vizir at, viii. 29
Shuttlecock:
  Pembroke, Cts of, calls, 'shuttlesomething,' i. 496
Shuttleworth, (?) James (1714–73), M.P.:
  Nourse angers Windsor by accusing, of pretended illness, i. 248
Shuttleworth, Thomas (b. ?1674) or Richard (1708–before 1748); absconding bank clerk:
  Mann almost catches, before his escape to Naples, iii. 76–7
Shutz. *See* Schutz
Shuvalov, Comtesse. *See* Saltykov, Ekaterina Petrovna (1743–1817)
Shuvalov, André (1744–89), Comte; Gen.:
  England visited by, vi. 460
  Mann entertains, in Florence, vi. 460
Shuvalov, Ivan Ivanovich (1727–97), called Comte:
  blameless career of, when given absolute power, vi. **289n**
  Catherine II said to be cicisbea of, vii. 149
  —— said to have made, a chief minister, vi. **59**
  Elizabeth of Russia's minion, vi. 59, 455, vii. 149
  ——'s supposed husband, vi. 289n
  England visited by, vi. 289, 455–6
  Florence visited by, vii. 149
  HW disappointed in, vi. 289
  HW knew, in Paris, vi. 455
  HW's esteem for, vi. 289n, 455–6
  HW to receive compliments of, vi. 565
  Italy may be visited by, vi. 456
  Mann entertains, vi. 564
  —— will expect, vi. 460
  Razumovskiĭ accompanies, vi. 456, 564–5
Shveidnitz. *See* Schweidnitz
Siam:
  ambassadors from and to, *see under* Ambassador
Siberia:
  Apraxin exiled to, v. 159
  Catherine II would rather plunder Constantinople than develop, ix. 545
  death preferable to exile in, vi. 68
  forces of, oppose Frederick II, v. 327
  HW compares Houghton (Norfolk) to, i. 495, ii. 68, 467, 481
  next door to the Russian Court drawing-room, vi. 55
  Peter III may banish Vorontsov to, vi. 11
  Pomerania worth more than, vi. 11
  Russian leaders recalled from, vi. 11, 59–60
Sibilla, giuoco della. *See* Giuoco
Sibley, James (d. by 1793), HW's footman:
  (?) illiterate, ix. 118
  (?) letter mistakenly posted by, ix. 118
Sibyl:

Domenichino's, i. 267-8, 313, 325
Sibylline Leaves:
  HW will not dispose, over Europe, ix. 105
Sicard, —— (d. 1752), French traitor:
  France demands, from Tripoli, iv. 319
Sicilies, two. *See* Naples; Sicily; Two Sicilies
Sicily:
  Bute would have written to HW from Otranto, had he visited, vii. 103
  Charles of Naples may take refuge in, ii. 453
  Cicero in, compared to Conway, viii. 526
  earthquake damage in, less than was represented, ix. 391
  grain not to be sent by, to Italy, till French and Spanish wants are filled, vii. 430
  honours of, may be conferred on Mann, ii. 484
  Inquisition suppressed in, ix. 383
  Leghorn bans ships from, because of plague, ii. 252
  Malta imports all supplies from, iv. 405
  Naples isolated from, because of plague, ii. 252
  Otranto not in, vii. 107
  Phelps's secret expedition into, v. 124
  plague in, *see under* Messina
  Pomfret, Cts of, describes tour of, v. 579
  rebellion in, viii. 39
  Wortley Montagu may embark from, for Egypt, vi. 77
Sida, Abp of. *See* Onorati, Bernadino
Sida Tunez Bey, son of Bey of Tunis. *See* Yūnus Bey
Sideboard:
  Brown, Sir Robert, saves money by not having orange or lemon on, ix. 609
Sidi Mahmūd Aga, envoy from Tripoli to Holland:
  Elizabeth brings, to Leghorn, vii. 24
Sidi Yannes. *See* Yūnus Bey
Sidney, Lady Dorothy (1617-84), m. 1 (1639) Henry Spencer, 1st E. of Sunderland; m. 2 (1652) Robert Smythe; 'Sacharissa':
  Smythe descended from, vii. 248
Sidney, Elizabeth (d. 1783), m. William Perry:
  marriage of, iv. 389n
Sidney, Mary (d. 1758), m. (1738) Sir Brownlow Sherard:
  co-heiress to Earls of Leicester, iv. 389n
Sidney, Sir Philip (1554-86), Kt:
  HW mentions, in *Catalogue of the Royal and Noble Authors*, v. 196
Sidney family, Earls of Leicester:
  co-heiress of, marries Perry, iv. 389n
Sidon:
  Arlington St's resemblance to, iv. 469
Siècle de Louis XIV, Le, . . . [and] *un précis du siècle de Louis XV. See under* Voltaire
Siena:
  Bichi, Mme, of, ii. 206

cantata and ball given for D. of York in theatre at, vi. 232
Carmelite friar from, vi. 438
coaches not to be hired at, iii. 232
cold very severe at, in winter, viii. 130
commissary of, welcomes D. of York, vi. 224
countess of, will not sit at table with actor, vi. 170
epidemic at, vi. 511
fen country makes air of, unwholesome, viii. 130
figure of, dressed in red velvet, at St John's day celebration, ii. 251
Fortini-Oxenden feud divides, iii. 374
Guercino painting at, iv. 263, 313
HW proposes, to D. and Ds of Gloucester, as winter residence, viii. 125, 130
Hervey to visit, vi. 430
inn at, vi. 223
lady from, calls on Princesse de Craon, i. 481
Leopold to visit, viii. 343
Mann gets marble from, for Chesterfield, iii. 423
—— hopes not to accompany Tuscan Court, to, vi. 511
—— plans Sir Robert Walpole's visit to, ii. 212-13
Oxenden may visit, to learn Italian, iii. 232
passeggio out of gates of, vi. 232
Spanish army blocks approach from, to Tuscany, i. 289
Strozzi fails to visit, i. 111
Te Deum sung in, v. 112
theatre at, burned, ii. 46
theatre, new, at, iv. 391
Tuscan Court pleased by shows at, vi. 515
Tuscan Court to go to, vi. 511
visitors to: Almada, vii. 26; Bruce, iv. 391; Damer, Hon. George, vi. 286; Gascoigne, vi. 286; Leopold, vi. 515; Mann, iv. 391, vi. 223, 228; Montemar, ii. 46; Orford, Cts of, viii. 70; Oxenden, iii. 232, 374; Rockingham, iv. 263; York, Cardinal, ix. 394; York, D. of, vi. 223-4, 228, 231-2
Young Pretender leaves, for Florence, vii. 318
Siette. *See* La Siette
'Sigismonda':
  Furoni's painting of, attributed to Correggio, v. 200
Silesia:
  arms of, on Hyndford's plate, ii. 89
  Austria hopes to regain, iv. 528, 576, v. 360
  Bohemian areas adjacent to, retained by Frederick II, v. 116
  borders of, in dispute, iv. 187
  Frederick II demands, i. 144
  —— may be given Holland or Flanders in lieu of, iii. 223

[Silesia, *continued*]

HW imagines Frederick II galloping to, ix. 190

Hohenfriedburg defeat in, iii. 58, 65

Hungarians invade, ii. 543, 547

Hyndford secures, to Frederick II instead of to Maria Theresa, ii. 89

Lobkowitz transferred to, iii. 58

Maria Theresa loses, ii. 521

—— may obtain, at expense of English and Dutch alliance, iii. 238

—— persuaded by Robinson to give up all of, to Frederick II, ii. 108

——'s attempt to recover, disastrous, iv. 588, v. 15, 502, 519, vi. 51–2

Prussian-Russian battle expected in, v. 72

Silesian loan:

Frederick II may demand, iv. 360

Prussian manifesto stops payment of interest on, iv. 348

Silhouette, Étienne de (1709–67), controller-general:

French trade and credit ruined by financial device of, to raise money, v. 349

Silhouette:

Huber's, of Ds of Grafton, v. 548, 554

Silistria:

Russians threaten, vii. 479, viii. 29

Silius, C. (d. A.D. 48):

Messalina marries, in her husband's lifetime, viii. 333

Silk:

brocaded, Mrs Rudd pays mercer for, viii. 153

cherry-coloured, Mann should not be paid with, vi. 226

coat of, v. 410

damask of, v. 447

Florence to send, to Constantinople, iii. 437

flowered, canonici and abbés forbidden to wear, v. 224

HW procures, for Mme Pucci, i. 159, 222, 416, ii. 112

hangings of, v. 468, 471, 481

stockings worn as sleeves are tipped with, ii. 109

waistcoat of, iv. 396

Silk merchant. *See* Dreier; Nutini

Sillery:

battle of, v. 416

Silva Gruenemberg, Odoardo de (ca 1693–1771), Marchese della Banditella; Spanish consul at Leghorn 1718–62:

Braitwitz hears from, i. **180**

Charles of Naples sends, to Mann with expostulations, iii. 57

Mann might have been compared by, to Telesephorus, iii. 383

—— negotiates with, iii. 65

——'s correspondence with, iii. 57

——'s negotiations with, approved by George II, iii. 86

—— thanked by, iii. 383

protest by, about passage of artillery, ii. 542

Richecourt belittles complaints of, ii. 542

Silver:

bell of, for inkstand, vii. 383

candlestick of, vii. 285

Cellini's chest of, vii. 427

coffee-pot of, *see under* Coffee-pot

double-plated, Mann wants dish-covers of, viii. 27, 32

écus of, given by Lady Mary Wortley Montagu to son, ii. 567

Electress leaves, to courtiers, ii. 169

flowers of, on riding-coat, vi. 3

glasses framed in, ii. 169

hoard of, in Mme Gavi's small coal, i. 223

Invincible carries, iii. 411

Jesuits', weighed, vii. 512–13

lamps of, ix. 55

Mann to buy, ii. 472

medals of, ii. 406, 424, 447, 478, v. 189, 201, 203

medals sold for their content of, ii. 478

pencil of, i. 194

penny of, ix. 15

picture-frame of, ii. 171

plated, wears badly, viii. 27

scarcity of, in Rome, i. 4

snuff-box of, ii. 553

standish of, ii. 126

suit laced with, i. 183

table and stands of, ii. 169

teaspoons of, v. 221

trunk of, for perfumes, x. 56

tubes of, iv. 203

Silver lace. *See under* Lace

Silver pharaoh. *See under* Faro

Silver plate:

cost of Fane's, ii. 472

Mann to buy, ii. 472

Silversmith:

Munro to consult, about double silver plated dish-covers, viii. 32

See also Demetrius; Siries, Cosimo; Siries, Louis

Silver stuff:

HW's suit of, for George III's wedding, vii. 285

Simbach:

battle of, ii. 230, 234, 249

Simiramis. *See* Semiramis

Simolin, Ivan Matveevich (1720–ca 1800), Russian minister to England 1779–85:

George III told by, about Russian-Turkish peace, ix. 486

Simon, St:

HW refers to Saville as, vii. 170

Simonet, ——, maître de ballet at Paris and London (fl. 1772–92):

(?) daughter of, ix. 585

Simonet, Mlle, dancer; æronaut:

balloon ascent by, with Blanchard, ix. 585

Simonet, Mme, dancer:
daughter of, ix. 585
Simonetta, Contessa. *See* Castelbarco, Teresa di
Simonetti, Francesco:
government post given to, vii. 294
Simonetti. *See also* Simonetta
Simonin. *See* Simolin
Simpson, Rev. Peter (ca 1710–80), (?) assistant at Mayfair Chapel:
(?) sermon by, iv. 241, 243
Sims, William (fl. 1778–1814), customs official:
Mann, John, to be succeeded by, viii. 368
Sinclair, Hon. James (d. 1762), army officer; M.P.:
Port l'Orient bungled by, iii. 456
Wentworth to be succeeded by, iii. 456
Singer; singers:
amateur, might walk at a coronation, viii. 86
bankers recruit, for English opera, i. 191
from Canterbury, Oxford, and the farces, to sing *Miserere*, i. 211
Gallini collects, in Italy, ix. 431
Italian: Conway, Bns, has, at assembly, i. 334; Pembroke, E. of, pursues, to Florence, ix. 497n; *William and Mary* visited by, i. 141
Mann may have to hire, for Holdernesse, iv. 259
poor, of Handel's oratorios, ii. 180, 186
See also Opera
Singing:
popularity of, in England, viii. 89
Sinigaglia:
Spaniards march to, ii. 16
Spanish invalids to sail to, ii. 76
Young Pretender at, vii. 225
Sinistri:
Mulinari nearly as big as, ii. 138
Sinopoli:
earthquake account mentions, ix. 376
Sinzendorff, Philipp Ludwig (1699–1747), Count von; cardinal; Bp of Breslau:
Old Pretender may receive, i. 11
Sion House, Middlesex:
Northumberlands build at, iv. 341
Siracusa. *See* Syracuse
Sir Charles Grandison. See under Richardson, Samuel
Sir Courtly Nice. See under Crowne, John
Sirens:
England imports, from Italy, when superannuated, viii. 149
Siries, Cosimo (d. 1789), Florentine jeweller:
(?) medal by, viii. 469–70, 478, 500
Siries, Louis (d. ? 1759), French silversmith at Florence:
Astley's copy mistaken by, for Guercino original, iv. 313–14
at Palazzo Vecchio, i. 213, iv. 475n, viii. 500
Correggio painting shown by, to Mann, iv. 314

edict will be resented by customers of, iv. 475
French goldsmith, buying and selling curiosities at the Palazzo Vecchio in Florence, iv. 475n
French silversmith settled at Florence, viii. 500n
HW's old acquaintance of Palazzo Vecchio, iv. 313, viii. 500
HW's patch box praised by, i. 414
Mann to order scissors from, i. 93, 99
medallist probably grandson of, viii. 500
razors to be made by, for Sultan of Turkey, iii. 437
spectacles blamed by, for mistake, iv. 313–14
stairs to rooms of, ix. 169
Siries, Luigi (1743–1811), Florentine jeweller:
(?) medal by, viii. 469, 478, 500
Siris. See under Berkeley, George
Siristori. *See* Serristori
Sismani, Principe di. *See* Corsini, Bartolommeo (1683–1752)
Sisson, (?)Jeremiah, of Beaufort Bldgs, Strand; scientific instrument-maker:
design of, for water-raising machine, v. 390
HW and James Mann hurry, to finish drawing, v. 384
HW delivers Perelli's letter to, v. 354, 359–60
HW's correspondence with, v. 407
'low indigent mechanic,' v. 407
Mann, James, to treat with, v. 414
model of machine to be sent by sea, v. 375–6
payments to, v. 384, 407, 414
Perelli praises performance of, v. 430, 432–3
——'s correspondence with, v. **348**, 354, 359–60, 375, 414, 432–3
Sittingbourne, Kent:
HW visits, i. 142
Six Letters from A—d B—r to Father Sheldon. See under Douglas, John
Six Overtures for Violins. See under Handel, George Frideric
Sixpences:
HW wins, at faro, iii. 494
Six Voyages. See under Tavernier, Jean-Baptiste
1641:
1770 treads in steps of, vii. 170
Sixtus V (Felice Peretti) (1521–90), pope 1585–90:
casino of, at Villa Negroni, viii. 7
Clement XIV imitates, vii. 157
Elizabeth supposedly excommunicated by, vi. 177
Italy unused to severity of, v. 395
treasure deposited by, in Castel St Angelo, vi. 446, 448
Villa Negroni, villa of, may be used by Ds of Kingston, vii. 567, viii. 14, 24–5, 31

Skating:
Omai learns, viii. 175
on Florentine ponds, viii. 434
Skavronska, Anna Karlovna (1723–75), m. (1742) Count Mikhail Ilarionovich Vorontsov:
appearance and costume of, masculine, vi. 193
Catherine II rejects proposal of, to surrender Order of St Catherine, vi. 65
Craon, Princesse de, quarrels with, v. 248–9, 259
Czarina Elizabeth's relative, v. 248, vi. 173
—— jealous of nephew's attentions to, vi. 173
Italy to be revisited by, vi. 173
Mann knew, at Florence, vii. 245
Skelton, Young Pretender's officer. See Sheridan, Sir Thomas
Skerrett, Maria (ca 1702–38), m. (ca 1738) Sir Robert Walpole, K.B., 1725; K.G., 1726:
daughter of, i. 320n, vi. 262n, ix. 418n, 464n
Leneve, Isabella, cares for daughter after death of, ix. 609n
marriage of, vi. 27
Skin diseases:
Pisa baths thought to cure, viii. 83
Skinner, Brinley (d. 1764), consul at Leghorn 1724–34:
Charles III snatches wig of, vii. 238
Skinner, Matthew (1689–1749), serjeant-at-law; M.P.:
rebel lords tried by, iii. 282
Skittles:
Chatsworth guests play, v. 433
Skreene. See Skrine
Skrine, Mrs. See Sumner, Jane
Skrine, William (ca 1672–1725); apothecary:
son of, iv. 145
Skrine, William (?1721–83), M.P. Callington 1774–80:
circumstances of, said to be distressed, ix. 386
extravagance of, in entertaining at Florence, iv. 145
obligated to Orford, ix. 158, 166
Orford, E. of, sends, to Callington borough, viii. 46
—— wishes, to assist in Mozzi affair, ix. 158, 162, 164, 166
Roman's letter to, enclosed by Mann to HW, vi. 447, 450
son of Bath apothecary, iv. 145
suicide of, ix. 385–6
wife's death will be a relief to, vi. 402
Skrymsher. See Boothby Skrymsher
Skyrockets:
HW would like to drink, iii. 249
Slaughter:
Mann's reflections on, ix. 282

Slave; slaves:
African, observe destruction of men-of-war by hurricane, ix. 109
'black boys' given to Mann and Dick by Russians, vii. 228
galley: at Leghorn, eat venison, iv. 83; escape from galleys, iv. 206; sent to work at Messina, ii. 262
Moroccan, accompany ambassador at Leghorn, viii. 469
Turkish girls, given to Lady Dick and Maria Louisa by Russians, vii. 228
Slavery:
Acton and sailors might be carried into, iv. 473
HW attacks, iv. 126
Montesquieu attacks, iv. 126
Turkish pirates subject captive seamen to, i. 16
Slave trade:
African Company's, debated in Parliament, iv. 126
England to assist France in, v. 526
Slavonians:
Mann grants commissions to, for their protection against French, ix. 249
sailors who capture Great Duchess of Tuscany, ix. 479
Sleep:
HW has lost little of, despite gout, ix. 620
HW's, 'marvellous,' ix. 558
Sleeve; sleeves:
lawn, Bp Hervey wears, ix. 455
long, to be worn by Venetian doge's nephew or grandson, i. 75
Mann wears, at baptism, i. 473
stockings worn as, ii. 109
Slingsby, Barbara (ca 1669–1721), m. 1 (1688) Sir Richard Mauleverer, 4th Bt; m. 2 (1693) John Arundell, 2d Bn Arundell; m. 3 (1708) Thomas Herbert, 8th E. of Pembroke:
relationships of, iv. 108n, ix. 178n
Slippers:
HW gives, to Princesse de Craon, i. 415
Montagu, Lady Mary Wortley, wears, vi. 3
of gold brocade, Bootle wears, at breakfast, iv. 184
Sloane, Sir Hans (1660–1753), cr. (1716) Bt; physician:
India ink, coloured, imported by, i. 436
museum of: HW a trustee of, iv. 358–9; offered for sale, after Sloane's death, iv. 358
Walpole, Lady, refused India ink by, i. 436
Sloop; sloops:
American, burned on the Delaware, viii. 386
English, puts in at Antibes, ii. 385
Gage dispatches, with news of Lexington battle, viii. 110
in English invasion of France, v. 204

Sluys:
Conway to visit, v. 261
French besiege, iii. 389
governor of, reprimanded for not admitting English troops, iii. 91
Smallpox:
Chute discusses, with Mme Sarrazin, i. 498
——'s joke on Primate of Lorraine's death from, i. 480, 498
deaths from, in Swedish royal family, i. 255
epidemic of, in London, iii. 224, iv. 434
French and Spanish fleets ravaged by, viii. 519, 527, 530
inoculation for, see under Inoculation
Italian peasants want, to reduce the number of their children, vi. 150
Lorenzi's daughter has, after inoculation, vi. 153
occurrences of, i. 148, 150, 255, 416, 468, 480, 498, ii. 65, 341, 510, iii. 224, 334, 467, iv. 137-8, 175, v. 42-3, vi. 126-7, 153, 525-6, 558, 561, vii. 238, 527, viii. 1-2, 5, 8, 13, 19, 330, ix. 413, 414
Octavius may have had, on the brain, ix. 414
prevalent in Florence, vi. 559
Smells:
Chute and HW enjoy, ii. 230
Smelt, Leonard (ca 1719-1800), Capt. in royal engineers; George IV's sub-governor:
resigns as George IV's sub-governor, viii. 217
Smerna; Smirnia. See Smyrna
Smissaert, Joan Carel (1684-1747), Lt.-Gen.:
witticism by, on being sent from England without orders, ii. 458
Smith, Capt. See Callis, Smith
Smith, Mr ——:
puny spark, iv. 23
St John, Vcts, accompanied by, iv. 23
Smith, Capt. John, Sackville's aide-de-camp:
boastful letters of, from army in France, v. 211
Smith, John, under-sheriff of Middlesex:
Wilkes cannot again be returned by, as M.P., vii. 110
Smith, Joseph (ca 1675-1770), English consul at Venice 1744-60:
Chute and HW amused by ignorance of, ii. 465
English newspapers probably shown by, to HW, i. 84
George III buys art collection and library of, vi. 107, 115, ix. 93
Gray draws money from, i. 82
HW's lack of influence with opera directors to be repeated by, ii. 211
library of, ii. 465n
Mann's correspondence with, i. 82, 88, 101, 195
—— sends letter through, to HW, i. 58, 86

paintings of, shown to Chute and HW, ii. 465
Pertici and 'tinca nera' sought by, at Venice, for English performances, ii. 198
titlepages alone known to, ii. 465
Smith, Joseph (ca 1733-90), Gen.:
booty of, at Tanjore, vii. 561
Smith, Margaret (d. 1814), m. (1760) Sir Charles Bingham, 7th Bt; cr. (1776) Bn and (1795) E. of Lucan:
artistic activities of, viii. 462, 475
daughter of, to wed, ix. 104, 108
daughters taught by, viii. 417
Florence visited by, viii. 417, 462
HW's neighbourhood visited by, viii. 517
HW's relations with, viii. 417, 462, 475
husband follows volatile leadership of, viii. 475
Mann loves, ix. 108
—— praised by, viii. 517
—— saw, with her daughter and niece, ix. 620
—— to entertain, at dinner, viii. 462-3
—— to take, to opera, viii. 418
painting executed by, for Mann, viii. 462
painting the pursuit of, at Rome, viii. 462
poetic turn of, viii. 475
(?) sarcophagus from Rome to be presented by, to HW, viii. 462, 475
Smith:
Young Pretender assumes name of, vii. 318
Smith. See also Smyth; Smythe
Smithfield:
earthquake effects expected in, iv. 130
Warburton measures ground in, for Wilkes's execution, vi. 185
Smithson, Lady Elizabeth. See Seymour, Lady Elizabeth (1716-76)
Smithson, Sir Hugh (d. 1733), 3d Bt:
said to be a coachman, iv. 124-5
Smithson, (afterwards Percy), Sir Hugh (1715-86), 4th Bt, 2d E. of Northumberland; n.c.: cr. (1766) D. of Northumberland; M.P.:
administration may be headed by, vi. 521
Cabinet councillor and chamberlain to Q. Charlotte, vi. 103
chaplains of, vi. 239
dukedom conferred upon, v. 191n, vi. 462
election of, iii. 425
etiquette of, iv. 341
extravagant construction by, iv. 341
father-in-law wants title to revert to, iv. 81
gallery of: HW condemns, iv. 340-1, 507, v. 88, 90, 96-7; HW sees, by candlelight, v. 88; Mann defends, to Galfridus Mann, iv. 340-1; Mann procures copies of Italian paintings for, iv. 328-9, 340-1, 352-3, 490, 507n, v. 88, 90, 96-7; Mann receives drawing of, v. 209; will be opened with masquerade, iv. 507
George III will not entail dukedom on children of, by another wife, viii. 99n

[Smithson, Sir Hugh, *continued*]
Gordon rioters pick pockets of, ix. 54
grandfather of, a coachman, iv. 124–5
HW does not know, well enough to recommend Muzell to him, v. 514
K.G., v. 27
Mann receives snuff-box from, v. 209, 222
——'s correspondence with, v. 209
marriage and peerages of, vii. 365n
may be prosecuted for hiring mob at Brentford, vii. 79
Middlesex Parliamentary seat of, vacated, iv. 125
mob forces, to drink Wilkes's health, vii. 7
mob pelts, vii. 99
Northumberland title goes to, iv. 124
Parliamentary act procured by, to boost his rent by erection of powder mills, vii. 365–6
political failure of, vii. 216
remarriage of, unlikely, viii. 99
Robinson gets Armagh archbishopric through influence of, vi. 276
Rockingham ministry shows civilities to, vi. 431
son of, v. 512, viii. 315n, ix. 422n
son of, marries Bute's daughter, vi. 302n
supper given by, for Cts of Yarmouth, v. 191
Swiss porters kept by, iv. 341
upper servants of, want to be stylish by wearing mourning for Ps Caroline, v. 165
Weymouth to succeed, as Lord Lieutenant of Ireland, vi. 302
wife of, does not inherit Percy estate, iv. 11n
Smith Stanley, Edward (1752–1834); styled Ld Strange or Ld Stanley; 12th E. of Derby, 1776; M.P.:
cook of, who protests against 3 A.M. suppers, asked how much he valued his life, viii. 310
fiancée to be entertained by, at fête champêtre at the Oaks, viii. **14**
wife of, to wed Dorset after her divorce, viii. 436
Smith Stanley, James (1717–71), styled Bn Strange; M.P.:
death of, leaves chancellorship of Duchy of Lancaster vacant, vii. 313
Egmont clashes with, iv. **32**
militia bill to be presented by, v. 552
Onslow's exemption from place tax sought by, v. 199
Tories usually joined by, iv. 32
Smitsart. *See* Smissaert
Smoking:
Stanislas I's, iv. 26
Smollett, Tobias George (1721–71), novelist:
Adventures of Peregrine Pickle, Lady Vane's memoirs in, i. 459n
capable of dealing with parties, not with factions, vi. 306

False Alarm attributed by, to Johnson, vii. 189
HW warns Mann against, vii. 198
History of England by, vi. 306, vii. 198n
settled at Pisa for health, vii. 189
Smugglers:
East India Company buys tea at Ostend to cheat, ix. 577–8
Smuggling:
Blakiston twice convicted of, iv. 261n
Haszlang conducts, ix. 55
of Burgundy wine, iv. 289
Smyrna:
Pars shut up in consul's house at, during plague, x. 48
Turkish cruelties to Christians at, vii. 232, 235
Smyth, Arthur (1706–71), Bp of Clonfert, 1752; of Down, 1753; of Meath, 1765; Abp of Dublin, 1766:
HW's financial dealings with, i. **10**
Mann to receive compliments of, i. 25
Naples visited by, i. 16, 23
Rome visited by, i. 10, 15, 16, 23, 25
Shrewsbury's servant discusses Young Pretender's departure with, i. 14
Venice the destination of, i. 23
Wiseman to be instructed by, i. 15
Smyth, Lady Georgiana. *See* Fitzroy, Lady Georgiana
Smythe, Maria Anne (1756–1837), m. 1 (1775) Edward Weld; m. 2 (1778) Thomas Fitzherbert; m. 3 (1785) George, P. of Wales:
George, P. of Wales's connection with: ix. 625n, 637; Mann tries to discredit rumours of, ix. 627; reported in Berlin gazette, ix. 628; reported in *Gazette de Leyde*, ix. 628–9
Smythe, Robert (d. before 1684):
Smythe, Bn, descended from, vii. 248
Smythe, Sir Sidney Stafford (1705–78), Kt; Bn of the Exchequer; M.P.:
becomes commissioner of the Great Seal, v. **25**
Methodist, and Sacharissa's descendant, vii. 248
to be Lord Keeper, vii. 248
Snakes:
taming of, iv. 454
See also Asp
Sneyd, Jeremiah (fl. 1770–91), 1st clerk in secretary of state's office:
continuance of, in secretary's office, unknown to Mann, ix. 272
HW hopes, will be more regular in transmitting letters, vii. 454
Mann offered services of, as Larpent's successor, vii. **443**
Snow:
England has: in late March, ix. 483; in October, ix. 613
Fiesole cut off by, viii. 347
Florence cut off by, from Rome, ix. 470

Florence imports, from Vallombrosa, iv. 25
French post impeded by, i. 207
HW kept in town by, ix. 258
in Florence: in April, i. 369; in March, ix. 628; plentiful, iii. 466; prevents use of coaches, vi. 385, 574, 575; streets covered, vi. 479
in Paris, vi. 396
near Florence: falls daily, iii. 471; in October, iv. 336
on Bologna mountains, v. 435, ix. 22
on Bologna road, ix. 2
on Florentine hills, in April, iii. 391
on Tuscan mountains: in April, ix. 397; in January, vi. 575, ix. 2; in late October, ix. 334, 441; in March, iii. 472; in May, i. 34
Orford, Cts of, turned back by, at Siena, viii. 70
Pisa covered by, in late March, vii. 294
Snow (vessel), French:
English brig captured by, v. 334
Snuff:
Florentines sacrifice, for lottery tickets, iv. 389
HW does not take, iv. 377
Mann lists advantages of, iv. 392
——'s headache may be caused by, iv. 376, 377, 392
—— tries to stop taking, iv. 376, 377, 389, 392
—— uses, to appear nonchalant, iv. 392
Snuff-box; snuff-boxes:
Barbantane supposed to have sent, to Mann, ix. 206
Capponi receives, from Modenese princess, i. 70
Catherine II gives, to Chesterfield, vii. 376
Choiseul's portrait frequently found on, in France, vii. 303
Coke, Lady Mary, brings, to HW, vi. 94
crystal, jewelled, given by Maria Theresa to Forrester, ii. 107
diamond: Catherine II said to have promised, to Mann, ix. 84; Maria Theresa gives, to Giustiniani, vi. 465
Electress gives, to Kaunitz, i. 48
Florence to send, to Constantinople, iii. 437
French excel, in designing, ix. 635
Gordon rioters snatch, from members of Parliament, ix. 54
HW's, balloon looks no bigger than, ix. 579
HW sends, to Mann, i. 436
HW to buy, in Rome, i. 29
HW to procure, for Mann in Naples, i. 26, 29
HW to show, to Rucellai, i. 30
horn, Frederick II gives, to Giustiniani, vi. 465
Mann procures, from Naples for Stone, i. 26, 29, ii. 115, 330, 445, 496n

Modenese princess gives, to Capponi and Mme Grifoni, i. 70
Neapolitan: HW and Galfridus Mann receive, ii. 496; sent by Mann to HW, ii. 330
Northumberland, D. of, gives, to Mann, v. 209
pillow no bigger than, i. 481
Serristori, Andrea, receives, from Modenese princess, i. 64, 70
silver, Uguccioni gives, to Granvilles, iii. 553
stone, given by Bp of Apamea to Kaunitz, i. 48
Suares, Mme, receives, from Modenese princess, i. 64
Wade's, stolen at gaming-house, iv. 110
with Zincke's portrait of Cts of Orford, HW receives, from Sharpe, to be sent to Mozzi, ix. 501
Wortley Montagu collects, iv. 226
Snuff shop:
Mann's abstinence from snuff will distress, iv. 389
Soap:
remedy beneficial to Horatio Walpole (1678–1757), iii. 510n, iv. 3
Sobervia, galleon:
in Spanish fleet, i. 286
Sobieska, Maria Clementina (1702–35), m. (1719) James Francis Edward Stuart, the 'Old Pretender':
bare-bone knees of, ix. 106
cost of funeral of, exclusive of mausoleum in St Peter's, v. 391
Mann calls, 'Santa Sobieski,' iii. 362
miracles of, will cause her to be declared a saint, v. 424
Orsolene convent the refuge of, from husband's tyranny, ix. 106
Sobieski, Johan. See John III
'Sobieski, Santa.' See Sobieska, Maria Clementina
Sobieskists, Polish:
HW pities, vii. 338
Sochet, Charles-René-Dominique (1727–94), called Chevalier Destouches; French naval officer:
Arbuthnot's clash with, ix. 150
Society for Arts and Sciences. See Society for the Encouragement of Arts, Manufactures, and Commerce
Society for the Encouragement of Arts, Manufactures, and Commerce:
establishment of, v. 173
HW neglects, viii. 284
Society for the Reformation of Manners:
HW proposes project for, v. 418
Society of Apothecaries:
garden of, at Chelsea, ii. 250
Society of Artists Associated for the Relief of their Distressed Brethren:
exhibit of, vii. 210–11

Socorro, Marqués del. *See* Solano y Bote, José

Socrates (469–399 B.C.), philosopher:
house of, compared to that of Ds of Queensberry, iv. 226, 235–6

Soderini, Signora. *See* Cenci, Porcia (ca 1700–72); Mignanelli, Prudenza (ca 1691–1775)

Södermanland, D. of. *See* Karl (1748–1818)

Sodi, Pietro, dancer:
opera performance of, pleases, ii. 104

Sofa, The. See Sopha

Sofa:
Fane likes to recline on, iii. 100

Soho:
ball at, vii. 193
St Anne's in, v. 140, 148
tailor in, Theodore of Corsica knows, v. 45

Soho Square:
Beckford's house in, vii. 205
Cornelys, Theresa, takes Carlisle House in, vii. 271
English court would not exile people to, vii. 298

Soissons, Bp of. *See* Fitzjames, François de

Solano, Joseph:
captured at Velletri, ii. 493

Solano y Bote, José (1726–1806), cr. (1784) Marqués del Socorro; Spanish naval officer:
said to return to Europe with Guichen, ix. 94

Solaro di Breglio, Roberto Ignazio (ca 1715–65), Sardinian minister to France 1758–65:
employed in Paris peace treaty, vi. 105

Soldier; soldiers:
Botta's solicitude for, vi. 124
elections invalid if supervised by, i. 252
England and America enlist, viii. 81
English: cuts ring from old woman's finger, v. 221; remark by, to French, v. 191; take to robbery when disbanded, iv. 111
foot, Mann receives letter through, i. 52
Frederick II forbids, to accept any more presents from a Madonna, ix. 499–500
hat retained and musket shouldered by, when delivering message, iii. 439–40
Joseph II encourages copulation to get more, ix. 280
Palliser's house protected by, viii. 442
physicians commit more deaths than, ix. 342
sbirri quarrel with, viii. 8–9
Sundon's election invalidated by presence of, i. 251–2
will not, like priests, be suppressed, ix. 237

'Soldiers at cards.' *See under* Van Dyck, Antony

Soleil, French privateer:
arrival in London of prisoners from, iii. 180
English ship captures, on way from Dunkirk to Montrose, iii. 173

Henry Benedict (Stuart)'s capture on, believed certain, iii. 173, 177

Soleil Royal, French ship:
Conflans forced to burn, v. 351
runs aground, v. 357

Solemeni. *See* Solimena

Solicitor-General:
Dunning resigns as, vii. 175, 180
Murray is, i. 250n, 344n, 494, ii. 118, iii. 283, 379
—— succeeds Strange as, ii. 118
—— to succeed Strange as, i. 494
Wedderburne becomes, vii. 269
Wilkes not proved by, to be author of *North Briton,* vi. 189
Yorke, Charles, may become, iv. 202
See also De Grey, Sir William (1719–81); Murray, William (1705–93); Norton, Sir Fletcher (1716–89); Strange, Sir John (1692–1754)

Solimena, Francesco (1657–1747), painter:
painting not by, left by Electress to Benedict XIV, ii. 171, 207

Solis de Folck de Cordona, Francesco (1713–75), cardinal, 1756:
Conclave entered by, vii. 113
'dried blackish parchment only covers his little bones,' viii. 69
reaches Conclave in dying condition, viii. 68–9

Solis y Sante (d. 1744), Don; Duque d'Atrisco; field marshal:
detachment of, ii. 443

Solitaire:
San Vitale gives, to Tesi, i. 70

Solomon (fl. ca 970 B.C.), king of Israel:
Churchill asks question about, iv. 367
Frederick II compared to, v. 94, vii. 539
HW has not sagacity of, vii. 555
HW's name for Louis XV, vii. 157
saying attributed to, vii. 198

Solomon I (d. 1784), king of western Georgia 1752–65, 1768–84:
Turkish warfare of, vi. 420

Soltyk, Kajetan (d. 1788), Bp of Kiev 1749–59, of Cracow 1759–88:
Russians remove, vi. 574

Soltykov, Count Petr Semenovich (ca 1700–72), Russian field marshal:
Prussian oath of allegiance taken back by, vi. 75

Somers, John (1651–1716), cr. (1697) Bn Somers; lord chancellor:
Swift disparages, in history, v. 185
Yorke's papers of, lost in fire, iv. 322, 331–2

Somerset, Ds of. *See* Fillol, Catherine; Finch, Lady Charlotte (d. 1773); Percy, Lady Elizabeth (ca 1667–1722); Stanhope, Anne (ca 1497–1587); Thynne, Frances (ca 1699–1754)

Somerset, D. of. *See* Seymour, Algernon (1684–1750); Seymour, Charles (1662–1748);

Seymour, Edward (ca 1500–52); Seymour, Sir Edward (1695–1757)

Somerset, Lady Anne (1741–63), m. (1759) Charles Compton, 7th E. of Northampton, 1758:
Bagot and physician accompany, to Rome, vi. 142
death of, vi. 150
Florence visited by, vi. 132
handsome, v. 294
health of, consumption, vi. 132, 142, 145
Mann tries to comfort, vi. 132
Naples to be visited by, vi. 132, 142
Northampton, E. of, to wed, v. **294**, 313

Somerset, Lord Charles Noel (1709–56), 4th D. of Beaufort, 1745:
brother succeeded by, iii. 26n, iv. 50n
daughter of, viii. 54n
Jacobites led by, i. **231**, iii. 26
Opposition meeting addressed by, at St Alban's Tavern, iv. 50
widow of, viii. 46n, 120, ix. 564n

Somerset, Lady Elizabeth (d. 1760):
mother loses, by consumption, vii. 372

Somerset, Lady Henrietta (1748–69), m. (1769) Sir Watkin Williams Wynn, 4th Bt:
mother loses, by consumption, vii. 372

Somerset, Henry (1707–45), 3d D. of Beaufort:
brother succeeds, iii. 26n, iv. 50n
divorce of, i. **452**–3, ii. 185, 199
Raphael painting may be bought by, ii. 239, 273
Talbot pitied by, i. 486
wife's accusation of impotence disproved by, before witnesses, ii. 185, 199

Somerset, Henry (1744–1803), 5th D. of Beaufort, 1756:
ball given by, at Paris, vi. 365
first of his family to forsake Jacobitism, vii. 174
lieutenancy of Welch counties contested by, with Morgan of Tredegar, vii. 174
Mastership of Horse to Q. Charlotte resigned by, vii. 174
sister of, v. 294

Somerset, Lady Mary Isabella (1756–1831), m. (1775) Charles Manners, styled M. of Granby 1770–9; 4th D. of Rutland, 1779:
beauty of, ix. 282
beauty of, not so striking to HW, viii. 54
Florence to be visited by, vii. 397
Granby to wed, viii. 54, 120–1, 148
mother accompanied by, at Pisa, vii. **372**, 397
Tuscan court favours, at Florence, vii. 406

Somerset, ship:
at Port Mahon, i. 285

Somerset:
descent of title of, ii. 522–3, iv. 124–5, 138–9

Somerset family:
Beaufort, D. of, the first member of, to forsake Jacobites, vii. 174

George II to perpetuate, with earldoms, iv. 81

Somerset House:
Frederick II may have to live at, vi. 38, 320
HW writes from, i. 230, 263
Karl Wilhelm Ferdinand gives levees and dinners at, vi. 197
Portuguese royal family may flee to, vi. 38, 95

Somersetshire:
man from, meets Pitt at Bath, vi. 425–6
Pynsent supposed to be from, vi. 276

Somodevilla y Bengocchea, Zenón de (1702–81), Marqués de la Ensenada, 1736:
Campillo to be succeeded by, as secretary at Madrid, ii. 253
Mann asked by, for passport to take furniture to Spain, ii. 253

Sonata:
Veracini's, includes 'Tweedside,' iv. 148

Sondes, Bn. *See* Watson, Hon. Lewis (1728–95)

Sondes, Vcts. *See* Tufton, Lady Margaret

Sonetto:
affair in Mann's garden satirized in, iii. 498–9, **502**

Sonnet; sonnets:
Frederick II writes, to Voltaire, v. 168, 171
political, Mann sends, to HW, i. 302
Surrey's, ii. **497**

Soor, in Bohemia:
Frederick II defeats P. Charles at, iii. 127

Soothsayers:
visions of, not revealed until fulfilled, vi. 562

Sootwater:
drawings in, viii. 524

Sopha, Le. See under Crébillon, Claude-Prosper Jolyot de

Sophi, of Persia:
etiquette for, vii. 550

Sophia (1777–1848), Ps:
father asks provision for, viii. 372
inoculation of, ix. 406

Sophia Matilda (1773–1844), of Gloucester, Ps:
birth of, vii. **483**
brother will probably not be preferred to, viii. 302
descendant of both HW and George I, ix. 248
father dotes on, viii. 86
father essential to welfare and happiness of, viii. 329
father may be amused by, viii. 306
father may take, to southern France, viii. 76
father's plight may arouse sympathy for, viii. 321
George III demands provision for, viii. 372, 376

[Sophia Matilda, *continued*]
  HW calls, 'a dear soul,' viii. 302
  HW sees, at Gloucester House, ix. 68
  Leopold sees, viii. 297
  less pretty than she was, viii. 332
  Mann called on by, viii. 297
  —— to be called on by, viii. 291
  mother angers, by snatching off cap to show her hair, viii. 297
  mother would have trouble in travelling with, if father died, viii. 326
  Ranelagh visited by, ix. 68
  recovers from inoculation, viii. 86
  to be inoculated, viii. 82
Sophie Karoline (1737–1817) of Brunswick-Wolfenbüttel, m. (1759) Friedrich Wilhelm, Margrave of Brandenburg-Bayreuth:
  (?) George III may wed, iv. 494
Sophie-Philippine-Élisabeth-Justine (1734–82), 'Madame Sophie,' daughter of Louis XV:
  Beauvilliers scratched by, from party list, vii. 115–16
  Du Barry, Comtesse, to be presented to, vii. 78
  expense of coffee and rouge for, iv. 500
  father nursed by, although she had never had smallpox, viii. 1–2
  health of: smallpox, viii. 13; smallpox, cured, viii. 13, 19
  Marie-Antoinette governed by, vii. 321; mother not addressed by, across father at dinner, iv. 340
Soprapporta; soprapporte:
  Mann offers HW views of Florence for, vii. 275, 287–8
'Soquxkin soqubut':
  Japanese term for 'heart,' iii. 308
Sora, Duca di. *See* Boncompagni, Gaetano (1707–77)
Sora, Duchessa di. *See* Boncompagni, Maria (1686–1745)
Sora:
  Francis III occupies, ii. 438
Sorba, Agostino Paolo Domenico (1715–71), Marchese; Genoese minister to France:
  born at Paris, vii. 363
  Choiseul instigated by, to invade Corsica, vii. 363
  death of, vii. 363
  Genoa proposes sending, to England to congratulate George III, v. 509
  Genoa told by, of French withdrawal from Corsican ports, vi. 536
Sorba, Giambattista (d. 1738), Genoese diplomatist; chargé d'affairs at Paris:
  son of, vii. 363
Sorbe. *See* Sorba
Sore leg:
  occurrences of, ii. 139, viii. 118, 480
Sore mouth:
  occurrences of, ii. 148, v. 543
Sore throat:

epidemic of, in England, i. 398n, v. 312, 362, 369, 416
  Wilmot cures, by lancing, v. 369
Sorgental. *See* Görgenthal
Soriano:
  earthquake account mentions, ix. 376
Sortes virgilianas:
  Mann's opinion of, i. 108
Sortes Walpolianæ:
  Chute designates HW's discoveries by serendipity as, iv. 407, 415
Sotomayor, Marqués de. *See* Masones de Lima y Sotomayor, Don Jaime
Soubise ('Soubize'), P. and Maréchal de. *See* Rohan, Charles de
Soubise, Princesse de. *See* Hesse-Rheinfels-Rotenburg, Anna Viktoria Maria Christina von
Soul, the:
  Stosch's witticisms on, i. 404
Soup:
  at Florentine dinner, iii. 357
  Mann eats, at dinner, i. 104
  scraps of paper, with holy words, made into, iv. 430
Sourdine:
  Brown marches to, ii. 488
Sousfermiers:
  France abolishes, iv. 500
South America:
  revolt in, would distract Spain from Gibraltar, ix. 292
Southampton, Bn. *See* Fitzroy, Charles (1737–97); Fitzroy, Hon. George Ferdinand (1761–1810)
Southampton, Bns. *See* Keppel, Laura (1765–98); Warren, Anne (d. 1807)
Southampton, E. of:
  Grafton, D. of, may inherit title of, viii. 5
  See also Wriothesley, Thomas (1607–67)
Southampton:
  Isenburg astonished by tide at, iv. 563
Southampton, English ship:
  (?) French and Spanish chase, into Plymouth, viii. 506
South Audley St, London:
  Portuguese king buys house for embassy in, iv. 164n
South Carolina. *See under* Carolina
Southerne, Thomas (ca 1660–1746), dramatist:
  Oroonoko, Imoinda in, iii. 18
South Pole:
  horrible metropolis may arise near, viii. 154
South Sea Bubble:
  East India Company speculation similar to, vi. 498, vii. 467
South Sea Company:
  English-Spanish negotiations over, iv. 197–8
  governor of, *see* Burrell, Peter
  Knight, cashier of, iii. 419n, viii. 174n
Southwark:
  Astley establishes amphitheatre in, for riding and rope-dancing, ix. 451n

East India Company stores tea in, ix. 577–8

fire in, ix. 577–8

Gordon rioters start fires in, ix. 57

HW will not pack up till the French are in, iv. 469

southward expansion of, viii. 228

Southwick, Hants, Whithed's seat:

burns down, iv. 185

HW was to have gothicized, iv. 185

Souvré ('Souvray'), Marquis de. See Le Tellier, François-Louis (1704–67)

Sovrano, Emanuel, Capt.:

captured at Velletri, ii. 493

Sowden, Rev. Benjamin (d. ca 1779), Presbyterian minister 1748– ca 1779 at Rotterdam:

Montagu, Lady Mary Wortley, entrusts MSS to, vi. 84

Soyres, François de (d. 1807):

Bauffremont recommended, to HW and D. of Richmond, ix. 518

Edgcumbe travels with, ix. 518, 551n

English well spoken and written by, ix. 519

HW recommends, ix. 518–19; 551n

HW told by, from Florence, that Mann is better, ix. 551

youngish French Protestant of good family who left the army, ix. 518

Spa:

Carteret (Granville) ordered by physicians to go to, iii. 26

Cholmondeley to visit, vii. 316

Cumberland, D. and Ds of, to go to, ix. 645

Orlov to visit, viii. 113

Poyntz, Mrs, to visit, vi. 164

visitors to: Bath, E. of, iv. 80; Cardigan, Cts of, i. 141; Pitt, Anne, viii. 405; Spencer, Bns, vi. 173

York, D. of, to visit sister at, vi. 524

'Spaccatavola' (dancer):

Pantolomina compared with, iii. 356

Spada, 'Conte' or 'Marquis':

Young Pretender accompanied by, at Florence, vii. 229

—— sends, to Leopold, ix. 102

Spagna, capitano della Piazza de. See Capitano

Spagnolet; Spagnoletto. See Ribera, José de

Spaight, ——, merchant of Carrickfergus:

Thurot captures, v. 376

Spain, Infant of. See Philip, Don

Spain, K. of. See Charles III (1716–88); Charles IV (1748–1819); Charles V (1500–58); Ferdinand VI (1713–59); Philip II (1527–98); Philip V (1683–1746)

Spain, Q. of. See Bourbon d'Orléans, Louise-Élisabeth de (1709–42); Elizabeth (1692–1766); Louisa Maria Theresa (1751–1819); Marie Amalie (1724–60)

Spain:

Acquaviva is protector of, iii. 339n

admiral of, Du Chaffault refuses precedence to, viii. 528

Aix treaty awaits accession of, iii. 485

Aix treaty not yet signed by, iii. 511

Aix treaty preliminaries do not mention, iii. 480

Algerian hostilities of, viii. 121–2, 179, ix. 26, 415–16

allodials claimed by, ii. 176

ambassadors from and to, see under Ambassador

ambassador to, not yet appointed, vi. 444

America may get underhand aid from, viii. 139, 271, 366, 459

American conquests of, less cruel than slave trade, iv. 126

America now a hindrance instead of a help to England in fighting, viii. 485

armada of: Elizabeth's medal on defeat of, v. 357; tapestry in House of Lords depicts, vii. 242

armaments said to be prepared by, viii. 98

army camp of, at San Roque, pestiferous, ix. 59

army of: Abruzzo approached by, ii. 438; Acquaviva sends Roman recruits to, ii. 542; advance of, reported from Rome, iii. 15; Alessandria the theatre of, iii. 36, 75, 120, 137, 226; Ambrose harasses, iii. 37; ammunition and artillery received by, despite English fleet, ii. 296; Apremont and other officers captured by, iii. 153–4; Aqui approached by, iii. 225; Aquila reached by, i. 265; Arezzo approached by, i. 289, 341, 350; Asti captured from, iii. 226; at Cartagena, may threaten Gibraltar, vii. 261; at Presidii, lack horses, i. 262; at Rome, ii. 531–4; Austrians defeat, at Campo Santo, ii. 161, 163–5, 312; Austrians may resist, in Lombardy, vii. 474; Austrians try to cut off, iii. 66; Barcelona the embarkation point of, i. 182, 192, 290, 312, 361, ii. 106; Birtles tells Haddock of approach of, i. 305–6; Bologna the theatre of, i. 289, 341, 350, 432, ii. 45, 55, 58, 76, 99, 154, 175, 199; Bomporto the theatre of, ii. 151, 189; Botta attacks, iii. 291; called 'Ligur-Napolispani,' iii. 82; campaign of, compared to country dances, ii. 55; cannon captured by, iii. 119–20; Castro and Ronciglione may be winter station of, i. 204; Charles III to send, to son, v. 335; Charles Emmanuel III attacks, near River Lambro, iii. 278–9; Charles Emmanuel III deters, from invading Tuscany, ii. 58; Charles Emmanuel III dislodged by, from Mont Castello and the Tanaro, iii. 120; Charles Emmanuel III may resist, in Lombardy, i. 266; Charles Emmanuel III not alarmed by junction of, iii. 47; Charles Emmanuel III said to have defeated, on the Var, ii. 466; Charles Emmanuel III's news intercepted by, iii.

[Spain, *continued*]

190; Charles Emmanuel III to pursue, iii. 292; Colligara reached by, ii. 151; convoys of, to Italy, i. 323, 350; courier robbed by, ii. 515–16; couriers may be intercepted by, iii. 156, 163–4; Cuneo the theatre of, ii. 519; deserters from, i. 349, 379, 427, 432, 455, 464, ii. 216, 412, 454, iii. 36, 231; Elizabeth Farnese's appointments to, insane, ii. 135; Empoli the theatre of, i. 341; encamped near Prati della Masone, i. 424; English at Leghorn to be respected by, i. 215; English fleet does not keep, from Italy, iii. 9; Europe Point said to be occupied by, ix. 324; expects reinforcements from Majorca and Barcelona, ii. 106; Faenza the theatre of, ii. 175; Fano the theatre of, ii. 7, 45, 55, 335, 339, 412; Farlo to be entered by, ii. 45; Ferrara the theatre of, i. 464, 500; Fleury may permit, to invade Tuscany, i. 205, ii. 42; Florence's gates to be passed by, i. 342; Florence threatened by, i. 342, 349, 365; Foligno the theatre of, i. 265, 289, ii. 18, 27, 42, 76, 174, 200, 331, 529, 542, iii. 15; Forlimpopoli the theatre of, ii. 257; Fossombrone the theatre of, ii. 18; France forbids, to enter Tuscany, i. 197–8, 214, iii. 7; France to give orders to, i. 265; Francis I orders Braitwitz to keep, out of Tuscany, ii. 66, 127, 134; Francis III of Modena commands, ii. 222, 228, 235; French troops withdrawn from, iii. 8; Garfagnano may be invaded by, iii. 65; Genoa abandoned and plundered by, iii. 305–6; Genoa aids, iii. 64–5; Genoa approached by, ii. 454, 554, 559, iii. 35, 36, 47, 292; vii. 469; Genoa invaded by, iii. 40, 51, 58; Genoese and Neapolitan barks thought to supply, iii. 56–7; Genoese provisions for, iii. 266; German cavalry to cut off, from Ferrara, iii. 197; German deserters bribed by, ii. 243; German troops oppose, ii. 200, 267; Gibraltar besieged by, *see under* Gibraltar; Gibraltar threatened by, v. 20, vii. 261; Imola the theatre of, i. 289, ii. 175; infantry of, outnumbers Lobkowitz's, ii. 312; invalids of, *see under* Invalid; Irish deserters give news of, ii. 432; kettle drums captured by, ii. 161, 189; La Cattolica the theatre of, ii. 58, 200, 331; large cannon lacked by, ii. 151; Leghorn might be menaced by, i. 196, 212, ii. 77; Licanians captured by, ii. 459–60; lives on biscuits, iii. 35; Loano reached by, iii. 559; Lobkowitz has insufficiently crushed, ii. 359; Lobkowitz may be pursued by, ii. 508; Lobkowitz pursued by, near Rome, ii. 530–4; Lobkowitz pursues, ii. 412–13; Lobkowitz's advance awaited by, ii. 335; Lobkowitz to drive, to Naples or Pesaro, ii. 405; Lodi pillaged by, iii. 267, 268–9; Lombardy may be invaded by, i. 180, 192, 198, 204, 208, 213, 214, 219, 229, 261, 266, 311, 323, 341, 349, ii. 45, 76, 547, iii. 22, 295, 367; Lucca approached by, iii. 35; Madrid to send orders to, i. 265–6; Maillebois joins, at Piacenza, iii. 266; Majorca said to be base of, against Minorca, vii. 261; Mann discusses, with Braitwitz, i. 182; Maria Theresa's hussars pursue, ii. 199; Martin demands that Charles III withdraw troops from, ii. 15, v. 564; Massa the theatre of, i. 314, 323; Mathews awaits, ii. 106; Mathews to protect Nice from, ii. 312; Mathews wants Charles Emmanuel III to coop up, in Tuscany, ii. 108; may be cut off from Naples, i. 500; may be transported from Antibes to Genoa, vii. 469; may embark at Naples, iii. 410; may retire to Naples, ii. 325, 397–8; Milan attempt abandoned by, iii. 225; Milan may be captured by, i. 198, iii. 119; miquelets in, i. 432, ii. 101; Miranda besieged by, vi. 38; Mirandola besieged by, i. 489; Modena besieged by, i. 455, 464, 465; Modena threatened by, i. 226, 379, 424, iii. 22, 30, 65, 156; money shortage prevents Traun from marching against, ii. 257; Montale the theatre of, iii. 30; Nádasdy pursues, iii. 244; Naples may not receive, ii. 412–13; Naples receives troops from, iii. 367; Neapolitans may join, i. 198, 265, 350, ii. 10; Neapolitans separated from, ii. 15, 66; near Rome, iii. 530–4, 546; Nice may be traversed by, ii. 395, 461; Nice reached by, iii. 9; Novi the theatre of, iii. 58; officers of, devout, i. 427; Oneglia the theatre of, ii. 454, 461, 559; Orbetello the theatre of, i. 178, 192, 198, 204, 214, 226, 239, 262, 265, 289, 350, 389, ii. 7, 16, 27, 243, 253, iii. 55; Pallavicini escaped by, iii. 244; Pallavicini exposes Milan to, iii. 120; Panaro valley the theatre of, i. 432, 455, 464, 472, 489, ii. 45, 55, 76, 151, 154, 164–5, 196, 197, iii. 30, 35; Papal states threatened by, ii. 444; Papal states traversed by, i. 261, 323; Parma captured from, iii. 244, 245; Parma threatened by, i. 198, 204, 214, ii. 454, iii. 22; 'patrimoine de St-Pierre' reached by, ii. 546; Pavia may be invaded by, iii. 41; Perugia the theatre of, ii. 42, 76, 542, iii. 11, 15; Pesaro the theatre of, i. 379, ii. 76, 174, 335, 339, 412, 419; Philip, Don, to command, at Nice, ii. 547; Philip, Don, to join, iii. 47; Piacenza occupied by, iii. 156, 258, 262, 266, 268, 275, 276; Piacenza threatened by, i. 198, 204, 214; Pironi confined by, ii. 253, 257; Po controlled by, iii. 276; Pontremoli and the Luneggiana threatened by, i. 289, ii. 76, iii. 35, 245; Presidii the theatre of, i. 192, 262, ii. 27, 325, 547, iii. 410; provisions stored by, in the Luneggiana and Tuscany, iii. 10;

Rimini the theatre of, i. 379, ii. 13, 16, 199, 216, 243, 253, 331; iii. 36; Ripalta captured from, iii. 262; Riviera di Ponente plundered by, iii. 306; Ronciglione occupied by, ii. 527; St Philip's in Minorca to be attacked by, ix. 229; St Philip's to be stormed by prisoners released for, ix. 180; San Giovanni the theatre of, ii. 154; San Lazaro (Piacenza) defeat of, iii. 265-7, 274; San Roque encampment of, ix. 59, 72; San Stefano the theatre of, i. 197; Sardinians may pursue, ii. 199-200; Sarzana threatened by, i. 314; Savoy campaign of, to decide Neapolitan plans, ii. 302; Seravalle the theatre of, iii. 84, 292; Sestri the theatre of, iii. 40; Sezi reached by, iii. 226; sickly, at Minorca, ix. 197; Sienese approach to Tuscany blocked by, i. 289; Sinigaglia the theatre of, ii. 16, 76; Spanish and Neapolitan letters to, captured, ii. 85-6; Spezia the theatre of, i. 182, 198, 206, 262, 289, 314, 323, 350, ii. 405, 413; standards captured by, ii. 189, iii. 119; supplies stored for, at Leghorn, iii. 10; taxes levied by, in Italy, ii. 344; tied up at Gibraltar, ix. 345; to receive artillery by way of Adriatic, iii. 30; Tortona the theatre of, iii. 36, 41, 75, 82, 267, 291-2; transports hired by, at Genoa and Leghorn, iii. 304; Traun may dislodge, ii. 253, 271; Traun's nephews captured by, ii. 154; Traun's troops too weak to attack, ii. 127; Traun tells Braitwitz not to fight, ii. 295; Turin threatened by, iii. 120; Tuscan area may be passed by, i. 226, 341, iii. 35, 58, 65; Tuscan negotiations with, i. 228; Tuscans may aid, iii. 10-11, 31; Tuscany said by Fleury to be safe from, i. 197-8, 205; Valenza may be captured by, iii. 120, 137; Velletri fortified by, ii. 454; Velluti to protest against route of, i. 341; victories of, in Lombardy, iii. 119-20; 'victory' claimed by, ii. 161; Villafranca captured by, ii. 437; Villettes asks Mann to report progress of, i. 265; Viterbo may be left by, to cross Tuscany to join Gages, iii. 58; Viterbo the theatre of, ii. 243, iii. 55, 58; Viviani deserts to, iv. 350

artillery of: at Algiers, viii. 121-2; at Genoa, ii. 244, 257; in Italy, ii. 27, 296, iii. 35-6, 147

Ascanio supports faction of, in Florence, i. 86-7

Assiento treaty with England, to be renewed by, iii. 480

Austrians may resist, in Lombardy, vii. 474

Banks tries to find islands not discovered by, vii. 436

barks of, i. 262, 350, 433, ii. 288

batteries of, see under Battery

Bavarian treaty with, reported, i. 183

Beauvau a grandee of, iii. 1

Bedford, D. of, tells Fane that he cannot go to, iv. 203

Benedict XIV acknowledges Francis I despite cabals of, iii. 183

—— fears cabals of, iii. 157-8

—— receives indemnity from, for right to appoint to its own benefices, v. 437

——'s advisers said to favour, ii. 56

—— said to be betrayed to, by Valenti, ii. 56, iii. 492

—— threatens, with excommunication, ii. 56, 344

'bombastly unsuccessful,' in war, ix. 338

Bourbons and Austria fought over, v. 199-200

bravado of, below par, ix. 351

Brest fleet said to be off coast of, iii. 274

Bristol ambassador to, v. 166, 175, 190, 194-5

—— assembles servants for post at, v. 202

—— returns from, v. 548-9, 558

——'s demands upon, v. 563-4

—— treated by, with derision, vi. 5

cardinals fear exclusion by, at next papal election, vi. 387

cardinals from: awaited at Conclave, vii. 95; reach Rome, vii. 113

Cartagena should not have been left in hands of, i. 96

Castellar recalled to, ii. 44

Castro and Ronciglione may be taken by, from papacy, vii. 36, 45, 413

Catherine II's manifestos illiterate enough to be from, vi. 71

cavalry of: convoy to bring, i. 323, 350; inferior to Lobkowitz's, ii. 312; to pass through Loreto, to Fano, ii. 45; to repass the Var, iii. 51

Charles III behaved better at Naples than at, v. 560

—— displeases, ix. 32

—— does not send couriers to, ii. 486

——'s departure to, v. 318, 335, 363

—— to be king of, v. 264, 270, 275, 335

—— to observe neutrality when called to throne of, v. 271

Charles Emmanuel III may be lured by, from Maria Theresa, i. 312

Choiseul's fall may displease, vii. 259

Clement XIII 'carted' by, vii. 32

—— relaxes Lenten rules for, vi. 5

——'s disputes with, over Jesuit expulsion, vi. 517-19, et passim

Clement XIV detaches Portugal from negotiations with, vii. 221

—— may disappoint, vii. 157

——'s negotiations with, over Jesuits, see under Jesuit

consuls from and to, see under Consul

corn shortages in, vi. 206

Corsican relations with, ii. 156

couriers from and to, see under Courier

Cours de l'Europe satirizes, i. 177

[Spain, *continued*]

court of: conceals destination of fleet, ix. 173–4; Mann calls publication of, about Minorca, a scurrilous performance, ix. 188–9; Montemar expected by, to relieve Modena, i. 501; neutrality said to be the policy of, iv. 498, viii. 463; tells Roman minister to disavow Young Pretender, vi. 399; *see also under* Charles III; Ferdinand VI; Philip V

Craon accuses England of alliance with, i. 180

Czarina's death should help England to defeat, vi. 1

defeat of, at Gibraltar, attributed to faithless allies, ix. 149

disarms, vii. 297

dress of, i. 399

Du Châtelet draws, into attack on Falkland Islands, vii. 258

Dutch ships may be searched by, ii. 116

Eliott's success against furious attack by, ix. 325

Elizabeth Farnese fonder of Naples than of, i. 291

—— must be infuriated by defeats of, ii. 331

England again permitted by, to use Channel, ix. 191

England assured by, of pacific intentions, v. 541

England captures quicksilver from, viii. 543

England denies right of search to, iii. 255

England does not frighten, v. 78

England does not know decision of, viii. 467

England excels, in avarice and cruelty, vii. 400

England feels that armada of, is bound for Lisbon, viii. 111

England makes head against, only by sufferance of Eastern powers, ix. 201

England may be baffled by underhand aid by, for America, viii. 139

England may be preferred by, to France, iii. 278

England resembles, in lust for gold, vii. 381

England said to have accepted mediation by, viii. 440

England saved by slowness of, in joining France, viii. 448

England's commercial relations with, iii. 480, 504, iv. 170–1, 197–8

England's feeble enemy, ix. 149

England should send Moors to invade, vi. 100

England's relations with: Assiento Treaty, iii. 480; English rejection of Spanish ultimatum, viii. 486; Ferdinand VI may improve, iii. 278; may yet be neutral, viii. 463; Portugal a factor in, vi. 99–100; predicted as harmonious, v. 544; quarrel over Falkland Islands, vii. 239–42, 245–6, 250–2,

255, 258, 359; Spanish bullying for France strains, v. 536; wanted by Pitt for discussion in House of Commons, v. 553; war possible, iv. 487, 491, v. 171–2, 260, 553–4, 555, viii. 17; Young Pretender may inflame, i. 14

England's wars and peace treaties with, *see* War, English-Spanish

England thought herself trampled on by, iii. 69

England too disunited for war with, to unify her, vi. 540

England will love to humble, now that Pitt rules, vi. 441

English army in, under Peterborough, ii. 180, viii. 482

English capture Central American fort of, viii. 543

English consuls in, reassured about English-Spanish relations, v. 544

English convention with, *see under* Convention

English fleet unable to interrupt Genoese commerce with, iii. 207

English-French naval disarmament pact rejected by, viii. 299–300

English-French war might be joined by, iv. 487, 491

English manufacturers solicited by, iv. 170–1

English messenger from Hanover to, iv. 498

English sailors must precede Sir James Gray at, v. 560

envoys from and to, *see under* Envoy

expedition by, from Cadiz to Minorca, would have little chance of success, ix. 59

expedition of, threatening Tuscany, *see under* Tuscany: Spanish expedition in

family compact of France and, *see* Bourbon family: family compact of

Farinelli said to have escaped from, ii. 119

Ferdinand ordered by, to admit no guests to his table, vii. 191

finances of, inadequate, vii. 244

fleet armed by, v. 494, viii. 412

fleet of: Algiers and Tunis preoccupy, viii. 120; Algiers to be attacked by, ix. 416; at Cadiz, not to join Brest fleet, ix. 72; at Spezia, may go to Barcelona and Toulon, i. 323; at Toulon, ii. 93, 360, 370; Brest fleet may be joined by, ix. 16; Cadiz, said to be retreat of, ix. 145, 344; cautious conduct of, ix. 147; Charles III orders, home to escape disease, viii. 530, 538; Charles III to be escorted by, from Naples, v. 324, 333; crippled, ix. 344; Darby braves, at Cadiz, ix. 147; Darby not opposed by, ix. 145, 147, 149; decisive battle avoided by, ix. 156; does not alarm English ministry viii. 101; English merchant fleets gobbled up by, ix. 78; English merchant ship seized by, near Majorca, ii. 354; Estaing said to

be taking, against Jamaica, ix. 345; fire-ships and bomb ships in, i. 286; Florentine Jacobites expect victory from, ii. 415; France may borrow, to besiege Minorca viii. 437, 443, 467; French fleet does not aid, against Darby, ix. 149; French fleet joins, viii. 502, ix. 73; French fleet may join, against Gibraltar, viii. 484; French fleet quarrels with, viii. 528; French fleet separates from, ii. 415, viii. 541; George II orders Haddock to intercept, i. 259, 260, 267, 269, 281, 306, 380, 405; Gibraltar left unblocked by, ix. 145; Gulf of Lyon alleged location of, i. 179; Haddock alarms, i. 322; Haddock keeps, at Cadiz, i. 219; Haddock to keep, at Barcelona, i. 259, 266–7, 290–1; Haddock too weak for, i. 269, 281; leaves Cadiz, i. 23; Lisbon said to be target of, viii. 111; list of ships in, i. 286; Mann must get Saunders to defeat, vi. 48; Ma-thews eluded by, at Majorca, ii. 244; may be sent to America, viii. 224; Minorca expects surprise from, viii. 114; off Gibral-tar and detains Dutch vessel, viii. 541; Rodney defeats, ix. 16, 17, 21, 24; Russian fleet to be intercepted by, ix. 415; size of, i. 286; Spezia gulf patrolled by, i. 317; to accompany French and Dutch to India, ix. 485–6; Toulon squadron joins, i. 269; very sickly, ix. 145; West Indies menaced by, i. 17, 20

fleet of France, and ('combined fleet'): at Brest, viii. 525; at mouth of Channel, ix. 297; avoids Hardy's, in Channel, viii. 506; Cadiz left by, ix. 82, 173, 181; Cape St Vincent said to be approached by, ix. 173, 181; disappears from Plymouth, viii. 511; dispersed by storm, ix. 336; does not en-gage Howe, ix. 337; Dutch fleet may have joined, ix. 188; English fleet plays hide-and-seek with, ix. 306; English fleet said to have defeated, i. 35; French fleet's sepa-ration from, ix. 197; French ships join, viii. 502; Gibraltar bay to have been closed by, ix. 16; Gibraltar to be captured by, before Howe's arrival, ix. 323; Howe at-tacked for not fighting, ix. 439n; in Chan-nel, ix. 182, 185, 186, 188; Mann hopes that English fleet will drive, from Minorca, ix. 205; Minorca attacked by, ix. 178–9, 180–1, 182; Minorca instead of Gibraltar the objective of, ix. 173–4; near Cartagena, ix. 174; now separated but could reas-semble, ix. 201; Plymouth approached by, viii. 506, 511; reported to have departed from English coast, ix. 302; reported to have returned to Brest ix. 186; thought to have gone home, ix. 191, 192; to engage Howe, ix. 326

fleets prepared by, vii. 474

Florentine adherents of, avoid Mann's parties, and want Ferdinand VI to send Don Philip, iii. 498

Florentine agent of, see Vernaccini, Ranieri

Florentine jewels claimed by, i. 238

France advised by, to refuse English peace terms, vi. 66, 76

France at odds with, ii. 416, vii. 322, ix. 32

France grudgingly aids, against Gibraltar, ix. 292

France invokes family compact to get aid from, v. 563–5, vi. 5, 95, viii. 478, 495

France is unlikely to aid, under family compact, vii. 244

France lures, by family pact, v. 563

France manages, in family pact, v. 4–5

France may aid, against Algiers, viii. 179

France may alienate England from, iii. 378, 393

France may be compelled by family com-pact to aid, vii. 244

France may be joined by, in spring of 1757, v. 20

France may borrow fleet from, to besiege Minorca, viii. 437, 443, 467

France may cede Minorca to, in return for alliance, iv. 545, 572, 575

France may induce, not to suppress Jesuits, vii. 372

France may sacrifice England to, at Aix treaty, iii. 511

France said to permit, to invade Tuscany, iii. 30–1, 38

France's alliance with: v. 536, 539, viii. 486; England asks terms of, v. 559; Eng-land ignorant of the terms of, v. 548; must be to England's disadvantage, v. 544; not countenanced at Naples, v. 551, 555; not yet announced, viii. 486; would align Europe towards France, v. 528; would de-feat England, viii. 448

France's peace negotiations with Charles Emmanuel III broken by, iii. 223

France's treaty with: England demands sight of v. 557; England does not know terms of, v. 548; must be to England's dis-advantage, v. 544

France to answer for, at Aix treaty, iii. 480

France to share San Domingo with, ix. 180

France will not be aided by, iv. 498

Francis I's election forbidden by, to be celebrated, iii. 183–4

Francis III will easily be reinstated by, iii. 156

French alliance by, would turn Europe towards France, iv. 528

French alliance with, not yet announced, viii. 486–7

French and Italian ministers in, dismissed, to England's advantage, vi. 420

French-Bavarian alliance may be affected by, i. 119

French-Bavarian treaty with, rumoured, i. 183

French guarantee may not save Tuscany from, ii. 502

[Spain, *continued*]

French junction with, would defeat England, viii. 448

French presumption may be checked by, viii. 396

French rifts with, ii. 416

French rift with England said to be disapproved by, viii. 375

French vessels mistaken for those of, i. 46

French victory may deflect, from peace, ix. 83

frigates of, *see under* Frigate

Fuentes delivers declaration of, to England, v. 559

Gabburri Mme, returns to, ii. 46

Gages ordered by, to attack Lobkowitz, iii. 15

galleys of, *see under* Galley

Genoa's alliance and negotiations with, ii. 455, 509, 546–7, 554–5, iii. 65, 237, 304, 343–5, 363–4

George II's orders may deter, from attacking Francis I's possessions, in Tuscany, i. 288

Gibraltar allowed by, to cool, ix. 345

Gibraltar and Minorca unlikely to be taken by inefficient fleet of, viii. 119

Gibraltar blockade abandoned by, ix. 59

Gibraltar may be besieged by, viii. 501

Gibraltar regarded by, as a point of national honour, iv. 575

Gibraltar's capture no longer hoped by, ix. 48, 331

Gibraltar siege exaggerated by accounts from, ix. 334

Gibraltar's prisoners from, may infect garrison with the itch, ix. 59

governor from, in West Indies, i. 7

grandee of, less dangerous than Irish papist, iv. 171

Grantham stays in, despite war declaration, viii. 487

Gray, Sir James, expected to be ambassador to, v. 150, 159, 165–6, 174, 556, vi. 107, 112

—— goes to, vi. 463

HW wants Mann to be minister to, v. 166

Havana may not be restored to, vi. 99–100

havocked world for gold, ix. 142

hostility disclaimed by, viii. 384

Huntingdon seeks embassy in v. 166, 175

inquisitors of, will not be able to oppress newly-discovered stars, ix. 614

Ireland may be invaded by, v. 539

Irish unrest said to be aroused by gold from, vi. 24

Italy devastated and taxed by, ii. 344

Italy will not be upset by succession of, v. 280

Jamaica said to have been captured by, viii. 196–7

Jesuits' expulsion from, after alleged plot, vi. 509–10, 513, 515–19, 535–6, vii. 136, 376, x. 49; *see also under* Charles III

Joseph II forbids Leopold to negotiate with, ix. 46

Keene asks for recall from, v. 159

—— must continue ambassador to, iv. 203

Labour in Vain mentions, ii. 18

Leghorn has no subjects of, vi. 351

'Leghorn' is Mann's code name for, ix. 43

Leopold forbidden to negotiate directly with, ix. 43

—— receives complaints from, concerning supplies sent to St Philip's, ix. 250

——'s accession announced to, vi. 345

——'s possible loss of grand ducal title enrages, vi. 330

——'s remonstrances to, viii. 509

letters from, to army, captured with courier, ii. 85

letters to Maria Louisa from, must be delivered by Spanish minister, ix. 334

Llano goes to Parma from, vii. 445

Lombardy may be exchanged by, for Tuscany, i. 206

Lombardy threatened by, ii. 295

Lombardy to be invaded by, through Nice, ii. 395

losses of, through family compact, vi. 95

Majorca filled by, with troops, vii. 261

manifesto of, tries to justify rupture with England, v. 563

Mann has Leopold and Maria Louisa urge Charles III to release, from war with England, ix. 43–4

—— hopes for English fleet to drive away, from Minorca, ix. 205

—— speculates on reactions of, to Young Pretender's separation from wife, ix. 100

man *or* men of war of, *see under* Man of war

Maria Amalia of Naples refuses to flee to, ii. 3

Maria Amalia of Parma's extravagance subject of complaints of, vii. 412

Maria Louisa brings dogs from, to Florence, vi. 330

——'s jewels from, vi. 481

——'s letters from father in, must be delivered by Spanish minister, ix. 334

Maria Theresa's designs on Naples known to, ii. 390

Massa claims of Cybo relinquished to, i. 35

Masserano dies on reaching, viii. 328n

Medici allodials in Tuscany claimed by, i. 238, ii. 176

Mexican revolts against, would guarantee peaceful policy in Europe, viii. 384

ministers from and to, *see under* Minister

Minorca cannot receive Russian war ships for fear of attack by, viii. 114

Minorca, if France cedes it to her, might be exchanged by, for Gibraltar iv. 575

Minorca may be attacked by, viii. 114, ix. 48

Minorcan news comes only from, ix. 205

Minorca's garrison prisoners in, ix. 430

Minorca's siege by, *see under* Minorca

miquelets of, ii. 100

Miranda siege indicates belligerency of, vi. 38

Modena may be allied with, i. 216

Moniño will oppose Court intrigues of, if detrimental to country's welfare, viii. 478

Montemar awaits advice from, before daring to return there, ii. 54

—— awaits orders from, ii. 27

—— recalled to, ii. 46

—— sends courier to, ii. 42

Mount Stuart does not go to, ix. 398n

—— promised ambassadorship to, ix. 345–6

munitions of, to be deposited in Corsica according to Genoese treaty with Villettes, ii. 271

Muzell to sail to, v. 527

Naples advises Gages to await orders from, after Charles Albert's death, iii. 8, 10, 11

Naples and Portugal not invaded by, vi. 1

Naples exchanges couriers with, weekly, vi. 349

Naples hopes that Sardinia can be bribed by, i. 145, 291

Naples ordered by, to send food to Tuscany, vi. 448

navy prepared by, at Cadiz, viii. 496

Neapolitan cardinals and nobles forbidden by, to celebrate Francis I's election, iii. 183–4

Neapolitan Court assures Gray that letters from, promise rapprochement with England, v. 551, 555

neutrality of: excuse to invade Ireland, v. 539; expected, viii. 467; Frederick II must be encouraged by, v. 271

O'Brien, Mrs, discloses Tencin's secrets to, but loses pension, iv. 28

Old Pretender acknowledges help of, by not celebrating Francis I's election, iii. 184

——'s pension from, vi. 387

Orsi expect defeat of, i. 427

Pallavicini formerly nuncio at, vii. 118

Papal states and Sicilies may export grain to, vii. 430

Parma to be supported by, in quarrel with Clement XIII, vii. 10

party of, at Florence: avoids Mann's parties, iii. 498; wants Don Philip, iii. 498

peace may leave, to mercy of Maria Theresa and Charles Emmanuel III, iii. 219

peace preliminaries to be ratified by, ix. 365

peace with, declared in House of Commons, iii. 268

Pensacola captured by, ix. 172

Peruvian cruelties of, outdone by English in India, vii. 387, 396–7

Peterborough hunts for army in, ii. 180, viii. 482

Phelps to be given post in, vi. 112

Pitt lures London with hope of plunder from, v. 549

—— should not want war with, v. 544, 549

——'s resignation will make, bolder, v. 538, 539

Pitt, George, may be transferred to, from Turin, vi. 500

Pius VI may fear, more than poison, viii. 86

Polish partition may inspire, to divide Milan with France and Sardinia, vii. 469

Porto Longone belongs to, vii. 131

ports of France and, surround those of Italy, ix. 352

Portugal may be attacked by, v. 559–60, vi. 1, 23–4, 31, viii. 253

Portugal's conquest means more to, than Havana's loss, vi. 48, 51, 92

Portugal's independence disappoints, vi. 95, 99

Portugal's war with, *see* War: Portuguese-Spanish

Portugal to exchange territories with, in Paraguay, v. 341

Portuguese campaign of: fails to live up to boastful manifestos, vi. 66; minimized by HW, vi. 23–4; pleases HW, vi. 31

Portuguese conquest by: may be pushed to exchange for Havana, vi. 99–100; would make France more insolent, vi. 76

Portuguese island seized by, viii. 309–10

Potosi's wealth can be procured by, only by digging, vii. 561–2

prisoners from and to, *see under* Prisoner

privateer from, captures English, i. 153

register ships of, i. 175, 208, 377, viii. 543

religion used by, as an excuse for plunder, ix. 400

reluctance of, for peace, gives enemies a chance to make gains, iii. 488

Rigaut de Barbezieux retires to, after sweetheart's death, v. 169

Rio Grande settlement of, attacked by Portuguese, viii. 223

Rochford wants post in, v. 166

Rome's revenue lowered by act of, in buying nomination to benefices, v. 349

Rosenberg's debts in, paid by Maria Theresa, vii. 294

royal family of, addicted to playing with tapestry, vii. 242

Russian change enrages, vi. 12

Sandwich rumoured to be ambassador to, vi. 103, 112

Sardinia may be allied with, i. 85, vii. 465

Sardinia not bribed by, i. 145

Savoy plundered by, iii. 505

Schaub buys pictures cheaply during wars in, v. 199–200

secretary of state of, *see* Secretary of State, Spanish

secret expedition of, will be abandoned if Sultana produces an heir, v. 494

[Spain, *continued*]

ship of: brings arms to Young Pretender, iii. 138; British sailor boards, viii. 543; English attack on, viii. 306–7; English captain throws cannon from, ii. 406; lacks *corpo santo*, ix. 26; lost on Irish coast, iii. 138; Scotland to have received arms and money from, iii. 134

ships of: at Genoa, i. 262, ii. 244, 257; captured, i. 175; cruise near the Gorgona, i. 182; Dutch ship detained by, viii. 541; English merchant ships watched by, ii. 354; may intercept English corn shipments to Italy, vi. 206; near Port Mahon, listed, i. 286

siege of Minorca not yet begun by, ix. 196

South American revolt might distract, from Gibraltar, ix. 292

Squillace's difficulties in, vi. 414–15

stocks rise and fall on news from, vii. 250

Tabuernigas flee from, i. 277–8

Te Deums not to be sung by, for victories in Naples, ii. 486

Te Deum sung by, for supposed victory, ii. 161, 163

threats of, vi. 12

Townshend, Charles, employed in, ix. 392n

treasure expected by, may make policy anti-war, viii. 375–6

treasure's arrival at, rumoured in Florence, i. 83

troop movements of, near Gibraltar, v. 20

troop shipments of, to Italy, not impeded by English fleet, iii. 9–10

troops of: 14,000, tied up at Gibraltar, ix. 345; on Majorca, may threaten Minorca, vii. 261

troops of France and, landed in Minorca, reported sickly, ix. 197

troops sent by, to Naples, iii. 367

Tuscan independence of, would please England, ii. 2

Tuscan neutrality with, preserved by Francis I, ii. 92

Tuscan regency does not welcome English protection for fear of antagonizing, ii. 37–8

Tuscans told by, that goods bound for England will be confiscated, viii. 508–9

Tuscany hopes for aid from, i. 144

Tuscany may be invaded by, when P. Charles invades France, ii. 285, 295

Tuscany said to be resigned to, by England, i. 180

Tuscany threatened by invasion from, *see under* Tuscany: Spanish invasion threatens

Tyrawley may get embassy in, v. 166

undependable, iv. 571, viii. 424

visitors to: Pitt, Thomas, and Lord Strathmore, v. 501; Young Pretender, iii. 377, 390, 392

Viviani gets envoy's credentials from, vi. 349

—— language-master at Court of, iv. 350

Wall probably tries to lure English manufacturers into service of, iv. 170–1

—— recalled by, to succeed Carvajal as secretary of state, iv. 426

Walpole, Sir Robert, advised England to cultivate, v. 121

war expenses of, futile, iii. 432

war waged by, differently from Frederick II, ix. 190

xebecs of, *see under* Xebec

Young Pretender disregarded by, vi. 399

—— may be assisted by, i. 14, iii. 97, 105, 130, 137–8, 330, 335

—— may be set up by, in Ireland, vii. 328

—— receives money and promise of pension from, iii. 392

—— said to be going to, i. 13, iii. 140, 198, 377–8

——'s departure may embroil, i. 119

——'s invasion not helped much by, iii. 105, 137–8, 139

——'s negotiation with, i. 15, iii. 97

——'s Polish attempt probably does not involve, vii. 338

—— will probably urge, to make Clement XIII give him royal honours, vi. 369

Spangles:

French fond of, as ornament, ix. 635

Spaniard; Spaniards:

Cartagena victory causes consternation among, i. 68

cocchiata given by, in Florence to lady, vi. 158

Conclave gets appeal from, over ship capture, i. 8

English captains damn, ii. 38

Spaniel; spaniels:

HW's, tanned black, *see* Rosette

King Charles: Dacre promises, to HW, vi. 479; Dacre's bitch miscarries, vi. 534, 546; HW alone has true small breed of, iii. 59; HW gets puppies, for Maria Louisa, vii. 40; HW has, iii. 71; HW jokes about Charles I's descendants as, iii. 71; HW promised, to Mari, ii. 293; HW promised, to the Tesi, ii. 280, 293, 351; HW's gift of, rejected by Duchesse de Mirepoix, vi. 534; HW tries to get, for Maria Louisa, vi. 479, 534, 546; Hertford's valet-de-chambre brings, to Mann, vii. 56; Mann asks HW to get, for Maria Louisa, vi. 438, 470; Mann has two, iii. 59; Maria Louisa asks Mann about, vi. 438, 519, 546; Maria Louisa receives from Mann, vii. 56; puppies about to have offspring, vii. 97; puppies on way to Mann for Maria Louisa, vii. 45, 48, 50, 54, 57, 66, 72, 79; puppies to be housebroken by Mann before being given to Maria Louisa, vii. 72; unprocurable after Halifax's death, ii. 293; Voelcker has smallest breed of, vii. 56

Spanish Gazette:

Mann sends HW abstract of, ix. 325–6

news of destruction of floating batteries confirmed by, ix. 329

Spanish Guards:
casualties of, at San Lazaro, iii. 267

Spanish language:
Carteret and his daughter speak, i. 278
Craon does not understand, i. 280
Pomfret, Cts of, does not speak, i. 277
(?) St-Germain's native tongue, x. 20

Sparrow, John; convict:
trial of, ix. 67

Sparta, Q. of:
character in *Ballet de la Paix*, ii. 496

Sparta:
Windham imbibes notions of, ix. 50

Speaker of House of Commons. *See under* Parliament: House of Commons

Speaking trumpet:
Craon, Princesse de, would need, to talk to Vorontovs at dinner, v. 248

Spears:
at SH, iv. 381

Spectacles:
Balmerinoch uses, to read speech, iii. 301
green, HW buys, from Scarlet, v. 131
HW reads without, v. 139, 157
La Condamine wears, in street, vi. 146
Siries blames his mistake upon, iv. 314

Spectator, The:
HW expected Pulteney's writings to resemble those in, iv. 374
Pinkethman's petition in, ii. 565
See also under Addison, Joseph; Cocchi, Raimondo

Spedale degli Innocenti:
Eleonora's bastards put in, ii. 40

Speed, Henrietta Jane (1728–83), m. (1761) Francesco Maria Giuseppe Giustino, Barone di la Perrière, Conte de Viry, 1766:
death of, sudden, viii. 328n
Gray makes, heroine of *Long Story*, viii. 328n
husband of, arrested but she can go where she pleases, viii. 328
husband's fall caused by intrigues of, to have him made prime minister, viii. 328n
Shelburne friend of, viii. 328n

Speke, Philippa, m. Edward Bridges, Mann's great-great-grandmother:
(?) Chute investigates, in Heralds' office, iv. 13

Spence, Joseph (1699–1768), divine; anecdotist:
Cocchi gives book to, iv. 438
Genoa visited by, i. 91
HW calls on, iv. 188
HW mentions, i. 475
HW to travel with, i. 86
Mann bored by pedantry of, i. 107
——'s correspondence with, i. 51
—— sends thanks to, i. 96
mother cherished by, iv. 188–9

mules counted by, with HW in chaise, i. 91

Parallel in the Manner of Plutarch, A,
Mann receives from HW, v. 289
Pope defended in pamphlet by, iv. 62n
Venice visited by, i. 86
works of, iv. 188n

Spence, Mrs Joseph. *See* Collier, Mirabella

Spence, English sloop:
Spanish galleys attacked by, i. 471

Spencer, Bns and Cts. *See* Poyntz, Margaret Georgiana (1737–1814)

Spencer, Cts. *See* Bingham, Hon. Lavinia (1762–1831)

Spencer, Charles (1706–58), 5th E. of Sunderland; 2d D. of Marlborough, 1733:
address of loyalty to George II moved by, in Parliament, ii. 399
alleged appointment of, ii. 556
brother of, iii. 272n, ix. 78n
command in Flanders may be given to, i. 353
daughter of, vi. 148n, viii. 524n
death of, v. 259
Devonshire succeeded by, as lord steward of the Household, iv. 67
English invasion of France led by, v. 204, 211
estate and will of, v. 259
Frederick, P. of Wales, does not speak to, at Carlton House, i. **337**
Gower succeeds, as lord privy seal, iv. 517
grandmother conciliated by resignations of, ii. 350
health of, in great danger, v. 251
land poor, v. 527
Lennox, Lady Georgiana Caroline, given away by, ii. 451
Lincoln receives officer's apology before, i. 412
Master of the Ordnance, iv. 517
Mastership of the Horse may go to, iv. 182–3
Richmonds friendly with, ii. 451
Rochefort inquiry conducted by, v. 155
sister of, v. 156n
Somers's papers preferred by, to be burned, iv. 331–2
teaspoons abandoned by, in retreat from St Malo, v. 221
troops commanded by, under Lord George Sackville, v. 198
Walpole, Sir Edward, told by, of son's bravery, v. 240

Spencer, Lord Charles (1740–1820), M.P.:
Harcourt may be succeeded by, as chamberlain to the Queen, vii. 66

Spencer, Charlotte, *See* Spenser, Charlotte

Spencer, Lady Diana (1734–1808), m. 1 (1757) Frederick St John, 2d Vct Bolingbroke (divorced, 1768); m. 2 (1768) Topham Beauclerk:
Beauclerk to wed, vi. 567

[Spencer, Lady Diana, *continued*]
  Bedchamber position to Q. Charlotte given to, v. **518**, vi. 104n
  Bedford, Ds of, gives watch to, for Q. Charlotte, vi. 104–5
  divorce of, vi. 567
  HW builds closet at SH for illustrations by, to *Mysterious Mother*, viii. 524
  Richmond House masquerade and fireworks attended by, vi. 148
Spencer, Lady Elizabeth (1737–1831), m. (1756) Henry Herbert, 10th E. of Pembroke:
  beautiful, vi. 9, 19
  daughter taken by, to Nice for health, ix. 497n
  husband asks, to elope with him and his mistress, vi. 16
  husband deserts, vi. 9–10
  husband leaves, at Nice, ix. 493
  husband may be charmed by, into forsaking La Rena, v. **156**
  husband wishes to take leave of, before joining army, but is repulsed, vi. 33
  husband writes begging letters to, while eloping with mistress, vi. 25
  Mann hoped that husband would make amends to, vi. 22
  —— pities, vi. 19
  Richmond's masquerade attended by, as a pilgrim, vi. 149
Spencer, George (1739–1817), 3d D. of Marlborough:
  chamberlain's office vacated by, for D. of Devonshire, vi. 130–1
  expense of, at Venice, vi. 6
  father's death benefits estate of, v. **259**
  Garter to be conferred upon, vi. 572
  lord chamberlain, vi. 103
  Master of the Horse, vi. 130
  Paduan house taken by, v. 512
  Russell, Lady Caroline, to wed, despite his dislike of her mother, vi. 73
  Sandwich opposed by, viii. 435
  sister of, vi. 9n
  Zanetti's gems said to have been bought by, at Venice, v. 561
Spencer, George John (1758–1834), styled Vct Althorp 1765–83; 2d E. Spencer, 1783; M.P.:
  arrived in England with his wife, ix. 632
  engagement of, ix. **104**, 108
  Italy visited by, with wife, ix. 613n, 618n
Spencer, Lady Georgiana (1757–1806), m. (1774) William Cavendish, 5th D. of Devonshire, 1764:
  beauty of, disparaged by HW, ix. 411
  Fox, C.J., supported by, in Westminster election, despite indecent abuse by Court party, ix. 489
  marriage of, vii. **562**, viii. 14
  Polignac, Duchesse de, exchanges presents with, ix. 427
Spencer, Lady Georgiana Caroline. *See* Carteret, Lady Georgiana Caroline

Spencer, Lady Henrietta Frances (1761–1821), m. (1780) Frederick Ponsonby, styled Vct Duncannon; 3d E. of Bessborough, 1793:
  Chartres, Duc de, displays horses' and dogs' copulations on buttons to, at dinner, ix. 409, 417
Spencer, Hon. John (1708–46), M.P.:
  arrested in Covent Garden bagnio, i. 505
  death of, due to brandy, beer, and tobacco, iii. 272
  Marlborough's heir, iii. 272, vi. 277n
  Pitt gets reversion of estate from, vi. 277
  wife of, ix. 78n
Spencer, John (1734–83), cr. (1761) Vct and (1765) E. Spencer; M.P.:
  becomes Vct, v. 490
  Bologna visited by, vi. 173
  daughter of, ix. 409n
  Dick to be proxy for, at christening of Cowper's child, viii. 233, 239
  entail of Sunderland estate broken by, vi. 277n
  (?) extravagance of, v. 200
  health of, bad, ix. 78
  Mann encloses letter to, vi. 336
  mother's jointure inherited by, ix. 78
  Northamptonshire's moderate petition disappoints, ix. 10
  Sacchi painting bought by, v. **172**
  (?) son's match disapproved by, ix. 104
  stepbrother will entertain, at Florence, vi. 173
Spencer, John (d. 1767), East India official:
  letter from, vii. 381
Spencer, Robert (1641–1702), 2d E. of Sunderland:
  James II's betrayal by, may be reenacted, ii. 458
Spencer, Lord Robert (1747–1831), M.P.:
  Fox, Hon. Stephen and Lady Mary, accompanied by, in dressing-room, vii. 392
  letter to, tells of house-breaking at HW's Arlington St house, vii. 295
  Mann entertains, at dinner, vii. 295
Spencer family:
  Beauclerk's marriage to Vcts Bolingbroke approved by, vi. 567
  Pembroke's elopement resented by, vi. 10
Spenser, Mr ——:
  extravagance of, v. 200
Spenser *or* Spencer, Charlotte (d. 1789):
  Devonshire, D. of, has daughter by, ix. 455n
Spenser. *See also* Le Despenser; Spencer
Speronara, Tuscan vessel:
  (?) launching of, vi. 548
Spezia, Gulf of:
  importance of, i. 309
  Spaniards patrol, i. 317
  Spanish expedition may aim for, i. 206
  two fleets in, i. 311
Spezia:
  English squadron guards, iii. 55

fleets said to leave, for Toulon, i. 323
France said to have demanded, of Genoa, iv. 277
French ships between Genoa and, i. 322
governor of, warns Genoa of arrival of Spanish fleet, i. 308–10
limit set to English ships which can stay at, iv. 588
Mann receives letter from, about attack on San Remo, iii. 121
Montemar said to have reached, i. 195
Pope's ship carried to, i. 16
Spanish army's landings at, i. 179, 182, 198, 314, 323, 350, ii. 405, 413
Spanish army leaves garrison at, i. 289
Spanish barks at, i. 262

Sphinx, French ship:
in Vilaine river, v. 351

Spider; spiders:
Sloane's museum contains, iv. 358–9

Spina, Jean, Cadet:
captured at Velletri, ii. 493

Spinach:
tarts of, i. 218

Spinage, John, magistrate:
(?) Wilkes applies to, vi. 138

Spindler, ——, Major (d. 1743):
killed at Campo Santo, ii. 164

Spinelli, ——, Marchese:
passport in name of, ii. 388

Spinelli, Ferdinando Maria (1728–95), cardinal, 1785; governor of Rome, 1778:
Pius VI urged by, to suppress Carnival, ix. 383

Spinelli, Gaetano (1688–1766), senator:
Walpole, Bns, cases of, opened by, i. 224

Spinelli, Giuseppe (1694–1763), cardinal, 1735:
Louis XV wants French candidate elected by, i. 20–1
Old Pretender visited by, at Albano, after Benedict XIV's audience, iv. 590
—— writes to, of grudge against Benedict XIV, iv. 590

Spinola, Marchesa. See Durazzo, Pauline (ca 1755–73)

Spinola, Giovanni Battista (1681–1752), cardinal, 1733:
votes for, at Papal election, i. 16–17

Spinola de la Cerda. See Cordova Spinola de la Cerda

Spiridov, Alexei Grigor'evich (fl. 1770–90), Russian naval officer:
escape of, at Tchesmé battle, vii. 227, 233
(?) on board *Winchelsea* at Leghorn, vii. 233

Spiridov, Grigorii Andreevich (1713–90), Russian naval officer, Kt:
Orlov notified by officer from, vii. **162**
Russian ship arrives with, at Port Mahon, vii. 162
ship of, blown up, vii. 227, 233, 234
ships of, at Port Mahon, vii. 185

Turkish fleet said to be burned by, at Lemnos, vii. 319

Spirit of lavender. See under Lavendar

Spirit of Patriotism. See St John, Henry (1678–1751): *Letters*

Spirits:
fœtuses preserved in, in Sloane's museum, iv. 359
Middlesex, Cts of, preserves miscarriage in, iii. 447

Spithead:
Brederode reaches, iii. 556

Spittle ('Spittal') Square, Bishopsgate St:
Rice lives in, iv. 397

Spleen:
English, Mann claims to have, iv. 404
English weakness, iv. 1

Sponge; sponges:
hot: Mann applies, to breast, iii. 8; Mann uses, for pain in stomach, vi. 469

Sponging:
eyes to be helped by, ii. 386

Spoons:
gold, for Leopold II's household, made from furnishings in Palazzo Pitti, ix. 231
Mann's, acquired from Fane, ii. 472

Sprimont, Nicholas (1716–71):
Chelsea china made by, vi. 121–2

Spring; springs:
to cables of Turkish fleet, vii. 234

Spring Garden:
HW escorts two ladies to Cts of Albemarle's in, viii. 442

Spry, Sir Richard (1715–75), Kt, 1773; naval officer:
Orford, Cts of, to be taken by, in ship from Naples to Marseille, vii. 2

Spry, Mrs William. See Pitt, Amelia

Spurs:
man wears, to London theatre, i. 172
Vorontsov wears, to dinner table, v. 248

Spy; spies:
English, French seize, at Brest, iii. 182n
French: Hawley hangs, iii. 201, 241; surgeon asks Hawley for corpse of, to dissect, iii. 201; Mann's, abbé is, at Rome, i. 113, 114, 140
St-Germain arrested as, iii. 181–2, x. 20, 21
Virrette arrested as, iii. 182n

Squares:
London's, new, viii. 228

Squib; squibs:
for Rodney, disturb HW's sleep, ix. 281
in London, for Amherst's capture of Montreal, v. 437
in London bonfires, after battle of Minden, v. 314
Jupiter lights, in English opera, iii. 370
mob throws, in London, viii. 442

Squillace, Marqués de. See Gregorio, Leopoldo de

Squillace, in Italy:
earthquake account mentions, ix. 376

Squire, Samuel (1713–66), rector of St Anne's, Soho; Bp of St David's, 1761:
dubious about HW's inscription, v. 140
Squire; squires:
country, in uniform, v. 311–12
Squirrel. *See* 'Hunt the squirrel'
Stables:
Leopold's, visited by Maria Amalia, ix. 301
Stade:
convention at, *see* Kloster-Zeven: convention of
Cumberland, D. of, should not have marched towards, v. 146
—— takes route of, to Hanover, v. 28
Stadtholder:
William of Orange becomes, iii. 394
Staff:
chamberlain's, v. 91, vi. 96
Devonshire, D. of, leaves, with Egremont, vi. 96
pilgrim's, i. 339
Stafford, Cts of. *See* Cantillon, Henrietta (d. 1761)
Stafford, E. of. *See* Stafford-Howard, William Matthias (1719–51)
Stafford, M. of. *See* Leveson-Gower, Granville (1721–1803)
Stafford, Francis; Young Pretender's tutor:
Young Pretender sends, to brother, ii. 377–8
—— to receive effects from, from Rome in France, ii. 433–4
Stafford, Henry (fl. 1744–64), Young Pretender's companion:
Bath's former 'creature,' iv. 9
Young Pretender said to be banished with, to Pont Beauvoisin, iv. 9
Stafford:
races at, v. 421
Stafford-Howard, Lady Henrietta Maria (d. 1756), m. (1748) Claude-Prosper Jolyot de Crébillon:
husband takes, to provinces, iv. 325
Stafford-Howard, Lady Mary Apolonia Scolastica (1721–69), m. (1744) Guy-Auguste de Rohan-Chabot, Comte de Chabot:
marriage of, ii. 430
Stafford-Howard, William Matthias (? 1719–51), 3d E. of Stafford:
England revisited by, before invasion threat, ii. 429
France preferred by, i. 135
France revisited by, for sister's wedding, ii. 429–30
HW on round of dinners with, i. 131
Histoire de Dom B——, bound by, like prayer-book, i. 273–4
(?) Knight, Mrs, has affair with, i. **126**
London and Paris to be residences of, ii. 277
marriage of, ii. 219, 277
returns to England, with stories of Primate of Lorraine, i. 273
wife left by, in France, ii. 430

Winnington entertains, with HW, ii. 283
—— jokes with, about Catholicism and fasting, ii. 283
Staffordshire:
Etruscan vases made in, vii. 211; *see also under* Wedgwood, Josiah
Leake and Stone in, iii. 178
Staffort. *See* Stafford
Stage:
elephant breaks, i. 358
England, like Athens, as fond of, as of the state, viii. 435
enlarged, for Venetian scene in opera, i. 302
HW thinks royalty are like actors on, ix. 552, 624
See also Opera; Theatre
Stage box:
George II occupies, at theatre, iv. 290
Stage-coach; stage-coaches:
HW receives message by, of E. of Orford's insanity, viii. 293
leave from Whitehorse Cellar, v. 313
Russian fleet as slow as, vii. 224
Stagione:
Mann's slow convalescence attributed to, viii. 479
Stahremberg. *See* Starhemberg
Stained glass:
at SH, iv. 371, 382, 391, 396, vii. 365
at the Vyne, iv. 485n
HW does not remember seeing, in Italy, iv. 111, 119
HW gets, from Flanders, iv. 199–200
HW vainly asks Mann to get, for SH, iv. 111, 119
Stainville, Comte de. *See* Choiseul-Stainville, Étienne-François de (1719–85)
Stainville, Marquis de. *See* Choiseul, François-Joseph de (1695–1769); Choiseul-Stainville, Jacques-Philippe de (d. 1789)
Stair, E. of. *See* Dalrymple, John, (1673–1747); Dalrymple, John (1749–1821); Dalrymple-Crichton, William (d. 1768)
Staircase:
at SH, *see under* SH
to Uffizi gallery, vi. 123
wooden, peculiar to England, vi. 143
Stairs. *See* Stair
Staley, Andrew (ca 1733–1813), King's messenger:
Stormont sends news of Louis XV by, viii. 1
Stamford, Cts of. *See* Bentinck, Lady Henrietta (1737–1827)
Stamford, E. of. *See* Grey, George Harry
Stamford:
Cottesmore near, ix. 222, 461, 546, 678
Stampa, Carlo Francesco (1685–1751), general:
Botta to succeed, iv. 320
death of, iv. 295
Francis I's commissary for Italy, iv. **24,** 295

Grand Duke of Tuscany's villa occupied by, iv. 116
'paragino' at Pisa, iv. 24
Richecourt disputes with, over chairs and stools, iv. 320
—— fears that Craon will be succeeded by, iv. 24
Stamp Act:
Buckingham grand jury links land tax with, vi. 494
England may see 'wisdom' of, viii. 208
Grenville, George, author of, vi. 401, ix. 279
repeal of; moved by Conway, ix. 252; voted, vi. 401, 408, 409–10
vipers hatched from, disliked by HW, ix. 213
Stamperia Bonducciana:
Arno Miscellany printed at, ix. 507, x. 46
Standards:
captured at Piacenza, iii. 267, 270
French: captured at Louisbourg and carried to St Paul's cathedral, v. 238; HW might wrap, in postscript, v. 518
of Blenheim, in Westminster Hall, ix. 337
recaptured from Spaniards, ii. 189
Spaniards capture, iii. 119
Spaniards send, to Madrid, ii. 161, 189
Standish:
HW keeps letter in, iii. 372
metal, HW's, at Arlington St, vii. 285
silver, Pomfret, Cts of, gives, to Uguccioni, ii. 126
Stands:
silver, left by Electress to Rinuccini, ii. 169
Stanhoe, Norfolk:
Walpole, Bn, has house at, ii. 249
Stanhope, Cts. *See* Hamilton, Grisel (ca 1719–1811)
Stanhope, Lady. *See* Delaval, Anne Hussey
Stanhope, Hon. Alexander (d. 1707); envoy to Spain and Holland:
d'Ayrolles clerk to, at The Hague, iii. 404
d'Ayrolles, Mme, mistress of, iii. 404
Stanhope, Anne (d. 1587), m. 1 (by 1535) Edward Seymour, E. of Hertford; cr. (1547) D. of Somerset; m. 2 Francis Newdigate:
husband disinherits stepsons of, in favour of her own son, iii. 523, iv. 139
Stanhope, Lady Caroline (1747–67), m. (1765) Kenneth Mackenzie, cr. (1766) Vct Fortrose and (1771) E. of Seaforth:
death of, from white lead, vi. 484
Stanhope, Charles (1673–1760); M.P.:
Crawford's servant rewarded by, iv. 110, 118–19
Pembroke taken home by, in chariot, iv. 108
Stanhope, Charles (1753–1816), styled Vct Mahon 1763–86; 3d E. Stanhope, 1786; M.P.:
ancestry of, viii. 67

defeated as Wilkes's candidate for Westminster, viii. 52
father-in-law attended by, viii. 371
'furious republican citizen of Geneva,' ix. 32
Gordon rioters prevailed upon by, to disperse, ix. 54
Mann, Horace II, opposes, at Maidstone meeting, ix. 32
marriage of, viii. 67
Marsham to have been opposed by, in Kent election, ix. 490, 494
Stanhope, Elizabeth (d. 1761), m. (1747) Welbore Ellis, cr. (1794) Bn Mendip:
husband of, v. 417n
marriage of, alienates her father, iii. 485
Stanhope, Hon. George (1717–54), army officer:
Argyll's aide-de-camp, i. 356
Stanhope, Lady Gertrude (ca 1696–1775), m. (1724) Sir Charles Hotham, 5th Bt:
Chesterfield's witticism to, when she invites him to Methodist retreat in Welsh mountains, viii. 90–1
death of, from fire, viii. 90
witty, but a Methodist, viii. 90
Stanhope, James (1673–1721), cr. (1717) Vct and (1718) E. Stanhope:
pension of, ii. 178
Port Mahon capture brings peerage to, v. 52
Stanhope, Hon. John (1705–48); M.P.:
Admiralty post assigned to, iii. **463,** iv. 12
Chesterfield's inheritance from, iv. 12
death of, iv. 12
Derby election after death of, iv. 19
witticism by, on Curzon's drippy nose, iv. 12
witty, viii. 90
Stanhope, Lady Lucy (1714–85):
Theodore of Corsica, 'admirer' of, ii. 192, 207–8, 221, 229
Stanhope, Mary (ca 1686–1762), m. (1707) Charles Fane, 1st Vct Fane:
death of, vi. 74
nervous disorders of, vi. 74
Stanhope, Philip (1714–86), 2d E. Stanhope, 1721:
address against use of Hanoverian troops proposed by, ii. 158, 178
brother of, i. **356**
Euclid deserted by, for matrimony, iii. 19
father's pension ends soon, ii. 178
mob incited by, i. 390
son of, viii. 52n, 67
Stanhope, Philip (1732–68), Chesterfield's illegitimate son:
allusion to graces in father's letters to, did him no good, ix. 337
Niccolini entertains, at dinner, iv. 174
Venice rejects, as English Resident, because of illegitimacy, vii. 325

Stanhope, Philip Dormer (1694–1773), 4th E. of Chesterfield:

assembly given by, at newly-completed house, iv. 302

bad actors and authors patronized by, iv. 142

Barnard's relations with, at Tunbridge, iii. 404

Bath visited by, iii. 463

Boughton Malherbe once owned by, iv. 166

brother calls on, at Blackheath, vi. 164

brother of, i. 279n, iii. 463, v. 417n, vi. 521n

brother's bequest to, iv. 12

brother's correspondence with, iv. 472

Case of the Hanover Forces by, ii. 123

Catherine II gives box to, in return for compliments to her ambassador, vii. 376

Cholmondeley answers, i. 230

Churchill attributes stale jokes to, ii. 131

Claude Lorrain painting bought by, vii. 466

Crébillon's *Sopha* put on sale by, at White's, i. 334

Dayrolles's relations with, iii. 404

death of, vii. 471

Derby election financed by, iv. 19

Devonshire succeeded by, as lord lieutenant of Ireland, ii. 550

Dublin gentleman praises 'humility' of, iii. 189–90

Dutch negotiations of, not likely to succeed, iii. 68–9

Fleury to be threatened by, i. 371

Fox discusses D. of Newcastle with, iv. 502

France said to be visited by, i. 371

Frederick, P. of Wales, impelled by, against Sir Robert Walpole, i. 329

French invasion feared by, viii. 391

French reception of, i. 232

French war not expected by, iv. 472

George II begrudges audience to, ii. 564

—'s levee attended by, ii. 102

Guasco intimate with, vi. 530

HW expects more from Pulteney's paper than from that of, iv. 374

HW says, has 'little title to fame,' iv. 166

Hague, The, gives cool reception to, x. 10

Hague, The, visited by, ii. 564

Hamilton and Elizabeth Gunning entertained by, iv. 302–3

Hammond favourite of, i. 275n, 451

Hanoverian dynasty attacked by, i. 230, ii. 123–4

Harrington may be succeeded by, as secretary of state, iii. 326

health of, deaf, iv. 207

Hervey 'lives shut up with,' i. 275

Holland and then Ireland to be visited by, ii. 562

Jones described by, to HW, iv. 214

letters of: lack wit, viii. 91; to son, ix. 337n

Lyttelton defends, i. 232

Mallet and Flobert meet at house of, v. 377

Mann astonished by, i. 133

—— doubtful about stability of, in office, iii. 338

—— fears cunning of, ii. 557

—— introduces HW's verses as those of, ii. 372

—— receives commissions from, iii. 422–3

Marchmont advanced by, iv. 5

—— supposed to have written apology for resignation of, iv. 6

Marlborough, Ds of, leaves legacy to, as 'patriot,' ii. 540

Milton translation by Mme du Boccage praised by, iv. 142

mother-in-law leaves nothing to, ii. 231

naval investigation proposed by, in Parliament, ii. 400

Newcastle may be jealous of, iii. 413

——'s quarrel with, iii. 463

New Ode, A, mentions, ii. 52

newspapers print farewell speech of, iii. 52

Nugent, Mrs, asks, to urge her husband to speak in Parliament, i. 254–5

Old Pretender's people exult in retirement of, iii. 475

Opposition still includes, ii. 102

Orford sells Houghton lantern to, iv. 163

Orford, Cts of (Bns Walpole), amuses, by mistakes in her letters to him, iii. 70

—— corresponds with, i. 409, iii. 61, 70

—— hopes to secure Clinton barony through, i. 360, 409

—— receives intelligence from, i. 371

—— would never be content with, iv. 439

Ormond visited by, at Avignon, to tell Pretender to persuade Jacobites to vote against Sir Robert Walpole, i. 232n, iii. 68–9

pedigree of, iv. 181, 195

Pelham must bring in, ii. 537

Phipps, Mrs, called on by, iii. 190

Pope's alterations to Bolingbroke's *Letters* reported by, iv. 61

presidency declined by, iv. 207

resignation of, as secretary of state: iii. 463; rumoured because Newcastle may be jealous, iii. 412–13

returns from Holland, iii. 52

Richecourt and Bns Walpole hope to manage English relations with Tuscany through, i. 387

Saint-Germain intimate with, x. 21

Sandwich may succeed, iii. 413, 422

secretaryship of state predicted for, by Gage, i. 296

Siena marble procured for, iii. 423

sister of, viii. 90–1

son did not benefit by allusions to *the graces* in letters of, ix. 337

son of, vii. 325

speech by, in House of Lords, i. 230, 232, ii. 356

Venice to receive minister selected by, iii. 453

Walpole, Sir Robert, greeted by, at House of Lords, i. 338

—— quotes, i. 232

—— talks to, at George II's levee, ii. 102

Westminster election bragged about by, to Lovel, i. 272

'When Fanny blooming fair,' Shirley, Lady Fanny, celebrated by, viii. 401n

widow of, viii. 283n, 412n

wife of, ix. 248n

Winnington's witticism on turncoat politics of, ii. 540

wit of, i. 270, iv. 507

witticisms by: on Carteret's marriage, ii. 424; on giving Hanover to Pretender to make him unpopular in England, ii. 123-4; on Henry Jones, iv. 214, 218; on Pembroke's conduct at Bridge Committee, iv. 108; on the Pelhams, iv. 214; on the presidency, iv. 214; on the Viscontina, i. 197; to Anne Pitt, on Pitt's speaking in a horizontal posture, vii. 177; to sister, when she invited him to Methodist 'seminary' in Welsh mountains, viii. 91

World contributions by, iv. 374, 395n

Stanhope, Sir Thomas (d. 1770), Kt, 1759; Capt.:

defeated in Derby election, iv. 19

Du Quesne and officers courteously treated by, v. 255

Stanhope, Hon. Sir William (1702-72), K.B., 1725; M.P.:

brother called on by, at Blackheath, vi. 164

brother's correspondence with, iv. 472

daughter's marriage alienates, iii. 485

deed for Shirley's separate maintenance to be carried by, from Florence to England, iv. 569

Frederick, P. of Wales, cool to, for his behaviour at Carlton House, i. **279**

heir not begotten by, vi. 418

Herbert, Mrs, shocked by, at Ps of Wales's reception, iii. 175

house and entertainment of, seem Florentine, iii. 485

jealous, vi. 170, 418

Mann told by, in Florence, about trials of deafness, v. 177

Naples to be visited by, v. 550

Naples visited by, vi. 418

Parliamentary debates hardly heard by, with ear trumpet, vi. 183

Petersham, Lady Caroline, entertained by, at ball, iii. 485

Petershams may inherit property from, iii. 485

Pope's house and garden altered by, v. 417-18, ix. 177-8

Prince Henry mistaken by, for wax child, iii. 175

returns to England, disgusted by Naples, vi. 418

son-in-law advises, v. 417

wife of, vi. 521n

wife parts with, at Blackheath, vi. 164

wife's relations with, vi. 164, 170

Wilkes chiefly intimate with, at Naples, vi. 292

witticisms by: on ear-cropping, vi. 183; to young wife on wedding night, vi. 164

witty, viii. 90

Stanhope, William (ca 1683-1756), cr. (1730) Bn and (1742) E. of Harrington:

brother of, iv. 110

Carteret less civil than, to Mann, ii. 363

circular letter by, to Trevor, i. 281

Cope promoted by, iii. 117

Cox bought off by, despite Bristow's and Frankland's opposition, iv. 156-7

daughter of, vi. 484

Dorset replaces, in Ireland, iv. 202

—— succeeds, as lord president, ii. 550

earldom given to, i. **333**

Frederick, P. of Wales, makes Elizabeth Chudleigh write to, for warrant as secretary at war, iii. 175

—— tells footman not to give letter to, except in Yonge's presence, iii. 175

Garter might be expected by, iv. 84

George II displeased with, iv. 202

—— does not make, K.G., iv. 72-3

——'s favour abandoned by, to please D. of Newcastle, v. 100

Granville said to resign seals to, ii. 556

Hanover visit of, with George II, ii. 363

Holdernesse's experience compared with that of, v. 100

Irish lord lieutenancy or Presidency of the Council may be offered to, iii. 327

Ligonier plays whist with, at Petersham, iii. 166

lord lieutenant of Ireland, iv. 156n, v. 100n

Mann asked by, to assist Nomis, ii. 110

—— hears from, of neutrality, i. 181

—— informed by, of George II's intention of going to England, iii. 99

—— receives letter from, giving George II's approval, iii. 86

—— sends news of Young Pretender's departure to, i. 113, 115, 119, 208

mob assaults, at Dublin, iv. 156

Newcastle, D. of, attacks, x. 10

—— may quarrel with, iv. 326

president of the council, i. 333

resignation of, as secretary of state, iii. 211, 326

resignations instigated by, iv. 207

secretaryship of state given back to, ii. 537

son of, iii. 43n, 294n

[Stanhope, William (ca 1683–1756), *continued*]
Suares recommended by, for preferment, ii. 455
Tabuerniga family receive pension through, i. 278
Stanhope, William (1719–79), styled Vct Petersham 1742–56; 2d E. of Harrington, 1756:
HW mentions, ii. 374
marriage of, iii. 294
Stanhope, Sir William, may leave property to, iii. 485
White's Club attended by, just before earthquake, iv. 140
wife of, i. 184n, 274n, ix. 508n
wife wakes, after earthquake, iv. 140
wounded at Fontenoy, iii. 43
Stanhope, Durham:
Keene gets living of, from Sir Robert Walpole, iv. 346
Stanhope family:
name of, becomes popular as Sir Robert Walpole's declines, i. 270
pedigree of, iv. 181, 195
Stanhope's rejection at Derby a blow to, iv. 19
wit of, iv. 12, viii. 90
Stanislas I (Leszczyński) (1677–1766), K. of Poland 1704–9; D. of Lorraine 1737–66:
Boufflers, Marquise de, mistress of, iv. 236, vi. 243, 270n
—— ridicules, in letters to husband, iv. 236
career of, vi. 402–4
chancellor of, *see* Chaumont, Antoine-Martin de, Marquis de la Galaisière
Craon favoured by, iv. 236
——'s correspondence with, iii. 467
—— watched by, in illness, iv. 92
Craon, Princesse de, given Queen's apartment by, iv. 116
—— may displace Marquise de Boufflers in affections of, iv. 26
—— may wed, iv. 116, 126, 132
Craons courted by, iii. 467
death of, from burns, vi. 402–3
Frederick Augustus II former rival of, vi. 403
funeral oration for, in Paris, vi. 403–4
granddaughters permitted to visit, when treasurer says expense seems justifiable, vi. 403
HW calls, 'best of beings,' vi. 254
Peter the Great and Charles XII prepared way for, vi. 404
Poland too stupid to reelect, vi. 402
Pomfret, E. of, 'nicknamed K. Stanislas' after, ii. **501**
smokes a pipe, iii. 467, iv. 26
still alive in Stanislas II's reign, vi. 253
wealth and bequests of, vi. 403
witticisms by: on daughter's gift of a nightgown, vi. 403; on Marquise de

Boufflers' intrigue with La Galaisière, vi. 244, 246; to lady who burned her arm, vi. 403
Stanislas II (Stanislas Augustus Poniatowski) (1732–98), K. of Poland 1764–95:
attack upon, must alarm other monarchs, vii. 359
chosen instead of Czartoryski, vi. 248n
Conway knew, vi. 248
Craven, Bns, shows HW's letter to, and he translates it into French, ix. 632–3
Czartoryski's cousin and friend, vi. **248**, ix. 633
English fleet might restore, vii. 475
Frederick II urges Catherine II to make, abdicate in favour of P. Henry, ix. 44–5
HW acquainted with, in England, vi. 253
kingdom of: may be more manageable after its partition, vii. 440; may be partitioned, vii. 419
Lind taken by, as preceptor to his nephew, vii. 565
made K. of Poland, vi. 253
Polish minister at Rome reports Young Pretender's alleged Polish trip to, vii. 352
Stanislas I alive during reign of, vi. 253, 404
unhappy, vii. 352
Stanley, Bn. *See* Smith Stanley, Edward (1752–1834)
Stanley, Bns. *See* Hamilton, Lady Elizabeth (1753–97)
Stanley, Edward (1689–1776), 11th E. of Derby:
regiment raised by, iii. 128
son of, v. 199n, 552n, vii. 313n
Stanley, Hans (1721–80), politician; M.P.:
Admiralty changes expected by, vi. 326
Bedford's dismissal affects, vi. 326–7
English courier sent to, with news of Pondicherry capture, v. 515
frigate awaits, at Leghorn, vi. 326
HW recommends, to Mann, vi. 292, 300, 304
HW warns Mann about conversation with, vi. 300, 304
Italy to be visited by, vi. 293, 300
lord of the Admiralty, vi. 292
Mann encloses letter to, to Paris, vi. 340
—— entertains, vi. 313, 326
may be ambassador to Russia, vi. 444
Paris mission of, v. 504, 514, 515, 536, vi. 92–3, 300
Rome but not Naples to be visited by, on way to Paris, vi. 327
Scarbrough succeeded by, as Cofferer, vi. 473
Virrette released by influence of, with Holdernesse, iii. **182n**
Stannaries:
warden of, Waldegrave was, vi. 126n
Stanno. *See* Stanhoe

Stansted House, Sussex:
(?) Northumberlands build at, iv. 341
Staples, Hon. Henrietta. *See* Moleswoth, Hon. Henrietta
Staples, (? John, d. 1789), lawyer:
Dingley assaulted by, vii. 98
Stapleton, Catherine (ca 1732–1802), m. Sir James Wright, Kt, 1766; cr. (1772) Bt:
George III's picture done by, for Mann and shown to Q. Charlotte, vi. 501, 503
Stapleton, Lady Georgiana Maria. *See* Fitzroy, Lady Georgiana Maria (b. 1785)
Stapleton, Mrs John Horace Thomas. *See* Fitzroy, Georgiana Maria
Stapleton, Walter (d. 1746), Brig.-Gen. in French service:
Kilmarnock's severity opposed by, iii. **285**
Perth aided by, iii. 259
Stapleton, Mrs William. *See* Keppel, Anna Maria (1759–1836)
Star; stars:
astronomers' theory about, iii. 71, v. 85
Cowper orders, from London, ix. 568
newly discovered, ix. 614
'Star and Garter,' tavern in Pall Mall:
Byron kills Chaworth in, vi. 284
Star and garter:
Vorontsov, Cts, wears, vi. 193
Star Chamber:
England seems as if fined in, vi. 274
Starhemberg, Georg Adam (1724–1807), Graf; cr. (1765) Fürst; ambassador from Austria to France:
Austrian-Dutch quarrel discussed by, at Paris, ix. 561
Maria Theresa sends, to Paris, v. **498**
recall of, arouses fear of war in France, vi. **404**
Staten Island:
Howe lands on, viii. 229, 241
State of Parties. See St John, Henry (1678–1751): *Letters*
States General. *See under* Holland
Statesman, The. See under Williams, Sir Charles Hanbury
Stationer. *See* Woodmason, James
Stationery:
Mann's expense allowance for, ii. 516
'Statira.' *See under* Lee, Nathaniel: *Alexander the Great*
Statius, Publius Papinius (ca 61–96), Latin poet:
secretary of militia reads, aloud to E. of Orford's guests, viii. 295
Statue; statues:
at Casa Feroni, i. 33
at Easton Neston, iv. 390
at Florentine Duomo, weep on catafalque, vi. 367
at Wilton, adorned with charcoal, ix. 178
casts of, to be exhibited in Richmond's garden room, v. 173

Corinthian, belittled by Roman sailors, iii. 264
Damer, Hon. Mrs, may want to copy, in Florence, ix. 184
Del Nero's, ii. 308, 326, 338, 347
export of, forbidden, iv. 465
Francavilla's, bought by Mann for Frederick, P. of Wales, *see under* Francavilla
HW's: bought at Rome, x. 7; Mann distressed by accidents to, iii. 13
in Capitol at Rome, iv. 470
in Florentine loggia, vi. 123–4
in Florentine Tribune, viii. 527
Leicester to obtain, from Rome, iv. 104
Louis XVI orders, of balloon operators, ix. 450
Lyttelton orders gesse of, iv. 539, 547, 554, v. 40
Mann advises Botta, about placing, vi. 124
of Cicero, in Pomfret collection, iv. 390
of Ganymede, ii. 153, 178, 303, 329, 561
of gesso, *see under* Gesso
of Henri IV, viii. 19, 36
of Hermaphrodite, *see* Hermaphrodite
of Leda and the Swan, iv. 547
of 'Livia,' *see under* Livia
of Louis XV at Bordeaux, i. 125
of Morpheus, ii. 153, 178, 303, 329, 561
of St Ignatius, vii. 513
of Venus, extracting a thorn, iv. 547
Pisans may erect, to Leopold, vii. 95
Pomfret's, presented to Oxford, iv. 390n, 470, 579, 562n
removed from *tribuna* in Uffizi gallery, ix. 170
Walpole, Sir Robert, needs, at Houghton, ii. 326
Wilton's, iv. 397–8
Statute of Lunacy:
HW and Sir Edward Walpole not to take out, for E. of Orford, viii. 294, ix. 126
Stavordale, Bn. *See* Fox-Strangways, Henry Thomas (1747–1802)
Stay; stays:
HW wears, as old woman, i. 359
Richecourt, Cts, wears, in England, iv. 365
Staymaker:
Lombard, Peter, said to have been, vii. 435
Steare, Staples, bookseller:
prosecuted as Wilkes's publisher, vii. 29
Steavens, Sarah (d. 1799), m. (1738) James West:
husband and brother of, iv. 371n
Steavens, Thomas (ca 1728–?59):
HW recommends, to Mann, iv. 371
Italy visited by, iv. 371
Mann's correspondence with, iv. 379
West's brother-in-law, iv. 371
witticism of, to Signora Capello, iv. **175**
Steavens. *See also* Stephens; Stevens
Stedman, Mrs John. See Moders, Mary

Steel:
buckles of, *see under* Buckles
from Woodstock, i. 302
HW sends, to Mann, i. 302
machine of, iv. 203
Steele, Sir Richard (1672–1729), essayist; dramatist; M.P.:
Conscious Lovers, HW prefers, to Moore's *Foundling*, iii. 465
Tender Husband, 'Biddy Tipkin' in, v. 438
Stefanucci, Orazio (1706–75), S.J.; authority on canon law:
imprisoned, vii. 526
treatise attributed to, vii. 517, 526–7
Stella:
discussion about, in *giuoco della sibilla*, iv. 477
Stephan:
Orford, Cts of, accompanied by, to England, iii. 50
—— to be accompanied by, iii. 46
Pomfret, Cts of, had, as valet-de-chambre, iii. 46
Stephen, St, of Hungary:
order of, *see* Order of St Stephen
Stephens, Joanna (d. 1774):
medicine of: Victoire, Mme, cured by, vi. 164; Walpole, Sir Robert, takes, ii. 552
Stephens, Peter (d.?1775), artist:
drawings printed by, at Rome, and given to Mann, iv. 427–8
Florence and Rome visited by, vii. 427
HW gets engraving of, vii. 423
mad, vii. 423
Mann has never seen prints by, vii. 427
——'s house said to have been frequented by, vii. 423
prints by, not to be had in Rome, vii. 429
views by; HW sees, at E. of Upper Ossory's, vii. 422–3; HW wants, from Mann, vii. 422–3
Stephens. *See also* Steavens; Stevens
Sterndale, John, printer:
House of Commons questions, vii. 555
Sterne, Laurence (1731–68), novelist; divine:
Tristam Shandy: HW sends, to Mann, v. 407; Mann's opinion of, v. 446, 520–1; Roxburghe lends, to Mann, v. 520–1
Patch's caricature of, vii. 5, 27, 33, 37
Stettin:
Frederick II's artillery was to have prevented fall of, vi. 12
Stevens, Dr (?) Sachaverell (d. 1768):
England called a 'mobocracy' by, v. 138
Stevenson, Samuel, mayor of Maidstone:
Holdernesse's letter to, v. 34
Steward, Capt. [?James or William Stewart]
Ireland to be visited by, to enter Parliament, vii. 1
Irish gentleman, vii. 27
Mann sends caricature and paper on Tuscany through, to HW and Shelburne, vii. 27–8
—— sends letter through, to HW, vii. 1
Steward; stewards: *See under* Servant
Stewart, ——:
arrested in Covent Garden bagnio, i. 505
Stewart, Archibald (1697–1780), M.P.; Provost of Edinburgh:
arrested, iii. 181
Wade with, iii. 175–6
Stewart, Archibald James Edward. *See* Douglas, Archibald James Edward
Stewart, Charles (d. 1764), 5th E. of Traquair:
arrest of, iii. 288
Barrymore, Cotton, and Williams converse with, about Old Pretender's affairs, iii. 381
evidence expected from, about plot, iii. 381, 391
Lovat's body paraded before dungeon of, iii. 387
Stewart, Lt Charles:
hostage in Marátha war, viii. 510
Stewart, Hon. Elizabeth. *See* Molesworth, Hon. Elizabeth (d. 1835)
Stewart, Hon. James (ca 1699–1768), army officer, M.P.:
conduct of, to be probed, v. 23
Panmure said to be replacing, iv. 562
Stewart, Hon. John (ca 1709–96), M.P.:
voted for, as commissioner, i. 438
Stewart, John (d. after 1788), cr. (1784) titular Bt; valet to Young Pretender:
Young Pretender attended by, vii. 318
—— sends, to Paris for daughter, ix. 513
Stewart, Mary (d. 1751), m. (1741) Kenneth Mackenzie, styled Lord Fortrose:
rebels joined by, iii. 233
Stewart, Mary (d. 1769), m. James O'Hara, 2d Bn Tyrawley:
husband of, i. 104
Stewart, Capt. Robert:
Braddock rescued by, iv. 495
Stewart, William (fl. 1731–43), paymaster of pensions:
Jeffries said to succeed, i. 494
Stewart. *See also* Stuart
Stick:
George II walks with, v. 256
HW able to walk without, in less than a month after attack of gout, viii. 70
Stiletto:
Italians no longer wield, vi. 254
Stilo ['Stillo']:
earthquake damages, ix. 376
Stilts:
man on, peers through second-story windows in London, i. 399
Stinsanacone:
earthquake account mentions, ix. 376
Stiria. *See* Styria
Stirling, E. of. *See* Alexander, William

Stirling:
Falkirk near, iii. 214
London's example followed by, with regard to Pitt, v. 546
Stirling Castle:
Cumberland, D. of, may relieve, before it is captured, iii. 204
Stirrup:
Joseph II unlikely to hold, for Clement XIII, vi. 555
Stitara. *See* Rolle, Margaret
Stockbridge:
Fox undermines Hay's leadership in, v. 23
Hay loses seat for, v. 73
Stock exchange. *See* Change Alley
Stockholm:
incendiaries from, said to have tried to burn Copenhagen arsenal, vii. 470
Vergennes ambassador at, viii. 17
Stockings:
cabriolets embroidered on, as clocks, iv. 483
Doncaster, Craon wears, as sleeves, ii. 109
grey, Montagu, Lady Mary Wortley, wears, vi. 3
ladies', cost of, ii. 281
thread, to be worn outside bootikins, viii. 494
Young Pretender's forces repair, at Perth, iii. 105
Stock-jobbers:
HW's reflections on, ix. 287
lies circulated by, viii. 412
Stock-jobbing:
'patriots' involved in, vi. 498
Stocks:
bolstered so that they are no longer fortune's weather-glass, viii. 464
Chute thinks of withdrawing his money from, viii. 210
East India, *see under* East India Company
English newspapers concerned with, vi. 174
fall: v. 74; on American-French alliance news, viii. 348, 364; on American war prospects, viii. 213; on French war prospect, viii. 179, 282, 361; on news of peace failure, vi. 81; on Spanish war prospect, vii. 239, 250, 282; on Young Pretender's invasion of England, iii. 186
French may buy, in England, to profit by rise at peace news, ix. 357
HW prefers a bronze to a fortune in, v. 558
invasion of Ireland and Jamaica would lower, v. 558
invasion threats hardly affect, ii. 393
Lunardi invests in, ix. 543
Mann's legacy from father invested in, v. 54–5, 61
peace not indicated by level of, ix. 354
peace treaty fails to raise, iii. 511
peace would raise, v. 497

Pompadour, Marquis de, buys, in England, to profit by rise at peace news, ix. 357
Pulteney said to increase, ii. 91
rise and fall, on news from Spain, vii. 250
rise of: indicates hopes of Spanish neutrality, viii. 463–4; shows hope of peace, iii. 483, v. 504, vi. 38
rise six per cent, ix. 139
rumours of Spanish war do not affect, viii. 98
Spanish treaty boosts, in England, iv. 198
Stoic:
HW does not imitate, vii. 365
Lucas has greater sangfroid than, ix. 307
'Stoic,' race horse:
HW sells, vii. 497
Stoicism:
HW's distresses sometimes distract him from, viii. 327
Stokes, Adrian (ca 1533–85):
portrait of, by Lukas de Heere, bought by HW at Oxford's sale, i. 373–4
Stolberg-Gedern, Gustav-Adolf (1722–57), P. of:
daughters of, ix. 427n, 538n
Stolberg-Gedern, Karoline Auguste of (1755–1829), m. 1 (1771) Charles-Bernard-Pascal-Janvier Fitzjames, Marquis de la Jamaïque, 4th D. of Berwick (attainted), 1785; m. 2 (1793) Dominique, Duque de Castelfranco:
England visited by, ix. 427
sister of, vii. 402
Stolberg-Gedern, Luise Maximiliane of (1752–1824), m. (1772) Charles Edward Stuart, the 'Young Pretender'; styled Cts of Albany:
Alfieri's affair with, ix. 397, 535, 538n
—— teaches and tempts, ix. 106–7
ancestry of, vii. 402, ix. 538n
beauty of: rivalled by Cts Cowper's, viii. 245; vastly faded, viii. 480
Bianchette convent the temporary refuge of, ix. 101–2, 108n
breakfast often taken by, with husband and Mme Orlandini, ix. 101
brother-in-law and Pius VI invite, to convent at Rome, ix. 106
brother-in-law consulted by, about leaving husband, ix. 101
brother-in-law protects, in Rome, ix. 108n, 150, x. 47–8
brother-in-law publishes intrigues of, with Alfieri, ix. 397
brother-in-law to lend coach to, ix. 107
calls not returned by, at Florence, ix. 535
convent can seldom be left by, in husband's lifetime, ix. 107
England may be visited by, to wed Alfieri, x. 48
erudition of, ix. 106
Grenville and other English in love with, viii. 102

[Stalberg-Gedern, Luise Maximiliane of, *cont.*]
Gustav III discouraged by, at Rome, from aiding her husband, ix. 475
HW wants print of, vii. 422, 427, 429
husband bars all access to room of, save from his own, viii. 245
husband blames his impotence on potion given by, to him at Mann's instigation, ix. 102
husband does not conceal his stench and temper from, viii. 480
husband guards, jealously, lest legitimacy of heir be dubious, viii. 94, 137, 245
husband ill-treats, ix. 100–1, 108n, 150, 538n
husband insists on royal honours for, against her wishes, vii. 406
husband meets, at Loreto, and conveys her to Macerata and Rome, vii. 406
husband separated from, ix. 100–1, 108n, 150, 396–7, 538n, x. 47–8
husband's recovery from illness will disappoint, ix. 395
husband tenderly treated by, viii. 137
income of, after separation from husband, ix. 536
Leopold protector of, against husband, ix. 101–2, 108n
Louis XVI gives pension to, ix. 150, 536
Louise, Princesse, may have produced, vii. 399
Maltzan, Baronne de, companion to, ix. 522
Marie-Antoinette's gracious letter to, ix. 150
marriage of, vii. 398–9, 402, 405–6
Orsolene convent at Rome to be occupied by, ix. 106
pitied in Florence at the time of her separation from husband, ix. 396
Pius VI to give half of husband's pension to, ix. 107
probably at Paris, viii. 102
probably not a Protestant, vii. 402
Roman visit of, called imprisonment by HW, ix. 115
Seymour attached to, with husband's consent, viii. 94, 102
sister of, ix. 402, 427
stepdaughter's arrival may cause, to repent of her elopement, ix. 535
visitors call on, in husband's theatre box, viii. 245
Walkinshaw, Clementina, pleads with, for daughter, x. 47
Stomach:
bleeding from, probably not caused by gout, ix. 560
Mann attributes HW's illness to, vi. 114
organic disorder of, v. 217
sickness of, viii. 244
See also Disorder in stomach and bowels; Dropsy in the stomach; Indigestion; Vomiting; Water in the stomach

Stomacher:
Charlotte's, of diamonds, v. 529
Stone, Andrew (1703–73), undersecretary of state; M.P.:
address to George II said to demand dismissal of, as George III's tutor, iv. 370
Argyll praises, for treatment of two Scotch place-seekers, iv. 366
Birtles's dispatches betrayed by, iv. 364
brother of, iv. 315, 505
Christ Church people flatter, iv. 261
death of, vii. 538
Dorléans book disclaimed by, iv. 344
George III's sub-governor, iii. 347n, iv. 246, 323
HW advises Mann not to give presents to, ii. 137
HW asks Mann for Roman gossip about, iv. 360
Harcourt calls, a Jacobite, iv. 344
—— fit to be a cipher to, iv. 246, 345
—— refuses to act with, iv. 343–4
Hayter and Harcourt oppose, over George III's tutorship, iv. 323, 343–4
Johnson contemporary with, iv. 345
Mann astonished at account of, ii. 381
—— hopes for payment of arrears through, ii. 516–17, iii. 56, 221, 490
—— neglected by, iii. 474, 483–4, 490, iv. 195
—— pays, for 'protection,' vii. 538
——'s present to, useless, ii. 115
Mann, Galfridus, says, is unfriendly to Mann, ii. 115
Murray urges Bp Hayter to promote, iv. 345
Newcastle consults, iii. 347
——'s favourite, iv. 505
——'s secretary, i. 6, 137n, iii. 347n, vii. 538n
Oswald brings fans to, i. 6
Ravensworth accuses, of toasting Old Pretender and Dunbar, iv. 360–1, 364
snuff-box for, i. 29, ii. 115, 330, 445, 496
treasurer to Augusta, Ps of Wales, vii. 538n
treasurer to Q. Charlotte, v. 517–18
unpopularity of, iv. 345
Whigs disown, iv. 345
Stone, Mrs Andrew. *See* Mauvillain, Hannah (ca 1710–82)
Stone, Dr George (ca 1708–64), Bp of Ferns and Leighlin 1740–3; of Kildare 1743–5; of Derry 1745–7; Abp of Armagh 1747–64:
Bedford rejects overtures of, v. 154
brother of, iv. 315, 505
'cardinalesque' inclinations of, iv. 315
credit of, decays, iv. 505
Cunningham aide-de-camp to, iv. 315
—— brought by, into Irish Parliament, iv. 316
death of, from drunkenness, vi. 269, 275

Dorset family would make, sole regent, iv. 316

epigram handed to, at dinner in Dublin Castle, iv. 316, 318

Irish unrest provoked by, v. 154, 474

Lorraine, Primate of, compared with, iv. 316, vi. 269

Newcastle's abandonment of, surprises Mann, iv. 505

nominated lord justice in Ireland, iv. 426

Pembroke's tennis games with, stopped because of blasphemy, iv. **109**

removal of, a 'peace-offering,' iv. 503

Stone, Staffs:

Cumberland, D. of, awaits rebels at, iii. 173, 178

Stone (anatomical):

Du Muy operated upon for, viii. 133

occurrences of, ii. 140, 538, 552, 566, iii. 16, 22, 29, iv. 418, vi. 27, 164

treatments for, ii. 552, vi. 164

Stone; stones:

artificial, gate piers of, vii. 311

black, of Dr Dee, vii. 286–7, 301

bridge of, at Henley, *see under* Henley

hard: box of, vi. 241, 243; Craon and Mann discuss, ii. 207

snuff-box of, i. 48

staircase should be built of, vi. 143

with vases, in Stosch's collection, v. 201

See also Gem; Jewel

'Stone-water':

Omai's name for ice, viii. 175

Stony Point on the Hudson:

Americans capture, viii. 519

British capture, viii. 500

Stools; stools:

Bayreuth, Margravine, provides very few of, for Florentine visitors, viii. 164

Richecourt and Stampa dispute over, iv. 320

sold out of Palazzo Vecchio, ix. 231

Stoppani, Giovanni Francesco (1695–1775), cardinal, 1754; nuncio:

Falkirk news sent to Rome by, iii. 214

Stopper:

golden, for Caroline's crystal hunting-bottle, ix. 464

Stop-watch. *See under* Watch

Store-ship:

English forced to burn, in attack on Charleston, viii. 236

Stork:

kite's fight with, in clouds, will be reproduced by rival aviators, ix. 543

Stormont, Vct. *See* Murray, David (ca 1689–1748); Murray, David (1727–96)

Stormont, Vcts. *See* Scott, Margery

Stosch, Bn. *See* Muzell, Heinrich Wilhelm (1723–82); Stosch, Philipp von (1691–1757)

Stosch, Heinrich Sigismund (1699–1747):

Mann sends corpse of, to Leghorn, iii. 358

Stosch, Philipp von (1691–1757), Bn; 'John Walton'; 'Cyclops':

arrears of pension sought by, iv. 53

Bentinck and Raymond make offers to, for Gladiator and Meleager, i. 264

brother of, dies, iii. 358

Buonaccorsi and Mann executors to, v. 149

Buonaccorsi inherits picture from, v. 149

cameos of: France buys, v. 201; Mann inherits, v. 149, ix. 650; numerous, v. 151; sent to HW by Mann, x. 56; to be sold separately, v. 186

cats disparaged by, i. 434

cats of, i. 164, 181, 434, 462

Chute gets from, a rare print by 'Marc Antonio' after Raphael, vii. 432

collection of: Benedict XIV might have bought, for Instituto at Bologna, v. 434; contains tracts about the Medici, v. 278; Frederick Augustus II covets, v. 434; George II's death may facilitate sale of, v. 445; HW desires items from, v. 188–9; marble fragment in, v. 192; nephew probably comes to England to sell, v. 427; nephew to sell, intact, v. 186; nothing yet sold from, v. 192; offered to Francis I, v. 149, 151; overrated, ix. 651; Richecourt may incorporate, by edict, v. 475; stones with vases not to be separated from, v. 201; would be more valuable if kings could compete for it, v. 434

Dalton buys modern medals from collection of, v. 478

death of, v. 149, 151

Del Nero does not employ, as English agent for his pictures, ii. 308

Description des pierres gravés, iv. 157n

drawings and prints of, v. 189, 202

Duncannon buys gladiator from, v. 151

—— corresponds with, about Meleager, iv. 159

—— gets intaglio from, for paying pension arrears, i. 212n, iv. 70, 159

Electress's wealth falsely reported by, ii. 206

England's spy on Old Pretender, i. 164n

English secret service at Rome managed by, v. 149

English visitors shown collection of, ii. 41, 62

Frederick II buys map collection of, ix. 651

—— feared by, ii. 308

Galla Placidia medal offered by, to HW, iv. 53, 70

Galli, Contessa, jokes about, i. 445

Gavi offered sum by, for Homer intaglio, iii. 489

gazettes relied on by, for news, ii. 308

Gazzetta letteraria exposes, i. 381–2

George II alone believes tales of, ii. 225

Gladiator intaglio of, i. 212n, 264, 302, ii. 369, iv. 157, 159, v. 151

[Stosch, Philipp von, *continued*]

Greek medals procured by, through Albani and Mann from estate of deceased Roman, ii. 478

HW could pity, for edict restricting sale of his collection, v. 475

HW mentions, v. 168

HW not indebted to, i. 439

HW offended at, for selling Gladiator to Duncannon, iv. 157, 159

HW's letter from, about pension arrears, iv. 36, 53

HW's transactions with, i. 416, 439, ii. 347

HW suggests giving Maltese cats to, to pay postage, i. 452

HW wants gladiator intaglio and Meleager of, i. 212n, 264, 302

HW wants items from collection of, v. 178, 189, 201-2

health of: apoplexy, v. 149; cut for the piles, i. 112, 404; inflammation of the bowels, v. 149

Houghton views coveted by, in return for carriage of medals and postage, i. 416

Ilay resembles, i. 420

intaglii cornered by, iv. 104

intaglii of: collected systematically, v. 186; numerous, v. 149

intaglio praised by, iii. 476

Kaunitz gets present from, by claiming relationship, i. 48–9

library of: v. 187; HW asks about state-papers and letters in, v. 278; sold to Vatican, v. 284

London Gazette gets false news from, ii. 206

Mann asked by, to punish editors of *Gazzetta letteraria* for insulting him, i. 382

—— called on by, ii. 308

—— congratulated by, on not having apoplexy, iii. 477

—— consults, about Cicciaporci's drawings, ii. 313

—— executor to, v. 149, 151

—— inherits cameo from, v. 149, ix. 650

—— sends news of HW's illness to, i. 51

—— thanked by, for sending brother's corpse to Leghorn, iii. 358

—— to tell, of Oxford's sale, i. 378

—— wants appointments of, as British secret agent, v. 149

—— will speak to, about Galla Placidia, iv. 70

maps collected by, v. 186

maps of: Benedict XIV not to buy, v. 186; catalogue printed of, v. 192

medals carried by, from Rome for HW, i. 416

medals of: bawdy, v. 160; bought by Dalton for George III, v. 231; HW insists on paying for, v. 215; HW receives prices of, v. 227; HW thanks Mann for, v. 203; sent by Albani, ii. 478

Meleager and Gladiator might be given up by, to escape criminal charges, ii. 369

Meleager of, i. 212n, 264, 302, iv. 159

Natter's correspondence with, through HW, iii. 243

nephew heir to, v. 149, 151

nephew of, v. 384n

nephew recalled by, from army, v. 149, 434

Newcastle might have heard from, of HW's and Mann's illnesses, i. 51

Old Pretender's movements to be reported by, to England, i. 9–10

pension of, i. 212n, iv. 53

Prideaux discusses collection and 'heathenish' remarks of, with HW, i. 378, 404

Prussian, i. 164n

Richecourt probably made edict forbidding export of antiquities to get collection of, iv. 465

Roman correspondent of, dies, ii. 380

Rome expels, i. 164n

soul said by: to be located in anus, i. 112, 404; to resemble glue, i. 378, 404

Valenti makes offer to, through Albani, v. 192

—— offers to buy map collection of, v. 186

weekly letters written by about Young Pretender, iv. 333

will of, v. 149, 151, 380

Young Pretender believed by, to be dead, iv. 333, 508

——'s departure not known to, ii. 380

youth mistreated by, ii. 369

Stosch, William. *See* Muzell, Heinrich Wilhelm (1723–82)

'Stoschino'. *See* Muzell, Heinrich Wilhelm

Stove; stoves:

earthenware for, ix. 645

German: Botta's room heated by, v. 370; Pitti palace furnished with, vi. 291, 576

Germans miss, in Florence, vi. 576

Stow, John (ca 1525–1605), chronicler:

Carte's history compared to *Survay* of, ii. 480

future imitators of, iv. 58

London's factions would tire patience of, vii. 330

Stowe:

visited by Ps Amelia, Ds of Bridgwater, and Sir R. Lyttelton, vi. 247

Strafford, Cts of. *See* Campbell, Lady Anne (ca 1715–85)

Strafford E. of. *See* Wentworth, Sir Thomas (1593–1641); Wentworth, William (1722–91)

Straits. *See* Gibraltar, Straits of

'Straizes,' Comte de:

England visited by, ix. 409

Stralsund:

Frederick II to besiege, v. 265

Strand, London:

Beaufort Buildings in, vii. 56

Campbell, bookbinder in, ix. 192

Fountain tavern in, i. 429n
Northumberland House in, iv. 507n
Vaillant, French bookseller in, v. 400
Strange, Bn. See Smith-Stanley, Edward (1752–1834); Smith-Stanley, James (1717–71)
Strange, Bns. See Hamilton, Lady Elizabeth (1753–97)
Strange, ——, merchant at Cadiz:
ship of, v. 269
Strange, Sir John (ca 1696–1754), Kt, 1740; Master of the Rolls; solicitor-general; M.P.:
chief justiceship may be given to, i. 494
death of, i. 494n
Frederick, P. of Wales, proposes opponent for, i. 299
Indemnity Bill supported by, i. 429
Master of the Rolls, i. 494n
Murray succeeds, as solicitor-general, i. 494, ii. 118
named in Secret Committee lists, i. 384
resigns because of ill health, ii. 118
Strange, John (1732–99), English resident at Venice, 1773–88:
conduct of, at Venice, justified by him in long and tedious letters which were unanswered, viii. 298
letters of, to Mann and Lynch about D. of Gloucester's recovery, are transposed, viii. 140
Mann's correspondence with, about D. of Gloucester, viii. 135–6, 140, 329
Rochford should have been told by, of D. of Gloucester's health, viii. 136
Strange, Sir Robert (1721–92), Kt, 1787; engraver:
Albano pilgrimage may be made by, v. 404
drawings by, v. 470, vi. 108
drawings engraved by, v. 470, vi. 108
HW recommends, to Mann, v. 404, 448, 461, vi. 108
Italy to be visited by, v. 404
Jacobite, v. 404, 461
Mann encloses letter to, viii. 24
—— promised by, to be prudent at Rome, v. 470
——'s advice from, about collecting virtu for George III, approved by HW, v. 497
—— tells: to deal with lady at Barbarini palace for Guido's Magdalen, v. 532–3; to look for art purchases at Rome and Naples, vi. 115
method invented by, for drawing in colours, vi. 108
permission granted to, to draw in Florentine palaces, v. 448
probably lives in St Martin's Lane, viii. 24
Strangways, Susanna (1689–1758), m. Thomas Horner:
(?) HW mentions, i. 475
Strasbourg, Abp of. See Rohan, Armand-Gaston-Maximilien de

Strasbourg:
visitors to, Gloucester, D. and Ds of, viii. 134
Strathallan, Vct. See Drummond, James Francis Edward
Strathfieldsaye, Hants:
Pitt, George, lives in, i. 468n
Strathmore, Cts of. See Cochrane, Susan (d. 1754)
Strathmore, E. of. See Lyon, Charles (1699–1728); Lyon, John (1737–76)
Straw:
hat of, iv. 430
streets littered with, to deaden noise outside windows of women who lie in, vii. 323
young men at St Alban's Tavern have streets littered with, vii. 323
'Strawberry, Counts of':
armorial achievements of, iv. 200
Strawberry Hill:
abbeys' and cathedrals' gloomth imparted to, iv. 372
air and tranquillity of, HW's requisites, ix. 257
'all brick and mortar,' iv. 368
armoury at, iv. 381, 396, 400
battlements of: HW may mount pop-guns on, v. 311; to be reared, iv. 199
Beauclerk Closet built to hold Lady Diana Beauclerk's illustrations for Mysterious Mother, viii. 524
bedchamber in Round Tower at, to be hung with brocatelle, v. 420
Bentley's view of, HW sends, to Mann, iv. 368, 377, 379, 386–7, 390
Blue Bedchamber at, iv. 381, 387
books at, iv. 382, see also under Library
Boufflers, Comtesse de, considers, unworthy of English solidity, vi. 270
bow window at, HW writes in, iv. 46, 68
'bow window room' at, see Blue Bedchamber
Breakfast Room at, iv. 382
Brentford election keeps HW from, vii. 73
cabinet and gallery at: Pitt, Thomas, draws Gothic ornaments for, vi. 25; to be finished in summer, v. 18
cabinet ('chapel,' 'Tribune') at: Caligula's bust to adorn, vi. 523, ix. 89, 90; cameo in, ix. 89; carpenters' strike delays completion of, vi. 49; cost of, v. 514; glass case in, ix. 90; HW to dedicate Cellini coffer in, vii. 425; HW to impart 'Catholic air' to, v. 306, vi. 136; HW wants Crébillon's and Marivaux's portraits for, iv. 324; Mann to enrich, with medal, viii. 470; Nivernais takes off his hat in, vi. 136; to be added, v. 238
chapel at: Donatello bas-relief for, vii. 450n, 456, 499, viii. 15; finished, viii. 15; sarcophagus from Rome would adorn, viii. 462

[Strawberry Hill, *continued*]

chimney fire at, vii. 201

China Closet at, iv. 382, 387

China Room at, ceiling copied from that at little Borghese villa, v. 471

Chute's bedchamber at, iv. 381

—— the presiding genius at, viii. 209

—— to describe, to Mann, iii. 497

cloister and Holbein Chamber added to, v. 238

cloister at: extends, v. 506; to be added, v. 238

closet at, furnished with porcelain specimens from all countries, ix. 591

closet, glazed, in Great North Bedchamber at, vii. 432

columbarium intended for, v. 157

construction expenses at, v. 420, 514

Conway describes, to Mann, iv. 290–1

—— sends coachmaker's apprentice to HW at, vii. 284, 286

cottage at, HW builds, vii. 128

cows at, iii. 414, iv. 380, ix. 532

Craon, Princesse de, would be pleased by, iv. 387

dampness of: disagrees with HW, viii. 277–8; may give rheumatism to HW, vi. 456–7

'Description' of, almost finished, ix. 531

eating-room and library to be built at, iv. 382

field at, mentioned by *Public Advertiser* as in need of draining, ix. 146

Fiesole hill compared with, iv. 193, 203

finished except for Great North Bedchamber, vii. 340

Frenchmen's opinion of, vii. 312

full of Mann's gifts, vii. 425

gallery and cabinet at, delayed by labour strike, vi. 49

gallery at: advances, v. 497, 506, 558, vi. 18; carpenters' strike delays, vi. 49; cost of, v. 514; eagle and Vespasian bust to adorn, v. 461; grows too magnificent for HW's humility, vi. 152; HW writes in, vi. 219; to be added, v. 238

garden at: altar to adorn recess in, iv. 325, 368–9, 372; HW supervises servants lopping trees in, viii. 48; Mann supposes, to be Gothic, iv. 368, 372; sepulchral altar installed near wood in, iv. 388; shrubs for, v. 113

gate at, has bell, viii. 211

Giberne restrained from calling at, iv. 97, 98

goldfish pond at, iv. 188, v. 361

Gothic gateway built in garden of, vii. 311

Gothic pretensions of, iv. 362

Great North Bedchamber at: Cellini's chest to be in glass closet in, vii. 432; chimney-back for, iv. 396; finishing touch to SH, vii. 432; HW builds, vii. 240; 'proceeds fast,' vii. 311

'grows near a termination,' iv. 368

HW adds to acreage of, iv. 16

HW assumes 'Burlington air' for, iv. 361

HW at: 'constantly,' iv. 324; for change of air, iv. 119, viii. 432, 436, ix. 284; for Easter, v. 75; for rest of season, iii. 435; for some days, vi. 98; for summer, vi. 422; in mid-winter to safeguard orange trees and goldfish, v. 361; to be near Galfridus Mann, iv. 525; when told of James Mann's death, vi. 225–6

HW better in London than at, vi. 451, 456–7, viii. 288

HW builds 'little Gothic castle' at, iv. 111

HW busy with, iv. 371, 396

HW calls: 'charming villa,' iii. 497; 'country palace,' ix. 262; 'Otranto,' vii. 350; 'Woden,' 'Thor,' 'Gothic Lares,' v. 433

HW cannot miss lilacs at, vi. 289

HW collects arms at, iv. 375, 396

HW describes, iv. 379–82, ix. 532

HW does not visit, because of Brentford elections and high water, vii. 73

HW exhausts hoards and collections at, vii. 432

HW expects to be robbed at, iv. 188

HW gives only a transient glance to, iv. 163

HW hardly has a chance to go to, v. 101

HW has completed: 'almost,' vi. 110; 'these three years,' viii. 100

HW hopes to find the grass green at, ix. 497

HW improves, into 'charming villa,' iii. 497

HW keeps Christmas at, iv. 16, 212, v. 558, viii. 55

HW lives at, in tranquillity and idleness, ix. 608

HW makes alterations at, iii. 486

HW may add gallery, tower, larger cloister, and cabinet to, v. 238, 306

HW must linger in London before going to, vi. 416

HW never stays long at, in wet weather, viii. 288

HW never wants amusement at, viii. 283

HW plans *terreno* at, iv. 131

HW prefers, to lands on the Ohio, v. 306

HW regrets that he cannot show, to Mann, iv. 53, viii. 103, ix. 532

HW's additions to, will not be interrupted by the French, v. 310

HW's contentment with, unusual in England, viii. 100–1

HW sees balloon from, ix. 579

HW's heirs will condemn, and pull it to pieces, viii. 27

HW's joy at revisiting, after long absence, vii. 554–5

HW's letter-writing improves at, iv. 53

HW's letter written in solitude and silence of, ix. 226

HW's 'little cockboat shall waft' him to, vi. 311

HW's planting at, 'vast,' iv. 53–4

HW supervises construction at, iv. 371

HW takes, iii. 414

HW threatens to send, to Mann, vii. 450

HW to bring Galfridus Mann to, iv. 525–6

HW to 'concentre my few remaining joys' at, on return to England, vi. 359–60, 365

HW to go to, if Parliament is dissolved, ix. 461

HW to read romances at, viii. 117

HW to receive company at, ix. 401

HW tormented by visitors to, ix. 423

HW to 'trifle' at, vii. 145

HW wants stained glass for, iv. 111

HW wants to retire to, vi. 359–60, 365, ix. 22, 33–4

HW writes at: from bow window, iv. 46, 68; from China Closet, iv. 382; from Gallery, vi. 219; from Round Drawing-Room, vii. 315

hall in, decked with saints and called Paraclete, iv. 372, 381

Hampton Court Park near, viii. 315

Henry VII's chimney-back at, iv. 395, 396

horses at, iv. 380

Houghton inspires HW to beautify, vii. 499

landscape effects at, iv. 53–4, 380, 386, vii. 315, 555, ix. 532

lane between Thames and, flooded with water, viii. 47

lease of, iii. 486

library at: Chute searches, iv. 64; HW and dogs retire to, vi. 257; HW to place books in, iv. 456; to be built, iv. 382

Mann advises HW not to visit, in winter, vi. 456–7, viii. 285

—— and Hamilton discuss, vi. 260

Mann congratulates HW on safe return to, iv. 42, vi. 562

—— envies, iv. 146, 443

—— expects HW to be at, vi. 411–12

—— fears that charms of, will keep HW from Florence, iv. 349

—— longs to see, iv. 377

—— must call, 'Strawberry Hill' not 'Twickenham,' iii. 486

—— sends ivy seeds to HW for, v. 457–8

——'s gifts convert, into a Galleria Reale, ix. 531

——'s letters at, vii. 73, ix. 185

——'s presents in every chamber of, viii. 15

——'s presents to be entered in catalogue of, ix. 90, 531

—— unable to collect ornaments for, except altar, iv. 365

—— urges HW not to retire to, ix. 33–4

—— will prefer Parliamentary news to that of, iv. 30

—— will share his melancholy with HW if he visits, v. 512

Mann, Horace II and Lady Lucy, may dine at, vii. 408

Mann, Horace II, has presumably sent HW's letters to, ix. 417

—— may call on HW at, ix. 659

meadows at, ix. 497

melancholy completely absent from, iv. 64

Morice lives near, ix. 159

Müntz stays at, v. 239

name of, chosen, iii. 486, 490

neighbourhood of, ix. 532

painting of marriage of Henry VII desired for, iv. 390

parlour at, iv. 380

Pars does washed drawings of, viii. 135, 144, x. 48

peach-coloured hangings unsuitable to solemnity of, v. 471

prints convey solemnity of, without the gayety of scenery, ix. 532

Red Bedchamber at, iv. 381

Refectory at, iv. 382

Richmond Park's disputes near, iv. 322–3

Robinson printer at, v. 120–1

Round Tower at: Bianca Cappello's portrait to hang in, v. 420; cost of, v. 514; finished, vii. 311; finishing, vii. 128; French prisoners might be confined in, v. 310; HW writes in bow-window of, near Bianca Cappello's picture, vii. 315; to be added, v. 238; to be furnished, when gallery is complete, v. 497

servants at, see under Servant

settees at, iv. 382, 387

sheep at, iii. 414, iv. 380, ix. 532

shrubs at, HW delights in, vii. 555

simplicity of, iv. 382

softens the decays of age, viii. 103

'source of elegancy and erudition,' v. 253

stained glass at: HW collects, iv. 111, 119, 371–2; 'long saints' in, iv. 372; Mann does not know where to find, iv. 119; Palmer glazier for, iv. 396; powder mill explosion breaks, vii. 365; red ivy would look well through, v. 457–8; sun makes, 'gorgeous,' ix. 532

staircase at, iv. 361, 368, 381

Suffolk, Cts of, HW's only sensible friend at, vi. 544

swans at, ix. 532

terrace at, iv. 16

too unfinished to entertain San Severino, iv. 372

towers at, arise, v. 506

tower to be added to, v. 238

trees at: 'blue' and 'green,' iv. 54; HW delights in, vii. 555; may be injured by wind, iv. 24; orange trees, v. 361, 369; trimming of, vii. 315, viii. 48

view from, iii. 496, iv. 16, 380, 382, vii. 315, 491, ix. 532

visitors to: Boufflers, Comtesse de, vi. 270; Chastellux, vii. 468; Chute, iii. 435, 442,

[Strawberry Hill, *continued*]
497, iv. 361, 381, 382, 456, vi. 257, 265, vii. 284, 310, 350, viii. 103, 209–10; Conway, vi. 322; Dacres, viii. 103; Frenchmen, who whisk through it, ix. 423; French people, who consider it one of the sights, ix. 427; George III and Q. Charlotte, vi. 426; Guines, vii. 311, 312; Hamilton, Sir William and Lady, vii. 339; Keppel, Bp, vi. 128; Lorenzi, iv. 87, 89; Mann, Edward Louisa, iii. 503, iv. 63, 64, 456; Mann, Galfridus, iii. 503, iv. 63, 64, 456; Mann, Horace II, viii. 490, 493, 497, ix. 532; Mann, Horace II, and party, ix. 154; Masserano, vii. 311; Muzell (Stosch), v. 427, 433; Nivernais, vi. 136; Rena, Contessa, vii. 107; Richmond, D. of, vi. 322; Seilern, vii. 311; Waldegrave, Cts, vi. 127–8; Waldegrave daughters, viii. 315; Whithed, iii. 442

windows at, *see* Strawberry Hill: stained glass at

workmen at, iv. 348, vi. 49

Yellow Bedchamber at, iv. 381

Strawberry Hill Press:
books from, HW would send: to Albani, in exchange for Herculaneum book, v. 262; to Charles of Naples in return for Herculaneum book, v. 131

constantly at work, v. 239

HW tells Mann of opening of, v. 120–1

HW wants Mann to have complete set of editions of, v. 278

HW will print only gift books at, v. 131

Lucan edition printed at, v. 472

Mann not to give books from, to Firmian, v. 278

—— receives *Fugitive Pieces* and *Royal and Noble Authors* from, v. 339

—— thanks HW for Spence's *Parallel* from, v. 289

—— will get ode from, if he captures a town, v. 266

rarity of products of, v. 278

'Strawberry King at Arms.' *See* Chute, John

Streamers:
gondola decked with, at Ranelagh, iv. 47

Street; streets:
London's: dirty, iii. 317; newly added, viii. 228; repaved, in summer, v. 427

present age prefers riding about, to roads or turf, ix. 317

Street cries:
in London, v. 154

Streetwalkers. *See* Whores

Strelitz:
Charlotte's marriage a sensation at, v. 525

Strickland, Elizabeth (d. 1821), m. (1781) Strickland Freeman, of Fawley Court, Bucks:
Conway's neighbour, ix. 576

Damer, Mrs models Isis head from, ix. 576

Strickland, William (1714–88), M.P.:
story told by, in Parliament, ii. 355

Strode, Mrs ——:
Mann and Mrs Morehead entertained by, iii. 477

Strohmfeld, Maj., Bn., gentleman of the Chamber to the D. of Östergötland:
(?) Mann sends HW's letter to Ds of Gloucester by, viii. 247

Stroke, apoplectic:
occurrence of, vii. 455

Stroke, paralytic:
occurrences of, v. 15, 21, 27, 29, 232, 234, 252, 432, vi. 72, vii. 43, 70, viii. 5, 55, 86–7, 230, 237, 283

Strongoli, island of:
earthquake account mentions, ix. 376

Strozzi, Principessa. *See* Strozzi, Giulia (1726–85); Strozzi, Teresa (1682–1748)

Strozzi, Ferdinando (1719–69), Principe:
marriage of, iii. 350

Strozzi, Filippo (1700–63), Duca di Bagnolo:
mother disowns, iii. 350

mother's museum probably robbed by, iii. 350

Strozzi, Girolamo (1724–81):
Bagnesi's duel with, ii. 133

Strozzi, Giulia (1726–85), m. (1747) Principe Ferdinando Strozzi:
marriage of, iii. 350

Strozzi, (?) Isabella (ca 1759–83):
(?) brother offered, to Mozzi as wife, ix. 130, 498

Strozzi, Lorenzo (d. 1802), Duca di Bagnolo:
sister offered by, to Mozzi as wife, ix. 130, 498

Strozzi, Ottavia (1709–48), m. (1728) Principe Filippo Corsini:
daughter of, ii. 121

Strozzi, Roberto (1717–80):
(?) Bocchineri's duel with, prevented, i. 111

Strozzi, Rosso (d. 1743), introduttore degl'ambasciadori at Florence:
Baldocci deputy to, ii. 146, 182

(?) ball given by, ii. 60, 166

death of, ii. 145

distant relatives heirs to, ii. 146

estate mismanaged by, ii. 145–6

Francis I's birthday to be celebrated in gala announced by, ii. 113

Frescobaldi, Mme, cicisbea of, ii. 145

grand master of the ceremonies and introducer of ambassadors, ii. 146

horses of, numerous but underfed, ii. 146

servants of, obliged to borrow sheets and shirts for him in last illness, ii. 146

Strozzi, Teresa (1682–1748), m. (1699) Principe Lorenzo Francesco Strozzi:
HW pities, iii. 361

museum of, robbed, iii. 349–50, 361n

sons of, iii. 350

Strozzi, Teresa (1747–1816), m. (1766) Giuseppe Luigi Riccardi:
(?) wedding dinner for, vi. 458

Strozzi, Casa:
family fracas in, over robbery, iii. 349

Strozzi, Palazzo:
concert not to be held in, i. 316
Struensee, Johann Friedrich (1737–72), Greve; physician:
arrest of, vii. 373, 385
Christian VII and Caroline Matilda ruled by, vii. **273**
execution of, vii. 392, 401, 409
opponents to accuse, of drugging Christian VII, vii. 380
probably a French tool, vii. 273
Strulbrug; Struldbrugs. *See under* Swift, Jonathan: *Gulliver's Travels*
Strutt, Samuel (d. 1785), clerk assistant to the House of Lords:
Chatham carried to house of, viii. 371
'Stuart, Mr':
Bute's pseudonym, vii. 103
Stuart, Lady Anne (1746–ca 1819), m. 1 (1764) Hugh Percy, styled Bn Warkworth 1750–66 and E. Percy 1766–86; 2d D. of Northumberland, 1786 (divorced, 1779); m. 2 (1780) Friedrich Karl Hans Bruno, Bn von Poellnitz:
grandfather's bequest to, v. 473
marriage of, vi. **302n**
mother's remark about, viii. 378
pregnant and to be divorced, viii. 378
uncle not told of disgrace of, viii. 381
weak, viii. 378
Stuart, Lady Augusta (1749–78), m. (1773) Capt. Andrew Corbet:
Findlater supposedly to marry, vii. 312
grandfather's bequest to, v. 473
Stuart, Capt. Benjamin:
(?) Mann's letter taken by, to HW, ix. 42, 49
(?) Murray sends, as courier from Minorca, ix. 42
(?) quarantined, ix. 42
Stuart, Lady Caroline (1750–1813), m. (1778) John Dawson, cr. (1785) E. of Portarlington:
grandfather's bequest to, v. 473
Stuart, Hon. Sir Charles (1753–1801), K.B., 1799; army officer; M.P.:
grandfather's bequest to, v. 473
Stuart, Charles Edward, 'the Young Pretender.' *See* Charles Edward
Stuart, Charlotte (1753–89), dau. of Young Pretender; Ds of Albany, 1784:
appearance of, resembles father's, ix. 535
calls to be returned by, ix. 535
educated in Paris convent, ix. 512, x. 47
father acknowledges, as his daughter and sole heiress, ix. 512–13, 516n
father joined by, just in time to reap inheritance, ix. 549
father registers, at Paris and Florence, as Ds of Albany, ix. 512–13, 516n, 521–2
father sends Stewart to Paris to fetch, to Florence, ix. 513
father's intended bequest to, ix. 512–13, 522
father's jewels worn by, ix. 536

father's only child, x. 47
father summons, to Florence, and has her called Ds of Albany, ix. 538n
father to marry, to Florentine cavaliere, ix. 513, 522
Fitzjames family do not acknowledge, lest they have to support her, ix. 516, x. 47
Fitzjames family will be caused no expense by, ix. 522
Florence expects, soon, ix. 521
Florence reached by, ix. 535, 538
Florentine ladies leave cards at door of, ix. 535
Florentine theatres visited by, in father's jewels, ix. 536
French Court said to grant tabouret to, as Duchess, ix. 537
Gem attends, at Paris, ix. 516, x. 47
grandfather offers to provide for, x. 47
HW wants to hear more about, ix. 520
Maria Louisa has not yet received, ix. 537
mother would disgrace, ix. 522
O'Donnel, Mrs, and Nairne accompany, as *dame de compagnie* and *écuyer*, ix. 536
on way to Florence, escorted by two ladies and two gentlemen, ix. 524
Pius VI allows father of, to make her a duchess but her uncle does not, ix. 552–3
—— writes congratulatory answer to letter of, ix. 550
Rohan, Abp, often visited by, ix. 513
stepmother may repent after arrival of, ix. 535
uncle does not answer letter of, ix. 549–50
uncle will not give jewels to, ix. 525–6
Stuart, Hon. Frederick (1751–1802), M.P.:
grandfather's bequest to, v. 473
Stuart, Henry Benedict, Cardinal York. *See* Henry Benedict
Stuart, James (1708–67), 8th E. of Moray:
rebel lords' condemnation shunned by, iii. 284
Stuart (later Stuart Wortley Mackenzie), James Archibald (1747–1818):
grandfather leaves reversion of estates to, on condition of taking name Wortley, v. 473
Stuart, James Francis Edward, 'the Old Pretender.' *See* James Francis Edward
Stuart, Lady Jane (1742–1828), m. (1768) Sir George Macartney, Kt, 1764; K.B., 1772; cr. (1776) Bn, (1792) Vct, and (1794) E. Macartney:
grandfather's bequest to, v. 473
Macartney marries, vii. 586
Stuart, John (Young Pretender's valet), *see* Stewart, John
Stuart, John (1713–92), 3d E. of Bute, 1723; prime minister:
appearance of: altered, and looks old, vii. 103; emaciated and looks older, vii. 312
Argyll's death leaves, the chief power in Scotland, v. 527n

[Stuart, John (1713–92), *continued*]

Augusta, Ps of Wales, implied by satiric print to be having affair with, v. 487

—— tells, to announce to Mann the P. of Saxe-Gotha's impending visit, vii. 328

Bedford and George Grenville joined by, in wanting troops sent to America, vi. 401

behaves moderately, despite recent good fortune, v. 527

brother considers Mann's delay in getting Bath ribbon a reflection on, vii. 52–3

brother may be involved in resignation of, vi. 133

brother of, v. 212, vi. 302n, viii. 401n

Cabinet Council includes, v. 443

cards of, labelled 'Mr Stuart,' vii. 103

caricature of, v. 93

Cider Tax causes downfall of, v. 129, 132

Clement XIII might be succeeded by, vii. 92

clergyman given rich living by, to get possession of Lady Mary Wortley Montagu's letters, vi. 85n

Dalton ordered by, to buy medals for George III, v. 478

daughters of, v. 416, 527, 531, vi. 302n, 586, vii. 312, viii. 378

England reached by, vii. 312

English disputes blamed on, vii. 83

English victory or defeat would make Pitt seem preferable to, vi. 48

father-in-law's death benefits, v. 527

Florence visited by, vii. 103, 107n

Fox will embarrass, vi. 93

friends of: indignant over Ps of Wales's exclusion from Regency, vi. 297; to compose new administration, vi. 521; warm, vi. 496

Garter installation of, at Windsor, vi. 37, 79

Garter not worn by, vii. 91, 96, 103

George II's death benefits, v. 527

George III advised by, to dismiss ministers, vi. 301–2

—— grants offices to friends of, vi. 307

—— might be saddled by, with Grenville ministry, vi. 396

—— 'sacrifices,' vi. 172, vii. 221

——'s favour retained by, vi. 129

——'s Groom of the Stole, v. 6, 13

—— should not have been involved by, in deep measures, vi. 134

——'s marriage blamed upon, vi. 53

——'s offer of Francavilla statues declined by, ix. 94

—— told by, that Orford bets on his having a child, v. 530–1

Grenville and Halifax insist on removal of, vi. 168

Grenville hopelessly offends, vi. 490

—— makes abject advances to, vi. 419

—— ministry affronts, by Regency Bill, vi. 299–300

—— ministry forbids George III to consult, vi. 302

——'s enmity with, vi. 92n

—— would have been preferred by, to Fox, as manager of House of Commons, vi. 92

Grub Street papers about, printed in Vienna court gazette, vi. 178

HW does not want to show, to Fleury, vi. 135

HW esteemed by, vii. 103

HW glad he had no letter from, vii. 107

HW would have received letter from, from Otranto, vii. 103, 107n

Halifax adjourns House of Lords before friends of, arrive, vi. 297n

Hardinge, Mrs, makes witticism about George III's choice of, v. 459–60

Hardwicke and Newcastle advise, to be secretary of state, v. 488

Hardwicke and Newcastle join, against Pitt, v. 539n

health of: broken past recovery, vii. 302; continental journey made for, vii. 42, 152; disorders in stomach and bowels, vii. 103; extremely ill, vii. 152; fever and sore throat, caught from daughter, v. 416; good, vii. 312; Mann sees little hope for, vii. 161; Naples air bad for, vii. 96; political aspect of, vii. 152; retirement caused by, vi. 128; said to be recovered, vii. 83

Holdernesse succeeded by, as secretary of state, v. 487

house of, in Audley Street, attacked by mob, vii. 7

House of Commons would, if possible, be managed by, in person, vi. 92

incognito of, vii. 91, 96, 103

itinerary of, vii. 103

Lee jealous of favour of, with Ps of Wales, v. 104

London's petitions hasten downfall of, vi. 129

(?) Mann asks questions of, about Wilkes's election, vii. 110

—— offers his house to, vii. 53, 96, 103

—— sends invitation to, through brother, vii. 42, 53, 103

Martin serves under, in Treasury, vi. 183n

may fall into Grenville's hands, vi. 489

may go abroad, vi. 168

ministerial changes attributed to influence of, vi. 431

minister in power, though out of office, vi. 133

ministry of, cannot endure at same time with two others, v. 465

mob hisses and pelts, vi. 102

Mortimer and D. of Suffolk compared with, vi. 53

'Murray' the pseudonym of, vii. 91, 96

Naples visited by, vii. 91, 96

Newcastle probably dismissed by, because peace seemed certain, vi. 38

Nivernais dines with, vi. 82

North Briton, accuses, of making George III tell a lie, vi. 136
obliging attitude of, v. 484
Opposition's boasts alarm, vi. 508
'persecuted,' vi. 395
Pitt (Chatham) and D. of Newcastle reconciled by, v. 97
Pitt (Chatham) attacks, vi. 395
—— does not receive keys from, vi. 130
—— may approach, closer, vi. 490
—— may become unpopular when allied to, vi. 433
—— promises to aid friends of, vi. 436
——'s alliance with, vi. 473
——'s friendship with, would please George III but alienate the people, vi. 440
——'s ministry advised by, from fear, vi. 159–60
—— the chief rival of, at George II's death, vii. 152
Pitt, Anne, friend of, viii. 378
regency measure pressed upon, vi. 294
regime of, probably ending, vi. 93
resort near Venice revisited by, for health, vii. 161
returns to London, vi. 219
Robinson said to owe archbishopric to influence of, vi. 276
Rockingham ministry's opposition to, will counteract Pitt's concessions to him, vi. 436
Rome visited by, vii. 83, 91, 96
Scotsmen not preferred by, v. 465, vi. 295
secretary of state's position may have been accepted by, in order to make a popular peace, v. 488
sole minister for a day or two, v. 448
son of, ix. 336n, 398n
Treasury headed by, vi. 37
Treasury resigned by, vi. 128–9
Treasury would have been given by, to Fox, vi. 134
turbulence stirred up by, vi. 209
Venice left by, for England, in poor health and spirits, vii. 297, 302
Waldegrave did not like, vi. 128
weekly papers abuse, especially for being Scotch, vi. 42
Wilkes writes *North Britons* against, vi. 60n
York, D. of, allies, with Bedford and Grenville, vi. 402
Yorke family may upset control of, vi. 98
Stuart, John (1744–1814), styled Vct Mount Stuart 1744–92, 4th E. of Bute, 1792; cr. (1796) M. of Bute, M.P.:
ambassadorship to Spain promised to, ix. 345–6
arrives in London, ix. 354
Dutens employed by, in Turin embassy, ix. 625n
envoy to Turin, ix. 336
'fracas of gallantry' may have caused departure of, from Turin, ix. 336, 346

Madrid may be the post of, ix. 363, 398
Mann receives accounts from, of destruction of floating batteries, ix. 325
—— receives letter of *congé* from, ix. 345
marriage of, vi. **465**
Northington may succeed, at Turin, ix. 336, 354
return of, to England, known by HW before Mann, ix. 345
servants dismissed by, and equipages sold, ix. 345
sister-in-law of, vi. 480
Turin left by, ix. 345–6, 354
Stuart, Lady Louisa (1757–1851):
grandfather's bequest to, v. 473
Stuart, Lady Mary (1740–1824), m. (1761) Sir James Lowther, 5th Bt, cr. (1784) E. of Lonsdale:
grandfather's bequest to, v. 473
marriage of, v. **527,** 531
Stuart, Hon. William (1755–1822), Bp of St David's, 1793; Abp of Armagh, 1800:
grandfather's bequest to, v. 473
Stuart. *See also* Stewart
Stuart family ('House of Stuart'):
adherents of, decry Q. Elizabeth, viii. 415
Albany, Cts of, gets nothing from, ix. 536
Benedict XIV might have exiled Virgin with, at Albano, vi. 227
Carlisle garrison has to swear never to fight against, iii. 166
conclusion of, 'wretched,' ix. 108
France tells Holland not to oppose, iii. 134
Guglielmi a former dependent of, vi. 392
historians may now forget, unless Cardinal York becomes pope, ix. 106
House of Hanover should learn by example of, to avoid despotism, viii. 140
Jewish customs might be imitated by, ix. 115
Lennox, Lady Sarah, descended from, v. 531
less harmful to England than Pelhams and Patriots are, iii. 456
Rome to entertain D. of York under very nose of, vi. 177
Sophia Matilda of Gloucester born on holiday of, vii. 483
strange termination of, vi. 325
Stuart, Charlotte, one of last chapters in history of, ix. 538
Walpole daughters marry into, v. 285
York, Cardinal, might marry in order to continue line of, ix. 115
York, D. of, must vex, by his welcome at Rome, vi. 237
Stuart Mackenzie, Lady Elizabeth. *See* Campbell, Lady Elizabeth (ca 1722–99)
Stuart Mackenzie, Hon. James (?1719–1800), politician; M.P.:
Amelia, Ps, entertains, vi. 579
Bute's resignation may involve, vi. 133

[Stuart Mackenzie, Hon. James, *continued*]
Charlotte, Q., to receive Mann's box of essences through, vi. 241, 243
couriers to, have long since departed, v. 465
Dutens employed by, in Turin embassy, ix. 625n
England reached by, viii. 401
fans might be sent by, from Turin, v. 462
Florence to be visited by, on way to Naples for health, vii. 337
Florence visited by, vii. 401
George III gets Smith's collection at recommendation of, vi. 115
—— promises to, to give Bath order to Mann, vi. 580, vii. 3, 5
——'s appointment of, to Venetian envoyship, v. 471–2, 508
Gordon rioters pick pockets of, ix. 54
Grafton's dealings with, about Mann's Bath ribbon, vi. 580, 587, vii. 41
Grenville ministry demands dismissal of, vi. 302
HW considers, 'a man of strict honour,' vi. 111
HW may intercede through relatives of wife of, for Mann, v. 452
HW sees, about Mann's Bath ribbon, vi. 579–80
HW talks with, about Mann, viii. 412
HW tells Mann to write to, vi. 111, 580, vii. 42, 49
HW told by, that Dick will bring Mann his Bath ribbon, vii. 41, 52
Italy may be visited by, vii. 53
Lee said to be succeeded by, as treasurer to Ps of Wales, v. 104–5, 110
Lyttelton may succeed, at Turin, v. 507–8
Mann corresponds with, about Francavilla statues, vii. 583
—— corresponds with, about getting Bath order, vi. 235–6, 314, 317, 469–70, 486, 582, vii. 1, 3, 4, 5, 14, 52, 53
—— might be helped by, to get Neapolitan post, vi. 107, 111
—— might offer services to, for collecting virtu for George III, v. 452
—— offers Bute a lodging through, vii. 53, 103
——'s delay in getting Bath ribbon considered by, a reflection on Bute, vii. 53
——'s friendship with, v. 212, 462, vi. 107, 111, viii. 381, 401
——'s pretensions not to be compared with those of, v. 472, 483
——'s protector, viii. 160
—— visited by, in Florence on way to Venice, viii. 381
—— would be warned by, of any danger, vi. 115
—— writes to, but does not mention Bath ribbon, vi. 580
niece's disgrace not known by, viii. 381

Privy Seal of Scotland obtained by, vi. 444, 453
Rockingham ministry shows civilities to, vi. 431
Shaw, Elizabeth, said to have flirted with, at ridotto, iii. 27
Turin post to go to, v. 212, 218
Venetian appointment not notified to, v. 511
Venice rejects, vii. 325
vice-chamberlain's post rumoured for, v. 452
Stucco:
gilt, used to ornament room in Uffizi gallery, ix. 170
Stuffs:
gold and silver, to enliven London, vi. 196
Stukeley, William (1687–1765), divine; antiquary:
Philosophy of Earthquakes, earthquake attributed by, to electricity, iv. 154, 158
Stura, valley of:
Austrians and Sardinians meet at, iii. 432
Sturgeon:
Clement XIII's fondness for, vi. 327, 331, 380, vii. 4
——'s major-domo gives, to D. of York, as Tiber product, vi. 229
Sturgis ('Sturgiss'), Rev. Samuel (ca 1701–43), fellow of King's College, Cambridge, 1723–36:
academician promised English paints by, i. 462
black wig of, i. 461
'blind' coffee-house frequented by, i. 462
clothes of, in Bns Walpole's cases, i. 224
Dashwood's correspondence with, i. 125
death of, ii. 197–9, 210, 217
Geneva and Aix inquired about by, i. 95
health of, jaundice, ii. 197–8
Leghorn merchants tell lies to, i. 462
Mann fears he may have to bury, ii. 198
Pannoni's avoided by, i. 462
Pasquale, not Cocchi, physician to, ii. 198
sent to Leghorn: i. 95, 107; for burial, ii. 199
Swiss coffee-house frequented by, i. 406
Walpole, Bn, friend of, i. 70n
Walpole, Bns, banishes, for debts, i. 95, 461
—— has, as lover, i. 70, 89–90, 461
—— has, tell lies at coffee-house, i. 406, 462
—— houses, i. 70–1
—— richer because of death of, ii. 217
—— tired of, ii. 198
Walpole, Sir Robert, denounced by, i. 406
Sturrock, William (d. 1765), Beauchamp's tutor:
Hertford, E. and Cts, write to, that they will provide for him for life, ii. 544
Sturt, Capt. See Stuart, Benjamin
Styptic:
newly-discovered, highwayman to test efficacy of, vi. 147

Styria:
Venice may be menaced by army in, iv. 176
Styx:
HW imagines Mexicans and Peruvians on shores of, ix. 109
Suard, Jean-Baptiste-Antoine (1733–1817); journalist:
Montagu, Mrs, retorts to, at meeting of Académie française, viii. 267
Suares de la Concha, Mme. *See* Valvasone, Maria Anna
Suares de la Concha, Baldassare (1692–1758), ball; postmaster general:
daughter says that her suitors are older than, ii. 197
HW's correspondence with, i. **49**
Scarperia dinner in honour of Modenese princess attended by, i. 56
son ordered by, to visit grandparents, i. 70
wife's illness, patiently borne by, iii. 226
Suares de la Concha, Ferdinando (1718–99), ball:
Friulian lady said to be engaged to, i. **416**
mother's illness does not disturb, iii. 226–7
Suares de la Concha, Francesco (1720–77), cavaliere ('Cecco;' 'Cecchino'):
arrival of, at Florence in disobedience of parental orders, i. 69–70
cane heads inquired about by, i. 117
carries letter from HW to Mme Grifoni, i. 78
'Cecca, la' pursued by, i. 70, 121, 128, 156
Chesupiades shared by, with Pepi, ii. 345
Demetrio not to be acted by, i. 99
Federici, Contessa, wooed by, ii. 345
Florentine gates guarded by, during plague, ii. 288, 295
grandfather to be visited by, at Friuli, i. 70
(?) Gray's odd behaviour with, i. 50
HW gives cane to, i. 117, 456
HW gives flutes to, ii. 12–13
HW may be visited in England by, ii. 108–9
HW's correspondence and friendship with, i. 72, 74, 103, 115, 147, 181, 456, ii. 108–9
HW's news of, pleases his mother, i. **39**
Harrington through Robinson recommends, for preferment, ii. 455
Mann called on by, ii. **108–9**
—— discusses Agdollo with, i. 149
—— discusses HW with, i. 72, 73
—— entertains: at concert, ii. 12–13; at supper, i. 104
—— expects letter of thanks from, for HW, i. 456
—— hears news of HW through, i. 50
——'s correspondence with, i. 52
—— seldom sees, i. 147
——'s opera box entered by, i. 81, 149
mother's brothers may assist, i. 161
mother's embarrassment explained by, i. 137
mother's illness does not disturb, iii. 226–7
Pepi's child attributed to, ii. 345

Pistoia visited by, i. 103
Serristori rebukes, i. 149
sister of, vi. 491
sunburned, i. 69
to play flutes at concert, ii. 12–13
Valvasone visit of, i. 70, 156, 181
Suares de la Concha, Giuseppe (d. 1755), Bp of San Miniato 1735–55:
bishopric resigned by, ii. 40
nieces' marriages to Richecourt and Rucellai suspected by, in ravings, ii. 40
nieces receive no dowries from, i. **138**
Richecourt's and Rucellai's persecutions make, mad, ii. 40
(?) Rucellai's persecution of, ii. 63
San Miniato left by, ii. 40
sister-in-law shown 'bawdy matters' by, ii. 40
Suares de la Concha, Maria Teresa (1723–1809) ('Teresina'), m. (1746) Conte Bernardo Pecori:
convent life contemplated by, ii. 138
Dal Borgo entertains, ii. 85
Demetrio to be acted by, for Modenese princess, i. 99, 100, 101
disappointed not to have Mann's opera box, i. 81
elderly suitors rejected by, ii. 197
grows beautiful, ii. 85
Guicciardini might marry, ii. 138
HW compliments family on engagement of, iii. 161
husband jealous of, iii. 311
husband not yet found for, ii. 526
Mann entertains: at concert, ii. 12–13; at supper, i. 104
——'s opera box to be occupied by, i. **69**
marriage of, iii. 227, 238
Maynard regrets that only Italian is spoken by, ii. 372
mother wants to marry, to Roberto Pandolfini, i. 137, 171, 202
Panciatichi may marry, ii. 197
Pecori to marry, iii. 136
—— will make, happy, iii. 145
Salimbeni constantly with, i. 101
sister's marriage no longer to be postponed in hopes of match for, iii. 84
uncle fears marriage of, to Richecourt or Rucellai, ii. 40
uncle has no dowry for, i. 138
uncle's madness may hinder marriage of, ii. 40
Suares de la Concha, Maria Vittoria (1725–1806), m. (1744) Pierfrancesco Carducci; 'Vittorina':
Carducci to wed, ii. 439, 526, iii. 84, 136
Demetrio to be acted by, for Modenese princess, i. 99, 100, 101
disappointed not to have Mann's opera box, i. 81
HW compliments family on marriage of, ii. 540

[Suares de la Concha, Maria Vittoria, *cont.*]
health of, measles, i. 444, 445
husband jealous of, iii. 145, 311
husband of, i. **38n**
Mann entertains: at concert, ii. 12–13; at supper, i. 104
——'s opera box to be occupied by, i. 69
Maria Louisa represented by, at reception for newly-wed Florentine girls, vi. 491
marriage of, iii. 145
Molinari woos, ii. 29, 138, 197
poverty of, iii. 145
pretty, ii. 29
Salimbeni constantly with, i. 101
to sing at concert, ii. 12
uncle fears marriage of, to Richecourt or Rucellai, ii. 40
uncle has no dowry for, i. 138
uncle's illness may hinder marriage of, ii. 40
Suares de la Concha family:
Bologna visited by, i. 444, 445
HW sends box and cane to, i. 416
HW sends compliments to, on daughter's marriage, ii. 540
HW suspects loyalty of, to Mann, i. 419
lotteries appropriate for, ii. 351
Mann entertains: and gives necklaces to them, i. 484; at farewell dinner, i. 161; at dinner, ii. 251
—— to give HW's compliments to, on daughters' espousals, iii. 161
Munich may be sought by, i. 161
Pisa visited by, iii. 227
Demetrio given by, for Modenese princess, i. 65, 99, 100, 101, 104
return of, to Florence, i. 55, 444, 456
uncle mourned by, ii. 439
Venice and Valvasone visited by, i. 156, 161, 171, 202
villa of: Carducci to wed Teresa Suares at, iii. 136; Dal Borgo villa near, ii. 85; Mann and Chute see *Demetrio* performed at, i. 120
Suarez; Suarres. *See* Suares de la Concha
Suave mari magno turbantis æquora ventis:
HW's 'old tune,' viii. 48
Subdeacon:
York, Cardinal, becomes, iii. 499
Subscription book:
HW's London parish circulates, iii. 167
Suckling ('Sucking'), Maurice (1726–78), naval captain, 1755; comptroller of the navy, 1775; M.P.; HW's cousin:
Fox tells Mann about, ii. **152**
Mann sends messages to, by Fox, ii. 182
on board *Newcastle,* at Leghorn, ii. 152, 182
Walpole, Sir Robert, great-uncle of, ii. 152, 182
Suckling, Mrs Maurice. *See* Walpole, Hon. Mary (1726–64)

Suckling, William (1730–98), comptroller of customs; HW's cousin:
address of, in New North St, Red Lion Square, viii. 209
Customs place described by, x. 53–4
HW does not receive Customs House document from, viii. 361
HW's and Sir Edward Walpole's cousin, viii. **178**
HW tells Mann to write to, telling him to execute collector's duties and pay HW and Sir Edward Walpole, viii. 231
Mann's correspondence with, about customs place, viii. 231, 237, 243, 252
——'s place in Custom House to be filled by, viii. 178, 184
—— to insert name of, in letter of attorney, viii. 209
Sudbrook, Ds of Argyll's villa:
Coke, Lady Mary, permitted to live at, vii. 538n
Sudbury:
borough of, advertises for a purchaser of election, v. 484
Vernon of, vi. 31
Sudermania. *See* Södermanland
Sudley, Vct. *See* Gore, Sir Arthur (1703–73); Gore, Arthur Saunders (1734–1809)
Sudley, Vcts. *See* Annesley, Catharine (d. 1770)
Suera, Baron, Russian official:
Orlov receives peace treaty from, viii. 40
Suez:
English caravan from, captured by Arabs, viii. 510
Suffield, Bns. *See* Hobart, Lady Caroline (1767–1850)
Suffocation:
Orford, Cts of, suffers from, ix. 112
Suffolk, Cts of. *See* Graham, Catherine (d. 1762); Hobart, Henrietta (ca 1681–1767); Trevor, Hon. Maria Constantia (1744–67)
Suffolk, Ds of. *See* Brandon, Lady Frances (1517–59)
Suffolk, D. of. *See* Pole, William de la (1396–1450)
Suffolk, E. of. *See* Howard, Charles (1675–1733); Howard, Henry (1739–79); Howard, Henry Bowes (1687–1757); Pole, William de la (1396–1450)
Suffolk, Earls of:
HW queries relationship of, to Dukes of Norfolk, vii. 485n
Suffolk:
Charlotte's ship reaches coast of, v. 528
Holt has estate in, iii. 196
invasion may land in, ii. 401
Keppel declines election offer from, ix. 86
Suffolk St, London:
Anhalt, P. of, lodges in, vi. 437
bawdy-house in, i. 331
La Condamine lodges in, vi. 146
Saxe-Gotha, P. of, lodges in, i. 331

Sugar:
  Beckford concerned with price of, vi. 39
  Carlisle citadel reproduced in, iii. 174–5
  HW should use, sparingly, on stewed fruit, vi. 114
  tax on, vi. 489
Sugar cane:
  hurricane damages, iv. 331
Sugar-figures:
  for dessert, Münchhausen, Bns, castrates, iv. 125, 144
Sugar plums:
  sugar 'citadel' pelted with, iii. 175
Suicide:
  HW calls, death 'à l'anglaise,' ix. 385–6
  HW's reflections on, iv. 461
  occurrences of, vii. 420, ix. 386, 407
  Orford attempts, vii. 495, 505, viii. 293
  out of fashion, iii. 229
  Powell's will convince French visitors of English fondness for self-murder, ix. 407
Suit; suits:
  crimson velvet, worn by Pomfret, iv. 390
  Francis I's, iii. 58–9
  HW's, of silver stuff, for George III's wedding, vii. 285
  Mann orders, from Lyon, vi. 357
  plain, Walpole, Richard, wears, iv. 342
  silver-laced, i. 183
  summer, made for Ashburnham, iii. 420
Sukey, sloop:
  Gage sends dispatches by, viii. 110
Sulivan, Laurence (ca 1713–86), M.P.:
  mob attacks, by mistake for Onslow, vii. 288
Sulivan, Lt Phillipe:
  captured at Velletri, ii. 492
Sulkowsky, Ps. See Mniszech, Louise
Sullivan, Maj.-Gen. John (1740–95):
  Long Island defeat of, viii. 249
Sully. See Béthune, Maximilien de
Sulphur:
  Mann, Lady Lucy, might go to Puzzuolo to breathe, viii. 190
  ointment of, vii. 460
Sultan, British ship:
  Howe to be joined by, viii. 411
Sulzbach, Elector of. See Karl Theodor
Sulzbach, Pfalzgräfin von. See Eleonore (1712–59)
Summer:
  deplorably wet, ix. 312
  HW dreads, in wartime because of danger to friends, viii. 529
  HW stores knowledge during, v. 368
  hot and dry in England, iv. 188
  marriages and deaths unfashionable in, vi. 251–2
  warmer in England than in Ireland, v. 121
Summer Assizes:
  Aylesbury's contest with Buckingham over, iv. 449n

Summer house:
  Radnor's, in Chinese style, iv. 382
Sumner, Jane (d. 1766), m. (1764) William Skrine:
  death of, at Rome, vi. 398, 402
  Sandwich, E. of, 'bestowed on the public,' vi. 402
Sun:
  Jupiter supposedly moves the earth towards, iv. 119–20, 143
  Mann fond of, iv. 143
Sunday:
  English clergyman refuses to attend opera on, ii. 162–3
  macaronies run races in evenings on, vii. 491
  Methodists do not play cards on, iv. 34
  Methodists object to opera attendance on, iv. 86
Sunderland, Cts of. See Sidney, Lady Dorothy (1617–84)
Sunderland, E. of. See Spencer, Charles (1706–58); Spencer, Robert (1641–1702)
Sunderland estate:
  Spencer, John, entails, on Pitt, vi. 277n
Sundermania. See Södermanland
Sundon, Bn. See Clayton, William
Sundon, Bns. See Dyve, Charlotte
Sunning Hill:
  Pitt, Thomas, visits, to drink waters, vi. 73
Superbe, French ship:
  sunk, v. 351
Superstitions:
  Mann's reflections on, ii. 59, iv. 429–30
Supper; suppers:
  after Florentine opera, avoided, ii. 303
  Aiguillon gives, for English prisoners, v. 251
  Amelia, Ps, gives, for Christian VII, vii. 48
  Arenberg entertained only at, ii. 97
  Corsi gives, for Eszterházys, iv. 350
  Craon's: i. 194; for English captains, ii. 98
  Craon, Princesse de, takes, at midnight, ii. 122
  Derby's cook resents serving, at 3 A.M., viii. 310
  Du Barry, Comtesse, gives, vii. 115
  Ferdinand of Naples gives, at Caserta, without tables, vii. 191
  Frederick, P. of Wales, gives, after son's christening, iii. 174–5
  George II takes, with family, iv. 539
  Gloucester, D. of, to have been entertained at, in Pisa theatre, vii. 357
  HW might eat stewed fruit for, vi. 114
  HW substitutes, for dinner, in France, vi. 396
  HW takes, in company, v. 368
  HW takes hartshorn and pears at, vi. 110, 114
  HW to leave ball before, ix. 22
  Leopold and Maria Louisa do not restrict guests at, vii. 191

[Supper; suppers, *continued*]
Leopold and Maria Louisa take, at 9 P.M., vi. 354
Leopold and Maria Louisa to give, at great theatre, for D. and Ds of Cumberland, ix. 645
Louis XV's expenses not all swallowed up by, iv. 500
Lucca serves, of 60 covers, for D. of York, vi. 222
Mann and Horace Mann II walk in moonlight before, viii. 517
Mann finds, too expensive, ii. 281
—— regularly entertains Pelham with Englishmen at, iv. 115
——'s diet at, i. 78
Northumberlands give, for Cts of Yarmouth, v. 191
Rohan, P. Camille de, gives, at Leghorn, for Leopold, vi. 556
St John prepares, at Craon's, v. 533
Sansedoni, Mme, gives, for D. of York, vi. 224
served at 12 at Robinson's ball, i. 185
Suffolk, Cts of, takes, in chamber with Lord Chetwynd, vi. 544
Tuscan Court gives, weekly, at Pisa, vii. 171, 191, 262
Whitehead's, at 'Bedford Head,' i. 211
Surat:
hurricane and flood reported at, ix. 428
Surfeit water:
Nugent takes, at night, i. 271
Surgeon; surgeons:
Acquaviva's, iii. 136
Beaufort's potency examined by, ii. 185
Benedict XIV's, *see* Ponzio
Capponi treated by, ii. 183
Chetwynd's wound dressed by, ii. 192
Clement XIV's *see* Laboussiere
commission on Filipe Antonio's imbecility consults, v. 329
Downe tells, to disregard pain, v. 466
English, for D. of Gloucester, throws Italian prescriptions away, vii. 393
Ferrers's body to be delivered to, v. 388, 403
French and German, Panciatichi not cured by, iv. 36
Greek, Cocchi's book on, iv. 179, 189, 437
HW has to have, for gout in arm, ix. 618
HW's, wants him to take the air too soon ix. 617
HW's, *see also* Watson, Henry (d. 1793)
HW to be treated by, i. 52
HW told by, about effects of castration, ii. 565
HW urged by, to take the air, ix. 626
Hawley asked by, for corpse of spy to dissect, iii. 201
Irish, Bolton, Ds of, picks up, at Tunbridge, and makes will in his favour, v. 365

Lobkowitz accompanied by, ii. 564
Mann given false encouragement by, ix. 567
——'s: alarmed by Mann's swollen feet, viii. 79; believes his rheumatism to be gout in head, viii. 479; feeds him ice creams and uses bleedings and senapisms, ix. 560; Mann tells, that he must get well, to entertain the Hollands, vi. 467; tells him that chalkstones are painful, ix. 626; *see also* Benevoli, Antonio
murderers' bodies delivered to, v. 388
papal, *see* La Bossier *or* Laboussiere, Carlo
Paris, Panciatichi's knee not cured by, iv. 36
St-Aignan's: Mann thinks to be valet-de-chambre, i. 81; St-Aignan recommends, to Mann, i. 81
'sensible young' in D. of Gloucester's suite, x. 50
Tencin in vain dissuaded by, from trip to Rome, i. 481
See also Benevoli, Antonio; Charlton, John; Cocchi, Antonio; Mick; Nesi, Francesco Maria; Page-surgeon; Pasquale, Gaetano; Patch, James
Surgeon-page. *See* Page-surgeon
Surgeon's Hall:
Ferrers's body dissected at, v. 403
Surgical instruments:
Benevoli lacks, i. 89, 341
Gloucester, D. of, presents, to hospital at Rome, viii. 129
Surprize, American privateer:
Prince of Orange captured by, viii. 302
Surrey, E. of. *See* Howard, Charles (1746–1815); Howard, Henry (ca 1517–47)
Surrey:
counter-protests signed in, ix. 10
High Sheriff of, *see* Saunderson, Edward
Keppel accepts election offer from, ix. 86
Mann family's estate possibly in, *see under* Sussex
Stanley's villa in, viii. 14
Surry. *See* Surrey
Survay of London. See under Stow, John
Surveyor of the Forests:
Legge succeeds Whitworth as, i. 493
Surveyor of the Roads:
Legge became, iii. 457n
See also Phillipson, John (d. 1756); Walker, Thomas (d. 1748)
Surveyor of the Royal Gardens. *See* Hervey, Hon. Thomas (d. 1775)
Surveyor of the Woods. *See* Phillipson, John
Susa, Vittorio Francesco (1692–1762), Marchese di:
captured, ii. 436
English captains entertained by, ii. 360
Villefranche commanded by, ii. 360
Susa:
governor of, Viry ordered to report to, twice a day, viii. 328
Viry arrested at, viii. 328

Sussex, D. of. *See* Augustus Frederick
Sussex, E. of. *See* Yelverton, George Augustus (1727–58)
Sussex:
Brest fleet near coast of, ii. 402
counter protest signed in, ix. 10
Mann family estate allegedly in, ii. 307, viii. 168, 173, 176, 181
Newcastle, D. of, kisses men of, at troop review, iii. 495
—— might be begging France for post in, v. 499
Temple, Mrs, in, iv. 180
Sutherland, Cts of. *See* Wemyss, Lady Elizabeth (d. 1747)
Sutherland, (?)Alexander:
Mann sends packet through, to HW, ix. 81, 87, 93
Minorca left by, for England, after rift with Murray, ix. 81
Sutherland, ship:
expected at Port Mahon, i. 285
Suttermans, Justus (1597–1681), painter:
(?) masquerader costumed like portrait by, i. 338
Sutton, Daniel (ca 1735–1819), inoculator:
European princes might be saved by, vi. 562
Sutton (formerly Manners), Lord Robert (1722–62); M.P.:
Robinson entertains, i. 222
Sutton, Dr Robert (?ca 1731–97), inoculator:
rumoured to be at Paris, viii. 2
Stormont said to have been asked to take, to Louis XV, viii. 2
Swallowfield, Berks, Dodd's seat:
HW to visit, i. 253
Swan; swans:
visible from SH, ix. 532
See also Leda and the Swan
Swares. *See* Suares de la Concha
Sweden, K. of. *See* Adolf Fredrik (1710–71); Charles XII (1682–1718); Fredrik I (1676–1751); Gustav III (1746–92); Gustavus (Vasa) I (1496–1560); Karl XIII (1748–1818)
Sweden, P. of. *See* Adolf Fredrik (1710–71)
Sweden, Q. of. *See* Christina (1626–89); Louise Ulrica (1720–82); Ulrica Leonora (1688–1741)
Sweden:
Adolf Fredrik heir to crown of, ii. 219, 278
Austrian alliance with, i. 446
captains from, at Leghorn, *see* Anckarloo, David; Fleetrood
Catalogue of French Books, A, satirizes, ii. 53
Choiseul 'buys,' vii. 133
Danish prince proposed as future king of, ii. 203n
Daun and Fermer may be joined by troops of, v. 247
fleet of, to enter Mediterranean, ix. 59
France informs, that she must make peace, v. 498

France's ally, iv. 571
Frederick I menaced by, v. 119, 247, 258, 327
French baffled in, vii. 157
French troops said to be going to, in English men of war, vii. 466
hesitant, v. 502
Loutherbourgh from, viii. 93
Maria Theresa's alliance with, vi. 564
revolution in, vii. 438
royal family of, smallpox deaths in, i. 255
Russian army imitated by that of, v. 312
Russia's war with, *see* War, Swedish-Russian
seamen of, on Prussian privateer, v. 349
secretary of legation of, at Rome, *see* Basquiat
Senate of, to choose bride for Adolf Fredrik, ii. 305
ship of, *see Esperance*
Thurot may enlist troops of, v. 347
troops of, approach Berlin but are repulsed, v. 247
Young Pretender said to be visiting, iv. 44
—— to be assisted by, iii. 311
Sweepstakes:
HW searches newspapers for accounts of, vii. 497
Sweetmeats:
Mann sends, to Mathews, ii. 195
Swelling. *See* Swollen ankles; Swollen body; Swollen feet; Swollen legs
Swiegel. *See* Schwichelt
Swift, Jonathan (1667–1745), dean of St Patrick's, Dublin; author:
Bolingbroke and Pope urge, to burn history of Anne's reign, v. 184
Caroline would have been praised by, as much as Q. Anne, if she could have helped him, ix. 8
Cork's *Remarks on the Life* of, iv. 454n, 457, v. 194
correspondence of, with Bolingbroke, Gay, and Bathurst, read by HW, ix. 6–8
Gulliver's Travels: HW alludes to, ii. 495; HW alludes to Struldbrugs in, vi. 110, 219; solemnity of, equalled by modern rumours, viii. 519
HW calls: 'malignant,' ix. 6; 'wild beast,' ix. 8
history by, of Q. Anne's last years: HW discusses, v. 184–5; Lucas the editor of, v. 200–1; Mann attributes, to Lord Cork, v. 194
letters of, disagreeably mention Cts of Suffolk, vi. 524, 543n, ix. 8
Love Song ('Mild Arcadians'), by, imitated in *Arno Miscellany*, ix. 507
Lyttelton's *Dialogues of the Dead* mention, v. 408
Memoirs . . . of Martin Scriblerus, characters in, iv. 214
new-coined words irritate, ix. 538

[Swift, Jonathan, *continued*]
Pomfret, Cts of, condemns humour of, i. 477
Pope in awe of, ix. 6
Queensberry, Ds of, mentioned in letters of, iii. 195n
witticism by, about Holland, viii. 523
Swiftsure, English ship:
Monmouth supported by, v. 193
Swimburn. *See* Swinburne
Swimmer. *See* Swymmer
Swinburne, Henry (1743–1803):
Florence left by, ix. 65
Mann sends rock crystals through, to HW, ix. 65
Swinburne, Mrs Henry. *See* Baker, Martha
Swinging:
Mann to use, for exercise, ii. 558
navy uses, for exercise, ii. 558
Swinny, Owen Mac (d. 1754), playwright:
George II's message to Frederick, P. of Wales, to be read by, i. 296
playhouse director, i. 296n
witticism by, on Cambric Bill, ii. 192
Swiss:
maladie du pays of, vi. 198
Swiss coffee-house. *See under* Coffee-house
Swisserland. *See* Switzerland
Swiss guards:
Florentine: captain of, accompanies Dumesnil to Electress, i. 236; Francis I orders sent, from Florence, iii. 82
French, Choiseul to give up, vii. 322, 363
Switzerland:
Buignon from, ix. 517n, 523
Burnaby raises troops in, ii. 215
Choiseul oppresses, vii. 130
English travellers swarm in, ix. 618
French ambassador alarms, with news of P. Charles's invasion, ii. 290
Gloucester, D. of, to visit, viii. 123
HW's servant Louis from, iv. 554
London servants from, to form a regiment, ii. 409
mercenary voting in, i. 470
Müntz from, v. 239
officials of, join Young Pretender, iii. 259
Palmerston's travels in, with Pars, x. 48
Pennsylvania's immigrants from, may form regiment, iv. 531
porters from, kept by Northumberlands, iv. 341
Prévost to visit relatives in, vii. 554
Richecourt said to visit, i. 125
troops of, at Rome, ii. 532
Villettes later becomes minister to, iii. 456n
—— sends courier through, ii. 385
Voltaire in, v. 51
See also Berne; Geneva; Grisons; Lausanne; Zurich
Swollen ankles:
occurrence of, viii. 280
Swollen body:
occurrence of, ix. 394

Swollen feet:
occurrence of, ix. 593
Swollen legs:
occurrences of, vii. 355, 369, viii. 137, 244, ix. 266, 442
Sword; swords:
Birmingham hopes to make, for American war, viii. 77
diamond-studded: gold, given by Catherine II to Gunning, vii. 508; Mathews receives, ii. 370
duel fought with, iv. 364
Flobert guards mistress's house with, v. 386
Irish Catholics forbidden to carry, iv. 289
Marlborough's, ii. 248
rioters seize, in Genoa, iii. 338
sailor tosses, to unarmed opponent, viii. 543
Swymmer, Mrs. *See* Astley, Arabella
Swymmer, Anthony Langley (? 1724–60), M.P.:
(?)Florence visited by, iv. 376
Sydenham, Humphrey (1694–1757):
Parliamentary debates by: on amendment to the Address, x. 23; on Scotch Bill, x. 31
Sydney, Bn and Vct. *See* Townshend, Rt Hon. Thomas (1733–1800)
Sykes, Sir Francis (1732–1804), cr. (1781) Bt; East India Co. official; M.P.:
excessive table allowance of, vii. 451–2
HW says, was originally waiter in a tavern, ix. 141
Haidar Ali thinks he has as much right as, to Indian diamonds, ix. 141
'Sylvia':
Berkeley, Lady Henrietta, and Vcts Belfield use, as nom-de-plume, ii. 220
Symptomatic fever. *See under* Fever
Symson (? Simpson), Rev. Peter, assistant at Mayfair Chapel:
(?) sermon by, iv. 241, 243
Syracuse, Bp of. *See* Testa, Francesco Maria (d. 1773)
Syringe; syringes:
Ponzio uses, on Benedict XIV, v. 37
templars take, to theatre, iii. 469
Syringe-baths:
Gloucester, D. of, takes, vii. 334
Szembeck, Barbe-Madeleine-Élisabeth de (ca 1709–62), m. 1 Jean Clément, Comte de Branicki; m. 2 (1736) Ulrik Frederik Woldemar Lowendal, Comte de Lowendal:
Coventry, Cts of, gives fan to, and is forced to take it back, iv. 338

T——, Miss:
HW mentions, iv. 292
Taaffe, Theobold, (ca 1708–80) M.P.:
Albemarle bails, but makes no defence for him, iv. 294
burgundy smuggled by, iv. 289
Coke's witticism about Parliamentary membership of, iv. 289
faro-banker for Duchesse de Mirepoix, iv. 288

French court receives, v. 473
galleys may be punishment of, iv. 288, 294
imprisoned with Wortley Montagu at Fort l'Évêque, Paris, for robbing Payba, iii. 450n, iv. 288, v. 473
member of Parliament, iii. **450n**, iv. 289
Newcastle, D. of, accompanied by, to Lewes races, iv. 289
Pompadour, Marquise de, receives turtles and pineapples from, iv. 289
religion forsaken by, to fight a duel in Ireland, iv. 289
White's Club does not include, iv. 289
Woffington, Margaret, makes bet with, iv. 289
Tabachiera. *See* Snuff-box
Tabernacle:
  by Donatello, *see under* Donatello
  in Palazzo Pitti oratory, iv. 489
Tabernego. *See* Tabuerniga
Table; tables:
  black and white (?marble), x. 7
  charge for casing, x. 4
  granite, x. 3, 7
  HW's, with drawers, in Arlington Street, vii. 285
  mosaic, ancient, x. 7
  Newcastle, D. of, takes, to Germany, iii. 484–5
  octagon, in Uffizi, removed, ix. 170
  oriental alabaster, x. 7
  porphyry, x. 7
  Rowley gives, to Mann, iii. 9
  scagliola, *see under* Scagliola
  silver, left by Electress to Rinuccini, ii. 169
  sold out of Palazzo Pitti, ix. 231
Tablettes. *See* Pocket-book
Tabor:
  people dance to, around maypole, iv. 47
Tabouret:
  Mirepoix, Duchesse de, does not have, at French court, iv. 28, 92, 144
  —— regains, through husband's dukedom, iv. 280–1
  Stuart, Charlotte, said to have, at French court, ix. 537
Tabuerniga, Marqués de (d. 1753):
  Carteret and his daughter shelter, i. 278
  Carteret, Bns, retorts to, about Lincoln, ii. 483
  flees from Spain, after offending Q. by supporting P. of the Asturias, i. 277–8
  Harrington procures pension for, i. 278
  Pomfret, Cts of, calls on, i. 277
  Ranelagh visited by, ii. 483
  returns to Spain after Philip V's death, i. 277n
Tabuerniga, Marquesa de. *See* Fuentes, ——
Tabuerniga, ——; brother of Marqués de Tabuerniga:
  Carteret and his daughter shelter, i. 278
  flees from Spain after offending Q. by supporting P. of the Asturias, i. 277–8

Harrington procures pension for, i. 278
returns to Spain to rescue fiancée, i. 278
Tacitus, Publius Cornelius (ca 55–ca117), historian:
  Gray's Latin inscription to be in style of, iv. 407
  (?) HW quotes, iii. 78
  HW quotes passage in, about mutineers, iv. 125
  Peter III's murder makes annals of, seem more credible, vi. 65
Taffanel, Clément de (1706–95), Marquis de la Jonquière; French naval officer:
  Anson's battle with, iv. 38
Tagliamento, river:
  overflowing of, v. 134
Tahiti ('Otaheite'):
  forgotten, viii. 21
  living with the young is like living in, ix. 538
  not exploited because it has no wealth, ix. 545
  Omai native of, viii. 175
Tailor; tailors:
  Albemarle ruins, iv. 270
  French furnish, to the age, vi. 15
  in Drury Lane farce, iv. 342
  in Soho, harbours Theodore of Corsica, v. 45
  Italian, Vaneschi brings, to London, i. 191
  journeymen, go on strike, vii. 30–1
  Montagu, D. of, places, on Great Wardrobe payroll, iv. 79
Talard. *See* Tallart
Talbot, Bns and Cts. *See* De Cardonnel, Mary
Talbot, Barbara (d. 1759), m. (1742) James Aston, 5th Bn Aston of Forfar:
  Boulogne visited by, i. 140
Talbot, Lady Cecil (1735–93), m. (1756) George Rice (? m. 2 Robert Wilson); Bns Dinevor, s.j., 1782:
  father's barony to revert to, ix. 86
Talbot, Charles (1660–1718), 12th E. of Shrewsbury, cr. (1694) D. of Shrewsbury:
  wife of, iv. 203n
Talbot, Charles (1685–1737), cr. (1733) Bn Talbot, lord chancellor 1733–7:
  son of, i. 385n
Talbot, Charles (ca 1722–66):
  Boulogne visited by, i. 140
Talbot, Francis (1727–1813):
  Boulogne visited by, i. 140
Talbot, George (1719–87), 14th E. of Shrewsbury:
  Boulogne visited by, i. 140
  Bulstrode tutor to, i. 140n
  Craon, Princesse de, attends tenebræ with, i. 4
  Dashwood ridicules religion of, ii. 79
  Mahony, Comtesse, to be accompanied by, i. 28
  Rome visited by, i. 4

[Talbot, George, *continued*]
servant of, talks with Smyth about Young Pretender's departure, i. 14
Talbot, Hon. Mrs George. *See* Fitzwilliam, Hon Mary
Talbot, Mrs Henry (?Catharine Clopton d. 1754):
Maclaine robs, iv. 168
Talbot, James (1726–90), Bp of Birtha:
Boulogne visited by, i. 140
Talbot, John (ca 1384–1453), cr. (1442) E. of Salop:
HW praises, ii. 357
Talbot, John (d. 1751):
Boulogne visited by, i. 140
Talbot, John (ca 1712–56), M.P.:
(?) HW's friend, iii. 176
Indemnity Bill supported by, i. 429
lord of trade, iv. 517
named in Secret Committee lists, i. **385,** 391
Parliamentary vote by, on privately-raised regiments, x. 19
(?) steward of Cheshire estate ordered by, to burn stock if rebels approach, iii. 176
Talbot, Lucy (d. 1787):
Boulogne visited by, i. 140
Talbot, Mary (d. 1753), m. (1749) Charles Dormer, 8th Bn Dormer:
Boulogne visited by, i. 140
Talbot, Thomas Joseph (1727–95), Bp of Acon, 1766:
Boulogne visited by, i. 140
Talbot, William (1710–82), 2d Bn Talbot, 1737, cr. (1761) E. Talbot:
Beaufort pities, for ill-tempered mistress and wife, i. 486
—— sues, ii. 185
Beaufort, Ds of, commits adultery with, i. 453
becomes Earl, v. 489, 490
becomes lord steward, v. 489
Bubb Dodington supported by, iv. 39
Dinevor title conferred on, to go to daughter's heirs, ix. 86
'Fountain' meeting attended by, i. **336**
Halifax to be succeeded by, in Board of Trade, v. 486
law suit will deprive, of wealth acquired by marriage, ii. 199
mob breaks lord steward's wand in hand of, vii. 98–9
Murray's testimony interrupted by, iii. 381
Newcastle, D. of, advised by, on Pitt's resignation, v. 540
Pitt, Elizabeth, mistress of, iv. 507n
Regency bill opposed by, iv. 248
wife separated from, i. 486
Wilkes fights with, vi. 137, 163
witticism by, about D. of Newcastle, vi. 79
Talbot family:
genealogy of, brings them no advantages, iv. 408

HW praises, ii. **357**
motto of, iv. 475
Tallart, Comte de. *See* Hostun, Camille d'
Tallow:
cheap in Florence, ii. 281
Tallow candles. *See under* Candle
Tallow-chandlers:
HW attributes rioters' window-breaking to glaziers and, ix. 343
mob of, riots in London, vii. 200
Talmond, Princesse de. *See* Jablonowska, Marie-Louise
Tamburro notturno. See under Rucellai
Tamerlane. See under Rowe, Nicholas
Tamerlano. See under Bernasconi, Andrea; Piovene, Conte Agostino
Tanaro, river:
Charles Emmanuel III and Austrians behind, iii. 84
Spaniards dislodge Charles Emmanuel III from posts along, iii. 120
Tancred and Sigismunda. See under Thomson, James
Tangier, Bay of:
St Esprit may have sunk in, iii. 82
Tanjore, 'King' of. *See* Tuljajī
Tanjore ('Tanjour'):
capture of, vii. 561
Tankerville, Cts of. *See* Colville, Camilla (1698–1775)
Tankerville, E. of. *See* Bennet, Charles (1697–1753); Grey, Ford (d. 1701)
Tanucci, Bernardo (1698–1783), statesman:
Charles of Naples confides in, v. 330
dissertation by, advocates a K. of Italy, v. 494–5
Gray to get billet from, v. **160**
—— told by, that Naples and Charles III want neutrality, vi. 5–6
Hamilton, Sir William, not on good terms with, vi. 547
Jesuits opposed by, x. 49
Neapolitans clamorous against, v. 329–30
Tuscan government hated by, vi. 448
Wilkes neglected by, vi. 292
Tapestry:
Arnaldi's, i. 56
Charles III may declare war from horse of, vii. 245
—— said to have flogged horse in, vii. 230–1
—— shoots at, vii. 237–8
—— should be left to enjoyment of, vii. 254
—— slaughtered animals in, vii. 241
Cumberland, D. of, receives, at Rome, vii. 566
Ferdinand VI tries to mount horses in, vii. 241
Ferdinand of Naples's pastimes worse than shooting birds or thrashing horses in, vii. 254
French, chairs covered with, vii. 285

of Armada's destruction, in House of Lords, vii. 242
York, D. of, receives, at Rome, vi. 229, 232
See also Hangings
Tapestry Hangings of the House of Lords. *See under* Morant, Philip; Pine, John
Tappia, Conte:
San Remo deputy, iii. 123
Tapping (for the dropsy):
Saxe subjected to, iii. 91
Tar:
sailor mends wooden leg with, viii. 283–4, 290
Southwark magazines of, catch fire, ix. 577
Tarascon. *See* Richard de Tarascon
Tariff. *See* Protecting Duties
'Tarinity':
Henley preaches on, ii. 465
Tarleton, Sir Banastre (1754–1833), cr. (1815) Bt; army officer; M.P.:
defeated in America, ix. 141
Taro, river:
armies of Austria and Spain separated by, iii. 245
Imperial army awaits Gages on banks of, iii. 236
Tart; tarts:
currant, Mann serves, to Contessa del Benino, i. 68
gooseberry: Hobart and Mann consume, iii. 261; Mann has, for dinner in garden, v. 10; Mann lives on, i. 57, 61; Mann sends, to Princesse de Craon, iii. 402
of duke cherries, iv. 260
spinach, i. 218
Tartan; tartans:
English use, as fire-ships, ii. 301
French, English capture, i. 408
French ship to be escorted by, back to Tripoli, vii. 24
Norris captures, ii. 455
Tartan, English cutter:
news brought by, v. 210
Tartar, English tartan:
sails to Minorca, ix. 249
Tartar:
Dashkov, Ps, is, vii. 248
Tartary:
forces of, oppose Frederick II, v. 327
Frenchman and Englishman would seem fellow-countrymen if they met in, ix. 555–6
ownership of portions of, inconsequential, vii. 420
Pomerania worth more than, vi. 11
Tartuffe. See under Molière
Tar-water:
Berkeley's *Siris* popularizes, ii. 452, 464–5
Mann, Galfridus, takes, v. 30, 36
newspapers print verses on Berkeley and, ii. 505
Tassels:
on Ds of Buckingham's funeral canopy, ii. 193

Tassi, Nicolli:
(?) Mann consults, ix. 120
(?) Mann opens Cts of Orford's will in presence of, ix. 114
Taste:
French, in small ornaments, excels English, ix. 635
HW's reflections on, as responsible for ill-advised alterations, ix. 177
in beauty and wit, alters, ix. 308
refined, Pope's garden spoiled by, ix. 177
Tatton, Katharine (d. 1729), m. 1 (1724) Edward Nevill, 15th Bn Abergavenny; m. 2 (1725) William Nevill, 16th Bn Abergavenny:
buried in Kensington Church, iv. 182
daughter of, iii. 63
Tattoo, of drums:
English royal family like, i. 410
Taube, Gräfin von. *See* Hoym, Gisela Erdmuth von
Taube, Evert Vilhelm (1737–99), Friherre, Swedish Army officer:
(?) Mann sends HW's letter to Ds of Gloucester by, viii. 247
Taunton, Somerset:
Maxwell M.P. for, iv. 441
Tauris:
archbishopric of, in Turkish hands, vi. 196
Tavanti, Signora. *See* Cocchi, Beatrice
Tavanti, Angelo (1714–82), Tuscan financier:
government post given to, vii. 294
Tavern; taverns:
American agitation descends from Parliament to, viii. 86
Carteret and Winchilsea never dine at, i. 335
dinners at, for Parliamentary candidates, i. 243
future dukes will frequent, iv. 155
Hamilton frequents, iv. 155
in Piccadilly, iii. 387n
Norsa keeps, iii. 284
Rockingham's friends and George Grenville dine at, vii. 115
Rumbold and Sykes formerly waiters at, ix. 141
See also Bedford Head; Fountain; Star and Garter
Tavernier, Jean-Baptiste (1605–89), Bn d'Aubonne, 1670:
Six voyages, (?)HW reads of temple in, viii. 433
Tavistock, Marchioness of. *See* Keppel, Lady Elizabeth (1739–68)
Tavistock, M. of. *See* Russell, Francis (1739–67); Russell, Francis (1765–1802)
Tavora, Francisco d'Assis de (1703–59), Marquês de Tavora:
alleged plot by, v. 250
Tavora, Dona Leonor de (1700–59), m. Francisco d'Assis de Tavora:
alleged plot by, v. 250

Tax; taxes:
called heavy, in House of Lords, ii. 158
Craon to pay, on future daughter-in-law's fortune, iii. 23
England expects additions to, viii. 448
England may see folly of imposing, on America, viii. 208
Ferrara's and Romagna's, ii. 344
Florentine: as high as they can be, vi. 254; on decedents' estates, v. 149, 151
French, of ten per cent, i. 115
Genoa does not levy, ii. 555
House of Commons considers, ix. 566, 573, 583
India subjected to, by East India Company's servants, vii. 451-2
inheritance: in Tuscany, acquittance needed for, ix. 521; on legacies in Tuscany, ix. 666
land: Buckingham grand jury thanks Parliament for lowering, vi. 494; continued, i. 390; diminution of, not irreparable, vi. 501; diminution of, proves unpopular, vi. 494; English country gentry try to avoid, by piling up the public debt, ix. 506; London opposes country squires' attempt to lower, vi. 487-8; ministry defeated in attempt to preserve, vi. 487-9; remonstrants may refuse to pay, vii. 197; Townshend refuses to pay, vii. 346
Londoners ignore, ix. 243
merchants thrive by, v. 549
ministry dispenses, for Scotland, iv. 311
new, in England, ix. 506, 566
North to lay, before House of Commons, ix. 254
on Electress's pensions to servants, iii. 23-4
on Irish absentees, vii. 524, 531
on tea, proposed, ii. 141-2
on tobacco, at Florence, iv. 389
on tradesmen's bills, iv. 183
Orford, Cts of, averse to, iv. 504-5
Parliament debates over, iii. 458
Parliament should heap, on advocates of American war, viii. 133-4
place tax, debated in House of Commons, v. 199
Portuguese officer prosecuted for not paying, vii. 166
Pulteney said to increase, ii. 91
Scottish, iv. 311
size of, in England, i. 401
Spanish army levies, on Italian towns, ii. 344
Tuscan collectors of, more diligent than under the Medici. vi. 254-5
Tuscan quarantine creates, ii. 297
See also Cider Tax; Sugar tax
Taxation:
North's peace terms disclaim, viii. 354
Taylor, Elizabeth (1729-1801), m. (1747) William Young, cr. (1769) Bt:
Florence visited by, iv. 327

from Kent, 'refined' in France, iv. 327
Taylor, John (1703-72), M.D.; quack oculist:
calls himself 'Chevalier,' v. 252
Florentine oculist outdoes, ii. 240
HW calls, quack, iv. 461n
HW's epigram on, v. 252, 255
Kilmorey, Vcts, recommends, to Albani, iv. 458
Walpole family's patronage boasted of by, at Rome, iv. 458, 461
Taylor, Mary (fl. ca 1751-3), housekeeper at Hampton Court:
visitors conducted by, iv. 272
Taylor, Robert (1710-62), physician:
Frederick, P. of Wales, attended by, iv. 232
Tchesmé:
battle of, vii. 226-8, 232-6
Russians do not follow up successes at, vii. 331
Turkish fleet burned in harbour of, vii. 234-5
Tea:
booths for, at Ranelagh, iv. 47
Bostonians dump, in harbour, vii. 550, viii. 13
dish of, Walpole, Sir Edward, takes, ix. 463
duty on, proposed by English ministers, ii. 141-2
East India Company buys, at Ostend to cheat smugglers, ix. 577-8
East India Company's stock of, at Southwark, catches fire, ix. 577-8
George II to hold cup for, at subscription masquerade, iv. 49
HW avoids, vii. 76
HW mentions, iv. 326
HW receives, from Mann, i. 12, 17, 19
Mann, Chute, and Whithed take, i. 428
Mann gives, to Vorontsov family, vi. 193
—— takes, under orange trees, i. 104
—— to take, with Chute and Whithed, i. 161
——unable to get, for HW, i. 59
New York rejects, viii. 13
seed of: Ginori content with small quantity of, ii. 235; Ginori thinks, is in Botanic Garden at Chelsea, ii. 183; HW to get, through brother at Chelsea, ii. 250; Mann wants, ii. 323; to be sought in Chelsea botanical garden, ii. 216; Walpole, Sir Edward, forgets to get, ii. 284
served at Robinson's ball, i. 185
smuggled, found in Haszlang's house, ix. 55
tax on, proposed, ii. 141-2
universal use of, ii. 142
Venice well stocked with, i. 59
Tea-kettle:
lamp of, only light in Cts of Coventry's sick-room, v. 451
ormolu, sold at auction, vii. 211-12

Teano, Principe di. *See* Gaetani, Michel-
angelo (ca 1689–1760)
Tea service:
of Chelsea china, vi. 121–2
Teaspoons, silver:
Marlborough abandons, in retreat from St-
Malo, v. 221
Tea tongs:
English may try to batter Calais with, v.
221
Teatro degl'Intrepidi (called Teatro della
Palla a Corda), Florence:
Mann serves sherbets before opening of, ix.
585, 592
masked balls given free at, for Archduke
and Archduchess from Milan, ix. 50
new theatre, opened with show about
Amerigo Vespucci, viii. 514
open in June 1785, ix. 585
(?) Young Pretender decorates box in, ix.
536
Teatro del Cocomero, Florence:
admission price to, iv. 357
Andromaca in prose given at, ii. 128
bad opera at, ii. 555
Bagnano not to give operas in, i. 56
burletta in, i. 128, iii. 356, 476
Fumagalli almost inaudible at, i. 423
Gloucester, D. of, attends, with Leopold
and Maria Louisa, vii. 405
Iphigenia at, ii. 128, 134
Leopold frequents, vi. 477
(?) little opera at, i. 80
Mann serves sherbets before opening of,
ix. 585, 592
Medici, Filippo, impresario at, ii. 178
open in June 1785, ix. 585
opera not to be given in, i. 56
operas at, i. 284
Via della Pergola in opposition to, iii. 356
Teatro della Pergola (at Florence):
Accademia dei nobili to give celebration
in, vi. 367
accademici deny use of, to Filippo de'
Medici, ii. 439
admission fee for, vii. 458
bad opera at, i. 128, 555
ball at, iii. 8, 115, 364, vi. 486
balls discontinued at, when masking is
forbidden, iv. 219
bal masqué at, vii. 456
Botta wants opera at, in autumn, vi. 166
boxes at, hung with damask, i. 60
Coke, Lady Mary, saw Botta at, vii. 552
Craon, Princesse de, attends opera in
Francis I's box at, i. 83
—— takes curtain-rising at, as compliment, iii. 358
—— to have attended, in mask, iii. 8
crowded because of masks, ii. 372
Cumberland, D. and Ds of, eat ices at
Mann's before going to, ix. 644
deserted, ii. 139, iv. 357

doormen of, inspect pies, iv. 219
empty without masking, iv. 216
English do not wear gala at, from pique
at Richecourt's neglect, v. 9
fat pies and meat dishes forbidden in, iv.
219
Francis I's box at, i. 60, 83
Fumagalli ineligible for, i. 423
Galli, Mme, has box at, iii. 505
Gloucester, Ds of, Joseph II, and Leopold
drive to, vii. 112
Gloucester, Ds of, to be attended at, by
Mann's servants with ice refreshments, viii.
291
HW imagines himself in, ii. 149
Hobart starts riot in, iii. 478
Holt and Monro attend, masked, iii. 400
illuminated, iii. 355
intermezzi worse than those at, iv. 210–11
Joseph II attends, vii. 108, 112
Karl Alexander visits ladies in boxes at,
iv. 376
Mann becomes cicisbeo in order to attend,
vi. 180
—— indifferent to maskings in, iv. 404
—— mistakenly takes Richecourt's box in,
i. 394
——'s box at: i. 48, 51, 60, 69, 81, 111,
136, 149, 239, 240, 394, ii. 29, 128–9, iii.
311; changed for Richecourt's, i. 240, 394,
ii. 129, 139; Feroni, Mme, and Suares
family conflict over, i. 81; Knight to use,
iii. 462; lined and matted to exclude cold,
ii. 128–9; shared by a lady, vi. 180; *see
also under* Theatre: Florentine: Mann's
boxes at
—— sees Mme Venturini at, ii. 392
—— sees Young Pretender at, ix. 467
—— serves sherbets before opening of, ix.
585, 592
—— takes Morice to, to hear Marchesi, ix.
435
—— to get second box at, for Mrs Garrick,
vi. 180
masked balls given free at, for Archduke
and Archduchess of Milan, ix. 50
masks to be permitted in, ii. 364
(?) open after Lent, vi. 224
open in June 1785, ix. 585
operas in, ii. 134, 555, iii. 356, iv. 357,
vi. 477; *see also under* Opera
San Vitale tells directors of, to arrest
Tesi's insulter, ii. 368
Sauveterre dances in, iii. 355–6
second opera in, to be improved by Manzuoli to attract Grand Duke, vi. 477
to be scene of *bal masqué* and supper for
D. and Ds of Cumberland, ix. 644–5
Young Pretender often sick in corridor of,
viii. 244
——'s box at: frequented by visitors to
his wife, viii. 245; furnished with couch,
viii. 244; lined with crimson damask, with

[Teatro della Pergola, *continued*]
velvet gold-laced cushion, ix. 536; Young Pretender sleeps in, viii. 244–5
Tebaldi, Signora. *See* Ganganelli, Porzia
Techen. *See* Teschen
Tedeschi, (?)Caterina, Italian singer:
Delaval flogs, on finding Guadagni in her bed, iv. 41, 55, vii. 278
——'s mistress, iv. 41
flogging of, would shock the Florentines, iv. 55
Tedeschino (?Giovanni Tedeschi), singer:
Salimbeni imitated by, i. 284
Te Deum; Te Deums:
abundance of, to celebrate alleged victories, v. 246
at Florence, for Francis I's election, iii. 115
Austrians sing, at Campo Santo, ii. 163
Botta does not order singing of, v. 317
—— does not sing, v. 435
England sings, for Frederick II, v. 319
English victories hard to crowd into a single, v. 333
for Maria Theresa's coronation, i. 100
for Prague coronation (of Maria Theresa), ii. 240, 241–2
France sings, for insignificant successes, v. 502
Francis I orders, to be sung in Tuscany, v. 112
French and Spanish supporters sing, for alleged victory, iii. 268
Incontri, Abp, and attendants whisper, in coach, v. 151–2
Leopold's arrival not to be celebrated by, at Florentine Duomo, vi. 334
Lorenzi has, sung in French convent for Dauphin's wedding, iii. 14
Mann may sing, in his chapel, viii. 216
Mantua sings, for Daun's defeat, v. 463
Paris celebrates with, for victory in Germany, vi. 90
Richelieu's army sings, on landing at Ciudadela, iv. 567
Spain not to sing, for victories in Naples, ii. 486
Spaniards sing, for supposed victory, ii. 161
sung at Florence for Maria Theresa's recovery, vi. 532
sung at Florence, Leghorn, Siena, and Pistoia, v. 112
sung at Madrid and Port Mahon, for Spanish landing on Minorca, ix. 189
sung in Florentine church, i. 100
Tuscan singing of, followed by orders of neutrality, v. 114
Teeth. *See* Tooth
Teissonière. *See* Dayrolles
Telescope:
diminishing end of: HW in old age looks through, ix. 616; SH should be viewed through, ix. 532

Telesephorus:
Mann might be compared to, iii. 383
Teller of Exchequer. *See* Exchequer
Tellier, Le. *See* Le Tellier
Temistocle. See under Metastasio; Porpora
Tempest, The. See under Shakespeare, William
Tempi, Marchesa. *See* Bentivoglio, Elisabetta (ca 1696–1771); Capponi, Maria Laura (1726–77)
Tempi, Marchese Ferdinando:
(?) Richecourt's orders to, about theatre, iv. 219
Tempi, Leonardo (1685–1752), Marchese:
ball to be given by, ii. **435**
daughter-in-law pleases, ii. 438–9
death of, iv. 298
Dini, Mme, has, as cicisbeo for 30 years, iv. 298
health of, apoplexy, iv. 298
(?) villa of, near Leghorn gate in Florence, visited by Ds of Modena and daughter, ii. 227–8
Tempi, Luca Melchior (1688–1762), nuncio at Brussels, 1737–44; at Lisbon, 1744–54; cardinal:
Riccardi to send gems to, to be sold in Portugal, iii. 94, 259, 349
Tempi, Luigi (1721–63), Marchese:
marriage of, ii. **435**, 438–9
(?) Salviati family related to, ii. 520
(?) Tesi, the, pursued by, ii. 520
wife pleases father more than, ii. 438–9
Tempi, Maria Maddalena (d. 1798), m. (1739) Niccolò Martelli:
ball given by, for brother's marriage, ii. 435, 438
Tempi family:
bereavement excludes, from Carnival diversions, iv. 298
Carteret's wedding too simple for, ii. 445
Templars:
Foundling upheld by, iii. 469
syringes taken by, to theatre, iii. 469
Temple, Cts. *See* Chambers, Anne (ca 1709–77); Nugent, Lady Mary Elizabeth (d. 1812)
Temple, E. *See* Grenville, George (1753–1813); Grenville-Temple, Richard (1711–79)
'Temple, Lord':
Young Pretender said to have dispatched, to his father, iii. 87
Temple, Henry (ca 1673–1757), cr. (1723) Vct Palmerston:
daughter-in-law of, iv. 180n
Limerick gets reversion of, i. 492
Temple, Henry (1739–1802), 2d Vct Palmerston:
Garrick to accompany, from Genoa to Florence, vi. 180
lord of the Admiralty, viii. 135, 144
Pars does volume of washed drawings for, viii. 135

——'s patron, viii. 135, 144, x. 48
Switzerland visited by, x. 48
Temple, Jane Martha (1672–1751), m. 1 (1692) John Berkeley, 3d Bn Berkeley of Stratton; m. 2 (1700) William Bentinck, 1st E. of Portland:
Pembroke treats, indecently, in law suit, iv. 109
Temple, Sir Richard (1675–1749), 4th Bt; cr. (1714) Bn and (1718) Vct Cobham; field marshal, M.P.:
Churchill's regiment acquired by, iii. 62
faction of: disbanded, iii. 194; may be dismissed, iii. 188
field marshal in command of troops in England, i. 457
Frederick, P. of Wales, impelled by, against Sir Robert Walpole, i. 329
nephew of, ii. 98
New Ode, A, satirizes, ii. 50
resignation of, ii. 356
William III promotes, x. 14
Temple, Hon. Richard (ca 1726–49), M.P.:
wife of, iv. 180n
Temple, Mrs Richard. See Pelham, Henrietta (1730–68)
Temple, Sir William (1628–99), cr. (1666) Bt:
E. of Norwich said by, to have outlived his reputation as a wit, ix. 308
Temple; temples:
Gothic or Chinese, in English landscape effects, iv. 166
Indian, richly decorated, has old baboon in shrine, viii. 433
Temple, the, London:
denizens of, disregard monarchs, vii. 497
Hull attorney in, viii. 78, 200
Malcolm, Sarah, washerwoman at, iii. 460n
Seymour-Conway sends letter to T. Tighe in, ix. 608
Sherlock master of, iv. 133n
Temple, the, Paris:
Sartine searches Conti at, vii. 453
Temple Bar:
Crassus the richest man on other side of, v. 558
London and House of Commons must be pacified by, vii. 283
mob intercepts merchants at, vii. 98
Temple de Terpsychore, Paris:
Guimard, Mlle, builds, vii. 322–3
'Tench, Mr':
Old Pretender's name for Sir Robert Walpole, i. 479
Tencin. See Guérin de Tencin
Ten Commandments:
England does not strangle, vi. 91
parody of, i. 313
Tender; tenders:
English capture Admiral Peroz's, i. 380–1
Townshend's, iii. 325
Tender Husband. See under Steele, Sir Richard

Tenducci, Giusto Ferdinando (ca 1736–ca 1800), singer:
England long despises, vii. 353
England to be revisited by, vii. 353
Gloucester, D. of, hears, in Florence, vii. 353
Tenebræ:
Craon, Princesse de, and Lord Shrewsbury attend, i. 4
Tenedos:
Elphinston sent to, to blockade Dardanelles, vii. 228
Teniers, David (1610–90):
HW wishes he knew nothing of, ii. 218
Van Dyck's imitation of, i. 373
Tennis:
Pembroke and the Primate of Ireland play, iv. 109
Selwyn's witticism on players at, iv. 155
Tennis ball:
Frederick, P. of Wales, injured by, iv. 240
Tent; tents:
Braitwitz demands, i. 293
in Mann's garden, v. 10
Leghorn officers live in, i. 303
prepared at San Martino for Leghorn troops, ii. 76
Turkish, captured by Russians, vii. 478–9
Tent-bed:
Downe offers, to Cts of Coventry, iv. 324
Tenures:
purchase of, to secure election, iv. 435–6
Teodosia, Abp of. See Manciforte Sperelli, Giovanni Ottavio
Teologo. See Theologian
Teresa (1515–82), saint:
Huntingdon, Cts of, compared to, v. 398
Maria Theresa's day, iii. 439
opera performed on day of, vi. 558–9
Teresa, ship:
in Spanish fleet, i. 286
Ternay ('Terney'). See Arzac de Ternay
Terpsichore, French frigate:
in Thurot's fleet, v. 372
Terra-cotta:
Damer, Hon. Mrs, models kittens and bridge keystones in, ix. 576
HW has cast in, of Livia statue, vi. 107
model of statue in, ii. 179, 190, 197, 200, 210
Proctor's model in, of Ixion, ix. 577
Terra del Sole:
Lobkowitz to pass through, iii. 11
Terray, Joseph-Marie (1715–78), abbé; controller-general:
appointed controller-general, vii. 164
banished, viii. 34–5
Choiseul opposes war plans of, vii. 258
French finances reformed by, vii. 192
mistress sacrificed by, vii. 339
resignation and subsequent reinstatement of, rumoured, vii. 284

Terreno. See under Mann, Sir Horace: house of
Terrible, English sloop:
    involved in war, iii. 235–6, 277, 336
Terrible, English war ship:
    destroyed, ix. 194
Terrick, Richard (1710–77), Bp of Peter-
    borough 1757–64; Bp of London 1764–77:
    English Roman Catholics persecuted by,
    vi. 394
    George III sends, to examine proofs of
    Gloucester's and Cumberland's weddings,
    vii. 483
    —— unable to heed plea of, against Soho
    ball, vii. 193
Terziarii:
    of Jesuits, vii. 503–4, viii. 50
Teschen:
    peace congress to meet at, viii. 454
Teshu Lama. *See* dPal-ldan ye-šes (1737–80)
Tesi, Vittoria (1700–75), actress:
    acting resumed by, iii. 355
    applauded by audience, iii. 452
    Chute and Mme Suares quarrel with, ii.
    322
    Corsi and Tempi pursue, ii. 520
    costume of, i. 40, ii. 263, 302, 361
    Craon gives banishment notice to, ii. 520–1
    Craon, Princesse de, called on by, ii. 263
    —— criticizes acting of, ii. 302
    —— envies costume and coiffure of, ii.
    263
    engaged for the Carnival, ii. 322
    fashion brought by, from Reggio, i. 110
    fee of, for singing, ii. 281
    gendarmes insult, at opera, ii. 368
    HW agrees with Princesse de Craon's
    opinion of, ii. 318
    HW cannot get dog for, ii. 280, 293, 334,
    351, 368
    HW discourages English projects of, iii.
    289, 293–4
    HW mentions, i. 43
    HW urged by, to make her prima donna
    in England, iii. 277
    Hildburghausen led by, as her hero, at
    Vienna, v. 194
    Juvrecourt scolds, for applying to Riche-
    court and not to him, ii. 368–9
    libels against, ii. 391
    Mann called on by, ii. 281
    —— dares not convey HW's messages to,
    iii. 304
    —— discourages, from going to England,
    iii. 305
    Neapolitan cantata to include, iii. 438
    opera for, rehearsed in Mann's house, ii.
    294
    opera in Florence ruined by ostentation of,
    ii. 361
    opera of: in Venice, a failure, ii. 280–1;
    in Florence, successful, ii. 302–3
    Parigi, the, 'creature' of, ii. 302
    'passed the bloom of her wrinkles,' v. 194

Petrillo dependant of, i. 130
    return of, to Florence, ii. 263
    Richecourt's amours revealed by, i. 45
    San Vitali breaks with, ii. 263
    —— brings coach horses and servants for,
    ii. 263
    —— dismissed by, ii. 520
    ——, dying lover of, gives presents to her,
    i. 70
    —— may buy Niccolini's jewels for, i. 135
    ——'s jewels worn by, ii. 263
    Suares, Mme, tries to promote opera for,
    ii. 280–1
    to sing at Venice, ii. 520–1
    Walpole, Bns, tells, that HW will forget
    to send her a dog, ii. 334
    Walsegg ['Walseck'] escorts, to burletta, i.
    130
    Williams's former flame, v. 194
Tessé, Comte de. *See* Froulay, René-Mans
    de (1736–1814)
Tessé, Comtesse de. *See* Noailles, Adrienne-
    Catherine de (1741–1814)
Test, The, weekly paper:
    Bubb Dodington said to be author of, v.
    38
    Pitt attacked by, v. 38
    Pitt, Elizabeth Villiers, sends brother's let-
    ters to, v. 46
Testa, Francesco Maria (d. 1773), Bp of Syra-
    cuse 1748–54; Abp of Monreale 1754–73:
    Malta refuses visitation from, iv. 405
Testas, Maria Anna (1715–95), m. Jan Nico-
    las Floris, Rijksgraaf van Nassau, Heer
    van Ouwerkerk:
    Cowper not allowed by, to use Auver-
    querque title, viii. 370
Tester:
    beds in Italian inns lack, ii. 315
    Mann anxious to hear that Louis XV has
    installed Comtesse du Barry under, vii. 90
Testoon; testoons:
    Florentine currency, ii. 348
    HW seeks, for Cts of Pomfret, i. 4
Tête naissante:
    Mesman exhibits, despite gray hair, viii.
    243–4
Teutschmaister:
    regiment of, ii. 164
Tewkesbury:
    borough of, trusts Gage, i. 255
Texel:
    Dutch fleet at, ix. 281, 311
Thaïs:
    HW would not distinguish between Frede-
    gonde and, viii. 35
Thamas Kouli-Kan, French ship:
    Noailles claims, after English seize it, viii.
    366
Thame:
    Damer, Mrs, makes bridge keystone mask
    of, ix. 576, 613

Thames, English ship:
French capture, v. 414–15

Thames River:
bridge built over, at Henley, ix. 576, 613
cannot be crossed at Richmond, viii. 47
Chute's trip on, from SH to London, iii. 497
England's Brenta, iii. 497
fleets could almost sail up, to Twickenham, because of deluges of rain, ix. 306
floods on, viii. 47
HW sighs for, vii. 491
HW's new terrace overlooks, iv. 16
HW walks by, v. 238
heat of, in hot spell, iv. 166
hot enough to bathe in, in February, viii. 442
Jacobites expect French expedition to go up, ii. 433
lane between SH and, flooded, viii. 47
Linton hardly needs, v. 129
'little turbulent ocean,' declaring its independence, ix. 306
Maltese cats to be drowned in, i. 482
masquerade to be held on, viii. 86
not easily crossed at Richmond, in high water, vii. 73
regatta to be held upon, viii. 112
Richmond's fireworks on, iv. 56, vi. 148–9
Robinson's letter mentions, v. 121
SH in an elbow of, ix. 532
SH overlooks, iii. 414
view of, from SH, iv. 380
Whitehall gardens slope to, iv. 56

Thames Street, London:
Ferdinand as popular as if born in, v. 227

Thanet, E. of. *See* Tufton, Sackville (1733–86); Tufton, Thomas (1644–1729)

Thatched House Tavern, near St James's:
Lord Mayor's guests escorted from, to Mansion House, vii. 200
Rockingham faction dines with Grenville at, vii. 115

Theatre; theatres:
English mania for, viii. 435
Florentine: closed for a year of mourning, vi. 340; closed on account of mourning, ii. 558; deserted, ii. 139; Florence unsociable during closing of, iii. 476–7; Gloucester, D. of, to attend, in Mann's coaches, viii. 291; Leopold amuses himself with masks at, in Carnevalino, viii. 343; Leopold disgusted with poor performances in, vi. 477; manager of, wants to give passion play in Lent, vii. 459; Mann does not attend, because of excessive cold, ix. 248; Mann enjoys evenings alone more than, v. 49; Mann's boxes at, decorated for D. and Ds of Cumberland, ix. 644; Mann's boxes at, offered to D. of Gloucester, viii. 291; Mann's boxes at, used by Lady Mary Coke, vii. 543; Mann's boxes at, Windham to use, ix. 33; Mann's boxes

at, *see also under* Teatro della Pergola; Mann's servants forbidden to go to, after his death, ix. 670; Maria Louisa attends, nightly, vi. 581; Maria Louisa dances at, vi. 491; masks everywhere in, ii. 391; masks not permitted in, ii. 139; not to open for a year, vi. 354; open, ix. 33; opening of, expected, ii. 113; 'smallest theatre,' Leopold attends low farces in, vi. 477; 'smallest theatre,' *nobili* act in, vi. 393; Stuart, Charlotte, appears at, in father's jewels, ix. 536; to be opened but Leopold and Maria Louisa will not be allowed to go to them, vi. 407; Young Pretender wants to decorate his boxes in, ix. 536; *see also* Teatro degl' Intrepidi; Teatro del Cocomero; Teatro della Pergola
HW never expects to die in, ix. 649
HW regards contemporary events as scenes in, ix. 387
HW thinks of kings and empresses as playing in, ix. 552
Italy's increased taste for, vii. 458
Leghorn: Langlois insulted in, iii. 365–6, 374; only theatre in Tuscany to be open for a year, vi. 354
London: audiences at, pelt candle-snuffers while waiting, viii. 348; Barry, Elizabeth, wears clogs to, i. 435; Bracegirdle, Mrs, wears pattens to, i. 435; deserted, iii. 177; England in 1778 like the half hour before the play begins at, viii. 348; Frederick, P. of Wales, attends, at Queensbury House, iii. 468–9; French, produces riots, iv. 100; George III attends, v. 461; Gunning sisters draw mobs to, iv. 311–12; HW attends, only twice in first five months of 1786, ix. 648; national calamities make no difference to attendance at, ix. 110; new, to be erected for people of fashion, ix. 317; Oldfield, Mrs, leaves, in chair, i. 435; pantomimes may be expelled from, ii. 538; Pertici wants engagement in, ii. 198; shut because of epidemic disorder, ix. 284; wild dukes in, iii. 317; *see also* Covent Garden Theatre; Drury Lane Theatre; Haymarket: King's Theatre in; Haymarket: little theatre in
Paris, mad foreigner wears ribbons of every order at, ix. 572
Pisan: ball and supper to have been given at, for D. of Gloucester, vii. 357; impresario of, has burletta performed, vii. 171; Mann to attend, vii. 72; new, vii. 353
Roman: furbished up by Benedict XIV, iv. 98; Pius VI rejects proposal to close, ix. 383; to reopen after Old Pretender's burial, vi. 385
Russian, head of, translated *Hamlet*, vi. 426
Scottish nobility and Cts of Dalkeith form, in Queensbury House, iii. 468

[Theatre; theatres, *continued*]
Sienese: burnt, ii. 46; new, iv. 391; York, D. of, hears cantata at, vi. 232
strolling companies make, in barns, viii. 371
Viennese, to be closed for a year, vi. 340
Westminster, used by D. of York, Lady Stanhope, and Delaval family, vi. 521
See also Actor; Opera; Plays; Shows
Théâtre des grecs. See under Brumoy, Pierre
Thebes, Abp of. *See* Borromeo, Vitaliano
Theobald, Lewis (1688–1744):
Thirlby gives notes to, for Shakespeare edition, iv. 215n
Theodore:
and Honoria, story of, ix. 247
Theodore, 'K. of Corsica.' *See* Neuhof, Théodore-Antoine, Bn de
Theologian:
Lami is, to Francis I, vi. 13
Maria Theresa gives Giustiniani patent as, vi. 465
Theresa, St. *See* Teresa
Therese (1723–43), of Bavaria:
Electress's bequest to, ii. 171
Thésée, French ship:
sunk, v. 351, 357
Thetford:
Conway M.P. for, vi. 238n
Thétis, French ship of India Company:
captured off Cape Finisterre, iii. 410
Thetis, man of war:
Mann receives news of Spanish fleet from, vi. 19
Thiers, Baron de. *See* Crozat, Louis-Antoine
Thinking:
equivalent to a headache to a man of quality, vi. 415
Thirlby, Styan (?1686–1753); Fellow of Jesus College, Cambridge:
career and publications of, iv. 215n
papers left by, to Sir Edward Walpole, iv. 215n
Theobald gets notes from, for Shakespeare edition, iv. 215n
Walpole, Sir Edward, gets customs place for, iv. 215n
—— wants, to write Sir Robert's life, iv. 215
Thirty-nine Articles:
clergy's adherence to, debated in Parliament, vii. 366, 376
Thisbe:
Coventry, Cts of, mispronounces, iv. 367
Thistle, Order of:
Carlisle invested with, by Charles Emmanuel III, vii. 59
—— obtains, vi. 554, vii. 14, 502
Cowper wants, vi. 555, vii. 502, 508, 511, 513
Dumfries receives, iv. 311
foreigner at Paris wears order of, viii. 361, ix. 572

Hyndford gets, i. 497
more than two Englishmen never receive, at one time, vi. 555
Northington receives, vii. 508, 511, 513, ix. 398n
Thistlethwayte, Alexander (?1717–71), M.P.:
bankrupt, vi. 268
brother leaves Norton estate to, iv. 238
brute, iv. **237,** 246
(?) Chute and Edward Louisa Mann write to, vi. 316
Chute urges, to pay Sophia Lucchi's fortune, vi. 268
Dagge authorized by, to write note to Galfridus Mann, vi. 265, 267
—— calls on, to get his signature to Lucchi paper, v. 420
—— engages, to pay Sophia Lucchi's fortune, v. 413
—— represents, as ready to pay Sophia Lucchi, vi. 278
—— threatens, with law suit, vi. 268
HW expects delays and evasions from, v. 421
inhuman, iv. 243
Lucchi, Angiola, gets annuity from, iv. 312n, vi. 265, 278–9
Mann writes to, about the Lucchi, iv. 330
Mann, Galfridus, more acceptable than Chute to, iv. 312
Whithed's bequest to Sophia Lucchi withheld by, iv. 246, 254, 312, vi. 265, 268, 278–9
Thistlethwayte, Rev. Robert (ca 1721–67):
brother dragged out by, to hunt, iv. **237**
brother's bequest to, iv. 238
brute, iv. 237, 246, 288
(?) Chute and Edward Louisa Mann write to, vi. 316
Chute urges, to pay Sophia Lucchi's fortune, vi. 268
country squire parson, vi. 268
Dagge authorized by, to write to Galfridus Mann, vi. 265, 267
—— engages, to pay Sophia Lucchi's fortune, v. 413
—— represents, as ready to pay Sophia Lucchi, vi. 278
—— threatens, with law suit, vi. 268
HW expects delays and evasions from, v. 421
inhuman, iv. 243
legal devices of, to avoid paying Sophia Lucchi's legacy, vi. 288
Lucchi, Angiola, gets annuity from, iv. 312n, vi. 265, 278–9
Mann, Galfridus, more acceptable than Chute to, iv. 312
money will be paid by, to Sophia Lucchi, v. 421
not docile, vi. 268
Whithed's bequest to Sophia Lucchi withheld by, iv. 246, 254, 312, vi. 265, 268, 278–9, 288–9

Thomas, St (fl. 1st cent. A.D.):
figure of, in painting of Henry VII's marriage, iv. 390n
Thomas, Sir Edmund (1712–67), 3d Bt, 1723; M.P.:
becomes lord of Trade, v. 490
petition against, i. 318
Thomas, John (1691–1766), Bp of Lincoln, 1744; of Salisbury, 1761:
Carteret makes, bishop, ii. 537–8
Keene dines with, when told of new bishopric, iv. 347
Walpole, Sir Robert, called on by, ii. 537
Thomas, John (1696–1781), Bp of Peterborough, 1747; of Salisbury, 1757; of Winchester, 1761:
George III's tutor, iv. 348
read prayers to George II at Leicester House, iv. 348
Thomas, John (1712–93), Bp of Rochester 1774–93:
Amelia, Ps, has use of gallery of, in Westminster Abbey, ix. 648
Thomas, Mary (d. 1832), m. (ca 1772) John Zoffany:
marriage of, perhaps bigamous, viii. 539
Thomas, Sir Noah (1720–92), M.D., 1753; Kt, 1775:
Chute treated by, viii. 210
consulted in Rockingham's last illness, ix. 287
Thomond, Cts of. See Seymour, Lady Elizabeth (1685–1734)
Thomond, E. of. See O'Brien, Henry (1688–1741); Wyndham-O'Brien, Percy (?1723–74)
Thompson, Rev. Anthony (d. 1756), English chargé d'affaires at Paris; Dean of Raphoe 1744–56:
Amelot notifies, of France's declaration of war against England, ii. 422
France's answer to, about Young Pretender, ii. 409
HW to hear Mann's news explained by, i. 115
Irish dean, ii. 422n
Mann's correspondence with, ii. 397, 404
——'s letters forwarded by, ii. 380, 397, 412
politeness expected from, despite war with France, ii. 283
Waldegrave's chaplain, ii. 422n
Thompson, B.B., mayor of Kingston-upon-Hull, 1779–80:
(?) Orford thanked by, ix. 355
Thompson, Edward (1696–1742), M.P.:
voted for, as commissioner, i. 437
Thompson, Richard, printer:
arrested, vii. 280
Thompson, Thomas (d. 1763), quack physician:
nerves treated by, iv. 389
Winnington treated by, iii. 249

Thompson. See also Thomson
Thomson, James ((1700–48), poet:
Seasons, The, HW prefers Lee to, iii. 27
Tancred and Sigismunda, iii. 27
'Thor':
HW's term for SH, v. 433
Thoresby, D. of Kingston's seat:
fire at, iv. 321
Thorn:
at Glastonbury, viii. 148
Thornton, Bonnell (1724–68), satirist:
City Latin by, satirizes bridge inscription, v. 449n
Thornton, William (?1712–65), M.P.:
Parliamentary debate by, on Scotch Bill, x. 32
Thorold, Charles:
Roman Catholicism abjured by, at St Martin's, London, to secure inheritance, vi. 380
Thorold, Jane (d. 1759), m. Col. Daniel Leighton; Bedchamber woman to Ps of Wales:
warrant request not signed by, iii. 175
Thorold, Sir Nathaniel (d. 1764), cr. (1741) Bt:
dies at Naples, vi. 380
Thou, Jacques-Auguste de (1553–1617), 'Thuanus':
Canterbury, Abp of, quotes, i. 301
Thoughts on the Cause of the Present Discontents. See under Burke, Edmund
Thoughts on the Difficulties and Distresses. See under King, John (ca 1753–1823)
Thrale, Mrs. See Salusbury, Hester Lynch
Thrale, Henry (ca 1729–81):
great brewer, ix. 633n
widow of, ix. 611n, 633n
Thread stockings. See under Stocking
Threads:
Charles III pulls wigs off with, vii. 238
Three Hours after Marriage. See under Pope, Alexander
Three Princes of Serendip, The, fairy tale:
serendipity derived from, iv. 407–8, x. 34–5
Throat. See Sore throat
Throne:
Bristol, E. of, revived by prospect of, vi. 450
Charlotte stands under, v. 531
Mogul's, of gold, ix. 545
Thrush:
Mann does not know meaning of, iv. 242
occurrences of, iii. 250, iv. 232
Thuanus. See Thou
Thubières. See Tubières
Thucydides (d. ca 400 B.C.), historian:
Boston may produce counterpart of, viii. 62
Thumasin, ——, Maj.:
captured at Velletri, ii. 491
Thun, Josef Maria von (d. 1763), Bp of Gurk, 1741; of Passau, 1761; Austrian minister at Rome, 1740:

[Thun, Josef Maria von, *continued*]

Acquaviva obtains Young Pretender's passports from, ii. 378

Benedict XIV hears news from, i. 282

—— rebukes, at audience, i. 201

——'s memorial from, fictitious answer to, i. 442, 445–6

Braitwitz communicates with, at Rome, i. 282

——'s correspondence with, ii. 42

English captain does not know how to address, ii. 461

English captains dine with, iii. 12

Licanian captures estimated by, ii. 460

Mann flattered by, ii. 461

—— informed by, of Young Pretender's escape from Rome, ii. 373, 380

—— receives courier from, ii. 453

—— satisfies demand of, for English naval help, ii. 471

——'s correspondence with, ii. 474, 476

Mathews's friendship to Austria doubted by, ii. 476

Pontano claimed by, from prison, ii. 56

Traun and Vienna to receive couriers from, ii. 56

Vienna refers letters of, to Lobkowitz, ii. 515

Young Pretender's departure prophesied by, i. 101

Thurlow, Edward (1731–1806), cr. (1778) Bn Thurlow; attorney-general 1771–8; lord chancellor, 1778:

administration might have been wrecked by, to satisfy Opposition, viii. 447

attorney-general, vii. 269

Bathurst succeeded by, as lord chancellor, viii. 385

Burke calls, 'iron Pluto,' ix. 684

George III confers with, ix. 683, 684, 685

—— consults, about C.J. Fox and George IV, ix. 381–2

—— insists on keeping, as chancellor, despite opposition of North and D. of Portland, ix. 381

—— refers Ds of Kingston's *nolle prosequi* to, viii. 162

——'s wishes to patch up administration seconded by, ix. 379

government to be assumed by, ix. 683

Great Seal may be given back to, ix. 460

HW thinks, will not succeed Rockingham, ix. 289

Kingston, Ds of, opposed by, at trial, viii. 193, 196

Mann's brother's will to be inspected by, viii. 258

Parliamentary reform resisted by, ix. 273

remains lord chancellor, ix. 262

ridiculous in House of Lords, ix. 407

Rockingham approached by, to form ministry, ix. 256

Roman Catholic toleration disliked by, ix. 66–7

thieves steal Great Seal from, ix. 481

weeps when with George III, ix. 684

Thurn-Valsassina, Gräfin. *See* Reischach, Gabriele

Thurn-Valsassina, Anton (1723–1806), Graf; army officer; Grand Maître 1771–90:

Barbantane writes to, viii. 394

brother and Leopold accompanied by, vi. **350**

captain of the *garde noble*, vi. 398

captain of the *garde noble* and *grand maître*, vii. 253

Gloucester, D. of, receives, vii. 35⅄

Mann told by, about sales of Grand Ducal furniture, ix. 231

Thurn-Valsassina, Franz (*or* Johann Franz Joseph) (1718–66), Graf; Tuscan Grand Chambellan 1765–6; army officer:

Botta at odds with, vi. 398

brother of, vi. 350

death of: HW admires Leopold for mourning, vi. 404; increases Lenten solemnity in Florence, vi. 400; soon after his marriage, vi. 398

diplomats call upon, at Florence, vi. **337**

Leopold's former governor, vi. 398

Lorenzi and Viviani excluded from antechamber of, vi. 346

Mann escorts Murray to apartment of, vi. 350

Thurot, François (1727–60), French naval capt.:

departure of, from Dunkirk, said to indicate beginning of invasion, v. 349

fleet of: captures Carrickfergus, v. 371–4; carried to Isle of Man, v. 376; English frigates capture, in Irish Channel, v. 376, 385–6; Gothenburg reached by, v. 346–7; Ostend said to be visited by, v. 349; raids Islay, v. 371–2; said to set sail, v. 338; Scotland threatened by, v. 328, 352

HW glad that Mann has got letter about, v. 389

Jennings might be carried off by, v. 381

killed, v. 376

newspapers describe birth and apostacy of, v. 381–2

re-embarkation of, from Carrickfergus, v. 376

Swedish troops might be enlisted by, v. 347

Thursday nights:

Mann's assemblies on: garden incident discredits, iii. 497–9, iv. 447; Mann cured by, of fever, ii. 300; Mann gives up, iii. 501; Mann's entertainments to be confined to, ii. 285–6; Mann's terreno illuminated on, iii. 490; opened by a concert, iii. 421; popular, ii. 289, 297, iii. 279

Richecourt gives assemblies on, iv. 446

Thynne, Frances (ca 1699–1754), m. (1715) Algernon Seymour, styled E. of Hertford; 7th D. of Somerset, 1748:

Bootle woos, iv. 183

HW imagines presents that would be given to, according to Italian customs, ii. 141

husband's letter to George II resigns pension of, as lady of the Bedchamber to Q. Caroline, i. **346**

son's death distresses, ii. 522

Sturrock's correspondence with, ii. 544

Thynne, Thomas (1734–96), 3d Vct Weymouth, 1751; cr. (1789) M. of Bath:

administration might have been wrecked by, to satisfy Opposition, viii. 447

Cabinet may be re-entered by, vii. 424

circular letter of: about French provocation and George III's messages to Parliament, viii. 373–4; about loss of 3 mails from Italy, viii. 468; about P. Octavius's birth and English victories, viii. 454

Conway to be succeeded by, as secretary of state, vi. 569, 571, 578

George III adds, to Bedchamber, v. **460**

good-natured, vi. 578

HW's letters may be opened during secretaryship of, vi. 570

Hillsborough succeeds, as secretary of state, viii. 533, 534

Irish lord lieutenancy resigned by, vi. 311

letter of, illegally printed, vii. 77

Longleat visited by, viii. 534

Murray's letters dispatched to, by Mann, viii. 380, 443

—— told by, that his secrets can be ciphered by Mann and conveyed by post, ix. 42

Noailles notifies, of American-French treaty, viii. 363–4

Northumberland to be succeeded by, as Lord Lieutenant of Ireland, vi. 303

Pitt thought to be in league with, vii. 259

Privy Seal coveted by, vii. 310

Rochford succeeded by, as secretary of state for southern province, viii. 142

Rockingham refuses Shelburne's request to ask Cabinet post for, ix. 261

Sandwich succeeds, as secretary of state, but in northern province, vii. 255

Seals resigned by, vii. 255, viii. 534

Shelburne succeeded by, as secretary of state, vii. 62

Tiara:

cardinals accept, though about to die, viii. 432

Charlotte's, of diamonds, v. 529

papal, Galluzzi's history may discredit, ix. 80

Tiber:

Atrisco tries to cross, ii. 443–4

Borghese's valet drowns in, iii. 444

bridge over, demolished, ii. 444, 525

fight at Ponte Molle on, ii. 531–2

Lobkowitz to bridge, ii. 437

Pius VI cannot cleanse Ds of Kingston with holy water from, viii. 126

Spaniards control, ii. 533

sturgeon from, vi. 229

Tiberius (Tiberius Claudius Nero Cæsar) (42 B.C.–A.D. 37), Roman Emperor A.D. 14–37:

Giovanni Gastone de' Medici, the counterpart of, i. 273n

Tibet, Lama of. See dPal-ldan ye-šes

Tibullus:

character in *Ballet de la Paix*, ii. 496

Tickell, Richard (1751–93):

Anticipation, drafts of speeches that would probably be made were printed in, viii. 528n

Ticket, Lottery. See Lottery ticket

Ticket, opera. See *under* Opera

Ticonderoga:

Americans said to be besieged in, viii. 261

Amherst takes, v. 326, 333

Burgoyne captures, viii. 323, 329

English defeat at: v. 233, 241, 246; Paris fireworks to celebrate, v. 246

Tide-waiters:

Newcastle, D. of, restores, to office, vi. 323

Tidone:

battle of, iii. 291, 302

Tie wig. See *under* Wig

Tiger; tigers:

element of, in human composition, vii. 192, 194, 201, 387

Zanetti's intaglio of: HW wants, v. 562; Mann often reminds Murray about, vi. 116; Murray has not found, vi. 14

Tighe, T. (of the Temple):

Seymour-Conway's letter sent to, with abbreviated address, ix. 608

Tiles:

Dutch, wallpaper imitates, at SH, iv. 382

storm injures, on New Year's Day, viii. 431

Tilliburdin. See Tullibardine

Tillot. See Du Tillot

Tillotson, Dr John (1630–94), Abp of Canterbury, 1691:

Birch's life of, iv. 282n

Russell, Lady Rachel, urges, to accept archbishopric, iv. 282n

Tilson, Christopher (1670–1742), M.P.:

death of, ascribed to examination by Secret Committee, i. 33

Fane succeeds, i. 33

Tilt Yard, the:

conversation at, x. 14

Timber:

France needs, for navy, ix. 4

French hope to get, from Corsica, vii. 47

See also Tree; Wood

Time:

HW's lessons from, viii. 301

Italian way of computing: i. 32n; changed at Florence to French, iv. 26

See also Old people

Times:

'make men, not men times,' vii. 514

Tin:

case of, with éloge of the deceased, put into tombs in Italy, v. 170

'Tinca nera.' *See* Pertici, 'Tinca Nera'

Tindal, Matthew (ca 1653–1738), deist:

Bolingbroke to be classed with, iv. 454

Tinker:

Clement XIV son of, vii. 117

Tinsel:

HW compares glory to, viii. 327

royal velvet and ermine might just as well be actor's, ix. 624

worn by humbler Florentine ladies, ix. 175

Tip; tips:

actors at Calais expect, vii. 519–20

Amalia's, i. 64–5

at christening, viii. 199, 219

Pulteney family niggardly about, iii. 443

York, D. of, gives, to Lucchese servants, vi. 222

'Tipkin, Biddy.' *See under* Steele, Sir Richard: *Tender Husband*

Tippet; tippets:

fur, Princesse de Craon wears, ii. 109

HW sends, to Pandolfini, i. 45, 47, 52

Tipping, Lady. *See* Cheeke, Anne (d. 1728)

Tipping, Letitia (d. 1779), m. (1725) Samuel Sandys, cr. (1743) Bn Sandys:

conundrum on 'queer arse' of, iii. 28

HW mentions, i. 475

Orford title of great-uncle of, i. **333**

Walpoles notified by, to quit house in Downing St, i. 478

Wilmington offers Downing St house to, i. 478

Tipping:

at brothel, viii. 413

English custom of, imitated by Duc and Duchesse de Mirepoix, iv. 89

women of fashion never practise, iv. 89

See also Tip; tips

Tisiphone:

East India Company should be corrected by, vii. 442

HW's name for Mrs Galfridus Mann, v. 129

HW's term for Maria Theresa, v. 498

Tissot, Simon-André (1728–97), Swiss physician:

Carlisle, Cts of, advised by, to go to Rome, vii. 447

Herbert, Lady Charlotte, to have consulted, at Lausanne, ix. 493

Morice's motions directed by, ix. 435

Tissue:

Craon's reception of *toison d'or* characterized by, i. 20

Edward I's, found perfect in his grave, viii. 4

Titchfield, M. of. *See* Bentinck, William Henry Cavendish (1738–1809)

Tithes:

Talbot takes, in kind, iii. 176

Titian (Tiziano Vecellio) (1477–1576), painter:

alleged Danæ by, bought by Young from Hugford, iv. 330

'Concert' (attributed to), vi. 179, 246, 291

England does not yet outdo, viii. 92

Jackson's prints imitate, iv. 381

painting by: in Pitti palace, banished because the figure's back is turned, vi. 179; of Venus, ill copied in Zoffany's painting of Tribune, viii. 527; of Venus, would not please Q. Charlotte, viii. 540

Vasari's portrait of Bianca Cappello worthy of, iv. 407

Title; titles:

HW's reflections on futility of, ix. 583

Title page:

Smith's reading does not go beyond, i. 467

Tito, Santi di (1536–1603), painter:

Mann has 'Last Supper,' by, copied for Chute, iv. 529

Titus Flavius Sabinus Vespasianus (40–81), Roman Emperor 79–81:

Jews enjoy their Ranelagh, when their Knightsbridge is occupied by, ix. 317

Tivoli:

Atrisco halts near, ii. 444

HW and Gray visit, i. 26

HW compares Twickenham to, iv. 16

temple at, copied for frieze of Houghton picture gallery, ii. 63

Toad-eater:

dowagers usually accompanied by, iii. 298

Toasts:

Hamiltons never make, to those beneath the rank of earl, iv. 339

Mann's, at Leghorn, iii. 151, 152

Tobacco:

duty on, at Florence, iv. 389

English addiction to, iii. 272

pigtail, Ferrers uses, on way to execution, v. 401

sparks of, might explode a bomb, v. 155

Tuscan trade in, iv. 389

Tobago:

taken by French, ix. 172

Tobit:

Castiglione's painting of, *see under* Castiglione, Benedetto

Tocha, La, ship:

in Spanish fleet, i. 286

Tocsin:

at Monte Santa Maria, iv. 423

Toft, Mary (ca 1701–63), 'rabbit-woman':

no successors to, ii. 124

Toilet; toilets:

Finch, Lady Charlotte, displays, at accouchement, iii. 442

gold, ii. 170

Toison d'Or:

Choiseul and Fuentes receive, v. 560

Craon receives, i. 11, 16, 20

Leopold II gives, to son, as Joseph II's deputy, vii. 55, 59

—— thinks that English honours are as common as, vii. 502

Maria Theresa bribes Gen. Brown with, v. 72

secretary of, *see* Nenny, Cornelius von

secretary to bring, from Vienna to Florence for Francis II, vii. 1

Toland, John (1670–1722); deist:

Bolingbroke to be classed with, iv. 454

Tollemache, Hon. George (1744–60):

godparents of, ii. 431

Tollemache, Lionel (1708–70), 4th E. of Dysart:

Ham House the residence of, v. 438n

son denied money by, to get married, v. 438–9

Tollemache, Lionel (1734–99), styled Lord Huntingtower 1740–70; 5th E. of Dysart, 1770:

Mann guesses that appearance of, outweighs his poverty, v. 446

Walpole, Charlotte, weds, v. 438–9

Tollendal, Comte de. *See* Lally, Thomas-Arthur

'Tom, HW's old'. *See* Barney, Tom

Tomb; tombs:

Italian, contain éloges, v. 170

sepulchral altar, *see under* Altar

Tom's Coffee House:

Edwin and Gage at, i. 296

Spectator mentioned by man at, iii. 565

Tonnay, Geoffroy de:

wife of, loved by Rigaut de Barbezieux, v. 169

Tonnelier. *See* Le Tonnelier

Tonson, Jacob jr (d. 1767), *or* Richard (d. 1772), M.P.:

Ashton's books sold by, iv. 165

HW meets, at Onslow's, iv. 165

Tonson (formerly Hull); William (1724–87), cr. (1783) Bn Riversdale; Irish M.P.:

peerage of, ix. 433

Tonsure:

abbé receives, i. 62

Tooke, Rev. John Horne (1736–1812), M.P.:

House of Commons accuses, of attacking Norton, vii. 555–6

Wilkes defeats, vii. 314

—— disputes with, vii. **263**, 274

Tooth; teeth:

Churchill loses, i. 271

Clement XIV's, fall out, viii. 43

Craon, Princesse de, loses, iv. 213

false, ii. 289

Goldsworthy, Martha Carolina, to cut, i. 351

Gondi, Mme, loses, ii. 86–7

man draws, and puts them in again, iv. 291–2

Norton's, pulled, ix. 40

Oglethorpe's, gone, ix. 570

Salimbeni loses, i. 116

——'s, fast again, i. 132

transplanting of, ii. 324

Turk, Martha, has, black, viii. 295

William Frederick, P., cuts, viii. 315

See also Dentistry

Tooth-ache:

occurrences of, ii. 324, iv. 87

Vorontsov, Mme, pretends to have, v. 248

Topaja, Villa della:

Craon to take Mann, Chute, and Whithed to, i. 443

Topaz; topazes:

George II gives, to maids of honour, iv. 112

Mann has seal cut on, for Rowley, iii. 9

Toppaia. *See* Topaja

Torbay:

Brest fleet near, ii. 398, 407

Darby reported at, ix. 186

—— returns to, ix. 182

Hardy's fleet at, viii. 500

Torch; torches:

Florentines use, to watch floods, iii. 131

Neapolitan cardinals forbidden by Spain to light, for Francis I's election, iii. 183

priests carry, at Electress's funeral, ii. 173

wax: Lorenzi illuminates windows with, iii. 14; Neapolitans told to use, in carrying out San Gennaro, viii. 541; Old Pretender does not use, to celebrate Francis I's election, iii. 184

Torgau:

battle of, v. 452, 456, 459, 463

Tories:

adherents gained by, in Parliament, iii. 4

appointed to Admiralty, i. 356, 363, 366

Argyll pleases, i. 366

army increases opposed by, in Parliament, i. 410

Beaufort's defection may affect, vii. 174

Berkeley, Norborne, is, v. 460

Country Girl, The, mentions, i. 24

country squires of, defeat land tax, vi. 489

Court aided by clergy and, to infatuate England, viii. 491

Deerhurst betrayed by, i. 211

Egmont not forgiven by, for desertion, iv. 32

Fazackerley a member of, vi. 42

Fox, C.J., by violence might provoke, against him and North, ix. 379

Fox, Henry, and Pitt hated by, iv. 510

Fox, Henry, will alienate, vi. 93

Frederick, P. of Wales, leagued with, iv. 3

George II rejects, i. 363, 365

George III appoints, to Bedchamber, v. 460

Gower treated with deference by, ii. 141

Haddock would anger, if he let Spanish fleet escape, i. 219

Hanoverian troops not discussed by, in House of Lords, ii. 141

in House of Commons, iii. 4

investigation of Port Mahon's fall languidly

[Tories, continued]
pursued by, for fear of uniting D. of Newcastle and Fox, v. 56
Labour in Vain mentions, ii. 20
Mathews opposed by, in Mediterranean investigation, for opposition to them in Monmouthshire election, iii. 33
Minorcan investigation to be used by,
against ministry, v. 77
Newdigate attended by, in Grosvenor Square
on way to Brentford election, ii. 25
new Opposition not liked by, iii. 370
newspaper of, ii. 33
Northey is, v. 460
North followed by, against Shelburne, ix.
379
opposition from: expected, ii. 564; in Parliament, iii. 202
Parliamentary voting avoided by, ii. 383,
ix. 19
Pelham must bring in, ii. 537
Pitt abandoned by, in demand for review
of Spanish negotiations, v. 553
—— supported by, in attempt to oust Hessian troops, v. 33–4
Pitt, George, belongs to, v. 460
positions refused by, ii. 550
preferment of, may upset government, v.
465
prerogative supported by, viii. 492
Prowse leads, iv. 32
public measures not opposed by, i. 390
Pulteney pretends to join, ii. 49
rancour of, hoodwinks English people, viii.
491
Strange usually votes with, iv. 32
subsidiary treaties opposed by, in House of
Commons, iv. 300
too contemptible to hold office, vi. 295
Wales, Ps of, suggested by, as regency
member, vi. 299
Walpole, Sir Robert, not to be persecuted
by, i. 336
—— resented by, i. 363
Whigs may detain Hessian troops to thwart,
v. 33–4
Whigs say, no longer exist, i. 337, 363
Tories, American (Loyalists):
Carlisle disapproves of sacrifice of, at peace
treaty, ix. 365
Cornwallis's surrender terms said to protect, ix. 211
English invasion of Carolina might be aided
by, viii. 157–8
Tornaquinci, Abate Giovanni Antonio (1680–
1764), Tuscan secretary of state:
aged 80 and very weak, v. 62
childish from old age, v. 107
custom house to be ordered by, to release
HW's picture, i. 162
Electress leaves annuity to, ii. 169
Francis I's letter from, without vowels, v.
62, 85
health of, put to bed and bled, v. 62

incapable of business, v. 84–5
Mann asks, about Silva's authority, i. 180
—— hears from, about Leghorn earthquake, i. 293
—— receives apologies from, for letter, iv.
146
——'s dispute with, over citizenship of
English at Leghorn, iv. 266–7
office of, i. 57
Pucci writes to, of English earthquake, iv.
143
Richecourt forces, to write severe letter to
Mann, iv. 146
—— formerly abused by, to Mann, iv. 267
——'s opposition to Mann discussed by,
with Rinuccini and Braitwitz, ii. 10
secretary of state and third of Regency, v.
62
valet-de-chambre of, used to get ten paul
pieces for issuing passports, v. 482
Vienna neglects, v. 107
Torre, La. *See* La Torre
Torre di Mezza Via:
camp at, ii. 531
Torreggiani, Marchesa. *See* Capponi, Maria
Settimia
Torreggiani *or* Torriggiani, Luca (d. 1770),
Marchese:
marriage of, iii. 506
Torreggiani, Luigi Maria (1697–1777), cardinal, 1753:
Almada's paper attacks, v. 423
book burned by order of, v. 476–7
Bourbon courts would exclude, from Papal
councils, vii. 16
Clement XIII aided by, against anti-Jesuit
champions, v. 475
congregation orders, to bid prelates pay no
royal honours to Young Pretender, vi. 392
Corsini subject of complaints of, to Clement
XIII, v. 425
courier from Lisbon expected by, v. 430
dying, iv. **463**
epitaph for, v. 436–7
foreign courts offended by, vii. 119
French, Neapolitan, and Spanish ministers
refuse to negotiate through, vii. 35
Jesuits befriended by, v. 436
Jesuits threaten to withdraw pension from,
if he does not make Clement XIII yield, v.
425
plot allegedly instigated by, with Acciaioli
and bastard brothers, against Portuguese
king, v. 475
Portuguese king offended by, v. 348, 425
Portuguese rupture with, permanent, v. 437
St-Odile refuses to wait in ante-chamber of,
vi. 573
York, Cardinal, receives billet from, vi. 388,
391
Torres y Morales, Rodrigo (ca 1687–1755),
admiral; Marqués de Matallana:
Cartagena abandoned by, with fleet and
treasure, on Vernon's approach, i. 71

treasure said to have been taken by, to Cadiz, i. 83

Torri, Flaminio (1621–61), painter:
Guido's pupil, i. 268, ii. 214
'Magdalen' by: Chute likes, i. 268; companion to Guido's head, i. 241, ii. 214; Penny sends, to Mann for HW, i. 268

Torriano, Lady. See Mann, Eleanor (d. 1789)

Torriano, Sir John (d. 1778), Kt, 1755:
caveat entered by, against James Mann's will, vi. 240, 241–2, 245, 247, viii. 271
father-in-law excludes, vii. 51, 112
Mann family quarrels with, vi. 245
wife of, vi. 242n

Torrigiani. See Torreggiani

Törring-Jettenbach, Ignatius Felix Joseph (ca 1679–1763), Graf von, general:
capture of, rumoured, i. 289
relief force of, dispersed, i. 289

Torrington, Vct. See Byng, Sir George (1664–1773); Byng, George (1740–1812); Byng, Pattee (1699–1747)

Torso:
Gaddi's, at Uffizi, ix. 170

Tort de la Sonde, Barthélemy (1738–1818), Guines's secretary:
Guines's law suit with, viii. 100

Tortoise:
Cumberland, D. of, compared with, iv. 121

Tortoise-shell:
snuffbox of, ix. 501

Tortola, West Indian island:
lands in, claimed by Mann family: Allet tells Mann about, viii. 168, 200, 220; Duane and Hull seek new grant for, viii. 200; HW never heard of, viii. 176; Mann, Edward, had grant of, viii. 168, 199–200; Mann, Edward Louisa, had no right to alienate, from family, viii. 173; Mann, Edward Louisa, inherits, from Edward Mann, viii. 173; Mann, Edward Louisa, leaves, to Mary Mann, viii. 168, 202; Mann, Horace II, consults Duane about, viii. 181; Mann, Mary, applies for grant of lands in, viii. 264; probably worthless during American crisis, viii. 206–7; revert to the Crown, viii. 202, 206, 264; visitor to, tells Mann of value of, viii. 169, 200

Tortona ('Tortonne'):
besiegers set fire to parts of, iii. 100
Charles Emmanuel III insists on evacuation of, iii. 279
Gages approaches, iii. 41, 84, 292
Genoese galleys try to supply provisions for, iii. 344
siege of: Charles Emmanuel III does not raise, iii. 100; French and Spaniards may begin, iii. 36, 75, 84; Maillebois announces, iii. 89
Spaniards may retire to, iii. 267
surrender of, iii. 100

Torture:
army officers at Metz broken upon wheel, v. 382–3

Corsican patriots, racked on the wheel by French, vii. 148
Damiens subjected to, v. 59, 79–80, vi. 147

'Tory,' HW's black spaniel:
wolf devours, in Alps, i. 257

Toscanelli, Francesco Antonio:
Dissertatio super controversiis . . . Cybo, i. 34

Tosier. See Tozier

'To the Earl of Bath.' See under Williams, Sir Charles Hanbury

Totila (d. 552), K. of the Ostrogoths:
Jackson's prints seem coeval with, iv. 381

Totnes:
mayor of, forwards to Sir Robert Walpole a letter from Frederick, P. of Wales, recommending candidate, i. 299

Touche, La. See Gervaise de la Touche

Touillet. See Trouillet

Toulon:
armament of, supposedly to aid Spain against Algiers, viii. 179
Boscawen might be forbidden to bombard, v. 302
——'s fleet cruises near, v. 297
capture of, unlikely, iii. 358
Clement XIV's ship takes D. of Cumberland to, vii. 566
convoy of, escapes, iii. 277
Corsica well situated to overlook, v. 37
English fleet should have blocked the French at, iv. 564–5
English invasion might threaten, v. 223
fleet of: alarms HW for Mann's safety, ii. 384; blown back, viii. 383; Boscawen demolishes, v. 326; Boscawen may engage, in battle, v. 318; Boscawen to bottle up, v. 292; England said to be destination of, v. 328; English fleet should have destroyed, iv. 564; English preparations against, vii. 478; estimated, i. 286, ii. 396; France alarmed lest Howe and Byron encircle, viii. 394; gets no treasure, i. 36; goes to America, viii. 386; Hawke watches, iv. 583; Mann surprised to see himself quoted on sailing of, viii. 380; Mathews said to have injured, ii. 402, 403; may be bound for Minorca, viii. 375, 380–1; may have gone to America to attack Howe, viii. 381; may intercept ship to Leghorn, vi. 88; may try to reach West Indies, v. 318; Philip, Don, may be accompanied by, i. 215; preparation of, iv. 540–1, 545, 558, v. 263–4, vii. 261; prepares to attack Russian fleet, vii. 474; reaches Barcelona, i. 190; returns, i. 46, iv. 581; said to have sailed, viii. 376; Saunders pursues, from Malta towards the Levant, v. 431; Spanish fleet joined by, i. 269; threatens to expel Hawke from Mediterranean, iv. 587; to be kept in reserve instead of attacking Boscawen, v. 303; to come out, ii. 443, iv. 545; to join Brest fleet, ii. 393, 396, 404, 423; Townshend avoids, iii. 324–5; see also under La Clue

[Toulon, *continued*]

France does not make war preparations at, vii. 244

French and Spanish fleets at, ii. 93

French and Spanish fleets plan Italian invasion from, ii. 370–1

French and Spanish fleets preparing to leave, ii. 359

French and Spanish fleets said to go to, from Spezia, i. 322–3

French assemble expedition at, ii. 106

French fleet goes to, from Hyères, i. 309

French may try to reach Corsica from, iv. 588

French transports at, iv. 545

French transports go to, for more troops, iv. 552

Fronsac brings news of St Philip's surrender to, iv. 572

La Clue reaches, v. 197

Lage's fleet at, iii. 253

letters from, received at Leghorn, viii. 461

Mathews approaches, ii. 447

—— bottles up French fleet at, ii. 15

—— may attack Court at, ii. 443

—— threatens, ii. 463

Medley leaves ships near, iii. 334

Mirepoix's letters from, v. 141

Noel goes to, to spy on French, iv. 536

Osborne's fleet menaces, v. 135

second squadron sails from, viii. 397

Stormont to visit, vii. 25

Townshend may command squadron off, iii. 376

trade at, interrupted, v. 123

Toulongeon, Comte de. *See* Chavignard, Anne-Théodore

Toulouse:

Mann, Horace II and Lady Lucy, visit, viii. 239, 251

Toulouse, Parliament of:

Beauvau thought to be improper person to suppress, vii. 321–2

Tounson, Robert:

Customs place granted to, x. 52

Toupet:

Charlotte, Q., refuses to curl, v. 528

Tour, La. *See* La Tour

Touraine, D. of. *See* Douglas, Archibald (ca 1370–1424)

Touriers:

Court preceded by, with baggage, vii. 108

Tournai:

battle of, since called battle of Fontenoy, iii. 42n

English capture, iii. 52

French besiege, iii. 39

French capture, iii. 61

governor of, *see* Dorth

Tournament; tournaments:

England celebrates with, iv. 71

Florence plans, for Maria Josefa, vi. 525

of bears, at Hanover, iv. 200

Temple not fond of, v. 346

Tournay. *See* Tournai

Tournelle, Marquise de la. *See* Mailly-Nesle, Marie-Anne de

Tourneur, Le. *See* Le Tourneur

Toussaint, Franz Joseph (d. 1762), Freiherr von ('All Saints'; 'All the Saints'):

bigot, iv. 445

Dumesnil accuses, of heresy for avoiding Mass, iii. 491

father-in-law of, i. 406

Florence suddenly visited by, to confer with Acton and Mill, iv. 97–8

Francis I and Richecourt reconciled by, i. 235, 490

Francis I's favourite, i. 189n, (?) 328, iii. 7, iv. 97

Mill recommended by, iii. 407

——'s scheme to destroy East India Company quashed by, iv. 101

orders from, to fire on Florence in case of insurrection, i. 349

Richecourt favoured by, i. 189n, 235, 490, ii. 363

Tuscany to be temporarily administered by, v. 107

Uguccioni hopes for preferment through, ii. 455

Walpole, Bns, said to court, through Richecourt, ii. 210

Wasner instigated by, to plead for Bns Walpole, ii. 194

Tower, at SH. *See under* Strawberry Hill

Tower Hill:

Mann hopes that Young Pretender will be hanged at, ii. 421

Tower of London:

Bastille no longer resembled by, vi. 312

Belle-Isle might be confined in, ii. 563

Burke says he deserves to be sent to, vii. 170

chaplain of, *see* Harby, Rev. Edward (ca 1700–61); Humphreys, Cornelius

constable of, *see* lieutenant of

curiosities of, i. 233

deputy lieutenant of, *see* Williamson, Adam

gentleman gaoler of, *see* Fowler, Abraham

'governor' of, *see* lieutenant of

Granville might be sent to, after another upheaval, iii. 213

guards from, disperse London mob, vii. 7

guns of: celebrate d'Estaing's defeat, viii. 545; Mann expects to hear, in honour of Eliott and Howe, ix. 340

HW jokes about being sent to, i. 233

Henry VIII's codpiece in, i. 233

Kelly escapes from, iii. 153n

lieutenant and constable of, *see* Cornwallis, Charles (1700–62); Cornwallis, Charles (1738–1805)

lions in, i. 233, vi. 135

London officials may be put in, for remonstrance, vii. 197

Lovat buried in, iii. 386n
mobs carry Sir Robert Walpole's effigy to, i. 390
prisoners in: Balmerinoch, Bn, iii. 281, 282, 296, 299; Cameron, Archibald, iv. 384; Cecil, William, ii. 408; Cromarty, E. of, iii. 272, 281; Crosby, Brass, vii. 291; Derwentwater, E. of, iii. 180–1; Ferrers, E., v. 374, 388, 397, 398–9, 408; Gordon, Lord George, ix. 62, 64, 90–1; Kelly, George, iii. 153n; Kilmarnock, iii. 281, 299; Kynnaird, Vct, iii. 241; Laurens, Henry, ix. 91, 212; Lovat, iii. 380, 387; Oliver, Richard, vii. 288; Pomfret, E. of, ix. 98; Sayre, viii. 138; Traquair, E. of, iii. 387; Tullibardine, M. of, iii. 106n; Walpole, Sir Robert, vi. 26; Wilkes, ix. 136
Richardson says that Sayre tried to bribe him to betray, viii. 138
Scrope does not dread, i. 458
Shah-Goest placed in, v. 378
shut at 7, iii. 138
Stair said to have patent from, ii. 224
undertaker of, see Allingham
Wales, P. and Ps of, embark at, i. 451
Walpole, Horatio (1678–1757), may go to, i. 299
Walpole, Sir Robert, may go to, i. 233, 299
—— refuses to send Sir William Wyndham to, vii. 289
Town crier. See under Crier
Towneley, Francis (1709–46):
rebels joined by, iii. 179
'Townley, Lady.' See under Vanbrugh, Sir John: Provoked Husband
Townsend, Isaac (ca 1685–1765), Adm.; M.P.:
Martinique fleet defeated by, in West Indies, iii. 186
Townsend, James (1737–87), alderman; sheriff; lord mayor; M.P.:
George III disrespectfully treated by, vii. 196
goods of, seized because he refuses to pay land tax, vii. 346
House of Commons's conduct charged by, to Ps of Wales's influence, vii. 289
London's remonstrance avowed by, vii. 198
memorials by, in newspapers, vii. 339
weavers pacified by, vii. 163
Wilkes contends with, for Middlesex elections, viii. 47
Townsend. See also Townshend
Townshend, Vcts. See Harrison, Etheldreda (ca 1708–88); Walpole, Dorothy (1686–1726)
Townshend, Lady Audrey (d. 1781), m. Robert Orme:
family disapproves of marriage of, iv. 495n
Townshend, Hon. Augustus (d. 1746):
captain of an Indiaman, i. 173
death of, iii. 277
Winnington's duel with, i. 172–3, 207

Townshend, Charles (1675–1738), 2d Vct Townshend; secretary of state:
guards sent by, to keep crowds away from plague house in London, ix. 423
marriage of, ix. 423n
secretary of state, v. 516n, vi. 211n, ix. 423
son of, iii. 320n, v. 138n, 516n, vi. 47n, 211n
son's education neglected by, iii. 169
Townshend, Charles (1700–64), 3d Vct Townshend, 1738:
death of, vi. 211
housemaid bears three children to, and inherits his money, vi. 211
long hair worn by, v. 138
mob raised and papers posted by, against Militia Bill, v. 138
Poyntz tutor to sons of, iv. 208n
sons of, iii. 468n, 566, iv. 33, v. 104n, 138, 552n, ix. 392n
wife separated from, i. 173
wife's witticism on vote of, at rebels' trial, iii. 285
Townshend, Rt Hon. Charles (1725–67), chancellor of the Exchequer:
administration to have been betrayed by, to Opposition, vi. 552
Admiralty post taken from, iv. 517
Admiralty to be headed by, vi. 130
Barrington succeeded by, as secretary at war, v. 490
brother of, v. 553n
brother pushes, into knavery, vi. 493
brother's caricature furnished by, with inscription, v. 78
chancellor of the Exchequer, vi. 443, 494, 498, 549
Churchill longed to satirize, vi. 261, 304
Conway influenced by, against Pitt's plans for East India Company, vi. 493
——'s preferment hurts, vi. 493
Dashwood succeeds, as treasurer of the Chambers, v. 490
death of, vi. 551–2
debate on East India Company's petition avoided by, vi. 495
dismissal claimed by, vi. 494
East India Company stock owned by, vi. 498
father's death confines, vi. 211
friends alone can be injured by, vi. 492
Garter installation attended by, at Windsor, vi. 86
HW hears from, about Lady Mary Wortley Montagu's MSS, vi. 85–6
health of: fever, putrid, vi. 551
Hillsborough to be succeeded by, as treasurer of the Chambers, v. 26
Holland succeeded by, as paymaster of the forces, vi. 304
jokes on deathbed, vi. 551
mother of, v. 24n

[Townshend, Rt Hon. Charles, *continued*]
North declines to succeed, as secretary of state, vi. 552
Parliamentary speech of: on seizure of Wilkes's papers, vi. 208; when brilliantly drunk, vi. 512
Pitt bids, to be chancellor of the Exchequer, not paymaster, and then changes, vi. 439–40, 442
—— names, for secretary of state, vi. 161
—— resented by, for making him chancellor of the Exchequer, vi. 493
——'s half-ally, disgruntled at Grenville's advancement, v. 553
Poyntz tutor to, iv. 208n
retires to the country in a rage, v. 104
Rockinghams may be led by, vi. 495
Sackville's appointment resented by, v. 104
St Alban's Tavern meetings attended by, v. 553
to be secretary at war, v. 486
wife of, iii. **468n**
'wild, romancing, indiscreet manner' of, vi. 494
witticism by, to mother about Bns Anson's virginity, v. 66
Yarmouth cannot re-elect, v. 26
Townshend, Charles (1728–1810), cr. (1797) Bn Bayning; M.P.:
Spanish position of, ix. 392n
treasurer of the Navy, ix. 392
Townshend, Hon. George (1715–69), naval officer; HW's cousin:
acquittal of, iii. 376
Admiralty lords suspend, iii. 324
Admiralty scolded by Charles Emmanuel III for court-martialling, iii. 332
Bastia bombarded by, iii. 157, 162, 169
Botta's peace terms condemned by, iii. 312
brother of, iii. 277
captains' prizes shared by, at Leghorn, iii. 277
Charles Emmanuel III pleased by conduct of, iii. 325
—— seeks cooperation of, against Genoa, iii. 292
—— to confer with, iii. 297
conferences of Corsican malcontents unknown to, iii. 183
Corsican rebels to have been aided by, iv. 274, 385, v. 37
Corsica's capture expected of, iii. 245
court martial of, iii. 245, 324, 332, 359–60, 361, 373, 378–9
disgrace of, iii. 324
eagle recommended by, at Port Mahon, iii. 268
eagle to be conveyed by, iii. 253
eagle would be thrown overboard by, iii. 263–4
education of, neglected, iii. 169, 190, 269
Florence to be visited by, iii. 42

French squadron should be demolished by, iii. 265
Genoese harmed by, iii. 157
Genoese to be harassed by, iii. 245, 292
Genoese to be threatened by, to save Corsican rebels, iii. 260
George II said to favour, iii. 374
HW comments on stupidity of, iii. 190
HW thanks Mann for news of, iii. 390
informed of nothing, iii. 171
Lage's fleet to be attacked by, near Genoa, iii. 253
——'s ships avoided by, iii. 324–5
Leghorn visited by, iii. 156, 169, 277
letter of, is used for evidence against him, iii. 324
Liechtenstein congratulated by, iii. 269
Mann advises, to write to D. of Newcastle, iii. 375–6
—— confers with, about eagle, iii. 253
—— gives exact description of Corsica to, v. 37
—— indirectly responsible for command being given to, iii. 146–7
—— regrets having recommended, to Sardinians, iii. 169–70
——'s correspondence with, iii. 42, 147, 156, 169–70, 216, 245, 292, 374
—— seeks further information about, iii. 350
—— to confer with, at Leghorn, iii. 183
—— tries to impel, towards Corsica, iii. 163
—— will ask, about pedestal for eagle, iii. 427
Mathews to be surpassed by, iii. 253
Medley not a friend to, iii. 374
—— not the prosecutor of, iii. 359
'plenipotentiary' in Corsica, iii. 182
Port Mahon visited by, iii. 207, 216
Rivarola does not assist, iii. 157
—— to be landed by, on Corsica, iii. 146
Rowley tells, to conquer Corsica, iii. 146
Sandwich causes court martial of, iii. 332, 361, 374
ship of, returned to him, iii. 375
ships left by, near Corsica, iii. 207
ships to be sent by, to Riviera di Ponente, iii. 292
snuff-box for Stone sent by, to England, ii. 445, 477
squadron of, near Genoa, iii. 253
squadron off Marseille and Toulon may be commanded by, iii. 376
Toulon convoy missed by, iii. 277
Villettes's correspondence with, iii. 183, 245
—— seeks interview with, iii. 292
Townshend, Hon. George (1724–1807), 4th Vct Townshend, 1764; cr. (1787) M. Townshend:
absurdity of, encourages Irish opposition, vii. 362

arrival of, from Germany awaited, v. 552
Art of Political Lying attacks, v. 78
Bristol succeeded by, as lord lieutenant of Ireland, vi. 549
brother pushed by, into knavery, vi. 493
Campbell, Lord Frederick, goes to Ireland as secretary to, vi. 549
caricatures by, of political figures, v. 77-8, 90, 93
carpenter and 'low fellows' live with, vii. 380
Conway succeeds, as lieutenant of ordnance, vi. 549
'Cotillon, The,' by, satirizes Irish, vii. 380
Cumberland, D. of, attacked by, iv. 33
—— has, as aide-de-camp, iv. 33
depicted on design for Wolfe's monument, v. 422
disappointed at not becoming marquess, vi. 493
Fox's presence resented by, v. 104
Gordon rioters threaten, ix. 53
Hague, The, visited by, ii. **566**
investigation of Port Mahon's fall languidly pursued by, for fear of uniting D. of Newcastle and Fox, v. 56
Irish Parliament prorogued by, vii. 166, 170
Irish will be imposed upon by, at first, vi. 549
lives with low associates, and satirizes chief Irishmen in ballad, vii. 380
lord lieutenant of Ireland, vi. 549, vii. 362n
Master of the Ordnance, ix. 53
Militia Bill promoted by, v. 137-8
militia's restorer, v. 552
mother gives ball for, on his coming of age, iii. 18
mother of, v. 24n
Poyntz tutor to, iv. 208n
Quebec expedition led by, v. 266-7
Quebec surrenders to, after Wolfe's death, vi. 16n
regiment to be raised by, for Dutch service, ii. 566
retires to the country in rage, v. 104
sister of, iv. 495n
son of, ix. 392n, 612n
'Treaty, The,' equals caricatures of, v. 93
'wrongheadedness' of, v. 267
Townshend, Henry (1736-62), army officer; M.P.:
death of, vi. 47
wounded, v. 516
Townshend, Hon. (afterwards Lord) John (1757-1833), M.P.:
lord of the Admiralty, ix. 392
Rolliad and other verses by, ix. 612n
Townshend, Hon. Thomas (1701-80); M.P.:
Gray, Sir James, aided by, in diplomatic career, iii. **444**, 453
son of, v. 516n, vi. 47n
Teller of the Exchequer, v. 516n

Townshend, Rt Hon. Thomas (1733-1800), cr. (1783) Bn and (1789) Vct Sydney; M.P.:
peace notified by, to city of London, ix. 355n
proposed as Speaker of House of Commons, vii. **180**
report by, of Godolphin's death, misinterpreted, ix. 583
secretary of state, ix. 355n, 583
Shelburne may succeed, as Home Secretary, ix. 487
Townshend, Hon. William (1702-38), M.P.:
son of, ix. 392n
Townshend. *See also* Townsend
Townshend family:
Orme's marriage to Lady Audrey Townshend not approved by, iv. 495n
Townshend, Vcts, breaks with, i. 173
Toynbee, Mrs Paget:
HW's letters edited by, x. 38, 39
Toys:
Du Quesne has, on shipboard, v. 255
from Paris, at Leghorn fair, vi. 423
Pius VI's nephew receives, in France on Princess's birth, viii. 470
Tozier, Grace (d. 1753), tavern keeper:
Wales, P. and Ps of, visit tavern of, i. 451
Traces:
long, on Electress's coach, iii. 370
Tracy, Thomas (?1716-70), M.P.:
Parliamentary debate by, over Scotch Bill, x. 31
Trade:
England loses, by American war, ix. 506
French, *see under* France
See also Commerce
Trade Bills:
Parliament debates over, iv. 135
Tradesmen:
bills of, may be taxed, iv. 183
luxury of, in England, vi. 455
lying is merely an expletive for, ix. 298
Tradrums:
high court, Serristori, Giovanna, wears, at baptism, i. 473
Traetta, Tommaso Michele Francesco Saverio (1727-79), composer:
Olimpiade, L', by, vi. 558
Tragedy; tragedies:
at Drury Lane Theatre, ill-played, vii. 82
Bayreuth, Margravine of, composes, iv. 478
Pertici undeserving of Garrick's praises for, iv. 357
Roman nobility act, at Frascati, iv. 481
Walpole, Bns, prefers, ii. 128
Train:
Craon, Princesse de, wears, at ceremony of the *doti,* ii. 196
of black crêpe: Kingston, Ds of, wears, vii. 556; Kingston, Ds of, might wear, at trial, viii. 187
Traitta *or* Trajitta. *See* Traetta

Trajan (Marcus Ulpius Trajanus) (ca 53–117), Roman emperor 98–117:
(?) medal of, i. 12
medal of father of, x. 7
medal of forum of, x. 7
Tranquillity:
advantages of, HW's reflections on, vii. 367
Transmigration of souls:
HW jokes about, v. 7
Transport; transports:
Americans capture, viii. 229
Dutch, escape English seizure, ix. 9
English: detained in the Downs, v. 130; Newcastle, D. of, hires, to take him to Holland, iii. 484; Rodney sends, to Gibraltar, ix. 16
French: at Dunkirk, ii. 407, iii. 103; at Toulon, iv. 545; Boscawen to 'swallow up,' iv. 483; captured by English privateers, iii. 230; French send, to Toulon from Minorca for more troops, iv. 552; Norris to burn, at Dunkirk, ii. 402; Parker defeats, ix. 21; take English troops to Gibraltar, iv. 581
Hanoverian troops to be taken away in, v. 13
lost in storm at Portsmouth, ix. 115
Neapolitan, escape with artillery, iii. 82
Pringle hostage for, ix. 309
Spaniards hire, at Genoa and Leghorn, iii. 304
Theodore's, dispersed, ii. 174
Transportation:
expenses of, i. 130
noblemen often fail to defray charges of, i. 474
See also Carriage; Cart; Chair; Chaise; Chariot; Coach; Frullone; Go-cart; Gondola; Hearse; Landau; Litter; Merlin: chair of; Mules; Phaeton; Post-chaise; Procaccia; Ship; Stage-coach; Vettura; Vis-à-vis; Voiture; Wagon
Transteverini; Transtiverains. See Trasteverini
Transubstantiation:
Maguire cannot swallow, i. 420
Trapp, Joseph (1679–1747), D.D.; poet, pamphleteer:
son of, i. 70
Trapp, Rev. Joseph (ca 1716–69), rector of Harlington and Strathfieldsaye:
Bouverie pays travelling expenses of, i. 70
Chute's fan displeases, i. 116–17
Florence visited by, i. 63, 67, 70
languages not known by, i. 70
Mann entertains, i. 70, 116–17
—— ridicules behaviour and costume of, i. 132
——'s little house occupied by, i. 67, 146, 154
Pisa visited by, i. 67
Rome to be visited by, i. 154
silent, i. 67, 70, 116

Traquair, E. of. See Stewart, Charles (d. 1764)
Traschieto. See Treschietto
Trasteverini:
Albani might arouse, iii. 114
Clement XIII's nephews may be stoned by, vi. 229
ready to rebel, ii. 462
Trattato della pubblica felicità. See under Muratori
Traun, Otto Ferdinand (1677–1748), Graf von Abensberg-Traun, Austrian field marshal:
accounts not received from, of battle, ii. 154
Alberoni's lands in the Plaisanterie seized by, ii. 199
Austrian-Sardinian negotiations awaited by, ii. 263
Bologna scene of military preparations of, ii. 55
Bologna threatened by army of, i. 500
Bologna to be occupied by, ii. 199
Bosville to join army of, ii. 309
Braitwitz hears from, that Spaniards will invade Tuscany when P. Charles invades France, ii. 285
—— ordered by: not to obey Francis I's orders, ii. 128; not to risk battles with Spaniards, ii. 295; to send troops to San Martino, ii. 85
Buon Porto, station of, when rejoined by Faenza detachment, ii. 66
Cesena visited by, ii. 13
Charles Emmanuel III checks ardour of, ii. 13
——'s and George II's intercessions might save, ii. 285
courier from, ii. 175
Craon's letter from, ii. 164–5
Dettingen victory exaggerated by, ii. 269
Faenza visited by, ii. 3
Gages may be forced to give up Bologna to, ii. 108
German troops withdrawn by, from Tuscan borders, ii. 134
Lobkowitz to replace, ii. 279–80, 285, 302
Lombardy to be defended by, ii. 263, 295
Lorraine's recovery expected by, ii. 285
Maria Theresa to get remonstrances from, to orders, ii. 128
Mathews wants, to coop up Spaniards in Tuscany, ii. 108
Milanese abbeys seized by, ii. 55
money demanded by, ii. 199
money shortage prevents, from marching against Spaniards, ii. 257
Montemar fears, i. 341
—— to be attacked by, with aid of Sardinian troops, i. 350
nephews of, captured by Spaniards, ii. 154
Panaro not to be crossed by, ii. 66
Panaro not to be left by, ii. 76
Ponte del Reno visited by, i. 500

regiment of, ii. 164

Spaniards deterred by fear of, from invading Tuscany, ii. 58

Spaniards may be dislodged by, ii. 58, 253, 257, 271

Thun sends courier to, ii. 56

troops of, too weak to make promised attack on Spaniards, ii. 127

Tuscany not to be defended by, ii. 295

Tuscany warned by, of Spanish invasion from Bologna, ii. 76

Zambeccari may be seized by, ii. 257

Travel:

Penthièvre, Duc de, takes only two posts a day, iv. 466

weapons needed as precaution for, iv. 312

see also Transportation

Travellers:

HW's reflections on, iv. 180

Travels and Adventures of Three Princes of Serendip. See under Chetwood, William

Travels through Different Cities . . . See under Drummond, Alexander

'Travendahl, Comte de':

Christian VII's assumed name, vii. 43n

Treasurer of the Chambers:

Arundel replaces Cotton as, iii. 256

Cotton succeeds Hobart as, ii. 551

Dashwood succeeds Charles Townshend as, v. 490

Elliot becomes, vi. 38

Hillsborough succeeds Arundel as, iv. 517

Townshend to succeed Hillsborough as, v. 26

See also Arundel, Richard; Cotton, Sir John Hind; Hobart, John (1723–93), styled Bn Hobart; Vice-Treasurer

Treasurer of the Household:

Bateman succeeds Berkeley as, v. 25

Berkeley succeeds Fitzwalter as, iv. 518

Shelley succeeds Edgcumbe as, vi. 470

Stone becomes, to Q. Charlotte, v. 517–18

Treasurer of the Navy. *See under* Navy

Treasury:

Bedford faction willing to let Grafton keep place in, vi. 538

board of: Legge opposes Hessian subsidy at meeting of, iv. 501; meets at Sir Robert Walpole's house, i. 391n

Bradshaw secretary of, viii. 56

Bubb Dodington resigns as lord of, i. 257n

Bute to be first lord of, vi. 37

—— would have given, to Fox, vi. 134

Carteret covets place in, ii. 265–6, 277

—— said to allow George II no power in, ii. 81

Cavendish, Lord John, leaves, vi. 444

changes in, i. 332, ii. 350, 551, iii. 211, 256, iv. 517, v. 24, 25, ix. 392

Compton appointed to, i. 337

Devonshire, D. of, first lord of, v. 17, 24, 74

Earle is lord of, i. 242n, 250n

Edgcumbe may get post in, ii. 356–7

Elliot succeeds James Grenville in, v. 490

Fane made clerk of, ii. 33

first lord of: Exchequer auditorship controlled by, iv. 233n; to be chosen, ii. 265, 277

Fox, C.J., dismissed as lord of, vii. 557

Fox, Henry, may succeed Pelham as head of, iv. 411, 419

—— to be lord of, ii. 350, 356

Furnese lord of, iv. 517, v. 172n

—— succeeds Legge as secretary of, i. 492–3

George II wants to dismiss people from, ii. 232

Grafton becomes head of, vi. 439, 443

Grenville, George, replaces Middlesex as lord of, iii. 419

—— to be first lord of, vi. 130

Grenvilles will not waive, to Rockingham, vii. 181

HW jokes about Mann's essences sweetening, ii. 292

Hessian treaty arrives at, iv. 493

Jeffries secretary to, ii. 321, 365

Legge lord of, iii. 256, 457n

—— replaced in, by D. of Newcastle, v. 103

—— secretary of, i. 492, iii. 457n

lords of, Mann, Mary, might apply to, for grant of Tortola lands, viii. 264

Lyttelton at, announces 'business at the House,' iii. 168

Mann does not understand Newcastle's position in, iv. 422

Martin secretary to, v. 25, vi. 183n

Middlesex to continue in, iii. 370

—— to join, ii. 365

money of, hoodwinks the English people, viii. 491

Murray may succeed Pelham as first lord of, iv. 411, 419

Newcastle takes charge of, iv. 417, 422

New Ode, A, satirizes, ii. 50

North and C.J. Fox propose Portland as first lord of, ix. 377, 379

Nugent a lord of, i. 254n, v. 24

Pelham, as first lord of, controls Exchequer auditorship, iv. 233n

—— first lord of, ii. 299, 313, iv. 233n, ix. 20n

—— may get post in, ii. 147, 265–6, 277

—— resigns as first lord of, iii. 211

—— resumes first lordship of, iii. 212

Pitt asks Newcastle to confine himself to, v. 91

—— may succeed Pelham as first lord of, iv. 411, 419

—— wants Temple as head of, vi. 161, 307, 433

Pitt, William II, may become first lord of, ix. 460

[Treasury, *continued*]

Portland, D. of, becomes first lord of, ix. 391

—— resigns post in, ix. 460n

Pulteney, E. of Bath, covets post in, ii. 265, 277, 299, iii. 211, 212

—— refuses post in, ii. 72, iii. 212

——'s appointees to, called 'dishclouts,' ii. 350

Rockingham becomes first lord of, ix. 261–2

—— succeeds George Grenville as first lord of, vi. 310

Sandys in, ii. 103

Scrope is secretary of, i. 467

Shelburne resigns as first lord of, ix. 377

——'s accession as first lord of, produces resignations, ix. 293–4

Temple refuses to become first lord of, vi. 307–8

vacancies in, vi. 38

Vane, lord of, iv. 39, 72

Villiers covets post in, iii. 458

Waldegrave might be first lord of, v. 98

Waller refuses post in, i. 332

Walpole, Sir Robert, first lord of, vi. 26–7

—— would not return to, ii. 142

West secretary to, iv. 371n, v. 25

Wilmington's impotence in, satirized in ballad, ii. 83

—— to head, i. 319, 332

Treaties:

Mann's reflections on, viii. 374

See under names of countries; see also Convention

'Treaty, The,' satiric print:

HW describes, and sends it to Mann, v. 93

Trebbia, the:

Charles Emmanuel III joined by Austrians at, iii. 269

Trebeck, Andrew (ca 1681–1758), D.D., rector of St George's, Hanover Square:

(?) Hamilton-Gunning marriage not performed by, iv. 303

Treby, George (ca 1684–1742), M.P.; lord of the Treasury, 1741:

Treasury post lost by, i. 332

Trecothick, Barlow (?1718–75), M.P., alderman:

London election candidate, vii. 5

London's remonstrance avowed by, vii. 198

Tredegar:

Morgan of, vii. 174

Tree; trees:

at Knole, sacrificed by Dorset, vii. 83

English, are often in full leaf by end of April, ix. 497

HW's interest, shifts to, from china, iv. 53–4, 70

HW's servants lop, at SH, viii. 48

HW thins, at SH, vii. 315

Northington orders cutting of, to spite son, vii. 368

storm injures, on New Year's Day, viii. 431

whirlwind at Rome injures, iv. 69

wind may injure, at SH, iv. 25

See also Cedar of Lebanon; Cypresses; Elm; Firs; Holly; Horsechestnut; Lime-trees; Oak; Olive tree; Orange trees; Palm tree; Pines; Thorn; Timber; Wood

Trenchard, John (?1668–1723), M.P.:

widow of, marries Gordon, his co-author in letters signed 'Cato,' iv. 167

Trenchard, Mrs John. *See* Blackett, Anne

Trent:

couriers from Germany pass through, twice a week, viii. 321

visitors to: Cholmondeley, viii. 319; Gloucester, D. and Ds of, viii. 317, 319, 321–3, 325–6, 329, 336–7, x. 50; Heywood, Col., viii. 317, 321, 337; Heywood, Mrs, viii. 323; Pitt, Anne, viii. 389

Winckelmann murdered at, vii. 113

Trentham, Vct. *See* Leveson-Gower, Granville (1721–1803)

Trentham, Vcts. *See* Egerton, Lady Louisa

Trenton, Battle of:

Hessians defeated in, viii. 285–6

Trepanning:

Tavistock undergoes, vi. 497

Trepid, Capt. Young's ship:

almost sunk, iv. 591

letter from, discredits Byng, iv. 591

Tre-Primati, Russian war ship:

at Leghorn, vii. 191

Treschietto, Marchese di. *See* Nay, Emmanuel-François-Joseph-Ignace de

Treschietto:

Richecourt's new title, iii. 385, 394

Tresconi (country dances):

Florentines offended by interruption to, iii. 365

Tresette:

Karl Friedrich's only game, iv. 148–9

Trevecca House, Talgarth, Wales:

Hotham, Lady Gertrude, invites Chesterfield to, viii. 91

Trevigar, Rev. Luke (1705–72), Fellow of Clare Hall, Cambridge; divine:

HW tutored by, in mathematics, v. 353

Trevisani, Angelo (1669–?1753), painter:

Correggio painting copied by, x. 7

Tre Visi, Villa de. *See* Palmieri, Villa

Trevor, Hon. Elizabeth (d. 1761), m. (1732) Charles Spencer, 2d D. of Marlborough:

Hague, The, to be visited by, ii. 209

Trevor, John (? 1717–43), M.P.:

Admiralty appointment of, i. 366

lacks estate and parts, i. 366

Pelhams' relative, i. 366

Trevor, Hon. John (1749–1824), 3d Vct Hampden, 1824; minister to the Diet at Ratisbon 1780–3; envoy extraordinary to Turin, 1783:

former German employments of, ix. 398

Turin post of, ix. 398, 595n

wife of, ix. 595n

Trevor, Mrs John. *See* Burton, Harriet (ca 1751–1829)

Trevor, Hon. Maria Constantia (1744–67), m. (1764), Henry Howard, 12th E. of Suffolk: death of, vi. 484

Trevor, Richard (1707–71), Bp of St David's, 1744; of Durham, 1752:
Canterbury archbishopric may go to, v. 185
death of, vii. 313

Trevor (later Hampden), Hon. Robert (1706–83), 4th Bn Trevor, 1764; cr. (1776) Vct Hampden; diplomatist:
daughter of, vi. 484
Harrington's circular letter to, i. 281
letter of, to Mann, described to Craon, ii. 427
Mann hears from: frequently, ii. 442; that French have captured two mails, iii. 143
—— sends case of drams to, iii. 177
—— sends citrons to, i. 413
retirement of, rumoured, iii. 351
sons of, ix. 398, 595n
superseded, as postmaster, vi. 311

Trevor (afterwards Hampden), Thomas (1746–1824), 2d Vct Hampden, 1783; M.P.:
Mann receives attentions from, at Florence, ix. 592
wife of, ix. 592, 595n

Treyssac de Vergy, Pierre-Henri (d. 1774):
Éon, Chevalier d', attacks, vi. 190
—— liberates, from prison, vi. 262
Guerchy accused by, vi. 262
Mann astonished by story of, vi. 273

Trial. *See under* Court martial; Rebel lords; *and names of the various defendants*

Trial, Bristol privateer:
San Zirioco captured by, iii. 134, 138

Trial, English sloop:
Dutch intercepted by, vi. 71

Trianon:
in disrepair, i. 127
Louis XV gives, to wife, i. 127

Tribune, in Uffizi gallery at Florence. *See under* Uffizi

Trichonium, Bp of. *See* La Ville, Jean-Ignace de

Tricolour cockade. *See* Cockade

Trident, the, Adm. Dennis's ship:
Gloucester, D. of, to entertain Grand Duke and Duchess on, vii. 353

Triennial Act. *See under* Parliament, British: acts of

Trier, Abp and Elector of. *See* Klemens Wenzel (1739–1812)

Trieste:
Austrian army to embark at, for Naples, ii. 3
corn must be shipped from, from Hungary to Italy, vi. 448
English attack expected at, v. 134

Florentine goods sent from Leghorn to, i. 380
German reinforcements to embark at, iii. 206, 220
Maria Theresa's maritime power established at, iv. 98, 102
——'s subsidy carried to, from England by Forrester, ii. 107
Venice to be eclipsed by, iv. 102

'Trifaldine, Cts.' *See under* Cervantes: *Don Quixote*

Trigge, Thomas (d. 1814), K.B., 1801; army officer:
Mann consigns packet to, viii. 380
Rome left by, for Florence on way to England, viii. 380

Trincalo. *See* Trinculo

Trincomalee, Ceylon:
English capture, ix. 277
French said to have retaken, ix. 393

'Trinculo, D.':
HW's name for D. of Newcastle, iv. 502
HW's name for sea captains, ii. 117

Trinità. *See* Ponte a Santa Trinità

Trinità del Monte, Rome:
Palazzo Medici on, iii. 113

Trinity, the:
Berkeley's *Siris* discusses, ii. 452, 465
Charlotte, William Pitt II, and George IV called, by HW, ix. 680
Italian painter includes Madonna in, vii. 459
Maguire cannot swallow doctrine of, ii. 420
pope's tiara symbolizes, iii. 358

Trinity College, Cambridge:
Bentley, Master of, iv. 368n, vii. 365n

Trino, near Turin:
Charles Emmanuel III at, iii. 156

Trinquemale. *See* Trincomalee

Triple alliance:
English fleet relies on, ii. 339
mis-spelling of, ii. 336, 339, 544
tricolour cockade for, ii. 336, 522, 544

Tripoli:
ambassador of, *see under* Ambassador
dey of, *see* Ali I (d. 1796) Karamanliya; Mehemmed Pāshā Karamānlī (d. 1754)
French demands refused by, iv. 319
French ship returns to, vii. 24
French ships may go from Malta to, iv. 320
minister from, to Holland, *see* Sidi Mahmūd Aga

Trip to Calais. See under Foote, Samuel

'Tristram Shandy':
Patch's caricature of: HW sure he has thanked Mann for, vii. 33; Mann sends, to HW by Capt. Steward, vii. 27; Mann's reasons for asking about, vii. 37

Tristram Shandy. See under Sterne, Laurence

Triton, French war ship:
in Mediterranean, v. 249

Tritons:
state coach adorned with, vi. 104

Triulzi, Ps. See Archinto, Maria

'Triumph of Bacchus.' See under Carracci, Annibale

'Trojan horse':
Mathews's horse called, ii. 453

Tron, Andrea (1712–85), procurator of St Mark; Venetian ambassador to Austria:
Ulfeld threatens, iv. 190

Tronchin, Théodore (1709–81), Swiss physician:
certainly a quack, vi. 154
charlatan, vi. 152
Northampton may consult, at Geneva, vi. 150, 152

Tronto, the:
Austrians cross, ii. 419, 438
Spaniards retreat to Naples by way of, ii. 412

Trooper:
De la Warr's, prophesies earthquake, iv. 137, 147, vii. 261

Troti, Angiolo (1503–63), called Bronzino; painter:
portrait by, bought by Mme Suares from Laurenzo, and given to Mann to be sold, i. 128
Vasari's portrait of Bianca Cappello attributed to, iv. 399

Trotti, Joachim-Jacques (1705–59), Marquis de la Chétardie, French ambassador to Russia 1739–42, 1743–4:
Anne of Russia said to have imprisoned, i. 20
Elizabeth of Russia demands her presents back from, ii. 495
Russia said to have dismissed, ii. 466, 495

Trouillet. See Raffron du Trouillet

Trousers:
red, English disputes should not be settled by, ix. 5

Troy:
HW will not hobble like Nestor to siege of, ix. 296
SH nearly as ruined as, vii. 365

True and Faithful Relation, A. See under Dee, John

Trumbull. See Turnbull

Trumpet; trumpets:
Cumberland, D. of, likes, iii. 20
George II's fondness for, v. 238
Prussians blow, prematurely at Kunersdorf battle, v. 331

Trumpet. See also Ear trumpet; Speaking trumpet

Trunk; trunks:
HW's: full of masquerade costumes, vii. 193; opened at Calais, i. 142, 161
Mann sends, to Cts of Pomfret, i. 129
Mozzi unpacks, ix. 435
silver, for perfumes, x. 56
Uguccioni writes to Cts of Pomfret about, i. 170

Truro:
Frederick, P. of Wales, quarrels with Falmouth over candidate for borough of, i. 451

Truth:
difficulty of establishing, in England, viii. 63–4
HW's reflections on, v. 167

Tryon, William (1729–88), colonial governor; army officer:
magazine burned by, viii. 309
Montgomery's victory over Carleton reported by, viii. 156

Tryton. See Triton

Tub; tubs:
fir trees planted in, at Ranelagh, iv. 47

Tubes:
silver, used to ventilate bed, iv. 203

Tubières de Grimoard de Pestel de Levy, Anne-Claude-Phillippe de (1692–1765), Comte de Caylus:
encaustic method of, v. 239
Stosch's cameos coveted by, v. 434

Tubières de Grimoard de Pestel de Levy, Charles de (ca 1698–1750), Marquis de Caylus:
Barnett defeats, ii. 15
Turkish ambassador entrusted to, ii. 15

Tuccoli, ——, Italian physician:
Gloucester, D. of, attended by, vii. 334, 337, 341, 342, 393

Tucker, Richard, receiver of hawkers and pedlars:
turned out of office, i. 420

Tuckfield, Margaret (ca 1678–1754), m. 1 (1704) Samuel Rolle; m. 2 John Harris of Hayne:
bequests of, iv. 418, 424
brother leaves fortune to, iv. 482n
daughter accuses, of having 'sold' her, iv. 439
daughter announces coming visit to, iii. 60
daughter coolly received by, iii. 139
daughter offered house by, iii. 104
daughter receives allowance from, iii. 224
daughter's education neglected by, ix. 121
daughter's jewels supposed to have belonged to, ix. 144, 148
daughter tells, about Walpole family, iii. 139
daughter wounds, by her misconduct, iii. 39
death of, iv. 418
grandson slights, iv. 482
London visit of, postponed till her daughter is out of the way, iii. 60
marriages of, i. 486, iv. 418n, 482n
'poor weak woman,' iii. 104, 132

Tuckfield, Roger (? 1685–1739), M.P.:
sister of, iv. 482n

Tuffnell, (?) John Jolliffe (d. 1794):
Florence visited by, i. 106

Tufton, Lady Anne (1693–1757), m. (1709) James Cecil, 5th E. of Salisbury, 1694:
Clifford title not left to, ii. 144
Tufton, Lady Catharine (1693–1734), m. (1709) Edward Watson, styled Vct Sondes:
Clifford title not given to, ii. 144
Tufton, Lady Isabella (d. 1764), m. 1 Lord Nassau Powlett; m. 2 Sir Francis Blake Delaval:
Foote arranges second marriage of, iv. 231
—— kept by, iv. 231
mad, iv. 231n
Tufton, Lady Margaret (1700–75), Bns de Clifford, s.j. 1734; m. (1718) Thomas Coke, cr. (1728) Bn Lovel and (1744) E. of Leicester:
Clifford barony bestowed on, ii. 144
family of, mad, iii. 457
Tufton, Lady Mary (1701–85), m. 1 Anthony Grey, styled E. of Harold; m. 2 (1736) John Leveson-Gower, 2d Bn Gower, cr. (1746) E. Gower:
(?) HW mentions, iv. 326
niece presented by, to Frederick, P. of Wales, iii. 447
remark by, about Frederick, P. of Wales's musical clock, iii. 447
Tufton, Lady Mary (1723–1806), m. (1763) Dr William Duncan, cr. (1764) Bt:
Florence visited by, viii. 105
husband leaves all to, recommending his nephew to her, viii. 41
Mann to tell, that English ladies weep no more, viii. 112
marriage of: perhaps platonic, viii. 41, 48–9; Selwyn's witticism on, viii. 49
tears of bereavement cause, to leave her callers, viii. 105
Tufton, Sackville (1733–86), 8th E. of Thanet:
Lowther contests Appleby election with, iv. 435
sister of, viii. 48n
'young Croesus,' iv. 435
Tufton, Thomas (1644–1729), 6th E. of Thanet:
daughter of, iv. 231n
Tufton family:
madness in, iii. 457
Tuljajī (d. 1787), Raja of Tanjore:
HW could learn about, ix. 117
Tullibardine, M. of. See Murray, William (1689–1746)
Tullie, Joseph (d. 1774), deputy usher of Exchequer:
estate of, in Yorkshire, vii. 498
Yorkshire farmer refuses to accept new guineas from, vii. 498
Tullybardine. See Tullibardine
Tuna. See Tunny Fish
Tunbridge Wells:
Bolton, Ds of, picks up Irish surgeon at, v. 365
Carteret, Bns, to visit, ii. 501

Chesterfield tries to establish Barnard as wit at, iii. 404
Chute and Whithed visit, iii. 436
fecundity supposedly increased by visits to, ii. 501
HW may visit, i. 452
HW might prefer, to Paris, vi. 492
Holdernesse abused for playing blindman's buff at private room at, iv. 346
Tunis, Bey of. See Ali II
Tunis:
bey's son revolts in, iv. 319
Spanish fleet may have its hands full at, viii. 120
Tunny fish:
Leopold to watch catching of, at Porto Ferrajo, vii. 131
Turchine:
monks of, iii. 123
Turcotti, Maria Giustina (1720–ca 1800); singer and impresario:
Arminio chosen by, i. 80
Mann's conversation with, iii. 317
Turenne, Maréchal Vicomte de. See La Tour d'Auvergne, Henri de (1611–75)
Turf:
present age prefers riding about streets to riding on, ix. 317
Turgot, Anne-Robert-Jacques (1727–81), Bn de l'Aulne; French controller-general:
Boynes replaced by, viii. 26
dismissed, viii. 140n, 208
HW praises, viii. 133, 140, 208
Maurepas jealous of, viii. 207
Turin:
academy at, Davison attends, iii. 407
Albani's messenger goes to, iii. 2
Anson's victory reported in letters to, iii. 415
Bartolommei to send news from, i. 342
Birtles to send Genoese courier to, ii. 375
Bristol, E. of, has no successor at, v. 191, 202–3
—— makes post at, too expensive for Mann, v. 175, 195
—— minister at, iii. 372n
—— prepares to leave, v. 195
Broglie wants to visit, to pay court to Victor Amadeus III, vii. 521
Carlisle might be envoy at, viii. 36
Charles Emmanuel III leaves, ii. 59, iii. 432
—— to return to, iii. 353
Coke, Lady Mary, well received at, vii. 560
Conti menaces, ii. 504
courier arrives at, almost naked, iii. 334
courier from: about Genoese campaign, iii. 451; arrives, iii. 358; awaited, iii. 335; just arrived, iii. 440; to Florence, discontinued, iii. 131
couriers sent to, ii. 411
Court of: awaits England's example in answering Leopold's letter, vi. 378; con-

[Turin, *continued*]

tributes patents only, to Corsican revolt, iv. 274; Corsican rebels should be protected by, iii. 258; English negotiations with, may be upset by Minorca's capture, iv. 576; expected Corsican conquest, iii. 215; French overtures to, iii. 218; Mann negotiates with, over Corsican rebels, iii. 276; to welcome D. of York, vi. 201; Townshend's appointment will please, iii. 147; Vienna court at odds with, iii. 478; Vienna court negotiates with, iii. 400–1; wants Mann to borrow money, iii. 215, iv. 386; wears tricolour cockade, ii. 544; Young Pretender not recognized at, iii. 143

Cumberland, D. of, avoids, because of English minister, vii. 525

dispatches deciphered at, iii. 12

dispatch from, sent by Mount Stuart, ix. 325

Dutens employed in English embassy at, ix. 625n

English visitors flock to Florence after festivities at, iv. 159, 160, viii. 131

express from, to carry battle news to England, ii. 436

fever in, prevalent, iii. 477

Florence communicates with, only through the Grisons, iii. 214

Fox wants Williams to have post at, iii. 16

'fracas' at, may have caused Mount Stuart's departure, ix. 336

French army to march upon, iii. 304

Fumagalli to be sent to England from, ii. 97

Genoa siege's raising rumoured at, iii. 422

Guasco brothers leave, vi. 529

Hamilton abandons Mme St-Gilles at, iv. 309

house rent at, v. 175

lady of, entertained by Mann, iii. 499

letter from, with news of Gibraltar, ix. 329

letters from, about Bergen-op-Zoom, iii. 440

Lobkowitz's son to bring father's dispatches to, ii. 486–7, 491

Lynch is English minister at, vii. 272, viii. 36

Lyttelton refuses to succeed Stuart-Mackenzie at, v. 507–9

Mann hears from, of English-French peace negotiations, vi. 89

—— hopes to hear of Bristol's successor at, v. 197

—— might be envoy at, v. 166, 175, 191, 195, 202, vi. 500

—— might visit, incognito, v. 266

——'s letters sent through Germany from, ii. 412

—— to decipher dispatch from, i. 428

—— writes to, for orders for Sardinian galleys to put to sea, iii. 236

Maria Theresa sends Bartolommei to, i. 196

messenger from Naples to, iv. 576

ministers of, at Paris and London, help in peace of Paris, vi. 105

Montemar may visit, i. 198

Mount Stuart leaves, ix. 336, 345, 354

Northington may succeed Mount Stuart as envoy at, ix. 336, 354

Orford declines post at, v. 195, 206

Pitt, George, envoy at, v. 548, vi. 2n, 500

—— to take Grafton's house at, vi. 2

Richelieu said to visit, iv. 576

Rochford envoy at, iv. 58, 420, 426

——'s new appointment vacates post at, iv. 461

Rochford, Cts of, to go to, iv. 58

sea engagement not reported from, ii. 403

Spaniards may besiege, iii. 120

Spanish invasion of Lombardy apprehended at, ii. 295

Stuart Mackenzie envoy at, v. 212, 218

—— may send fans from, v. 462

Townshend's instructions to come from, iii. 245

Trevor envoy to, ix. 398, 595n

Trino near, iii. 156

Villettes minister at, ii. 60n, iii. 150, 183, iv. 76

—— sends courier from, through Germany, ii. 389, 397

Viry's secret correspondence at, viii. 328n

visitors to: Almada, v. 436; Bartolommei, i. 195–6; Bute, vii. 103; Coke, Lady Mary, vii. 543, 545, 553, 556, 559, 560; Conway, iv. 293, 304; Ferdinand of Naples, ix. 586; Fumagalli, ii. 97; Gloucester, D. of, vii. 370, viii. 252; Grafton, D. and Ds of, v. 537, 554, 557, vi. 2, 34; Mann, Horace II, viii. 129; Mathews, Adm., ii. 215, 360, 370; Money, iii. 12; Montagu, Lady Mary Wortley, i. 91; Orford, Cts of, vii. 120; Penthièvre, iv. 466; Phelps, vi. 112; Philipps, i. 138; Raper, i. 138; Richecourt, i. 95; Richecourt, Comte and Comtesse de, iv. 45; Wentworth, iii. 401, 406; York, D. of, vi. 193, 201, 204, 244

wedding, royal, at, iv. 159

Williams may succeed Villettes as minister to, iii. 347, 456, 465, 466

Wright would probably want post at, if Mann rejects it, vi. 503

Turinetti, Ercole (1717–81), Marchese di Priero e Pancalieri, imperial envoy to Rome:

Benedict XIV sends for, iii. 157

Viennese couriers awaited by, iii. 158

Turinetti, Giovanni Antonio (1687–1757), Marchese di Priero e Pancalieri, imperial ambassador to Venice:

Maria Theresa's letter to, threatens Venice with diplomatic break, iv. 190

memorial delivered by, to Venice, iv. 161

Turk, Martha (ca 1737–1791); 3d E. of Orford's mistress:
age of, forty, viii. 295
HW calls, 'housemaid,' ix. 133
HW describes, viii. 295
HW's attention to, in E. of Orford's
former illness, viii. 294
HW urged by, not to remove E. of Orford
from Eriswell, viii. **293**
keeper retained for E. of Orford at request of, viii. 296
Orford, E. of, has slept with, for 20
years, viii. 295
—— joins his forehead to, every evening
at table, viii. 295
—— praises Dr Monro to, viii. 372
Walpole, Sir Robert, makes plans which
are baffled by, ix. 133
Turkey, Sultana of:
pregnant, v. 494
Turkey, Sultan ('Grand Signor') of. *See*
Abdul-Hamid (1725–89); Mahmoud I
(1696–1754); Mustafa III (1717–74)
Turkey:
anti-Russian grumbling of, more audible
in England than in Italy, ix. 436
archbishopric of Tauris in hands of, vi.
196
armaments prepared by, v. 493
armament will be abandoned by, if Sultana produces an heir, v. 494
army of, in wretched condition, vii. 173
Austria and Russia may dismember, ix.
399
Austria, Prussia, and Russia may combine
against, ix. 359, 436
Catalogue of French Books, A, satirizes,
ii. 53
Catherine II and Joseph II said to have
been mollified by compliance of, to their
demands, ix. 409–10
Catherine II attacked by, at Choiseul's instigation, vii. 133–4, 143
—— duped by, vii. 438
—— may give, to son, vii. 236
—— may turn from, to Denmark, vii. 273
——'s destruction of, would harm the
faithful, vii. 169
——'s war against, miscarries, vii. 157
—— to defend usurpations in, ix. 436
cavalry of, to have been remounted, vii.
160
Choiseul might espouse quarrel of, viii. 11
—— must abandon or aid, vii. 202
——'s intrigues a disadvantage to, vii. 259
Christians at Smyrna cruelly treated by,
vii. 233, 235
Constantinople's approaches fortified by,
vii. 331
costume of, iv. 362, vi. 148
courier from India travels to port in, v.
523

England angers, by letting Russian fleet
cross the English Channel, vii. 479
England will be glad of diverting news
of, vii. 121
English intervention against France will
distress, vii. 479
Fane said to be ambassador to, iii. 99–100
fleet of: Elphinston attacked by, at Napoli
di Romania, vii. 234; Ibrahim commands,
vii. 234; Russians destroy, vii. 226–8, 232–5,
236, 239, 249; said to be burned at
Lemnos, vii. 319
France incited, against Russia, vii. 307, 338
France may aid, against Austria, Prussia,
and Russia, ix. 359
France may incite, against Joseph II, ix.
46
France said to threaten Joseph II if he
makes war on, ix. 415
France unpopular in, as cause of war with
Russia, vii. 202
French merchant ships intercepted by Rus-
sians on way to, vii. 307
French to assist, with advisors and tech-
nicians, vii. 185
frigates of, *see under* Frigate
Giovanni Gastone's collection sent to, iii.
437
girls from, *see* Girls: Turkish
Golitsyn defeated by, vii. 140
Greeks do not aid Russia against, vii. 222
Greeks flee to Venice to escape vengeance
of, vii. 226
Greeks will be sacrificed to, by Russians,
vii. 212
Grotius and Puffendorf will be taught to
people of, vii. 88
HW asks about, and compares it to Babylon, vii. 212
HW prefers Grand Signior of, to Catherine II, vii. 195
janizaries of, may precipitate war, ix. 360
Louis XV and French ministers vainly encourage, vii. 331
Malta fears, v. 493–4
man *or* men of war of, *see under* Man
of war
Maria Theresa forbids Knights of Malta
to fight, v. 505
—— need not fear, v. 494
Orlov, Alexis, the scourge of, at sea, viii.
114
Orlov, Grigoriĭ, conducts Russian negotiations with, vii. 441
pirates from, feared by Pope's seamen, i.
16
Pitt might encourage, to be impertinent,
in order to use armament, v. 537
Polish confederates not aided by, vii. 319
religion forces Roman Catholic countries
to oppose, ii. 428
Rome prays for, in war with Russia, vii.
140

[Turkey, *continued*]
Russia attacked by, vii. 133–4, 143
Russia battles with, over Bender, vii. 154–5, 160, 245
Russian fleet might frighten, into peace, vii. 149, 192
Russian fleet to attack, vii. 148–9
Russian invasion of, disliked by France, vii. 204
Russian negotiations with, vii. 469–70
Russian relations with, v. 247–8
Russians capture military chest and tents from, vii. 479
Russians defeat, before Golitsyn's recall, vii. 146
Russians force, from Moldavia and Volakia, vii. 154–5
Russians haggle with, over villages in Morea, vii. 224
Russian squadron may move to Malta to scare, vii. 189
Russia's war with, *see under* War, Russian-Turkish
Russia unlikely to wrest Holy Land from, vii. 194–5
sedition in, possible, vii. 155, 159–60
Tuscany's treaty with, iii. 437
Venice threatened by, v. 494
war or peace in, intermittent, vii. 432
Turkey; turkeys:
come from the Orient, ix. 609n
English capture, in France, iii. 327
geese to race with, v. 7
HW does not eat, at Christmas, iii. 16
Leneve, Isabella, counts, after Houghton dinner, ix. 609
small: HW thinks, should be called 'turkey-pouts,' ix. 609n; served as second course at dinner, but seldom eaten, ix. 609
Turkey cock:
Orford, Cts of, resembles, iii. 224
Turkey Company:
Wright's offers from, v. 21
Turkey handkerchiefs. *See under* Handkerchief
Turkey leather. *See under* Leather
Turkey merchant:
Clephane's correspondence with, about Cartagena, i. 71
Laws, Capt., tells, of English loss at Cartagena, i. 71
Turks:
Catherine II compels HW to sympathize with, vii. 116
Crawford fights against, in Hungary, iv. 110
Lorraine, Primate of, defends amorous practices of, i. 273
Louis XV negotiates with, ii. 543
St Stephen knights to win prizes from, to pay for church, vi. 259
Turk's Island:
French capture of, vi. 252

Turnbull, George (ca 1703–48), L.L.D.; author; divine:
health of: poor, iii. 232; possible consumption, iii. 184–5; probably hopeless, iii. 192
'pandle,' iii. 232
Rome to be visited by, iii. 232
Walpole, Horatio (1723–1809) accompanied by in Italy as tutor, iii. 184–5, 192
Turner, Lady. *See* Leigh, Cassandra (1723–70)
Turner, ——, china merchant:
large price asked by, for jar cracked by earthquake, iv. 155
Turner, ——, m. Rev. Dr John Gardiner:
son of, not by Bn Walpole, ii. 522
Turner, Sir Charles (ca 1665–1738), cr. (1727) Bt:
wife of, ii. 182
Turner, Charles (ca 1726–83), cr. (1782) Bt, M.P.:
chariot of, overturned in Gordon Riots, ix. 54
Turner, Mrs Charles. *See* Walpole, Mary (1673–1701)
Turner, Cholmley (1685–1757), M.P.:
named in Secret Committee lists, i. 384
Secret Committee not attended by, i. 401
Turner, Edith (1642–1733), m. Alexander Pope:
birth of son of, satirized in *New Lesson for Pope*, ii. 34
Spence's mother's ghost will be pursued by that of, iv. 189
Turner, Sir Edward (1719–66), 2d Bt, 1735; M.P.:
Spanish privateer said to have captured, between Dover and Calais, i. 153
Turner, Sir Gregory (1748–1805) (after 1775 Page-Turner), 3d Bt, 1766; M.P.:
Mann to be accompanied by, at investiture, vii. 60
Turner. *See also* Garth-Turnour; Turnor
Turnips:
Chute lives on, ii. 100
HW not interested in, ii. 47
Turnkey:
at Newgate, iv. 312
Turnor, Edmund (ca 1755–1829), M.P.:
HW recommends, as friend of Thomas Walpole II, to Mann, viii. 488
Turnor, Sir William, Kt, 1686:
Wright friend of, i. 423
Turnor. *See also* Turner
Turnpike:
Bedford and Grafton dispute over, iv. 549
Brown, Sir Robert, avoids fees for, ix. 609n
messengers numerous upon, after Parliament's dissolution, viii. 45
Turnpike Bill. *See under* Parliament: acts of
'Turnstile, The.' *See* 'Treaty, The'
Turnur. *See* Turner; Turnor

Turpentine:
Southwark magazines of, catch fire, ix. 577
Turtle:
Egremont looks forward to dinners of, vi. 159
Taaffe brings, to Marquise de Pompadour, iv. 289
Turton, John (1735–1806), physician:
alarmed about Morice, ix. 202
Tuscan architecture. *See under* Architecture
Tuscan Council, at Vienna:
Alberti appointed to, iv. 220
Tuscany, Grand Duchess of. *See* Marguerite-Louise (1645–1721); Maria Louisa (1745–92); Maria Theresa (1717–80); Martelli, Camilla (d. 1590)
Tuscany, Grand Duke of. *See* Cosimo I (1519–74); Cosimo II (1590–1621); Cosimo III (1642–1723); Ferdinando I (1549–1609); Ferdinando II (1610–70); Ferdinando III (1769–1824); Francesco I (1541–87); Francis I (1708–65); Giovanni Gastone (1671–1737); Leopold II (1747–92)
Tuscany:
Acquaviva tells Montemar to invade, i. 266
Algeria makes peace with, iv. 472, ix. 270
Algerian corsairs prey on trade of, iv. 472–3
Algeria's war with, iv. 472, 487–8
ancient people of, addicted to divination, iv. 477
Antinori rules, v. 90
army of: Franchini drummed out of, v. 510; leaves for Austrian service, v. 179–80; *see also* Tuscany: troops of
art shipments from, must have export licenses, iv. 465, v. 208
Austria dominates, ix. 505, 554
Austria forgets the money accumulating in, v. 102
Austrian artillery permitted to pass through, ii. 541–2
Austria's connection with, to increase, ix. 128
Bandini and Old Pretender's underling pass through, from Rome, ii. 380
Barbary states the only official enemy of, v. 349
Benedict XIV reconciled with, iv. 446
—— to settle disputes about, with St-Odile, iv. 305
Bientina lake protected by dikes from overflowing into, iv. 515
borders of, manned under pretence of guarding against plague, ii. 270, 285
Botta commands troops in, for Francis I, v. 471n
—— to govern, v. 125
bread shortage in, vi. 448, ix. 318
Charles III and Gages threaten, ii. 509
Charles III may declare war on, iii. 65
—— once acknowledged as Great Prince of, v. 494–5, vi. 406

Charles, P., possibly to rule, ii. 2, 30, 331, 336, v. 556
Charlotte, Ps, may govern, iii. 49, 207, iv. 29, 178, 355
china factory in, ix. 598, 635, 645
Clement XIII bullied by, about ecclesiastical immunities, vi. 449
cloth unobtainable in, save from England, iv. 205
corn expensive in, vi. 452
corn plentiful in, but money is not, vi. 486
corn sought by, in England and Hungary, vi. 446, 448
Corsican news depresses, vii. 130
Corsican women banished to, vii. 245
Corsica receives notice from, by felucca, ii. 263
council of, in Vienna, iv. 220
court of: *accesso* a dignity conferred by, vi. 531; at Pisa, vi. 417, 422, 511, 515, vii. 149, 325, 352, viii. 188, ix. 334, 436; at Porto Ferrajo, vii. 131; attends two playing societies, vi. 393; Barbantane does not acknowledge pretensions of habitués of, vi. 481; Beaufort, Ds of, and family, favoured by, vii. 406; Botta explains altered ceremonies of, vi. 378; Boufflers's friends not so well received as he by because no foreign minister presented them, vi. 474; Charlotte's brother well received by, vi. 437–8; Cumberland, Ds of, may embarrass, vii. 501–2; drawing-room at, for Archduke and Archduchess of Milan, ix. 50; drawing-room not held in, ix. 340; English visitors at, served punch, vi. 430; English visitors irritated by procedure of, vi. 482, 483; etiquette of, vi. 367, 378, ix. 334, 340; etiquette of, at Pisa, vii. 171, 191, 262; etiquette of, excludes Dick, vii. 395; etiquette of, too much for untitled visitors, vi. 467; fine clothes not required at, ix. 340; gala apartement at, ix. 301; gala at, vi. 467; gala day routine of, vi. 367; Gloucester, Ds of, received by, before any other court did so, vi. 297; grandees of, must all be invited to meet visiting sovereigns, viii. 164; Guasco accepted by, vi. 531; Herveys well received by, vi. 430; Holy Week ceremonies of, worthy of Vienna, vi. 412; Huntingdon favoured by, vii. 406, 446; imitates that of Vienna, vi. 390; Kingston, Ds of, may shun, viii. 398; Kingston, Ds of, sends respectful message to, viii. 7; Lappeggi preferred by, to Castello and Petraia, vi. 412; Leghorn's preparations for, vi. 417, 422; Leghorn to be visited by, vi. 417; less exacting than any other in Europe, ix. 340; Mann does not follow, to Pisa, ix. 334; Mann goes to, only to deliver letters or present strangers, ix. 340; Mann presents Lord Robert Manners at,

[Tuscany, *continued*]

ix. 282; Mann's truculence to, would be backed by Pitt, vi. 483; Mann to accompany, to Pisa and perhaps to Siena, vi. 511; Mann to present English visitors at, viii. 250–1; Maria Josefa's wedding to be celebrated by, vi. 556; mourns for Ps Charlotte, vii. 533; no longer follows Francis I's ceremonies, vi. 378; no public days, levees, or drawing-rooms at, ix. 340; Pisa shows for, uninteresting, vi. 515; Poggio a Caiano the residence of, vii. 296; Poggio a Caiano to be visited by, vii. 325; Rena must be excluded by, vii. 119; resides at Poggio Imperiale, viii. 7, ix. 301; returns from Vienna, viii. 250; returns to Pisa from Leghorn, vii. 80; Salviati made Grand Chambellan by, vi. 467; Siena may be visited by, vi. 511; Sienese shows please, vi. 515; Spanish minister attends, at Pisa, ix. 334; to visit Vienna, vii. 214; Vienna court prescribes etiquette to, for Maria Louisa's churching, vi. 486–7; Vienna to regulate mourning for, vi. 337, 340; Vienna will lecture, for extravagance, vii. 134–5; will soon find travelling too expensive, vii. 134

Craons may help Old Pretender's sons across, i. 15

Cristiani may rule, iv. 335

crops in, destroyed by drought, ix. 314, 318

Cumberland, D. of, may visit only Leghorn in, vii. 53

Cuneo's capture would endanger, ii. 513

Del Monte banditti terrorize, iv. 446

desertion expected from, ii. 120

disloyalty of, caused by dislike of Richecourt, iii. 11

divination popular in, iv. 477

edict by, for Del Montes' arrest or death, iv. 446

Electress's death frees Francis I from interference in, ii. 160

England given credit by, for coming independence, vi. 123

England opposed by, despite trade benefits, iv. 581

England quarrels with, over Wright, v. 20–1

England reported to have resigned, to Spain, i. 182

England would prefer, to be independent of Spain or Austria, ii. 2

English china compared to that of, ix. 635

English cloth contraband in, iv. 205

English-commanded ship of, rescued from Prussian privateer, v. 349

English corn kept from, by embargo, vi. 460, 462

English fleet to go to, v. 114

English fleet to protect, ii. 27, 37–8, iii. 10

English fleet well received by, v. 128

English privateers almost provoke, to war, v. 335

English relations with, may be guided by Richecourt and Bns Walpole through Chesterfield, i. 387

English ships carry flag of, when carrying French goods, v. 269, 273–4

English trade beneficial to, v. 36, 108, 269

envoys from and to, *see under* Envoy

Etruscan vases said to have been discovered in, vi. 561

famine expected in, from heat and drought, ix. 314, 318

famine threatens, vi. 446, 448

fathers in, post notices that they will not pay sons' debts, viii. 237

finances of, loan sought from Jews at Leghorn, vi. 448

first minister of, Rosenberg to replace Botta as, vi. 447–8, 453–4

flag of, v. 269, 273, 278

fleet of, consists of three ships, iv. 487

Fleury about to permit Spanish invasion of, ii. 42

—— said to oppose Spanish invasion of, i. 197–8, 205, 230

Flobert banished from, v. 377

floods in, i. 109, iv. 220, vii. 274, 378, 383

Foligno gives access to, i. 261

France guarantees safety of, i. 120, 205, 206, 214, 229, 230, 281, 288, 290, ii. 502, 509

France said to have ordered Gages not to invade, iii. 7

France said to permit Spain to invade, iii. 30–1, 38

France to keep Francis I in, away from German influence, i. 152

Franchini banished from, v. 511

Francis I and Leopold vainly try to drain marshy tract in, viii. 343

Francis I denudes, of troops, i. 180

—— does not want troops of, at Leghorn, iii. 11

—— may get Naples instead of, ii. 331

—— may visit, on way to Naples, ii. 3

—— neglects, v. 90

—— not alarmed over, i. 216

—— orders, to prepare, ii. 364

—— orders Braitwitz to keep Spaniards out of, ii. 66, 127, 134

—— orders Te Deums to be sung in, v. 112

—— reproves, for method of chastising Del Monte family, iv. 437

—— said to have excluded English ships from ports of, i. 36

——'s interests in, endangered by Richecourt's opposition to English fleet, ii. 329

——'s only interest in, is to get money, i. 406

——'s troops sent to borders of, to preserve neutrality, ii. 541
—— to lose, to Don Philip, i. 196
—— trusts France's guarantee of neutrality of, ii. 509
—— uncertain about France's guarantee, i. 288
—— unlikely to relinquish, iv. 178
—— will still get revenue from, even when son reigns at Florence, vi. 255
Francis III of Modena may invade, ii. 295
French guarantee of, may cease if England joins with Austria, i. 288
French propaganda in, viii. 416
Gages crosses, iii. 40–1
—— may call Francis I to account for mobilization in, ii. 127
—— may invade, ii. 509, 556, 559, iii. 35–6, 38
—— prepares invasion of, while awaiting new orders from Madrid, iii. 10
—— promises not to invade, iii. 38
——'s march to Genoa may endanger, iii. 53
—— to enter Lombardy to isolate, iii. 31
galleys and war ships lacked by, vi. 259
Genoa receives disavowal from, of captain's action, ii. 263
George II assures, of protection, i. 281
——'s intention to protect, known to Regency Council, ii. 27, 38
George III might not consider, worthy of a minister plenipotentiary, vii. 293
German troops sent from, i. 154, 214, 229
German wars not to involve, v. 112
Giovanni Gastone governs, through Giuliano, v. 62
Goldsworthy says that Francis I, Mann, and Regency Council belittle danger of, ii. 106–7
government of, may be taken away from Richecourt, ii. 310
government posts in, never vacated, iv. 210
grenadiers to be contributed by, to Austrian army, v. 15
HW hopes secretaries of state in, do not open letters, viii. 38
HW may ask Sandwich to defend, ii. 561
Hancarville proposes to furnish, with fresh fish, vii. 448
Hanoverian negotiations said to be about, iv. 178
harvest in, ix. 318
health magistrates of, ii. 270
Hervey, Bp, 'hovers around,' ix. 651
horses in, all employed by new court, v. 336
imperial fiefdom of, makes it liable to contribute troops, v. 15
influenza in, ix. 304
Inquisition to be re-established in, iv. 420, 445, 446, 448

Jesuits' revenues in, small, vii. 508
Jesuits suppressed in, by Leopold, vii. 508, 512–13
Joseph II favours, ix. 137
—— to renounce, to brother, vi. 123
'Julianism' of, v. 62
Karl Joseph expected by, as Grand Duke, iv. 178, 295, v. 556
lack of defences and money exposes, to any enemy, iii. 120
law courts in, more lax than in England, ix. 131
laws of: Act of Succession, iv. 466; edict against export of antiquities, iv. 465, 208
Leopold officially takes possession of, vi. 412
—— proclaimed as Grand Duke of, vi. 329, 330
—— rides around, as a private gentleman would on his estate, viii. 343
—— to be ruler of, v. 556, vi. 123, 125
Lestock ordered to defend, i. 405
Lobkowitz cannot save, and aid Charles Emmanuel III too, ii. 512
—— leaves artillery with, ii. 529–30
—— may enter, ii. 339
—— may retreat through, ii. 508
—— not to retreat through, ii. 520
—— ordered by Vienna to bring his army into, iii. 11
—— preserves, ii. 343
——'s retreat to Lombardy may expose, ii. 502, 508
Lorraine faction depend on Francis I's favours to people of, v. 125
Lorrainers hated by, iv. 581
Lucca could conquer, iii. 120
Lucca may be flooded by, iv. 514–15, 521–2
Madrid treaty expected to aid, iv. 294
Mann advised by HW not to quit post at, iv. 409
—— disputes in, over prizes from the Levant and French West Indies, v. 280–1
——'s disputes with, over seizure of English ships carrying Tuscan flag, v. 269, 273
——'s MS account of, for George III, sent to Shelburne through Capt. Steward, vii. 27–8, 37, ix. 230
Maria Theresa may send troops to, iv. 320
—— may want a few troops from, v. 175
——'s army protects, ii. 352
—— wants aid from, ii. 359
—— will lose, ii. 521
Martin's squadron to protect, from invasion, ii. 26
Mathews does not understand situation in, ii. 98
—— may land marines in, ii. 26
—— to defend, ii. 296
—— wants Charles Emmanuel III and Traun to coop up Spaniards in, ii. 108

[Tuscany, *continued*]

Migazzi gets orders from, to oppose Dumesnil's consecration, iii. 492

Milan may be exchanged for, i. 290

minister of, to France, warned by Fleury, i. 290

ministers from and to, *see under* Minister

mobilization in, under pretence of guarding against the plague, ii. 285

Montemar demands passage through, i. 226, 228, 280, 289–90, ii. 46

—— may invade, ii. 16

——'s army may leave garrison in, i. 228–9, 289

Murray cannot get aid from, ix. 196–7

Naples and Rome shut off from, for fear of plague, ii. 270

navy of, Mann opposes English sailors' enlisting in, iv. 472

Neapolitan ambitions of Viennese court may endanger, ii. 390

Neapolitan cavalry to return through, iii. 297

Neapolitan troops may invade, ii. 295, iii. 346

Neapolitan troops rumoured to be invading, iii. 364

neutrality of: disputed at Leghorn, ii. 438; follows singing of Te Deum, v. 114; Francis I preserves, i. 456, ii. 92, 339, 361, 541, v. 114; has hitherto protected it, ii. 361; irritates Mathews, ii. 339, 361; preserved even after Charles VI's death, v. 112; Richecourt proclaims, in spite of his probable distrust, ii. 513; will be preserved, v. 176

Niccolini banished from, iv. 2

nobility of: classified, vi. 350–1, 360n; inferior to English M.P.s, vi. 483; to be classified as *patrizii* and *nobili*, iv. 192–3

orders awaited by, from Vienna, v. 85

passports for: invalid, v. 482; Modena, Ds of, wants, ii. 223; Montemar and Castellara want, ii. 44; Young Pretender obtains, ii. 378

peeress of, given niggardly present by husband on giving birth to an heir, viii. 233

people of, may aid Spanish army, iii. 11, 31

Philip, Don, might become Grand Duke of, i. 196, 380, 389

pickets of, ii. 100

Pisa baths are Mann's favourite place in, iv. 158

plague precautions of, futile, ii. 295

Port Mahon packet-boat almost destroyed by government of, viii. 416

post office of, ix. 564

Protestant girls in, converted by priests, vi. 249–50

publication rules of, violated by edition of Montesquieu's letters, vi. 530

quarantines in, futile, ii. 295

rainfall in, excessive, iv. 149

Richecourt carries away money of, iii. 115

—— muzzles discontent in, iv. 77

——'s letters intercepted by Spaniards may endanger neutrality of, ii. 516

—— will leave, in a state of Julianism, v. 62

Rome does not yet treat, severely, iv. 458

Rome's agreement with, iv. 420–1

Rome's authority in, resisted, vii. 504

Rosenberg's debts in, not paid, vii. 294

Russian fleet awaited by, vii. 159

secretary of state of, *see* Secretary of State, Tuscan

secretary of war of, *see* Secretary of War, Tuscan

ships fly colours of, for self-protection, v. 269

ships of: English men of war capture, v. 269; load French goods for the Levant, v. 273; Prussian privateer captures, v. 330, 349; respected by all but Algerians, ix. 270; to carry books to HW, ix. 138

Spain notifies, that goods sent to England will be confiscated, ix. 509

Spain orders Naples to send food to, despite Tanucci's dislike, vi. 448

Spain suspects, of intercepting courier, ii. 85–6

Spaniards and Neapolitans march through, to join Gages, iii. 65

Spaniards cannot help knowing preparations of, ii. 359

Spaniards may cross, to join Don Philip, iii. 2

Spaniards may enter: iii. 24–5; from Genoa, ii. 454; from Perugia, iii. 10

Spaniards may exchange Lombardy for, i. 206

Spaniards may invade, when P. Charles invades France, ii. 285, 295

Spaniards may invade Genoa by way of, iii. 36

Spaniards to cross Pietra Santa in, iii. 35

Spaniards unlikely to molest, ii. 58

Spanish aid hoped by, i. 144

Spanish army crosses, at Pietra Santa, iii. 40

Spanish invalids from Viterbo to cross, to join Gages, iii. 47, 55, 58

Spanish invasion diverted from, to Lombardy, iii. 22

Spanish invasion of: depends on Don Philip's success, ii. 312; prevented, ii. 108

Spanish invasion threatens, i. 179–81, 192–3, 195, 196, 197–9, 204–5, 207, 213–15, 226, 228–9, 230, 238, 259, 261–2, 265–7, 269, 280–2, 288, 289–91, 314, 322–3, 349, 427, ii. 16, 26, 27, 37, 58, 76, 92, 98, 100, 105, 127–8, 129, 175–6, 295–6, 297, 312, 361, 454, iii. 10–11, 24, 25, 35–6, 53, 245

Spanish troops negotiate with, i. 228–9

Stainville may rule, iv. 29

state papers of, of Medici period, not accessible, v. 284

taxes in, *see under* Tax

Theodore wants English newspapers in, iv. 378

titles of, not acknowledged by Barbantane, vi. 481

tobacco trade in, iv. 389

Toulon squadron may threaten, i. 190

Toussaint to administer, temporarily, v. 107

Traun not to defend, ii. 295

—— warns, ii. 76

—— withdraws German troops from borders of, ii. 134

tribute may no longer be paid by, to Barbary states, vi. 259

troops for, said to assemble in Lombardy, iv. 320

troops of: at Cortona, iv. 437; desert, ii. 100, iv. 424; Francis I orders, to keep active, ii. 100; Frederick II's witticism about, v. 224; Leghorn to be guarded by, ii. 530, iii. 2; Lobkowitz to be joined by, iii. 11; mobilized for defence, ii. 530; Prato and Pistoia to be stations of, ii. 98, 100; to join Austrian army, v. 15; to stay in garrison at Vienna, v. 195–6; to take oath to Maria Theresa at Linz, v. 180

Turkey's treaty with, iii. 437

Vienna connections of, must interest it in events on the Scheldt, ix. 544

Vienna ministers neglect, v. 102

villas of, disparaged by HW, iv. 165–6

Viviani expects Spaniards to conquer, i. 129

vulnerable, ii. 435

war preparations of, will be halted by non-cooperation of English fleet, ii. 370

war ship of, at Leghorn, vii. 108

woods of, Cargil and Hamilton live in, v. 457

Wright may seek appointment to, vi. 499

York, D. of, tours through, in coach, vi. 220–5

Young Pretender crosses, ii. 378

—— may retire to, iv. 93

—— to cross, i. 13, 15

Tutor; tutors ('governors'):

Christian IV's nephew's, i. 339

Christian VII does not have, vii. 40

English: HW's opinion of, iv. 170, 454; Jacobite sympathies of, iii. 112

Tver, Abp and Bp of. *See* Levshin, Petr Georgievich (1737–1812)

Tweeddale, Marchioness of. *See* Carteret, Hon. Frances (d. 1788)

Tweeddale, M. of. *See* Hay, John

'Tweedsside':

Veracini always plays air of, when Mann is present, iv. 148

Twelfth Night:

Winchilsea gambles at court on, ii. 565

Twickle. *See* Wassenaer

Twickenham:

auctions at, v. 121–2

Chute and Whithed visit HW at, iii. 442

Chute to visit, iii. 435

Duane is HW's neighbour in, ix. 216

fleets could almost sail to, in floods, ix. 306

Francklin is HW's tenant at, iv. 374

Giles is HW's neighbour at, viii. 247, 255n

HW not to lead militia of, v. 300, 307, viii. 98

HW settles in, iii. 414

HW's 'metropolis,' iii. 496

HW's stay at, enables him to see Galfridus Mann, iii. 442

Ham House near, v. 439n

Kneller's 'Cave' at, ii. 36

land scarce and villas abundant at, iv. 16

lane at, flooded with water, viii. 47

Mann must not use name of, for SH, iii. 486

military preparations at, viii. 512

old gentlewomen HW's only company at, ix. 530

Pitt, Thomas, receives call at, from Strathmore, vi. 152

—— takes house at, vi. 18, 25

Pope's garden at, v. 417, ix. 177

——'s residence at, mentioned in *New Lesson for Pope*, ii. 35–6

powder mills explode near, vii. 365

Radnor lives at, v. 1n

Robinson's letter mentions, v. 121

SH view posted at, to go to Florence, iv. 379–80

Tuscany as ignorant as, of Dutch events, ix. 544

'unpolitical village,' ix. 589

view of, from SH, iv. 380, ix. 532

Waldegrave, Cts, takes house at, vi. 136

Twickenham Park:

HW often sees Mrs Noel at Ds of Montrose's at, ix. 187, 312, 319, 320

Twickle. *See* Wassenaer

Twisleton, Thomas (ca 1735–1788), 7th Bn Saye and Sele, 1781:

barony of Saye and Sele adjudged to, ix. 165

Two Sicilies, K. of. *See* Ferdinand IV (I)

Two Sicilies:

Montemar conquers, i. 427

protest against nomination of king of, v. 330

Twysden, Frances (1753–1821), m. (1770) George Bussy Villiers, 4th E. of Jersey:

beauty of, in miniature, ix. 411

Paris to be visited by, ix. 411

Tyburn:

Cameron dislikes ignominy of, iv. 384

Derwentwater to be hanged at, iii. 181

Ferrers's execution at, v. 402–3

house-breakers incur risk of, vii. 301

Townshend, Vcts, enjoys hangings at, from her villa nearby, vi. 165

'Tyler, Wat':
Conway's nickname for HW, ii. 539, 559
Tylney, E. See Child, Richard (1680–1750);
Tylney, John (1712–84)
Tylney (before 1734, Child), John (1712–84),
2d E. Tylney, 1750:
Abano visited by, to avoid nephew's death
throes, viii. 22
brother of, iv. 483n
brother's misfortune shocks, iv. 355–6
codicils probably to be cancelled by, viii.
23
death of, greatly affects Mann, ix. 533–4,
537
dinner given by, for Mann's investiture, vii.
60, 63–4
Florence to be visited by, viii. 23, 312
Florence visited by, iv. 355–6
Florentine house to be re-occupied by, vii.
468
Fuentes, Conde and Condesa de, do not
attend ball given by, at Wanstead, v. 417
HW entertained by, at ball, v. 417
HW praises, v. 417
health of, nose-bleed, viii. 145
heir wanted by, viii. 182
Jermy, as his banker, leaves legacy to, ix.
206
jewels bought from Lady Orford and given
to niece by, ix. 144
legacies of, to Mann and Chase, ix. 534
Leopold's comptroller has beer and punch
served to, vi. 379
lives in pompous style, viii. 312
Longs accompany, viii. 312
Mann accompanied by: at investiture, vii.
60; to receive Karl Alexander, iv. 376
—— intimate with, for years, ix. 533, 537
—— tells, that HW caused his promotion,
vi. 376
Naples visit deferred by, viii. 145
Neapolitan possessions of, to be sold for
servants' benefit, ix. 534
Orford, Cts of, occupies Florentine house
of, vii. 468
public ball to be given by, at Naples, viii.
280–1
Rome and Naples to be visited by, viii. 251
servants of, have new laced clothes, vii.
60, 63–4
spacious fine house occupied by, in Naples,
viii. 280
will of, courier takes, to nephew and heir,
ix. 533
Wilton does statue of Bacchus for, iv. 397–8
Tympany:
Pomfret, Cts of, beats time on, iv. 584
—— exhibits, iv. 579
Type, printer's:
Florentine, ix. 507
Tyranny:
HW's reflections on, vii. 100, 452
Mann's reflections on, vii. 518

Tyrants:
HW comments on, ix. 214
HW considers, a proof of an hereafter, viii.
103–4
only successful when they reign in the
hearts of the people, vii. 100
Tyrawley, Bn. See O'Hara, James
Tyrawley, Bns. See Stewart, Mary (d. 1769)
Tyrconnel, E. of. See Carpenter, George
Tyre, Abp of. See Baiardi, Ottavio Antonio
(1694–1764)
Tyre:
Arlington St's resemblance to, iv. 469
Tyrol:
German troops to march to, i. 154
Tyrrel, Dr. ——:
Gondi, Mme, treated by, ii. 87
mercurial unctions administered by, for
scurvy, ii. 87

Ubaldini, Contessa. See Antaldi, Lavinia
Ubaldini, Monsieur ——:
(?) Chute and Whithed occupy 'dull' apart-
ment of, i. 146
Ubaldini, Maria Ottavia (d. 1744), m. (1702)
Pier Filippo Uguccioni; Electress's mistress
of the household:
dies about a year after Electress, iii. 23
Electress discusses her health with, ii. 172
——'s bequests to, ii. 169–70, iii. 23
son of, ii. 170
Ubaldo (called Mignon or Velluti) (d. 1750),
rector of the college of Scolopi:
(?) Medici bastard, ii. 39
Ucalegon:
HW quotes allusion to, vii. 34n
Uccellatori, Gli. See under Gassmann, Florian;
Goldoni, Carlo
Udine:
diocese of, to be created, iv. 191
Venice offers to transfer patriarchate to, iv.
206
Udny, John (1727–1800), English consul at
Venice ca 1761–76, at Leghorn, 1776–ca
1800:
Dick succeeded by, as consul at Leghorn,
viii. 233, 251
dispatches from Gen. Murray brought to
Florence by, ix. 233
Mann's accounts with, relating to Minorca's
siege, ix. 303, 429–31
——'s letter from, about D. of Gloucester,
viii. 311
—— tells: to collect provisions at Florence
for Minorca, viii. 380; to send express
about naval actions near Gibraltar, ix. 9
Mann, Horace II, turns over envoy's duties
to, ix. 676
Pleydell writes to, about D. of Gloucester,
viii. 311
Tuscany demands satisfaction from, in case
of Port Mahon packet-boat, viii. 417

unable to assist Murray, ix. 197
Venetian consulship exchanged by, for one at Leghorn, viii. 233
Uffizi Gallery, at Florence:
Act of Accession provides against scattering the treasures of, v. 466
armoury converted into bad rooms for, ix. 170
Bianchi sets fire to, and robs it of a gold foot, ix. 65
bronzes in, fill several rooms, ix. 170
Bruce, Miss, offended by pictures in, iv. 145
'Cabinet de Madame,' ix. 170
Cellini's gold lamina in, vii. 407
Charles III's tour of, v. 500
china in, rearranged, ix. 170
Cicero bust in, iv. 86
Cocchi, Raimondo, an antiquarian in, v. 152
Conway introduced to Bianchi in, iv. 290
corridors in, resemble upholsterer's shop, ix. 171
crowded with modern painters' portraits, ix. 170
drawings of, executed for HW at Mann's order, i. 58, 68, ii. 133, 181, 202, 214, 292, 303
fire at, vi. 67–8, 71, ix. 65
Francis I has not as yet stripped, iii. 83
Gaddi torso in, ix. 170
Giovanni Gastone's bust in, ix. 170
HW would be glad to have longer account of, when it appears, ix. 531
Laocoön in, vi. 67, 71, ix. 171
Leopold disperses Niobe group in, ix. 170–1, 203, 530–1
—— increases contents of, ix. 230
Mann's old apartment near, i. 381
—— tired by, though carried up stairs, ix. 171
medals in: Conway studies, iv. 290, 297; remain unchanged, ix. 170
new staircase made to, from Loggia, vi. 123, ix. 169–70
Pitt, Anne, considered a connoisseuse at, vii. 457
proposal to plunder, i. 193
Richecourt fears that the Spaniards may rob, ii. 295
scaffali (bookcases) in, taken away, ix. 170
Siries's rooms in, ix. 169
transformation of, ix. 169–71
treasures of, not removed, i. 380
Tribune in: Crew to take designs of, to HW, ii. 274; crystal vase from ix. 169, x. 56; HW deplores violation of, ix. 177; Mann wants to give, to HW, i. 324; perforated, ix. 170; rock crystal and other 'rubbish' sold from, ix. 65; Venus in, compared by Young to his alleged Titian, iv. 331; Zoffany sent to do a view of, vii. 430, 436n, 519, viii. 33–4, 539–40; Zoffany's painting of, criticized by HW, viii. 526–7;

Zoffany's painting of, will record its former state, ix. 177; Zoffany's view of, too crowded with portraits of English travellers then in Florence, viii. 34; Zoffany transfers paintings to, from Pitti, viii. 540
visitors to, Brand, iv. 471; Bruce, Miss, iv. 145; Charles III, v. 500; Conway, iv. 290; Damer, Mrs, ix. 203; Huntingdon, iv. 457; Pitt, Thomas, v. 500–1; Vorontsov and postmaster, v. 249
Walpole, Sir Robert, would enjoy, ii. 212
Wilton guides Huntingdon in, iv. 457
Zoffany had right to take down any painting in, viii. 540
Ughi, Maria Minerva (1731–1822), m. (1750) Luigi or Louis Roland, Conte Lorenzi:
Louis XV reverenced by, when playing kings at cards, iv. 276
Madonna di Loreto visited by, to induce pregnancy, iv. 437
marriage of, to take place, iv. 192
'Paris doll,' v. 501
Ughi, Scipione (1670–1746), or Piero (1676–1744):
Modenese princess told by, that he had danced with her, i. 66
Ugo. See Franchini, Ugo
Uguccione. See Uguccioni
Uguccioni, Signora. See Ubaldini, Maria Ottavia
Uguccioni, ——:
confirmed as nun, ii. 45
Uguccioni, Giovanni Battista Maria (1710–82), senator, 1761; 'Bistina':
abbé writes epithalamiums for, ii. 510
alarm of, over probable reception of his poem and presents, ii. 553–4
Alamanni friend of, ii. 127
believes Cts of Pomfret's boast about her ancestry, iv. 78
Bosville, Mrs, assisted by, ii. 242, 251
brothers of, leave Mann to tell him of Cts Granville's death, iii. 151
canary birds coupled by, at Casa Cannonoci, ii. 446
cantata and epithalamium sent by, to England, ii. 510, 545
Carteret wedding shocks, by its simplicity, ii. 445
compliments expected by, on Carteret wedding, ii. 446
diamond-studded picture of Cts Granville expected by, ii. 554
English visit of, would flatter Bns Carteret and Cts of Pomfret, ii. 467
epithalamium of, must be rewritten, ii. 522
expense of shipping Cts of Pomfret's furniture will ruin, i. 130
Fermor, Lady Juliana, and Miss Shelley will be loved by, iv. 70
Fermor, Lady Sophia (Cts Granville) corresponds with, iii. 151
—— tells, about matrimonial plans, iv. 70

[Uguccioni, Giovanni Battista Maria, *cont.*]
—— will shock, by her death, iii. 133, 148
Fermor, William, missed by, at Leghorn, ii. 509–10
Fermor family idolized by, ii. 509
Granvilles' gifts from, ii. 553
Lestevenons repulse, i. 217
Mann contradicts guess of, about Cts of Orford, iii. 75
—— sees Cts Granville's letters to, iii. 151
—— to get Chute and Whithed introduced by, at Baronessa Ricasoli's, i. 129
—— told by, that Cts of Pomfret wants her furniture sent on, i. 129
—— to tell, that Cts Granville still has conversazioni, ii. 537
mother's inheritance mentioned by, ii. 170
Orford, Cts of, recommends Guise and Valtravers to, iv. 393
—— will probably ask, to get her a house, iv. 393
poems of, would provide Pomfrets with paper, ii. 510, 554
Pomfret, Cts of, corresponds with, i. 129, 170, 217, ii. 126, 196, iii. 61
—— gives silver standish to, ii. 126
—— to translate mottoes by, for pictures, ii. 545
—— will not be welcomed by, iv. 102
Pomfret family's return to Florence wished by, iv. 70
Pomfret family will keep, busy, iv. 97
Pomfrets friendly with, ii. 467n
preferment hoped by, through Carteret's marriage to Lady Pomfret's daughter, ii. 455, 554
religion might be changed by, to get English preferment, ii. 554
Walpole, Bns, has affair with, i. 448
Ugurgieri Malavolti, Signora. *See* Chigi Zondadari, Cecilia
Uhlefeld *or* Uhlefeldt. *See* Ulfeld
Ulcer:
Gloucester, D. of, thought to have, in large intestine, vii. 337
Ulfeld, Corfiz Anton (1699–1760), Graf; Austrian statesman:
Magnan sent by, to Francis I, ii. 564
Venetian ambassador told by, that Maria Theresa demands change in their policy, iv. 189–90
Ulla, La. *See* La Ulla
Ulrica Leonora (1688–1741), Q. of Sweden, 1719–41:
death of, puts English into mourning, i. 255
smallpox prevalent in family of, i. 255
Ulysses:
Putello acts part of, iii. 355
Umbria:
Lobkowitz to go to, ii. 529
Uncles:
HW's reflections on, ix. 331

Unction:
Dumesnil receives, as bishop, iii. 492
extreme: Benedict XIV receives, v. 37, 81; Botta receives, vi. 13; Dauphin receives, vi. 364; Electress has, ii. 160; Old Pretender receives, v. 391, 392, vi. 379; Richecourt's daughter has, v. 43; Young Pretender has, ix. 468, 482n
mercurial, ii. 87
Under-doorkeeper of House of Commons:
insolence of, i. 245
Under-petticoat:
beaver, lined with scarlet shag, given by Braitwitz to Mme Vitelli, ii. 333
HW wears, as old woman, ii. 359
Undersecretary of state. *See* Wood, Robert
Undertaker; undertakers:
Brown, Sir Robert, bargains with, over consumptive daughter's funeral, ix. 609n
Cameron not disturbed by, iv. 384
escutcheon placed by, on Mrs Edwards's door, iv. 4
Ferrers's scaffold hung by, with black, v. 402
for petitions, in English counties, vii. 163
HW's term for Daun, v. 432
of Tower of London, *see* Allingham
Unhappy Favourite, The. See under Banks, John
Uniform; uniforms:
blue and red, laced, worn by Mill and Davison, iii. 407
country squires wear, v. 312
English ladies wear their husbands', viii. 384
for *calcio* at Leghorn, vi. 423
Joseph II wears, without ensigns, vii. 108
of Jacobite forces, iii. 299
whimsical, English at Venice wear, when attending opera at Padua, v. 513
white worn by troops at Bologna border, ii. 85–6
Unigenitus, bull of:
Benedict XIV's senility exhibited in, v. 44–5
HW might amuse himself with, in Paris, v. 337
Louis XV's assassin may have been motivated by, v. 48
University; universities:
Bingham, Hon. Richard, too young for, at 15, viii. 462
books have imprimatur of, ii. 480
HW scoffs at degrees taken at, ix. 316
Uomo nero:
HW asks meaning of, iv. 291, 298
Upholsterer; upholsterers:
crowds of, at sales at Palazzo Pitti, ix. 231
Gibson is, iv. 224
Upholsterer's shop:
corridors in Uffizi gallery resemble, ix. 171
Upper Brook St, London,:
Molesworth's house in, burns, vi. 138

Upper Ossory, Cts of. *See* Liddell, Hon. Anne (ca 1738–1804)

Upper Ossory, E. of. *See* Fitzpatrick, John (1745–1818)

Upton, Mrs ——:
Braddock ill-treats, for not giving him enough money, iv. 492–3

Urbino:
duchy of, Clement XIV from, vii. 117

Urfé, Honoré d' (1568–1625), author:
Astrée, L', HW to resemble shepherd in, iii. 414

Urinal:
Tesi seems to be using, ii. 361

Urine, suppression of:
occurrences of, viii. 39

Urn; urns:
alabaster, *see under* Vase
antique Roman sepulchral, *see under* Altar
glass, bought by HW, x. 7
HW buys, at Rome, x. 7
HW's sepulchral, for Galfridus Mann's monument: designed by Bentley and placed in Linton church, v. 128, 142, 157, 249–50; Mann frames design of, for his bedside, v. 253
HW's sepulchral, for Mann, placed in Linton church, ix. 666, 668, 670, 671, 678
Mann presents, to Ds of Gloucester, viii. 453
—— procures, for Sir Robert Walpole, i. 24
of Clodia, bought by HW, x. 7

Urquhart, Chevalier Adam:
Young Pretender drives away, x. 47

Urrutia, Don Rodrigo, Capt. of the *Poder*:
rescue of, ii. 414

Ursuline convent at Rome:
Wortley Montagu, Mary, enters, vi. 113

Usher, Capt. Arthur (d. 1763):
death of, in fire, while visiting sister on return from Jamaica, vi. 138
negroes of, suspected of starting fire, vi. 141

Usher, Mary Jenney (ca 1723–63), m. (1744) Richard Molesworth, 3d Vct Molesworth:
burned to death, in fire at house in Upper Brook St, vi. 138, 139, 140, 143, 145, ix. 242
husband persuaded by, to give annuity to his brother, vi. 140

Usher of the Black Rod. *See* Molyneux, Sir Francis

Usher of the Black Rod in Ireland. *See* Dayrolles

Usson, Comtesse d'. *See* Poll, Margarethe Cornelia van de

Usson, François-Armand d' (1716–78), Marquis de Bonac; French ambassador to Holland 1751–6:
Rouillé writes through, to Fox, iv. 524

Usson de Bonac, Pierre-Chrysostome d' (1724–82), Comte d'Usson; French ambassador to Sweden 1774–82:
arrival of, in England, vi. 135

envoy to Sweden, married to Dutchwoman, vi. 135n

Hervey, Bns, often entertains, vi. 135

Usurers:
caution should be taught to, in moneylending to noblemen's sons, viii. 237
interest reduction opposed by, iv. 111
Mann has little pity for, iv. 242
rapine by, in England, viii. 231

Usury:
Walker's, iii. 511n

Utica:
Pomfret, Cts of, mistakes Attica for, iv. 579

Utrecht, treaty of:
Aix treaty has Dunkirk demolished according to terms of, iii. 481, 527
Dutch do not forget, iii. 68
English M.P.s accused of trying to reproduce, x. 10
Pynsent opposed, vi. 277, 284

Utrecht Gazette. *See* Gazette d'Utrecht

Vacation:
Londoners used to be lively after long, ix. 558

Vado:
English ships at, iii. 10
Mathews at, ii. 438
Medley takes house at, iii. 432

Vado Bay:
English fleet to be open to, iv. 588
France said to have demanded, of Genoa, iv. 277

Vaillant, Paul (ca 1715–1802), bookseller:
HW patronizes, v. 400
HW's correspondence with, v. 400
sheriff at Ferrers's execution, v. 400–2
Sheriff's Account of Earl Ferrers's Behaviour, v. 400–2
Strand shop of, thronged with curiosity-seekers, v. 400

Vairasse, Denis (fl. 1665–81):
Histoire des Sevarambes, L', v. 552n

Valantano, Madonna di. *See* Madonna

Valdagno:
Mann, Horace II and Lady Lucy, visit, viii. 114–15, 118, 122–3
Schio near, viii. 122
waters of, agree with Lady Lucy Mann, viii. 122

Valence. *See* Valenza

Valencia de Alcantara:
English troops capture, vi. 78

Valenciennes:
Louis XV and Noailles at, ii. 441

Valentano, Madonna di. *See* Madonna

Valentano, 'Prophetesses' of. *See* Poli, Anna Teresa; Renzi, Bernardino

Valenti, ——, dancer:
England visited by, iii. 455
Narni dances with, in Florentine opera, iii. 455

Valenti, Silvio (1690–1756), called Valenti Gonzaga; cardinal, 1738; Papal secretary of state 1740–56:
Benedict XIV assembles cardinals in apartment of, ii. 444
—— consults, about Young Pretender, iv. 22
—— governed by, under Acquaviva's tuition, iii. 114, 158, 330
—— indemnifies, for loss of abbeys, ii. 55
—— said to be betrayed by, to France, Spain, and Austria, iii. 492
——'s secretary of state, ii. 55, iii. 144
Colonna may become *camerlingo* after death of, iv. 589
death of, expected, iv. 463
Mann translates English addresses for benefit of, iii. 144
Maria Theresa's general seizes abbeys of, ii. 55
—— will blame, for Pontano's arrest, ii. 56
paralyzed, iv. 463
St-Odile asks, about Benedict XIV's claim to Monte Santa Maria, iv. 428
Spanish sympathies of, iii. 114
Stosch receives offer from, for map collection, v. 186, 192
translations of Cts of Pomfret's letters sent to, ii. 558
Venetians reject, for low birth, until he becomes Gonzaga, iv. 409, vii. 325
Valentia, Vct. *See* Annesley, Arthur (1744–1816), Annesley, George (1771–1844)
Valentia, Vcts. *See* Lyttelton, Hon. Lucy Fortescue (d. 1783)
Valentini, Regina (1722–1808), m. (ca 1743) Pietro Mingotti; singer:
Cumberland, D. of, favours, iv. 557
Vaneschi disputes with, iv. 557
Valenza:
Charles Emmanuel III to besiege, iii. 237
Sardinians capture, iii. 253, 258
Spaniards threaten, iii. 120, 137
'Valere,' character in Italian comedy:
Lincoln resembles, ii. 103
Valet. *See under* Servants
Valet-secretary, Mann's. *See* Palombo, Domenico
Valle, Andrea. *See* Valle, Filippo
Valle, Filippo della (1697–1770), sculptor:
HW dissatisfied with Livia statue executed by, ii. 292, 303
Livia statue by: payment for, x. 5; to be done, i. 317; to be varnished, ii. 116
Mann's communications with, about Livia statue, ii. 161, 175, 177, 214, vi. 107, 114–15
——'s payment to, for statue, ii. 175, 177, 214
model by, for Livia statue: HW's, decays, vi. 98; Valle may sell, ii. 178–9
mould by, for Livia statue: HW wants another cast from, vi. 98; Mattei, Duke, receives, vi. 115–16

Parker not trusted by, ii. 152
—— to threaten, to get statue finished, i. 317
slowness of, enrages Mann, ii. 127
statue not to be sent by, till paid for, ii. 152
Vallée, La. *See* Valle
Valletort, Vct. *See* Edgcumbe, Richard (1764–1839)
Valletort, Vcts. *See* Hobart, Lady Sophia (1768–1806)
Valli. *See* Valle
Vallombrosa:
Hugford at, i. 482, iv. 23
Mann has never visited, iv. 329
Milton's mention of, arouses English interest, iv. 317
Paoli, Clemente, at, vii. 130, 159
print of: HW sees, at Barrett-Lennard's, iv. 317; Mann to send, to HW, iv. 320, 329
scagliola tables to be sent from, iv. 23
snow imported from, for sherbets, iv. 25
Vallory. *See* Valori
Valltravers. *See* Valtravers
Val Montone:
Neapolitan troops at, ii. 447
Valombrosa. *See* Vallombrosa
Valory, Guy-Louis-Henri (1692–1774), Marquis de; French minister to Prussia:
Frederick II wants, as minister, iv. 541–2
Valory. *See also* Valle
Valtravers, (?) Johann Rudolf (fl. 1747–64), diplomatist:
Florence visited by, iv. 393
Guise's governor, iv. 393
Orford, Cts of, recommends, to Uguccioni, iv. 393
Valvasone, Contessa di. *See* Verità, Eurizia
Valvasone, Carlo Luigi di (1698–1773):
nephew may be aided by, i. 161
nephew to see, i. 70
Valvasone, Clemente Giuseppe di (1699–1744), Col.:
death of, ii. 439
nephew may be aided by, i. 161
nephew to see, i. 70
Valvasone, Ferdinando di (1702–49):
nephew may be aided by, i. 161
nephew to see, i. 70
Valvasone, Gabriele Carlo di (1705–85):
nephew may be aided by, i. 161
nephew to see, i. 70
Valvasone, Maria Anna di (1697–1773), m. (1716) Ball Baldassare Suares de la Concha:
Amorevoli negotiates with Mann through, i. 101, 112
antiquated head-dress of, iv. 148
ball to be given by, i. 56
'Bronzino' bought by, from Laurenzo, and sent to Mann to be sold, i. 128–9
brother-in-law shows 'bawdy matters' to, ii. 40

brother-in-law's madness concealed by, ii. 41

brothers of, to help her son, i. 161

Cerchi, cavaliere, related to, i. 123

Charles Albert may be sought by, i. 161

Chute and Mann entertained by, at play, i. 120

Chute, Mann, and Whithed secured by, to back Tesi's opera, ii. 280–1

daughter's dowry worries, i. 137

daughter's match expected by, ii. 138

daughter's match imagined by, i. 202

daughter's suitor may be cloyed by, ii. 29

daughter wanted by, to marry Roberto Pandolfini, i. 137, 171, 202

Demetrio performed at house of, i. 65, 100, 104, 120

'easy of access,' iii. 84

Electress's funeral procession passes house of, ii. 173

emerald earrings of, in pawn, i. 484

family of, at Valvasone, i. 202

Florentines all to flock to, i. 101

Frederick Augustus buys pictures from, iii. 392

HW asks about, i. 402

HW questions loyalty of, to Mann, i. 419

HW sends news about son and sister of, i. **39**

health of: issue of blood, iii. 226, 238, 243; toothache, ii. 324

Hobart may be enjoyed by, iii. 63

jewels pawned by, i. 137, 484

ladies to be brought by, to Mann's garden, i. 498

Mann expects letter of thanks from, for HW, i. 456

—— gives news of HW to, i. 39

—— goes to Electress's funeral from house of, ii. 173

—— hears from, about Salimbeni, i. 116, 132

—— receives mistaken news from, iii. 75

——'s emerald earrings seized by, i. 484

——'s guests counted by, ii. 1

——'s opera box sometimes occupied by, i. 69, 81, ii. 29, iii. 311

——'s relations with, strained, i. 81, ii. 242

——'s social relations with, i. 101, 104, 120, 484, ii. 1, 98, 275, 281, 353

—— visited by, with diversions, in his illness, i. 101

Maynard talks French with, ii. 372

—— to be introduced to, by Mann, ii. 367

Modenese princess gives étui and snuff-box to, i. 64

Modenese princess to be treated at villa of, with comedy, i. 65

—— ushered in by, i. 56

once handsome, now horrible, vii. 306

Orford, Cts of, said by, to have received husband's letter, iii. 47

papers sought by, ii. 29

parties avoided by, because her jewels are in pawn, i. 137

Pisan lady conducted by, ii. 353

Richecourt said by, to have received letters from Cts of Orford, iii. 64

Salimbeni and Amorevoli brought by, to Mann, i. 101

Salimbeni's accident described by, i. 116, 132

Scarperia dinner in honour of Modenese princess attended by, i. 56

sister of, i. 39n, ii. 25n, 246n

son ordered by, to visit her parents at Friuli and wait for her there, i. 70

son presents 'la Cecca' to, i. 128

son's offer of preferment refused by advice of, ii. 455

Tesi quarrels with, ii. 322

——'s opera may be produced through efforts of, ii. 280, 281

Verona ladies served by, ii. 286

Villio buys pictures from, iii. 392

Violante, Principessa, subject of stories of, iii. 311

Walpole, Horatio (1723–1809), enjoys, iii. 84

Worsley cicisbeo to, v. 460

Valvasone, Maria Cristina di (1705–47), m. (1721) Marchese Orazio Francesco Pucci:

(?) Chute and Whithed to be polite to, i. 42

family of, ii. 25n

Giovanardi accompanies, i. (?) 42, ii. 273

—— advises, i. 46

—— assists and is assisted by, ii. 54

—— may give refuge to, at Bologna, i. 158, 171

—— visited by, near Modena, ii. 54

HW asks if Ds of Modena is to take, to France, ii. 246

HW commends Mann's advice to, i. 171

HW inquires about fate of, after fall of Modena, ii. 31

HW mentions, i. 42

HW politely treated by, i. 39

HW's correspondence with, ii. 25, 31, 54, 68

HW sends silks to, i. 159, 222, 416, ii. 112

HW to receive compliments of, i. 158

Mann's correspondence with, i. 158, 416

—— sends compliments to, i. 42

Modena, Ds of, not accompanied by, ii. 273

Modena visited by, ii. 112

Modenese duchess's Bedchamber woman, ii. 25n, 246n

Modenese D. and Ds quarrel with, i. 158

namesake of, ii. 112

raffle of china won by, i. 159

Rangoni rejected by, as cicisbeo, i. 46

success of, at Reggio, i. 46

Valvasone, Massimiliano di (b. 1708):

nephew may be aided by, i. 161

nephew to see, i. 70

Valvasone, Nicolò Cesare (1666–1745), Conte di:
daughters of, ii. 25n
grandson to have visited, at Friuli, i. 70
Valvasone, Valenzio di (1703–between 1746 and 1760):
nephew may be aided by, i. 161
nephew to see, i. 70
Valvasone, near Friuli:
Suares family visits, i. 202
Valverde, Duca di. See Gravina, ——; Reggio e Branciforte, Don Luigi
Van Berckel; Van Berghen. See Berckel
Vanbrugh, Charles (d. 1745), Ensign:
mortally wounded at Fontenoy, iii. 43
Vanbrugh, Capt. Giles Richard (d. 1746):
drowned, iii. 378–9
Goldsworthy's brother-in-law, iii. 379
Vanbrugh, Sir John (1664–1726), Kt, 1714; dramatist; architect:
HW ridicules architecture of, viii. 93
Provoked Husband: Cibber's preface to, vii. 132n; HW quotes Lady Townley's remark in, vii. 210, ix. 476
Provoked Wife, Christian VII attends performance of, vii. 57
Vanbrugh, Philip (1682–1753), naval captain; naval commissioner:
daughter to live with, at Plymouth, ii. 158
Vanbrugh, Philippia (ca 1716–77), m. (1734) Burrington Goldsworthy, consul at Leghorn 1736–54 and at Cadiz 1754–62:
absurdities of, i. 351
Albizzi, 'the little,' calls on, i. 316
Barrett-Lennard, Mrs, will be tired by, iv. 93
children misinformed by, i. 351
Chute irritated by, i. 372
——'s joke about, i. 351, 373, iv. 93, 298
concert to be attended by, i. 316
Craon calls on, i. 314
Craon, Princesse de, called on by, i. 316
—— calls on, i. 316
Del Benino, Contessa, calls on, i. 316
England may be visited by, with her children, i. 262
England to be visited by, ii. 13, 31
father to be visited by, at Plymouth, ii. 158
Galli, Contessa, helps, i. 351
Grifoni, Mme, calls on, i. 316
HW commends Mann's kindness to, i. 334
HW disliked by, i. 146
HW meets, at Ds of Richmond's, ii. 158, 188
HW misses, at Bedford House, vi. 17
HW's apartment at Mann's house occupied by, i. 314
HW thinks English journey of, useless, ii. 31
husband's gout encourages, iv. 335
Italian learned by, at Leghorn, v. 353n
Leghorn house of, prepared, i. 381

Leghorn situation described by, i. 313
letter from, to Mann, i. 395, 420, iv. 335
maids of, misbehave, i. 395
Mann calls, 'horrid fool,' 'unconnected,' and 'fiddle faddle,' i. 316
Mann leaves, with Chute and Whithed, i. 313
—— longs for departure of, i. 316, 351, 362, 371, 381
—— pays court to, at Leghorn theatre, i. 260
——'s house left by, i. 395, 401–2
—— to be visited by, iv. 93
—— to shelter, at Florence, i. 293, 306
—— visited by, i. 313, 343, 381
—— would have good post given to husband of, to deter from Florentine promotion, ii. 13–14
'pert little unbred thing,' ii. 158
Pomfret, Cts of, corresponds with, i. 420
Richmond, Ds of, has, as companion, i. 186, 334n
—— invites, for a visit, ii. 158
Richmonds to be urged by, to intercede for her husband, ii. 13
servants of, i. 306, 313
verbs disliked by, v. 353n
Wachtendonck cicisbeo to, i. 146–7, 186n
—— leaves coach and horses to, i. 110
—— pays, i. 147, 186
—— praised by, i. 105
—— relinquishes picture of, at priests' demand, i. 109
——'s death may make, anxious to leave, i. 138
Wager, Sir Charles, said to be uncle of, i. 302n
—— will aid, ii. 13, 31
Walpole, Bns, tells rumour to, i. 361
'young fellows' call on, i. 314
Vance, Abbé de:
Lorenzi tells story about irregular baptism of, to Mann, i. 62
Vandals. See Goths and Vandals
Vandelli, Joseph:
captured at Velletri, ii. 493
Vandeput, Sir George (ca 1717–84), 2d Bt:
Crowle counsel for, iv. 224
petition of, presented by Egmont, iv. 224
Vandermeer. See Montvandermeer
Vandières, Marquis de. See Poisson, Abel-François
Van Dorth. See Dorth
Van Dyck, Sir Anthony (1599–1641), Kt, painter:
cat in style of, i. 495
Cipriani's paintings to replace those by, at Houghton, ix. 316
'Clinton's' portrait attributed to, ix. 151, 227, 240, 292, 298, 304, 501, 504
costumes of, imitated by masqueraders, i. 339, vii. 193

Orford, E. of, complained of having too many pictures by, ix. 418
'Soldiers at Cards' by, bought by HW at Oxford's sale, i. 373
Walpole family's full-length portraits by, sold for a song, iv. 261
Van Dyke. *See* Van Dyck
Vane, Vcts. *See* Hawes, Anne; Hawes, Frances
Vane, Hon. Frederick (1732–1801), M.P.:
Pulteney's legacy to, vi. 560
Vane, Gilbert (1678–1753), 2d Bn Barnard:
son of, iv. 39n
Vane, Hon. Gilbert (d. 1772), Ensign, 1732; Lt-Col., 1745:
German officers will not serve with, unless he fights duel with Rich, i. 486
Vane, Sir Henry (1589–1655), Kt, 1611:
Wentworth enrages, by taking Raby title, i. 333n
Vane, Hon. Henry (ca 1705–58), 3d Bn Barnard, 1753; cr. (1754) E. of Darlington; M.P.:
afterwards E. of Darlington, ii. 18n, iv. 39n
Cholmondeley succeeds, as vice-treasurer of Ireland, ii. 551
confusion of, iv. 4
Country Girl, The, satirizes, ii. 23
dismissed as lord of the Treasury, iv. 517
Edgcumbe may be succeeded by, as Irish paymaster general, i. 487, 492
HW's opinion of, iv. 39
Labour in Vain satirizes, ii. 18–20
New Ode, A, satirizes, ii. 51
paymaster, iv. 517
Petersham, Lady Caroline, coupled with name of, iv. 140
Potter succeeds, as joint paymaster, v. 25
promotion of, as vice-treasurer of Ireland, satirized in *Labour in Vain,* ii. 18n
Pulteney gives position to, ii. 72n
——'s 'toad-eater,' i. 487, iv. 39
Treasury appointment of, iv. 39
Treasury duties of, interrupted by care of Ds of Newcastle's pig, iv. 72
Williams, Sir Charles Hanbury, satirizes, ii. 321
Vane, Henry (?1726–92), 2d E. of Darlington:
Cleveland's bequest to, vii. 5
Pulteney's legacy to, vi. 560
Vane, Hon. Raby (1736–69), M.P.:
Pulteney's legacy to, vi. 560
Vane, William Holles (1714–89), 2d Vct Vane, 1734:
Churchill's remark to, i. 139
entail of Newcastle estate broken by, i. 209–10
wife idolized by, i. 459
wife of, iv. 230n
wife's divorce from, wished by Berkeley, i. 459
wife wanted back again by, i. 209–10
Vaneschi, Francesco (fl. 1732–56), Abbate:
Bonducci reports English success, operas,

cheating of Lord Middlesex, change of religion, and marriage by, ii. 198
—— wants to succeed, ii. 198
Calais visited by, i. 141
Cumberland, D. of, disputes with, over opera house, iv. 557
death of, reported, ii. 198, 210
excessive charges by, i. 191, 216
HW travels with, i. 141
Holdernesse entertains, ii. 131
London opera to discard, i. 358
low English woman married by, ii. 210
Middlesex and Raymond cheated by, at Lucca, i. 216
Mingotti and Ricciarelli dispute with, iv. 557
opera by, parodied by Crudeli, i. 200
opera directors dominated by, i. 191
tailor brought by, from Italy, i. 191
yacht visited by, i. 141
Vaneschi, Mme ——:
Amorevoli used to keep, ii. 210
Holdernesse entertains, ii. 131
marriage of, ii. 210
Van Heck, Daniel (fl. 1740–50), postal director at Leyden:
delays caused by sending letters through, iii. 145–6, 257
Van Hoey, Abraham (1684–1766), Dutch ambassador to France:
Dutch minister at Paris, iii. 264n
Holland asked by, if he should celebrate French victories in Flanders, iii. 91
Kilmarnock spurns intercessions of, iii. 285
letters of: Mann asks about, ii. 337; printed in English press, iii. 271
Paris visited by, iii. 264
Vanities:
HW receives, because he never seeks them, ix. 68
Vanity:
Mann considers essential, to Court life, vi. 407
——'s reflections on, iv. 150
Vanloo, Jean-Baptiste (1684–1745), painter:
portrait by, of Vcts Townshend, i. 174
Vanneck, Elizabeth (d. 1760), m. (1750) Hon. Thomas Walpole:
death of, from fever and sore throat, v. 416
Vanneck, Sir Gerard William (?1743–91), 2d Bt, 1777; M.P.:
alleged daughter of, v. 416n
Vanneck, Sir Joshua (d. 1777), cr. (1751) Bt:
daughter of, v. 416n
Vanni, Gobbo:
Babi paid by, for Florentine appearance, ii. 526
Vannini, Attilia *and* Giovanni, inn of, at Florence:
Elector Palatine receives Leopold's visit at, viii. 164
(?) Young Pretender stays at, vii. 225

Vansittart, Henry (1732–?70), governor of Bengal; M.P.:
ship of, lost, vii. 282
Vanvitelli, Luigi (1700–73), architect:
Dicharazione dei disegni del reale palazzo di Caserta: awaits shipment at Leghorn, v. 318; HW receives, v. 363; HW thanks Mann for, v. 327; Hamilton might be jealous of Mann over, vi. 547; Mann gets, and hopes to get further ones, vi. 547; Mann sends bill of lading for, to HW, v. 324, vi. 545, 547, 555, 559, 561, 562; Mann trying to get, for HW, v. **272**
Var, *or* Varo, river:
Austrian crossing of: accomplished, iii. 336; Genoese should have been disarmed before, iii. 345; in retreat, iii. 363; Maillebois will make the Austrians regret, iii. 334; Mann awaits news of, iii. 330
Charles Emmanuel III said to have defeated the Spaniards near, ii. 466
——— urges Austrians to drive French across, iii. 436
English ships at mouth of, iii. 336
French crossing of: Austrians would be embarrassed by, iii. 367; Boufflers predicts, iii. 406; in retreat, burning bridges, iii. 323; may not be possible, iii. 405–6; to intercept Austrian expedition for Genoa, iii. 374, 376; under Belle-Isle, iii. 363, 409; would encourage Neapolitan advances, iii. 378
Spanish cavalry to repass, iii. 51
Varese:
revenues of, vi. 331
Simonetti, Cts, becomes princess of, vi. 331
Varo, the. *See* Var
Vasari, Giorgio (1511–74), biographer; architect; painter:
portrait by, of Bianca Cappello: HW installs, in Arlington St house, iv. 407; HW thanks Mann for, iv. 403; HW to frame, with Latin inscription and grand ducal coronet, iv. 407; HW used to admire, at Casa Vitelli, iv. **398**, 402–3, 404; Mann hangs, in his bedchamber, iv. 398; Mann sends, to HW, iv. 398, 402–3, 404, 407, 414, x. 56
Vase; vases:
alabaster, from Volterra: Conway's, procured by Mann, iv. 321, 329; Dashwood's, procured by Mann through HW at Dashwood's request, i. 249, 287, 351, 369, ii. 214; Fox's, for Holland House, procured by Mann, iv. 569, 582, v. 49, 97, 118, 123, 132, 134, 139, 148, 155, 178, 187, 189, 212, 218; HW's, for Wolterton, procured by Mann, ii. 47; Hyde's, arrive, vi. 13; Hyde's, ready and waiting shipment from Italy, v. 524; Lyttelton's procured by Mann, iv. 539, 547, 554, 557, 582; Mann gets, weekly, i. 394–5
alabaster pieces seldom big enough for 4-ft vases, iv. 582
antique, bought by, HW, x. 4

bronze, HW buys, at Oxford's sale, i. 374
Etruscan: alleged discovery of, in Tuscany, v. 561, vi. 6; Hamilton does book about, x. 46; Hamilton's collection of, purchased by Parliament for British Museum, x. 46; made in Staffordshire, vii. 211
from Ginori's factory: HW receives, from Mann, ix. 635, x. 56; Mann orders, for HW, ix. 598; take 4 months to make, ix. 645
HW buys, at Rome, x. 7
HW to buy, at Mead's sale, iv. 470
of citrons, i. 322
of rock crystal, see *under* Rock crystal
on eagle's pedestal, iii. 122
on Stosch's sculptured gems, v. 189, 201
Vasil'chikov, Alexander Semenovich:
Catherine II's new favourite, vii. 441, 444
Vassal, Elizabeth, m. Hon. Gen. John Barrington:
(?) Kingston, Ds of, attended by, viii. 192
Vassalage, feudal:
privately-raised regiments will help restore, x. 15
Vassari. *See* Vasari
Vassor. *See* Le Vassor
Vatican:
air of, pestiferous in hot months, viii. 462
Austrians occupy heights near, ii. 533
balcony of, Benedict XIV gives public benediction from, v. 103
Charles of Naples dines at, ii. 533
Clement XIII at, during D. of York's visit to Monte Cavallo, vi. 228
Clement XIV poisoned at, viii. 49
———'s body brought to, viii. 43
HW asks whether, is hung with sackcloth, ix. 237
Mann has library at, searched for Richard I's poem, v. 157, 169–70
——— should threaten Florentines with thunder of, if they do not welcome Garrick, vi. 177
——— to get copies of paintings in, iv. 328
Petrarch's and Bembo's notes on MS at, v. 169
Raphael's loggias in, vii. 298
Stosch's library bought by, viii. 284
Vauban, Marquise de. *See* Puget, Henriette de
Vaudreuil, Comte de. *See* Rigaud, Louis-Philippe de (ca 1691–1763)
Vaudreuil, Marquis de. See Rigaud, Pierre-François de (1698–1765)
Vaudreul. *See* Vaudreuil
Vaughan, George (fl. 1730–47), sedan-chair maker:
Frederick, P. of Wales, dismisses, for voting for Trentham, iv. 122
witticism by, on Frederick, P. of Wales's chair, iv. 122, 144
Vaughan, Hannah (1711–68), m. ——— Pritchard; actress:
plays acted by, iii. 342

Vaughan, Sir John (ca 1731–95), K.B., 1792; Lt-Gen., 1782:
  ingratitude of George III and Lord North towards, ix. 218
Vaughan, Lady Rachel. *See* Wriothesley, Lady Rachel (ca 1637–1723)
Vauguion; Vauguyon. *See* La Vauguyon
Vaulting:
  by Accademia dei nobili, vi. 367
Vaux, Comte de. *See* Jourda, Noël de (1705–88)
Vaux, Ann (d. 1767), m. 1 (1737) William Penn; m. 2 (1767) Alexander Durdin:
  Burdett accompanies and abandons, in Paris, iv. 20
Vauxhall, London:
  diversions at, must be curtailed by inclement weather, iv. 69
  Gunning sisters pursued at, by mobs, iv. 260
  HW avoids, i. 434
  HW prefers, to Ranelagh because of water approach and better garden, i. 434
  link-boys' saying at, iv. 91
  Mann's garden compared to, ii. 478, 485, 497, iv. 427
  Newcastle's dessert imitates, iv. 126
  operas eclipsed by, i. 421
  Ranelagh to rival, i. 401
  visitors to: Christian VII, vii. 41; HW, i. 450; Walpole, George, i. 450
Vecchiarelli, Isabella (ca 1681–1761), m. Scipio Publicola, Principe di Santa Croce:
  Craon, Princesse de, met by, i. 3
Veers, Daniel Diederick (b. ca 1718), impostor:
  borrows from bankers in Paris, Lyon, Marseille, and Genoa, iii. 507, 510n
  Niccolini not present to detect, iv. 7
  Onslow's son impersonated by, in Florence, iii. 505, 510n
  signatures forged by, iii. 507
Vegetable; vegetables:
  Mann, Horace II, has diet of, ix. 353
  Pembroke lives upon, iv. 109
Vegetable Staticks. See under Hales, Stephen
Veglia:
  'Grogrum' gives, ii. 333
Veigel, Eva Maria. *See* 'Violette'
Veil:
  black: Kingston, Ds of, might wear, at trial, viii. 187; Kingston, Ds of, wears, viii. 6; Waldegrave, Cts, wears, vii. 193
  red, worn by Mrs George Pitt at masquerade, iv. 49
Velletri:
  Charles of Naples at, ii. 447, 454, 487, 489, 490, 504
  —— retires to, ii. 533
  Francis III of Modena at, ii. 454, 487
  Lobkowitz blamed by Mann for Charles's escape at, ii. 514–15
  ——'s attack on, ii. 486–94, 504, 514
  Spaniards and Neapolitans fortify, ii. 454

Spaniards fear repetition of attack on, ii. 533
Vellum:
  leaves of, in pocket book, i. 194
Velluti, Ferdinando (1681–1763), Barone del Galluccio:
  Montemar to confer with, i. 228, 314, 323
  Spaniards' route to be protested by, i. 341
Velluti. *See also* Filippo, Ubaldo
Velmonte. *See* Val Montone
Velvet:
  black, Florentine husband gives coupon of, to wife on birth of heir, viii. 233
  breeches of, ii. 334
  brocade of, ii. 169
  cap of, black, ii. 85
  carpet of, ix. 536
  coffin of, vi. 216
  crimson, Pomfret wears suit of, iv. 390
  cushion of, ix. 536
  disrespect shown to wearers of, v. 94
  Edward I's, found perfect in his grave, viii. 4
  gown of, black, Bagnolese wears, ii. 128
  green, bag of, used by secretaries of state and Lord Treasurer, ii. 225
  muffeteens of, vi. 3
  red: Buckingham, Ds of, has robes of, i. 254; figure of Siena dressed in, for St John's Day celebration, ii. 251
  royal garments of, might just as well be buckram and tinsel, ix. 624
  violet-coloured, mantle of, v. 529
  yellow, Montagu, Lady Mary Wortley, wears, vi. 17
Vence:
  French forces at, iii. 336
Venereal disease:
  Keysar's pills to cure, viii. 451n
  occurrences of, i. 444, iv. 36, 447, vi. 551
Venerosi Pesciolini, Signore Michele:
  (?) Santa Maria faction at Pisa led by, ix. 582
Venetian; Venetians:
  Cerretesi taken by, to Oxford and Blenheim, ii. 166
Venetian mask. *See under* Mask
Venetian noble:
  Catalans wish to capture, i. 132
Venetian prints:
  Jackson's, at SH, iv. 375, 380–1
Venetian song:
  Salimbeni and Amorevoli sing, in Mann's garden, i. 240
Vengeance, English war ship:
  escapes to Ireland, ix. 152
  in danger, v. 350
Venice:
  (?) air of, benefits HW, i. 77
  airs of, *see* Airs, Venetian
  ambassadors from and to, *see under* Ambassador
  arsenal at, busy preparing regatta for D. of York, vi. 241

1024INDEX

INDEX

[Venice, *continued*]

Ascension Day festivities of: Craons to attend, i. 25, iv. 29; Cumberland, D. of, to attend, vii. 559; England might copy, viii. 112; English visitors to flock to, vi. 292, vii. 296–7; Gloucester, D. and Ds of, to attend, 291; Joseph II and Leopold to attend, vii. 108, 111, viii. 95, 105; Maria Louisa to attend, vii. 205; Pitt, Thomas, to attend, v. 500; to be rivalled at Florence on St John's Day, ii. 462; York, D. of, to attend, vi. 204, 224, 232

Austrian minister to, named by Guadagni, vii. 272

barcaroles of, iv. 177, vii. 249

Bavarian troops said to be visible from, i. 108

beheading at, of man who stole a cup from a church, i. 85

Benedict XIV abused even by boatmen of, iv. 177

—— demands complete submission from, iv. 206

—— quarrels with, over Attems' appointment to Aquileia, iv. 160–1, 163, 165, 173, 176, 177, 189–91, 198

Bethel's asthma cured at, ii. 65, 117

Bonaichi flees to, i. 148

Bonaventuri flees from, to Florence, iv. 414

Boothby to get passports at, v. 481

bride of, abducted by Pembroke, vii. 152

Brown, Sir Robert, gets fortune as merchant, at, ix. 609

Capello recalled by, from Rome, iv. 161, 176

Cappello, Bianca, made daughter of the Republic by, iv. 399, 415

carnival at, i. 134

Chesterfield to select minister to, iii. 453

Chute suggested by Mann for post at, iii. 444, 448, 458

Clement XIII's election as pope will heal Rome's breach with, v. 219

——'s family honoured by, v. 230

——'s ridiculous letters to, v. 236–7

Compagni and Libri's correspondent at, i. 422

consuls from and to, *see under* Consul

Cornaro daughter made daughter of the Republic by, iv. 399, 415

courier from India to, v. 523

Craon, Princesse de, would dislike fleeing to, i. 178

custom house officer in, i. 64

Dixon in service of, vii. 296

doge and senate of, told by Lady Mary Wortley Montagu, that she will reconcile them with George II, i. 98

doge of, *see* Foscarini, Marco (1695–1763); Grimani, Pietro (d. 1752); Pisani, Luigi (1663–1741)

doges of, rule harmlessly, v. 105, 126

doge's salary at, i. 75

Du Tillot may succeed Montallegre at, vii. 325

edict of, against Rome, vii. 56

election at, for doge and procurator, i. 75–7

Eleonora Luisa dies at, ii. 62n

England to receive delegates from, to congratulate George II, v. 508–9

English peer demanded by, as resident, vii. 325

English visitors at, soon to come in crowds to Florence, vi. 41

fanali wanted from, i. 59, 73, 76, 87

Ferrara may be garrisoned by, i. 380

fireworks at, for doge's election, i. 76

floods in territory of, v. 134

Florence full of letters from, ii. 553

Florentine opera lures Sir James Gray from, iii. 433

Francis I's agent at, sends rumours of English-French war, ii. 44

Francis III and Don Philip said to have retreated to, iii. 269

Francis III may finish carnival at, ii. 161

Gaetani at, collects notices of great men, vi. 14, 35

George III buys art collection from Smith at, vi. 107, ix. 93

——'s letter to, accrediting Northampton, vi. 150

——'s portrait to be sent from, to Mann, vi. 501

Gloucester, D. of, made ill by heat and nauseous air of, viii. 314

—— not to take house at, viii. 252

—— to visit, vii. 370

gondoliers at, i. 64, iv. 177

Gray, Sir James, feigns illness before departure from, iv. 370

—— said to have accepted post at, with reluctance, iii. 472

—— stays in, in hope of shift to Berlin, iii. 444

—— temporarily leaves, iii. 433, 438

—— will not leave, iii. 457

Greek refugees flee to, vii. 226, 235

HW mentions, i. 43

HW's letter comes by way of, iii. 348

Hartington and Smyth set out for, i. 23

Holdernesse not improved by stay at, iii. 435

Holdernesses expect child at, iii. 41

Holdernesse to leave Sir James Gray at, as resident, ii. 431–2, iii. 41

Inquisition at, iv. 198, 420

Joseph II invades, viii. 37

letters from: reach Florence on Wednesdays only, viii. 136; report D. of Gloucester's death, viii. 136

library of St Mark at: Chute has seen, ii. 63; to be copied for ceiling of Houghton picture gallery, ii. 63

manifest prepared by, for circulation in European courts, iv. 176

Mann hears rumour from, of Murray's transfer to Constantinople, vi. 356
—— hopes Cts of Orford will prefer, to Florence, iii. 369
—— hopes not to be sent to, ii. 244
—— receives letter from, i. 108
—— regrets that HW's portrait was not painted for him at, ii. 243
—— will write to, about Zanetti's cameo, vi. 6
Mantuan duke might be bullied by, iv. 409
Mari leaves, i. 226
Maria Theresa may arouse France by threats to, iv. 176
—— negotiates with, iv. 189–90
—— told by Benedict XIV not to attack, iv. 177
—— threatens, but does not harm, iv. 173
—— wants, to accept Attems, iv. 160–1
Marlborough said to have bought Zanetti's gems at, v. 561, vi. 6
masking at, i. 77
masquerade of, imitated at Ranelagh, iv. 46
Methodists would have gondoliers at, singing hymns, iv. 177
Middlesex may be ambassador to, ii. 289
ministers from and to, see under Minister
minister to be sent by, to England, ii. 244
Modenese ducal family to flee to, i. 442
Montagu, Lady Mary Wortley, gives copies at, of her letters, vi. 141
—— leaves her clothes at, vi. 4
Murray usually takes company from, to opera at Padua, v. 513
neutrality promised by, i. 226
Niccolini may live at, iv. 24
Northampton leaves for Geneva, vi. 150, 154
——'s official entry at, vi. 142, 150, 154
—— to go to, as minister, v. 505
nunciature and dataria shut up by, iv. 173
nuncio at, see under Nuncio
opera scene depicts, i. 302
Orford, Cts of, has house at, iii. 50
—— may settle at, iii. 46, 50
Orlov receives courier from, vii. 204
Pasquali at, seeks books on music for HW, v. 477, 482
patriarchate might be transferred by, to the Udine, iv. 206
Paul V's quarrel with, iv. 198
Pierson brings pictures from, viii. 570
Pius VI threatens, with interdiction, viii. 189
post from, to Florence, i. 88, 190, iii. 439
Prussian minister at, desires peace, i. 483
quarantine on borders of, ii. 122
Richecourt may visit, iii. 47
—— sends valuables to, ii. 513
Rome and Vienna get couriers from, iv. 190

Rome gets no more money from, for benefices, iv. 173
Rome's quarrels with, iv. 160–1, 163, 165, 173, 176, 177, 189–91, 198, 206, 420, v. 219, 230, vii. 56, viii. 189
rumour of Austrian-Prussian peace comes from, i. 134
St Mark's library at, ii. 63
San Barnaba, poor nobles at, i. 75
San Lorenzo, Riva nun leaves, ii. 86
senate of: Benedict XIV distrusts, iv. 206; censures Capello, iv. 177; dismisses nuncio, iv. 173, 176; Grimani's family lose votes in, i. 76; Mann to send memorial to, iv. 198; Wotton's relations with, iv. 198
ship of: captured by English, iii. 81; gives information to Cornish, ii. 414
Smith 'merchant of,' ii. 465
——'s collection at, packed by Dalton, vi. 107, 115
—— tries to hire Pertici and 'tinca nera' at, for English theatre, ii. 198
'snug' for love affairs, i. 108
Stanhope rejected by, as English resident, because of illegitimacy, vii. 325
Strange justifies his conduct at, in letters, viii. 298
SH's view resembles, iii. 497
Stuart Mackenzie gets equipment for embassy at, v. 508
—— said to be rejected by, vii. 325
Suares family to visit, i. 156, 161, 171
tea plentiful in, i. 59
Tesi performs in opera at, ii. 280, 520–1
Trieste to eclipse, iv. 102
Turkish threat incites, to prepare for war, v. 494
Udny transferred from, to Leghorn, viii. 233
Ulfeld sends courier to, iv. 190
Valenti rejected by, for low birth, iv. 409, vii. 325
vessel of, with English engineers, intercepted by French frigate off Corsica on way from Leghorn to Minorca, viii. 476–7
Vienna court threatens, for defying Benedict XIV, iv. 176
visitors to: Bethel, ii. 65, 117; Brown, Lady, ix. 246; Bute, vii. 103, 161, 297, 302; Cholmondeley, vii. 349; Chute, i. 74, 101, iii. 257, 268; Craven, Bns, ix. 632, 654; Dalton, vi. 107, 115; Damer brothers, vi. 287; Dick, Mr and Mrs, vi. 142, 154; Earl Marischal, iii. 379; Elcho, iii. 148, 379; Eleonora, Ps, i. 74, 77; Francis III, ii. 222, iv. 76; Gloucester, D. and Ds of, viii. 125, 130, 134, 305, 314–15; Gray, Thomas, i. 43, 82, 445; HW, i. 54, 58, 64, 72, 74–7, 84–5, 86, 88, 94; Hervey, iii. 148; Lee, Capt., iv. 364; Lincoln, i. 41, 61, 72, 86; Magnan, iii. 563; Modena, Ds of, ii. 222; Montagu, Lady Mary Wortley, i. 92, 98; Murray, Lord George, iii. 379; Nicco-

[Venice, *continued*]
lini, iv. 24; Pembroke, vii. 119; Pitt,
Thomas, v. 512; Pomfrets, i. 35, 41; Riche-
court, i. 195; Schulenburg, iii. 50–1;
Spence, i. 86; Stuart-Mackenzies, viii. 381;
(?) Walpole, Bns, i. 107, 115, 125, 134;
Whithed, i. 74, 101, iii. 257, 268; *see also
under* Ascension Day festivities of
Walpole, Bns, wears costume of, i. 317
Walpole, Sir Robert, to be subject of
panegyric to be in work published at, vi.
14, 35
Wright, Sir James, takes post at, vi. 499
Young Pretender said not to be well re-
ceived at, i. 98
Venison:
HW serves, at SH, iv. 89
Italian contempt of, iv. 83
Lorenzi says, is as good as beef, iv. 89
Newcastle procures, from New Park, i. 506
pasty of, vi. 322
slaves get, from Pisa forest, iv. 83
Ventimiglia:
Ambrose blockades, iii. 37
Austrians and Piedmontese retreat to-
wards, iii. 409
French capture castle of, iii. 422
Leutrum to besiege, iii. 436–7, 441
Spanish stores at, destroyed by Charles
Emmanuel III's troops, iii. 58
Ventletrap:
price of, v. 173
Venturelli, Gregorio:
Dissertatio super controversiis . . . Cybo, i.
34
Venturi, Neri (1702–58), senator, 1734:
new Regency member, v. 125
Venturi Gallerani, Ottavia, m. (1716) Ottavio
Sansedoni:
(?) dying, iv. 429
Venturini, Signora. *See* Behan, ——
Venturini, Leonardo (fl. 1738–59), bookseller
and publisher of Lucca:
England visited by, ii. 391
wife met by, at Boulogne, and brought to
Lucca, ii. 392
Venus:
bronze statue of, bought by HW, x. 7
Francavilla's statue of, vi. 583
HW's name for the Tedeschi, iv. 41
statue of, extracting thorn from foot, iv.
547
Titian's, viii. 527, 540
Venus, English war ship:
in danger, v. 350
Venus de' Medici:
compared to alleged Titian, iv. 331
gesso of: HW wants, iii. 34; Mann to get,
for Lyttelton, iv. 539, 547, 554
Wilton copies, for Rockingham, iv. 397
Zoffany's painting of Tribune omits, viii.
527

'Venus Disarming Cupid.' *See under* Cam-
biaso, Luca
Veracini, Francesco Maria (1690–ca 1750),
musician and composer:
sonata performed by, iv. 148
Verazano. *See* Verrazzano
Verb; verbs:
Goldsworthy, Mrs, ignorant of, v. 353
Verberil. *See* Rigaut de Barbezieu
Vercelli:
robbery near, iii. 334
Vercellini, Frans, Lt:
captured at Velletri, ii. 493
Verdea, wine of. *See under* Wine
Verdigris:
Mann's 'accident' from, viii. 8, 15
Vere, Bn. *See* Beauclerk, Aubrey (1740–1802);
Beauclerk, Lord Vere (1699–1781)
Vere, Bns. *See* Chambers, Mary (d. 1783);
Ponsonby, Lady Catherine (1742–89)
Vere, Lady Diana de (d. 1742), m. (1694)
Charles Beauclerk, cr. D. of St Albans:
Hampton Court paintings of beauties in-
clude, i. 295n
sons attend funeral of, at Windsor, i. 295
Vere family:
pedigree of, iv. 181
Vergennes, Comte de. *See* Gravier, Charles
(1718–87)
Vergy. *See* Treyssac de Vergy
Véri, Joseph-Alphonse de (1724–99), auditor
of the Rota:
Guasco excluded by, vi. 575
Verna, La ('the Vernia'):
Paoli, Clemente, seeks retreat at, vii. 130
Vernacci, Mme. *See* Brandi, Gaetana
Vernaccini, Abate Francesco, (fl. 1783–5),
Neapolitan agent in Tuscany:
news received by, ix. 375
Vernaccini, Abate Ranieri (d. 1759), Spanish
agent in Tuscany 1741–59:
Castellar tells, to threaten Regency with
blockade, i. 349
Craon pressed by, for answer, i. 280
——'s letter from, i. 241–2
Gages's correspondence with, ii. 324
Montemar sends courier to, i. 226
—— to receive pistols from, i. **207**
Regency council receives Neapolitan memo-
rial from, about allodials, ii. 177
Salas communicates with, i. 215
sends news to Montemar, i. 238
Vienna court sends packet to, by Craon,
iii. 292–3
Vernaci. *See* Del Vernaccia
Vernaci, Mme. *See* Brandi, Gaetana
Vernaroli, Ipolite, Col.:
captured at Velletri, ii. 493
Vernet, Joseph (*or* Claude-Joseph) (1714–
89), painter:
Patch studied under, vii. 275
Verney, John (1738–1816), 14th Bn Wil-
loughby de Broke, 1752:

Gordon rioters assault, ix. 53–4

Vernio, Conte di. *See* Bardi, Carlo

Vernon, Edward (1684–1757), Adm., 1745; M.P.:
American war may produce successor to, iv. 449
Ascanio, Père, disparages, i. 86
birthday of, i. 196, 211, v. 171
Cartagena should not have been relinquished by, i. 96
coast patrol organized by, iii. 110
disgrace of, iii. 188, 244, 253
Estevenon, Mme, discusses, i. 200
forgotten in England, i. 390
HW knows inside information of, about West Indies, iii. 494
HW parodies, i. 76
habeas corpus suspension opposed by, ii. 408
Ipswich near home of, iii. 494n
letters to, published by him, iii. 459, 472
Mann curious to hear about reception of, in England, ii. 151
Martin to succeed, iii. 188
Mathews may be succeeded by, ii. 312
merchant knocks down, ii. 143
name of, removed from list of admirals, iii. 244, 253
Philipps receives letter of complaint from, about provisions, iii. 168
places named by, i. 175
portrait of, on ale-house signs, ii. 423, iii. 255
privateers pursued by, iii. 173
Pulteney's letter to, on Portobello capture, iii. 459
returns to England, no longer popular, ii. 135
revered by sea captains but hated by army officers, ii. 151
Rome depreciates success of, i. **7**
Santiago to be attacked by, i. 175
(?) speech by, reported in *Berne Gazette*, ii. 206
Torres pursued by, at Cartagena, i. 71
unpopular with Mediterranean fleet, ii. 312
Vernon, Henry, boasts of relationship to, i. 126, iv. 305
victory of: not repeated, i. 466; should please George II and Sir Robert Walpole, i. 7; Walpole party's victory instead of, i. 362
Warren as absurd as, iv. 33
Wentworth's quarrel with, i. 175, ii. 143
Wilkes compared with, vii. 8

Vernon (after 1715, Venables Vernon), George (1710–80), cr. (1762) Bn Vernon; M.P.:
peerage granted to, vi. 31

Vernon, Lady Harriet *or* Henrietta. *See* Wentworth, Lady Henrietta

Vernon, Henrietta (d. 1828), m. 1 (1764) Richard Grosvenor, 1st Bn Grosvenor; cr.

(1784) E. Grosvenor; m. 2 (1802) Lt-Gen. George Porter (after 1819, de Hochepied), Bn de Hochepied:
Cumberland, D. of, has affair with, vii. 165, 345n
husband discards, vii. 165

Vernon, Henry (1718–65), of Hilton Park; M.P.:
Bolingbroke introduces, to Duchesse du Maine, i. **126**
Cotton travelled with, ii. 342
joke to, about 'uncle,' i. 126, 135, iv. 305
marriage of, ii. 342
money squandered by, on clothes and opera girl, i. 126
relationship to Admiral Vernon claimed by, i. 126, iv. 305
wagers laid by, on Cartagena capture, i. 126

Vernon, Henry (1748–1814):
Craven, Bns, has adventures with, ix. 632
—— said to be cousin of, ix. 632
interference of, in Bns Craven's quarrel with Horace Mann II, ix. 616

Vernon, Matthew; mercer:
alleged Jacobite toasts at house of, iv. 361

Vernon, Richard (1726–1800), M.P.; sportsman:
Bedford, D. of, visited by, at Woburn, iv. 301
black-balled by his friends at White's, iv. 300–1

Verona:
Bellotto's views of, attributed to Canaletto, vii. 298–9
Dunbar said to visit, i. 113
Leopold to meet Joseph II at, viii. 105
Maffei writes from, i. 150
Mann entertains ladies from, ii. 286
Podestà's son of, is Cts of Orford's lover, i. 196
Richecourt and Bns Walpole to meet at, i. 107
visitors to: Gloucester, D. and Ds of, viii. 314, x. 50; Walpole, Bns, i. 107, 134, 150; Young Pretender said to visit, i. 113

Verracini. *See* Veracini

Verrazzano, Neri da' (1683–1745), senator, 1736:
Electress's executor, ii. 168

Verres, Caius (d. 43 B.C.), Roman magistrate:
Clive compared with, vii. 530

Verrio, Antonio (ca 1639–1707), painter:
Marriot, Mrs, painted by, as Fury, iv. 212

Versailles:
American-French treaty of alliance signed at, viii. 362
bread riots at gates of, viii. 106
cabinet of, upholds William Pitt II, ix. 485
Clement XIV's treatment of threats from, vii. 221

[Versailles, *continued*]

Court of: carts Clement XIII, vii. 32; should wait for end of campaign before making peace, v. 504–5; willing to make peace, v. 360; *see also* France: court of

Deane openly countenanced at, viii. 253

Du Barry, Comtesse, eclipses beauties and duchesses of, vii. 75

Du Châtelet's conduct may offend, vii. 127

Dunn in favour at, vi. 7

England might have been captured and sent to, v. 300

epigrams exhaled at, ix. 496

Fort l'Évêque close to, v. 473

Fox, C.J., has partisans at, ix. 495

French cardinals send an express to, protesting against Cavalchini's appointment, v. 224

Genoese doge and senate go to, iii. 312–13, v. 386

guards at, die of heat, iv. 166

HW sees beast of Gevaudan at, vi. 289n

Hervey, Bp, declines to go to, as peace delegate, ix. 454

Joseph II perhaps rebuffed by, viii. 278

La Chalotais's trial at, vii. 206

Louis XV, Comtesse du Barry, and Maupeou almost alone at, vii. 298

Louis XVI besieged at, by mob, viii. 112

Mirepoix, Duchesse de, has no tabouret at, iv. 144

news report from, iii. 259

Paoli at, vii. 31

Parliament of Paris to compromise with, vii. 265

Poussin paintings only surpassed in size by those at, v. 209

pride and meanness of, vii. 142

Richelieu sends courier to, for aid, vii. 329

treaty of, iv. 565, 570, 578, 582, v. 229

Verskovis, James Francis (d. ca 1750), Flemish carver:

HW employs, iii. 420–1

returns to Rome, to carve for the English, iii. 421

Vertot, René Aubert de (1655–1735), historian:

English ministerial changes resemble *Revolutions* of, iii. 213, vi. 158, 169

Vertue, George (1684–1756), engraver; antiquary:

benefit tickets for Eva Violette designed by, iv. 74n

Vescovich, Count Antonio, Dalmatian leader:

Mann commissions, ix. 249

Vesey, Sir John Denny (ca 1709–61), 2d Bt, cr. (1750) Bn Knapton; M.P.:

peerage granted to, iv. 136

Vespa, Giuseppe (1727–1804), cr. (1802) Freiherr von Vespa; court physician to Maria Louisa:

Leopold and Maria Louisa accompanied by, vii. 220

Maria Louisa may choose, vi. 460

Vespasian (Titus Flavius Sabinus Vespasianus) (9–79), Roman Emperor 69–79:

bust of: bill of lading for, x. 6; bill of lading for pedestal for, v. 521, 533, 538; Caligula's bust superior to, vi. 523; casing expense for, x. 4; considered the fourth or fifth bust of Rome, vi. 523; HW hopes that Spaniards do not capture ship carrying pedestal for, v. 559; HW likes pedestal for, vi. 17–18, 25; HW's eagle confronts, iii. 420, v. 461; HW wants altar as pedestal for, v. 461, 471, 514; HW wants to know price of pedestal for, vi. 9; large, v. 471; Mann fears that HW does not like pedestal for, vi. 20; Mann seeks altar for pedestal of, v. 470, 482, 512; Mann surprised to hear that pedestal for, has not arrived, vi. 6; Parker sends, x. 4; pedestal for, approved by HW, v. 525; pedestal for, being repaired by workmen, v. 521; pedestal for, in same ship with Hyde's vases, vi. 13; pedestal for, on shipboard awaiting convoy, v. 524

Vespucci, Amerigo (1451–1512), Italian navigator:

Florentine theatre opens with show about return of, from conquest of America, viii. 514

Vessel. See Ship

'Vesta, Temple of':

HW calls Anne Pitt's house, viii. 15

Vestale, La, French frigate:

Vilaine entrance defended by, v. 351

Vestal virgin:

urn of, x. 8

Vestimento:

Scarlatti, Signorita, gives, i. 53

Vestments:

discovered in Cumberland's baggage, iii. 242

embroidered, Mann hopes to exchange, for Correggio picture, i. 199

Vestr'Allard. *See* Vestris, Marie-Jean-Augustin

Vestris, Mme. *See* Heinel, Anne-Frédérique

Vestris, Gaetano Apollino Baldassare (1729–1808); called Vestris; dancer:

'reigning bubble' in England, ix. 134

Vestris, Maria Teresa Francesca (1726–1808), actress:

Walpole, Horatio (1723–1809), described by, iv. 22

Vestris, Marie-Jean-Augustin (1760–1842); called Vestr'Allard; dancer:

Allegranti is applauded more than, ix. 243

benefit for, better attended than opera for hurricane sufferers, ix. 134

'reigning bubble' of London, ix. 134

'Vesuve, Comte de':

Mann may be given title of, ii. 484

Vesuvius:

English politics compared to, vi. 567

eruption of: HW surprised that Mann does

not mention, viii. 515; Hamilton describes, vii. 339n, viii. 529, 541, x. 46; sketch of, sent to HW by Mann, viii. 514, 520, 541
HW compares Frederick II and Joseph II to, viii. 38
Hamilton burned by, to a cinder, vii. 339
'out of humour,' vi. 422
Vettura (carriage *or* fly):
slow conveyance, ix. 677
Viaggiatori felici, I. See under Anfossi, Pasquale
Via Larga, in Florence:
Botta reviews troops in, v. 179
Viareggio:
Montemar visits, ii. 59
Viaticum:
York, Cardinal, administers: to Old Pretender, v. 390; to Young Pretender, ix. 627
Vicar of Conclave. *See* Colonna, Marcantonio
Vicars, Robert, Lt:
captured at Velletri, ii. 492
Vice; vices:
'orthodox,' drinking and avarice are, iv. 134
Vice-admiralty Court:
at Gibraltar, v. 273
Vice-chamberlain:
Finch, Hon. William, is, i. 468n, iii. 389n
—— succeeds Lord Sidney Beauclerk as, i. 493–4
Stuart-Mackenzie may become, v. 452
to Q. Charlotte, Fitzroy, Charles, becomes, vii. 66
Villiers succeeds Hon. William Finch as, vi. 311
Vice-chancellorship of Santa Chiesa:
Archinto receives, iv. 590
Benedict XIV appoints Colonna to, iv. 589
Old Pretender wants son to have, iv. 589–90, v. 8
Vice-legate:
at Avignon, *see* Acquaviva, Pasquale
at Bologna, *see* Molinari, Giovanni Carlo
Vice-treasurer:
Charlotte's, Grenville, James, resigns, as, vii. 180
Vice-treasurer of Ireland. *See under* Ireland
Vichy-Champrond, Marie de (1696–1780), m. (1718) Jean-Baptiste-Jacques-Charles du Deffand de la Lande, Marquis de Chastres:
death of, at Paris, ix. 90
Gleichen first met HW at home of, viii. 171
HW might hint to, that there is corn at Genoa and Leghorn, viii. 106
HW's friendship and correspondence with, ix. 90
HW told by, of Frenchmen's opinion of SH, vii. 312

HW to revisit Paris to see, vi. **484,** vii. 311
HW urged by, to revisit Paris, viii. 120
HW wants iris roots for, vii. 323
impetuosity of, characteristic of bygone French, viii. 498
Mann hopes that HW has had an entertaining visit with, viii. 130
modern French not understood by, ix. 538
Victoire-Louise-Marie-Thérèse (1733–99); ('Mme Victoire'); dau. of Louis XV:
Beauvilliers scratched by, from party list, vii. 115–16
Du Barry, Comtesse, to be presented to, vii. 78
expense of coffee and rouge for, iv. 500
father devoted to, vi. 164
father nursed by, although she had never had smallpox, viii. 1–2
Marie-Antoinette governed by, vii. 321
mother and sisters not addressed by, across father at dinner, iv. **340**
Orléans, Bp of, talks with, and she betrays him to Louis XV, vii. 321
Poyntz, Mrs, cures, of stone, by Mrs Stephens' medicine, vi. 163–4
Stanislas I visited by, vi. 403
Victor Amadeus II (1666–1732), K. of Sardinia 1718–30:
morganatic marriage of, vi. 144
Raphael painting would have been bought by, ii. 235
Victor Amadeus III (1726–96), styled D. of Savoy, 1730; K. of Sardinia, 1773:
Adélaïde, Mme, said to marry, iii. 218–19
Broglie wants to pay court to, vii. 521
Corsica may go to, viii. 26
George III persuades, to pardon Viry, viii. 328n
Mann praised by, through Gorsegno, iii. **170**
Milan coveted by, vii. 469
Sardinian army directed by, iii. 344
wedding of, iv. 159
Victoria. *See* La Victoria
Victory, English ship:
expense of, ii. 521
lost, with Sir John Balchen and crew, ii. 521, 543
Victory:
peace preferable to, vi. 85
Vienna:
Albani's messenger goes to, iii. 2, 114
Althan to go to, with Lobkowitz's dispatches, ii. 486, 489, 491
America is connected with by ignorant Florentines, v. 236
Antinori neglected by, v. 107
Austrian army complains to, of lack of artillery carriages, iii. 406
Austrian-Prussian peace not reported from, i. 134
Bagard's dismissal ordered by, i. 368, 406

[Vienna, *continued*]

balls allowed at, despite mourning for Madame Royale, iii. 14

bank of, Francis III ensures money in, vi. 144

Bartolommei formerly minister at, i. 195

Bavarian elector expected to besiege, i. 143, 151, 155

Benedict XIV writes letter to, ii. 55

Botta goes to, v. 424, vi. 87

—— ordered by, to give precedence to nuncio, vi. 44

——'s credit at, secure, vi. 254

——'s plea to Francis I may not reach, in time, vi. 267

——'s proposals rejected at, vi. 13

——'s retirement finally approved by, vi. 448

Braitwitz sends remonstrances to, ii. 128

'brother at,' *see* Joseph II

Catherine II's manifesto reaches Florence from, vi. 74

ceremonial for Maria Louisa's churching established at, vi. 486–7

Charles III sends courier to, with message to Joseph II and Maria Theresa, vii. 446

——'s neutrality statement to appease, v. 271

Charles, P., invites James to, for Joseph II's wedding, v. 462

—— retires to, i. 430

Charles Emmanuel III awaits answers from, iii. 393

—— sends courier to, iii. 312

Choiseul in letter disparages his post at, v. 242, 307

Conclave sends courier to, to complain of Bourbon cardinals, viii. 79

convent of Saliciennes to be founded in, by French ladies, iv. 333–4

Corsican disappointment depresses, vii. 130

council of war at, Daun's orders from, v. 96

councils held in, v. 72

courier from: awaited, ii. 168, iii. 313, 455; dispatches of, not divulged, ii. 182; forbids Leopold to negotiate with Spain, ix. 46; to England, with peace news, i. 472

couriers to: about Dumesnil's arrest, iii. 492; from Rome, iii. 158; seeks Francis I's orders, iii. 298

court gazette of: Mann to show mourning notice in, for George II, to Botta, v. 463; reprints Grub St papers, vi. 178

court of: alarmed, v. 195; Albani's and Thun's letters referred by, to Lobkowitz, ii. 515; apprehensive about Peter III, vi. 14; Brown may be told by, not to press the French, iii. 436; Catherine II's accession disliked by, vi. 75; Charles of Naples unlikely to allow, to take Naples from him, v. 280; Charles Emmanuel III cannot be expected by, to be too loyal, iii.

156; Coke, Lady Mary, no longer suspects, vii. 560; commissaries might be appointed by, to suppress Jesuits, vii. 135; contributes patents only to Corsican revolt, iv. 274; Corsican conquest expected by, iii. 215; Corsican rebels trusted promises of, iii. 258; Cumberland, Ds of, may embarrass, vii. 502; dislikes Russian invasion of Morea, vii. 204–5; England should have joined, to keep Corsica out of French hands, viii. 437; England still treats, politely, v. 462; English court unlikely to complain to, about Niccolini, iii. 19; Europe organized by, to destroy Prussia, v. 15; France may appease, by Sardinian concessions, iv. 576; France may give less aid to, v. 187; French court may be overshot by, v. 141; hears of Peter III's dethronement, before express arrives, vi. 62–3; ignores Lobkowitz's weakness, ii. 515; instigates Martin's ultimatum to Charles III, vi. 565; Jesuits' dissolution may be delayed by, to secure total suppression, vii. 477; Kaunitz inclines, towards Bourbons, vii. 54; Lorenzi scolded by, v. 475; Neapolitan conquest wanted by, ii. 390; not so sure of Catherine II's friendship, vi. 75; observes no law but that of pride, vi. 395; Parma suspects, of trying to usurp it, vi. 379; Peace of Füssen concealed by, iii. 38; Rodt supposed to bring secret of, to Conclave, v. 215; shame-proof, vi. 2; spreads report that English will attack Trieste, v. 134–5; Tesi's banishment from Florence ordered by, ii. 520; threatens Venice for defying Benedict XIV, iv. 176; Turin court's relations with, ii. 228, iii. 400–1, 478; unwilling to make peace till Silesia is regained, v. 360; wants Mann to borrow money, iv. 386; will want to advance to Naples, iii. 306; woos Ferdinand VI, iii. 292; would be edified by Holy Week in Florence, vi. 412; would spend its last florin rather than yield to Frederick II, vi. 87

Cowper to go to, from Frankfurt, ix. 661

Craon gets courier from, iii. 292–3

——'s disavowal of Richecourt's enmity to Ginori to impress Court of, ii. 216

——'s medical excuse to visit Pisa to be reported to, i. 342

Craven, Bns, to go to, ix. 655

Cristiani summoned to, iv. 335

Dal Pozzo, Mme, avoids, i. 80

daughter's birth to Leopold and Maria Louisa disappoints, vi. 481

Daun's defeat causes consternation in, v. 456

——'s retirement reported from, v. 470

devil more feared at, than anywhere else, iv. 334

dispatches sent to, about English at Leghorn, iv. 277

dispensation sent to, for P. Charles's wedding, ii. 330

Du Châtelet's haughtiness at, vii. 127

England may substitute Prussia for, as ally, iii. 238

English-French peace hoped by, to be deferred, vi. 87

English march on Rhine rumoured from, ii. 290

etiquette of, does not allow early announcement of pregnancy, vi. 427

express from, to England, announcing Young Pretender's departure, ii. 404

Florence gets information from, i. 40, 121, 143, 151, ii. 553, iii. 441, v. 90, 107, vi. 10, viii. 454

Francis I announces from, that Botta will rule Tuscany, v. 125

—— blamed by people of, i. 143

—— invites Craons to, iv. 25

——'s ministers ignore affairs of, i. 155

Francis II to be educated at, ix. 474, 499

Frederick II may threaten, ii. 512, v. 95

freemasons suppressed at, ii. 226

French minister expected at, i. 151

French treaty with, see Versailles, Treaty of

Gavi's prosecution transferred to, i. 491

——'s release ordered from, i. 368

Genoese doge and senators to go to, vi. 312–13

George II's death to be mourned by, v. 462

German gazetteers told to get all military news from, v. 310

Germans at, would faint at Joseph II's and Leopold's informality, vii. 112

Germans find Florentine climate as bad as that of, vi. 575

Ginori's mission to, i. 395, 406, 490, ii. 122, 138

—— to replace Bartolommei at, i. 395, 406, 490

Grantham ambassador at, like his father, ix. 296n

Grune's rumoured appointment to, i. 144, 151

Guadagni omnipotent at, through Francis I's cicisbea, vii. 272, 278–9

HW averse to any detachment from, vi. 333

HW, if a commander-in-chief, would dash to, to make peace, v. 285

hope in, about war success, v. 519–20

Ingenhousz inoculates archdukes at, vii. 91

inhabitants of, would stone Wraxall, ix. 138

Irish Lorrainer goes to, to protest to Francis I, v. 125

Joseph II sends courier to, vii. 111

—— taken from, i. 155

—— to return to, vi. 556, viii. 312

Kaunitz orders James to leave, v. 462

——'s alleged stud of horses at, i. 49

Khevenhüller to defend, i. 151

Kingston, Ds of, rebuffed at, viii. 398

Kinský brings Order of Marie-Thérèse to Leopold from, vi. 362

Langlois affair sent to, by courier, iii. 374

Leghorn governor tells, of Saunders's approach, v. 507

Leopold and Francis II visit, ix. 505

Leopold and Maria Louisa avoid burletta for fear of reprimand from, vi. 393

Leopold and Maria Louisa may be forbidden by, to attend theatre, vi. 407

Leopold asks permission from, for trip to Rome, vii. 91

—— awaits instructions from, vi. 337, 350, 353, 356

—— hears from D. of Gloucester at, about marriage, vii. 308

—— hopes for remission from, of orders to go to Parma, vii. 413

—— probably told by, how to receive D. of Gloucester, viii. 129

—— receives private messenger from, every fortnight, ix. 44

Lobkowitz ordered by, to enter Tuscany, iii. 11

——'s army not reinforced by, iii. 22

——'s expedition promised from, ii. 271

Lorenzi hears English news from, i. 325

Louisbourg's capture probably causes sensation at, v. 235

Lucca sends emissary to, to complain of floods, iv. 515

Magnan sends letters to, by courier, iii. 220

—— sent to, by George II, ii. 564

——'s plan for Corsican rebellion submitted to, iv. 274, 386

Mann, Horace II, to visit, viii. 374

Maria Theresa orders Francis I to return to, i. 316

masking to be allowed in Florence if there is no bad news from, vi. 559

mass said at, for those killed in a whole campaign, v. 333

Mathews to send couriers to, ii. 325

Mauduit's *Considerations* appear at, v. 469

Maximilian Joseph of Bavaria sent to, x. 10

Migazzi gets orders from, to oppose Dumesnil's consecration, iii. 492

minister of, at Florence, is plenipotentiary, vii. 293

ministers at odds at, v. 102

mob of, tries to honour Paoli on supposed visit, vii. 140

Modenese treaty with, iv. 393–4, 400

mourning at, for Duchesse de Lorraine, iii. 14

mourning directions expected from, on Electress's death, ii. 175

mourning rigorously enforced at, vi. 354

Niccolini may be visiting, iii. 7

[Vienna, *continued*]

Niccoli's iniquity discovered in, iv. 335

nuncio may be dismissed from, i. 56

nuncio's status at, vi. 319

orders awaited from, about Electress's effects, ii. 176

orders may have been received from, about announcing Leopold's accession, vi. 345

Orford, Cts of, may visit, iii. 48

Orsi disappointed at French not capturing, i. 481

panduri to be placed outside of, i. 144

Paris, Abp of, asked to send nuns to, iv. 333–4

Pius VI asks leave of Joseph II to visit him in, ix. 239

——'s visit to, ix. 250, 384

Prague disaster concealed at, v. 242

preparations for defence of, i. 143–4

Priero to go to, iii. 158

Protestant girls' case contested in, vi. 250

Pucci's letter mentions no orders from, v. 116

Richecourt blamed for Tuscany's poor relations with, iv. 267

—— complains to George II through, ii. 328

—— permitted to visit, whenever he pleases, iv. 392

—— prepares for trip to, iv. 327, 334

—— refused leave to visit, iv. 252

—— sends courier to, ii. 314

—— shines dimly at, iii. 219

——'s influence at, said to have declined, iv. 463

——'s intrigues at, iii. 322

——'s rebuffs from, iv. 284

——'s return from, will be awaited by Cts of Orford, iii. 144

—— summoned to, i. 89, 95

—— to refer Mann's letter about jurisdictions to, iii. 1

—— wants money to take to, iv. 488

Richecourts of Turin to visit, iv. 45

Richmond, Mrs, sends to, iii. 290

Robinson, Sir Thomas, English minister at, i. 497n, iv. 202, 417n, ix. 296n

Rosenberg visits, to get his debts paid, vii. 220

Russian manifesto forwarded from, to Florence, vi. 74

St Joseph's Day at, vi. 371

St-Odile opposes Richecourt in, iv. 305, 308

Sankt Pölten near, i. 194

Seckendorf discloses plan to, v. 266

secretary of *toison d'or* to come to Florence from, vii. 1

siege of, represented in dance at Florentine opera, ix. 360

Simonetti, Mme, makes plans at, for Modena heiress, vi. 201

Stainville has no place at, iv. 29

Stanislas II sends letter to his 'sister' at, ix. 633

Stormont to have post in, vi. 130

—— to return to, vii. 18, 25

theatres at, closed for a year for mourning, vi. 340

Thun sends courier to, ii. 56

Thurn, Comtesse, left at, vii. 253

Tornaquinci neglected by, v. 107

Toussaint sends orders from, i. 349

Tuscan council in, iv. 220

Tuscan court awaits orders from, before admitting visitors, vi. 337, 340

Tuscan court imitates, vi. 390, 412

Tuscan court will be lectured by, for extravagance, vii. 134–5

Tuscan regency defends Langlois case to, iii. 366

Tuscan regency mentions Mann's rumoured promotion to, vi. 346

Tuscan regency sends courier to, iv. 423

Tuscan regents neglected by, v. 107

Tuscan troops to form garrison at, v. 195–6

Tuscany awaits orders and officials from, v. 85

Tuscany's link with, must interest it in the Scheldt, ix. 544

Venice sends couriers to, iv. 190

Villiers may become minister to, iii. 16–17

visitors to: Botta, vi. 246; Chute, iii. 207, 279; Coke, Lady Mary, vii. 553; Craon, Princesse de, vi. 324; Dumesnil, iii. 491; Forrester, ii. 107; Gloucester, D. of, vii. 332; Hamilton, Sir William and Lady, vii. 448; Hildburghausen, v. 194; Lee, viii. 390; Leopold and Maria Louisa, vii. 205, 214, 220, 332, viii. 240, 250, 370, 389, 409; Löwenstein, iii. 306; Magnan, ii. 564; Mill, iii. 407, 454; Pius VI, ix. 283, 384; Richecourt, i. 89, 95, iii. 144, 192, 219, 290, 322, iv. 327, 334, 335, 421, 488, v. 80; Schulenburg, iii. 50; Scottish gentlemen, iii. 290; Simonetti, Cts vi. 126, 201; Tesi, ii. 521, v. 194; Vorontsov, vi. 180; Whithed, iii. 207, 279

Walpole, Bns, might follow Richecourt to, i. 89, 95, 125

Vieri, Abbé. *See* Véri, Joseph-Alphonse de

Vieri, Girolamo (d. 1742), Auditor:

daughter supported by, i. 473

death of, from falling picture, i. 473, 481

Vieri, Maria Maddalena (d. 1794), m. (1731) Conte Giovanni Francesco del Benino:

Buckingham's story would be enjoyed by, ii. 307

Del Monte comforts, i. 473

——'s affair with, i. 33, 123, ?156, 473

father of, dies, i. 473, 481

father supports and keeps, from husband's treatment, i. 473

Goldsworthy, Mrs, called on by, i. 316

HW to receive compliments of, i. 37, 68

husband of: a beast, i. 473; put under *pupilli*, i. 122

Mann entertains, at coffee, i. 33

—— serves currant tarts to, i. 68

——'s party not to be attended by, i. 498

Vierpyl, Simon (ca 1725–1810), sculptor; art dealer:

(?)Chute employs, to purchase eagle, iii. 101

(?)Mann employs, to get sepulchral *ara*, iv. 352

Mann helped by, at Rome in finding art objects, iv. 391

Vies des Pères:

Lorraine, Primate of, suggests, as title of *Portier des Chartreux*, i. 274

Vieumenil. *See* Viomenil

Vieux Colombier, Rue du, Paris:

Miséricorde convent in, x. 47

Vigna, Casa. *See* Pisa: Mann's house at

Vignerot du Plessis, Louis-François-Armand (1696–1788), Duc de Richelieu; Maréchal de France:

Adélaïde, Mme, advised by, to receive Comtesse du Barry, vii. 87

army under: aids Soubise, v. 137, 146, 159; embarrasses Frederick II's strategy, v. 146; may attack Minorca, iv. 545; may invade England, iii. 187, 509

becomes maréchal, iii. 510

Byng's behaviour not to be estimated by, v. 61

——'s squadron cannot stop land operations of, iv. 558

Charles Emmanuel III to be visited by, at Turin on way to France, iv. 576

Ciudadela magistrates surrender on board ship of, iv. 552

Du Barry the pimp of, vii. 75

Du Barry, Comtesse, entertains, at supper, vii. 115

financial misconduct of, attacked, v. 172, 193–4, 195

Genoa to be evacuated by, iii. 510

Germans force, to fight in winter, v. 158, 176

Gibraltar reinforcements spur, to desperate attack on Minorca, iv. 576

Hanover electorate plundered by, v. 172n, vii. 329

Jesuits said to have been restored by, vii. 316

Kloster-Zeven convention concluded by, with D. of Cumberland, v. 136n

Louis XV asked by, to permit Comtesse du Barry's presentation, vii. 115

Parliament of Bordeaux intimidates, vii. 329

pavilion built by, with Hanover spoils, v. 172n, vii. 329

Port Mahon captured by, iv. 552

retreats to Fronsac, and sends to Versailles for help, vii. 329

son-in-law sent by, to Madrid, iv. 572

son of: boasts of father's amours and lack of Latin, iv. 339; sent to Paris with news, iv. 572

Te Deum sung by, on landing in Minorca, iv. 567

Voltaire sends letter of, to Byng, v. 51, 61

winter quarters must be left by, to aid Soubise, v. 158

wrinkles of, vii. 329

York, Cardinal, rebuked by, iii. 509–10

Vignerot du Plessis-Richelieu, Emmanuel-Armand (1720–88), Duc d'Aiguillon:

Avignon may not be relinquished by, vii. 527

becomes prime minister, vii. 314

Broglie an adherent of, vii. 283

——'s quarrel with, vii. 521

cabinet post to go to, vii. 265

Choiseul may be succeeded by, vii. 79, 85, 258

correspondence in Guines's case published by, viii. 90

Du Barry, Comtesse, often visited by, vii. 321

—— retires to estate of, at Rueil, viii. 2

—— said to have been betrayed by, viii. 12

English prisoners entertained by, at supper, v. 251, 255

friends of, imply that Choiseul wanted war, vii. 258

HW's opinion of, vii. 323

jaundiced by vexation, vii. 207

Jesuits may be befriended by, vii. 260

La Chalotais drives, to demand a trial, vii. 206–7

Lambert's toast must have made bad impression on, v. 255

Louis XV does not favour, much, vii. 321

Louis XVI's attitude towards, conjectured, viii. 18

Mann asks about, viii. 10

Marlborough's teaspoons returned by, v. 221

Maupeou opposes, vii. 453

mother of, vi. 524n

mother told by, to visit Mme du Barry, vii. 338

pacific policy of, his only virtue, viii. 11

Parliament of Bretagne restored in spite of, vii. 134

parliaments detest, vii. 259

Princes of the Blood to be reconciled by, to spite Maupeou, vii. 399

SH makes HW pity, vii. 315

Vergennes replaces, as prime minister, viii. 17

Vignerot du Plessis-Richelieu, Louis-Antoine-Sophie (1736–91), Duc de Fronsac; Duc de Richelieu, 1788:

father's amours and lack of Latin proclaimed by, iv. 339

news of St Philip's surrender brought by, from Minorca to Toulon and Paris, iv. 572

Vignolles, Marie-Charlotte de, m. Charles Sarrazin:
cannon reverberations from Modena allegedly heard by, i. 443
Chute discusses smallpox with, i. 498
Craon and friends banish, from quadrille médiateur games, ii. 329
Craon's guests told by, not to mention son's death, i. 463
Craon, Princesse de, discussed by, with Mann, ii. 175
—— entertains, i. 414, 498
—— has, as companion, i. 436n
—— tired of compliments of, ii. 362
—— tires, by illnesses, ii. 122
Craons dismiss, ii. 361
daughter in Lorraine to take care of, ii. 361
daughter of, iii. 452
faro played by, ii. 318
HW asks if Princesse de Craon's suppers make, impatient for cards, iii. 161
HW imagines comment of, on Mrs Bosville, ii. 298
income of, ii. 361
India ink praised by, i. 414, 436
Juvrecourt son-in-law of, i. **193,** ii. 368
'Lorraine lady,' i. 436n
Mann, Chute, and Whithed forced by, to play quadrille médiateur, ii. 132, 148
quadrille médiateur craved by, ii. 122, 148, 329
quadrille médiateur of, will suffer after her dismissal, ii. 361
to retire to Lorraine, ii. 361
wig of: clawed aside when gambling, ii. 318; HW remembers, iii. 452; will suffer after her dismissal, ii. 361
Vigo:
Watson reports action at, v. 297
Vilaine River:
French ships driven up, v. 351, 359
Vilette, Mme de. See Des Champs de Marcilli
Vilette, seigneur de. See Le Vallois, Philippe
Villa; villas:
Florentine, architecture of, iv. 166, 191
Italians never spend both spring and autumn in the same, vi. 456
Mann hankers for, iv. 25, 160, 193
views of, HW receives and dislikes, iii. 185, iv. 166
Villafranca (Villefranche):
battle at, ii. 435–7, 441
Charles Emmanuel III to attack, iii. 313
French blockade of, v. 264
frigate sails from, to pursue pirates, ix. 480
garrison of, iii. 323
Lobkowitz to avenge loss of, by taking Naples, ii. 437
Mathews to leave, ii. 360
Medley receives letter at, from Townshend, iii. 359

——'s fleet at, iii. 334
Noel goes to, to spy on French, iv. 536
one of England's last available Mediterranean ports, iv. 575
Sardinians abandon, ii. 436
sea engagement not reported at, ii. 403–4
seaman at, reports victory to Florence, i. 471
Susa commander of, ii. 360
Villa Medici. See under Medici
Villa Patrizzi. See under Patrizzi
Villa Petraia. See under Petraia
Villars, Maréchale de. See La Rocque de Varengeville, Jeanne-Angélique de (d. 1763)
Villars, Claude-Louis-Hector (1653–1734), Duc de; Maréchal de France:
minuet danced by, supported by aides-de-camp, iv. 159
pun by, on Milan, iv. 159
Villars, Honoré-Armand (1702–70), Duc de:
York, D. of, entertained by, at ball at country house, vi. 553
Villa Suares:
Mann does not want to spend night at, ii. 333
Modenese princess to be entertained at, i. 99, 100
Ville, Abbé de la. See La Ville
Ville de Paris, La, ship:
de Grasse's ship, taken by Rodney, ix. 278
Villefranche. See Villafranca
Villeggiature:
Clement XIV passes, at Castel Gandolfo, vii. 526
Florence deserted during, ii. 64, 329
Florentines prolong, till St Martin's summer, iv. 451
Ville-Issey, Bn de. See Jadot, Jean-Nicolas (1710–61)
Villette. See Vilette
Villette de Murçay, Marthe-Marguerite de (1673–1729), m. (1686) Jean-Anne de Tubières de Grimoard de Pestel de Lévi, Marquis de Caylus:
Mann quotes, vii. 406
Villettes, Arthur (ca 1702–76), English secretary of embassy at the court of Savoy 1734–41, Resident 1741–9; minister to Switzerland 1749–62:
Birtles's correspondence with, iii. 65
Botta's peace terms condemned by, iii. 312
Charles Emmanuel III persuaded by, about Corsican rebels, iii. 260
——'s accounts of battle to be forwarded by, to England, ii. 155
——'s attitude reported by, to be favourable, i. 265
—— sends, to confer with fleet, iii. 64
——'s intentions doubted by, i. 312
——'s picture given to, iv. 76
—— summons, to approve his evacuation of Chambéry, ii. 142
—— to be notified by, of Young Pretender's departure, i. 14

Chute and Whithed laugh at, ii. 279
cipher not used by, ii. 385
Cooper assured by, iii. 81
Corsican rebellion approved by, iii. 276
courier cannot be sent by, through France, ii. 385
couriers of: carry incomplete news, iii. 335; dispatched at every opportunity, iii. 436; go faster than Mann's, iii. 305; reaches England, ii. 417; sent from Turin through Germany, ii. 389, 397; will disappoint England, iii. 363
courier's robbery concealed by, iii. 334
England hears little of, ii. 293
England visited by, before settling at Berne, iv. 76, 90
English fleet off Genoa to be visited by, iii. 64
English minister at Turin, ii. 60n, iii. 456n
fleet's movements not announced to, iii. 334
Florence visited by, iii. 64
Fumagalli's capture at Turin requested of, iii. 96–7
Genoa visited by, ii. 271
Genoese news reported by, iii. 367, 436
Gorsegno's conduct upheld by, iii. 478
—— tells, at Charles Emmanuel III's quarters, about English captain's disloyalty, iii. 150
HW has nothing to do with, iv. 90
HW traces Mann's illness to tiring qualities of, ii. 60
Hyères visit refused by, ii. 271
illness of, at Turin, prevents Gorsegno from consulting him, iii. 150
letters of: immoderately long, ii. 508, iii. 237, 245, 312, 426, 465, 466; pompous, ii. 279, 385, iii. 183, 476; quoted by Mann, iii. 237; use ciphers, ii. 59, 97
Lombard victories to be reported by, iii. 291
Mann angry with, for diverting courier, ii. 404
—— asked by, to borrow money from Leghorn merchants, iii. 215
—— awaits return of, with orders for Cooper, iii. 81
—— confers with, iii. 64
—— corresponds with Gorsegno since visit of, to fleet, iii. 150
—— dislikes possible replacement of, by Williams, iii. 466
—— expects to hear from, i. 342
—— involved by, in Corsican intrigues, iii. 260–1
—— may assist, at fleet conference at Leghorn, i. 443
—— mistakenly writes name of, for Villiers, ii. 25
—— plagued by, ii. 293
—— receives from, a letter from Nice, ii.
413

——'s correspondence with, ii. 16, 59, 79, 385, 404, 413, iii. 237, 374
—— sends letters through, ii. 385
——'s plan for Corsican conquest forwarded by, to England, iv. 386
—— to notify, of Young Pretender's departure, i. 13–14
—— will enjoy Williams's letters more than those of, iii. 465
Mathews may be summoned by, ii. 16
—— not to act too suddenly on advice of, ii. 26–7
——'s correspondence with, ii. 26, 37
—— sees, at Genoa, ii. 271
——'s treaty with Genoa aided by, ii. 271, 455, 529
—— to confer with, ii. 240–1
minister to Switzerland, iii. 456n
Money's dispatches said by, to assure English fleet's continuing to threaten Genoa, iii. 12
Montemar's motives interpreted by, ii. 16
plans to be announced by, iii. 353
Port Mahon reached by, on way to see Rowley, iii. 81
Rochford to meet, at Paris, iv. 76
San Lazaro victory may be announced by, iii. 265
Savona attack will be described by, iii. 476
servant of, takes news to England, iii. 431
solemnity of, iv. 76
Spaniards commented on by, ii. 279
successor to Wentworth desired by, iii. 451
Townshend's correspondence with, iii. 183, 245
—— to be interviewed by, iii. 292
Turin left by, iv. 76
Wentworth's mission advised by, iii. 401–2
Williams may succeed, at Turin, iii. 347, 456, 465, 466
Villiers, Vct. See Mason-Villiers, George (1751–1800)
Villiers, Vcts. See Seymour-Conway, Lady Gertrude (1750–93)
Villiers, Barbara (1641–1709), m. 1 (1659) Roger Palmer, cr. (1661) E. of Castelmaine; m. 2 (1705) Robert Feilding; cr. (1670) Ds of Cleveland, s.j.; Charles II's mistress:
granddaughter of, ix. 508
Yarmouth, Cts of, the successor of, iv. 90
Villiers, Lady Elizabeth (d. 1782), m. 1 (1739) Aland John Mason; m. 2 (1763) Gen. Charles Montagu; cr. (1746) Vcts, (1767) Cts Grandison:
son of, vii. 323
wealthy Irish peeress, vii. 323
Villiers, George (1592–1628), cr. (1616) Vct Villiers; (1617) E., (1618) M., and (1623) D. of Buckingham:
HW satirizes, ii. 357
James I's letters to, i. 357

Villiers, George (1628–87), 2d D. of Buckingham, 1628:
Protestant miracles affirmed by, to James II's emissary, ii. 306
Rehearsal, The: Champion, The, quotes, ii. 33; revolutions should be as bloodless as in, vii. 236
Villiers, George Bussy (1735–1805), styled Vct Villiers 1742–69; 4th E. of Jersey, 1769:
becomes lord of the Admiralty, v. 490
Finch, Hon. William, succeeded by, as vice-chamberlain, vi. 311
Hyde brother of, vii. 313n
wife of, ix. 411n
Villiers, Thomas (1709–86), cr. (1756) Bn Hyde, and (1776) E. of Clarendon, n.c.:
Admiralty post may be obtained by, iv. 12
Admiralty post taken from, v. 25
Berlin post refused by, iii. 458
character of, iii. 458, iv. 17
Frederick II said to have requested, as English minister, iv. 541
——'s letters from, printed, iv. 17
—— succeeds with, at Dresden treaty, iv. 541
Frederick Augustus II of Poland makes peace through, i. **499**
'gazetted,' iv. 17
Granville's conversation with, iv. 17
Gray, Sir James, congratulated by, iii. 444, 453
HW discusses election with, at Granville's, iv. 17
HW to tell, that his alabaster vases are ready and awaiting shipment from Italy, v. 524
lord of the Admiralty, iii. 458n, iv. 17
Mann mistakenly writes 'Villettes' for, ii. 25
superseded, as postmaster, vi. 311
to be Chancellor of the Duchy of Lancaster, vii. 313
Treasury post coveted by, iii. 458
vases for: arrive, vi. 13; ready and awaiting shipment, v. 524
Vienna post may go to, iv. 17–18
witticism by, on P. Charles's victories, i. **499**, ii. 25
Villiers, William (ca 1712–69), 3d E. of Jersey:
brother of, iii. 458n
son of, vi. 311n
Villinghausen:
battle of, v. 515
Villio, Amilius, Graf, Polish ambassador to Venice 1712–63:
Florentine pictures sought by, for K. of Poland, iii. 392
Vilmanstrand:
battle at, i. 155
Vilshoven:
Austrians capture, i. 288
Vimeur, Jean-Baptiste-Donatien de (1725–1807), Comte de Rochambeau:

Arbuthnot alleged to have fought with, ix. 150
expected arrival of, encourages Americans, ix. 70
Vincennes:
Young Pretender imprisoned at, iv. 8, 22, 44
Vincent, ——:
HW must remember, ii. 111
Lorraine, Primate of, ruins, ii. 111
Nomis accompanied by, ii. 111
Vincent, Lady. *See* Astley, Arabella
Vincent, Augustine (ca 1584–1626), herald:
MS baronage by, quoted by HW, iv. 138
Vincent, Nicholas, naval officer:
misbehaviour of, v. 296
Vinci, Jacopo, lawyer:
Electress's will attested by, ii. 173
Vindication of a Late Pamphlet . . . Hanover Troops:
publication of, ii. 141
Vine, the. *See* Vyne, the
Vine; vines:
Florentine vineyards', injured by floods and cold, v. 510
frost said to have killed, in France and Italy, vi. 514
Mann's lamp standards covered with, ii. 479
Vinegar:
Lorraine officials sell, at Florence, ii. 270
used against plague, ii. 270
Vingt-et-un:
Gloucester, D. of, plays, with entourage, vii. 352
Vins, Joseph Nicolaus de (1732–98), Freiherr; Austrian Maj.-Gen.:
Prussians defeat, viii. 405
Vintimiglia. *See* Ventimiglia
Vintimille, Marquise de. *See* Mailly-Nesle, Pauline-Félicité de
Vintimille, Charles-Emmanuel-Marie-Madelon de (1741–1810), Marquis de Luc:
birth of, i. 125
Vintimille. *See also* Ventimiglia
Violante, ——, Italian athlete:
death of, from broken neck, ix. 451
descent of, from St Martin's steeple, ix. 450
Violante Beatrix (1673–1731) of Bavaria, m. 1689) Ferdinando de' Medici, Grand Prince:
Suares, Mme, tells stories about, iii. 311
'Violette,' Eva Maria Veigel (1724–1822), called, m. (1749) David Garrick:
Burlington, Cts of, may have spoiled, vi. 180
Bury causes riot to get more dances from, iv. 74n
career of, iv. 74n
Chute and Whithed dislike dancing of, iii. 342
hip hurt by, on road, vi. 203
Italy to be visited by, vi. 164
Mann's expectations of, vi. 170, 191

—— to get second theatre box for, vi. 180
—— will be embarrassed to present, to Florentine nobility, vi. 170, 180
marriage of, iv. 74
Naples visited by, vi. 203
Nardi's quarrel with, iii. **293**
Newcastle concerned about, iv. 74n
plays danced in by, iii. 342
will be called 'the Violetta' in Florence, vi. 180
Violin; violins:
Craon distracted by, from his cards, i. 417
Nardini plays, vi. 537
St-Germain plays, iii. 181, x. 20
Viomenil, Bn de. See Du Houx, Antoine-Charles (1728–92)
Virepoyl. See Vierpyl
Virgil (Publius Vergilius Maro) (70–19 B.C.), Roman poet:
Æneid: HW paraphrases, vii. 453; HW quotes, ii. 431, iii. 134, 161, v. 213, vii. 163; preserved by Virgil's executors, iv. 62
Eclogues, Williams, Sir Charles Hanbury, quotes, ii. 48
English schoolboy's study of, their only way of telling the seasons apart, vii. 305
Georgics: Philippi of, Holdsworth wrote dissertation on, iii. 139n; Young Pretender's medal quotes, i. 19
Mexico may produce counterpart of, viii. 62
Virgin and Child, Domenichino's painting of. See under Domenichino
Virginia:
Albemarle governor of, iv. 156n
Arnold joins Cornwallis in, ix. 167
Cornwallis to invade, viii. 158
events may be expected in, viii. 206
French encroachments threaten, iv. 440, 448, 495
governorship of: disputed, vii. 43–4; vacant by Albemarle's death, iv. 461
HW's vision of future senate in, vii. 210
SH more important to HW than boundaries of, v. 306
troops in, disbanded, iv. 455
Virgin Mary. See Mary, Virgin
Virgin of the Seven Sorrows. See under Pergolesi
Virieu-Beauvoir, François-Xavier (ca 1709–82), Comte de; army officer; Lt in the government of Le Havre:
Rodney's alleged notice to, v. 310
Virrette, ——, Swiss:
St-Germain's toad-eater, denounced and released, iii. 182n
Virtu:
Conway and Stormont absorbed in, iv. 298
Dalton advises George III about, v. 478
George III collects, v. 477–8, vi. 108
Mann should cater to George III's taste in, v. 452, 456–7, vi. 111

—— unwilling to procure, for George III, v. 456–7, 497, vi. 115
Virtue:
disbelieved or without authority now, ix. 373
HW's reflections on, v. 541
want of, HW's reflections on, viii. 362
Virtue, Temple of. See Honour and Virtue
Viry, Contessa di. See Montagu, Augusta (d. 1849); Speed, Henrietta Jane (1728–83)
Viry, Francesco Giuseppe (d. 1766), Conte di; Sardinian diplomatist:
employed in Paris peace treaty, vi. 105
Sardinian minister to England, viii. 328n
Viry, Francesco Maria Giuseppe Giustino di (1736–1813), Barone de la Perrière, Conte di Viry, 1766; diplomatist:
arrest of, at Susa, viii. **328**
marriage of, in England, viii. 328n
pardon of, viii. 328n
Sardinian ambassador to France, viii. 328n
secret correspondence by, at Turin, to become prime minister, viii. 328n
Vis-à-vis:
Englishwoman's child and nurse enter Florence in, drawn by nags and driven by old English coachman, viii. 260
Visconti, Caterina, opera singer; 'Viscontina':
'admired more than liked,' i. 190
Calais visited by, i. 141
captain of yacht demands song from, i. 141
Chesterfield jokes about age and weight of, i. 197
Conway, Bns, to have, sing at assembly, i. 334
deteriorates, iii. 437
HW travels with, i. 141
Holdernesse entertains, ii. 130
London opera directors retain, i. 421
London opera directors said to dismiss, i. 398, 423
Mann pities, i. 240
Pomfret, Cts of, discusses, i. **72**
salary of, i. 191
unpopular in England, i. 211
Visconti, Fulvia (d. 1777), m. Marchese Antonio Giorgio Clerici:
(?) child wanted by, ii. 252
Florence visited by, ii. 251–2
Lucca baths to be visited by, ii. 252
Visigoths:
HW compares English to, iv. 99
Visions:
HW knows texture of, too well, vii. 554
HW says, are never 'pure from annoy,' ix. 532
HW's fondness for, ix. 133
HW's reflections on, viii. 103, 194
mortals impelled by, to action, viii. 521
must be made to the last, ix. 604
ought to be cultivated, even if in vain, viii. 327

[Visions, *continued*]
playthings for boys, viii. 324
Visitation:
convent of, at San Remo, iii. 123
Visits:
'en blanc,' iv. 584, viii. 275
hours for, viii. 426
Visor:
Wilkes's squint imitated in, at masquerade, vii. 193
Vitelli, Mme. *See* Frescobaldi, Maria Anna (d. 1776)
Vitelli, Agnese, m. (1711) Francesco Maria Bagnesi:
(?) Modenese princess gives presents to, i. 64
Vitelli, Clemente (d. 1790), Marchese:
villa and furniture of town house sold by, to pay mother's dowry, iv. 399
Vitelli, Niccolò (1687–1747):
HW sees Bianca Cappello portrait in palace of, iv. 398, 402n
widow of, follows Braitwitz to Naples, iv. 399
Vitelli, Casa:
furniture of, sold, iv. 399
HW sees portrait of Bianca Cappello at, iv. 398, 402n, 404
Vitelli family:
falling to decay, iv. 402n
Vitellius, Aulus (A.D. 15–69), Roman emperor, A.D. 69:
medal of, bought by HW, x. 7
Viterbo:
Austrians at, ii. 527, 534
Gages assembles troops at, ii. 556
Gloucester, D. of, entertained at, by Clement XIV's staff, vii. 388
Montemar, Clarelli, and Ferretti to attend meeting at, i. 214–15
Neapolitans on way to Lombardy from, recalled to Naples, iii. 237
Spaniards from, to join Gages, iii. 58
Spanish baggage arrives at, ii. 243
Spanish invalids at, form army, iii. 55
Vitimillia. *See* Ventimiglia
Vitto Pittagorico. *See* Cocchi, Antonio: *Del Vito Pittagorico*
Vittorio Amadeo. *See* Victor Amadeus
Viviani, Marchese Luigi (1709–80), Neapolitan agent at Florence; Neapolitan minister to Tuscany, 1758; Spanish envoy to Tuscany 1765–80:
Baiardi's *prodromo* presented by, to Mann, v. 142
Botta to be assured by, of Neapolitan-Spanish neutrality, v. 270–1
—— told by, that Havana would not be captured, vi. 89
Charles III promotes, from chargé d'affaires to envoy, vi. 349–50
courier's non-appearance explained by, v. 463

deserts to Spaniards on Montemar's arrival, iv. 350
Eszterházys entertained by, at festino, iv. 350–1
Fogliani recommends, to Richecourt, iv. 350–1
furniture of, sold to pay debts, iv. 351
HW met, at Craon's, iv. 350
HW wants invisible architect of, at SH, iv. 372
intimate at Casa Craon, i. 238–9
language master at Spanish court, ii. 129, iv. 350
low credentials of, exclude him from chambellan's antechamber, vi. 346
Madrid visited by, ii. 129
Mann should have bought *Antiquities of Herculaneum* from, v. 299
—— told by: about Charles III's behaviour on wife's death, v. 441–2; about Spanish-Portuguese clash, viii. 223; about Young Pretender, i. 116
—— to write letter to England citing, as reason for promoting Mann, vi. 351
ministerial dinner to be given by, vi. 355, 362
Montemar's pimp, i. 239
Neapolitan-Spanish weekly courier service received by, vi. 349
Porta San Gallo shown by, to San Severino, iv. 372
Regency to tell, to have Del Monte seized, iv. 437
Spaniards joined by, i. 238–9, ii. 129
Spanish Court sends South American news to, viii. 223
Squillace writes to, that Havana's capture is not expected, vi. 100
wants to be Spanish minister to Francis I, ii. 129
will be *ministre de famille* at Leopold II's wedding, vi. 319
Viviani, Ottavio (b. 1679) *or* Stefano (b. 1681), painters:
landscapes by, x. 7
Viziers:
Williams's verses about, vii. 236
Vizir. *See* Grand Vizir
Vocabolario . . . della Crusca:
Kaunitz receives, from Ginori, i. 49
Vocabulary:
HW's reflections on change in, from one generation to another, ix. 538
Vœlcker, (?) George (d. 1770), (?) valet to George II:
dogs bred by, vii. 56
Voiture:
Beauchamp's, may be drawn by mules, vi. 336
Volakia. *See* Wallachia
Volcano:
at Messina, ix. 374
See also Vesuvius

Voltaire (François-Marie Arouet) (1694–1778):
'À Madame Lullin,' vii. 306
Byng receives from, Richelieu's letter, v. 51, 61
Candide imitation falsely attributed to, v. 514, 520
Catherine II's apologist, vi. 253, 570, vii. 195, 208, 515
——'s 'ascent' called 'a family squabble' by, ix. 194, 206
Congreve ridiculed by, for preferring rank of gentleman to that of author, v. 486
Craufurd calls on, and finds that he knows no Greek, vi. 40
death of: viii. 387; while railing at Shakespeare, viii. 536; will be Europe's good night, viii. 55
despots decorated by, ix. 613–14
Écossoise, authorship of, admitted, v. 520
England first popularized by, in France, viii. 267
epigram by, on George II and Frederick II, v. 31
epistle of, to Querini, Mann sends, to HW, iv. 329
Essai sur les mœurs quoted, vii. 387, 523
Frederick II does not need, to show him how to write, v. 157
—— hymned by, vii. 515
—— probably pays, in base metal, vii. 515
——'s addresses should be corrected by, ii. 500
——'s friend, viii. 387
—— should make a dialogue of the dead with, viii. 149
——'s verses to, in *Cologne Gazette*, v. 180
——writes sonnets to, v. 171
Graftons call on, on first visit to Geneva, vi. 40
Gray's opinion of, vii. 515
HW quotes passage from, about Charles V, vii. 523
HW's comments on Clement XIII welcoming the D. of York will be echoed by, vi. 180
Homer the subject of, despite ignorance of Greek, vi. 40
Italian poet attacks, for pillaging and reviling Shakespeare, viii. 536
Jesuits the butt of writings by, v. 383, vii. 515
Lyttelton calls, an exile, v. 486
—— receives letter from, written from his hovel in France, v. 486
'meteor of the reading world,' viii. 387
Montagu, Mrs, hears invective by, against Shakespeare at Académie française, viii. 267
only European author who one wishes should write, vii. 515
Paris visited by, viii. 356
Poland's ravagers hymned by, vii. 515
Prédiction supposedly by, ridicules *La Nouvelle Héloïse*, v. 514

Pucelle by: circulated in MS, and then published as *La Jeanne*, iv. 548; HW criticizes, iv. 555; Mann supposes Wilkes's *Essay on Woman* to resemble, vi. 192; Voltaire alters, before printing it, iv. 548
Relation de la maladie . . . du jésuite Berthier, v. 383
Siècle de Louis XIV, Le, Calvinism subject of epigram in, i. 429n
Siècle de Louis Quinze, Précis du, vi. 85, vii. 85
sovereigns panegyricized by, for pay, vii. 195
statement by, that culture has softened human manners, vii. 387
'unpoisoner' of bygone criminals, vi. 65, 253
verses by: to centenarian lady, vii. 306; to Frederick II, v. 171, 180
visits never returned by, vi. 40
Walpole, Bns, discusses, with Andreasi, iii. 555
writings not produced by, recently, viii. 62
Volterra, Bp of. *See* Dumesnil, Joseph (d. 1781)
Volterra:
Acciaioli's villa near, iv. 160
alabaster of, not big enough for large vases, iv. 582
alabaster vases or urns of, *see under* Vase
bishopric of, has high revenue, iii. 491
chancellor and notary of, avoid Dumesnil, iii. 493
Dumesnil's attempt to occupy see of, iii. 490–3
Mann gets vases from, weekly, i. 394
Pisan cavaliere sent to, for indiscreet talk about Spaniards, ii. 46
Vomiting:
occurrences of, i. 37, ii. 153
Vorese. *See* Varese
Vorontsov, Cts. *See* Skavronska, Anna Carlovna
Vorontsov, Alexander Romanovich (1741–1805):
ambassador to England, vi. 55
credentials received by, vi. 61
uncle tells, to thank George III for Mann's attentions, vi. 203
Vorontsov, Mikhail Illarionovich (1714–67), vice-chancellor of Russia 1744–58; chancellor 1758–63:
at Florence in Princesse de Craon's time, iii. 184, v. 248
Bestuzhev could never live near, vi. 11
—— should have replaced, vi. 62
Botta asked by, to get house in Florence for 50 people, vi. 180
Catherine II probably hated by, vi. 195
Craon, Princesse de, quarrels with, v. 259
Craons to entertain, iii. 184
entourage of, almost equalled by Modenese princess's, vi. 201

[Vorontsov, Mikhail Illarionovich, *continued*]
Florence to be revisited by, vi. 191, 202, 204
Francis I orders, to be well received at Florence, iii. 184
Frederick II should have been warned against, vi. 61
Halifax tells English diplomats in Italy to welcome, vi. 173
health of, out of order, vi. 194
hypochondria of, vi. 202
Italy to be revisited by, vi. 173
Ivan VI dethroned by, vi. 62
Keith discusses Russian-Turkish relations with, v. 247
Mann attends disastrous dinner with, v. 248
—— entertains, at George III's command, vi. 180, 193–4, 204
Naples to be visited by, for health, iii. 184
nephew and niece of, vi. 55
nephew told by, to thank George III for Mann's attentions, vi. 203
nieces of, vi. 68
Peter III may banish, to Siberia, vi. 11
Pisa visited by, vi. 202, 204
Porter's conduct condemned by, v. 248
postmaster the only companion of, in Florence, v. 249
Russian revolution feared by, vi. 202, 205
'soul' of the Russian ministry, v. 247
Uffizi often visited by, v. 249
Vienna visited by, vi. 180
wears boots and spurs to dinner table, v. 248
Vorontsova, Ekaterina Romanova (1743–1810), m. (ca 1758–60) Mikhail Illarionovich Dashkov:
announcement not made by, until successful, vi. 66
Catherine II aided by, vi. **65**
——'s former favourite, but now disgraced, vii. 242
England visited by, to put her son in school, vii. 242, 245
HW meets and describes, vii. 248–9
Mann knew relatives of, at Florence, vii. 245
Quaker meeting attended by, vii. 249
Sermon prêché . . . sur la tombe de Pierre, a translation by, vii. 249
sister's confidence to, revealed to Catherine II, vi. 68
songs rendered by, vii. 249
verses by, on print of Catherine II, vii. 242
Vorontsova, Countess Elisaveta Romanovna:
brother of, vi. 55
Catherine II said to have declined surrender from, of Order of St Catherine, vi. 58–9
Peter III keeps, as mistress, despite alleged impotence, vi. 57
——'s intention to imprison Catherine II told by, to sister, vi. 68

——'s mistress, vi. 55, 65
—— would have married, vii. 215
Vortices:
Descartes's theory of, once fashionable, iv. 154
Voting:
for pay, HW's reflections on, ix. 275
Voyage d'Italie. See under Richard, Abbé
Voyage et les aventures des trois princes de Sarendip, Le. See under Mailly, Chevalier de
Voyer, Marc-Antoine-René de (1722–87), Marquis de Paulmy; Marquis d'Argenson's son:
(?)Ashburnham jealous of, iii. 454
Voyer, Marc-Pierre de (1696–1764), Comte d'Argenson; French war minister:
disgrace of: desirable, v. 59; rumoured, v. 56
government ministry given to, ii. **32**
letters of, in favour of Jacobites, iii. 271
Louis XV receives remonstrances from, about Young Pretender's arrival, ii. 415
Louis XV's and Mme de Pompadour's love of peace induces, to try to separate them, iv. 530
Louis XV's devotion to Rome demanded by, as bulwark of monarchy, v. 48
religious faction led by, v. 56
(?) son of, iii. 454
Voyer, Marc-René (1722–82), Marquis de Voyer; Comte d'Argenson's son:
armament for siege taken by, past Lyon, iv. 536
(?) Ashburnham jealous of, iii. 454
Voyer, René-Louis (1694–1757), Marquis d' Argenson:
(?)son of, iii. 454
witticism by, on Vandières's attempt to get *cordon bleu*, iv. 228
Vrillière. *See* La Vrillière
Vulture; vultures:
Austrian and Russian eagles become, viii. 55
HW and Mann resemble, in their correspondence, ix. 327
HW's term for Joseph II, ix. 410
Worsley compared with, i. 249
Vyne, the:
chapel at: Mann to get Last Supper painting for, iv. 485, 489, 529, 539; Sandys builds, iv. 485n; stained glass in, iv. 485n
Chute ill at, v. 1
—— the last of the male line of his family at, viii. 209n
—— visits, at brother's death, iv. 433
Chute, Anthony, owns, i. 234n, iii. 458n
HW encourages improvements to, iv. 449
HW to visit Chute at, iv. 449, v. 1
Whithed ill at, iv. 237–8
Vyner, Robert (ca 1685–1777), M.P.:
Parliamentary debates by: on privately-raised regiments, x. 15; on Scotch bill, x. 31, 32

W——t——e, Mrs:
(?) Maclaine's mistress, iv. 169
Waasner Twickle. *See* Wassenaer
Wachtendonck, Karl Franz (ca 1694–1741), Bn von:
body coach of, i. 110
Braitwitz to succeed, temporarily, i. 117
Corsini, Cardinal, entertains, i. 106
cousin of, maid of honour to Maria Theresa, procures Richecourt's disgrace, i. 490
death and burial of, i. 109–10, 117
death of, may make Goldsworthys anxious to leave, i. 138
disguises himself to meet Ps Triulzi, i. 489–90
Florence visited by, i. 40, 95
Goldsworthy, Mrs, cicisbea to, i. 146, 186n
—— paid by, i. 146–7, 186
—— praises, i. 105
Goldsworthys excluded from death-bed of, i. 109
ill with malignant fever, i. 105, 109
Maria Theresa's troops at Leghorn commanded by, i. 467n
Osorio contrasted with, i. 186
priests banish pictures and install altars at bedside of, i. 109
Richecourt returns to Florence after death of, i. 468
—— said to have been frightened by, from Florence by a duel challenge, i. 467
——'s disgrace said to be procured by, i. 106, 108, 490
—— tells story about, i. 489–90
state coach of, i. 260
Walpole, Bns, rails at, i. 107
Walsegg not to imitate, i. 130
Waddington, Edward (ca 1670–1731) Bp of Chichester, 1724:
Maddox chaplain to, ii. 246
Wade, George (1673–1748), Gen.; field marshal; M.P.:
Arenberg quarrels with, ii. 441
army of, iii. 128
cavalry of, pursues rebels, iii. 186
Cumberland, D. of, sends Conway to hurry, after fleeing rebels, iii. 179
disgrace and defeat of, rumoured at Florence, iii. 190
Drummond sends proposal to, for exchanging prisoners, iii. 187, 202
Durand sends express to, iii. 166
Edinburgh provost sees, at Newcastle, iii. 175–6
field marshal, ii. 366
generosity of, to poor gentleman, iv. 110
George II and council approve answer of, to Drummond, iii. 202
George II criticizes, ii. 494
—— limits the troops allotted to, iii. 117
—— receives, ii. 556
HW prefers, to Stair, ii. 494

Handasyd sent by, to take Edinburgh, iii. 159
Hawley to accompany army of, to Scotland, iii. 193
health drunk to, at Leghorn, iii. 152
Hessians and British army from Flanders to join, in Yorkshire, iii. 126–7
independence of government orders demanded by, iii. 166
Mann expects rebels to be crushed by, iii. 149
Marlborough might be rivalled by, ii. 456
named in Secret Committee lists, i. 385
Newcastle left by, iii. 153, 159, 165
noblemen's regiments more effective than army of, in Yorkshire, x. 14
Ostend artillery demanded from England by, iii. 69
quartermaster captured by, iii. 167
rebels avoid, iii. 159
rebels to be opposed by, iii. 117, 165, 166
Scotland to be approached by, from Doncaster, iii. 137
snuff-box stolen from, at gaming-house, iv. 110
Stair may keep, from army command, iii. 127
Wetherby approached by, iii. 173–4
Wager, Lady. *See* Earning, Martha
Wager, Sir Charles (ca 1666–1743), Kt, 1709; Adm.; M.P.:
administration not to be influenced by, ii. 31
Admiralty post refused by, i. 346
Bible misquoted by, i. 333
called an old woman, i. 346
death of, ii. 245–6
English doggedness in sea battles praised by, ii. 410
Gashry nephew of, ii. 81n
Goldsworthy may be aided by, ii. 13, 31, 246
Gordon given ship by, i. 298
Jackson hopes for preferment after death of, i. 218
'niece' of, i. 302n
resignation of, i. 333
Wages and salaries:
cardinal's, from Apostolic Chamber, vii. 118
Cocchi's, v. 194
cook's, at Florence, iii. 357
Giberne's, as secretary, i. 190
Languedoc governor's, vii. 322
librettists', i. 191
lieutenant-general's, vi. 560
Lorenzi's secretary's, i. 157
of *Directeur des places fortifiées*, vii. 283
opera singers', i. 191
Palombo's, i. 156
Sharpe's, as Cts of Orford's agent, ix. 492
tailor's, i. 191
travelling companion's, v. 503
valet-secretary's, i. 172, 190

Wagons:
Hermione treasure carried in, vi. 66
Kingston, Ds of, sends treasure in, to Leghorn, viii. 404
open, German, Joseph II enters Florence
in, vii. 108
visible from SH, iv. 380
Wainscot:
Kingston, Ds of, leaves pistol-mark in, viii.
198
of House of Commons, ix. 35
Waistcoat; waistcoats:
Balmerinoch doffs, at execution, iii. 302
black, *Hamlet* ghost wears, iv. 209
cabriolets painted on, iv. 483
Charles Emmanuel III once the only king
in Europe to fight in his, v. 277
Fitzgerald's, lined with gum, ix. 631
flannel: French army does not have, v. 435;
worn by Balmerinoch, iii. 299
Frederick, P. of Wales, puts on, iv. 232
HW sends, to Mann, i. 152, 193, 433, 473
laced: Maclaine steals and sells, iv. 168;
Walpole, Horatio (1723–1809), wears, iv.
342
lace for, copied from Greek frieze, vi. 218
Maclaine takes, to pawnbroker, iv. 168
Mann wears: at baptism, i. 473; in cold
spell, iii. 391
plaid, Frederick, P. of Wales, wears, iv. 131
silk, laced, worn by Palmer, iv. 396
silver, borrowed by Pamfili, iii. 445
trimmed, Walpole, Hon. Thomas, wears,
iv. 342
white, men wear, at Reggio fair, vi. 148
Waiters. *See under* Servants
Wake, Mrs. *See* Bennet, Camilla
Wake, William (1657–1737), Abp of Canter-
bury 1716–37:
death of, iii. 503n
Waldaise, ——, Capt.:
captured at Velletri, ii. 491
Waldeck, Karl August Friedrich (1704–63),
Fürst von; field marshal:
army in Flanders led by, iii. **240**
resignation of, after dispute with D. of
Cumberland, iii. 428–9
Venice said to secure services of, against
Austria, iv. 176
Waldeck, castle of:
Conway captures, vi. 55–6
Waldegrave, Bns. *See* Fitzjames, Henrietta
(ca 1667–1730)
Waldegrave, Cts. *See* Leveson-Gower, Lady
Elizabeth (d. 1784); Waldegrave, Lady
Elizabeth Laura (1760–1816); Walpole, Maria
(1736–1807)
Waldegrave, Lady. *See* Fitzjames, Henrietta
Waldegrave, Lady Anna Horatia (1762–1801),
m. (1786) Hon. Hugh Seymour-Conway,
later Lord Hugh Seymour:
Ancaster, D. of, dies before marrying, viii.
494, 498–9, ix. 75

——'s relatives tell, that he would have
married her, viii. 494
beautiful, viii. 498
Churchill, Sophia, less beautiful than, ix.
132
cousin's beauty thought to surpass that of,
ix. 508
father survived by, vi. **127**
fiancé's relationship to, ix. 632n, 647
fortune of, ix. 132
HW engrossed with, viii. 315
HW gets news from, about mother and
stepfather, viii. 147
HW praises, ix. 632
HW sees, at Gloucester House, ix. 68
HW wants to marry Hon. Horatio Walpole
to, ix. 132–3
marriage of, results in HW's meeting
George IV at her father-in-law's and at
Leicester House, ix. 647
mourning to be worn by, for D. of Ancaster, viii. 494
Ranelagh visited by, ix. 68
Seymour-Conway, Capt. Hugh, to wed, ix.
632
sister less beautiful than, ix. 68
stepfather lodges, at Hampton Court Park
near SH, viii. 315
Walpole, Hon. Mrs Robert, less beautiful
than, ix. 410
Waldegrave, Lady Charlotte Maria (1761–
1808), m. (1784) George Henry Fitzroy,
styled E. of Euston, 4th D. of Grafton,
1811:
Churchill, Sophia, as handsome as, ix. 132
cousin's beauty thought to surpass that of,
ix. 508
Egremont was engaged to, ix. 68, 74–5, 77,
544n
father survived by, vi. **127**
fortune of, ix. 132
handsome, ix. 132
HW engrossed by, viii. 315
HW gets news from, about mother and
stepfather, viii. 147
HW sees, at Gloucester House, ix. 68
HW wants to marry Hon. Horatio Walpole
to, ix. 132–3
less beautiful than her sisters but more
popular with men, ix. 68
marriage of, ix. 544, 554
Ranelagh visited by, ix. 68
stepfather lodges, at Hampton Court Park
near SH, viii. 315
Walpole, Hon. Mrs Robert, less beautiful
than, ix. 410
Waldegrave, Lady Elizabeth. *See* Leveson-
Gower, Lady Elizabeth (d. 1784)
Waldegrave, Lady Elizabeth Laura (1760–
1816), m. (1782) George Waldegrave, 4th
E. Waldegrave, 1784:
Carmarthen, M. of, unable to marry, ix. 75
Churchill, Sophia, less beautiful than, ix.
132

cousin marries, ix. 75n, 274, 410n

cousin's beauty thought to surpass that of, ix. 508

father survived by, vi. **127**

fortune of, ix. 132

HW engrossed by, viii. 315

HW gets news from, about mother and stepfather, viii. 147

HW mentions, ix. 272

HW sees, at Gloucester House, ix. 68

HW's letters censored by, x. 38–9, 42

HW wants to marry Hon. Horatio Walpole to, ix. 132–3

mother tells, of praying and weeping, viii. 323

pregnant, ix. 571

Ranelagh visited by, ix. 68

sister less beautiful than, ix. 68

stepfather lodges, at Hampton Court Park, near SH, viii. 315

Walpole, Hon. Mrs Robert, less beautiful than, ix. 410

Waldegrave, Frances, Lady. *See* Braham, Frances Elizabeth Anne

Waldegrave, Geoffrey Noel (b. 1905), 12th E. Waldegrave:

HW's MSS owned by, x. 44

Waldegrave, George (1751–89), styled Vct Chewton (1763–84); 4th E. Waldegrave, 1784; M.P.:

cousin marries, ix. 75n, 274, 410n, 584

HW praises, ix. 584

Waldegrave, George Edward (1816–46), 7th E. Waldegrave, 1835:

HW's MSS owned by, x. 40, 43

Waldegrave, Lady Henrietta (1717–53), m. 1 (1734) Hon. (later Lord) Edward Herbert; m. 2 (1739) John Beard:

daughter of, iii. **468**

generations of the family of, vi. 485, ix. 571

HW's footnote about, altered, x. 38

inoculated for smallpox, vi. 127

Waldegrave, James (1684–1741), 2d Bn Waldegrave, 1689; cr. (1729) E. Waldegrave; ambassador to Austria 1727–30, to France, 1730–40:

death of, stops son's marriage project with Lady Maria Walpole, v. 285

generations of family of, vi. 485, ix. 571

Magnan meets, in Paris, ii. 564

Old Pretender's nephew, i. 336

Thompson formerly chaplain to, ii. 422

Walpole, Sir Robert, to be impeached for appointing, i. 336

Young Pretender's possible journey through France to be stopped after remonstrance by, i. **14**

Waldegrave, James (1715–63), 2d E. Waldegrave, 1741:

Bute not liked by, vi. 128

Churchill, Lady Mary, might have married, v. 285

daughter inherits sagacity and good sense of, ix. 68

daughters of, viii. 315n, 498n, ix. 68, 410n, 632n

death of, from smallpox, vi. 126–8, 131

foreign gazettes predict removal of, iv. 355

George II gives Garter to, alone, v. 110, vi. 572n

——'s favourite, iv. 246, 505

——'s lord of the Bedchamber, iv. 246n

George III's governor, iv. 345, 347–8, 355, v. 285n, vi. 126n, 128

German gazette announces dismissal of, from George II despite George II's and Newcastle's favour, iv. 505

HW played with, in holidays, ca 1729, ix. 570

HW's school-fellow, ix. 570

income of, mostly dies with him, vi. 128

lived with his grandmother, ix. 570

ministry under Fox considered hopeless by, v. 99

Newcastle, D. of, said to favour, iv. 505

person of, unpleasant, (?) v. 98, vi. 127

posts refused by, vi. 131

seal of, given by wife to successor, vi. 164

teller of Exchequer, vi. 126n

to be first lord of Treasury, v. 98

Walpole, Maria, to marry, v. 284–5, 287

Warden of the Stannaries, iv. 246, vi. 126n

wife of, v. 98n, 240n

Waldegrave, Hon. John (1718–84), 3d E. Waldegrave, 1763; army officer; M.P.:

anxiety over military campaign of, v. 316

HW played with, in holidays, ca 1729, ix. 570

HW's school-fellow, ix. 570

inoculated for smallpox, vi. 127

lived with his grandmother, ix. 570

marriage of, assisted by Sandwich, iv. 258

Master of the Horse to Q. Charlotte, vii. 176, 180

mob pelts, by mistake, iv. **156**

Rochefort inquiry conducted by, v. 155

sister-in-law gives husband's seal to, vi. 164

son of, ix. 75n, 274n

Waldegrave, Hon. John James (1785–1835), 6th E. Waldegrave, 1794:

birth of, expected, ix. 571

HW's letters inherited by, x. 38–9, 42, 43

Waldegrave, Lady Laura. *See* Waldegrave, Lady Elizabeth Laura

Waldegrave family:

George IV gives dinner for, ix. 647

HW has seen 6 generations of, vi. 485

transcripts of HW's letters censored by, x. 38, 39, 42

Waldemar Christian (1622–56), Graf von Schleswig-Holstein, P. of Denmark:

(?) masquerader costumed like portrait of, i. 338

Wale, Samuel (d. 1786); artist:

drawing by, of eagle, iv. 485

Wales, P. of:
George III becomes, iv. 239, 246
Young Pretender proclaimed as, ii. 552
See also Frederick Louis; George III; George IV
Wales, Ps of. *See* Augusta (1719–72) of Saxe-Gotha
Wales:
counties in, Beaufort tries to wrest lieutenancy of, from Morgan, vii. 174
election in, disputed, iv. 394, 401
inhabitants of, all interrelated, i. 344
marches of, London as lawless as, ix. 620
Methodist 'seminary' in mountains of, viii. 90–1
north of, rebels will perish if they flee to, iii. 179
rebel army in, would have to be supplied from Ireland, iii. 160
Williams a Jacobite of, iii. 310n
Walker, Thomas (ca 1664–1748), customs commissioner; Surveyor of Crown Lands; M.P.:
death of, iii. 511
Newmarket frequented by, iii. 511n
surveyor of the roads and usurer, iii. 511n
Walpole, Sir Robert, and Lord Godolphin courted by, iii. 5
Walkinshaw, Catherine (1715–94):
Bedchamber woman to Augusta, Ps of Wales, ix. 516
Walkinshaw, Clementina Maria Sophia (ca 1726–1802); 'Cts of Alberstroff':
daughter not to be accompanied by, ix. 522
family of, ix. 516
Gem, Dr, attends, ix. 516, x. 47
HW and Mann call, 'Mrs Walsingham,' ix. 512, 538n
Young Pretender's daughter by, ix. 512–14, 516, 521–2, x. 46–7
Wall, Mr and Mrs ——:
son of, iv. 171n
Wall, Richard (1694–1778), Gen.; Spanish secretary of state, and ambassador to England:
birth and parentage of, iv. 171n
Charles III expresses confidence in, v. 347
English manufacturers said to be lured by, to Spain, iv. 170–1
English-Spanish commercial relations discussed by, iii. 504
fashionable in England, iv. 51, 426
Gondomar resembles, iv. 52
Irish Catholic, iv. 171, v. 347n
recalled to Spain, iv. 426
Spanish ambassador to England, iii. 504, iv. 426n, v. 347n
to be secretary of state for foreign affairs in Spain, iv. 426
witticism by, to Grossatesta, at *Peace in Europe* serenata, iv. 51–2
Wall; walls:
English estates no longer concealed by, iv. 166

Wallace, James (1729–83); M.P.:
counsel for Ds of Kingston, viii. 192, 196
Wallachia ('Volakia'):
Turks lose, to Russia, vii. 155
Waller, Edmund (1606–87), poet:
engravings to works of, i. 358
'Sacharissa' of, vii. 248
Waller, Edmund (ca 1699–1771), M.P.:
Bubb Dodington defended by, in Parliament, i. 354–5
Case of the Hanover Forces by, ii. 123
Court party not joined by, ii. 118
Lincoln replaces, as Cofferer, iii. 347
lordship of the Treasury refused by, i. 332
named in Secret Committee lists, i. 385
naval investigation proposed by, in Parliament, ii. 399–400, 427
Parliamentary motion proposed by, to ask George II to give up Hanover troops, ii. 355
Ralph's *Of the Use and Abuse of Parliaments* attributed to, ii. 464
Sandys succeeded by, as Cofferer, i. 385n, ii. 551
Wallingford:
election at, i. 400
Wallis:
regiment of, ii. 164
Wallmoden, Frau von. *See* Wendt, Amalie Sophie Marianne von
Wallmoden, Adam Gottlieb (1704–1756) Oberhauptman von:
wife's son said to resemble, ii. 524
Wallmoden, Johann Ludwig von (1736–1811), 'Master Louis,' reputed son of George II; Graf von Wallmoden-Gimborn, 1783; field marshal:
father's alleged resemblance to, ii. 524
Florence visited by, vi. 327, 354
George II resembled by, vi. 327
Mann introduces, at Court, vi. 350
—— to entertain, at dinner, vi. 327
messenger sent by, to summon servants from Rome, vi. 357
returns to Germany by way of Rome, vi. 362
Walloon Guards (Gardes Vallones):
at Campo Santo, ii. 154, 164
at Leghorn, iii. 55
at Rome, ii. 532
casualties in: at Campo Santo, ii. 154; at Piacenza, iii. 267, 270
Wallop, John (1690–1762), cr. (1720) Vct Lymington and (1743) E. of Portsmouth:
Isle of Wight command to be taken from, ii. 457
Wallpaper:
blue and white, striped, at SH, iv. 382
Dutch tiles imitated on, at SH, iv. 382
Gothic fretwork, in SH hall, iv. 380, 381
green, in SH closet, iv. 382
Mann, Galfridus, has, for Mann's room, iv. 367

pink, HW uses, at Rigby's, iv. 166
red, in SH bedchamber, iv. 381
stone-colour Gothic, in SH parlour, iv. 380
yellow, in SH bedchamber, iv. 381
Walmoden. *See* Wallmoden
Walpole, Bns. *See* Rolle, Margaret (1709–81);
see also Walpole of Wolterton, Bns
Walpole, Lady. *See* Shorter, Catherine (ca
1682–1737); Skerrett, Maria (ca 1702–38)
Walpole, Lady Anne. *See* Osborne, Lady Anne
Walpole, Burwell (1675–90):
death of, vi. 26
Walpole, Catherine (ca 1703–22), dau. of Sir
Robert Walpole:
death of, vi. 27
Walpole, Charlotte (1738–89), HW's niece;
m. (1760) Lionel Tollemache, styled Lord
Huntingtower; 5th E. of Dysart, 1770:
father of, i. **209**
father's bounty to, viii. 349
Huntingtower marries, v. 438–40, 446
sister less handsome than, v. 239
sister visited by, v. 439
Walpole, Dorothy (1686–1726), m. (1713)
Charles, 2d Vct Townshend:
husband of, ix. 423n
son, of, iii. 320n
Walpole, Lady Anne, brings up, v. 353n
Walpole, Edward (1674–98):
death of, vi. 26
Walpole, Hon. Sir Edward (1706–84), K.B.,
1753; HW's brother; M.P.:
Ædes Walpolianæ arouses jealousy of, iv.
41–2, 55
appearance of: beautiful without a wrinkle,
ix. 462; face unwrinkled, viii. 148; HW
claims, looks younger than his own, viii.
529; sleek, young, and in good colour, viii.
529
Ashton intimate with, iv. 215, 218
Bath order esteemed by, vi. 390
Boothby recommended by, to Mann, v. 431,
482
Chelsea residence of, ii. 250, 284
children generously treated by, iii. 349
clerk of the Pells, and K.B., i. 209n, ix.
462n, x. 52
Coke family quarrel patched up by, iii. 457
Customs House place of, viii. 276, x. 52–4
daughter inherits impetuosity of, viii. 125
daughter's letter exhibited by, vii. 415
daughter's marriage settlements entrusted
by, to HW, v. 285
daughter of, i. 209, v. 239–40, 284–5, 439n,
vi. 94n, 127n, ix. 410n, 466n, 508n
death of: ix. 466; delays HW's payment to
Croft, ix. 473; makes HW next heir to E. of
Orford, ix. 477n; Mann condoles with HW
upon, ix. 466; may soon occur, ix. 462–3
diet of, ix. 463
empty title would be inherited by, on
nephew's death, vii. 510–11

English visitors to Florence tell, that sister-
in-law's health is bad, vii. 505, 512
father scolded in letter by, accusing HW
of bringing Middleton, iv. 215
father's estate should go to Cholmondeleys
after deaths of HW and, ix. 132
father's retirement wished by, i. 253, 319
father sups with, after long Parliamentary
session, i. 294
fortune of, ample, ix. 466
fortunes of HW and, not paid by Orford
after mother's death, ix. 315–16
Fox asks, to employ Windsor tradesmen,
iv. 42
—— receives call from, iv. 42
Frederick, P. of Wales, to be attended by,
at levee, i. 338, 369
Frogmore the home of, iv. 42
generosity of, ix. 466
Gloucester, Ds of, cannot persuade, to call
on her husband, vii. 461
—— informs, of her marriage, vii. 415
—— speaks tenderly of, viii. 297
Gloucester, D. of, fails to call on, vii. 423,
427
HW acts with, in care of nephew, vii. 461
HW arouses jealousy of, iv. 41, 55
HW 11 years younger than, viii. 529
HW formally asked by, to look after E.
of Orford's affairs, vii. 496
HW impresses age of, upon nephew, viii.
372
HW notifies, of inheritance from uncle, iv.
403
(?) HW notifies, of Orford's recovery, viii.
368
HW persuades, to let Customs House clerks
rise by seniority, viii. 358
HW quarrels with, over Castle Rising, iii.
419
HW's coolness with, aggravated by Ashton,
iv. 215
HW's indebtedness from, must be felt by
him, v. 287
HW's letter to Mann about E. of Orford
seen and approved by, vii. 483
HW's place in Customs House expires with,
viii. 178
HW's references to, censored, x. 38
HW's relations with, iv. 218
HW surprised that Order of the Bath
should be accepted by, vi. 381
HW to call on, ix. 123
health of: appetite partly restored by the
bark, ix. 463; aversion to solid food, ix.
462; Mann condoles with HW on, ix. 469;
perfect for many years, ix. 462; unvaried
from 30 to 77, ix. 466
Houghton visited by, i. 88
Howe, Hon. Caroline, not to wed, i. **209,**
240
Huntingtower asks, for daughter's hand, v.
439

[Walpole, Hon. Sir Edward, *continued*]
Ilay to be asked by, about cobalt and zinc, ii. 250

inquiries of, about cobalt and zinc, ii. 284

Jebb's letter to, about D. of Gloucester's illness, viii. 319

Keppel, Mrs, given estate, house, and coach by, viii. 349, 352

K.B., i. 209n, vi. 27, 381n, 390

law to be obeyed literally by, in E. of Orford's case, viii. 295

letter by, about D. of Gloucester's illness, x. 50–1

Mann asks about attitude of, to daughter's match, vii. 396, 403

——'s correspondence with, v. 431

——'s letter of attorney required by, for Customs House petition, viii. 209

—— to send paints to, iii. 368–9

Mann, John, employed by, in Customs House, viii. 358

Marlborough tells, of son's bravery, v. 240

mistress tires, i. 240

modern miracles in painting and music disparaged by, ix. 577

Orford expects, will not press for payment of fortune for fear of being disinherited, ix. 316, 322–3

—— not to cause action by, viii. 316

—— said to have disinherited, vii. 496

——'s disposal of Rolle lands not to be opposed by, ix. 148, 156–7

—— should be matter of indifference to, after guarding against consequences of his confederates, viii. 303

——'s parasites sow distrust against, viii. 372–3

——'s relations with, vii. 461

—— to send mourning ring to, ix. 124

—— unlikely to be survived by, viii. 372, ix. 316

Orford, Cts of, leaves son to care of HW and, vii. 464, 487–94, 514

—— wanted by, to look after her son, vii. 470–1, 476, 481–2, 485–6

Orford estate not coveted by, ix. 125

paints, iii. 368

Pitt called on by, iii. 371

St Albans notified by, not to expect support against Fox, iv. 42

seclusion of, vii. 460–1

Shorter estate shared by, iv. 403

sister-in-law's death will not affect, ix. 123

son-in-law of, dies, viii. 348

son of, v. 240, vii. 300, 307

statute of lunacy not to be taken out by, for E. of Orford, viii. 294, ix. 126

Suckling cousin of, viii. 178

—— to pay moneys to, viii. 231, 237

tea seed forgotten by, ii. 284

tea seed to be procured by, ii. 250

temper of, unhappy, iv. 218

Thirlby gets Customs place through, iv. 215n

—— leaves papers to, iv. 215n

—— lives with, iv. 215n

—— wanted by, to write Sir Robert Walpole's life, iv. 215

town house of, given to Mrs Keppel, viii. 349

will of, leaves most to Mrs Keppel, ix. 466

Windsor estate of, viii. 349

witticism by, on Bubb Dodington, i. 258

Walpole, Edward (1737–71), Lt-Col.; HW's nephew:

bravery of, at St Malo, v. 240, 246

death of, vii. 300, 307

drinking and gaming the vices of, vii. 300

father of, i. 209

Walpole, George (1730–91), 3d E. of Orford, 1751; HW's nephew:

actions of, influenced by low rogues, ix. 124–5

agent of, desires agreement with Sharpe on mother's estate, ix. 150–1

balloon ascent encouraged by, ix. 596

Battie attends, vii. 540, 546, ix. 126

Bedchamber duties of, ix. 226

Bedchamber resigned by, ix. 266

Beevor attends, at Eriswell, viii. 293, 295, 296

bets made by, at Newmarket, vii. 503

bond of, turned over by Horace Mann II to Hull, viii. 78

Boone chosen by, to represent Ashburton, viii. 46–7

—— the only grateful friend of, viii. 292

boroughs of: Sharpe recommends sale of, viii. 52–3; tended by Lucas, ix. 462

broth the only nourishment of, viii. 505

Carder, Mrs, improves opinion of, of Mozzi, ix. 168

Catherine II may buy Houghton pictures from, viii. 427–8, 434, 440–1

—— may not pay whole sum to, for Houghton pictures, viii. 502

caveat by, against mother's will, ix. 124, 126, 137, 143, 167, 195, 493, 504, 509

Cheltenham visited by, iv. 273

Chute tries to marry, to Margaret Nicoll, iv. 256–7, 273

Cipriani does paintings for, ix. 247

——'s pictures vaunted by, though he had sold his others, ix. 418

claims of, against mother's estate: asserted by Lucas, ix. 143, 157, 186, 217, 333, 335, 341; chiefly repayment of fines on renewal of leases, ix. 335; exceed her estate's claims against him, ix. 412; for plate and jewels, ix. 158; HW does not know, ix. 176; not to be ready soon, ix. 191; should be made in justice to father's creditors, ix. 158

Clinton barony cannot be transmitted by, ix. 165

Clinton barony to be claimed by, ix. 151, 157, 240, 304
Clinton's alleged portrait desired by, ix. 151, 227, 240, 304
commission of lunacy would deprive, of his positions, vii. 482
Cony called 'prime minister' of, ix. 131
—— employed by, vii. 560
—— entrusted by, with his affairs, viii. 310–11
contradictions of, called by HW 'emanations of his malady,' ix. 195
Court attended by, vii. 460
creditors of: settlement by, viii. 246, 272; should get claims before harpies strip him, viii. 84; suit of, against him, may be terminated by him, viii. 246; told by Lucas that they may expect large sum from Mozzi, ix. 286, 439
daughter of, by weeding girl, ix. 355
death of, without children: would involve reversion of barony of Clinton, ix. 165; would leave empty title to uncle, vii. 510–11
debts contracted by father to be compounded by, ix. 148
debts of, vii. 510, 549, viii. 78, 82, 440–1, ix. 155, 158
delay in settling mother's affairs welcomed by, ix. 247
Devon and Dorset estates to be bequeathed by, to the Rolles, ix. 148, 156–7
Devon and Dorset estates to have been visited by, ix. 227
disposition and habits of, iv. 482, vii. 560, viii. 295
division of money held by Hoare unlikely to suit, ix. 426
Dorsetshire estate to be sold by, ix. 148
Duane rejected by, ix. 265
engaging when present, provoking when absent, iv. 482, viii. 54
England reached by, according to papers, iv. 251
English might forget mother's alienation from, ix. 396
Eriswell 'hovel' of, viii. 293, ix. 227
Eriswell revisited by, ix. 227
executor of father's estate, ix. 446
farm of: let for less than HW could have got, ix. 172; let to a jockey, viii. 52; near Newmarket, vii. 495
father allows, to ride cousin's horses, ii. 70
father's death would injure, iii. 496, iv. 233
father's debts unpaid by, viii. 440, ix. 158
finances of: greatly improved by HW, vii. 540, 549, viii. 294, 301, ix. 140, 172; HW not again to manage, viii. 53, 294, 301, 307–8, ix. 143; need attention, vii. 471, 481–2, 488–90, 497–8, 503, 509–11, 515, 521–2, 523, 528–9
fines on renewal of leases paid to mother instead of, ix. 335

Florence might be visited by, iii. 511
footman of, committed to prison for getting bastard, ix. 355
friend of: lost at sea, v. 206; tells HW not to release him, vii. 541
Geneva to be stopping-place of, iv. 7
George III bets with, on having a child before Sir James Lowther, v. 530–1
goes into country, vii. 551, viii. 372
Gordon, Lord George, as mad as, ix. 355
grandfather contrasted with, ix. 418
grandfather's acts all undermined by, viii. 502–3, ix. 132
grandfather said to have left fortune to, iv. 247
grandfather's creditors make agreement with, viii. 300–1
grandfather's debts compounded by, viii. 440–1
grandmother's bequest to, iv. 418, 424, 436
grandmother slighted by, iv. 482
Greek and Latin not to the taste of, iv. 481
groom advises, to rub his body with sulphur and hellebore, vii. 460
HW acts fairly towards, ix. 125
HW advertises recovery of, viii. 368
HW advised Horace Mann II to sue, viii. 82, 84
HW advised sale of pictures by, to pay father's and grandfather's debts, viii. 434, 440–1
HW and Sir Edward Walpole not to take action over, viii. 316
HW and Sir Edward Walpole not to take out statute of lunacy for, viii. 294, ix. 126
HW and Sir Edward Walpole should be indifferent to, viii. 303, 376
HW and Sir Edward Walpole want mother to take care of, vii. 470–1, 476, 481–2, 485–6
HW as counsel for, must not betray his interests, ix. 265
HW asks if Mann has been paid by, for mother's tomb, ix. 427
HW as nominee of, cannot altogether side with Mozzi, ix. 462
HW as referee for, cannot complain of lawyer's delays, ix. 289
HW became referee in Mozzi's affair only to save honour of, from public courts, ix. 445
HW called on by, vii. 551
HW cannot give Mozzi advice against, ix. 298
HW condemns Lucas for advising, to contest Cts of Orford's will, ix. 315
HW consulted on epitaph by, for mother, ix. 195
HW consults Sharpe about, vii. 496, 503, 545–6
HW declares to, that he will be motivated only by fairness, ix. 217

[Walpole, George, *continued*
HW disappointed in, iv. 482, vii. 121
HW dismissed by, vii. 3–4, ix. 172
HW does not approve advice given by lawyers to, ix. 147
HW does not approve contest of mother's will by, ix. 216
HW does not covet fortune of, ix. 125
HW does not reply to letter from, ix. 247
HW does not wish to inform, of objections to mother's will, ix. 125
HW during difficulties of, says that Sir Edward Walpole looks the younger uncle, viii. 529
HW expects to be dropped as referee by, because of plain dealing, ix. 184
HW fears, would object to Camden as referee, ix. 216
HW fears appearing too favourable to, ix. 216
HW forgets, as fast as possible, viii. 440
HW formally asked to look after affairs of, vii. 496
HW given no cause by, for tenderness, viii. 372–3
HW glad that Mann did not force mother of, to discuss him, viii. 320
HW has housed, at High Beech, viii. 300
HW has probably offended, ix. 477
HW heir to, ix. 477n
HW invited by, to Houghton, vii. 554
HW not eager to advise, ix. 195
HW notifies, of mother's death, ix. 121, 122
HW paid by, his legacy from Sir Robert Walpole, ix. 637
HW pities, for mother's behaviour, iv. 439
HW praises, i. 450, iii. 510–11, iv. 6–7, 19, 247, 254
HW preaches to, viii. 372–3
HW quotes from his reply to, ix. 516
HW regrets claim made by, ix. 519
HW's conduct of affairs of, vii. 494, 496–8, 503, 505, 510–11, 516, 521–2, 523, 529, 537, 540–1, 546, 548–9, 554, 560, 565, viii. 3–4, 19, 294, 301, 307–8, ix. 140, 143, 172
HW's conduct towards, acknowledged in words but not in practice, ix. 171–2
HW's correspondence with, vii. 467, ix. 121, 122, 124, 131, 140, 195, 247, 445, 516
HW's correspondence with mother about, vii. 470, 472, 476, 477, 478, 485, 486, 487–8, 493, 495, 509, 512, 514, 515–16, 517, 519, 523, 524, 525, 529, 531–2, 534, 537, 541, 544, 545, 548, 552, 557, 558, 560, 563, viii. 52, 58, 66, 70, 83
HW's ideas never approved by, or his lawyers, ix. 315
HW's letter about, seen and approved by Sir Edward Walpole, vii. 483
HW's letter condemning Sharpe and Lucas will not be shown to, ix. 315
HW's relations with, after mother's death,

ix. 121, 122, 123–4, 126, 136–7, 147–8, 155, 156–7, 157–8, 164–5, 216, 315, 350–1, 511, 515
HW's sale of horses and dogs may be disapproved by, vii. 540
HW surprised that hot weather does not cause, to relapse, viii. 407
HW's visit to, at Houghton, vii. 560, viii. 295
HW takes, to Vauxhall, i. 450
HW tells Monro to quit, when it is safe to do so, viii. 368
HW thinks as little as possible of, viii. 378
HW thinks claim of, wrong, ix. 265
HW to act justly towards, ix. 289
HW to seek Camden's and Conway's advice about, ix. 125
HW tries to dislodge parasites of, viii. 320
HW wants to keep mother on good terms with, vii. 557
HW will not again go to, unless he is brought to town, viii. 296
HW will not pay for serving, viii. 311
HW will not trouble himself about, viii. 502
habits of, intemperate, vii. 560
Hamilton's interference in boroughs of, displeases HW, vii. 548
Hampstead house occupied by, vii. 495
health of: apothecary, mistress, and physicians predict continuance of insanity, viii. 294; Beevor says, is better, viii. 296; eruption, vii. 460; fever, viii. 293; ill, iv. 273; insanity, vii. 460–1, 463, 467, 468, 471, 472, 476, 482, 485, 488–90, 492–3, 495, 505, 521, 529, viii. 293–6, 324, 327, 330, 332, 349, ix. 137; insanity of, a warning against marriage into insane families, ix. 424n; insanity pronounced incurable by Jebb and Battie, ix. 126; keeper cures, with apothecary's draught, viii. 372; malady induces contradictory conduct, ix. 195; recovers, vii. 539–41, 544, 546, 548, 554, 560, 563, 565, viii. 367, 372; recovery of, keeps HW from bothering with elections, viii. 38; recovery of, Mann thinks indicated, ix. 156; relapse expected by, viii. 372; supposed recovery of, doubted by HW, ix. 195–6; swelled leg may drain head, ix. 266
Hoare accepts Mozzi's order to pay, ix. 509, 511
honourable intentions of, defeated by bad advisers, ix. 181
Houghton being refurnished by, with modern pictures, ix. 247, 316
Houghton decorated with 'scratches' by, ix. 247
Houghton destroyed by, ix. 195
Houghton exterior 'improved' by, viii. 427–8
Houghton pictures must be preserved by, iv. 268

Houghton pictures not prized by, v. 208, ix. 418

Houghton pictures sold by, viii. 427–8, 434, 440–1, 451, 502, 541, ix. 108, 121, 133, 164, 316, 418

Houghton plundered by, ix. 132

Houghton's sale contemplated by, iv. 265

Hull, Mayor of, thanks, because his militia begot so many children there, ix. 355

indifference of, vii. 230

indolence and inattention of, iv. 418

ingratitude of, towards HW, innocently increased by Mann, ix. 136–7

inn on Newmarket road visited by, vii. 460

in the country, viii. 17

James treats, vii. 460

Jebb attends, at Eriswell, viii. 294

—— treats, vii. 495, 540, viii. 294, ix. 126

jockeys and grooms help ruin estate of, vii. 511

Knight recommended by, to Mann, iii. 462

lawyers of: delay settlement of affairs with Mozzi, ix. 161; do not communicate with HW, ix. 265; may be quickened by Mozzi's presence, ix. 307; object to Duane as referee, ix. 235; see also Cony, Carlos; Lucas, Charles

letters written by, on recovery, vii. 539

Lucas and Sharpe would probably favour, ix. 421–2

Lucas delays in transmitting demands of, upon Mozzi, ix. 172

—— expects, will consent to Duane as referee, ix. 216

—— instigated, to contest mother's will, ix. 315, 510

—— may seek approval of, for Duane's nomination, ix. 216, 217

—— profits by indolence of, ix. 456

—— reproved by, for delay, ix. 168, 181

——'s apparent zeal in cause of, well paid, ix. 200

—— says, has claims on his mother, ix. 143

—— the emissary of, ix. 227

—— to be tossed in blanket by, ix. 322, 328

—— to visit, ix. 286

—— to warn, against acquiescing in mother's will, ix. 126

—— to write to, ix. 472

Mackreth said to have lent money to mother of, thereby becoming M.P. for Castle Rising, viii. 53n

major-general's rank demanded by, viii. 372

Mann confers with mother about, vii. 468, 500–1, 503, 515–16, 517, viii. 17, 318, 353, 368, 376

—— encloses letter for, ix. 226

—— has had no connection with, ix. 136

—— hopes physique of, will be better than Gardiner's, ii. 507

—— hopes that HW will not ruin his health taking care of, viii. 303

—— never mentions, to his mother, viii. 23

—— not to complain about, to mother, viii. 47

—— paid by, for mother's tomb, ix. 436

—— pleased at HW's changed opinion of, iv. 6–7, 26

—— receives letter from: about Cts of Orford's papers, ix. 163, 181; about monument, ix. 219

—— sends drawing to, of mother's monument, ix. 350

—— to inform Mozzi of inheritance of, ix. 126

—— to receive mourning ring from, ix. 124, 206

—— urges HW to forget, viii. 513

—— will obey commands of: ix. 137; concerning mother's monument, ix. 206

—— wishes HW to explain to, about arms for mother's monument, ix. 240

—— writes to, ix. 163

Mann, Horace II, corresponds with, concerning father's debts, ix. 148, 155, 158

——'s bond from, viii. 78

—— sues, viii. 82, 84

Mann family fortunes involved in those of, iv. 250, vii. 496

marriage might improve finances of, iv. 250

marriage of, prevented by great-uncle, vii. 367

Martinelli writes letter to, ix. 554–5

militia given onions by, ix. 11

militia led by Windham under, ix. 11n

militia plagued by, viii. 451

militia taken by: to Hull, ix. 355; to Portsmouth, v. 300

militia to be commanded by, viii. 372

Monro diagnoses condition of, viii. 316

—— praised by, to Martha Turk, viii. 372

—— reports recovery of, to HW, viii. 367–8

monument to be erected by, for mother, ix. 195, 213, 219

Morice is HW's fellow-labourer in affairs of, ix. 171

mother and grandmother slighted by, iv. 482

mother and HW unable to rescue, from scoundrels, viii. 58

mother avoided by, vii. 224

mother cannot well disinherit, iv. 433

mother condemns: for ingratitude to her and HW, viii. 57; for lack of taste in Latin and Greek, iv. 481

mother corresponds with Sharpe about, vii. 464, 472, 476, 486, 491–4, 501, 503, 509–10, 514, 516, 525, 548, viii. 57

mother describes, to Mrs Richmond, iii. 192

mother fears that recovery of, will not be lasting, viii. 376

mother gives, power over her boroughs, viii. 46

mother leaves, to care of HW and Sir Edward Walpole, vii. 464, 487–8, 492–3, 496, 514, viii. 305

[Walpole, George, *continued*]

mother likes, though continuing to rob him, iv. 247

mother may meet, in England, vii. 121

mother may not know condition of, viii. 330

mother may take, to Italy, iv. 247

mother neglected by, during lifetime, but now to be honoured by monument, ix. 195

mother never inquires after, viii. 322, 347, 374

mother never inspired by, to tenderness, viii. 376

mother not to know of HW's break with, viii. 17

mother resembled by, i. **450**

mother ruins estate of, iv. 239

mother's affairs to be honourably settled by, ix. 144

mother's claims on, presented in 'case,' ix. 162

mother's correspondence with, vii. 558–9, viii. 541–2, ix. 180

mother's correspondence with Mann about, vii. 472, 476–8, 487, 534, 541, 544, 545, 552, 558, viii. 305

mother's death brings great estate to, ix. 125, 158

mother's disposition in favour of Mozzi approved by, ix. 168, 181

mother sees, vii. 230

mothers' estate and jointure inherited by, ix. 125

mother's estate to be given to Rolle family by, ix. 148, 156

mother should have left money in London to, Sharpe thinks, ix. 154–5

mother should sacrifice jointure to, instead of demanding arrears, iv. 486

mother shows concern for, iv. 479, 481, 486

mother slighted by, iv. 482

mother's memory respected by, ix. 168

mother's monument may be forgotten by, because HW did not oppose it, ix. 213

mother's monument to be superintended by Mann, ix. 195, 345, 350

mother's perishable property hardly of interest to, Mann thinks, ix. 169

mother's portrait should not be given by, to Mozzi, ix. 502

mother's will not to be disputed by, ix. 124, 172

mother's will omits name of, ix. 120, 122

mother too far away to aid, vii. 460

mother wants Pringle to examine, vii. 488

mother wounds, by her misconduct, iii. 39

mourning rings to be presented by, to his uncles and Mann, ix. 124

Mozzi advised to divide sum equally with, ix. 419

—— assured by, of satisfaction, ix. 181

—— authorizes payment to, by Hoare, ix. 498, 504

—— favoured by HW over, ix. 265

—— gives 'Clinton's' portrait to, ix. 298n

—— imprudently irritates lawyers of, ix. 216

—— might be unpopular in England for getting inheritance away from, ix. 396, 404

—— ought to be considerately treated by, ix. 147

—— receives release from, through Mann, ix. 527

—'s affair with, ix. 163, 439–41, 444–7, 448, 504, 509–11

—'s business with, to be settled when mother's will is proved, ix. 167

—'s compromise with, proposed, ix. 471–2

—'s conduct pleases, ix. 156

—'s dealings with, ix. 158, 166–7

—— sends list to, of things taken to Italy by his mother, ix. 151, 156

—'s letter from, ix. 186, 322

—'s letter from: called by HW 'gross, indecent and absurd,' ix. 328; 'indecent,' ix. 330

—'s letter to: approved by HW, ix. 319; approved by Mann, ix. 300, 301–2; not read by HW, ix. 176

—'s offer answered by, ix. 495

—— to grant wishes of, ix. 163

—— to meet demands of, ix. 144

—— to pay, through Hoare, ix. 492

—— to send HW list of demands of Cts of Orford on, ix. 158

—— turns mother of, from going to England from Calais to meet him, vii. 158

—— wants release from, for acting as his mother's executor, ix. 498

—— wishes to know demands of, ix. 161

—— writes to, with Mann's approval, ix. 300, 301–2

never in London, except to fulfil duties as Lord of Bedchamber, ix. 226

New Park visited by, in holidays, ii. 70

Nicoll match rejected by, iv. 256–7, 262, 265, 273, 278, 425, 431, 435, v. 285, viii. 301

North administration supported by, ix. 266

Orford deeds sought by, ix. 160

Orford jointure deficiency possibly under scrutiny by, ix. 176

parents' intercourse restricted after birth of, iii. 203

parsonage rented by, at Eriswell near Barton Mills, viii. 293

paternity of, dubious, vii. 548–9, ix. 132

physicians despised by, viii. 294

physicians of, want his friends kept away from him, vii. 482

Piddletown visited by, ix. 227

plover's eggs annually sent to HW by, ix. 143

portrait claimed by, that of a Clinton, ix. 240

'posthumous piety' of, ix. 227

rangerships to be taken away from, ix. 266
rents of mother's estate collected by, ix. 144
resigns as Groom of Bedchamber, ix. 266
ring for Mann probably forgotten by, ix. 206
Rockingham's turkey-geese match with, v. 7
Rolle estate and Walpole estate inherited by, with power to cut off entail, ix. 164n
Rolle family's Dorsetshire estate might be sold by, ix. 148
ruined, iv. 238–9
sailing taken up by, viii. 38
sale of Houghton pictures by, declared necessary to pay uncle's fortunes, but they are unpaid, ix. 316
sale of pictures by, ix. 247
satisfied in respect to mother's jewels, ix. 168
secretary of militia compelled by, to read Statius aloud, viii. 295
servants of, persist in pilfering, vii. 521
Sharpe laments conduct of, viii. 53
—'s expresses about borough elections unanswered by, viii. 46
—— surprised by Mozzi's employment of him when connected with, ix. 320, 333
—— thinks Mozzi should divide Cts of Orford's money in England with, ix. 154–5, 157, 160, 217, 335, 426
—— would probably favour, ix. 421–2
Shirley's portrait perhaps claimed by, ix. 227
Skrine and Boone chosen by, to represent his boroughs, viii. 46–7
Skrine desired by, to act as agent in affairs with Mozzi, ix. 163–4
—— obligated to, ix. 158
—— partial to, ix. 166
squanders money on whores and parasites, viii. 513
steward of, see Withers, William
suicidal attempts of, vii. 495, 505, viii. 293–4
sum to be claimed by, had been settled in advance by lawyers, HW thinks, ix. 335
sycophants of: divert him from pursuing just thoughts, ix. 148; impertinent to HW, ix. 143; incite him to affront HW, ix. 509; keep outsiders away from him, ix. 137; prejudice him against HW, ix. 125; sow mistrust against uncles, viii. 372–3; 'vultures,' vii. 521; would just have stolen more if his mother had died earlier, ix. 108
thoughtless, iv. 26
to be lord of the Bedchamber, iv. 470
to go into the country, vii. 551–2
Turin post declined by, v. 206
Turin post once requested by, v. 195, 206
Turk, Martha, has slept with, for 20 years, viii. 295
—— joins forehead to, at table in evening, viii. 295
—— the Delilah of, viii. 372

uncles do not covet estate of, ix. 125
uncles' fortunes not paid by, after mother's death, ix. 316, 322–3
uncles not expected by, to press for payment of their fortunes, lest they be disinherited, ix. 316
uncles' relations with, vii. 461
uncles said to be disinherited by, vii. 496, ix. 477
Van Dyck's portrait of Clinton sent to, ix. 501
Walpole, Horatio (1723–1809), gets angry letter from, about footman, ix. 355
Walpole, Hon. Horatio (1752–1822), invites, to be his son's godfather, ix. 418
—— should be heir to, ix. 132
——, with wife, invited by, to Houghton, in 'frantic' letter, ix. 418
whispers to country gentlemen at Houghton, viii. 295
'wild boy,' iii. 496, iv. 26
will of, HW not to influence, ix. 164
Windham will not be surprised at conduct of, ix. 11
Withers receives letter from, viii. 367
world believes, to be in his senses, viii. 46
Zincke's portrait of mother left to, to do as he pleases, ix. 504
Walpole, Horatio (1678–1757), cr. (1756) Bn Walpole of Wolterton; M.P.; HW's uncle:
ambition and dirt of, iv. 556
Amsterdam Gazette attributes naval investigation proposal to, ii. 427
Amigoni and Astley paint family of, iv. 341–2
avarice of, iv. 42, 81, v. 56–7, 62
bathing and fires avoided by, ii. 47
boasts jokingly about son, iii. 168
Bolingbroke's Letters to be answered by, iv. 62, 76
breeches shrugged by, i. 484
brother advised by, to decline pension, ii. 465
brother fetched by, from Houghton to Chelsea, i. 386
brother imitated by, iii. 469
brother not allowed by, to visit Ranelagh, ii. 8
brother's estate to be diverted by, from brother's grandchildren, v. 52
brother urged by, to resign, i. 319
Chesterfield not likely to be more successful than, in Dutch negotiations, iii. 68
Chetwynd's duel with, ii. 191–2, 207
childish, v. 52
cleanliness and warmth avoided by, ii. 47n
Common Sense prints satire on, i. 469–70
conundrum on Teller's and Auditor's places held by, iii. 28
cured at 75, iv. 291
death of, v. 56

[Walpole, Horatio (1678–1757), *continued*]
descendant of, also a descendant of his brother, ix. 418
Devonshire fails to get peerage for son of, iv. 66–7
drams addressed to, by mistake, iii. 238
Earle seconded by, i. **243**
Edinburgh capture reported by, to HW, iii. 108
Frederick, P. of Wales, to be attended by, at levee, i. 338, 369
Gower's stormy correspondence with, iv. 563
grandson of, Orford bound to make, his heir, ix. 132
HW advises Mann to write to, iii. 484
HW calls, 'old buffoon,' iii. 469
HW has cut all acquaintance with, since Nicoll affair, iv. 425
HW not found very tractable by, viii. 458
HW receives marriage-settlements from, iv. 250
HW's narrative about Nicoll affair should stay unpublished because of, iv. 278
HW's neglect from nephews would please, vii. 367
HW's political thermometer, i. 467
HW's quarrel with, v. 311n
HW tells, that he looks as if on way to Aix-la-Chapelle, ii. 305
HW to speak to, again, about Mann's theory about Young Pretender, iii. 210
health of: bed-ridden, iii. 504; better, iii. 510; going off, iii. 496; mended by soap and limewater, iii. 510n, iv. 3
Houghton visited by, ii. 305
house of, at Wolterton, visited and described by HW, ii. 47
House of Commons cannot spare, iii. 469
House of Commons tells, to 'withdraw,' i. 431
impeachment of, drawn up, i. 336, 344
indefatigable and healthy, iv. 250
Leheup brother-in-law to, iii. 111n
Magnan not heartily recommended by, ii. 563–4
—— said to be protégé of, ii. 548–9
—— writes to, ii. 549, 563
Mann aided by, in seeking salary arrears, iii. 474, v. 483
—— congratulates, on son's wedding, iv. 22
—— defends, i. 491
—— has seen, ii. 70
—— obtains expense arrears through, iii. 220
——'s correspondence with, iv. 22, 24–5
—— thinks, should be prime minister, iv. 419, 425, 431
—— to send orange flower water and dried orange flowers to, iv. 255
Mann, Robert, 'baited' by, to provide for Mann, ii. 308

nephew's estate aided by efforts of, iv. 250, 255
Newcastle, D. of, approached by, about Mann's salary arrears, iii. 474
—— asked by, to conceal rumour of sham Pretender, iii. 174, 199
Norwich election expenses mortify, v. 56
orange flower water liked by, iii. 330, iv. 255
Orford, E. of, cheated by, of marrying an heiress, iv. 273, vii. 367
Orford entail broken by, defrauding brother's descendants, vii. 367
Parliamentary debate by, on privately-raised regiments, x. 16
peerage given to, iv. 556, 563
peerage rumoured for, i. 430–1, 469–70, iii. 478, iv. 3
Pelham, Lady Catherine, to receive orange flower water from, iii. 330
Pitt attacked by, over naval appropriations, iii. 168–9
—— thanked by, iii. 371
Ranelagh visited by, with HW, ii. 8
Receipt to Make a Lord written about, i. 469–70
settlements made by, at son's wedding, iii. 469
soap 'mends,' iv. 3
son of, iii. 414n, 469n, vii. 141n, ix. 410n
son's horses put to grass in New Park by, ii. 70
speaks in Parliament for first time since brother's fall, i. 467
speeches of, on Aix treaty, iv. 3
'stumping along,' ii. 305
tailor in Drury Lane farce resembles, iv. 342
Tower of London rumoured to become prison of, i. 299
treaty with Saxony opposed by, in Parliament, iv. 300, 304–5
unjust uncle, vii. 497
whist parties sought by, iv. 250
widow of, ix. 385n
wife called 'Pug' by, ii. 47n
wig snatched off by, to show his gray hair, iii. 169
Winnington's speech frightens, i. 484
witticism by, on Perceval and Edwin, i. 27
Walpole, Hon. Horatio (Horace) [HW] (1717–97), 4th E. of Orford, 1791:
acquaintances of, are a few retired elderly folk, ix. 542
age of 32 admitted by, as 'elderly,' iv. 119
ambition never felt by, ix. 262
ancestors of, often met violent deaths, iv. 65
apologies by, for false humility, vii. 528
appearance of: as wrinkled as Methusaleh, viii. 176; bones 'no bigger than a lark's', viii. 71; fatter, viii. 148; looked charmingly

a month ago, viii. 176; 'old lean face,' vi. 136; 'very fat,' iv. 57; 'wrinkled parchment,' viii. 148; wrinkles, ix. 332
aversion of: to affectation, viii. 213; to ambition, viii. 100–1; to asking favours, vi. 479–80; to asking political favours, v. 79; to changing friends, vii. 425; to Christmas, ii. 367; to clergy, viii. 71, ix. 441; to country life, i. 443; to Court functions, ix. 307–8; to Court life, ix. 247; to diversions, viii. 86; to embarking on new scenes, vi. 111; to exultation, viii. 446; to Genoese, ii. 179; to gifts, ix. 655; to gifts from all but closest friends, viii. 475; to House of Commons, vi. 348; to lawyers, viii. 71, ix. 441; to ostentation, vi. 480; to Parliament, viii. 101; to philosophers, vi. 151; to physicians, v. 368, vi. 110, viii. 71, 74, ix. 441; to piddling politics, vii. 420; to politics, vi. 110, 300, 304, 308–9, 316, 348, 359, 363, 436, 550, 570, 572, 578, vii. 41, 129, 145, viii. 117, 351, ix. 140, 310, 311–12, 365, 476, 483, 604; to priests, viii. 71; to public places and active people, viii. 76; to questioning of wills, ix. 123; to removing landmarks, ix. 541; to royalty, v. 449; to sights, iv. 40; to slavery, iv. 126, vii. 462; to war, ii. 422–3, vi. 81, ix. 106, 108, 188, 365
basis of political pronouncements of, explained, ix. 30
came into the world at 5 years old, ix. 558
catalogue printed by, *see Ædes Walpolianæ*
character preferred by, to fortune, ix. 125
cheated sometimes, by tradesmen, v. 497
closet of curiosities fitted up by, i. 213, 241, 322, 324
costume of: at Birthday ball, i. 176, 185, 208; at masquerade, i. 359, ii. 167, vii. 193; discussed by women at opera, ii. 180; winter clothes ordered, ix. 541
Damer, Mrs, loved by, like own child, ix. 184
dances, i. 185, iii. 18
death of: HW anticipates inventory at time of, ix. 165; HW reconciled to thought of, ix. 201; will be like extinction of one lamp in an illumination, viii. 250; will not matter to the world, ix. 213
decay of faculties observed by, which prevents him from exposing himself, ix. 332
diet of: hartshorn and pears for supper, vi. 110, 114; stewed fruit might be part of, vi. 114; tea and wine avoided, vii. 76
disclaims power of prophecy, ix. 252
discriminating in his likes, iii. 442
emolument never asked by, though friends are in government, ix. 312
family affairs the chief occupation of, viii. 317
family's fall from prominence will not distress, i. 248

family views of, cut off by sale of Houghton pictures, ix. 164
favourite child, ix. 558
female relatives' spirits must be kept up by, when husbands are at war, viii. 507
finances of: annuities sold for 10 times more than he can pay, viii. 310; as ample as he wishes, viii. 283; currency in Arlington St house, vii. 284; Customs place, x. 52–3; 'dabs' saved to put in stocks, v. 497; father's family leaves or gives him a total of £7,000, ix. 637; father's legacy paid to, in full but without full interest, ix. 637; father's legacy to, not paid, iv. 250, ix. 315–16; Orford, 2d E. of, paid part of father's legacy to, ix. 637; SH construction expenses saved out of his income, v. 420; Suckling to remit money from Customs House place, viii. 231
first speech by, in Parliament, i. 376–7, 404
fondnesses of: anecdotes, iv. 27; antiquarianism, v. 140; essences, ii. 214; facts, ix. 146; masquerades, vii. 193; reading, v. 156; tranquillity, vii. 273, 367, viii. 327, ix. 331; visions, viii. 103, 194–5, 327, ix. 133, 604
habits of: abstinence, vi. 257; amuses himself with his own memory, ix. 559; at Houghton, ii. 36; attends Parliament constantly, but never stays long, i. 344; avoids everything that could disturb him, ix. 332; bad man of business, ix. 166; cautious in making decisions regarding property, ix. 166; cold baths, i. 452; comes home at 10 P.M. because of lack of things to do, vi. 550; diffidence with friends never felt by him, ix. 201; dines alone, early, ix. 460; dipping head in pail of cold water, v. 168; does not go out until 8 P.M., ix. 461; drinks nothing but cold water, viii. 423; during siesta-time, always drove about deserted Florence, ix. 558; face and neck washed in cold water upon awaking, viii. 423; faro-playing, v. 368; forgives political enemies but never forgets private friends, x. 28; grown indolent, ix 332; hardly stirs out of house, ix. 209–10; has neither quarrels nor enemies, ix. 310; haunts auctions, v. 368; hunting, brewing, reaping, and drinking avoided by, ii. 8; in league with all the sober virtues, ix. 338; laughs at all serious characters, iii. 4; lies abed all morning, v. 368; loo played till 2 or 3 A.M., v. 368; masks, in Venice, to avoid dancing, i. 77; never drinks liqueurs, v. 222; new acquaintance not sought or encouraged by, ix. 338; newspaper reading, vii. 497; plays biribis but does not mask or dance at Reggio, i. 46; political disinterestedness, v. 79, ix. 210, 260, 276; presents no longer accepted by, ix. 193; prowls about bridge at Florence after supper, i. 473; public places avoided by,

[Walpole, Hon. Horatio (1717–97), *continued*]
except Gloucester House, ix. 242, 247;
reading by candlelight, v. 139, 147; reading in a chaise, v. 139; reads little, ix.
542; reads till 3 A.M., vi. 523; recluse
life, ix. 242; regimen, temperance, and
cold habitually employed to resist gout,
ix. 242; renounces dining abroad, ix. 22;
retires early, in spite of fashionable late-
ness of hours, ix. 247; rises before eleven,
i. 335; sups in company, v. 368; snuff
avoided, iv. 377; visitors drop in around
8 P.M., ix. 617
happiness of, accounted for, ix. 331–2
health of: able to stamp with both feet
on marble hearth, viii. 71, 80; appetite
perfect and slumber marvellous, ix. 558;
as broken as if he was 100, ix. 570; bark
benefits, viii. 521, 532; between life and
death, ix. 348; bled, ii. 200, 213, ix. 280;
bled for influenza, ix. 297; bootikins beneficial to, vii. 76, 231, 241, 246, 310, 450,
viii. 67, 70–1, 80, 268, 272, 281–2, 421,
463, 479, 494, ix. 149, 242; bootikins used
by, for rheumatism of shoulder, viii. 463;
breast inflammation feared, viii. 426, 433;
breast weak, ix. 552; carried by servants
to bed, vi. 316, vii. 241, ix. 347; chalkstones, ix. 242; chalkstones from finger,
ix. 617–18; 'codicil' of gout, ix. 284; cold,
i. 197, 218, ii. 94, 115, 147, 174, 365, 546,
v. 139, vi. 42, 285, 348, 506, vii. 450; cold
and fever, ii. 200, 213; cold, fever, and
oppression on breast, ix. 280; cold, followed by gout, ix. 343; cough, ii. 135,
vii. 450, ix. 555; declines, vii. 537; disorder of, merely nervous, vi. 484; extremely but not dangerously ill, ix. 350;
eye improves, viii. 501; eyes, ii. 135, 148,
365, 386, v. 139; eyes cured by rum,
elder-flower water, and cold douches, v.
167–8, 177; eyesight conserved for worthy
books, ix. 542; eyes 'worn out,' v. 156;
eye trouble, diagnosed by Cocchi, v. 147,
163; fatigued after taking the air, ix. 558;
feet not quite recovered, viii. 227; fever,
i. 402, vi. 285; fever remedied by gout,
ix. 283; fingers lame in right hand, ix.
370; forbidden to speak, viii. 426, 433;
good, ix. 185, 297, 312, 323, 332; gout,
v. 432, 440, vi. 38, 46, 110, 114, 116, 117,
257, 266, 309, 316, 322–3, 332, 340, 348,
359, 361, 450, 454, vii. 61, 67, 240–1, 243,
246, 251–2, 440, 443, 447, 450, 454, 458,
459–60, 462, 464, 465, 471, 474, 476, 494,
555, viii. 55, 66, 70–1, 80, 83, 174, 178,
184, 189, 268, 270, 272, 274, 278, 279–80,
421, 422, 425, 426, 428, 432, 433, 436, 521,
532, 533, 542, ix. 149, 171, 201, 235, 242,
248, 280, 283, 284, 290, 297, 343, 347–8,
350, 351, 354, 358, 370, 402, 551, 555, 558,
560, 561, 615, 617, 622–3; gout, shortest
fit in many years, ix. 242; gout, shortest

fit in ten years, ix. 235; gout as a result
of being bled for influenza, ix. 297; gout
attributed to nerves, vi. 116, 117; gout becomes annual instead of biennial, viii. 272;
gout if cured might be succeeded by worse
ailments, ix. 402; gout in bowels, ix. 555;
gout in head, for half an hour, never in
stomach, viii. 422; gout never suffered by,
in stomach, ix. 551; gout of, compared to
Parliamentary ailments, ix. 402; gout
tendency makes a winter in Paris impossible, viii. 117; gout thrown out by, in
several joints, viii. 521; gout would return,
if in House of Commons, vii. 66; gouty
pain in hand, ix. 184; HW exaggerates
badness of, to escape social functions, ix.
22, 332, 595, 611, 647; HW guards, to
prevent decrepitude, not to prolong life,
ix. 5; hand muffled up, ix. 552; hand
shakes, ix. 539; hands lame, ix. 552,
629; hardened against cold, viii. 288; has
to be fed, viii. 274; headache, i. 221, vi.
506, vii. 194, ix. 648; inflammation of the
eyes, ii. 117, v. 131, 139, 147, viii. 501,
513; inflammation of the lungs suspected,
ii. 149; influenza, ix. 297; insomnia, viii.
342; joints of right hand cannot be
moved, ix. 354; limbs broken to pieces
by gout, ix. 321; London suits, better than
SH, vi. 451, 456–7, ix. 277–8, 288; loses
use of several joints of fingers, ix. 201;
Mann fears that late hours in Parliament
may shatter, ii. 114, v. 28; Mann's, compared to, viii. 532; Mann urges that letters
be omitted when it is too painful to
write, ix. 1; Mann, Horace II, reports, as
perfect, ix. 425; nerves, i. 452, ix. 49;
nerves affected by damp, viii. 288; nerves
very sensitive, viii. 272; nervous in the
morning, ix. 539; nervousness, ix. 201;
Orford's illness affects, viii. 373; pain in
breast and stomach, vi. 110; pain in eyes,
v. 139; pain in stomach, vi. 461, 468;
pains in stomach and limbs, vi. 450, 454;
paralytic disorder attributed to HW by
gazetteer, vi. 459; perspires immoderately
and constantly, viii. 423; quinsy, i. 51, 52,
54–5, 66, v. 369; recovered, vi. 50; relapses caused by venturing out too soon,
ix. 617; rheumatic fever, ix. 428; rheumatism, vi. 450, vii. 460, ix. 166, 570;
rheumatism in arm, ix. 432; rheumatism
in shoulder, ix. 463, 497; rheumatism possibly caused by SH damps, vi. 456–7;
right hand still weak, ix. 5; robust, vi.
396; sea air benefits, viii. 227, 311, 318;
sleeps as soon as fever has gone, ix. 620;
SH's dampness provokes gout, vi. 451,
viii. 277–8, 288; sufficient for HW's needs,
ix. 332; totters when going down stairs,
viii. 81; voice lost, ii. 135, viii. 426, 428;
vomitings, vi. 454; weakness in the breast,
ix. 350; weakness on the breast, 30 years

ago, viii. 80; weak on his feet, viii. 327, 337, 342; well as ever, vi. 136
house of, *see under* Arlington Street; Berkeley Square; Strawberry Hill; Windsor
house of, never properly aired before his return, ii. 343
house sought by, i. 334
ignorance of, of mechanics and geometry, v. 352–3
indifference of, to peace-time treaties, iv. 395–6
in minority, and unlikely to hear news, vi. 256
learning of, disparaged by him, v. 368
letter of: addressed in another's hand, viii. 72; demanding his letters from Mann, Mann keeps, iv. 397; from Paris, not to be specifically answered by Mann, viii. 127; sent to Paris by private hand, viii. 137; takes seven weeks to reach Florence, ix. 313; to Cts of Orford, Mann keeps copy of, vii. 532
letters of: amount to over 800, since he started writing to Mann, ix. 520; arrive with great speed, v. 322; barren in summer, ix. 503; burnt when spread out on hearth to dry, vi. 512, 525; contain nothing of consequence, and what anybody is welcome to see, ix. 185; contain only what HW believes to be true, ix. 186; copies of, about E. of Orford's affairs, made by HW, vii. 523; dates of, for 1760, v. 450; deaths and marriages the sources of, vi. 251–2; 'delightful and instructive,' Mann calls, ix. 281; depend upon generals and admirals, ix. 327; dictated, viii. 423, 426, 428, ix. 350, 615, 616; discuss kingdoms and rulers because common acquaintances are lacking, v. 329, viii. 206; dwindling, except for a few business and antiquarian ones, ix. 584; Gloucester, Ds of, says, are mere excuses for lack of anything to say, ix. 527; grow shorter, ii. 560; HW and Mann no longer have little events in common, to fill, v. 295; HW asks Mann to return, v. 60, 316, 324, 554, vi. 422, 451, vii. 94, 265, ix. 184, 380, 487; HW begs Mann not to entrust, to sots like Dering, v. 374–5; HW cautious to write only truths in, viii. 412, ix. 186; HW forgets by what messenger Mann is returning, vi. 73; HW gags pen for those that cross sea, ix. 257; HW indifferent about who opens, vi. 257; HW means what he says in, viii. 493; HW prides himself on keeping up, despite difficulties, ii. 479–80; HW promises to return, to Mann, iv. 23; HW re-reads, vii. 94; HW sends, by private hand, vi. 294, 308, viii. 137, ix. 309; HW's motives in writing, v. 263; HW will record great events in, though Mann no longer knows the background, v. 551–2; HW would like to stop

writing, from weariness of describing human folly, v. 545–6; *hors d'œuvre,* HW calls, ix. 167; inconsequential details will not be noticed in, ix. 97–8; indifference not a good ingredient in, ix. 312; information, not general topics, to be the staple of, viii. 456; in Mann's behalf, not answered, vi. 363; intervals between, make Mann anxious about HW's health, viii. 87; journals, not history, vi. 441; 'kind of history,' vii. 265; Leopold may open, ix. 412n; less frequent from Paris than from London, vi. 409; limited to topics of interest to posterity, viii. 451; long continuance of, to Mann, vi. 274; long continuance of, would never have been predicted, ix. 556; long on the road, ix. 333; Mann always impatient for, viii. 374; Mann calls, witty, i. 270; Mann cherishes and rereads, iii. 508, iv. 15, 83, 456; Mann compares, to Mme de Sévigné's, iv. 83; Mann could not bear to exchange, for anyone else's, ix. 76; Mann depends on, for explanation of public events, viii. 408; Mann finds, necessary to his tranquillity, viii. 388, 390, 396; Mann hopes, will continue even if there is nothing to say, iv. 397; Mann may have read a paragraph of, to Dering, v. 383; Mann needs, for recovery, ix. 607; Mann praises, ii. 425; Mann reads, first, of those in packets, vi. 326, ix. 333; Mann returns by Brand, iv. 441, 456, 471, 485; Mann returns, by Cardini, vi. 477, 483, 490; Mann returns, by Dixon, vii. 296, 309; Mann returns, by Giles, viii. 246, 247–8, 250, 260, 266; Mann returns, by Knightley, vii. 491; Mann returns, by Horace Mann II, viii. 100, 165, 379, 413, 493, 522, 530, ix. 198, 411, 417, 498, 521, 540, 621, 668; Mann returns, by Muzell, v. 413; Mann returns, by Phelps, v. 113, 118, 124; Mann returns, by Schutz, iv. 15, 23, 54; Mann returns, by Strathmore, v. 565, vi. 88, 141, 145, 152; Mann's anxiety to get, and pleasure in reading them, viii. 106; Mann's gratitude for, ix. 657; Mann's greatest consolation and instruction, viii. 396; Mann's reasons for valuing, iv. 283; Mann too weak to answer, ix. 662; Mann unprovoked by delays in, but merely worried about HW's health, viii. 232; Mann wants, back, iii. 508, iv. 15, 218, 397; Mann weeps over, ix. 662; Mann will be punctual in returning, ix. 395; may be opened now that his niece is married to D. of Gloucester, vii. 537; may seem grave but are really foolish, vi. 373; merit of, is not novelty, but confirmation of what is in newspapers, ix. 185–6; middle period of, the most agreeable because of England's victories, viii. 356, 484; more unreserved from Paris than when written from England, viii. 123,

[Walpole, Hon. Horatio (1717–97), *continued*]
134; must be copied, when concerned with
E. of Orford's affairs, vii. 523; must contain absurdities, iv. 74; newspapers may
anticipate, but Mann probably opens letters first, viii. 370; newspapers will inform Mann more quickly than, viii. 385;
often written by proxy, ix. 584; ordinary
small events too trivial to be discussed
in, to Mann, vii. 432; posterity's probable attitude to, vi. 303; proportioned to
frequency of political events, ix. 47; rarer
and less informing, ix. 484; rather eras
than journals, ix. 108; ready to be sent
back to him by any sober traveller, vii.
277; reports given in, for no more than
they are worth, viii. 386; restricted to
facts, ix. 79, 146; shorter, since more
frequent, viii. 450; shorter than Mann's,
ii. 560; sixty written between end of 1773
and 18 Sept. 1776, viii. 248; skim the
current of facts, and mark them for
Mann's information, ix. 79; sole source of
Mann's news from England, vi. 122, 502;
sometimes coloured when sent by the
post, viii. 493; style of, changes with politics, vi. 441; to Mme du Deffand, faithful, ix. 90; to relations, concerning sister-
in-law's death, ix. 122–3; transcription of,
x. 36–44; trifling and superficial, HW considers, ix. 146; uncensored, now that they
pass through Conway's office, vi. 309; uniform in sum total, viii. 379; Vertot's works
resemble, vi. 158; write themselves and
are not composed, viii. 97, written in
bow-window of Round Tower, vii. 315;
written only out of decorum, viii. 226
letter-writing in French difficult for, iii. 53
liberty and honour of England the only
objects of, ix. 311–12
life of, uniform to its first and only
principles, viii. 493
long life of, would never have been predicted in his childhood or youth, ix. 556
Mann chills, by refusal to come to England, viii. 176, 182–4, 194
—— does not receive all writings of, vi.
273
—— may need his former gifts to, to furnish Linton, viii. 175–6
—— promises to accept payment for commissions of, ix. 465
——'s arrival in England impatiently
awaited by, viii. 173–4
—— says he adores, viii. 425, 433, 438
——'s commissions forgotten by, ix. 468
——'s friendship with, like that of Orestes
and Pylades, vi. 274, vii. 309, viii. 283,
ix. 5, 9, 312, 615
——'s house inhabited by, for 13 months,
i. 143n
——'s inviolable affection for, ix. 192
——'s only friend, in England, viii. 166

——'s relations with: v. 72, 79, 89, vi.
280; friendship of long standing, ix. 332;
HW hopes to be his gazetteer, not his
philosopher, ix. 332
—— tells, to put cotton in his ears when
putting his head in water, v. 177
—— the 'dearest friend' of, i. 249
—— thinks, is made for the world, ix. 34
—— understands hints of, about lack of
credit in England, vi. 370
memory of: long, vi. 484–5; retentive of
trifles, v. 471; still good though his pen
grows old, vii. 216
military details not understood by, ix. 153
mind of: little and apt to fluctuate, viii.
379; naturally more gay than in moral
phase induced by nephew, viii. 301
narrative by, about Nicoll affair, iv. 273,
278, 435
nature gave, a statesman's head but no
ambition, vi. 550
nephews and nieces of, number 56, ix. 571
nephews of: HW does not interfere with
their pleasing themselves, ix. 331; HW has
little joy in, ix. 331
never good at detailing, viii. 351
not allowed to see company, ix. 552
opera subscription shared by, i. 358
Parliamentary motion by, iv. 222, 227
Parliamentary vote by, on privately-raised
regiments, x. 19
philosophic only when at ease, viii. 327
philosophy of, iv. 256, v. 539, vi. 359–60,
viii. 209–10, 213, 301, 327, 373
political rôle of, that of prompter rather
than actor, vi. 522
political secrets unknown to, ix. 185
portrait of, *see under* Reynolds, Sir Joshua
pride the one vice of, vii. 528–9
print of, Mann, Horace II, calls, a perfect
likeness, ix. 10
private intelligence from foreign courts
unavailable to, viii. 278
received no favours from any minister
except his father, ix. 276
reflections of, *see* Actors; Affluent, the;
Age, old; Age, present; Ambition; Ancestors and descendants; Ancestry; Architecture; Artists, modern; Assassins; Attor-
neys; Balloons, Beauty; Bishops; *Bon Ton;*
British Empire, Chance; Childhood;
Churchmen; City; Clergyman; Collections;
Common sense; Conquerors; Correspondence; Cosmetics; Country; Country life;
Courts; Crime; Cross devout people; Cures;
Death; Debts; Dissipation; Divines; Di-
vorce; Doctrines; Dreams; Dress; Dullness;
Eighteenth Century; Eloquence; Enemies;
England: comic nature of; England: deg-
redation of; England: eighteenth-century;
England: folly of; England: madness of;
England: political changes in; Equity; Ex-
perience; Faction; Fame; Fashion; Fidelity;

Folly; Fools; Freedom; Friends; Futility; Futurity; Gallantry; Genealogy; Generals; George I: HW's reflections on having descendants in common with; Glory; Gossip; Government; Gratitude; Grief; Hebrew priesthood; History; Honour; Human nature; Hypocrisy; Illness; Imperialism; Indifference; Jesuits: suppression of; Kings; Lawyers; Liberty; Life; Love; Lovematches; Man; March; Martyrs; Matrimony; Matter; Medicine; Ministers; Mirror; Mischief; Mistress; Monarchs; Mystery; Natural children; Newspapers; Nineteenth century; Nonsense; Old people; Pain; Parents; Passions; Patience; Patriotism; Peace; Physicians; Pleasure; Poets; Politicians; Politics; Posterity; Prayer; Predictions; Preferment; Pride; Princes; Propagation; Prophecy; Prosperity; Prudence; Public, the; Reality; Reason; Relativism; Religion; Retirement; Revolutions; Riches; Riots; Royalty; Sacrilege; Science; Scientific discoveries; Scrofula; Self-criticism; Self-knowledge; Self-love; Sixty; Slavery; Soldiers; Stage; Stock-jobbers; Suicide; Taste; Time; Times; Titles; Tranquillity; Travellers; Truth; Tyranny; Uncles; Virtue; Visions; Vocabulary; Voting; War; Warfare; Wisdom; Woman; Women, old; Women's spitefulness; World; Young people; Youth and old age
relative laughs violently at remarks of, when ill, vi. 455
religious opinions of, i. 85
retirement of, from the world, vi. 111
rôle of, as observer, iv. 503
seldom a lucky prophet, vi. 131
sentiments of, well known, ii. 186
Shorter estate shared by, iv. 403
smells enjoyed by, ii. 214, 230
society of, very narrow, ix. 99
speeches by, i. 376, ii. 406, iv. 222, 227, x. 25–8
spirits of: less nimble than formerly, but never low, ix. 312; scarce serve 'to rock the cradle of reposing age,' viii. 120
spirits still retained by, viii. 176
temper of, his weakness, vii. 522, 525
verses by: on earthquake, iv. 140; on Lady Bingley, iv. 141; on Lady Caroline Petersham, iv. 140–1; on Sandys's peerage, ii. 357–8, 372; on Wolterton, ii. 47n; satire on clergy, iv. 134
voice of: nearly gone, i. 252, ii. 135; seldom used, ii. 149
voting by, in Parliament, iii. 154, iv. 126, x. 19
walking avoided by, vi. 333, viii. 342
wishes of, mostly disinterested, ix. 399
works of: Mann delighted to contribute towards, iii. 508; see also under individual titles

Walpole, Horatio (1723–1809), 2d Bn Walpole of Wolterton, 1757; cr. (1806) E. of Orford, n.c.; M.P.; 'Pigwiggin'; HW's cousin:
Astley's painting of, in laced coat and waistcoat, iv. 342
avarice of, iv. 42, 81
family estate not likely to be dissipated by, iii. 505
father-in-law may get peerage for, iii. 469, iv. 66–7
father jokingly boasts about, in Parliament, iii. 168
father offended at Mann's failure to congratulate him on marriage of, iv. 22
father puts horses of, to graze at New Park, ii. 70
Florence to be visited by, iii. 42
good-natured, ix. 132
HW breaks all relations with family of, iv. 425
HW complains of bad breath of, iii. 72
HW formally asked by, to look after E. of Orford's affairs, vii. 496
(?) HW notifies, of Orford's recovery, viii. 368
HW told by, about P. of Orange's court, iii. 418
health of, fever and pain in bowels, iii. 192
Heathcote resembles, iv. 80–1
Houghton visited by, ii. 70
King's Lynn election left for, iii. 413–14, 418
King's Lynn seat vacated by peerage of, v. 57
Mann calls, 'Pig Wigging,' iii. 42
—— not to lodge, iii. 42, 59, 72
——'s conversazioni attended by, iii. 83–4
——'s correspondence with, iii. 42
——'s porter repels, iii. 59
—— to take notice of nuptials of, iii. 478
—— would be obliged to air his house if it had been occupied by, iii. 72
marriage of, approaching, iii. 469
Orford's angry letter to, about footman committed to prison, ix. 355
'procreated in . . . bed of money and avarice,' iv. 81
returns to England, iii. 418
Rome to be visited by, with Turnbull, iii. 232
Rome visited by, iii. 239
son of, ix. 418n
son of marries Sophia Churchill, ix. 172–3
son's match reluctantly approved by, ix. 132
Suares, Mme, liked by, iii. 84
travel improves, iii. 239
Turnbull tutor to, iii. 184–5, 192
uncle gives horse to, ii. 70
wife of, miscarries, iv. 42

Walpole, Hon. Horatio (1752–1822), 2d E.
of Orford, n.c., 1809; M.P.:
HW's opinion of, ix. 132
HW tries to marry a Waldegrave daughter
to, ix. 132–3
heir-apparent to both branches of family,
ix. 132
marriage of: ix. 172–3; a love-match, ix.
132
Orford, E. of, invited by, to be his son's
godfather, ix. 418
—— invites, to Houghton in 'frantic' letter, ix. 418
son born to, ix. 418
Walpole, Horatio (1783–1858), styled Bn
Walpole 1809–22; 3d E. of Orford, n.c.,
1822:
birth of, ix. 418
HW hopes, will be the heir of the family,
ix. 418
Orford, E. of, to be godfather to, ix. 418
Walpole, Mrs Horatio. See Churchill, Sophia
(d. 1797); Lombard, Mary Magdelaine (d.
1783)
Walpole, Laura (ca 1734–1813), m. (1758)
Hon. Frederick Keppel, Bp of Exeter;
HW's niece:
daughter of, ix. 410n, 508
daughter pardoned by, for elopement, ix.
508
father gives Windsor estate, house, and
coach to, viii. 348–9, 352
father leaves bulk of fortune to, ix. 466
father of, i. 209
(?) HW visited by, in illness, vi. 455
husband of, vi. 94n
husband of, dies, viii. 348
marriage of, v. 239, vii. 484n
marries a Stuart descendant, v. 285
Walpole, Lady Maria (Mary) (ca 1725–1801),
m. (1746) Col. Charles Churchill; HW's
half-sister:
Amor's name intrigues, ii. 505
Champion, The, mentions, as Sir Robert
Walpole's natural daughter, ii. 33
comet played by, with HW and Miss
Leneve, ii. 33
Court presentation of, ii. 330
daughter of, ix. 418n
daughters of, v. 279, viii. 320, ix. 132
effigy of, carried by mob, i. 390–1
father gives George II's diamond to, ix.
464
father tended by, in illness, ii. 449
favourite child, x. 28
fifth son born to, just after attendance
at opera and ball, v. 278–9
Fitzwilliam may marry, i. 177
France visited by, iv. 324–5, 339–40, vi. 262
French manners shock, iv. 339–40
HW accuses, of loving Monticelli, i. 487
HW discussed in presence of, ii. 180–1,
196

HW jokingly offers, to Chute, i. 257
harpsichord of, at Houghton, ii. 317
Hartington may marry, i. 176–7
Houghton visited by, i. 36
Legge wanted to marry, iii. 458
Leneve, Isabella, cares for, after mother's
death, v. 353n, ix. 609n
Mann seeks Pergolesi's Olimpiade for, iii.
95
—— sends flowers to, i. 254
Mann, Mary, visits, i. 359
marriage of, ii. 455, iii. 104, 132, 221,
239, v. 353n, vi. 27
musical ability of, ii. 316–17
Nancy to become home of, vi. 244
Norsa, Miss, might contaminate, ii. 249
opera attended by, ii. 180–1, 196
papal bull for legitimating if she married Pretender's son, i. 139
Patapan said to be courting, ii. 299
rank of earl's daughter given to, i. 320,
330, 348
Richmond visited by, i. 330, 359
son born to, iii. 371, 465, v. 278–9
Waldegrave might have married, v. 285
Willes a guardian to, x. 28
Walpole, Maria (1736–1807), HW's niece, m.
1 (1759) James Waldegrave, 2d E. Waldegrave; m. 2 (1766) William Henry, D. of
Gloucester:
accounts of, from Rome, are favourable,
viii. 179
affronts resented by, viii. 125
Albano the summer home of, at Albani's
villa, viii. 214, 247–8
Aldobrandini villa to be occupied by, viii.
186, 190
Ansbach visited by, ix. 413n
appearance of: beauty dimmed by grief,
vi. 136; better, viii. 335; fallen away and
shrunken, viii. 332; HW praises, v. 239–
40, 285; HW thought Mann would be
struck by, viii. 299; marred by anxiety,
viii. 326; more sublime than her daughter's, viii. 498; still attracts attention, ix.
68
bereavement of, may be easily consoled,
vi. 132
Boltons to give ball for, ix. 22
Bordeaux voyage may be undertaken by,
viii. 360
Boufflers, Comtesse de, wants to see, vi.
136
brother-in-law receives husband's seal
from, as sign that she is not pregnant, vi.
164
Carpenter, Lady Almeria, lady of Bedchamber to, ix. 638n
child expected by, in March 1776, viii. 171
Cholmondeley a cousin of, viii. 319n
Christine meets, at public places only,
viii. 190

Coke, Lady Mary, envies success of, vii. 530, 538, viii. 179n

courier sent by, to England, for Jebb and Adair, viii. 314, 317

court intrigues avoided by, ix. 140

court of, numerous, ix. 22

Cumberland's marriage must mortify, vii. 345

daughter born to, vii. 483

daughter gets consent of to break off match, ix. 75

daughter of, married, ix. 274

daughter resembles, ix. 410

daughter's engagement announced to, by courier, ix. 632

daughters of: viii. 315n, 498, ix. 68, 410n, 632; inherit her beauty but not her good fortune, ix. 75; rejected by Bns Walpole for her son, ix. 132

daughter told that praying and weeping are sole occupations of, viii. 323

death of, might result from husband's, viii. 144

dignity has not expelled the good nature of, viii. 299

English at Rome attentive to, viii. 190

English people in France shun, viii. 125

English visitors received by, at Rome, with great affability, viii. 247

Exeter, Bp of, tells, about husband's, will, vi. 128

father cannot be persuaded by, to call on her husband, vii. 461

father of, i. 209

father praised by, viii. 297

father's bounty to, viii. 349

father's impetuosity inherited by, viii. 125

father's letters from: about husband's illness, x. 50; announcing her marriage to D. of Gloucester, vii. 415

Florence avoided by, on way to Naples, resulting in 4 accidents, ix. 675

Florence not visited by, on way to Rome, viii. 174

Florence to be visited by: on way back to Rome, viii. 298, 312; on way from Rome, viii. 290

Florence visited by, viii. 296–7

France pays great attentions to, viii. 125

Geneva visited by, on way to Italy, ix. 314

Genoa visited by, ix. 628, 637, 638

Gloucester, D. of, escorts, to Soho ball, dressed as Elizabeth Woodville, vii. 193

good behaviour of, should excuse her marriage, vii. 437–8

HW advises, to submit entirely to George III, vii. 434

HW and Bp Keppel talk politics before, vi. 164–5

HW and Lady Hesketh meet at house of, vii. 467

HW asks, for permission to call on her husband, vii. 433

HW begs Mann not to entertain, at Florence, ix. 624

HW calls on, at the Pavilions, vii. 433–4

HW has had but one letter from, since start of her journey, viii. 147–8

HW occasionally goes to town to see, viii. 335

HW praised by, to Mann, viii. 297

HW recommends, to Mann, viii. 125, 131

HW sees, at Gloucester House, ix. 68

HW should conciliate D. of Gloucester for the sake of, vii. 417

HW's letter from: about declaration of her marriage, vii. 433; about husband's illness, viii. 319; about Lady Lucy Mann, viii. 191; about Pius VI's courtesies, viii. 174

HW's letter to: acknowledged in letter to Mann, viii. 250; delivered by D. of Östergotland's officer, viii. 247; two, to Venice, viii. 134

HW's relationship to, makes inquiries about Octavius's death improper, ix. 413n

HW suggests Siena as winter residence for, viii. 125

HW told by: about Cowper, ix. 641; in letter, that his letters are mere excuses for lack of anything to say, ix. 527

HW uneasy about pregnancy of, during husband's illness, viii. 144, 148

HW urges, to take husband to Italy at once, viii. 82

HW writes to, to prevent visit to Rome, viii. 125

handsomest woman in England, now that Cts of Coventry is dead, vi. 128

health of: fever and sore throat, v. 416; Mann will keep HW informed about, viii. 172; perfect, viii. 201; perfect constitution, viii. 335; perfectly well, viii. 190; permits her to go out, at Rome, viii. 184; slight indisposition, viii. 144, 164; very well, viii. 170; well, viii. 181

Heywood fails to tell Mann of situation of, viii. 317

—— might have been civil to uncle of, vii. 429

Heywood, Mrs, Bedchamber woman to, viii. 323n

—— not seen by, for 3 weeks, viii. 323

house taken by, at Twickenham, vi. 136

husband (first) of: v. 98n; dies, vi. 126–8, 131–2

husband (second) of: essential to her welfare and happiness, viii. 329; may take her to southern France, viii. 76; physicians of, encourage her slightly, about his health, viii. 321; plight of, may arouse sympathy for her, viii. 321; tells her to travel home with his body, viii. 326

Iron's Hill Lodge in New Forest visited by, viii. 360

[Walpole, Maria, *continued*]

Italian capitals will probably be avoided by, for fear of embarrassing monarchs, viii. 130–1

jointure of, vi. 127

Kilgore, Mrs, attends, in child bed, viii. 201

Kingston, Ds of, may avoid Rome during sojourn there of, viii. 220

Lago di Garda to be visited by, for summer, viii. 291

Leopold sees, viii. 297

Louis XVI invites, to Paris, viii. 125

Mann afraid to inquire about, at Rome, viii. 181

—— asks HW to remember him to, viii. 352, 376, 389

—— congratulates, on George III's reconciliation, ix. 65

—— does not owe visit from, to HW, viii. 299

—— hopes to hear of establishment for, ix. 77

—— impressed by beauty of, but still more by her affability and condescension, viii. 306

—— prevented by gout from paying attentions to, at Florence, viii. 290

—— receives gracious answer to his note to, viii. 247, 250

——'s call from, in Florence, viii. 291, 297

——'s correspondence with, viii. 201, 247, 250, ix. 202–3

——'s servants to attend, at theatre, with ice refreshments, viii. 291

—— sympathizes with HW over situation of, vii. 396

—— tells nephew to pay respects to, at Rome, viii. 131

—— told by, that HW would see urns presented to her by Mann at Florence with husband's permission, viii. 453

—— will not give offence elsewhere by attentions to, viii. 290

—— will probably mention passage of, through Florence, viii. 163

Mann, Horace II, awaits, at Florence, ix. 677

—— cordially received by, at Rome, ix. 674

—— probably not known by, to be at Genoa, ix. 638

—— receives regrets from, for rebuff at Genoa, ix. 674

—— to have audience with, viii. 163–4

Maria Louisa receives, though she had determined not to, viii. 298

marriage (first) of, vii. 284–5, 287

marriage (second) of: announced to HW, vii. 433; announced to her father, vii. 415; declared to Bp of Exeter, vii. 484; displeasing to HW, viii. 125; HW believes, vii. 302; known to Leopold, vii. 308; may

result in HW's letters being opened, vii. 537; not foreseen by Sir Robert Walpole, ix. 133; unhappy, ix. 674

Milan visited by, ix. 628, 632, 641

name of, as illegitimate child, vii. 435

Naples visited by, ix. 675

North Briton attacks D. of Gloucester for marrying, vii. 165

'now Lady Waldegrave in all the forms,' v. 294

Orford, Cts of, graciously received by, viii. 164, 170, 222

Padua visited by, viii. 144

physicians give no hope to, for husband's recovery, viii. 74, 76

physicians slightly encourage, about husband's health, viii. 321

Pius VI and Roman nobility attentive to, viii. 190

Pius VI appoints Ps Falconieri to wait upon, viii. 164

—— courteous to, viii. 174

Poggio Imperiale visited by, to see Tuscan grand ducal family, viii. 297

pregnant, v. 313, 337, vi. 128, vii. 442, 452, viii. 130, 171, 214

Ranelagh visited by, ix. 68

receives compliments on daughter's wedding, ix. 274

Roman journey probably already started by, viii. 144

Roman ladies offend, viii. 247

Roman ladies offended by postponement of reception by, viii. 164

Rome may be visited by, viii. 82, 290, ix. 618, 623

Rome visited by, viii. 163–4, 170–1, 174, 181, 184, 186, 190, 201, 214, 222, 247, 252, ix. 674

sister visits, v. 439

son born to, viii. 171, 178

Strasbourg visited by, viii. 134

SH visited by, after husband's death, vi. 127–8

transcripts of HW's letters about, altered by daughter, x. 38

Trent visited by, viii. 317, 319, 337

Tuscany the first court to receive, thanks to Mann, viii. 297–8

Venetian ambassador's house at Lago di Garda may be taken by, for summer, viii. 290, 291, 305

Venice visited by, viii. 125, 134, 291, 305

Waldegrave to wed, v. 285

warm and hurt by indignities, viii. 125

weeps but does not oppose husband's martial schemes, viii. 401

weeps when HW and Bp of Exeter discuss politics, vi. 165

Weymouth visited by, ix. 203

Walpole, Mary (1673–1701), m. (1689) Sir Charles Turner, cr. (1727) Bt:

grandson of, ii. 182

Walpole, Mary (ca 1705–32), HW's sister; m. (1723) George Cholmondeley, styled Vct Malpas 1725–33; 3d E. of Cholmondeley, 1733:
husband of, vii. 217n
posterity of, should follow HW and Sir Edward in succession to father's estate, ix. **132**
son of, iii. 177n, iv. 554n, vi. 210n, vii. 316n, viii. 524n, ix. 418
Walpole, Hon. Mary (1726–64 *or* 66), m. (1764) Maurice Suckling; HW's cousin:
(?) bad breath of, iii. 72
Mann sends pastels to, iii. 369
Walpole, Lady Rachel. *See* Cavendish, Lady Rachel (1725–1805)
Walpole, Hon. Richard (1728–98), HW's cousin; M.P.:
plain suit worn by in picture at Wolterton, iv. 342
Walpole, Robert (1650–1700), M.P.; HW's grandfather:
account-book of, i. **505–6**
death of, vi. 26
Nottingham ale purchased by, i. 506
son receives money from, i. 506
son succeeds, in estate of over £2000 yearly, vi. 25–6
wig purchased by, from Wilkins, i. 506
Walpole, Sir Robert (1676–1745), K.B., 1725; K.G., 1726; cr. (1742) E. of Orford; HW's father:
abuse of, stops, ii. 119
accident of, on Houghton stairs, ii. 277, 290
accusers of, to be indemnified, i. 425
Admiralty post held by, under P. George of Denmark, vi. 26
alleged corruption of, refuted by HW's small inheritance from him, ix. 637
Amelia, Ps, fishes with, at New Park, ii. 449
America's readiness to revolt foreseen by, as chance for foreign interference, viii. 523
Anne's speeches written by, vi. 26
anniversary of birth of, ix. 604
Anstruther to forward painting to, ii. 144
Arenberg expected by Mann to see, ii. 115, 137
Argyll prevents, from employing Hume-Campbell and Marchmont, iv. 5
——'s rudeness expected by, at House of Lords, i. 338
Arlington St house rented by, for HW, ii. 137
Ashton eulogizes, iii. 29, 40
—— no longer loyal to HW after death of, iv. 164
Augusta mistakes Sir Robert Rich for, ii. 219
aunt of, v. 353n
Austrian ambassador at London said to oppose, i. 325
'author of all the happiness' of Mann, i. 349
autobiography never written by, iv. 88
Baltimore tells, that Frederick, P. of Wales, does not refuse to see him, ii. 8
Barnard leads opposition to, vi. 252n
Bath, Order of, revived by, vi. 26, 381
Bath knighthood conferred on, vi. 26, 381n
Bathurst prejudiced against, ix. 7–8
Bedford, Berkshire, and Halifax cut, at House of Lords, i. 338
Benedict XIV's ignorance about, v. 125–7, 138
biographical sketch of, by HW, vi. 25–7
Biron compared to, by HW, ii. 467, 481
birthday of, ii. 298
bishops call on, ii. 537–8
Blakiston pardoned by, for smuggling, iv. 261n
Bland calls on, ii. 244
'Blunderer,' nickname for, i. 234
body of, to be opened after death, x. 12
Bolingbroke, Pulteney, and Old Pretender excluded by, ix. 605
Bolingbroke's falsely boasted abilities annihilated by, ix. 7
——'s ingratitude to, iv. 452
——'s *Letters* treat, leniently, iv. 60–1
——'s opposition may make, a 'martyr,' iv. 455
—— would have replaced, iv. 452, 455
Bootle warned by, i. 234
Bragge tells, that Correggio painting at Parma is not original, ii. 355
brags like any bridegroom, ii. 272
brother afraid to let, go to Ranelagh, ii. 8
brother and Selwyns advise, to decline pension, ii. 465
brother imitates, iii. 469
brother of, i. 344n, 469n, iii. 414n, 469n
brother's descendant also descended from, ix. 418
brother tries to divert estate of, from grandchildren, v. 52, vii. 367
Bubb Dodington attacked by, i. 297
Buckingham, Ds of, leaves legacy to, ii. 213
burnt in effigy, ix. 605
Burrell attached to, viii. 499
business no longer performed by, i. 339
busts in collection of, at Houghton, ii. 326
Bute gets more abuse than, vi. 42
Cambridge tutor of, ii. 64
Campbell in Admiralty of, iii. 256
Canterbury, Abp of, quotes Thuanus to, i. 301
Capello talks Latin with, at Lady Brown's, ii. 459
Carlton House thought to be closed to visits of, ii. 8
Caroline recommends Butler's book to, iv. 167

[Walpole, Sir Robert, *continued*]

Carteret and Newcastle keep, in ignorance of foreign affairs, ii. 30

Carteret said to threaten removal of appointees of, ii. 81

——'s civilities to HW probably intended for, ii. 527–8

—— sends to, a letter from daughter-in-law, i. 441

——'s remark about levees of, ii. 349

—— thanks: for aid in carrying Hanover troops measure, ii. 382; for coachman in Newcastle's presence, i. 506

Cerretesi entertained by, at Chelsea, i. 503, ii. 14

chairman of Secret Committee on Q. Anne's last administration, vi. 26

Champion, The, may be prosecuted by, for mentioning his natural daughter, ii. 33

chancellor of Exchequer, vi. 26

chariot cannot be used by, ii. 538

Chelsea depository for pictures of, ii. 249

Chelsea to be visited by, i. 386

Chesterfield quoted and discussed by, i. 232

—— talks with, at George II's levee, ii. 102

Chetwynd accused of wanting to hang, ii. 191

Cholmondeley's correspondence with, ii. 260

Churchill told by, about Hedon election, i. 221

—— would not have dared to approach, about marriage, iii. 132

Chute, Anthony, entertained by, i. 301

Chute, Francis, and Robinson voted out of Hedon after fall of, i. 234n

Chute, Francis, praised by, i. 234

Chute, John, attached to, i. 408

Clutterbuck employed but distrusted by, i. 391n

——'s succession to Onslow compared by, to Roxburghe's of Montrose, i. 391n

coachman of, i. 503, ii. 20–2

Cobham faction called 'nepotism' by, i. 451

Cocchi warned by Rucellai not to defend, ii. 133

Coke cites foreigners' respect for, i. 298

Coke visits, at Houghton, ii. 254

collection of, Mann eager to add to, i. 228

Collins's *Peerage* the best source of facts about, vi. 24

colonies conciliated by, viii. 513–14

'committeeing' of, not possible, i. 366

consternation over Patapan's accident amuses, ii. 71

Cork's political connections opposed to, iv. 456–7

—— visits, at Houghton, iv. 456

corpulency of, ii. 219

Correggio painting considered by, ii. 351, 355, 373

Court attendance by, i. 330, 502, ii. 14, 102

Craon's offer for daughter-in-law's expulsion rejected by, i. 326, 359

creditors of, defrauded by Cruwys, ix. 440

customs officials respect HW because of, i. 142

Customs place granted to, by George I, x. 52–3

Danvers's witticism on, i. 232

Dashwood cites foreigners' contempt for, i. 298

daughter (illegitimate) of, jilted by Keene, iv. 346

daughter-in-law accuses, of having 'bought' her, iv. 439

daughter-in-law disparages, i. 406, 423, 448

daughter-in-law expects: to be beheaded, i. 444; to flee to Florence, i. 450n

daughter-in-law expects Carteret to be eager to vex, i. 460–1

daughter-in-law has jewels rented by, for George II's coronation, v. 536

daughter-in-law not allowed by, to take earrings out of the country, ix. 148

daughter-in-law's conduct indifferent to, i. 326

daughter-in-law's expectations on death of, iii. 37, 53

daughter-in-law's infidelities known to, i. 425

daughter-in-law's letter to Carteret shown to, i. 441

daughter of, iii. 104n, 177n, iv. 554n, v. 285n, vi. 27, 210n, 262n, vii. 217n, 316n, viii. 524n, ix. 418n, 464n

daughter tends, in illness, ii. 449

death of: iii. 24, vi. 27, ix. 606, x. 12; daughter-in-law gets no mourning for, iii. 42; one of HW's heaviest blows, vi. 226; painless, iii. 32; Riccardi's letter forgotten because of, iii. 73; said to enrich daughter-in-law, iii. 37, 53; should not encourage daughter-in-law to go to England, iii. 38, 46, 48, 49; showed that there was little equity in a point of honour, viii. 155; son's title before, ix. 226; to be communicated to Mann by Galfridus Mann, iii. 24, 31, 34

debts and legacies of, iii. 32

debts of, vii. 510

Del Nero's statues might be bought by, ii. 308, 326

descendants of: defrauded by his brother, v. 52, vii. 367; will not all be deprived of his fortune, ix. 132, 418

Devonshire, D. of, likes, i. 176

disgrace of: i. 234n; cannot injure wife, i. 245–6; pleases daughter-in-law, i. 360, 367, 393–4

Domenichino painting desired by, to be sent by man of war, ii. 79, 89, 123, 144

Domenichino painting expected to please, ii. 57

Domenichino painting impatiently awaited by, ii. 63, 79, 89, 144, 181
Domenichino painting inquired about by, i. 442
Domenichino painting may come in Dutch ship at wish of, ii. 89, 123
Domenichino painting pleases, ii. 303, 308, 351
Domenichino painting surely will go to, i. 241
Domenichino painting will be respected for being in the collection of, ii. 285
Dorset discusses Hedon election with, i. 221
dukedom suggested for, ii. 142, 188
Edgcumbe intimate friend of, i. 399n, v. 259n, ix. 518
—— visits: at Houghton, ii. 25; with son, at Houghton, ii. 245
Egmont's election triumph during ministry of, iv. 31
election of committee chairman lost by party of, i. 242-3
Electress's affair to be told to, i. 241
Ellis shown by, over Houghton, ii. 25
employment of able people by, opposed because of their low rank, iii. 448
enemies of: convinced by his small estate that he did not plunder England, iii. 32; exposed after his death, iii. 459-60; HW 'in love' with, because they seemed patriotic, v. 541
England's greatest man, iv. 254
English naval actions in Mediterranean not blamed on, ii. 205
engraving of, in Ædes Walpolianæ, iii. 511
estate inherited by, vi. 26
estates of, should go to Cholmondeleys after sons' deaths, ix. 132
Europe would have been saved by, from wars, ii. 513
'every man has his price' said to be the maxim of, i. 343n, ix. 606
exchequer chest of, vii. 285
Excise causes clamour in time of, vi. 129
excused from returning calls when prime minister, viii. 228
exercise abandoned by, ii. 449
fall of, coincides with England's, v. 138
family ruined by, out of excessive vanity, vii. 497
father gives money to, i. 506
father's account-book found by, i. 505
first commoner to become K.G. since Charles II's restoration, vi. 27
fishes at New Park, ii. 449
Fitzwilliam attached to, i. 320n
Fleury friendly with, vi. 135
Florentine and Leghorn gossip about, i. 146
Florentine disrespect for, condemned by Mann to Richecourt, ii. 10–11
Florentines fear return of, to power, ii. 557

Florentines regard, as Maria Theresa's enemy, i. 406
Fox, Capt., knows, ii. 152, 190
Fox, C.J., compared with, ix. 275-6, 437
France may be refuge of, i. 360
Francis I considers, as a friend, ii. 11
Frederick, P. of Wales, graciously receives, on account of speech, ii. 409, 425
—— notified by, of resignation plans, i. 319
—— said by ballad to have procured fall of, ii. 80
—— to demand impeachment of, i. 329
Furnese an enemy of, v. 172n
—— puts high price on Sacchi painting wanted by, v. 173
gallery for pictures erected by, at Houghton from HW's directions, ii. 63
Gardiner not encouraged by, ii. 509, 563
Garter conferred on, vi. 27, vii. 391
Garter ribbon of, ii. 219
George I converses with, in Latin, i. 503n
—— gives Bolingbroke's memorial to, iv. 455
—'s relations with, in last year of reign, iv. 455
George II consults, on Cabinet Council's move against Carteret, ii. 536
—— cordial to, at levee, i. 502, ii. 14, 102
—— embraces, at close of ministry, i. 319, 348
—— gives cracked diamond to, iv. 112
—— gives diamond and crystal bottle to, but not money for Houghton, ix. 463-4
—— loves and laments, i. 339
—— may not permit, to retire, i. 287
—— persuaded by: to insist on Pulteney's going to House of Lords, i. 485n; to write financial offers to Frederick, P. of Wales, i. 296n
—— said to have summoned, from Houghton, ii. 553
—'s gracious reception of Cts of Orford ungrateful to memory of, iii. 72
—'s impotence after fall of, satirized in ballad, ii. 80-4
—'s pension to, at first declined and later requested, i. 329n, ii. 465
—'s reliance upon, satirized in ballad, i. 187-9
—'s rewards to, disprove Florentine attacks, ii. 11
—— still relies on, ii. 401
—— supported by, against George I, vi. 26
—— warned by, against father's carelessness about health, iv. 232
Gibson breaks with, over Quaker Bill, iii. 503n
—— said to be 'pope' of, i. 278
Gloucester's marriage not foreseen by, ix. 133
Godolphin favours, vi. 26

[Walpole, Sir Robert, *continued*]
Gordon, Sir William, opposes, over Chippenham election, i. 298, iii. 302
Grafton visits, at Houghton, ii. 245, 254
granddaughter of, to marry a Walpole, ix. 132
grandson baffles views of, ix. 133
grandson compounds debts of, viii. 440-1
grandson contrasted with, ix. 418
grandson said to have received fortune from, iv. 247
grandson sells pictures collected by, ix. 133
grandson signs agreement with creditors of, viii. 301
grandson undermines all the acts of, viii. 502
grandson would benefit more by Nicoll match than from, iv. 257
great chair of, at Houghton, ii. 68
greatgranddaughter of, to marry Wyndham's grandson, ix. 68
Guards would not have been sent by, to the polls, ix. 489
Gumley secures post through, ii. 25
HW an infant when ministry of, began, ix. 558
HW asks, about Mediterranean situation, i. 212
HW came into society at 5 years old, thanks to position of, viii. 228, ix. 558
HW cannot get used to new name of, i. 331
HW consults, about Mann's mourning problems, ii. 191
HW desired by, to return to England, i. 55
HW does not inherit wisdom of, viii. 67n
HW hurried by, to Parliament, ii. 394
HW jokes to, about old Horatio Walpole's gait in Houghton Gallery, ii. 305
HW laughs with, over raising of Prague siege, ii. 68
HW may accompany, to Houghton, i. 452
HW may not continue to live with, i. 478
HW may request, to intercede for Mann with Mann's father, i. 27
HW not to tell, of Mann's shipment till its arrival, ii. 202
HW not treated partially by, i. 270
HW reaches England at end of 'happy reign' of, viii. 356
HW received no favours from any minister except, ix. 276
HW recommends Jackson to, i. 186
HW refutes charges of corruption against, ix. 605-6, 637
HW rises early to meet, i. 335
HW's biographical sketch of, sent to Mann for Lami, vi. 25-7, 35
HW's cases from Florence directed to, ii. 177
HW's correspondence with, i. 146
HW's illness might alarm, i. 51-2

HW's legacy from, iv. 250, ix. 315, 637
HW speaks of Mann to, i. 373
HW spent last 3 summers of life of, at Houghton, vii. 121
HW's presence must have helped, ii. 105
HW's reverence for, increases with age, viii. 507
HW's sources of information as good as those of, ii. 48
HW suspected by brother of getting Middleton to write life of, iv. 215
HW takes, to Ranelagh for first time, ii. 8
HW to consult, about possible danger to Mann's position, ii. 31, 382
HW to describe opinion of, about Domenichino painting, ii. 292
HW to help hang pictures of, ii. 218
HW told by Winchilsea to tell story to, ii. 565
HW told he is older than, i. 294
HW wants: to buy Correggio painting, i. 166-7, 373; to buy Domenichino painting, i. 166-7
habits of, at Houghton, ii. 36
Haddock's tactics explained by, i. 219
Hanover troops debate not joined by, ii. 356
Hardwicke's *Walpoliana* about, sent to Mann, ix. 458, 463-4
Hare former tutor of, ii. 64
Hare-Naylor family invited by, to dinner, ii. 63-4
Hartington entertained by, i. 176
—— supports party of, i. 247
health of: ague and looseness, i. 164; apoplexy rumoured, i. 211; bled, ii. 200; bloody water, ii. 538; cold, ii. 159, 449; cold and fever, ii. 200, 213; fall on stairs, ii. 277, 290; fever, i. 164, iii. 16; fever, slow, ii. 159; flux of water, iii. 16; good as ever, i. 231, 263; 'indisposition,' ii. 140; insomnia, i. 171; Mann alarmed by, i. 194, 208; Mann urges HW to preserve, i. 284; medicines taken by, ii. 555, 566, iii. 13; recovered, i. 169, 211, 294; stone in bladder, ii. 538, 555, 558, 566, iii. 16, 21, 22, 29, vi. 27
healths drunk by, to Stair and Carteret, ii. 259-60
Hervey, Bns, courts, after shunning him during defeats, i. 276
Hervey, (?George), visits, at Houghton, ii. 25
Holland states-general compliments, i. 344, 370
Houghton endangered by sums spent by, at Houghton, iii. 32
Houghton's fate and Ds of Gloucester's marriage not foreseen by, ix. 133
Houghton should have been proportionate to fortune of, iii. 496
Houghton's illustrious founder, ix. 132

Houghton's remotest wing may be inhabited by, ii. 449

Houghton the monument of, ix. 195

Houghton to be occupied by, i. 452, 495, ii. 7–8, 442, 458

Houghton trip must be made by, in litter, ii. 538

Houghton visited by, i. 142, 375, 386, 390, 403, ii. 25, 31–3, 36, 88–9, 341, 458, 467, 481

house of, in Arlington Street: again thronged with applicants, ii. 381–2; HW describes, ii. 137; Mann asks about, ii. 114; opposite his former house there, i. 478; Walpole, Sir Robert, to move to, i. 440, 478

house of, in Downing St: i. 127, 478, 491, 494–5; accepted by him only as first lord of Treasury, i. 478; filled with refugees from fire, i. 496; HW's art objects sent to, x. 6; things moved from, to Houghton, i. 495

House of Commons managed by, against Dr Sacheverel, vi. 26

House of Lords attended by, i. 335, 338

House of Lords to be entered by, i. 319, 325, 333

Hulse attends, iii. 16, 22

Hume-Campbells court and then shun, iv. 5

hunts at Richmond on Saturdays, i. 247n

Hyndford's treachery to Maria Theresa satirized by, ii. 89

Ilay said to have betrayed, i. 347

——'s betrayal not believed by, i. 347n

—— shows Old Pretender's letter to Argyll to, i. 479

impeachment of: drawn up, i. 336; not openly hinted by Pulteney and Carteret, i. 329; Parliamentary speeches hint at, i. 354; talked about, i. 114, 366

Italian matters never interesting to, ii. 30

Italian singers enjoyed by, i. 274

Italian tour of, rumoured, i. 417, 426, ii. 145, 202, 211–13, 237, 254

Jacobites and Patriots join in opposing, vi. 93

Jacobites expect House of Commons to thwart, i. 203

Jamaica remittance might have been arranged by, i. 411

Jurin's medicine used by, ii. 552, 566, iii. 13

Keene, Benjamin, attacked in time of, iv. 198n

—— highly regarded by, v. 166

Keene, Edmund, gets preferment from, to marry his illegitimate daughter, iv. 346

Kendal, Ds of, hates, iv. 455

Kilmarnock pensioned by, iii. 284

King's Lynn corporation revere **memory** of, v. 57, 62

King's Lynn elects, M.P., vi. 26

Labour in Vain mentions, ii. 19

Lami wants panegyric of, for publication, vi. 13, 15

Lanfranco painting not wanted by, ii. 275, 296–7, 311

Laocoön of, at Houghton, ii. 326

last words of, x. 12

Latin the only foreign tongue spoken by, i. 503

Legge appointed by, iii. 457n

—— calls on, ii. 245

—— loses esteem of, by courting his daughter, iii. 458

Leghorn merchants not thought by, to be safe from Spaniards, i. 209

Leghorn rumoured to be visited by, on man of war, ii. 145

Leicester owes earldom to, ii. 441

Leneve, Isabella, lived with, to take care of daughter, v. 316, 353n, ix. 609n

lenient measures preferred by, vii. 86

levees of, i. 318, ii. 349

Leviathan compared to, by mad parson, i. 197

Lincoln visits, at Houghton, ii. 245, 248, 254

London clubs drink health of, ii. 142

London sojourn of, soon to end, ii. 211

London streets and squares confuse, when he returns calls, viii. 228

lord justice during kings' absences, vi. 26

Lovel tells, of Montemar's rumoured arrest, ii. 29

—— visits, at Houghton, ii. 254

Lyttelton moves for secret committee against, ii. 117

—— tells Bolingbroke not to publish reflections against, iv. 59

madwoman gives speech to, as Q. Elizabeth, when he comes down from St James for Parliament opening, viii. 361

Magnan said to have been employed by, ii. 548

Mann admires, ii. 478

Mann, Chute, and Whithed thanked by, for helping to secure Domenichino, i. 256–7

Mann congratulates, through HW, i. 348–9

—— discusses, with Richecourt, ii. 10–11

—— hopes, will retire, i. 287

—— hopes that art shipment will be approved by, ii. 200

—— identified with party of, in Florence, i. 393, ii. 363

—— pleased by opinion of, concerning Bns Walpole, ii. 4

—— procures urns and bronzes for, i. 24

—— regrets not having bought Parker's collection for, ii. 273

—— respects the prophecies of, iii. 148

——'s account of Corsica pleases, i. 163

—— said by Richecourt to be tool of, ii. 67

—— says, is only man who could run England despite opposition, v. 106

[Walpole, Sir Robert, *continued*]
—— sends *bronzo* to, ii. 177, 298, 303, 312
—— sends excuses to, for diverting courier, i. 113
——'s excuse for writing to HW is to convey news to, ii. 415
——'s fidelity to, iii. 99
——'s respect for, viii. 513
——'s safety assured by, ii. 394
—— sure that political crisis will not arouse, from retirement, ii. 557
—— thanked by: for *bronzo*, ii. 298; for getting Domenichino painting, i. 256–7
—— to be provided for by, in case Florence is captured, i. 196
—— to bequeath his Sabine to, ii. 93
—— wants Newcastle to be approached through, about salary arrears, ii. 517
—— wants to know opinion of, on new ministry, iii. 6
—— wonders how his conduct impresses, i. 119
Mann, Edward Louisa, esquire of the Bath for, viii. 146
—— suffered financial loss through, viii. 287
Mann, Horace II, disparages, vii. 340
Mann, Robert, calls on, ii. 244–5
Mann family owes all to, despite his unpaid debts, viii. 292
Maria Theresa owes present English aid to efforts begun by, ii. 126
——'s interests said to be endangered by hostility of, i. 325–6, 367, 404, 406, ii. 5, 126, 363, 382
Mathews directed by Winchilsea to take care of shipments for, ii. 330
——'s attachment to, ii. 153
medals, satirical, of, i. 189, 229, 426, ii. 45, v. 202
melancholy of, i. 171
melon seeds sent to, by Mann, i. 34, 38
ministry of: introduced HW at an early age to great figures, vi. 484; to end, i. 318
mobs carry effigies of, i. 390
mobs more violent in time of, iv. 48
mob would have been anticipated by, vii. 99
Money ordered by, to look up HW on way home, i. 108, 115
Monro, old Dr, highly regarded by, iii. 210
——'s appointment as travelling physician due to, iii. 210
Montagu, D. of, proposed by, as generalissimo, iv. 79
Montagu, Lady Mary Wortley, writes to, i. 98
Monticelli often dines with, i. 487
Morley said to receive money from, for Wallingford election, i. 400
Morris's *Essay* dedicated to, ii. 464
motto of, *see Fari quæ sentiat*
Museum Florentinum to be sent to, ii. 329
musicians despised by, i. 487

name of, declines, as Stanhopes grow popular, i. 270
Navy treasurer, vi. 26
negotiations in peacetime said to be overdone by, iv. 396
nephew of, iii. 320n
new attacks on, threatened, i. 95–6, 114
Newcastle and Carteret do not inform, of foreign affair, ii. 30
Newcastle discusses HW's attendance at Granville's assembly with, ii. 562
—— jealous of, ii. 535
—— said to have betrayed, ii. 82
—— sends Dettingen news to, ii. 258
——'s ministerial guests rescued by coachman of, i. 503
Newdigate, Sir Roger, and Tories met by, in Grosvenor Square, ii. 25
new ministers greeted by, at Court, i. 502
new ministers speak to, at George II's levee, ii. 102
New Ode, A, prefers, to new ministers, ii. 49–52
new Secret Committee proposal does not involve, ii. 118
newspapers exaggerate illness of, i. 165
newspapers mention illness of, ii. 140
Niccolini wants to sell Bns Walpole's jewels to, i. 217
Nugent's alleged bigamy ignored by, i. 271n
Old Coachman, The, mentions, ii. 22
old politicians hate Egmont because of, iv. 32
Old Pretender excluded by, ix. 605
——'s handwriting known to, i. 479
——'s offers to, seen and endorsed by George II, i. 479n
——'s party may be encouraged by Frederick, P. of Wales's defeat of, ii. 361
Onslow hails Parliamentary triumph over, ii. 540
opiates taken by, iii. 16, x. 12
opponents of, propose his retirement, i. 299
Opposition in time of, not so harmless, viii. 442
Opposition meeting against at Fountain, i. 329
Ormond to tell Old Pretender to influence Jacobites against, i. 232n
Oswald, George, to be authorized by, to pay for picture, i. 228
Oswald, James, deserts, i. 299
Oxford's overtures rejected by, vi. 26
Parliamentary career of, vi. 26–7
Parliamentary motion to remove, fails, i. 142n, 232n
Parliamentary shift said to be feared by, i. 203
Parliament ending pleases, i. 502
Parliament opening attended by, from St James's Palace, viii. 361

Parliament said to have been bribed by, ix. 605–6

party of: Coke, Fitzwilliam and Hartington support, i. 247; Dashwood and Quarendon oppose, i. 247; Onslow might have voted for, i. 251

Patapan interests, ii. 71

—— said to be 'familiar' of, ii. 299

Patriots cannot be conciliated by, i. 330–1

Paxton called secretary to, i. 417

paymaster of the forces, vi. 26

peace negotiations of, between England and Prussia, described by Mann to Riche-court, ii. 4–5

peerage granted to, i. 318, 325, vi. 27

Pelham 'friend and élève of,' i. 329n

—— not to replace, i. 319

—— secures pension for, i. 329n

——'s ingratitude to, attacked by Willes, iii. 471

—— visits, at Houghton, ii. 245, 248, 254

Pembroke would have been made K.G. by, iv. 109

Penny's letter read to, by HW, i. 257

perpetuation of family the great object of, ix. 156–7

pictures no longer collected by, i. 339–40, 462

pictures of: placed at Houghton in hopes they would stay there, viii. 441; that were not at Houghton, are sold, iv. 261, 268; three sales of, viii. 441; too numerous for Houghton, i. 340, ii. 249

pictures recommended to, by HW, i. 166–7

Pitt acquits, in speech, iii. 370

Pope never reviled, ix. 6

porter of, told to shoo away mob, ii. 96

prime ministry would never be accepted again by, ii. 142

prize-taking by ships would have been regulated by, iv. 54, v. 415

prophecy by: about foreign involvement in American revolt, viii. 523; about rebellions, iii. 118, 148, viii. 356, ix. 606; about ships' prizes, v. 415

proxy sent by, to House of Lords, ii. 159

Prussian peace negotiations kept secret by, until completion, ii. 5

public benefactions of, discarded like his pictures, viii. 503

Pulteney at odds with, over Hedon election, i. 220–1

—— attacked by, i. 297

—— discusses debates with, i. 299

—— excluded by, ix. 605

—— joked about by, ii. 25

—— might have executed, iv. 65

——'s motion for examination of foreign negotiations defeated by, i. 250

——'s speech answered by, i. 231

——'s triumph over, satirized, ii. 91

—— tries to undermine, by making Ver-non's fleet inactive, iii. 459

quieta non movere maxim of, iv. 409, vi. 111, vii. 289, 304, 359, ix. 434, 506, 529, 541, 603

Ranby attends, ii. 538, x. 12

Ranelagh visited by, ii. 8

Raphael painting not to be bought by, without more information, ii. 250, 254

reading and writing disliked by, iv. 88

religion of, 'fixed,' iv. 167

reminiscences said to have been written by, iv. 77, 88

resignation of, as prime minister: i. 332; approved by Mann, ii. 151; daughter-in-law expects congratulations on, i. 371; desired by his sons, i. 253, 319; followed by offers of dukedoms to others, v. 26

responsibility for Bavarian, Spanish and Swedish wars disclaimed by, i. 231–2

Richcourt's insulting remarks about, ii. 4–5

Richmond, D. of, defends, in House of Lords, i. 330

—— not a personal friend of, i. 319

—— tells, of resigning mastership of the horse, i. 319

Richmond (New Park) depository for pic-tures of, ii. 249

Richmond (New Park) to be visited by, i. 330, 333

Richmond (New Park) visited by, i. 164, 247n, 335, 358, ii. 136, 430, 449, 455

Rinuccini ascribes Richecourt's disgrace to, i. 108

Robinson, Luke, suffers for, iii. 371

Robinson, Sir Thomas's, ball not attended by, i. 185

Ross saved by, from unwelcome post in West Indies, i. 244

Rowley resembles, ii. 506

—— would respect letter from, asking for Gardiner's promotion, ii. 507

rumoured to be on man of war at Leg-horn, ii. 145

St James's not visited by, i. 403

Sandys angry with, for taking Orford title, i. 333

—— orders, to vacate Downing St house, i. 495

—— ridiculous as successor to, iv. 518

—— succeeds, in Exchequer post, ii. 118n

Sandys, Mrs, tells, to quit Downing St house, i. 478

Saturday sessions of Parliament intended to injure, i. 247

sayings attributed to: about every man having his price, i. 343n, ix. 606; about majority essential for ministry's mainten-ance, vii. 190; about ministers seeing too much of human badness, iv. 77, 88

Scottish and Cornish Parliamentary vote overthrows, i. 346n

Scottish partisans of, to defend him, i. 338

Scrope will not betray, i. 459

[Walpole, Sir Robert, *continued*]

Scully said to be preparing house for, in Florence, i. 426

secretary at war, vi. 26

Secret Committee friends expected by, to desert him, i. 429

Secret Committee may consist of friends of, i. 375

Secret Committee proposal arouses, i. 297

Secret Committee report does not mention, i. 425

Secret Committee to investigate: defeated, i. 362–4, 379, 388; fails to harm, i. 390, 420, 421, vi. 27; voted on, i. 383–6

self-seeking politicians revile, because he brought prosperity to England not to them, ix. 6–7

Selwyn, Mrs, listens to, i. 339

Shippen's price unknown to, i. 343n

sings ballad and laughs at Prague campaign in his great chair at Houghton, ii. 68

sister-in-law charges, for his grandson's riding her son's horses, ii. 70

sister of, iii. 320n, ix. 423n

snores before his curtains are drawn, i. 171

son of, iv. 233n, v. 121, 126, 127, vi. 27, ix. 462n

son scolds, for letting HW bring Middleton to Houghton, iv. 215

son's contemplated marriage to Caroline Howe not opposed by, i. 209

son's death ruins estate of, iv. 239

son's match with Margaret Rolle arranged by, iv. 439, ix. 156–7

sons sup with, after long Parliamentary session, i. 294

son stores pictures for, ii. 249

Spain recommended by, for friendly relations, v. 121

speech by: answering Pulteney, i. 231–2; in defence of his administration, i. 297; on address to George II, ii. 409

Stanhoe depository for pictures of, ii. 249

statues needed by, ii. 326

steward to, *see* Oswald, George

Sturgis opposed to, i. 406

succession to ministry of, iv. 518

successors should have imitated wise measures of, viii. 513

Suckling great-nephew of, ii. 152, 182

Sundon, Bns, discussed by, with HW, i. 276

—— discusses Bp Gibson with, at dinner, i. 278

—— proposes partnership with, i. 277

Swift's history belittles, v. 185

Theodore of Corsica falsely claims friendship of, ii. 187–8, 190, 210, 233

—— never had connections with, ii. 210, 225

——'s alleged relations with Carteret surprising to, ii. 210, 225

Thomas, Bishop, calls on, ii. 537–8

three last summers of life of, spent by HW at Houghton, vii. 121

Tories oppose further prosecution of, i. 336

Totnes mayor forwards letter to, i. 299

Tower of London rumoured to become prison of, i. 299

Tower of London the prison of, vi. 26

Townshend persecuted because related to, iii. 332

Townshend, Vcts, hates followers of, ii. 497

treasury and navy posts of, vi. 26–7

treasury board meets at house of, after his resignation of ministry, i. 391n

Turk, Martha, baffles plans of, ix. 133

Tuscan helplessness to be described to, i. 267

Tweeddale joins discontented Whigs during administration of, iii. 195n

Vernon's published correspondence vindicates, iii. 459–60, 472

——'s success should please, i. 7

virtues of, contrasted with HW's weaknesses, vii. 522, 523, 525

Waldegrave's appointment by, mentioned in impeachment, i. 336

Walker toad-eater to, iii. 511n

Walpole, Horatio (1723–1809), receives horse from, ii. 70

Whigs always supported by, vi. 26

Whitehead, Paul, comments on health of, i. 252

wife of, iii. 310n, vi. 27, viii. 71n

Willes, Edward, supported by, for Exeter bishopric, i. 279

Willes, Sir John, obligated to, iii. 471

—— principal friend of, x. 28

—— visits, at Houghton, ii. 25

Wilmington supplanted by, ii. 50n

Windham a Whig of the type of, viii. 524

Winnington's dismissal of Robert Mann violates promise to, ii. 497

——'s only superior, iii. 249

witticisms by: on Argyll's deserting Oxford's administration, x. 11; on being eunuch, i. 274; on Newcastle's dinner guests, i. 506; on Smissaert's remark, ii. 458; to Ranby, on deathbed, x. 12

would not return to the Treasury, ii. 142

Wyndham leads opposition against, ix. 68n

—— not sent by, to the Tower, vii. 289

Zanetti cheats, vi. 562

Walpole, Robert (1701–51), cr. (1723) Bn Walpole; 2d E. of Orford, 1745; HW's brother:

Amelia, Ps, receives call from, iv. 29

—— succeeds, as Ranger of New Park, Richmond, iv. 233, 322

arms of, inaccurately placed on proposed monument for wife, ix. 226

auditor of the Exchequer, i. 299n, iii. 285, 496n, iv. 233n, x. 52

Bath knighthood conferred on, iv. 233n, vi. 27, 381n

Bath order esteemed by, vi. 390

Chesterfield buys Houghton lantern from, iv. 163

creditors of, should get money returned by Mozzi, ix. 446

Cruwys employed by, ix. 440n

Customs place for lifetime of, x. 52–3

death of: iv. 238, 243; attributed to 'carbuncular state of blood,' iv. 413; would be fatal to HW, George Walpole, and Galfridus Mann, iv. 233; would ruin his family, iii. 496

debts of: estate unable to pay off, iii. 496; son adds to, vii. 510; son not legally bound to pay, viii. 440, ix. 155; son repudiates, ix. 155, 158; to be compounded by son, ix. 148

decree obtained by, ix. 186

diamond earrings (given to wife) later sold by, ix. 148

Exchequer house of: adjoins House of Commons, i. 299n; filled with father's pictures, ii. 249

father's retirement wished by, i. 253, 319

father sups with, after long Parliamentary session, i. 294

Frederick, P. of Wales, talks to, i. 386

—— to be attended by, at levee, i. 338, 369

gallery of, in Westminster Hall, iii. 285

Gardiner claims to be the son of, ii. 507, 522, 543

—— to receive letter from, ii. 522

—— writes to, through Mann, ii. 507

George I makes, Bn and K.G., vi. 27

George II notifies, about reversion of New Park rangership, iv. 125

government posts of, sinking, iii. 496

HW explains reference to son of, iv. 19

HW receives condolence calls on death of, iv. 246

HW receives part of father's legacy from, ix. 637

HW's enemy, iii. 496

HW's financial relations with, iii. 447–8

HW should send letter from, in Gardiner's behalf, ii. 509

health of: boil, iv. 233; improved, iii. 504; precarious, iii. 496, 505; recovered, iii. 510, iv. 6, 29; thrush, iv. 233, 242

Houghton closed by, for economy, iii. 40

Houghton visited by, ii. 88

invalids carried by, to Parliament, i. 299

jewels taken from wife by, ix. 162

lantern bought by, at Cholmondeley sale, iv. 163

lawyers given fees by, in preparation for wife's arrival, iii. 61

Luxborough chosen by, for Parliamentary member, iii. 419

Mann hopes that wife does not worry, iii. 132

—— hopes that wife will not be divorced by, iii. 80

——'s fidelity to, iii. 99

—— thanked by, through HW for news, iii. 61

Mann, Edward Louisa, suffered financial loss through, viii. 287

Mann, Galfridus, asked by, to ask Mann for proofs of wife's infidelity, iii. 200

Mann family, though inconvenienced by debts of, owes all to his father, viii. 292

marriage of: ix. 121; arranged by his father, ix. 156–7

marriage settlements of, ix. 440n

master of the Buckhounds, iii. 496, iv. 233n

mistress of, see Norsa, Hannah

physicians and bark rejected by, iv. 233

posts held by, iv. 233n

ranger of New Park, Richmond, i. 503n, iv. 125, 233n

Rowley would respect letter from, asking for Gardiner's promotion, ii. 507

Shukburghs recommended by, to Mann, iv. 160

son allowed by, to ride cousin's horses, ii. 70

son executor of estate of, ix. 446

Stanhoe house of, ii. 249

Sturgis friend of, i. 70n

visitors to, in illness, iii. 510

wife cherishes harsh letter from, iii. 50

wife claims jointure from time of death of, ix. 162

wife considers, best of his family, iii. 139

wife expects letter from, iii. 37

wife got few jewels from, ix. 148

wife may force, to return her estate to her, iii. 49–50

wife of, iv. 481n, v. 536n

wife restricts intercourse with, after son's birth, iii. 203

wife said to have received letter from, iii. 47, 49

wife's allowance from, iii. 88, 219, 224

wife's divorce would alienate property from, iii. 88

wife should be locked up by, iii. 192

wife's intercepted letters among papers of, iv. 247–8

wife's jewels mostly retained by, when she went abroad, ix. 472

wife's jointure said to be in arrears since death of, vii. 512

wife's motions indifferent to, iii. 61

wife's negotiations with, iii. 202–3, 224, 290, 348

wife's portrait by Zincke probably for, ix. 501

wife's schemes to be told to, by HW, i. 389–90

wife to ask for legal separation from, iii. 111

wife to make composition with, iii. 202

[Walpole, Robert (1701–51), *continued*]
wife wounds, by her misconduct, iii. 38–9
will drawn by, iv. 238
Walpole, Hon. Robert (1736–1810), English minister to Portugal; HW's cousin:
Amigoni's and Astley's paintings of, iv. 341, 342
beautiful wife brought home by, ix. 410–11, 417
Orford, Cts of, sees, in Paris, vii. **141**
wife's beauty makes, jealous, ix. 417
Walpole, Mrs Robert. *See* Shorter, Catherine
Walpole, Hon. Mrs Robert. *See* Grosett, Diana (d. 1784)
Walpole, Susan (1687–1763), m. Anthony Hamond; HW's aunt:
HW mentions, i. 140
Walpole, Hon. Thomas (1727–1803), banker; HW's cousin:
Amigoni's and Astley's paintings of, iv. 341, **342**
Cordon, Marchesa di, rescued by, ix. 55
HW asked by: to look after E. of Orford's affairs, vii. 496; to recommend son's friend to Mann, viii. 488
home of, in Lincoln's Inn Fields, ix. 55
Walpole, Thomas (1755–1840), diplomatist: HW's cousin:
HW's affection for, viii. 488
Turnor, friend of, recommended by HW to Mann, viii. 488
Walpole, Mrs Thomas. *See* Vanneck, Elizabeth (d. 1760)
Walpole estate:
Orford, 3d E. of, has right to leave, to whom he pleases, ix. 164n
Walpole family:
allied with Hamonds and Hostes, ii. 238n
arms of, to be on Cts of Orford's monument, ix. 226, 240
Chelsea once the home of, viii. 198
Cocchi respects, i. 387
fishing enjoyed by, ii. 256
Fitzroys make another match with, ix. 544
Gardiner to get advancement through, ii. 507, 509
George II's disavowal of civilities to Cts of Orford a just satisfaction to, iii. 144
gossip about, i. 146
HW asked by, to look after E. of Orford's affairs, vii. 496, 552
HW hopes to restore, vii. 497
HW outlives glory of, ix. 310
HW's hopes for, often disappointed, viii. 373
HW's inheritance or gifts from, ix. 637
HW's satisfaction in serving, his only reward for taking care of E. of Orford, viii. 303
HW twice expunged thoughts of, from his memory, viii. 301
HW will not cheat in behalf of, vii. 528
jewels of, ix. 144
Magnan boasts of protection from, ii. 548

Mann's respect for, iv. 486
Mann, Edward Louisa, lost money through, viii. 287
Mann family always taught to revere, vii. 353, 354
Mann family must always treat, with delicacy, viii. 78
Mann family's indebtedness to, i. 348
Monticelli often entertained by, i. 487
Orford inherits estate of, ix. 164n
—'s death would ruin, vii. 461
—— to deprive, of Dorsetshire estate, ix. 156–7
Orford, Cts of, disparages, i. 387, 406
—— not notified by, of Sir Robert Walpole's death, iii. 42
—— now mentions, with regard, iv. 479, 481, 486–7
—— said to have received nothing from, ix. 130
—— said to have taken deeds of, to Italy, ix. 160
perpetuation of, was Sir Robert's great object, ix. 156–7
Pett owes promotions to, ii. 509
pictures of, not valued enough by Lady Orford to be taken to Italy, ix. 227
Richecourt disparages, i. 387, 393–4, 404
Rome unlikely to honour recommendations by, iv. 461
Rowley esteems, ii. 507
Scully said to be preparing house for, in Florence, i. 426, 450, ii. 14
Stuart descendants marry daughters of, v. 285
Taylor boasts of patronage of, iv. 458, 461
Van Dyck portraits of, sold for a song, iv. 201
Walpole, Sir Robert, ruined, by excessive vanity, vii. 497
Walpole family, of Wolterton:
parsimony of, ii. 42
Walpole of Wolterton, Bns. *See* Cavendish, Lady Rachel (1727–1805); Lombard, Mary Magdelaine (ca 1695–1783)
'Walpoliana':
HW's letters may be dignified with the title of, iv. 215
Walpoliana. See under Yorke, Philip, 2d E. of Hardwicke
Walsegg ['Walseck'], Otto (d. 1743), Graf von; Gen.:
Electress called on by, at Florence, i. 130
Leghorn to be post of, i. 130
Petrillo insults, at burletta, i. 130
size of, i. 130
Tesi escorted by, i. 130
Walsingham, Bn. *See* De Grey, William (1719–81)
Walsingham, Cts of. *See* Schulenburg, Petronille Melusine de
'Walsingham, Mrs'. *See* Walkinshaw, Clementina

Walsingham, Capt. Henry. *See* Boyle, Hon. Henry (d. 1756)

Walsingham. *See also* Boyle-Walsingham

Walter. *See* Rolle-Walter

Walthers. *See* Wolters

Walton, Sir George (1665–1739), Kt, 1721; Adm., 1734:
    letter by, announcing naval victory, v. 297

Walton, Henry (d. 1764), farmer:
    Wilkes said to inherit money from, vi. 281

'Walton, John.' *See* Stosch, Philipp von

Walworth, Sir William (d. 1385), Kt, 1381; lord mayor of London:
    Harley the counterpart of, vii. 6

Wand; wands:
    lord steward's, vii. 99
    white, great officers break, over grave of old king, v. 445

Wandsworth Hill:
    Pitt visits Mrs George Pitt at, vi. 572

Wangenheim, Wilhelmina Sophia von (d. 1750), m. (1715) Gerlach Adolf, Freiherr von Münchhausen:
    sugar-figures castrated by, iv. 125, 144

Wanstead:
    Karl Friedrich mobbed on way to, iv. 155

Wanstead House, Essex, E. Tylney's seat:
    HW pleased by ball at, v. 417
    Muzell to visit, v. 427
    Orford, Cts of, to lodge at, vii. 120
    Tylney always intended to leave, to Long family, viii. 23

Wantley, Dragon of:
    Gevaudan beast compared with, vi. 289

Wanton Wife of Bath, The, ballad:
    HW alludes to, ii. 8, 23

Waple, John (d. 1763), accountant general of the Court of Chancery:
    Lucchis' money in name of, vi. 267

Wapping:
    coal-heavers terrorize, vii. 33
    punch to be drunk at, to celebrate Cherbourg capture, v. 227

War; wars:
    Algerian-Spanish, iv. 480, vii. 118, 120, 121–2, ix. 26, 416
    Algerian-Tuscan: iv. 472–3, ix. 270; Regency threatens, vi. 259; Tuscany cannot support, iv. 487
    American-English: address for peace fails by only one vote, ix. 244; American army in, said to mutiny, ix. 135; American defeat in, might precipitate French war, viii. 316; American deputies must be received by Howe to negotiate peace for, viii. 270; American losses in, might force them to submit, viii. 274; American retreat probably a wise move, viii. 282; Americans make no blunders in, viii. 124; Americans said to be determined upon, viii. 226; America unlikely to make peace overtures for, viii. 387; Bennington battle, viii. 335; Birmingham wants, to increase munitions manufacture, viii. 77; British defeats in south, viii. 141; Burgoyne's successes, viii. 323; Burgoyne's surrender, viii. 339–40, 344, 345; campaign in, seems to be over for the winter, viii. 278; Canadian operations in, viii. 156–7, 161, 185; Carlisle objects to sacrifice of loyalists by peace treaty for, ix. 365; Catherine II offers troops to England for, viii. 127; Charleston attack, viii. 236; Clinton-Cornwallis controversy over, ix. 370; commissaries and threats to conciliate, viii. 148; Conway moves address for peace in, ix. 244, 251–2, 259; Cornwallis's operations would be facilitated by naval victory over French, ix. 150; Cornwallis's successes, short-lived, ix. 151–2, 158; Cornwallis's surrender, ix. 209, 212; criminals increase as result of, ix. 316; definitive peace treaty to be signed for, ix. 426–7; Delaware River contests in, viii. 347, 386; Dutch war provoked by, ix. 211, 541; Eden and Carlisle stay to negotiate peace for, viii. 419–20; end of, will save thousands of lives and millions of money, ix. 209; England almost at last gasp in, ix. 201; England deserves to suffer the heavy consequences of, ix. 506; England loses trade by, ix. 506; England lowered by, ix. 433; England may hire Russians for, viii. 127, 324; England may sue for peace in, through France, viii. 324; England not brought to her senses by, viii. 310; England rendered by, impotent to keep Austria from taking Holland, ix. 541; England's loss of two armies in, almost unprecedented, ix. 210; England tries to raise a great army for, from Hesse and Brunswick, viii. 175; England will be ruined by, viii. 127; England will get nothing from, except its history, forty millions of debt, and three other wars, ix. 211; English army hardly sets out for, viii. 193–4, 197; English conquest of Lake Champlain, viii. 261; English country gentlemen promoted, but balk at its expense, ix. 5; English credit endangered by, ix. 310; English-French war to be joined to, viii. 348, 349; English inability to continue, will result in war with France, viii. 335; English national debt doubled by, ix. 434; English peace terms for, virtually allow American independence, viii. 354; France may forestall English peace efforts for, viii. 368–9; France may intervene in, viii. 268, 523; France spreads news of any English reverses in, viii. 250, 345; Franklin said to have made peace proposals for, viii. 281; French invasion of England would embarrass America in peace treaty of, viii. 392; French war grew out of, ix. 211; Gage a general in, vii. 44n; gazettes and Stormont optimistic over, viii. 306; Georgia campaigns, ix. 306; HW

[War; wars, *continued*]

augured ill of, viii. 355; HW cannot discover merit of system which started, ix. 143; HW condemns, viii. 452; HW disapproves of persistence in, ix. 139; HW expects, to be long, viii. 158, 484; HW foresaw miserable conclusion of, ix. 89; HW hopes, will die of old age, ix. 308; HW's dire predictions about, not unfulfilled, viii. 282; HW's predictions at beginning of, ix. 370; HW unable to grieve over termination of, ix. 209; Howe attacked for receiving American deputies for, viii. 270; Howe said to be making peace negotiations for, viii. 261; 'implicit submission' no longer to be demanded, ix. 210; inquiry into conduct of, debated in Parliament, viii. 351, 474; *London Gazette* tells lies about, viii. 232; loses popularity in England, viii. 205; Mann hopes for accommodation in, viii. 352; Mann's theories about English failure in, ix. 76; ministers responsible for, should be held answerable, if peace terms are humiliating, ix. 347; naval activity in, viii. 229; newspapers lie about, viii. 231-2; newspapers print rubbish during, ix. 146; news sources lacking for, viii. 185; New York campaigns, viii. 229-30, 241, 242-3, 248-9, 255-6, 261; North's peace terms for, viii. 348, 354, 358; Opposition should have opposed, more strongly, viii. 491; other wars may result from, viii. 287; outbreak of, viii. 109-11; Parliamentary debate over, after Burgoyne's defeat, viii. 341; Parliament eagerly promotes, viii. 81; Parliament may virtually send declaration of, viii. 74-5; Parliament to vote seamen for, viii. 127; Parliament unable to raise money for, viii. 465; peace articles for, published, ix. 362; peace commissioners fail to stop, viii. 400; peace for, not yet concluded, ix. 354, 355; peace in, delayed, viii. 285, 351; peace in, negotiations for, viii. 359, 362, 387, ix. 279, 311, 341-2, 352; peace in, would make HW happy, ix. 252; peace preliminaries for, signed, ix. 356; peace proposals for, to be passed by Parliament, viii. 359; peace treaty for, broken off, ix. 259; peace treaty in, said to be signed, ix. 346; Penn attempts mediation in, viii. 128; Percy may bring accommodation for, viii. 313, 315; politicians to blame for, viii. 490; Portuguese-Spanish clash may complicate, viii. 224; post-war hatred will be nourished by, viii. 287; progress of, nothing but miscarriages and drawn battles, ix. 164; prolonged frenzy of, endangers England's credit, ix. 309-10; Rhode Island campaign, viii. 281; Shelburne uses 'reciprocity' at time of peace after, ix. 519n; Spanish war added to, viii. 484, ix. 211; troops in winter quarters, viii. 349;

Yorktown ends 'another volume of,' ix. 211
Austrian-Bavarian: peace said to be concluded for, iii. 34, 37; progress of, i. 151, 194, 203, 289, 315-16; Walpole, Sir Robert, disclaims responsibility for, i. 231
Austrian-Dutch: compromise may avert, ix. 554, 562; conciliation to avert, ix. 593, 607; Dutch dykes opened in preparation for, ix. 543; European gazetteers disappointed by lack of, ix. 607; France and Prussia may join in, ix. 544; France may aid Holland in, ix. 545, 561; laid aside, ix. 556; Maestricht siege rumoured in, ix. 566; Vergennes involved in, ix. 561
Austrian-French: over Spain, v. 199-200; peace preliminaries of, iii. 487; progress of, i. 183, 194, 203, 289, 315-16, 451, 457, 466, 472, 481, ii. 58; said to have begun, i. 119
Austrian-Genoese: declared, iii. 75; may not be declared, iii. 58; peace terms for, iii. 305-6; termination of, iii. 312, 314-16
Austrian-Prussian: accommodation unlikely for, viii. 409; armies too close to avoid, viii. 398; armistice vainly sought to end, viii. 403; battles in, viii. 404; Charles, P., spoils peace for, iii. 127-8; ended, i. 456, 472, 482-3, ii. 5; ending of, favours Frederick II, vi. 119; England expects outbreak of, viii. 393; George II may arrange peace for, i. 76, 87; Joseph II deterred from, viii. 401; Joseph II keeps Frederick II at bay in, viii. 450; large armies accomplish little in, viii. 414; Leopold expects news of, viii. 389; letters from Vienna announce peace for, viii. 454; Maria Theresa halts, ix. 104; outbreak of, possible, viii. 389; peace after, belatedly known to Mann, i. 496-7; peace for, expected, vi. 118; peace for, not expected, i. 121, 144; peace rumoured for, i. 134, iii. 38; peace still expected for, viii. 407; progress of, vi. 51-2, 60
Austrian-Saxon, may end, i. 466-7
Austrian-Spanish, progresses slowly, in Italy, iii. 441; *see also under* Spain: army of commerce an excuse for, vi. 39
costliness of: England loses fifteen millions a year by, ix. 317; HW's reflections on, viii. 75; ruinous to England, ix. 201
costs England millions, while they lose, ix. 190-1
Danish-Russian, opening of, vi. 82
Dutch-English: American war provoked, ix. 541; armistice in, rumoured, ix. 188; begins in Mediterranean, ix. 120; continuance of, preferred by English to confession of mistake, ix. 143; definitive peace treaty not yet to be signed for, ix. 426-7; Dutch wealth and settlements hurt by, ix. 150; end of, in sight, ix. 266-7; England captures Ceylon settlement in, ix. 277; England makes headway in, only by suf-

ferance of eastern European powers, ix. 201; English manifesto on, sent by Hillsborough to Mann, ix. 112; Feilding's seizure of convoy may precipitate, ix. 3–4; grew out of American war, ix. 211; Holland a feeble enemy in, ix. 149; Holland might abandon, unless profitable, ix. 292; hopes for accommodation for, cease, ix. 108; lie given to English in reply to manifesto, ix. 142; *London Gazette* announces, ix. 104–5; Mann thinks, can be averted, ix. 8–9; newspapers print rubbish during, ix. 146; no declaration of, v. 266; peace not likely for, ix. 486; peace preliminaries signed for, ix. 437; peace still hoped for, ix. 116; preferable to war with Ireland, ix. 5; privateers delighted at prospect of, ix. 108; prizes taken by English in, repaid through wreck on Dutch coast, ix. 134–5; probably averted, ix. 5; reconciliation for, expected, ix. 266–7; suspension of arms in, ix. 357; threatened, v. 260; victories in, expected, ix. 279; victory at St Eustatius may bring peace in, ix. 139

Dutch-French: expected, iii. 24; neutrality treaty said to conclude, iii. 67–8; peace preliminaries for, signed at Aix, iii. 479; peace treaty for, signed, iii. 511; said to be declared, ii. 448–9; Wassenaer supposedly brings Dutch peace terms for, iii. 216

England's quadruple: managed deplorably for seven years, ix. 347; peace in, mentioned, ix. 272, 276

English-French: America may be saved by, viii. 268; American defeat might precipitate, viii. 316; American forts fought over in, iv. 506; American-French treaty precipitates, viii. 354–5; America now England's enemy in, viii. 485; American war to be joined to, viii. 349, 484; American war will alter course of, viii. 287; armistice for, iii. 480; begins, iv. 484; begun at sea, according to HW's predictions, viii. 395; Belle-Isle the author of, ii. 563; Berlin to arrange accommodation to prevent, iv. 541; blockade rules in, against neutral ships, v. 273–4; Bute may have become secretary of state in order to put an end to, v. 488; Canadian battle will probably decide, v. 327; Carolina's conquest endangered by, viii. 500; Catherine II and Maria Theresa might make peace for, viii. 519–20; Choiseul's return to power would reopen, viii. 1; continuance of, preferred by English to confession of mistake, ix. 143; couriers from Paris about peace for, vi. 105; declaration of, expected, ii. 394, 422, iv. 504–5; declaration of, sent to Florence by Pucci, ii. 442; declared conditionally, iv. 526; ending of, in sight, v. 497–8; England

excels France in privateering aspect of, viii. 422, 448; England fears, viii. 226; England on brink of, viii. 350; England the first to fire cannon in, iv. 488; England to declare, iv. 556; England will continue, in Germany, v. 456; English fleet prepares for, iv. 468; English inability to continue American war will bring on, viii. 335; English naval preparations possibly for, viii. 253; English victory in, unprecedented when on other side of Rhine, ii. 218; Europe regards, with ungrateful indifference, iv. 585; expected in 1742, i. 345; extends from Pondicherry to Canada, v. 290; Ferdinand's victory will tend to revive, vi. 47, 81; foreign correspondence will be hampered by, iv. 526; France a feeble enemy in, ix. 149; France disposed towards, viii. 273; France does not make preparations for, at Toulon, vii. 244; France imitates England's piddling style of waging, viii. 480; France prepares for, iv. 540; France prepares for, though claiming to be peaceful, viii. 262; France refuses to end, v. 534; France rejects English terms for ending, v. 526–7; France ruins her trade and army by, ix. 7; France says, must begin, iv. 523; France seems determined on, viii. 375; France suspends declaration of, viii. 332; France too cautious to declare, iv. 490; France wages, differently from Frederick II, ix. 190; France wants peace for, vi. 83; France will start, when England is sufficiently undone, viii. 300; Franco-Spanish naval preparations against Russia almost precipitate, vii. 474–5; Frederick II tries to avert, iv. 528; French account of naval clash in, viii. 402; French aid to America may precipitate, viii. 316; French avoid decisive battle in, ix. 156; French bankruptcy may be produced by trade ruin in, v. 122–3; French Court not keen for, viii. 384; French dread Howe's fleet in, ix. 313; French should be discouraged from, by defeats in Germany, v. 317; French trade suffers from, v. 122–3, viii. 455; Genoa professes impartiality in, iv. 581; George II said to have declared, ii. 44; Germany the theatre of, vi. 35, 43; grew out of American war, ix. 211; HW does not expect ending of, vi. 92; HW dreads, viii. 342; HW ends letters with wishes for peace in, ix. 337; HW's bitter expectations from, viii. 364; Hanoverian invasion might deter France from peace overtures in, v. 502; hinted at, in Louis XV's alleged letter, i. 114; Howe may bring on, by victories in America, viii. 256; in America, may break out, iv. 448; inexplicable conduct of French in, ix. 147; in Germany always fatal to French in winter campaigns, iv. 589; in Germany at a stand, v. 291, 440; in Germany, En-

[War; wars, *continued*]

glish rôle in, ended, v. 306; in Germany, not yet over, v. 549; in Germany, Parliament opposes, v. 553, vi. 7; in Germany, seems less interesting than Portuguese war, vi. 41; in Germany, subject of debate in England, v. 549, 553, vi. 2, 7, 14–15, 30–1; in Germany, tires England, v. 466, vi. 2; in Germany, wanes, v. 312, 500; in Germany, will be continued by England, v. 456; in India, may spread to Europe, iv. 448; Jersey not captured in, ix. 127–8; lack of declaration of, may facilitate peace, viii. 399, 414; languor of, ix. 48; Leghorn merchants anticipate ending of, vi. 69; London approves of, iv. 493; Louis XV's escape from assassination may distract France from, v. 48; Mann terrified by prospect of, viii. 357; Mann will learn peace news of, before HW, ix. 347; Maria Theresa unlikely to stop, v. 389, 502, vi. 23; Martinique's capture and Peter III's accession do not hasten end of, vi. 23; military lull in Germany may indicate ending of, v. 500; naval clash may begin, viii. 361; negotiations might still prevent, except in America, iv. 488; Newcastle's dismissal and courteous French answer indicate possible ending of, vi. 38; newspapers print rubbish during, ix. 146; Nivernais warns France that adherents of, gain ground in England, vi. 89; northern monarchs must despise, ix. 6; not yet declared despite French embargo, viii. 365–6; peace articles for, published, ix. 362; peace celebrations for, iv. 46–50, vi. 163; peace congress for, to settle India's ownership, v. 527; peace delegates for, v. 504, vi. 55, 69–70, 72, 73, 90, 92–3, ix. 279, 454–5; peace difficulties in, unintelligible to Mann, vi. 99; peace for, cannot await Havana's capture, vi. 69; peace for, concluded, vi. 116; peace for, not yet concluded, ix. 354, 355; peace for, opposed, iii. 448–9, vi. 89, 116; peace for, sincerely wanted by, D. of Bedford, vi. 92; peace for, to be adhered to, despite change in English administration, ix. 372; peace in, hoped for, ix. 183; peace in, seems certain, vi. 38, ix. 346–7; peace negotiations for, iii. 448–9, v. 546, vi. 54–5, 60, 65–6, 81; peace negotiations for, said to be broken off, iii. 440–1, 464, vi. 81; peace negotiations for, to begin, ix. 279; peace overtures for, from France, v. 497–8; peace overtures for, through Van Hoey, iii. 264; peace preliminaries for, negotiated at Paris by Fitzherbert, ix. 311; peace preliminaries for, signed, iii. 479–80, ix. 356, 357; peace preliminaries for, to be ratified by France, ix. 362, 365; peace proposals for, supposedly made by Franklin, viii. 281; peace prospects for, v. 360–1, ix. 342, 359, 366–7; peace

prospects for, nearer because of change in English administration, ix. 276; peace rumours for, iii. 218, 225, v. 365–6, 368–9, 504, 513, vi. 81, viii. 465, ix. 359; peace rumours for, implied by cessation of German war, v. 500; peace terms (definitive) for, not expected till Parliament meets, vi. 78; peace terms for, rejected by France, v. 526–7; peace terms for, unpopular in England, ix. 367–8, 373–4; peace terms from France for, rumoured from France, ix. 359; peace treaty (definitive) for, awaited, vi. 118; peace treaty for, not taken up in Parliament, iv. 30; peace treaty for, should be influenced by Gibraltar's defence and Rodney's victory, ix. 352; peace treaty for, signed, iii. 511, vi. 95, ix. 426–7; peace treaty for, unpopular with English at Florence, ix. 382; peace would have spared France losses in, v. 534; Pitt content to manage, under D. of Newcastle, v. 448; politicians to blame for, viii. 490; possibility of, vii. 156; progress of, nothing but miscarriages and drawn battles, ix. 164; Rome discusses possibility of, i. 24; rumoured, from Venice to Florence, ii. 44; Spain may join, iv. 491; Spain said to have advised France to continue, vi. 76; Spain will not be involved in, iv. 487; Spanish war added to, viii. 482–4; stock prices fluctuate according to, v. 497, 504, vi. 81, viii. 179, 282, 361; suspension of arms rumoured for, ii. 245; to be fought in Germany, vi. 35, 43; unavoidable though unwanted, iv. 482–3; undeclared despite hostilities, ii. 276, 283, viii. 390–1, 399, 412; undeclared war of succour, ii. 247; victory in, would be too dearly bought, ix. 336; Vienna hopes that peace will not be made for, vi. 87

English-Neapolitan: Bourbon family pact may necessitate declaration of, vi. 565; shipping disputes may precipitate, iii. 65

English-Russian, threatened, ix. 118

English-Spanish: added to American and French wars, viii. 482–4; America now England's enemy in, viii. 485; American war will alter course of, viii. 287; averted, v. 172, vii. 297, 304; believed to be averted, vii. 244–5; Bourbon family compact would have riveted, vii. 274; Carolina's conquest endangered by, viii. 500; Charles III does not intend, viii. 492; Charles III may declare, vii. 244–5, viii. 489; Charles III reluctantly declares, viii. 483; conduct of navies in, inexplicable, ix. 147; continuance of, preferred by English to confession of mistake, ix. 143; declaration of, v. 560–1, vi. 5, viii. 491; definitive peace treaty to be signed for, ix. 428; England fears, viii. 226; English administration not blamed for, viii. 491; expense and futility of, ii. 423, iii. 432; fallen into lethargy, ix. 145; first

effects of, viii. 496; forgotten in England, i. 390; France said to have been advised by Spain to continue, vi. 76; French letters predict, vii. 252–3; George III's refusal to appease America causes, viii. 490; grew out of American war, ix. 211; HW's letters will be made heavy by, v. 558; languor of, ix. 48; Leopold convinces Joseph II of folly of, ix. 58; Mann hopes, may be averted, v. 555; Mann persuades Leopold and Maria Louisa to urge Charles III to stop, ix. 42–4, 46; Mann pities George III for having to face, v. 538; Mann's fear of, viii. 357, 476; may result, without either Court wanting it, v. 554; newspapers print rubbish during, ix. 146; Orsi faction wants, concluded by peace, i. 263; outbreak of, likely, v. 536–7; peace in, attacked by newspapers, vii. 274; peace in, declared, vii. 269–70; peace in, hoped for, ix. 183; peace preliminaries for, ix. 356–7, 365; peace said to be made in, i. 180, 182, 380, ii. 107, ix. 145; peace signed for, vi. 95–6; Peterborough's conduct in, ii. 180, viii. 482; Pitt reverses his stand on, iv. 222; Pitt should avoid, v. 544; Pitt's resignation may precipitate, v. 537–8; politicians to blame for, viii. 490; Portugal the battlefield of, vi. 34–5, 43; preparations for, vii. 241–2; progress of, nothing but miscarriages and drawn battles, ix. 164; Repnin said to be going to England to avert, viii. 487; rumours of, iv. 491, ix. 98; Spain a feeble enemy in, ix. 149; Spain's reluctance to make peace in, gives English ships a chance to continue, iii. 488–9; Spain wages, differently from Frederick II, ix. 190; Spain will start when England is enough undone, viii. 300; Spanish avoid decisive battle in, ix. 156; Spanish compliance alone can avert, vii. 246; Spanish fleet may precipitate, viii. 111, 114; Spanish manifesto tries to justify, v. 563–4; threatened, viii. 459, 495; Torrington's prowess in, iv. 569n; Walpole, Sir Robert, disclaims responsibility for, i. 231

European, may arise from East Indian and West Indian disputes, iv. 448
European improvements in techniques of, ix. 105–6, 141–2
excuses offered by nations for waging, vi. 39
Frederick II makes, fashionable for kings, v. 277
French-Prussian: ending of, rumoured, v. 153, 159; Frederick II suggests negotiations to end, v. 366; prolongation of, in winter, distresses French troops, v. 254
French-Sardinian, peace negotiations for, broken off, iii. 441
Genoese-Sardinian: declared, iii. 75; termination of, iii. 312–14; to be declared, iii. 58
HW calls, demon of blood, ix. 188

HW comments on lack of news in, ix. 190–1
HW considers, a tragedy, ix. 365
HW detests, vi. 39, 81, ix. 106, 108
HW says that the world will never long be free from, ix. 546
human devastation of, HW's reflections on, vi. 81
inaction in, the worst fault in war, v. 519
Indians start, in America, vi. 177
Marlborough's general retorts to alderman's foolish remark about labour of, v. 198, viii. 29, 414, ix. 340
Modenese-Spanish, may begin over Massa, i. 35
modern aggressors wage, without pretending that it is holy, ix. 400
peace not so catching as, ix. 188
plague may be added to, for destruction of mankind, ix. 304–5
politeness of, v. 255
Portuguese-Spanish: German war less promising than, vi. 40; outbreak of, expected, viii. 223–4, 253; peace in, vi. 95, 99; progress of, vi. 41, 48, 66, viii. 223–4; Spain pushes, vi. 78; Spain said to have begun, vi. 34; Spain wantonly provokes, vi. 18–19; Tyrawley derides, vi. 70
Prussian-Russian: Elizabeth of Russia's answer to proposal for ending, v. 368–9; Elizabeth of Russia unlikely to stop, v. 389; Russian defeat in, alleged, v. 315; see also under Peter III of Russia
religion used as excuse for, vi. 39
rules of, French accuse English of violating, by use of fireworks, v. 283
Russian-Swedish: peace treaty for, ii. 275; Vilmanstrand captured in, i. 155; Walpole, Sir Robert, disclaims responsibility for, i. 232
Russian-Turkish: accommodation for, may be reached, vii. 161; battle of Tchesmé in, vii. 226–8, 232–3; begins, vii. 70; Catherine II declares, ix. 415; Choiseul dictates gazette article on, vii. 143; contestants in, agree to do nothing, viii. 34; declaration of, v. 247–8; Dick receives Order of St Anne after termination of, viii. 96; ends without any signal action, viii. 55; fears of, said to be removed, ix. 350; Fox, C.J., said to be responsible for peace in, ix. 486; France blamed by Turkey for causing, vii. 202; France may be involved in, ix. 359–60; France persuades Turkey to begin, vii. 70; HW knows nothing about, ix. 427; Joseph II may be prevented by, from coming to Italy, ix. 350; Joseph II to be umpire for, ix. 415; peace comes soon after resumption of hostilities in, viii. 33; peace made in, vii. 420; peace negotiations for, broken off, vii. 172–3, 438, 441; peace treaty for, announced, viii. 40; Pugachev may have contributed to ending of, viii. 35; resembles an armistice, viii. 28; resembles Chancery suit,

[War; wars, *continued*]
vii. 432; Rome prays for Turkey's success in, vii. 140; rumours of, ix. 420, 616n; Russians at Pisa rejoice over ending of, viii. 84; Russians capture Turkish beggage, vii. 479; Russian victory in, followed by invasion of Silistria, vii. 478–9; Russia's allies insist on conclusion of, viii. 33; Rutherfurd and Dick act as Russian commissaries during, viii. 453; Sultan averse to, but people and janizaries may precipitate it, ix. 360; Turkish instigators of, might be beheaded, vii. 159; Turkish peace negotiations may end, vii. 469–70; Turks lose provinces in, vii. 160
winter quarters not resorted to, in modern, v. 316–2, ix. 105

War, Council of (at Florence):
Richecourt president of, iv. 392

Warasdins:
Lobkowitz reinforced by, iii. 30

Warbeck, Perkin (1474–99), pretender:
Young Pretender may be impersonated by a, iii. 227, 270

Warburton, Jane (ca 1683–1767), m. (1717) John Campbell, 2d D. of Argyll:
(?)HW mentions, v. 503
Sudbrook the villa of, vii. 538n

Warburton, William (1698–1779), Dean of Bristol, 1757; Bp of Gloucester, 1759–79:
agnosticism of, vi. 196
Churchill dedicates sermons to, vi. 261–2
notes of, to Pope's *Essay on Man*, parodied in Wilkes's *Essay on Woman*, vi. 184
Pope to be defended by, iv. 62
speech of, against Wilkes, vi. 185
Wilkes's sacrifice wanted by, vi. 196

Ward, Joshua (1685–1761), quack doctor, M.P.:
HW describes cures by, v. 362–3
HW wants Mann to give a more accurate description to, v. 363
Mann inquires about remedy of, v. 358
—— tells HW not to consult, v. 386

Warden of the Stannaries:
Waldegrave replaces Thomas Pitt as, iv. 246–7
—— was, vi. 126n

Warder of Tower of London:
at execution of rebel lords, iii. 302

Ware, Isaac (d. 1766):
Plans, Elevations, and Sections . . . of Houghton, Mann receives, i. 416

Wareham:
election at, iii. 458

Warfare:
western, contrasted by HW with eastern, ix. 201

Warkworth, Bn. *See* Percy, Hugh (1742–1817)

Warkworth, Bns. *See* Stuart, Lady Anne (1746–ca 1819)

Warkworth Castle:
Northumberlands build at, iv. 341

Warner, Betty:

Warwick induces, to break oath to deceased protector, ii. 540

Warrant; warrants:
for Byng's execution, v. 63
for Sayre's arrest, defective, viii. 138
for secretary at war's position, iii. 175
general: outcry against, in counties, vi. 559; Parliament discusses, vi. 274, 283; 'sent to devil,' vi. 312

Warre, Jane (ca 1705–91), m. (1730) Sir Robert Grosvenor, 6th Bt:
Molesworth, Henrietta, stays at house of, vi. 145

Warren, Anne (d. 1807), m. (1758) Charles Fitzroy, cr. (1780) Bn Southampton:
Richmond's masquerade attended by, in Turkish dress, vi. 148
son's elopement not forgiven by, ix. 508
thirteen children of, ix. 508

Warren, Edward (d. 1760), Irish army officer in Tuscany:
health of, colic, i. 223
Modenese princess escorted by, through fortress, i. 66
Prujean and Elizabeth Pitt friends of, iv. 499
Regency council questions, i. 223

Warren, Elizabeth Harriet (ca. 1760–1826), m. (1777) Thomas James Bulkeley, 7th Vct Bulkeley:
Florence visited by, ix. 618n

Warren, Sir Peter (ca 1703–52), K.B., 1747; Vice-Adm.; M.P.:
Admiralty candidate, iv. 17
Anson and Vernon compared with, iv. 33
Cape Breton's conqueror, iv. 33
daughter of, vi. 148n
knighted, iii. 414
Navy Bill opposed by, iv. 33
ships captured by, off Cape Finisterre, iii. 410

Warren, Richard (1731–97), M.D.:
Gloucester, D. of, attended by, viii. 74
Kingston, Ds of, subject of testimony by, at House of Lords, viii. 151
Rockingham attended by, in last illness, ix. 287–8

Warrington Bridge:
demolished, iii. 173

Warsaw:
courier from, to Rome, about Cardinal of Bavaria's bishoprics, vi. 119
Durini lately nuncio at, viii. 11
English fleet should sail to, to restore Poland, vii. 475
peace expected by, vii. 438
Polish minister at Rome sends express to, vii. 352
visitors to, Craven, Bns, ix. 632

War ships. *See* Man of war; Ship of war

Wars of the Roses:
uncomfortable period to live in, viii. 117

Warth, Comtesse de la. *See* Chudleigh, Elizabeth, Ds of Kingston

Warwick, Cts of. *See* Hamilton, Elizabeth
Warwick, E. of. *See* Grenville, Francis (1719–73); Rich, Edward Henry (1698–1721)
Warwick, Earls of:
English merchants in India imitate, vi. 211–12
Warwick:
races at, v. 427
Warwick, ship:
at Leghorn, i. 455
at Port Mahon, i. 285
Warwickshire:
Conway to visit, v. 228
HW intends visit to Cts of Hertford in, v. 128
HW to visit Hertford in, iv. 265, v. 226, 228
HW visits, vii. 57
Washed drawing. *See under* Drawing
Washerwoman:
dies in St Martin's roundhouse, i. 504
See also under Servants
Washington, George (1732–99), Gen.; President of the United States 1789–97:
casualties of army of, viii. 339
Congress appoints, 'generalissimo,' viii. 120
Cornwallis's army surrenders to, ix. 208–9
defeat of, not total, viii. 349
distinguished in the last war, viii. 120
Fabius and Camillus imitated by, viii. 287
French capture, and engage him not to serve for a year, iv. 449–50
HW calls, 'dictator,' viii. 338
Howe apparently not to dislodge, viii. 320, 323–4
—— defeats, at Brandywine and Germantown, viii. 331, 338–9
—— fails to encircle in Westchester county, viii. 268–9
—— finds, too well entrenched to be attacked, viii. 352
—— retreats after advancing towards, viii. 323–4
——'s alleged defeat of, doubted by HW, viii. 334–5
——'s army not increased by battles with, viii. 336
——'s defeat may be considered best objective of, viii. 347–8
—— twice 'gazes at,' viii. 386
—— twice marches to, without attacking him, viii. 414
Howes said to have been prevented by, from crossing Delaware to Philadelphia, viii. 327
letter of, expresses enjoyment of cannonballs, iv. 450
Monmouth battle must be disappointment to, viii. 408
New England forces may join, to besiege Clinton, viii. 342
New Jersey said to be the station of, viii. 338–9

Speaker's mace not respected by, viii. 356
supposed revolt of troops under, ix. 135
talents of, conceded by both sides, viii. 282
two generals said to be court-martialled by, viii. 406
Washington family:
'frantic race,' v. 397
Wasner, Johann Ignaz (ca 1688–1767), Freiherr von; Austrian minister to England, 1741:
English Opposition said to work with, i. 325–6
footman of, brings letter to HW, iii. 29
George II may be influenced by, i. 325
Granville confers with, on Charles VI's death, x. 10
HW will not relinquish Riccardi's jewels to, iii. 74
Richecourt and Toussaint said to have urged, to intercede for Bns Walpole, ii. 194
Wasp:
HW sees, in April, ix. 392
Wassenaer, Unico Wilhelm (1696–1766), Graaf von; Heer von Opdam, Twickel, etc.; Director of the Dutch East India Co.:
Holland said to have sent, with peace terms to Paris, iii. 216
Wassenaer Obdam, Carel George (1733–1800), Rijksgraaf van; Heer van Twickel:
Joseph II to receive, ix. 593
Watch; watches:
Arundel takes, to Italy, v. 339
captured at Dettingen, ii. 261
chain for, v. 296
Deard reduces price of, v. 314
enamelled, Bedford, Ds of, sends, to Vcts Bolingbroke, for Q. Charlotte, vi. 104–5
Ferdinand VI's mania for, vii. 241
Florence to send, to Constantinople, iii. 437
George II gives: to Cts of Albemarle, iv. 111; to Elizabeth Chudleigh, iv. 57
gold, Mann, Mrs Galfridus, tries unsuccessfully to save, from highwayman, ix. 343–4
Gordon rioters snatch, from members of Parliament, ix. 54
HW sends, to Mme Grifoni, i. 415–16
makers of, *see* Deards, John *and* William; Ellicot, John; Gray, Benjamin *and* Robert
Pius VI's nephew receives, in France at Princess's birth, viii. 470
prices of, v. 295–6, 302
repeating: Amalia of Modena gives, at Florence, i. 64–5, 70
stop: Ferrers gives, to Vaillant, v. 401; key to, fits pocket-book, v. 402
woman's repeating, procured by HW for Mann to give to Santini for his sister-in-law, v. 293, 295–6, 302, 303–4, 306, 311, 313, 327, 337, 343, 347, 355, vii. 306
Watchman; watchmen:
highwayman nearly kills, iv. 188
Leveson-Gower and Rigby imitate, iv. 135
of Bristol, iv. 470

Watch seal; watch seals:
HW copies design for device for, v. 314, 322
price of, v. 314

Water:
armies lack, ii. 471
bad, at Petraia, i. 481
Boscawen's fleet gets, at Gibraltar, v. 307, 318
Chute takes, with turnips, ii. 100
cold: gout treated by bathing feet in, vi. 266, 313, 322, 335–6; gout treated by drinking, vi. 110, 114, 266, 322, 335, 459, vii. 246, 252, viii. 423, 430; HW dips his head in, every morning, v. 168
cold spring, for sponging eyes, ii. 386
Florentine mills lack, ix. 318
hot: Mann puts his feet in, to induce gout, viii. 457; Mann urged to put his feet into, to cure cold and headache, viii. 190; Walpole, Bns, soaks legs in, ii. 153
Leghorn's supply of, injured by earthquake, i. 304
machine for raising, see under Machine
Mann's panacea, inside and out, vi. 459
—— takes, iced, viii. 430
Mann, Horace II, takes, ix. 353
nerves 'cured' by, iv. 389
Orford, Cts of, cannot swallow, ix. 102
'rainwater from Paris,' iii. 414
sold on Neapolitan streets during drought, viii. 479
toast drunk in, in Parliament, i. 354
See also Bristol water; Hungary water; Iron-pear-tree water; Orange flower water

Water-colour:
Liotard's, iv. 362

Wateridge:
expense of, Florence to Leghorn, i. 130

Water in the stomach:
Rockingham may have died of, ix. 287

Watermen:
pun by, on Pembroke's death, iv. 108

Water music. See under Music

Waters, Charles; Cts of Orford's maître d'hôtel:
writes to Florence for a house, iv. 476

Water-works:
popular despite cold season in London, i. 434

Watson, ——:
Florence visited by, i. 106

Watson, Adm. See Walton, Sir George

Watson, Charles (1714–57), naval officer:
Princess Louisa commanded by, iii. 410

Watson, Henry (d. 1793), surgeon:
HW has, for his hand, ix. 617, 618
HW urged by, to take the air, ix. 617, 626

Watson, Lewis (ca 1714–45), 2d E. of Rockingham:
HW falls into lap of, at opera, i. 412

Watson (formerly Monson), Hon. Lewis (1728–95), cr. (1760) Bn Sondes; M.P.:

Bocchineri, Mme, gives venereal disease to, iv. 36, 447
Hoare does Ganymede for, iv. 86
Mann visited by, iv. 36

Watson, Thomas (1715–46), 3d E. of Rockingham, 1745:
death of, iii. 224

Watson-Wentworth, Charles (1730–82), styled Vct Higham 1734–46 and E. of Malton 1746–50; 2d M. of Rockingham, 1750; prime minister:
administration of, in 1765–6: America and Europe saved by firmness of, vi. 401; American disputes to be referred by, to Parliament, vi. 407, 408; Fox's and Mackenzie's sacrifices demanded by, vi. 302; Mann admires wisdom of, vi. 406–7, 408; Pitt charges, with perfidy, vi. 425; Pitt's inability to include Grenvilles strengthens, vi. 436; Pitt turns against, vi. 413–14; to include members of House of Commons, vi. 311; triumphant in Parliament, vi. 381–2
administration of, in 1782: announced, ix. 261, 262; Burke and Fox only able members of, ix. 295; called in Paris malheureux pour la France, ix. 287; cannot be as bad as predecessor, ix. 264, 276; change from, causes Cholmondeley to resign ambassadorship, ix. 333; change to, was for the better, but did not last, ix. 310; did not survive his death, ix. 310; disposed towards independence for America, ix. 285; HW gives, time to breathe, before sending Mann news of, ix. 272–3; HW predicts jolt of, ix. 273, 275; Mann's acquaintance with members of, ix. 270–1; may be maintained if it can make a tolerable peace, ix. 264; measures of, triumphant, ix. 285–6; popularity of, probably transient, ix. 275; Wray named by, as Westminster candidate, ix. 284–5
administration may be led by, vii. 182
administration refused by, vi. 543
administration to be accepted by, after negotiations with Bedfords and Grenvilles, vi. 538
Bedfords to be reconciled with, by disgusts and D. of Newcastle, vi. 549
both terms of, as prime minister, very short, ix. 288
breach between Shelburne Whigs and those of, not healed when they took office, ix. 294
brother of, died of convulsions, ix. 288
Burke, 'governor' of, vii. 209
Cabinet requested by, is granted, ix. 261–2
Cavendish, Lord John, friend of, ix. 293
constitutional demands of, granted, ix. 261
Conway urged by, to resign, vi. 471–2
Court offends, by appointing another person to treat with him, ix. 261, 380
Court side taken by, in voting, vi. 507–8
death of: not sudden, ix. 287; produces new scene, ix. 293; split administration, ix.

310; while prime minister, ix. 287–8; will have more consequences than his actions would have had, ix. 288

Devonshire, 4th D. of, by dying, placed, at head of Whigs, ix. 288

Devonshire, 5th D. of, might succeed, ix. 289

faction of: angry at all, vi. 567; Bedford faction meets, at Newcastle House, vi. 541–2; Bedford faction quarrels with, vi. 565; Burke's pamphlet severs, from supporters of Bill of Rights, vii. 209; dine at tavern with G. Grenville, vii. 115; fluctuate between Conway and George Grenville, vi. 495; Fox, C.J., and Cavendishes govern remnant of, ix. 379; Grenville, George, opposes, vi. 566, 567, 568; Grenville faction does not merge with, vi. 504; Grenville faction does not tell, of reason for motion in House of Lords, vi. 507; Grenville faction unites with, for East India Company's petition, vi. 495; meet at Fitzwilliam's, ix. 294 295–6; Newcastle, D. of, to unite, with Bedford faction, vi. 566; not numerous, ix. 295; Pitt's faction deserted by, vii. 199; Richmond deserts, ix. 294, 295; Townshend, Charles, may lead, vi. 495; warn him of snare laid by Shelburne, ix. 261

Fitzwilliam the nephew and 'Octavius' of, ix. 294

George III and Shelburne negotiate without consent of, ix. 372n

George III arrogantly treated by, in negotiations, vi. 539, 543

——'s brothers promised increased pensions by, vi. 424

——'s negotiations with, over new ministry, vi. 538–9

—— tells, that D. of Cumberland's death will make no difference, vi. 364

Gower may succeed, ix. 289

Grafton writes to, about George III's intentions, vi. 539

Grenville, George, breaks with, vi. 542

—— compared with, vi. 489

—— may get, in his clutches, vi. 539

—— not likely to acknowledge leadership of, vi. 504

—— succeeded by, as first commissioner of the Treasury, vi. 310

Grenvilles negotiate with, vi. 538–9

Grenvilles will not allow, to head Treasury, vii. 181

Guercino painting at Siena acquired by, through Mann, iv. 263, 268, 272–3, 313–14

HW deems, unable to get Bath ribbon for Mann, vi. 359n

HW mentions, iv. 326

HW not to tell, that his painting has been copied, iv. 314

HW's opinion of, vi. 359n, ix. 288

HW told by, about purchase of Guercino painting, iv. 272–3

health of: abscess, ix. 288; constitution bad, ix. 288; hypochondria, ix. 288; water in stomach, ix. 287

no man in public life had fewer enemies, ix. 288

Opposition not to be joined by, though he opposes, vi. 464, 549

Orford's turkey-geese match with, v. 7

Parliamentary motion by, vii. 180

Parliamentary Opposition too quiet to need, as leader in London, vii. 546

Parliamentary reforms opposed by, ix. 29–30

Parliament's dissolution by, would leave Wilkes in control, vii. 181

parts of, not great, ix. 288

Pitt (Chatham) calls on, though he had formerly been ejected from his house, vii. 181

—— must depend on, vii. 246

——'s coolness with, viii. 350

Portland rumoured to be successor to, ix. 289, 295

—— the logical successor to, ix. 372

prime ministry alone would satisfy, vi. 504, viii. 493

resignation by, as lord of the Bedchamber, v. 99, vi. 97

resigns, as first lord of the Treasury, vi. 431–2

Richmond may succeed, ix. 289

Sandwich attacked by, in House of Lords, ix. 221

seceding Whigs of, called Junto, ix. 294

Serristori, Mme, has, as cicisbeo, iv. 284

Shelburne asks, to give posts to Gower and Weymouth, ix. 261

—— rumoured as successor to, ix. 293

—— supports, as prime minister, ix. 261

silly enough to do mischief, vi. 505

spoke in Parliament only by necessity, ix. 288

terms of, deemed to invade rights of Crown, ix. 257

Thurlow negotiates with, to form ministry, ix. 256

—— unlikely to succeed, ix. 289

to be K.G., v. 368

Treasury headed by, ix. 262

virtues and amiability of, produced party esteem and friends' love, ix. 288

Wilton copies statue of Venus for, iv. 397

Woburn visited by, to confer with Bedford faction, vi. 538

Yorke, Charles, induced by, to reject Seals, vii. 175, 178

—— the oracle of, vi. 494

Yorke family attached to, vii. 178

Watson-Wentworth, Thomas (1693–1750), cr. (1734) E. of Malton, and (1746) M. of Rockingham; M.P.:

death of, from excessive claret, iv. 208

[Watson-Wentworth, Thomas (1693–1750), cont.]
express from, in Yorkshire, announces successes against rebels, iii. 186
regiment raised by, iii. 128, x. 13
Rockingham title goes to, iii. 110, 186n,
244
Yorkshire defence meeting headed by, iii.
110
Watson-Wentworth, Hon. Thomas (1720–34):
death of, from convulsions, ix. 288
HW remembers, at Eton, ix. 288
Wax:
bas relief of, v. 105
black, used in mourning on letters, i. 164
candles of, see under Candle
Florentines offer, to Mann for coronation
celebration, v. 533
insertion of, beneath broken seal, will enable re-sealing of letter, iv. 56
Lucan, Bns, models in, viii. 475
mask of, covers Clement XIV's disfigured
face, viii. 43
models in, by Cellini, ix. 215n
Stanhope, Sir William, thinks that Prince
Henry Frederick is a model in, iii. 175
torches of, iii. 14, 184, viii. 541
Venice to give present of, to D. of York,
vi. 241
Waxwork:
monarchs like to sit to a maker of, vii. 539
Rackstrow's, HW does not want to show,
to Fleury, vi. 135
Way of the World, The. See under Congreve,
William
Weakness on the breast:
occurrences of, viii. 80, ix. 350
Weald:
of Kent, vi. 117
Wealth:
London's evils aggravated by, vii. 151
See also Money; Riches
Weapons:
prohibited, in Florence, i. 136–7
See also Gun; Pistol
Weather-glass:
fortune's, viii. 464
HW's letters may be affected by, viii. 379
Weather house:
political change suggestive of that of, vi.
98
Weavers:
Bedford, D. of, mobbed and wounded by,
vi. 301
colours displayed by, vi. 301
George II offered 1000 men by, iii. 180
George III petitioned by, vi. 301
House of Lords rejects bill for relief of,
vi. 301
House of Lords surrounded by, vi. 301
insurrection of, in London, vi. 301
Piccadilly blocked by a mob of, vii. 6
riots against execution of, vii. 163
starving in England, vii. 476

Wedderburn, Alexander (1733–1805), cr. (1780)
Bn Loughborough, (1801) E. of Rosslyn;
solicitor-general, 1771; M.P.:
Burke's breach with, made up, viii. 341
East Indian Company officer questioned by,
about Grand Lama's letter, ix. 14–15
flippancies of, severely handled by succes-
sors, ix. 285
Kingston, Ds of, opposed by, at trial, viii.
193
solicitor-general, vii. 269
Wedding; weddings:
Lorenzi enjoys, iv. 92
Mann will tell HW about, ii. 56
of poor Florentine girls, vi. 491
opera interfered with by, ii. 59–60
Wedding clothes:
Ferrers wears, to execution, v. 399
Wedding coach. See under Coach
Wedding gown:
Elizabeth Chudleigh's, vii. 93
Wedding ring. See under Ring
Wedell, Gen. Karl Heinrich (1712–82):
Russians said to be defeated by, v. 315
Wedgwood, Josiah (1730–95), potter:
Etruscan vases of, vii. 211
Hamilton's portrait in Staffordshire ware
of, x. 46
Weedemans, hautboy player:
Holdernesse entertains, ii. 131
Weeding-girl. See under Servants
Weeds, garden:
Methodists may talk of, iv. 81
Weeds, widows':
Craon, Princesse de, will try to look well
in, iv. 418
Kingston, Ds of, may wear, at trial, viii.
187
Morehead, Mrs, wears, for Hunt, iii. 477
Weekends:
English will not come to town on, v. 118
English will not sacrifice, vii. 259
fashionable to leave London for the coun-
try on, iv. 63–4
Weemyss. See Wemyss
Weepers:
Dutch and English wear, for Princess
Royal, v. 266
Lothian wears, for son, iii. 281
Mann wears, for Ps Caroline, v. 165, 174
Pomfret shuns, after father's death, iv. 390
Weidel. See Wedell
Weld, Edward (1705–61), of Lulworth Castle:
arrest of, iii. 134
Weld, Edward (d. 1775):
widow of, ix. 628
Weld, Mrs Edward. See Smythe, Maria Anne
Welderen, Cts van. See Whitwell, Anne
Welderen, Jan Walrad (1725–1807), Count
van; Dutch envoy to England 1762–80:
anti-French, vii. 269–70
Choiseul's designs on Holland not believed
by, vii. 270

leaves England for Holland, ix. 108
marriage of, vii. 269n
Well:
Harcourt dies in, viii. 328
Wells, Phillis (d. 1742):
death of, i. 504
Welshmen:
Williams Wynn tells, that George II was not at Dettingen, ii. 305–6
Wemyss, David (1721–87), styled Lord Elcho; titular 5th E. of Wemyss, 1756:
cruelty of, iii. 272
grandfather's will should have prevented, from joining Jacobites, iii. 148–9
health of, salivation, iii. 248
Hervey friendly to, at Venice, iii. 148
Lincoln implored by, for pardon, iii. 272
Mann has seen, at Florence, iii. 118, 148
—— hopes, will not escape, iii. 149
Paris the refuge of, iii. 272
silly, iii. 118, 148
Venice visited by, iii. 148, 379
Young Pretender joined by, iii. 118
Wemyss, Lady Elizabeth (ca 1718–47), m. (1734) William Sutherland, 17th E. of Sutherland:
Cromarty in bed with, iii. 296
Wemyss (later Charteris), Francis (1723–1808), titular 6th E. of Wemyss, 1787:
grandfather leaves estate to, on condition of his not turning Jacobite, iii. 148–9
Wemyss, James (1699–1756), 4th E. of Wemyss:
son of, iii. 118n, 272n
Wen:
Francis III's, iv. 75
Wendover:
borough of, i. 425
election for, i. 397
Wendt, Amalie Sophie Marianne von (1704–65), m. (1727) Oberhauptmann Gottlieb Adam von Wallmoden; cr. (1740) Cts of Yarmouth; George II's mistress:
Albemarle, Cts of, friend of, iv. 112
—— influences, iv. 269
Bouverie buys peerage from, iii. 419
death of, vi. 362
Delorain, Cts of, supplanted by, in George II's affections, ii. 71
dessert depicts, with George II, v. 191
George II does not permit, to show special favour to Cts of Orford, iii. 111
—— goes abroad with, i. 188
——'s bequest to, v. 450
——'s devotion to, satirized in ballad, ii. 81
——'s mistress, v. 191n, 443n
Giberne's picture shown to, by his mother, iv. 90
—— will not be approved by, iv. 95, 98
HW mentions, iv. 326
HW's witticism to, on robbery of watch, iv. 112
health of: ague, iv. 88; beyond recovery, vi. 357; cancer in breast, vi. 354

Lorenzi asks about, iv. 96–7
Mirepoix visits, iv. 96
Northumberlands give supper for, v. 191
Pitt said to have lived with, i. 146
on the wane, iv. 212
Orford, Cts of, not taken by, to Court, iii. 111
Ranelagh proprietor influences, to persuade George II to order jubilee-masquerade, iv. 47
palace rooms unobtainable for, iv. 88
son of, ii. 524n
summoned on George II's death, v. 443
Schwichelt and Frechapelle fight duel over, iv. 184
Theodore of Corsica said to be 'uncle' of, ii. 187, 216
Wentworth, Bn and Vct. See Noel, Edward (1715–74)
Wentworth, Diana (1722–95), m. (1739) Godfrey Bosville:
archbishop complains about, ii. 286
Chute describes promiscuous behaviour of, ii. 286
Craon complains to Mann about, ii. 286
English reputation at Florence lowered by, ii. 309
family of, ii. 242
Florence visited by, to produce heir, ii. 238–9
husband grants separation to, ii. 309
husband tells, to follow Prole, ii. 286
Mann called on by, ii. 238
—— to entertain, ii. 275
Prole's affair with, ii. 251, 263, 298
—— to be joined by, ii. 286, 309
Uguccioni assists, ii. 242, 251
York the home of, ii. 242
Wentworth, Lady Henrietta (d. 1786), m. (1743) Henry Vernon:
Kingston, Ds of, seen by, at Colisée in Paris, viii. 242
lady of the Bedchamber to Ps Amelia, viii. 242n
marriage of, ii. 342
Wentworth, (?)Hugh (d. ?1787), army officer:
Florence visited by, ii. 146
from Mathews's ship, ii. 146
HW does not know, ii. 166
Lincoln resembles, ii. 146, 166
Mann must entertain, ii. 146
Wentworth, Sir Thomas (1593–1641), cr. (1628) Vct Wentworth, (1640) E. of Strafford:
HW satirizes, ii. 357
HW would like to have seen trial of, vi. 284
perishes before his cause succeeds, vii. 200
Sandys's hatred of Sir Robert Walpole over Orford title resembles Vane's hatred of, for taking Raby title, i. 333n
Wentworth, Thomas (?1693–1747), army officer, M.P.:

[Wentworth, Thomas, *continued*]
advice by, on privately-raised regiments, x. 14
Austrian-Sardinian negotiations to be mediated by, iii. 401
Austrians hate, for favouring Piedmontese, iii. 451
Austrians to be spurred on by, iii. 406
Austrians to receive proposal from, about capture of Genoa, iii. 417
courier of, iii. 417
Holland visited by, to demand troops, ii. 400
'Jamaica general,' ii. 242
niece of, ii. 242
Piedmontese want a successor to, iii. 451
Santiago land attack refused by, i. **175**
Sinclair to succeed, iii. 456
Turin visited by, iii. 401, 406
Vernon will be challenged by, ii. 143
Wentworth, Sir William (1686–1763), 4th Bt, 1706; M.P.:
daughter of, ii. 242
Wentworth, William (1722–91), 2d E. of Strafford, 1739:
HW describes Wentworth Castle, the seat of, v. 429n
HW dines with, i. **320**
HW's intimate friend, v. 452n, vii. 425
HW to visit, in Yorkshire, v. 429, vi. 247, vii. 425
scagliola pictures in box sent to, i. 396, ii. 131
sister of, ii. 342, viii. 242n
Wentworth-Fitzwilliam. *See* Fitzwilliam
Weobly, Herefordshire:
election of, disputed in Parliament, iv. 31
Werpup, Georg Anthon (d. 1765), Hanoverian Baron:
Hanoverian who attended Q. Charlotte to England, vi. 306
killed near Rome by overturn of chaise, vi. 306
Wesel:
siege of, raised, v. 444
Weser, river:
Cumberland, D. of, forced to cross, v. 109
French army crosses, v. 117
Wesley, Rev. John (1703–91), founder of Methodism:
(?)Indian's conversation with, i. 477
West, Mrs. *See* Burnet, Elizabeth
West, Benjamin (1738–1820), historical painter:
HW's opinion of, vii. 211, viii. 93
Houghton pictures to be appraised by, viii. 441
Poussin imitated by, in historical paintings, vii. 210–11
prices of, vii. 211
West, Lady Henrietta Cecilia (1727–1817), m. (1762) James Johnston:

Mann has 'flirtation' with, at Florence, viii. 85
West, James (1703–72), M.P.; politician:
Antiquarian Society member, iv. 371n
brother-in-law of, iv. 371
HW gives to, a letter to Mann, recommending Steavens, iv. 379
HW informs, of income from Customs place, x. 53
Martin succeeds, as secretary of the Treasury, v. 25
M.P. for St Alban's, iv. 371n
named in Secret Committee lists, i. **385**
Pelham's secretary, iv. 371
reversion secured by, for himself and his son, v. 26
secretary to the Treasury, i. 385n, iv. 371n
treasurer to the Royal Society, iv. 371n
voted for, as commissioner, i. 437
West, James (1742–95), M.P.:
reversion secured for, by father, v. 26
West, Mrs James. *See* Steavens, Sarah
West, John (1693–1766), 7th Bn de la Warr, cr. (1761), E. de la Warr:
earldom granted to, v. 490
regiment of, i. **353**
subscription masquerade attended by, dressed as Q. Elizabeth's porter, iv. 49
trooper of, prophesies earthquake, iv. 137, 147, vii. 261
trooper's wife talks to, about husband's insanity, iv. 137
West, Hon. John (1729–77), styled Vct Cantelupe, 1761; 2d E. De La Warr, 1766; army officer:
Ancaster succeeded by, as Q. Charlotte's Master of the Horse, vi. 473
Cumberland, D. of, takes, to Hanover, v. 78
West, Richard (ca 1691–1726), lord chancellor of Ireland, M.P.:
son of, i. 468n
West, Richard (1716–42):
Ashton's poem on death of, i. 468–70
buried at Hatfield, i. 468n
ode by, on death of Q. Caroline, published in Dodsley's miscellanies, i. 468n
poetic genius of, i. 468n
West, Temple (1713–57), naval officer; Cobham's nephew; Rear-Adm. 1755; Vice-Adm., 1756:
acquittal of, desired, iv. 583
Admiralty post given to, iv. 25
Hawke and Saunders sent to Gibraltar to punish, iv. 562
Mann explains Tuscan situation to, ii. 98
—— visited by, in Florence, with naval captains, ii. **98**, 99
Westenra, Jane (d. 1788), m. (1734) John Monckton, 1st Vct Galway:
brag to be played by, out of town to avoid earthquake, iv. 137
West India merchants. *See under* Merchant

West Indian; West Indians:
  boroughs contested by, v. 484
  elderly, tells Mann about Tortola lands, viii. 169, 200
West Indies:
  Albemarle's letters from, not made public, vi. 77–8
  American navy half-starves, viii. 229
  Byron may save, if unhurt by d'Estaing, viii. 447–8
  climate of, will not permit English wounded to recover, ix. 278
  Clinton said to have embarked and disembarked troops for, viii. 424
  department of: not relinquished by Pitt, v. 104; to be restored to Pitt as secretary of state, v. 488
  endangered, viii. 431, 490
  England captures wealth in, iii. 92
  England overruns, v. 326, vi. 16
  English capture Dominica in, v. 516
  English expeditions in, i. 175, 291, ii. 251–2, 278–9, iv. 491
  English fleet for, gobbled up by Spaniards, ix. 77–8, 83
  English fleet from, arrives safely, viii. 391–2, 410, 501
  English ministerial supporters do not want to go to war for, iv. 468
  French: American colonies send grain to, vi. 486; prizes from, disputed by England with the Dutch, v. 280
  French and Spanish fleets unite in, ix. 73
  French fleet may attack, viii. 386
  French fleet sails from Brest to, ix. 220
  French losses in, to be greater than expected, ix. 286
  French may know about undivulged English successes in, iii. 487–8, 494
  governor from Spain in, i. 7
  governors in, wicked, v. 13
  HW's interests too narrow to include, vii. 550–1
  La Clue may try to reach, with Toulon fleet, v. 318
  Martin from, vi. 183n
  naval battles in, ix. 52, 277–8, 284
  news from, awaited, v. 291
  Payne from, vii. 272
  probably saved, viii. 535
  regiment for, debated in Parliament, iv. 531
  Rodney may have gone to, ix. 17, 24, 99
  Ross saved from post in, i. 244
  Spanish fleet sails to, i. 17, 20
  Townshend defeats Martinique fleet in, iii. 186
  turnpike bill would be more upsetting than, to Parliament, vii. 455
  war in: HW expected to report upon, iv. 455; may spread to Europe, iv. 448
  Young from, iv. 327
  See also Barbados; Cuba; Dominica; Guade-
lupe; Havana; Jamaica; Martinique; Porto
Rico; Saint Christopher's; Saint Vincent;
San Domingo; Tortola
West Looe:
  HW mentions, v. 89
Westminster, E. of. See Murray, Hon. Alexander (1712–78)
Westminster, High Bailiff of. See Corbett, Thomas; Leigh, Peter; Lever, John
Westminster:
  abbot of, supposed to be in a painting of Henry VII's marriage, iv. 390
  Blakiston leads independent electors of, iv. 261n
  Court candidates elected by, iii. 425
  Court party cannot find candidate for, i. 257
  crowd at, awaits Wilkes, vii. 13
  election at: almost contested, ix. 284–5; Bedford, D. of, pays for, iv. 112–13; Court institutes scrutiny for, in favour of Wray, to exclude C.J. Fox, ix. 563n; Fox, C.J., candidate for, ix. 11; Fox, Henry, and Pitt demand investigation of delay in scrutiny at, iv. 122–3; Gower pays for scrutiny at, iv. 113; Hood and C.J. Fox returned for, ix. 563; Hood's candidacy for, withdrawn, ix. 285; House of Commons examines, ix. 502; Mann, Horace II, eager about, ix. 505; Middlesex election bodes ill for, iv. 131; Mountmorres defeated as Wilkes's candidate for, viii. 52; Northumberland, Ds of, wins, for her son and Lord Thomas Clinton, viii. 51–2; Parliament to settle, i. 220, 233, 246, 247, 250, 272, 298, 322; Perceval carries, i. 272, iv. 31; satiric prints of, ix. 496; scrutiny of, iv. 107–8, 113, 122–3, 156, 223–4; scrutiny of, demolished, ix. 562; scrutiny of, provoked by royal vengeance, ix. 565; Sundon's, contested, i. 246, 250–2; Trentham to be rechosen at, iv. 100n; Trentham wins, iv. 107, 156
  Fox, C.J., elected by, though a petition is presented against him, ix. 488n
  —— has partisans at Amsterdam and Versailles as well as, ix. 495–6
  —— opposes Wray and Hood in, ix. 489, 490–1
  illuminated for Keppel's arrival, viii. 443–4, 446
  Independent Electors of, iii. 387, iv. 223
  Parliamentary members from, vote for address, ii. 125
  petitions from: presented by Cooke and Egremont, iv. 223–4, 235; presented by Pulteney, i. 232–3, 298; voted at meeting, ix. 10–11
  Pitt, William II, nominated by, ix. 278
  punch to be drunk at, to celebrate Cherbourg capture, v. 227
  remonstrance to Parliament being prepared by, ix. 218

[Westminster, *continued*]

Sandys vacates seat for, in Parliament, vii. 206

theatre in, used by D. of York, Lady Stanhope, and Delavals, vi. 521

Wilkes in political control of, viii. 45

Westminster Abbey:

ambassadors lie unburied in, vi. 216

Charlotte's retiring chamber behind altar at, v. 535

Coke, Lady Mary, visits burial vaults in, when Ps Louisa dies, viii. 14

dedicated to St Peter, viii. 382n

Edward I's grave opened by Chapter of, viii. 4

Garrick to be buried in, viii. 435

Gay's monument in, iii. 195n

George III's coronation in, v. 534–6

Handel's jubilee in, ix. 647–8

Henry VII's chapel, Walpole, Lady, commemorated by monument in, i. 212n, ii. 347, vi. 98n

Pitt may be buried in, viii. 382

revenues derived from Coronation spectators at, v. 536

Richmond's corpse exhumed from, iv. 182

Rochester, Bp of, has gallery in, ix. 648

tombs in: HW does not want to show, to Fleury, vi. 135; shown to visitors, iv. 181–2

visitors to: Abergavenny, iv. 181; Selwyn, iv. 181

Westminster Association:

Jebb the orator of, ix. 36n

Westminster Bridge:

pier of, sinks, iv. 108

Westminster Hall:

approach to House of Commons through, i. 300

constables, horse guards, and foot guards to protect, during Wilkes's trial, vii. 12

coronation banquet in, v. 535

deeds for breaking Linton entail to be presented at, viii. 258, 259

Ferrers tried in, v. 367, 387–9

Fox, C.J., harangues meeting at, for voting a petition, ix. 10–11

gallery in, belongs to 2d E. of Orford, iii. 284–5

Jebb's rôle at, ix. 23, 36

Kingston, Ds of, may be tried in, viii. 87, 151, 187

—— tried in, viii. 191–3, 195–6

law suit in, over wager on D. of Cumberland's weight, iv. 208–9

Middlesex's trial in, iv. 4–5

Montagu, D. of, forced to produce wife at, ix. 564n

rebel lords tried in, iii. 280–6

standards of Blenheim hung in, ix. 337

trophies in, ii. 248

Wilkes's trial in, vii. 11–13, 29–30

Westminster School:

Dashkov to enter, vii. 242

Johnson, Bp, former Master of, iv. 345

Molesworth studies at, vi. 140

Murray and Stone at, iv. 345

Westmorland, Cts of. *See* Cavendish, Mary (1698–1778)

Westmorland, E. of. *See* Fane, John (1685–1762)

Westmorland:

militia of, in Carlisle, iii. 159

Weston, Stephen (1665–1742), Bp of Exeter, 1724:

death of, i. 279

Westphalia:

army in, will mutiny in cold weather, v. 435

Belle-Isle may march to, x. 23

Crown Point politically situated in, v. 369

English reverses in, v. 544

Hanover may raise recruits in, v. 195

Lippe-Bückeburg leaves, vi. 43

peace of, France pretends to be guardian of, v. 96

'Wet brown paper.' *See under* Paper

Wetherby, Yorks:

Wade approaches, iii. 173–4

Weymouth, Vct. *See* Thynne, Thomas (1734–96)

Weymouth, Vcts. *See* Bentinck, Lady Elizabeth Cavendish

Weymouth:

election at, i. 420, 475

English expedition sails from, v. 244

visitors at, D. and Ds of Gloucester, ix. 203

Whaley, John (1710–45), poet:

poem of, in *Ædes Walpolianæ*, iv. 69

Wheat:

price of, rises in England, vi. 455

Wheble, John (1746–1820), publisher of the *Middlesex Journal*:

arrest of, vii. 279–80

Wheel; wheels:

at D. of Richmond's fireworks, iv. 56

of chaise, iv. 483

officers broken upon, v. 382

Wheelchairs:

gout-sufferers use, at Stowe, vi. 247

Wheeler, Mrs John. *See* Winnington, Anne

'When Fanny blooming fair.' *See under* Stanhope, Philip Dormer, E. of Chesterfield

Wherry:

Howe does not lose one, ix. 337

Whey:

Walpole, Sir Edward, takes, ix. 463

See also Goat's whey

Whifield. *See* Whitefield

Whig; Whigs:

Argyll pleases, by leaving Court, i. 366

Balchen firm as, ii. 458

Broad Bottom coalition dupes, i. 337

Conway unattached to either faction of, ix. 294

Cotton professes to be, i. 363

Fox supported by, iv. 412

George II to cherish, i. 339
Grant clan leans towards, iii. 233
HW settled as, ix. 40
Hampden a 'buffoon,' iv. 224
Hessian troops may be detained by, from wish to thwart Pitt and Tories, v. 34
Jacobites defeated by, in after-rebellion elections, iii. 425
Johnson, Bp, disowned by, iv. 345, 346, 361
Lestock upheld by, iii. 33
London, Middlesex, and Westminster vote for, iii. 425
Minorcan investigation to be used by, in favour of ministry, v. 77
Morgan an adherent of, vii. 174
Murray and Stone disowned by, iv. 345, 361
old, George III refuses to accept, ix. 386n
Pelham attacked, for trying to dismiss Hanover troops, iii. 17
Pitt's faction of, do not join Court, ii. 118
Pulteney pretends to join, ii. 49–50
Pynsent belongs to, vi. 284
reverses may invigorate, iii. 118
Rockingham's, seceding, called junto, ix. 294
—— succeeded Devonshire as leader of, ix. 288
Shelburne's, opposed those of Rockingham, ix. 294
Tories' non-existence affirmed by, i. 337, 363
Tweeddale among the discontented, iii. 195n
union of, saves Parliament in 1742, i. 118
Walpole, Sir Robert, always loyal to, vi. 26
Windham is, of old school, viii. 524
young, led by Hartington, iv. 223
Whig families:
credit lost by, in their own counties, ix. 488
Whiggism:
HW's, old-fashioned, vi. 257
Oxfordshire election a revival of, iv. 435
Whig-Patriots:
to come into power, i. 319
See also Patriots
Whips:
coachmen crack, in Florence, i. 488
Whisk. See Whist
Whiskers:
Wortley Montagu wears, vi. 113
See also Beard
Whisperer:
author of, see Moore, William
Mann borrows 6 numbers of, from Leghorn, vii. 219
Wales, Ps of, denounced by, vii. 196
Whist:
Choiseul and Comtesse du Barry play, with Louis XV, vii. 157
dull, vi. 555

English supposed to know, naturally, vi. 430
fashionable in London, ii. 119, 124, 130, 148
French imitate, from England, vi. 555
HW has not yet learned to play, ii. 119
HW tries to supersede, with bilboquet, ii. 204
Italians said to seek English company in order to play, iv. 175
Mann forgets how to play, vi. 430
—— pretends not to know, iv. 160
Maria Louisa plays, with Mann and Mrs Hervey, vi. 430
—— plays, with Vcts Sudley, vii. 203
Orford, Cts of, plays, iii. 111
played: at Petersham, iii. 166; at Richmond Green, iv. 63; by ladies at Stanhope's, iii. 485
Shukburghs addicted to, iv. 160
Tyrawley comments on, ii. 148
Walpole, Horace (1678–1757), seeks parties at, iv. 250
White's Club members play, in country on weekends, iv. 63
Whistles:
at Craon's house, solemn, i. 79
Whiston, William (1667–1752), divine:
HW satirizes, in verse, iv. 134
unlucky to die before present era, vii. 81
Whitchester, Lord. See Scott, John (1745–9)
White, Mrs:
HW's hostess at Brandon, ii. 318
wig worn by, over shaved forehead, ii. 318
White, John (1699–1769), M.P.:
Parliamentary debate by, on privately-raised regiments, x. 18
White:
Newton said to have called, offensive to eyesight, ii. 228
White boys (Irish 'levellers'):
disturbances by, vi. 24
France said to have instigated rebellion of, in Ireland, vi. 414
Irish, coal-heavers all are, vii. 33
Whitefield, Rev. George (1714–70), Methodist divine:
England tolerates, ix. 23
Ferrers's conversion sought by, v. 398
HW satirizes, in verse, iv. 134
Huntingdon, Cts of, sends, to Ferrers, v. 398
Townshend, Vcts, makes witticism on, iv. 52, 70
Venice might be converted by, after its quarrel with Benedict XIV, iv. 163, 177
Whitehall:
fire at, i. 496
France makes peace overtures to, v. 499
garden at, slopes to Thames, iv. 56
HW could not have endured Lord George Sackville's ordeal at, v. 387
Richmond's fireworks at, iv. 56, vi. 148

[Whitehall, *continued*]
——'s garden in, to have exhibit of casts from statues, v. 173
——'s masquerade at, vi. 148–9
Whithed takes Pembroke's house in, iv. 142

Whitehall Evening Post:
HW's illness reported in, vi. 459, 461
(?)Mann takes, vi. 326
ships' prizes mentioned in, iii. 441

Whitehall Palace:
Burlington, Kent, and others responsible for alterations in plans of, v. 363–4
Jones's plan for, imitated at Caserta, v. 363

'White Hart,' inn at Windsor:
couples visit, in chaises, iii. 298

Whitehaven:
American privateer attacks, viii. 377

Whitehead, Paul (1710–74), poet:
'infamous but not despicable,' i. 252
Manners by, i. **211,** 252
supper given by, at 'Bedford Head,' i. 211
Walpole, Sir Robert, angers, by being in good health, i. 252
World contributions by, iv. 395n

Whitehorse Cellar, Piccadilly:
stage coaches leave from, v. 313

White's Club:
Almack's eclipses, as gaming centre, vii. 187
Arthur of, iv. 135
bet-book at, says that Burdett will be hanged, iv. 20
bets made at, over dying man, iv. 185
Chesterfield puts Crébillon's *Sopha* on sale at, i. 334
chocolate house the first meeting place of club of, ix. 483n
dinner at, extravagant, iv. 260
frequenters of: Bath, iv. 63; Bedford, ii. 124n; HW, iii. 261; Hobart, iii. 261; Janssen, ii. 124n; Lonsdale, iv. 63; Montford, iv. 169
gamblers at, i. 36
HW preferred Newmarket to politics as a topic at, ix. 483
in St James's St, iv. 168, ix. 483n
Jeffries the contribution of, to politics, ii. 365
Maclaine's lodging near, on St James's St, iv. 168
—— visited by Montfort and other members of, iv. 169
Mackreth a former waiter at, viii. 53n
Mirepoix sends card inviting chess-players of, iv. 289
Onslow rails at, ii. 289
parsons scandalized by bets at, about earthquake, iv. 131
Petersham loses at, iv. 140
Pope mentions, ii. 124n
Rumbold a former waiter at, ix. 400
suppers at, elegant, iii. 261

Taaffe and Wortley Montagu do not belong to, iv. 289
two clubs at, iv. 289
Vernon black-balled at, iv. 301
whist-players of, play whist in country on weekends, iv. 63

Whitewashing:
of churches, ii. 480, viii. 527

Whitfield, Anne (d. 1723), m. (1713) Archibald Campbell, cr. (1706) E. of Ilay:
husband buries, under stairs, i. 506

Whitfield. *See also* Whitefield

Whitham, Anne (ca 1761–1824), m. (1780), Gen. James Murray:
escapes to Leghorn from Minorca, ix. 179, 180
husband recommends, to Mann, ix. 349
pregnant, ix. 364

Whitham. *See also* Whittam

Whithed (formerly Thistlethwayte), Francis (1719–51), M.P.:
Accademia to be attended by, ii. 187
Albani introduced to, by Mann, iii. 59
—— introduces, to Roman society, iii. 59
——'s protection alone keeps, at Rome, iii. 196
—— to receive letter of thanks from, iii. 197
Austrian brutality disgusts, iii. 279
authorship of literary piece suspected by, ii. 411
bequests of, iv. 238, 251
Bologna visited by: iii. 257; to examine Domenichino painting, i. 227–8, 235, 240, 241, 312–13
brother drags, out to hunt, iv. 237
brothers of, obstruct his bequest to Lucchi family, iv. 312n
Carmelite friar's story to be told by, to HW, iv. 128
Casa Ambrogi residence of, ii. 109
Castello visited by, i. 443, ii. 1
Chute alarmed by fit of, ii. 109
——brings up, iv. 238
—— helps administer will of, iv. 246
—— laments, iv. 256
—— little obliged to, vi. 268
——persuades, to provide for Lucchi family, vi. 265
—— tries to marry fiancée of, to Orford, iv. 256
—— would have made, his heir, iv. 238
'Chutehed,' iii. 420, 435
Cocchi attends, ii. 109
—— diagnoses death of, iv. 244
Correggio painting thought by, to cost more than HW expects, ii. 370
Craon constantly invites, to play quadrille, ii. 101
—— entertains, ii. 132
—— invites, to Petraia, Castello and Topaja, i. 443

(?)Craon, Princesse de, called on by, at Petraia, i. 443

Craons to entertain, ii. 372

Craons visited by, at Petraia, ii. 1

Creti's painting disliked by, ii. 303

Dagge recommended to, vi. 268

Dal Borgo entertains, ii. 85

daughter born to, ii. 406

daughter of, see Lucchi, Sophia

daughter's picture sent to, by Mann, iv. 244

death of, iv. 237–8, 243

Del Sarto painting criticized by, ii. 214

departure of: from Florence, iii. 257; imminent, iii. 47, 252

diet of, i. 218

Dunbar tells Romans that Chute is tutor to, iii. 136

England disappoints, iii. 329

English captains' gratitude to Mann witnessed by, ii. 115

English weddings reported to, ii. 455

'excessively good' to HW, i. 365

Firenzuola, the, tires, i. 241

Florentine house of, see Ambrogi, Casa

Ginori, Mme, to entertain, i. 161

Giogo, the, crossed by, i. 241, 257

Giuseppe and Riviera's discussion of Young Pretender overheard by, at Petroni's assembly, iii. 85

Goldsworthy, Mrs, with, i. 313

good-natured, iii. 443

HW and Anthony Chute discuss, i. 301

HW and Sir Robert Walpole thank, for helping to secure Domenichino painting, i. 257

HW asks, to await his return to Florence, ii. 482

HW asks about, ii. 123

HW asks about cicisbea of, ii. 497

HW asks Chute to remember him to, i. 365

HW blames, for anti-Jacobite behaviour at Rome, iii. 139

HW congratulates, on increase of his family, iii. 350, 425

HW considered plumper by, iii. 317

HW finds, in London, iii. 316

HW gets false notions from, about Mann's health, iii. 382

HW glad that Mann has regained, iii. 209

HW impatient to see in England, ii. 410, iii. 224, 272

HW regrets that Mann is soon to lose, iii. 224

HW relieved by indolence of, in letter-writing, iii. 442

HW reproached by, for being so English, iii. 339

HW's absence from cocchiata regretted by, ii. 1

HW sends regards to, i. 143, 177, 346, 392, 421, 440, ii. 194, 277, 343, 401, 425, 432, 529, iii. 210, 214

HW's letter to Mann read by Mann to, i. 312, ii. 132

HW's letter to Mann relieves depression of, caused by courier, iii. 197

HW thanks, i. 340

HW to consult, about Young Pretender's movements, iii. 378

HW told by, about Chute's sister, iv. 19

HW to receive news from, about eagle, iii. 197

HW to receive regards of, i. 218, 294, 382, 418, 428, 474, ii. 68, 101, 264, iii. 56, 84, 239

HW to tell: about affair in Mann's garden, iii. 499; about Albani's dismissal, iii. 475

HW visited by, at SH, iii. 442

HW will laugh with, over Ashburnham's failure, iii. 420

HW wishes, were safely out of Rome, iii. 161

Hampshire election won by, iii. 420

Hampshire to be visited by, iii. 435

health of: bled, ii. 109, iv. 237; clap, ii. 197; cough, iv. 237; fever, common, ii. 138; fit, ii. 109; gout, iii. 221, 232

Hervey's conversation with, iii. 372

Hobart liked by, iii. 275, 507

—— replaces, iii. 261

——'s correspondence with, iii. 365, 382

Houghton plans enjoyed by, i. 428

house of, burned, iv. 185

'infinitely improved,' iii. 329

in love and wants a whore, i. 491

itinerary of: from Florence to England, iii. 257; from Florence to Rome, iii. 48–9; from Vienna to Berlin, iii. 279

Jacobite lies contradicted by, iii. 135–6

Jacobites might molest, at Rome, iii. 113

lady discusses Young Pretender with, at Rome, iii. 97

lean and silent, i. 112

leaner and 'pretty,' iii. 317

lean, pale, deaf, and silent, i. 117

Leghorn may be visited by, ii. 27

Lovat's picture sent by, to Mann, iii. 391

Lucchi, Angiola, arranges masses for, iv. 254

—— bears child to, ii. 333, 368, 406, vi. 268n

Lucchi family recommended by, to Chute, vi. 265

Lucchi family's bequests from, revealed to them by Mann, iv. 251

Mann asks about whereabouts of, i. 101

—— borrows money from, for Craon, ii. 134

—— brags to, of conversation with Richecourt, ii. 12

—— called on by, i. 161, ii. 140

—— cheered by company of, iii. 196

[Whithed, Francis, *continued*]
—— consults, about model of HW's statue, ii. 179
—— entertains: at dinner, ii. 17; at supper, i. 218; at tea, i. 428
—— excludes, during Theodore's visit, ii. 187
—— expects, at Florence, i. 97, 106, 235, 240
—— grieved at being dropped by, iii. 443
—— lodges, at his house, iii. 197
—— praises, i. 283-4
—— recommends Moretti to, iv. 46
—— regrets loss of, iii. 48, 257, 261, 263
——'s answer to Pucci's remonstrance approved by, ii. 325
——'s 'apartment over the river' to be occupied by, i. 146, 154
——'s correspondence with, iii. 257, 279, 322, 436, 453, 462
——'s devotion from, i. 343
—— sends regards to, iii. 467, iv. 93, 162
——'s guests entertained by, at Casa Ambrogi, ii. 386
——'s hospitality to be attested by, iii. 349
——'s sale of coffee pot to Mathews advised by, ii. 472
—— summons, to read HW's letter, ii. 132
—— to call on, ii. 109
—— to have tea with, i. 161
Mann, Galfridus, accompanies, to select Cholmondeley's pictures, iii. 405
—— procures seeds for, iv. 25
—— writes of death of, iv. 243
Mathews and Villettes laughed at by, ii. 279
mistress of, *see* Lucchi, Angiola
Modena, Princesses of, discuss HW with, iii. 257
'more agreeable than Christmas,' ii. 367
name changed by, from Thistlethwayte, vi. 268n
Naples visited by, iii. 171
Nicoll, Margaret, to have married, iv. 241, 256
Old Pretender said to be offended at, iii. 136
opera attended by, ii. 322, iii. 372
paintings collected by, iv. 142
Parliament entered by, iii. 446-7
Patapan again to be godfather to expected child of, ii. 333
Pembroke's house in Whitehall taken by, iv. 142
Petroni's assembly attended by, iii. 85
Pisa visited by, ii. 455
portrait of, in pastel: offered to HW by Mann, viii. 222; painted for Mann, ii. 243
(?) Pucci, Mme, to receive civilities from, i. 42
Riccardi's *festino* attended by, i. 146
Rivera's accusations against English fleet heard by, iii. 120

Roman letter to Goldsworthy amuses, iii. 226
Rome left by: for Florence, iii. 196; too soon, iii. 210
Rome soon to be revisited by, iii. 171
Rome visited by, iii. 48-9, 84, 85, 97, 113, 135-6, 141-2, 171, 196, 209
Sarrazin, Mme, forces, to play quadrille médiateur, ii. 132
seat of, *see* Southwick
Stanhope's house admired by, iii. 485
Strozzi family troubles known to, iii. 350
Suares, Mme, persuades, to back Tesi's opera, ii. 281
subscriber to concert at Florence, ii. 13
Topaja may be visited by, i. 443
Tunbridge visited by, iii. 436
Ubaldini's apartment occupied by, i. 146
Uguccioni to introduce, at Baronessa Ricasoli's, i. 129
valet robs, of money and clothes, ii. 4, 10
Venice visited by, i. 74, 101, iii. 268
Vienna visited by, iii. 207 257, 279
Violette's dancing disliked by, iii. 342
will of: iv. 238, 246, 254; seen by Chute and Galfridus Mann, iv. 251
Winchester assizes to be attended by, iv. 237
Young Pretender hated by, iii. 318
——'s invasion called by, a hoax, iii. 97
——'s progress denied by, at Rome, iii. 142
Whitmore, John (b. ca 1729), Oxford scholar: to be imprisoned for treason, iv. 6
Whitmore, Sir Thomas (1711-73), K.B., 1744; M.P.:
Bath knighthood given to, ii. 451
Whitsuntide:
exodus from London during, i. 450
Whittam (*or* Whitham), William, King's messenger:
arrested, vii. 280-1
Whitwell, Anne (1721-96), m. (1759) Jan Walrad, Count van Welderen:
Anne of Orange's maid of honour, vii. 269n
leaves England for Holland, ix. 108
Whitwell, John. *See* Griffin, Sir John Griffin
Whitworth, Francis (1684-1742), M.P.:
Legge succeeds, as surveyor of the forests, i. 493
Whore; whores:
aliases used by, vii. 520
Arbuthnot rebukes, ii. 70
'capering Madonna' in Italy, ii. 70
Damer, Hon. John, sups with four, at Bedford Arms, viii. 234
Moore's, in coffin chained to his, iv. 181
Orford, E. of, squanders money on, viii. 513
poxed, Lincoln robbed and infected by, vii. 378

'Treaty, The', implies that Cts of Lincoln was, v. 93

Whithed wants, i. 491

Wicquefort, Abraham van (1606–82):
Ambassadeur et ses fonctions, L': tale for new edition of, vii. 125

'Widdrington,' character in *Chevy Chace:*
Pitt resembles, vii. 264

Widows:
French opera singers omit powder when they act parts of, ii. 496

Wig; wigs:
Adonis: Mann wears, in portrait, viii. 27; Maron substitutes, in painting, for Mann's usual wig, viii. 32; old senators keep, with their robes, for days of ceremony, in Rome and Florence, viii. 32; suited only for younger men, viii. 27

black: Sturgis wears, i. 461; Wachtendonck disguises himself with, i. 489

bob, English visitors wear, in Florence, i. 132

brown bob, White, Mrs, wears, ii. 318

Cenci's, too spruce for Clement XIII to make him cardinal, v. 334

Charles III snatches, from visitors, vii. 238

Francis III pulls, down to nose, iv. 57

——'s, hung on his wen, iv. 75

full-bottom, out of style, ii. 148

Giovanni Gastone's, ix. 170

Gordon wears flannel under, i. 298

great, Mann to wear at Electress's, i. 83

iron, Wortley Montagu brings, from Paris, iv. 226

Parliament members stripped of, by Gordon rioters, ix. 54

periwigs, Norfolk ladies think it fashionable to wear, ii. 318

Sarrazin, Mme, must comb, herself, ii. 361

—— wore, ii. 318, iii. 452

tie, Sandwich wears, ii. 561

tied, physicians wear, viii. 71

Tyrawley's, from Paris, v. 191

vast, Brown, Sir Robert, sells, in Venice, ix. 609n

Walpole, Horatio (1678–1757), snatches off, iii. 169

Walpole, Robert, buys, from Wilkins, i. 506

white, old gallants wear, ii. 501

white with four tails, Skinner wears, vii. 238

See also Periwig

Wight, Isle of. *See* Isle of Wight

Wilbraham, Randle (? 1695–1770), M.P.; Deputy Steward of Oxford University:
Balmerinoch seeks, as counsel, iii. 287

Wilcocks, Joseph (1673–1756), Bp of Gloucester, 1721, of Rochester, 1731:
fit for nothing but death, ii. 201

York archbishopric predicted for, ii. 201

York archbishopric refused by, ii. 203n

Wilcox. *See* Wilcocks

Wilczek, Johann Joseph (1738–1819), Austrian minister to Tuscany:
Petraia occupied by, vii. 296

rank of, vii. 293

Wildair, Sir Harry. *See under* Farquhar, George: *Constant Couple*

Wilhelm (1682–1760), Landgrave of Hesse-Cassel 1730–60:
army command given to, i. 345

Wilhelm (1741–2), of Hesse-Cassel:
birth of, i. 255

Wilhelm (1743–1821), Landgrave of Hesse-Cassel, 1785; Elector of Hesse-Cassel, 1803:
Orford, Cts of, fondles, iii. 70

Wilhelmine Amalie (1673–1742), of Brunswick-Lüneburg, m. (1699) Joseph I, Holy Roman Emperor, 1705:
mourning for, i. 392, 433

Wilkes, John (1727–97), politician:
absent from presentation of new London remonstrance, vii. 216

addresses to constituents dated by, from Newgate, vii. 82

alderman for ward of Farringdon Without, vii. 81

alderman's dignity may have lulled, into prudence, vii. 208

alderman's post wanted by, vii. 206

always revives from his embers, viii. 45

Amherst and Christian VII eclipse, vii. 58

amnesty unlikely for, vi. 305

appeal of, to constituents, vii. 37

associates of, quarrel with one another, vii. 297

at end of his reckoning, vii. 270

at top of the wheel, viii. 55

attorney-general asked by, for writ of error, vii. 12

Augusta, Ps of Wales, abused by, vii. 340n

banishment of, silences Temple, vi. 290

Beauchamp asked by, to deliver message in Florence, vi. 281–2

Beckford was political firebrand instead of, vii. 223

Berlin and Italy to be visited by, vi. 272

Botta criticizes Lorenzi's attentions to, vi. 282

Brentford election kept quiet by, vii. 6

Bull in election with, viii. 48

Burke's and Saville's martyrdoms more respectable than that of, vii. 170

chamberlain of London, viii. 535

Chastellux known by, at Paris, vii. 28

—— talks with, in King's Bench Prison, vii. 28

Chief Justice abused by, in speech, vii. 12–13

Choiseul has probably tampered with, vii. 143

Churchill dies during visit to, at Calais, vi. 261

[Wilkes, John, *continued*]

——'s death deprives, of materials of history, vi. 281

——'s works to be edited by, vi. 261, 292

conversation and writing of, praised, vi. 136

Conway's defence of, results in his own dismissal, vi. 238n

Court of Aldermen set aside election of, vii. 84

Court of Common Pleas delivers, though Court of King's Bench may prosecute him, vi. 137

cries in favour of, at opening of Parliament, vii. 167

Croÿ discusses English freedom of speech with, vi. 137

Drury Lane Theatre club attended by, vi. 185

dull in Parliament, vi. 136

Dun threatens, vi. 189

ear-cropping may be punishment of, vi. 183

English liberties upheld by, vii. 81

English must see unworthiness of, vii. 122

English should chastise, vii. 239

Éon's 'father,' vi. 262

Essay on Woman: HW has never seen, though it lies in House of Lords, vi. 194–5; House of Lords to try, vi. 199; Mann surprised at failure to reprint, vi. 204; Mann wants copy of, vi. 192; March encourages Kidgell to inform against, vii. 73n; published by Kidgell, vi. 187; Sandwich denounces, in House of Lords, vi. 184–5; Wilkes reads, to Sandwich and Le Despenser, vi. 185

fails to appear before House of Commons, vi. 198

fame of, would never have been predicted, vii. 152

Forbes challenges, in Paris, vi. 162–3, 170, 174–5

foreign gazettes make much of affair of, vii. 80

forgotten, vii. 120

France preferred by, to martyrdom, vi. 194

French endure presence of, though he abused them in print, vi. 272

friends of, in House of Commons, petition against Luttrell, vii. 114–15

George III defeated by, ix. 565

—— lodges complaint against, in Parliament, vi. 182

—— orders Temple to remove, from militia of Buckinghamshire, vi. 138

——'s closet might be entered by, vii. 317

ghost of, in a sea of claret and port, vii. 5

Glynn, counsel and nominee of, vii. 30, 78

Gordon riots handled by, with zeal and spirit, ix. 63

grazier said to have left money to, vi. 281

HW asked by mob if he is for, vii. 194

HW asks about activities of, in Rome, vi. 290

HW calls: 'Alderman Catiline,' vii. 82; 'St Beelzebub,' vii. 170

HW compares: with Jack Cade, viii. 536; with Masaniello, vii. 317, viii. 535; with Rienzi, vii. 8, viii. 536; with Sacheverell, vi. 263, 360; with Vernon, vii. 8

HW could convince, that Bute wanted to become pope, vii. 92

HW glad that Methodism was not embraced by, vii. 87

HW hints to Choiseul's friend that Pitt might be restored by, vii. 143

HW sees, in hackney chair, vii. 5

handbills by, vii. 77

Harley opposes, vii. 6, 13

Holland House gives public breakfast to support Luttrell against, ix. 11

Horne disputes with, vii. 263, 274, 314

Houghton collection recommended by, to Parliament for purchase, viii. 304

House of Commons and City of London embroiled over, vii. 279

House of Commons did not dare to allow, to appear before them, vii. 303

House of Commons expels, vi. 183, 199; vii. 86, 97

House of Commons summons, before bar, vii. 73, 84, 281

House of Commons to choose Luttrell instead of, vii. 105

House of Lords argues writs of error of, vii. 83

House of Lords refuses to hear, vii. 77

Italy to be visited by, vi. 263

Junius papers ascribed to, vii. 248, 339

King's Bench Court commits, vii. 19, 22

King's Bench Court may fine or imprison, vii. 8

King's Bench Court tries, in Westminster Hall, vii. 11–13, 29

King's Bench Prison entered by, vii. 19, 28

ladies eclipse, vii. 92

legal punishment difficult to apply to such mob heroes as, vii. 143–4

letters of, to Middlesex electors and to his ward, vii. 213

London city banquets and sermons attended by, vii. 208

London election defeats, vii. 5–6

London, Middlesex, and Westminster politically controlled by, viii. 45

London visited by, when Parliament dissolved, vii. 5

Lord Mayor's election won by, viii. 45, 48

Lorenzi and Botta discuss coming visit of, with Mann, vi. 282

Louis XVI may be French equivalent of, viii. 62

Luttrell takes place of, in House of Commons, vii. 344

manifestos by, against House of Commons, vii. 205

Mann amazed at defiance of, vi. 200

—— asks how often House of Commons can reject, after his election, vii. 96, 110

—— glad of anything that draws attention away from, vii. 138

—— glad to hear that release of, produced no crisis, vii. 213

—— hopes, will never sit in House of Commons, vii. 96

—— hopes that flight of, will end controversies, vi. 203

—— hopes that Parliament will humble, vii. 296

—— impatient for sequel to affair of, vii. 16

—— not surprised by political shifts of, ix. 23

—— pleased by disappointment of, vii. 88

—— satisfied with behaviour of, in Florence, vi. 281

Mansfield threatened by *North Briton* for persecuting, vii. 28

March, Sandwich, and Temple demanded by, at bar of House of Commons, vii. 73–4, 77

Martin's duel with, vi. 183–4, 192, 198

—— told by, that Paris visit is just to see his daughter, vi. 198

masquerader dresses as, vii. 193

memorials by, in newspapers, vii. 339

Middlesex elects, vii. 6–7, 86, 97, 104–5, viii. 51

Middlesex sheriffs summon, vii. 475

mistress supposed to have robbed, vi. 305

mob of, does damage, vii. 6–7

mob tries to carry, from prison to Parliament, vii. 20

Mountmorres and Mahon defeated as Westminster candidates of, viii. 51

Naples visited by, to write history, vi. 281, 292, 305

never mentioned but in debates on Middlesex election, vii. 186

North Briton: Bute's conduct may justify, vi. 396; Bute will furnish matter for further issues of, vi. 402; condemned to be burnt, but rescued by mob at Cheapside, vi. 187–8; Finch, Lady Charlotte, will not be abused by, vi. 72; Forbes objects to, vi. 162; George III lodges complaint against Wilkes for, vi. 182; George III, with D. of Gloucester and D. of Cumberland, attacked by, vi. 165; HW encloses, from magazine, vi. 196; HW will have copy of, made for Mann, vi. 194; Junius's attacks exceed, vii. 165; Mann thanks HW for, vi. 204; Mann wants copy of, vi. 192; Mansfield threatened by, for persecution of Wilkes, vii. 28; riot over burning of, considered to be a revolution, vi. 200, 209; Russians unlikely to waste time imi-

tating writings of, vi. 60; Sandwich's writings as libellous as, vi. 323; Solicitor-General cannot prove Wilkes to be author of, vi. 189; Vergy's French imitation of, vi. 262; *Whisperer* and *Parliamentary Spy* more virulent than, vii. 196; Wilkes sent to Tower because he accused Bute in, of making George III tell a lie, vi. 136; Wilkes writes, against Bute, vi. 60n

Paoli might join, vii. 142

papers of, said to be illegally seized, vi. 207

Paris visited by, vi. 198, 365

Parliamentary representation wished by, to be reformed, viii. 187

Parliamentary seat to be demanded by, vii. 206

Parliament debates over legality of seizing papers of, vi. 207

Parliament's ending may deprive, of opportunity to vent his rage, vii. 214

Parliament would be controlled by, if Pitt or Rockingham dissolved it, vii. 181

party of: squabbles over Lord Mayor's appointment, vii. 520; strangely crumbled, vii. 208

Pitt and Grenville quarrel with, in print, vii. 163

Pitt attacks, vii. 251

printer released by, vii. 280

public speaking not the field of, vii. 86

Pynsent's bequest not believed by, vi. 281

release of, from prison, vii. 205

remonstrance presented by, to throne, in good form, viii. 89

ridiculous, vii. 246, 251

rigour against, ill-advised, vii. 86

riots allegedly fomented by, vii. 26

riots in favour of, vi. 187–8

Rome visited briefly by, vi. 292

Sayre a sheriff under, viii. 138

Scots oppose, vii. 8, 99, 317n

Scots put different meaning on '45' than that of, vii. 30

search of secretaries of state's houses demanded by, vi. 138

sentence of: considered mild by Mann, vii. 37; does not arouse mob's sympathy, vii. 33

sent to Tower because of *North Briton* No. 45, vi. 136

sheriff of London, vii. 314, 317, 360

Stanhope, Sir William, intimate with, at Naples, vi. 292

star of, dimmed, vii. 194

subscription for benefit of, vii. 92

successor will be named by, for Middlesex, vii. 82

supporters of Bill of Rights not approved by, vii. 114

Talbot fights, for abuse, vi. 137, 163

Tanucci neglects, at Naples, vi. 292

Temple friend of, vi. 138, 304

[Wilkes, John, *continued*]
——'s reconciliation with Halifax and Sandwich will interest, vi. 303–4
to appear before bar of House of Commons, vii. 82
too worthless to keep mob's respect, vii. 15
Townshend contends with, for Middlesex election, viii. 47
unpopular at Buckingham House, vi. 159
'virtue' of, more popular than Pitt's eloquence, vii. 163
Warburton's speech against, vi. 185
Westminster seat may be filled by nominee of, vii. 206
Weymouth's letter sent by, to printer, vii. 77
will be harmless in House of Commons, vii. 8
Wilmot upholds verdict against, vii. 83
Winckelmann said to have left gold medals to, vii. 113
witticism by: at Calais to Cröy on liberty of the press, vi. 137; on Lord George Germain, viii. 187
Wood prosecuted by, in Court of Common Pleas, vi. 188
wound of: prevents his appearing before House of Commons, vi. 198; recovers, vi. 186
writs of error of, to be tried before House Lords, vii. 83
Wilkes, Mary (1750–1802):
father goes to Paris just to see, vi. 198
Wilkes. *See also* Wilks
Wilkins, ——:
Walpole, Sir Robert, buys wig of, i. 506
Wilkinson, Capt. Andrew (d. 1785), of the *Glasgow*:
L'Oiseau's engagement with, v. 292
Tuscans complain about, v. 288
Wilkinson, Anne (1738–1803), m. (1771) Thomas Pitt, cr. (1784) Bn Camelford:
courier sent by, to husband at Naples, viii. 486
husband takes, to Italy, viii. 411
messenger of, delivers Mann's letters to HW, viii. 498
Wilkinson, John, M.D.; F.R.S., 1764:
marine belt of, vi. 332
Wilkinson, Pinckney (?1693–1784); M.P.:
son-in-law takes, to Italy, viii. 411
Wilkinson, Mrs William. *See* Amphlett, Christina
Wilks, Samuel, examiner of East India Correspondence:
Sykes brings, as witness, vii. 452
Will; wills:
Court of Chancery often sets aside, vi. 578
gratitude not to be expected from beneficiaries of, viii. 27
Mann astonished that lawyers so readily undertake to break, viii. 30

questioning of, disliked by HW, ix. 123
Spanish officers make, i. 427
Thomond cannot bring himself to make, viii. 25
Willemstad:
English army may escape by, ii. 457
Willes, Edward (ca 1693–1773), D.D.; Bp of St David's, 1742, of Bath and Wells, 1743: 'decipherer,' i. **279**
Exeter bishopric desired by, i. 279–80
Walpole, Sir Robert, supports, i. 280
Willes, Edward (1723–87), M.P.; judge of the Court of King's Bench:
Wilkes appears before, vii. 12
Willes, Sir John (1685–1761), Kt, 1737, Chief Justice of Common Pleas; M.P.:
becomes commissioner of the Great Seal, iv. 25
Buckingham Assizes Bill aims at, x. 27–8
court martial's dispute with, iii. 328
Grenvilles oppose, over Buckingham assizes, iii. 470–1
insurrections suppressed by, iv. 585
lawyers' army led by, iii. 180
lord chancellor's post refused by, iii. 212
on circuit, ii. 25
Walpole, Sir Robert, entrusts daughter to, x. 28
—— visited by, at Houghton, ii. 25
Willes, John (? 1721–84), M.P.:
Pelham's speech against father answered by, iii. 471
Willes. *See also* Wills
William, P. *See* William IV; William Augustus (1721–65); William Frederick (1776–1834); William Henry (1743–1805)
William I (the Conqueror) (1027–87), K. of England 1066–87:
Clinton title dates from time of, ii. 126
William III (1650–1702), K. of England 1688–1702:
Argyll and Cobham promoted by, x. 14
counsel for accused prisoners authorized in reign of, iii. 396
England's conquest by, not repeated in Nassau's attack on Jersey, viii. 472
factions bribed by, ix. 605
France threatened by, with Courtenay's claims, iii. 310
France to be humbled by, ix. 605
HW remembered half the remaining Court of, ix. 558
HW ridicules alleged virtues of reign of, ix. 605
Halifax's poem on the Boyne mentions, ii. 266
Hamilton gets retort from, about Scotland, iii. 103
health drunk to memory of, at Leghorn, iii. 152
Kelly confined in Tower since plot against, iii. 153n
naval operations in reign of, v. 223

Rochford and Grantham not allowed by: to take Nassau name, viii. 360; to use Nassau arms, viii. 370
Seymour, Sir Edward, retorts to, about D. of Somerset, ii. 523
Shebbeare writes against, v. 39n
Tamerlane acted on birthday of, iii. 333
William IV (1765–1837), K. of England 1830–7:
father requests provision for, viii. 371
Garter given to, ix. 273
Leghorn may be visited by, ix. 590
peerage withheld from, ix. 684
sails from England to Mediterranean, ix. 590
William I (1533–84), P. of Orange:
(?) witticism by, about fancies of unmarried girls and unmilitary men, viii. 414
William IV (1711–51), P. of Orange 1732–51; Stadtholder, 1747:
authority of, tottering, iv. 279
Burdett discovers alleged plot against, iv. 20
Cumberland, D. of, may be envied by, iii. 346
death of: iv. 279, 283, 285; postpones English festivities, iv. 280
health of: Aix waters taken, iv. 279; imposthume in head, iv. 283
Holland prevented by, from accepting neutrality, iii. 408
Karl Friedrich nephew of, iv. 148
made Stadtholder, iii. 394, 408
Mann had expected achievements from, iii. 408
Walpole, Horatio (1723–1809) describes court of, iii. 418
William V (1748–1806), P. of Orange 1751–95; Stadtholder:
Austria, Prussia, and France might limit, to a little kingdom near The Hague, ix. 539
birth of, iii. 469
blue ribbon conferred on, iv. 311
William, merchant vessel:
(?) capture of, v. 264
William and Mary, yacht:
Calais visited by, to await Lady Cardigan, i. 141
Italian singers visit, i. 141
William Augustus (1721–65), D. of Cumberland:
Aberdeen occupied by, iii. 228
Aberdeen station of, while awaiting supplies, iii. 233
'affronted,' vi. 303
aide-de-camps of: accompany him to Edinburgh, iii. 204; accompany him to Hulst, iii. 395
Albemarle (Bury) a favourite of, iv. 269, 460, vi. 94n, 366n
—— aide-de-camp to, iii. 177, 204, 218
—— escorted by, at Windsor, iv. 460
—— lord of the Bedchamber to, iv. 74n, 459n
Albemarle, Ds of, congratulated by, in Drawing-Room, vi. 94
alderman's witticism on butcheries of, iii. 288
Amelia, Ps, and Francis III discuss corpulency of, iv. 57
army adores, iii. 174, 204
army applications to come through, iii. 302
army command resigned by, v. 145
army left by, ii. 327
army of: Boyd in, iii. 285; in Netherlands, iii. 389; of observation in Hanover, v. 73; to be joined by him, ii. 217; to be led against rebels, iii. 166–7; to meet at Stone, iii. 173
assistants of, iii. 19–20
Augusta, Ps of Wales, urges, to linger on George III's wedding night, v. 530
Austrian appointment of P. Charles in Flanders offends, iii. 288
baggage of, returned from Scotland, iii. 242
Bath, E. of, may want to injure, iii. 347
Bedford, D. of, supported by, iv. 113, 201
—— visited by, at Woburn, iv. 89
Bedford faction favoured by, iv. 120, 207
birthday of, i. 398
Braddock's slowness irritates, iv. 492
brave: at Fontenoy, iii. 44; at Hastenbeck, v. 119; at Laeffeld, iii. 426
Breda revisited by, iii. 446
brother-in-law may envy, iii. 346
brother not imitated by, v. 145
Carlisle captured by, iii. 193
Charles, P., may be replaced by, in Flanders, iii. 324
Charlotte given away by, at wedding, v. 529
Constitutional Queries attacks, iv. 222, 234
Conway aide-de-camp to, iii. 26, 177, 204, 218
Conway and Hawley sent by, iii. 179
Conway told by, that ministers seek to prevent his going to Scotland, iii. 204
corpulence of, ii. 268, iv. 49, 57, 121, 208–9, v. 432
Court would not get much quarter from, vi. 102
Cromarty receives rents of, iii. 284
Culloden laurels of, iii. 246–9
Culloden news sent by, iii. 247
Danish princess supposed to marry, iii. 20
death of: vi. 363–4; announced in Leyden gazette, vi. 370; rumoured, vi. 256
defeat of: irretrievable, v. 125; rumoured, iii. 253
Dettingen behaviour of, praised, ii. 258, 259, 279
disappointments of, in the Low Countries, iii. 409

[William Augustus, *continued*]
 discipline of, strict, iii. 464
 Douglas, 'Mother,' calls, 'Great Sir,' iii. 52
 drums and trumpets enjoyed by, iii. 20
 'Duke of Wales' the nickname of, iii. 52n
 Dunmore subordinate to, iii. 20
 Dutch perform orders of, iii. 346
 Edinburgh insults, iii. 288
 Edinburgh to be visited by, on way to relieve Stirling Castle, iii. 204
 Elibank to be sued by, iii. 284
 England expects return of, iii. 255–6, 271, 442, 495
 England reached by, v. 144
 English habit worn by, at masquerade, iv. 49
 falls down at ball, iv. 121
 Fawkener secretary to, iii. 26, 382n, 456n
 fireworks watched by, iv. 48
 Flemish campaign may be conducted by, iii. 240
 Florentines condemn, i. 360
 Fontenoy defeat must mortify, iii. 42
 —— makes, as popular with men as he is with low women, iii. 52
 Fortrose with, iii. 233
 Fox attached to, iv. 224, 412
 —— breaks with, vi. 102, 134
 —— favoured by, v. 93n
 —— urged by, to remain Secretary at War, iv. 39
 France sends seasoned troops against, v. 94
 Frederick II must be envied by, v. 432
 French army approached by, v. 117
 French defeat, at Hastenbeck, v. 119
 French enmity to, used as excuse to thrash French actor, ii. 305
 French landing to be prevented by, iii. 187
 Garter of, to go to Albemarle, vi. 366
 generalissimo's post makes, happy, iii. 19–20
 George II accompanies, at his Parliament entrance, i. 398
 —— believes, to be paying his own expenses, iv. 373
 —— might recall, if Young Pretender proved to be a sham, iii. 174, 199
 —— orders, to sign Kloster-Zeven Convention, but disavows it, v. 136n
 —— receives, badly, v. 145
 —— said to give Hanover to, at instance of Parliament and P. of Wales, i. 328
 ——'s bequests to, v. 450
 ——'s gifts of jewels and money to, v. 450
 —— to be accompanied by: to Flanders, ii. 62; to Hanover, ii. 209
 George III compliments, on Albemarle's success, vi. 94
 —— gives Bath ribbon of, to second son, vi. 578
 —— grants offices to friends of, vi. 307
 —— hates, vi. 364
 —— names, captain general, vi. 302

 —— omits, from Regency, vi. 295
 —— said to be disliked by, vi. 163
 ——'s attentions to, v. 443, 449
 ——'s regency plans opposed by, vi. 299
 —— unites with, in hating ministers, vi. 364
 Granville's and Bolton's appointments probably distasteful to, iv. 207
 Great Wardrobe furnishes the Palace for, iv. 373
 HW compliments, in epilogue to *Tamerlane*, iii. 351
 HW mentions, iv. 292
 HW played with, at Leicester House, in childhood, ix. 647
 HW talks with, at masquerade, i. 359
 Hague, The, visited by, iii. 68
 Hanover to be administered by, iv. 249
 Hanover to be visited by, to command army of observation, v. 73, 78
 Hawley and Braddock please, by their brutality, iv. 492
 Hawley the favourite general and executioner of, iv. 73
 health drunk to, at Leghorn, iii. 152
 health of: declining, vi. 288; erysipelas, vi. 256; ill, ii. 279; salivation needed, iii. 483; shivering fit, ii. 268; stroke of the palsy, v. 432; wound in leg, ii. 258, 268, 340, v. 432
 Hervey's conduct praised by, x. 30
 Hervey, Felton, groom of the Bedchamber to, ii. 69n
 Holland to be visited by, iii. 464
 Holland visited by, iii. 340, 351
 Hulst secretly visited by, before its surrender, iii. 395
 Inverness occupied by, iii. 247
 Jacobites claim to have wounded, iii. 261
 Keppel, Hon. William, aide-de-camp to, iv. 459
 Kilmarnock falsely charged by, iii. 299–300
 Kloster-Zeven convention concluded by, with Richelieu, v. 136n
 Könisegg serves, iii. 19–20
 Laeffeld battle fought by, iii. 423–4
 Ligonier to be subordinate to, iii. 20, 167
 limps, ii. 340
 London may give honours to, iii. 288
 London saved by, from rebel army, iii. 178
 Lyttelton collects depositions against, iv. 240
 —— ill-treated by, iv. 33
 Mann admires philosophy of, vi. 291
 —— asked by, for map of Rome, iv. 459
 —— cheered by expulsion of rebels from England by, iii. 214
 —— hopes, will subdue Scotland, iii. 205, 257
 —— hopes for military success by, v. 96
 —— hopes that rebels will be terrified by, iii. 218

—— questions tactics of, at Hastenbeck, **v.** 146

—— would have given half his share of Leghorn toasts to, iii. 151

Mann, James, favoured by, v. 50

Mary, Ps, to visit, iii. 295

Mathews's cockade arouses curiosity of, ii. 522

military experience sought by, iii. 39

Mingotti favoured by, iv. 557

minority led by, in House of Lords, vi. 187

Münchhausen rebuked by, v. 145

Mutiny Bill receives vote of, iv. 38

name of, disperses armies, iii. 209, 213

Newcastle, D. of, at odds with, iv. 120

—— sees troop review prepared by, iii. 495

——'s followers will desert to, v. 93

Newmarket gambling led by, iv. 373

Newmarket visited by, vi. 288, 297

nose-blowing forbidden under windows of, iii. 464

Old Pretender survives, vi. 404

omnipotent, but uses nothing but machines, iv. 417

opera house taken by, iv. 557

Opposition might be countenanced by, iv. 300

Opposition persuaded by, to form ministry, vi. 310

(?) Orford, Cts of, disapproves of German campaign of, v. 96

Parliamentary debates expose arbitrary conduct of, iv. 33

Parliament entered by, i. 398

peace negotiations to be watched by, iii. 446

Pelham gets ordnance for, iv. 120

Pitt confers with, iv. 102

—— rejects proposals of, to form ministry, vi. 302

—— wants, to be head of army, vi. 161

Pitt, Mrs George, loved by, iv. 58

Portuguese princess mentioned as wife for, v. 341–2

Poyntz family aided by, iv. 208

Poyntz governor of, iii. 242n, iv. 208, vi. 163n

—— treasurer of, iii. 242n

Pringle discusses Galfridus Mann's illness with, iv. 529

—— physician to, iv. 525, 529

prisoners taken by, iii. 274

Prussian princess may wed, ii. 62

Ranelagh attended by, i. 434

rebels awaited by, at Stone, iii. 178

rebels do not forgive, iii. 296

rebels flee from, iii. 208–9, 239

rebels pursued by, iii. 185, 197, 213, 222

recalled, v. 136, 150

Regency Bill opposed by, iv. 249, 263

Regency controlled by, iv. 491

Regency includes, iv. 483

Regency said to be headed by, iv. 125

Remembrancer attacks, iv. 73

resentment of, complicates debate over Regency Bill, vi. 299

return of, from Scotland awaited, iii. 255–6, 271

rewards for, iii. 255–6

Richmond says that his children will precede grandchildren of, iii. 20

——'s masquerade attended by, vi. 149

Rivett, friend and manager of, iv. 19

Rochford, Cts of, loved by, iv. 58

Sackville sent by, to Saxe about Maestricht siege, iii. 481

Sandwich gives ball for, iv. 121

—— supported by, iv. 201

Scotland hates, iii. 288

Scotland rather than London may be destination of, iii. 193

Scotland the station of, in the rebellion, iii. 271, 273, 288, 382n, iv. 240

Scottish bill ignored by, iv. 311

Scottish disloyalty criticized by, iii. 228

scouting party sent out by, iii. 233

severity of, to rebels, iii. 288

Stade route followed by, to Hanover, v. 78

Stade the ill-judged refuge of, v. 146

Townshend, Hon. George, aide-de-camp to, turns against him, iv. 33

unpopularity of: iv. 240, 243, 322; keeps him from being regent, iv. 249

Vaneschi disputes with, over opera house, iv. 557

Waldeck at odds with, iii. 428–9

Wales, P. of, receives visit of, iii. 288

weight of, subject of wager and law suit, iv. 208–9

Wilson, Nanny, mistress to, iii. 52n

York, D. of, would precede, in prayers for royal family, v. 449

William Frederick (1776–1834), 2d D. of Gloucester, 1805:

Bayreuth, Margrave of, godfather to, viii. 181

birth of: viii. 171–2; announced to HW, viii. 178; authenticated, viii. 172; may drive Lady Mary Coke to Bedlam, viii. 179

christened at Rome, in presence of English colony, viii. 181

descendant of both HW and George I, ix. 248

father asks Margrave of Bayreuth to be godfather to, viii. 171

father essential to welfare and happiness of, viii. 329

father's plight may arouse sympathy for, viii. 321

George III demands provision for, viii. 372, 376

HW and D. of Gloucester will probably not prefer, to sister, viii. 302

HW sees, at Gloucester House, ix. 68

health of: inoculated, ix. 203; teeth cut, viii. 315; well, viii. 171–2, 181

[William Frederick, *continued*]

Leopold sees, viii. 297

Mann kisses, viii. 306

—— sees, in mother's arms, viii. 297

—— to be called on by, viii. 291

mother would have trouble in travelling with, if father died, viii. 326

pretty boy, viii. 332

Ranelagh visited by, ix. 68

William Henry (1743–1805), cr. (1764) D. of Gloucester:

accounts of, from Rome, are favourable, viii. 179

Adair and Jebb may enable, to finish his journey, viii. 329

Albani's villa left by, for Rome, viii. 247–8

Albano to be summer home of, at Albani's house, viii. 214

Aldobrandini villa to be occupied by, viii. 190

Ansbach visited by, ix. 413n

attendants of: have no confidence in Mann, vii. 370; impertinent to Mann, vii. 377; unworthy, vii. 357, 364, 384; vainly try to regain Mann's favour, vii. 384

baggage of, goes by sea to England, vii. 407

balls frequented by, v. 67

Bayreuth, Margrave of, asked by, to be godfather to child, viii. 171

Bernis gives dinner for, vii. 389

birth of, ii. **341**, 358

Boltons to give ball for, ix. 22

Bordeaux voyage may be undertaken by, viii. 360

Bracciano, Duca di, entertains, at concert, vii. 388

Caroline Matilda's disgrace must distress, vii. 384

Carpenter, Lady Almeria, probably caused Horace Mann II's rebuff from, ix. 638

Cato acted by, v. 327

character of, to be respected, vii. 361

Charlotte led by, to wedding, v. 529

Charlton the surgeon of, vii. 334

children of, to be inoculated before leaving England, viii. 82

Cholmondeley accompanies, from Genoa, vii. 335

—— attends, to Florence, vii. 353

——'s rudeness to Mann caused by that of, vii. 395

—— tells Mann to tell Leopold of plans of, to revisit, Florence, vii. 397

—— to accompany, throughout tour, vii. 343, 349, 370

—— told by, to visit Florence, vii. 337

—— totally attached to, vii. 357

Christine meets, at public places only, viii. 190

Clement XIV invites, to Rome, and tells nuncio to court him, vii. 343, 348

——'s hospitality to, vii. 388–9

—— talks with, in Monte Cavallo garden, vii. 389

Coke, Lady Mary, disapproves of marriage of, vii. 530, 538, viii. 179n

confidence of, in air of Rome, not shared by many, viii. 84

constitution of, always alarming, viii. 350

consuls visited by, at Genoa and Leghorn, vii. 347

courier sent by, to Mann, vii. 331

Court attendance denied to, vii. 433, 437

Court intrigues avoided by, ix. 140

court of, numerous, ix. 22

(?) Covent Garden play attended by, vi. 199

Cumberland, D. and Ds of, may be ill-received by foreign courts because of misbehaviour of, vii. 502

Cumberland, D. of, distresses, by marriage, vii. 395

—— may not be known by, to have married, vii. 355

—— should not involve, in his politics, viii. 74

daughter doted on by, viii. 86

daughter will probably be preferred by, to son, viii. 302, 306

death of: expected, vii. 374; might have occasioned his wife's, viii. 144; rumoured from Venice, viii. 136; rumoured in London, vii. 343–4; twice falsely announced in newspapers, ix. 623

desires to be home, vii. 377

Dick lodges, at Leghorn, vii. 332, 335, 347

—— notified by, through Rainsford, of marriage, vii. 437

—— often seen by HW since return of, viii. 335

—— preferred by, to Mann, as companion, vii. 395

—— promised Bath knighthood by, but George III can no longer be asked for it, viii. 85

dukedom and allowance conferred upon, vi. 264

England reached by, viii. 332

England to be destination of, to avoid Italian heat, viii. 311

England to be revisited by, viii. 314

English at Rome attentive to, viii. 190

English packets for, all pass through Mann's hands, vii. 370

English people in France shun, viii. 125

English travellers admitted to kiss the hand of, viii. 163

equerries, Cholmondeley, Lee, and Jervis accompany, to Florence, vii. 353

equerries of, *see also* Heywood; Rainsford essential to daughter's, son's, and wife's welfare, viii. 329

family may be taken by, to southern France, viii. 76

Ferdinand of Naples and republic of Lucca invite, vii. 348

fireworks watched by, iv. 48
Florence avoided by, viii. 174, ix. 675
Florence to be visited by, viii. 290, 290–1, 298, 312
Florence visited by, vii. 353, 405, viii. 290–1, 296–8
foreign trip of, delayed until he is too ill to travel, viii. 74
France pays great attentions to, viii. 125
Frederick II declines offer by, of army service, viii. 401, 404, 407, 409, 411
Friedrich II of Hesse exchanges visits with, viii. 275
Garter conferred on, vi. 37
Garter installation of, at Windsor, vi. 79
Geneva visited by, on way to Italy, ix. 314
Genoa visited by, vii. 331–2, 347, ix. 628, 638
George III and Rockingham promise increased allowance to, vi. 424–5, 428
George III demands provision for children of, viii. 372, 376
—— does not require, to remarry, vii. 484
—— notified by, of marriage, vii. 433, 437
—— omits, from Regency, vi. 295
—— reconciled with, ix. 62–3, 65
—— rejoices at recovery of, vii. 347
——'s affection for, vii. 437
——'s attitude aggravates illness of, x. 50
——'s brotherly letter cures, viii. 326
—— sends Adair and Jebb to attend, vii. 356
——'s kind letter answered by, with his own hand, viii. 329
——'s kind messages will relieve broken heart of, viii. 323
Giustiniani called on by, to thank him for civilities to D. of York, vii. 287
Gore family neighbours of, at Castel Gandolfo, viii. 251
great ladies of Rome do not altogether please, viii. 247
HW advises, to submit entirely to George III, vii. 434
HW begs Mann not to entertain, in Florence, ix. 624
HW believes that Cts Waldegrave is married to, vii. 302
HW calls, 'naturally obliging,' vii. 358
HW calls on, at the Pavilions, vii. 433–4
HW declines to convey Mann's invitation to, vii. 302
HW disliked by, vii. 404, 549
HW feels, should be out of England, viii. 117
HW has had no letters from, during his journey, viii. 148
HW hears of son's birth from, viii. 178
HW makes proper excuse for absence from, vii. 421
HW pleased by recovery of, vii. 349
HW restored to favour of, viii. 184

HW's cool relations with, caused by HW's disapproval of his marriage, vii. 434
HW sees, at Gloucester House, viii. 335, ix. 68
HW's failure to visit, may be resented, vii. 416–17
HW suggests Siena as winter residence for, viii. 125, 130
HW urges Mann to pay court to, viii. 125
HW vexed by rudeness of entourage of, to Mann, vii. 363–4
(?) HW wrote two letters to, to Venice, viii. 134
health of: alarms HW, vii. 361; almost well, viii. 332; asthma, vii. 303, 348, 355, 369, viii. 360, x. 50–1; better, vii. 375; bones, rattle in his skin, viii. 326; colic, vii. 332; cough, viii. 82, 86, 350, 360; diarrhœa, vii. 332, 334, 336, 342, 369; dysentery, viii. 314, 317, 319, 321, 322–3, 325–6; extremely well, viii. 117; fever, vii. 334; fever and bloody flux, viii. 135; flux, viii. 314; flux, bloody, vii. 336; good accounts of, vii. 377, viii. 329; grows fat, viii. 214; hæmorrhoids, x. 50; heats destroy, and damps bad for it, viii. 360; lame, viii. 335; Leghorn apothecary provides drugs for, vii. 393; Mann distrusts air of Rome for, viii. 84; mother's death and sister's disgrace do not injure, vii. 388; much better, vii. 384, 388; out of danger, vii. 336, 346–7, viii. 76, 140; out of order, viii. 350; perfect, viii. 190, 201, 214; permits journey to Rome, viii. 144; physicians fear effects of autumn campaign on, viii. 401; physicians slightly encouraged by, viii. 321, 322–3; probably improved by 'wholesome' illness, viii. 148; quite recovered, viii. 144; Rome fixed upon as favourable to, despite HW's dissuasion, viii. 130; seriously ill, ix. 677; shivering fits, viii. 76; small returns of his disorder, viii. 275; surgeon-page thinks, is past crisis, viii. 315; swelled legs, vii. 355, 369; swollen from groin to foot, viii. 326; syringe-baths for, vii. 334; ulcer suspected, in large intestine, vii. 337; Venice's heat and nauseous air affect, viii. 314; very ill, viii. 74; very well, viii. 170; well, viii. 163, 181
heart not sense lacked by, in mistreating Mann, vii. 500
Hertford presents Mann's offer to, but it is declined, vii. 302–3, 304
Heywood ought to have been civil to HW without knowledge of, vii. 429
household of, must be exhausted by fatigue and anxiety, viii. 319–20
house reserved for, in Rome, viii. 312
inn at Florence to be the home of, ix. 677
Italian capitals will probably be shunned by, lest monarchs be embarrassed by his wife, viii. 130–1
itinerary of: from Gibraltar to Leghorn,

[William Henry, *continued*]
vii. 294; from Naples, vii. 370; from Rome to England, viii. 252
Joseph II to meet, at Milan, viii. 331
Joseph II might have Leopold make Siena agreeable to, viii. 125
—— visited by, ix. 164
Kingston, Ds of, may be deterred from Rome by presence of, viii. 220
Lago di Garda to be visited by, for summer, viii. 291
Leghorn visited by, vii. 332-3, 333-7, 341-3, 347-9, 353, 393-4, 404, 405
Leopold asks, to get honours for Cowper, vii. 502
—— exchanges messages and visits with, viii. 291, 297-8
—— expected to meet, at Milan, viii. 331
—— informed by, at Vienna, about marriage, vii. 308
—— invited, to Florence, at Vienna, viii. 332
—— probably told by Vienna how to treat, viii. 129
——'s and Maria Louisa's social relations with, vii. 294, 304, 331, 332-3, 335, 342, 348, 352-3, 355-6, 357, 405, viii. 291, 297-8
letter from, to England, written in his own hand, viii. 141
lodge in New Forest visited by, viii. 360
Louis XVI invites, to Paris, viii. 125
Lucca invites, vii. 348
Luttrells' newspaper articles inflame George III against, viii. 77
Mann advises HW to call on, vii. 416-17, 421, 426-7, 437-8
—— afraid to inquire about, at Rome, viii. 181
—— asks HW to convey his gratitude to, viii. 352
—— called on by, when ill, viii. 291, 302
—— encouraged by efforts of, to hope for Bath Knighthood, vi. 314
—— gets gracious messages from, from Rome, viii. 170, 184, 201
—— has not asked if Italy will be revisited by, viii. 76
—— insists upon consultation with Italian physicians over health of, vii. 393
—— kisses hand of, vii. 336, 394
—— might have paid more attention to, in illness, viii. 141
—— moves furniture to Pisa for use of, vii. 342
—— offers coaches and theatre boxes to, viii. 291
—— prevented by gout from paying attentions to, at Florence, viii. 290
—— receives order from, to send him weekly gazette from Florence, viii. 396
——'s coaches seldom used by, vii. 395
——'s coolness from: attributed to bad attendants, viii. 297, 384; attributed to ill

health and family troubles, viii. 395-6; cancelled by warmth at Florence, viii. 297; caused by Dick, vii. 367, 404; changed graciously, vii. 405, viii. 247; unjustifiable, vii. 377
—— sends respects to, viii. 171, 247, 352, 376, 389
——'s house at Pisa arranged for occupancy by, vii. 342, 347-8, 358, 363-4, 377, 394-5
——'s name probably not mentioned by, to HW, viii. 453
——'s note from, announcing departure from Rome for Florence, viii. 291
——'s servants dismissed from, vii. 348, 394
——'s troublesome guest, vii. 500
—— tells nephew to pay respects to, at Rome, viii. 131
—— thanks, at Leghorn, for consenting to visit his Pisa house, vii. 347
—— told by: of value of a change of air, viii. 329; to expect visit from his wife and family, viii. 291, 297
—— wants HW to invite, to spend Florentine visit in his house, vii. 294
—— will heed HW's advice about behaviour to, viii. 131
—— will not give offence elsewhere by attentions to, viii. 290
—— will probably mention passage of, through Florence, viii. 163
Mann, Horace II, awaits, at Florence, ix. 676-7
—— cordially received by, at Rome, ix. 674
—— does not tell HW about rebuff from, ix. 637
—— received by, at Rome, viii. 163
—— receives regrets from, for rebuff at Genoa, ix. 674
—— repulsed by, at Genoa, ix. 628, 637, 638
Maria Louisa plays loo with, vii. 352
marriage of: v. 284n, vii. 537; announced, vii. 415; authenticated, vii. 483; declared to equerries, vii. 484; must make Parliamentary debate over Royal Marriage Bill very painful, vii. 396; *North Briton* attacks, vii. 165; not foreseen by Sir Robert Walpole, ix. 133; Royal Marriage Act caused by, ix. 629; unhappy, ix. 674; unwitnessed, vii. 484
Meek attends, vii. 337, 342
Milan visited by, ix. 628, 632
Molini attends, vii. 394
mother's illness must distress, vii. 355, 358, 377, 395
Naples visited by, vii. 336, 342, 348, 370, 375, 377, 384, ix. 675
Neapolitan and Roman experiences of, 'piteous,' vii. 405
newspapers call, 'D. of Lancaster,' vi. 264
nightgown worn by, when receiving Count Thurn, vii. 352

Orford, Cts of, did not like, when he was at Florence, viii. 175

—— graciously received by, viii. 170, 222

Padua visited by, viii. 135–6, 144, 314

'page-surgeon' attends, vii. 393, viii. 315

Pisa visited by, vii. 336, 342, 347–8, 352–3, 355, 356–7, 394–5, 404, 502

Pius VI courteous to, viii. 174, 190

—— pleased by gift from, of surgical instruments for hospital at Rome, viii. 129

Pleydell accompanies, viii. 311

plumper than when at Rome, viii. 332

Poggio Imperiale visited by, to see Tuscan grand ducal family, viii. 297

post-chaise used by, viii. 314

preparations and leave-takings by, for death, vii. 336

Quaker would not have been well-received by, viii. 53

quinze the favourite game of, vii. 356

Ranelagh visited by, ix. 68

return of, to England, strongly urged, viii. 252

Richmond's masquerade not attended by, vi. 148

Rochford has not told Mann how to behave to, in case of Florentine visit, viii. 129

Roman assemblies attended by, viii. 163

Roman nobility attentive to, viii. 174, 190

Romans insulted by, vii. 566

Roman visit of, deferred, vii. 357, 370, viii. 140, 141, 144

Rome approached by, though he seemed unlikely to want to revisit it, viii. 129

Rome considered by, the best winter residence, viii. 290

Rome to be visited by, vii. 384, viii. 82, 123, 130, ix. 618, 623

Rome visited by, vii. 396, 405, viii. 163–4, 170, 174, 181, 184, 186, 190, 201, 214, 222, 247, 252, 290, 291, 332, ix. 674

sails on frigate commanded by Jervis, vii. 353

St James's Palace to be home of, iv. 239

Saxony, Electress of, discusses Ds of Kingston with, viii. 25

secretary of state's office sends packets to, at Genoa, vii. 328

sister's disgrace will distress, vii. 384

son born to, viii. 171–2

son held by, for Mann to kiss, viii. 306

stepdaughters lodged by, at Hampton Court Park, viii. 315

Strasbourg the last place whence news of, reached HW, viii. 134

Switzerland to be visited by, viii. 123

takes proper exercise, viii. 163

Thurn received by, vii. 352

travels slowly in *vettura* from Rome to Florence, ix. 677

Trent visited by, viii. 314–15, 317, 319–20, 321, 322–3, 325, 329, 336–7, x. 50

Udny's letter about, viii. 311

Venetian ambassador's house at Lago di Garda may be taken by, for summer, viii. 290

Venice not to be visited by, viii. 252

Venice to be visited by, at Ascension, viii. 291

Venice visited by, viii. 125, 130, 134, 305, 314

Verona visited by, viii. 314

vingt-et-un played by, viii. 352

visitors not seen by, vii. 335

Viterbo entertainment of, vii. 388

votes in House of Lords, vi. 521

Waldegrave, Cts, escorted by, at Soho ball, dressed as Edward IV, vii. 193

Waldegrave, Lady Laura, given in marriage by, ix. 274

warm and hurt by indignities, viii. 125

Weymouth visited by, ix. 203

wife accepts Mann's urns with consent of, viii. 453

wife of, v. 240n, 284n

wife of, cannot persuade her father to call on him, vii. 461

wife told by, to travel home with his body, viii. 326

wife weeps but does not oppose martial schemes of, viii. 401

winter to be spent by, at Rome, viii. 82, 117

York, D. of, dying at Monaco, may be imitated by death of, at Leghorn, vii. 345

——'s memory highly regarded by, vi. 581

—— writes to: about making Mann a knight of the Bath, vi. 235, 241, 318, 581; a letter to be shown to George III, vi. 561

younger daughter of, dies after inoculation, viii. 86

Young Pretender met by, in Genoa street, vii. 343, 345

William, Charlotte (b. before 1780), m. —— Heaton; natural dau. of 5th D. of Devonshire:

Devonshire, D. of, said to be father of, ix. 444, 455

father pays Lady Elizabeth Foster to go to France with, ix. 459n

Foster, Lady Elizabeth, accompanies, at Florence, ix. 444

—— governess to, ix. 455, 459

Williams, Miss. *See* William, Charlotte

Williams, Benjamin, HW's printer:

(?) runs away, v. 300

Williams, Sir Charles Hanbury, (1708–59), K.B., 1744; diplomatist; author; M.P.:

Austrian minister and Russian minister negotiate with, iv. 186–7

Bath knighthood obtained by, despite Pelham's opposition, ii. 451

Bath visited by, ii. 104

Berlin post may be assigned to, iii. 341

Capuchin, The, HW transcribes, for Mann, ii. 71–3

[Williams, Sir Charles Hanbury, *continued*]
Country Girl, The: HW quotes, ii. 22–4;
Mann disparages, ii. 42
Country Maid, The, author of, ii. 48
daughter of, v. 53, 312n, 429n
Dresden to be station of, iii. 347
England revisited by, iv. 90, v. 53, 183
envoy to Prussia, iv. 51
epigram by, on Egmont's opposition to
Mutiny Bill, iv. 51
fashionable, iv. 198
Finch family called 'black, funereal,' in ode
by, v. 345n
Fox and Lady Caroline Lennox married at
house of, ii. 451
Fox's friend, ii. 90n, 451, v. 54n
—— wants, to go to Turin, iv. 16
granddaughter of, ix. 577
Hamburg lady (Mlle John) has affair with,
v. 183, 194
health of: aphrodisiac deranges, v. 183;
fever, v. 190; insanity suspected, v. 183,
190; venereal disease, ii. 104
Isabella, or the Morning, Leicester described
in, ix. 308n
Jamaica remittance agreement witnessed by,
i. 411
Labour in Vain: HW quotes, ii. 18–20;
Mann disparages, ii. 42
letters and verses of, admired, iv. 186
Mann dislikes appointment of, to Turin,
iii. 466
——'s praises heard by, in Germany, iv. 90
—— will prefer letters of, to Villettes', iii.
465
Mengs considered by, equal to Carlo Maratti, iv. 352
—— recommended by, to Mann, iv. 330–1,
352
ministry dislike, iv. 16
Montagu embroiled with, v. 53
New Ode, A: given false ending to hide its
authorship by, ii. 52n; HW transcribes, ii.
48–51; Mann likes, ii. 78
odes on Pulteney attributed to, ii. 70
Ode . . . to the Earl of Bath, An, HW
transcribes, ii. 73–5
Old Coachman, The: HW quotes, ii. 20–2;
Mann disparages, ii. 42
'Pandæmonium, The,' HW quotes, vii. 236
Parliamentary vote by, on privately-raised
regiments, x. 19
paymastership of marines resigned by, iii.
341
return of, from Russia, v. 53, 183
returns, on ill-success of Anglo-Russian
negotiations, v. 53
Secret Committee may examine, i. 411
1741 by, i. 346–7
Statesman, The, attributed to, ii. 90–1
Tesi ancient favourite of, v. 194
'To the Earl of Bath,': HW quotes, ii.
320–1; pleases Mann, ii. 334

Townshend, Vcts, discusses Anson with, iii.
13
Turin post may go to, iii. 347, 456, 465, 466
Winnington friend of, iii. 250
witticism by, on Pitt's resignation of Bedchamber, iii. 27
World contributions by, iv. 395n
Williams, Charlotte Hanbury (1738–90), m.
(1759) Hon. Robert Boyle Walsingham:
later Walsingham:
daughter of, ix. 577n
Williams, Edmund (d. 1752), Capt.:
investigation of, iii. 25, 32–3
Williams, Lady Frances. *See* Coningsby, Lady
Frances
Williams, Frances Hanbury (1735–59), m.
(1754) William Anne Holles Capel, 4th E.
of Essex:
ball given by, for D. of York, v. 53–4
death of, v. 312, 429
Lyttelton tells, not to meddle in politics,
v. 54
Rochford, Cts of, entertains, at ball, v. 57
York, D. of, attracted by, v. 53–4
—— object of song rendered by, v. 57
Williams, John, Piccadilly innkeeper:
Independents denounced by, iii. 387n
Independents should be prosecuted, for
beating, iii. 399
Williams, (?) John (d. before 1775):
HW sends letter to Mann through, i. 5
HW thanks Mann for civilities to, i. 12
Williams, Peter; inn-keeper; 'groom':
(?) Ferrers may have injured, v. 395
Williams, Sir William Peere (ca 1730–61); 2d
Bt, 1758; M.P.:
death of, v. 505
Williamson, Adam (1676 or 7 – 1747), Lt-Gen.;
deputy lieutenant of the Tower of London:
Balmerinoch ill-treated by, iii. 301
Lovat offers to marry his son to the niece
of, iii. 380
paper sent to, in behalf of rebel lords, iii.
286
Williamstadt. *See* Willemstad
Williams Wynn, Sir Watkin. *See under* Wynn
Willingmi, English ship:
Leghorn visited by, from Newfoundland,
viii. 246
Willington, [?Edward Pearce]; engineer:
captured by the French, viii. 476n
Willoughby de Broke, Bn. *See* Verney, John
(1738–1816)
Willoughby de Eresby, Bns. *See* Bertie, Lady
Priscilla Barbara Elizabeth (1761–1828)
Will-o-wisp:
peace compared to, vii. 255
Wills, Lt-Gen. Sir Charles (1666–1741), K.B.:
HW mentions, iv. 441
Wills, Haughton (ca 1710–82):
Mann sends medals through, to HW, v.
209, 215, 233

Wilmington, E. of. *See* Compton, Sir Spencer

Wilmot, Edward (1693–1786), cr. (1759) Bt; physician:
Frederick, P. of Wales, attended by, iv. 232
Pelham, Lady Catherine, saved by lancing by, v. 369

Wilmot, John (1647–80), 2d E. of Rochester:
HW 'transposes' lines by, ii. 482
wit of, would be approved only in one half-century, ix. 308

Wilmot, Sir John Eardley (1709–92), Kt, 1755; chief justice of common pleas 1766–71:
becomes commissioner of Great Seal, iv. 25
health of, will not let him accept Seals, vii. 175
Pratt succeeded by, as Chief Justice of Common Pleas, vi. 443
Seals may be thrust upon, vii. 179
verdict against Wilkes upheld by, vii. 83
Vergy makes deposition before, vi. 262

Wilson, Nanny:
Cumberland, D. of, takes, as his mistress from Drury Lane stage, iii. 52

Wilton, —— (senior):
son receives article from, iv. 392

Wilton, Joseph (1722–1803), sculptor:
Adventurer said to mention, iv. 395n
Capezzoli lives with, vii. 567
design submitted by, for Wolfe's tomb, v. 428
father of, sends him the article mentioning him, iv. 392
Inspector article praises, iv. 397
Mann encloses letters to, from two poor fathers, vi. 418
—— has, in his house, iv. 391
——'s correspondence with, iv. 520
sculpture by, iv. 397–8
World article thought by Mann to praise, iv. 392, 395, 397

Wilton:
bridge at, Pembroke designs, iv. 109
Pembroke the owner of, vi. 9
statues at, adorned with charcoal, ix. 178

Wiltshire:
Pynsent said to be from, vi. 276
to present petition, vii. 132

Wilzeck. *See* Wilczek

Wimpole, Cambs, Hardwicke's seat:
Hardwicke may retire to, iv. 202

Wimpsey, Joseph, banker:
bankruptcy of, vii. 426

Winchelsea, ship:
at Leghorn, i. 455
Leghorn reached by, vii. 233

Winchelsea. *See also* Winchilsea

Winchester, Bp of. *See* Hoadly, Benjamin (1676–1761); North, Hon. Brownlow (1741–1820); Thomas, John (1696–1781)

Winchester, Dean of. *See* Pearce, Zachariah (1690–1774)

Winchester, E. of. *See* Le Despenser, Hugh (1261–1326)

Winchester:
Whithed to attend assizes at, iv. 237

Winchilsea, E. of. *See* Finch, Daniel (1689–1769); Finch, George (1752–1826)

Winchilsea family:
Granville, Cts, entertains, ii. 527

Winckelmann, Johann Joachim (1717–68); archæologist:
in Albani's service, vii. 113
murdered at Trent, vii. 113
Wilkes said to have inherited gold medals from, vii. 113
will of, sent to Mann by Albani, vii. 113

Wind:
in England, viii. 431
French fleet dispersed by, viii. 535
high, in Florence, iv. 25
Mann depressed by, iv. 234
Rome hurt by, iv. 69

Windam; Windham. *See also* Wyndham

'Windham, Mr':
Mann's code name for Joseph II, ix. 42–3

Windham, William (1750–1810), statesman; M.P.:
balloon ascent made by, ix. 579
Brussels visited by, on return to England, ix. 79
Cholmondeley a friend of, viii. 524
departure of, for Italy, deferred, viii. 527
English victories distress, ix. 50
George III indiscreetly discussed by, ix. 524
Gordon rioters will not reconcile Mann with, ix. 55
HW recommends, to Mann, viii. 521, 524
HW regrets that his recommendation of, was so unrewarding to Mann, ix. 79, 518
HW satisfied of virtue of, but not of his knowledge of the world, ix. 40
HW sees, and hears Mann praised, ix. 97
HW sorry that Mann sees so little of, ix. 40
HW takes Mann's remarks about, too seriously, ix. 523–4
health of, recovered, ix. 97
Italian language distasteful to, ix. 50
Italy to be visited by, for health, viii. 521, 524
languages studied by, at Florence, ix. 33
loss of Gibraltar and Port Mahon wished by, as blow to government, ix. 50
Mann avoided by, for being George III's minister, ix. 40n
—— does not see, as much as was expected, ix. 33, 523–4
—— enjoys meeting, ix. 2–3
—— lately saw, in Italy, ix. 398
——'s dinners and conversazioni attended by, as spectator, ix. 33
—— will see, in theatre boxes, ix. 33
morose notions of Spartan teachers imbibed by, ix. 50

[Windham, William, *continued*]
M.P. for Norwich, viii. 524n, ix. 579
Norfolk gentleman of considerable estate, viii. 521, 524
Norfolk militia gets resignation from, as Lt-Col., because of E. of Orford's trouble-making, ix. 11n
Northington's secretary in Ireland, viii. 521n, ix. 398
Orford's conduct will not surprise, ix. 11
patriotism of, may be morose, ix. 40
sentiments suppressed by, in deference to Mann, ix. 50
temper of, sour, ix. 50
Whig of the old school, viii. 524
Windows:
coach: mob holds flambeaux to, vii. 194; of glass, vii. 6, 49, 201-2
Frenchman encourages English mob to break, vii. 111
HW rings for candles, lest mob break, as they did two years before, ix. 563
HW's, broken by mob, ix. 343
illumination of, at Florence, for birth of Cowper's son, viii. 232
Italian: of paper, in Florence, viii. 232; unglazed in Montaigne's time, viii. 16
Mann's: broken by wind, iv. 25; on garden side, made into doors, i. 499
mob breaks, after Westminster election, ix. 563, 564, 565
North's and Germain's broken by mob, viii. 442
Norton's, broken by mob, vii. 305
See also Stained glass
Windsor, Vcts. *See* Clavering, Alice (d. 1776)
Windsor, Hon. Alice Elizabeth, (1749-72), m. (1768) Francis Seymour-Conway, styled Vct Beauchamp, 2d M. of Hertford, 1794:
Beauchamp to wed, vi. 480
death of, vii. 381
Windsor, Hon. Catharine (d. 1742 *or* 3), m. (1741) Matthijs Lestevenon de Berkenroode:
Florence visited by, i. **200**, 217
Haddock and Vernon discussed by, i. 200
Italy bores, i. 200-1
Mann's attentions refused by, i. 217, 248
Pomfret, Cts of, sister of, i. 200
Uguccioni repulsed by, i. 217
Windsor, Hon. Charlotte Jane (1746-1800), m. (1766) John Stuart, styled Vct Mount Stuart, 4th E. of Bute, 1792; cr. (1796) M. of Bute:
marriage of, vi. 465
Windsor, Herbert (1707-58), 2d Vct Windsor, 1738, M.P.:
daughter of, vii. 381n
Nourse challenges, unsuccessfully, i. 248
—— rebuked by, for slandering Shuttleworth, i. **248**
rebel lords condemned by, iii. 284
sister will be delighted by ingenuity of, iii. 303

Windsor, Other Hickman (1751-99), 6th E. of Plymouth, 1771:
fat, sweet-tempered and indolent, vii. 378
Hertford sends letter through, to Mann, vii. 373
Windsor:
Albemarle attends D. of Cumberland at, iv. 460
Belle-Isle imprisoned near, at great expense, iii. 18
Charlotte, Q., charmed with, vi. 79
Fox asks Sir Edward Walpole to employ tradesmen at, iv. 42
Garter installation at, vi. 79, 80
Garter obligations concerning, iv. 72-3
George III and Charlotte visit Eton from, vi. 83
HW's house at: HW could send cheese and hare from, iii. 331; HW seems to prefer to the Birthday, iii. 348-9; HW to spend summer in, iii. 297; Mann congratulates HW on, iii. 307; within Castle, iii. 298
Keppel, Augustus, not elected at, due to George III's opposition, ix. 86
Keppel, Frederick, a canon of, v. 239
—— becomes dean of, v. 239n
races at, HW will not attend, iii. 298
royal apartment at, said to be given to pregnant young lady, iv. 278
royal family at, for Bute's and Gloucester's Garter installations, vi. 79
St Albans, Ds of, buried at, i. 295
visitors to: Beauclerk, Lords Henry, Sidney, and Vere, i. 295
Walpole, Sir Edward, gives estate at, to Mrs Keppel, viii. 349
—— to support Fox in borough of, iv. 42
White Hart inn at, iii. 298
Windsor Castle:
HW's house within, iii. 298
housekeeper of, *see* Chudleigh Elizabeth; Marriot, Mrs
housekeeper's revenues at, large, iv. 213
Windsor chair. *See under* Chair
Wine:
Aleatico and Verdea: Beauchamp owes HW for, vii. 302; Beauchamp wants, from Mann, vii. 200, 204; bill of lading for, vii. 215, 279
booths for, at Ranelagh, iv. 47
Chute shuns, ii. 149
——'s temperate use of, brings on gout, ii. 100
clergyman tells Mann to drink, to bring on gout, vi. 335
Cori has bottle of, i. 254
Cyprus, Hobart prefers, as restorative, iii. 261
elections usually bring consumption of, viii. 45
England could have grown grapes for, in hot summer, viii. 407
Ferrers denied, on way to execution, v. 401

——'s allowance of, in prison, shortened, v. 397

Florence: for Fox, sent in chests by Mann, v. 156, 164, 187, 189, 304, 309, 313, 353, 375, 383; Grifoni, Mme, displeases HW by offer of, ii. 348, 366, 527; HW's drams mistaken for Fox's, v. 353; Mazzei to sell, in England, v. 495; Pembroke buys, from the Rena, v. 156

French, improve by crossing the sea, v. 233

glass of, figuratively thrown by Lord Mark Ker in gentleman's face, vi. 162

gout driven to stomach by, viii. 423

HW avoids, vi. 257, vii. 76

HW may receive, from Mann, i. 12

HW tries, for gout cure, vi. 322

Lucca gives, to D. of York, vi. 221

Mann dilutes, at dinners, i. 155, vi. 469

—— has avoided, i. 78, vi. 469

—— serves, to Vorontsov family, vi. 193

—— used to drink too much, at meals, i. 78

of Verdea, like cider, vii. 204

sailors often tamper with shipments of, v. 304

tax on, would be less burdensome than one on tea, ii. 142

York, D. of, receives, at Rome, vi. 228

—— takes extra dose of, on St Andrew's day, ix. 100

Wine merchant:
Garrick used to be, i. 435
Rena, Contessa, wife of, vii. 106n

Winkleman. See Winckelmann

Winnington, Anne, m. John Wheeler:
brother avoided by, iii. 250
Methodism of, iii. 250

Winnington, Henrietta (d. 1761), m. (1736) Hon. Samuel Masham, 2d Bn Masham, 1758:
Thompson consulted by, in brother's illness, iii. 249-50

Winnington, Thomas (1696-1746), politician; M.P.:
abstains from voting, in Parliament, i. 484
address against rank for officers of privately-raised regiments to be procured by, iii. 154
anecdote by, about Cts of Abercorn and Ds of Devonshire calling women 'ugly,' i. 478
Bubb Dodington answered by, i. 354-5
Carteret's maxim questioned by, ii. 535
death of, iii. 249-50, 257
does not speak, in debate over privately-raised regiments, iii. 158
Gage discusses his son with, i. 255
George II asks, to recall Pelham ministry, iii. 212
HW entertained by, ii. 283
Hulse and Thompson consulted by, iii. 250
Lincoln entertained by, ii. 283
Mann, Robert, dismissed by, ii. 479, 496-7

Nugent rebuked by, i. 431

Parliamentary debates by: on amendment to the Address, x. 22, 23; on privately-raised regiments, x. 16, 17, 18

Parliamentary vote by, on privately-raised regiments, x. 19

paymaster and cofferer of the forces, i. 172n

paymastership to go to, ii. 349-50, 356

Pembroke, Cts of, amuses, by her euphemisms, i. 496

Pitt answered by, ii. 351

Quarendon's witticism to, on Bell's release, i. 503

resigns as paymaster, iii. 211

Stafford entertained by, ii. 283

Townshend's duel with, i. 172, 207

Townshend, Vcts, 'cicisbea' of, i. 173, 207, 264

—— entertained by, i. 496

—— induces, to dismiss Robert Mann in spite of promise to Sir Robert Walpole, ii. 497

Williams's friend, iii. 250

witticisms by: comparing Betty Warner's lovers to the Ds of Marlborough's legatees, ii. 540; on Churchill daughter, ii. 481; on girl who loved her own sex, iv. 53; on Pitt's and Chesterfield's turncoat politics, ii. 540; on Pitt's renouncing P. of Wales, iii. 27; on prudery, i. 496; on Walpole, Horatio (1678-1757), iii. 28; to Stafford, about Catholicism and fasting, ii. 283

Worcester's instructions to, ii. 103

Winstanley, Robert (1710-1804):
(?) observation by, in coffee-house, on recent crime, iv. 317-18

Winter:
of 1775-6, worst in HW's recollection, viii. 174
Parliament session equivalent to, in HW's opinion, ix. 358
sets in at Florence in October, ix. 334
unfavourable to gout-sufferers, viii. 185
warm but stormy in England, iv. 16

Winter clothes:
Belle-Isle does not provide, for army, v. 435
Florentines clad in, in April, ix. 397
Florentines wear, in October, iv. 336
Florentines wearing, in June, ix. 281
HW comes to London to order, ix. 541

Winter quarters:
Frederick II goes into, v. 18
French army goes into, v. 355
modern fighters do not go into, ix. 105

Winterton, Bn and E. of. See Garth-Turnour, Edward-Turnour (1734-88)

Wintzingerode, Hans Sigismund (1717-71), German army officer:
to be witness at Lord George Sackville's court martial, v. 366

Wiquefort. See Wicquefort

Wire:
Charles III snatches wigs with, vii. 238
for bell, vii. 392
Wirtemborg; Wirtembergh. *See* Württemberg
Wirts. *See* Würtz
Wirtzbourg. *See* Würzburg
Wisdom:
HW thinks, merely consists in making remarks on the folly of others, ix. 540
Wiseman (?Wyseman), Mr:
HW cannot find, i. (?)15, 18, 21, 23
HW discusses (?) Young Pretender's movements with, i. 18
Mann's correspondence with, i. 18
Smyth to instruct, in case of Young Pretender's departure, i. 15
Wit:
HW disclaims, i. 270
Italian language lacks word for, v. 127
taste in, changes, ix. 308
Witches:
French opera singers omit powder when they act the parts of, ii. 496
pinching of, to loosen their charms, iii. 19
Witham:
Charlotte, Q., visits E. of Abercorn at, v. 528
Wither, Henrietta Maria (d. 1790), m. 1 Thynne Worsley; m. 2 Edmund Bramston:
Cowper's annuity to, vii. 416
Elliot, Lady Frances, leaves small legacy to, vii. 416
Withers, William, E. of Orford's steward:
(?) HW urged by, not to move E. of Orford, viii. 293
(?) Orford writes to, viii. 367
Wittel, Gaspar Adriaensz van (1653–1736), called Gaspare Vanvitelli *or* Gasparo dagli Occhiali: HW buys paintings by, x. 8
Woburn, seat of D. of Bedford:
Bedford, D. of, acts plays at, iii. 309n
—— would never relinquish, iii. 255
fender at, vi. 218
Pitt sends Gower to, with overtures to D. of Bedford, vi. 472
visitors to: Cumberland, D. of, iv. 89; Guerchy, vi. 218; HW, iv. 281; Rockingham, vi. 538; Vernon, iv. 301
Woden:
HW's term for SH, v. 433
Woffington, Margaret (ca 1714–60), actress:
Cæsar takes, v. 157
Cholmondeley weds sister of, iii. 340
Darnley keeps, i. 176
Foundling well acted by, iii. 465
HW criticizes, i. 176
Sir Harry Wildair performed by, i. 176
Taaffe's bet with, iv. 289
Woffington, Mary (ca 1729–1811), m. (1746) Rev. Hon. Robert Cholmondeley:
marriage of, iii. 340
Wolcot, Dr John (1738–1819); 'Peter Pindar':
Bozzi and Piozzi: advertised to be published, ix. 638; Boswell and Mrs Piozzi satirized in,
ix. 638, 640–1; Mann would rather see, than Mrs Piozzi's anecdotes, ix. 643
Wolf; wolves:
German princes hunt, ix. 364
'Tory' devoured by, i. 257
Wolfe, Gen. James (1727–59); Maj.-Gen.:
Conway not befriended by, v. 267
death of, v. 338, vi. 16n, viii. 185
HW's opinion of, v. 267
letters of, despairing, v. 336
Louisbourg siege shows abilities of, v. 267
Maria Theresa should have, instead of Daun, v. 428
Montgomery less successful than, viii. 185
monument for, designed, v. 421–2, 428, 436
Quebec expedition headed by, v. 266–7
Townshend succeeds, vi. 16n
Wolley, Edward (ca 1604–84), Bp of Clonfert, 1665:
Charles II's remark about, vi. 57, viii. 52
Wolsey, Thomas (?1475–1530), cardinal:
hat of, HW receives, viii. 174
masqueraders dressed as, vii. 193
Wolters, Dirk ('Richard') (1713–71), banker:
(?) Veers imitates writing of, iii. 507
Wolterton, Norfolk:
HW expects owner's duel to appear on fresco at, ii. 192
HW's verses on, ii. 47n
HW visits, ii. 47, iii. 72
picture at, of Walpole of Wolterton family, iv. 341–2
Woman of the Bedchamber. *See under* Bedchamber
Women:
abandoned, of quality, Mann's visitors limited to, iv. 454
addicted to brag and Methodism, iv. 41
Clement XIII orders, to cover their faces in churches, v. 292
English: are no longer merely gallant, but become streetwalkers, viii. 427; get little joy from religion in old age, iv. 378
Florentine, compared to those of York and Edinburgh, iv. 427
Florentine archbishop orders, to uncover their breasts in church, v. 292
Francis II taken from care of, before they could give him foolish prejudices, ix. 282
French, act in Genoese opera, iii. 505
Italian: act in Genoese opera, iii. 505; shave their bodies, iii. 437; soon lose beauty, vii. 306
Italians punish lightly, iv. 356
letters of, superior to men's, iv. 282
Methodism attracts, iv. 41, 82
milk of, viii. 321
old: HW thinks that living with, is worse than living out of the world, ix. 542; religion used by, as cloak for scandal-mongering, ix. 584
power of, over husbands, HW's reflections on, viii. 208
scandal by, HW's reflections on, ii. 62

spitefulness of, HW's reflections on, ii. 506

Wood, Robert (?1717–71), archæologist; politician; M.P.:
future travellers' descriptions of England's ruins will resemble books of, viii. 62
Lyttelton, Richard, rejects offer transmitted by, v. 507–8, 511
Mann's friendship with, authorizes application for higher rank, v. 453
—— writes to, requesting promotion, v. 453, 454–5, 463, 483
(?) Orford, Cts of, tells, of her plans and grievances, iv. **476**
Pitt's approaches from, for Mann, v. 455, 483, vi. 469
Ruins of Baalbec and *Ruins of Palmyra* by, HW praises, v. 173
Wilkes wins damages from, in Court of Common Pleas, vi. 188

Wood:
lacking at Florence, to build *casotti,* ii. 270
Lorraine officials sell, ii. 270
sailor mends leg of, viii. 283–4, 290
Soubise, Princesse de, will get, from husband, v. 178
staircases should not be built of, vi. 143
See also Timber; Tree

Woodcock; woodcocks:
English travellers compared to, iv. 265, 271
Pembroke, Cts of, calls 'bird of the wood,' i. 495–6

Woodfall, Henry Sampson (1739–1805), printer:
imprisoned, for printing libel on Norton, vii. 555, 556

Woodfall, William, printer:
arrested, vii. 280

Woodmason, James (fl. 1773–ca 1798) stationer:
children of die in fire, ix. 242

Woodmason, James (1773–?82):
(?) dies in fire, ix. 242

Woodmason, Mary (1774–?82):
(?) dies in fire, ix. 242

Woodmason, Mary Magdalen, wife of James Woodmason:
children of, die in fire caused by her candle, ix. 242

Woodstock:
HW receives steel from, i. 302

Woodville, Elizabeth (1437–92), m. 1 (ca 1452) Sir John Grey; m. 2 (1464) Edward IV of England:
Waldegrave, Cts, dresses as, at ball, vii. 193

Woolcot. *See* Wolcott

Woolsacks:
Lord Chancellors sometimes carried to, ix. 347

Woolterton. *See* Wolterton

Woolwich:
Cromarty, Cts of, visits, to see captured son, iii. 272

Wootton, Sir Harry. *See* Wotton, Sir Henry

Wootton, John (ca 1682–1764), painter:
Patapan to be painted by, ii. 220

Wootton, Norfolk:
HW imagines himself married to heiress of, ii. 238

Worcester, Bp of. *See* Hough, John (1651–1743); Hurd, Richard (1720–1808); Johnson, James (1705–74); Maddox, Isaac (1697–1759); North, Hon. Brownlow (1741–1820)

Worcester:
Charles II not attended to, by Highlanders, iii. 107
instructions of, to Sandys and Winnington, ii. 103
music festival at, Coventry to attend, iv. 338
paste of, superior to all but that of Saxony for porcelain, ix. 635
Pitt and Legge receive freedom of, v. 87
shoemaker at, exhibits shoe made for Cts of Coventry, iv. 324
to present petition, vii. 132

Worcester, Battle of:
Charles II lectured by Kirk of Scotland on eve of, vii. 386

Work-box:
HW mentions, iv. 375

Workmen:
fright of, when Mann's greenhouse collapses, iv. 94
George III sees, fall off scaffold at Kew, iv. 240
Mann enjoys watching, iv. 357

World, The:
Chesterfield to contribute to, iv. 374
HW contributes to, iv. 373–4, 385, 399–400
HW lists contributors to, iv. 395n
HW's articles in, may show Chute's influence, iv. 385
Mann welcomes issues of, iv. 385, 392, 395, 399–400
Pulteney, E. of Bath, contributes to, about Newmarket, iv. 374
Theodore of Corsica benefited by papers in, iv. 373–4
Wilton thought by Mann to be praised in, iv. 392, 395, 397

World:
grows more intrepid, ix. 105
HW forsakes, except for amusement, vi. 359
HW holds to, by but few threads, ix. 116
HW's reflection on, as 'a comedy to those who think, a tragedy to those who feel,' vii. 387, 397
HW thinks, can be cured of any folly but not of being foolish, ix. 642
insanity of, HW's reflections on, vi. 570
senility of, HW's reflections on, ix. 47
See also Life

Worlidge, Thomas (1700–66), painter and etcher:
HW mentions, iv. 427

Worming:
Patapan undergoes, ii. 317
Worms, treaty of:
Austrian conquest of Naples said to be promised by, ii. 444
Charles Emmanuel III granted Finale by, ii. 360
England disregards, iii. 481
English fleet rejoices at, ii. 336
English fleet relies on triple alliance of, ii. 339
Genoese fear consequences of, ii. 546–7, 554
Lomellini invokes clause of, iii. 67
Maria Theresa promised English naval help at, ii. 470
—— to observe terms of, iii. 481
Mathews expects his cockade by, ii. 522
Parliamentary debate over, expected, ii. 383
signed, ii. 311
Woronzow. See Vorontsov
Worseley; Worsely. See Worsley
Worsley, Lady. See Fleming, Seymour Dorothy
Worsley, Frances (1694–1743), m. (1710), John Carteret, 2d Bn Carteret, 1695; 1st E. Granville, 1744:
daughters of, vi. 275n
death of, ii. 255
Hague, The, to be visited by, ii. 209
husband discussed by, i. 258
plump, ii. 209
Worsley, Sir Richard (1751–1805), 7th Bt; M.P.:
connivance of, in wife's prostitution, ix. 246
jury awards shilling damages to, ix. 246
North's pleasantry on, ix. 246
wife accused of adultery by, ix. 245
wife leaves, ix. 228
Worsley, Sir Robert (?1669–1747), 4th Bt, 1676; M.P.:
daughter of, i. 258n, ii. 209n
Worsley, Sir Thomas (1728–68), 6th Bt, 1756:
relative of, vi. 476
Worsley, Thomas, of Pidford:
(?) Cardini, servant of, vi. 477, 483, 490–1
(?) HW's letters to be taken by, back to England from Italy, vi. 476–7
Naples visited by, vi. 476–7
Worsley, Thomas (1710–78), equerry to George II; surveyor-general of board of works; M.P.:
architectural taste of, v. 460
death of, from self-starvation, viii. 428
George III's equerry, v. 460
Mann's acquaintance with, i. 287, viii. 428
——'s death reported by, to HW, i. 249, 286–7
Master of the Board of Works, v. 460, viii. 428n
Suares, Mme, has, as cicisbeo, v. 460
Worsley, Mrs Thynne. See Wither, Henrietta Maria

Wortley-Mackenzie, James Archibald. See Stuart, James Archibald (1747–1818)
Wortley Montagu, Edward (1678–1761); M.P.; ambassador to Turkey 1716–17:
avarice of, v. 472n
death of: v. 472, 527; benefits Bute, v. 473, 527
HW calls, 'old Avidien,' v. 472
Pope satirizes, v. 472n
son gets small allowance from, iv. 226
wealth and bequests of, v. 472–3, 483
Wortley Montagu, Edward (1713–76), traveller; M.P.:
adventures of, better than his writings, v. 472n
Albemarle bails, but makes no defence for him, iv. 294
Ashe, Elizabeth, thought to have married, iv. 289
Coke's witticism about Parliamentary membership of, iv. 289
daughter said to be placed by, in Roman convent, vi. 113
Ethiopia to be visited by, from Italy, vi. 113
extravagance of, iv. 226, 235
faro-banker to Duchesse de Mirepoix, iv. 288
father almost disinherits, v. 472–3
father gives small allowance to, iv. 226
galleys may be punishment of, iv. 288, 294
imprisoned with Taaffe at Fort l'Évêque, Paris, for robbing Payba, iii. 450n, iv. 287–8, 294, v. 473n
iron wig brought by, from Paris, iv. 226
mother does not supply, iv. 235
mother leaves one guinea to, vi. 81
mother's conversation with, at Geneva, iii. 567
Parliament entered by, iii. 450
Rome visited by, to embark at Naples or Sicily for Egypt in search of antiquities, vi. 76–7
Royal Society elects, iv. 226
snuff-boxes collected, and shoe-buckles worn by, with frock, iv. 226
whiskers and Ethiopian costume worn by, vi. 113
White's Club does not include, iv. 289
Wortley Montagu, Mrs Edward jr. See Ashe, Elizabeth; Wortley Montagu, Sally
Wortley Montagu, Mary (1718–94), m. (1736) John Stuart, 3d E. of Bute:
children of, unfortunate, viii. 378
daughter's misconduct mentioned to, viii. 378
father's bequest to, v. 473
HW pities, because of her eccentric mother, v. 472, vi. 4
HW praises, v. 472
HW praises award of peerage to, v. 490
Mann informed by, through HW, that Anne Pitt goes to Pisa, vii. 557

mob throws stones into chamber of, vii. 7
mother bequeathes manuscripts to, vi. 84
mother's bequest to, vi. 72
mother's letters will be closely guarded by, vi. 84, 141
Pitt, Anne, friend of, viii. 378
Wortley Montagu, Mary (b. ca 1750), natural dau. of Edward Wortley Montagu jr:
convent at Rome entered by, vi. 113
Wortley Montagu, Sally (d. 1776), wife of Edward Wortley Montagu jr:
father-in-law's will refers to, v. 472
Wotton, Sir Henry (1568–1639), Kt, 1603; diplomatist:
Boughton Malherbe once owned by, iv. **166**
definition by, of an ambassador's function, v. 276
HW disparages, iv. 166
Venetian senate's relations with, iv. 198
Wraxall, Nathaniel William (1751–1831), cr. (1813) Bt; M.P.:
Parliamentary speech of, as translated in foreign gazettes, must offend sovereigns, ix. 137–8
Wray, Sir Cecil (1734–1805), 13th Bt, 1752; army officer; M.P.:
Court institutes Westminster scrutiny in favour of, ix. 563n
Fox, C.J., and Hood oppose, in Westminster, ix. 489
named by new ministers as Parliamentary candidate for Westminster, ix. **284**
very unknown, ix. 284
Wray. See also Wrey
Wrey, Sir Bourchier (? 1715–84), 6th Bt, 1726; M.P.:
Banks, Margaret, receives opera ticket from, iii. 234
Mann knew, in Florence, iii. 238
Orford, Cts of, cousin of, iii. 238
—— lodges, iii. 224, 238
—— writes to, at Exeter, iii. 224
Wrey family:
Bourchiers united with, iii. 238
Wright, Lady. See Stapleton, Catherine (ca 1732–1802)
'Wright, Mrs.' See Coleman, Sarah
Wright, ——:
Florence to be visited by, i. 423
friend of Sir William Turnur and Sir Erasmus Philipps, i. 423
imprisoned, on suspicion of attacking Lucca, i. 449–50, 460
Wright, Capt. Fortunatus (d. 1757), merchant and privateer:
Corbet's correspondence with, iii. 384
English privateer in Mediterranean commanded by, v. 20–1
French vow to capture, with special fleet, v. 21
prisoners gently treated by, v. 21
prizes taken by, to Porto Ferrajo, v. 69

Silva compliments Mann for forcing, to give up captured prize, iii. 383–4
Turkey Company makes offer to, v. 21
Tuscan government quarrels with England over, v. 20
Wright, Sir James (d. 1803); Kt, 1766; cr. (1772) Bt; British Resident at Venice 1766–74:
ivy admired by, in Boboli gardens, v. **457**
Mann assured by, of innocence of trying to supplant him, vi. 510
—— 's correspondence with, about possible transfer, vi. 499–500, 502–3, 510
—— sends ivy seeds to, v. 457
uncle asks George III to appoint, to Naples or Florence, vi. 500
Venice reached by, vi. 499
Wright, Sir Martin (ca 1693–1767), Kt, 1745; judge of King's Bench:
Murray remanded by, iv. 249–50
Wright, Thomas (d. 1797), printer:
arrested, vii. 280
Wrinkles:
HW's, ix. 332
HW thinks, are negligible if one is not in pain, ix. 540
Wriothesley, Lady Rachel (ca 1637–1723), m. 1 (ca 1653) Francis Vaughan, styled Bn Vaughan; m. 2 (1669) William Russell, styled Bn Russell:
letters of, HW wants D. of Bedford to print, iv. 282–3
Tillotson urged by, to accept archbishopric, iv. 282n
Wriothesley, Thomas (1607–67), 4th E. of Southampton, 1624:
daughter of, iv. 282n
lord treasurer, iv. 282n
Wrist:
Mann has weakness in, iv. 401
Writing:
HW's, is just for his own amusement, ix. 584
Mann fatigued by, ix. 597
Writing-box:
HW keeps bank-notes in, at Arlington St, vii. 285
Morice puts cameo in, ix. 94
Mozzi shows Cts of Orford's, to Mann, to be opened in lawyer's presence, ix. 114
Writ of error; writs of error:
Wilkes applies to attorney-general for, vii. 12
—— 's, argued before House of Lords, vii. 83
Wrottesley, Elizabeth (1745–1822), m. (1769) Augustus Henry Fitzroy, 3d D. of Grafton:
Grafton to marry, vii. 121
Wrottesley, Sir John (1744–87), 8th Bt, 1769; M.P.; army officer:
news of D. of York's death taken by, to England, from Monaco, vi. 554
Paris visited by, vi. 554

[Wrottesley, Sir John, *continued*]
York, D. of, supposedly has, as Groom of the Bedchamber, vi. 554n
Wrottesley, Lady Mary. *See* Leveson-Gower, Lady Mary (d. 1771)
Wrought Silks and Velvets Bill:
rejected, vi. 301
Württemberg, D. of. *See* Karl Eugen (1728–93)
Württemberg, Q. of. *See* Charlotte Augusta Mary
Württemburg:
Cowper said to be proud of a paltry order from, ix. 646
troops of, defeated, v. 355
Würtz von Rudenz, Wolfgang Ignatz (ca 1685–1774), Marchese di San Pasquale:
captured at San Lazaro, iii. 267
Würzburg, Bp of. *See* Seinsheim, Adam Friedrich von (d. 1779)
Wyatt, James (1746–1813), architect:
HW prefers, to Adam, viii. 93
Wymondefold, Mrs. *See* Knight, Hon. Henrietta
Wyndham, Sir Charles (1710–63), 4th Bt, 1740; 2d E. of Egremont, 1750; M.P.:
address of loyalty to George II seconded by, in Parliament, ii. 399
appetite of, vi. 158–9
Augsburg to have been the post of, v. 540
brother dies at same age as, viii. 25
brother of, vi. 311n
'convert,' ii. 399
death and property of, vi. 158–9
Devonshire, D. of, leaves key and staff with, vi. 96
earldom to revert to, iv. 81
Egremont title goes to, iv. 124
extravagance of, v. 200
Granville tries to get Northumberland title for, iv. 12, 81
health of: apoplectic lethargy, vi. 17; recovered, vi. 33
Mann anxious to hear of successor to, vi. 23
——'s letter to, describes Spain's motives, vi. 100
Melcombe may succeed, as secretary of state, vi. 17
secretary of state, v. 72, 75–6, 98, 540, 541, vi. 17, 23, 96
Somerset, D. of, leaves borough and estate to, iii. 11
supposed Maratti painting bought by, v. 172
well bred, v. 541
Wilkes complains to, vi. 138
Wyndham, Hon. Charles William (1760–1828), M.P.:
(?) arrest of, for riot, ix. 565
Worsley, Lady, has affair with, ix. 228
Wyndham, Sir Edward (ca 1667–95); 2d Bt:
grandson dies at same age as, viii. 25

Wyndham, Elizabeth (d. 1769), m. (1749) Hon. George Grenville:
brother of, vi. 311n
grandfather's legacy to, iii. 11
Wyndham, George O'Brien (1751–1837), 3d E. of Egremont, 1763:
HW sees, at Gloucester House, ix. 68
person and fortune of, ix. 68
Ranelagh visited by, ix. 68
uncle's real estate goes to, viii. 25
Waldegrave, Lady Charlotte Maria, engaged to, ix. 68, 74–5, 77, 544
Wyndham, Henry Penruddocke (1736–1819), M.P.:
Bubb Dodington's memoirs published by, ix. 503n
Wyndham, Lady Katharine. *See* Seymour, Lady Katharine (d. 1731)
Wyndham, Thomas (ca 1693–1777), M.P.:
Bubb Dodington's heir, ix. 80
Wyndham, Sir William (?1688–1740), 3d Bt; M.P.:
Bolingbroke's letter to, iv. 452
Chancellor of Exchequer in Q. Anne's reign, and opponent of Sir Robert Walpole, ix. 68n
grandson of, to marry Sir Robert Walpole's great-granddaughter, ix. 68
Jacobitism of, iv. 60
son dies at same age as, viii. 25
son of, ii. 399, v. 24n
Walpole, Sir Robert, refuses to send, to the Tower, vii. 289
Wyndham-O'Brien (formerly Wyndham), Percy (?1723–74), cr. (1756) E. of Thomond; cofferer; M.P.:
death of, viii. 25
grandfather's legacy to, iv. 11
lord of the Treasury, iv. 517, v. 24
peerage granted to, v. 24
resignation of, as cofferer, vi. 311
Treasury post left by, v. 24
uncle leaves estate to, v. 24n
will not made by, viii. 25
Wynn, Lady Henrietta. *See* Somerset, Lady Henrietta
Wynn, Sir Watkin Williams (?1693–1749), 3d Bt, 1740; M.P.:
defeated in Welsh election, ii. 401
French insurrection might be led by, iii. 310
George II said by, to be absent from Dettingen, ii. 305–6
Jacobite, of Wales, iii. 310n
Lee seconded by, i. 243
Lovat's trial attended by, iii. 381
named in Secret Committee lists, i. 385
Opposition assembly addressed by, at St Alban's Tavern, iv. 50
Parliamentary debate by, on privately-raised regiments, x. 17
Parliament entered by, after his petition about Denbighshire election, i. 343–4

Traquair converses with, about Old Pretender's affairs, iii. 381
Welsh races attended by, ii. 305
Wynn, Sir Watkin Williams (1748–89), 4th Bt, 1749; M.P.:
dinner given by, at country house, vii. 64
Mann to be accompanied by, at investiture, vii. 60
Patch paints, x. 45
Poussin painting bought by, vii. 466
Wynne, William (d. 1815), Kt, 1748; barrister:
counsel for Ds of Kingston, viii. 193, 196

Xavier, ship:
in Spanish fleet, i. 286
Xebec; xebecs:
English have, on Corsican coast, iii. 232
Spanish: Benedict XIV allows, to enter, ii. 291; Benedict XIV does not permit, to unload, ii. 296, 300; blockaded at Genoa, ii. 257; crews flee from, ii. 301; driven back by Mathews's ships, when about to return, ii. 301; escape of, from Civita Vecchia, ii. 296, 300–1; escape of, from Majorca to Civita Vecchia, ii. 287, 300; repelled from Orbetello, ii. 287
Turkish, defeated by Russians, vii. 234
See also Postillion
Xenophon (b. ca 430 B.C.), Greek historian and general:
New York may produce counterpart of, viii. 62
Ximenes d'Aragona, Marchesa di. *See* Scarlatti-Rondinelli, Elena Vittoria
Ximenes d'Aragona, Ferdinando (d. 1816), Marchese d'Esch, Priore di Romagna:
England to be visited by, vii. 25
mother of, vii. 25

Yacht *or* Yatch:
Caroline Matilda to travel in, vii. 409
HW sails to Dover in, i. 142
Newcastle, D. of, finds, too small for his travelling gear, iii. 484–5
of Ds of Kingston, Russian admiralty told to take care of, viii. 333
See also Charlotte; William and Mary
Yarmouth, Cts of. *See* Wendt, Amalie Sophie Marianne von (1704–65)
Yarmouth, E. of. *See* Seymour-Conway, Francis (1743–1822)
Yarmouth:
Carteret puts in at roadstead of, ii. 80
Pitt and Legge receive freedom of, v. 87
Townshend, Charles, cannot be re-elected from, v. 26
Yarmouth, English ship:
French ships pursued by, iii. 411
Yatch. *See* Yacht

Yates, Sir Joseph (1722–70), Kt, 1763; judge of the court of King's Bench:
Wilkes appears before, vii. 12
Yellow fever:
Alexander and Cæsar would look badly after, v. 290
Yelverton, George Augustus (1727–48), 2d E. of Sussex, 1731; M.P.:
lord of the Bedchamber to George III, iv. 247
Yeomen of the guard:
Berkeley said to get position in, ii. 143
changes in command of, i. 457, 492, ii. 551, v. 25
Dorset succeeds Falmouth as captain of, ix. 241
Edgcumbe captain of, ix. 518n
HW calls, 'band of pensioners,' ix. 241
See also Bathurst, Allen (1684–1775), Bn Bathurst; Hobart, John (1723–93), Bn Hobart
Yertzin, 'Countess,' of Mecklenburg-Strelitz:
HW mentions, vi. 239
Yonge, Sir George (1733–1812), 5th Bt, 1755; M.P.:
resignation of, from Admiralty, vii. 180
Yonge, Sir William (ca 1693–1755), 4th Bt, 1731; M.P.:
Bedford attacks, i. 336
Cornish petition presented by, i. **233**
death of, iv. 518
Earle proposed by, i. 243
Frederick, P. of Wales, wants Harrington to receive letter in presence of, iii. 175
impeachment of, intended, i. 344
Parliamentary bill proposed by, iii. 396
Parliamentary committee headed by, iii. 387n
Parliamentary debate by, on privately-raised regiments, x. 13, 15, 16, 17, 18
Parliamentary speech by, i. 297
vice-treasurer of Ireland, iii. 155, 256, iv. 518
Yorick:
Hamlet's soliloquy on, ix. 7
York, Abp of. *See* Blackburne, Lancelot (1658–1743); Gilbert, John (1693–1761); Herring, Thomas (1693–1757); Hutton, Matthew (1693–1758); Markham, William (1719–1807)
York, Cardinal. *See* Henry Benedict Maria Clement (Stuart)
York, Ds of. *See* Hyde, Anne
York, D. of. *See* Edward Augustus (1739–67); Frederick Augustus (1763–1827); Richard (1473–83)
York, Dukes of:
bagnios and taverns will be frequented by, iv. 15
York:
archbishopric of: Herring receives, ii. 201n, 203; refused by several bishops, ii. 203
Bosville, Mrs, lives at, ii. 242

[York, *continued*]
Christian VII to visit, vii. 41
—— unable to see races at, vii. 48
Cope's defeat becomes known at, iii. 126
election at, i. 301
London's example followed by, with regard to Pitt, v. 546
physician from, joins rebels, iii. 180
women of, compared to those of Florence, iv. 427
York Buildings Co.:
miners settled by, at Strontean, x. 31
Yorke, Miss —— (d. 1759):
death of, v. 312
Yorke, Hon. Charles (1722–70), lord chancellor, 1770; M.P.:
attorney-general, vi. 263, 268, 443
bereavements of, v. 312
death of: after kissing George III's hand as lord chancellor, vii. 178; already forgotten, vii. 187
father's death confines, vi. 211
George III and Grafton offer post of lord chancellor to, vii. 178
Grafton influenced by acceptance or refusal of, vii. 182
Grenville, George, anxious about 'trimming' of, vi. 494
(?) HW mentions, iv. 326
lord chancellor's post coveted by, vii. 175, 178
lord chancellor's post first declined and then accepted by, vii. 174, 175–6, 178, 188
Norton opposes promotion of, vii. 176
—— succeeded by, as attorney-general, vi. 443
opinion of, on Cts of Orford's claim, ix. 162, 169, 186
Parliamentary speech of, on seizure of Wilkes's papers, vi. 208
Parliament not attended by, on first day of session, vii. 178
patent of precedence accepted by, over De Grey, vi. 268–9
resigns: as attorney-general, vi. 443; since he cannot be chancellor, vi. 443–4
Rockingham has attachment of, vii. 178
Rockingham's oracle, vi. 494
Rockingham the obstacle to lord chancellorship for, vii. 175
solicitorship suggested for, iv. **202**
Somers's papers in collection of, lost in fire, iv. 321–2, 331–2
Yorke, Mrs Charles. *See* Freeman, Catherine (d. 1759)
Yorke, Hon. Elizabeth (1725–60), m. (1748) George Anson, cr. (1747) Bn Anson:
death of, v. 416, 429
husband's relations with, iv. 13
minuets illegally danced by, at Sandwich's ball, iv. 121
witticisms about virginity of, iv. 13, v. 66

Yorke, Hon. John (1728–1801), M.P.:
becomes lord of Trade, v. 490
Parliament not attended by, on first day of session, vii. 178
Yorke, Hon. Sir Joseph (1724–92), K.B., 1761; cr. (1788) Bn Dover; army officer; diplomatist; M.P.:
Ferdinand's victory announced by, v. 314
George II hears false victories announced by, v. 319
Hanover might be ceded by, if England lost the war, v. 499
Mann might correspond with, at The Hague, v. **129**
—— told by, about Dutch-English trade pact, v. 269
not yet returned from Holland, ix. 116
Parliament not attended by, on first day of session, vii. 178
Rockingham has attachment of, vii. 178
Stormont may be replaced by, at Paris, viii. 179
Yorke, Lady Margaret (1731–69), m. (1749) Sir Gilbert Heathcote, 3d Bt, 1759:
marriage of, iv. 80
Yorke, Philip (1690–1764), cr. (1733) Bn Hardwicke and (1754) E. of Hardwicke; lord chancellor 1737–56; M.P.:
address against use of Hanoverian troops opposed by, ii. 159
Amelia, Ps, denies Richmond Park ticket to, iv. 322
Anson follows, iv. 135
—— would have navy treasurership according to demands of, v. 93
ballad satirizes, ii. 82–3
Bath's Court presentation arouses jealousy of, iv. 80
bill against clandestine marriages gets support of, iv. 383
Bootle's appointment approved by, on condition that Glenorchy receive post, i. 487
Bute advised by, to be secretary of state, v. 488
Bute and D. of Newcastle join, against Pitt, v. 539n
Byng re-investigation opposed by, in House of Lords, v. 64–5
——'s courage contrasted to behaviour of, v. 67
country visit of, v. 74
daughter of, iv. 121n, v. 416n
death of, vi. 211
English success attributed by HW to loss by, of absolute power, v. 499
faction of, v. 27
Fox hated by, iv. 412, v. 87
—— opposed by, iv. 383
George III talks with, at levee, v. 530
HW did not admire, vii. 265
Harcourt's complaints to be heard by, iv. 343

House of Lords formerly subservient to, vi. 109–10

'immensely rich,' vi. 211

jealousy of, iv. 80, 412

Jones nephew of, v. 26

mace of, i. 174

Mann must now read manifesto of, v. 286

Mansfield upheld by, against Pratt, v. 205

may be lord president, iv. 3, 202

may be lord privy seal, v. 92–3, 541

may be lord treasurer, iv. 412

may retire to Wimpole, iv. 202

Newcastle may be joined by, in opposition, vi. 98, 107, 109

Newcastle-Pitt coalition announced by, at Kensington, v. 103

Newcastle prevented by, from joining Fox, v. 87

—— to be succeeded by, as High Steward of Cambridge, iv. 19

newspapers laud, iii. 293

Northington abuses, vi. 109

opinion of, on Ferrers's will, v. 398

Pitt's popularity alarms, v. 87

preferment awaited by, v. 104

rebel lords tried by, iii. 280–1, 283, 287, 293

resigns as lord chancellor, iii. 211, iv. 3, v. 17, 25

Robinson to entertain, i. 174

Sandys succeeds, as Speaker of House of Lords, v. 25

Seals refused but Presidency or Privy Seal might be accepted by, v. 92–3

Seymour, Sir Edward, denied Somerset title by, iv. 139

Shebbeare attacks, v. 39

son of, ii. 351

temptations resisted by, vi. 104

war would be conducted by, as slowly as Chancery suit, v. 261

Westminster election returns said by, to be illegally made out, i. 272

Yorke, Philip (1720–90), styled Vct Royston 1754–64; 2d E. of Hardwicke, 1764; M.P.:

Address seconded by, ii. 351

brother advised by, about becoming lord chancellor, vii. 178

father-in-law of, i. 487

Grub St kennels searched by, for anecdotes about Sir Robert Walpole, ix. 464

HW apologizes for being 'squab' about Mann's commission for, v. 539

HW calls, oaf, ix. 463

HW refuses to bother about picture for, v. 538

'historically curious and political,' v. 129

later E. of Hardwicke, v. 538n

Mann did not want HW to speak to, about picture, v. 545

—— might send unusual documents to, v. 129

——'s letters from: about Jesuits' corres-

pondence relating to Gunpowder Plot, ix. 458; with anecdotes of Sir Robert Walpole, ix. 458

—— tries to get painting for, v. 532–3

Parliament not attended by, on first day of session, vii. 178

Rockingham has attachment of, vii. 178

Sandwich contests Cambridge high stewardship with, vi. 219

Walpoliana: HW attacks errors in, ix. 463–4; sent by him to Florence, ix. 458, 463

Yorke, Mrs Philip. See Campbell, Jemima (1722–97)

Yorke family:

avarice of, vi. 269

HW has no connection with, v. 538

Mauduit's book inspired by faction of, v. 458

minority may be joined by, in East Indian dispute, vi. 473

Opposition never joined by, unless with hope of success, vi. 98

Rockingham's adherents, vii. 178

very powerful, v. 129

Yorke, Charles, wanted by, to become lord chancellor, vii. 178

York House:

style of, to return, ii. 316

Yorkshire:

coin-clipping prevalent in, vii. 498

committee of, Saville tries to humour, ix. 18

Danby from, viii. 94

HW visits, iv. 585, vii. 57, 425

Herring and Malton head defence meeting in, iii. 110

Herring's speech to, on threatened invasion, iii. 126

inn at, crowd waits at, to see Ds of Hamilton enter post-chaise, iv. 317

Malton sends express from, iii. 186

may present petition, vii. 132

Muzell to visit clergyman in, v. 427

Piers a rich gentleman of, viii. 148

Rokeby in, viii. 282n

Russian fleet on coast of, vii. 146

Strafford, E. of, in, vii. 425

troops from Flanders to land in, iii. 134

Tullie has estate in, vii. 498

Wade to be joined in, by Hessians and army from Flanders, iii. 126–7

Wetherby in, iii. 173–4

Yorktown, Virginia:

Cornwallis's surrender at, ix. 208–9, 210–11, 212

Young, Lady. See Taylor, Elizabeth

Young, Edward (1683–1765), poet:

HW denies saying of, that fame is mankind's universal passion, ix. 545

Revenge, The, theatrical company acts, iii. 468

Young, Edward (1689–1773), Bath King-of-Arms:
daughter of, i. 431n, iv. 58n
Young, James (d. 1789), Capt.:
Byng accused by, iv. 586, 590–1
Trepid, ship of, almost sunk, iv. 591
Young, Lucy (ca 1723–73), m. (1740) William Henry Nassau de Zuylestein, 4th E. of Rochford, 1738:
Augusta, Ps of Wales, had, as maid of honour, i. 431n, iv. 58n
ball given by, v. 57
beauty of, faded, iv. 378
Cumberland, D. of, in love with, iv. 58
——, with D. of York, interrupts duet of, with Cts of Essex, v. 57
Florence to be visited by, iv. 370, 376
Friedrich Wilhelm of Hesse in love with, iv. 58
gaiety of, iv. 76
HW describes, iv. 58
HW wishes Mann were more struck by beauty of, iv. 389
husband no longer faithful to, iv. 378
Mann entertains, at Florence, iv. 378
marriage of, i. 431
subscription masquerade attended by, in vast beauty, iv. 49
Turin to be residence of, iv. 58, 76
Young, Margaret (fl. 1760–86), HW's housekeeper at SH:
HW told by, to see balloon, ix. 579
Young, Margaret Caroline (ca 1745–79), m. (ca 1762) Valentine Rudd:
acquittal of, after refusing her lawyer a clear story, viii. 152–4
reluctant mercer paid by, for brocaded silk, viii. 153–4, 167
Young, Sir William (1725–88), cr. (1769) Bt; Lt-Gov. of Dominica:
boasts of his wealth, iv. 331
Florence visited by, iv. 327, 331
organ and electrical instruments bought by, iv. 331
pictures bought by, iv. 331
sugar cane of, damaged by hurricane, iv. 331
weekly concert given by, in Florence, iv. 327
West Indian, iv. 327
Young, Mrs William. *See* (?) Taylor, Elizabeth
Younge. *See* Yonge
Younger, Elizabeth (d. 1762), m. Hon. John Finch:
marriage and daughter of, iii. 389
Young people:
conversational difficulties with: HW's reflections on, vii. 350–1, 364–5; Mann's reflections on, vii. 357
HW's reflections on, ix. 307–8
Youth:
death begins with end of, vi. 462
See also Youth and Old Age

Youth and Old Age:
HW's reflections on, ii. 498–9, vi. 462, vii. 237, 364–5, viii. 219, 359, ix. 109, 332, 502
See also Age, old
Ypres:
communication with, reopened, ii. 416
French almost capture, ii. 456
Maria Theresa said to have given, to the French, v. 117
siege of, delayed, ii. 463
Yunus Bey (d. 1756), son of Bey of Tunis:
rebellion of, iv. 319
Yvery, history of house of. *See under* Perceval, John (1683–1748)
Yvetot. *See* 'Roi d'Yvetot'

Zaballi, Abate:
Mann entertains, i. 104
Zabern, Rohan's château:
Hussars seize, ii. 293
Zacchiroli, Abbé Francesco:
Description de la galerie royale de Firenze, (?) HW requests from Mann, ix. 531
Zagorola:
Lobkowitz marches to, ii. 447
Załuski, Józef Jedrzej (1702–74), Bp of Kiev, 1759:
Russians remove, vi. 574
Zambeccari, ——, m. Count Pironi:
brother's intercession liberates, from Spanish captors, ii. 257
Zambeccari, Conte, Spanish minister at Bologna:
Montemar said by, to be going to Naples, ii. 2
Regency council's reply sent to, by Vernaccini, i. 281
sister liberated by, ii. 257
Traun may seize, ii. 257
Zambeccari, Francesco, Mgr:
alleged Domenichino painting owned by, acquired by HW through Mann, i. 167, 199, 226–7, 240, 241, 256–7, 267–8, 442, 462, ii. 57–8, 67, 285
Bolognese pronunciation of name of, i. 167n
collection of, at Bologna, to be sold, i. 167
HW visits house of, to see Domenichino painting, ii. 308
receipt given by, for Domenichino painting, ii. 57–8, 67
rich, i. 227
Zamperini, Anna Maria (b. ca 1752), Venetian singer:
Hobart prefers, to Lavinia Guadagni, vii. 271
——'s mistress, vii. 271
Zanetti, Conte Antonio Maria (1680–1757), collector:
cameo owned by, of tiger: HW wants, v. 562; Mann often reminds Murray of, vi. 116; Mann will write to Venice about, vi. 6; Murray has not found, vi. 14

Marlborough said to have bought gems of, v. 561-2, vi. 6
Regent of France employs, to buy pictures, v. 562n
Walpole, Sir Robert, cheated by, v. 562

Zanetti, Conte Antonio Maria (1706 or 1716-78):
Marlborough's purchases from, v. 561-2, vi. 6

Zanovitch, Premislos (b. ca 1747), 'Prince Scanderbeck'; sharper:
Lincoln cheated by, vii. 368, 378

Zarlino, Gioseffe (1517-90), musicologist:
Opere, Mann to send, to Hawkins, v. 467

Zatta ('Zattee'):
melon variety, iv. 170

Zeal:
convert-making, HW lacks, viii. 281

Zecchins:
exchange in, unfavourable to English in Florence, iii. 433

Zell, Ds of. See Desmier d'Olbreuse, Éléonore (1639-1722)

Zell:
Caroline Matilda said to go to, vii. 409

Zen, Alois (b. ca 1734), sharper:
Lincoln cheated by, vii. 368, 378

Zennoni, Don. See Somodevilla y Bengoechea, Zenón de

Zeno, Apostolo (1668-1750):
Gianguir by, ii. 96, 104

Zerbst. See Anhalt-Zerbst

Zinc:
Ginori wishes, from England, for painting china, ii. 184, 202, 216, 250, 283-4, 323
Mann, Galfridus, thinks, is mineral water, ii. 216
pewter by-product, ii. 323
Walpole, Sir Edward, hears that, is in Lancashire, ii. 284
—— to ask Ilay for, ii. 250

Zincke, Christian Friedrich (1685-1767), enamel-painter:
Cowley's miniature by, in HW's collection, vi. 523
(?) miniature by, ii. 347
Orford, Cts of, painted by, on snuffbox, ix. 501-2, 504

Zingari (gipsies):
Monte Santa Maria inhabited by, iv. 424, 428

Zingho. See Zinc

Zingist. See under Dow, Alexander

Zinzendorff. See Sinzendorff

Zipoli, Catterina, singer:
Caffarelli's witticism to, iii. 438

Zocchi, Giuseppe (1711-67), painter:
Mann sends view of Florence by, to HW, i. 57, 58

Zoffanii. See Zoffany

Zoffany, Mrs. See Eiselein, Maria Juliana Antonia; Thomas, Mary

Zoffany, John (1733-1810), painter:
Charlotte said to have sent, to Florence to paint Tribune scene, viii. 540
gates of Florentine baptistery to be copied by, in gesses, vii. 430
George III sends, to Florence to do view of Tribune, vii. 430, 436n, 519, viii. 33-4, 539
HW criticizes, vii. 435-6. viii. 92-3, 526-7, 529, 539
HW goes to studio of, to see picture of Tribune at Florence, vii. 519
'Hogarth of Dutch painting,' viii. 92-3
Italians think, was hanged for bigamy, viii. 539
Mann criticizes, viii. 33-4
——'s portrait to be inserted by, into painting of Tribune, vii. 519
—— tortured by, to appear before Leopold and Maria Louisa to be painted, viii. 540
Mann, Horace II, testifies to good likeness by, of Mann, viii. 529
many portraits painted by, at Florence, viii. 33-4
may return to England or go to Russia, viii. 92
painting by, of Florentine Tribune: Florentine criticisms of, viii. 539; has faulty perspective, viii. 539; increased in value by alterations in Tribune, ix. 177
painting by, of Holy Family, at Royal Academy exhibit, viii. 92
Patch's engravings charm, vii. 430
position of Queen's painter enables, to take down any picture in Florentine galleries, viii. 540

Zondadari. See Chigi Zondadari

Zorndorf:
Austrians, Russians, and Prussians all sing Te Deums for alleged victory at, v. 246, 317
battle of, v. 236, 237, 241
Russians give and accept no quarter at, v. 255

Zuccari, Federico (1542 or 3-1609), painter:
paintings by, in Caprarola palace, illustrated in Illustri fatti Farnesiani, ix. 403n

Zuccari, Taddeo (1529-66), painter:
paintings by, in Caprarola palace, illustrated in Illustri fatti Farnesiani, ix. 403n

Zucchero. See Zuccari

Zulestein:
William III compels E. of Rochford to take name of, instead of Nassau, viii. 360

Zulestein. See also Nassau de Zuylestein

Zung, Francisco, Col.:
captured at Velletri, ii. 493

Zurich:
canton of, prepares against invasion, ii. 290

Zweibrücken Birkenfeld, Pfalzgräfin von. See Maria Franziska Dorothea (1724-94)